MW01679959

American Heritage® Roget's Thesaurus

OFFICE EDITION

Houghton Mifflin Harcourt
Boston • New York

Words are included in this thesaurus on the basis of their usage. Words that are known to have current trademark registrations are shown with an initial capital and are also identified as trademarks. No investigation has been made of common-law trademark rights in any word, because such investigation is impracticable. The inclusion of any word in this thesaurus is not, however, an expression of the publisher's opinion as to whether or not it is subject to proprietary rights. Indeed, no definition in this thesaurus is to be regarded as affecting the validity of any trademark.

American Heritage and the eagle logo are registered trademarks of American Heritage Inc. Their use is pursuant to a license agreement with American Heritage Inc.

Reference Permissions
Houghton Mifflin Harcourt Publishing Company
222 Berkeley Street, Boston, MA 02116

Visit our websites: hmhco.com *and* ahdictionary.com

ISBN: 978-0-544-16666-0

Manufactured in the United States of America

1 2 3 4 5 6 7 8 9 10 - DOC - 20 19 18 17 16 15 14

Guide to the Thesaurus

The *American Heritage Roget's Thesaurus* is designed for quick and easy access to the best synonyms for a particular context. Concise definitions identify the central meaning shared by each group of synonyms, while a system of main entries and handy cross-references eliminates the open-ended searching associated with many thesauruses.

Entry Order Headwords are listed alphabetically in boldface type and are followed by an italic part-of-speech label. If a headword has more than one part of speech, each additional part of speech appears boldface and indented within the same entry. Phrasal verbs (two-word verbs consisting of a verb and an adverb or preposition) are listed in alphabetical order, also boldface and indented, directly under the base verb:

> **smile** *noun.* A facial expression marked by an upward curving of the lips ▶ grin, simper, smirk. [*Compare* **sneer.**]
> **smile** *verb.* To curve the lips upward in expressing amusement, pleasure, or happiness ▶ beam, grin, simper, smirk. ***Idioms:*** break into a smile, crack (or flash or give) a smile.
> **smile on** *or* **upon** *verb.* To lend supportive approval to ▶ countenance, encourage, favor. [*Compare* **approve, support.**]

Synonym Lists Synonyms are presented in lists following the definition to which they belong; they are introduced by the symbol ▶.

> **absent-minded** *adjective.* So lost in thought as to be unable to remember or attend to things ▶ absent, abstracted, bemused, distracted, distrait, far away, forgetful, inattentive, lost, oblivious, preoccupied, scatterbrained. *Slang:* spaced-out, spacy. ***Idioms:*** a million miles away, gathering wool, lost (or off) in space, out of it. [*Compare* **careless, detached, dreamy, negligent.**]

Most of the synonyms in a list are also entered individually at their own alphabetical place in the thesaurus as cross-references. Many words appear in more than one synonym list, and so are cross-referenced to more than one main entry.

> **forgetful** *adjective.* —*See* **absent-minded, careless.**

Note that many of the entries in the thesaurus contain both main-entry lists (which are generally grouped first in the entry) and cross-references, listed as *See Also* cross-references at the end of the entry, as in the example for **blink:**

> **blink** *verb.* To open and close one or both eyes rapidly ▶ bat, flutter, nictitate, twinkle, wink. —*See also* glitter, renege, surrender (1).
> **blink at** *verb.* To pretend not to see ▶ connive at, disregard, ignore, overlook, pass over, wink at. ***Idioms:*** be blind to, close (*or* shut) one's eyes to, let go (*or* pass), look the other way, make allowances for, sweep under the rug, turn a blind eye (*or* deaf ear) to.
> **blink** *noun.* A brief closing of the eyes ▶ bat, flutter, nictitation, wink. —*See also* **flash** (1), **flash** (2).

Senses and Definitions The main entries in this thesaurus are organized into defined senses, as in a dictionary. Each sense begins with a brief definition stating the meaning that is shared by the entry word and its synonyms. If an entry has more than one sense for any part of speech, the senses are numbered. Numbering begins again, if needed, for each new part of speech. In the entry for **breach,** the noun has two numbered senses; the verb has only one sense and is unnumbered:

> **breach** *noun.* **1.** An act of breaking a law or of nonfulfillment of an obligation ▶ contravention, delinquency, dereliction, infraction, infringement, malfeasance, nonfeasance, negligence, transgression, trespass, violation. [*Compare* **crime.**] **2.** An interruption in friendly relations ▶ alienation, break, breakdown, collapse, disaffection, estrangement, falling out, fissure, rent, rift, rupture, schism, split. [*Compare* **argument.**] —*See also* **crack** (2).
> **breach** *verb.* To make a hole or other

opening in ▶ break (through), gap, hole, perforate, pierce, punch (through), puncture. *Slang:* bust (through). [*Compare* **cut.**] —*See also* **violate** (1).

When an entry with only one part of speech has a single sense that is a cross-reference, the definition is omitted as unnecessary. The definition for such a sense will be found at the main entry to which the cross-reference points:

boaster *noun.* —*See* **braggart.**

braggart *noun.* One given to boasting ▶ blusterer, boaster, brag, braggadocio, bragger, swaggerer, vaunter. Informal: blowhard. *Slang:* blower, windbag. [*Compare* **egotist, showoff.**]
braggart *adjective.* —*See* **boastful.**

Cross-References There are three distinct types of cross-references between synonym lists. A cross-reference introduced by the word *See* leads from a *cross-reference entry* to the full *main-entry list,* as described above. If the word you have looked up contains a *See* cross-reference, you know that you will find the complete list of synonyms for that sense, including all labeled terms and idioms, at the entry to which the cross-reference points.

A second kind of cross-reference leads from a multi-sense entry to a main entry elsewhere in the alphabetical list. These are the *See Also* cross-references listed at the end of an entry and described above.

A third kind of cross-reference, enclosed in brackets and introduced by the word *Compare,* leads from a synonym list at a main entry to one or more other, closely related main entries elsewhere in the thesaurus. If you have already found the right synonym for your purpose, you may not choose to follow a *Compare* cross-reference. However, if you want to consider other synonyms for entries with similar but somewhat different meanings, the *Compare* cross-references will help you broaden your search:

anchor *noun.* A device for supporting or holding in place ▶ brake, dowel, grapnel, kedge, mooring, wedge. [*Compare* **bond, cord, fastener, nail.**] —*See also* **press.**
anchor *verb.* —*See* **fasten.**

nail *verb.* —*See* **capture, fasten, hit.**
nail *noun.* A bolt or shaft hammered or

drilled in place, used to support or hold together ▶ bolt, peg, pin, rivet, screw, spike, stud, tack. [*Compare* **anchor, cord, fastener.**]

Labels All words requiring status labels are clearly tagged at the boldface entry word and in synonym lists. The usage labels *Informal* and *Slang* indicate levels of usage and styles of expression that may not be appropriate in all contexts. *Informal* generally applies to those words that are commonly used in the spoken language and in ordinary writing but that may not be appropriate in formal or official contexts. The word *buddy,* for example, carries an *Informal* label in the synonym list at **friend.** *Slang,* on the other hand, is a style of language characteristic of very casual speech. The *Slang* label appears at words and special senses of words that have an exceptionally vivid, humorous, irreverent, or sarcastic flavor. For example, at the synonym list at **eat,** the word *chow down* is labeled *Slang.*

The dialect label *Chiefly Regional* indicates that a term is indigenous to one or more geographic areas within the United States. For example, the words *chaw,* a synonym of **chew,** and *poorly,* a synonym of **sick,** are labeled *Chiefly Regional* because they are more commonly used in some parts of the country than in others.

Core Synonym Paragraphs These paragraphs, located at the end of a main entry, explain the different nuances of meaning among a selected group of synonyms.

There are two kinds of synonym paragraphs. The first consists of a group of undiscriminated, alphabetically ordered words sharing a single, irreducible meaning. These synonyms are presented in illustrative examples following a core definition, as in the Core Synonym paragraph for **luxury.**

The second kind of paragraph consists of fully discriminated synonyms ordered in a way that reflects their relationships. A brief sentence explaining the initial point of comparison of the words is given, followed by an explanation of their connotations and varying shades of meaning, along with illustrative examples, as in the paragraph for **lethargy.**

A

A-1 *adjective. See* **A-one.**

aback *adverb.* Without adequate preparation ▶ short, unawarely, unawares. ***Idioms:*** by surprise, off guard.

abandon *verb.* **1.** To give up or leave completely ▶ abdicate, cast aside, cede, demit, desert, forfeit, forgo, forsake, forswear, hand over, lay aside, lay down, leave, maroon, quit, quitclaim, relinquish, render, renounce, resign, sacrifice, surrender, throw over, waive, yield. ***Idioms:*** back out on, leave in the lurch, run out on, walk out on. [*Compare* **defect, discard, empty.**] **2.** To cease trying to continue ▶ break off, desist, discontinue, give up, leave off, quit, remit, stop. *Informal:* knock off, swear off. *Slang:* lay off. ***Idioms:*** call it a day, call it quits, have done with, throw in the towel (*or* sponge). [*Compare* **stop.**] **3.** To yield oneself unrestrainedly, as to an impulse ▶ deliver, relinquish, surrender. ***Idioms:*** give oneself up (*or* over). *—See also* **drop** (4).

abandon *noun.* **1.** A complete surrender of inhibition ▶ abandonment, incontinence, unrestraint, wantonness, wildness. [*Compare* **enthusiasm, ease, freedom.**] **2.** A careless, often reckless regard for consequences ▶ blitheness, carelessness, heedlessness, thoughtlessness. [*Compare* **temerity.**]

✚ **CORE SYNONYMS:** *abandon, surrender, relinquish, yield, resign, cede, waive, renounce.* These verbs mean giving something up or leaving someone or something completely. *Abandon* and *surrender* both imply no expectation of recovering what is given up; *surrender* also implies the operation of compulsion or force: *abandoned all hope for a resolution; surrendered control of the company. Relinquish* may connote regret: *can't relinquish the idea. Yield* implies giving way, as to pressure, often in the hope that such action will be temporary: *had to yield ground. Resign* suggests formal relinquishing (*resigned their claim to my land*) or acquiescence arising from hopelessness (*resigned himself to forgoing his vacation*). *Cede* connotes formal transfer, as of territory: *ceded the province to the victorious nation. Waive* implies a voluntary decision to dispense with something, such as a right: *waived all privileges.* To *renounce* is to relinquish formally and usually as a matter of principle: *renounced worldly goods.*

---

abandoned *adjective.* **1.** Having been given up and left alone ▶ bereft, derelict, deserted, desolate, forlorn, forsaken, jilted, lorn, marooned, outcast, rejected, relinquished. ***Idioms:*** left holding the bag, left in the lurch, out in the cold, out on a limb. [*Compare* **empty, lonely, unreserved.**] **2.** Lacking in moral restraint ▶ dissipated, dissolute, fast, licentious, profligate, rakish, unbridled, unconstrained, uncontrolled, ungoverned, uninhibited, unrestrained, wanton, wild. [*Compare* **corrupt, unscrupulous.**]

abandonment *noun.* **1.** A giving up of a possession, claim, or right ▶ abdication, quitclaim, relinquishment, renunciation, resignation, sacrifice, surrender, waiver. **2.** The act of forsaking ▶ dereliction, desertion. *—See also* **abandon** (1), **defection.**

abase *verb. —See* **debase, disgrace, humble.**

abasement *noun. —See* **degradation** (1).

abash *verb. —See* **embarrass.**

abashment *noun. —See* **embarrassment.**

abate *verb. —See* **decrease, deduct, subside.**

abatement *noun. —See* **decrease, deduction** (1), **waning.**

abbé *noun. —See* **cleric.**

abbot *noun. —See* **cleric.**

abbreviate *verb.* —*See* **shorten.**

abdicate *verb.* —*See* **abandon** (1).

abdication *noun.* —*See* **abandonment** (1).

abduct *verb.* To seize and detain a person unlawfully ▶ kidnap, snatch, spirit away, take hostage. [*Compare* **seize, steal.**]

abecedarian *noun.* —*See* **beginner.**

aberrance *or* **aberrancy** *noun.* —*See* **abnormality.**

aberrant *adjective.* —*See* **abnormal, errant** (2).

aberration *noun.* —*See* **abnormality, deviation.**

abet *verb.* —*See* **help, promote** (2).

abetment *noun.* —*See* **help.**

abettor *or* **abetter** *noun.* —*See* **accessory, assistant.**

abeyance *noun.* The condition of being temporarily inactive ▶ dormancy, intermission, latency, quiescence, suspension, remission. [*Compare* **break, rest.**]

abeyant *adjective.* —*See* **latent.**

abhor *verb.* —*See* **hate.**

abhorrence *noun.* —*See* **despisal, disgust, hate** (1), **hate** (2).

abhorrent *adjective.* —*See* **offensive** (1).

abide *verb.* —*See* **endure** (1), **endure** (2), **live**[1], **remain.**

abide by *verb.* —*See* **follow** (4).

abiding *adjective.* —*See* **continuing.**

ability *noun.* **1.** Natural or acquired skill or talent ▶ adeptness, art, command, craft, expertise, expertness, knack, mastery, proficiency, skill, technique. *Informal:* know-how, savvy. [*Compare* **dexterity, talent.**] **2.** Physical, mental, financial, or legal power to perform ▶ capability, capacity, competence, competency, faculty, might. [*Compare* **energy, power.**]

✚ **CORE SYNONYMS:** *ability, art, craft, expertise, knack, know-how, technique.* These nouns denote natural or acquired skill or talent: *a tricky solo passage that showcases a pianist's ability; the art of rhetoric; pottery that reveals an artist's craft; political expertise; a knack for teaching; mechanical know-how; a precise diving technique.*

---

abjuration *noun.* —*See* **retraction.**

abjure *verb.* —*See* **break** (5), **retract** (1).

ablaze *adjective.* —*See* **burning.**

able *adjective.* Having sufficient ability or resources ▶ capable, competent, good, skilled, skillful. [*Compare* **dexterous, expert, gifted, qualified.**]

able-bodied *adjective.* —*See* **healthy, lusty.**

ablution *noun.* —*See* **purification** (2).

abnegate *verb.* —*See* **deny.**

abnegation *noun.* —*See* **denial** (1).

abnormal *adjective.* Departing from the normal ▶ aberrant, anomalistic, anomalous, atypic, atypical, deviant, divergent, irregular, preternatural, unnatural. [*Compare* **eccentric, unusual.**]

abnormality *noun.* The condition of being abnormal ▶ aberrance, aberrancy, aberration, anomaly, deviance, deviancy, deviation, exception, irregularity, oddity, preternaturalness, unnaturalness. [*Compare* **defect, deformity, difference, eccentricity.**]

abnormally *adverb.* —*See* **unusually.**

abode *noun.* —*See* **home** (1).

abolish *verb.* To put an end to ▶ abrogate, annihilate, annul, cancel, extinguish, invalidate, negate, nullify, set aside, vitiate, void. *Informal:* ax. [*Compare* **cancel, eliminate, stop, suppress.**] —*See also* **annihilate.**

abolition *or* **abolishment** *noun.* An often formal act of putting an end to ▶ abrogation, annihilation, annulment, cancellation, defeasance, invalidation, negation, nullification, voidance. [*Compare* **annihilation, repeal.**]

abominable *adjective.* —*See* **damned, offensive** (1).

abominate *verb.* —*See* **despise, hate.**

abomination *noun.* —*See* **hate** (1), **hate** (2).

aboriginal *adjective.* —*See* **domestic** (3), **indigenous.**

abound *verb.* —*See* **teem**[1].

about *adverb.* —*See* **approximately, backward.**

about-face *verb.* To turn sharply around ▶ double (back), reverse. ***Idiom:*** turn on one's heels.

about-face *noun.* —*See* **reversal** (1).

aboveboard *adjective.* —*See* **frank, honest.**

abracadabra *noun.* —*See* **gibberish, spell**[2].

abrade *verb.* —*See* **chafe, erode, scrape** (1).

abrasion *noun.* A mark or shallow cut made by contact with an object ▶ scrape, scratch, scuff, striation. [*Compare* **cut, furrow, impression.**]

abrasive *adjective.* —*See* **rough** (1).

abrasiveness *noun.* —*See* **irregularity.**

abridge *verb.* —*See* **shorten.**

abridgment *noun.* —*See* **synopsis.**

abrogate *verb.* —*See* **abolish.**

abrogation *noun.* —*See* **abolition.**

abrupt *adjective.* **1.** Rudely informal ▶ bald, bluff, blunt, brief, brusque, crusty, curt, gruff, short, short-spoken. [*Compare* **impudent, rude.**] **2.** Unexpectedly sudden ▶ hurried, precipitant, precipitate, sharp, sudden, unannounced. ***Idioms:*** from out of nowhere (*or* the blue), without warning. [*Compare* **quick, rash.**] —*See also* **steep**[1] (1).

✚ **CORE SYNONYMS:** *abrupt, curt, gruff, brusque, blunt, bluff, crusty.* These adjectives mean rudely informal or discourteous. *Abrupt* and *curt* denote usually rude briefness: *an abrupt end to the conversation; a curt letter of rejection. Gruff* implies roughness or surliness but does not necessarily suggest rudeness: *a gruff reply. Brusque* emphasizes rude abruptness: *a brusque manner. Blunt* stresses utter frankness and usually a disconcerting directness: *a blunt refusal. Bluff* refers to unpolished, unceremonious manner but usually implies hearty good nature: *a bluff and courageous sailor. Crusty* suggests a rough and forbidding manner that sometimes conceals benevolence of spirit: *a crusty old gentlemen who feeds stray cats.*

---

abscond *verb.* —*See* **escape** (1).

abscond with *verb.* —*See* **steal.**

absence *noun.* **1.** Failure to be present ▶ cut, nonappearance, nonattendance, truancy, truantry. *Informal:* hooky. [*Compare* **emptiness, nothingness.**] **2.** The condition of lacking something ▶ dearth, lack, want. [*Compare* **need, shortage.**]

absent *adjective.* Not present ▶ away, elsewhere, gone, missing, nonattendant, nonexistent, off, out, truant. ***Idioms:*** AWOL, gone fishing, playing hooky. [*Compare* **empty.**] —*See also* **absent-minded.**

absent-minded *adjective.* So lost in thought as to be unable to remember or attend to things ▶ absent, abstracted, bemused, distracted, distrait, faraway, forgetful, inattentive, lost, oblivious, preoccupied, scatterbrained. *Slang:* spaced-out, spacy. ***Idioms:*** a million miles away, gathering wool, lost (*or* off) in space, out of it. [*Compare* **careless, detached, dreamy, negligent.**]

absent-mindedness *noun.* —*See* **trance.**

absolute *adjective.* Having and exercising complete political power and control ▶ absolutistic, arbitrary, autarchic, autarchical, autocratic, autocratical, despotic, dictatorial, monocratic, totalitarian, tyrannic, tyrannical, tyrannous. [*Compare* **influential, powerful, strong.**] —*See also* **definite** (3), **implicit** (2), **perfect, pure, unconditional, utter**[2].

absolutely *adverb.* Without question ▶ categorically, certainly, definitely, doubtless, doubtlessly, indubitably, positively, surely, undoubtedly, unquestionably. ***Idioms:*** beyond (*or* without) a doubt, beyond the shadow of a doubt.

[*Compare* **considerably, really, unusually, very.**] —*See also* **completely** (1), **yes.**

absolution *noun.* —*See* **exculpation, forgiveness.**

absolutism *noun.* **1.** A political doctrine advocating the principle of absolute rule ▶ authoritarianism, autocracy, despotism, dictatorship, totalitarianism. [*Compare* **subjugation.**] **2.** A government in which all power is vested in a single leader or party ▶ autarchy, autocracy, despotism, dictatorship, monocracy, one-party rule, tyranny.

absolutistic *adjective.* —*See* **absolute.**

absolve *verb.* —*See* **clear** (3), **excuse** (1).

absorb *verb.* **1.** To occupy the attention of ▶ consume, employ, engage, engross, immerse, involve, monopolize, occupy, preoccupy, tie up. [*Compare* **charm, grip.**] **2.** To take in and incorporate, especially mentally ▶ assimilate, digest, drink in, grasp, imbibe, incorporate, learn, sponge up, take up. *Informal:* soak up. [*Compare* **know, understand.**] —*See also* **drink** (3).

✚ **CORE SYNONYMS:** *absorb, consume, engross, monopolize, preoccupy.* These verbs mean to occupy someone's attention: *study that absorbs all her time; was consumed by fear; engrossed herself in her reading; a service monopolized by one company; was preoccupied with financial worries.*

---

absorbed *adjective.* —*See* **busy** (1), **rapt.**

absorbent *or* **absorptive** *adjective.* Having a capacity or tendency to absorb or soak up ▶ assimilative, bibulous, imbibing, permeable, retentive, spongy.

absorption *noun.* **1.** The process of absorbing and incorporating ▶ assimilation, digestion, incorporation, intake, osmosis. [*Compare* **mastery.**] **2.** Total occupation of the attention or of the mind ▶ engagement, engrossment, enthrallment, immersion, involvement, preoccupation, prepossession.

absquatulate *verb.* —*See* **escape** (1).

abstain *verb.* —*See* **refrain.**

abstain from *verb.* —*See* **avoid.**

abstemious *adjective.* —*See* **temperate** (2).

abstemiousness *noun.* —*See* **moderation.**

abstinence *noun.* —*See* **temperance** (1), **temperance** (2).

abstinent *adjective.* —*See* **ascetic.**

abstract *adjective.* —*See* **deep** (2), **theoretical** (1), **theoretical** (2).

abstract *noun.* —*See* **synopsis.**

abstract *verb.* —*See* **detach, review** (1).

abstracted *adjective.* —*See* **absent-minded.**

abstraction *noun.* —*See* **detachment** (1), **trance.**

abstruse *adjective.* —*See* **ambiguous** (1), **deep** (2), **obscure** (1).

absurd *adjective.* —*See* **foolish.**

absurdity *noun.* —*See* **foolishness, scream** (2).

abundance *noun.* A great deal ▶ bounty, mass, mountain, much, plenty, plethora, profusion, wealth, world. *Informal:* barrel, heap, lot, mess, pack, peck, pile. [*Compare* **excess, flood.**] —*See also* **plenty.**

abundant *adjective.* —*See* **generous** (2).

abundantly *adverb.* —*See* **considerably.**

abuse *verb.* **1.** To treat wrongfully or harmfully ▶ exploit, ill-treat, ill-use, impose on (*or* upon), maltreat, mishandle, mistreat, misuse, oppress, persecute, use, victimize, wrong. ***Idioms:*** kick around, knock about (*or* around), take advantage of, treat like dirt. [*Compare* **injure, insult, violate.**] **2.** To use improperly ▶ exploit, misapply, misappropriate, mishandle, mistreat, misuse, pervert. —*See also* **revile.**

abuse *noun.* **1.** Improper use or handling ▶ ill-usage, misapplication, misappropriation, mishandling, misuse, perversion. [*Compare* **degradation.**] **2.** Physically harmful treatment ▶ ill-treatment, maltreatment, mishandling, mistreatment, misusage. —*See also* **vituperation.**

✤ **CORE SYNONYMS:** *abuse, mistreat, ill-treat, maltreat.* These verbs mean to treat wrongfully or harmfully. *Abuse* applies to injurious or improper treatment: "*We abuse land because we regard it as a commodity belonging to us*" (Aldo Leopold). *Mistreat, ill-treat,* and *maltreat* all share the sense of inflicting injury, often intentionally: "*I had seen many more patients die from being mistreated for consumption than from consumption itself*" (Earl of Lytton). *The army had orders not to ill-treat the prisoners.* "*When we misuse* [a language other than our native language], *we are in fact trying to reduce its element of foreignness. We let ourselves maltreat it as though it naturally belonged to us*" (Manchester Guardian Weekly).

---

abusive *adjective.* Of, relating to, or characterized by verbal abuse ▶ contumelious, invective, opprobrious, scurrilous, sharp-tongued, vituperative. [*Compare* **disdainful, impudent.**]

abut *verb.* —*See* **adjoin.**

abutting *adjective.* —*See* **adjoining.**

abysm *noun.* —*See* **deep.**

abysmal *adjective.* Open wide ▶ abyssal, cavernous, gaping, yawning. [*Compare* **broad, open.**] —*See also* **deep** (1), **terrible.**

abyss *noun.* —*See* **deep.**

academic *adjective.* —*See* **didactic, educational** (1), **pedantic, theoretical** (1).

accede *verb.* —*See* **assent.**

accelerate *verb.* —*See* **speed.**

accent *noun.* Special attention given to something considered important ▶ accentuation, emphasis, stress, weight. [*Compare* **importance, notice.**] —*See also* **tone** (2).

accent *or* **accentuate** *verb.* —*See* **emphasize.**

accentuation *noun.* Special attention given to something considered important ▶ accent, emphasis, stress, weight. [*Compare* **importance, notice.**]

accept *verb.* **1.** To receive something offered willingly and gladly ▶ embrace, take (up), welcome. ***Idioms:*** receive with open arms, take (*or* fold) to one's bosom. [*Compare* **acquire, take.**] **2.** To admit to one's possession, presence, or awareness ▶ have, receive, take. [*Compare* **absorb.**] **3.** To allow admittance, as to a group ▶ admit, intromit, let in, receive, take in. ***Idioms:*** welcome aboard (*or* on board), take (*or* welcome) into the fold. [*Compare* **permit.**] —*See also* **assent, believe** (1), **endure** (1), **understand** (1).

acceptable *adjective.* **1.** Worthy of being accepted or allowed ▶ admissible, allowable, permissible, unobjectionable, unexceptionable. *Slang:* kosher. **2.** Adequate to satisfy a need, requirement, or standard ▶ adequate, all right, average, common, decent, fair, fairish, goodish, moderate, modest, palatable, passable, popular, reasonable, respectable, satisfactory, sufficient, tolerable. *Informal:* OK, tidy. [*Compare* **appropriate.**]

acceptance *noun.* **1.** The act of accepting or adopting ▶ acquiescence, adoption, agreement, assent, consent, embracement, espousal, nod, yes. *Informal:* OK. ***Idioms:*** stamp (*or* seal) of approval. [*Compare* **confirmation, permission.**] **2.** Favorable reception or regard ▶ acknowledgement, approbation, approval, credit, esteem, favor, recognition, regard, welcome. [*Compare* **praise.**] —*See also* **patience.**

acceptant *adjective.* —*See* **receptive.**

acceptation *noun.* —*See* **meaning.**

accepted *adjective.* Generally approved or agreed upon ▶ admitted, conventional, customary, established, orthodox, received, recognized, sanctioned, time-honored, traditional. [*Compare* **common, ordinary.**]

accepting *adjective.* —*See* **patient.**

access *noun.* —*See* **admission, outburst.**

access *verb.* To gain entry into a computer network or database ▶ enter, log in (*or* on). ***Idioms:*** gain access (*or* admittance *or* entry), get connected.

accessible *adjective.* Easily approached ▶ approachable, responsive, welcoming. —*See also* **convenient** (2), **open** (4).

accession *noun.* —*See* **addition** (1).

accessory *noun.* One who assists a lawbreaker in a wrongful or criminal act ▶ abettor, accomplice, confederate, conspirator. ***Idiom:*** partner in crime. —*See also* **attachment.**

accessory *adjective.* —*See* **auxiliary** (1).

accident *noun.* An unexpected and usually undesirable event ▶ casualty, contretemps, misadventure, mischance, misfortune, mishap, reversal, setback. [*Compare* **collision, disaster.**] —*See also* **chance** (1), **chance** (2), **crash** (2).

accidental *adjective.* Occurring unexpectedly ▶ adventitious, casual, chance, contingent, fluky, fortuitous, inadvertent, incidental, odd, serendipitous, unanticipated, unexpected, unintended, unplanned. [*Compare* **chance, random.**] —*See also* **unintentional.**

✚ **CORE SYNONYMS:** *accidental, fortuitous, contingent, incidental, adventitious.* These adjectives apply to what happens unexpectedly or unintentionally. *Accidental* primarily refers to what occurs by chance: *an accidental meeting.* It can also mean subordinate or nonessential: "*Poetry is something to which words are the accidental, not by any means the essential form*" (Frederick W. Robertson). *Fortuitous* stresses chance even more strongly: "*the happy combination of fortuitous circumstances*" (Sir Walter Scott). *Contingent* describes what is possible but uncertain because of unforeseen or uncontrollable factors: "*The results of confession were not contingent, they were certain*" (George Eliot). *Incidental* refers to a minor or unanticipated result or accompaniment: "*There is scarcely any practice which is so corrupt as not to produce some incidental good*" (Enoch Mellor). *Adventitious* applies to something acquired or added externally, sometimes by accident or chance: "*The court tries to understand 'whether the young man's misconduct was adventitious or the result of some serious flaw in his character'*" (Harry F. Rosenthal).

---

acclaim *verb.* —*See* **honor** (1), **praise** (1).

acclaim *or* **acclamation** *noun.* —*See* **praise** (1).

acclamatory *adjective.* —*See* **complimentary** (1).

acclimate *or* **acclimatize** *verb.* —*See* **adapt, harden** (1).

acclimated *or* **acclimatized** *adjective.* —*See* **accustomed** (1).

acclimation *or* **acclimatization** *noun.* —*See* **adaptation.**

acclivity *noun.* —*See* **ascent** (2).

accolade *noun.* A memento received as a symbol of excellence or victory ▶ award, cup, prize, trophy. —*See also* **compliment, distinction** (2), **praise** (1), **reward.**

accolade *verb.* —*See* **praise** (1).

accommodate *verb.* To have the room or capacity for ▶ contain, hold. —*See also* **adapt, compromise, harmonize** (1), **lodge, oblige** (1).

✚ **CORE SYNONYMS:** *accommodate, contain, hold.* These verbs mean to have the room or capacity for: *The restaurant accommodates 50 customers. The book contains some amusing passages. This pitcher holds two pints.*

---

accommodating *adjective.* —*See* **obliging.**

accommodation *noun.* —*See* **adaptation, compromise.**

accommodations *noun.* Steps taken in preparation for an undertaking ▶ arrangements, plans, preparations, provisions.

accompaniment *noun.* —*See* **concomitant, enhancement.**

accompanist *noun.* —*See* **concomitant.**

accompany *verb.* To be with or go with ▶ attend, chaperon, companion, company, convoy, escort. ***Idioms:*** go hand in hand with, hang around (*or* out) with, tag along with. [*Compare* **guide.**] —*See also* **supplement.**

✚ CORE SYNONYMS: *accompany, escort, chaperon.* These verbs mean to be with or to go with another or others. *Accompany* suggests going with another on an equal basis: *She went to Europe accompanied by her colleague. Escort* stresses protective guidance: *The party chairperson escorted the candidate through the crowd. Chaperon* specifies adult supervision of young persons: *My mom helped chaperon the prom.*

---

accompanying *adjective.* —*See* **concurrent.**

accomplice *noun.* —*See* **accessory.**

accomplish *verb.* To obtain a goal or objective by effort ▶ achieve, arrive at, attain, come to, fulfill, gain, get to, reach, realize. *Informal:* hit on. *Slang:* score. ***Idiom:*** bring to pass. [*Compare* **fulfill.**] —*See also* **effect, perform** (1).

✚ CORE SYNONYMS: *accomplish, reach, achieve, attain, gain.* These verbs mean to obtain a goal or objective by effort. *Accomplish* and *reach* are the least specific: *accomplished the goal; reached a definitive conclusion. Achieve* suggests the application of skill or initiative: *achieved national recognition. Attain* implies the impelling force of ambition, principle, or ideals: *trying to attain self-confidence. Gain* connotes considerable effort in surmounting obstacles: *gained the workers' trust.*

---

accomplished *adjective.* Proficient as a result of practice and study ▶ finished, polished, practiced. [*Compare* **able, expert.**]

accomplishment *noun.* Something that is completed or attained successfully ▶ achievement, acquirement, acquisition, arrival, attainment, coup, deed, effort, endeavor, exploit, feat, masterstroke, realization, success, successfulness, triumph, tour de force. [*Compare* **conquest, goal, performance.**] —*See also* **fulfillment** (1).

✚ CORE SYNONYMS: *achievement, exploit, feat, masterstroke, realization, triumph.* These nouns mean something completed or attained successfully: *feats of bravery; achievements of diplomacy; military exploits; a masterstroke of entrepreneurship; a realization of the director's vision; the triumph of winning the championship.*

---

accord *verb.* To let have as a favor, prerogative, or privilege ▶ award, concede, give, grant, vouchsafe. [*Compare* **yield.**] —*See also* **agree** (1), **agree** (2), **confer** (2).

accord *noun.* —*See* **agreement** (1), **agreement** (2), **harmony** (1), **treaty.**

accordance *noun.* —*See* **agreement** (2), **conferment.**

accordant *adjective.* —*See* **agreeable, unanimous.**

accost *verb.* To approach for the purpose of speech ▶ greet, hail, salute. [*Compare* **encounter, interrupt, welcome.**]

accouchement *noun.* —*See* **birth** (1).

account *noun.* **1.** A statement of causes or motives ▶ explanation, justification, rationale, rationalization, reason. [*Compare* **answer, apology, belief.**] **2.** A precise list of fees or charges ▶ bill, check, invoice, reckoning, statement, tally. *Informal:* damage, tab. **3.** A measure of those qualities that determine merit, desirability, usefulness, or importance ▶ valuation, value, worth. [*Compare* **cost, importance.**] —*See also* **esteem, story** (1), **use** (2).

account *verb.* —*See* **regard.**

account for *verb.* To offer reasons for or a cause of ▶ explain, justify, rationalize. [*Compare* **clarify, resolve.**]

accountability *noun.* —*See* **responsibility.**

accountable *adjective.* —*See* **explainable, liable** (1).

accouter *or* **accoutre** *verb.* —*See* **furnish.**

accouterments *or* **accoutrements** *noun.* —*See* **outfit.**

accredit *verb.* —*See* **attribute, authorize, confirm** (3).

accreditation *noun.* —*See* **confirmation** (1).

accretion *noun.* —*See* **buildup** (2).

accrue *verb.* —*See* **accumulate.**

acculturate *verb.* To fit for companionship with others, especially in attitude or manners ▶ civilize, humanize, socialize.

acculturation *noun.* —*See* **adaptation.**

accumulate *verb.* To bring together so as to increase in mass or number ▶ accrue, agglomerate, aggregate, amass, assemble, build up, collect, cumulate, garner, gather, hive, heap up, mass, pile up, roll up. [*Compare* **assemble, increase, save.**]

✤ **CORE SYNONYMS:** *accumulate, collect, assemble, amass.* These verbs mean to bring or come together so as to increase in mass or number: *Accumulate* applies to the increase of like or related things over an extended period: *They accumulated enough capital to invest. Old newspapers accumulated in the basement. Collect* frequently refers to the careful selection of like or related things that become part of an organized whole: *She collects stamps as a hobby. Tears collected in his eyes. Assemble* implies a definite and usually close relationship. With respect to persons, the term suggests convening out of common interest or purpose: *Assembling an able staff was more difficult than expected. The reporters assembled for the press conference.* With respect to things, *assemble* implies gathering and fitting together components: *The curator is assembling an interesting exhibit of Stone Age artifacts. Amass* refers to the collection or accumulation of things, often valuable things, to form an imposing quantity: *Their families had amassed great fortunes. Rocks had amassed at the bottom of the glacier.*

---

accumulation *noun.* **1.** A quantity accumulated ▶ aggregation, amassment, assemblage, buildup, collection, congeries, cumulation, gathering, mass. [*Compare* **heap.**] **2.** The act of accumulating ▶ agglomeration, buildup, conglomeration. [*Compare* **increase.**] —*See also* **buildup** (2), **deposit** (2).

accumulative *adjective.* Increasing, as in force, by successive additions ▶ additive, cumulative.

accuracy *or* **accurateness** *noun.* Freedom from error ▶ correctness, definitude, exactitude, exactness, meticulousness, preciseness, precision, rightness. —*See also* **veracity.**

accurate *adjective.* Conforming exactly to fact ▶ actual, correct, errorless, exact, factual, faithful, precise, right, rigorous, true, veracious, veridical. ***Idioms:*** on the button (*or* money *or* nose), spot on. [*Compare* **literal, perfect, sure.**] —*See also* **careful** (2).

accursed *adjective.* —*See* **damned.**

accusation *noun.* A charging of someone with a misdeed ▶ arraignment, crimination, charge, denouncement, denunciation, finger-pointing, impeachment, imputation, incrimination, inculpation, indictment, recrimination.

accusatorial *or* **accusatory** *adjective.* Containing, relating to, or involving an accusation ▶ denunciative, denunciatory, incriminating, incriminatory, inculpatory. [*Compare* **insinuating.**]

accuse *verb.* To make an accusation against ▶ arraign, blame, charge, denounce, impeach, incriminate, inculpate, indict, tax, recriminate. *Slang:* finger. ***Idioms:*** hang (*or* pin) something on, point the finger at, put the finger on. [*Compare* **implicate.**]

accused *noun.* A person against whom an action is brought ▶ defendant, respondent.

accuser *noun.* **1.** One that accuses ▶ arraigner, denouncer, indicter, recriminator. **2.** One that makes a formal complaint, especially in court ▶ claimant, complainant, plaintiff.

accustom *verb.* To make familiar through constant practice, use, or habit ▶ condition, familiarize, habituate, inure, wont. [*Compare* **adapt.**]

accustomed *adjective.* **1.** Adapted to the existing environment and conditions ▶ acclimated, acclimatized, adapted, conditioned, hardened, inured, seasoned, toughened. **2.** Subject to a pattern or habit of behavior ▶ chronic, habitual, routine. **3.** In the habit ▶ habituated, used, wont. —*See also* **common** (1).

ace *noun.* A key resource to be used at an opportune moment ▶ trump, trump card. *Informal:* clincher. ***Idiom:*** ace in the hole. —*See also* **expert.**

ace *adjective.* —*See* **excellent.**

ace *verb.* —*See* **defeat.**

acerbic *adjective.* —*See* **biting, bitter** (1), **sour.**

acerbity *noun.* —*See* **sarcasm.**

acetous *adjective.* —*See* **sour.**

ache *verb.* To experience or express compassion ▶ commiserate, condole, feel, sympathize. ***Idioms:*** be (*or* feel) sorry, have one's heart ache (*or* bleed) for someone, have one's heart go out to someone. [*Compare* **comfort, pity.**] —*See also* **desire, hurt** (2).

ache *noun.* —*See* **pain.**

achievable *adjective.* —*See* **possible.**

achieve *verb.* —*See* **accomplish, effect, perform** (1).

achievement *noun.* —*See* **accomplishment.**

aching *or* **achy** *adjective.* —*See* **painful.**

acicula *noun.* —*See* **point** (1).

acicular *or* **aciculate** *or* **aciculated** *adjective.* —*See* **pointed.**

acid *or* **acidic** *adjective.* —*See* **biting, sour.**

acidity *noun.* —*See* **sarcasm.**

acidulous *adjective.* —*See* **sour.**

acknowledge *verb.* **1.** To admit to the reality or truth of ▶ admit, avow, concede, confess, grant, own (up). *Slang:* fess up. *Chiefly Regional:* allow. [*Compare* **assent.**] **2.** To express recognition of ▶ admit, recognize. [*Compare* **confirm.**]

✚ **CORE SYNONYMS:** *acknowledge, admit, own, avow, confess, concede.* These verbs mean to admit the reality or truth of something, often reluctantly. To *acknowledge* is to accept responsibility for something one makes known: *He acknowledged his mistake. Admit* implies reluctance in acknowledging one's acts or another point of view: *"She was attracted by the frankness of a suitor who . . . admitted that he did not believe in marriage"* (Edith Wharton). *Own* stresses personal acceptance and responsibility: *She owned that she feared for the child's safety. Avow* means to assert openly and boldly: *"Old Mrs. Webb avowed that he, in the space of two hours, had worn out her pew more . . . than she had by sitting in it forty years"* (Kate Douglas Wiggin). *Confess* usually emphasizes disclosure of something damaging or inconvenient to oneself: *I have to confess that I lied to you.* To *concede* is to intellectually accept something, often against one's will: *The lawyer refused to concede that the two cases had similarities.*

---

acknowledgment *noun.* **1.** The act of admitting to something ▶ admission, avowal, concession, confession, recognition. ***Idiom:*** owning up. **2.** Favorable notice, as of an achievement ▶ credit, recognition. —*See also* **acceptance** (2), **appreciation.**

acme *noun.* —*See* **climax.**

acolyte *noun.* —*See* **devotee.**

acquaint *verb.* To make known socially ▶ familiarize, introduce, present. —*See also* **inform** (1).

acquaintance *noun.* Personal knowledge derived from participation or observation ▶ conversance, experience, familiarity. [*Compare* **awareness.**]

acquainted *adjective.* Having good knowledge of something ▶ conversant, familiar, schooled, versant, versed. ***Idiom:*** up on. [*Compare* **accustomed.**] —*See also* **informed.**

acquiesce *verb.* —*See* **assent, surrender** (1).

acquiescence *noun.* —*See* **acceptance** (1), **obedience.**

acquiescent *adjective.* —*See* **obedient, passive, willing.**

acquirable *adjective.* —*See* **available.**

acquire *verb.* —*See* **develop** (1), **get** (1), **learn** (1).

acquirement *noun.* —*See* **accomplishment.**

acquisition *noun.* —*See* **accomplishment, addition** (1).

acquisitive *adjective.* —*See* **curious** (2), **greedy.**

acquisitiveness *noun.* —*See* **greed.**

acquit *verb.* —*See* **act** (1), **clear** (3).

acquittal *noun.* —*See* **exculpation.**

acreage *noun.* —*See* **land, lot** (1).

acres *noun.* —*See* **land.**

acrid *adjective.* —*See* **biting, bitter** (1).

acridity *noun.* —*See* **sarcasm.**

acrimonious *adjective.* —*See* **resentful.**

acrimony *noun.* —*See* **resentment.**

across *adjective.* —*See* **transverse.**

act *noun.* **1.** Something done ▶ action, deed, doing, performance, thing, work. [*Compare* **accomplishment.**] **2.** A display of insincere behavior ▶ acting, affectation, disguise, dissemblance, dissimulation, masquerade, pretense, sham, show, simulation. [*Compare* **affectation, façade, pose.**] **3.** A short theatrical piece within a larger production ▶ sketch, skit. [*Compare* **satire.**] —*See also* **bit**[1] (4), **law** (2).

act *verb.* **1.** To conduct oneself in a specified way ▶ acquit, bear, behave, carry, comport, demean, deport, do, handle, quit. [*Compare* **appear.**] **2.** To behave insincerely or take on as a false appearance ▶ affect, assume, counterfeit, dissemble, dissimulate, fabricate, fake, feign, play-act, pose, pretend, put on, sham, simulate. ***Idioms:*** make believe, put on an act. [*Compare* **disguise, fake.**] **3.** To play the part of ▶ do, dramatize, enact, impersonate, perform, play, play-act, portray, represent. —*See also* **function, stage.**

act on *verb.* —*See* **influence.**

act up *verb.* —*See* **malfunction, misbehave.**

acting *noun.* The art and occupation of an actor ▶ dramatics, stage, theater, theatrics. —*See also* **act** (2).

acting *adjective.* —*See* **temporary** (1).

action *noun.* —*See* **act** (1), **battle, behavior** (1), **lawsuit, motion, plot** (1).

activate *verb.* To set in motion ▶ actuate, spark, start, turn on. [*Compare* **energize, provoke.**] —*See also* **mobilize.**

active *adjective.* In action or full operation ▶ alive, functioning, going, humming, operating, operative, running, ticking, working. *Slang:* purring. ***Idioms:*** going full blast (*or* force *or* tilt), in high gear. [*Compare* **busy.**] —*See also* **energetic.**

activity *noun.* Energetic physical action ▶ exercise, exertion, workout. [*Compare* **energy.**] —*See also* **agitation** (3), **motion.**

actor *or* **actress** *noun.* A theatrical performer ▶ player, thespian, trouper. [*Compare* **fake, lead, mimic.**] —*See also* **participant.**

actual *adjective.* Occurring or existing in act or fact ▶ existent, extant, real, true.

[*Compare* **physical.**] —*See also* **accurate, authentic** (1).

✦ **CORE SYNONYMS:** *actual, real, true, existent.* These adjectives mean not being imaginary but occurring or existing in act or fact. *Actual* means existing and not merely potential or possible: *"rocks, trees . . . the* actual *world"* (Henry David Thoreau). *Real* implies authenticity, genuineness, or factuality: *Don't lose the bracelet; it's made of real gold. She showed real sympathy for my predicament. True* implies consistency with fact, reality, or actuality: *"It is undesirable to believe a proposition when there is no ground whatever for supposing it true"* (Bertrand Russell). *Existent* applies to what has life or being: *Much of the beluga caviar existent in the world is found near the Caspian Sea.*

actuality *noun.* Something demonstrated to exist or known to have existed ▶ event, fact, phenomenon, reality. ***Idioms:*** hard (*or* cold *or* plain) fact. [*Compare* **information.**] —*See also* **certainty, existence.**

actualization *noun.* The condition of being in full force or operation ▶ being, effect, force, realization. [*Compare* **exercise.**]

actualize *verb.* To make real or actual ▶ bring about, make happen, materialize, realize. ***Idioms:*** bring to pass, carry (*or* put) into effect. [*Compare* **effect, produce.**]

actually *adverb.* In point of fact ▶ as a matter of fact, indeed, in fact, really. —*See also* **now** (1), **really.**

actuate *verb.* To set in motion ▶ activate, start, turn on. [*Compare* **energize, provoke.**] —*See also* **use.**

acumen *noun.* —*See* **discernment.**

acuminate *adjective.* —*See* **pointed.**

acumination *noun.* —*See* **point** (1).

acute *adjective.* —*See* **clever** (1), **critical** (2), **high** (3), **pointed, sharp** (3), **urgent** (1).

acutely *adverb.* —*See* **very.**

acuteness *noun.* —*See* **discrimination** (1).

adage *noun.* —*See* **proverb.**

adamant *adjective.* —*See* **stubborn** (1).

adapt *verb.* To make or become suitable to a particular situation or use ▶ acclimate, acclimatize, accommodate, adjust, conform, fashion, fit, remodel, shape, suit, tailor. ***Idioms:*** get used to, learn to live with (*or* accept). [*Compare* **change, convert.**]

✦ **CORE SYNONYMS:** *adapt, accommodate, adjust, conform, fit, tailor.* These verbs mean to make suitable to or consistent with a particular situation or use: *adapted themselves to city life; can't accommodate myself to the new requirements; adjusting their behavior to the rules; conforming her life to accord with her moral principles; fitting the punishment to the crime; tailored the report for the needs of the committee.*

adaptable *adjective.* Capable of adapting or being adapted ▶ adaptive, adjustable, elastic, flexible, malleable, pliable, pliant, supple, versatile. [*Compare* **changeable, obedient.**]

adaptation *noun.* The act or process of adapting ▶ acclimation, acclimatization, accommodation, acculturation, adaption, adjustment, conditioning, conformation. [*Compare* **change.**] —*See also* **variation.**

adapted *adjective.* —*See* **accustomed** (1).

adaption *noun.* —*See* **adaptation.**

adaptive *adjective.* —*See* **adaptable.**

add *verb.* To combine numbers to form a sum ▶ add up, cast, foot (up), sum (up), tot (up), total, totalize. [*Compare* **calculate, count.**] —*See also* **attach** (2).

add up *verb.* —*See* **amount.**

added *adjective.* —*See* **additional.**

addendum *noun.* —*See* **addition** (1).

addiction *noun.* Compulsive physiological and psychological need for a habit-forming substance ▶ craving, compulsion, dependence, drug abuse, enslavement, fixation, susbstance abuse. [*Compare* **custom.**]

addition *noun.* **1.** Something tending to augment something else ▶ accession, acquisition, addendum, augmentation. [*Compare* **attachment.**] **2.** The act or process of adding ▶ summation, sums, totalization. [*Compare* **calculation.**] —*See also* **extension** (2).

additional *adjective.* Being an addition ▶ added, extra, fresh, further, more, new, other, supplemental, supplementary. [*Compare* **auxiliary.**]

additionally *adverb.* In addition ▶ also, besides, further, furthermore, likewise, more, moreover, still, too, yet. ***Idioms:*** as well, for good measure, not to mention, on top of, to boot, to say nothing of.

additive *adjective.* Increasing, as in force, by successive additions ▶ accumulative, cumulative.

additive-free *adjective.* —*See* **natural** (1).

addle *verb.* —*See* **confuse** (1).

addled *or* **addlepated** *adjective.* —*See* **confused** (1).

add-on *noun.* —*See* **enhancement, extension** (2).

address *verb.* **1.** To talk to an audience formally ▶ lecture, prelect, sermonize, speak. [*Compare* **converse.**] **2.** To bring an appeal or request to the attention of ▶ appeal, apply, approach, petition. [*Compare* **appeal, request.**] **3.** To mark a written communication with its destination ▶ direct, superscribe. [*Compare* **ticket.**] —*See also* **apply** (1), **deal** (1), **send** (1).

address *noun.* —*See* **bearing** (1), **home** (1), **speech** (2), **tact.**

addresses *noun.* —*See* **advances.**

adduce *verb.* —*See* **cite.**

adept *adjective.* —*See* **expert.**

adept *noun.* —*See* **expert.**

adeptness *noun.* —*See* **ability** (1).

adequacy *noun.* An adequate quantity ▶ enough, sufficiency.

adequate *adjective.* —*See* **acceptable** (2), **sufficient.**

adhere *verb.* —*See* **bond, follow** (4).

adherence *noun.* —*See* **bond** (3).

adherent *noun.* —*See* **devotee, follower.**

adherents *noun.* The steadfast believers in a faith or cause ▶ congregation, faithful, fold. [*Compare* **follower, assembly.**]

adhesion *noun.* —*See* **bond** (3).

adhesive *adjective.* —*See* **sticky** (1).

ad hoc *adjective.* —*See* **temporary** (2).

adieu *noun.* —*See* **departure.**

ad interim *adjective.* —*See* **temporary** (1).

adipose *adjective.* —*See* **fatty.**

adjacent *adjective.* —*See* **adjoining, close** (1).

adjoin *verb.* To be contiguous or next to ▶ abut, border, bound, butt, flank, impinge, join, meet, neighbor, touch, verge. [*Compare* **border.**] —*See also* **attach** (1).

adjoining *adjective.* Sharing a common boundary ▶ abutting, adjacent, bordering, conjoining, conterminous, contiguous, neighboring, next.

adjourn *verb.* —*See* **defer**[1]**.**

adjournment *noun.* —*See* **delay** (1).

adjudicate *or* **adjudge** *verb.* —*See* **judge.**

adjudication *noun.* —*See* **ruling.**

adjunct *noun.* —*See* **attachment.**

adjure *verb.* —*See* **appeal** (1), **command** (1).

adjust *verb.* To alter for proper or accurate functioning ▶ align, attune, calibrate, fine-tune, fix, modulate, regulate, set, temper, tweak, tune (up). [*Compare* **fix, tinker.**] —*See also* **adapt.**

adjustable *adjective.* —*See* **adaptable.**

adjustment *noun.* —*See* **adaptation.**

adjutant *noun.* —*See* **assistant.**

ad-lib *verb.* —*See* **improvise** (1).

ad-lib *noun.* Something improvised ▶ extemporization, impromptu, improvisation. [*Compare* **makeshift.**]

ad-lib *adjective.* —*See* **extemporaneous.**

admeasure *verb.* —*See* **distribute.**

admeasurement *noun.* —*See* **distribution** (1).

administer *verb.* **1.** To have charge of the affairs of others ▶ administrate, captain, control, dictate, direct, dominate, govern, head, lead, manage, reign, rule, run. ***Idioms:*** be at the helm, be in the driver's seat, hold sway over, hold the reins. [*Compare* **command, supervise.**] **2.** To oversee the provision or execution of ▶ administrate, carry out, dispense, execute. [*Compare* **conduct.**] **3.** To provide as a remedy ▶ apply, dispense, dose, give, medicate, prescribe, treat, vaccinate. *Informal:* doctor. [*Compare* **cure, dress, drug.**] **4.** To mete out by means of some action ▶ deal, deliver, give.

administrable *adjective.* Capable of being governed ▶ controllable, governable, manageable, rulable. [*Compare* **loyal, obedient.**]

administrant *noun.* —*See* **executive.**

administrate *verb.* —*See* **administer** (1), **administer** (2).

administration *noun.* —*See* **exercise** (1), **government** (1), **government** (2), **management.**

administrative *adjective.* Of, for, or relating to administration or administrators ▶ directorial, executive, governmental, managerial, ministerial, organizational, supervisory.

administrator *noun.* —*See* **executive.**

admirable *adjective.* Deserving honor, respect, or admiration ▶ commendable, creditable, deserving, estimable, exemplary, honorable, laudable, meritorious, praiseworthy, reputable, respectable, venerable, worthy. [*Compare* **choice, excellent, honest, marvelous.**]

admiration *noun.* —*See* **esteem.**

admire *verb.* To have a feeling of great awe and rapt admiration ▶ marvel, wonder. ***Idioms:*** be agog (*or* agape *or* awestruck). [*Compare* **gaze, stagger.**] —*See also* **value.**

admirer *noun.* —*See* **beau** (1), **fan**[2].

admissible *adjective.* —*See* **acceptable** (1).

admission *noun.* The act of admitting or the state of being admitted ▶ access, admittance, entrance, entrée, entry, ingress, introduction, intromission. [*Compare* **acceptance, permission.**] —*See also* **acknowledgment** (1).

admit *verb.* To express recognition of ▶ acknowledge, recognize. [*Compare* **confirm.**] —*See also* **accept** (3), **acknowledge** (1), **permit** (3).

admittance *noun.* —*See* **admission.**

admitted *adjective.* —*See* **accepted.**

admix *verb.* —*See* **mix** (1).

admixture *noun.* —*See* **mixture.**

admonish *verb.* —*See* **chastise, warn.**

admonishing *adjective.* Giving warning ▶ admonitory, cautionary, monitory, warning.

admonition *or* **admonishment** *noun.* —*See* **rebuke, warning.**

admonitory *adjective.* Giving warning ▶ admonishing, cautionary, monitory, warning.

ado *noun.* —*See* **agitation** (3).

adolescence *noun.* —*See* **youth** (1).

adolescent *noun.* —*See* **teenager.**

adolescent *adjective.* —*See* **childish.**

adopt *verb.* To take, as another's idea, and make one's own ▶ appropriate, assume, embrace, espouse, take on, take up. [*Compare* **act, seize.**] —*See also* **confirm** (3), **pass** (6).

adoption *noun.* —*See* **acceptance** (1), **confirmation** (1), **exercise** (1).

adorable *adjective.* —*See* **delightful.**

adoration *noun.* The act of adoring, especially reverently ▶ idolization, reverence, veneration, worship. [*Compare* **honor, praise.**] —*See also* **devotion, love** (1).

adore *verb.* **1.** To feel deep devoted love for ▶ love, worship. ***Idioms:*** be soft (*or* stuck *or* sweet) on, place (*or* put) on a pedestal, worship the ground someone walks on. **2.** To like or enjoy enthusiastically ▶ be big on, be crazy about, be hot on, be into, be keen on, be mad about, be nuts about, be wild about, delight (in), dote on (*or* upon), love. *Slang:* eat up, get off on. —*See also* **like[1], revere.**

adorn *verb.* **1.** To furnish with decorations ▶ bedeck, bejewel, deck (out), decorate, dress (up), embellish, emblazon, festoon, garnish, gild, ornament, trim. *Slang:* doll up, gussy up. **2.** To endow with beauty and elegance by way of a notable addition ▶ beautify, embellish, enhance, grace, set off.

adornment *noun.* Something that adorns ▶ decoration, embellishment, garnishment, garniture, ornament, ornamentation, trim, trimming.

adrift *adjective.* —*See* **lost** (1).

adroit *adjective.* —*See* **dexterous.**

adroitness *noun.* —*See* **dexterity.**

adscititious *adjective.* Not part of the real or essential nature of a thing ▶ adventitious, incidental, inessential, supervenient. [*Compare* **irrelevant, unnecessary.**]

adulate *verb.* —*See* **flatter** (1).

adulation *noun.* —*See* **flattery.**

adulator *noun.* —*See* **sycophant.**

adult *adjective.* —*See* **mature.**

adulterant *noun.* —*See* **contaminant.**

adulterate *verb.* —*See* **contaminate, dilute.**

adulterated *adjective.* —*See* **impure** (2).

adulteration *noun.* —*See* **contamination.**

adulterator *noun.* —*See* **contaminant.**

adulterer *noun.* —*See* **philanderer.**

adumbrate *verb.* —*See* **draft** (1), **foreshadow, obscure, shade** (2).

advance *verb.* **1.** To cause to move forward or upward, as toward a goal ▶ drive, forward, foster, further, promote, propel, push. [*Compare* **drive, improve.**] **2.** To move forward ▶ come (along), get along, march, move (up), press (on), proceed, progress, push (on). [*Compare* **plunge.**] —*See also* **lend, offer** (1), **promote** (1), **propose, rise** (3).

advance *noun.* Forward movement ▶ advancement, furtherance, headway, march, procession, progress, progression, stride. [*Compare* **accomplishment, progress.**] —*See also* **increase** (2).

advance *adjective.* Going before ▶ antecedent, anterior, earlier, precedent, preceding, previous, prior.

✚ **CORE SYNONYMS:** *advance, forward, foster, further, promote, propel.* These verbs mean to cause to move forward or upward, as toward a goal: *advance a worthy cause; forwarding their own interests; fostered friendly relations; furthering your career; efforts to promote sales; a speech that propelled the candidate to victory.*

◀ **ANTONYM:** *retard*

---

advanced *adjective.* —*See* **complex** (1), **old** (2), **progressive** (1).

advancement *noun.* A progression upward in rank ▶ elevation, jump, preferment, promotion, raise, rise, upgrade. [*Compare* **increase.**] —*See also* **advance, development, improvement** (1), **progress.**

advances *noun.* Personal approach to gain acquaintance, favor, or an agreement ▶ addresses, approach, attentions, moves, overture, proposition. [*Compare* **feeler, offer.**]

advantage *noun.* **1.** A factor conducive to superiority and success ▶ handicap, head start, odds, start, toehold, vantage. *Informal:* jump. **2.** Something beneficial ▶ avail, benefit, blessing, boon, favor, gain, profit. [*Compare* **help, luck, patronage.**] **3.** A dominating position, as in a conflict ▶ better, bulge, draw, drop, edge, leverage, superiority, upper hand, vantage, whip hand. *Informal:* inside track, jump, leg up. —*See also* **interest** (1), **use** (2).

advantage *verb.* —*See* **profit** (2).

advantageous *adjective.* —*See* **beneficial, profitable.**

advantages *noun.* —*See* **amenities** (1).

advent *noun.* The act of arriving ▶ appearance, arrival, coming. [*Compare* **entrance.**]

adventitious *adjective.* Not part of the real or essential nature of a thing ▶ adscititious, incidental, inessential, supervenient. [*Compare* **irrelevant, unnecessary.**] —*See also* **accidental.**

adventure *noun.* An exciting or unusual undertaking ▶ emprise, enterprise, escapade, experience, odyssey, venture. [*Compare* **feat, journey, trip.**]

adventure *verb.* —*See* **gamble** (2), **venture.**

adventurer *noun.* **1.** One who seeks adventure ▶ daredevil, quester, venturer. [*Compare* **builder.**] **2.** A freelance fighter ▶ mercenary, soldier of fortune. [*Compare* **fighter, soldier.**] **3.** One who speculates for quick profits ▶ gambler, speculator, operator.

adventuresome *adjective.* —*See* **adventurous.**

adventuresomeness *noun.* —*See* **daring.**

adventurous *adjective.* Taking or willing to take risks ▶ adventuresome, audacious, bold, daredevil, daring, enterprising, venturesome, venturous. [*Compare* **brave, rash**[1].] —*See also* **dangerous.**

✚ **CORE SYNONYMS:** *adventurous, adventuresome, audacious, daredevil, daring, venturesome.* These adjectives mean inclined to undertake risks: *adventurous pioneers; an adventuresome prospector; an audacious explorer; a daredevil test pilot; daring acrobats; a venturesome investor.*

---

adventurousness *noun.* —*See* **daring.**

adversarial *adjective.* —*See* **opposing.**

adversary *noun.* —*See* **opponent.**

adverse *adjective.* Not encouraging life or growth ▶ hostile, inhospitable, unfavorable. [*Compare* **severe.**] —*See also* **harmful, opposing, unfavorable** (1).

adversity *noun.* —*See* **misfortune.**

advert *verb.* —*See* **refer** (1).

advertise *verb.* —*See* **announce, promote** (3).

advertisement *noun.* —*See* **publicity.**

advertising *noun.* The act or profession of promoting something, as a product ▶ ballyhooing, billing, promoting, promotion, publicity, publicizing. *Informal:* plugging. —*See also* **publicity.**

advice *noun.* An opinion as to a decision or course of action ▶ counsel, direction, guidance, pointer, recommendation, suggestion, tip. ***Idiom:*** word to the wise. [*Compare* **command, deliberation, warning.**] —*See also* **news.**

✚ **CORE SYNONYMS:** *advice, counsel, recommendation, suggestion.* These nouns denote an opinion as to a decision or course of action: *The speaker had sound advice for the unemployed. I accepted my attorney's counsel. The committee will follow your recommendation. The teacher offered several suggestions for improving my essay.*

---

advisable *adjective.* Worth doing, especially for practical reasons ▶ best, desirable, expedient, politic, practicable, recommendable, well, wisest. [*Compare* **appropriate, sensible.**]

advise *verb.* To give recommendations to someone about a decision or course of action ▶ counsel, direct, guide, recommend, steer. *Informal:* mentor. ***Idiom:*** give a piece of advice. [*Compare* **guide, propose, warn.**] —*See also* **confer** (1), **inform** (1).

✚ **CORE SYNONYMS:** *advise, counsel, direct, recommend.* These verbs mean to suggest a particular decision or course of action: *His friends advised him to go abroad. She will counsel her friend to be prudent. The technician directed them to read the manual. The waiter recommended that I try the halibut.*

---

advised *adjective.* —*See* **deliberate** (2), **informed.**

advisement *noun.* Careful thought ▶ consideration, deliberation, study. [*Compare* **attention, examination, scrutiny.**]

adviser *or* **advisor** *noun.* One who advises another ▶ consultant, counselor, guide, guru, mentor. [*Compare* **assistant, expert, lawyer.**]

advisory *adjective.* Giving advice ▶ consultative, consultatory, consulting, consultive, counseling, recommendatory. [*Compare* **cautionary, educational.**]

advisory *noun.* A report giving information ▶ bulletin, notice. [*Compare* **report, warning.**]

advocacy *noun.* —*See* **patronage** (1).

advocate *noun.* One that argues for or defends a cause ▶ booster, champion, defender, promoter, proponent, supporter, upholder, vindicator. [*Compare* **lawyer, patron, sponsor.**] —*See also* **representative.**

advocate *verb.* —*See* **support** (1).

aegis *noun.* —*See* **patronage** (1).

aeon *noun. See* **eon.**

aerate *verb.* To expose to circulating air ▶ air, freshen, ventilate, wind.

aerial *adjective.* Of or relating to air ▶ airy, atmospheric, pneumatic. —*See also* **high** (1).

aesthetic *or* **esthetic** *adjective.* Relating to or appreciative of the arts ▶ artistic, creative. *Informal:* artsy, arty. —*See also* **cultural.**

affability *noun.* —*See* **amiability.**

affable *adjective.* Characterized by kindness and warm, unaffected courtesy ▶ courteous, gracious, hospitable. [*Compare* **attentive, courteous.**] —*See also* **amiable.**

affair *noun.* **1.** Something that concerns or involves one personally ▶ business, concern, interest, lookout. **2.** Something to be done, considered, or dealt with ▶ business, matter, thing. [*Compare* **business, problem, task.**] —*See also* **love** (3), **party.**

✦ **CORE SYNONYMS:** *affair, business, concern, lookout.* These nouns denote something that involves one personally: *I won't comment on that; it's not my affair. Please mind your own business. This situation is none of your concern. It's your lookout to file your application on time.*

---

affect[1] *verb.* —*See* **influence, move** (1).

affect *noun.* —*See* **emotion.**

affect[2] *verb.* —*See* **act** (2).

affectation *noun.* Behavior that is assumed rather than natural ▶ affectedness, artificiality, air, airs, mannerism, pose, pretense, simulation, theatricism. [*Compare* **façade, posture.**] —*See also* **act** (2).

✦ **CORE SYNONYMS:** *affectation, pose, air, airs, mannerism.* These nouns refer to personal behavior assumed for effect. An *affectation* is artificial behavior, often adopted in imitation of someone, that is perceived as being unnatural: "*His* [Arthur Rubinstein's] *playing stripped away . . . the affectations and exaggerations that characterized Chopin interpretation before his arrival*" (Michael Kimmelman). *Pose* denotes an attitude adopted to call favorable attention to oneself: *His humility is only a pose. Air,* meaning a distinctive but intangible quality, does not always imply sham: *The director had an air of authority.* The plural form *airs,* however, suggests affectation and self-importance: *The movie star was putting on airs. Mannerism* denotes an idiosyncratic trait or quirk, often one that others find obtrusive and distracting: *His mannerism of closing his eyes as he talked made it seem as if he were deep in thought.*

---

affected *adjective.* —*See* **artificial** (2), **concerned.**

affectedness *noun.* —*See* **affectation.**

affecting *adjective.* Exciting a deep, usually somber response ▶ heart-rending, impressive, moving, poignant, stirring, touching. [*Compare* **pitiful.**]

✤ **CORE SYNONYMS:** *affecting, moving, stirring, poignant, touching.* These adjectives mean exciting or capable of exciting a deep, usually somber emotion. *Affecting* applies especially to what is heart-rending or bittersweet: *an affecting photo of the hostages' release. Moving* is the most general of these terms: *"A . . . widow . . . has laid her case of destitution before him in a very moving letter"* (Nathaniel Hawthorne). Something *stirring* excites strong, turbulent, but not unpleasant feelings: *a stirring speech about patriotism. Poignant* suggests the evocation of keen, painful emotion: *"Poignant grief cannot endure forever"* (W.H. Hudson). *Touching* emphasizes sympathy or tenderness: *a touching eulogy.*

affection *noun.* —*See* **emotion, love** (1).

affectional *or* **affective** *adjective.* Relating to, arising from, or appealing to the emotions ▶ emotional, emotive.

affectionate *adjective.* Feeling or expressing fond feelings or affection ▶ caring, devoted, doting, fond, loving, tender.

affectivity *noun.* —*See* **emotion.**

affectless *adjective.* —*See* **expressionless.**

affianced *adjective.* —*See* **engaged.**

affidavit *noun.* A formal declaration of truth or fact given under oath ▶ deposition, testimony, witness.

affiliate *verb.* —*See* **associate** (1), **pass** (6).

affiliate *noun.* —*See* **associate** (1), **branch** (3).

affiliation *noun.* —*See* **association** (1).

affinity *noun.* —*See* **inclination** (1), **likeness** (1).

affirm *verb.* —*See* **assert, confirm** (1), **confirm** (3).

affirmation *noun.* —*See* **assertion, confirmation** (1).

affirmative *adjective.* —*See* **favorable** (2).

affirmative *adverb.* —*See* **yes.**

affix *verb.* —*See* **attach** (1), **attach** (2), **fix** (3).

afflict *verb.* To cause great pain or suffering to ▶ agonize, excruciate, kill, pain, plague, rack, scourge, smite, strike, torment, torture, wound. [*Compare* **distress, hurt, traumatize.**]

✤ **CORE SYNONYMS:** *afflict, agonize, rack, torment, torture.* These verbs mean to bring great pain or suffering to someone: *He was afflicted with arthritis. I was agonized to see her suffering. The patient was racked with cancer. She is tormented by migraine headaches. The refugee was tortured by painful memories.*

afflicted *adjective.* —*See* **miserable.**

affliction *noun.* —*See* **burden**[1] (1), **curse** (3), **distress, sickness, trial** (1).

afflictive *adjective.* —*See* **painful.**

affluence *noun.* —*See* **wealth.**

affluent *adjective.* —*See* **rich** (1).

afford *verb.* —*See* **offer** (2).

affray *noun.* —*See* **fight** (1).

affright *verb.* —*See* **frighten.**

affright *noun.* —*See* **fear.**

affront *verb.* —*See* **insult, offend** (1).

affront *noun.* —*See* **disrespect, indignity.**

afghan *noun.* —*See* **wrap.**

aficionado *noun.* —*See* **fan**[2]**.**

afield *adverb.* Not in the right way or on the proper course ▶ amiss, astray, awry, wrong.

afire *or* **aflame** *adjective.* —*See* **burning.**

a fortiori *adverb.* —*See* **even** (2).

afraid *adjective.* Filled with fear or terror ▶ aghast, alarmed, apprehensive, fearful, fearsome, frightened, funky, horrified, panicky, panic-stricken, petrified, scared, terrified, timid, timorous, tremulous. *Informal:* spooked. *Slang:* chicken. ***Idioms:*** frightened (*or* scared) to death, scared stiff. [*Compare* **fearful.**]

✦ **CORE SYNONYMS:** *afraid, apprehensive, fearful, frightened, scared.* These adjectives mean filled with fear or terror: *afraid of snakes; feeling apprehensive before surgery; fearful of criticism; frightened by thunder; children who were scared of the dark.*

afresh *adverb.* —*See* **anew.**

after *adverb.* —*See* **later.**

after *adjective.* Following something else in time ▶ later, posterior, subsequent, ulterior. [*Compare* **following.**]

afterlife *noun.* —*See* **immortality.**

aftermath *noun.* —*See* **effect** (1).

aftermost *adjective.* —*See* **last**[1] (2).

afterward *or* **afterwards** *adverb.* —*See* **later.**

afterworld *noun.* —*See* **eternity** (2).

again *adverb.* —*See* **anew.**

against *adjective.* —*See* **indisposed.**

agape *adjective.* —*See* **open** (1).

age *noun.* **1.** Old age ▶ agedness, elderliness, maturity, old age, senectitude, senescence, seniority, years. [*Compare* **senility.**] **2.** A particular time notable for its distinctive characteristics ▶ day, epoch, era, period, time, times.

age *verb.* To grow old ▶ get along, get on. ***Idiom:*** advance in years. —*See also* **mature.**

✦ **CORE SYNONYMS:** *age, period, epoch, era.* These nouns refer to a particular time notable for its distinctive characteristics. *Age* is the most general: *the Elizabethan Age; the age of Newton; the Iron Age. Period* denotes the prevalence of a specified culture, ideology, or technology (*artifacts of the pre-Columbian period*) or a distinct developmental phase (*Picasso's blue period*). *Epoch* refers to a time that is regarded as being remarkable or memorable: "*We enter on an epoch of constitutional retrogression*" (John R. Green). An *era* is a period of time notable because of new or different aspects or events: "*How many a man has dated a new era in his life from the reading of a book*" (Henry David Thoreau).

aged *adjective.* Brought to full flavor and richness by aging ▶ mellow, ripe. [*Compare* **mature.**] —*See also* **old** (2).

agedness *noun.* —*See* **age** (1).

ageism *noun.* Discrimination based on age ▶ discrimination, intolerance, prejudice. [*Compare* **hate.**]

ageless *adjective.* Existing unchanged forever ▶ eternal, timeless. [*Compare* **endless.**] —*See also* **vintage.**

✦ **CORE SYNONYMS:** *ageless, eternal, timeless.* These adjectives mean existing unchanged forever: *the ageless themes of love and revenge; eternal truths; timeless beauty.*

agency *noun.* —*See* **agent, branch** (3).

agenda *noun.* —*See* **list**[1]**, program** (1).

agent *noun.* That by which something is done or caused ▶ agency, channel, instrument, instrumentality, intermediary, means, mechanism, medium, organ. [*Compare* **go-between, representative.**] —*See also* **spy.**

age-old *adjective.* —*See* **old** (1).

ages *noun.* A long time ▶ blue moon, eon, eternity, forever, long, years. ***Idioms:*** dog's age, coon's age, donkey's years, forever and a day, forever and ever, a month (*or* week) of Sundays.

agglomerate *verb.* —*See* **accumulate.**

agglomeration *noun.* The act of accumulating ▶ accumulation, buildup, conglomeration. —*See also* **heap** (1).

aggrandize *verb.* —*See* **exaggerate, exalt, increase.**

aggrandizement *noun.* —*See* **exaltation, increase** (1).

aggravate *verb.* —*See* **annoy, intensify.**

aggravation *noun.* —*See* **annoyance** (1), **annoyance** (2).

aggregate *noun.* —*See* **total, whole.**

aggregate *verb.* —*See* **accumulate, amount.**

aggregation *noun.* —*See* **accumulation** (1).

aggress *verb.* —*See* **attack** (1).

aggression *noun.* Hostile or warlike behavior or attitude ▶ aggressiveness, bellicoseness, belllicosity, belligerence, combativeness, contentiousness, hostility, militance, pugnaciousness, pugnacity, saber-rattling, truculence, truculency, warmongering. [*Compare* **hate.**] —*See also* **attack.**

aggressive *adjective.* Inclined to act in a way that shows hostility or an eagerness to fight ▶ bellicose, belligerent, combative, contentious, hawkish, hostile, militant, pugnacious, quarrelsome, scrappy, truculent, warlike, warmongering. —*See also* **assertive.**

✚ **CORE SYNONYMS:** *aggressive, belligerent, bellicose, pugnacious, contentious, quarrelsome.* These adjectives mean having or showing hostility or an eagerness to fight. *Aggressive* and *belligerent* refer to a tendency to hostile behavior: *The aggressive prisoner was placed in a solitary cell. A belligerent reporter badgered the politician. Bellicose* and *pugnacious* suggest a natural disposition to fight: *"All successful newspapers are ceaselessly querulous and bellicose"* (H.L. Mencken). *A good litigator needs a pugnacious intellect. Contentious* implies chronic argumentativeness: *"His style has been described variously as abrasive and contentious, overbearing and pompous"* (Victor Merina). *Quarrelsome* suggests bad temper and a perverse readiness to bicker: *"The men gave him much room, for he was notorious as a quarrelsome person when drunk"* (Stephen Crane).

aggressiveness *noun.* —*See* **aggression.**

aggressor *noun.* One who starts a hostile action ▶ assailant, assailer, assaulter, attacker, provoker. [*Compare* **opponent.**]

aggrieve *verb.* —*See* **distress.**

aghast *adjective.* —*See* **afraid.**

agile *adjective.* —*See* **dexterous.**

agility *or* **agileness** *noun.* The quality or state of being agile ▶ deftness, dexterity, dexterousness, nimbleness, quickness, spryness, swiftness. [*Compare* **energy, haste.**]

aging *adjective.* —*See* **old** (2).

agitate *verb.* **1.** To cause to move to and fro violently ▶ churn, convulse, rock, shake, whip, worry. [*Compare* **disorder, disturb, upset.**] **2.** To impair or destroy the composure of ▶ bewilder, bother, discompose, disorient, disquiet, distract, disturb, flurry, fluster, jar, perturb, rock, ruffle, shake (up), toss, unsettle, upset. *Informal:* rattle, throw (off). ***Idioms:*** throw out of kilter (*or* whack). [*Compare* **confuse, distress, nonplus.**] —*See also* **arouse.**

✚ **CORE SYNONYMS:** *agitate, churn, convulse, rock, shake.* These verbs mean to cause to move to and fro violently: *land agitated by tremors; a storm churning the waves; buildings and streets convulsed by an explosion; a hurricane rocking trees and houses; an earthquake that shook the ground.*

agitated *adjective.* Marked by unrest or disturbance ▶ convulsed, disturbed, flustered, stormy, tempestuous, tumultuous, turbulent, restless, unsettled. ***Idioms:*** all shook up, all worked up, in a ferment (*or* spin *or* state *or* stir). [*Compare* **confused, disorderly, unruly.**] —*See also* **anxious.**

agitating *adjective.* —*See* **disturbing.**

agitation *noun.* **1.** A condition of being agitated or disturbed; a confused or emotional situation ▶ commotion, convulsion, disorder, disturbance, ferment, helter-skelter, ruckus, scene, stir, Sturm und Drang, tempest, tumult, turbulence, turmoil, unrest, uproar. *Informal:* flap, to-do. *Slang:* hoo-ha, stink. [*Compare* **disorder, display, restlessness.**] **2.** A state of discomposure ▶ disconcertment, dither, fluster, flutter, hurry-scurry, perturbation, tumult, turmoil, twitter, upset. *Informal:* lather, stew. *Slang:* tizzy. [*Compare* **anxiety, confusion, worry.**] **3.** Agitated, excited movement and activity ▶ ado, bustle, commotion, excitement, flurry, fuss, stir, whirl, whirlpool. *Informal:* state.

agitator *noun.* One who agitates, especially politically ▶ firebrand, fomenter, incendiary, inciter, instigator, malcontent, rabble-rouser, troublemaker. [*Compare* **aggressor, extremist.**]

agnate *adjective.* —*See* **kindred.**

agnostic *noun.* —*See* **skeptic.**

ago *adjective.* —*See* **past.**

agog *adjective.* —*See* **eager.**

agonize *verb.* —*See* **afflict, brood.**

agonizing *adjective.* —*See* **tormenting.**

agony *noun.* —*See* **distress.**

agrarian *adjective.* —*See* **country.**

agree *verb.* **1.** To be compatible, suitable, or in correspondence ▶ accord, belong, check, chime, comport, conform, consist, correspond, dovetail, fit, go (together), harmonize, match (up), square, tally. *Informal:* jibe. [*Compare* **suit.**] **2.** To come to an understanding or to terms ▶ accord, coincide, concur, get together, harmonize. ***Idioms:*** be of one mind, see eye to eye. —*See also* **assent.**

✚ **CORE SYNONYMS:** *agree, conform, harmonize, accord, correspond, square.* These verbs all indicate a compatibility between people or things. *Agree* may indicate mere lack of incongruity or discord, although it often suggests acceptance of ideas or actions and thus accommodation: *We finally agreed on a price for the house. Conform* stresses correspondence in essence or basic characteristics, sometimes as a result of established standards: *Students are required to conform to the rules. Harmonize* implies the combination or arrangement of elements in a pleasing whole: *The print on the curtains harmonized with the striped sofa. Accord* implies harmony, unity, or consistency, as in essential nature: "*The creed* [upon which America was founded] *was widely seen as both progressive and universalistic: It accorded with the future, and it was open to all*" (Everett Carll Ladd). *Correspond* refers to similarity in form, nature, function, character, or structure: *The Diet in Japan corresponds to the American Congress. Square* stresses exact agreement: *The testimony of the witness squared with the plaintiff's version of the events.*

---

agreeability *noun.* —*See* **amiability.**

agreeable *adjective.* In keeping with one's needs or expectations ▶ accordant, compatible, concordant, conformable, congenial, congruous, consistent, consonant, correspondent, corresponding, harmonious. [*Compare* **fit, similar.**] —*See also* **amiable, favorable** (2), **obliging, pleasant, willing.**

agreeableness *noun.* —*See* **amiability.**

agreed *adverb.* —*See* **yes.**

agreeing *adjective.* —*See* **unanimous.**

agreement *noun.* **1.** An often written acceptance of terms between parties ▶ accord, arrangement, bargain, bond, charter, compact, contract, convention, covenant, deal, pact, understanding. [*Compare* **compromise.**] **2.** The act or state of agreeing or conforming ▶ accord, accordance, concord, concordance, chime, concert, conformance, conformation, conformity, congruence, congruity, consensus, consonance, correspondence, harmonization, harmony, keeping, rapport, tune, unanimity, unanimousness, unison, unity. ***Idiom:*** meeting of the minds. [*Compare* **understanding.**] —*See also* **acceptance** (1), **treaty.**

✚ **CORE SYNONYMS:** *agreement, bargain, compact, contract, covenant, deal.* These nouns denote an acceptance, often bound in writing, of terms between parties: *signed the purchase and sale agreement; kept my end of the bargain and mowed the lawn; made a compact to correspond regularly; a legally binding contract to install new windows; a cov-*

enant for mutual defense; ignored the requests that weren't part of the deal.

---

ahead *adverb.* —*See* **early, forward.**

aid *noun.* —*See* **assistant, help, relief** (2).

aid *verb.* —*See* **help, oblige** (1).

aide *noun.* —*See* **assistant.**

ail *verb.* —*See* **worry.**

ailing *adjective.* —*See* **sick** (1).

ailment *noun.* —*See* **disease, sickness.**

aim *verb.* **1.** To direct something, such as a weapon or a remark, often toward a target ▶ cast, direct, head, lay, level, point, set, train, turn, zero in. [*Compare* **guide.**] **2.** To strive toward a goal ▶ aspire, seek. ***Idioms:*** go (*or* grab) for the brass ring, keep one's eyes on the prize, set one's sights on. —*See also* **bear** (5), **intend.**

aim *noun.* —*See* **intention, thrust.**

✚ **CORE SYNONYMS:** *aim, direct, level, point, train.* These verbs mean to turn something toward an intended goal or target: *aimed the camera at the guests; directing my eyes on the book; leveled criticism at the administration; pointing a finger at the suspect; trained the gun on the intruder.*

---

aimless *adjective.* Without aim, purpose, or intent ▶ desultory, directionless, errant, pointless, purposeless, rambling, rudderless, wandering, undirected. [*Compare* **erratic, futile, random.**]

air *noun.* **1.** The gaseous mixture enveloping the earth ▶ atmosphere, ether. **2.** The celestial regions as seen from the earth ▶ firmament, heavens, sky. ***Idiom:*** wild blue yonder. **3.** A general impression produced by a predominant quality or characteristic ▶ ambiance, atmosphere, aura, feel, feeling, mood, smell, tone. *Slang:* vibe, vibration. [*Compare* **environment, shade.**] —*See also* **affectation, bearing** (1), **melody, wind[1].**

air *verb.* **1.** To expose to circulating air ▶ aerate, freshen, ventilate, wind. **2.** To utter publicly ▶ disclose, divulge, express, put, state, vent, ventilate, voice. ***Idiom:*** come out with. [*Compare* **announce, say.**]

✚ **CORE SYNONYMS:** *air, vent, express, voice.* These verbs mean to utter publically. To *air* is to show off one's feelings, beliefs, or ideas: *They aired their differences during dinner.* To *vent* is to unburden oneself of a strong pent-up emotion: *"She was jealous . . . and glad of any excuse to vent her pique"* (Edward G.E.L. Bulwer-Lytton). *Express,* a more comprehensive term, refers to both verbal and nonverbal communication: *found the precise words to express her idea; expressed his affection with a hug; "expressing emotion in the form of art"* (T.S. Eliot). *Voice* denotes the expression of outlook or viewpoint: *The lawyers voiced their satisfaction with the verdict.*

---

airing *noun.* A show that is aired on television or radio ▶ broadcast, program. —*See also* **expression** (1).

airless *adjective.* **1.** Lacking fresh air ▶ close, stale, stifling, stuffy, suffocating, unventilated. [*Compare* **moldy.**] **2.** Lacking movement of air ▶ breathless, breezeless, stagnant, still, windless. ***Idioms:*** dead (*or* flat) calm. [*Compare* **still.**]

airs *noun.* —*See* **affectation.**

airy *adjective.* **1.** Of or relating to air ▶ aerial, atmospheric, pneumatic. **2.** Having little weight; not heavy ▶ fluffy, light, lightweight, weightless. ***Idioms:*** light as air (*or* a feather). [*Compare* **immaterial.**] **3.** Exposed to or characterized by the presence of freely circulating air or wind ▶ blowy, breezy, gusty, ventilated, windblown, windswept, windy. —*See also* **high** (1), **lighthearted, sheer[2].**

ajar *adjective.* —*See* **open** (1).

akin *adjective.* —*See* **kindred, like[2].**

alabaster *adjective.* —*See* **fair[1]** (3).

alacrity *noun.* —*See* **haste** (1).

à la mode *adjective.* —*See* **fashionable.**

alarm *noun.* A signal that warns of imminent danger ▶ alarum, alert, heads up, high sign, red flag, warning. [*Compare* **omen.**] —*See also* **fear.**
alarm *verb.* —*See* **dismay, frighten, warn.**
alarmed *adjective.* —*See* **afraid.**
alarming *adjective.* —*See* **fearful.**
alarmist *noun.* One who needlessly alarms others ▶ Chicken Little, panicmonger, scaremonger. ***Idiom:*** one who cries wolf. [*Compare* **pessimist.**]
alcoholic *adjective.* —*See* **hard** (3).
alcoholic *noun.* —*See* **drunkard.**
alehouse *noun.* —*See* **bar** (2).
alert *adjective.* Vigilantly attentive ▶ attentive, bright-eyed, heedful, intent, observant, open-eyed, regardful, vigilant, wakeful, wary, watchful, wide-awake. ***Idioms:*** all ears (*or* eyes), on guard, on one's toes, on the ball, on the lookout, on the qui vive. [*Compare* **aware, wary.**] —*See also* **clever** (1).
alert *noun.* —*See* **alarm.**
alert *verb.* —*See* **warn.**

✚ CORE SYNONYMS: *alert, heedful, watchful, vigilant.* These adjectives mean very attentive. *I remained alert to career opportunities. Please be heedful of the traffic signs. The watchful parents protected their toddler. The ranger kept a vigilant eye out for forest fires.*

---

alertness *noun.* The condition of being alert ▶ caution, vigilance, wakefulness, wariness, watchfulness. [*Compare* **care.**]
alibi *noun.* —*See* **excuse** (1).
alien *adjective.* Not part of the essential nature of a thing ▶ foreign, extraneous, extrinsic. [*Compare* **irrelevant.**] —*See also* **foreign** (1).
alien *noun.* —*See* **foreigner.**
alienate *verb.* —*See* **estrange, isolate** (1).
alienation *noun.* —*See* **breach** (2), **grant, isolation.**
alight[1] *verb.* To come ashore from a seacraft ▶ debark, disembark, land, light. —*See also* **land** (2).
alight on *or* **upon** *verb.* —*See* **encounter** (1).
alight[2] *adjective.* —*See* **burning.**
align *verb.* —*See* **adjust, ally, equalize, even, line.**
alignment *verb.* —*See* **arrangement** (1).
alike *adjective.* —*See* **like**[2]**.**
alikeness *noun.* —*See* **likeness** (1).
aliment *noun.* —*See* **food.**
alimentary *adjective.* —*See* **nutritious.**
alimentation *noun.* —*See* **living.**
alimony *noun.* —*See* **living.**
alive *adjective.* Having or exhibiting existence or life ▶ animate, animated, around, breathing, existent, existing, extant, live, living, subsisting, vital. ***Idioms:*** alive and kicking, among the living. [*Compare* **lively.**] —*See also* **active, aware, busy** (2).

✚ CORE SYNONYMS: *alive, live, living, animate, animated, vital.* These adjectives mean possessed of or exhibiting life. *Alive, live,* and *living* refer principally to organisms that are not dead: *the happiest person alive; a live canary; living plants. Animate* applies to living animal as distinct from living plant life: *Something animate was moving inside the box. Animated* suggests renewed life, vigor, or spirit: *The argument became very animated. Vital* refers to what is characteristic of or necessary to the continuation of life: *You must eat to maintain vital energy.*

◀ ANTONYM: *dead*

---

alky *noun.* —*See* **drunkard.**
all *adjective.* —*See* **complete** (1).
all *noun.* —*See* **whole.**
all *adverb.* —*See* **completely** (1).
all-around *adjective.* —*See* **general** (2), **versatile.**
allay *verb.* —*See* **pacify, relieve** (1).
allegation *noun.* —*See* **assertion.**
allege *verb.* —*See* **assert.**
alleged *adjective.* —*See* **supposed.**
allegiance *noun.* —*See* **fidelity.**

allegiant *adjective.* —*See* **faithful.**
allegorize *verb.* —*See* **embody** (1).
allegory *noun.* —*See* **embodiment.**
alleviate *verb.* —*See* **relieve** (1).
alleviation *noun.* —*See* **relief** (1).
alley *noun.* —*See* **way** (2).
alliance *noun.* An association for a common cause or interest ▶ bloc, cartel, coalition, combination, combine, confederacy, confederation, consortium, faction, federation, league, monopoly, organization, party, pool, ring, syndicate, trust, union. [*Compare* **assembly, band**[2]**, force, union.**] —*See also* **association** (1).
allied *adjective.* Closely connected by or as if by a treaty ▶ aligned, confederated, federated, unified. —*See also* **kindred.**
all-inclusive *adjective.* —*See* **detailed, general** (2).
allocate *verb.* —*See* **appropriate, distribute.**
allocation *noun.* —*See* **allotment, distribution** (1).
allocution *noun.* —*See* **speech** (2).
allot *verb.* —*See* **appropriate, distribute.**
allotment *noun.* That which is allotted ▶ allocation, allowance, apportionment, distribution, division, dole, lot, measure, part, portion, quantum, quota, ration, share, split. *Informal:* cut. *Slang:* divvy. [*Compare* **cut.**] —*See also* **arrangement** (1), **distribution** (1).
all-out *adjective.* —*See* **intense, utter**[2]**.**
all-overs *noun.* —*See* **jitters.**
allow *verb.* —*See* **acknowledge** (1), **distribute, permit** (1), **permit** (2), **permit** (3).
allowable *adjective.* —*See* **acceptable** (1).
allowance *noun.* —*See* **allotment, permission.**
alloy *noun.* —*See* **mixture.**
  alloy *verb.* —*See* **mix** (1).
alloyed *adjective.* —*See* **impure** (2).
all-purpose *adjective.* —*See* **versatile.**
all right *adjective.* —*See* **acceptable** (2), **healthy.**
  all right *adverb.* —*See* **yes.**
all-right *adjective.* —*See* **good** (1).
all-round *adjective.* —*See* **general** (2), **versatile.**
all the same *adverb.* —*See* **still** (1).
allude to *verb.* —*See* **hint, refer** (1).
allure *verb.* —*See* **attract, seduce.**
  allure *noun.* —*See* **attraction.**
allurement *noun.* —*See* **attraction, lure** (1).
allurer *noun.* —*See* **seducer** (1).
alluring *adjective.* —*See* **desirable, seductive.**
allusion *noun.* —*See* **hint** (2).
allusive *adjective.* Tending to bring a memory, mood, or image, for example, subtly or indirectly to mind ▶ connotative, evocative, impressionistic, reminiscent, suggestive. [*Compare* **designative, symbolic.**]
alluvion *noun.* —*See* **flood.**
alluvium *noun.* —*See* **deposit** (2).
ally *verb.* To be formally associated, as by treaty ▶ align, confederate, federate, league. ***Idioms:*** band together, join forces, team up. [*Compare* **combine.**] —*See also* **associate** (1).
  ally *noun.* —*See* **associate** (1).
almost *adverb.* —*See* **approximately.**
alms *noun.* —*See* **donation.**
almsman *or* **almswoman** *noun.* —*See* **beggar** (1).
aloha *interjection.* —*See* **hello.**
alone *adverb.* Without the presence or aid of another ▶ single-handedly, singly, solely, solitarily, solo. ***Idioms:*** by oneself, all by one's lonesome. [*Compare* **separately.**] —*See also* **solely.**
  alone *adjective.* —*See* **solitary, unique.**
aloneness *noun.* —*See* **solitude.**
aloof *adjective.* —*See* **cool, detached** (1).
aloofness *noun.* —*See* **apathy, detachment** (2), **inhospitality.**
already *adverb.* —*See* **earlier** (1).
also *adverb.* —*See* **additionally.**
alter *verb.* —*See* **change** (1), **change** (2), **distort, sterilize** (2).

alterable *adjective.* —*See* **changeable** (1).

alteration *noun.* —*See* **change** (1), **variation.**

altercate *verb.* —*See* **argue** (1).

altercation *noun.* —*See* **argument.**

alter ego *noun.* —*See* **friend.**

alternate *verb.* To take turns ▶ interchange, rotate, shift.

alternate *noun.* —*See* **substitute.**

alternation *noun.* Occurrence in successive turns ▶ interchange, rotation, shift.

alternative *noun.* —*See* **choice, variation.**

altitude *noun.* The distance of something from a given level ▶ elevation, height, loftiness, tallness. [*Compare* **ascent.**]

alto *adjective.* —*See* **low** (1).

altogether *adverb.* —*See* **completely** (1).

altruism *noun.* —*See* **benevolence.**

altruistic *adjective.* Of or concerned with charity ▶ benevolent, charitable, eleemosynary, philanthropic. —*See also* **benevolent** (1).

always *adverb.* —*See* **forever.**

amalgam *or* **amalgamation** *noun.* —*See* **mixture.**

amalgamate *verb.* —*See* **associate** (1), **mix** (1).

amaranthine *adjective.* —*See* **endless** (2).

amass *verb.* —*See* **accumulate.**

amassment *noun.* —*See* **accumulation** (1).

amateur *noun.* One lacking professional skill and ease in a particular pursuit ▶ dabbler, dilettante, layperson, nonprofessional, smatterer, uninitiate. *Informal:* duffer. [*Compare* **beginner, fan.**]

✚ **CORE SYNONYMS:** *amateur, dabbler, dilettante, nonprofessional.* These nouns mean one engaging in a pursuit but lacking professional skill: *a musician who is a gifted amateur, not a professional; a dabbler in the stock market; a sculptor but a mere dilettante; a nonprofessional athlete.*

◀ **ANTONYM:** *professional*

amateurish *adjective.* Lacking the required professional skill ▶ crude, dilettante, dilettantish, inexpert, nonprofessional, unprofessional, unskilled, unskillful. [*Compare* **inefficient.**]

amativeness *noun.* —*See* **desire** (2), **love** (2).

amatory *adjective.* —*See* **erotic.**

amaze *verb.* —*See* **surprise.**

amaze *noun.* —*See* **wonder** (1).

amazement *noun.* —*See* **wonder** (1).

amazing *adjective.* —*See* **astonishing.**

ambassador *noun.* —*See* **representative.**

ambiance *or* **ambience** *noun.* —*See* **air** (3), **environment** (2).

ambiguity *noun.* An expression or term liable to more than one interpretation ▶ double-entendre, equivocality, equivocation, equivoque, tergiversation. —*See also* **equivocation, vagueness.**

ambiguous *adjective.* **1.** Lacking certainty or clarity ▶ abstruse, borderline, chancy, clouded, cryptic, doubtful, dubious, dubitable, enigmatic, equivocal, inconclusive, indecisive, indeterminate, obscure, perplexing, problematic, questionable, recondite, uncertain, unclear, unsure, woolly. *Informal:* iffy. ***Idioms:*** at issue, in doubt, in question, up in the air. [*Compare* **indefinite, unclear.**] **2.** Liable to more than one interpretation ▶ ambivalent, cloudy, double-edged, equivocal, inexplicit, nebulous, obscure, two-edged, uncertain, unclear, vague.

✚ **CORE SYNONYMS:** *ambiguous, equivocal, obscure, recondite, abstruse, cryptic, enigmatic.* These adjectives mean lacking certainty or clarity. *Ambiguous* indicates the presence of two or more possible meanings: *Frustrated by ambiguous instructions, I was unable to assemble the toy.* Something *equivocal* is unclear or misleading: "*The polling had* *a complex and equivocal message for potential female candidates"* (David S. Broder). *Obscure* implies lack of clarity of expression: *Some say that Kafka's style is obscure and complex. Recondite* and *abstruse* connote the erudite obscurity of the scholar: *"some recondite problem in historiography"* (Walter Laqueur). *The students avoided the professor's abstruse lectures. Cryptic* suggests a sometimes deliberately puzzling terseness: *The new insurance policy is full of cryptic terms.* Something *enigmatic* is mysterious and puzzling: *The biography struggles to make sense of the artist's enigmatic life.*

---

ambiguousness *noun.* —*See* **vagueness.**

ambit *noun.* —*See* **circumference, range** (1).

ambition *noun.* A strong desire to achieve something ▶ ambitiousness, aspiration, emulation. [*Compare* **drive, enthusiasm, thirst.**] —*See also* **dream** (3), **intention.**

ambitious *adjective.* Full of ambition ▶ aspiring, desirous, determined, driven, emulous, enterprising, highflying, hustling, overambitious. ***Idioms:*** on the fast track, on the make. [*Compare* **assertive, diligent.**]

ambitiousness *noun.* A strong desire to achieve something ▶ ambition, aspiration, emulation. [*Compare* **drive, enthusiasm, thirst.**]

ambivalent *adjective.* —*See* **ambiguous** (2), **doubtful** (2).

amble *verb.* —*See* **stroll.**

amble *noun.* —*See* **walk** (1).

ambrosial *adjective.* —*See* **delicious.**

ambulance chaser *noun.* —*See* **lawyer.**

ambulate *verb.* —*See* **walk.**

ambuscade *verb.* —*See* **ambush.**

ambuscade *noun.* An attack or stratagem for capturing or tricking an unsuspecting person ▶ ambush, trap. [*Compare* **deceit, trick.**]

ambush *verb.* To attack suddenly and without warning ▶ ambuscade, bushwhack, raid, surprise, waylay. ***Idioms:*** lay (*or* set) a trap for, lie in wait for. [*Compare* **attack, catch.**] —*See also* **lurk.**

ambush *noun.* An attack or stratagem for capturing or tricking an unsuspecting person ▶ ambuscade, trap. [*Compare* **deceit, trick.**]

✦ CORE SYNONYMS: *ambush, ambuscade, bushwhack, waylay.* These verbs mean to attack suddenly and without warning, especially from a concealed place: *guerrillas ambushing a platoon; highway robbers ambuscading a stagecoach; a patrol bushwhacked by poachers; a truck waylaid by robbers.*

---

ameliorate *verb.* —*See* **improve.**

amelioration *noun.* —*See* **improvement** (1), **progress.**

amenability *or* **amenableness** *noun.* —*See* **obedience, openness, responsibility.**

amenable *adjective.* —*See* **liable** (1), **obedient, receptive, willing.**

amend *verb.* —*See* **correct** (1), **improve, revise.**

amendatory *adjective.* —*See* **corrective.**

amendment *noun.* —*See* **improvement** (1), **revision.**

amends *noun.* —*See* **compensation.**

amenities *noun.* **1.** Anything that increases physical comfort ▶ advantages, comforts, conveniences, facilities, resources, services. **2.** Social courtesies ▶ civility, courteousness, courtesy, graciousness, pleasantry, politeness, proprieties, urbanity. [*Compare* **amiability, manners, tact.**]

✦ CORE SYNONYMS: *amenities, comforts, conveniences, facilities.* These nouns denote something that increases physical comfort or that facilitates work: *an apartment with amenities like air conditioning; a suite with all the comforts of home; a kitchen with modern conveniences; a school with excellent facilities.*

---

amenity *noun.* —*See* **amiability.**

amerce *verb.* To impose a fine on ▶ fine, mulct, penalize. [*Compare* **punish.**]

amercement *noun.* A sum of money levied as punishment for an offense ▶ fine, mulct, penalty. [*Compare* **punishment.**]

amiability *or* **amiableness** *noun.* The quality of being pleasant and friendly ▶ affability, agreeability, agreeableness, amenity, congeniality, congenialness, cordiality, cordialness, friendliness, geniality, genialness, kindness, pleasantness, sociability, sociableness, sweetness, warmth. [*Compare* **amenity, benevolence.**]

amiable *or* **amicable** *adjective.* Pleasant and friendly in disposition ▶ affable, agreeable, approachable, companionable, congenial, cordial, friendly, genial, good-natured, good-tempered, likable, neighborly, pleasant, sociable, sweet, warm, warm-hearted. [*Compare* **benevolent, obliging, social.**]

✚ **CORE SYNONYMS:** *amiable, cordial, genial, good-natured, sociable.* These adjectives mean pleasant and friendly in disposition: *amiable to guests; a cordial welcome; a genial guide; a good-natured roommate; enjoyed a sociable chat.*

---

amigo *noun.* —*See* **friend.**

amiss *adjective.* Having a defect or defects ▶ defective, blemished, faulty, flawed, imperfect. [*Compare* **shabby, trick.**] —*See also* **confused** (2).

amiss *adverb.* Not in the right way or on the proper course ▶ afield, astray, awry, wrong.

amity *noun.* —*See* **friendship.**

amnesty *noun.* —*See* **forgiveness.**

amoral *adjective.* —*See* **unscrupulous.**

amorist *noun.* —*See* **gallant.**

amorous *adjective.* —*See* **erotic, lascivious.**

amorousness *noun.* —*See* **eroticism, love** (2).

amorphous *adjective.* —*See* **shapeless.**

amount *verb.* To come to in number or quantity ▶ add up, aggregate, come, number, reach, run, sum up, total (up). —*See also* **equal** (1).

amount *noun.* —*See* **import, quantity** (3), **total.**

amour *noun.* —*See* **love** (3).

amour-propre *noun.* —*See* **egotism, pride.**

ample *adjective.* Having plenty of room ▶ capacious, commodious, roomy, spacious. [*Compare* **big.**] —*See also* **broad** (1), **full** (3), **generous** (2), **sufficient.**

amplification *noun.* —*See* **increase** (1).

amplify *verb.* —*See* **broaden, elaborate, elevate** (2), **increase.**

amplitude *noun.* —*See* **bulk** (1), **size** (2).

amply *adverb.* —*See* **considerably.**

amputate *verb.* —*See* **cripple.**

amuck *adjective.* Out of control ▶ runaway, unbridled, uncontrolled. ***Idioms:*** out of hand, running wild. [*Compare* **abandoned, loose.**]

amulet *noun.* —*See* **charm.**

amuse *verb.* To occupy in an agreeable or pleasing way ▶ charm, cheer, divert, entertain, recreate, regale. [*Compare* **absorb, cheer.**] —*See also* **delight** (1).

✚ **CORE SYNONYMS:** *amuse, entertain, divert, regale.* These verbs refer to actions that provide pleasure, especially as a means of passing time. *Amuse,* the least specific, implies directing attention away from serious matters: *I amused myself with a game of solitaire. Entertain* suggests acts undertaken to furnish amusement: "*They* [timetables and catalogs] *are much more entertaining than half the novels that are written*" (W. Somerset Maugham). *Divert* implies distraction from worrisome thought or care: "*I had neither Friends or Books to divert me*" (Richard Steele). To *regale* is to entertain with something enormously enjoyable: "*He loved to regale his* *friends with tales about the many memorable characters he had known as a newspaperman"* (David Rosenzweig).

amusement *noun.* Something that amuses, entertains, or pleases ▶ delight, disport, distraction, diversion, enjoyment, entertainment, fun, hobby, pastime, play, pleasure, recreation, sport, treat. *Slang:* jollies, kicks. [*Compare* **gaiety.**]

amusing *adjective.* —*See* **delightful, funny** (1), **pleasant.**

analogize *verb.* —*See* **liken.**

analogous *adjective.* —*See* **like²**.

analogue *noun.* —*See* **parallel.**

analogy *noun.* —*See* **likeness** (1), **parallel.**

analysis *noun.* The separation of a whole into its parts for study ▶ anatomization, anatomy, breakdown, dissection, reduction, subdivision. —*See also* **examination** (1), **examination** (2), **logic.**

analytical *or* **analytic** *adjective.* —*See* **logical** (1).

analyze *verb.* To separate into parts for study ▶ anatomize, break down, dissect, reduce, resolve, subdivide, take apart. —*See also* **examine** (1).

✚ **CORE SYNONYMS:** *analyze, anatomize, dissect.* These verbs mean to separate into constituent parts for study: *analyze a chemical substance; a book that anatomizes 19th-century European history; medical students dissecting cadavers.*

anarchy *noun.* —*See* **disorder** (2), **license** (2).

anathema *noun.* —*See* **curse** (1), **hate** (2).

anathematize *verb.* To invoke evil upon ▶ curse, damn, hex, imprecate. [*Compare* **charm.**]

anatomize *verb.* —*See* **analyze.**

anatomy *or* **anatomization** *noun.* —*See* **analysis.**

ancestor *noun.* **1.** A person from whom one is descended ▶ antecedent, ascendant, father, forebear, forefather, foremother, mother, parent, primogenitor, progenitor. **2.** One that precedes, as in time ▶ antecedent, forerunner, precursor, predecessor, progenitor, prototype.

✚ **CORE SYNONYMS:** *ancestor, forebear, forefather, progenitor.* These nouns denote a person from whom one is descended: *ancestors who were farmers; land once owned by his forebears; laws handed down from our forefathers; our progenitors' wisdom.*

◀ **ANTONYM:** *descendant*

ancestral *adjective.* Of or from one's ancestors ▶ familial, genealogical, hereditary, inherited, patrimonial.

ancestry *noun.* One's ancestors or their character or one's ancestral derivation ▶ birth, blood, bloodline, descent, derivation, extraction, family, family tree, genealogy, line, lineage, origin, parentage, pedigree, race, roots, seed, stock. [*Compare* **kin, progeny.**]

anchor *noun.* A device for supporting or holding in place ▶ brake, dowel, grapnel, kedge, mooring, wedge. [*Compare* **bond, cord, fastener, nail.**] —*See also* **press.**

anchor *verb.* —*See* **fasten.**

anchorage *noun.* —*See* **harbor.**

anchorman *or* **anchorwoman** *noun.* —*See* **press.**

ancient *adjective.* —*See* **early** (1), **old** (1).

ancient *noun.* —*See* **senior** (2).

ancient history *noun.* —*See* **antiquity.**

ancillary *adjective.* —*See* **auxiliary** (1).

androgynous *noun.* Being neither distinguishably masculine nor feminine ▶ degendered, epicene, genderless, gender-neutral, gender-nonspecific, sexless, ungendered. [*Compare* **effeminate, masculine.**]

androgyny *noun.* The quality of being androgynous ▶ epicenism, gender-neutrality, sexlessness. [*Compare* **effeminacy, masculinity.**]

anecdote *noun.* —*See* **yarn.**

anemic *adjective.* —*See* **pale** (2), **sick** (1).

anesthetic *adjective.* —*See* **callous.**

anesthetize *verb.* —*See* **drug** (1).

anew *adverb.* Once more ▶ afresh, again, once again, over again. ***Idioms:*** from the beginning (*or* start *or* top).

anfractuous *adjective.* —*See* **indirect** (1), **winding.**

angel *noun.* —*See* **innocent** (1), **patron, rescuer, sponsor.**

angelic *or* **angelical** *adjective.* —*See* **innocent** (1).

anger *noun.* A strong feeling of displeasure or hostility ▶ animosity, choler, fury, furor, indignation, irateness, ire, outrage, rage, resentment, wrath, wrathfulness. *Informal:* dander. [*Compare* **enmity, hate, annoyance.**]

anger *verb.* **1.** To cause to feel or show anger ▶ burn (up), enrage, exasperate, incense, infuriate, irritate, madden, provoke, rile. *Informal:* tee off, tick off. *Slang:* piss off, p.o. ***Idioms:*** bend out of shape, get one's dander up, get on one's nerves, make one hot under the collar, make one's blood boil, make one's fur fly, put one's back up, rub one the wrong way. [*Compare* **annoy, offend.**] **2.** To be or become angry ▶ blow up, boil over, bristle, burn, explode, flare up, foam, fume, rage, seethe, storm. *Informal:* steam. ***Idioms:*** blow a fuse, blow a gasket, blow one's stack (*or* top), breathe fire, fly off the handle, foam (*or* froth) at the mouth, get hot under the collar, have a cow, hit the ceiling (*or* roof), lose one's temper, see red, throw a fit. [*Compare* **boil.**] —*See also* **offend** (1).

✚ **CORE SYNONYMS:** *anger, rage, fury, ire, wrath, resentment, indignation.* These nouns denote strong feelings of marked displeasure or hostility. *Anger,* the most general, is strong displeasure: *vented my anger by denouncing the supporters of the idea. Rage* and *fury* imply intense, explosive, often destructive emotion: *smashed the glass in a fit of rage; directed his fury at the murderer. Ire* is a term for anger most frequently encountered in literature: "*The best way to escape His ire/Is, not to seem too happy*" (Robert Browning). *Wrath* applies especially to anger that seeks vengeance or punishment: *saw the flood as a sign of the wrath of God. Resentment* refers to indignant smoldering anger generated by a sense of grievance: *deep resentment among the union employees that led to a strike. Indignation* is righteous anger at something wrongful, unjust, or evil: "*public indignation about takeovers causing people to lose their jobs*" (Allan Sloan).

---

angle¹ *verb.* —*See* **fish** (1).

angle² *noun.* —*See* **bend, viewpoint, wrinkle** (2).

angle *verb.* —*See* **bend** (2), **bias** (2), **swerve.**

angry *adjective.* Feeling or showing anger ▶ annoyed, boiling, choleric, cross, enraged, exacerbated, fuming, furious, huffy, incensed, indignant, inflamed, infuriated, irate, ireful, irritated, livid, mad, nettled, peeved, rabid, raging, seething, vexed, wrathful. *Informal:* sore. *Slang:* het up. ***Idioms:*** at the boiling point, bent out of shape, fit to be tied, foaming (*or* frothing) at the mouth, hot under the collar, in a rage (*or* temper), in a towering rage, seeing red, up in arms.

✚ **CORE SYNONYMS:** *angry, furious, indignant, infuriated, irate, ireful, livid, mad, wrathful.* These adjectives mean feeling or showing marked displeasure or hostility: *an angry retort; a furious scowl; an indignant denial; infuriated commuters who were stuck in traffic; irate protesters; ireful words; a livid disciplinarian; mad at a friend; a wrathful act.*

---

angst *noun.* —*See* **anxiety** (1).

anguish *noun.* —*See* **distress, grief.**

anguish *verb.* —*See* **distress, grieve.**

anguishing *adjective.* —*See* **tormenting.**

angular *adjective.* —*See* **thin** (1).

anhydrous *adjective.* —*See* **dry** (1).

anima *noun.* —*See* **spirit** (2).

animal *adjective.* —*See* **sensual** (2).

animalism *or* **animality** *noun.* —*See* **sensuality** (1).

animalize *verb.* —*See* **corrupt.**

animate *verb.* **1.** To make alive ▶ enliven, quicken, vitalize, vivify. [*Compare* **energize, provoke.**] **2.** To make lively or animated ▶ brighten, enliven, light (up), perk up. —*See also* **elate, encourage** (1), **fire** (1).

animate *adjective.* —*See* **alive.**

animated *adjective.* —*See* **alive, cheerful, lively.**

animating *adjective.* —*See* **invigorating.**

animation *noun.* —*See* **elation, energy, spirit** (1).

animosity *noun.* —*See* **anger, enmity.**

animus *noun.* —*See* **enmity.**

annals *noun.* A chronological record of past events ▶ archive, chronicle, historical record, history. [*Compare* **story.**]

annex *verb.* —*See* **attach** (2).

annex *noun.* —*See* **extension** (2).

annihilate *verb.* To destroy all traces of ▶ abolish, blot out, clear, eradicate, erase, expunge, exterminate, extinguish, extirpate, kill, liquidate, obliterate, remove, root (out *or* up), rub out, snuff out, stamp out, uproot, wipe out. ***Idioms:*** do away with, make an end of, put an end to, put to bed. [*Compare* **abolish, overwhelm.**] —*See also* **abolish, destroy** (1), **massacre.**

✚ **CORE SYNONYMS:** *annihilate, exterminate, extinguish, extirpate, eradicate, obliterate.* These verbs mean to destroy all traces of: *a squadron that was annihilated in the attack; exterminated the cockroaches in the house; criticism that extinguished my enthusiasm; policies that attempt to extirpate drug abuse; scientists working to eradicate deadly diseases; a magnet that obliterated the data on the floppy disk.*

---

annihilation *noun.* Utter destruction ▶ eradication, extermination, extinction, extinguishment, extirpation, liquidation, obliteration. [*Compare* **defeat** —*See also* **abolition, destruction.**

annotation *noun.* —*See* **commentary.**

announce *verb.* To bring to public notice or make known publicly ▶ advertise, annunciate, blaze, blazon, broadcast, bruit, declare, herald, noise (about *or* around), proclaim, promulgate, propagate, publish, trumpet. ***Idioms:*** issue a statement, make public (*or* known), spread the word. [*Compare* **gossip, reveal, spread.**] —*See also* **proclaim.**

✚ **CORE SYNONYMS:** *announce, advertise, broadcast, declare, proclaim, promulgate, publish.* These verbs mean to bring to public notice or make known publicly: *announced a cease-fire; advertise a forthcoming concert; broadcasting their opinions; declared her political intentions; proclaiming his beliefs; promulgated a policy of nonresistance; publishing the marriage banns.*

---

announcement *noun.* The act of announcing ▶ annunciation, broadcasting, communication, declaration, notification, proclamation, promulgation, publication. —*See also* **message.**

annoy *verb.* To trouble the nerves or peace of mind of, especially by repeated vexations ▶ aggravate, bother, bug, chafe, disturb, exasperate, fret, gall, get (to), irk, irritate, molest, nettle, peeve, pester, provoke, put out, rankle, rile, ruffle, vex. ***Idioms:*** drive one bananas (*or* crazy *or* nuts), drive one up a wall, get in one's hair, get on one's nerves, get under one's skin, try one's patience.

[*Compare* **agitate, distress, insult.**] —*See also* **harass, offend** (1).

✚ CORE SYNONYMS: *annoy, irritate, bother, irk, vex, provoke, aggravate, peeve, rile.* These verbs mean to trouble a person's nerves or peace of mind, especially by repeated vexations and often evoking moderate anger: *Annoy* refers to mild disturbance caused by an act that tries one's patience: *The sound of the printer annoyed me. Irritate* is somewhat stronger: *I was irritated by their constant interruptions. Bother* implies imposition: *In the end, his complaining just bothered the supervisor. Irk* connotes a wearisome quality: *The city council's inactivity irked the community. Vex* applies to an act capable of arousing anger or perplexity: *Hecklers in the crowd vexed the speaker. Provoke* implies strong and often deliberate incitement to anger: *His behavior provoked me to reprimand the whole team. Aggravate* is a less formal equivalent: *"Threats only served to aggravate people in such cases"* (William Makepeace Thackeray). *Peeve,* also somewhat informal, suggests a querulous, resentful response to a mild disturbance: *Your flippant answers peeved me.* To *rile* is to upset and to stir up: *It riled me to have to listen to such lies.*

annoyance *noun.* **1.** The act of annoying or the state of being annoyed ▶ aggravation, bother, botheration, bothering, exasperation, harassment, irritation, pestering, provocation, vexation. [*Compare* **distress.**] **2.** Something that annoys ▶ aggravation, besetment, bother, irritant, irritation, nuisance, pain, peeve, pest, plague, thorn, torment, trial, vexation. *Informal:* hassle, headache. ***Idioms:*** pain in the neck (*or* butt), thorn in one's side.

annoyed *adjective.* —*See* **angry.**

annoying *adjective.* —*See* **disturbing.**

annul *verb.* —*See* **abolish, cancel** (1).

annular *adjective.* —*See* **round** (1).

annulment *noun.* —*See* **abolition.**

annulus *noun.* —*See* **circle** (1).

annunciate *verb.* —*See* **announce.**

annunciation *noun.* —*See* **announcement, message.**

anoint *verb.* —*See* **oil.**

anointed *adjective.* —*See* **divine** (2).

anomalous *or* **anomalistic** *adjective.* —*See* **abnormal.**

anomaly *noun.* —*See* **abnormality.**

anonymity *noun.* —*See* **obscurity.**

anonymous *adjective.* Having an unknown or withheld authorship or agency ▶ nameless, unacknowledged, uncredited, unidentified, unknown, unnamed, unsigned. [*Compare* **obscure.**]

anorak *noun.* —*See* **coat** (1).

answer *verb.* To speak or act in response, as to a question ▶ field, rejoin, reply, respond, retort, return, riposte. [*Compare* **acknowledge.**] —*See also* **satisfy** (1), **solve** (1).

answer *noun.* **1.** Something spoken or written in return, as to a question or demand ▶ comeback, rejoinder, repartee, reply, response, return, retort, riposte. **2.** A solution, as to a problem ▶ determination, explanation, key, resolution, result, solution. [*Compare* **discovery.**]

✚ CORE SYNONYMS: *answer, respond, reply, retort.* These verbs mean to act in response, as to a question. *Answer, respond,* and *reply* are the most general. *Please answer my question. Did you expect the president to respond personally to your letter? The opposing team scored three runs; the home team replied with two of their own. Respond* also denotes a reaction, either voluntary (*A bystander responded to the victim's need for help*) or involuntary (*I responded in spite of myself to the antics of the puppy*). To *retort* is to answer verbally in a quick, caustic, or witty manner: *She won the debate by retorting sharply to her opponent's questions.*

answerability *noun.* —*See* **responsibility.**

answerable *adjective.* —*See* **liable** (1).

antagonism *noun.* —*See* **enmity, opposition** (1).

antagonist *noun.* —*See* **opponent.**

antagonistic *adjective.* —*See* **contrary, opposing, unfavorable** (1).

antagonize *verb.* —*See* **estrange.**

ante *noun.* —*See* **bet.**

ante *verb.* —*See* **contribute** (1).

antecede *verb.* —*See* **precede.**

antecedence *noun.* —*See* **precedence.**

antecedent *adjective.* —*See* **advance, past.**

antecedent *noun.* That which produces an effect ▶ cause, determinant, occasion, reason. [*Compare* **impact, origin, stimulus.**] —*See also* **ancestor** (1), **ancestor** (2).

antedate *verb.* —*See* **precede.**

antediluvian *adjective.* —*See* **early** (1), **old** (1).

anterior *adjective.* —*See* **advance, past.**

anthropic *adjective.* —*See* **human.**

anthropoid *adjective.* —*See* **human, humanlike.**

anthropomorphic *or* **anthropomorphous** *adjective.* —*See* **humanlike.**

antic *noun.* —*See* **prank**[1].

antic *adjective.* —*See* **eccentric.**

anticipant *adjective.* —*See* **expectant.**

anticipate *verb.* —*See* **expect** (1), **foresee, prevent.**

anticipated *adjective.* —*See* **due** (2).

anticipation *noun.* **1.** The condition of looking forward to something, especially with eagerness ▶ expectance, expectancy, expectation, high hopes, hopefulness. [*Compare* **desire.**] **2.** Something that is expected ▶ expectation, likelihood, promise, prospect. [*Compare* **chance, theory.**]

anticipatory *or* **anticipative** *adjective.* —*See* **expectant.**

anticlimax *noun.* —*See* **disappointment** (2).

antidotal *adjective.* —*See* **curative.**

antidote *noun.* —*See* **cure.**

antipathetic *adjective.* —*See* **offensive** (1), **opposing.**

antipathy *noun.* —*See* **enmity, hate** (1).

antipode *or* **antipodes** *noun.* —*See* **opposite.**

antipodean *or* **antipodal** *adjective.* —*See* **opposite.**

antiquated *adjective.* —*See* **old-fashioned, old** (1).

antique *adjective.* —*See* **old-fashioned, old** (1), **vintage.**

antiquity *noun.* Ancient times ▶ ancient history, distant past, prehistory, protohistory, time immemorial, time out of mind. ***Idiom:*** mists of time. [*Compare* **past.**]

antiseptic *adjective.* —*See* **clean** (1), **sterile** (1).

antiseptic *noun.* —*See* **purifier.**

antithesis *noun.* —*See* **opposite, opposition** (1).

antithetical *adjective.* —*See* **opposite.**

antonym *noun.* —*See* **opposite.**

antonymic *or* **antonymous** *adjective.* —*See* **opposite.**

antsy *adjective.* —*See* **edgy.**

anxiety *noun.* **1.** A troubled or anxious state of mind ▶ angst, anxiousness, apprehension, care, concern, concernment, disquiet, disquietude, distress, nervousness, stress, solicitude, unease, uneasiness, worriment, worry. [*Compare* **agitation, fear, restlessness.**] **2.** An exaggerated concern ▶ complex, neurosis, phobia. *Informal:* hang-up. [*Compare* **obsession.**]

✚ **CORE SYNONYMS:** *anxiety, worry, care, concern, solicitude.* These nouns refer to a troubled or anxious state of mind. *Anxiety* suggests feelings of fear and apprehension: *"Feelings of resentment and rage over this devious form of manipulation cannot surface in the child . . . . At the most, he will experience feelings of anxiety, shame, insecurity, and helplessness"* (Alice Miller). *Worry* implies persistent doubt or fear: *"Having* *come to a decision the lad felt a sense of relief from the worry that had haunted him for many sleepless nights"* (Edgar Rice Burroughs). *Care* denotes a state of mind burdened by heavy responsibilities: *The old man's face was worn with care. Concern* stresses serious thought combined with emotion: *"Concern for man himself and his fate must always form the chief interest of all technical endeavors"* (Albert Einstein). *Solicitude* is active and sometimes excessive concern for another's well-being: *"Animosity had given way . . . to worried solicitude for Lindbergh's safety"* (Warren Trabant).

---

anxious *adjective.* In a state of anxiety, uneasiness, or emotional distress ▶ agitated, apprehensive, concerned, distraught, distressed, disturbed, impatient, nervous, overcome, overwrought, rattled, shaken, shaken-up, solicitous, stressed, troubled, uneasy, unnerved, unsettled, upset, worried. *Informal:* stressed-out. *Slang:* het up. ***Idioms:*** ill at ease, on tenterhooks. [*Compare* **afraid, eager, edgy.**]

anxiousness *noun.* —*See* **anxiety** (1).

anyway *adverb.* —*See* **still** (1).

A-one *or* **A-1** *adjective.* —*See* **excellent.**

apace *adverb.* —*See* **fast.**

apart *adverb.* —*See* **separately.**

apart *adjective.* —*See* **solitary.**

apartment *noun.* An often rented living space in a building ▶ condominium, co-op, efficiency, flat, loft, pied-à-terre, rental, suite, studio, walk-up. *Informal:* condo.

apathetic *adjective.* Lacking interest ▶ blasé, detached, disinterested, impassive, incurious, indifferent, lethargic, listless, phlegmatic, supine, unconcerned, uninterested, unresponsive. [*Compare* **cold, cool, languid.**]

apathy *noun.* Lack of emotion or interest ▶ aloofness, callousness, coldness, coolness, detachment, disinterest, impassiveness, impassivity, incuriosity, incuriousness, indifference, insensibility, insensibleness, insouciance, lassitude, lethargy, listlessness, nonchalance, phlegm, stolidity, stolidness, unconcern, uninterest, unresponsiveness.

ape *verb.* —*See* **imitate.**

ape *noun.* —*See* **mimic, oaf.**

apéritif *noun.* —*See* **appetizer.**

aperture *noun.* —*See* **hole** (2).

apex *noun.* —*See* **climax, point** (1).

aphonic *adjective.* —*See* **mute.**

aphorism *noun.* —*See* **proverb.**

aphoristic *adjective.* —*See* **pithy.**

aphrodisiac *adjective.* —*See* **erotic.**

aping *noun.* —*See* **mimicry.**

apish *adjective.* —*See* **imitative** (1).

aplomb *noun.* —*See* **balance** (2), **confidence.**

apocalypse *noun.* —*See* **revelation.**

apocalypticist *noun.* —*See* **pessimist** (2).

apocryphal *adjective.* —*See* **false, mythical.**

apogee *noun.* —*See* **climax.**

apologetic *adjective.* —*See* **sorry.**

apologia *noun.* —*See* **apology** (1).

apologize *verb.* —*See* **defend** (2).

apology *noun.* **1.** A statement that justifies or defends something, such as a past action or policy ▶ apologetic, apologia, defense, justification, plea, vindication. [*Compare* **explanation.**] **2.** A statement of acknowledgment expressing regret or asking pardon ▶ excuse, mea culpa, regrets. [*Compare* **acknowledgment.**]

✚ **CORE SYNONYMS:** *apology, apologia, defense, justification.* These nouns denote a statement that justifies or defends something, such as a past action or policy: *arguments that constituted an apology for capital punishment; published an apologia expounding their version of the events; a defense based on ignorance of the circumstances; an untenable justification for police brutality.*

---

apoplexy *noun.* —*See* **seizure** (1).

apostasy *noun.* —*See* **defection.**

apostate *noun.* —*See* **defector.**
apostatize *verb.* —*See* **defect.**
apostle *noun.* A person doing religious or charitable work in a foreign country ▶ evangelist, missionary, missioner. [*Compare* **cleric, representative.**]
apothegm *noun.* —*See* **proverb.**
apotheosis *noun.* —*See* **exaltation.**
apotheosize *verb.* —*See* **exalt.**
appall *verb.* —*See* **disgust, dismay.**
appalling *adjective.* —*See* **fearful, ghastly** (1), **outrageous, terrible.**
apparatus *noun.* Something attached as a permanent part of something else ▶ fitting, fixture, installation. [*Compare* **attachment.**] —*See also* **device** (1), **gadget, outfit.**
apparel *noun.* —*See* **dress** (1).
apparel *verb.* —*See* **dress** (1).
apparent *adjective.* **1.** Readily seen, perceived, or understood ▶ clear, clear-cut, conspicuous, crystal clear, distinct, evident, glaring, manifest, marked, noticeable, observable, obvious, patent, plain, pronounced, self-evident, unmistakable, visible. [*Compare* **definite, perceptible, sharp.**] **2.** Appearing as such but not necessarily so ▶ external, ostensible, ostensive, outward, seeming, superficial. [*Compare* **probable.**]

✚ **CORE SYNONYMS:** *apparent, clear, clear-cut, distinct, evident, manifest, obvious, patent, plain.* These adjectives mean readily seen, perceived, or understood: *angry for no apparent reason; a clear danger; clear-cut evidence of tampering; distinct fingerprints; evident hostility; manifest pleasure; obvious errors; patent advantages; making my meaning plain.*

---

apparently *adverb.* On the surface ▶ evidently, externally, ostensibly, ostensively, outwardly, seemingly, superficially. ***Idioms:*** as far as one can tell (*or* see), on the face of it, to all appearances.
apparition *noun.* —*See* **appearance** (2), **ghost.**
appeal *verb.* **1.** To make an earnest or urgent request ▶ adjure, ask (for), beg, beseech, crave, entreat, implore, petition, plead, pray, request, seek, solicit, sue, supplicate. **2.** To bring an appeal or request to the attention of ▶ address, apply, approach, petition. [*Compare* **request.**] —*See also* **attract.**
appeal for *verb.* —*See* **demand** (1).
appeal *noun.* An earnest or urgent request ▶ application, entreaty, imploration, imploring, importunity, petition, plea, prayer, requisition, supplication. [*Compare* **question.**] —*See also* **attraction, demand** (1).

✚ **CORE SYNONYMS:** *appeal, beg, crave, beseech, implore, entreat.* These verbs mean to make an earnest request. *Appeal* has the broadest application: *The emcee of the marathon appealed to the listeners to make a donation. Beg* and *crave* mean to ask in a serious and sometimes humble manner, especially for something one cannot claim as a right: *I begged her to forgive me. The attorney craved the court's indulgence. Beseech* emphasizes earnestness and often implies anxiety: *Be silent, we beseech you. Implore* intensifies the sense of urgency and anxiety: *The child implored the teacher not to be angry. Entreat* pertains to persuasive pleading: *"Ask me no questions, I entreat you"* (Charles Dickens).

---

appealer *noun.* One that asks a higher authority for something, as a favor or redress ▶ appellant, petitioner, suitor.
appealing *adjective.* —*See* **attractive.**
appear *verb.* **1.** To come into view ▶ come out, emerge, issue, loom, materialize, show (up), turn up. ***Idioms:*** come to light, make (*or* put in) an appearance, meet the eye. **2.** To give the impression of being ▶ feel, look, seem, sound. ***Idioms:*** have all the earmarks of being, give the idea (*or* impression) of being, strike one as being. [*Compare* **resemble.**] —*See also* **begin.**

✤ CORE SYNONYMS: *appear, emerge, issue, loom, materialize, show.* These verbs mean to come into view: *a ship appearing on the horizon; a star that emerged from behind a cloud; a diver issuing from the water; a peak that loomed through the mist; a job offer that materialized overnight; a shirtsleeve showing at the edge of the jacket.*

appearance *noun.* **1.** The way something or someone looks ▶ aspect, guise, look, looks, features, mien, semblance, stamp, visage. [*Compare* **face.**] **2.** The act of coming into sight ▶ apparition, emergence, manifestation, materialization, turning up. ***Idiom:*** coming into view. **3.** The act of arriving ▶ advent, arrival, coming. [*Compare* **entrance.**] **4.** The character projected or given by someone to the public ▶ image, impression. [*Compare* **façade.**]

appease *verb.* —*See* **pacify, satisfy** (2).

appellant *noun.* One that asks a higher authority for something, as a favor or redress ▶ appealer, petitioner, suitor.

appellation *or* **appellative** *noun.* —*See* **name** (1).

append *verb.* —*See* **attach** (1), **attach** (2).

appendage *noun.* —*See* **attachment.**

appertain *verb.* —*See* **apply** (2).

appetence *or* **appetency** *noun.* —*See* **desire** (1).

appetite *noun.* A desire for food or drink ▶ hunger, ravenousness, stomach, taste, thirst. ***Idioms:*** a stomach for, the munchies. [*Compare* **voracity.**] —*See also* **desire** (1), **desire** (2).

appetizer *noun.* A food or drink served before a meal ▶ amuse bouche, apéritif, hors d'oeuvre, starter, tapa. [*Compare* **refreshment.**]

appetizing *adjective.* —*See* **delicious.**

applaud *verb.* To express approval audibly, as by clapping ▶ cheer, clap, root. ***Idioms:*** give a big hand (*or* welcome), give an ovation, give someone a hand, put one's hands together. —*See also* **praise** (1).

✤ CORE SYNONYMS: *applaud, cheer, root.* These verbs mean to express approval or encouragement, especially audibly: *applauded at the end of the concert; cheered when the home team scored; rooting for the underdog in the tennis championship.*

applause *noun.* Approval expressed by clapping ▶ hand, ovation, plaudit. ***Idiom:*** round of applause. —*See also* **praise** (1).

apple-polish *verb.* —*See* **fawn.**

apple-polisher *noun.* —*See* **sycophant.**

apple-polishing *noun.* —*See* **flattery.**

applesauce *noun.* —*See* **nonsense.**

appliance *noun.* —*See* **device** (1).

applicability *noun.* —*See* **relevance.**

applicable *adjective.* —*See* **relevant, usable.**

applicant *noun.* A person who applies for or seeks something, such as a job or position ▶ aspirant, candidate, hopeful, petitioner, seeker. [*Compare* **competitor.**]

application *noun.* A document used in applying, as for a job ▶ form, paper, sheet. —*See also* **appeal, diligence, duty** (2), **exercise** (1), **relevance.**

apply *verb.* **1.** To devote oneself or one's efforts ▶ address, bend, buckle down, concentrate, dedicate, devote, direct, exert, focus, give, turn. ***Idiom:*** keep one's nose to the grindstone. [*Compare* **commit, engage.**] **2.** To be pertinent ▶ appertain, bear on (*or* upon), concern, pertain, refer, relate. ***Idioms:*** have a bearing on, have to do with. **3.** To bring an appeal or request to the attention of ▶ address, appeal, approach, petition. [*Compare* **appeal, request.**] **4.** To ask for employment, acceptance, or admission ▶ petition, put in. —*See also* **administer** (3), **resort, use.**

appoint *verb.* To select for an office or position ▶ assign, designate, elect, make, name, nominate, tap. [*Compare* **authorize, choose.**] *—See also* **furnish.**

✦ **CORE SYNONYMS:** *appoint, designate, name, nominate, tap.* These verbs mean to select for an office or position: *was appointed chairperson of the committee; expects to be designated leader of the opposition; a new police commissioner named by the mayor; to be nominated as her party's candidate; was tapped for fraternity membership.*

appointment *noun.* The act of appointing to an office or position ▶ assignment, designation, election, installation, naming, nomination. [*Compare* **confirmation.**] *—See also* **engagement** (1), **position** (3).

apportion *verb. —See* **distribute.**

apportionment *noun. —See* **distribution** (1).

apposite *adjective. —See* **relevant.**

appositeness *noun. —See* **relevance.**

appraisal *or* **appraisement** *noun. —See* **estimate** (1).

appraise *verb. —See* **estimate** (1), **test** (1).

appreciable *adjective. —See* **perceptible, understandable.**

appreciate *verb. —See* **enjoy, value.**

appreciation *noun.* A being grateful ▶ acknowledgment, gratefulness, gratitude, indebtedness, thankfulness, thanks. *—See also* **esteem.**

appreciative *adjective.* Showing or feeling gratitude ▶ grateful, thankful. [*Compare* **obliged.**]

apprehend *verb. —See* **arrest, know** (1), **perceive, understand** (1).

apprehensible *adjective. —See* **understandable.**

apprehension *noun.* Intellectual hold ▶ comprehension, grasp, grip, hold, understanding. [*Compare* **knowledge.**] *—See also* **anxiety** (1), **arrest, fear.**

apprehensive *adjective. —See* **afraid, anxious.**

apprentice *noun. —See* **beginner, student.**

apprise *verb. —See* **inform** (1).

approach *verb.* **1.** To come near in space or time ▶ close in on, converge on, gain on, near. ***Idioms:*** be around the corner, close the gap, come close to, come within spitting distance, draw near to (*or* nigh), stare one in the face. **2.** To bring an appeal or request to the attention of ▶ address, appeal, apply, petition. [*Compare* **appeal, request.**] *—See also* **rival, start** (1).

approach *noun.* **1.** A method used for making, doing, or accomplishing something ▶ attack, blueprint, course, design, game plan, idea, layout, line, means, modus operandi, plan, procedure, process, project, schema, scheme, strategy, tack, tactic, technique. ***Idiom:*** course of action. [*Compare* **line, way.**] **2.** The act or fact of coming near ▶ coming, convergence, imminence, nearness. [*Compare* **advance, appearance.**] *—See also* **advances.**

✦ **CORE SYNONYMS:** *approach, blueprint, design, plan, project, scheme, strategy.* These nouns denote a method or program for making, doing, or accomplishing something: *an encouraging approach to reducing the high school dropout rate; a blueprint for reorganizing the company; social conventions of human design; has no vacation plans; an urban renewal project; a new scheme for conservation; a strategy for survival.*

approachable *adjective.* Easily approached ▶ accessible, responsive, welcoming. [*Compare* **convenient.**] *—See also* **amiable.**

approaching *adjective.* In the relatively near future ▶ coming, due, forthcoming, upcoming. ***Idioms:*** around the corner, on the horizon. [*Compare* **close.**] *—See also* **imminent.**

approaching *adverb. —See* **approximately.**

approbate *verb. —See* **permit** (2).

approbation *noun. —See* **acceptance** (2), **permission, praise** (1).

approbatory *adjective.* —*See* **complimentary** (1).

appropriate *adjective.* Suitable for a particular person, condition, occasion, or place ▶ apt, becoming, befitting, comely, comme il faut, correct, decent, decorous, de rigueur, felicitous, fit, fitting, nice, proper, right, respectable, seemly, tailor-made. ***Idiom:*** cut out for. [*Compare* **beneficial, opportune, relevant.**] —*See also* **convenient** (1), **just.**

appropriate *verb.* To set aside or apart for a specified purpose ▶ allocate, allot, assign, budget, designate, earmark, set apart, set aside. [*Compare* **distribute.**] —*See also* **adopt, plagiarize, seize** (1).

✤ CORE SYNONYMS: *appropriate, allocate, allot, designate, earmark.* These verbs mean to set aside for a specified purpose: *appropriated funds for public education; allocated time for recreation; allotted fifty minutes for taking the test; designated a location for the new hospital; money earmarked for a vacation.*

appropriation *noun.* Money or other resources granted for a particular purpose ▶ budget, grant, subsidy, subvention. —*See also* **seizure** (2).

approval *noun.* —*See* **acceptance** (2), **confirmation** (1), **permission.**

approve *verb.* To be favorably disposed toward ▶ countenance, favor, hold with. *Informal:* go for. ***Idioms:*** be in favor of, take kindly to, think highly (*or* well) of. [*Compare* **assent, value.**] —*See also* **confirm** (3), **permit** (2).

approving *adjective.* —*See* **favorable** (2).

approximate *verb.* —*See* **estimate** (2), **rival.**

approximate *adjective.* —*See* **loose** (3).

approximately *adverb.* Near to in quantity or amount ▶ about, almost, approaching, around, circa, nearly, practically, roughly, some. ***Idioms:*** for all practical purposes, for the most part, give or take a little, in all (*or* everything) but name, in the ballpark (*or* neighborhood) of, on the order of, pretty much. [*Compare* **fairly, usually.**]

approximation *noun.* —*See* **estimate** (2).

appurtenance *noun.* —*See* **attachment.**

apropos *adjective.* —*See* **relevant.**

apt *adjective.* —*See* **appropriate, inclined.**

aptitude *noun.* —*See* **intelligence, talent.**

aptness *noun.* —*See* **talent.**

aquiver *adjective.* —*See* **tremulous.**

arbiter *noun.* —*See* **judge** (2).

arbitrary *adjective.* Based on individual judgment or discretion ▶ discretionary, judgmental, personal, subjective, unscientific. [*Compare* **random.**] —*See also* **absolute, capricious.**

arbitrate *verb.* To intervene between disputants in order to bring about an agreement ▶ mediate, moderate. [*Compare* **confer.**] —*See also* **judge.**

arbitration *noun.* —*See* **compromise.**

arbitrator *noun.* —*See* **judge** (2).

arc *verb.* —*See* **bend** (1).

arc *noun.* —*See* **bend.**

arcadian *adjective.* Charmingly simple and carefree ▶ idyllic, pastoral. [*Compare* **fresh, still.**] —*See also* **country.**

arcane *adjective.* —*See* **mysterious, obscure** (1).

arced *adjective.* —*See* **bent.**

arch[1] *verb.* —*See* **bend** (1), **stoop.**

arch *noun.* —*See* **bend.**

arch[2] *adjective.* —*See* **mischievous.**

archaic *adjective.* —*See* **old** (1), **old-fashioned.**

arched *adjective.* —*See* **bent.**

archenemy *noun.* —*See* **opponent.**

archetypal *or* **archetypical** *adjective.* —*See* **ideal, original, typical.**

archetype *noun.* —*See* **epitome, original.**

archfiend *noun.* —*See* **fiend.**

architect *noun.* —*See* **originator.**

archive *noun.* A chronological record of past events ▶ annals, chronicle, historical record, history. [*Compare* **story.**] —*See also* **depository.**

arciform *adjective.* —*See* **bent.**

arctic *adjective.* —*See* **cold** (1).

ardent *adjective.* —*See* **eager, enthusiastic, hot** (1), **passionate.**

ardor *noun.* —*See* **enthusiasm** (1), **love** (2), **passion.**

ardorless *adjective.* —*See* **frigid.**

arduous *adjective.* —*See* **burdensome, difficult** (1), **rough** (3).

arduously *adverb.* —*See* **hard** (2).

area *noun.* **1.** A sphere of activity, experience, study, or interest ▶ arena, bailiwick, circle, department, domain, field, orbit, province, realm, scene, subject, terrain, territory, world. *Slang:* bag, turf. [*Compare* **branch, range.**] **2.** A part of the earth's surface ▶ belt, district, locality, neighborhood, quarter, region, section, sector, tract, zone. *Informal:* neck of the woods. [*Compare* **field, territory.**] —*See also* **locality, neighborhood** (1), **size** (1).

✚ **CORE SYNONYMS:** *area, bailiwick, domain, field, province, realm, territory.* These nouns denote a sphere of activity, experience, study, or interest: *an expert in the area of corporate law; considers biochemistry to be her bailiwick; the domain of quantum physics; the field of comparative literature; the province of politics; the realm of constitutional law; the territory of historical research.*

---

arena *noun.* —*See* **area** (1).

argot *noun.* —*See* **dialect, language** (2).

arguable *adjective.* —*See* **debatable.**

argue *verb.* **1.** To engage in a quarrel ▶ altercate, bicker, brawl, broil, caterwaul, contend, dispute, fall out, feud, fight, quarrel, quibble, row, spar, spat, squabble, tiff, wrangle. *Informal:* hassle, tangle. ***Idioms:*** be at loggerheads, cross swords, have a brush with, have it out, have words, lock horns, mix it up. [*Compare* **conflict, contest, haggle.**] **2.** To put forth reasons for or against something, often excitedly ▶ contend, debate, dispute, moot, plead. ***Idioms:*** make a case for, put up an argument. [*Compare* **appeal, assert.**] —*See also* **assert, discuss, indicate** (1).

argue into *verb.* —*See* **persuade.**

✚ **CORE SYNONYMS:** *argue, quarrel, wrangle, squabble, bicker.* These verbs denote verbal exchange expressing conflict. To *argue* is to present reasons or facts in order to persuade someone of something: *"I am not arguing with you—I am telling you"* (James McNeill Whistler). *Quarrel* stresses hostility: *The children quarreled over whose turn it was to wash the dishes. Wrangle* refers to loud, contentious argument: *"audiences . . . who can be overheard wrangling about film facts in restaurants and coffee houses"* (Sheila Benson). *Squabble* suggests petty or trivial argument: *"The one absolutely certain way of bringing this nation to ruin . . . would be to permit it to become a tangle of squabbling nationalities"* (Theodore Roosevelt). *Bicker* connotes sharp, persistent, bad-tempered exchange: *The senators bickered about the president's tax proposal for weeks.*

---

argument *noun.* A discussion, often heated, in which a difference of opinion is expressed ▶ altercation, bicker, clash, contention, controversy, debate, difficulty, disagreement, dispute, falling out, feud, fight, fireworks, fracas, fuss, misunderstanding, polemic, quarrel, row, run-in, set-to, spat, squabble, tiff, words, wrangle. *Informal:* hassle, rhubarb, tangle. ***Idiom:*** war of words. [*Compare* **conflict, deliberation, uproar.**] —*See also* **logic, objection, reason** (1), **subject.**

✚ **CORE SYNONYMS:** *argument, dispute, controversy.* These nouns refer to a discussion, often heated, in which a difference of opinion is expressed: *Argument* stresses the advancement by each side of facts and reasons intended to persuade the other side: *Emotions are seldom swayed by argument. Dispute* implies animosity: *A dispute arose among union members about the terms of the new contract. Controversy* applies especially to major differences of opinion involving large groups of people: *The use of nuclear power is the subject of widespread controversy.*

---

argumentative *adjective.* Given to or characterized by arguing ▶ cantankerous, combative, contentious, disagreeable, disputatious, eristic, factious, feisty, hotheaded, litigious, polemic, polemical, quarrelsome, scrappy. ***Idiom:*** having a chip on one's shoulder. [*Compare* **aggressive, ill-tempered.**]

✚ **CORE SYNONYMS:** *argumentative, combative, contentious, disputatious, quarrelsome, scrappy.* These adjectives mean given to or fond of arguing: *an argumentative child; a combative teenager; a contentious mood; a disputatious lawyer; a quarrelsome drinker; a scrappy litigator.*

---

aria *noun.* —*See* **melody.**

arid *adjective.* —*See* **dry** (2), **dull** (1).

arise *verb.* —*See* **begin, rise** (1), **rise** (2), **stand** (1), **stem.**

aristocracy *noun.* —*See* **society** (1).

aristocratic *adjective.* —*See* **noble.**

arithmetic *noun.* Arithmetic calculations ▶ computation, figures, numbers. [*Compare* **addition, calculation.**]

ark *noun.* —*See* **cover** (1).

arm *noun.* —*See* **branch** (1), **branch** (3), **extension** (2).

arm *verb.* —*See* **gird.**

armada *noun.* A group of warships operating under one command ▶ fleet, flotilla.

armchair *adjective.* —*See* **theoretical** (1).

armistice *noun.* —*See* **truce.**

armpit *noun.* —*See* **pit**[1]**.**

army *noun.* —*See* **crowd.**

aroma *noun.* **1.** The quality of something that may be perceived by the olfactory sense ▶ odor, scent, smell. [*Compare* **fragrance, stench.**] **2.** A distinctive yet intangible quality ▶ atmosphere, flavor, savor, smack. [*Compare* **quality.**] —*See also* **fragrance.**

aromatic *adjective.* —*See* **fragrant, spicy.**

aromatize *verb.* To fill with a pleasant odor ▶ perfume, scent.

around *adverb.* —*See* **approximately, backward.**

around *adjective.* —*See* **alive.**

around-the-clock *adjective.* —*See* **continual.**

arouse *verb.* To induce or elicit a reaction or emotion ▶ agitate, awake, awaken, kindle, raise, rouse, stir (up), waken. [*Compare* **provoke.**] —*See also* **fire** (1), **wake**[1]**.**

✚ **CORE SYNONYMS:** *arouse, rouse, stir.* These verbs mean to induce or elicit a reaction or emotion. To *arouse* means to awaken, as from inactivity or apathy; *rouse* means the same, but more strongly implies vigorous or emotional excitement: "*In a democratic society like ours, relief must come through an aroused popular conscience that sears the conscience of the people's representatives*" (Felix Frankfurter). "*The oceangoing steamers . . . roused in him wild and painful longings*" (Arnold Bennett). To *stir* is to cause activity, strong but usually agreeable feelings, trouble, or commotion: "*It was him as stirred up th' young woman to preach last night*" (George Eliot). "*I have seldom been so . . . stirred by any piece of writing*" (Mark Twain).

---

arraign *verb.* —*See* **accuse.**

arraigner *noun.* One that accuses ▶ accuser, denouncer, indicter, recriminator.

arraignment *noun.* —*See* **accusation.**

arrange *verb.* **1.** To put into a deliberate order ▶ array, codify, collocate, deploy, dispose, marshal, methodize, order, organize, range, regiment, regulate, sort, systemize, systematize. [*Compare* **classify, line.**] **2.** To plan the details or arrangements of ▶ blueprint, lay out, map (out), organize, plan, prepare, schedule, set out (*or* up), work out. ***Idioms:*** get (*or* put) into shape. [*Compare* **design, draft.**] —*See also* **compromise, harmonize** (2), **settle** (1), **settle** (2).

✚ **CORE SYNONYMS:** *arrange, marshal, order, organize, sort, systematize.* These verbs mean to put things or people in a deliberate order: *arranging figures numerically; had to marshal all relevant facts for presentation; ordered the plants by genus; organized the fundraiser; sorted the sweaters by color; systematized the assorted files.*

arrangement *noun.* **1.** The act or condition of being arranged ▶ allotment, alignment, assortment, categorization, classification, codification, deployment, disposal, disposition, distribution, format, formation, grouping, harmonization, layout, lineup, orchestration, order, ordering, organization, positioning, ranking, sequence, setup. **2.** The way in which one is placed or arranged ▶ attitude, pose, position, posture. —*See also* **agreement** (1), **compromise, system.**

arrangements *noun.* Steps taken in preparation for an undertaking ▶ accommodations, plans, preparations, provisions.

arrant *adjective.* —*See* **utter[2].**

array *verb.* —*See* **arrange** (1), **dress up.**

array *noun.* An impressive or ostentatious exhibition ▶ display, manifestation, pageant, panoply, parade, pomp, show, spectacle. —*See also* **attire, group.**

✚ **CORE SYNONYMS:** *array, display, panoply, parade, pomp.* These nouns denote an impressive or ostentatious exhibition: *an array of diamond rings; a tasteless display of wealth; a panoply of medals; a parade of knowledge and virtue; ceremonial pomp.*

arrears *or* **arrearage** *noun.* —*See* **debt** (1), **debt** (2).

arrest *verb.* To take into custody as a prisoner ▶ apprehend, seize. *Informal:* nab, pick up. *Slang:* bust, collar, cuff, haul up, pinch, pull in, run in. ***Idioms:*** take charge (*or* hold) of. [*Compare* **catch, take.**] —*See also* **grip, stop** (2).

arrest *noun.* A seizing and holding by law ▶ apprehension, seizure. *Slang:* bust, collar, pickup, pinch. [*Compare* **catch.**] —*See also* **detention.**

arresting *adjective.* —*See* **noticeable.**

arrival *noun.* **1.** The act of arriving ▶ advent, appearance, coming. [*Compare* **entrance.**] **2.** One that arrives ▶ comer, newcomer, visitor. [*Compare* **addition, company.**] —*See also* **accomplishment.**

arrive *verb.* **1.** To come to a particular place ▶ breeze in, check in, come, drop in, get in, make it, pop in, pull in, reach, roll in (*or* up), show up, turn up. *Slang:* blow in. ***Idioms:*** arrive (*or* come) onto the scene, make (*or* put in) an appearance, make the scene. **2.** To gain success ▶ get ahead, get on, rise, succeed. ***Idioms:*** go far, go places, make good, make it. —*See also* **happen** (1).

arrive at *verb.* —*See* **accomplish.**

arrogance *noun.* The quality of being arrogant ▶ braggodocio, disdainfulness, haughtiness, hauteur, hubris, insolence, loftiness, lordliness, overbearingness, pomposity, pompousness, presumption, pride, pridefulness, priggishness, proudness, self-importance, self-satisfaction, smugness, superciliousness, superiority. [*Compare* **egotism, impudence.**]

arrogant *adjective.* Overly convinced of one's own superiority and importance ▶ disdainful, haughty, high-and-mighty, hubristic, insolent, lofty, lordly, overbearing, overweening, prideful, priggish, proud, self-important, self-satisfied, smug, supercilious, superior. *Informal:* high-hat, snooty, swellheaded. ***Idioms:*** full of oneself, on one's high horse. [*Compare* **dictatorial, egotistic, pompous, snobbish.**]

✚ **CORE SYNONYMS:** *arrogant, proud, haughty, disdainful, supercilious.* These adjectives refer to one who is overly convinced of one's own superiority and importance. One who is *arrogant* is overbearing and demands excessive power or consideration: *an arrogant and pompous professor, unpopular with students and colleagues alike. Proud* can suggest justifiable self-satisfaction but often implies conceit: "*There is such a thing as a man being too proud to fight*" (Woodrow Wilson). *Haughty* suggests proud superiority, as by reason of high status: "*Her laugh was satirical, and so was the habitual expression of her arched and haughty lip*" (Charlotte Brontë). *Disdainful* emphasizes scorn or contempt: "*Nor* [let] *grandeur hear with a disdainful smile,/The short and simple annals of the poor*" (Thomas Gray). *Supercilious* implies haughty disdain and aloofness: "*His mother eyed me in silence with a supercilious air*" (Tobias Smollett).

---

arrogate *verb.* —*See* **seize** (1).

arrogation *noun.* —*See* **seizure** (2).

art *noun.* Deceitful cleverness ▶ artfulness, artifice, cleverness, craft, craftiness, cunning, deceitfulness, deviousness, disingenuousness, foxiness, guile, shrewdness, slyness, wiliness. [*Compare* **deceit, dishonesty, stealth.**] —*See also* **ability** (1), **business** (2).

artery *noun.* —*See* **vessel** (2).

artful *adjective.* Deceitfully clever ▶ calculating, crafty, cunning, designing, double-dealing, foxy, guileful, scheming, sharp, shrewd, sly, tricky, wily. [*Compare* **shrewd, stealthy, underhand.**] —*See also* **dexterous.**

artfulness *noun.* —*See* **art.**

article *noun.* —*See* **element** (2), **item, object** (1).

article of faith *noun.* —*See* **doctrine.**

articulacy *or* **articulateness** *noun.* —*See* **eloquence.**

articulate *adjective.* —*See* **eloquent, oral.**

articulate *verb.* —*See* **combine** (1), **pronounce, say.**

articulation *noun.* —*See* **expression** (1), **voicing.**

artifice *noun.* —*See* **art, trick** (1).

artificial *adjective.* **1.** Made by humans, often in imitation of something else ▶ ersatz, imitation, manmade, manufactured, mock, pretend, simulated, synthetic. *Informal:* pretend. [*Compare* **counterfeit, fake.**] **2.** Not genuine or sincere ▶ affected, contrived, feigned, insincere, phony, pretended, stagy, studied. *Slang:* phony-baloney. [*Compare* **pompous.**]

✚ **CORE SYNONYMS:** *artificial, synthetic, ersatz, simulated.* These adjectives refer to what is made by humans rather than natural in origin. *Artificial* is broadest in meaning and connotation: *an artificial sweetener; artificial flowers. Synthetic* often implies the use of a chemical process to produce a substance that will look or function like the original, often with certain advantages: *synthetic rubber; a synthetic fabric.* An *ersatz* product is a transparently inferior imitation: *ersatz coffee; ersatz mink. Simulated* often refers to a fabricated substitute or imitation of a costlier substance: *simulated diamonds.*

---

artificiality *noun.* —*See* **affectation, insincerity.**

artisan *noun.* —*See* **maker.**

artistic *adjective.* Relating to or appreciative of the arts ▶ aesthetic, creative. *Informal:* artsy, arty. —*See also* **inventive.**

artless *adjective.* Free from guile, cunning, or deceit ▶ guileless, ingenuous, innocent, naive, natural, simple, unaffected, unsophisticated, unstudied, unworldly. [*Compare* **frank, genuine, innocent.**] —*See also* **rustic.**

✤ **CORE SYNONYMS:** *artless, naive, simple, ingenuous, unsophisticated, natural, unaffected, guileless.* These adjectives mean free from guile, cunning, or deceit. *Artless* stresses absence of plan or purpose and suggests unconcern for or lack of awareness of the reaction produced in others: *a child of artless grace and simple goodness. Naive* sometimes connotes a credulity that impedes effective functioning in a practical world: *"this naive simple creature, with his straightforward and friendly eyes so eager to believe appearances"* (Arnold Bennett). *Simple* stresses absence of complexity, artifice, pretentiousness, or dissimulation: *"Those of highest worth and breeding are most simple in manner and attire"* (Francis Parkman). *"Among simple people she had the reputation of being a prodigy of information"* (Harriet Beecher Stowe). *Ingenuous* denotes childlike directness, simplicity, and innocence; it connotes an inability to mask one's feelings: *an ingenuous admission of responsibility. Unsophisticated* indicates absence of worldliness: *the astonishment of unsophisticated tourists at the tall buildings. Natural* stresses spontaneity that is the result of freedom from self-consciousness or inhibitions: *"When Kavanagh was present, Alice was happy, but embarrassed; Cecelia, joyous and natural"* (Henry Wadsworth Longfellow). *Unaffected* implies sincerity and lack of affectation: *"With men he can be rational and unaffected, but when he has ladies to please, every feature works"* (Jane Austen). *Guileless* signifies absence of insidious or treacherous cunning: *a guileless, disarming look.*

artlessness *noun.* The absence of guile, cunning, or deceit ▶ guilelessness, ingenuousness, innocence, naiveté, naturalness, simpleness, simplicity, unsophistication, unworldliness. [*Compare* **honesty.**]

arty *or* **artsy** *adjective.* **1.** *Informal* Relating to or appreciative of the arts ▶ aesthetic, artistic, creative. **2.** *Informal* Pretentiously artistic ▶ *Informal:* artsy-craftsy.

as *conjunction.* —*See* **because.**

ascend *verb.* To move upward along a surface or slope ▶ clamber, climb, go up, mount, scale, scramble. —*See also* **rise** (2), **rise** (3).

ascendance *or* **ascendancy** *noun.* —*See* **dominance.**

ascendant *adjective.* —*See* **dominant** (1).

ascendant *noun.* —*See* **ancestor** (1).

ascension *noun.* —*See* **ascent** (1).

ascent *noun.* **1.** The act of rising or moving upward ▶ ascension, climb, climbing, lift, mounting, rise, rising. [*Compare* **increase.**] **2.** An upward path or surface ▶ acclivity, grade, gradient, inclined plane, rise, slant, slope. [*Compare* **elevation, hill.**]

ascertain *verb.* —*See* **discern, discover.**

ascertainment *noun.* —*See* **discovery.**

ascetic *adjective.* Renouncing material comforts and pleasures ▶ abstinent, austere, monkish, puritan, puritanical, self-denying. [*Compare* **meager, temperate.**]

ascribe *verb.* —*See* **attribute, fix** (3).

aseptic *adjective.* —*See* **dull** (1), **sterile** (1).

asepticism *noun.* —*See* **dullness.**

ashen *or* **ashy** *adjective.* —*See* **pale** (1).

ashes *noun.* The substance of the body, especially after decay or cremation ▶ clay, cremains, dust, remains.

aside *noun.* —*See* **comment, digression.**

asinine *adjective.* —*See* **foolish.**

ask *verb.* **1.** To put a question to someone ▶ cross-examine, examine, inquire, interrogate, query, question, quiz, pump. *Informal:* grill. ***Idiom:*** give someone the third degree. **2.** To seek an answer to a question ▶ pose, put, raise. [*Compare* **say.**] **3.** To request that someone take part in or be present at a particular occasion ▶ bid, invite, summon. ***Idioms:*** extend an invitation to, request the presence of. [*Compare* **request.**] —*See also* **appeal** (1), **demand** (2).

✦ **CORE SYNONYMS:** *ask, question, inquire, query, interrogate, examine, quiz.* These verbs mean to put a question to or seek information from someone. *Ask* is the most neutral term: *The coach asked me what was wrong. Question* implies careful and continuous asking: *The prosecutor questioned the witness in great detail. Inquire* refers to a simple request for information: *The committee will inquire how it can be of help. Query* usually suggests settling a doubt: *The proofreader queried the spelling of the word. Interrogate* applies especially to official questioning: *The detectives interrogated the suspects. Examine* refers particularly to close and detailed questioning to ascertain a person's knowledge or qualifications: *Only lawyers who have been examined and certified by the bar association are admitted to practice. Quiz* denotes the informal examination of students: *The teacher quizzed the pupils on the state capitals.*

askance *adverb.* —*See* **skeptically.**
asleep *adjective.* —*See* **dead** (1), **dead** (2), **sleeping.**
aspect *noun.* —*See* **appearance** (1), **expression** (4), **face** (3), **viewpoint.**
asperity *noun.* —*See* **difficulty.**
asperse *verb.* —*See* **malign.**
aspersion *noun.* —*See* **indignity, libel.**
asphyxiate *verb.* —*See* **choke.**
aspirant *noun.* One who aspires ▶ aspirer, dreamer, hopeful, seeker. *Informal:* wannabe. —*See also* **applicant.**
aspiration *noun.* A strong desire to achieve something ▶ ambition, ambitiousness, emulation. [*Compare* **drive, enthusiasm, thirst.**] —*See also* **dream** (3).
aspire *verb.* To strive toward a goal ▶ aim, seek. ***Idioms:*** go (*or* grab) for the brass ring, keep one's eyes on the prize, set one's sights on. —*See also* **desire.**
aspiring *adjective.* —*See* **ambitious.**
ass *noun.* —*See* **fool.**
assail *verb.* —*See* **attack** (1), **beat** (1), **revile.**
assailability *noun.* —*See* **exposure.**
assailable *adjective.* —*See* **vulnerable.**
assailant *or* **assailer** *noun.* —*See* **aggressor.**
assailment *noun.* —*See* **attack.**
assassin *noun.* —*See* **murderer.**
assassinate *verb.* —*See* **murder.**
assassination *noun.* —*See* **murder.**
assault *noun.* —*See* **attack.**
assault *verb.* To compel another to participate in or submit to a sexual act ▶ force, molest, rape, ravish, violate. —*See also* **attack** (1), **beat** (1).
assaulter *noun.* —*See* **aggressor.**
assay *verb.* —*See* **attempt, estimate** (1), **test** (1).
assay *noun.* —*See* **test** (1).
assemblage *noun.* —*See* **accumulation** (1), **assembly.**
assemble *verb.* To come, bring, or call together ▶ call, cluster, collect, congregate, convene, convoke, forgather, gather, get together, group, muster, round up, send for, summon. [*Compare* **mobilize.**] —*See also* **accumulate, make.**

✦ **CORE SYNONYMS:** *assemble, convene, convoke, muster, summon.* These verbs mean to come, bring, or call together: *assembled the troops; convened a meeting; will convoke the legislature; mustering the militia; summoned a witness.*

assembler *noun.* —*See* **maker.**
assembly *noun.* A number of persons who have come or been gathered together ▶ assemblage, body, company, conclave, conference, congregation, congress, convention, convocation, council, crowd, forum, galaxy, gathering, group, meeting, muster, rally, troop.

Informal: get-together. [*Compare* **attendance, band**[2]**, crowd, force.**] —*See also* **convention.**

assent *verb.* To respond affirmatively; receive with agreement or compliance ▶ accede, accept, acquiesce, agree, concur, consent, nod, subscribe, yes. [*Compare* **acknowledge, agree, approve, permit.**]

assent *noun.* —*See* **acceptance** (1), **permission.**

✦ **CORE SYNONYMS:** *assent, agree, accede, acquiesce, consent, concur.* These verbs denote an affirmative response to or acceptance of something, as another person's views, proposals, or actions. *Assent* implies agreement, especially as a result of deliberation: *They readily assented to our suggestion. Agree* and *accede* are related in the sense that assent has been reached after discussion or persuasion, but *accede* implies that one person or group has yielded to the other: *"It was not possible to agree to a proposal so extraordinary and unexpected"* (William Robertson). *"In an evil hour this proposal was acceded to"* (Mary E. Herbert). *Acquiesce* suggests passive assent because of inability or unwillingness to oppose: *I acquiesced in their decision despite my misgivings. Consent* implies voluntary agreement: *Our parents consented to our marriage. Concur* suggests that one has independently reached the same conclusion as another: *"I concurred with our incumbent in getting up a petition against the Reform Bill"* (George Eliot).

---

assenting *adjective.* —*See* **favorable** (2), **unanimous.**

assert *verb.* To put into words positively and with conviction ▶ affirm, allege, argue, asseverate, aver, avouch, avow, claim, contend, declare, enounce, enunciate, hold, insist, maintain, profess, say, state, swear. ***Idiom:*** have it. [*Compare* **announce, confirm, stipulate, support.**] —*See also* **claim.**

assertion *noun.* The act of asserting positively or something so asserted ▶ affirmation, allegation, asseveration, averment, avowal, claim, contention, declaration, profession, statement. [*Compare* **announcement, assumption.**]

assertive *adjective.* Bold or confident in assertion ▶ aggressive, emphatic, forceful, insistent, in-your-face. *Informal:* go-ahead. [*Compare* **definite, dictatorial, frank.**]

assess *verb.* To establish and apply as compulsory ▶ exact, impose, levy, put. —*See also* **estimate** (1).

assessed *adjective.* —*See* **calculated.**

assessment *noun.* —*See* **estimate** (1), **tax.**

assessor *noun.* —*See* **critic** (1).

asset *noun.* —*See* **spy, virtue.**

assets *noun.* —*See* **capital** (1), **resources.**

asseverate *verb.* —*See* **assert.**

asseveration *noun.* —*See* **assertion.**

assiduity *or* **assiduousness** *noun.* —*See* **diligence.**

assiduous *adjective.* —*See* **diligent.**

assign *verb.* To appoint and send to a particular place ▶ post, set, station. [*Compare* **position.**] —*See also* **appoint, appropriate, attribute, distribute, fix** (3), **transfer** (1).

assignation *noun.* —*See* **engagement** (1).

assignment *noun.* —*See* **appointment, distribution** (1), **grant, task** (1).

assimilate *verb.* —*See* **absorb** (2), **liken.**

assimilation *noun.* —*See* **absorption** (1).

assimilative *adjective.* —*See* **absorbent.**

assist *verb.* —*See* **help, oblige** (1).

assist *noun.* —*See* **help.**

assistance *noun.* —*See* **help.**

assistant *noun.* A person who assists someone else, especially a person who assumes some of the duties of a superior ▶ abettor, adjutant, aid, aide, attendant, auxiliary, coadjutant, coadjutor, deputy, help, helper, lieutenant, reliever, second, succorer. *Slang:* gofer. ***Idioms:*** man (*or* girl) Friday, right-hand man (*or* woman), second in command. [*Compare* **associate, follower, minor, subordinate.**]

assistant *adjective.* —*See* **auxiliary** (1).

✚ CORE SYNONYMS: *assistant, aide, coadjutant, coadjutor, helper, lieutenant, second.* These nouns denote a person who holds a position auxiliary to another and assumes some of the superior's responsibilities: *an editorial assistant; a senator's aide; the general's coadjutant; a bishop's coadjutor; a teacher's helper; a politician's lieutenant; a prizefighter's second.*

---

assize *noun.* —*See* **law** (2).

associate *verb.* **1.** To unite or be united in a relationship ▶ amalgamate, affiliate, ally, bind, combine, conjoin, connect, federate, incorporate, join, link, relate. [*Compare* **band, combine.**] **2.** To be with as a companion ▶ be friendly, be intimate, consort, fall in with, fraternize, hang around, hobnob, pal (around), run (around), take up with, troop. *Slang:* hang out. ***Idioms:*** have relations, keep company, rub elbows (*or* shoulders). **3.** To come or bring together in one's mind or imagination ▶ bracket, connect, correlate, couple, identify, link. [*Compare* **equal, liken.**]

associate *noun.* **1.** One who is united in a relationship with another ▶ affiliate, ally, cohort, colleague, compatriot, confederate, copartner, fellow, partner. [*Compare* **peer**[2].] **2.** One who shares interests or activities with another ▶ chum, companion, comrade, crony, fellow, mate. *Informal:* bud, buddy, pal. *Slang:* sidekick. ***Idiom:*** partner in crime. [*Compare* **friend.**] —*See also* **concomitant.**

✚ CORE SYNONYMS: *associate, partner, colleague, ally, confederate.* These nouns denote one who is united in a relationship, as in a venture, with another. An *associate* is the most general term: *ate lunch with her business associates every Wednesday.* A *partner* participates in a relationship in which each member has equal status: *a partner in a law firm.* A *colleague* is an associate in an occupation or profession: *a colleague and fellow professor.* An *ally* is one who associates with another, at least temporarily, in a common cause: *countries that were allies in World War II.* A *confederate* is a member of a confederacy, league, or alliance or sometimes a collaborator in a suspicious venture: *confederates in a scheme to oust the chairman.*

---

association *noun.* **1.** The state of being associated ▶ affiliation, alliance, combination, conjunction, connection, cooperation, partnership. [*Compare* **friendship, relation.**] **2.** Something, such as a feeling or idea, associated with a specific person or thing ▶ connection, connotation, impression, suggestion. —*See also* **conference** (2), **union** (1).

assort *verb.* —*See* **classify.**

assorted *adjective.* —*See* **various.**

assortment *noun.* A collection of various things ▶ conglomeration, gallimaufry, hodgepodge, jumble, medley, mélange, miscellany, mishmash, mixed bag, mixture, olio, patchwork, potpourri, salmagundi, variety. *Slang:* grab bag. [*Compare* **combination, mixture, odds and ends.**] —*See also* **arrangement** (1).

assuage *verb.* —*See* **pacify, relieve** (1).

assuagement *noun.* —*See* **relief** (1).

assume *verb.* To take upon oneself ▶ incur, shoulder, tackle, take on, take over, undertake. [*Compare* **endure, take.**] —*See also* **act** (2), **adopt, don, seize** (1), **suppose** (1).

assumed *adjective.* Being fictitious and not real, as a name ▶ made-up, pretended, pseudonymous. [*Compare* **false, fictitious.**]

assuming *adjective.* —*See* **impudent.**

assumption *noun.* Something taken to be true without proof ▶ axiom, assertion, given, lemma, postulate, postulation, premise, presumption, presupposition, speculation, supposition. [*Compare* **assertion, theory.**] —*See also* **impudence, seizure** (2).

assumptive *adjective.* —*See* **impudent, presumptive.**

assurance *noun.* —*See* **confidence, optimism, promise** (1), **safety, sureness.**

assure *verb.* —*See* **convince, guarantee** (2).

assured *adjective.* —*See* **confident, optimistic, sure** (1).

assuredly *adverb.* —*See* **yes.**

assuredness *noun.* —*See* **decision** (2), **sureness.**

astir *adjective.* —*See* **busy** (2).

astonish *verb.* —*See* **surprise.**

astonishing *adjective.* So remarkable as to be difficult to believe ▶ amazing, astounding, awe-inspiring, dumbfounding, fabulous, fantastic, flabbergasting, incredible, marvelous, miraculous, overwhelming, phenomenal, prodigious, staggering, stunning, stupendous, unbelievable, wonderful, wondrous. *Informal:* mind-blowing, mind-boggling. [*Compare* **exceptional, rare.**]

astonishment *noun.* —*See* **marvel, wonder** (1).

astound *verb.* —*See* **surprise.**

astounding *adjective.* —*See* **astonishing.**

astray *adverb.* Not in the right way or on the proper course ▶ afield, amiss, awry, wrong.

astray *adjective.* —*See* **lost** (1).

astringent *adjective.* —*See* **biting.**

astronomical *adjective.* —*See* **enormous, heavenly** (2).

astute *adjective.* —*See* **discriminating, shrewd.**

astuteness *noun.* —*See* **discernment, discrimination** (1).

asylum *noun.* —*See* **cover** (1), **home** (3), **refuge** (1).

asymmetric *or* **asymmetrical** *adjective.* —*See* **irregular.**

asymmetry *noun.* —*See* **irregularity.**

atelier *noun.* An artist's workspace ▶ studio, workroom, workshop.

atheism *noun.* Lack of belief in God ▶ disbelief, faithlessness, godlessness, impiety, irreligion, unbelief.

atheist *noun.* One who does not believe in God ▶ heathen, infidel, nonbeliever, pagan.

atheistic *adjective.* Not believing in God ▶ disbelieving, faithless, godless, impious, irreligious, ungodly. [*Compare* **doubtful.**]

athirst *adjective.* —*See* **eager.**

athletic *adjective.* —*See* **muscular.**

atingle *adjective.* —*See* **thrilled.**

atmosphere *noun.* **1.** The gaseous mixture enveloping the earth ▶ air, ether. **2.** A distinctive yet intangible quality ▶ aroma, flavor, savor, smack. [*Compare* **quality.**] —*See also* **air** (3), **environment** (2).

atmospheric *adjective.* Of or relating to air ▶ aerial, airy, pneumatic.

atomize *verb.* —*See* **crush** (2), **disintegrate.**

atone *noun.* —*See* **purify** (1).

atonement *noun.* The act of making amends ▶ expiation, penance, reconciliation, reparation. [*Compare* **compensation, purification.**]

atrium *noun.* —*See* **court** (1).

atrocious *adjective.* —*See* **offensive** (1), **outrageous, tormenting.**

atrociousness *noun.* —*See* **outrageousness.**

atrocity *noun.* —*See* **outrage, outrageousness.**

atrophy *noun.* —*See* **deterioration** (1).

atrophy *verb.* —*See* **deteriorate.**

attach *verb.* **1.** To join one thing to another ▶ adjoin, append, affix, clamp, clip, connect, couple, fasten, fuse, fix, moor, secure. [*Compare* **bond, combine, join.**] **2.** To add as a supplement or an appendix ▶ add (on), affix, annex, append, subjoin.

attachment *noun.* A subordinate element added to another entity ▶ accessory, adjunct, appendage, appurtenance, supplement. [*Compare* **addition.**] —*See also* **bond** (3), **love** (1).

✚ **CORE SYNONYMS:** *attachment, appendage, appurtenance, adjunct, accessory.* These nouns denote subordinate elements added to another entity. An *attachment* adds a function to the thing to which it is connected: *The food processor has an attachment for kneading dough.* An *appendage* supplements without being essential: "*. . . and the complete absence of appendages at the stern decreases hull resistance*" (R.J.L. Dicker). An *appurtenance* belongs naturally as a subsidiary attribute, part, or member: "*an internationally known first-class hotel . . . equipped with such appurtenances as computers, word processors, copiers and telex*" (Oscar Millard). An *adjunct* is added as an auxiliary but is often self-sustaining: "*Intelligence analysts . . . believe that of all the countries of the Middle East, none use terrorism more effectively as an adjunct to diplomacy . . .*" (Elaine Sciolino). An *accessory* is usually nonessential but desirable: *Our new car has such accessories as air conditioning and a sunroof.*

attack *verb.* **1.** To set upon with violent force ▶ aggress, assail, assault, beset, bombard, charge, fall on (*or* upon), go at, have at, march against, rush, sail into, storm, strike. *Informal:* light into, pitch into. *Slang:* lay into, tear into. ***Idioms:*** gang up on, have a go at, let have it, open up on. [*Compare* **ambush, contend, raid.**] **2.** To start work on vigorously ▶ dive into, go at, plunge into, set to work, tackle, wade in (*or* into). ***Idioms:*** get a move on, get cracking (*or* moving), hop to it, look lively, roll up one's sleeves. [*Compare* **start.**]

attack *noun.* The act of attacking ▶ aggression, assailment, assault, attempt, drive, offense, offensive, onrush, onset, onslaught, storming, strike. [*Compare* **advance, charge, siege.**] —*See also* **approach** (1), **seizure** (1).

✚ **CORE SYNONYMS:** *attack, bombard, assail, storm, assault, beset.* These verbs mean to set upon with violent force, physically or figuratively. *Attack* applies to offensive action, especially to the onset of planned aggression: *The commandos attacked the outpost at dawn. Bombard* suggests showering with bombs or shells (*The warplanes bombarded the town*) or with words (*The celebrity was bombarded with invitations*). *Assail* implies repeated attacks: *Critics assailed the author's second novel. Storm* refers to a sudden, sweeping attempt to achieve a victory: "*After triumphantly storming the country,* [the President] *is obliged to storm Capitol Hill*" (The Economist). *Assault* usually implies sudden, intense violence: *Muggers often assault their victims on dark streets. Beset* suggests beleaguerment from all sides: *The fox was beset by hunters and hounds.*

attackable *adjective.* —*See* **vulnerable.**

attacker *noun.* —*See* **aggressor.**

attain *verb.* —*See* **accomplish, get** (1).

attainable *adjective.* —*See* **available, possible.**

attainment *noun.* A quality that makes a person suitable for a particular position or task ▶ credential, endowment, qualification, skill. —*See also* **accomplishment, fulfillment** (1).

attempt *verb.* To make an attempt to do or make ▶ assay, endeavor, essay, seek, strive, struggle, try (for). *Informal:* shoot for (*or* at). ***Idioms:*** give a whirl, go to all lengths, have a go at, have (*or* make *or* take) a shot at, have a try at, make a grab (*or* stab) at, take a crack at, try one's hand at, have (*or* take) a whack at. [*Compare* **aspire, presume, start.**]

attempt *noun.* A trying to do or make something ▶ bid, crack, effort, endeavor, essay, go, offer, stab, trial, try, undertaking. *Informal:* shot, whirl. *Slang:* take. [*Compare* **effort.**] *—See also* **attack.**

attend *verb.* **1.** To occur as a consequence ▶ ensue, follow, result. [*Compare* **stem.**] **2.** To work and care for ▶ do for, minister to, serve, wait on (*or* upon). [*Compare* **help, work.**] **3.** To make an effort to hear something ▶ hark, hearken, heed, listen. ***Idioms:*** be all ears, give (*or* lend) an ear. *—See also* **accompany, hear, tend².**

attendance *noun.* The condition or fact of being present ▶ occurrence, presence. [*Compare* **existence.**]

attendant *noun.* *—See* **assistant, concomitant.**

attendant *adjective.* *—See* **concurrent.**

attending *adjective.* *—See* **concurrent, following** (2).

attention *noun.* Concentration of the mental powers on something ▶ attentiveness, concentration, consideration, contemplation, heedfulness, intentness, preoccupation, regardfulness. [*Compare* **alertness, care, diligence.**] *—See also* **notice** (1).

attentions *noun.* *—See* **advances.**

attentive *adjective.* Full of polite concern for the well-being of others ▶ considerate, courteous, gallant, neighborly, polite, regardful, respectful, solicitous, thoughtful. [*Compare* **benevolent, friendly.**] *—See also* **alert.**

✚ CORE SYNONYMS: *attentive, thoughtful, considerate, solicitous.* These adjectives mean full of polite concern for the well-being of others. *Attentive* suggests devoted, assiduous attention: *a good editor who is attentive to detail.* Although *thoughtful* and *considerate* are often used interchangeably, *thoughtful* implies a tendency to anticipate needs or wishes, whereas *considerate* stresses sensitivity to another's feelings: *a thoughtful friend who brought me soup when I was sick; considerate, quiet neighbors. Solicitous* implies deep concern that often verges on anxiety or expresses itself in exaggerated and sometimes cloying attentiveness: *was annoyed by a solicitous and meddlesome cousin.*

attentiveness *noun.* *—See* **attention, consideration** (1).

attenuate *verb.* To become diffuse ▶ rarefy, thin. *—See also* **dilute, enervate.**

attenuate *or* **attenuated** *adjective.* Marked by great diffusion of component particles ▶ rare, rarefied, thin.

attenuation *noun.* *—See* **debilitation.**

attest *verb.* *—See* **certify, confirm** (1), **indicate** (1), **testify.**

attestant *or* **attester** *or* **attestor** *noun.* One who testifies, especially in court ▶ deponent, testifier, witness.

attestation *noun.* *—See* **confirmation** (2).

attire *noun.* Showy and elaborate clothing or apparel ▶ array, finery, frippery, regalia. *Slang:* get-up, glad-rags, Sunday best. ***Idiom:*** go-to-meeting clothes. *—See also* **dress** (1).

attire *verb.* *—See* **dress up, dress** (1).

attitude *noun.* **1.** A general cast of mind with regard to something ▶ feeling, sentiment. [*Compare* **idea.**] **2.** The way in which one is placed or arranged ▶ arrangement, pose, position, posture. *—See also* **posture** (1), **posture** (2).

attitudinize *verb.* *—See* **impersonate, pose** (1).

attorney *noun.* *—See* **lawyer.**

attract *verb.* To direct or impel to oneself by some quality or action ▶ allure, appeal, draw, entice, lure, magnetize, take. *Informal:* pull. ***Idioms:*** catch one's eye, pique one's interest. [*Compare* **charm.**] *—See also* **grip.**

attraction *noun.* The power or quality of attracting ▶ allure, allurement, appeal, attractiveness, call, captivation, charisma, charm, draw, enchantment, enticement, fascination, glamour, gravitation, lure, magnetism, witchery. *Informal:* pull. *—See also* **lure** (1).

attractive *adjective.* Pleasing to the eye or mind ▶ appealing, bewitching, captivating, charismatic, charming, cute, desirable, enchanting, engaging, enticing, fascinating, fetching, glamorous, graceful, lovely, magic, magical, magnetic, pretty, sweet, taking, tempting, well-favored, winning, winsome. [*Compare* **delightful, seductive.**] *—See also* **beautiful, becoming.**

attractiveness *noun.* *—See* **attraction.**

attribute *verb.* To regard as belonging to or resulting from another ▶ accredit, ascribe, assign, charge, credit, refer. [*Compare* **accuse.**] *—See also* **fix** (3).

attribute *noun.* An object or expression associated with and serving to identify something else ▶ emblem, metaphor, signifier, symbol, token. [*Compare* **expression, sign, term.**] *—See also* **quality** (1).

✦ **CORE SYNONYMS:** *attribute, ascribe, credit, assign, refer.* These verbs mean to regard as belonging to or resulting from another. *Attribute* and *ascribe,* often interchangeable, have the widest application: *The historian discovered a new symphony attributed to Mozart. The museum displayed an invention ascribed to the 15th century. Credit* frequently applies to an accomplishment or virtue: *"Some excellent remarks were made on immortality, but mainly borrowed from and credited to Plato"* (Oliver Wendell Holmes, Sr.). *Assign* and *refer* are often used to classify or categorize: *Program music as a genre is usually assigned to the Romantic period. "A person thus prepared will be able to refer any particular history he takes up to its proper place in universal history"* (Joseph Priestley).

---

attrition *noun.* *—See* **penitence.**

attune *verb.* *—See* **adjust, harmonize** (1).

atypical *or* **atypic** *adjective.* *—See* **abnormal, unusual.**

atypically *adverb.* *—See* **unusually.**

au courant *adjective.* *—See* **contemporary** (2).

auction *noun.* *—See* **deal** (1).

audacious *adjective.* *—See* **adventurous, brave, impudent.**

audacity *or* **audaciousness** *noun.* *—See* **daring, impudence.**

audience *noun.* **1.** The body of persons who admire a public personality, especially an entertainer ▶ following, public. [*Compare* **fan[2].**] **2.** A chance to be heard ▶ audition, hearing, listen. ***Idiom:*** one's day in court. **3.** Someone who sees something occur ▶ eyewitness, seer, viewer, witness.

audit *noun.* *—See* **examination** (1).

audit *verb.* *—See* **examine** (1).

audition *noun.* **1.** A chance to be heard ▶ audience, hearing, listen. ***Idiom:*** one's day in court. **2.** The sense by which sound is perceived ▶ ear, hearing.

augment *verb.* *—See* **gain** (1), **increase, supplement.**

augment *noun.* *—See* **increase** (1).

augmentation *noun.* *—See* **addition** (1), **increase** (1).

augur *verb.* *—See* **foreshadow, prophesy.**

augur *noun.* *—See* **prophet.**

augural *adjective.* *—See* **prophetic.**

augury *noun.* *—See* **magic** (1), **omen, prophecy.**

august *adjective.* *—See* **exalted, grand.**

auld lang syne *noun.* *—See* **past.**

au naturel *adjective.* *—See* **nude.**

aura *noun.* *—See* **air** (3).

aureate *adjective.* *—See* **oratorical.**

aurora *noun.* *—See* **dawn.**

auspex *noun.* *—See* **prophet.**

auspices *noun.* *—See* **patronage** (1).

auspicious *adjective.* *—See* **favorable** (1), **opportune.**

austere *adjective.* *—See* **ascetic, bare** (1), **bleak** (1).

austerity *noun.* *—See* **severity.**

autarchic *or* **autarchical** *adjective.* *—See* **absolute.**

autarchist *noun.* —*See* **dictator.**

autarchy *noun.* —*See* **absolutism** (2).

authentic *adjective.* **1.** Not counterfeit or copied ▶ actual, bona fide, certified, confirmed, genuine, good, indubitable, legitimate, original, proved, real, tested, true, undoubted, unquestionable, verified, veritable. *Slang:* legit, kosher. ***Idioms:*** honest to goodness, for real, real live, sure enough, the real McCoy, the real thing, true to life. [*Compare* **actual, certain.**] **2.** Worthy of belief, as because of precision or faithfulness to an original ▶ authoritative, convincing, credible, faithful, true, trustworthy, valid. [*Compare* **accurate, definitive, dependable.**]

✚ **CORE SYNONYMS:** *authentic, bona fide, genuine, real, true, undoubted, unquestionable.* These adjectives mean not counterfeit or copied: *an authentic painting by Corot; a bona fide transfer of property; genuine crabmeat; a real diamond; true courage; undoubted evidence; an unquestionable antique.*

◀ **ANTONYM:** *counterfeit*

authenticate *verb.* —*See* **confirm** (1), **prove.**

authentication *noun.* —*See* **confirmation** (2).

authenticity *noun.* —*See* **veracity.**

author *noun.* —*See* **originator.**

author *verb.* —*See* **publish** (2).

authoritarian *adjective.* Characterized by or favoring absolute obedience to authority ▶ autocratic, despotic, dictatorial, totalitarian, tyrannic, tyrannical. [*Compare* **absolute.**] —*See also* **dictatorial.**

authoritarian *noun.* One who imposes or favors absolute obedience to authority ▶ autocrat, despot, dictator, martinet, totalitarian, tyrant. —*See also* **dictator.**

authoritarianism *noun.* —*See* **absolutism** (1), **tyranny.**

authoritative *adjective.* **1.** Having or arising from authority ▶ conclusive, formal, imperial, official, ruling, sanctioned, standard, supreme. [*Compare* **administrative.**] **2.** Exercising authority ▶ commanding, dominant, lordly, masterful. —*See also* **authentic** (2), **definitive.**

authority *noun.* The right and power to command, decide, rule, or judge ▶ carte blanche, command, control, domination, dominion, jurisdiction, mandate, mastery, might, omnipotence, power, prerogative, rule, sovereignty, superiority, supremacy, sway. *Informal:* muscle, say-so. —*See also* **dominance, expert, permission.**

authorization *noun.* —*See* **permission.**

authorize *verb.* To give authority to ▶ accredit, commission, empower, enable, entitle, license, qualify. [*Compare* **appoint, elect, legalize.**] —*See also* **permit** (2).

✚ **CORE SYNONYMS:** *authorize, accredit, commission, empower, license.* These verbs mean to give someone the authority to act: *authorized her partner to negotiate on her behalf; a representative who was accredited by his government; commissioned the real-estate agent to purchase the house; was empowered to make decisions during the president's absence; a pharmacist licensed to practice in two states.*

autochthonous *adjective.* —*See* **domestic** (3), **indigenous.**

autocracy *noun.* —*See* **absolutism** (1), **absolutism** (2), **tyranny.**

autocrat *noun.* —*See* **authoritarian, dictator.**

autograph *verb.* —*See* **sign.**

automatic *adjective.* —*See* **perfunctory, spontaneous.**

autonomous *adjective.* —*See* **free** (1), **independent** (1).

autonomy *noun.* —*See* **freedom, independence.**

auxiliary *adjective.* **1.** Giving or able to give help or support ▶ accessory, aiding, ancillary, assistant, assisting, collateral, cooperating, helping, contributory, subsidiary, supporting, supportive. [*Compare* **minor, subordinate.**] **2.** Used or held in reserve ▶ backup, emergency, reserve, secondary, standby, supplemental, supplementary. [*Compare* **additional.**]
auxiliary *noun.* —*See* **assistant.**

avail *verb.* —*See* **profit** (2).
avail *noun.* —*See* **advantage** (2), **use** (2).

available *adjective.* Capable of being obtained or used ▶ acquirable, attainable, gettable, obtainable, procurable. ***Idioms:*** at (*or* on) hand, at one's disposal, on tap, to be had, within reach. [*Compare* **convenient, open, unoccupied.**] —*See also* **single.**

avant-garde *noun.* —*See* **forefront.**
avant-garde *adjective.* —*See* **progressive** (1).

avarice *or* **avariciousness** *noun.* —*See* **greed.**

avaricious *adjective.* —*See* **greedy.**

avenge *verb.* To exact revenge for or from ▶ get, pay back, pay off, redress, repay, requite, vindicate. *Informal:* fix. ***Idioms:*** even the score, get back at, get even with, give a taste of one's own medicine, pay back in kind (*or* in one's own coin), pay off old scores, settle a score, settle (*or* square) accounts, take an eye for an eye. [*Compare* **punish, retaliate.**]

avenging *adjective.* —*See* **vindictive.**

avenue *noun.* —*See* **way** (2).

aver *verb.* —*See* **assert.**

average *adjective.* Relating to or occupying a middle position on a scale of evaluation ▶ fair, indifferent, mediocre, medium, middling, tolerable. —*See also* **acceptable** (2), **common** (1), **ordinary.**
average *noun.* Something, as a type, number, quantity, or degree, that represents a midpoint between extremes ▶ mean, median, medium, midpoint, norm, par. [*Compare* **center.**] —*See also* **usual.**

✚ **CORE SYNONYMS:** *average, medium, mediocre, fair, middling, indifferent, tolerable.* These adjectives indicate a middle position on a scale of evaluation. *Average* and *medium* apply to what is midway between extremes and imply both sufficiency and lack of distinction: *a novel of average merit; an orange of medium size. Mediocre* stresses the undistinguished aspect of what is average: "*The caliber of the students . . . has gone from mediocre to above average*" (Judy Pasternak). What is *fair* is passable but substantially below excellent: *in fair health. Middling* refers to a ranking between average and mediocre: *gave a middling performance. Indifferent* most commonly suggests neutrality: "*His home, alas, was but an indifferent attic*" (Edward Everett Hale). Something *tolerable* is merely acceptable: *prepared a tolerable meal.*

---

averageness *noun.* —*See* **usualness.**

averment *noun.* —*See* **assertion.**

averse *adjective.* —*See* **indisposed.**

averseness *noun.* —*See* **indisposition.**

aversion *noun.* —*See* **hate** (1), **hate** (2), **indisposition, opposition** (1).

avert *verb.* —*See* **prevent, turn** (2).

aviator *noun.* A person who flies an airplane ▶ flier, pilot. *Slang:* flyboy.

avid *adjective.* —*See* **eager, greedy, voracious.**

avidity *or* **avidness** *noun.* —*See* **greed, voracity.**

avocation *noun.* —*See* **business** (2).

avoid *verb.* To keep away from ▶ abstain from, burke, bypass, circumvent, dodge, duck, elude, escape, eschew, evade, get around, lay off, refrain from, shun, stay off. ***Idioms:*** fight shy of, give a wide berth to, have no truck with, keep at arm's length, keep clear of, keep one's distance from, let well enough alone, stay clear of, steer clear of. [*Compare* **evade, skirt.**]

✣ **CORE SYNONYMS:** *avoid, escape, shun, eschew, evade, elude.* These verbs mean to keep away from persons or things. *Avoid* always involves an effort to keep away from what is considered dangerous or difficult: *avoiding strenuous exercise. Escape* can mean to get free or to remain untouched or unaffected by something unwanted: *"Let no guilty man escape, if it can be avoided"* (Ulysses S. Grant). *Shun* refers to keeping clear of what is unwelcome or undesirable: *"Family friends . . . she shunned like the plague"* (John Galsworthy). *Eschew* involves staying clear of something because to do otherwise would be unwise or morally wrong: *"Eschew evil, and do good"* (Book of Common Prayer). *Evade* implies adroit maneuvering and sometimes implies dishonesty or irresponsibility: *tried to evade jury duty.* To *elude* is to get away from artfully: *eluded their pursuers.*

avoidance *noun.* —*See* **escape** (2).
avoirdupois *noun.* —*See* **heaviness.**
avouch *verb.* —*See* **assert, confirm** (1).
avow *verb.* —*See* **acknowledge** (1), **assert.**
avowal *noun.* —*See* **acknowledgment** (1), **assertion.**
await *verb.* —*See* **expect** (1), **lurk.**
awaiting *adjective.* —*See* **expectant.**
awake *adjective.* Not in a state of sleep or unable to sleep ▶ unsleeping, wakeful, wide-awake. [*Compare* **restless.**] —*See also* **aware.**
awake *or* **awaken** *verb.* —*See* **arouse, wake**[1].
award *verb.* **1.** To let have as a favor, prerogative, or privilege ▶ accord, concede, give, grant, vouchsafe. [*Compare* **yield.**] **2.** To bestow a reward on ▶ guerdon, honor, reward. —*See also* **confer** (2), **donate, gift.**
award *noun.* A memento received as a symbol of excellence or victory ▶ accolade, cup, prize, trophy. [*Compare* **medal.**] —*See also* **distinction** (2), **donation, reward.**
aware *adjective.* Marked by comprehension, cognizance, and perception ▶ alive, awake, cognizant, sensible, sentient, wise. *Informal:* with-it. *Slang:* hip. ***Idioms:*** in the know (*or* swim), on to, up on. [*Compare* **alert, informed, sensitive.**]

✣ **CORE SYNONYMS:** *aware, cognizant, sensible, awake.* These adjectives mean marked by comprehension, cognizance, and perception. *Aware* implies knowledge gained through one's own perceptions or by means of information: *Are you aware of your opponent's hostility? I am aware that the legislation passed. Cognizant* is a formal equivalent of *aware: "Our research indicates that the nation's youth are cognizant of the law"* (Jerry D. Jennings). *Sensible* implies knowledge gained through intuition or intellectual perception: *"I am sensible that the mention of such a circumstance may appear trifling"* (Henry Hallam). To be *awake* is to have full consciousness of something: *"as much awake to the novelty of attention in that quarter as Elizabeth herself"* (Jane Austen).

awareness *noun.* The condition of being aware ▶ cognizance, consciousness, mindfulness, perception, realization, recognition, sense. [*Compare* **alertness.**]
awash *adjective.* —*See* **full** (1).
away *adjective.* —*See* **absent.**
awe *noun.* —*See* **wonder** (1).
awe *verb.* —*See* **surprise.**
awe-inspiring *adjective.* —*See* **astonishing, grand.**
awesome *adjective.* —*See* **excellent, exceptional, grand.**
awful *adjective.* —*See* **terrible.**
awful *adverb.* —*See* **very.**
awfully *adverb.* —*See* **very.**
awkward *adjective.* **1.** Lacking dexterity and grace in physical movement ▶ butterfingered, cloddish, clumsy, gawky,

graceless, inept, lubberly, lumpish, maladroit, stumbling, uncoordinated, ungainly, ungraceful. *Slang:* klutzy. ***Idioms:*** all thumbs, having two left feet. **2.** Difficult to handle or manage ▶ bulky, clumsy, ungainly, unhandy, unmanageable, unwieldy. [*Compare* **heavy, unruly.**] **3.** Characterized by embarrassment and discomfort ▶ constrained, embarrassed, embarrassing, self-conscious, uncomfortable, uneasy. ***Idiom:*** ill at ease. [*Compare* **delicate, unpleasant.**] —*See also* **unfortunate** (2), **unskillful.**

awry *adverb.* Not in the right way or on the proper course ▶ afield, amiss, astray, wrong.

ax *noun.* —*See* **dismissal.**

ax *verb.* —*See* **abolish, dismiss** (1).

axial *adjective.* —*See* **central.**

axiom *noun.* —*See* **assumption, law** (3), **moral, proverb.**

axis *noun.* —*See* **center** (3).

aye *noun.* An affirmative vote or voter ▶ yea, yes.

aye *adverb.* —*See* **yes.**

B

babble *verb.* To talk rapidly, incoherently, or indistinctly ▶ blather, burble, chatter, gabble, gibber, jabber, jibber-jabber, prate, prattle, rant, rave. [*Compare* **speak, stammer.**] —*See also* **burble, chatter** (1).

babble *noun.* Empty or foolish talk ▶ blarney, blather, blatherskite, double talk, drivel, gabble, gibberish, gobbledygook, jabber, jabberwocky, jargon, jibber-jabber, nonsense, prate, prattle, twaddle. *Slang:* hot air. [*Compare* **nonsense.**] —*See also* **burble, chatter.**

babe *noun.* —*See* **baby** (1), **beauty, darling** (1), **innocent** (2).

babel *noun.* —*See* **noise** (1).

baby *noun.* **1.** A very young child ▶ babe, babe in arms, bambino, cherub, infant, neonate, newborn, nursling, papoose, toddler, tot. *Informal:* preemie. ***Idiom:*** bundle of joy. **2.** A childish or pampered person ▶ crybaby, milksop, milquetoast, mollycoddle, namby-pamby. *Informal:* softy. *Slang:* cream puff. ***Idioms:*** mama's boy (*or* girl). [*Compare* **weakling.**] —*See also* **darling** (1).

baby *verb.* To treat indulgently ▶ cater (to), coddle, cosset, humor, indulge, mollycoddle, overindulge, pamper, spoil. [*Compare* **adore, defer**^{2}.]

CORE SYNONYMS: *baby, pamper, indulge, humor, spoil, coddle, mollycoddle.* These verbs mean to treat someone indulgently, as by catering excessively to his or her desires or feelings. *Baby* suggests the indulgence and attention one might give to an infant: *"I should like to be made much of, and tended—yes, babied"* (Adeline D.T. Whitney). To *pamper* is to gratify appetites, tastes, or desires: *"He was pampering the poor girl's lust for singularity and self-glorification"* (Charles Kingsley). *Indulge* suggests a kindly or excessive lenience in yielding especially to wishes or impulses better left unfulfilled: *"You musn't think because I indulge you in some things that you can keep everyone waiting"* (Theodore Dreiser). *Humor* implies compliance with or accommodation to another's mood or idiosyncrasies: *"Human life is . . . but like a forward child, that must be played with and humored a little to keep it quiet till it falls asleep"* (William Temple). *Spoil* implies excessive indulgence that adversely affects the character, nature, or attitude: *"He seems to be in no danger of being spoilt by good fortune"* (George Gissing). *Coddle* and *mollycoddle* point to tender, overprotective care that often leads to weakening of character: *"I would not* coddle *the child"* (Samuel Johnson). *Stop mollycoddling me; I'm a grown person.*

---

babyish *adjective.* Of or like a baby ▶ cherubic, childlike, infantile, infantine. *Informal:* kidlike. [*Compare* **innocent.**] —*See also* **childish.**

baby-sit *verb.* —*See* **tend**[2]**.**

back *noun.* The part farthest from the front ▶ back end, back side, end, hind end, rear, stern, tag end, tail, tail end.

back *verb.* **1.** To move in a reverse direction ▶ back away (*or* off), backpedal, backtrack, back up, fall back, retreat, retrocede, retrograde, retrogress, reverse. ***Idiom:*** retrace one's steps. [*Compare* **flinch, recede, retreat.**] **2.** To present evidence in support of ▶ back up, bolster, buttress, corroborate, substantiate, support, sustain, vouch (for). [*Compare* **prove.**] **3.** To act as a patron to ▶ patronize, sponsor, support. [*Compare* **donate.**] —*See also* **confirm** (1), **finance, support** (1).

back away *or* **off** *verb.* —*See* **back** (1).

back down *or* **away** *or* **out** *verb.* —*See* **renege.**

back down *or* **off** *verb.* —*See also* **weaken.**

back up *verb.* —*See* **back** (1).

back *adjective.* Located in the rear ▶ hind, hinder, hindmost, hindermost, posterior, rear, rearward. —*See also* **remote** (1).

back *adverb.* —*See* **backward.**

backbite *verb.* —*See* **malign.**

backbone *noun.* —*See* **courage.**

backbreaking *adjective.* —*See* **burdensome.**

backcountry *noun.* —*See* **country.**

backdrop *noun.* —*See* **scene** (1), **scene** (2).

backer *noun.* —*See* **patron, sponsor.**

backfire *verb.* To produce an unexpected and undesired result ▶ boomerang. ***Idiom:*** blow up in one's face. [*Compare* **fail.**] —*See also* **explode** (1).

background *noun.* —*See* **history** (2), **scene** (2).

backhanded *adjective.* —*See* **indirect** (1).

backing *noun.* —*See* **capital** (1), **confirmation** (2), **endorsement, patronage** (1).

backlog *noun.* —*See* **hoard.**

backpack *verb.* To travel about or journey on foot ▶ hike, march, tramp, trek. [*Compare* **journey, walk.**]

backpack *noun.* —*See* **pack** (1).

backpedal *verb.* —*See* **back** (1), **renege.**

backset *noun.* A change from better to worse ▶ reversal, reverse, setback. [*Compare* **misfortune, relapse.**]

backside *noun.* —*See* **buttocks.**

backslide *verb.* —*See* **relapse.**

backslide *or* **backsliding** *noun.* —*See* **relapse.**

backstairs *adjective.* —*See* **secret** (1).

back talk *noun.* Insolent talk ▶ mouth. *Informal:* lip, sass. [*Compare* **impudence.**]

back-to-back *adjective.* —*See* **consecutive.**

backtrack *verb.* —*See* **back** (1).

backup *adjective.* —*See* **auxiliary** (2).

backward *adjective.* **1.** Having only a limited ability to learn and understand ▶ dense, dull, feeble-minded, half-witted, simple, simple-minded, slow, slow-witted, thick-witted, weak-minded. *Informal:* soft. *Slang:* dim, dimwitted. ***Idioms:*** not playing with a full deck, soft in the head. [*Compare* **stupid.**] **2.** Behind others in progress or development ▶ lagging, underdeveloped, undeveloped. **3.** Moving or directed toward the rear ▶ rearward, retrograde, retrogressive. **4.** Clinging to obsolete ideas ▶ reactionary, unprogressive. [*Compare* **conservative.**] —*See also* **depressed** (2), **ignorant** (2), **shy**[1]**.**

backward *adverb.* Toward the back ▶ about, around, back, backwards, rearward.

backwardness *noun.* —*See* **ignorance** (1), **shyness.**

backwards *adverb.* —*See* **backward.**

backwoods *noun.* A dense growth of trees and underbrush covering an area

▶ forest, timberland, woodland, woods. [*Compare* **wilderness.**] —*See also* **country.**

bacterium *noun.* —*See* **germ** (1).

bad *adjective.* **1.** Of low or lower quality ▶ bum, coarse, common, dissatisfactory, inadequate, inferior, low-grade, low-quality, mean, mediocre, poor, second-class, second-rate, shabby, subpar, substandard, unsatisfactory. *Slang:* bush-league. ***Idioms:*** below par, not up to scratch (*or* snuff). [*Compare* **defective, shabby, shoddy, terrible.**] **2.** Marred by decay ▶ decayed, flyblown, foul, overripe, putrescent, putrid, rancid, rotten, spoiled, worm-eaten, wormy. [*Compare* **filthy, moldy, offensive.**] —*See also* **evil, fateful** (1), **harmful, unpleasant, unruly.**

bad *noun.* Whatever is destructive or harmful ▶ badness, evil, ill, worse. [*Compare* **harm.**]

badge *noun.* —*See* **decoration, sign** (1).

badger *verb.* —*See* **harass.**

badinage *noun.* —*See* **ribbing.**

badlands *noun.* —*See* **desert[1].**

badmouth *verb.* —*See* **belittle, malign.**

bad name *noun.* —*See* **disgrace.**

badness *noun.* Whatever is destructive or harmful ▶ bad, evil, ill, wrong. [*Compare* **harm.**]

bad odor *noun.* —*See* **disgrace.**

bad-tempered *adjective.* —*See* **ill-tempered.**

baffle *verb.* To put at a loss as to what to say or do ▶ confound, mystify, nonplus, perplex. *Informal:* flummox, stick, stump, throw. *Slang:* beat. [*Compare* **confuse, embarrass.**] —*See also* **frustrate.**

baffle *noun.* —*See* **brake.**

baffled *adjective.* —*See* **confused** (1).

bafflement *noun.* —*See* **daze.**

bag *noun.* A flexible container for carrying items ▶ pouch, sack, tote (bag). *Chiefly Regional:* croker sack, crocus sack, gunnysack, poke, tow bag, tow sack. —*See also* **area** (1), **forte, purse, suitcase.**

bag *verb.* —*See* **bulge, capture, catch** (1), **get** (1).

baggage *noun.* —*See* **slut.**

bag lady *noun.* —*See* **pauper.**

bail[1] *noun.* One who posts bond ▶ bailsman, bondsman. —*See also* **pawn[1].**

bail[2] *verb.* —*See* **dip** (2).

bail out *verb.* To catapult oneself from a disabled aircraft ▶ eject, jump. —*See also* **escape** (1).

bailiwick *noun.* —*See* **area** (1).

bailsman *noun.* One who posts bond ▶ bail, bondsman.

bait *noun.* Something that leads one into danger or entrapment ▶ decoy, lure. [*Compare* **trap, trick.**] —*See also* **lure** (1).

bait *verb.* To arouse hope or desire without affording satisfaction ▶ tantalize, tease. ***Idiom:*** make one's mouth water. [*Compare* **charm, flirt.**] —*See also* **harass.**

bake *verb.* —*See* **burn** (3), **cook.**

baked *adjective.* —*See* **drugged.**

baker *noun.* A person who prepares food for eating ▶ chef, cook, culinary artist.

baking *adjective.* —*See* **hot** (1).

balance *noun.* **1.** A stable state of opposing forces ▶ counterpoise, equilibrium, equipoise, poise, stasis. [*Compare* **equivalence, stability.**] **2.** A stable emotional state ▶ aplomb, collectedness, composure, coolness, equanimity, imperturbability, imperturbableness, levelheadedness, nonchalance, poise, sang-froid, self-possession, steadiness, unflappability. *Slang:* cool. [*Compare* **calm, reserve.**] **3.** Satisfying arrangement marked by even distribution of elements, as in a design ▶ harmony, proportion, symmetry. [*Compare* **agreement.**] **4.** A remaining part ▶ leavings, leftover, leftovers, pickings, remainder, remains, remnant, residue, rest. [*Compare* **end, surplus, trace.**]

balance *verb.* **1.** To put in balance ▶ counterbalance, equalize, even (out), level (off), poise, stabilize, steady. [*Compare* **equalize.**] **2.** To act as an equalizing force to ▶ compensate, counteract, counterbalance, counterpoise, countervail, make up, offset, oppose, set off. [*Compare* **harmonize.**] **3.** To rest on a narrow or insecure surface ▶ perch, poise, roost, teeter. [*Compare* **sway.**] —*See also* **cancel** (2), **compare.**

balanced *adjective.* **1.** Neither favorable nor unfavorable ▶ even, fifty-fifty, nip and tuck. **2.** Characterized by or displaying symmetry, especially correspondence in scale or measure ▶ proportional, proportionate, regular, symmetric, symmetrical. [*Compare* **even, parallel.**] **3.** Having components that are pleasingly combined ▶ concordant, congruous, harmonious, symmetrical. [*Compare* **pleasant.**] —*See also* **fair**[1] (1), **sensible.**

bald *adjective.* —*See* **abrupt** (1), **bare** (1), **bare** (3).

balderdash *noun.* —*See* **nonsense.**

bald-faced *adjective.* —*See* **impudent.**

baleful *adjective.* —*See* **fateful** (1).

balk *verb.* —*See* **frustrate.**

balky *adjective.* —*See* **contrary.**

ball *noun.* A spherical object ▶ globe, orb, sphere, spheroid. [*Compare* **circle, drop.**] —*See also* **dance.**

ballad *noun.* —*See* **song.**

balloon *verb.* To increase or expand suddenly, rapidly, or without control ▶ explode, mushroom, snowball. [*Compare* **increase.**] —*See also* **bulge, swell.**

ballot *verb.* To cast a vote ▶ poll, vote. ***Idioms:*** exercise one's civic duty, go to the polls.

ballot *noun.* A list of candidates proposed or endorsed by a political party ▶ lineup, ticket, slate.

balloter *noun.* One who votes ▶ elector, voter. ***Idiom:*** member of the electorate.

ball up *verb.* —*See* **botch, confuse** (3).

ballyhoo *noun.* —*See* **publicity.**

ballyhoo *verb.* —*See* **promote** (3).

balm *noun.* —*See* **ointment.**

balminess *noun.* —*See* **foolishness.**

balmy *adjective.* Free from extremes in temperature ▶ clement, mild, moderate, temperate. [*Compare* **pleasant.**] —*See also* **foolish, gentle** (2).

baloney *noun.* —*See* **nonsense.**

bambino *noun.* —*See* **baby** (1).

bamboozle *verb.* —*See* **deceive.**

ban *verb.* —*See* **censor** (2), **exclude, forbid.**

ban *noun.* —*See* **curse** (1), **forbiddance.**

banal *adjective.* —*See* **trite.**

banality *noun.* —*See* **cliché, insipidity.**

bananas *adjective.* —*See* **insane.**

band[1] *noun.* A long narrow piece, as of material ▶ bandeau, belt, cincture, cinch, fillet, girdle, riband, ribbon, sash, strap, strip, stripe, strop, swatch, swath, tape. —*See also* **circle** (1), **stripe.**

band *verb.* —*See* **encircle, streak.**

band[2] *noun.* A group of people acting together in a shared activity ▶ cohort, company, corps, party, troop, troupe, unit. [*Compare* **alliance, assembly, force, union.**] —*See also* **gang, group.**

band *verb.* To form a united group ▶ combine, come together, flock (together), gang (together), group, join (together), league, unite. ***Idiom:*** join forces. [*Compare* **ally, assemble, associate, combine.**]

✚ **CORE SYNONYMS:** *band, company, corps, party, troop, troupe.* These nouns denote a group of people acting together in a shared activity or for a common purpose: *a band of laborers; a company of ballet dancers; a corps of drummers; a party of tourists; a troop of students on a field trip; a troupe of actors.*

---

bandage *verb.* —*See* **dress** (2).

bandeau *noun.* —*See* **band**[1].

banderole *noun.* —*See* **flag**[1].

bandit *noun.* —*See* **thief.**

bandsman *noun.* —*See* **player** (2).

bandy *verb.* —*See* **discuss, exchange.**

bane *noun.* —*See* **curse** (3), **destruction, poison, ruin** (1).

baneful *adjective.* —*See* **harmful.**

bang *verb.* To strike together or handle noisily ▶ clang, clap, clash, crack, crash, ding, knock, rap, slam, smack, smash, thump, thwack, whack. [*Compare* **hit, slap, thud.**] —*See also* **beat** (1), **blast** (1), **crack** (2).

bang up *verb.* —*See* **batter.**

bang *noun.* A forceful movement causing a loud noise ▶ crash, slam, smash, wham. —*See also* **blast** (1), **blow²**, **crack** (1), **thrill.**

bang *adverb.* —*See* **directly** (3).

banish *verb.* To force to leave a country or place by official decree ▶ deport, exile, expatriate, expel, extradite, ostracize, transport. [*Compare* **eject, exclude, forbid.**] —*See also* **dismiss** (2), **dismiss** (3).

✚ **CORE SYNONYMS:** *banish, exile, expatriate, deport, transport, extradite.* These verbs mean to send away from a country or state. *Banish* applies to forced departure from a country by official decree: *The spy was found guilty of treason and banished from the country. Exile* specifies voluntary or involuntary departure from one's own country because of adverse circumstances: *The royal family was exiled after the uprising. Expatriate* pertains to departure that is sometimes forced but often voluntary and may imply change of citizenship: *She was expatriated because of her political beliefs. Deport* denotes the official act of expelling an alien: *The foreigner was deported for entering the country illegally. Transport* pertains to sending a criminal abroad, usually to a penal colony: *Offenders were transported to Devil's Island. Extradite* applies to the delivery of an accused or convicted person to the state or country having jurisdiction over him or her: *The court will extradite the terrorists.*

banishment *noun.* —*See* **exile.**

bank¹ *noun.* —*See* **heap** (1).

bank *verb.* —*See* **heap** (1).

bank² *verb.* To place money in an account ▶ deposit, invest, lay away, salt away. *Informal:* sock away. [*Compare* **conserve, save.**]

bank on *verb.* —*See* **depend on** (1).

bank *noun.* —*See* **depository.**

bankable *adjective.* —*See* **profitable.**

banking *noun.* The management of money ▶ finance, investment, money management.

bankroll *verb.* —*See* **finance.**

bankroll *noun.* —*See* **capital** (1).

bankrupt *verb.* —*See* **destroy** (1), **ruin.**

bankrupt *noun.* —*See* **pauper.**

bankrupt *adjective.* —*See* **empty** (2), **poor.**

bankruptcy *noun.* The condition of being financially insolvent ▶ failure, insolvency, ruin, ruination. [*Compare* **poverty.**]

banned *adjective.* —*See* **forbidden.**

banner *noun.* —*See* **flag¹.**

banner *adjective.* —*See* **excellent.**

banneret *noun.* —*See* **flag¹.**

banquet *noun.* A large, elaborately prepared meal ▶ feast, junket. *Informal:* feed, spread.

bantam *adjective.* —*See* **little.**

banter *noun.* —*See* **ribbing.**

banter *verb.* —*See* **joke** (2).

baptize *verb.* —*See* **name** (1).

bar *noun.* **1.** Something that blocks entry or passage ▶ barricade, barrier, block, blockage, bottleneck, clog, dam, encumbrance, hindrance, hurdle, impediment, obstacle, obstruction, snag, sticking point, stop, stumbling block, wall. [*Compare* **catch, disadvantage.**] **2.** A public establishment that sells alcoholic drinks and often food, often from a counter ▶ alehouse, cocktail lounge, inn, lounge, nightclub, pub, public house, roadhouse, saloon, tavern, wine bar. *Informal:* juke joint, watering hole. —*See also* **court** (2), **fastener, rod, stripe.**

bar *verb.* —*See* **enclose** (1), **exclude, forbid, obstruct, streak.**

✚ **CORE SYNONYMS:** *bar, barrier, obstacle, obstruction, block, hindrance, im-*

pediment, snag. These nouns refer to something that blocks entry or passage or that slows progress. *Bar* and *barrier* convey that which confines or prevents exit or entry: "*Tyranny may always enter—there is no charm, no bar against it—the only bar against it is a large resolute breed of men*" (Walt Whitman). "*Literature is my Utopia . . . . No barrier of the senses shuts me out from the sweet, gracious discourse of my book friends*" (Helen Keller). *Obstacle* applies to something that literally or figuratively stands in the way of progress: "*We combat obstacles in order to get repose*" (Henry Adams). An *obstruction* makes passage or progress difficult: *A sandbar is an obstruction to navigation. Block* suggests obstruction that effectively prevents all passage: *I had a mental block and couldn't remember the date. Hindrance* and *impediment* are applied to something that interferes with or delays passage or progress: "*an attachment that would be a hindrance to him in any honorable career*" (Thomas Hardy). *The report stated that overcrowded classrooms are an impediment to learning.* A *snag* is an unforeseen or hidden, often transitory obstacle: *Due to an unanticipated snag in plans, the project was delayed.*

---

barb *noun.* —*See* **crack** (3), **spike.**

barbarian *noun.* —*See* **boor, fiend.**

barbarian *adjective.* —*See* **coarse** (1), **uncivilized.**

barbaric *adjective.* —*See* **coarse** (1), **uncivilized.**

barbarism *noun.* —*See* **corruption** (3).

barbarity *noun.* —*See* **cruelty, outrage.**

barbarous *adjective.* —*See* **cruel, uncivilized.**

barbecue *verb.* —*See* **cook.**

barbed *adjective.* —*See* **thorny** (1).

bard *noun.* —*See* **poet.**

bare *adjective.* **1.** Without addition, decoration, or qualification ▶ austere, bald, bare-bones, classic, dry, plain, plain-Jane, plain vanilla, severe, simple, spare, spartan, stark, unadorned, undecorated, unvarnished, vanilla. [*Compare* **rustic.**] **2.** Just sufficient ▶ mere, scant, scanty. [*Compare* **insufficient, meager.**] **3.** Without the usual covering ▶ bald, barren, hairless, leafless, naked, nude. [*Compare* **open.**] —*See also* **empty** (1), **nude.**

bare *verb.* To remove the clothing or covering from ▶ denude, disrobe, divest, expose, flay, peel, strip, unclothe, uncover, undress. [*Compare* **skin.**] —*See also* **reveal.**

bare-bones *adjective.* —*See* **bare** (1).

barefaced *adjective.* —*See* **impudent.**

barely *adverb.* By a very little; almost not ▶ hardly, just, scarce, scarcely. ***Idioms:*** by a hair (*or* whisker), by the skin of one's teeth. [*Compare* **approximately, merely, only.**]

bareness *noun.* —*See* **emptiness** (2), **nudity.**

barf *verb.* —*See* **vomit.**

bargain *noun.* Something offered or bought at a low price ▶ find. *Informal:* buy, deal. *Slang:* steal. —*See also* **agreement** (1), **deal** (1).

bargain *verb.* —*See* **contract** (1), **haggle.**

bargain for *or* **on** *verb.* —*See* **expect** (1).

bargain-basement *adjective.* —*See* **cheap.**

barge in *verb.* —*See* **interrupt** (2), **intrude.**

bark *verb.* —*See* **crack** (2), **snap** (3).

bark *noun.* —*See* **crack** (1).

barm *noun.* —*See* **foam.**

barmy *adjective.* —*See* **foamy.**

barnyard *adjective.* —*See* **obscene.**

baronial *adjective.* —*See* **grand.**

baroque *adjective.* —*See* **complex** (1), **ornate.**

barracks *noun.* Usually temporary living accommodations ▶ lodgings, rooms, quarters. *Slang:* crash-pad. [*Compare* **apartment, home.**]

barrage *noun.* A concentrated outpouring, as of missiles, words, or blows ▶ bombardment, broadside, burst, cannonade, crossfire, discharge, fire, flak, fusillade, hail, rain, salvo, shower, storm, volley. [*Compare* **attack, blast, flood.**]

barrage *verb.* To direct a barrage at ▶ blitz, bomb, bombard, cannonade, fusillade, pelt, pepper, shell, shower. [*Compare* **attack, overwhelm.**]

✦ CORE SYNONYMS: *barrage, bomb, bombard, pelt, pepper, shell, shower.* These verbs mean to direct a concentrated outpouring at something or someone: *barraged the speaker with questions; bombed the village from the air; bombarded the box office with ticket orders; pelted the speaker with tomatoes; peppered the senator with protests; shelled the fortification; showered the child with gifts.*

barred *adjective.* —*See* **forbidden.**

barrel *noun.* —*See* **abundance, vat.**

barrel *verb.* —*See* **rush.**

barren *adjective.* **1.** Unable to produce offspring ▶ childless, impotent, infertile, sterile, unfruitful. **2.** Unable to support vegetation or crops ▶ dead, desert, desolate, infertile, lifeless, sterile, unfruitful, unproductive, waste. [*Compare* **bleak, dry.**] —*See also* **bare** (3), **empty** (1), **empty** (2), **futile.**

barren *noun.* —*See* **desert**[1]**.**

barrenness *noun.* —*See* **emptiness** (2), **futility, nothingness** (2), **sterility** (2).

barrens *noun.* —*See* **desert**[1]**.**

barricade *noun.* —*See* **bar** (1), **bulwark, defense.**

barricade *verb.* —*See* **obstruct.**

barrier *noun.* A solid structure that separates one area from another ▶ partition, screen, wall. [*Compare* **border.**] —*See also* **bar** (1).

barter *noun.* —*See* **change** (2), **deal** (1).

barter *verb.* —*See* **change** (3).

basal *adjective.* —*See* **constitutional, elementary, radical.**

base[1] *noun.* **1.** A center of organization, supply, or activity ▶ camp, command post, complex, depot, headquarters, home, home base, home office, installation, post, station. [*Compare* **center.**] **2.** The lowest or supporting part or structure ▶ basis, bed, bottom, cornerstone, foot, footing, foundation, ground, groundwork, pedestal, seat, stand, substratum, substructure, underpinning. [*Compare* **stage, support.**] —*See also* **basis** (1), **theme** (1).

base *verb.* To provide a basis for ▶ build, construct, establish, found, ground, model, predicate, rest, root, undergird, underpin. [*Compare* **depend, support.**] —*See also* **position.**

base[2] *adjective.* —*See* **shoddy, sordid.**

baseborn *adjective.* —*See* **illegitimate, lowly** (1).

baseless *adjective.* Having no basis in fact ▶ groundless, idle, meritless, unfounded, unproved, unwarranted. [*Compare* **empty, false.**]

✦ CORE SYNONYMS: *baseless, groundless, idle, unfounded, unwarranted.* These adjectives mean being without a basis or foundation in fact: *a baseless accusation; groundless rumors; idle gossip; unfounded suspicions; unwarranted jealousy.*

baselessly *adverb.* Without basis or foundation in fact ▶ groundlessly, unwarrantedly, unfoundedly.

baseness *noun.* —*See* **corruption** (2).

bash *verb.* —*See* **hit, slam** (1).

bash *noun.* —*See* **blast** (3), **blow**[2]**, party.**

bashful *adjective.* —*See* **shy**[1]**.**

bashfulness *noun.* —*See* **shyness.**

basic *adjective.* —*See* **elemental, elementary, essential** (2), **radical.**

basic *noun.* —*See* **element** (1).

basically *adverb.* —*See* **essentially.**

basin *noun.* The region drained by a river system ▶ drainage basin, watershed. —*See also* **depression** (1), **vat.**

basis *noun.* **1.** An underlying support, as for an argument, action, or belief ▶ base, cornerstone, footing, foundation, fundamental, ground, grounds, groundwork, keystone, root, rudiment, underpinning. [*Compare* **cause, origin, support.**] **2.** A justifying fact or consideration ▶ foundation, justification, reason, warrant. [*Compare* **account, apology.**] **3.** An established position from which to operate or deal with others ▶ footing, standing, status, terms. [*Compare* **place.**] *—See also* **base**[1] (2).

✚ **CORE SYNONYMS:** *basis, foundation, grounds, groundwork.* These nouns pertain to an underlying support, as for an argument, action, or belief. *Basis* is the most general term: "*Healthy scepticism is the basis of all accurate observation*" (Arthur Conan Doyle). *Foundation* often stresses firmness of support for something of relative magnitude: "*Our flagrant disregard for the law attacks the foundation of this society*" (Peter D. Relic). *Grounds* signifies a justifiable reason: *The lawyer outlined the grounds for the divorce. Groundwork* usually has the sense of a necessary preliminary: "*It* [the Universal Declaration of Human Rights] *has laid the groundwork for the world's war crimes tribunals*" (Hillary Rodham Clinton).

bask *verb. —See* **luxuriate.**
basket *noun.* **1.** A container made of interwoven material ▶ creel, hamper, pannier. [*Compare* **container.**] **2.** The contents of a basket ▶ basketful, bushel. **3.** The goal in the game of basketball ▶ bucket, field goal, hoop, net, swish, swisher.
bass *adjective. —See* **low** (1).
bastard *adjective. —See* **illegitimate.**
bastardize *verb. —See* **corrupt.**
baste *verb. —See* **beat** (1).
bastion *noun. —See* **bulwark, fort.**
bat[1] *verb. —See* **blink.**
bat *noun. —See* **blink.**
bat[2] *noun. —See* **bender.**
batch *noun. —See* **group.**
bate *verb. —See* **subside.**
bathe *verb.* **1.** To make moist ▶ dampen, moisten, wash, wet. **2.** To flow against or along ▶ lap, lave, lip, wash. [*Compare* **flow.**] *—See also* **clean** (1).
bathetic *adjective. —See* **sentimental.**
bathos *noun. —See* **sentimentality.**
baton *noun. —See* **stick** (1).
batten *verb.* To make a large profit ▶ cash in, profit. *Slang:* clean up. ***Idioms:*** make a killing, make out like a bandit. *—See also* **prosper.**
batter *verb.* To injure or damage, as by abuse or heavy wear ▶ bang up, knock about (*or* around), maim, mangle, manhandle, maul, mutilate, ravage, rough up, scuff, work over. ***Idioms:*** play (*or* wreak) havoc (on *or* with). [*Compare* **abuse, damage, deform.**] *—See also* **beat** (1).

✚ **CORE SYNONYMS:** *batter, maim, mangle, maul, mutilate.* These verbs mean to damage, injure, or disfigure as by abuse or heavy wear: *a house battered by a hurricane; a construction worker maimed in an accident; machinery that mangled the worker's fingers; a tent mauled by a hungry bear; mutilated the painting with a razor.*

battle *noun.* An encounter between opposing military forces ▶ action, belligerency, brush, clash, combat, conflict, confrontation, encounter, engagement, hostilities, skirmish, sortie, strife, struggle, war, warfare. [*Compare* **competition, conflict, fight.**] *—See also* **competition** (1).
battle *verb. —See* **contend.**
battle-ax *or* **battle-axe** *noun. —See* **scold, witch** (2).
battle cry *noun. —See* **cry** (2).
batty *adjective. —See* **insane.**
bauble *noun. —See* **novelty** (3).
bawd *noun. —See* **harlot.**
bawdiness *noun. —See* **obscenity** (1).
bawdry *noun. —See* **obscenity** (2).
bawdy *adjective. —See* **obscene.**

bawl *verb.* To cry loudly, as an upset baby does ▶ caterwaul, holler, howl, squall, wail, yowl. [*Compare* **scream.**] *—See also* **cry, shout.**

bawl out *verb.* *—See* **chastise.**

bawl *noun.* *—See* **roar.**

bawling *noun.* *—See* **cry** (1).

bay[1] *noun.* A body of water partly enclosed by land but having a wide outlet to the sea ▶ bight, gulf, sound. [*Compare* **channel, harbor, inlet.**]

bay[2] *noun.* *—See* **howl.**

bay *verb.* *—See* **howl.**

bayonet *verb.* *—See* **cut** (1).

bazaar *noun.* *—See* **exhibition.**

be *verb.* *—See* **exist.**

be into *verb.* *—See* **enjoy.**

bead *noun.* *—See* **drop** (1).

beak *noun.* The horny projection forming a bird's jaws ▶ bill, mandible, nib. *—See also* **nose** (1).

beam *noun.* **1.** A narrow line of light or other radiant energy ▶ finger, ray, shaft, stream. **2.** A sturdy horizontal structural support ▶ crossbeam, crosstie, girder, I-beam, joist, lintel, rafter, tie beam, timber, trestle, viga. [*Compare* **column, support.**]

beam *verb.* To emit a bright light ▶ blaze, burn, gleam, glow, incandesce, radiate, shine. [*Compare* **glare, glitter, illuminate.**] *—See also* **smile.**

beamy *adjective.* *—See* **bright.**

bean *noun.* *—See* **head** (1).

bear *verb.* **1.** To hold the weight of ▶ carry, hold (up), shoulder, support, sustain, uphold. **2.** To keep steadily in mind ▶ cherish, entertain, harbor, nourish, nurse. [*Compare* **ponder, think.**] **3.** To have as a visible characteristic ▶ carry, display, exhibit, have, possess, wear. [*Compare* **display, show.**] **4.** To give birth to ▶ bring forth, deliver, have. *Chiefly Regional:* birth. ***Idioms:*** be brought abed (*or* to bed) of. **5.** To proceed in a specified direction ▶ aim, go, head, make, set out, start out, strike out, turn. *Informal:* light out. [*Compare* **go, start, turn.**] *—See also* **act** (1), **bring** (1), **carry** (1), **carry** (2), **endure** (1), **produce** (1), **push** (1).

bear on *or* **upon** *verb.* *—See* **apply** (2).

bear out *verb.* *—See* **confirm** (1), **prove.**

bear up *verb.* To withstand stress or difficulty ▶ endure, hold up, stand up. ***Idioms:*** bite the bullet, grin and bear it, keep a stiff upper lip, make the best of it, take one's medicine, take it (lying down). [*Compare* **carry on, endure.**]

bearable *adjective.* Capable of being tolerated ▶ endurable, sufferable, supportable, tolerable.

beard *verb.* *—See* **defy** (1).

bearer *noun.* *—See* **messenger.**

bearing *noun.* **1.** Behavior that reveals one's personality or state of mind ▶ address, air, demeanor, manner, mien, poise, presence, style. [*Compare* **appearance, behavior, posture.**] **2.** The compass direction in which a ship or aircraft moves ▶ course, heading, vector. [*Compare* **direction.**] **3.** One's place and direction relative to one's surroundings ▶ bearings, location, orientation, position, situation, whereabouts. *—See also* **impact, relevance.**

beast *noun.* *—See* **fiend.**

beastly *or* **beastlike** *adjective.* Similar to a beast in behavior ▶ bestial, brutish. [*Compare* **cruel, savage, uncivilized.**]

beat *verb.* **1.** To hit heavily and repeatedly ▶ assail, assault, bang, baste, batter, belabor, bludgeon, buffet, club, cudgel, drub, flail, hammer, maul, pelt, pound, pummel, smash, thrash, thresh, whale. *Informal:* lambaste, lather, thump. *Slang:* clobber. ***Idioms:*** knock the daylights (*or* stuffing *or* tar) out of, rain blows on, tan someone's hide. [*Compare* **batter, hit, slap.**] **2.** To punish with blows or lashes ▶ birch, cane, flagellate, flay, flog, hide, horsewhip, lash, scourge, strap, thrash, whip. *Informal:* trim. *Slang:* lay into, lick. **3.** To shape, break, or flatten with repeated blows ▶ forge, hammer, pound, stamp. [*Compare* **even.**] **4.** To indicate time or rhythm ▶

count, tap (out). ***Idioms:*** keep time, mark time. **5.** To make rhythmic contractions, sounds, or movements ▶ drum, flutter, hammer, palpitate, pound, pulsate, pulse, tap, throb, thump, tick. **6.** To combine or process ingredients by stirring ▶ blend, cream, fold (in), mix, stir, whip, whisk. [*Compare* **combine, mix.**] —*See also* **baffle, deceive, defeat, flap** (1), **surpass.**

beat down *verb.* —*See* **break** (2), **glare** (2).

beat off *verb.* —*See* **repel.**

beat *noun.* **1.** A stroke or blow that produces a sound ▶ bump, clunk, knock, pound, rap, smack, thud, thump, whack. [*Compare* **blow**^{2}.] **2.** An area regularly covered, as by a policeman or reporter ▶ circuit, round, rounds, route, territory. [*Compare* **circle.**] **3.** A rhythmic contraction or sound ▶ drumbeat, palpitation, pounding, pulsation, pulse, throb, throbbing, tick, ticktock. —*See also* **rhythm.**

beat *adjective.* —*See* **tired** (1).

✚ **CORE SYNONYMS:** *beat, baste, batter, belabor, buffet, hammer, lambaste, pound, pummel, thrash.* These verbs mean to hit heavily and repeatedly with violent blows: *was mugged and beaten; basted him with a stick; was battered in the boxing ring; rioting students belabored by police officers; buffeted him with her open palm; hammered the opponent with his fists; lambasted every challenger; troops pounded with mortar fire; pummeled the bully soundly; thrashed the thief for stealing the candy.*

---

beatification *noun.* —*See* **exaltation.**

beating *noun.* A punishment dealt with blows or lashes ▶ caning, flagellation, flaying, flogging, hiding, lashing, pounding, thrashing, whipping. *Informal:* trimming. *Slang:* licking. —*See also* **defeat.**

beatitude *noun.* —*See* **happiness, holiness.**

beau *noun.* **1.** A man who courts a woman ▶ admirer, courter, suitor, swain, wooer. [*Compare* **gallant.**] **2.** A man who is vain about his clothes ▶ coxcomb, dandy, fop, peacock, swell. —*See also* **boyfriend.**

beau ideal *noun.* —*See* **model.**

beautiful *adjective.* Having qualities that delight the eye ▶ attractive, beauteous, comely, exquisite, fair, good-looking, gorgeous, handsome, lovely, pretty, pulchritudinous, ravishing, sightly, statuesque, stunning. ***Idiom:*** easy on the eyes. [*Compare* **attractive, seductive.**]

✚ **CORE SYNONYMS:** *beautiful, lovely, pretty, handsome, comely, fair.* These adjectives apply to those qualities that delight the eye. *Beautiful* is most comprehensive: *a beautiful child; a beautiful painting; a beautiful mathematical proof. Lovely* applies to what inspires emotion rather than intellectual appreciation: *"They were lovely, your eyes"* (George Seferis). What is *pretty* is beautiful in a delicate or graceful way: *a pretty face; a pretty song; a pretty room. Handsome* stresses poise and dignity of form and proportion: *We were taken to a very large, handsome paneled library. "She is very pretty, but not so* extraordinarily *handsome"* (William Makepeace Thackeray). *Comely* suggests wholesome physical attractiveness: *"Mrs. Hurd is a large woman with a big, comely, simple face"* (Ernest Hemingway). *Fair* emphasizes freshness or purity: *"In the highlands, in the country places,/Where the old plain men have rosy faces,/And the young fair maidens/Quiet eyes"* (Robert Louis Stevenson).

◀ **ANTONYM:** *ugly*

---

beautify *verb.* To endow with beauty and elegance ▶ embellish, enhance, grace, set off. [*Compare* **adorn.**]

beauty *noun.* A person regarded as physically attractive ▶ Adonis (for a man), belle (for a woman), dreamboat, eyeful, goddess (for a woman), lovely, stunner, Venus (for a woman), vision. *Slang:* babe, dish, doll, fox, hotty, hunk (for a man), knockout, looker, stud (for a man). *—See also* **virtue.**

becalm *verb. —See* **pacify.**

because *conjunction.* For the reason that ▶ as, for, inasmuch as, seeing as, since. ***Idioms:*** on account of the fact that, in consequence of the fact that, in view of the fact that.

because of *preposition.* By the cause of ▶ as a result of, by reason of, by virtue of, due to, in consequence of, in view of, on account of, owing to, through.

beckon *verb. —See* **gesture.**

becloud *verb. —See* **obscure.**

become *verb.* **1.** To come to be ▶ change (to *or* into), come (to be), develop (into), get (to be), grow (to be), turn (to *or* into), wax. **2.** To look good on or with ▶ enhance, flatter, suit. ***Idiom:*** put in the best light. *—See also* **suit** (1).

becoming *adjective.* Pleasingly suited to the wearer ▶ attractive, fetching, flattering, perfect, well-suited. [*Compare* **attractive.**] *—See also* **appropriate.**

bed *verb. —See* **lodge, retire** (1).

bed *noun. —See* **base**[1] (2).

bedaub *verb. —See* **dirty, smear.**

bedaze *verb. —See* **daze** (1).

bedazzle *verb.* To confuse with bright light ▶ blind, daze, dazzle.

bedeck *verb. —See* **adorn** (1), **dress up.**

bedevil *verb. —See* **harass.**

bedim *verb. —See* **obscure.**

bedraggled *adjective. —See* **shabby.**

bedtime *noun. —See* **night.**

beef *noun. —See* **brawn, complaint.**

beef *verb. —See* **complain.**

beef up *verb. —See* **increase.**

beefy *adjective. —See* **muscular.**

beetle *verb. —See* **bulge.**

befall *verb.* To take place by chance ▶ betide, chance, hap, happen. *—See also* **happen** (1).

befit *verb. —See* **justify** (2), **suit** (1).

befitting *adjective. —See* **appropriate, convenient** (1).

befog *verb. —See* **obscure.**

before *adverb.* Until then ▶ beforehand, earlier. *—See also* **earlier** (1), **earlier** (2).

beforehand *adverb.* Until then ▶ before, earlier. *—See also* **earlier** (1), **early.**

befoul *verb. —See* **denigrate, dirty.**

befuddle *verb. —See* **confuse** (1), **drug** (2).

befuddlement *noun. —See* **daze.**

beg *verb.* To ask for as charity; solicit money or favors ▶ bum, cadge. *Informal:* panhandle. *Slang:* mooch, scrounge. ***Idioms:*** hit someone up for, pass the cup (*or* hat), touch someone for. [*Compare* **freeload.**] *—See also* **appeal** (1), **demand** (2).

✚ **CORE SYNONYMS:** *beg, bum, cadge, mooch, panhandle.* These verbs mean to ask for or obtain by charity: *begging for change; bummed a ride to the stadium; cadged a meal; mooching food; homeless people forced to panhandle.*

---

beget *verb.* To be the biological father of ▶ father, get, sire. *—See also* **breed.**

begetter *noun. —See* **father, originator.**

beggar *noun.* **1.** One who begs habitually or for a living ▶ almsman, almswoman, cadger, mendicant. *Informal:* panhandler. *Slang:* bummer, mooch, moocher. [*Compare* **parasite.**] **2.** One who humbly entreats ▶ petitioner, prayer, suitor, suppliant, supplicant. *—See also* **pauper.**

beggarly *adjective. —See* **poor.**

beggary *noun.* The condition of being a beggar ▶ mendicancy, mendicity. *—See also* **poverty.**

begin *verb.* To come into being ▶ appear, arise, commence, crop up, dawn, emerge, originate, start. ***Idioms:*** raise (one's) head, see the light of day. [*Compare* **cause, stem.**] *—See also* **start** (1).

beginner *noun.* One who is just starting to learn or do something ▶ abecedarian, apprentice, cub, fledgling, freshman, greenhorn, initiate, learner, neophyte, newcomer, novice, novitiate, tenderfoot, tyro. *Slang:* newbie, rookie. [*Compare* **amateur.**]

beginning *noun.* The act of bringing or being brought into existence ▶ commencement, conception, inauguration, inception, incipience, incipiency, initiation, introduction, invention, launch, leadoff, opening, origination, start. *Informal:* kickoff. [*Compare* **foundation.**] —*See also* **birth** (2), **origin.**

beginning *adjective.* Of or occurring at the start of something ▶ early, inaugural, inceptive, incipient, initial, initiatory, introductory, leadoff, opening, starting. [*Compare* **first, introductory.**] —*See also* **elementary.**

begird *verb.* —*See* **encircle.**

begrime *verb.* —*See* **dirty.**

begrudge *verb.* ▶ covet, envy, grudge.

begrudging *adjective.* —*See* **envious.**

beguile *verb.* —*See* **charm** (1), **deceive.**

beguiling *adjective.* —*See* **seductive.**

behave *verb.* —*See* **act** (1), **function.**

behavior *noun.* **1.** The manner in which one behaves ▶ action, actions, comportment, conduct, deportment, form, manner, style, way, ways. [*Compare* **bearing, custom, manners.**] **2.** The way in which something functions ▶ functioning, operation, performance, reaction, working, workings.

✚ **CORE SYNONYMS:** *behavior, conduct, deportment.* These nouns refer to the manner in which one behaves. *Behavior* is the most general: *The children were on their best behavior. Conduct* applies to actions considered from the standpoint of morality and ethics: *"Life, not the parson, teaches conduct"* (Oliver Wendell Holmes, Jr.). *Deportment* more narrowly pertains to actions measured by a prevailing code of social behavior: "[Old Mr. Turveydrop] *was not like anything in the world but a model of Deportment*" (Charles Dickens).

---

behemoth *noun.* —*See* **giant.**

behemoth *adjective.* —*See* **enormous.**

behest *noun.* —*See* **command** (1), **demand** (1).

behind *adverb.* So as to fall behind schedule ▶ behindhand, late, slow. ***Idiom:*** behind time. —*See also* **late.**

behind *noun.* —*See* **buttocks.**

behindhand *adjective.* —*See* **late** (1).

behold *verb.* —*See* **see** (1).

beholden *adjective.* —*See* **obliged** (1).

beholder *noun.* —*See* **watcher** (1).

being *noun.* The condition of being in full force or operation ▶ actualization, effect, force, realization. [*Compare* **exercise.**] —*See also* **essence, existence, human being, thing** (1).

bejewel *verb.* —*See* **adorn** (1).

belabor *verb.* To discuss at great or excessive length ▶ dwell on, harp on, labor. ***Idiom:*** run into the ground. [*Compare* **elaborate, exaggerate.**] —*See also* **beat** (1).

belated *adjective.* —*See* **late** (1).

belatedly *adverb.* —*See* **late.**

belatedness *noun.* The quality or condition of not being on time ▶ lateness, slowness, tardiness, unpunctuality.

belay *verb.* —*See* **stop** (2).

belch *verb.* —*See* **erupt.**

beldam *or* **beldame** *noun.* —*See* **witch** (2).

beleaguer *verb.* —*See* **besiege, harass.**

beleaguerment *noun.* A prolonged encirclement of an objective by hostile troops ▶ besiegement, blockade, investment, siege. [*Compare* **attack.**]

belie *verb.* —*See* **distort, refute.**

belief *noun.* **1.** Something believed or thought to be true ▶ conviction, estimate, estimation, feeling, idea, judgment, mind, notion, opinion, persuasion, position, sentiment, view. [*Compare* **assumption, deduction, posture, viewpoint.**] **2.** Mental acceptance of the truth or actuality of something ▶ credence, credit, faith. —*See also* **doctrine, trust.**

✚ **CORE SYNONYMS:** *belief, opinion, view, sentiment, feeling, conviction, per-*

suasion. These nouns signify something a person believes or thinks to be true. A *belief* is a conclusion to which one subscribes strongly: *"Our belief in any particular natural law cannot have a safer basis than our unsuccessful critical attempts to refute it"* (Karl Popper). *Opinion* is applicable to a judgment based on grounds insufficient to rule out the possibility of dispute: *"A little group of willful men, representing no opinion but their own, have rendered the great Government of the United States helpless and contemptible"* (Woodrow Wilson). *View* stresses individuality of outlook: *"My view is . . . that freedom of speech means that you shall not do something to people either for the views they have or the views they express"* (Hugo L. Black). *Sentiment* and especially *feeling* stress the role of emotion as a determinant: *"If men are to be precluded from offering their sentiments on a matter which may involve the most serious and alarming consequences . . . reason is of no use to us"* (George Washington). *"There needs protection . . . against the tyranny of the prevailing opinion and feeling"* (John Stuart Mill). *Conviction* is belief that excludes doubt: *"the editor's own conviction of what, whether interesting or only important, is in the public interest"* (Walter Lippmann). *Persuasion* applies to a confidently held opinion: *"He had a strong persuasion that Likeman was wrong"* (H.G. Wells).

---

believability *noun.* —*See* **verisimilitude.**

believable *adjective.* Worthy of being believed ▶ credible, creditable, plausible, reasonable, valid. [*Compare* **convincing, sound^2.**]

✚ **CORE SYNONYMS:** *believable, credible, plausible, reasonable, valid.* These adjectives mean worthy of being believed or accepted: *a believable excuse; a credible assertion; a plausible pretext; testimony from an eyewitness that gave a reasonable account of the accident; a valid explanation.*

---

believe *verb.* **1.** To regard something as true or real ▶ accept. *Slang:* buy, swallow. ***Idioms:*** have no doubt about, feel certain (*or* sure) of, take for granted. **2.** To have confidence in the truthfulness of ▶ credit, trust. ***Idioms:*** give credence to, have faith (*or* trust *or* confidence) in, take at one's word. [*Compare* **depend on.**] **3.** To have an opinion ▶ conceive, consider, deem, hold, opine, think. *Informal:* figure, judge. ***Idioms:*** be convinced, be of the opinion. [*Compare* **guess, infer, suppose.**] **4.** To view in a certain way ▶ feel, hold, sense, think. [*Compare* **perceive, regard.**]

believe in *verb.* —*See* **depend on** (1).

believer *noun.* —*See* **devotee, follower.**

belittle *verb.* To represent or speak of as small or insignificant ▶ decry, denigrate, deprecate, depreciate, derogate, discount, disparage, downgrade, minimize, run down, slight, talk down. *Informal:* badmouth, pooh-pooh. *Slang:* put down. ***Idioms:*** make light (*or* little) of. [*Compare* **denigrate, humble, ridicule, snub.**]

✚ **CORE SYNONYMS:** *belittle, minimize, decry, disparage, depreciate, derogate, downgrade.* These verbs mean to think, write, or speak of as being small, insignifcant, or of little importance. *Belittle* and *minimize* mean to make less important, but *minimize* strongly implies the minimum level: *He belittled the child's attempts to draw. She tried to minimize my accomplishment.* To *downgrade* is to minimize in importance or estimation: *My rival downgraded the painting, calling it superficial. Decry* implies open denunciation or condemnation: *A staunch materialist, he decries economy. Disparage* often implies the communication of a low opinion by indirection: *Some critics disparage psychoanalysis as being a pseudoscience.* To *depreciate* is to assign a lower than usual value to someone or something: *Some musicologists depreciate Liszt's compositions. Derogate* implies a detraction that impairs: *People often derogate what they don't understand.*

---

belittlement *noun.* The act or an instance of belittling ▶ denigration, deprecation, depreciation, derogation, detraction, disparagement, minimization.

belittling *adjective.* —*See* **disparaging.**

bell *verb.* —*See* **ring²**.

belle *noun.* —*See* **beauty.**

bellicose *adjective.* —*See* **aggressive, military** (1).

bellicosity *or* **bellicoseness** *noun.* —*See* **aggression, fight** (2).

belligerence *noun.* —*See* **aggression, fight** (2).

belligerency *noun.* —*See* **battle, fight** (2).

belligerent *adjective.* Engaged in warfare ▶ clashing, combatant, fighting, hostile, militant, warring. ***Idioms:*** at war, under arms. [*Compare* **military.**] —*See also* **aggressive.**

belligerent *noun.* One who engages in a combat or struggle ▶ combatant, fighter, soldier, warrior. [*Compare* **aggressor, soldier.**]

bellow *verb.* —*See* **shout.**

bellow *noun.* —*See* **roar, shout.**

belly *verb.* —*See* **bulge.**

bellyache *verb.* —*See* **complain.**

bellyache *noun.* —*See* **complaint.**

bellyacher *noun.* —*See* **grouch.**

belong *verb.* —*See* **agree** (1).

belongings *noun.* —*See* **effects, holdings.**

beloved *adjective.* —*See* **darling.**

beloved *noun.* —*See* **darling** (1).

belowground *adjective.* —*See* **underground.**

belt *noun.* —*See* **area** (2), **band¹**, **blow²**, **drink** (2), **drop** (4), **territory.**

belt *verb.* —*See* **drink** (1), **encircle, hit.**

bemire *verb.* —*See* **dirty.**

bemoan *verb.* —*See* **deplore** (1), **grieve.**

bemuse *verb.* —*See* **daze** (1).

bemused *adjective.* —*See* **absent-minded, confused** (1).

bemusement *noun.* —*See* **trance.**

benchmark *noun.* —*See* **standard.**

bend *verb.* **1.** To deviate or cause to deviate from a straight line in a smooth, continuous manner ▶ arc, arch, bow, crook, curve, hook, loop, round, turn. [*Compare* **wave, wind².**] **2.** To move or cause to move in a bent or angular direction ▶ angle, deflect, flex, refract, reflect, turn, warp. [*Compare* **glance, swerve.**] **3.** To curve or yield under pressure ▶ bow, buckle, give, kink, sag, warp. [*Compare* **cave in, deform.**] —*See also* **apply** (1), **distort, stoop.**

bend *noun.* Something bent or curved ▶ angle, arc, arch, bow, crescent, crook, curvature, curve, flexure, fold, hairpin, hook, horseshoe, oxbow, round, turn, turning, U-turn. [*Compare* **curl.**]

✚ **CORE SYNONYMS:** *bend, crook, curve, round.* These verbs mean to deviate or to cause to deviate from a straight line in a smooth, continuous manner: *bent his knees and knelt; crooked an arm around the package; a bird that curved its talons around the branch; rounding the lips to articulate an "o."*

◀ **ANTONYM:** *straighten*

---

bendability *noun.* —*See* **flexibility** (1).

bendable *adjective.* —*See* **malleable.**

bender *noun. Slang* A drinking bout ▶ bacchanal, bacchanalia, binge, brannigan, carousal, carouse, drunk, spree. *Slang:* bat, beer blast, booze, jag, souse, tear, toot. [*Compare* **binge, blast.**]

bending *adjective.* —*See* **bent.**

benediction *noun.* **1.** A short prayer said at meals ▶ blessing, grace, thanks, thanksgiving. [*Compare* **prayer¹.**] **2.** The act of praying ▶ invocation, prayer, supplication. [*Compare* **appeal.**]

benefaction *noun.* —*See* **donation, favor** (1).

benefactor *or* **benefactress** *noun.* —*See* **donor, patron.**

benefic *adjective.* —*See* **beneficial.**

beneficence *noun.* —*See* **benevolence, donation, favor** (1).

beneficent *adjective.* —*See* **beneficial, benevolent** (1).

beneficial *adjective.* Affording benefit or advantage ▶ advantageous, benefic, beneficent, benignant, constructive, contributive, favorable, fruitful, good, helpful, profitable, propitious, toward, salubrious, salutary, useful, valuable, worthwhile. [*Compare* **effective.**]

✚ **CORE SYNONYMS:** *beneficial, profitable, advantageous.* These adjectives apply to what promotes a favorable result, advantage, or gain. *Beneficial* is said of what enhances well-being: *a trade agreement beneficial to all countries. Profitable* refers to what yields material gain or useful compensation: *profitable speculation on the stock market.* Something *advantageous* affords improvement in relative position or in chances of success: *found it socially advantageous to entertain often and well.*

◀ **ANTONYM:** *detrimental*

benefit *noun.* —*See* **advantage** (2), **interest** (1), **use** (2).

benefit *verb.* To derive advantage ▶ capitalize, gain, profit. ***Idiom:*** do well. —*See also* **profit** (2).

✚ **CORE SYNONYMS:** *benefit, capitalize, profit.* These verbs mean to derive advantage from something: *benefited from the stock split; capitalized on his adversary's blunder; profiting from her experience.*

benevolence *noun.* Kindly, charitable interest in others ▶ altruism, beneficence, benignancy, benignity, charitableness, charity, goodwill, grace, humanity, kindheartedness, kindliness, kindness, philanthropy. ***Idioms:*** the goodness (*or* kindness) of one's heart. [*Compare* **amiability, consideration, generosity.**] —*See also* **favor** (1).

benevolent *adjective.* **1.** Characterized by kindness and concern for others ▶ altruistic, beneficent, benign, benignant, good, goodhearted, helpful, kind, kindhearted, kindly. [*Compare* **amiable, generous, humanitarian, selfless.**] **2.** Of or concerned with charity ▶ altruistic, charitable, eleemosynary, philanthropic.

✚ **CORE SYNONYMS:** *benevolent, kind, kindly, kindhearted, benign.* These adjectives mean having or showing kindness and concern for others. *Benevolent* suggests charitableness and a desire to promote the welfare or happiness of others: *a benevolent contributor. Kind* and *kindly* are the least specific: *thanked her for her kind letter; a kindly gentleman. Kindhearted* especially suggests an innately kind disposition: *a kindhearted teacher. Benign* implies gentleness and mildness: *benign intentions; a benign sovereign.*

benighted *adjective.* —*See* **ignorant** (2).

benightedness *noun.* —*See* **ignorance** (1).

benign *adjective.* —*See* **benevolent** (1), **favorable** (1), **harmless.**

benignancy *noun.* —*See* **benevolence.**

benignant *adjective.* —*See* **beneficial, benevolent** (1).

benignity *noun.* —*See* **benevolence, favor** (1).

bent *adjective.* Deviating from a straight line ▶ angled, arced, arched, arciform, bending, bowed, crooked, curled, curved, curvilinear, curving, doubled, flexed, folded, hooked, looped, recurved, rounded, warped. [*Compare* **curly.**] —*See also* **intent.**

bent *noun.* —*See* **disposition, inclination** (1), **talent.**

benumb *verb.* —*See* **daze** (1), **deaden, paralyze.**

benumbed *adjective.* —*See* **dead** (2).

bequeath *verb.* To convey something from one generation to the next ▶ hand down, hand on, pass (along *or* on), transmit. —*See also* **donate, leave[1]** (1).

bequest *noun.* Something bestowed voluntarily ▶ gift, present, presentation. *Slang:* freebie. [*Compare* **grant.**] —*See also* **donation.**

berate *verb.* To reprimand loudly or harshly ▶ bawl out, rate. *Informal:* tell off. ***Idioms:*** give hell to, give it to. —*See also* **chastise.**

berating *noun.* —*See* **tirade.**

bereft *adjective.* —*See* **abandoned** (1), **empty** (2).

berth *noun.* —*See* **position** (3).

berth *verb.* —*See* **lodge.**

beseech *verb.* —*See* **appeal** (1).

beset *verb.* —*See* **attack** (1), **besiege, harass, surround.**

besetment *noun.* —*See* **annoyance** (2).

besides *adverb.* —*See* **additionally.**

besiege *verb.* To surround with hostile troops ▶ beleaguer, beset, blockade, invest, siege. ***Idiom:*** lay siege to. [*Compare* **attack, surround.**] —*See also* **enclose** (2), **harass.**

✚ **CORE SYNONYMS:** *besiege, beleaguer, blockade, invest, siege.* These verbs mean to surround with hostile troops or forces: *besiege a walled city; an enclave beleaguered by enemy attack; blockaded the harbor; investing a fortress; a castle sieged by invaders.*

---

besiegement *noun.* —*See* **siege.**

besmear *verb.* —*See* **denigrate, smear.**

besmirch *verb.* —*See* **denigrate, dirty, disgrace.**

besoil *verb.* —*See* **dirty.**

besot *verb.* —*See* **drug** (2).

besotted *adjective.* —*See* **drunk, infatuated.**

bespatter *verb.* —*See* **denigrate, dirty, splash** (1), **stain.**

bespeak *verb.* —*See* **book, indicate** (1).

bespeckle *verb.* —*See* **speckle.**

bespoke *adjective.* —*See* **custom.**

bespoken *adjective.* —*See* **engaged.**

besprinkle *verb.* —*See* **speckle, sprinkle.**

best *adjective.* **1.** Surpassing all others in quality, achievement, or desirability ▶ finest, first, foremost, greatest, highest, leading, nicest, optimal, optimum, preeminent, superlative, supreme, top, unsurpassed. [*Compare* **choice, exceptional, primary, unique.**] **2.** Much more than half ▶ better, biggest, greater, larger, largest, most. —*See also* **advisable.**

best *noun.* **1.** The finest or most preferable part of something ▶ choice, cream, crème de la crème, elite, flower, pick, prize, top. ***Idioms:*** cream of the crop, flower of the flock, pick of the bunch (*or* crop *or* litter), top of the line, top of the heap. **2.** Friendly greetings ▶ regards, respects.

best *verb.* —*See* **defeat, surpass.**

bestain *verb.* —*See* **stain.**

bestial *adjective.* Similar to a beast in behavior ▶ beastlike, beastly, brutish. [*Compare* **cruel, savage, uncivilized.**]

bestiality *noun.* —*See* **corruption** (1), **cruelty.**

bestialize *verb.* —*See* **corrupt.**

bestow *verb.* —*See* **confer** (2), **donate, lodge.**

bestowal *or* **bestowment** *noun.* —*See* **conferment.**

bestride *verb.* To sit or stand with a leg on each side of ▶ straddle, stride.

bet *noun.* Something risked on an uncertain outcome ▶ ante, kitty, pool, pot, stake, stakes, venture, wager. —*See also* **gamble.**

bet *verb.* To make a bet ▶ gamble, game, lay, play, wager. ***Idioms:*** ante (*or* pony) up, feed the pot (*or* kitty), lay odds (*or* a wager), put money on something, put up or shut up, show the color of one's money. —*See also* **expect** (1), **gamble** (2).

✚ **CORE SYNONYMS:** *bet, ante, kitty, pot, stake, wager.* These nouns denote something valuable risked on an uncertain outcome: *placed a $50 bet in the first race; raising the ante in a poker game; threw another quarter into the kitty; won the whole pot at cards; played for high stakes; laid a wager on who would win.*

---

bête noire *noun.* —*See* **hate** (2).

bethink *verb.* —*See* **remember** (1).

betide *verb.* To take place by chance ▶ befall, chance, hap, happen. —*See also* **happen** (1).

betimes *adverb.* —*See* **early, intermittently.**

betoken *verb.* —*See* **foreshadow, indicate** (1).

betray *verb.* **1.** To be treacherous to ▶ cross up, double-cross, turn in. *Informal:* knife. *Slang:* rat (on *or* out), sell out. ***Idioms:*** play someone false, sell down the river, stab in the back. [*Compare* **abandon, disappoint, inform.**] **2.** To disclose in a breach of confidence ▶ blab, divulge, expose, give away, let out, reveal, tell, uncover, unveil. *Informal:* leak, spill. ***Idioms:*** let slip, let the cat out of the bag, spill the beans, tell all. [*Compare* **reveal.**] —*See also* **deceive.**

betrayal *noun.* An act of betraying ▶ backstabbing, double cross, double-dealing, treachery. *Slang:* sellout. [*Compare* **treason.**] —*See also* **faithlessness.**

betrayer *noun.* One who betrays ▶ Benedict Arnold, double-crosser, double-dealer, Judas, quisling, snake, traitor. *Slang:* rat. ***Idiom:*** snake in the grass. [*Compare* **creep, informer, defector.**]

betroth *verb.* —*See* **pledge** (1).

betrothal *noun.* The act or condition of being pledged to marry ▶ engagement, espousal, troth.

betrothed *adjective.* —*See* **engaged.**

betrothed *noun.* —*See* **intended.**

better[1] *adjective.* Of greater excellence than another ▶ finer, nicer, preferable, superior, worthier. —*See also* **best** (2).

better *adverb.* To a greater extent ▶ more. ***Idioms:*** more fully, to a greater degree.

better *noun.* One who stands above another in rank ▶ elder, senior, superior. *Informal:* higher-up. [*Compare* **chief.**] —*See also* **advantage** (3).

better *verb.* —*See* **improve, surpass.**

better[2] *noun. See* **bettor.**

better half *noun.* —*See* **spouse.**

betterment *noun.* —*See* **improvement** (1), **progress.**

bettor *or* **better** *noun.* —*See* **gambler** (1).

between *adjective.* —*See* **middle.**

beveled *adjective.* —*See* **oblique.**

beverage *noun.* —*See* **drink** (1).

bevy *noun.* —*See* **flock, group.**

bewail *verb.* —*See* **deplore** (1), **grieve.**

beware *verb.* To be careful ▶ look out, mind, watch out. ***Idioms:*** be on guard, be on the lookout, keep an eye peeled, take care (*or* heed).

bewilder *verb.* —*See* **agitate** (2), **confuse** (1), **daze** (1).

bewildered *adjective.* —*See* **confused** (1).

bewilderedness *noun.* —*See* **daze.**

bewilderment *noun.* —*See* **complexity, daze.**

bewitch *verb.* —*See* **charm** (1), **charm** (2).

bewitching *adjective.* —*See* **attractive, magic, seductive.**

bias *verb.* **1.** To cause to have a prejudiced view ▶ jaundice, prejudice, prepossess, turn (against), warp. [*Compare* **indoctrinate, influence.**] **2.** To alter or present material so as to favor a particular viewpoint ▶ doctor, fiddle (with), massage, skew, slant, tailor. *Informal:* angle. [*Compare* **distort.**]

bias *noun.* An inclination for or against that inhibits impartial judgment ▶ one-sidedness, partiality, partisanship, preconception, prejudice, prepossession, slant, tendentiousness. —*See also* **inclination** (1).

bias *adjective.* —*See* **oblique.**

✚ **CORE SYNONYMS:** *bias, jaundice, prejudice, warp.* These verbs mean to cause to have a prejudiced view: *His experiences biased his outlook. Dishonest leaders have jaundiced her view of politics. Lying has prejudiced the public against them. Bitterness has warped your judgment.*

biased *adjective.* Exhibiting bias ▶ discriminatory, one-sided, opinionated, partial, partisan, preconceived, predisposed, prejudiced, prejudicial, prepossessed, skewed, slanted, tendentious. [*Compare* **intolerant, narrow, unfair.**] —*See also* **oblique.**

bibelot *noun.* —*See* **novelty** (3).

bibulous *adjective.* —*See* **absorbent, drunk.**

bicker *verb.* —*See* **argue** (1).

bicker *noun.* —*See* **argument.**

bid *verb.* **1.** To request that someone take part in or be present at a particular occasion ▶ ask, invite, summon. ***Idioms:*** extend an invitation to, request the presence of. [*Compare* **appeal, request.**] **2.** To make an offer of ▶ offer. *Informal:* go. —*See also* **command** (1), **compete.**

bid *noun.* A spoken or written request for someone to take part or be present ▶ call, invitation, summons. *Informal:* invite. [*Compare* **request.**] —*See also* **attempt, offer.**

biddable *adjective.* —*See* **obedient.**

bidding *noun.* —*See* **command** (1).

biddy *noun.* —*See* **witch** (2).

bide *verb.* —*See* **endure** (2), **remain.**

biff *verb.* —*See* **hit.**

biff *noun.* —*See* **blow**^{2}**.**

biform *adjective.* —*See* **double** (2).

bifurcate *verb.* —*See* **branch.**

big *adjective.* Above average in amount, size, or scope ▶ biggish, considerable, extensive, good, goodly, great, healthy, king-size, large, large-scale, largish, outsize, queen-size, respectable, significant, sizable, substantial. *Informal:* tidy. [*Compare* **bulky, enormous, grand.**] —*See also* **generous** (1), **important, mature, pregnant** (1).

✚ **CORE SYNONYMS:** *big, extensive, great, large, sizable.* These adjectives mean being notably above the average in amount, size, or scope: *The developers built a big shopping mall. The hurricane caused extensive damage. We saw a great ocean liner pull into the harbor. A large boulder blocked the road. The executive made a sizable fortune in the stock market.*

◀ **ANTONYM:** *small*

Big Brother *noun.* —*See* **dictator.**

biggest *adjective.* —*See* **best** (2).

biggish *adjective.* —*See* **big.**

big gun *noun.* —*See* **dignitary.**

big head *or* **bigheadedness** *noun.* —*See* **egotism.**

bigheaded *adjective.* —*See* **egotistic** (1).

big-hearted *adjective.* —*See* **generous** (1).

big-heartedness *noun.* —*See* **generosity.**

big house *noun.* —*See* **jail.**

bight *noun.* A body of water partly enclosed by land but having a wide outlet to the sea ▶ bay, gulf, sound. [*Compare* **channel, harbor, inlet.**]

big-league *adjective. Informal* Being among the leaders in one's field ▶ big-name, blue-chip, celebrity, leading, major, major-league. *Informal:* bigtime, heavyweight. [*Compare* **famous, important, primary.**]

big name *noun.* —*See* **celebrity, dignitary.**

bigness *noun.* —*See* **size** (2).

bigoted *adjective.* —*See* **intolerant** (1).

bigotry *noun.* Irrational suspicion or hatred of a particular group, race, or religion ▶ discrimination, intolerance, prejudice. [*Compare* **hate.**]

big shot *noun.* —*See* **dignitary.**

big-ticket *adjective.* —*See* **costly.**

bigtime *or* **big-time** *adjective.* —*See* **big-league, important.**
big-timer *noun.* —*See* **dignitary.**
big wheel *noun.* —*See* **boss, dignitary.**
bigwig *noun.* —*See* **dignitary.**
bile *noun.* —*See* **temper** (1).
bilge *noun.* —*See* **nonsense.**
biliousness *noun.* —*See* **temper** (1).
bilk *verb.* —*See* **cheat** (1).
bilk *noun.* —*See* **cheat** (2).
bill[1] *verb.* To present with a request or demand for payment ▶ charge, dun, invoice, solicit.
bill *noun.* —*See* **account** (2), **law** (2), **program** (2), **sign** (2).
bill[2] *noun.* **1.** The horny projection forming a bird's jaws ▶ beak, mandible, nib. **2.** The projecting rim on the front of a cap ▶ brim, eyeshade, peak, visor.
billboard *noun.* —*See* **sign** (2).
billet *noun.* —*See* **position** (3).
billet *verb.* —*See* **lodge.**
billingsgate *noun.* —*See* **vituperation.**
billion *noun.* —*See also* **heap** (2).
binary *adjective.* —*See* **double** (2).
bind *verb.* To make fast or firmly fixed, as by means of a cord or rope ▶ fasten, knot, secure, tie (up). —*See also* **associate** (1), **commit** (2), **dress** (2), **fasten.**
bind *noun.* —*See* **predicament, problem.**
binder *noun.* —*See* **fastener.**
binding *noun.* —*See* **bond** (2), **fastener.**
bine *noun.* —*See* **shoot.**
binge *noun.* A period of uncontrolled self-indulgence ▶ debauch, fling, orgy, rampage, riot, saturnalia, splurge, spree. *Slang:* jag. [*Compare* **blast.**] —*See also* **bender.**

✦ **CORE SYNONYMS:** *binge, fling, jag, orgy, rampage, spree.* These nouns denote a period of uncontrolled self-indulgence: *a gambling binge; had one last fling before beginning a new job; a crying jag; an eating orgy; rioters on a rampage; a shopping spree.*

biome *noun.* —*See* **environment** (3).
biosphere *noun.* —*See* **environment** (3).
bird *noun.* —*See* **hiss** (2).
bird *verb.* —*See* **hiss** (2).
birdbrained *adjective.* —*See* **giddy** (2), **stupid.**
bird-dog *verb.* —*See* **follow** (3).
birth *noun.* **1.** The act or process of bringing forth young ▶ accouchement, birthing, childbearing, childbirth, delivery, labor, lying-in, nativity, parturition, travail. **2.** The initial stage of a developmental process ▶ beginning, commencement, dawn, embarkation, genesis, inception, nascence, nascency, onset, opening, origin, outset, spring, start. *Informal:* day one, square one. —*See also* **ancestry, nobility.**
birth *verb.* —*See* **bear** (4).

✦ **CORE SYNONYMS:** *birth, beginning, dawn, genesis, nascence, outset, start.* These nouns denote the initial stage of a developmental process: *the birth of a new nation; the beginning of a new era in technology; the dawn of civilization; the genesis of quantum mechanics; the nascence of classical sculpture; had clear objectives from the outset of the project; laid down the rules at the start of the retreat.*

birthing *noun.* —*See* **birth** (1).
birthplace *noun.* —*See* **origin.**
birthright *noun.* Any special privilege accorded a firstborn ▶ heritage, inheritance, legacy, patrimony. —*See also* **right.**
bishop *noun.* —*See* **cleric.**
bit[1] *noun.* **1.** A tiny amount ▶ crumb, dab, dash, dot, dram, drop, fragment, grain, iota, jot, little, minim, mite, modicum, molecule, morsel, nip, ort, ounce, particle, pinch, scrap, scruple, shard, shred, smidgen, snip, snippet, speck, tad, tittle, trifle, whit. [*Compare* **flake, part, shade.**] **2.** A small portion of food ▶ bite, crumb, dollop, morsel, mouthful, piece, scrap, slice, sliver, swallow, taste, tidbit. [*Compare* **drop.**] **3.** A

rather short period ▶ interval, space, spell, time, while. [*Compare* **flash.**] **4.** *Informal* A characteristic behavior or performance ▶ act. *Slang:* number, routine, shtick. —*See also* **item.**

bit² *noun.* —*See* **brake.**

bit *verb.* —*See* **restrain.**

bitch *verb.* —*See* **complain.**

bitch *noun.* —*See* **complaint.**

bitchy *adjective.* —*See* **malevolent.**

bite *verb.* —*See* **chew, erode, hurt** (2).

bite *noun.* —*See* **bit¹** (2), **edge, refreshment.**

biting *adjective.* So sharp as to cause mental pain ▶ acerbic, acid, acidic, acrid, astringent, catty, caustic, corrosive, cutting, harsh, mordacious, mordant, pungent, scathing, scorching, searing, sharp, sharp-tongued, slashing, stinging, trenchant, truculent, venomous, vitriolic, waspish, withering. [*Compare* **ill-tempered, resentful, sarcastic.**] —*See also* **sharp** (3).

bits and pieces *noun.* —*See* **odds and ends.**

bitter *adjective.* **1.** Having a sharp, unpleasant, alkaline taste or smell ▶ acerbic, acrid, brackish, briny, harsh, pungent. [*Compare* **sour.**] **2.** Painfully intense ▶ brutal, cruel, hard, harsh, penetrating, punishing, racking, relentless, rigorous, rough, severe, stinging, tough. [*Compare* **bleak, intense, sharp.**] **3.** Difficult to accept or bear ▶ disagreeable, distasteful, galling, indigestible, painful, unpalatable, unpleasant. [*Compare* **disturbing, unbearable, vexatious.**] —*See also* **resentful.**

✚ **CORE SYNONYMS:** *bitter, acerbic, acrid, sour.* These adjectives mean having a sharp, unpleasant, alkaline taste or smell: *a bitter cough syrup; an acerbic green apple; acrid smoke; a sour lemon.*

bitterness *noun.* —*See* **resentment, sarcasm.**

bizarre *adjective.* Conceived or done with no reference to reality or common sense ▶ antic, fantastic, fantastical, far-fetched, grotesque. —*See also* **eccentric, exotic.**

bizarrely *adverb.* —*See* **unusually.**

blab *verb.* —*See* **betray** (2), **chatter** (1), **gossip.**

blab *noun.* —*See* **chatter, gossip** (2).

blabber *verb.* —*See* **chatter** (1).

blabber *noun.* —*See* **chatter.**

blabby *adjective.* Inclined to gossip ▶ gossipy, talebearing, taletelling.

black *adjective.* **1.** Of the darkest color ▶ blue-black, coal-black, ebon, ebony, inky, jet, jet-black, jetty, onyx, pitch-black, pitchy, raven, sable, sooty. **2.** Having little or no light ▶ dark, inky, lightless, moonless, pitch-dark, starless, sunless, unlit. [*Compare* **shady.**] —*See also* **dark** (2), **dirty, evil, gloomy, malevolent.**

black *verb.* —*See* **dirty.**

black out *verb.* —*See* **censor** (2), **faint.**

blackball *verb.* —*See* **exclude, veto.**

blacken *verb.* —*See* **denigrate, dirty.**

black eye *noun.* A bruise surrounding the eye ▶ *Informal:* mouse. *Slang:* shiner. [*Compare* **bruise.**] —*See also* **stain.**

blackjack *verb.* —*See* **coerce.**

blackleg *noun.* —*See* **cheat** (2).

blacklist *verb.* —*See* **exclude.**

black look *noun.* —*See* **frown.**

blackmail *verb.* —*See* **extort.**

blackout *noun.* ▶ faint, fainting spell, swoon, syncope.

black-tie *adjective.* —*See* **formal.**

blade *noun.* The cutting part of a sharp instrument ▶ edge, knife blade, knife-edge, razor, razorblade.

blah *adjective.* —*See* **boring, depressed** (1), **dull** (1).

blahs *noun.* —*See* **depression** (2).

blamable *adjective.* —*See* **blameworthy.**

blame *noun.* Responsibility for an error or crime ▶ blameworthiness, culpability, fault, guilt, onus. *Slang:* rap. [*Compare* **burden¹, error, responsibility.**] —*See also* **criticism.**

blame *verb.* —*See* **accuse, criticize** (1), **fix** (3).

✣ **CORE SYNONYMS:** *blame, fault, guilt.* These nouns denote a sense of responsibility for an error or crime. *Blame* stresses censure or punishment for a lapse or misdeed for which one is held accountable: *The police laid the blame for the accident on the driver. Fault* is culpability for wrongdoing or failure: *It is my own fault that I wasn't prepared for the exam. Guilt* applies to willful wrongdoing and stresses moral culpability: *The prosecution presented evidence of the defendant's guilt.*

---

blamed *adjective.* —*See* **damned.**

blameful *adjective.* —*See* **blameworthy.**

blameless *adjective.* —*See* **exemplary, innocent** (2).

blameworthy *adjective.* Deserving blame ▶ blamable, blameful, censurable, culpable, guilty, red-handed, reprehensible. ***Idioms:*** at fault, in error (*or* the wrong), to blame. [*Compare* **liable.**]

✣ **CORE SYNONYMS:** *blameworthy, blamable, blameful, censurable, culpable, guilty, reprehensible.* These adjectives mean meriting reproof or punishment: *blameworthy behavior; blamable but understandable resentment; blameful impulsiveness; censurable misconduct; culpable negligence; guilty deeds; reprehensible arrogance.*

◀ **ANTONYM:** *blameless*

---

blanch *verb.* —*See* **cook, pale.**

bland *adjective.* Without definite or distinctive characteristics ▶ colorless, indistinctive, neutral. [*Compare* **boring.**] —*See also* **flat** (2), **insipid, ordinary.**

blandish *verb.* —*See* **coax, flatter** (1).

blandishment *noun.* —*See* **flattery.**

blandness *noun.* —*See* **dullness, insipidity.**

blank *adjective.* —*See* **empty** (1), **expressionless, vacant.**

blanket *noun.* —*See* **coat** (2).

blanket *verb.* —*See* **cover** (1).

blanket *adjective.* —*See* **general** (1).

blankness *noun.* —*See* **emptiness** (1), **emptiness** (2), **nothingness** (2).

blare *verb.* —*See* **shout.**

blaring *adjective.* —*See* **loud.**

blarney *noun.* —*See* **babble, flattery.**

blasé *adjective.* —*See* **apathetic.**

blaspheme *verb.* To use profane or obscene language ▶ curse, damn, swear. *Informal:* cuss. —*See also* **revile.**

blasphemous *adjective.* Showing irreverence and contempt for something sacred ▶ impious, profane, sacrilegious.

blasphemy *noun.* —*See* **sacrilege, swearword.**

blast *noun.* **1.** An explosive noise ▶ bang, boom, crash, crump, reverberation, rumble, roar, sonic boom, thunder. [*Compare* **clash, crack, noise.**] **2.** A violent release of confined energy ▶ blowout, blowup, burst, detonation, discharge, eruption, explosion, flare-up, fulmination. [*Compare* **barrage.**] **3.** *Slang* A big, exuberant party ▶ celebration, shindig, shindy. *Informal:* wingding. *Slang:* bash, blowout. [*Compare* **bender, binge.**] —*See also* **wind**[1].

blast *verb.* **1.** To make an explosive noise ▶ bang, boom, crash, roar, rumble, thunder. [*Compare* **crack.**] **2.** To spoil or destroy ▶ blight, corrode, corrupt, dash, nip, scorch, shrivel, wither. [*Compare* **destroy, ruin.**] **3.** To discharge a gun or firearm ▶ blast away, fire (away *or* off), pop (off), shoot (away *or* off). ***Idioms:*** go bang-bang, open fire, take a shot (*or* potshot). —*See also* **explode** (1), **slam** (1).

✣ **CORE SYNONYMS:** *blast, blight, dash, nip, wreck.* These verbs mean to spoil, destroy, or ruin something: *actions that blasted the chance for peace; hopes blighted by ill wishes; ambitions dashed by lack of funds; plans nipped in the bud; a life wrecked by depression.*

---

blasted *adjective.* —*See* **bleak** (1), **damned.**

blatancy *noun.* —*See* **impudence.**

blatant *adjective.* —*See* **impudent, obvious, vociferous.**

blather *noun.* —*See* **babble, nonsense.**

blather *verb.* —*See* **babble.**

blatherskite *noun.* —*See* **babble.**

blaze[1] *noun.* **1.** The visible signs of combustion ► conflagration, fire, flame, flare-up. **2.** An intense blinding light ► dazzle, flare, glare.

blaze *verb.* —*See* **beam, burn** (2), **glare** (2).

blaze[2] *verb.* —*See* **announce.**

blazing *adjective.* —*See* **brilliant, burning, passionate.**

blazon *verb.* —*See* **announce.**

bleach *verb.* —*See* **pale.**

bleak *adjective.* **1.** Marked by cold and unpleasant conditions ► austere, blasted, dour, exposed, forbidding, foul, grim, hard, harsh, inclement, nasty, raw, severe, stark, unsheltered, windswept. [*Compare* **barren, bitter, lonely.**] **2.** Offering little encouragement ► dark, depressing, dim, dismal, downbeat, discouraging, gloomy, inauspicious, pessimistic, unencouraging, unpromising, unpropitious. [*Compare* **doubtful, unfavorable.**] —*See also* **gloomy.**

blear *verb.* —*See* **obscure.**

blear *adjective.* —*See* **unclear.**

bleary *adjective.* —*See* **tired** (1), **unclear.**

bleed *verb.* —*See* **drain** (1), **ooze.**

bleep *verb.* —*See* **censor** (1).

blemish *verb.* —*See* **damage, deform.**

blemish *noun.* —*See* **defect, deformity, stain.**

blemished *adjective.* Having a defect or defects ► amiss, defective, faulty, flawed, imperfect. [*Compare* **shabby, trick.**]

blench *verb.* —*See* **flinch.**

blend *verb.* —*See* **beat** (6), **harmonize** (2), **mix** (1).

blend *noun.* —*See* **harmony** (1), **mixture.**

bless *verb.* To make sacred by a religious rite ► consecrate, hallow, sanctify. [*Compare* **exalt.**] —*See also* **devote.**

blessed *adjective.* —*See* **damned, holy.**

blessedness *noun.* —*See* **happiness, holiness.**

blessing *noun.* A short prayer said at meals ► benediction, grace, thanks, thanksgiving. [*Compare* **prayer[1]**.] —*See also* **advantage** (2), **endorsement.**

blight *verb.* —*See* **blast** (2), **decay.**

blight *noun.* —*See* **decay.**

blind *adjective.* **1.** Having little or no sight ► blinded, dim-sighted, eyeless, legally blind, sightless, stone-blind, unseeing, unsighted, visionless, visually impaired. **2.** Concealed from view ► hidden, secluded, screened, secret. ***Idioms:*** out of sight, out of view. [*Compare* **hidden.**] **3.** Unwilling or unable to perceive ► dull, insensible, obtuse, purblind, uncomprehending, undiscerning, unnoticing, unperceptive, unseeing. [*Compare* **ignorant.**] —*See also* **drunk.**

blind *verb.* To confuse with bright light ► bedazzle, daze, dazzle.

blind alley *noun.* A course leading nowhere ► cul-de-sac, dead end.

blindness *noun.* The condition of not being able to see ► legal blindness, sightlessness, visual impairment.

blink *verb.* To open and close one or both eyes rapidly ► bat, flutter, nictitate, twinkle, wink. —*See also* **glitter, renege, surrender** (1).

blink at *verb.* To pretend not to see ► connive at, disregard, ignore, overlook, pass over, wink at. ***Idioms:*** be blind to, close (*or* shut) one's eyes to, let go (*or* pass), look the other way, make allowances for, sweep under the rug, turn a blind eye (*or* deaf ear) to.

blink *noun.* A brief closing of the eyes ► bat, flutter, nictitation, wink. —*See also* **flash** (1), **flash** (2).

✦ **CORE SYNONYMS:** *blink, nictitate, twinkle, wink.* These verbs mean to open and close an eye or the eyes rapidly: *a dog blinking lazily at the fire; a reptile that nictitated as it closed in on its prey; twinkled, then laughed and responded; winked conspiratorially at his friend.*

---

bliss *noun.* —*See* **delight, happiness, heaven.**

blissful *adjective.* —*See* **delightful.**

blister *verb.* —*See* **slam** (1).

blister *noun.* —*See* **burn, welt.**

blistering *adjective.* —*See* **hot** (1).

blithe *adjective.* —*See* **careless, lighthearted.**

blitheness *noun.* A careless, often reckless regard for consequences ▶ abandon, carelessness, heedlessness, thoughtlessness. [*Compare* **temerity.**] —*See also* **merriment** (1).

blithesome *adjective.* —*See* **cheerful.**

blithesomeness *noun.* —*See* **merriment** (1).

blitz *noun.* —*See* **charge** (1).

blitz *verb.* —*See* **barrage.**

blitzkrieg *noun.* —*See* **charge** (1).

bloat *verb.* —*See* **swell.**

bloc *noun.* An association for a common cause or interest ▶ coalition, league, organization. [*Compare* **association.**] —*See also* **public** (1).

block *verb.* To cut off from sight ▶ block out, blot (out), conceal, curtain, hide, obscure, obstruct, screen, shroud, shut off (*or* out). [*Compare* **disguise, hide, wrap.**] —*See also* **fill** (2), **obstruct, veto.**

block in *or* **out** *verb.* —*See* **draft** (1).

block *noun.* —*See* **bar** (1), **head** (1).

✚ **CORE SYNONYMS:** *block, hide, obscure, obstruct, screen, shroud.* These verbs mean to cut off from sight: *a tree that blocked the view; a road hidden by brush; mist that obscured the mountain peak; skyscrapers obstructing the sky; a fence that screens the alley; a face shrouded by a heavy veil.*

---

blockade *noun.* A prolonged encirclement of an objective by hostile troops ▶ beleaguerment, besiegement, investment, siege. [*Compare* **attack.**]

blockade *verb.* —*See* **besiege, obstruct.**

blockage *noun.* —*See* **bar** (1).

blockhead *noun.* —*See* **dullard.**

blockheaded *adjective.* —*See* **stupid.**

blocky *adjective.* —*See* **bulky** (1), **stocky.**

blond *or* **blonde** *adjective.* —*See* **fair[1]** (2).

blood *noun.* —*See* **ancestry, murder, nobility.**

bloodbath *noun.* —*See* **massacre.**

bloodcurdling *adjective.* —*See* **horrible.**

bloodless *adjective.* —*See* **callous, pale** (1), **pale** (2).

bloodletting *noun.* —*See* **massacre.**

bloodline *noun.* —*See* **ancestry.**

bloodshed *noun.* —*See* **massacre.**

bloodstain *verb.* To cover with blood ▶ bloody, ensanguine, incarnadine.

bloodsucker *noun.* —*See* **parasite.**

bloodsucking *adjective.* —*See* **parasitic.**

bloodthirsty *adjective.* —*See* **murderous.**

blood vessel *noun.* —*See* **vessel** (2).

bloody *adjective.* Of or covered with blood ▶ bleeding, blood-soaked, bloodstained, gory, hemorrhaging. [*Compare* **ghastly.**] —*See also* **damned, murderous.**

bloody *verb.* To cover with blood ▶ bloodstain, ensanguine, incarnadine.

bloody-minded *adjective.* —*See* **murderous.**

bloom[1] *noun.* **1.** A time of vigor, youth, or peak condition ▶ blossom, efflorescence, florescence, flower, flush, heyday, prime, salad days. **2.** A fresh rosy complexion ▶ blush, color, flush, glow. [*Compare* **color, complexion.**] —*See also* **flower.**

bloom *verb.* **1.** To bear flowers ▶ blossom, blow, bud (out), burgeon, effloresce, flower, open (up *or* out). ***Idioms:*** burst into flower (*or* bloom). **2.** To grow rapidly ▶ blossom, flourish, thrive. [*Compare* **increase.**]

✚ **CORE SYNONYMS:** *bloom, blossom, efflorescence, florescence, flower, flush, prime.* These nouns denote a condition or time of vigor, youth, or peak condition: *beauty in full bloom; the blossom of a great romance; the efflorescence of humanitarianism; the florescence of Greek civilization; in the flower of youthful enthusiasm; in the flush of their success; the prime of life.*

---

bloom² *noun.* —*See* **rod.**

bloomer *noun.* —*See* **blunder.**

blooming *adjective.* —*See* **ruddy.**

blooper *noun.* —*See* **blunder.**

blossom *noun.* —*See* **bloom¹** (1), **flower.**

blossom *verb.* To grow rapidly ▶ bloom, flourish, thrive. [*Compare* **increase.**] —*See also* **bloom¹** (1).

blot *noun.* —*See* **smear, stain.**

blot *verb.* —*See* **block, cancel** (1), **denigrate, disgrace.**

blot out *verb.* —*See* **annihilate.**

blotch *noun.* —*See* **smear.**

blotch *verb.* —*See* **stain.**

blotto *adjective.* —*See* **drunk.**

blow¹ *verb.* **1.** To be in a state of motion, as air or wind ▶ bluster, breathe, freshen, gust, puff, rise, stir, sweep. ***Idioms:*** come (*or* kick *or* spring) up. **2.** To move in or on the wind ▶ drift, flap, float, flutter, fly, sail, stream, waft, wave. **3.** To come open or fly apart suddenly and violently, as from internal pressure ▶ blow out, burst, explode, pop. *Slang:* bust. **4.** To manifest strong winds and precipitation ▶ blow up, set in, squall, storm. [*Compare* **rain.**] —*See also* **boast, botch, explode** (1), **go** (1), **pant, treat** (2), **waste.**

blow in *verb.* —*See* **arrive** (1).

blow up *verb.* —*See* **anger** (2), **increase, swell.**

blow *noun.* —*See* **boast, storm, wind¹.**

blow² *noun.* A sudden heavy stroke ▶ bang, bonk, buffet, bust, chop, clout, crack, hit, jab, lick, pound, punch, slug, sock, stroke, swat, swing, swipe, thump, thwack, welt, whack, wham, whop. *Informal:* bash, biff, bop, clip, wallop. *Slang:* belt, conk, haymaker, knuckle sandwich, paste, roundhouse. [*Compare* **slap.**] —*See also* **shock¹.**

blow³ *verb.* —*See* **bloom¹** (1).

blow-by-blow *adjective.* —*See* **detailed.**

blower *or* **blowhard** *noun.* —*See* **braggart.**

blowout *noun.* —*See* **blast** (2), **blast** (3), **defeat.**

blowup *noun.* —*See* **blast** (2), **outburst.**

blowy *adjective.* —*See* **airy** (3).

blubber¹ *verb.* —*See* **cry.**

blubber² *noun.* Adipose tissue ▶ fat, lard, suet, tallow. [*Compare* **oil.**]

blubbering *noun.* —*See* **cry** (1).

bludgeon *verb.* —*See* **beat** (1), **intimidate.**

blue *adjective.* —*See* **depressed** (1), **gloomy, racy, sorrowful.**

blue blood *noun.* —*See* **nobility, society** (1).

blue-blooded *adjective.* —*See* **noble.**

blue-chip *adjective.* —*See* **big-league.**

bluecoat *noun.* —*See* **police officer.**

blue moon *noun.* —*See* **ages.**

bluenose *noun.* —*See* **prude.**

bluenosed *adjective.* —*See* **prudish.**

blue-pencil *verb.* —*See* **censor** (1).

blueprint *noun.* —*See* **approach** (1), **draft** (1).

blueprint *verb.* —*See* **arrange** (2), **design** (1), **design** (2).

blue-ribbon *adjective.* —*See* **excellent.**

blues *noun.* —*See* **depression** (2).

bluff *verb.* —*See* **deceive.**

bluff *adjective.* —*See* **abrupt** (1).

blunder *verb.* To move heavily or clumsily ▶ bumble, clump, flounder, galumph, hulk, lumber, lump, lurch, stump, stumble. [*Compare* **stagger,**

stumble.] —*See also* **botch, err, muddle.**

blunder *noun.* A stupid, clumsy mistake ▶ bobble, bungle, faux pas, foozle, fumble, muff, solecism, stumble. *Informal:* blooper, boner, boo-boo, fluff, no-no. *Slang:* bloomer, clinker, goof, howler. [*Compare* **mess, error.**]

✤ **CORE SYNONYMS:** *blunder, bumble, flounder, lumber, lurch, stumble.* These verbs mean to move heavily or clumsily: *blundered about the dark room; flies bumbling against the screen; floundered up the muddy trail; a wagon lumbering along an unpaved road; twisted her ankle and lurched home; stumbled but regained his balance.*

---

blunderer *noun.* A clumsy, inept person ▶ botcher, bungler, dub, foozler, lubber. *Informal:* sad sack. *Slang:* klutz, screwup. ***Idiom:*** bull in a china shop. [*Compare* **boor, oaf.**]

blunt *adjective.*—*See* **abrupt** (1), **dull** (3).

blunt *verb.* —*See* **deaden, dull.**

blur *verb.* —*See* **drug** (2), **obscure.**

blurry *adjective.* —*See* **unclear.**

blurt *verb.* —*See* **exclaim.**

blush *verb.* To become red in the face ▶ color, crimson, flush, glow, mantle, redden. ***Idioms:*** go red (*or* crimson *or* scarlet), turn red as a beet.

blush *noun.* A fresh rosy complexion ▶ bloom, color, flush, glow. [*Compare* **color, complexion.**]

bluster *verb.* —*See* **blow**[1] (1), **boast, shout.**

bluster *noun.* —*See* **roar.**

blustery *adjective.* —*See* **rough** (2).

board *verb.* To go aboard a means of transport ▶ catch, take. *Informal:* hop. —*See also* **lodge.**

boards *noun.* —*See* **stage** (1).

boast *verb.* To talk with excessive pride ▶ bluster, brag, crow, gasconade, puff (up), swagger, swell (up), vaunt. *Informal:* blow. ***Idioms:*** blow one's own horn (*or* trumpet), pat oneself on the back, shoot off one's mouth (*or* face), sing one's own praises, talk big. [*Compare* **exaggerate, exult, strut.**] —*See also* **command** (2).

boast *noun.* Boastful talk or behavior ▶ boasting, brag, braggadocio, bragging, bravado, fanfaronade, gasconade, vaunt. *Informal:* blow, fish story. *Slang:* gas. [*Compare* **bombast.**]

✤ **CORE SYNONYMS:** *boast, brag, crow, vaunt.* These verbs mean to talk with excessive pride about oneself or something related to oneself. *Boast* is the most general: "*We confide* [that is, have confidence] *in our strength, without boasting of it; we respect that of others, without fearing it*" (Thomas Jefferson). *Brag* implies exaggerated claims and often an air of insolent superiority: *You shouldn't brag about your grades. Crow* stresses exultation and often loud rejoicing: *No candidate should crow until the votes have been counted. Vaunt* suggests ostentatiousness and lofty extravagance of expression: "*He did not vaunt of his new dignity, but I understood he was highly pleased with it*" (James Boswell).

---

boaster *noun.* —*See* **braggart.**

boastful *adjective.* Characterized by or given to boasting ▶ blustering, bombastic, braggart, cocky, puffed up, swollen, vaunting. ***Idioms:*** full of gas (*or* hot air). [*Compare* **arrogant, egotistic, pompous.**]

boat *noun.* A conveyance that travels over water ▶ bark, barque, craft, ship, vessel, watercraft.

boatman *noun.* —*See* **sailor.**

bob *verb.* —*See* **bow**[1] (1), **float** (1).

bode *verb.* —*See* **foreshadow, threaten** (1).

bodiless *adjective.* —*See* **immaterial.**

bodily *adjective.* Of or relating to the body ▶ corporal, corporeal, fleshly, incarnate, mortal, personal, physical, somatic. [*Compare* **perceptible, physical, real.**]

✚ **CORE SYNONYMS:** *bodily, corporal, corporeal, fleshly, physical, somatic.* These adjectives mean of or relating to the body: *a bodily organ; a corporal defect; corporeal suffering; fleshly frailty; physical robustness; a somatic symptom.*

body *noun.* **1.** The human body excluding the head and limbs ▶ midsection, torso, trunk. **2.** The physical frame of a dead person or animal ▶ bones, cadaver, carcass, corpse, mummy, relics, remains. *Slang:* stiff. *—See also* **assembly, constitution, force** (3), **group, human being, object** (1), **quantity** (3), **system.**

body forth *verb.* *—See* **embody** (1).

body politic *noun.* *—See* **state** (1).

boff *or* **boffo** *or* **boffola** *noun.* *—See* **hit.**

bog *noun.* *—See* **swamp.**

bog *verb.* *—See* **hinder.**

bog down *verb.* *—See* **hinder.**

bogey *or* **bogeyman** *noun.* *—See* **ghost.**

boggle *verb.* *—See* **botch, stagger** (2).

bogle *noun.* *—See* **ghost.**

bogus *adjective.* *—See* **counterfeit.**

boil *verb.* To be in a state of turmoil or excitement ▶ bubble, burn, churn, effervesce, ferment, froth, percolate, seethe, simmer, smolder. *—See also* **anger** (2), **burn** (3), **cook.**

boil away *verb.* *—See* **evaporate.**

boil down *verb.* To reduce in complexity or scope ▶ pare (down), simplify, streamline. ***Idioms:*** reduce to the basics (*or* essentials *or* bare bones). [*Compare* **explain.**] *—See also* **shorten.**

boil *noun.* *—See* **welt.**

boilerplate *noun.* Written material used to fill space in a publication ▶ filler. [*Compare* **item.**]

boiling *adjective.* *—See* **hot** (1).

boisterous *adjective.* *—See* **vociferous.**

bold *adjective.* *—See* **adventurous, brave, impudent, noticeable, steep**[1] (1).

boldfaced *adjective.* *—See* **impudent.**

boldness *noun.* *—See* **daring, impudence.**

bollix up *verb.* *—See* **botch.**

bolster *verb.* *—See* **back** (2), **defend** (2), **support** (2).

bolt *verb.* To move suddenly and involuntarily ▶ jump, start. [*Compare* **bump, jerk.**] *—See also* **fasten, gulp, run** (2), **rush.**

bolt *noun.* A sudden and involuntary movement ▶ jump, start, startle. [*Compare* **jerk, recoil.**] *—See also* **nail.**

bomb *noun.* *—See* **failure** (1).

bomb *verb.* *—See* **barrage, fail** (1).

bombard *verb.* *—See* **attack** (1), **barrage.**

bombardment *noun.* *—See* **barrage.**

bombast *noun.* Pretentious, pompous speech or writing ▶ claptrap, fire and brimstone, fustian, grandiloquence, magniloquence, orotundity, rant, turgidity. [*Compare* **gibberish, nonsense, oratory.**]

bombastic *adjective.* *—See* **boastful, oratorical.**

bombed *adjective.* *—See* **drunk.**

bombshell *noun.* *—See* **shock**[1].

bona fide *adjective.* *—See* **authentic** (1).

bond *noun.* **1.** Something that physically confines the legs or arms ▶ ball and chain, chains, fetter, handcuffs, hobble, irons, leg irons, manacle, restraint, shackle, straitjacket, trammel. [*Compare* **brake, restraint.**] **2.** That which unites or binds ▶ binding, cinch, girth, hitch, holdfast, knot, ligament, ligature, link, nexus, splice, tie, vinculum, yoke. [*Compare* **band, joint.**] **3.** The close physical union of two objects ▶ adherence, adhesion, attachment, cohesion. *—See also* **agreement** (1), **cord, pawn**[1].

bond *verb.* To form a tight bond ▶ adhere, cleave, cling, cohere, stick. ***Idioms:*** hold tight (*or* fast), stick (*or* cling) tight, stick like glue (*or* a bur). [*Compare* **attach.**] *—See also* **pawn**[1].

bondage *noun.* *—See* **slavery.**

bondservant *noun.* *—See* **slave.**

bondsman *noun.* One who posts bond ▶ bail, bailsman.

bone-dry *adjective.* —*See* **dry** (1).

boneheaded *noun.* —*See* **stupid.**

boneheadedness *noun.* —*See* **stupidity.**

boner *noun.* —*See* **blunder.**

bone up *verb. Informal* To apply one's mind to the acquisition of knowledge, especially when pressed for time ▶ lucubrate, study. *Informal:* cram, grind. ***Idioms:*** burn the midnight oil, hit the books. [*Compare* **examine.**]

bong *verb.* —*See* **ring²**.

bonk *noun.* —*See* **blow²**.

bonkers *adjective.* —*See* **insane.**

bonny *adjective.* —*See* **good** (1).

bonus *noun.* —*See* **reward.**

bony *adjective.* —*See* **thin** (1).

boo *noun.* —*See* **hiss** (2).

boo *verb.* —*See* **hiss** (2).

boob *noun.* —*See* **dullard, fool.**

boobishness *noun.* —*See* **foolishness.**

booby trap *noun.* —*See* **trap** (1).

boodle *noun.* —*See* **bribe, plunder.**

boogie *verb.* —*See* **dance.**

book *noun.* A printed and bound work ▶ booklet, edition, hardcover, paperback, tome, volume. [*Compare* **publication.**] —*See also* **script** (2).

book *verb.* To cause to be set aside, as for one's use, in advance ▶ arrange for, bespeak, engage, reserve. [*Compare* **hire, lease.**] —*See also* **list¹**.

✚ **CORE SYNONYMS:** *book, bespeak, engage, reserve.* These verbs mean to cause something to be set aside in advance, as for one's use or possession: *will book a hotel room; made sure their selections were bespoken; engaged a box for the opera season; reserving a table at a restaurant.*

---

booking *noun.* A commitment, as for a performance by an entertainer ▶ date, engagement. *Slang:* gig.

bookish *adjective.* Devoted to study or reading ▶ scholarly, studious. [*Compare* **educated, intellectual, learned.**] —*See also* **pedantic.**

boom *verb.* —*See* **blast** (1), **prosper, rumble** (1).

boom *noun.* —*See* **blast** (1).

boomerang *verb.* To produce an unexpected and undesired result ▶ backfire, boomerang. ***Idiom:*** blow up in one's face. [*Compare* **fail.**]

booming *adjective.* —*See* **flourishing, loud.**

boomy *adjective.* —*See* **flourishing.**

boon¹ *noun.* —*See* **advantage** (2).

boon² *adjective.* —*See* **cheerful.**

boondocks *or* **boonies** *noun.* —*See* **country.**

boor *noun.* An unrefined, rude person ▶ barbarian, cad, chuff, churl, Philistine, troglodyte, vulgarian, yahoo. *Informal:* caveman, slob. [*Compare* **blunderer, clodhopper, oaf.**]

✚ **CORE SYNONYMS:** *boor, barbarian, churl, vulgarian, yahoo.* These nouns denote an unrefined, rude person: *listened to the boor talk about himself all night; a barbarian bewildered by the art exhibit; offended by the churl's lack of manners; refused to invite the vulgarian to the party; acted like a yahoo at the restaurant.*

---

boorish *adjective.* —*See* **coarse** (1).

boost *verb.* To increase in amount ▶ hike, jack (up), jump, raise, up. [*Compare* **increase.**] —*See also* **elevate** (1), **help, increase, promote** (3), **steal.**

boost *noun.* —*See* **encouragement, increase** (2), **increase** (1), **lift.**

booster *noun.* —*See* **advocate.**

boot *noun.* —*See* **dismissal, ejection, thrill.**

boot *verb.* —*See* **dismiss** (1), **eject** (1), **vomit.**

booth *noun.* A small, often makeshift structure for the display and sale of goods ▶ counter, stand, stall. [*Compare* **store.**]

bootleg *verb.* —*See* **smuggle.**

bootlegger *noun.* A person who engages in smuggling ▶ contrabandist, runner, smuggler. *Slang:* mule.
bootless *adjective.* —*See* **futile.**
bootlessness *noun.* —*See* **futility.**
bootlick *verb.* —*See* **fawn.**
bootlicker *noun.* —*See* **sycophant.**
booty *noun.* —*See* **plunder.**
booze *noun.* —*See* **bender.**
booze *verb.* —*See* **drink** (2).
boozed *or* **boozy** *adjective.* —*See* **drunk.**
boozehound *or* **boozer** *noun.* —*See* **drunkard.**
bop *verb.* —*See* **hit.**
bop *noun.* —*See* **blow²**.
border *noun.* **1.** A line or area where something ends or abruptly changes ▶ brim, brink, curb, edge, edging, fringe, hem, limit, lip, margin, perimeter, periphery, rim, threshold, verge. [*Compare* **circumference.**] **2.** The line or area separating geopolitical units ▶ borderland, borderline, boundary, frontier, march, marchland. [*Compare* **limit, outskirts.**]
border *verb.* To put or form a border on ▶ bound, edge, fringe, margin, rim, skirt, verge. —*See also* **adjoin.**
border on *or* **upon** *verb.* —*See* **rival.**

✦ **CORE SYNONYMS:** *border, margin, edge, verge, brink, rim, brim.* These nouns refer to the line or narrow area where something ends or abruptly changes. *Border* refers either to the boundary line (*a fence along the border of the property*) or to the area immediately inside (*a frame with a wide border*). *Margin* is a border of more or less precisely definable width: *the margin of the page. Edge* refers to the bounding line formed by the continuous convergence of two surfaces: *sat on the edge of the chair. Verge* is an extreme terminating line or edge: *the sun's afterglow on the verge of the horizon.* Figuratively, it indicates a point at which something is likely to begin or to happen: *an explorer on the verge of a great discovery. Brink* denotes the edge of a steep place: *stood on the brink of the cliff.* In an extended sense it indicates the likelihood or imminence of a sudden change: *on the brink of falling in love. Rim* most often denotes the edge of something circular or curved: *a crack in the rim of the lens. Brim* applies to the upper edge or inner side of the rim of something shaped like a basin: *lava issuing from the brim of the crater.*

bordering *adjective.* —*See* **adjoining.**
borderland *noun.* —*See* **border** (2).
borderline *noun.* —*See* **border** (2).
borderline *adjective.* —*See* **ambiguous** (1).
bore¹ *verb.* —*See* **cut** (1), **dig.**
bore² *verb.* To make weary with dullness or tedium ▶ fatigue, stultify, tire, weary. ***Idioms:*** bore out of one's mind, bore to death (*or* distraction *or* tears), put to sleep. [*Compare* **annoy, tire.**]
bore *noun.* —*See* **drip** (2).
boreal *adjective.* —*See* **cold** (1).
boredom *noun.* The condition of being bored ▶ ennui, listlessness, tediousness, tedium. *Informal:* blahs, doldrums. [*Compare* **apathy, dullness, monotony.**]
boring *adjective.* Arousing no interest or curiosity ▶ deadly, drear, dreary, dry, dull, humdrum, irksome, monotonous, stuffy, tedious, tiresome, uninteresting, unvaried, weariful, wearisome, weary. *Informal:* blah, ho-hum. *Slang:* draggy. [*Compare* **dull, insipid, trite.**] —*See also* **ordinary.**

✦ **CORE SYNONYMS:** *boring, monotonous, tedious, irksome, tiresome, humdrum.* These adjectives refer to that which arouses no interest or curiosity. *Boring* implies feelings of listlessness and discontent: *I had never read such a boring book.* What is *monotonous* bores because of lack of variety: "*There is nothing so desperately monotonous as the sea*" (James Russell Lowell). *Tedious* suggests dull slowness or long-windedness: *Traveling by plane avoids spending tedious days on the train. Irksome* describes what is demanding of time and effort and yet is dull and often unrewarding: *"I know and feel what an irksome task the writing of long letters is"* (Edmund Burke). Something *tiresome* fatigues because it seems to be interminable or to be marked by unremitting sameness: *"What a tiresome being is a man who is fond of talking"* (Benjamin Jowett). *Humdrum* refers to what is commonplace, trivial, or unexcitingly routine: *My quiet cousin led a humdrum existence.*

---

borough *adjective.* —*See* **city.**

borrow *verb.* —*See* **plagiarize.**

bosom *noun.* The seat of a person's innermost emotions and feelings ▶ breast, heart, soul. ***Idioms:*** the bottom (*or* cockles) of one's heart, one's heart of hearts.

bosom *adjective.* —*See* **intimate**[1] **(1).**

boss *noun.* Someone who directs and supervises workers ▶ director, foreman, foreperson, forewoman, head, manager, overseer, superintendent, superior, supervisor, taskmaster, taskmistress. *Informal:* straw boss. *Slang:* big cheese, big wheel, chief. [*Compare* **executive.**] —*See also* **chief.**

boss *verb.* To command in an arrogant manner ▶ dictate, dominate, domineer, order, rule, tyrannize. ***Idioms:*** boss around, lord it over, throw one's weight around. [*Compare* **command.**] —*See also* **supervise.**

boss *adjective.* —*See* **excellent.**

bossy *adjective.* —*See* **dictatorial.**

botch *verb.* To ruin through clumsiness or ineptness ▶ ball up, blunder, boggle, bungle, butcher, foul up, fumble, gum up, mangle, mess up, mishandle, mismanage, muddle, muff, spoil, wreck. *Informal:* bollix up, flub, muck up. *Slang:* blow, goof up, louse up, screw up, snafu. ***Idioms:*** make a mess (*or* muck *or* hash) of. [*Compare* **damage, destroy.**]

botch *noun.* —*See* **mess (1).**

✚ **CORE SYNONYMS:** *botch, bungle, fumble, muff.* These verbs mean to ruin through inept or clumsy handling: *botch a repair; bungle an interview; fumbled my chance to apologize; muffed the painting job.*

---

botcher *noun.* —*See* **blunderer.**

bother *noun.* Needless trouble ▶ botheration, fuss, pother, red tape, rigmarole. *Informal:* hassle, headache. [*Compare* **agitation, inconvenience.**] —*See also* **annoyance (1), annoyance (2).**

bother *verb.* —*See* **agitate (2), annoy, hurt (3), worry.**

botheration *noun.* —*See* **annoyance (1), bother.**

bothering *noun.* —*See* **annoyance (1).**

bothersome *adjective.* —*See* **disturbing.**

bottleneck *noun.* —*See* **bar (1).**

bottle up *adjective.* —*See* **repress.**

bottom *noun.* **1.** A side or surface that is below or under ▶ underneath, underpart, underside, undersurface. **2.** A very low or lowest level, position, or degree ▶ low, minimum, nadir, rock bottom. —*See also* **base**[1] **(2), buttocks, center (3).**

bottom *adjective.* Opposite to or farthest from the top ▶ lowermost, lowest, nethermost, undermost.

boulevard *noun.* —*See* **way (2).**

bounce *verb.* To reverse direction after striking something ▶ bounce back, rebound, reflect, snap back, spring back. [*Compare* **bend, glance.**] —*See also* **bound**[1]**, bump, dismiss (1), eject (1).**

bounce back *verb.* —*See* **echo, recover (2).**

bounce *noun.* **1.** A bouncing movement ▶ bound, hop, rebound. **2.** The ability to recover quickly from depression or discouragement ▶ buoyancy, elasticity, flexibility, resilience, resiliency. —*See also* **bound¹** (2), **dismissal, ejection, flexibility** (1), **spirit** (1).

bouncy *adjective.* —*See* **lively.**

bound¹ *verb.* To move in a lively way ▶ bounce, hop, jump, leap, skip, skitter, spring, trip. [*Compare* **gambol.**]

bound *noun.* **1.** A bouncing movement ▶ bounce, hop, rebound. **2.** A sudden lively movement ▶ bounce, hop, jump, leap, skip, spring.

bound² *verb.* —*See* **adjoin, border, determine, limit.**

bound *noun.* —*See* **limits.**

bound³ *adjective.* —*See* **obliged** (2).

boundary *noun.* —*See* **border** (2).

boundless *adjective.* —*See* **endless** (1), **incalculable.**

boundlessness *noun.* —*See* **infinity** (1).

bounds *noun.* —*See* **limits.**

bounteous *adjective.* —*See* **generous** (2).

bounteousness *noun.* —*See* **generosity, plenty.**

bountiful *adjective.* —*See* **generous** (1), **generous** (2).

bountifulness *noun.* —*See* **generosity, plenty.**

bounty *noun.* —*See* **abundance, generosity, reward.**

bouquet *noun.* Cut flowers or foliage arranged or worn for display ▶ boutonniere, corsage, garland, lei, nosegay, posy, wreath. [*Compare* **flower.**] —*See also* **fragrance.**

bout *noun.* —*See* **competition** (2), **turn** (1).

boutique *noun.* A retail establishment where merchandise is sold ▶ emporium, outlet, shop, store.

bow¹ *verb.* **1.** To incline the head or body, as in greeting, consent, courtesy, submission, or worship ▶ bob, curtsy, genuflect, kneel, kowtow, nod, salaam. **2.** To conform to the will or judgment of another ▶ defer, submit, yield. ***Idioms:*** give ground, give way. [*Compare* **humor.**] —*See also* **stoop, succumb, surrender** (1).

bow *noun.* An inclination of the head or body, as in greeting, consent, courtesy, submission, or worship ▶ curtsy, genuflection, kowtow, nod, obeisance, salaam.

bow² *verb.* —*See* **bend** (1), **bend** (3).

bow *noun.* —*See* **bend.**

bow³ *noun.* —*See* **front.**

bowdlerize *verb.* —*See* **censor** (1).

bowed *adjective.* —*See* **bent.**

bowels *noun.* —*See* **viscera.**

bowl *verb.* —*See* **throw.**

bowl over *verb.* —*See* **stagger** (2).

bowl *noun.* —*See* **throw.**

box¹ *noun.* —*See* **package, predicament.**

box *verb.* —*See* **enclose** (1).

box² *verb.* —*See* **hit, slap.**

box *noun.* —*See* **slap.**

boxer *noun.* A contestant in a boxing match ▶ fighter, prizefighter, pugilist. [*Compare* **fighter.**]

box office *noun.* The amount of money collected as admission, especially to a sporting event ▶ gate, receipts, take.

boy *noun.* A young male person ▶ boychild, lad, stripling, youth. *Informal:* junior, son. *Slang:* homeboy, little shaver, nipper. [*Compare* **child.**] —*See also* **fellow.**

boycott *verb.* —*See* **exclude.**

boyfriend *noun.* A man who is a woman's romantic partner ▶ beau, inamorato. *Informal:* fellow, main man. *Slang:* old man. [*Compare* **darling, lover.**]

bozo *noun.* —*See* **fool.**

brace *verb.* —*See* **gird, support** (2), **tense.**

brace *noun.* —*See* **couple, support.**

bracer *noun.* —*See* **tonic.**

bracing *adjective.* —*See* **invigorating.**

bracket *noun.* —*See* **class** (2), **support.**

bracket *verb.* —*See* **associate** (3), **support** (2).

brackish *adjective.* Containing salt ▶ briny, saline, salty. —*See also* **bitter** (1).

brag *verb.* —*See* **boast.**

brag *noun.* —*See* **boast, braggart.**

brag *adjective.* —*See* **excellent.**

braggadocio *noun.* —*See* **arrogance, boast, braggart.**

braggart *noun.* One given to boasting ▶ blusterer, boaster, brag, braggadocio, bragger, swaggerer, vaunter. *Informal:* blowhard. *Slang:* blower, windbag. [*Compare* **egotist, showoff.**]

braggart *adjective.* —*See* **boastful.**

braid *verb.* —*See* **weave.**

braid *noun.* —*See* **web.**

brain *noun.* The seat of the faculty of intelligence and reason ▶ head, mind. *Informal:* gray matter. [*Compare* **imagination.**] —*See also* **mind** (2).

braincase *noun.* ▶ brainpan, cranium, skull. [*Compare* **head.**]

brainchild *noun.* —*See* **invention** (2).

brainless *adjective.* —*See* **foolish, mindless, stupid.**

brainlessness *noun.* —*See* **stupidity.**

brainpan *noun.* The bony framework of the head ▶ braincase, cranium, skull. [*Compare* **head.**]

brainpower *or* **brains** *noun.* —*See* **intelligence.**

brainsick *adjective.* —*See* **insane.**

brainsickness *noun.* —*See* **insanity.**

brainstorm *noun.* A sudden exciting thought ▶ inspiration, bright idea. *Informal:* brain wave. [*Compare* **idea.**]

brainstorming *noun.* —*See* **thought.**

brainwash *verb.* —*See* **indoctrinate** (2).

brainwashing *noun.* —*See* **propaganda.**

brain wave *noun. Informal* A sudden exciting thought ▶ brainstorm, bright idea, inspiration. [*Compare* **idea.**]

brainwork *noun.* —*See* **thought.**

brainy *adjective.* —*See* **intelligent.**

braise *verb.* —*See* **cook.**

brake *noun.* A device for slowing or stopping motion ▶ baffle, bit, bridle, checkrein, curb, damper, drag, leash, rein, restraint, snaffle. [*Compare* **bond, restraint.**] —*See also* **anchor.**

brake *verb.* —*See* **restrain.**

brambly *adjective.* —*See* **thorny** (1).

branch *noun.* **1.** Something resembling or analogous to a tree branch ▶ arm, division, extension, fork, offshoot, ramification, subdivision, tributary. [*Compare* **division.**] **2.** An area of academic study that is part of a larger body of learning ▶ discipline, field, specialty. [*Compare* **area.**] **3.** An administrative unit, as of government or company ▶ affiliate, agency, arm, bureau, chapter, department, division, office, organ, section, wing. —*See also* **brook**[1], **stick** (1).

branch *verb.* To separate into branches or branchlike parts ▶ bifurcate, branch out (*or* off), diverge, diversify, divide, fork, part, radiate, ramify, split, subdivide. [*Compare* **deviate, scatter.**]

✚ **CORE SYNONYMS:** *branch, arm, fork, offshoot.* These nouns denote something resembling or analogous to a tree branch: *a branch of a railroad; an arm of the sea; the western fork of the river; an offshoot of a mountain range.*

---

brand *noun.* —*See* **kind**[2], **mark** (1).

brand *verb.* To cause to feel embarrassment, dishonor, and often guilt ▶ mortify, reproach, shame, stigmatize. ***Idioms:*** put to shame, put to the blush. [*Compare* **belittle, denigrate, embarrass, humble.**] —*See also* **mark** (1).

brandish *verb.* To wield boldly and dramatically ▶ flourish, sweep, wave. [*Compare* **handle.**] —*See also* **display.**

brand-new *adjective.* —*See* **new.**

brannigan *noun.* —*See* **bender.**

brash *adjective.* —*See* **impudent, rash**[1], **tactless.**

brashness *noun.* —*See* **impudence, temerity.**

brass *noun.* —*See* **impudence.**

brassbound *adjective.* —*See* **stubborn** (1).

brass hat *noun.* —*See* **chief.**

brass ring *noun. Slang* A person or thing worth catching ▶ *Informal:* catch. ▶ plum, prize. [*Compare* **treasure.**]

brass-tacks *adjective.* —*See* **pithy.**

brassy *adjective.* —*See* **impudent.**

brat *noun.* —*See* **urchin.**

brattle *verb.* To make or cause to make a succession of short, sharp sounds ▶ chatter, clack, clank, clatter, rattle. [*Compare* **knock, shake.**]

bravado *noun.* —*See* **boast.**

brave *adjective.* Having or showing courage ▶ audacious, bold, courageous, dashing, dauntless, doughty, fearless, fortitudinous, gallant, game, gritty, hardy, heroic, intrepid, mettlesome, nervy, plucky, spirited, stout, stouthearted, unafraid, undaunted, unflinching, valiant, valorous. *Informal:* spunky. *Slang:* gutsy, gutty. *Regional:* bodacious. [*Compare* **adventurous, rash[1]**.]

brave *verb.* —*See* **defy** (1), **venture.**

✚ **CORE SYNONYMS:** *brave, courageous, fearless, intrepid, bold, audacious, valiant, valorous, mettlesome, plucky, dauntless, undaunted.* These adjectives mean having or showing courage, especially under difficult or dangerous conditions. *Brave,* the least specific, is frequently associated with an innate quality: "*Familiarity with danger makes a brave man braver*" (Herman Melville). *Courageous* implies consciously rising to a specific test by drawing on a reserve of inner strength: *The courageous soldier helped the civilians escape from the enemy. Fearless* emphasizes absence of fear and resolute self-possession: "*world-class* [boating] *races for fearless loners willing to face the distinct possibility of being run down, dismasted, capsized, attacked by whales*" (Jo Ann Morse Ridley). *Intrepid* sometimes suggests invulnerability to fear: *Intrepid pioneers settled the American West. Bold* stresses readiness to meet danger or difficulty and often a tendency to seek it out: "*If we shrink from the hard contests where men must win at the hazard of their lives . . . then bolder and stronger peoples will pass us by*" (Theodore Roosevelt). *Audacious* implies extreme confidence and boldness: "*To demand these God-given rights is to seek black power—what I call audacious power*" (Adam Clayton Powell, Jr.). *Valiant* suggests the bravery of a hero or heroine: "*a sympathetic and detailed biography that sees Hemingway as a valiant and moral man*" (New York Times). *Valorous* applies to the deeds of heroes and heroines: "*The other hostages* [will] *never forget her calm, confident, valorous work*" (William W. Bradley). *Mettlesome* stresses spirit and love of challenge: "*her horse, whose mettlesome spirit required a better rider*" (Henry Fielding). *Plucky* emphasizes spirit and heart in the face of unfavorable odds: "*Everybody was . . . anxious to show these Belgians what England thought of their plucky little country*" (H.G. Wells). *Dauntless* refers to courage that resists subjection or intimidation: "*So faithful in love, and so dauntless in war,/There never was knight like the young Lochinvar*" (Sir Walter Scott). *Undaunted* suggests persistent courage and resolve: "*Death and sorrow will be the companions of our journey . . . . We must be united, we must be undaunted, we must be inflexible*" (Winston S. Churchill).

◀ **ANTONYM:** *cowardly*

---

bravery *noun.* —*See* **courage.**

brawl *noun.* —*See* **fight** (1).

brawl *verb.* To exchange blows with another person ▶ fight. *Slang:* rumble. ***Idioms:*** duke it out, mix it up, slug it out. [*Compare* **wrestle.**] —*See also* **argue** (1).

brawn *noun.* Solid and well-developed muscles ▶ bulk, muscle, muscularity, physique. *Informal:* beef. [*Compare* **constitution.**] —*See also* **strength.**

brawny *adjective.* —*See* **muscular.**

bray *verb.* —*See* **crush** (2).

brazen *or* **brazenfaced** *adjective.* —*See* **impudent.**

brazenness *noun.* —*See* **impudence.**

breach *noun.* **1.** An act of breaking a law or of nonfulfillment of an obligation ▶

contravention, delinquency, dereliction, infraction, infringement, malfeasance, nonfeasance, negligence, transgression, trespass, violation. [*Compare* **crime.**] **2.** An interruption in friendly relations ▶ alienation, break, breakdown, collapse, disaffection, estrangement, falling out, fissure, rent, rift, rupture, schism, split. [*Compare* **argument.**] —*See also* **crack** (2).

breach *verb.* To make a hole or other opening in ▶ break (through), gap, hole, perforate, pierce, punch (through), puncture. *Slang:* bust (through). [*Compare* **cut.**] —*See also* **violate** (1).

✚ **CORE SYNONYMS:** *breach, infraction, violation, transgression, trespass, infringement.* These nouns denote an act of breaking a law or regulation, or of failing to fulfill a duty, obligation, or promise. *Breach* and *infraction* are the least specific: *Revealing the secret would be a breach of trust. Infractions of the rules will not be tolerated.* A *violation* is committed willfully and with complete lack of regard for legal, moral, or ethical considerations: *In violation of her contract, she failed to appear. Transgression* most often applies to divine or moral law: "*The children shall not be punished for the father's transgression*" (Daniel Defoe). *Trespass* implies willful intrusion on another's rights, possessions, or person: "*In the limited and confined sense* [trespass] *signifies no more than an entry on another man's ground without a lawful authority*" (William Blackstone). *Infringement* is most frequently used to denote encroachment on another's rights: "*Necessity is the plea for every infringement of human freedom*" (William Pitt the Younger).

---

bread *noun.* —*See* **food, living, money** (1).

bread and butter *noun.* —*See* **living.**

breadth *noun.* The extent of something from side to side ▶ broadness, expanse, wideness, width. [*Compare* **distance.**]

break *verb.* **1.** To crack or split into two or more fragments by means of force or strain ▶ crack (apart *or* open), fracture, rift, rive, shatter, shiver, smash, splinter, sunder. ***Idioms:*** break (*or* crack) asunder, break in two, smash to bits (*or* pieces *or* smithereens). [*Compare* **burst, crush, destroy, disintegrate.**] **2.** To severely impair someone's spirit, health, or will ▶ beat down, crush, destroy, overwhelm, ruin, shatter. **3.** To give way mentally and emotionally ▶ break down, collapse, crack, crumble, crumple, fall, fold, snap. **4.** To be made public ▶ come out, get out, out, transpire. *Informal:* leak (out). come to light (*or* notice). [*Compare* **air, announce, appear.**] **5.** To discontinue (a habit, for example) ▶ abjure, cut out, forswear, give up, leave off, renounce, stop. *Informal:* swear off. *Slang:* kick. [*Compare* **abandon.**] **6.** To interrupt regular activity for a short period ▶ recess. *Informal:* knock off. ***Idioms:*** take a break, take a breather, take five (*or* ten). [*Compare* **rest**[1].] —*See also* **breach, collapse** (1), **communicate** (1), **crack** (1), **decipher, demote, disobey, divide, gentle, malfunction, penetrate, ruin, violate** (1).

break apart *verb.* —*See* **disintegrate, divide.**

break away *verb.* To withdraw from an association or federation ▶ pull out, secede, splinter (off), withdraw. *Informal:* split (away). [*Compare* **quit.**]

break down *verb.* To take something apart ▶ disassemble, dismantle, take down. —*See also* **analyze, decay, destroy** (1), **disintegrate, malfunction.**

break in *verb.* To enter forcibly or illegally ▶ burglarize, invade, trespass. [*Compare* **rob, steal.**] —*See also* **domesticate, interrupt** (2).

break off *verb.* To bring an activity or relationship to an end suddenly ▶ cease, discontinue, interrupt, suspend, terminate. —*See also* **abandon** (2), **separate** (1).

break out *verb.* To become manifest suddenly and in full force ▶ be triggered (*or* sparked). (*or* **touched off**), burst (forth *or* out), erupt, explode, flare (up), irrupt. —*See also* **escape** (1).

break up *verb.* —*See* **disintegrate, divide, laugh, scatter** (2), **separate** (1).

break *noun.* A cessation of continuity or regularity ▶ discontinuance, discontinuation, discontinuity, disruption, interruption, pause, suspension. [*Compare* **stop.**] —*See also* **breach** (2), **crack** (2), **escape** (1), **gap** (2), **opportunity, rest**[1] (1).

✦ **CORE SYNONYMS:** *break, crack, fracture, splinter, shatter, smash.* These verbs mean to crack or split into two or more fragments by means of force or strain. *Break* is the most general: *The window was broken by vandals. I broke my arm when I fell. That delicate ornament will break easily.* To *crack* is to break, often with a sharp snapping sound, without dividing into parts: *I cracked the coffeepot, but it didn't leak. The building's foundation cracked during the earthquake. Fracture* applies to a break or crack in a rigid body: *She fractured her skull in the accident. Splinter* implies splitting into long, thin, sharp pieces: *Repeated blows splintered the door.* To *shatter* is to break into many scattered pieces: *The bullet shattered the mirror upon impact. Smash* stresses the force of a blow or impact and suggests complete destruction: *He angrily smashed the vase against the wall.*

---

breakable *adjective.* —*See* **fragile.**

breakage *noun.* —*See* **damage.**

breakdown *noun.* **1.** A sudden sharp decline in mental, emotional, or physical health ▶ collapse. *Informal:* crackup. [*Compare* **infirmity.**] **2.** A cessation of proper functioning ▶ collapse, failure, malfunction, outage. —*See also* **analysis, breach** (2), **collapse** (2), **decay.**

breaker *noun.* —*See* **wave.**

break-in *noun.* The act of entering a building or room with the intent to commit theft ▶ breaking and entering, burglary, forced entry, trespass. [*Compare* **larceny.**]

breakneck *adjective.* —*See* **fast** (1).

breakout *noun.* —*See* **eruption, escape** (1).

breast *noun.* The seat of a person's innermost emotions and feelings ▶ bosom, heart, soul. ***Idioms:*** the bottom (*or* cockles) of one's heart, one's heart of hearts.

breastwork *noun.* —*See* **bulwark.**

breath *noun.* The act or process of breathing ▶ exhalation, expiration, inhalation, inspiration, respiration, suspiration, wind. —*See also* **breeze** (1), **shade** (2), **spirit** (2).

breathe *verb.* **1.** To take a breath or breaths ▶ breathe in (*or* out), exhale, expire, inhale, inspire, respire, suspire. ***Idiom:*** draw breath. [*Compare* **pant.**] **2.** To tell in confidence ▶ confide, share, unbosom, whisper. [*Compare* **communicate, reveal, say.**] —*See also* **blow**[1] (1), **exist.**

breather *noun.* —*See* **rest**[1] (1).

breathing *adjective.* —*See* **alive.**

breathless *adjective.* —*See* **airless** (2).

breech *noun.* —*See* **buttocks.**

breed *verb.* To give life to; have offspring ▶ beget, engender, father, hatch, increase, multiply, parent, procreate, proliferate, propagate, reproduce, spawn. [*Compare* **produce.**] —*See also* **grow.**

breed *noun.* —*See* **kind**[2].

breeding *noun.* Training in the proper forms of social and personal conduct ▶ education, upbringing. [*Compare* **courtesy, manners.**] —*See also* **culture** (3), **reproduction.**

breeze *noun.* **1.** A gentle wind ▶ breath, cat's-paw, draft, eddy, puff, whiff, zephyr. [*Compare* **wind**[1].] **2.** *Informal* An easily accomplished task ▶ cakewalk, child's play, cinch, picnic, pushover, snap, walkaway, walkover.

Slang: duck soup. ***Idioms:*** piece of cake, walk in the park. [*Compare* **runaway.**]

breeze *verb. Informal* To progress quickly and effortlessly ▶ coast, sail, skate, zip. *Informal:* romp, waltz.

✚ CORE SYNONYMS: *breeze, cinch, pushover, snap.* These nouns denote a task that is easily accomplished: *The exam was a breeze. Chopping onions is a cinch with a food processor. Winning the playoffs was no pushover. The child's card game was a snap to learn.*

breezeless *adjective.* —*See* **airless** (2).

breezy *adjective.* —*See* **airy** (3), **lively.**

brew *noun.* —*See* **combination, drink** (1).

brew *verb.* —*See* **threaten** (2).

brewing *adjective.* —*See* **imminent.**

bribe *noun.* Money or a favor given as an inducement to dishonest behavior ▶ fix, graft, payola, soap, sop. *Informal:* hush money, payoff. *Slang:* boodle, grease, kickback, protection.

bribe *verb.* To give or promise a bribe to ▶ buy (off), corrupt, fix, suborn. *Informal:* pay off. ***Idioms:*** cross someone's palm, grease someone's palm (*or* hand), take care of.

bric-a-brac *noun.* —*See* **novelty** (3).

bridal *noun.* —*See* **wedding.**

bridle *noun.* —*See* **brake.**

bridle *verb.* —*See* **restrain.**

bridled *adjective.* —*See* **restricted.**

brief *adjective.* Expressed in few words ▶ abbreviated, abridged, compendious, compressed, concise, condensed, crisp, curt, laconic, lean, short, succinct, summary, terse, thumbnail, trenchant. [*Compare* **pithy.**] —*See also* **abrupt** (1), **quick, transitory.**

brief *noun.* —*See* **message, synopsis.**

briery *adjective.* —*See* **thorny** (1).

brig *noun.* —*See* **jail.**

brigade *noun.* —*See* **detachment** (3).

brigand *noun.* —*See* **thief.**

bright *adjective.* Giving off or reflecting much light ▶ beaming, beamy, brilliant, effulgent, fulgent, glowing, incandescent, irradiant, lambent, lucent, luminescent, luminous, lustrous, radiant, refulgent, shining, shiny. [*Compare* **brilliant, glossy, sparkling.**] —*See also* **cheerful, clear** (2), **clever** (1), **colorful** (1), **favorable** (1), **intelligent.**

✚ CORE SYNONYMS: *bright, brilliant, radiant, lustrous, lambent, luminous, incandescent, effulgent.* These adjectives refer to what gives off or reflects much light. *Bright* is the most general: *bright sunshine; a bright blue. Brilliant* implies intense brightness and often suggests sparkling or gleaming light: *a brilliant color; a brilliant gemstone.* Something *radiant* emits or seems to emit light in rays: *a radiant sunrise; a radiant smile.* A *lustrous* object reflects an agreeable sheen: *thick, lustrous auburn hair. Lambent* applies to a soft, flickering light: *"its tranquil streets, bathed in the lambent green of budding trees"* (James C. McKinley). *Luminous* especially refers to something that glows in the dark: *a luminous watch dial. Incandescent* stresses burning brilliance: *Flames consist of incandescent gases. Effulgent* suggests splendid radiance: *"The crocus, the snowdrop, and the effulgent daffodil are considered bright harbingers of spring"* (John Gould).

brighten *verb.* To make lively or animated ▶ animate, enliven, light (up), perk up. —*See also* **clear** (1).

bright-eyed *adjective.* —*See* **alert.**

bright idea *adjective.* A sudden exciting thought ▶ brainstorm, inspiration. *Informal:* brain wave. [*Compare* **idea.**]

brilliance *noun.* **1.** Exceptional brightness and clarity ▶ brilliancy, effulgence, fire, luminosity, radiance. **2.** Liveliness and vivacity of imagination ▶ brilliancy, fire, genius, inspiration. [*Compare* **intelligence, invention.**] —*See also* **glitter** (2), **glory.**

brilliant *adjective.* Extremely or harshly bright ▶ blazing, blinding, dazzling, glaring, glary, pulsing, throbbing. [*Com-

pare **sparkling.**] —*See also* **bright, favorable** (1), **glorious, glossy, intelligent.**

brim *noun.* —*See* **bill**[2] (2), **border** (1), **limit** (1).

brimful *or* **brimming** *adjective.* —*See* **full** (1).

bring *verb.* **1.** To cause to come along with oneself ▶ bear, carry, convey, fetch, take (along), transport. [*Compare* **carry.**] **2.** To achieve a certain price ▶ bring in, fetch, get, go for, realize, sell for. —*See also* **cause.**

bring about *verb.* —*See* **cause, effect.**

bring around *or* **round** *verb.* —*See* **convince, persuade, revive** (2).

bring down *verb.* —*See* **overthrow.**

bring forth *verb.* —*See* **bear** (4), **produce** (1).

bring in *verb.* —*See* **return** (3).

bring off *verb.* —*See* **effect.**

bring on *verb.* —*See* **cause.**

bring out *verb.* —*See* **publish** (1).

bring up *verb.* To take care of and educate a child ▶ foster, parent, raise, rear. [*Compare* **nurture.**] —*See also* **broach, refer** (1).

brink *noun.* —*See* **border** (1).

briny *adjective.* Containing salt ▶ brackish, saline, salty. —*See also* **bitter** (1), **marine** (1).

briny *noun.* —*See* **ocean.**

brio *noun.* —*See* **spirit** (1).

brisk *adjective.* —*See* **energetic, fast** (1).

bristle *verb.* —*See* **anger** (2), **teem**[1].

bristly *adjective.* —*See* **hairy, thorny** (1).

brittle *adjective.* —*See* **fragile.**

broach *verb.* To put forward a topic for discussion ▶ bring up, introduce, moot, put forth, raise. [*Compare* **name, propose, refer.**]

✚ **CORE SYNONYMS:** *broach, introduce, moot, raise.* These verbs mean to bring forward a point, topic, or question for consideration or discussion: *broach the subject tactfully; introduce a tax bill before the legislature; an idea that was mooted before the committee; raised the problem of dropouts with the senior faculty.*

---

broad *adjective.* **1.** Of large extent or expanse ▶ ample, expansive, extended, extensive, outspread, outstretched, spacious, spread out, wide. [*Compare* **widespread.**] **2.** Spread out over a large area ▶ far-flung, widespread. —*See also* **broad-minded, general** (2), **loose** (3), **obscene, obvious.**

broadcast *verb.* —*See* **announce, plant.**

broadcast *noun.* A show aired on television or radio ▶ airing, program.

broaden *verb.* To make or become broader or more comprehensive ▶ amplify, dilate, distend, enlarge, expand, extend, spread (out), widen. [*Compare* **increase, lengthen, spread.**]

broadening *noun.* —*See* **expansion.**

broad-minded *adjective.* Not narrow or intolerant; respectful of others' views ▶ accepting, broad, humanistic, liberal, open-minded, progressive, tolerant. [*Compare* **fair**[1], **liberal, tolerant.**]

✚ **CORE SYNONYMS:** *broad-minded, broad, liberal, open-minded, tolerant.* These adjectives mean having or showing an inclination to respect views and beliefs that differ from one's own: *a broad-minded judge; showed broad sympathies; a liberal cleric; open-minded impartiality; a tolerant attitude.*

◀ **ANTONYM:** *narrow-minded*

---

broadness *noun.* The extent of something from side to side ▶ breadth, expanse, wideness, width. [*Compare* **distance.**]

broadside *noun.* —*See* **barrage.**

broad-spectrum *adjective.* —*See* **general** (2).

Brobdingnagian *adjective.* —*See* **enormous.**

broil[1] *verb.* —*See* **burn** (3), **cook.**

broil[2] *verb.* —*See* **argue** (1).

broiling *adjective.* —*See* **hot** (1).

broke *adjective.* —*See* **poor.**

broken-down *adjective.* —*See* **shabby.**
brokenhearted *adjective.* —*See* **depressed** (1).
broker *noun.* —*See* **go-between.**
bromide *noun.* —*See* **cliché.**
bromidic *adjective.* —*See* **trite.**
Bronx cheer *noun.* —*See* **hiss** (2).
Bronx cheer *verb.* —*See* **hiss** (2).
brood *verb.* To focus the attention on something moodily and at length ▶ agonize, dwell, fret, fuss, mope, worry. *Informal:* stew. ***Idiom:*** eat one's heart out. [*Compare* **ponder, sulk.**]
brood *noun.* The offspring, as of an animal or bird, for example, that are the result of one breeding season ▶ litter, spawn, young. —*See also* **flock, progeny.**

✚ **CORE SYNONYMS:** *brood, dwell, fret, mope, stew, worry.* These verbs mean to focus the attention on something moodily and at length: *brooding about his decline in popularity; dwelled on her defeat; fretted over the loss of his job; moping about his illness; stewing over her upcoming trial; worrying about the unpaid bills.*

---

brook[1] *noun.* A small stream ▶ arroyo, bayou, bourne, creek, feeder, rill, rivulet, runnel, tributary, watercourse. *Chiefly Regional:* branch, kill, run.
brook[2] *verb.* —*See* **endure** (1).
brother *noun.* —*See* **friend.**
brotherhood *noun.* —*See* **company** (3).
brouhaha *noun.* —*See* **disorder** (2), **sensation** (2), **vociferation.**
browbeat *verb.* —*See* **intimidate.**
browbeater *noun.* —*See* **bully.**
brown *adjective.* —*See* **dark** (2).
brown *verb.* —*See* **cook.**
brownnose *verb.* —*See* **fawn.**
brownnose *or* **brownnoser** *noun.* —*See* **sycophant.**
brown study *noun.* —*See* **trance.**
browse *verb.* **1.** To look through reading matter casually ▶ dip into, flip through, glance at (*or* over *or* through), leaf (through), look through (*or* over), riffle (through), run through, scan, skim, thumb (through). ***Idiom:*** pass (*or* run) one's eyes over. [*Compare* **examine.**] **2.** To feed on vegetation ▶ crop, forage, graze, nibble (at), pasture. [*Compare* **chew.**]
bruise *noun.* An injury that does not break the skin ▶ black-and-blue mark, contusion. [*Compare* **black eye, harm.**]
bruise *verb.* To make a bruise or bruises on ▶ contuse. ***Idioms:*** beat (*or* leave) black-and-blue. [*Compare* **hurt.**]
bruiser *noun.* —*See* **thug.**
bruit *verb.* —*See* **announce.**
brume *noun.* —*See* **haze.**
brunet *adjective.* —*See* **dark** (2).
brush[1] *noun.* Light and momentary contact with another person or thing ▶ flick, graze, kiss, rub, skim. —*See also* **battle.**
brush *verb.* To make light and momentary contact with, as in passing ▶ flick, graze, kiss, rub (against *or* along), shave, skim. [*Compare* **caress, rub, touch.**]

✚ **CORE SYNONYMS:** *brush, flick, graze, shave, skim.* These verbs mean to make light and momentary contact with something, as in passing: *Her arm brushed mine. I flicked the paper with my finger. The knife blade grazed the countertop. A taxi shaved the curb. The oar skims the pond's surface.*

---

brush[2] *noun.* A dense growth of shrubs ▶ brake, brushwood, bushes, canebrake, chaparral, scrub, shrubbery, thicket, underbrush, undergrowth.
brusque *adjective.* —*See* **abrupt** (1).
brutal *adjective.* —*See* **bitter** (2), **cruel.**
brutality *noun.* —*See* **cruelty.**
brutalize *verb.* —*See* **corrupt.**
brute *noun.* —*See* **fiend.**
brutish *adjective.* —*See* **bestial, uncivilized.**
bubble *noun.* —*See* **burble, dream** (2).
bubble *verb.* —*See* **boil, burble, foam.**
bubbly *adjective.* —*See* **lively.**
buck *verb.* —*See* **contest, defy** (1).

buck up *verb.* —*See* **encourage** (2).

bucket *verb.* —*See* **rush.**

bucket *noun.* —*See* **basket** (3).

buckle *verb.* To fall in ▶ cave in, collapse, crumple, give, go. ***Idiom:*** give way. [*Compare* **fall.**] —*See also* **bend** (3), **fasten, succumb.**

buckle down *verb.* —*See* **apply** (1).

buckle *noun.* —*See* **fastener.**

buckram *adjective.* Rigidly constrained or formal; lacking grace and spontaneity ▶ starchy, stiff, stilted, wooden. [*Compare* **cool, forced, prudish.**]

bucolic *adjective.* —*See* **country.**

bud[1] *noun.* —*See* **germ** (2).

bud *verb.* —*See* **bloom**[1] (1).

bud[2] *noun.* —*See* **friend.**

buddy *noun.* —*See* **associate** (2), **friend.**

budge *verb.* To move or cause to move slightly ▶ move, shift, stir.

budget *noun.* Money or other resources granted for a particular purpose ▶ appropriation, grant, subsidy, subvention. —*See also* **overhead, quantity** (3).

budget *verb.* —*See* **appropriate.**

budget *adjective.* —*See* **cheap.**

buff[1] *verb.* —*See* **gloss**[1].

buff *adjective.* —*See* **muscular.**

buff[2] *noun.* —*See* **fan**[2].

buffet *noun.* —*See* **blow**[2].

buffet *verb.* —*See* **beat** (1).

buffoon *noun.* —*See* **fool.**

bug *noun.* —*See* **defect, fan**[2], **germ** (1), **sickness.**

bug *verb.* To monitor telephone calls with a concealed device connected to the circuit ▶ tap, wiretap. —*See also* **annoy.**

bugbear *noun.* —*See* **hate** (2).

buggy *adjective.* —*See* **insane.**

build *verb.* To make or form a structure ▶ carpenter, construct, erect, frame, knock together, put up, raise, rear. —*See also* **base**[1], **increase, make.**

build in *verb.* To construct as an integral part ▶ include, incorporate, integrate.

build up *verb.* —*See* **accumulate, gain** (1), **increase, promote** (3).

build *noun.* —*See* **constitution.**

builder *noun.* A person or business that builds something ▶ carpenter, constructor, contractor, erector, mason. [*Compare* **maker.**] —*See also* **developer.**

building *noun.* Something built, especially for human use ▶ construction, edifice, erection, pile, structure.

building block *noun.* —*See* **part** (1).

buildup *noun.* **1.** The act of accumulating ▶ accumulation, agglomeration, conglomeration. **2.** The result or product of building up ▶ accretion, accumulation, development, enlargement, growth, multiplication, proliferation, sprawl, spread. —*See also* **accumulation** (1), **increase** (1), **publicity.**

built-in *adjective.* Serving as a nondetachable part of a larger unit ▶ component, constituent, incorporated, integral. —*See also* **constitutional.**

bulge *verb.* To curve outward past the normal or usual limit ▶ bag, balloon, beetle, belly, jut, overhang, pouch, project, protrude, protuberate, stand out, stick out. —*See also* **swell.**

bulge *noun.* —*See* **advantage** (3), **projection.**

✚ **CORE SYNONYMS:** *bulge, balloon, belly, jut, project, protrude.* These verbs mean to curve, spread, or extend outward past the normal or usual limit: *The lawyer's wallet bulged with money. Our expenses are ballooning. The sail bellied in the wind. A pipe jutted from the side of the building. Braces can fix teeth that project from the mouth at an angle. A sconce protruded from the wall.*

---

bulk *noun.* **1.** Great amount or dimension ▶ amplitude, magnitude, mass, size, volume. **2.** The greatest part or portion ▶ mass, preponderance, preponderancy, weight. [*Compare* **center.**] —*See also* **brawn, quantity** (3).

bulky *adjective.* **1.** Of large, often awkward size and weight ▶ blockish, blocky, cumbersome, cumbrous, heavy, hefty, lumpish, lumpy, massive, oversize, oversized, ponderous, voluminous. [*Compare* **big, heavy.**] **2.** Having a large body, especially in girth ▶ full-figured, heavy, hefty, hulking, hulky, husky, plus-sized, stout, sturdy. [*Compare* **fat, muscular, stocky.**] —*See also* **awkward** (2).

bull *noun.* —*See* **nonsense, police officer.**

bulldoze *verb.* —*See* **intimidate, muscle.**

bulldozer *noun.* —*See* **bully.**

bulletin *noun.* A report giving information ▶ advisory, notice. [*Compare* **report, warning.**] —*See also* **item, message.**

bullheaded *adjective.* —*See* **stubborn** (1).

bullheadedness *noun.* —*See* **stubbornness.**

bull session *noun.* —*See* **conversation.**

bully *noun.* One who is habitually cruel to smaller or weaker people ▶ browbeater, bulldozer, hector, intimidator, persecutor, tease, tormentor. [*Compare* **tough.**]

bully *verb.* —*See* **intimidate.**

bully *adjective.* —*See* **excellent.**

bulwark *noun.* A structure used as a defense against an attack ▶ barricade, bastion, breastwork, earthwork, parapet, rampart. [*Compare* **base, fort.**]

✚ CORE SYNONYMS: *bulwark, barricade, breastwork, earthwork, rampart, bastion, parapet.* These nouns refer literally to structures used as a defense against attack. A *bulwark* can be a mound of earth, an embankment, or a wall-like fortification. *Barricade* usually implies hasty construction to meet an imminent threat. *Breastwork* denotes a low defensive wall, especially a temporary one hurriedly built. *Earthwork* is a defensive construction of earth. A *rampart,* the main defensive structure around a guarded place, is permanent, high, and broad. A *bastion* is a projecting section of a fortification from which defenders have a wide range of view and fire. *Parapet* applies to any low fortification, typically a wall atop a rampart. Of these words, *bulwark* and *bastion* are the most frequently used to refer figuratively to something regarded as being a safeguard or a source of protection: *"The only sure bulwark of continuing liberty is a government strong enough to protect the interests of the people, and a people strong enough and well enough informed to maintain its sovereign control over its government"* (Franklin D. Roosevelt). *A free press is one of the bastions of a democracy.*

---

bum[1] *noun.* —*See* **pauper, wastrel** (2).

bum *verb.* —*See* **beg, idle** (1).

bum out *verb.* —*See* **depress.**

bum *adjective.* —*See* **bad** (1).

bum[2] *noun.* —*See* **buttocks.**

bumble[1] *verb.* —*See* **blunder, muddle.**

bumble[2] *verb.* —*See* **hum.**

bumble *noun.* —*See* **hum.**

bumbling *adjective.* —*See* **unskillful.**

bummer *noun. Slang* A great disappointment or regrettable fact ▶ crime, pity, shame. ***Idiom:*** a crying shame. —*See also* **beggar** (1), **killjoy.**

bump *verb.* To proceed with sudden, abrupt movements ▶ bounce, jar, jerk, jiggle, jolt, jounce, lurch, rattle. [*Compare* **shake.**] —*See also* **collide, demote, eject** (1).

bump into *verb.* —*See* **encounter** (1).

bump off *verb.* —*See* **murder.**

bump *noun.* **1.** An unevenness or elevation on a surface ▶ burl, excrescence, gnarl, growth, hump, knob, knot, lump, node, nodule, nub, outgrowth, protuberance. [*Compare* **projection.**] **2.** A small raised area of skin, as from a blow or sting ▶ bunch, knot, lump, swelling. *Informal:* boo-boo. *Slang:* goose egg. [*Compare* **welt.**] —*See also* **beat** (1), **collision, hill.**

bumpiness *noun.* —*See* **irregularity.**

bumpkin *noun.* —*See* **clodhopper.**

bumpy *adjective.* —*See* **rough** (1).

bunch *noun.* —*See* **bump** (2), **circle** (3), **group, heap** (2), **quantity** (2).

bundle *noun.* —*See* **fortune, group, package.**

bundle *verb.* —*See* **wrap** (1).

bundle up *verb.* To put on warm clothes ▶ wrap, wrap up.

bung *noun.* —*See* **plug.**

bungle *verb.* —*See* **botch, muddle.**

bungle *noun.* —*See* **blunder.**

bungler *noun.* —*See* **blunderer.**

bungling *adjective.* —*See* **inefficient, unskillful.**

bunk[1] *verb.* —*See* **lodge.**

bunk[2] *or* **bunkum** *noun.* —*See* **nonsense.**

buns *noun.* —*See* **buttocks.**

Bunyanesque *adjective.* —*See* **enormous.**

buoy *verb.* —*See* **elate, support** (2).

buoyancy *noun.* The ability to recover quickly from depression or discouragement ▶ bounce, elasticity, flexibility, resilience, resiliency.

buoyant *adjective.* —*See* **lighthearted.**

burble *verb.* To flow with or make a soft liquid sound ▶ babble, bubble, gurgle, lap, murmur, purl, ripple. [*Compare* **trickle, wash.**] —*See also* **babble.**

burble *noun.* A soft liquid sound ▶ babble, bubble, gurgle, lap, murmur, purl, ripple.

burden[1] *noun.* **1.** A source of persistent worry or hardship ▶ affliction, albatross, cross, drag, drain, millstone, onus, strain, tax, trial, tribulation, weight. *Informal:* headache, pain. ***Idioms:*** royal headache (*or* pain), weight (*or* load) on one's mind. [*Compare* **care, curse, difficulty.**] **2.** Something carried or transported ▶ ballast, cargo, encumbrance, freight, haul, lading, load, weight. —*See also* **duty** (1).

burden *verb.* To weigh down or place a heavy load on ▶ charge, cumber, encumber, freight, lade, load, oppress, saddle, strain, tax, try, weight. [*Compare* **fill, hinder.**]

✚ **CORE SYNONYMS:** *burden, affliction, cross, trial, tribulation.* These nouns denote a source of persistent worry or hardship: *the burden of a guilty conscience; indebtedness that is an affliction; a temper that is your cross; a troublemaker who is a trial to the teacher; suffered many tribulations in rising from poverty.*

---

burden[2] *noun.* —*See* **import, thrust.**

burdensome *adjective.* Requiring great bodily, mental, or spiritual strength ▶ arduous, backbreaking, crushing, formidable, grinding, grueling, heavy, laborious, onerous, oppressive, overpowering, overtaxing, rigorous, rough, severe, taxing, toilsome, tough, trying, weighty. [*Compare* **difficult.**] —*See also* **disturbing.**

✚ **CORE SYNONYMS:** *burdensome, onerous, oppressive, arduous, grueling, rigorous.* These adjectives apply to what imposes a severe test of bodily or spiritual strength. *Burdensome* is associated with both mental and physical hardship: *The burdensome task of preparing her tax return awaited her. Onerous* connotes the figuratively heavy load imposed by something irksome or annoying: *My only onerous duty was having to clean the bathroom.* Something *oppressive* weighs one down in body or spirit: *"Old forms of government finally grow so oppressive that they must be thrown off"* (Herbert Spencer). *Arduous* and *grueling* emphasize the expenditure of sustained and often exhausting labor: *Becoming a doctor is an arduous undertaking. Digging ditches is grueling work. Rigorous* implies the imposition of severe and uncompromising demands: *"Yet out of this unflattering, rigorous realism . . . Swift made great art"* (M.D. Aeschliman).

---

bureau *noun.* —*See* **branch** (3).

bureaucratic *adjective.* —*See* **governmental.**

burg *noun.* —*See* **city.**

burgeon *verb.* —*See* **bloom**[1] (1), **increase.**

burgess *or* **burgher** *noun.* —*See* **citizen.**

burglar *noun.* —*See* **thief.**

burglarize *verb.* To enter forcibly or illegally ▶ break in, invade, trespass. [*Compare* **steal.**] —*See also* **rob.**

burglary *noun.* The act of entering a building or room with the intent to commit theft ▶ break-in, breaking and entering, forced entry, trespass. —*See also* **larceny.**

burial *noun.* An act of placing a body in a grave or tomb ▶ burying, entombment, inhumation, interment, sepulture. [*Compare* **funeral.**]

buried *adjective.* —*See* **hidden** (1), **ulterior** (1), **underground.**

burke *verb.* —*See* **avoid, repress.**

burlesque *noun.* —*See* **satire.**

burlesque *verb.* —*See* **imitate.**

burly *adjective.* —*See* **muscular.**

burn *verb.* **1.** To undergo or cause to undergo damage by fire ▶ burn down (*or* up), carbonize, incinerate, char, scorch, sear, singe. *Slang:* torch. ***Idioms:*** burn to a crisp, go up in flames (*or* smoke), reduce to ashes (*or* cinders). **2.** To undergo combustion; be on fire ▶ blaze, crackle, combust, flame, flare, hiss, roar. [*Compare* **smolder.**] **3.** To feel or look hot ▶ bake, boil, broil, burn up, roast, steam, swelter. ***Idiom:*** be on fire. **4.** To cause to become sore or inflamed ▶ inflame, irritate, sting. —*See also* **anger** (1), **anger** (2), **beam, boil, cheat** (1), **deceive, hurt** (2).

burn off *verb.* —*See* **evaporate.**

burn out *verb.* —*See* **tire** (2).

burn *noun.* Damage that results from burning ▶ blister, char, scorch, sear, singe. —*See also* **cheat** (1), **pain.**

✚ **CORE SYNONYMS:** *burn, scorch, singe, sear, char.* These verbs mean to undergo or cause something to undergo damage by means of fire or intense heat. *Burn,* the most general, applies to the effects of exposure to a source of heat or to something that can produce a similar effect: *burned the muffins in the oven. Scorch* involves superficial burning that discolors or damages the texture of something: *scorched the shirt with the iron. Singe* specifies superficial burning and especially the deliberate removal of projections such as feathers from a carcass before cooking: *singed my eyelashes when the fire flared up; singed the chicken before roasting it. Sear* applies to surface burning of organic tissue: *seared the lamb over high heat.* To *char* is to use fire to reduce a substance to carbon or charcoal: *wood charred by the fire.*

burning *adjective.* On fire ▶ ablaze, afire, aflame, alight, blazing, conflagrant, fiery, flaming. ***Idioms:*** in a blaze, in flames. —*See also* **hot** (1), **passionate, urgent** (1).

burnish *verb.* —*See* **gloss**[1].

burnish *noun.* —*See* **gloss**[1].

burnout *noun.* —*See* **exhaustion.**

burr *noun.* —*See* **hum.**

burr *verb.* —*See* **hum.**

burrow *noun.* A place used as an animal's dwelling ▶ den, hole, lair. [*Compare* **cave.**]

burrow *verb.* —*See* **dig.**

burst *verb.* To break open or fly apart suddenly, as from internal pressure ▶ blow (out), explode, pop, rupture. *Slang:* bust. ***Idiom:*** give way. —*See also* **break out, explode** (1).

burst out *verb.* —*See* **exclaim.**

burst *noun.* —*See* **barrage, blast** (2), **eruption, outburst.**

bursting *adjective.* —*See* **eager, full** (1).

bury *verb.* To place a corpse in or as if in a grave ▶ entomb, inhume, inter, lay, sepulcher. ***Idioms:*** lay (*or* put) to rest. —*See also* **hide**[1].

bush *noun.* —*See* **wilderness.**

bushed *adjective.* —*See* **tired** (1).

bushel *noun.* The contents of a basket ▶ basket, basketful. —*See also* **heap** (2).

bush-league *adjective.* —*See* **bad** (1), **minor** (1).

bushwhack *verb.* —*See* **ambush.**

business *noun.* **1.** Commercial, industrial, or professional activity in general ▶ commerce, enterprise, industry, trade, trading, traffic. **2.** Activity pursued as a livelihood ▶ art, avocation, calling, career, craft, employment, handicraft, job, line, métier, occupation, practice, profession, pursuit, specialty, trade, vocation, walk of life, work. *Slang:* dodge, racket. [*Compare* **position.**] **3.** Something to be done, considered, or dealt with ▶ affair, matter, thing. [*Compare* **problem, task.**] **4.** Something that concerns or involves one personally ▶ affair, concern, interest, lookout. —*See also* **ability** (1), **company** (1), **patronage** (2).

✚ **CORE SYNONYMS:** *business, industry, commerce, trade, traffic.* These nouns apply to commercial, industrial, or professional activity in general. *Business* pertains broadly to commercial, financial, and industrial activity: *He decided to go into the oil business. Industry* entails the production and manufacture of goods or commodities, especially on a large scale: *She is a leader in the computer industry. Commerce* and *trade* refer to the exchange and distribution of goods or commodities: *Congress regulates interstate commerce. The entrepreneur was involved in the domestic fur trade. Traffic* pertains in particular to businesses engaged in the transportation of goods or passengers: *The city renovated the docks to attract shipping traffic. Traffic* may also suggest illegal trade: *The federal agents discovered a brisk traffic in stolen goods.*

---

businesslike *adjective.* —*See* **serious** (1).

businessperson *noun.* —*See* **dealer.**

buss *verb.* —*See* **kiss.**

buss *noun.* —*See* **kiss.**

bust[1] *verb. Slang* To come open or fly apart suddenly and violently, as from internal pressure ▶ blow (out), burst, explode, pop. —*See also* **arrest, breach, demote, gentle, hit, malfunction, ruin.**

bust *noun.* —*See* **arrest, blow[2], disappointment** (2), **failure** (1).

bust[2] *noun.* —*See* **sculpture.**

busted *adjective.* —*See* **poor.**

bustle *verb.* —*See* **rush.**

bustle *noun.* —*See* **agitation** (3).

bustling *adjective.* —*See* **busy** (2).

busy *adjective.* **1.** Involved in activity or work ▶ absorbed, at work, employed, engaged, occupied, taken up (with), working. ***Idiom:*** in the middle (of). [*Compare* **rapt.**] **2.** Full of lively activity ▶ alive, astir, bustling, crawling, hectic, humming, restless, swarming, teeming. *Informal:* hopping. [*Compare* **active, frantic.**] **3.** Excessively filled with detail ▶ cluttered, crowded, fussy, overloaded. [*Compare* **detailed, elaborate, ornate.**] —*See also* **curious** (1).

busy *verb.* To make busy ▶ employ, engage, occupy. [*Compare* **absorb, involve.**]

busybody *noun.* A person who meddles or pries into the affairs of others ▶ interloper, meddler, quidnunc. *Informal:* kibitzer. *Slang:* buttinsky, nosy parker, yenta. [*Compare* **gossip, snoop.**]

but *adverb.* Nothing more than ▶ just, merely, only, simply. [*Compare* **barely, solely.**]

butcher *noun.* —*See* **murderer.**

butcher *verb.* —*See* **botch, massacre.**

butchery *noun.* —*See* **massacre.**

butt[1] *verb.* —*See* **adjoin, drive** (2), **push** (1).

butt in *verb.* —*See* **meddle.**

butt *noun.* —*See* **push.**

butt[2] *noun.* **1.** One that is fired at, attacked, or abused ▶ mark, target. **2.** An object of amusement or laughter ▶ jest, joke, laughingstock, mockery. ***Idiom:***

figure of fun. [*Compare* **fool.**] *—See also* **dupe, object** (2).

butt³ *noun. —See* **buttocks, end** (3).

butte *noun. —See* **hill.**

butter up *verb. —See* **flatter** (1).

buttery *adjective. —See* **flattering.**

buttinsky *noun. —See* **busybody.**

buttocks *noun.* The part of the body on which one sits ▶ breech, derrière, fundament, hindquarters, posterior, rump, seat. *Informal:* backside, behind, bottom, bum, butt, hind end, rear, rear end. *Slang:* booty, buns, can, duff, fanny, heinie, kiester, tail, tush, tushy.

button-down *or* **buttoned-down** *adjective. —See* **conventional.**

buttress *noun. —See* **support.**

buttress *verb. —See* **back** (2), **support** (2).

buxom *adjective. —See* **shapely.**

buy *verb.* To acquire in exchange for money ▶ pay for, purchase. *Slang:* score. [*Compare* **get, spend.**] *—See also* **believe** (1), **bribe.**

buy *noun.* **1.** Something bought or capable of being bought ▶ purchase. [*Compare* **effects.**] **2.** *Informal* Something offered or bought at a low price ▶ bargain, find. *Informal:* deal. *Slang:* steal.

buyer *noun. —See* **consumer.**

buzz *verb. —See* **hum, telephone.**

buzz *noun.* A telephone communication ▶ call, ring. *—See also* **hum, thrill.**

by-and-by *noun.* Time that is yet to be ▶ future, futurity, hereafter, tomorrow. ***Idiom:*** time to come. [*Compare* **approach, possibility.**]

bygone *adjective. —See* **old** (1), **past.**

bylaw *noun. —See* **law** (1).

bypass *noun. —See* **escape** (2).

bypass *verb. —See* **avoid, skirt.**

bypast *adjective. —See* **past.**

byproduct *noun. —See* **derivative.**

bystander *noun. —See* **watcher** (1).

byword *noun. —See* **proverb.**

byzantine *adjective. —See* **complex** (1).

C

cabal *noun. —See* **plot** (2).

cabal *verb. —See* **plot** (2).

cabalistic *adjective. —See* **mysterious, obscure** (1).

cabbage *noun. —See* **money** (1).

cabin *noun. —See* **hut.**

cable *noun. —See* **cord.**

cache *noun. —See* **depository, hoard.**

cache *verb.* To have or put in a customary place ▶ keep, put, store. *—See also* **hide¹.**

cachinnate *verb. —See* **laugh.**

cachinnation *noun. —See* **laugh.**

cackle *verb. —See* **laugh.**

cackle *noun. —See* **laugh.**

cacophonous *or* **cacophonic** *or* **cacophonical** *adjective. —See* **inharmonious** (2).

cacophony *noun. —See* **noise** (1).

cad *noun. —See* **boor.**

cadaver *noun. —See* **body** (2).

cadaverous *adjective. —See* **ghastly** (2), **haggard, pale** (1).

cadence *noun. —See* **rhythm.**

cadenced *adjective. —See* **rhythmical.**

cadency *noun. —See* **rhythm.**

cadge *verb. —See* **beg.**

cadger *noun. —See* **beggar** (1).

caducity *noun.* The condition of being senile ▶ anecdotage, anility, dotage, sanility. [*Compare* **age.**]

cage *verb. —See* **enclose** (1).

cage *noun.* An enclosure for confining an animal or bird ▶ coop, cote, crate, hutch, kennel, pound, run, stall. [*Compare* **pen².**]

cagey *adjective. —See* **shrewd.**

caitiff *adjective. —See* **cowardly.**

caitiff *noun. —See* **coward.**

cajole *verb. —See* **coax.**

cake *verb. —See* **harden** (2).

cake *noun. —See* **lump¹.**

cakewalk *noun. —See* **runaway** (1).

calaboose *noun. —See* **jail.**

calamitous *adjective. —See* **disastrous.**

calamity *noun. —See* **disaster.**

calculate *verb.* To ascertain by mathematics ▶ cast, cipher, compute, figure, reckon. ***Idioms:*** crunch numbers, do the math (*or* numbers). [*Compare* **add, count, measure.**] —*See also* **estimate** (1).

✚ CORE SYNONYMS: *calculate, compute, reckon, cipher, figure.* These verbs refer to the use of mathematical methods to determine a result. *Calculate,* the most comprehensive, often implies a relatively high level of abstraction or procedural complexity: *The astronomer calculated the planet's position. Compute* applies to possibly lengthy arithmetic operations: *computing fees according to time spent. Reckon, cipher,* and *figure* suggest the use of simple arithmetic: *reckoned the number of hours before her departure; had to be taught to read and to cipher; trying to figure my share of the bill.*

calculated *adjective.* Planned, weighed, or estimated in advance ▶ assessed, considered, contrived, deliberate, designed, devised, figured, formulated, intentional, predetermined, premeditated, schemed. —*See also* **deliberate** (2).

calculating *adjective.* Coldly planning to achieve selfish aims ▶ conniving, designing, manipulative, scheming. —*See also* **artful.**

calculation *noun.* The act, process, or result of calculating ▶ cast, computation, figuring, reckoning. —*See also* **caution.**

calendar *noun.* —*See* **program** (1).

calendar *verb.* To enter on a schedule ▶ docket, program, slate, schedule. [*Compare* **list**[1].]

calender *verb.* —*See* **press** (2).

caliber *noun.* Degree of excellence ▶ class, grade, quality. [*Compare* **degree.**] —*See also* **merit.**

calibrate *verb.* —*See* **adjust.**

call *verb.* To describe with a word or term ▶ characterize, denominate, designate, label, name, style, tag, term, title. [*Compare* **describe.**] —*See also* **assemble, name** (1), **predict, shout, telephone, visit.**

call down *verb.* —*See* **chastise.**

call for *verb.* —*See* **demand** (1), **demand** (2), **justify** (2).

call forth *verb.* —*See* **evoke.**

call off *verb.* To decide not to continue ▶ cancel. *Slang:* scrap, scratch, scrub. [*Compare* **defer, drop.**]

call up *verb.* —*See* **imagine, mobilize.**

call *noun.* **1.** A telephone communication ▶ buzz, ring. **2.** A spoken or written request for someone to take part or be present ▶ bid, invitation, summons. *Informal:* invite. [*Compare* **request.**] —*See also* **attraction, cause** (2), **demand** (1), **shout, visit** (1).

caller *noun.* A person or persons visiting one ▶ company, guest, visitant, visitor.

call girl *noun.* —*See* **harlot.**

calligraphic *adjective.* Of or relating to representation by means of writing ▶ graphic, scriptural, written.

calligraphy *noun.* —*See* **script** (1).

calling *noun.* An inner urge to pursue an activity or perform a service ▶ mission, vocation. [*Compare* **dream, duty, fate.**] —*See also* **business** (2).

callous *adjective.* Lacking compassion or mercy ▶ anesthetic, bloodless, cold-blooded, cold-hearted, compassionless, hard, hard-boiled, hardened, hard-hearted, heartless, insensate, insensible, insensitive, merciless, obdurate, pitiless, remorseless, soulless, stonyhearted, thick-skinned, uncaring, uncompassionate, unfeeling, unmerciful, unpitying, unsympathetic, untouched. ***Idioms:*** hard (*or* tough) as nails. [*Compare* **cold, severe.**]

call to arms *or* **call to battle** *noun.* —*See* **cry** (2).

calm *adjective.* Not excited or agitated ▶ collected, composed, cool, cool-headed, detached, easygoing, even, even-tempered, imperturbable, mellow, nonchalant, peaceful, placid, poised, possessed, serene, tranquil, unflappable, unruffled. ***Idiom:*** cool as a cucumber. —*See also* **still.**

calm *noun.* Lack of emotional agitation ▶ calmness, peace, peacefulness, placidity, placidness, quietude, repose, serenity, tranquillity. ***Idiom:*** peace of mind. [*Compare* **balance.**] —*See also* **stillness.**

calm *verb.* —*See* **pacify.**

✤ **CORE SYNONYMS:** *calm, cool, composed, collected, unruffled, nonchalant, imperturbable, detached.* These adjectives indicate absence of excitement or agitation, especially in times of stress. *Calm* is the most general: *The calm police officer helped to prevent the crowd from panicking. Cool* usually implies merely a high degree of self-control, but it may also indicate aloofness: "*Keep strong, if possible. In any case, keep cool. Have unlimited patience*" (B.H. Liddell Hart). "*An honest hater is often a better fellow than a cool friend*" (John Stuart Blackie). *Composed* implies serenity arising from self-discipline: *The dancer was composed as she prepared for her recital. Collected* usually suggests self-possession: *The witness remained collected throughout the questioning. Unruffled* emphasizes calm despite circumstances that might elicit agitation: "*with contented mind and unruffled spirit*" (Anthony Trollope). *Nonchalant* describes a casual manner that may suggest, sometimes misleadingly, a lack of interest or concern: *He reacted to the news in a nonchalant manner. Imperturbable* stresses unshakable calmness usually considered as an inherent trait: "*A man . . . /Cool, and quite English, imperturbable*" (Lord Byron). *Detached* implies aloofness resulting either from lack of active concern or from resistance to emotional involvement: *He sat through the service with a detached air.*

---

calmness *noun.* —*See* **calm, stillness.**

calumniate *verb.* —*See* **malign.**

calumniation *noun.* —*See* **libel.**

calumnious *adjective.* —*See* **libelous.**

calumny *noun.* —*See* **libel.**

camaraderie *noun.* —*See* **company** (3), **friendship.**

camouflage *verb.* —*See* **conceal, disguise.**

camp *noun.* —*See* **base**[1] (1).

campaign *noun.* —*See* **drive** (1).

campestral *adjective.* —*See* **country.**

campiness *noun.* —*See* **theatricalism.**

can *noun.* —*See* **buttocks, jail.**

can *verb.* —*See* **dismiss** (1), **preserve** (1).

canal *noun.* —*See* **vessel** (2), **way** (2).

canard *noun.* —*See* **lie**[2]**.**

cancel *verb.* **1.** To cross out or remove ▶ annul, blot (out), cross (off *or* out), delete, efface, erase, expunge, obliterate, rub (out), scratch (out *or* off), strike (out *or* off), undo, vacate, wipe (out), x (out). [*Compare* **drop, lift.**] **2.** To make ineffective by applying an opposite force or amount ▶ balance, compensate, counteract, counterbalance, counterpoise, countervail, negate, neutralize, nullify, offset, outweigh, redeem, set off. [*Compare* **abolish, balance.**] **3.** To decide not to continue ▶ call off. *Slang:* scrap, scratch, scrub. [*Compare* **defer, drop.**] —*See also* **abolish.**

✤ **CORE SYNONYMS:** *cancel, erase, expunge, efface, delete.* These verbs mean to cross out, remove, or invalidate something. To *cancel* refers to invalidating by or as if by drawing lines through something written: *canceled the postage stamp; canceled the reservation. Erase* is to wipe or rub out, literally or figuratively: *erased the equation from the blackboard; erased any hope of success. Expunge* and *efface* imply thorough removal: *expunged their names from the list; tried to efface prejudice from his mind.* To *delete* is to remove matter from a manuscript or data from a computer application: *deleted expletives from the transcript; deleted the file with one keystroke.*

---

cancellation *noun.* —*See* **abolition, erasure.**

candid *adjective.* —*See* **frank.**

candidate *noun.* —*See* **applicant, comer** (2).

candidness *noun.* —*See* **honesty.**

candy *verb.* —*See* **sweeten.**

cane *noun.* —*See* **stick** (2).

cane *verb.* —*See* **beat** (2).

canker *noun.* —*See* **poison.**

canker *verb.* —*See* **corrupt, poison.**

cannonade *verb.* —*See* **barrage.**

cannonade *noun.* —*See* **barrage.**

canny *adjective.* —*See* **economical, shrewd.**

can of worms *noun.* —*See* **problem.**

canon *noun.* —*See* **doctrine, law** (1).

canonical *adjective.* —*See* **conventional.**

canonization *noun.* —*See* **exaltation.**

canoodle *verb.* —*See* **caress.**

cant[1] *noun.* —*See* **inclination** (2).

cant *verb.* —*See* **incline.**

cant[2] *noun.* —*See* **dialect, language** (2).

cantankerous *adjective.* —*See* **argumentative, ill-tempered.**

cantankerousness *noun.* —*See* **temper** (1).

canter *verb.* —*See* **run** (1).

canter *noun.* —*See* **run** (1).

canvass *noun.* A gathering of information or opinion from a variety of sources or individuals ▶ count, poll, survey.

canyon *noun.* —*See* **valley.**

cap *noun.* Something that covers, especially to prevent contents from spilling ▶ cover, covering, lid, top. [*Compare* **plug.**] —*See also* **climax, limit** (1).

cap *verb.* To put a topping on ▶ crest, crown, tip, top, top off. —*See also* **climax, cover** (1).

capability *noun.* —*See* **ability** (2).

capable *adjective.* —*See* **able.**

capacious *adjective.* Having plenty of room ▶ ample, commodious, roomy, spacious. [*Compare* **big, broad.**] —*See also* **full** (3).

capacity *noun.* The ability or power to seize or attain ▶ compass, grasp, range, reach, scope. [*Compare* **influence.**] —*See also* **ability** (2).

caper *noun.* —*See* **prank**[1]**.**

caper *verb.* —*See* **gambol.**

capillary *noun.* —*See* **vessel** (2).

capital *noun.* **1.** Money or property used to produce more wealth ▶ assets, backing, capitalization, financing, funding, grubstake, principal, resources, risk capital, stake, venture capital. *Informal:* bankroll. [*Compare* **funds, grant, money.**] **2.** The monetary resources of a government, organization, or individual ▶ finances, funds, money, moneys. —*See also* **resources.**

capital *adjective.* —*See* **excellent, primary** (1).

capitalist *noun.* One who is occupied with or expert in large-scale financial affairs ▶ financier. *Informal:* moneyman.

capitalization *noun.* —*See* **capital** (1).

capitalize *verb.* —*See* **benefit, finance.**

capitulate *verb.* —*See* **succumb, surrender** (1).

capitulation *noun.* The act of submitting or surrendering to the power of another ▶ giving up, submission, surrender. [*Compare* **obedience.**]

caprice *noun.* —*See* **fancy.**

capricious *adjective.* Marked by whim or impulse ▶ arbitrary, changeable, erratic, fickle, flighty, freakish, impulsive, inconsistent, inconstant, mercurial, shifty, temperamental, ticklish, uncertain, unpredictable, unstable, unsteady, vagrant, variable, volatile, wayward, whimsical. [*Compare* **changeable, spontaneous.**]

✚ **CORE SYNONYMS:** *capricious, arbitrary, impulsive, whimsical.* These adjectives mean determined by whim or impulse rather than judgment or reason: *a capricious refusal; an arbitrary decision; an impulsive purchase; a whimsical remark.*

---

capsize *verb.* —*See* **overturn.**

capsized *adjective.* —*See* **upside-down.**

captain *noun.* The person in charge of a ship ▶ commander, shipmaster, skipper. —*See also* **chief.**

captain *verb.* —*See* **administer** (1).

captious *adjective.* —*See* **critical** (1).

captivate *verb.* —*See* **charm** (1), **grip.**

capture *verb.* To obtain possession or control of ▶ catch, gain, get, net, secure, take, win. *Informal:* bag. *Slang:* cop, nail. [*Compare* **arrest, get, seize.**] —*See also* **grip, occupy** (2).

capture *noun.* —*See* **catch** (1).

carbon copy *noun.* —*See* **copy** (1).

carcass *noun.* —*See* **body** (2).

card *noun.* —*See* **character** (5), **joker, program** (2).

cardinal *adjective.* —*See* **primary** (1).

cardsharp *noun.* —*See* **cheat** (2).

care *noun.* **1.** Cautious attentiveness ▶ carefulness, caution, gingerliness, heed, heedfulness, mindfulness, regard, wariness, watchfulness. [*Compare* **diligence, prudence.**] **2.** The function of watching, guarding, or overseeing ▶ charge, custody, guardianship, keeping, protection, safeguard, safekeeping, superintendence, supervision, trust, tutelage, ward. [*Compare* **conservation, patronage.**] **3.** A cause of distress or anxiety ▶ concern, stressor, trouble, worry. [*Compare* **anxiety, burden[1].**] —*See also* **anxiety** (1), **caution, thoroughness, treatment.**

care *verb.* To have an objection ▶ mind, object.

care for *verb.* —*See* **enjoy, tend[2].**

✚ **CORE SYNONYMS:** *care, charge, custody, keeping, supervision, trust.* These nouns refer to the function of watching, guarding, or overseeing: *left the house keys in my care; has charge of all rare books in the library; had custody of his children; left the canary in the neighbors' keeping; assumed supervision of the students; documents committed to the bank's trust.*

---

careen *verb.* —*See* **stagger** (1).

career *noun.* —*See* **business** (2), **history** (2).

carefree *adjective.* —*See* **lighthearted.**

careful *adjective.* **1.** Cautiously attentive ▶ conscious, heedful, mindful, observant, regardful, watchful. **2.** Marked by attentiveness to every detail ▶ accurate, fastidious, fussy, meticulous, painstaking, punctilious, scrupulous, solicitous. [*Compare* **deliberate, detailed, thorough.**] —*See also* **conservative** (2), **wary.**

✚ **CORE SYNONYMS:** *careful, heedful, meticulous, painstaking, scrupulous, observant, mindful, fastidious, punctilious.* These adjectives mean cautiously attentive, especially to details. *Careful* and *heedful* suggest circumspection and solicitude: *A careful examination of the gem showed it to be fake. The hikers were heedful of the danger posed by the thunderstorm. Meticulous* and *painstaking* stress extreme care: *"He had throughout been almost worryingly meticulous in his business formalities"* (Arnold Bennett). *Repairing the fine lace entailed slow and painstaking work. Scrupulous* suggests care prompted by conscience: *"Cynthia was scrupulous in her efforts to give no trouble"* (Winston Churchill). *Observant* and *mindful* imply diligence in observing a law, custom, duty, or principle: *A good driver is mindful of the speed limit. The doctor was observant of each patient's symptoms. Fastidious* implies concern, often excessive, for the requirements of taste: *"Your true lover of literature is never fastidious"* (Robert Southey). *Punctilious* specifically applies to minute details of conduct: *"The more unpopular an opinion is, the more necessary is it that the holder should be somewhat punctilious in his observance of conventionalities generally"* (Samuel Butler).

◀ **ANTONYM:** *careless*

---

carefulness *noun.* —*See* **care** (1), **caution, thoroughness.**

careless *adjective.* Lacking concern, attention, or regard ▶ blithe, feckless, forgetful, heedless, inadvertent, inattentive, inobservant, irresponsible, insouciant, mindless, nonchalant, reckless, thoughtless, unconcerned, unheeding, unmindful, unthinking. [*Compare* **apathetic, lighthearted, negligent, rash.**] —*See also* **messy** (1).

✚ **CORE SYNONYMS:** *careless, heedless, thoughtless, inadvertent.* These adjectives apply to what is marked by a lack of concern, attention, or regard. *Careless* often implies negligence: "*It is natural for careless writers to run into faults they never think of*" (George Berkeley). *Heedless* often suggests recklessness: "*We have always known that heedless self-interest was bad morals; we know now that it is bad economics*" (Franklin D. Roosevelt). *Thoughtless* applies to actions taken without due consideration: "*But thoughtless follies laid him low/And stain'd his name*" (Robert Burns). *Inadvertent* implies unintentional lack of care: *With an inadvertent gesture, the child swept the vase off the table.*

◀ **ANTONYM:** *careful*

carelessness *noun.* A careless, often reckless disregard for consequences ▶ abandon, blitheness, heedlessness, thoughtlessness. [*Compare* **temerity.**]

caress *verb.* To touch or handle affectionately ▶ cuddle, fondle, pat, pet, stroke. *Informal:* canoodle. [*Compare* **neck, snuggle.**]

✚ **CORE SYNONYMS:** *caress, cuddle, fondle, pet.* These verbs mean to touch or handle affectionately: *caressed the baby's forehead; cuddled the kitten in his arms; fondling the dog's ears; petting her pony.*

caretaker *noun.* One who is legally responsible for the care and management of the person or property of an incompetent or a minor ▶ conservator, custodian, guardian, keeper. [*Compare* **representative.**]

careworn *adjective.* —*See* **haggard.**

cargo *noun.* —*See* **burden**[1] (2).

caricature *noun.* —*See* **mockery** (2), **satire.**

caricature *verb.* —*See* **imitate.**

caring *adjective.* —*See* **affectionate.**

carnage *noun.* —*See* **massacre.**

carnal *adjective.* —*See* **sensual** (2).

carnality *noun.* —*See* **sensuality** (1).

carnival *noun.* —*See* **celebration** (1).

carol *verb.* —*See* **sing.**

carol *noun.* —*See* **song.**

carom *verb.* —*See* **glance** (1).

carousal *or* **carouse** *noun.* —*See* **bender.**

carp *verb.* —*See* **complain, quibble.**

carp at *verb.* —*See* **criticize** (1), **nag.**

carp *noun.* —*See* **complaint.**

carper *noun.* —*See* **critic** (2).

carpet *verb.* —*See* **cover** (1).

carping *adjective.* —*See* **critical** (1).

carriage *noun.* —*See* **posture** (1), **transportation.**

carrier *noun.* —*See* **messenger.**

carrot *noun.* —*See* **lure** (1).

carry *verb.* **1.** To move while supporting ▶ bear, cart, convey, haul, lug, pack, transport. *Informal:* tote. *Slang:* schlep. [*Compare* **send.**] **2.** To hold on one's person ▶ bear, have, possess. *Informal:* pack. [*Compare* **hold.**] **3.** To have as a condition or a consequence ▶ entail, involve. **4.** To have for sale ▶ deal (in), keep, offer, stock. [*Compare* **sell.**] —*See also* **act** (1), **bear** (1), **bear** (3), **bring** (1), **communicate** (1), **communicate** (2), **conduct** (3), **extend** (1), **pass** (6).

carry away *verb.* —*See* **enrapture.**

carry off *verb.* —*See* **kill**[1], **steal.**

carry on *verb.* To engage in (a war or campaign, for example) ▶ carry out, conduct, wage. [*Compare* **oppose.**] —*See also* **conduct** (1), **endure** (1), **misbehave, participate, rave.**

carry out *verb.* **1.** To engage in (a war or campaign, for example) ▶ carry on, conduct, wage. [*Compare* **oppose.**] **2.** To be responsible for or guilty of an error or crime ▶ commit, do, perpetrate. *Informal:* pull off. [*Compare* **perform.**] —*See also* **administer** (2), **effect, enforce, follow** (4).

carry through *verb.* —*See* **effect.**

✚ **CORE SYNONYMS:** *carry, convey, bear, transport.* These verbs mean to move while supporting. *Carry* is the most general: *The train carries baggage, mail, and passengers.* The term can also refer to conveyance through a channel or medium: *Nerve cells carry and receive nervous impulses. Convey* often implies continuous, regular movement or flow: *The assembly line conveyed the truck's components.* The word also means to serve as a medium for delivery or transmission: *A fleet of trucks will convey the produce to the market. Bear* strongly suggests the effort of supporting an important burden: *The envoy bore the sad news. Transport* is largely limited to the movement over a considerable distance: *Huge tankers are used to transport oil.*

---

cart *verb.* —*See* **carry** (1).

carte blanche *noun.* —*See* **authority.**

cartel *noun.* ▶ bloc, coalition, organization. [*Compare* **association.**]

carton *noun.* —*See* **package.**

carve *verb.* —*See* **cut** (2), **engrave** (1).

carving *noun.* —*See* **sculpture.**

Casanova *noun.* —*See* **gallant, philanderer.**

cascade *verb.* —*See* **flow** (2).

cascade *noun.* —*See* **flow.**

case *noun.* —*See* **character** (5), **condition** (1), **example** (1), **frame, lawsuit, problem, reason** (1), **subject, wrapper.**

case *verb.* —*See* **examine** (1).

caseharden *verb.* —*See* **harden** (1).

cash *noun.* —*See* **money** (1).

cash in *verb.* To make a large profit ▶ batten, profit. *Slang:* clean up. ***Idioms:*** make a killing, make out like a bandit.

cashier *verb.* —*See* **dismiss** (1).

casing *noun.* —*See* **frame, wrapper.**

cask *noun.* —*See* **vat.**

Cassandra *noun.* —*See* **pessimist** (2).

cast *verb.* —*See* **add, aim** (1), **calculate, choose** (1), **design** (1), **fish** (1), **shed**[1] (1), **throw.**

cast about *or* **around** *verb.* —*See* **seek** (1).

cast aside *verb.* —*See* **abandon** (1).

cast down *verb.* —*See* **lower**[2].

cast out *verb.* —*See* **dismiss** (3), **dismiss** (2).

cast *noun.* **1.** A hollow device for shaping a fluid or plastic substance ▶ form, matrix, mold. **2.** The act, process, or result of calculating ▶ calculation, computation, figuring, reckoning. —*See also* **chance** (2), **color** (1), **expression** (4), **form** (1), **inclination** (1), **kind**[2], **sculpture, throw.**

caste *noun.* —*See* **class** (2).

castigate *verb.* —*See* **chastise, punish.**

castigation *noun.* —*See* **punishment.**

castle in the air *noun.* —*See* **dream** (2).

castrate *verb.* —*See* **cripple, sterilize** (2).

casual *adjective.* —*See* **accidental, easygoing, everyday.**

casualness *noun.* —*See* **ease** (1).

casualty *noun.* A loss of life, or one who has lost life, usually as a result of accident, disaster, or war ▶ death, fatality, kill, loss. —*See also* **accident, victim.**

casuistry *noun.* —*See* **fallacy** (2).

catachresis *noun.* —*See* **corruption** (3).

cataclysm *noun.* —*See* **disaster, revolution** (2).

cataclysmic *adjective.* —*See* **disastrous.**

catacomb *noun.* —*See* **grave**[1].

catalog *noun.* —*See* **list**[1], **program** (1), **program** (2).

catalog *verb.* —*See* **classify, list**[1].

catalyst *noun.* An agent that stimulates or precipitates a reaction or change ▶ ferment, leaven, leavening, reactant, yeast. —*See also* **stimulus.**

cataract *noun.* —*See* **flood.**

catastrophe *noun.* —*See* **collapse** (2), **disaster.**

catastrophic *adjective.* —*See* **disastrous.**

catcall *noun.* —*See* **hiss** (2).

catcall *verb.* —*See* **hiss** (2).

catch *verb.* **1.** To gain control of or an advantage over by or as if by trapping ▶ bag, enmesh, ensnare, ensnarl, entangle, entrap, net, snare, tangle, trammel, trap, web. *Informal:* hook. [*Compare* **seize, take.**] **2.** To get hold of something moving ▶ clutch, grab, seize, snag, snatch. *Informal:* nab. ***Idiom:*** lay hands on. [*Compare* **grasp.**] **3.** To become stuck or entangled ▶ fix, hook, lodge, snag, stick. [*Compare* **fix.**] **4.** To have a sudden overwhelming effect on ▶ seize, strike, take. [*Compare* **move.**] **5.** To go aboard a means of transport ▶ board, take. *Informal:* hop. **6.** *Informal* To succeed in communicating with ▶ contact, reach. *Informal:* get. ***Idioms:*** catch up with, get hold of, get in touch with, get through to, get to, make contact with. —*See also* **capture, contract** (2), **fasten, hit, see** (1), **understand** (1).

catch up *verb.* To come up even with another ▶ overtake, pull alongside, pull even. [*Compare* **approach, equalize.**] —*See also* **grip, involve** (1).

catch *noun.* **1.** The act of catching, especially a sudden taking and holding ▶ capture, clutch, grab, seizure, snatch. [*Compare* **arrest, hold.**] **2.** *Informal* A person or thing worth catching ▶ plum, prize. *Slang:* brass ring. **3.** *Informal* A tricky or unsuspected condition ▶ hitch, rub, snag. [*Compare* **bar, disadvantage, trick.**] —*See also* **fastener, treasure.**

✚ **CORE SYNONYMS:** *catch, enmesh, ensnare, entangle, entrap, snare, tangle, trap.* These verbs mean to gain control of or an advantage over by or as if by trapping: *caught in a web of lies; enmeshed in the neighbors' dispute; ensnared an unsuspecting customer; became entangled in her own contradictions; entrapped by a convincing undercover agent; snared by false hopes; tangled by his own duplicity; trapped into incriminating himself.*

---

catching *adjective.* —*See* **contagious.**

catechism *or* **catechization** *noun.* —*See* **test** (2).

catechize *verb.* To subject to a test of knowledge or skill ▶ examine, quiz, test. [*Compare* **ask.**] —*See also* **indoctrinate** (1).

categorical *adjective.* —*See* **definite** (1).

categorically *adverb.* —*See* **absolutely.**

categorization *noun.* —*See* **arrangement** (1).

categorize *verb.* —*See* **classify.**

category *noun.* —*See* **class** (1).

cater *verb.* **1.** To comply with the wishes or ideas of another ▶ cater to, gratify, humor, indulge. [*Compare* **defer**[2].] **2.** To place food before someone ▶ serve, wait on (*or* upon). [*Compare* **give, distribute.**] —*See also* **baby.**

caterwaul *verb.* —*See* **argue** (1), **bawl.**

caterwaul *noun.* —*See* **noise** (1).

catharsis *noun.* —*See* **purification** (1), **purification** (2).

cathartic *adjective.* —*See* **eliminative.**

cathartic *noun.* —*See* **purifier.**

catholic *adjective.* —*See* **universal** (1).

catholicon *noun.* Something believed to cure all human disorders ▶ cure-all, elixir, panacea. [*Compare* **cure.**]

catlike *adjective.* —*See* **stealthy.**

catnap *noun.* —*See* **nap.**

catnap *verb.* —*See* **nap.**

cat's cradle *noun.* —*See* **tangle.**

cat's-paw *noun.* —*See* **dupe, pawn**[2].

catty *adjective.* —*See* **biting.**

caulking *noun.* —*See* **filler** (1).

cause *noun.* **1.** That which produces an effect ▶ antecedent, determinant, occasion, reason. [*Compare* **impact, origin, stimulus.**] **2.** A basis for an action or a decision ▶ call, grounds, justification, mainspring, motivation, motive, necessity, occasion, reason, spring, wherefore, why. ***Idiom:*** why and wherefore. [*Compare* **account, basis.**] **3.** A goal served with great or uncompromising dedication ▶ crusade, holy war, jihad. [*Compare* **drive.**] —*See also* **lawsuit.**

cause *verb.* To be the cause of ▶ bring, bring about, bring on, effect, effectuate, generate, induce, ingenerate, inspire, lead to, make, occasion, precipitate, prompt, provoke, result in, secure, set off, stir (up), touch off, trigger. ***Idioms:*** bring to pass (*or* effect), give rise to. [*Compare* **begin, develop, produce, start.**]

✚ **CORE SYNONYMS:** *cause, reason, occasion, antecedent.* These nouns refer to something that produces an effect. A *cause* is an agent or condition that permits the occurrence of an effect or leads to a result: *"He is not only dull in himself, but the cause of dullness in others"* (Samuel Foote). *Reason* refers to what explains the occurrence or nature of an effect: *There was no obvious reason for the accident. Occasion* is a situation that permits or stimulates existing causes to come into play: *"The immediate occasion of his departure . . . was the favorable opportunity . . . of migrating in a pleasant way"* (Thomas De Quincey). *Antecedent* refers to what has gone before and implies a relationship—but not necessarily a causal one—with what ensues: *Some of the antecedents of World War II lie in economic conditions in Europe following World War I.*

---

caustic *adjective.* —*See* **biting.**

causticity *noun.* —*See* **sarcasm.**

caution *noun.* Careful forethought to avoid harm or risk ▶ calculation, care, carefulness, chariness, gingerliness, precaution, wariness. —*See also* **alertness, care** (1), **prudence, warning.**

caution *verb.* —*See* **warn.**

cautionary *adjective.* Giving warning ▶ admonishing, admonitory, monitory, warning.

cautious *adjective.* —*See* **conservative** (2), **deliberate** (3), **wary.**

cave *or* **cavern** *noun.* A hollow beneath the earth's surface ▶ dugout, grotto, tunnel. [*Compare* **hole.**]

cave in *verb.* —*See* **buckle, collapse** (1).

caveat *noun.* —*See* **example** (2), **warning.**

cavernous *adjective.* Open wide ▶ abysmal, abyssal, gaping, yawning. [*Compare* **broad, open.**] —*See also* **hollow** (2).

cavil *verb.* —*See* **quibble.**

caviler *noun.* —*See* **critic** (2).

caviling *noun.* —*See* **quibbling.**

cavity *noun.* —*See* **depression** (1), **hole** (1).

cavort *verb.* —*See* **gambol.**

cease *verb.* To bring an activity or relationship to an end suddenly ▶ break off, discontinue, interrupt, suspend, terminate. —*See also* **disappear** (2), **lapse, stop** (2), **stop** (1).

cease *noun.* —*See* **stop** (2).

cease-fire *noun.* —*See* **truce.**

ceaseless *adjective.* —*See* **continual, endless** (2).

ceaselessness *noun.* —*See* **endlessness.**

cede *verb.* —*See* **abandon** (1), **transfer** (1).

ceiling *noun.* —*See* **limit** (1).

celebrate *verb.* **1.** To mark a day or an event with ceremonies of respect, festivity, or rejoicing ▶ commemorate, keep, observe, solemnize. [*Compare* **sanctify.**] **2.** To show joyful satisfaction in an event, especially by merrymaking ▶ feast, party, rejoice, revel. ***Idioms:*** beat the drum, have a ball, jump for joy, kick up one's heels, kill the fatted calf, let one's hair down, live it up, make merry, paint the town red, whoop it up. [*Compare* **exult, rejoice, revel.**] —*See also* **honor** (1).

✦ CORE SYNONYMS: *celebrate, observe, keep, commemorate, solemnize.* These verbs mean to mark a day or an event with ceremonies of respect, festivity, or rejoicing. *Celebrate* often emphasizes the joy or reverence associated with an event: *We held a surprise party to celebrate her birthday. Observe* stresses compliance or respectful adherence to that which is prescribed: *observe the speed limit; observe the Sabbath. Keep* implies actions such as the discharge of a duty or the fulfillment of a promise: *keep one's word; keep personal commitments.* To *commemorate* is to honor the memory of a past event: *a ceremony that commemorated the career of a physician. Solemnize* implies dignity and gravity in the celebration of an occasion: *solemnized the dignitary's funeral with a 21-gun salute.*

celebrated *adjective.* —*See* **famous.**

celebration *noun.* **1.** A joyous or festive occasion ▶ carnival, festival, festivity, fete, fiesta, holiday, jubilee, red-letter day, revel, revels. **2.** The act of observing a day or an event with ceremonies ▶ commemoration, keeping, observance, solemnity, solemnization. [*Compare* **ceremony, memorial.**] **3.** The act of showing joyful satisfaction in an event ▶ festivity, jollification, jubilation, merrymaking, pageantry, rejoicing, revelry. —*See also* **blast** (3), **merriment** (2), **party, praise** (1).

celebratory *adjective.* —*See* **merry.**

celebrity *noun.* A famous person ▶ figure, hero, heroine, idol, legend, lion, luminary, name, notable, personage, personality, star, superstar. *Informal:* big name. [*Compare* **dignitary.**] —*See also* **fame.**

✦ CORE SYNONYMS: *celebrity, hero, luminary, name, notable, personage.* These nouns refer to a person who is famous: *a social celebrity; the heroes of science; a theatrical luminary; a big name in sports; a notable of the concert stage; a personage in the field of philosophy.*

celerity *noun.* —*See* **haste** (1).

celestial *adjective.* —*See* **divine** (1), **heavenly** (1), **heavenly** (2).

celibacy *noun.* —*See* **chastity.**

celibate *adjective.* —*See* **chaste.**

cement *verb.* —*See* **harden** (2).

censor *verb.* **1.** To examine and remove objectionable or improper material from a publication ▶ bowdlerize, cut, edit, expurgate, sanitize, screen. *Informal:* bleep, blue-pencil, red-pencil. [*Compare* **examine.**] **2.** To keep from being published or transmitted ▶ ban, black out, hush (up), kill, silence, stifle, suppress, withhold. ***Idioms:*** keep (*or* put) a lid on. [*Compare* **forbid, repress, silence.**]

censorious *adjective.* —*See* **critical** (1).

censurable *adjective.* —*See* **blameworthy.**

censure *noun.* —*See* **criticism.**

censure *verb.* —*See* **chastise, criticize** (1), **deplore** (1).

censurer *noun.* —*See* **critic** (2).

center *noun.* **1.** A place of concentrated activity, influence, or importance ▶ focus, headquarters, heart, hotbed, hub, locus, seat. **2.** A point or area equidistant from all sides of something ▶ median, middle, midpoint, midst, navel, omphalos. **3.** A point of origin or crucial factor ▶ axis, bottom, core, cynosure, focus, heart, hub, nave, nucleus, pivot, quick, root. [*Compare* **crisis, germ.**] —*See also* **heart** (1).

center *verb.* —*See* **concentrate.**

center *adjective.* —*See* **central.**

✦ CORE SYNONYMS: *center, focus, headquarters, heart, hub, seat.* These nouns refer to a place of concentrated activity or importance: *a great cultural center; the focus of research efforts; a company's headquarters; a town that is the heart of the colony; the hub of a steel empire; the seat of government.*

central *adjective.* At, in, near, or being the center ▶ axial, center, centric, equidistant, focal, inmost, innermost, medial, median, mid, middle, middlemost, midmost, nuclear. [*Compare* **convenient.**] —*See also* **middle, primary** (1).

centric *adjective.* —*See* **central.**

cerebral *adjective.* —*See* **intellectual, mental.**

cerebrate *verb.* —*See* **think** (1).

cerebration *noun.* —*See* **thought.**

ceremonial *adjective.* —*See* **ritual.**

ceremonial *noun.* —*See* **ceremony** (1).

ceremonious *adjective.* Fond of or given to ceremony ▶ conventional, courtly, dignified, formal, official, punctilious, solemn, stately. [*Compare* **gracious, prudish, serious.**] —*See also* **ritual.**

ceremoniousness *noun.* —*See* **ceremony** (2).

ceremony *noun.* **1.** A formal act or set of acts prescribed by ritual ▶ ceremonial, custom, liturgy, observance, office, ordinance, rite, ritual, service, solemnity, tradition. **2.** Strict observance of social conventions ▶ ceremoniousness, etiquette, form, formality, protocol, punctiliousness. [*Compare* **custom, manners.**] —*See also* **ritual.**

certain *adjective.* **1.** Bound to happen ▶ ineluctable, inescapable, inevitable, irresistible, necessary, sure, unavoidable. ***Idioms:*** in the cards, sure as shooting. [*Compare* **fated, irrevocable, set.**] **2.** Established beyond a doubt ▶ conclusive, decisive, hard, inarguable, incontestable, incontrovertible, indisputable, indubitable, irrefutable, positive, sure, unassailable, undeniable, undisputable, unquestionable, unquestioned. [*Compare* **authentic, decided, implicit.**] —*See also* **definite** (3), **several, sure** (1), **sure** (2).

✣ **CORE SYNONYMS:** *certain, inescapable, inevitable, sure, unavoidable.* These adjectives mean bound to happen: *soldiers who knew they faced certain death; facts that led to an inescapable conclusion; an inevitable result; sudden but sure retribution; an unavoidable accident.*

---

certainly *adverb.* —*See* **absolutely.**

certainty *noun.* The quality of being actual or factual ▶ actuality, cinch, fact, reality, sure thing, truth. ***Idioms:*** matter of fact, the case. —*See also* **sureness.**

certification *noun.* An assumption of responsibility, as one given by a manufacturer, for the quality, worth, or durability of a product ▶ guarantee, guaranty, surety, warrant, warranty. —*See also* **confirmation** (1).

certify *verb.* To confirm formally as true, accurate, or genuine ▶ attest, swear (to), testify, verify, witness. ***Idiom:*** bear witness. [*Compare* **prove.**] —*See also* **confirm** (3), **guarantee** (1).

certitude *noun.* —*See* **confidence, sureness.**

cessation *noun.* —*See* **end** (1), **stop** (1), **stop** (2).

cesspool *or* **cesspit** *noun.* —*See* **pit**[1].

chachka *noun.* —*See* **novelty** (3).

chafe *verb.* To make the skin raw by friction ▶ abrade, excoriate, fret, irritate, gall, rub. [*Compare* **scrape.**] —*See also* **annoy.**

chaff *verb.* —*See* **joke** (2).

chaff *noun.* —*See* **ribbing.**

chagrin *noun.* —*See* **embarrassment.**

chagrin *verb.* —*See* **embarrass, offend** (1).

chain *noun.* —*See* **cord, series.**

chain *verb.* —*See* **fasten, hamper**[1].

chains *noun.* —*See* **bond** (1).

chalet *noun.* —*See* **villa.**

challenge *noun.* An act of taunting another to do something bold or rash ▶ dare, gauntlet, provocation. —*See also* **defiance** (1), **objection.**

challenge *verb.* To call on another to do something bold ▶ dare, defy. ***Idiom:*** throw down the gauntlet. —*See also* **claim, contest, defy** (1), **object, rival.**

challenger *noun.* —*See* **competitor.**

challenging *adjective.* —*See* **difficult** (1).

champ *verb.* —*See* **chew.**

champ *noun.* —*See* **winner.**

champion *adjective.* —*See* **excellent, victorious.**

champion *verb.* —*See* **support** (1).

champion *noun.* A person revered especially for noble courage ▶ hero, heroine, paladin. ***Idiom:*** knight in shining armor. —*See also* **advocate, winner.**

championship *noun.* —*See* **patronage** (1).

chance *noun.* **1.** An unexpected random event ▶ accident, fluke, fortuity, hap, happenchance, happenstance, hazard. [*Compare* **event.**] **2.** The random, unintended, or unpredictable element of an event or the force regarded as the cause of such an event ▶ accident, cast, coincidence, contingency, fortuitousness, fortuity, fortune, hap, hazard, lottery, luck, serendipity. ***Idiom:*** luck of the draw. [*Compare* **fate, gamble.**] **3.** The likeliness of a given event occurring ▶ likelihood, odds, possibility, probability, prospects. —*See also* **opportunity, risk.**

chance *verb.* To take place by chance ▶ befall, betide, hap, happen. —*See also* **gamble** (2), **venture.**

chance on *or* **upon** *verb.* —*See* **encounter** (1).

chance *adjective.* —*See* **accidental, random.**

chancy *adjective.* —*See* **ambiguous** (1), **dangerous.**

change *verb.* **1.** To make different ▶ alter, modify, mutate, shade, shake up, spice up, turn, vary. [*Compare* **adapt, renew, revise, revolutionize.**] **2.** To become different ▶ alter, change over, develop, evolve, fluctuate, modify, mutate, shift, turn, vacillate, vary. [*Compare* **convert.**] **3.** To give up in return for something else ▶ barter, commute, exchange, interchange, shift, substitute, switch, trade, transpose. *Informal:* swap. [*Compare* **reciprocate.**]

change *noun.* **1.** The process or result of making or becoming different ▶ alteration, development, evolution, fluctuation, modification, mutation, permutation, shift, variation, vicissitude. [*Compare* **adaptation, renewal.**] **2.** The act of exchanging or substituting ▶ barter, commutation, exchange, interchange, reciprocation, reciprocity, shift, substitution, switch, trade, transposition. *Informal:* swap. —*See also* **conversion** (1), **transition.**

changeable *adjective.* **1.** Capable of or liable to change ▶ alterable, commutative, convertible, fluctuant, fluid, inconstant, kaleidoscopic, labile, modifiable, mutable, permutable, reversible, transformable, transmutable, uncertain, unsettled, unstable, unsteady, variable, variant, varying. [*Compare* **malleable.**] **2.** Changing easily, as in expression ▶ fluid, mobile, plastic. [*Compare* **unstable.**] —*See also* **capricious.**

changeless *adjective.* —*See* **unchanging.**

changelessness *noun.* The condition of being without change or variation ▶ consistency, constancy, evenness, firmness, fixedness, flatness, immutability, invariableness, invariance, permanence, regularity, sameness, steadiness, unchangingness, unfailingness, uniformity. [*Compare* **continuation, endlessness.**]

change of heart *noun.* —*See* **reversal** (1).

changeover *noun.* —*See* **conversion** (1).

channel *verb.* —*See* **concentrate, conduct** (3).

channel *noun.* A narrow body of water, usually connecting two larger bodies ▶ narrows, neck, reach, strait. [*Compare* **bay[1], harbor, inlet.**] —*See also* **agent, furrow, way** (2).

chant *verb.* —*See* **sing.**

chaos *noun.* —*See* **disorder** (1), **disorder** (2), **disorderliness.**

chaotic *adjective.* —*See* **confused** (2).

chap *noun.* —*See* **fellow.**

chaperon *or* **chaperone** *verb.* —*See* **accompany.**

chaperon *or* **chaperone** *noun.* A guide or companion whose purpose is to ensure propriety or restrict activity ▶ companion, escort. [*Compare* **guide.**]

chaplain *noun.* —*See* **cleric.**

chapter *noun.* A particular subdivision of a written work ▶ part, passage, section, segment. —*See also* **branch** (3).

char *verb.* —*See* **burn** (1).

char *noun.* —*See* **burn.**

character *noun.* **1.** The combination of emotional, intellectual, and moral qualities that distinguishes an individual ▶ complexion, disposition, makeup, nature, personality, temperament. [*Compare* **disposition, identity, psychology.**] **2.** Moral or ethical strength ▶ fiber, honesty, honor, integrity, principle, probity, uprightness. [*Compare* **good.**] **3.** A statement attesting to personal qualifications, character, and dependability ▶ recommendation, reference, testimonial. [*Compare* **endorsement.**] **4.** Public estimation of someone ▶ name, report, reputation, repute. *Informal:* rep. [*Compare* **image, status.**] **5.** A person who is appealingly odd or curious ▶ eccentric, oddity, original. *Informal:* card, case, oddball. *Slang:* flake. [*Compare* **crackpot.**] **6.** A person portrayed in fiction or drama ▶ part, persona, personage, role. **7.** A conventional mark used in a writing system ▶ figure, letter, mark, sign, symbol. —*See also* **dignitary, quality** (1).

✦ **CORE SYNONYMS:** *character, disposition, temperament, personality, nature.* These nouns refer to the combination of emotional, intellectual, and moral qualities that distinguishes an individual. *Character* especially emphasizes moral and ethical qualities: *"Education has for its object the formation of character"* (Herbert Spencer). *Disposition* is approximately equivalent to prevailing frame of mind or spirit: *"A patronizing disposition always has its meaner side"* (George Eliot). *Temperament* applies broadly to the sum of physical, emotional, and intellectual components that affect or determine a person's actions and reactions: *"She is . . . of a serene and proud and dignified temperament"* (H.G. Wells). *Personality* is the sum of distinctive traits that give a person individuality: *possessed a cheerful and outgoing personality. Nature* denotes native or inherent qualities: *"It is my habit,—I hope I may say, my nature,—to believe the best of people"* (George W. Curtis).

---

character assassination *noun.* —*See* **libel.**

characteristic *adjective.* —*See* **special.**

characteristic *noun.* —*See* **quality** (1).

characterization *noun.* —*See* **representation.**

characterize *verb.* —*See* **call, distinguish** (2), **represent** (2).

charade *noun.* —*See* **façade** (2).

charbroil *verb.* —*See* **cook.**

charge *verb.* **1.** To cause to be filled, as with a particular mood or tone ▶ fill, imbue, impregnate, permeate, pervade, saturate, suffuse, transfuse. [*Compare* **steep**[2].] **2.** To place a trust upon ▶ entrust, trust. [*Compare* **authorize.**] **3.** To put explosive material into a weapon ▶ load, prime, ready. —*See also* **accuse, attack** (1), **attribute, bill**[1], **burden**[1], **command** (1), **commit** (2), **fill** (1).

charge in *verb.* —*See* **intrude.**

charge with *verb.* —*See* **impose on.**

charge *noun.* **1.** A swift advance or attack ▶ blitz, blitzkrieg, onslaught, raid, rush. [*Compare* **attack, invasion.**] **2.** A person who relies on another for support ▶ dependent, ward. —*See also* **accusation, care** (2), **command** (1), **cost** (1), **detention, duty** (1), **kick, management, mission** (1), **toll**[1] (1).

✦ **CORE SYNONYMS:** *charge, imbue, impregnate, permeate, pervade, saturate,* *suffuse.* These verbs mean to cause to be filled, as with a particular mood or tone: *an atmosphere charged with excitement; poetry imbued with lyricism; a spirit impregnated with lofty ideals; optimism that permeates a group; letters pervaded with gloom; a play saturated with imagination; a heart suffused with love.*

chariness *noun.* —*See* **caution.**

charisma *noun.* —*See* **attraction.**

charitable *adjective.* Of or concerned with charity ▶ altruistic, benevolent, eleemosynary, philanthropic. [*Compare* **benevolent.**] —*See also* **humanitarian, tolerant.**

✚ CORE SYNONYMS: *charitable, benevolent, eleemosynary, philanthropic.* These adjectives mean of, concerned with, providing, or provided by charity: *a charitable foundation; a benevolent fund; eleemosynary relief; philanthropic contributions.*

charitableness *noun.* —*See* **benevolence, tolerance.**

charity *noun.* —*See* **benevolence, donation, mercy, tolerance.**

charlatan *noun.* —*See* **fake.**

charm *verb.* **1.** To please greatly or irresistibly ▶ beguile, bewitch, captivate, enchant, entrance, fascinate, win over. [*Compare* **delight, seduce.**] **2.** To act upon with or as if with magic ▶ bewitch, enchant, ensorcell, enthrall, entrance, hypnotize, mesmerize, spell, spellbind, vamp, voodoo, witch. [*Compare* **enrapture.**] —*See also* **amuse.**

charm *noun.* A small object worn or kept for its supposed magical power ▶ amulet, fetish, grigri, juju, mascot, mojo, obeah, periapt, phylactery, talisman. [*Compare* **magic.**] —*See also* **attraction, spell[2].**

✚ CORE SYNONYMS: *charm, beguile, bewitch, captivate, enchant, entrance, fascinate.* These verbs mean to attract strongly or irresistibly: *manners that charmed the old curmudgeon; delicacies that beguile even the most discerning gourmet; a performance that bewitched the audience; a novel that captivates its readers; children who enchanted their grandparents; music that entrances its listeners; a celebrity who fascinated the interviewer.*

◀ ANTONYM: *repel*

charmer *noun.* —*See* **seducer** (1).

charming *adjective.* —*See* **attractive, delightful.**

chart *noun.* An orderly columnar display of data ▶ table, tabulation. [*Compare* **list[1].**]

chart *verb.* —*See* **design** (1), **plot** (1).

charter *verb.* To engage the temporary use of something for a fee ▶ hire, lease, rent. [*Compare* **lease.**]

charter *noun.* —*See* **agreement** (1), **law** (1).

chary *adjective.* —*See* **economical, wary.**

chase *verb.* —*See* **court** (2), **drive** (3), **follow** (3), **hunt, pursue** (1).

chase *noun.* The following of another in an attempt to overtake and capture ▶ hot pursuit, hunt, pursuit.

chasm *noun.* —*See* **deep, gap** (1).

chaste *adjective.* Morally beyond reproach, especially in sexual conduct ▶ celibate, continent, decent, modest, moral, pure, virgin, virginal, virtuous. ***Idiom:*** pure as the driven snow. [*Compare* **innocent.**]

chasten *verb.* To castigate for the purpose of improving ▶ chide, correct. —*See also* **chastise.**

chastise *verb.* To criticize for a fault or an offense ▶ admonish, berate, call down, castigate, censure, chasten, chide, dress down, jump (on *or* all over), lecture, objurgate, rap, rebuke, reprimand, reproach, reprove, scold, tax, upbraid. *Informal:* bawl out, lambaste, tell off. *Slang:* chew out. ***Idioms:*** blow up at, bring (*or* call *or* take) to task, call on the carpet, give hell (*or* it) to, haul (*or* rake) over the coals, jump down someone's throat, lay someone out in lavender, let someone have it. [*Compare* **criticize, revile, slam.**] —*See also* **punish.**

✚ CORE SYNONYMS: *chastise, scold, upbraid, berate, reprove, rebuke, reprimand, reproach.* These verbs mean to criticize for a fault or an offense. *Chastise* means to criticize severely: *chastised the students for talking during class. Scold* implies reproof: *parents who scolded their child for being rude. Upbraid* generally suggests a well-founded reproach, as one leveled by an authority: *upbraided by the supervisor for habitual tardiness. Berate* suggests scolding or rebuking at length: *an angry customer who berated the clerk. Reprove* usually suggests gentle criticism and constructive intent: *With a quick look, the teacher reproved the child for whispering in class. Rebuke* and *reprimand* both refer to sharp, often angry criticism: *"Some of the most heated criticism . . . has come from the Justice Department, which rarely rebukes other agencies in public"* (Howard Kurtz). *"A committee at* [the university] *asked its president to reprimand a scientist who tested gene-altered bacteria on trees"* (New York Times). *Reproach* usually refers to regretful or unhappy criticism arising from a sense of disappointment: *wrote a letter reproaching the reporter for failing to give a balanced account of the debate.*

chastisement *noun.* —*See* **punishment.**

chastity *noun.* The condition of being chaste ▶ celibacy, decency, innocence, modesty, morality, purity, virginity, virtue, virtuousness.

chat *verb.* —*See* **converse**[1].

chat *noun.* —*See* **chatter, conversation.**

chattel *noun.* —*See* **effects, slave.**

chatter *verb.* **1.** To talk rapidly and incessantly on trivial matters ▶ babble, blab, blabber, chitchat, clack, drivel, jabber, natter, palaver, patter, prate, prattle, rattle (on), run on, tattle. *Informal:* go on, ramble (on), spiel, yammer. *Slang:* chin wag, gab, gas, jaw, yak. ***Idioms:*** bend someone's ear, run off at the mouth, shoot the breeze (or bull). [*Compare* **speak.**]—*See also* **babble. 2.** To make or cause to make a succession of short, sharp sounds ▶ brattle, clack, clank, clatter, rattle. [*Compare* **knock, shake.**] —*See also* **gossip.**

chatter *noun.* Incessant and usually inconsequential talk ▶ babble, blab, blabber, chat, chitchat, clack, drivel, jabber, palaver, patter, prate, prattle, small talk, tattle. Informal: yammer. *Slang:* gab, gas, yak. [*Compare* **speech.**]

chatty *adjective.* —*See* **conversational, talkative.**

chauffeur *noun.* A person who operates a motor vehicle ▶ driver, motorist, operator.

chauffeur *verb.* —*See* **drive** (1).

chaw *verb.* —*See* **chew.**

cheap *adjective.* Low in price ▶ bargain-basement, budget, dirt-cheap, economy, frugal, inexpensive, low, low-cost, low-priced. ***Idiom:*** for a song. [*Compare* **meager.**] —*See also* **shoddy, stingy.**

cheapen *verb.* —*See* **debase, depreciate.**

cheapskate *noun.* —*See* **miser.**

cheat *verb.* **1.** To get money or something else from someone by deceitful trickery ▶ bilk, burn, cozen, defraud, fleece, game, gull, hoax, mulct, overcharge, rook, swindle, victimize. *Informal:* chisel, flimflam, shortchange, take, trim. *Slang:* clip, con, diddle, do, gouge, nick, rip off, scalp, scam, skin, soak, stick, sting. ***Idioms:*** load the dice, stack the cards (or deck), take someone for a ride, take someone to the cleaners. [*Compare* **deceive, pirate, steal.**] **2.** To be sexually unfaithful to another ▶ philander. *Informal:* fool around, mess around, play around. *Slang:* two-time. —*See also* **deceive.**

cheat *noun.* **1.** An act of cheating ▶ burn, deceit, fraud, hoax, humbug, masquerade, swindle, victimization. *Informal:* flimflam. *Slang:* con, grift, scam, sting. **2.** A person who cheats ▶ bilk, blackleg, cardsharp, cheater, cozener, deceiver, defrauder, dodger, knave, masquerader, rook, sharper, swindler, trickster, victimizer. *Informal:* chiseler, crook, flimflammer. *Slang:* diddler, grifter, scammer, shill. [*Compare* **fake.**]

cheater *noun.* —*See* **cheat** (2), **philanderer.**

check *noun.* —*See* **account** (2), **examination** (1), **restraint, stop** (1).

check *verb.* —*See* **agree** (1), **examine** (1), **frustrate, repel, restrain, stop** (2), **stop** (1), **test** (1).

check in *verb.* —*See* **arrive** (1).

check out *verb.* —*See* **die.**

checked *adjective.* —*See* **restricted.**

checklist *noun.* —*See* **list**[1]**.**

checkmate *verb.* —*See* **defeat, frustrate.**

checkmate *noun.* —*See* **defeat.**

checkup *noun.* —*See* **examination** (1), **examination** (2).

cheek *or* **cheekiness** *noun.*—*See* **impudence.**

cheeky *adjective.* —*See* **disrespectful, impudent.**

cheer *noun.*—*See* **happiness, praise** (1).

cheer *verb.* To express approval audi-bly, as by clapping ▶ applaud, clap, root. ***Idioms:*** give a big hand (*or* welcome), give an ovation, give someone a hand, put one's hands together. —*See also* **amuse, delight** (1), **encourage** (1), **encourage** (2), **praise** (1).

cheerful *adjective.* Being in or showing good spirits ▶ animated, blithesome, boon, bright, cheery, chipper, convivial, exhilarated, gay, glad, gleeful, happy, jocund, jolly, jovial, joyful, lighthearted, merry, mirthful, sunny. ***Idiom:*** on top of the world. [*Compare* **lighthearted, lively.**] —*See also* **merry, optimistic.**

✚ **CORE SYNONYMS:** *glad, happy, cheerful, lighthearted, joyful.* These adjectives mean being in or showing good spirits. *Glad* often refers to the feeling that results from the gratification of a wish or from satisfaction with immediate circumstances: *"Some folks rail against other folks, because other folks have what some folks would be glad of"* (Henry Fielding). *Happy* applies to a pleasurable feeling of contentment: *"Ask yourself whether you are happy, and you cease to be so"* (John Stuart Mill). *Cheerful* suggests characteristic good spirits: *a cheerful volunteer. Lighthearted* stresses the absence of care: *"He whistles as he goes, lighthearted wretch,/Cold and yet cheerful"* (William Cowper). *Joyful* suggests lively, often exultant happiness: *the joyful laughter of children.*

◀ **ANTONYM:** sad

cheerfulness *noun.* —*See* **happiness, optimism.**

cheering *adjective.* —*See* **encouraging.**

cheerless *adjective.* —*See* **gloomy, sorrowful.**

cheery *adjective.*—*See* **cheerful, merry.**

cheesy *adjective.* —*See* **shoddy.**

chef *noun.* A person who prepares food for eating ▶ baker, cook, culinary artist.

chef-d'oeuvre *noun.* An outstanding and ingenious work ▶ magnum opus, masterpiece, masterwork. [*Compare* **accomplishment, composition, treasure.**]

chemical-free *adjective.* —*See* **natural** (1).

cherish *verb.* —*See* **bear** (2), **value.** To care enough to keep someone in mind remember, think about, think of.

cherub *noun.* —*See* **baby** (1), **innocent** (1).

cherubic *adjective.* —*See* **babyish.**

chew *verb.* To seize and grind with the teeth bite, champ, chomp, chump, crump, crunch, gnash, gnaw, masticate, munch, nibble, ruminate. *Chiefly Regional:* chaw. [*Compare* **browse, eat.**]

chew out *verb.* —*See* **chastise.**

chew on *or* **over** *verb.* —*See* **ponder.**

✚ **CORE SYNONYMS:** *chew, bite, champ, chomp, gnaw.* These verbs mean to seize and tear or grind something with the teeth: *I chewed on a piece of candy. She bit into a ripe apple. The horse was champing at its bit. The cow is chomping its hay. His dog was gnawing a bone.*

---

chic *adjective.* —*See* **exclusive** (3), **fashionable.**

chic *noun.* —*See* **elegance.**

chicanery *noun.* —*See* **dishonesty** (2).

chichi *adjective.* —*See* **exclusive** (3).

chick *noun.* —*See* **girl.**

chicken *noun.* —*See* **coward.**

chicken *adjective.* —*See* **afraid, cowardly.**

chicken feed *noun.* —*See* **peanuts.**

chickenhearted *or* **chicken-livered** *adjective.* —*See* **cowardly.**

chickenheartedness *noun.* —*See* **cowardice.**

chide *verb.* To castigate for the purpose of improving ▶ chasten, correct. —*See also* **chastise.**

chief *noun.* One who governs or leads ▶ boss, captain, chieftain, commander, director, elder, emir, emperor, general, governor, head, headman, hierarch, king, kingpin, leader, lord, majesty, master, monarch, overlord, potentate, prince, queen, ringleader, ruler, sachem, sagamore, sheik, sovereign, suzerain. *Slang:* brass hat, honcho. ***Idioms:*** cock of the block (*or* walk). [*Compare* **dictator.**] —*See also* **boss.**

chief *adjective.* —*See* **dominant** (1), **primary** (1).

chieftain *noun.* —*See* **chief.**

child *noun.* **1.** A young person between birth and puberty ▶ innocent, juvenile, moppet, preadolescent, preteen, tot, whelp, youngster. *Informal:* kid, young'un. [*Compare* **baby.**] **2.** One who is not yet legally of age ▶ juvenile, minor, underage person. [*Compare* **youth.**] —*See also* **innocent** (2), **progeny.**

childbirth *or* **childbearing** *noun.* —*See* **birth** (1).

childhood *noun.* The stage of life between birth and puberty ▶ innocence, early years, preadolescence, prepubescence. [*Compare* **youth.**]

childish *adjective.* Of or characteristic of a child, especially in immaturity ▶ adolescent, babyish, childlike, immature, infantile, juvenile, puerile, sophomoric. [*Compare* **foolish.**]

childless *adjective.* —*See* **barren** (1).

childlike *adjective.* —*See* **babyish, childish.**

child's play *noun.* —*See* **breeze** (2).

chill *noun.* —*See* **cold.**

chill *adjective.* —*See* **cold** (1), **cool.**

chill out *verb.* —*See* **rest**[1] (1).

chilliness *noun.* —*See* **cold.**

chilly *adjective.* —*See* **cold** (1), **cool.**

chime *verb.* —*See* **agree** (1), **ring**[2].

chime in *verb.* —*See* **interrupt** (2).

chime *noun.* —*See* **agreement** (2).

chimera *noun.* —*See* **dream** (2).

chimeric *or* **chimerical** *adjective.* —*See* **illusive, imaginary.**

chink *noun.* —*See* **crack** (2).

chintzy *adjective.* —*See* **gaudy.**

chin wag *verb.* —*See* **chatter** (1).

chip *noun.* —*See* **flake.**

chip *verb.* —*See* **flake.**

chip in *verb.* —*See* **contribute** (1), **contribute** (2), **interrupt** (2).

chipper *adjective.* —*See* **cheerful, lively.**

chisel *verb.* —*See* **cheat** (1), **engrave** (1).

chiseler *noun.* —*See* **cheat** (2).

chitchat *noun.* —*See* **chatter.**

chitchat *verb.* —*See* **chatter** (1).

chivalric *adjective.* —*See* **gallant.**

chivalrous *adjective.* —*See* **gallant, gracious** (2).

chivalry *or* **chilvalrousness** *noun.* Respectful attention, especially toward women ▶ gallantry. [*Compare* **consideration, courtesy.**]

chock-full *or* **chock-a-block** *adjective.* —*See* **full** (1).

choice *noun.* The act, power, or right of choosing ▶ alternative, decision, discretion, election, free will, option, pick, preference, selection, volition. *Informal:* druthers. [*Compare* **voice, will.**] —*See also* **best** (1), **elect.**

choice *adjective.* **1.** Of fine quality ▶ exceptional, fine, first-class, first-rate, high-grade, premium, prime, select, sterling, superior, top-drawer, top-grade, top-of-the-line. [*Compare* **best, excellent, exceptional.**] **2.** Singled out in preference ▶ chosen, elect, exclusive, select. [*Compare* **favorite.**] —*See also* **delicate** (1).

✚ **CORE SYNONYMS:** *choice, alternative, option, preference, selection, election.* These nouns denote the act, power, or right of choosing. *Choice* implies broadly the freedom to choose from a set: *The store offers a wide choice of vegetables. I had no choice in the matter. Alternative* emphasizes choice between only two possibilities or courses of action: *"An unhappy alternative is before you, Elizabeth . . . . Your mother will never see you again if you do not marry Mr. Collins, and I will never see you again if you* do" (Jane Austen). *Option* often stresses a power or liberty to choose that has been granted: *The legislature outlined several tax options. Preference* indicates choice based on one's values, bias, or predilections: *We were offered our preference of wines. Selection* suggests a variety of things or persons to choose from: *The video store had a wide selection of foreign films. Election* especially emphasizes the use of judgment: *The university recommends careful consideration in the election of a major.*

---

choke *verb.* To stop breathing or to stop the breathing of ▶ asphyxiate, gag, smother, stifle, strangle, strangulate, suffocate, throttle. —*See also* **fail** (1), **fill** (2), **obstruct, repress, suppress.**

choke off *verb.* —*See* **suppress.**

choke *noun.* —*See* **plug.**

choked *adjective.* —*See* **overcrowded.**

choler *noun.* —*See* **anger.**

choleric *adjective.* —*See* **angry, testy.**

chomp *verb.* —*See* **chew.**

choose *verb.* **1.** To make a choice from a number of alternatives ▶ cast, cull, decide (on), elect, go with, opt (for), pick (out), select, single (out), take, vote (for), weigh, will. **2.** To have an inclination to ▶ desire, like, please, prefer, want, will, wish. ***Idioms:*** have a mind, see fit.

choosy *adjective.* —*See* **fussy.**

chop *verb.* —*See* **cut** (3).

chop down *verb.* —*See* **drop** (3).

chop *noun.* —*See* **blow²**.

choppiness *noun.* —*See* **irregularity.**

chops *noun.* —*See* **mouth** (1).

chore *noun.* —*See* **task** (1), **task** (2).

chortle *verb.* —*See* **laugh.**

chortle *noun.* —*See* **laugh.**

chosen *adjective.* Singled out in preference ▶ choice, elect, exclusive, select. [*Compare* **excellent, favorite.**]

chosen *noun.* —*See* **elect.**

chow *noun.* —*See* **food.**

chow down *verb.* —*See* **eat** (1).

christen *verb.* —*See* **name** (1).

chronic *adjective.* **1.** Subject to a disease or habit for a long time ▶ confirmed, habitual, habituated, inveterate. [*Compare* **stubborn.**] **2.** Of long duration ▶ continuing, lingering, persistent, prolonged, protracted. [*Compare* **confirmed, continuing.**] **3.** Subject to a habit or pattern of behavior ▶ accustomed, habitual, routine.

✚ **CORE SYNONYMS:** *chronic, confirmed, habitual, inveterate.* These adjectives mean having long had a habit or a disease: *a chronic complainer; a confirmed alcoholic; a habitual cheat; an inveterate smoker.*

---

chronicle *noun.* A chronological record of past events ▶ annals, archive, chronicle, historical record. *—See also* **story** (1).

chronicle *verb.* *—See* **list**[1].

chronological *adjective.* *—See* **consecutive.**

chubby *adjective.* *—See* **fat** (1).

chuck *verb.* *—See* **discard, eject** (1), **throw, vomit.**

chuck *noun.* *—See* **throw.**

chuck-full *adjective. See* **chock-full.**

chuckle *verb.* *—See* **laugh.**

chuckle *noun.* *—See* **laugh.**

chuff *noun.* *—See* **boor.**

chug *or* **chugalug** *verb.* *—See* **drink** (2).

chum *noun.* *—See* **associate** (2), **friend.**

chumminess *noun.* *—See* **friendship.**

chummy *adjective.* *—See* **intimate**[1] (1).

chump[1] *noun.* *—See* **drip** (2), **dullard.**

chump[2] *verb.* *—See* **chew.**

chunk *noun.* *—See* **lump**[1].

chunky *adjective.* *—See* **stocky.**

church *adjective.* Of or relating to a church or to an established religion ▶ churchly, ecclesiastical, religious, spiritual. [*Compare* **clerical, divine, holy, ritual.**]

churchman *or* **churchwoman** *noun.* *—See* **cleric.**

churl *noun.* *—See* **boor, miser.**

churlish *adjective.* *—See* **coarse** (1), **ill-tempered.**

churn *verb.* *—See* **agitate** (1), **boil.**

chutzpah *or* **hutzpah** *noun.* *—See* **impudence.**

cinch *noun.* *—See* **band**[1], **breeze** (2), **certainty.**

cinch *verb.* *—See* **guarantee** (2).

cincture *noun.* *—See* **band**[1].

cincture *verb.* *—See* **encircle.**

cinerarium *noun.* *—See* **grave**[1].

cipher *noun.* *—See* **nonentity.**

cipher *verb.* *—See* **calculate.**

circa *adverb.* *—See* **approximately.**

circle *noun.* **1.** A round closed plane shape or figure ▶ annulus, band, circlet, cirque, circuit, crown, disk, gyre, halo, hoop, ring, round, roundlet, wheel, wreath, zodiac. [*Compare* **ball, circumference, loop.**] **2.** A course, process, or journey that ends where it began or repeats itself ▶ circuit, cycle, orbit, round, tour, turn. **3.** A small group of friends or associates ▶ clique, coterie, crew, crowd, group, in-group, set. *Informal:* bunch, gang. [*Compare* **crowd, group.**] *—See also* **area** (1), **range** (1), **revolution** (1).

circle *verb.* *—See* **encircle, surround, turn** (1).

circlet *noun.* *—See* **circle** (1).

circuit *noun.* *—See* **beat** (2), **circle** (1), **circle** (2), **circumference, conference** (2), **journey, loop, revolution** (1).

circuitous *adjective.* *—See* **indirect** (1).

circular *adjective.* *—See* **indirect** (1), **round** (1).

circular *noun.* An announcement distributed on paper to a large number of people ▶ flier, handbill, leaflet, notice.

circulate *verb.* *—See* **flow** (1), **spread** (2). To become known far and wide ▶ get around, go around, spread, travel. ***Idioms:*** go (*or* make) the rounds.

circulation *noun.* *—See* **distribution** (2), **publication** (1), **revolution** (1).

circumference *noun.* A line around a closed figure or area ▶ ambit, circuit, compass, perimeter, periphery. [*Compare* **border, circle, limits.**]

✢ **CORE SYNONYMS:** *circumference, circuit, compass, perimeter, periphery.* These nouns refer to a line around a closed figure or area: *the circumference of the earth; followed the circuit around the park; stayed within the compass of the schoolyard; the perimeter of a rectangle; a fence around the periphery of the property.*

---

circumlocution *noun.* *—See* **wordiness.**

circumlocutionary *adjective.* *—See* **wordy** (1).

circumlocutory *adjective.* *—See* **indirect** (1), **wordy** (1).

circumnavigate *verb.* —*See* **encircle, skirt.**

circumscribe *verb.* —*See* **determine, encircle, limit.**

circumscribed *adjective.* —*See* **restricted.**

circumscription *noun.* —*See* **restraint, restriction.**

circumspect *adjective.* —*See* **deliberate** (3), **wary.**

circumspection *noun.* —*See* **prudence.**

circumstance *noun.* **1.** Something that takes place ▶ episode, event, experience, happening, incident, occasion, occurrence, thing. [*Compare* **event.**] **2.** One of the conditions or facts attending an event and having some bearing on it ▶ condition, detail, fact, factor, particular. [*Compare* **element, quality.**] —*See also* **event** (1).

✚ **CORE SYNONYMS:** *circumstance, occurrence, happening, event, incident, episode.* These nouns refer to something that takes place or comes to pass. *Cirmcumstance, occurrence,* and *happening* are the most general: *"Billy had found Alice, thus bringing about the odd circumstance of their renewing their acquaintanceship"* (Eleanor H. Porter). *The sunrise is an everyday occurrence. The reporter dismissed the report as a happening of no great importance. Event* usually signifies a notable occurrence: *major world events reported on the evening news. "Great events make me quiet and calm; it is only trifles that irritate my nerves"* (Victoria). *Incident* may apply to a minor occurrence: *a small incident blown out of proportion.* The term may also refer to a distinct event of sharp identity and significance: *a succession of exciting incidents.* An *episode* is an incident in the course of a progression or within a larger sequence: *"Happiness was but the occasional episode in a general drama of pain"* (Thomas Hardy).

---

circumstances *noun.* —*See* **conditions.**

circumstantial *adjective.* —*See* **detailed, gracious** (2).

circumstantiate *verb.* —*See* **prove.**

circumstantiation *noun.* —*See* **confirmation** (2).

circumvent *verb.* —*See* **avoid, skirt.**

circumvention *noun.* —*See* **escape** (2).

circumvolution *noun.* —*See* **revolution** (1).

circumvolve *verb.* —*See* **turn** (1).

cirque *noun.* —*See* **circle** (1).

cistern *noun.* —*See* **vat.**

citadel *noun.* —*See* **fort.**

citation *noun.* A written or printed notification of a legal infraction ▶ ticket. —*See also* **distinction** (2), **reference** (1).

cite *verb.* To bring forward as proof or support ▶ adduce, invoke, lay, present, produce. [*Compare* **offer.**] —*See also* **name** (2), **name** (1).

citizen *noun.* A person owing loyalty to and entitled to the protection of a given state ▶ burgess, burgher, freeman, national, subject, taxpayer. [*Compare* **inhabitant.**]

✚ **CORE SYNONYMS:** *citizen, national, subject.* These nouns denote a person owing allegiance to a nation or state and entitled to its protection: *an American citizen; a Nigerian national; a French subject.*

---

city *noun.* A large and important town ▶ borough, megalopolis, metropolis, municipality. *Informal:* burg, town. [*Compare* **village.**]

city *adjective.* Of, in, or belonging to a city ▶ civic, local, metropolitan, municipal, urban.

civic *adjective.* —*See* **city, popular.**

civil *adjective.* —*See* **courteous** (1), **popular, profane** (2).

civility *noun.* —*See* **amenities** (2), **courtesy.**

civilization *noun.* The total product of human creativity and intellect ▶ culture, Kultur, society. *—See also* **culture** (2), **culture** (3).

civilize *verb.* To fit for companionship with others, especially in attitude or manners ▶ acculturate, humanize, socialize.

civilized *adjective.* *—See* **cultured.**

civilizing *adjective.* *—See* **cultural.**

clabber *verb.* *—See* **coagulate.**

clack *verb.* **1.** To make a light, sharp noise ▶ click, snap. [*Compare* **crackle.**] **2.** To make or cause to make a succession of short, sharp sounds ▶ brattle, chatter, clank, clatter, rattle. [*Compare* **knock, shake.**] *—See also* **chatter** (1).

clack *noun.* A light, sharp noise ▶ click, crackle, snap. [*Compare* **crack.**] *—See also* **chatter.**

clad *verb.* *—See* **face** (2).

claim *verb.* To defend, maintain, or insist on the recognition of ▶ assert, challenge, demand, postulate, vindicate. ***Idioms:*** have dibs on, lay claim to, stake a claim. *—See also* **assert, demand** (1).

claim *noun.* **1.** A legitimate or asserted right to demand something as one's due ▶ pretense, pretension, title. *Slang:* dibs. **2.** A right or legal share in something ▶ interest, portion, stake, title. [*Compare* **cut, right.**] *—See also* **assertion, debt** (1), **demand** (1).

✚ **CORE SYNONYMS:** *claim, pretense, pretension, title.* These nouns refer to a legitimate or asserted right to demand something as one's due: *had a legal claim to the property; makes no pretense to scholarliness; justified pretensions to the presidency; has no title to our thanks.*

---

claimant *noun.* One that makes a formal complaint, especially in court ▶ accuser, complainant, plaintiff.

clamber *verb.* *—See* **ascend.**

clammy *adjective.* Slightly wet ▶ damp, dank, dewy, moist. [*Compare* **sticky, wet.**]

clamor *noun.* *—See* **noise** (1), **roar, vociferation.**

clamor *verb.* *—See* **shout.**

clamorous *adjective.* *—See* **loud, vociferous.**

clamp *noun.* *—See* **fastener.**

clamp *verb.* *—See* **attach** (1), **fasten.**

clampdown *noun.* Forceful subjugation, as against an uprising ▶ crackdown, lockdown, repression, suppression. [*Compare* **oppression, restraint.**]

clan *noun.* *—See* **family** (2).

clandestine *adjective.* *—See* **secret** (1).

clandestinely *adverb.* *—See* **secretly.**

clandestinity *or* **clandestineness** *noun.* *—See* **secrecy.**

clang *verb.* *—See* **bang.**

clang *noun.* *—See* **clash.**

clangor *noun.* *—See* **noise** (1).

clank *verb.* To make or cause to make a succession of short, sharp sounds ▶ brattle, chatter, clack, clatter, rattle. [*Compare* **knock, shake.**]

clap *verb.* To express approval audibly, as by clapping ▶ applaud, cheer, root. ***Idioms:*** give a big hand (*or* welcome), give an ovation, give someone a hand, put one's hands together. *—See also* **bang, crack** (2), **slap.**

clap *noun.* *—See* **crack** (1).

claptrap *noun.* *—See* **bombast, nonsense.**

clarification *noun.* *—See* **explanation, purification** (1).

clarifier *noun.* *—See* **purifier.**

clarify *verb.* **1.** To make clear or clearer ▶ clear (up), define, elucidate, illuminate, illustrate, simplify. ***Idioms:*** shed (*or* throw) light on *or* upon. [*Compare* **explain, show.**] **2.** To remove impurities from ▶ clean, cleanse, purify, refine. [*Compare* **clean.**]

clarity *noun.* The quality of being clear and easy to perceive or understand ▶ clearness, comprehensibility, distinctness, explicitness, intelligibility, legibility, limpidity, limpidness, lucidity, lucidness, pellucidity, pellucidness, perspicuity, perspicuousness, plainness, preciseness, precision, simplicity. *—See also* **purity, visibility.**

clash *verb.* —*See* **bang, conflict, contend.**

clash *noun.* A loud, harsh striking noise ▶ clang, crash, slap, smack, smash, whack. [*Compare* **blow², crack, slam.**] —*See also* **argument, battle, conflict.**

clasp *noun.* —*See* **embrace, fastener, hold** (1).

clasp *verb.* —*See* **embrace** (1), **grasp.**

class *noun.* **1.** A subdivision of a larger group ▶ category, classification, department, division, family, genre, group, order, set. [*Compare* **kind.**] **2.** A division of persons or things by quality, rank, or grade ▶ bracket, caste, grade, hierarchy, league, level, order, range, rank, school, stratum, tier. [*Compare* **place.**] **3.** Degree of excellence ▶ caliber, grade, quality. [*Compare* **degree.**] —*See also* **elegance.**

class *verb.* —*See* **classify.**

classic *adjective.* —*See* **bare** (1), **typical, vintage.**

classical *adjective.* —*See* **typical, vintage.**

classification *noun.* —*See* **arrangement** (1), **class** (1).

classified *adjective.* —*See* **confidential** (3).

classify *verb.* To arrange or organize according to class ▶ assort, catalog, categorize, class, coordinate, distribute, divide, grade, group, pigeonhole, place, range, rank, rate, separate, size, sort (out), stereotype, stratify. [*Compare* **arrange, position.**]

classy *adjective.* —*See* **elegant, exclusive** (3), **fashionable.**

clatter *verb.* To make or cause to make a succession of short, sharp sounds ▶ brattle, chatter, clack, clank, rattle. [*Compare* **knock, shake.**]

clay *noun.* The substance of the body, especially after decay or cremation ▶ ashes, cremains, dust, remains. —*See also* **earth** (1).

clean *adjective.* **1.** Free from dirt, stain, or impurities ▶ antiseptic, cleanly, fresh, immaculate, scrubbed, spick-and-span, spotless, stainless, unsmirched, unsoiled, unsullied. ***Idioms:*** clean as a whistle, squeaky clean. [*Compare* **neat, sterile.**] **2.** Not lewd or obscene ▶ decent, inoffensive, modest, wholesome. *Informal:* G-rated. [*Compare* **correct, ethical.**] **3.** According to the rules ▶ fair, sporting, sportsmanlike, sportsmanly. —*See also* **dexterous, innocent** (1), **innocent** (2), **perfect.**

clean *adverb.* —*See* **completely** (1).

clean *verb.* **1.** To rid of dirt, stains, trash, or other impurities ▶ bathe, cleanse, launder, lave, rinse, wash. [*Compare* **scrape, refine.**] **2.** To remove impurities from ▶ clarify, cleanse, purify, refine. —*See also* **tidy** (1), **tidy** (2).

clean out *verb.* —*See* **empty, ruin.**

clean up *verb. Slang* To make a large profit ▶ batten, cash in, profit. ***Idioms:*** make a killing, make out like a bandit.

✚ **CORE SYNONYMS:** *clean, antiseptic, cleanly, immaculate, spotless.* These adjectives mean free from dirt, stain, or impurities: *clean clothing; antiseptic surgical instruments; a cleanly pet; an immaculate tablecloth; a spotless kitchen.*

◀ **ANTONYM:** *dirty*

---

cleaner *noun.* —*See* **purifier.**

cleaning *noun.* —*See* **purification** (1).

cleanliness *noun.* —*See* **purity.**

cleanly *adjective.* —*See* **clean** (1).

cleanly *adverb.* —*See* **fair¹.**

cleanness *noun.* —*See* **purity.**

cleanse *verb.* To remove impurities from ▶ clarify, clean, purify, refine. —*See also* **clean** (1), **purify** (1).

cleanser *noun.* —*See* **purifier.**

cleansing *noun.* —*See* **purification** (1).

clear *adjective.* **1.** Free from what obscures or dims ▶ crystal, crystal clear, crystalline, hyaline, limpid, lucid, pellucid, see-through, translucent, transparent. [*Compare* **filmy, sheer.**] **2.** Free from clouds or mist ▶ bright, cloudless, fair, fine, sunny, unclouded. **3.** Free from obstructions ▶ free, open, unbarred, unblocked, unhindered, unimpeded, unobstructed, unplugged. [*Compare* **passable.**] —*See also* **apparent** (1), **decided, definite** (1), **empty** (1), **obvious, perfect, pure, sharp** (2).

clear *verb.* **1.** To become brighter or fairer ▶ brighten, clear up, kindle, illuminate, lighten. **2.** To rid of obstructions ▶ free, open, remove, unblock. [*Compare* **rid.**] **3.** To free from a charge or imputation of guilt ▶ absolve, acquit, discharge, exculpate, exonerate, justify, purge, vindicate. ***Idiom:*** get off the hook. [*Compare* **forgive.**] **4.** To pass by or over safely or successfully ▶ hurdle, negotiate, surmount. —*See also* **annihilate, clarify** (1), **empty, extricate, rid, pass** (6), **return** (3), **settle** (3), **tidy** (1).

clear *adverb.* —*See* **completely** (1).

clear out *verb.* —*See* **run** (2).

clear up *verb.* —*See* **solve** (1).

✚ **CORE SYNONYMS:** *clear, limpid, lucid, pellucid, transparent.* These adjectives mean free from what obscures or dims: *clear, sediment-free claret; limpid blue eyes; lucid air; a pellucid brook; transparent crystal.*

---

clearance *noun.* —*See* **elimination.**

clear-cut *adjective.* —*See* **apparent** (1), **decided, definite** (1).

clearing *noun.* ▶ field, meadow, pasture. [*Compare* **lot.**]

clearness *noun.* —*See* **clarity, visibility.**

clear-sightedness *noun.* —*See* **discernment.**

cleavage *noun.* —*See* **crack** (2).

cleave[1] *verb.* —*See* **crack** (1), **cut** (2).

cleave[2] *verb.* —*See* **bond.**

cleft *noun.* —*See* **crack** (2).

clemency *noun.* —*See* **mercy.**

clement *adjective.* Free from extremes in temperature ▶ balmy, mild, moderate, temperate. [*Compare* **pleasant.**] —*See also* **tolerant.**

clench *verb.* —*See* **grasp.**

clench *noun.* —*See* **hold** (1).

clergyman *or* **clergywoman** *noun.* —*See* **cleric.**

cleric *noun.* A person ordained for service in a Christian church ▶ abbé, abbot, bishop, chaplain, churchman, churchwoman, clergyman, clergywoman, clerical, clerk, curate, deacon, divine, ecclesiastic, minister, monk, parson, pastor, preacher, prelate, priest, rector, vicar. *Informal:* padre, reverend.

clerical *adjective.* Of or relating to the clergy, especially in a Christian church ▶ ecclesiastical, episcopal, ministerial, pastoral, priestly, sacerdotal. [*Compare* **spiritual.**]

clerical *noun.* —*See* **cleric.**

clerk *noun.* —*See* **cleric, seller.**

clever *adjective.* **1.** Mentally quick and original ▶ acute, alert, bright, ingenious, intelligent, inventive, keen, quick, quick-thinking, quick-witted, resourceful, sharp, sharp-witted, shrewd, smart. ***Idioms:*** nobody's fool, on the ball (*or* beam), quick on the uptake, sharp as a tack, smart as a whip. [*Compare* **artful, intelligent, shrewd.**] **2.** Exhibiting or employing wit or originality ▶ humorous, scintillating, smart, sparkling, witty. [*Compare* **funny, sarcastic.**] —*See also* **dexterous.**

✚ **CORE SYNONYMS:** *clever, ingenious, shrewd.* These adjectives refer to mental adroitness or to practical ingenuity and skill. *Clever* is the most comprehensive: "*Everybody's family doctor was remarkably clever, and was understood to have immeasurable skill in the management and training of the most skittish or vicious diseases*" (George Eliot). *Ingenious* implies originality and inventiveness: "*an ingenious solution to the storage problem*" (Linda Greider). *Shrewd* emphasizes mental astuteness and practical understanding: "*a woman of shrewd intellect*" (Leslie Stephen).

---

cleverness *noun.* —*See* **art, dexterity, intelligence.**

cliché *noun.* A trite expression or idea ▶ banality, bromide, commonplace, platitude, saw, stereotype, truism. ***Idiom:*** old chestnut.

✚ **CORE SYNONYMS:** *cliché, bromide, commonplace, platitude, truism.* These nouns denote an expression or idea that has lost its originality or force through overuse: *a short story weakened by clichés; the old bromide that we are what we eat; uttered the commonplace "welcome aboard"; a eulogy full of platitudes; a once-original thought that has become a truism.*

---

clichéd *adjective.* —*See* **trite.**

click *noun.* A light, sharp noise ▶ clack, crackle, snap. [*Compare* **crack.**]

click *verb.* To make a light, sharp noise ▶ clack, snap. [*Compare* **crackle.**] —*See also* **relate** (2), **succeed** (2).

client *noun.* —*See* **consumer.**

clientele *or* **clientage** *noun.* —*See* **patronage** (3).

climacteric *noun.* —*See* **crisis.**

climacteric *adjective.* —*See* **urgent** (1).

climactic *adjective.* Of or constituting a climax ▶ crowning, culminating, peak. [*Compare* **last.**] —*See also* **dramatic** (2).

climate *noun.* —*See* **environment** (2), **temper** (3).

climax *noun.* The highest point or state ▶ acme, apex, apogee, cap, crest, crown, culmination, fastigium, height, meridian, peak, pinnacle, pitch, roof, summit, top, vertex, zenith. *Informal:* payoff. [*Compare* **face.**] —*See also* **crisis.**

climax *verb.* To reach or bring to a climax ▶ cap (off), crescendo, crest, crown, culminate, peak, top (off *or* out).

✚ **CORE SYNONYMS:** *climax, summit, peak, pinnacle, acme, apex, zenith.* These nouns all mean the highest point. *Climax* refers to the point of greatest strength, effect, or intensity that marks the endpoint of an ascending process: *The government's collapse was the climax of a series of constitutional crises. Summit* denotes the highest level attainable: *"This* [appointment] *had been the summit of Mr. Bertram's ambition"* (Sir Walter Scott). *Peak* usually refers to the uppermost point: *"It was the peak of summer in the Berkshires"* (Saul Bellow). *Pinnacle* denotes a towering height, as of achievement: *The articulation of the theory of relativity catapulted Einstein to the pinnacle of his profession. Acme* refers to an ultimate point, as of perfection: *The artist's talents were at their acme when this work was created. Apex* is the culminating point: *The military regime represented the apex of oppression and intimidation. Zenith* is the point of highest achievement, most complete development, or greatest power: *"Chivalry was then in its zenith"* (Henry Hallam).

---

climb *verb.* —*See* **ascend, rise** (2), **rise** (3).

climb *noun.* —*See* **ascent** (1).

climbing *verb.* —*See* **ascent** (1).

clinch *verb.* —*See* **decide, embrace** (1), **guarantee** (2).

clinch *noun.* —*See* **embrace.**

clincher *noun. Informal* A key resource to be used at an opportune moment ▶ ace, trump, trump card. ***Idiom:*** ace in the hole.

cling *verb.* —*See* **bond.**

clinging *adjective.* Fearful of the loss of position or affection ▶ clutching, green-eyed, jealous, possessive. [*Compare* **envious.**] —*See also* **tight** (1).

clink *noun.* —*See* **jail.**

clinker *noun.* —*See* **blunder, failure** (1).

clip¹ *verb.* —*See* **cheat** (1), **cut** (3), **hit.**

clip *noun. Informal* Rate of motion or performance ▶ pace, speed, tempo, velocity. —*See also* **blow².**

clip² *verb.* —*See* **attach** (1), **fasten.**

clip *noun.* —*See* **fastener.**

clippers *noun.* —*See* **shears.**

clique *noun.* —*See* **circle** (3).

cloaca *noun.* —*See* **pit¹.**

cloak *noun.* —*See* **veil, wrap.**
cloak *verb.* —*See* **clothe, conceal, disguise, wrap** (2).
cloak-and-dagger *adjective.* —*See* **secret** (1).
clobber *verb.* —*See* **beat** (1), **overwhelm** (1).
clobbering *noun.* —*See* **defeat.**
clock *verb.* To record the speed or duration of ▶ time. [*Compare* **measure.**]
clod *noun.* —*See* **dullard, lump**[1]**.**
cloddish *adjective.* —*See* **awkward** (1), **stupid.**
cloddishness *noun.* —*See* **stupidity.**
clodhopper *noun.* A clumsy, unsophisticated person ▶ bumpkin, hick, peasant, rustic, yokel. *Informal:* hillbilly. *Slang:* hayseed, rube. [*Compare* **boor, oaf.**]
clog *noun.* —*See* **bar** (1).
clog *verb.* —*See* **delay** (1), **fill** (2), **obstruct.**
cloister *verb.* To put into solitude ▶ isolate, seclude, sequester, sequestrate. [*Compare* **enclose, imprison, isolate.**]
clomp *verb.* —*See* **thud.**
clone *verb.* —*See* **copy, mimic.**
clone *noun.* —*See* **double.**
close *adjective.* **1.** Not far from another in space, time, or relation ▶ adjacent, contiguous, immediate, near, nearby, neighboring, nigh, proximate. ***Idioms:*** a stone's throw, at hand, next to, under one's nose, within an inch, within hailing (*or* spitting) distance. [*Compare* **adjoining.**] **2.** Consistent with correctness, accuracy, or completeness ▶ exact, faithful, full, rigorous, strict. [*Compare* **careful, thorough.**] **3.** Almost even ▶ nip and tuck, tight. ***Idiom:*** neck and neck. —*See also* **airless** (1), **confidential** (2), **intimate**[1] (1), **stingy, taciturn, thick** (2), **tight** (4).
close *verb.* **1.** To move a door, for example, in order to cover an opening ▶ clench, seal, shut, slam. **2.** To come together from different directions ▶ converge, join, meet, unite. [*Compare* **combine.**] —*See also* **conclude, enclose** (1), **fill** (2).
close in *verb.* —*See* **enclose** (2).
close off *verb.* —*See* **isolate** (1).
close out *verb.* To get rid of by selling ▶ dispose of, dump, sell off, unload.
close *noun.* —*See* **court** (1), **end** (1), **end** (2).
close *adverb.* To a point near in time, space, or relation ▶ closely, hard, near, nearby, nigh.

✚ **CORE SYNONYMS:** *close, immediate, near, nearby, nigh, proximate.* These adjectives mean not far from another in space, time, or relationship: *an airport close to town; her immediate family; his nearest relative; a nearby library; our nighest neighbor; the proximate neighborhood.*

◀ **ANTONYM:** *far*

---

closed-door *adjective.* Belonging or confined to a particular person or group as opposed to the public or the government ▶ personal, private, privy. [*Compare* **confidential, secret.**]
close-fisted *adjective.* —*See* **stingy.**
closely *adverb.* —*See* **close.**
close-minded *adjective.* —*See* **intolerant** (1).
close-mouthed *adjective.* —*See* **taciturn.**
closeness *noun.* —*See* **friendship, thickness.**
closet *verb.* —*See* **enclose** (1).
closing *adjective.* —*See* **last**[1] (1).
closing *noun.* —*See* **end** (1), **end** (2).
closure *noun.* —*See* **end** (1).
clot *verb.* —*See* **coagulate.**
clot *noun.* —*See* **lump**[1]**.**
clothe *verb.* To cover as if with clothes ▶ cloak, coat, drape, jacket, mantle, robe, shawl, vest. —*See also* **dress** (1), **wrap** (2).

✚ **CORE SYNONYMS:** *clothe, cloak, drape, mantle, robe.* These verbs mean to cover as if with clothes: *trees clothed in leafy splendor; mist that cloaks the* *mountains; a beam draped with cobwebs; a boulder mantled with moss; snow robing fields and gardens.*

---

clothing *or* **clothes** *noun.* —*See* **dress** (1).

cloud *noun.* —*See* **crowd.**

cloud *verb.* —*See* **denigrate, drug** (2), **obscure.**

cloudburst *noun.* —*See* **rain.**

clouded *adjective.* —*See* **ambiguous** (1), **murky** (1).

cloudiness *noun.* —*See* **vagueness.**

cloudless *adjective.* —*See* **clear** (2).

cloud nine *noun.* —*See* **heaven.**

cloudy *adjective.* —*See* **ambiguous** (2), **murky** (1), **unclear.**

clout *noun.* —*See* **blow**[2], **influence.**

clout *verb.* —*See* **hit.**

clown *noun.* —*See* **joker.**

clown *verb. Informal* To make jokes; behave playfully ▶ jest, joke, quip. *Informal:* clown around, fool around, horse around. ***Idioms:*** crack wise, play the fool. [*Compare* **play.**]

cloy *verb.* —*See* **satiate.**

club *noun.* —*See* **union** (1).

club *verb.* —*See* **beat** (1).

clue *noun.* —*See* **hint** (2), **tip**[3].

clueless *adjective.* —*See* **ignorant** (1), **ignorant** (3).

clump *noun.* —*See* **group, lump**[1].

clump *verb.* —*See* **blunder, thud.**

clumsy *adjective.* —*See* **awkward** (1), **awkward** (2), **tactless, unskillful.**

clunk *noun.* —*See* **beat** (1).

clunk *verb.* —*See* **thud.**

clunker *noun.* —*See* **failure** (1).

cluster *noun.* —*See* **group.**

cluster *verb.* —*See* **assemble.**

clutch[1] *verb.* —*See* **catch** (2), **grasp.**

clutch *noun.* —*See* **catch** (1), **crisis, hold** (1), **purse.**

clutch[2] *noun.* —*See* **group.**

clutching *adjective.* Fearful of the loss of position or affection ▶ clinging, green-eyed, jealous, possessive. [*Compare* **envious.**]

clutter *noun.* —*See* **disorder** (1).

clutter *verb.* —*See* **disorder.**

cluttered *adjective.* —*See* **busy** (3).

coach *verb.* —*See* **educate.**

coach *noun.* —*See* **educator.**

coaction *noun.* —*See* **cooperation.**

coactive *adjective.* —*See* **cooperative.**

coadjutant *or* **coadjutor** *noun.* —*See* **assistant.**

coagulate *verb.* To change or be changed from a liquid into a soft, semisolid, or solid mass ▶ clot, congeal, curdle, gelatinize, jell, jelly, set, stiffen. *Chiefly Regional:* clabber. [*Compare* **harden.**]

✚ **CORE SYNONYMS:** *coagulate, clot, congeal, curdle, jell, jelly, set.* These verbs mean to change or be changed from a liquid into a soft, semisolid, or solid mass: *egg white coagulating when heated; blood clotting over the wound; gravy congealing as it cools; milk that had curdled; used pectin to jell the jam; jellied consommé; allowed the aspic to set.*

---

coalesce *verb.* —*See* **combine** (1), **mix** (1).

coalition *noun.* —*See* **alliance, unification.**

coarse *adjective.* **1.** Lacking in delicacy or refinement ▶ barbarian, barbaric, boorish, churlish, common, crass, crude, gross, ill-bred, indelicate, inelegant, philistine, plebeian, rough, rude, tasteless, unbecoming, uncivilized, uncouth, uncultivated, uncultured, unpolished, unrefined, vulgar. *Informal:* tacky. [*Compare* **abrupt, improper, rustic.**] **2.** Consisting of or covered with large particles ▶ grainy, granular, gravelly, gritty, rough, sabulous, sandy. —*See also* **bad** (1), **obscene, rough** (1).

coarseness *noun.* —*See* **irregularity, obscenity** (1).

coast *verb.* To ride or be pulled on a sled in the snow ▶ sled, sledge, sleigh-ride, slide. ***Idioms:*** go sledding (*or* coasting *or* sleigh-riding). —*See also* **breeze, glide** (1).

coat *noun.* **1.** An outer garment that has sleeves ▶ anorak, jacket, mackintosh, overcoat, parka, raincoat, slicker, sport coat, sport jacket, sports coat, sports jacket, suit coat, suit jacket, trench coat, windbreaker. **2.** A layer of material covering something else ▶ blanket, coating, covering, crust, dusting, layer, overlay, sheet. [*Compare* **face, finish, skin.**]

coat *verb.* —*See* **clothe, cover** (1), **finish.**

coating *noun.* —*See* **coat** (2).

coax *verb.* To persuade or try to persuade by gentle persistent urging or flattery ▶ blandish, cajole, honey, wheedle. *Informal:* soft-soap, sweet-talk. [*Compare* **flatter.**] —*See also* **persuade.**

cock *noun.* —*See* **faucet.**

cock-and-bull story *noun.* —*See* **lie**[2].

cockcrow *noun.* —*See* **dawn.**

cockeyed *adjective.* —*See* **drunk, foolish.**

cocktail lounge *noun.* —*See* **bar** (2).

cocky *adjective.* —*See* **boastful.**

coddle *verb.* —*See* **baby, cook.**

codify *verb.* —*See* **arrange** (1).

coequal *noun.* —*See* **peer**[2].

coequal *adjective.* —*See* **equal.**

coequality *noun.* —*See* **equivalence.**

coerce *verb.* To compel by threats ▶ blackjack, dragoon, force. *Informal:* hijack, strong-arm. [*Compare* **intimidate.**] —*See also* **force** (1).

coercion *noun.* —*See* **force** (1).

coercive *adjective.* Accomplished by force ▶ forced, forcible, violent. *Informal:* strong-arm.

coercively *adverb.* With force and violence ▶ forcibly, violently. ***Idioms:*** against one's will, by force, under duress.

coetaneous *adjective.* —*See* **contemporary** (1).

coeval *adjective.* —*See* **contemporary** (1).

coeval *noun.* One of the same time or age as another ▶ contemporary.

coexistent *or* **coexisting** *adjective.* —*See* **contemporary** (1).

cogency *noun.* The power of an argument to convince or compel agreement ▶ force, forcefulness, justice, persuasiveness, weight. ***Idiom:*** sound reason. [*Compare* **eloquence, veracity, verisimilitude.**]

cogent *adjective.* —*See* **convincing, sound**[2].

cogitate *verb.* —*See* **ponder, think** (1).

cogitation *noun.* —*See* **thought.**

cogitative *adjective.* —*See* **thoughtful.**

cognate *adjective.* —*See* **kindred.**

cognizable *adjective.* —*See* **perceptible.**

cognizance *noun.* —*See* **awareness, notice** (1).

cognizant *adjective.* —*See* **aware.**

cognomen *noun.* —*See* **name** (1).

cohere *verb.* —*See* **bond.**

coherence *noun.* —*See* **consistency.**

coherent *adjective.* —*See* **understandable.**

cohesion *noun.* —*See* **bond** (3), **consistency.**

cohort *noun.* —*See* **associate** (1), **band**[2], **follower.**

coil *verb.* —*See* **wind**[2].

coil *noun.* —*See* **curl, loop.**

coin *verb.* —*See* **invent.**

coincide *verb.* To occur at the same time ▶ concur, harmonize, synchronize. —*See also* **agree** (2).

coincidence *noun.* —*See* **chance** (2).

coincident *adjective.* —*See* **concurrent.**

cold *adjective.* **1.** Marked by a low temperature ▶ arctic, boreal, chill, chilly, cool, freezing, frigid, frosty, gelid, glacial, icy, nippy, polar, shivery, wintry. ***Idioms:*** bitter (*or* bitterly) cold. **2.** Lacking feeling or emotion ▶ cold-blooded, dispassionate, dry, emotionless, impassible, impassive, indifferent, insensible, insensitive, insusceptible, matter-of-fact, neutral, passionless, phlegmatic, stolid, thick-skinned, unaffected, unemotional, unmoved, unresponsive, unimpressionable, unsusceptible. [*Compare* **apathetic, callous.**] —*See also* **cool, frigid, unconscious.**

cold *noun.* Lack of warmth ▶ chill, chilliness, coldness, coolness, frigidity, frigidness, frostiness, frozenness, iciness, nip, wintriness.

✚ **CORE SYNONYMS:** *cold, arctic, chilly, cool, frigid, frosty, gelid, glacial, icy.* These adjectives mean marked by a low or an extremely low temperature: *cold air; an arctic climate; a chilly day; cool water; a frigid room; a frosty morning; gelid seas; glacial winds; icy hands.*

◀ **ANTONYM:** *hot*

---

cold-blooded *adjective.* —*See* **callous, cold** (2).
cold feet *noun.* —*See* **fear.**
cold-hearted *adjective.* —*See* **callous.**
coldness *noun.* —*See* **cold, inhospitality.**
coldshoulder *verb.* —*See* **snub.**
cold shoulder *noun.* —*See* **snub.**
collaborate *verb.* —*See* **cooperate.**
collaboration *noun.* —*See* **cooperation.**
collaborative *adjective.* —*See* **cooperative.**
collapse *verb.* **1.** To suddenly lose all health or strength ▶ break (down), cave in, crack, drop, give out, succumb. *Informal:* crack up. *Slang:* conk out. ***Idiom:*** give way. [*Compare* **fade, faint, tire.**] **2.** To undergo sudden financial failure ▶ crash, fail, go under. *Informal:* fold. ***Idioms:*** go bankrupt, go belly up, go broke, go bust, go down the tubes, go on the rocks, go to the wall. [*Compare* **fail, ruin.**] **3.** To undergo capture, defeat, or ruin ▶ fall, go down, go under, topple. [*Compare* **succumb, surrender.**] —*See also* **break** (3), **buckle.**
collapse *noun.* **1.** A sudden sharp decline in mental, emotional, or physical health ▶ breakdown. *Informal:* crackup. [*Compare* **infirmity.**] **2.** An abrupt disastrous failure ▶ breakdown, catastrophe, crash, debacle, disaster, smash, smashup, wreck. [*Compare* **failure.**] **3.** A disastrous defeat or ruin ▶ fall, downfall, waterloo. [*Compare* **defeat.**] —*See also* **breach** (2).
collar *noun.* —*See* **arrest, fastener.**
collar *verb.* —*See* **arrest.**
collate *verb.* —*See* **compare.**
collateral *adjective.* Lying in the same plane and not intersecting ▶ parallel. ***Idiom:*** side by side. —*See also* **auxiliary** (1), **minor** (1).
collateral *noun.* —*See* **pawn**[1].
collateralize *verb.* —*See* **pawn**[1].
collation *noun.* —*See* **contrast, refreshment.**
colleague *noun.* —*See* **associate** (1), **peer**[2].
collect[1] *verb.* —*See* **accumulate, assemble, compose** (4).
collect[2] *noun.* —*See* **prayer**[1] (2).
collected *adjective.* —*See* **calm.**
collectedness *noun.* —*See* **balance** (2).
collectible *adjective.* —*See* **due** (1).
collection *noun.* —*See* **accumulation** (1), **group.**
collective *adjective.* —*See* **cooperative.**
collide *verb.* To come together with force ▶ bump, crash, knock, hit, impact, run into, slam, strike. [*Compare* **crash.**] —*See also* **conflict, contend.**
collision *noun.* A violent forcible contact ▶ bump, concussion, crash, foul, hit, impact, jar, jolt, knock, percussion, shock, smash. [*Compare* **crash, slam.**]

✚ **CORE SYNONYMS:** *collision, concussion, crash, impact, jar, jolt, shock.* These nouns denote violent forcible contact between two or more things: *the midair collision of two light planes; the concussion caused by an explosion; a crash involving two cars; the impact of a sledgehammer on pilings; felt repeated jars as the train ground to a halt; a series of jolts as the baby carriage rolled down the steps; experienced the physical shock of a sudden fall.*

---

collocate *verb.* —*See* **arrange** (1).
collocation *noun.* —*See* **expression** (3).
colloquial *adjective.* —*See* **conversational.**

colloquium *noun.* —*See* **conference** (1).
colloquy *noun.* —*See* **conversation.**
collude *verb.* —*See* **plot** (2).
collusion *noun.* —*See* **plot** (2).
colonist *or* **colonial** *noun.* —*See* **settler.**
colonize *verb.* —*See* **occupy** (2).
colonizer *noun.* —*See* **settler.**
colony *noun.* —*See* **possession.**
colophon *noun.* —*See* **mark** (1).
color *noun.* **1.** That aspect of things that is caused by differing qualities of the light reflected or emitted by them ▶ cast, hue, shade, tinge, tinct, tint, tone, undertone, wash. **2.** Something that imparts color ▶ colorant, coloring, dye, dyestuff, paint, pigment, stain, tincture. [*Compare* **finish.**] **3.** Skin tone, especially of the face ▶ coloring, complexion. **4.** A fresh rosy complexion ▶ bloom, blush, flush, glow. —*See also* **verisimilitude.**
color *verb.* **1.** To impart color to ▶ dye, emblazon, imbue, pigment, stain, tincture, tinge, tint, wash. [*Compare* **finish.**] **2.** To give a deceptively attractive appearance to ▶ gild, gloss (over), gloze (over), overlay, sugarcoat, varnish, veneer, whitewash. ***Idioms:*** paper over, put a good face on. [*Compare* **disguise, extenuate.**] —*See also* **blush, distort.**
colorant *noun.* —*See* **color** (2).
colorfast *adjective.* Retaining original color ▶ fast, indelible.
colorful *adjective.* **1.** Full of color ▶ bright, deep, fluorescent, gay, rich, vibrant, vivid. [*Compare* **bright.**] **2.** Evoking strong mental images through distinctiveness ▶ graphic, picturesque, striking, vivid. —*See also* **descriptive, multicolored.**
coloring *noun.* Skin tone, especially of the face ▶ color, complexion. [*Compare* **bloom.**] —*See also* **color** (2).
colorless *adjective.* Without definite or distinctive characteristics ▶ bland, indistinctive, neutral. [*Compare* **boring.**] —*See also* **dull** (1), **pale** (1).
colorlessness *noun.* —*See* **dullness.**
colors *noun.* —*See* **flag**[1].
colossal *adjective.* —*See* **enormous.**
coltish *adjective.* —*See* **lively.**
column *noun.* A sturdy vertical structural support ▶ pier, pilaster, pillar, post, shaft, stud. [*Compare* **beam, support.**] —*See also* **line.**
columnist *noun.* —*See* **press.**
comatose *adjective.* —*See* **unconscious.**
comb *verb.* —*See* **scour**[2].
combat *verb.* —*See* **contend, oppose.**
combat *noun.* —*See* **battle, opposition** (1).
combatant *noun.* One who engages in a combat or struggle ▶ belligerent, fighter, soldier, warrior. [*Compare* **aggressor, soldier.**]
combatant *adjective.* —*See* **belligerent.**
combative *adjective.* —*See* **aggressive, argumentative.**
combativeness *noun.* —*See* **aggression, fight** (2).
combination *noun.* The result of combining ▶ brew, composite, compound, conjugation, entente, hybrid, incorporation, merger, unification, union, unity. [*Compare* **assortment, mixture.**] —*See also* **alliance, association** (1).
combine *verb.* **1.** To bring or come together into a united whole ▶ articulate, coalesce, compound, concrete, conjoin, conjugate, connect, consolidate, couple, integrate, join, link, marry, meld, unify, unite, wed, yoke. [*Compare* **mix, harmonize.**] **2.** To make a part of a united whole ▶ embody, incorporate, integrate. —*See also* **associate** (1), **band**[2], **cooperate.**
combine *noun.* —*See* **alliance.**

✚ **CORE SYNONYMS:** *combine, join, unite, link, connect.* These verbs mean to bring or come together into a united whole. *Combine* suggests the mixing or merging of components, often for a specific purpose: *The cook combined various ingredients. "When bad men* *combine, the good must associate"* (Edmund Burke). *Join* applies to the physical contact or union of at least two separate things and to the coming together of persons, as into a group: *The children joined hands. The two armies joined together to face a common enemy. "Join the union, girls, and together say* Equal Pay for Equal Work" (Susan B. Anthony). *Unite* stresses the coherence or oneness of the persons or things joined: *The volunteers united to prevent their town from flooding. The strike united the oppressed workers. Link* and *connect* imply a firm attachment in which individual components nevertheless retain their identities: *The study linked the high crime rate to unemployment. The reporter connected the police chief to the scandal.*

---

combined *adjective.* —*See* **cooperative, impure** (2).

combust *verb.* —*See* **burn** (2).

come *verb.* To have as one's home or place of origin ▶ hail, originate. [*Compare* **descend, stem.**] —*See also* **advance** (2), **amount, arrive** (1), **become** (1), **happen** (1), **stem.**

come across *verb.* —*See* **contribute** (1), **encounter** (1).

come around *or* **round** *verb.* —*See* **recover** (2), **visit.**

come back *verb.* —*See* **return** (1).

come between *verb.* —*See* **estrange.**

come by *verb.* —*See* **get** (1), **visit.**

come in *verb.* To complete a race or competition in a specified position ▶ finish, place, run. —*See also* **enter** (1).

come into *verb.* To receive from one who has died ▶ inherit. ***Idioms:*** be (*or* fall) heir to.

come on *verb.* —*See* **encounter** (1).

come off *verb.* —*See* **succeed** (2).

come out *verb.* **1.** To be made public ▶ break, get out, out, transpire. *Informal:* leak (out). ***Idioms:*** come out of the closet, come to light. [*Compare* **air, announce.**] **2.** To make one's formal entry, as into society ▶ debut. ***Idiom:*** make one's bow. —*See also* **appear** (1).

come over *verb.* —*See* **visit.**

come through *verb.* —*See* **survive** (1).

come to *verb.* —*See* **accomplish, strike** (2).

come together *verb.* —*See* **band**[2].

comeback *noun.* A return to former prosperity or status ▶ recovery, reestablishment, restoration. [*Compare* **renewal, revival.**] —*See also* **answer** (1).

comedian *noun.* —*See* **joker.**

comedic *adjective.* —*See* **funny** (1).

comedown *noun.* —*See* **descent.**

comedy *noun.* —*See* **humor.**

come-hither *adjective.* —*See* **seductive.**

comely *adjective.* —*See* **appropriate, beautiful.**

come-on *noun.* —*See* **lure** (1).

comer *noun.* **1.** One that arrives ▶ arrival, newcomer, visitor. [*Compare* **addition, company.**] **2.** One showing much promise ▶ candidate, hopeful, prospect, rising star, up-and-comer.

comestible *adjective.* Fit to be eaten ▶ eatable, edible, esculent, palatable.

comestibles *noun.* —*See* **food.**

comeuppance *noun.* —*See* **due.**

comfort *verb.* To give support in time of grief or pain ▶ condole, console, reassure, solace, soothe, succor. [*Compare* **encourage, feel, help, relieve.**]

comfort *noun.* A consoling in time of grief or pain ▶ consolation, reassurance, solace, succor. [*Compare* **help, pity.**] —*See also* **ease** (1), **prosperity** (2).

✚ **CORE SYNONYMS:** *comfort, console, reassure, solace.* These verbs mean to give support in time of grief or pain: *comforted the distressed child; consoling a recent widow; reassured them that everything would be all right; solaced myself with a hot cup of coffee.*

---

comfortable *adjective.* Affording pleasurable ease ▶ cozy, easeful, easy, restful, snug, soothing. *Informal:* comfy, cushy, homey, soft. —*See also* **prosperous, sufficient.**

✚ **CORE SYNONYMS:** *comfortable, cozy, snug, restful.* These adjectives mean affording pleasurable ease. *Comfortable* implies the absence of sources of pain or distress: *It's important to wear comfortable shoes on the hike.* The word may also suggest peace of mind: *I felt comfortable with the decision. Cozy* suggests homey and reassuring ease: *She sat in a cozy nook near the fire. Snug* brings to mind the image of a warm, secure, compact shelter: *The children were snug in their beds. Restful* suggests a quiet conducive to tranquillity: *He spent a restful hour reading.*

◀ **ANTONYM:** *uncomfortable*

comfortless *adjective.* —*See* **gloomy, uncomfortable.**

comforts *noun.* —*See* **amenities** (1).

comfy *adjective.* —*See* **comfortable.**

comic *adjective.* —*See* **funny** (1).

comic *noun.* —*See* **joker.**

comical *adjective.* —*See* **funny** (1).

comicalness *noun.* —*See* **humor.**

coming *adjective.* **1.** In the relatively near future ▶ approaching, due, forthcoming, upcoming. ***Idioms:*** around the corner, on the horizon. [*Compare* **close, imminent.**] **2.** Showing great promise ▶ promising, up-and-coming. ***Idiom:*** on the way up. [*Compare* **encouraging.**] —*See also* **following** (1), **future.**

coming *noun.* **1.** The act of arriving ▶ advent, arrival, appearance. [*Compare* **entrance.**] **2.** The act or fact of coming near ▶ approach, convergence, imminence, nearness. [*Compare* **advance, appearance.**]

coming-out *noun.* The instance or occasion of being presented for the first time to society ▶ debut, presentation.

command *verb.* **1.** To give orders to ▶ adjure, bid, call, charge, dictate, direct, enjoin, instruct, order, summon, tell. ***Idioms:*** call the shots, say the word. [*Compare* **boss, govern.**] **2.** To have at one's disposal ▶ boast, enjoy, have, hold, own, possess. ***Idiom:*** have at the ready. —*See also* **dominate** (1), **dominate** (2).

command *noun.* **1.** An order ▶ behest, bidding, charge, commandment, dictate, dictation, direction, directive, fiat, imperative, injunction, instructions, mandate, order, word, writ. [*Compare* **law, ruling.**] **2.** The capacity to lead others ▶ lead, leadership. —*See also* **ability** (1), **authority, dominance, domination, government** (1).

commandeer *verb.* —*See* **seize** (1).

commander *noun.* The person in charge of a ship ▶ captain, shipmaster, skipper. —*See also* **chief.**

commanding *adjective.* Exercising authority ▶ authoritative, dominant, lordly, masterful. [*Compare* **administrative.**] —*See also* **dominant** (1), **noticeable.**

commandment *noun.* —*See* **command** (1).

command post *noun.* —*See* **base**[1] (1).

comme il faut *adjective.* —*See* **appropriate.**

commemorate *verb.* **1.** To honor or keep alive the memory of ▶ memorialize. [*Compare* **immortalize.**] **2.** To mark a day or an event with ceremonies of respect, festivity, or rejoicing ▶ celebrate, keep, observe, solemnize. [*Compare* **sanctify.**]

commemoration *noun.* Something, as a structure or custom, serving to honor or keep alive a memory ▶ memorial, monument, remembrance. [*Compare* **testimonial.**] —*See also* **celebration** (2).

commemorative *adjective.* Serving to honor or keep alive a memory ▶ memorial, monumental.

commence *verb.* —*See* **begin, start** (1).

commencement *noun.* —*See* **beginning, birth** (2).

commend *verb.* To pay a compliment to ▶ compliment, congratulate, felicitate, praise. ***Idioms:*** pay tribute to, raise a glass to, take off one's hat to. [*Compare* **honor.**] *—See also* **entrust** (1), **praise** (1).

commendable *adjective.* *—See* **admirable.**

commendation *noun.* *—See* **compliment, distinction** (2), **praise** (1).

commendatory *adjective.* *—See* **complimentary** (1).

commensurate *or* **commensurable** *adjective.* *—See* **proportional** (1).

comment *noun.* An expression of fact or opinion ▶ aside, editorial, note, obiter dictum, observation, reflection, remark, word. [*Compare* **expression.**] *—See also* **commentary.**

comment *verb.* To state facts, opinions, or explanations ▶ commentate, editorialize, note, observe, opine, reflect, remark. [*Compare* **say.**]

✚ **CORE SYNONYMS:** *comment, observation, remark.* These nouns denote an expression of fact or opinion: *made an unpleasant comment about my friend; a casual observation about the movie; an offensive personal remark.*

---

commentaries *noun.* *—See* **memoir.**

commentary *noun.* Critical explanation or analysis ▶ annotation, comment, criticism, critique, exposition, exegesis, interpretation, note, notice, review. [*Compare* **explanation.**]

commentate *verb.* *—See* **comment.**

commentator *noun.* *—See* **critic** (1), **press.**

commerce *noun.* *—See* **business** (1).

commingle *verb.* *—See* **mix** (1).

comminute *verb.* *—See* **crush** (2).

commiserate *verb.* To experience or express compassion ▶ ache, condole, feel, sympathize. ***Idioms:*** be (*or* feel) sorry, have one's heart ache (*or* bleed) for someone, have one's heart go out to someone. [*Compare* **comfort, pity.**]

commiseration *noun.* *—See* **pity** (1).

commiserative *adjective.* *—See* **sympathetic.**

commission *noun.* *—See* **license** (3), **mission** (1).

commission *verb.* *—See* **authorize.**

commit *verb.* **1.** To be responsible for or guilty of an error or crime ▶ carry out, do, perpetrate. *Informal:* pull off. [*Compare* **perform.**] **2.** To be morally bound to do ▶ bind, charge, obligate, oblige, pledge. ***Idiom:*** be duty bound. [*Compare* **force, pledge.**] **3.** To place officially in confinement ▶ consign, institutionalize. *Informal:* send up. [*Compare* **imprison.**] *—See also* **entrust** (1), **pledge** (2).

commitment *noun.* *—See* **duty** (1), **engagement** (1), **promise** (1).

committed *adjective.* *—See* **faithful, obliged** (2).

commix *verb.* *—See* **mix** (1).

commixture *noun.* *—See* **mixture.**

commodious *adjective.* Having plenty of room ▶ ample, capacious, roomy, spacious. [*Compare* **big, broad.**]

commodity *noun.* *—See* **good** (2).

common *adjective.* **1.** Occurring or encountered regularly ▶ accustomed, average, commonplace, customary, daily, everyday, familiar, frequent, general, habitual, normal, ordinary, regular, routine, typical, usual, widespread, wonted. [*Compare* **intermittent, ordinary, prevailing.**] **2.** Belonging to, shared by, or applicable to all alike ▶ communal, conjoint, cooperative, general, joint, mutual, public, shared. [*Compare* **open.**] *—See also* **acceptable** (2), **bad** (1), **coarse** (1), **general** (1), **lowly** (1), **notorious, ordinary.**

common *noun.* A tract of land set aside for public use ▶ green, lawn, park, plaza, square. [*Compare* **reservation.**]

✚ **CORE SYNONYMS:** *common, ordinary, familiar.* These adjectives describe what is regularly or frequently encountered. *Common* applies to what takes place often, is widely used, or is well known: *The botanist studied the common dandelion.* The term also implies coarseness or a lack of distinction: *My wallet was stolen by a common thief. Ordinary* describes something usual that is indistinguishable from others, sometimes derogatorily: *A ballpoint pen is adequate for ordinary purposes. The critic gave the ordinary performance a mediocre review. Familiar* applies to what is well known or quickly recognized: *Most children can recite familiar nursery rhymes.*

---

commonalty *or* **commonality** *or* **commoners** *noun.* The common people ▶ commons, crowd, hoi polloi, masses, mob, multitude, plebs, plebeians, populace, proletariat, public, rank and file, ruck, third estate. ***Idioms:*** the great unwashed, men (*or* women) in the street. [*Compare* **riffraff.**]

commonly *adverb.* —*See* **usually.**

commonplace *adjective.* —*See* **common** (1), **ordinary, trite.**

commonplace *noun.* —*See* **cliché, usual.**

commons *noun.* —*See* **commonalty.**

common sense *noun.* The ability to make sensible decisions ▶ judgment, mother wit, reason, sense, wisdom. *Informal:* gumption, horse sense. [*Compare* **discernment, prudence.**]

commonsensical *or* **commonsensible** *adjective.* —*See* **sensible.**

commotion *noun.* —*See* **agitation** (1), **agitation** (3), **disorder** (2).

communal *adjective.* —*See* **common** (2), **popular.**

communalize *verb.* To place under government or group ownership or control ▶ nationalize, socialize.

communicable *adjective.* —*See* **contagious, outgoing.**

communicate *verb.* **1.** To make known ▶ break, carry, convey, disclose, divulge, get across, impart, pass, report, reveal, tell, transmit. [*Compare* **air, announce, inform.**] **2.** To spread a disease to others ▶ carry, convey, give, infect, pass, spread, transfer, transmit. —*See also* **express** (1), **relate** (2), **say.**

communication *noun.* **1.** The exchange of ideas by writing, speech, or signals ▶ communion, conference, conversation, correspondence, discussion, exchange, intercommunication, interaction, intercourse, interface. [*Compare* **conversation, deliberation.**] **2.** A situation allowing exchange of ideas or messages ▶ contact, correspondence, intercommunication, touch. —*See also* **announcement, message.**

communicative *adjective.* —*See* **conversational, outgoing.**

communion *noun.* —*See* **communication** (1).

communiqué *noun.* —*See* **message.**

community *noun.* —*See* **neighborhood** (1), **public** (1), **village.**

commutation *noun.* —*See* **change** (2).

commutative *adjective.* —*See* **changeable** (1).

commute *verb.* —*See* **change** (3).

comp *noun. Informal* A free ticket entitling one to transportation or admission ▶ pass. *Slang:* freebie.

compact[1] *adjective.* —*See* **little, pithy, stocky, thick** (2).

compact *verb.* —*See* **constrict** (1), **squeeze** (1).

compact[2] *noun.* —*See* **agreement** (1).

compactness *noun.* —*See* **thickness.**

companion *noun.* —*See* **associate** (2), **concomitant, mate.**

companion *verb.* —*See* **accompany.**

companionable *adjective.* —*See* **amiable, social.**

companionless *adjective.* —*See* **solitary.**

companionship *noun.* —*See* **company** (3), **friendship.**

company *noun.* **1.** A commercial organization ▶ business, concern, conglomerate, corporation, enterprise, establishment, firm, house, monopoly, multinational, partnership. *Informal:* outfit. [*Compare* **alliance.**] **2.** A person or persons visiting one ▶ caller, guest, visitant, visitor. **3.** A pleasant association among people ▶ brotherhood, camaraderie, companionship, comradeship, fellowship, sisterhood, society. [*Compare* **friendship.**] —*See also* **assembly, band**[2]**.**

company *verb.* —*See* **accompany.**

comparable *adjective.* Estimated by comparison ▶ comparative, relative. —*See also* **like**[2]**.**

comparative *adjective.* Estimated by comparison ▶ comparable, relative.

compare *verb.* To examine in order to note the similarities and differences of ▶ balance, collate, contrast, counterpoint, counterpose, juxtapose, weigh. —*See also* **equal** (1), **liken.**

comparison *noun.* —*See* **contrast, likeness** (1).

compass *noun.* The ability or power to seize or attain ▶ capacity, grasp, range, reach, scope. [*Compare* **influence.**] —*See also* **circumference, range** (1).

compass *verb.* —*See* **know** (1), **surround, understand** (1).

compassion *noun.* —*See* **pity** (1).

compassionate *adjective.* —*See* **humanitarian, sympathetic.**

compassionless *adjective.* —*See* **callous.**

compatible *adjective.* —*See* **agreeable.**

compatriot *noun.* A person who is from one's own country ▶ countryman, countrywoman, fellow citizen, kinsman, kinswoman. —*See also* **associate** (1).

compeer *noun.* —*See* **peer**[2]**.**

compel *verb.* —*See* **force** (1).

compellation *noun.* —*See* **name** (1).

compelled *adjective.* —*See* **obliged** (2).

compelling *adjective.* —*See* **convincing, urgent** (1).

compendious *adjective.* —*See* **brief.**

compensate *verb.* To give compensation to ▶ indemnify, pay, recompense, recoup, redress, reimburse, remit, remunerate, reward, repay, requite. [*Compare* **settle.**] —*See also* **balance** (2), **cancel** (2).

compensation *noun.* Something to make up for loss or damage ▶ amends, damages, indemnification, indemnity, offset, payment, quittance, recompense, recoupment, redress, reimbursement, remuneration, reparation, repayment, requital, restitution, reward, satisfaction, settlement, setoff. —*See also* **due, wage.**

✚ **CORE SYNONYMS:** *compensation, reparation, redress, amends, restitution, indemnity.* These nouns refer to something given to make up for loss, suffering, or damage. *Compensation* is the most general term: *I received a free ticket to another concert in compensation for the concert that had been canceled. Reparation* implies recompense given to one who has suffered at the hands of another: *"reparation for our rights at home, and security against the like future violations"* (William Pitt). *Redress* involves setting an injustice right; the term may imply retaliation or punishment: *"There is no grievance that is a fit object of redress by mob law"* (Abraham Lincoln). *Amends* usually implies the giving of satisfaction for a minor grievance or lesser injury: *How can I make amends for losing my temper? Restitution* is the restoration of something taken illegally: *"He attempted to enforce the restitution of the Roman lands and cities"* (George P.R. James). *Indemnity* implies repayment or reimbursement: *Homeowners demanded indemnity for the damages caused by the riot.*

---

compensatory *or* **compensative** *adjective.* Affording compensation ▶ reimbursable, remunerative.

compete *verb.* To strive against others for victory ▶ contend, contest, bid, emulate, play, race, rival, vie. ***Idioms:*** give a run for one's money, take on. [*Compare* **contend.**]

✚ **CORE SYNONYMS:** *compete, contest, vie.* These verbs mean to seek to strive against others for victory: *Local hardware stores can't compete with discount outlets. I contested with other bidders for the antique. The top three students vied for the title of valedictorian.*

---

competence *or* **competency** *noun.* —*See* **ability** (2).

competent *adjective.* —*See* **able, sufficient.**

competition *noun.* **1.** A vying with others for victory or supremacy ▶ battle, contention, contest, corrivalry, race, rivalry, strife, striving, struggle, tug of war, war, warfare. [*Compare* **conflict.**] **2.** A test of skill or ability ▶ bout, contest, event, fight, game, match, meet, tournament, tourney, trial. [*Compare* **test, tilt.**] —*See also* **competitor.**

competitive *adjective.* Given to competition ▶ cutthroat, dog-eat-dog, emulous, rivalrous. [*Compare* **argumentative.**]

competitor *noun.* One that competes ▶ challenger, competition, contender, contestant, corrival, emulator, opponent, rival. [*Compare* **opponent.**]

complain *verb.* To express feelings of pain, dissatisfaction, or resentment ▶ carp, fuss, grouch, grumble, grump, grunt, moan, mutter, murmur, nag, repine, snivel, whimper, whine. *Informal:* crab, gripe, grouse, holler, kick, squawk, yammer. *Slang:* beef, bellyache, bitch, kvetch. ***Idioms:*** bitch and moan, have a bone to pick, kick up a fuss (*or* row), make a fuss (*or* stink). [*Compare* **object, quibble.**]

complainant *noun.* One that makes a formal complaint, especially in court ▶ accuser, claimant, plaintiff.

complainer *noun.* —*See* **grouch.**

complaint *noun.* An expression of pain or dissatisfaction ▶ carp, fuss, grievance, grouch, grumble, grunt, murmur, mutter, squawk, whimper, whine. *Informal:* gripe, grouse, yammer. *Slang:* beef, bellyache, bitch, kick, kvetch, stink. ***Idiom:*** bone to pick. —*See also* **disease, objection, objection, sickness.**

complaisance *noun.* —*See* **obedience.**

complaisant *adjective.* —*See* **obedient, obliging.**

complement *noun.* —*See* **enhancement, mate.**

complement *verb.* —*See* **perfect, supplement.**

complementary *or* **complemental** *adjective.* Supplying mutual needs or offsetting mutual lacks ▶ correlative, interdependent, interrelated, mutual, reciprocal, supplemental, symbiotic. [*Compare* **agreeable.**]

complete *adjective.* **1.** Including every constituent or individual ▶ all, entire, full, gross, intact, integral, perfect, round, total, whole. **2.** Not shortened by omissions ▶ full-length, unabbreviated, unabridged, uncensored, uncut, unedited, unexpurgated. [*Compare* **continual.**] **3.** Having reached completion ▶ closed, concluded, consummated, done, ended, executed, finished, over, performed, terminated, through. —*See also* **thorough, utter**[2]**.**

complete *verb.* —*See* **conclude, perfect, supplement.**

✚ **CORE SYNONYMS:** *complete, whole, all, entire, gross, total.* These adjectives mean including every constituent or individual: *the complete vacation package included airfare, hotel, and car rental; a whole town devastated by an earthquake; all the class going on a field trip; entire shipments lost by the distributor; gross income; the total cost.*

◀ **ANTONYM:** *partial*

---

completely *adverb.* **1.** To the fullest extent ▶ absolutely, all, altogether, dead, downright, entirely, flat, fully, just, perfectly, purely, quite, thoroughly, totally, utterly, well, wholly. *Informal:* clean, clear. ***Idioms:*** hook, line, and sinker, in toto, root and branch, through and through, to the nth degree. [*Compare*

absolutely, considerably, really, unusually, very.] **2.** In a painstakingly complete manner ▶ comprehensively, exhaustively, intensively, thoroughly. ***Idioms:*** backwards and forwards, down to the ground, from soup to nuts, in and out, up and down.

completeness *noun.* The state of being entirely whole ▶ entirety, fullness, integrity, oneness, totality, wholeness.

completion *noun.* —*See* **end** (1), **fulfillment** (1).

complex *adjective.* **1.** Difficult to understand because of intricacy ▶ advanced, baffling, baroque, bewildering, byzantine, complicated, confounding, confusing, convoluted, crabbed, daedal, Daedalian, difficult, elaborate, entangled, inextricable, intricate, involute, involved, knotty, labyrinthine, mazy, mystifying, perplexing, puzzling, sophisticated, tangled, tortuous. [*Compare* **ambiguous, incomprehensible, mysterious.**] **2.** Consisting of two or more parts ▶ composite, compound, manifold, multiple, multiplex. [*Compare* **various.**]

complex *noun.* **1.** An entity composed of interconnected parts ▶ conglomerate, group, network, syndrome, system, tissue, web. [*Compare* **mixture.**] **2.** An exaggerated concern ▶ anxiety, neurosis, phobia. *Informal:* hang-up. [*Compare* **anxiety, obsession.**] —*See also* **base**[1] (1).

✚ **CORE SYNONYMS:** *complex, complicated, intricate, involved, tangled, knotty.* These adjectives mean difficult to understand because of intricacy. *Complex* implies a combination of many associated parts: *The composer transformed a simple folk tune into a complex set of variations. Complicated* stresses elaborate relationship of parts: *The party's complicated platform confused many voters. Intricate* refers to a pattern of intertwining parts that is difficult to follow or analyze: "*No one could soar into a more intricate labyrinth of refined phraseology*" (Anthony Trollope). *Involved* stresses confusion arising from the commingling of parts and the consequent difficulty of separating them: *The movie's plot was criticized as being too involved. Tangled* strongly suggests the random twisting of many parts: "*Oh, what a tangled web we weave,/When first we practice to deceive!*" (Sir Walter Scott). *Knotty* stresses intellectual complexity leading to difficulty of solution or comprehension: *Even the professor couldn't clarify the knotty point.*

---

complexion *noun.* Skin tone, especially of the face ▶ color, coloring. [*Compare* **bloom, color.**] —*See also* **character** (1), **disposition.**

complexity *noun.* Something complex ▶ bewilderment, complication, elaborateness, entanglement, intricacy, perplexity. [*Compare* **tangle.**]

compliance *or* **compliancy** *noun.* An act of willingly carrying out the wishes of others ▶ obedience, observance. —*See also* **obedience.**

compliant *adjective.* —*See* **obedient.**

complicate *verb.* To make complex, intricate, or perplexing ▶ embarrass, embroil, entangle, involve, knot, obfuscate, perplex, ravel, snarl, tangle, vex. [*Compare* **confuse.**]

complicated *adjective.* —*See* **complex** (1), **difficult** (1), **elaborate.**

complication *noun.* —*See* **complexity, difficulty.**

compliment *noun.* An expression of admiration or congratulation ▶ accolade, commendation, congratulations, felicitations, praise, tribute. *Informal:* congrats. ***Idiom:*** pat on the back. —*See also* **praise** (1).

compliment *verb.* To pay a compliment to ▶ commend, congratulate, felicitate, praise. ***Idioms:*** pay tribute to, raise a glass to, take off one's hat to.

[*Compare* **honor.**] —*See also* **drink** (4), **praise** (1).

complimentary *adjective.* **1.** Serving to compliment ▶ acclamatory, approbatory, commendatory, congratulatory, encomiastic, eulogistic, laudatory. **2.** Costing nothing ▶ free, gratis, gratuitous. ***Idioms:*** as a freebie, for free, for nothing, on the house.

comply *verb.* —*See* **follow** (4).

component *noun.* —*See* **part** (1).

component *adjective.* —*See* **built-in.**

comport *verb.* —*See* **act** (1), **agree** (1).

comportment *noun.* —*See* **behavior** (1).

compose *verb.* **1.** To form by artistic effort ▶ create, design, draft, indite, orchestrate, pen, produce, score, write. [*Compare* **invent.**] **2.** To devise and set down ▶ draft, draw up, formulate, frame. **3.** To be the constituent parts of ▶ form, make up. [*Compare* **contain.**] **4.** To bring one's emotions under control ▶ calm down, collect (oneself), contain (oneself), control (oneself), cool (down), simmer down. *Slang:* chill (out). ***Idiom:*** cool it. [*Compare* **calm.**] —*See also* **make, publish** (2).

composed *adjective.* —*See* **calm.**

composite *adjective.* —*See* **complex** (2).

composite *noun.* —*See* **combination, mixture.**

composition *noun.* **1.** Something that is the result of creative effort ▶ creation, invention, opus, output, piece, production, work, writing. [*Compare* **invention, masterpiece.**] **2.** A relatively brief discourse written especially as an exercise ▶ essay, paper, theme. —*See also* **compromise.**

compos mentis *adjective.* Mentally healthy ▶ lucid, normal, rational, sane. ***Idioms:*** all there, in one's right mind, of sound mind. [*Compare* **healthy.**]

composure *noun.* —*See* **balance** (2).

compound *verb.* —*See* **combine** (1).

compound *adjective.* —*See* **complex** (2).

compound *noun.* —*See* **combination.**

comprehend *verb.* —*See* **contain** (1), **know** (1), **understand** (1).

comprehensibility *noun.* —*See* **clarity.**

comprehensible *adjective.* —*See* **understandable.**

comprehension *noun.* Intellectual hold ▶ apprehension, grasp, grip, hold, understanding. [*Compare* **knowledge.**]

comprehensive *adjective.* —*See* **detailed, general** (2).

comprehensively *adverb.* —*See* **completely** (2).

compress *verb.* —*See* **constrict** (1), **squeeze** (1).

compressed *adjective.* —*See* **thick** (2).

compression *noun.* —*See* **constriction.**

comprise *verb.* —*See* **contain** (1).

compromise *noun.* A settlement of differences through mutual concession ▶ accommodation, arbitration, arrangement, composition, concession, give-and-take, mediation, settlement, trade-off. [*Compare* **agreement.**]

compromise *verb.* To make a concession ▶ accommodate, arrange, concede, settle. ***Idioms:*** come to an understanding, give and take, go fifty-fifty, make a deal, meet someone halfway, steer a middle course, strike a bargain. [*Compare* **agree, settle.**] —*See also* **endanger.**

compulsion *noun.* —*See* **force** (1), **obsession.**

compulsory *adjective.* —*See* **required.**

compunction *noun.* —*See* **penitence, qualm.**

compunctious *adjective.* —*See* **sorry.**

computation *noun.* **1.** The act, process, or result of calculating ▶ calculation, cast, figuring, reckoning. **2.** Arithmetic calculations ▶ arithmetic, figures, numbers. [*Compare* **addition.**]

compute *verb.* —*See* **calculate.**

comrade *noun.* —*See* **associate** (2), **friend.**

comradeship *noun.* —*See* **company** (3), **friendship.**

con *verb.* To commit to memory ▶ learn, memorize. ***Idioms:*** learn by heart (*or* rote). [*Compare* **learn, remember.**] —*See also* **cheat** (1), **examine** (1).

con *noun.* —*See* **cheat** (1), **criminal.**

concatenation *noun.* —*See* **series.**

concave *adjective.* —*See* **hollow** (2).

concavity *noun.* —*See* **depression** (1).

conceal *verb.* To prevent something from being known ▶ camouflage, cloak, cover (up), enshroud, hide, hush (up), mask, obscure, screen, shroud, veil. ***Idioms:*** keep in the dark, keep under cover, keep under one's hat, keep under wraps. [*Compare* **disguise.**] —*See also* **block, hide**[1]**.**

concealed *adjective.* —*See* **hidden** (1), **ulterior** (1).

concealment *noun.* —*See* **secrecy.**

concede *verb.* To let have as a favor, prerogative, or privilege ▶ accord, award, give, grant, vouchsafe. [*Compare* **yield.**] —*See also* **acknowledge** (1), **compromise, surrender** (1).

conceit *noun.* —*See* **egotism, fancy.**

conceited *adjective.* —*See* **egotistic** (1).

conceivable *adjective.* Capable of being anticipated, considered, or imagined ▶ earthly, imaginable, likely, mortal, possible, thinkable. ***Idioms:*** humanly possible, within the bounds (*or* range *or* realm) of possibility. [*Compare* **possible.**]

conceivably *adverb.* —*See* **maybe.**

conceive *verb.* —*See* **believe** (3), **design** (1), **imagine, understand** (1).

concentrate *verb.* To direct toward a common center ▶ center, channel, concenter, converge, focalize, focus, hone in, zero in. [*Compare* **assemble.**] —*See also* **apply** (1).

concentrated *adjective.* **1.** Not diffused or dispersed ▶ exclusive, intensive, undivided, unswerving, whole. [*Compare* **thick.**] **2.** Having a high concentration of the distinguishing ingredient ▶ potent, stiff, strong. [*Compare* **straight.**] —*See also* **intense.**

concentration *noun.* —*See* **attention, intensity, junction.**

concept *noun.* —*See* **doctrine, idea.**

conception *noun.* —*See* **beginning, idea.**

conceptual *adjective.* —*See* **imaginary, theoretical** (1), **theoretical** (2).

conceptualization *noun.* —*See* **theory** (1), **thought.**

conceptualize *verb.* —*See* **think** (1).

concern *verb.* —*See* **apply** (2), **worry.**

concern *noun.* **1.** Something that concerns or involves one personally ▶ affair, business, interest, lookout. **2.** A cause of distress or anxiety ▶ care, stressor, trouble, worry. [*Compare* **anxiety, burden**[1]**.**] —*See also* **anxiety, company** (1), **consideration** (1), **curiosity** (1), **importance, qualm.**

concerned *adjective.* Having concern ▶ affected, connected, engaged, interested, involved. —*See also* **anxious, sympathetic.**

concernment *noun.* —*See* **curiosity** (1), **importance.**

concert *noun.* —*See* **agreement** (2), **cooperation, harmony** (1).

concert *verb.* —*See* **cooperate.**

concerted *adjective.* —*See* **cooperative.**

concertize *verb.* To make music ▶ perform, play, render.

concession *noun.* —*See* **acknowledgment** (1), **compromise.**

conciliate *verb.* To reestablish friendship between ▶ make up, reconcile, reunite. —*See also* **pacify.**

conciliation *noun.* A reestablishment of friendship or harmony ▶ rapprochement, reconcilement, reconciliation, settlement. [*Compare* **agreement, atonement, compromise.**]

conciliatory *adjective.* —*See* **peaceable.**

concise *adjective.* —*See* **brief.**

conclave *noun.* —*See* **assembly, convention.**

conclude *verb.* To bring or come to a natural or proper end ▶ close, complete, consummate, end, finish, play out, see through, terminate, wind up, wrap up. [*Compare* **abolish, stop.**] —*See also* **decide, infer, settle** (2), **settle** (1).

✚ **CORE SYNONYMS:** *conclude, complete, close, end, finish, terminate.* These verbs mean to bring or come to a natural or proper end. *Conclude, complete,* and *finish* suggest the final stage in an undertaking: *The author concluded the article by restating the major points. "Nothing worth doing is completed in our lifetime"* (Reinhold Niebuhr). *"Give us the tools, and we will finish the job"* (Winston S. Churchill). *Close* applies to the ending of something ongoing or continuing: *The band closed the concert with an encore. End* emphasizes finality: *We ended the meal with fruit and cheese. Terminate* suggests reaching an established limit: *The playing of the national anthem terminated the station's broadcast for the night.* It also indicates the dissolution of a formal arrangement: *The firm terminated my contract yesterday.*

concluded *adjective.* —*See* **complete** (3).

concluding *adjective.* —*See* **last**[1] (1).

conclusion *noun.* A position arrived at by reasoning from premises ▶ deduction, inference, judgment. [*Compare* **belief.**] —*See also* **decision** (1), **end** (1), **end** (2).

conclusive *adjective.* —*See* **authoritative** (1), **certain** (2), **decisive, definitive.**

conclusively *adverb.* In conclusion ▶ finally, last, lastly, ultimately. ***Idioms:*** at last, in the end. [*Compare* **ultimately.**]

concoct *verb.* —*See* **design** (1), **invent.**

concoction *noun.* —*See* **invention** (2).

concomitant *noun.* One that accompanies another ▶ accompaniment, accompanist, associate, attendant, companion. [*Compare* **associate.**]

concomitant *adjective.* —*See* **concurrent.**

concord *noun.* An identity or coincidence of interests, purposes, or sympathies among the members of a group ▶ oneness, solidarity, union, unity. [*Compare* **alliance, union.**] —*See also* **agreement** (2), **harmony** (1), **treaty.**

concordance *noun.* —*See* **agreement** (2).

concordant *adjective.* Having components pleasingly combined ▶ balanced, congruous, harmonious, symmetrical. [*Compare* **harmonious, pleasant.**] —*See also* **agreeable, unanimous.**

concordat *noun.* —*See* **treaty.**

concourse *noun.* —*See* **crowd, junction.**

concrete *adjective.* —*See* **physical, real** (1).

concrete *verb.* —*See* **combine** (1), **harden** (2).

concretize *verb.* —*See* **embody** (1).

concupiscence *noun.* —*See* **desire** (2).

concupiscent *adjective.* —*See* **lascivious.**

concur *verb.* To occur at the same time ▶ coincide, harmonize, synchronize. —*See also* **agree** (2), **assent, cooperate.**

concurrent *adjective.* Occurring or existing at the same time ▶ accompanying, attendant, attending, coexisting, coincident, concomitant, contemporary, contemporaneous, parallel, simultaneous, synchronic, synchronous. —*See also* **contemporary** (1).

✚ **CORE SYNONYMS:** *concurrent, contemporary, contemporaneous, simultaneous, synchronous, coincident, concomitant.* These adjectives mean occurring or existing at the same time. *Concurrent* implies parallelism in character or length of time: *The mass murderer was given three concurrent life sentences. Contemporary* is used more often of persons, *contemporaneous* of events and facts: *The composer Salieri was contemporary with Mozart. A rise in interest rates is often contemporaneous with an increase in inflation. Simultaneous* more narrowly specifies occurrence of events at the same time: *The activists organized simultaneous demonstrations in many major cities. Synchronous* refers to correspondence of events in time over a short period: *The dancers executed a series of synchronous movements. Coincident* applies to events occurring at the same time without implying a relationship: "*The resistance to the Pope's authority . . . is pretty nearly coincident with the rise of the Ottomans*" (John Henry Newman). *Concomitant* refers to coincidence in time of events so clearly related that one seems attendant on the other: *He is an adherent of Freud's theories and had a concomitant belief in the efficacy of psychoanalysis.*

---

concurrently *adverb.* At the same time ▶ simultaneously, synchronously, together. ***Idioms:*** all at once, all together. [*Compare* **together.**]

concussion *noun.* —*See* **collision.**

condemn *verb.* To pronounce judgment against ▶ convict, damn, doom, proscribe, sentence. ***Idioms:*** pass judgment (*or* sentence) on, seal someone's doom (*or* fate). [*Compare* **criticize, punish, slam.**] —*See also* **deplore** (1).

✚ **CORE SYNONYMS:** *condemn, damn, doom, sentence.* These verbs mean to pronounce judgment against one found to be guilty or undeserving: *condemned the dissident to hard labor; damned the murderer to everlasting misery; an attempt that was doomed to failure; sentenced the traitor to life in prison.*

---

condemnable *adjective.* —*See* **deplorable.**

condemnation *noun.* —*See* **criticism, disapproval, vituperation.**

condemned *adjective.* Sentenced to terrible, irrevocable punishment ▶ damned, doomed, fallen, fated, foredoomed, hellbound, lost, reprobate, sentenced. ***Idiom:*** gone to blazes.

condensation *noun.* Moisture accumulated on a surface through sweating or condensation ▶ lather, perspiration, sweat, transudation. —*See also* **synopsis.**

condense *verb.* To make thick or thicker, especially through evaporation or condensation ▶ inspissate, reduce, thicken. [*Compare* **coagulate.**] —*See also* **shorten.**

condescend *verb.* **1.** To bring oneself down to a level considered inappropriate to one's dignity ▶ deign, descend, lower, sink, stoop, vouchsafe. ***Idioms:*** come down a peg, slum it. **2.** To treat in a superciliously indulgent manner ▶ patronize. *Informal:* high-hat. ***Idioms:*** lord it over, speak (*or* talk) down to. [*Compare* **insult, snub.**]

✚ **CORE SYNONYMS:** *condescend, deign, stoop.* These verbs mean to bring oneself down to a level considered inappropriate to one's dignity: *won't condescend to acknowledge his rival's greeting; didn't even deign to reply; stooped to contemptible methods to realize their ambitions.*

---

condescension *or* **condescendence** *noun.* Superciliously indulgent treatment, especially of those considered inferior ▶ haughtiness, patronization, snobbery. *Informal:* snootiness. [*Compare* **arrogance.**]

condiment *noun.* —*See* **flavoring.**

condition *noun.* **1.** Manner of being or form of existence ▶ case, mode, situation, state, status. **2.** Something indispensable ▶ essential, must, necessary, necessity, need, precondition, prerequisite, requirement, requisite, sine qua non. ***Idiom:*** be-all and end-all. [*Compare* **element, standard.**] —*See also*

circumstance (2), place (1), provision, shape.
condition *verb.* —*See* **accustom.**

✤ **CORE SYNONYMS:** *condition, situation, state, status.* These nouns denote the manner of being or form of existence of a person or thing: *a jogger in healthy condition; a police officer responding to a dangerous situation; an old factory in a state of disrepair; the uncertain status of the peace negotiations.*

---

conditional *adjective.* Depending on or containing a condition or conditions ▶ conditioned, contingent, dependent, provisional, provisory, relative, specified, stipulated, subject, tentative. [*Compare* **qualified.**]

✤ **CORE SYNONYMS:** *conditional, contingent, dependent, relative, subject.* These adjectives mean determined or to be determined by something else: *conditional acceptance of the apology; assistance contingent on need; a water supply dependent on rainfall; the importance of a discovery as relative to its usefulness; promotion subject to merit.*

---

conditioned *adjective.* —*See* **accustomed** (1), **conditional, qualified.**
conditioning *noun.* —*See* **adaptation, practice.**
conditions *noun.* Existing surroundings that affect an activity ▶ circumstances, context, environment, estate, setting, surroundings. *Slang:* scene. [*Compare* **air, environment.**]
condolatory *adjective.* —*See* **sympathetic.**
condole *verb.* To experience or express compassion ▶ ache, commiserate, feel, sympathize. ***Idioms:*** be (*or* feel) sorry, have one's heart ache (*or* bleed) for someone, have one's heart go out to someone. [*Compare* **pity.**] —*See also* **comfort.**
condolence *noun.* —*See* **pity** (1).
condonable *adjective.* —*See* **pardonable.**
condonation *noun.* —*See* **forgiveness.**
condone *verb.* —*See* **forgive.**
conduce *verb.* —*See* **contribute** (2).
conducive *adjective.* Tending to contribute to a result ▶ contributive, contributory, helpful, participatory. [*Compare* **auxiliary.**]
conduct *verb.* **1.** To control the course of an activity ▶ carry on, control, direct, engineer, handle, manage, operate, run, steer. *Slang:* quarterback. [*Compare* **administer, maneuver.**] **2.** To engage in (a war or campaign, for example) ▶ carry on, carry out, wage. [*Compare* **oppose.**] **3.** To serve as a conduit ▶ carry, channel, convey, mediate, pass on, transfer, transmit. [*Compare* **carry, send.**] —*See also* **guide, lead.**
conduct *noun.* —*See* **behavior** (1), **management.**

✤ **CORE SYNONYMS:** *conduct, direct, manage, control, steer.* These verbs mean to control the course of an activity. *Conduct* can apply to the guidance, authority, and responsibility of a single person: *The chairperson conducted the hearing.* It can also refer to the coordinated actions of a group: *The elections were conducted fairly. Direct* stresses regulation to assure proper planning and implementation: *The seasoned politician directed a brilliant political campaign. Manage* suggests the manipulation of a person, a group, or, often, a complex organization: *It takes skill to manage a hotel. Control* stresses regulation through restraint and also connotes domination: *Our vice president controls the firm's personnel policies. Steer* suggests guidance that controls direction or course: *I deftly steered the conversation away from politics.*

---

conductor *noun.* —*See* **guide.**
confab *noun.* —*See* **conversation.**
confab *verb.* —*See* **converse**[1].
confabulate *verb.* —*See* **converse**[1].
confabulation *noun.* —*See* **conversation.**

confabulator *noun.* —*See* **conversationalist.**

confabulatory *adjective.* —*See* **conversational.**

confederacy *noun.* —*See* **alliance.**

confederate *noun.* —*See* **accessory, associate** (1).

confederate *verb.* —*See* **ally.**

confederation *noun.* —*See* **alliance, union** (1).

confer *verb.* **1.** To meet and exchange views to reach a decision ▶ advise, consult, debate, deliberate, negotiate, parley, talk. *Informal:* huddle, powwow. [*Compare* **converse, discuss.**] **2.** To give formally or officially ▶ accord, award, bestow, give (away), grant, hand out, impart, present.

conference *noun.* **1.** A meeting for the exchange of views ▶ colloquium, discussion, forum, panel, parley, roundtable, seminar, summit, symposium, workshop. *Informal:* powwow. *Slang:* rap session. **2.** A group of athletic teams that play each other ▶ association, circuit, division, league, loop. [*Compare* **union.**] —*See also* **assembly, communication** (1), **conferment, convention, deliberation** (1).

conferment *or* **conferral** *noun.* The act of conferring, as of an honor ▶ accordance, bestowal, bestowment, conference, grant, presentation.

confess *verb.* —*See* **acknowledge** (1).

confession *noun.* —*See* **acknowledgment** (1), **religion.**

confessor *noun.* One in whom secrets are confided ▶ confidant, confidante, intimate, repository. [*Compare* **friend.**]

confidant *or* **confidante** *noun.* One in whom secrets are confided ▶ confessor, intimate, repository. —*See also* **friend.**

confide *verb.* To tell in confidence ▶ breathe, share, unbosom, whisper. [*Compare* **communicate, reveal, say.**] —*See also* **entrust** (1).

confide in *verb.* —*See* **depend on** (1).

confidence *noun.* A firm belief in one's own powers ▶ aplomb, assurance, certitude, self-assurance, self-confidence, self-possession. [*Compare* **balance, courage.**] —*See also* **sureness, trust.**

✚ **CORE SYNONYMS:** *confidence, assurance, aplomb, self-confidence, self-possession.* These nouns denote a firm belief in one's own powers, abilities, or capacities. *Confidence* is the most general: *"You gain strength, courage and confidence by every experience in which you really stop to look fear in the face"* (Eleanor Roosevelt). *Assurance* even more strongly stresses certainty and can suggest arrogance: *How can you explain an abstruse theory with such assurance? Aplomb* implies calm poise: *"It is native personality, and that alone, that endows a man to stand before presidents or generals . . . with* aplomb*"* (Walt Whitman). *Self-confidence* stresses trust in one's own self-sufficiency: *"The most vital quality a soldier can possess is self-confidence"* (George S. Patton). *Self-possession* implies composure arising from control over one's own reactions: *"In life courtesy and self-possession . . . are the sensible impressions of the free mind, for both arise . . . from never being swept away, whatever the emotion, into confusion or dullness"* (William Butler Yeats).

---

confident *adjective.* Having a firm belief in one's own powers ▶ assured, poised, secure, self-assured, self-confident, self-possessed. [*Compare* **brave.**] —*See also* **optimistic, sure** (1).

confidential *adjective.* **1.** Known about by very few ▶ inside, private, privy, secret. *Informal:* hush-hush. [*Compare* **secret.**] **2.** Indicating intimacy and mutual trust ▶ close, familiar, innermost, intimate, inward, personal. **3.** Of or being information available only to authorized persons ▶ classified, privileged, restricted, sensitive, top secret.

configuration *noun.* —*See* **form** (1).

configure *verb.* —*See* **make.**

confine *verb.* —*See* **enclose** (1), **imprison, limit.**

confined *adjective.* —*See* **narrow** (1), **restricted.**

confinement *noun.* —*See* **detention, restriction.**

confines *noun.* —*See* **limits.**

confining *adjective.* —*See* **tight** (4).

confirm *verb.* **1.** To assure the certainty or validity of ▶ affirm, attest, authenticate, avouch, back (up), bear out, corroborate, declare, evidence, justify, substantiate, sustain, testify (to), validate, verify, warrant. [*Compare* **acknowledge, certify, legalize, prove.**] **2.** To make firmer in a particular conviction or habit ▶ fortify, harden, reinforce, strengthen. [*Compare* **back, establish.**] **3.** To accept officially ▶ accredit, adopt, affirm, approve, certify, endorse, pass, ratify, sanction. [*Compare* **accept.**] —*See also* **prove.**

✚ **CORE SYNONYMS:** *confirm, corroborate, substantiate, authenticate, validate, verify.* These verbs mean to affirm the certainty or validity of something. *Confirm* implies removal of all doubt: "*We must never make experiments to confirm our ideas, but simply to control them*" (Claude Bernard). *Corroborate* refers to supporting something by means of strengthening evidence: *The witness is expected to corroborate the plaintiff's testimony.* To *substantiate* is to establish by presenting substantial or tangible evidence: "*one of the most fully substantiated of historical facts*" (James Harvey Robinson). *Authenticate* implies the establishment of genuineness of something by the testimony of an expert: *Never purchase an antique before it has been authenticated. Validate* refers to establishing the validity of something, such as a theory, claim, or judgment: *The divorce validated my parents' original objection to the marriage. Verify* implies proving by comparison with an original or with established fact: *The bank refused to cash the check until the signature was verified.*

confirmation *noun.* **1.** An act of confirming officially ▶ accreditation, adoption, affirmation, approval, certification, endorsement, passage, ratification, sanction, verification. [*Compare* **acceptance.**] **2.** That which confirms ▶ attestation, authentication, avouchment, backing, circumstantiation, corroboration, demonstration, documentation, evidence, justification, proof, substantiation, sustainment, testament, testimonial, testimony, validation, verification, warrant. [*Compare* **testimony.**]

confirmed *adjective.* **1.** Firmly established by long standing ▶ deep-rooted, deep-seated, entrenched, established, hard-shell, incorrigible, incurable, indelible, ineradicable, ingrained, inveterate, irradicable, old-line, rooted, set, settled, vested. [*Compare* **firm[1], fixed.**] **2.** Subject to a disease or habit for a long time ▶ chronic, habitual, habituated, inveterate. [*Compare* **stubborn.**]

confiscate *verb.* —*See* **seize** (1).

confiscation *noun.* —*See* **seizure** (2).

conflagrant *adjective.* —*See* **burning.**

conflagration *noun.* The visible signs of combustion ▶ blaze, fire, flame, flare-up.

conflict *noun.* A state of disagreement and disharmony ▶ clash, confrontation, contention, difference, difficulty, discord, disagreement, discord, discordance, disharmony, dissension, dissent, dissentience, dissidence, dissonance, faction, friction, inharmony, schism, strife, variance, warfare. [*Compare* **opposition.**] —*See also* **battle.**

conflict *verb.* To fail to be in accord ▶ clash, collide, contradict, contrast, differ, disaccord, disagree, discord, diverge, jar, mismatch, oppose, vary. ***Idioms:*** go (*or* run) counter to.

✚ **CORE SYNONYMS:** *conflict, discord, strife, contention, dissension, clash, variance.* These nouns refer to a state of disagreement and disharmony. *Conflict* suggests antagonism of ideas or interests that often results in hostility or divisiveness: *conflict between smoking and nonsmoking factions. Discord* is a lack of harmony often marked by bickering and antipathy: *family discord. Strife* usually implies a struggle, often destructive, between rivals or factions: *political strife. Contention* suggests a dispute in the form of heated debate or quarreling: *lively contention among the candidates. Dissension* implies difference of opinion that disrupts unity within a group: *rampant dissension among the staff. Clash* involves irreconcilable ideas or interests: *a personality clash. Variance* usually suggests discrepancy or incompatibility: *actions at variance with his principles.*

---

conflicting *adjective.* —*See* **discrepant, incongruous, inharmonious** (1), **opposing.**

confluence *noun.* —*See* **junction.**

conflux *noun.* —*See* **junction.**

conform *verb.* —*See* **adapt, agree** (1), **conventionalize, follow** (4), **harmonize** (1).

conformable *adjective.* —*See* **agreeable, obedient.**

conformance *noun.* —*See* **agreement** (2).

conformation *noun.* —*See* **adaptation, agreement** (2).

conformist *adjective.* —*See* **conventional.**

conformity *noun.* —*See* **agreement** (2).

confound *verb.* To take one thing mistakenly for another ▶ confuse, mistake, mix up. —*See also* **baffle, confuse** (1), **embarrass.**

confounded *adjective.* —*See* **confused** (1), **damned.**

confront *verb.* To meet face-to-face, especially defiantly ▶ encounter, face, front, meet. ***Idiom:*** stand up to. [*Compare* **contest, defy.**]

confrontation *noun.* A face-to-face, usually hostile meeting ▶ duel, encounter, face-off, mano a mano, meeting, showdown. [*Compare* **argument, fight.**] —*See also* **battle, conflict.**

confuse *verb.* **1.** To cause to be unclear in mind or intent ▶ addle, befuddle, bewilder, confound, discombobulate, disorient, dizzy, fuddle, jumble, mix up, muddle, mystify, perplex, puzzle. *Informal:* throw. ***Idioms:*** make one's head reel (*or* swim *or* whirl). [*Compare* **agitate, complicate, daze.**] **2.** To take one thing mistakenly for another ▶ confound, mistake, mix up. **3.** To put into total disorder ▶ ball up, cross up, disorder, garble, jumble, mess up, muddle, muddy, scramble, snarl. *Slang:* snafu. ***Idioms:*** make a hash (*or* mess) of, play havoc with. [*Compare* **complicate, disorder.**] —*See also* **embarrass.**

✦ **CORE SYNONYMS:** *confuse, addle, befuddle, discombobulate, fuddle, muddle, puzzle.* These verbs mean to cause to be unclear in mind or intent: *heavy traffic that confused the driver; problems that addle my brain; a question that befuddled even the professor; was discombobulated by all of the possibilities; a complex plot line that fuddled my comprehension; a student who was muddled by endless facts and figures; behavior that really puzzled me.*

---

confused *adjective.* **1.** Mentally uncertain ▶ addled, addlepated, baffled, befuddled, bemused, bewildered, confusional, confounded, discombobulated, disconcerted, disoriented, dizzy, dumbfounded, flustered, haywire, lost, muddle-headed, mystified, nonplused, perplexed, punch-drunk, puzzled, stuck, stumped, turbid. *Informal:* mixed-up. ***Idioms:*** at a loss, at sea, in a fog (*or* haze *or* state *or* tizzy). [*Compare* **agitated, ignorant.**] **2.** Characterized by physical confusion ▶ amiss, chaotic, deranged, disarranged, disarrayed, disordered, disorganized, disrupted, disturbed, garbled, helter-skelter, higgledy-piggledy, jumbled, messy, muddled, pell-mell, scrambled, snarled, topsy-turvy, unsettled, unsystematic, upside-down, willy-nilly. *Informal:* mixed-up. *Slang:* snafu. ***Idiom:*** at sixes and sevens. [*Compare* **complex, messy.**]

confusedness *noun.* —*See* **disorder** (1).

confusion *noun.* —*See* **daze, disorder** (1), **disorder** (2), **embarrassment, misunderstanding.**

confute *verb.* —*See* **refute.**

con game *noun.* —*See* **trick** (1).

congeal *verb.* —*See* **coagulate, harden** (2).

congener *noun.* —*See* **parallel.**

congenial *adjective.* —*See* **agreeable, amiable, pleasant.**

congeniality *or* **congenialness** *noun.* —*See* **amiability.**

congenital *adjective.* —*See* **constitutional, innate.**

congeries *noun.* —*See* **accumulation** (1).

congest *verb.* —*See* **fill** (2).

congested *adjective.* —*See* **overcrowded.**

conglomerate *noun.* —*See* **company** (1), **complex** (1).

conglomeration *noun.* —*See* **assortment.** The act of accumulating ▶ accumulation, agglomeration, buildup. [*Compare* **increase.**]

congrats *noun.* —*See* **compliment.**

congratulate *verb.* To pay a compliment to ▶ commend, compliment, felicitate, praise. ***Idioms:*** pay tribute to, raise a glass to, take off one's hat to. [*Compare* **honor.**]

congratulation *noun.* —*See* **compliment.**

congratulatory *adjective.* —*See* **complimentary** (1).

congregate *verb.* —*See* **assemble.**

congregation *noun.* The steadfast believers in a faith or cause ▶ adherents, faithful, fold. [*Compare* **follower, assembly.**] —*See also* **assembly.**

congress *noun.* —*See* **assembly, convention, union** (1).

congruity *or* **congruence** *noun.* —*See* **agreement** (2), **consistency.**

congruous *adjective.* Having components pleasingly combined ▶ concordant, balanced, harmonious, symmetrical. [*Compare* **pleasant.**] —*See also* **agreeable.**

conjectural *adjective.* —*See* **supposed.**

conjecture *noun.* —*See* **guess, theory** (1).

conjecture *verb.* —*See* **guess.**

conjectured *adjective.* —*See* **untried.**

conjoin *verb.* —*See* **associate** (1), **combine** (1).

conjoining *adjective.* —*See* **adjoining.**

conjoint *adjective.* —*See* **common** (2).

conjugal *adjective.* —*See* **marital.**

conjugality *noun.* —*See* **marriage.**

conjugate *verb.* —*See* **combine** (1).

conjugation *noun.* —*See* **combination.**

conjunction *noun.* —*See* **association** (1).

conjuration *noun.* —*See* **magic** (1), **magic** (2).

conjure *verb.* —*See* **evoke.**

conjure up *verb.* —*See* **imagine.**

conjurer *noun.* —*See* **wizard.**

conjuring *noun.* —*See* **magic** (2).

conk *noun.* —*See* **blow²**, **head** (1).

conk *verb.* —*See* **hit.**

conk out *verb.* —*See* **collapse** (1), **malfunction.**

connatural *or* **connate** *adjective.* —*See* **constitutional, innate, kindred.**

connect *verb.* To come together by arrangement ▶ hook up, get together, meet (up), rendezvous. —*See also* **associate** (1), **associate** (3), **attach** (1), **combine** (1), **relate** (2).

connected *adjective.* —*See* **concerned.**

connection *noun.* **1.** Something, such as a feeling or idea, associated with a specific person or thing ▶ association, connotation, impression, suggestion. [*Compare* **hint.**] **2.** An acquaintance who is in a position to help ▶ contact, source. [*Compare* **go-between.**] —*See* *also* **association** (1), **joint** (1), **pusher, relation** (1).

conniption *or* **conniption fit** *noun.* —*See* **temper** (2).

connivance *noun.* —*See* **plot** (2).

connive *verb.* —*See* **plot** (2).

connive at *verb.* —*See* **blink at.**

conniving *adjective.* Coldly planning to achieve selfish aims ▶ calculating, designing, manipulative, scheming. [*Compare* **artful.**]

connoisseur *noun.* —*See* **expert.**

connotation *noun.* Something, such as a feeling or idea, associated with a specific person or thing ▶ association, connection, impression, suggestion. [*Compare* **hint.**] —*See also* **meaning.**

connotative *adjective.* Tending to bring a memory, mood, or image, for example, subtly or indirectly to mind ▶ allusive, evocative, impressionistic, reminiscent, suggestive. [*Compare* **designative, symbolic.**]

connote *verb.* —*See* **mean**[1]**.**

connubial *adjective.* —*See* **marital.**

connubiality *noun.* —*See* **marriage.**

conquer *verb.* —*See* **defeat, occupy** (2).

conquering *adjective.* —*See* **victorious.**

conqueror *noun.* One that conquers ▶ conquistador, master, subduer, subjugator, surmounter, vanquisher, victor, winner. —*See also* **winner.**

conquest *noun.* The act of conquering ▶ knockout, subjugation, triumph, victory, win. [*Compare* **accomplishment, defeat.**]

✚ **CORE SYNONYMS:** *conquest, victory, triumph.* These nouns denote the act of conquering, as by winning a war, struggle, or competition. *Conquest* connotes subduing, subjugating, or achieving control over: *"Conquest of illiteracy comes first"* (John Kenneth Galbraith). *Victory* refers especially to the final defeat of an enemy or opponent: *"Victory at all costs, victory in spite of all terror, victory however long and hard the road may be"* (Winston S. Churchill). *Triumph* denotes a victory or success that is especially noteworthy because it is decisive, significant, or spectacular: *preaching the eventual triumph of good over evil.*

---

conquistador *noun.* —*See* **conqueror.**

consanguine *or* **consanguineous** *adjective.* —*See* **kindred.**

conscience *noun.* —*See* **decency** (1).

conscienceless *adjective.* —*See* **unscrupulous.**

conscientious *adjective.* —*See* **diligent, ethical.**

conscientiousness *noun.* —*See* **diligence.**

conscious *adjective.* —*See* **careful** (1), **deliberate** (1).

consciousness *noun.* —*See* **awareness, spirit** (2).

conscript *verb.* To enroll compulsorily in military service ▶ draft, impress, induct, levy.

conscription *noun.* —*See* **draft** (2).

consecrate *verb.* To make sacred by a religious rite ▶ bless, hallow, sanctify. [*Compare* **exalt.**] —*See also* **devote.**

consecrated *adjective.* —*See* **divine** (2), **holy.**

consecution *noun.* —*See* **series.**

consecutive *adjective.* Following one after another in an orderly pattern ▶ back-to-back, chronological, numerical, sequent, sequential, serial, seriate, successional, successive. ***Idioms:*** in order, in turn. [*Compare* **following, gradual.**]

consensual *adjective.* —*See* **unanimous.**

consensus *noun.* —*See* **agreement** (2).

consent *verb.* —*See* **assent, permit** (2).

consent *noun.* —*See* **acceptance** (1), **permission.**

consequence *noun.* —*See* **effect** (1), **importance.**

consequent *adjective.* —*See* **following** (2), **logical** (2).

consequential *adjective.* —*See* **following** (2), **important, influential, pregnant** (2).

conservancy *noun.* —*See* **conservation.**

conservation *noun.* The careful guarding of an asset ▶ conservancy, husbandry, maintenance, management, preservation, protection. [*Compare* **care, defense, economy.**]

conservational *noun.* —*See* **preservative.**

conservative *adjective.* **1.** Favoring traditional view and values, especially as a political philosophy ▶ neoconservative, orthodox, right, rightist, right-wing, Tory, traditionalist, traditionalistic. *Informal:* neocon. [*Compare* **ultraconservative.**] **2.** Kept within sensible limits ▶ careful, cautious, discreet, guarded, moderate, modest, reasonable, restrained, temperate. —*See also* **conventional, preservative.**

conservative *noun.* One with poltically conservative views ▶ neoconservative, orthodox, rightist, rightwinger, Tory, traditionalist. *Informal:* neocon. [*Compare* **ultraconservative.**]

conservator *noun.* One who is legally responsible for the care and management of the person or property of an incompetent or a minor ▶ caretaker, custodian, guardian, keeper. [*Compare* **representative.**]

conserve *verb.* To protect an asset from loss or destruction ▶ husband, preserve, save. [*Compare* **defend.**] —*See also* **preserve** (1), **scrimp.**

consider *verb.* To receive an idea and think about it in order to form an opinion about it ▶ entertain, hear of, think about, think of. —*See also* **believe** (3), **deal** (1), **discuss, look** (1), **ponder, regard, value.**

considerable *adjective.* —*See* **big, important.**

considerably *adverb.* To a considerable extent ▶ abundantly, amply, expansively, extensively, far, largely, much, quite, significantly, sizably, spaciously, substantially, well. ***Idioms:*** by a long shot (*or* way), by a wide margin, by far. [*Compare* **absolutely, completely, really, unusually, very.**]

considerate *adjective.* —*See* **attentive, obliging.**

consideration *noun.* **1.** Thoughtful attention to others ▶ attentiveness, concern, helpfulness, hospitality, kindness, loving kindness, regard, solicitousness, solicitude, sweetness, tenderness, thoughtfulness, warm-heartedness. [*Compare* **amiability, benevolence, generosity.**] **2.** Careful thought ▶ advisement, deliberation, study. [*Compare* **examination, scrutiny.**] —*See also* **attention, deliberation** (1), **esteem.**

considered *adjective.* —*See* **calculated, deliberate** (2).

consign *verb.* To place officially in confinement ▶ commit, institutionalize. *Informal:* send up. [*Compare* **imprison.**] —*See also* **entrust** (1), **send** (1).

consignment *noun.* —*See* **delivery.**

consist *verb.* To have an inherent basis ▶ dwell, exist, inhere, lie, repose, reside, rest. [*Compare* **endure, live.**] —*See also* **agree** (1).

consistency *or* **consistence** *noun.* Logical agreement among parts ▶ coherence, cohesion, congruence, congruity, uniformity. [*Compare* **agreement, proportion.**] —*See also* **changelessness.**

consistent *adjective.* —*See* **agreeable, unchanging.**

consistently *adverb.* —*See* **usually.**

consolation *noun.* ▶ comfort, reassurance, solace, succor. [*Compare* **help, pity.**]

console *verb.* —*See* **comfort.**

consolidate *verb.* —*See* **combine** (1).

consolidated *adjective.* —*See* **thick** (2).

consolidation *noun.* —*See* **unification.**

consonance *noun.* —*See* **agreement** (2), **harmony** (1).

consonant *adjective.* —*See* **agreeable, harmonious** (2), **unanimous.**

consort *noun.* —*See* **spouse.**

consort *verb.* —*See* **associate** (2).

consortium *noun.* —*See* **alliance.**

conspicuous *adjective.* —*See* **apparent** (1), **noticeable.**
conspiracy *noun.* —*See* **plot** (2).
conspirator *noun.* —*See* **accessory.**
conspire *verb.* —*See* **plot** (2).
constable *noun.* —*See* **police officer.**
constancy *noun.* —*See* **changelessness, fidelity.**
constant *adjective.* —*See* **continual, faithful, firm**[1] (3), **unchanging.**
consternate *verb.* —*See* **dismay.**
consternation *noun.* —*See* **fear.**
constituency *noun.* —*See* **patronage** (3).
constituent *adjective.* —*See* **built-in.**
constituent *noun.* —*See* **part** (1).
constitute *verb.* To be the constituent parts of ▶ compose, form, make up. [*Compare* **contain.**] —*See also* **equal** (1), **establish** (2), **found.**
constitution *noun.* The physical characteristics of a person ▶ body, build, figure, form, frame, habit, habitus, make, makeup, physique, shape. [*Compare* **character, form.**] —*See also* **foundation.**
constitutional *adjective.* Forming an essential element, as arising from the basic structure of an individual ▶ basal, built-in, congenital, connate, connatural, elemental, immanent, inborn, inbred, indigenous, indwelling, ingrained, inherent, innate, intrinsic, native, natural. ***Idioms:*** in one's blood, runs in the family. [*Compare* **confirmed, elemental, innate.**] —*See also* **essential** (2).
constitutional *noun.* —*See* **walk** (1).
constitutive *adjective.* —*See* **essential** (2).
constrain *verb.* To check the freedom and spontaneity of ▶ constrict, cramp, inhibit. —*See also* **force** (1), **restrain.**
constrained *adjective.* —*See* **awkward** (3), **obliged** (2), **reserved.**
constraint *noun.* —*See* **force** (1), **reserve** (1), **restraint, restriction.**
constrict *verb.* **1.** To make smaller or narrower by binding or squeezing ▶ compact, compress, constringe, contract, narrow, shrink, tighten. [*Compare* **decrease, shorten.**] **2.** To check the freedom and spontaneity of ▶ constrain, cramp, inhibit. [*Compare* **restrain.**] —*See also* **squeeze** (1).
constriction *noun.* The act or process of constricting ▶ compression, contraction, narrowing, shrinkage, squeeze. [*Compare* **decrease.**]
constringe *verb.* —*See* **constrict** (1), **squeeze** (1).
construct *verb.* —*See* **base**[1] (2), **build, make.**
construable *adjective.* —*See* **explainable.**
construction *noun.* Something built, especially for human use ▶ building, edifice, erection, pile, structure. —*See also* **explanation.**
constructive *adjective.* —*See* **beneficial, effective** (1).
constructor *noun.* —*See* **builder.**
construe *verb.* To understand in a particular way ▶ interpret, read, take. ***Idioms:*** read between the lines, see in a special light, take to mean. —*See also* **explain** (1), **translate.**
construe *noun.* —*See* **translation.**
consuetude *noun.* —*See* **custom.**
consul *noun.* —*See* **representative.**
consult *verb.* —*See* **confer** (1).
consultant *noun.* —*See* **adviser.**
consultation *noun.* —*See* **deliberation** (1).
consulting *adjective.* —*See* **advisory.**
consume *verb.* **1.** To engulf completely ▶ desolate, devastate, devour, dispatch, eat (up), ravage, swallow (up), waste. *Informal:* polish off, put away. ***Idioms:*** do away with, lay waste. [*Compare* **annihilate, destroy.**] **2.** To be depleted ▶ exhaust, go, spend. ***Idiom:*** go down the drain. —*See also* **absorb** (1), **eat** (1), **erode, exhaust** (1).
consumer *noun.* One who buys goods and services ▶ buyer, client, customer, patron, purchaser, shopper, user.
consummate *verb.* —*See* **conclude.**

consummate *adjective.* —*See* **definitive, perfect, utter[2].**

consummation *noun.* —*See* **end** (1), **fulfillment** (1).

consumption *noun.* The act of consuming ▶ depletion, expenditure, usage, use, utilization. [*Compare* **use.**]

contact *noun.* **1.** A coming together or touching ▶ contingence, taction, touch. [*Compare* **brush[1], touch.**] **2.** A situation allowing exchange of ideas or messages ▶ communication, correspondence, intercommunication, touch. [*Compare* **communication.**] **3.** An acquaintance who is in a position to help ▶ connection, source. —*See also* **go-between.**

contact *verb.* To succeed in communicating with ▶ reach. *Informal:* catch, get. ***Idioms:*** catch up with, get hold of, get in touch with, get through to, get to.

contagion *noun.* —*See* **contaminant, poison.**

contagious *adjective.* Capable of transmission by infection ▶ catching, communicable, infectious, pestilent, pestilential, taking, transferable, transmittable, virulent.

contain *verb.* **1.** To have as a part ▶ comprehend, comprise, consist of, embody, embrace, encompass, have, include, involve, subsume, take in. **2.** To be filled by ▶ have, hold. [*Compare* **constitute.**] **3.** To have the room or capacity for ▶ accommodate, hold. —*See also* **compose** (4), **enclose** (1).

✚ CORE SYNONYMS: *contain, include, comprise, comprehend, embrace, involve.* These verbs mean to have as a part of something larger. *Contain* is the most general: *This CD contains some of my favorite songs. Include* often implies an incomplete listing: *"Through the process of amendment, interpretation and court decision I have finally been included in 'We, the people'"* (Barbara C. Jordan). *Comprise* usually implies that all of the components are stated: *The book comprises 15 chapters. Comprehend* and *embrace* usually refer to the taking in of subordinate elements: *My field of study comprehends several disciplines. This theory embraces many facets of human behavior. Involve* usually suggests inclusion as a logical consequence or necessary condition: *"Every argument involves some assumptions"* (Brooke F. Westcott).

---

container *noun.* An object, such as a carton, can, or jar, in which material is held or carried ▶ holder, receptacle, repository, vessel. [*Compare* **depository, package.**]

contaminant *noun.* One that contaminates ▶ adulterant, adulterator, contagion, contamination, contaminator, disease, impurity, infection, pestilence, poison, pollutant, pollution, taint. [*Compare* **contamination, poison.**]

contaminate *verb.* To make impure, unclean, or inferior by contact or mixture ▶ adulterate, corrupt, debase, doctor, foul, infect, load, poison, pollute, sophisticate, taint. [*Compare* **corrupt, dilute, dirty.**] —*See also* **corrupt.**

✚ CORE SYNONYMS: *contaminate, adulterate, debase, doctor, load.* These verbs mean to make impure, unclean, or inferior by adding foreign substances to something: *contaminated the river with industrial waste; adulterate coffee with ground acorns; silver debased with copper; doctored the wine with water; rag paper loaded with wood fiber.*

---

contaminated *adjective.* —*See* **impure** (2).

contamination *noun.* The state of being contaminated ▶ adulteration, corruption, defilement, dirtiness, foulness, impurity, infection, pollution, sophistication, uncleanliness, uncleanness, unwholesomeness. [*Compare* **decay, dirtiness.**] —*See also* **contaminant.**

contaminative *adjective.* —*See* **unwholesome** (2).

contaminator *noun.* —*See* **contaminant.**

contemn *verb.* —*See* **despise.**

contemplate *verb.* —*See* **intend, look** (1), **ponder.**

contemplative *adjective.* —*See* **thoughtful.**

contemplation *noun.* An act of directing the eyes on an object ▶ look, regard, sight, view. [*Compare* **gaze, watch.**] —*See also* **attention, thought.**

contemporaneous *adjective.* —*See* **concurrent, contemporary** (1).

contemporary *adjective.* **1.** Belonging to the same period of time ▶ coetaneous, coeval, coexistent, concurrent, contemporaneous, synchronal, synchronic, synchronous. **2.** Characteristic of recent times or informed of what is current ▶ au courant, current, cutting-edge, latest, latter-day, modern, modernistic, present, recent, state-of-the-art, topical, up-to-date, up-to-the-minute, ultramodern. [*Compare* **fashionable, new.**] —*See also* **concurrent, present**[1].

contemporary *noun.* **1.** One of the same time or age as another ▶ coeval. **2.** A person of the present age ▶ modern.

contempt *noun.* —*See* **defiance** (2), **despisal, hate** (1).

contemptible *adjective.* —*See* **offensive** (1).

contemptuous *adjective.* —*See* **disdainful, disrespectful.**

contend *verb.* To strive in opposition ▶ battle, clash, collide, combat, duel, encounter, engage, fence, fight, grapple, joust, meet, scuffle, spar, strive, struggle, take on, tilt, tussle, war, wrestle. ***Idioms:*** lock horns with, go to the mat with. [*Compare* **confront, oppose.**] —*See also* **argue** (1), **argue** (2), **assert, compete.**

contender *noun.* —*See* **competitor.**

content *adjective.* Having achieved satisfaction, as of one's goal ▶ fufilled, gratified, happy, satisfied.

content *verb.* —*See* **satisfy** (2).

contentedness *noun.* The condition of being satisfied ▶ contentment, fulfillment, gratification, satisfaction. [*Compare* **happiness, satiation.**] —*See also* **happiness.**

contention *noun.* —*See* **argument, assertion, competition** (1), **conflict, theory** (2).

contentious *adjective.* —*See* **aggressive, argumentative, debatable.**

contentiousness *noun.* —*See* **aggression, fight** (2).

contentment *noun.* The condition of being satisfied ▶ contententdness, fulfillment, gratification, satisfaction. [*Compare* **happiness, satiation.**] —*See also* **happiness.**

conterminous *adjective.* —*See* **adjoining.**

contest *noun.* —*See* **competition** (1), **competition** (2).

contest *verb.* To take a stand against ▶ buck, challenge, dispute, oppose, resist, traverse. ***Idiom:*** go against. [*Compare* **confront, object, oppose.**] —*See also* **compete.**

contestable *adjective.* —*See* **debatable.**

contestant *noun.* —*See* **competitor.**

context *noun.* —*See* **conditions, environment** (2).

contexture *noun.* —*See* **texture.**

contiguous *adjective.* —*See* **adjoining, close** (1).

continence *noun.* —*See* **temperance** (1).

continent *adjective.* —*See* **chaste, temperate** (2).

contingence *noun.* A coming together or touching ▶ contact, taction, touch. [*Compare* **brush**[1], **touch.**]

contingency *noun.* —*See* **chance** (2), **possibility** (1).

contingent *adjective.* —*See* **accidental, conditional, probable.**

continual *adjective.* Existing or occurring without interruption or end ▶ around-the-clock, ceaseless, constant, continuous, endless, eternal, everlasting, incessant, interminable, never-ending, nonstop, ongoing, perennial, perpetual, persistent, relentless, round-the-clock, timeless, unbroken, unceasing, undying, unending, unfailing, uninterrupted, unremitting. [*Compare* **ageless, continuing, endless, unchanging.**]

✦ **CORE SYNONYMS:** *continual, continuous, constant, ceaseless, incessant, perpetual, eternal, perennial, interminable.* These adjectives mean occurring repeatedly over a long period of time. *Continual* is chiefly restricted to what is intermittent or repeated at intervals: *The continual banging of the shutter in the wind gave me a headache. Continuous* implies lack of interruption: *The horizon is a continuous line. Constant* stresses steadiness or persistence and unvarying nature: *The constant ticking of the clock lulled him to sleep. Ceaseless* and *incessant* pertain to uninterrupted activity: *The ceaseless thunder of the surf eroded the beach. The toddler asked incessant questions. Perpetual* emphasizes both steadiness and duration: *The ambassador had a perpetual stream of visitors. Eternal* refers to what is everlasting, especially to what is seemingly without temporal beginning or end: *"That freedom can be retained only by the eternal vigilance which has always been its price"* (Elmer Davis). *Perennial* describes existence that goes on year after year, often with the suggestion of self-renewal: *The candidates discussed the perennial problem of urban poverty. Interminable* refers to what is or seems to be endless and is often applied to something prolonged and wearisome: *After an interminable delay, our flight was canceled outright.*

---

continually *adverb.* Without stop or interruption ▶ ceaselessly, constantly, continuously, endlessly, forever, incessantly, interminably, nonstop, perpetually, persistently, relentlessly, steadily, unceasingly, unfailingly, unremittingly. *Slang:* 24-7. ***Idioms:*** around (*or* round) the clock, all the time, seven days a week. [*Compare* **forever, usually.**]

continuance *noun.* —*See* **continuation** (1).

continuation *noun.* **1.** Uninterrupted existence or succession ▶ continuance, continuity, continuum, durability, duration, endurance, permanence, persistence, persistency, survival. [*Compare* **endlessness, stability.**] **2.** A continuing after interruption ▶ renewal, resumption, resurgence, revival. [*Compare* **revival.**]

continue *verb.* To begin or go on after an interruption ▶ pick up, proceed, renew, reopen, restart, resume, take up. —*See also* **endure** (2), **extend** (1).

continuing *adjective.* Existing or remaining in the same state for an indefinitely long time ▶ abiding, durable, enduring, lasting, long-lasting, long-lived, long-standing, maintaining, old, perdurable, perennial, permanent, persevering, persistent, persisting. [*Compare* **continual, endless, unchanging.**] —*See also* **chronic** (2).

continuity *noun.* —*See* **continuation** (1).

continuous *adjective.* —*See* **continual.**

continuum *noun.* —*See* **continuation** (1).

contort *verb.* —*See* **deform.**

contortion *noun.* —*See* **deformity.**

contour *noun.* —*See* **form** (1).

contrabandist *noun.* A person who engages in smuggling ▶ bootlegger, runner, smuggler. *Slang:* mule.

contract *noun.* —*See* **agreement** (1).

contract *verb.* **1.** To enter into a formal agreement ▶ bargain, covenant, stipulate. ***Idioms:*** shake hands on, sign on the dotted line, strike a bargain. [*Compare* **agree, pledge, settle.**] **2.** To become affected with a disease ▶ catch, develop, get, incur, sicken, take. *Informal:* pick up. ***Idiom:*** come down with.

[*Compare* **develop, get.**] —*See also* **constrict** (1), **pledge** (2).

contraction *noun.* —*See* **constriction.**

contractor *noun.* —*See* **builder.**

contradict *verb.* —*See* **conflict, deny.**

contradiction *noun.* —*See* **denial** (1), **opposite, opposition** (1).

contradictory *adjective.* —*See* **contrary, discrepant, opposite.**

contradictory *noun.* —*See* **opposite.**

contradistinction *noun.* —*See* **opposition** (1).

contraindicated *adjective.* —*See* **unwise.**

contralto *adjective.* —*See* **low** (1).

contraposition *noun.* —*See* **opposition** (1).

contrapositive *noun.* —*See* **opposite.**

contraption *noun.* —*See* **device** (1), **gadget.**

contrariness *or* **contrariety** *noun.* —*See* **opposition** (1).

contrary *adjective.* Marked by a disposition to oppose ► antagonistic, balky, contradictory, contrarious, difficult, froward, hostile, impossible, inimical, ornery, perverse, wayward. [*Compare* **opposing.**] —*See also* **different, opposite.**

contrary *noun.* —*See* **opposite.**

contrast *verb.* —*See* **compare, conflict, differ.**

contrast *noun.* The act or state of being contrasted ► collation, comparison, counterpoint, juxtaposition. —*See also* **difference.**

contrasting *adjective.* —*See* **different, discrepant, opposite.**

contravene *verb.* —*See* **deny, violate** (1).

contravention *noun.* —*See* **breach** (1).

contretemps *noun.* —*See* **accident.**

contribute *verb.* **1.** To give in common with others ► ante, chip in, donate, give, subscribe. *Informal:* kick in. *Slang:* come across with. ***Idiom:*** do one's bit. [*Compare* **give.**] **2.** To help bring about a result ► chip in, conduce, partake, participate, share. ***Idioms:*** have a hand in, take part. [*Compare* **advance, help, participate.**] —*See also* **donate.**

contribution *noun.* —*See* **donation.**

contributive *adjective.* Tending to contribute to a result ► conducive, contributory, helpful, participatory. [*Compare* **auxiliary.**]

contributor *noun.* —*See* **donor, patron.** A person instrumental in the growth of something, especially in its early stages ► creator, producer. [*Compare* **developer.**]

contributory *adjective.* —*See* **auxiliary** (1). Tending to contribute to a result ► conducive, contributive, helpful, participatory.

contrite *adjective.* —*See* **sorry.**

contriteness *noun.* —*See* **penitence.**

contrition *noun.* —*See* **penitence.**

contrivance *noun.* —*See* **device** (1), **gadget, invention** (2).

contrive *verb.* —*See* **design** (1), **invent.**

contrived *adjective.* Not natural or spontaneous ► effortful, forced, labored, strained. [*Compare* **awkward, stiff.**] —*See also* **calculated.**

control *verb.* —*See* **administer** (1), **compose** (4), **conduct** (1), **dominate** (1), **govern.**

control *noun.* —*See* **authority, dominance, domination, government** (1), **reserve** (1), **restraint.**

controllable *adjective.* Capable of being governed ► administrable, governable, manageable, rulable. [*Compare* **loyal, obedient.**]

controlled *adjective.* —*See* **reserved, restricted.**

controlling *adjective.* —*See* **dominant** (1), **repressive.**

controversy *noun.* —*See* **argument.**

controvert *verb.* —*See* **deny.**

contumacious *adjective.* —*See* **defiant.**

contumacy *noun.* —*See* **defiance** (2).

contumelious *adjective.* —*See* **abusive, impudent.**

contumely *noun.* —*See* **indignity, vituperation.**

contuse *verb.* To make a bruise or bruises on ▶ bruise. ***Idioms:*** beat (*or* leave) black-and-blue. [*Compare* **hurt.**]

contusion *noun.* An injury that does not break the skin ▶ black-and-blue mark, bruise. [*Compare* **black eye, harm, trauma.**]

conundrum *noun.* —*See* **mystery.**

convalesce *verb.* —*See* **recover** (2).

convalescence *noun.* The process or period of a return to health ▶ rally, recovery, recuperation.

convene *verb.* —*See* **assemble.**

convenience *noun.* Unrestricted freedom to choose ▶ discretion, leisure, pleasure, will.

conveniences *noun.* —*See* **amenities** (1).

convenient *adjective.* **1.** Suited to one's needs or purpose ▶ appropriate, befitting, expedient, fit, good, handy, meet, proper, suitable, tailor-made, useful. [*Compare* **beneficial, opportune.**] **2.** Being within easy reach ▶ accessible, handy, nearby, ready. ***Idioms:*** at one's fingertips, at the ready, close (*or* near) at hand, close by. [*Compare* **available, central, close.**]

convention *noun.* A formal assemblage of the members of a group ▶ assembly, conclave, conference, congress, convocation, council, meeting, session, synod. —*See also* **agreement** (1), **assembly, culture** (2), **custom, doctrine, treaty.**

conventional *adjective.* Conforming to established practice or standards ▶ button-down, canonical, conformist, conservative, doctrinaire, doctrinal, establishmentarian, normal, orthodox, received, regular, standard, stereotyped, straight, time-honored, traditional, typical, usual. *Slang:* square, uncool. [*Compare* **common, ordinary, prevailing.**] —*See also* **accepted, ceremonious.**

conventionalize *verb.* To make conventional ▶ conform, homogenize, normalize, regularize, standardize, stereotype, stylize, traditionalize.

converge *verb.* To come together from different directions ▶ close, join, meet, unite. [*Compare* **combine.**] —*See also* **concentrate.**

converge on *verb.* —*See* **approach** (1).

convergence *noun.* The act or fact of coming near ▶ approach, coming, imminence, nearness. [*Compare* **advance, appearance.**] —*See also* **junction.**

conversance *noun.* Personal knowledge derived from participation or observation ▶ acquaintance, experience, familiarity. [*Compare* **awareness.**]

conversant *adjective.* Having good knowledge of something ▶ acquainted, familiar, schooled, versant, versed. ***Idiom:*** up on. [*Compare* **accustomed, informed.**]

conversation *noun.* Spoken exchange ▶ chat, colloquy, confabulation, converse, dialogue, discourse, discussion, heart-to-heart, interlocution, interview, pillow talk, speech, talk, tete-a-tete. *Informal:* bull session, confab, talkfest. *Slang:* gabfest, jaw, rap. [*Compare* **chatter, gossip.**] —*See also* **communication** (1).

conversational *adjective.* In the style of conversation ▶ chatty, chitchatty, colloquial, communicative, confabulatory, cozy, informal. —*See also* **talkative.**

conversationalist *or* **conversationist** *noun.* One given to conversation ▶ confabulator, dialogist, discourser, interlocutor, talker. [*Compare* **speaker.**]

converse[1] *verb.* To engage in spoken exchange ▶ buttonhole, chat, confabulate, discourse, speak, talk. *Informal:* confab, visit. [*Compare* **chatter, confer, say.**] —*See also* **discuss.**

converse *noun.* —*See* **conversation.**

✦ **CORE SYNONYMS:** *converse, speak, talk, discourse.* These verbs mean to engage in spoken exchange. *Converse* stresses interchange of thoughts and ideas: "*With thee conversing I forget all time*" (John Milton). *Speak* and *talk,* often interchangeable, are the most general: *He ate without once speaking to his companion. "On an occasion of this kind it becomes more than a moral duty to speak one's mind. It becomes a pleasure"* (Oscar Wilde). *I want to talk with you about vacation plans. "Let's talk sense to the American people"* (Adlai E. Stevenson). *Discourse* usually refers to formal, extended speech: *"striding through the city, stick in hand, discoursing spontaneously on the writings of Hazlitt"* (Manchester Guardian Weekly).

---

converse² *adjective.* —*See* **opposite.**

converse *noun.* —*See* **opposite.**

conversion *noun.* **1.** The process or result of changing from one use, function, or appearance to another ▶ change, changeover, metamorphosis, mutation, shift, transfiguration, transformation, translation, transmogrification, transmutation, transubstantiation, turn. [*Compare* **change.**] **2.** A fundamental change in one's beliefs ▶ metanoia, rebirth, regeneration. [*Compare* **revival.**]

convert *verb.* To change into a different form, substance, or state ▶ denature, metamorphose, morph, mutate, reshape, transfigure, transform, translate, transmogrify, transmute, transpose, transubstantiate. [*Compare* **change.**] —*See also* **convince.**

✣ **CORE SYNONYMS:** *convert, metamorphose, transfigure, transform, transmogrify, transmute.* These verbs mean to change into a different form, substance, or state: *convert stocks into cash; misery that was metamorphosed into happiness; a gangling adolescent who was transfigured into a handsome adult; transformed the bare stage into an enchanted forest; a boom that transmogrified the sleepy town into a bustling city; impossible to transmute lead into gold.*

---

convertible *adjective.* —*See* **changeable** (1).

convey *verb.* —*See* **bring** (1), **carry** (1), **communicate** (1), **communicate** (2), **conduct** (3), **express** (1), **mean¹**, **say**, **transfer** (1).

conveyance *noun.* —*See* **delivery**, **grant**, **transportation.**

conveyer *noun.* —*See* **messenger.**

convict *verb.* —*See* **condemn.**

convict *noun.* —*See* **criminal.**

conviction *noun.* —*See* **belief** (1), **sureness.**

convince *verb.* To cause another to believe or feel sure about something ▶ assure, bring around (*or* round), convert, persuade, satisfy, sell (on), turn, win over. [*Compare* **dispose, prove.**] —*See also* **persuade.**

convincing *adjective.* Serving to convince ▶ cogent, compelling, effective, efficacious, forceful, forcible, persuasive, satisfactory, telling. [*Compare* **believable, definite, sound².**] —*See also* **authentic** (2).

convivial *adjective.* —*See* **cheerful, merry, social.**

conviviality *noun.* —*See* **merriment** (2).

convocation *noun.* —*See* **assembly, convention.**

convoke *verb.* —*See* **assemble.**

convoluted *adjective.* —*See* **complex** (1), **winding.**

convoy *verb.* —*See* **accompany.**

convulse *verb.* —*See* **agitate** (1).

convulsion *noun.* A condition of anguished struggle and disorder ▶ paroxysm, throes, spasm. —*See also* **agitation** (1), **revolution** (2), **seizure** (1).

cook *verb.* To prepare food for eating by the use of heat ▶ bake, barbecue, blanch, boil, braise, broil, brown, charbroil, coddle, deep-fry, fricassee, fry, griddle, grill, pan-broil, pan-fry, parboil, poach, roast, sauté, sear, simmer, steam, stir-fry, stew, toast. —*See also* **distort.**

cook up *verb.* —*See* **invent.**

cook *noun.* A person who prepares food for eating ▶ baker, chef, culinary artist.

cooking *noun.* —*See* **food.**

cool *adjective.* Not friendly, sociable, or warm in manner ▶ aloof, chill, chilly, detached, distant, formal, frigid, frosty, glacial, icy, impersonal, offish, remote, reserved, reticent, solitary, standoffish, unapproachable, uncommunicative, undemonstrative, withdrawn. [*Compare* **cold.**] —*See also* **calm, cold** (1), **marvelous.**

cool *verb.* —*See* **compose** (4).

cool *noun.* —*See* **balance** (2).

cooler *noun.* —*See* **jail.**

cool-headed *adjective.* —*See* **calm.**

coolness *noun.* —*See* **apathy, balance** (2), **cold.**

coop *noun.* —*See* **cage, jail.**

coop up *verb.* —*See* **enclose** (1).

cooperate *verb.* To work together toward a common end ▶ collaborate, combine, concert, concur, join, unite. ***Idioms:*** act in concert, join forces, pull together, team up. [*Compare* **ally, combine.**]

cooperation *noun.* Joint work toward a common end ▶ coaction, collaboration, concert, synergy, teamwork. [*Compare* **agreement, alliance.**] —*See also* **association** (1).

cooperative *adjective.* Working together toward a common end ▶ coactive, collaborative, collective, combined, concerted, group, joint, synergetic, synergic, synergistic, united. —*See also* **common** (2).

coordinate *verb.* —*See* **classify, harmonize** (1), **harmonize** (2).

cop *noun.* —*See* **police officer.**

cop *verb.* —*See* **capture, steal.**

cop out *verb.* —*See* **renege.**

copartner *noun.* —*See* **associate** (1).

cope with *verb.* ▶ deal with, handle, treat.

copious *adjective.* —*See* **generous** (2).

coplanar *adjective.* —*See* **even** (2).

copper *noun.* —*See* **police officer.**

copy *noun.* **1.** Something closely resembling another ▶ carbon copy, counterpart, ditto, duplicate, facsimile, image, likeness, photocopy, reduplication, replica, replication, reproduction, simulacrum. [*Compare* **double, parallel.**] **2.** An inferior substitute imitating an original ▶ ersatz, imitation, pinchbeck, reprint, simulation. *Informal:* knockoff. [*Compare* **counterfeit.**]

copy *verb.* To make a copy of ▶ clone, ditto, duplicate, imitate, photocopy, replicate, reprint, reproduce, simulate. *Informal:* knock off. [*Compare* **counterfeit, imitate, plagiarize.**] —*See also* **follow** (5).

copycat *noun.* —*See* **mimic.**

coquet *verb.* —*See* **flirt** (2).

coquetry *noun.* ▶ dalliance, flirtation.

coquette *noun.* A woman who is given to flirting ▶ flirt, tease. *Informal:* vamp. [*Compare* **seductress.**]

coquettish *adjective.* ▶ coy, flirtatious, flirty.

cord *noun.* A band or fiber used to bind, tie, connect, or support ▶ bond, cable, chain, cordage, fetter, guy, lace, lacing, line, noose, rope, string, thong. [*Compare* **band, fastener, thread.**]

cordage *noun.* —*See* **cord.**

cordial *adjective.* —*See* **amiable.**

cordiality *or* **cordialness** *noun.* —*See* **amiability.**

cordon *verb.* —*See* **enclose** (1).

core *noun.* —*See* **center** (3), **heart** (1).

cork *noun.* —*See* **plug.**

cork *verb.* —*See* **fill** (2).

corkscrew *verb.* —*See* **wind**[2]**.**

corky *adjective.* —*See* **lively.**

corner *noun.* —*See* **predicament.** Exclusive control or possession ▶ monopoly. [*Compare* **domination.**]

cornerstone *noun.* —*See* **base**[1] (2), **basis** (1).

cornucopia *noun.* —*See* **plenty.**

corny *adjective.* —*See* **sentimental, trite.**

corollary *noun.* —*See* **effect** (1).

corporal *adjective.* —*See* **bodily.**

corporation *noun.* —*See* **company** (1).
corporeal *adjective.* —*See* **bodily, physical.**
corporeality *noun.* —*See* **tangibility.**
corps *noun.* —*See* **band²**, **detachment** (3), **force** (3).
corpse *noun.* —*See* **body** (2).
corpulent *adjective.* —*See* **fat** (1).
corpus *noun.* —*See* **quantity** (3).
corral *verb.* —*See* **enclose** (1).
corral *noun.* —*See* **pen²**.
correct *verb.* **1.** To make right what is wrong ▶ amend, emend, fix, mend, rectify, redress, reform, remedy, repair, revise, right, straighten (up *or* out). ***Idioms:*** put right (*or* to rights), set right (*or* to rights). [*Compare* **cure, fix.**] **2.** To castigate for the purpose of improving ▶ chasten, chide. [*Compare* **chastise.**] —*See also* **punish.**
correct *adjective.* —*See* **accurate, appropriate.**

✥ **CORE SYNONYMS:** *correct, rectify, remedy, redress, reform, revise, amend.* These verbs mean to make right what is wrong. *Correct* refers to eliminating faults, errors, or defects: *I corrected the spelling mistakes. Rectify* stresses the idea of bringing something into conformity with a standard of what is right: *The omission of her name from the list will be rectified. Remedy* involves removing or counteracting something considered a cause of harm or damage: *He took courses to remedy his abysmal ignorance. Redress* refers to setting right something considered immoral or unethical and usually involves making reparation: *The wrong is too great to be redressed. Reform* implies broad change that improves form or character: *"Let us reform our schools, and we shall find little reform needed in our prisons"* (John Ruskin). *Amend* implies improvement through alteration or correction: *"Whenever* [the people] *shall grow weary of the existing government, they can exercise their constitutional right of amending it, or their revolutionary right to dismember or overthrow it"* (Abraham Lincoln).

---

correction *noun.* —*See* **punishment.**
correctional *adjective.* —*See* **punishing.**
corrective *adjective.* Tending to correct ▶ amendatory, emendatory, reformative, reformatory, remedial, reparative. [*Compare* **curative.**]
corrective *noun.* —*See* **cure.**
correctly *adverb.* —*See* **fair¹**.
correctness *noun.* —*See* **accuracy, decency** (2), **veracity.**
correlate *verb.* —*See* **associate** (3), **harmonize** (2).
correlate *noun.* —*See* **parallel.**
correlation *noun.* —*See* **relation** (1).
correlative *noun.* —*See* **parallel.**
correlative *adjective.* —*See* **complementary.**
correspond *verb.* —*See* **agree** (1), **equal** (1).
correspondence *noun.* A situation allowing exchange of ideas or messages ▶ communication, contact, intercommunication, touch. —*See also* **agreement** (2), **communication** (1), **letter, likeness** (1).
correspondent *noun.* —*See* **parallel, press.**
correspondent *adjective.* —*See* **agreeable.**
corresponding *adjective.* —*See* **agreeable, like²**, **proportional** (1).
corrival *noun.* —*See* **competitor.**
corrivalry *noun.* —*See* **competition** (1).
corroborate *verb.* —*See* **back** (2), **confirm** (1), **prove.**
corroboration *noun.* —*See* **confirmation** (2).
corrode *verb.* —*See* **blast** (2), **erode.**
corrosive *adjective.* —*See* **biting, harmful.**
corrosiveness *noun.* —*See* **sarcasm.**
corrugate *verb.* —*See* **wave** (1).
corrupt *verb.* To ruin morally ▶ animalize, bastardize, bestialize, brutalize, canker, contaminate, debase, de-

bauch, defile, demoralize, deprave, infect, pervert, poison, pollute, soil, stain, suborn, subvert, taint, vitiate, warp. [*Compare* **damage, debase.**] —*See also* **blast** (2), **bribe, contaminate, decay.**

corrupt *adjective.* **1.** Utterly reprehensible in nature or behavior ▶ debased, degenerate, depraved, miscreant, perverse, perverted, rotten, unhealthy, villainous. [*Compare* **disgraceful, evil, offensive, sordid.**] **2.** Open to bribery or dishonesty ▶ bribable, dishonest, dishonorable, mercenary, praetorian, profiteering, venal. *Informal:* crooked. ***Idioms:*** on the pad, on the take. [*Compare* **underhand, unscrupulous.**] —*See also* **erroneous.**

✚ **CORE SYNONYMS:** *corrupt, debase, debauch, deprave, pervert, vitiate.* These verbs mean to ruin morally: *was corrupted by limitless power; debased himself by pleading with the captors; a youth debauched by drugs and drink; indulgence that depraves the moral fiber; perverted her talent by putting it to evil purposes; a proof vitiated by a serious omission.*

---

corruption *noun.* **1.** Degrading, immoral acts or habits ▶ bestiality, criminality, debauchery, depravity, flagitiousness, immorality, impurity, perversion, rottenness, turpitude, vice, villainousness, villainy, wickedness. [*Compare* **cheat, crime.**] **2.** Departure from what is legally, ethically, and morally correct ▶ baseness, corruptness, depravity, dishonesty, improbity, jobbery, malfeasance, venality. *Informal:* crookedness. [*Compare* **disobedience, evil.**] **3.** A misused or incorrect term ▶ barbarism, catachresis, impropriety, malapropism, misusage, solecism. —*See also* **contamination.**

corruptive *adjective.* —*See* **harmful, unwholesome** (2).

corruptness *noun.* —*See* **corruption** (2).

corsage *noun.* —*See* **bouquet.**

coruscate *verb.* —*See* **glitter.**

coruscation *noun.* —*See* **flash** (1).

cosmic *adjective.* —*See* **heavenly** (2), **universal** (1).

cosmopolitan *adjective.* Experienced in the ways of the world; lacking natural simplicity ▶ sophisticated, worldly, worldly-wise. [*Compare* **experienced, shrewd, suave.**] —*See also* **universal** (1).

cosmos *noun.* —*See* **universe.**

cosset *verb.* —*See* **baby.**

cost *noun.* **1.** An amount paid or to be paid for a purchase ▶ charge, disbursement, expenditure, expense, outlay, payment, price. *Informal:* tab. [*Compare* **toll, wage.**] **2.** The expenditure at which something is obtained ▶ expense, price, sacrifice, toll. *Informal:* damage.

cost *verb.* To require a specified price ▶ go for, sell for. ***Idiom:*** set someone back. [*Compare* **bring, demand.**]

costive *adjective.* —*See* **stingy.**

costly *adjective.* Of great value or price ▶ dear, expensive, high, high-priced, inestimable, invaluable, precious, priceless, rich, valuable, worthy. *Informal:* big-ticket, pricey. ***Idioms:*** beyond price, of great price, worth its weight in gold. [*Compare* **steep**[1].]

costs *noun.* —*See* **overhead.**

costume *noun.* —*See* **disguise, dress** (2).

costume *verb.* —*See* **dress** (1).

cote *noun.* —*See* **cage.**

coterie *noun.* —*See* **circle** (3).

cotillion *noun.* —*See* **dance.**

cottage *noun.* —*See* **villa.**

cotton *verb.* —*See* **relate** (2).

couch *verb.* —*See* **lie**[1] (1), **phrase.**

council *noun.* —*See* **assembly, convention.**

counsel *noun.* —*See* **advice, deliberation** (1), **lawyer.**

counsel *verb.* —*See* **advise.**

counseling *adjective.* —*See* **advisory.**

counselor *noun.* —*See* **adviser, lawyer.**

count *verb.* **1.** To be of significance or importance ▶ import, matter, signify, weigh. **2.** To note items one by one in order to get a total ▶ enumerate, number, numerate, reckon, score, tally, tell. [*Compare* **add, calculate, measure.**] **3.** To indicate time or rhythm ▶ beat, tap. ***Idioms:*** keep time, mark time.

count off *verb.* —*See* **enumerate.**

count on *verb.* —*See* **depend on** (1), **expect** (1).

count out *verb.* —*See* **exclude.**

count *noun.* **1.** A noting of items one by one ▶ enumeration, numeration, reckoning, score, tally. [*Compare* **calculation, total.**] **2.** A gathering of information or opinion from a variety of sources or individuals ▶ canvass, poll, survey.

✚ **CORE SYNONYMS:** *count, import, matter, signify, weigh.* These verbs mean to be of significance or importance: *an opinion that counts; actions that import little; decisions that really matter; thoughts that signify much; considerations that weigh with her.*

---

countenance *noun.* —*See* **expression** (4), **face** (1), **face** (3).

countenance *verb.* **1.** To lend supportive approval to ▶ encourage, favor, smile on (*or* upon). [*Compare* **approve, support.**] **2.** To be favorably disposed toward ▶ approve, favor, hold with. *Informal:* go for. ***Idioms:*** be in favor of, take kindly to, think highly (*or* well) of. [*Compare* **assent, value.**]

counter *adjective.* —*See* **discrepant, opposite.**

counter *noun.* A small, often makeshift structure for the display and sale of goods ▶ booth, stand, stall. [*Compare* **store.**] —*See also* **opposite.**

counter *verb.* —*See* **oppose, retaliate.**

counteract *verb.* —*See* **balance** (2), **cancel** (2).

counterattack *verb.* —*See* **retaliate.**

counterattack *or* **counteraction** *noun.* —*See* **retaliation.**

counterbalance *verb.* —*See* **balance** (1), **balance** (2), **cancel** (2).

counterblow *noun.* —*See* **retaliation.**

counterfactual *adjective.* —*See* **false.**

counterfeit *verb.* To make a fraudulent copy of ▶ fabricate, fake, falsify, forge. [*Compare* **copy.**] —*See also* **act** (2).

counterfeit *adjective.* Fraudulently or deceptively imitative ▶ bogus, ersatz, fabricated, factitious, fake, false, forged, fraudulent, phony, sham, spurious, suppositious, supposititious. [*Compare* **artificial.**]

counterfeit *noun.* A fraudulent imitation ▶ fabrication, fake, falsification, forgery, phony, sham. [*Compare* **copy.**]

counterfeiter *noun.* ▶ fabricator, faker, falsifier, forger.

countermand *verb.* —*See* **lift** (3), **retract** (1).

countermand *noun.* —*See* **retraction.**

countermeasure *noun.* —*See* **cure.**

counterpart *noun.* One that has the same functions and characteristics as another ▶ equivalent, opposite number, vis-à-vis. —*See also* **mate, parallel.**

counterpoint *noun.* —*See* **contrast.**

counterpoint *verb.* —*See* **compare.**

counterpoise *noun.* —*See* **balance** (1).

counterpoise *verb.* —*See* **balance** (2), **cancel** (2).

counterpose *verb.* —*See* **compare.**

counterproductive *adjective.* —*See* **ineffectual** (1).

countervail *verb.* —*See* **balance** (2), **cancel** (2).

countless *adjective.* —*See* **incalculable.**

country *adjective.* Of or relating to the countryside ▶ agrarian, arcadian, bucolic, campestral, georgic, pastoral, provincial, rural, rustic. *Informal:* hick.

country *noun.* A remote or rural area ▶ backcountry, backwoods, countryside, God's country, hinterland. *Informal:* sticks. *Slang:* boondocks, boonies, hicksville. [*Compare* **desert**[1], **wilderness.**] —*See also* **state** (1), **territory.**

✚ **CORE SYNONYMS:** *country, rural, bucolic, rustic, pastoral.* These adjectives mean typical of the countryside as distinguished from the city. *Country* is the most general: *I left New York City to visit my country cousins. Rural* applies to sparsely settled or agricultural country: "*I do love quiet, rural England*" (George Meredith). *Bucolic* is often used pejoratively or facetiously of country people or their manners: "*The keenest of bucolic minds felt a whispering awe at the sight of the gentry*" (George Eliot). *Rustic* frequently suggests a lack of sophistication or elegance, but it may also connote artless and pleasing simplicity: "*some rustic phrases which I had learned at the farmer's house*" (Jonathan Swift). *The hiker slept in a charming, rustic cottage. Pastoral,* which evokes the image of shepherds, sheep, and verdant countryside, suggests serenity: *The train passed through pastoral landscapes en route to Oxford.*

---

countryman *or* **countrywoman** *noun.* A person who is from one's own country ▶ compatriot, fellow citizen, kinsman, kinswoman.

countryside *noun.* —*See* **country.**

coup *noun.* —*See* **accomplishment.**

couple *noun.* Two items of the same kind together ▶ brace, couplet, doublet, duet, duo, dyad, match, pair, span, two, twosome, yoke. [*Compare* **several.**]

couple *verb.* —*See* **associate** (3), **attach** (1), **combine** (1).

couplet *noun.* —*See* **couple.**

coupling *noun.* —*See* **joint** (1).

courage *noun.* The quality of mind enabling one to face danger or hardship resolutely ▶ backbone, braveness, bravery, courageousness, dauntlessness, doughtiness, fearlessness, fortitude, gallantry, gameness, hardihood, hardiness, heart, heroism, intestinal fortitude, intrepidity, intrepidness, mettle, nerve, pluck, pluckiness, prowess, spine, spirit, stoutheartedness, undauntedness, valiance, valiancy, valiantness, valor. *Informal:* grit, spunk, spunkiness. *Slang:* guts, gutsiness, moxie. [*Compare* **daring, decision, temerity.**]

courageous *adjective.* —*See* **brave.**

courageousness *noun.* —*See* **courage.**

courier *noun.* —*See* **messenger.**

course *noun.* The compass direction in which a ship or aircraft moves ▶ bearing, heading, vector. —*See also* **approach** (1), **direction, life, series, way** (2).

course *verb.* —*See* **flow** (1).

court *noun.* **1.** A roofless area partially or entirely enclosed by walls or buildings ▶ atrium, close, courtyard, enclosure, patio, quad, quadrangle, yard. **2.** A judicial assembly ▶ bar, forum, judicature, judiciary, tribunal.

court *verb.* **1.** To behave so as to bring on danger, for example ▶ invite, provoke, solicit, tempt. ***Idioms:*** ask (*or* go looking) for it. [*Compare* **attract, provoke.**] **2.** To attempt to gain the affection of ▶ chase, pursue, run after, spark, woo. *Informal:* romance. ***Idiom:*** make a play for. [*Compare* **appeal, flirt, see.**]

courteous *adjective.* **1.** Characterized by good manners ▶ civil, genteel, gentlemanly, mannerly, polite, well-bred, well-mannered, well-spoken. [*Compare* **ceremonious, cultured, suave.**] **2.** Characterized by kindness and warm, unaffected courtesy ▶ affable, gracious, hospitable. [*Compare* **amiable.**] —*See also* **attentive.**

✦ **CORE SYNONYMS:** *courteous, polite, mannerly, civil, genteel.* These adjectives mean conforming to or characterized by good manners. *Courteous* implies courtliness and dignity: "*If a man be gracious and courteous to strangers, it shows he is a citizen of the world*" (Francis Bacon). *Polite* and *mannerly* imply consideration for others and the adherence to conventional social standards of good behavior: "*It costs nothing to be polite*" (Winston S. Churchill). *The child was scolded by the teacher for not being more mannerly. Civil* suggests only the barest observance of accepted social usages; it often means merely neither polite nor rude: *If you can't be friendly, at least be civil. Genteel*, which originally meant well-bred, now usually suggests excessive and affected refinement: *"A man, indeed, is not genteel when he gets drunk"* (James Boswell).

◀ **ANTONYM:** *discourteous*

---

courteousness *noun.* —*See* **amenities** (2), **courtesy.**

courter *noun.* —*See* **beau** (1).

courtesan *noun.* —*See* **harlot.**

courtesy *noun.* Well-mannered behavior toward others ▶ civility, courteousness, genteelness, gentility, mannerliness, politeness, politesse. [*Compare* **consideration, manners.**] —*See also* **amenities** (2), **favor** (1).

courtier *noun.* —*See* **sycophant.**

courtliness *noun.* —*See* **elegance.**

courtly *adjective.* —*See* **ceremonious, elegant, gracious** (2).

courtyard *noun.* —*See* **court** (1).

cove *noun.* —*See* **harbor.**

covenant *noun.* —*See* **agreement** (1), **promise** (1).

covenant *verb.* —*See* **contract** (1), **pledge** (1).

cover *verb.* **1.** To extend over the surface of ▶ blanket, cap, carpet, coat, overlay, overspread, pave, plate, spread. [*Compare* **finish.**] **2.** To journey over ▶ cross, go, make, traverse. *Informal:* do. [*Compare* **cross, journey.**] —*See also* **conceal, defend** (1), **face** (2), **go** (4).

cover for *verb.* —*See* **substitute.**

cover *noun.* **1.** Something that physically protects, especially from danger ▶ ark, asylum, covert, coverture, harbor, haven, port, protection, refuge, retreat, safe house, sanctuary, screen, shelter. [*Compare* **defense, fort, hide-out.**] **2.** Something that covers, especially to prevent contents from spilling ▶ cap, covering, lid, top. [*Compare* **plug.**] —*See also* **façade** (2), **substitute, veil, wrapper.**

✚ **CORE SYNONYMS:** *cover, shelter, retreat, refuge, asylum, sanctuary.* These nouns refer to places affording protection, as from danger, or to the state of being protected. *Cover* suggests something that conceals: *traveled under cover of darkness. Shelter* usually implies a covered or enclosed area that protects temporarily, as from injury or attack: *built a shelter out of pine and hemlock boughs. Retreat* applies chiefly to a secluded place to which one retires for meditation, peace, or privacy: *a rural cabin that served as a weekend retreat. Refuge* suggests a place of escape from pursuit or from difficulties that beset one: *"The great advantage of a hotel is that it's a refuge from home life"* (George Bernard Shaw). *Asylum* adds to *refuge* the idea of legal protection or of immunity from arrest: *"O! receive the fugitive and prepare in time an asylum for mankind"* (Thomas Paine). *Sanctuary* denotes a sacred or inviolable place of refuge: *political refugees finding sanctuary in a monastery.*

---

coverage *noun.* —*See* **extent.**

covering *noun.* Something that covers, especially to prevent contents from spilling ▶ cap, cover, lid, top. [*Compare* **plug.**] —*See also* **coat** (2), **wrapper.**

covert *adjective.* —*See* **hidden** (1), **secret** (1), **ulterior** (1).

covert *noun.* A hiding place ▶ den, hideaway, hide-out, lair. —*See also* **cover** (1).

covertly *adverb.* —*See* **secretly.**

covertness *noun.* —*See* **secrecy.**

covet *verb.* To feel envy toward or for ▶ begrudge, envy, grudge. —*See also* **desire.**

covetous *adjective.* —*See* **envious, greedy.**

covetousness *noun.* —*See* **envy, greed.**

cow *verb.* —*See* **intimidate.**

coward *noun.* An ignoble, uncourageous person ▶ caitiff, craven, cur, dastard, funk, milksop, milquetoast, mouse, poltroon, recreant, sissy. *Informal:* nervous Nellie, scaredy-cat. *Slang:* chicken, fraidy cat, yellow-belly. [*Compare* **defector, sneak, weakling.**]

cowardice *noun.* Ignoble lack of courage ► chickenheartedness, cowardliness, cravenness, dastardliness, faintheartedness, funk, poltroonery, pusillanimity, recreance, spinelessness, unmanliness, white feather. *Slang:* gutlessness, yellowness, yellow streak. [*Compare* **fear.**]

cowardliness *noun.* —*See* **cowardice.**

cowardly *adjective.* Ignobly lacking in courage ► caitiff, chickenhearted, chicken-livered, craven, dastardly, fainthearted, lily-livered, pusillanimous, recreant, sissy, spineless, supine, unmanly, weak-kneed. *Slang:* chicken, gutless, wimpy, yellow, yellow-bellied. [*Compare* **afraid.**]

cower *verb.* —*See* **flinch.**

coxcomb *noun.* A man who is vain about his clothes ► beau, dandy, fop, peacock, swell.

coy *adjective.* Given to flirting ► coquettish, flirtatious, flirty. —*See also* **shy[1].**

coyness *noun.* —*See* **shyness.**

cozen *verb.* —*See* **cheat** (1), **deceive.**

cozener *noun.* —*See* **cheat** (2).

cozy *adjective.* —*See* **comfortable, intimate[1]** (1).

crab *noun.* —*See* **grouch.**

crab *verb.* —*See* **complain.**

crabbed *adjective.* —*See* **complex** (1), **ill-tempered.**

crabby *adjective.* —*See* **ill-tempered.**

crack *verb.* **1.** To undergo partial breaking ► break, cleave, crackle, craze, fissure, fracture, rift, rupture, split. [*Compare* **cut, tear[1].**] **2.** To make a sudden, sharp noise ► bang, bark, clap, pop, snap. [*Compare* **blast, crackle, snap.**] —*See also* **bang, break** (1), **collapse** (1), **decipher, open** (1).

crack up *verb.* —*See* **break** (3), **collapse** (1), **crash.**

crack *noun.* **1.** A sudden sharp, explosive noise ► bang, bark, clap, detonation, explosion, pop, rat-a-tat-tat, report, snap. [*Compare* **blast, crackle, snap.**] **2.** A partial opening caused by splitting and rupture ► breach, break, chink, cleavage, cleft, cranny, crevice, fault, fissure, fracture, niche, rift, rupture, split. [*Compare* **cut, hole.**] **3.** A flippant or sarcastic remark ► barb, dig, jest, quip. *Slang:* wisecrack. [*Compare* **joke.**] —*See also* **attempt, blow[2], flash** (2).

crack *adjective.* —*See* **expert.**

crackdown *noun.* Forceful subjugation, as against an uprising ► clampdown, lockdown, repression, suppression. [*Compare* **oppression, restraint.**]

cracked *adjective.* —*See* **insane, open** (1).

crackerjack *adjective.* —*See* **expert.**

crackerjack *noun.* —*See* **expert.**

crackle *verb.* To make a series of short, sharp noises ► crepitate, splutter, sputter. [*Compare* **crack, hiss, snap.**] —*See also* **burn** (2), **crack** (1).

crackle *noun.* A light, sharp noise ► clack, click, snap. [*Compare* **crack.**]

crackpot *noun.* A person regarded as strange, eccentric, or crazy ► crazy, eccentric, lunatic. *Informal:* crank, loon, loony. *Slang:* cuckoo, ding-a-ling, freak, kook, nut, screwball, space cadet, weirdie, weirdo. [*Compare* **character.**]

crackup *noun. Informal* A sudden sharp decline in mental, emotional, or physical health ► breakdown, collapse. [*Compare* **infirmity.**] —*See also* **crash** (2).

craft *noun.* **1.** A conveyance that travels over water ► bark, barque, boat, ship, vessel, watercraft. **2.** The technique, style, and quality of working ► craftsmanship, work, workmanship. [*Compare* **approach.**] —*See also* **ability** (1), **art, business** (2), **dishonesty** (2).

craftiness *noun.* —*See* **art, dishonesty** (2).

craftsmanship *noun.* The technique, style, and quality of working ▶ craft, work, workmanship. [*Compare* **approach.**]
crafty *adjective.* —*See* **artful.**
craggy *or* **cragged** *adjective.* —*See* **rough** (1).
cram *verb. Informal* To study or work hard, especially when pressed for time ▶ lucubrate, study. *Informal:* bone up, grind. ***Idioms:*** burn the midnight oil, hit the books. [*Compare* **examine.**] —*See also* **crowd, fill** (1).
cramp[1] *noun.* —*See* **pain.**
cramp[2] *noun.* —*See* **restraint.**
cramp *verb.* To check the freedom and spontaneity of ▶ constrain, constrict, inhibit. [*Compare* **restrain.**]
cramped *adjective.* —*See* **tight** (4).
cranium *noun.* The bony framework of the head ▶ braincase, brainpan, skull. [*Compare* **head.**]
crank *noun.* —*See* **crackpot, grouch.**
crank up *verb.* —*See* **elevate** (2).
crankiness *noun.* —*See* **temper** (1).
cranky *adjective.* —*See* **eccentric, ill-tempered.**
cranny *noun.* —*See* **crack** (2).
crap *noun.* —*See* **filth, nonsense.**
crapehanger *noun.* —*See* **pessimist** (2).
crappy *adjective.* —*See* **shoddy.**
crapulence *noun.* Unpleasant physical and mental effects following overindulgence in alcohol ▶ hangover, katzenjammer. *Informal:* head. —*See also* **drunkenness.**
crapulous *or* **crapulent** *adjective.* —*See* **drunk.**
crash *verb.* To wreck a vehicle ▶ rear-end, sideswipe, smash, total, wreck. *Informal:* crack up, pile up. —*See also* **bang, blast** (1), **collapse** (2), **collide, malfunction, retire** (1).
crash *noun.* **1.** A forceful movement causing a loud noise ▶ bang, slam, smash, wham. **2.** A wrecking of a vehicle ▶ accident, rear-ender, sideswipe, smash, smashup, wreck. *Informal:* crackup, fender-bender, pileup. —*See also* **blast** (1), **clash, collapse** (2), **collision.**
crash *adjective. Informal* Designed to meet emergency needs as quickly as possible ▶ *Informal:* hurry-up, rush.
crashing *adjective.* —*See* **utter**[2].
crass *adjective.* —*See* **coarse** (1).
crate *noun.* —*See* **cage, package.**
crave *verb.* To have a greedy, obsessive desire ▶ hunger, itch, lust, thirst. [*Compare* **desire.**] —*See also* **appeal** (1).
craven *adjective.* —*See* **cowardly.**
craven *noun.* —*See* **coward.**
cravenness *noun.* —*See* **cowardice.**
craving *noun.* —*See* **desire** (1).
crawl *verb.* **1.** To move along in a crouching or prone position ▶ creep, sinuate, slide, snake, squiggle, squirm, undulate, waggle, wiggle, worm, wriggle, writhe. ***Idiom:*** go on all fours. **2.** To advance slowly ▶ creep, drag, inch, poke. ***Idiom:*** go at a snail's pace. [*Compare* **trudge.**] —*See also* **teem**[1].
crawl *noun.* A very slow rate of speed ▶ creep, footpace, slow motion. ***Idiom:*** snail's pace.
crawling *adjective.* —*See* **busy** (2), **slow** (1).
craze *verb.* —*See* **crack** (1), **derange.**
craze *noun.* —*See* **enthusiasm** (2), **fashion.**
craziness *noun.* —*See* **foolishness, insanity.**
crazy *adjective.* —*See* **enthusiastic, foolish, insane.**
crazy *noun.* —*See* **crackpot.**
cream *noun.* —*See* **best** (1), **ointment.**
cream *verb.* —*See* **beat** (6), **foam, overwhelm** (1).
creaming *noun.* —*See* **defeat.**
cream puff *noun.* —*See* **baby** (2), **weakling.**
crease *noun.* —*See* **fold** (1), **wrinkle** (1).
crease *verb.* —*See* **fold, wrinkle.**
create *verb.* —*See* **compose** (1), **found, produce** (1).
creation *noun.* —*See* **composition** (1), **foundation, myth** (2), **universe.**

creative *adjective.* Relating to or appreciative of the arts ▶ aesthetic, artistic. *Informal:* artsy, arty. *—See also* **inventive.**

creativeness *noun. —See* **invention** (1).

creativity *noun. —See* **imagination, invention** (1).

creator *noun. —See* **developer, originator.**

creature *noun. —See* **human being.**

credence *noun.* Mental acceptance of the actuality of something ▶ belief, credit, faith. [*Compare* **trust.**]

credential *noun.* A quality that makes a person suitable for a particular position or task ▶ attainment, endowment, qualification, skill.

credibility *or* **credibleness** *noun. —See* **verisimilitude.**

credible *adjective. —See* **authentic** (2), **believable.**

credit *noun.* Mental acceptance of the actuality of something ▶ belief, credence, faith. [*Compare* **trust.**] *—See also* **acceptance** (2).

credit *verb.* To have confidence in the truthfulness of ▶ believe, trust. ***Idioms:*** give credence to, have faith (*or* trust *or* confidence) in, take at one's word. [*Compare* **depend on.**] *—See also* **attribute.**

creditability *or* **creditableness** *noun. —See* **verisimilitude.**

creditable *adjective. —See* **admirable, believable.**

credo *noun. —See* **doctrine.**

credulous *adjective. —See* **gullible.**

creed *noun. —See* **doctrine, religion.**

creek *noun. —See* **brook[1].**

creel *noun.* A container made of interwoven material ▶ basket, hamper, pannier. [*Compare* **container.**]

creep *verb.* To advance slowly ▶ crawl, drag, inch, poke. ***Idiom:*** go at a snail's pace. [*Compare* **trudge.**] *—See also* **crawl** (1), **sneak.**

creep *noun.* **1.** A very slow rate of speed ▶ crawl, footpace, slow motion. ***Idiom:*** snail's pace. **2.** *Slang* A repulsive, despicable, or immoral person ▶ insect, jackal, lowlife, reptile, snake, weasel. *Slang:* louse, maggot, rat, skunk, sleaze, sleazebag, slimeball, toad, troll, worm. [*Compare* **betrayer, informer, sneak.**]

creepy *adjective. —See* **weird.**

crème de la crème *noun. —See* **best** (1), **society** (1).

crepitate *verb.* To make a series of short, sharp noises ▶ crackle, splutter, sputter. [*Compare* **crack, hiss, snap.**]

crescendo *verb. —See* **climax.**

crescent *noun. —See* **bend.**

crest *noun. —See* **climax.**

crest *verb.* To put a topping on ▶ cap, crown, tip, top (off). [*Compare* **cover.**] *—See also* **climax.**

cretin *noun. —See* **dullard, fool.**

crevice *noun. —See* **crack** (2).

crew *noun. —See* **circle** (3), **crowd, force** (3).

crib *verb. —See* **plagiarize, steal.**

crib *noun. —See* **translation.**

cribber *noun.* One who reproduces another's work without permission ▶ pirate, plagiarist, plagiarizer. [*Compare* **forger.**]

crime *noun.* **1.** An act that violates public law ▶ felony, illegality, malefaction, misdeed, misdemeanor, offense, tort. [*Compare* **breach.**] **2.** A wicked act or wicked behavior ▶ deviltry, diablerie, evil, evildoing, immorality, iniquity, misdeed, offense, peccancy, sin, wickedness, wrong, wrongdoing. [*Compare* **corruption, cruelty, outrage.**] **3.** A great disappointment or regrettable fact ▶ pity, shame. *Slang:* bummer. ***Idiom:*** a crying shame. *—See also* **injustice** (1).

criminal *adjective.* **1.** Of, involving, or being a crime ▶ felonious, illegal, illegitimate, illicit, lawless, unlawful, wrongful. [*Compare* **forbidden.**] **2.** Contrary to accepted, especially moral conventions ▶ illicit, unlawful.

criminal *noun.* One who commits a crime ▶ convict, culprit, delinquent, desperado, felon, gangster, lawbreaker, malefactor, offender, outlaw, perpetrator, scofflaw, transgressor. *Informal:* crook, mobster. *Slang:* con, perp. [*Compare* **evildoer, fugitive, larcenist, thug.**]

criminality *noun.* —*See* **corruption** (1).

criminate *verb.* To cause to appear involved in or guilty of a crime or fault ▶ incriminate, implicate, inculpate. [*Compare* **accuse.**]

crimination *noun.* —*See* **accusation.**

crimp *verb.* —*See* **fold, wrinkle.**

crimp *noun.* —*See* **fold** (1).

crimson *verb.* —*See* **blush.**

cringe *verb.* —*See* **fawn, flinch.**

cringe *noun.* —*See* **recoil.**

crinkle *verb.* —*See* **fold, wrinkle.**

crinkle *noun.* —*See* **fold** (1), **wrinkle** (1).

cripple *verb.* To deprive of a limb or bodily member or its use ▶ amputate, castrate, dismember, maim, mangle, mutilate. [*Compare* **batter, cut.**] —*See also* **disable** (1).

crisis *noun.* A decisive point ▶ climacteric, climax, clutch, crossroads, crunch, crux, exigence, exigency, head, juncture, pass, turning point, zero hour. ***Idiom:*** moment of truth. [*Compare* **predicament.**] —*See also* **emergency.**

✦ **CORE SYNONYMS:** *crisis, crossroads, exigency, head, juncture, pass.* These nouns denote a decisive or critical point: *a military crisis; government policy at the crossroads; had predicted the health-care exigency; a problem that is coming to a head; negotiations that had reached a crucial juncture; things rapidly coming to a desperate pass.*

crisp *adjective.* —*See* **brief.**

crisscross *verb.* —*See* **cross** (2).

criterion *noun.* —*See* **standard.**

critic *noun.* **1.** A person who evaluates and reports on the worth of something ▶ appraiser, assessor, commentator, judge, pundit, reviewer. **2.** A person who finds fault ▶ blamer, carper, caviler, censurer, criticizer, faultfinder, hypercritic, mudslinger, nagger, niggler, nitpicker, pettifogger, quibbler. *Informal:* Monday morning quarterback. [*Compare* **scold.**]

critical *adjective.* **1.** Inclined to judge too severely ▶ captious, carping, censorious, faultfinding, hypercritical, judgmental, nagging, overcritical, reproachful. [*Compare* **severe.**] **2.** Keenly perceptive or discerning ▶ acute, discerning, discriminating, incisive, keen, penetrating, perceptive, probing, sensitive, sharp, trenchant. [*Compare* **careful, clever, intelligent, shrewd.**] —*See also* **essential** (1), **urgent** (1).

criticism *noun.* The act or an instance of finding fault ▶ blame, censure, condemnation, denunciation, finger-pointing, judgment, reprehension, reprobation. *Informal:* flak, guilt trip, pan. *Slang:* knock. [*Compare* **disapproval, rebuke.**] —*See also* **commentary.**

criticize *verb.* **1.** To find fault with ▶ blame, carp at, censure, fault, judge, rap, reprove, scapegoat. *Informal:* guilt-trip, pan, zing. *Slang:* knock, put down. ***Idioms:*** find fault with, lay (*or* put) a guilt trip on, pick apart (*or* to pieces), point the finger at, speak ill of. [*Compare* **chastise, malign, slam.**] **2.** To write a critical report on ▶ critique, review. [*Compare* **estimate.**]

criticizer *noun.* —*See* **critic** (2).

critique *noun.* —*See* **commentary.**

critique *verb.* To write a critical report on ▶ criticize, review. [*Compare* **estimate.**]

croak *verb.* —*See* **die, gasp.**

croaker *noun.* —*See* **pessimist** (2).

croaky *or* **croaking** *adjective.* —*See* **hoarse.**

crocked *adjective.* —*See* **drunk.**

crone *noun.* —*See* **witch** (2).

crony *noun.* —*See* **associate** (2), **friend.**

crook *noun.* —*See* **bend, cheat** (2), **criminal, stick** (2).

crook *verb.* —*See* **bend** (1).

crooked *adjective.* —*See* **bent, corrupt** (2), **dishonest, irregular.**

crookedness *noun.* —*See* **corruption** (2), **dishonesty** (1), **irregularity.**

croon *verb.* —*See* **sing.**

crooner *noun.* —*See* **vocalist.**

crop *noun.* —*See* **harvest.**

crop *verb.* —*See* **browse** (2), **cut** (3), **gather.**

crop up *verb.* —*See* **begin.**

cross *noun.* —*See* **burden**[1] (1).

cross *verb.* **1.** To go or extend across ▶ ford, pass, span, track, transit, traverse. **2.** To pass through or over ▶ crisscross, crosscut, cut across, decussate, intersect. [*Compare* **close.**] —*See also* **cancel** (1), **cover** (2), **frustrate.**

cross up *verb.* —*See* **betray** (1), **confuse** (3), **destroy** (1).

cross *adjective.* —*See* **angry, ill-tempered.**

crossbeam *noun.* —*See* **beam** (2).

crosscut *verb.* —*See* **cross** (2).

cross-examine *verb.* —*See* **ask** (1).

cross-examiner *noun.* —*See* **inquirer.**

cross-eyed *adjective.* Marked by or affected with a squint ▶ squint-eyed, squinty, strabismal, strabismic.

crossfire *noun.* —*See* **barrage.**

crossing *adjective.* —*See* **transverse.**

crossing *noun.* —*See* **journey.**

crossroads *noun.* —*See* **crisis, junction.**

crosstie *noun.* —*See* **beam** (2).

crosswise *or* **crossways** *adjective.* —*See* **transverse.**

crouch *verb.* —*See* **stoop.**

crow *verb.* —*See* **boast, exult** (1).

crow *noun.* —*See* **witch** (2).

crowd *noun.* An enormous number of persons gathered together ▶ army, cloud, concourse, crew, crush, drove, flock, gaggle, herd, horde, host, legion, mass, mob, multitude, pack, press, rout, ruck, scores, stable, swarm, throng, troop. [*Compare* **band**[2], **flock, group.**] —*See also* **assembly, circle** (3), **commonalty.**

crowd *verb.* To move into an area or space in large numbers ▶ cram, crush, flock, flood, jam, pile, pour, press, squeeze, swarm, throng, troop. —*See also* **fill** (1), **push** (1).

✦ **CORE SYNONYMS:** *crowd, crush, flock, horde, mob, press, throng.* These nouns denote an enormous group of people gathered close to one another: *a crowd of well-wishers; a crush of autograph seekers; a flock of schoolchildren; a horde of demonstrators; a mob of hard-rock enthusiasts; a press of shoppers; throngs of tourists.*

---

crowded *adjective.* —*See* **busy** (3), **thick** (2), **tight** (4).

crown *noun.* —*See* **circle** (1), **climax, head** (1).

crown *verb.* To put a topping on ▶ cap, crest, tip, top (off). [*Compare* **cover.**] —*See also* **climax.**

crowning *adjective.* ▶ climactic, culminating, peak. [*Compare* **last.**]

crow's-foot *noun.* —*See* **wrinkle** (1).

crow's nest *noun.* —*See* **lookout** (2).

crucial *adjective.* —*See* **decisive, important, primary** (1), **urgent** (1).

crucible *noun.* —*See* **trial** (1).

crucify *verb.* To subject another to extreme physical cruelty, as in punishing ▶ harrow, rack, torment, torture. ***Idioms:*** put on the rack (*or* wheel), put the screws to. [*Compare* **punish.**]

crud *noun.* —*See* **filth.**

crude *adjective.* Being in a natural state ▶ native, raw, rough, rude, unprocessed, unrefined, virgin. [*Compare* **wild.**] —*See also* **amateurish, coarse** (1), **rough** (4), **rude** (1).

crude *noun.* —*See* **oil.**

✦ **CORE SYNONYMS:** *crude, native, raw, unrefined.* These adjectives mean in a natural state and not yet processed for use: *crude rubber; native iron; raw cotton; unrefined sugar.*

---

cruel *adjective.* Characterized by or inflicting suffering or pain ▶ barbarous, brutal, ferocious, fierce, grim, inhuman, inhumane, merciless, pitiless, ruthless, sadistic, savage, truculent, vicious.

[*Compare* **fiendish, malevolent, murderous.**] —*See also* **bitter** (2).

✦ **CORE SYNONYMS:** *cruel, fierce, ferocious, barbarous, inhuman, savage, vicious.* These adjectives mean predisposed to inflict violence, pain, or hardship, or to find satisfaction in the suffering of others: *a cruel tyrant; a fierce warrior; a ferocious attack dog; a barbarous crime; inhuman treatment of captured soldiers; a savage outburst of temper; a vicious kick.*

---

cruelty *noun.* The quality or condition of being cruel ▶ barbarity, bestiality, brutality, ferocity, fiendishness, fierceness, grimness, inhumanity, mercilessness, pitilessness, ruthlessness, sadism, savagery, truculence, truculency. [*Compare* **crime, malevolence.**]

cruise *noun.* —*See* **journey.**

crumb *noun.* —*See* **bit**[1] (1), **bit**[1] (2).

crumble *verb.* —*See* **break** (3), **decay, disintegrate.**

crummy *adjective.* —*See* **shoddy.**

crump *verb.* —*See* **chew.**

crumple *verb.* —*See* **break** (3), **buckle, wrinkle.**

crumple *noun.* —*See* **fold** (1).

crunch *verb.* To rub together noisily ▶ gnash, grind. —*See also* **chew.**

crunch *noun.* —*See* **crisis.**

crusade *noun.* A goal served with great or uncompromising dedication ▶ cause, holy war, jihad. —*See also* **drive** (1).

crush *verb.* **1.** To press forcefully so as to reduce to a pulpy mass ▶ flatten, mash, mush, pulp, smash, squash. [*Compare* **squeeze.**] **2.** To break up into tiny particles ▶ atomize, bray, comminute, granulate, grind, levigate, mill, pestle, pound, powder, pulverize, smash, triturate. [*Compare* **break.**] **3.** To extract from by applying pressure ▶ express, press, squeeze. —*See also* **break** (2), **crowd, destroy** (1), **overwhelm** (1), **overwhelm** (2), **push** (1), **suppress.**

crush *noun.* —*See* **crowd.** An extravagant, short-lived romantic attachment ▶ *Informal:* infatuation, thing. ***Idiom:*** passing fancy. [*Compare* **love, obsession.**]

✦ **CORE SYNONYMS:** *crush, mash, pulp, smash, squash.* These verbs mean to press forcefully so as to reduce to a pulpy mass: *crushed the rose geranium leaves; mashed the sweet potatoes; pulped raspberries through a sieve; smashed the bamboo stems with a hammer; squashed the wine grapes.*

---

crust *noun.* —*See* **coat** (2), **impudence.**

crusty *adjective.* —*See* **abrupt** (1).

crutch *noun.* —*See* **support.**

crux *noun.* —*See* **crisis.**

cry *verb.* To shed tears ▶ bawl, blubber, howl, keen, lament, mewl, pule, sniffle, snivel, sob, squall, wail, weep, whimper, whine, yowl. ***Idioms:*** cry one's eyes out, turn on the waterworks. [*Compare* **bawl, grieve.**] —*See also* **exclaim, shout.**

cry up *verb.* —*See* **promote** (3).

cry *noun.* **1.** A fit of crying ▶ bawling, blubbering, lament, lamentation, plaint, sobbing, tears, wailing, weeping, whimpering, whining. [*Compare* **howl.**] **2.** A rallying term used by proponents of a cause ▶ battle cry, call to arms, call to battle, motto, rallying cry, slogan, war cry, watchword. —*See also* **demand** (1), **shout.**

✦ **CORE SYNONYMS:** *cry, weep, wail, keen, whimper, sob, blubber.* These verbs mean to make inarticulate sounds of grief, unhappiness, or pain. *Cry* and *weep* both involve the shedding of tears; *cry* more strongly implies accompanying sound: "*She cried without trying to suppress any of the noisier manifestations of grief and confusion*" (J.D. Salinger). "*I weep for what I'm like when I'm alone*" (Theodore Roethke). *Wail* refers primarily to sustained, inarticulate mournful sound: "*The women . . . began to wail* *together; they mourned with shrill cries"* (Joseph Conrad). *Keen* suggests wailing and lamentation for the dead: *"It is the wild Irish women keening over their dead"* (George A. Lawrence). *Whimper* refers to low, plaintive, broken or repressed cries: *The condemned prisoner cowered and began to whimper for clemency. Sob* describes weeping or a mixture of broken speech and weeping marked by convulsive breathing or gasping: *"sobbing and crying, and wringing her hands as if her heart would break"* (Laurence Sterne). *Blubber* refers to noisy shedding of tears accompanied by broken or inarticulate speech: *"When he drew out what had been a fiddle, crushed to morsels in the greatcoat, he blubbered aloud"* (Emily Brontë).

---

crybaby *noun.* —*See* **baby** (2).
crying *adjective.* —*See* **urgent** (1).
crypt *noun.* —*See* **grave**[1].
cryptic *adjective.* —*See* **ambiguous** (1), **mysterious.**
crystal *adjective.* —*See* **clear** (1).
crystal clear *adjective.* —*See* **apparent** (1), **clear** (1).
crystalline *adjective.* —*See* **clear** (1).
cuckoo *noun.* —*See* **crackpot.**
cuckoo *adjective.* —*See* **enthusiastic, insane.**
cuddle *verb.* —*See* **caress, snuggle.**
cudgel *noun.* —*See* **beat** (1).
cue *noun.* —*See* **hint** (2).
cue in *verb.* —*See* **inform** (1).
cuff *verb.* —*See* **slap.**
cuff *noun.* —*See* **slap.**
cul-de-sac *noun.* A course leading nowhere ▶ blind alley, dead end.
cull *verb.* —*See* **choose** (1), **glean.**
culminate *verb.* —*See* **climax.**
culminating *adjective.* ▶ climactic, crowning, peak. [*Compare* **last.**]
culmination *noun.* —*See* **climax, fulfillment** (1).
culpability *noun.* —*See* **blame.**
culpable *adjective.* —*See* **blameworthy.**
culprit *noun.* —*See* **criminal.**
cult *noun.* —*See* **religion.**
cultivate *verb.* —*See* **grow, nurture, promote** (2), **till.**
cultivated *adjective.* —*See* **cultured.**
cultivation *noun.* —*See* **culture** (3).
cultrate *adjective.* —*See* **pointed.**
cultural *adjective.* Promoting culture ▶ advancing, aesthetic, civilizing, cultivating, edifying, enlightening, fostering, humanizing, refining. [*Compare* **intellectual.**]
culture *noun.* **1.** The total product of human creativity and intellect ▶ civilization, Kultur, society. **2.** Behavior patterns, traits, and products considered as an expression of a certain people or period ▶ civilization, convention, custom, ethos, folkways, lifestyle, mores, society, tradition. **3.** Excellent taste resulting from intellectual development ▶ breeding, civilization, cultivation, enlightenment, refinement, sophistication. [*Compare* **courtesy, education, elegance.**]
culture *verb.* —*See* **till.**
cultured *adjective.* Characterized by discriminating taste and broad knowledge as a result of development or education ▶ civilized, cultivated, educated, highbrow, polished, refined, sophisticated, urbane, well-bred. [*Compare* **courteous, delicate, suave.**]
cumber *verb.* —*See* **burden**[1].
cumbersome *or* **cumbrous** *adjective.* —*See* **bulky** (1).
cumshaw *noun.* —*See* **gratuity.**
cumulate *verb.* —*See* **accumulate.**
cumulation *noun.* —*See* **accumulation** (1).
cumulative *adjective.* Increasing, as in force, by successive additions ▶ accumulative, additive.
cumulus *noun.* —*See* **heap** (1).
cunning *adjective.* —*See* **artful.**
cunning *noun.* —*See* **art.**
cupidity *noun.* —*See* **greed.**
cupola *noun.* —*See* **lookout** (2).
cur *noun.* —*See* **coward.**

curate *noun.* —*See* **cleric.**

curative *adjective.* Serving to cure ▶ antidotal, healing, medicinal, remedial, restorative, therapeutic. [*Compare* **corrective, tonic.**]

curative *noun.* —*See* **cure.**

curatorial *adjective.* —*See* **preservative.**

curb *noun.* —*See* **brake, restraint.**

curb *verb.* —*See* **restrain.**

curdle *verb.* —*See* **coagulate, decay.**

cure *noun.* An agent used to restore health ▶ antidote, corrective, countermeasure, curative, elixir, medicament, medication, medicine, nostrum, physic, remedy, restorative, treatment. [*Compare* **drug.**]

cure *verb.* To restore to health ▶ heal, rehabilitate, remedy, salve. *Informal:* doctor. [*Compare* **administer, fix, revive.**] —*See also* **prepare, preserve** (1).

cure-all *noun.* Something believed to cure all human disorders ▶ catholicon, elixir, panacea. [*Compare* **cure.**]

cureless *adjective.* —*See* **hopeless.**

curio *noun.* —*See* **novelty** (3).

curiosity *noun.* **1.** Mental acquisitiveness ▶ concern, concernment, curiousness, inquisitiveness, interest, interestedness, regard. ***Idiom:*** thirst for knowledge. **2.** Undue interest in the affairs of others ▶ curiousness, inquisitiveness, intrusiveness, meddlesomeness, prying. *Informal:* nosiness, snoopiness. —*See also* **mystery.**

curious *adjective.* **1.** Unduly interested in the affairs of others ▶ busy, inquisitive, inquisitorial, interfering, interposing, intrusive, meddlesome, meddling, obtrusive, officious, prying. *Informal:* nosy, snoopy. **2.** Eager to acquire knowledge ▶ acquisitive, inquiring, inquisitive, interested, intrigued, investigative, questioning, speculative. [*Compare* **eager, enthusiastic.**] **3.** Agreeably curious, especially in an old-fashioned or unusual way ▶ funny, odd, quaint. —*See also* **eccentric, funny** (3).

✚ **CORE SYNONYMS:** *curious, inquisitive, snoopy, nosy.* These adjectives apply to persons who are unduly interested in the affairs of other people. *Curious* most often implies an avid desire to know or learn, though it can suggest prying: *A curious child is a teacher's delight. A curious neighbor can be a nuisance. Inquisitive* frequently suggests excessive curiosity and the asking of many questions: *"Remember, no revolvers. The police are, I believe, proverbially inquisitive"* (Lord Dunsany). *Snoopy* suggests underhanded prying: *The snoopy hotel detective spied on guests in the lobby. Nosy* implies impertinent curiosity likened to that of an animal using its nose to examine or probe: *My nosy colleague went through my mail.*

---

curiously *adverb.* —*See* **unusually.**

curiousness *noun.* —*See* **curiosity** (1), **curiosity** (2).

curl *verb.* —*See* **wave** (1), **wind²**.

curl up *verb.* To take repose, as by sleeping or lying quietly ▶ lie (down), recline, repose, rest, stretch (out). [*Compare* **nap, sleep.**]

curl *noun.* Something with a curled or spiral shape ▶ coil, curlicue, frizzle, kink, lock, ringlet, spiral, swirl, twist, whorl, winding. [*Compare* **bend.**]

curly *adjective.* Shaped like or having curls ▶ coiled, frizzled, helical, kinky, spiral, swirly, twisted, twisty, whorled. [*Compare* **bent.**] —*See also* **wavy.**

currency *noun.* —*See* **money** (1).

current *adjective.* —*See* **contemporary** (2), **present¹**, **prevailing.**

current *noun.* —*See* **flow.**

currently *adverb.* —*See* **now** (1).

curse *noun.* **1.** A denunciation invoking a wish or threat of evil or injury ▶ anathema, ban, damnation, execration, hex, imprecation, malediction, oath. *Slang:* whammy. [*Compare* **spell².**] **2.** Something or someone believed to bring bad luck ▶ evil eye, hex, hoodoo, Jonah. *Informal:* jinx. [*Compare* **charm,**

magic.] **3.** A cause of suffering or harm ▶ affliction, bane, evil, ill, misery, plague, scourge, sorrow, woe. [*Compare* **burden[1], disaster.**] —*See also* **swearword.**

curse *verb.* **1.** To invoke evil upon ▶ anathematize, damn, hex, imprecate. [*Compare* **charm.**] **2.** To bring bad luck or evil to ▶ hex, hoodoo. *Informal:* jinx. **3.** To use profane or obscene language ▶ blaspheme, damn, curse. *Informal:* cuss. —*See also* **afflict.**

cursed *adjective.* —*See* **damned.**

cursive *noun.* —*See* **script** (1).

cursory *adjective.* —*See* **perfunctory, superficial.**

curt *adjective.* —*See* **abrupt** (1), **brief.**

curtail *verb.* —*See* **shorten.**

curtailment *noun.* —*See* **decrease.**

curtains *noun.* —*See* **death** (1).

curtsy *noun.* —*See* **bow[1].**

curtsy *verb.* —*See* **bow[1]** (1).

curvaceous *adjective.* —*See* **shapely.**

curvature *noun.* —*See* **bend.**

curve *noun.* —*See* **bend.**

curve *verb.* —*See* **bend** (1), **wave** (1).

curved *or* **curvilinear** *adjective.* —*See* **bent.**

curving *adjective.* Having bends, curves, or angles ▶ bending, crooked, curved. [*Compare* **bent.**]

curvy *adjective.* —*See* **shapely, wavy, winding.**

cushy *adjective.* —*See* **comfortable.**

cusp *noun.* —*See* **point** (1).

cuspate *or* **cuspated** *adjective.* —*See* **pointed.**

cuspidate *or* **cuspidated** *adjective.* —*See* **pointed.**

cuss *verb.* **1.** *Informal* To use profane or obscene language ▶ blaspheme, curse, damn, swear. **2.** To hurl strong deprecations, curses, or insults at ▶ *Informal:* cuss at, cuss out, mouth off at, swear at. [*Compare* **curse, insult, revile.**]

cuss *noun.* —*See* **swearword.**

custodian *noun.* One who is legally responsible for the care and management of the person or property of an incompetent or a minor ▶ caretaker, conservator, guardian, keeper. [*Compare* **representative.**]

custody *noun.* —*See* **care** (2), **detention.**

custom *noun.* A habitual way of behaving ▶ consuetude, convention, form, habit, habitude, manner, observance, practice, praxis, precedent, routine, usage, usance, use, way, wont. [*Compare* **addiction, approach, behavior, fashion.**] —*See also* **ceremony** (1), **culture** (2), **patronage** (2), **patronage** (3).

custom *adjective.* Made according to the specifications of the buyer ▶ bespoke, custom-built, customized, custom-made, made-to-order, tailored, tailor-made. ***Idiom:*** made-to-measure.

✚ **CORE SYNONYMS:** *custom, habit, practice, usage, use, wont, habitude.* These nouns denote patterns of behavior established by continual repetition. *Custom* is behavior as established by long practice and especially by accepted conventions: "*No written law has ever been more binding than unwritten custom supported by popular opinion*" (Carrie Chapman Catt). *Habit* applies to a behavior or practice so ingrained that it is often done without conscious thought: "*Habit rules the unreflecting herd*" (William Wordsworth). *Practice* denotes an often chosen pattern of individual or group behavior: "*You will find it a very good practice always to verify your references, sir*" (Martin Joseph Routh). *Usage* refers to an accepted standard for a group that regulates individual behavior: "*laws . . . corrected, altered, and amended by acts of parliament and common usage*" (William Blackstone). *Use* and *wont* are terms for customary and distinctive practice: "*situations where the use and wont of their fathers no longer meet their necessities*" (J.A. Froude). *Habitude* refers to an individual's behaving in a certain way rather than a specific act:

"*His real habitude gave life and grace/To appertainings and to ornament*" (William Shakespeare).

customarily *adverb.* —*See* **usually.**
customariness *noun.* —*See* **usualness.**
customary *adjective.* —*See* **accepted, common** (1).
custom-built *adjective.* —*See* **custom.**
customer *noun.* —*See* **consumer.**
customized *or* **custom-made** *adjective.* —*See* **custom.**
customs *noun.* —*See* **tax.**
cut *verb.* **1.** To penetrate with a sharp edge ▶ bayonet, bore, drill, gash, gore, gouge, hack, impale, incise, indent, knife, lacerate, lance, nick, notch, pierce, prick, punch, puncture, ream, scarify, slash, slit, spear, stab, stick, sting, transfix. [*Compare* **breach, crack, penetrate.**] **2.** To separate into parts with or as if with a sharp-edged instrument ▶ carve, cleave, dice, dissever, quarter, sever, slice, slit, snip, split. [*Compare* **divide.**] **3.** To decrease, as in length or amount, by or as if by severing or excising ▶ chop, clip, crop, cut back, cut down, lop, lower, mow, pare, prune, reap, scythe, shave, shear, sickle, skive, slash, snip, trim, truncate. [*Compare* **decrease, drop, shorten.**] **4.** To fail to attend on purpose ▶ duck, shirk, truant. *Informal:* skip. ***Idioms:*** go AWOL, play hooky (*or* truant). [*Compare* **avoid.**] —*See also* **censor** (1), **dilute, snub, swerve.**
cut across *verb.* —*See* **cross** (2).
cut back *verb.* —*See* **cut** (3).
cut down *verb.* —*See* **cut** (3), **drop** (3), **kill[1].**
cut in *verb.* —*See* **interrupt** (2), **intrude.**
cut off *verb.* To block the progress of and force to change direction ▶ head off, intercept. —*See also* **isolate** (1), **kill[1].**
cut out *verb.* To take the place of another against the other's will ▶ displace, force out, supplant, usurp. [*Compare* **assume, occupy, seize.**] —*See also* **break** (5), **go** (1).
cut up *verb.* —*See* **criticize** (1), **misbehave, shred, slam** (1).
cut *adjective.* —*See* **dilute.**
cut *noun.* **1.** An opening made by a sharp object ▶ gash, gouge, groove, incision, nick, notch, score, slash, slice, slit, split. [*Compare* **impression, prick, scrape.**] **2.** A part severed from a whole ▶ paring, piece, portion, shaving, slab, slice, sliver, snip, snippet, wedge. [*Compare* **flake, part.**] **3.** A deliberate slight ▶ rebuff, snub, spurn. *Informal:* cold shoulder, go-by. —*See also* **absence** (1), **allotment, decrease, taunt.**
cut-and-dried *adjective.* —*See* **ordinary.**
cutback *noun.* —*See* **decrease.**
cute *adjective.* —*See* **attractive, delightful.**
cutoff *noun.* —*See* **end** (1), **limit** (1), **stop** (1).
cutthroat *noun.* —*See* **murderer.**
cutthroat *adjective.* —*See* **competitive, murderous.**
cutting *adjective.* —*See* **biting.**
cutting edge *noun.* —*See* **forefront.**
cutting-edge *adjective.* —*See* **contemporary** (2).
cutup *noun.* —*See* **rascal.**
cycle *noun.* —*See* **circle** (2).
cyclic *adjective.* —*See* **periodic.**
cyclopean *adjective.* —*See* **enormous.**
cynic *noun.* A person who expects only the worst from people ▶ misanthrope, misanthropist, pessimist. [*Compare* **skeptic.**]
cynical *adjective.* —*See* **distrustful, sarcastic.**
cynicism *noun.* —*See* **distrust, sarcasm.**
cynosure *noun.* —*See* **center** (3).

D

dab *verb.* —*See* **smear, tap[1]** (1).
dab *noun.* —*See* **bit[1]** (1).

dabbler *noun.* —*See* **amateur.**
dab hand *noun.* —*See* **expert.**
dacha *noun.* —*See* **villa.**
dad *or* **daddy** *noun.* —*See* **father.**
daedal *or* **Daedalian** *adjective.* —*See* **complex** (1).
daffiness *noun.* —*See* **foolishness.**
daffy *adjective.* —*See* **foolish, insane.**
daft *adjective.* —*See* **foolish, insane.**
daftness *noun.* —*See* **foolishness.**
daily *adjective.* —*See* **common** (1), **everyday.**
dainty *adjective.* —*See* **delicate** (1), **fussy.**
dainty *noun.* —*See* **delicacy.**
dais *noun.* —*See* **stage** (1).
dale *noun.* —*See* **valley.**
dalliance *noun.* **1.** The practice of flirting ▶ coquetry, flirtation. **2.** A usually brief romance entered into lightly or frivolously ▶ fling, flirtation. [*Compare* **love.**]
dally *verb.* To treat lightly or flippantly ▶ flirt, play, toy, trifle. —*See also* **delay** (2), **flirt** (2), **hesitate.**
dam *verb.* —*See* **obstruct.**
dam *noun.* —*See* **bar** (1).
damage *noun.* Harm done to property or a person ▶ breakage, destruction, deterioration, disfigurement, impairment, injury, wastage, wreckage. [*Compare* **decay, destruction, ruin.**] —*See also* **account** (2), **harm.**
damage *verb.* To spoil the soundness or perfection of ▶ blemish, detract from, disserve, flaw, harm, hurt, impair, injure, mar, prejudice, tarnish, vitiate. [*Compare* **abuse, batter, botch, deform.**]
damages *noun.* —*See* **compensation.**
damn *verb.* **1.** To invoke evil upon ▶ anathematize, curse, hex, imprecate. [*Compare* **charm.**] **2.** To use profane or obscene language ▶ blaspheme, curse, swear. *Informal:* cuss. —*See also* **condemn.**
damn *adjective.* —*See* **damned.**
damnation *noun.* —*See* **curse** (1).
damned *adjective. Informal* So annoying or detestable as to deserve condemnation ▶ abominable, accursed, blasted, blessed, bloody, confounded, cursed, damn, darn, execrable, infernal. *Informal:* blamed, dang, danged, doggone, gosh-darn. *Slang:* freaking. *Regional:* dadblame, dadblasted, dadburn, dadgum, gol-durn, durn. [*Compare* **vexatious.**] —*See also* **condemned, utter**[2].
damp *adjective.* Slightly wet ▶ clammy, dank, dewy, moist. [*Compare* **sticky, wet.**] —*See also* **rainy.**
damp *verb.* —*See* **extinguish, muffle.**

✚ **CORE SYNONYMS:** *damp, moist, dank.* These adjectives mean slightly wet. *Damp* and *moist* both mean slightly wet, but *damp* often implies an unpleasant coldness: *firewood that rotted in the cold, damp cellar; a moist breeze that blew in from the ocean. Dank* emphasizes disagreeable, often unhealthful wetness: *a dank cave.*

---

dampen *verb.* To make moist ▶ bathe, moisten, wash, wet. —*See also* **depress, hinder, muffle.**
damsel *noun.* —*See* **girl.**
dance *verb.* To move rhythmically to music, using patterns of steps or gestures ▶ foot, step. *Slang:* boogie, hoof. ***Idioms:*** cut a rug, foot it, get down, trip the light fantastic. —*See also* **gambol.**
dance *noun.* A party or gathering for dancing ▶ ball, cotillion, formal, hoedown, masquerade, mixer, prom, promenade, rave. *Informal:* hop, sock-hop. [*Compare* **party.**]
dancer *noun.* A person who dances, especially professionally ▶ chorine, chorus boy, chorus girl, terpsichorean. *Slang:* hoofer.
dander[1] *noun.* —*See* **anger, temper** (1).
dander[2] *or* **dandruff** *noun.* Scaly pieces of dry skin that have been shed ▶ furfur, scale, scurf. [*Compare* **flake.**]
dandy *adjective.* —*See* **excellent, good** (1), **marvelous.**

dandy *noun.* A man who is preoccupied with or vain about his clothing and appearance ▶ beau, coxcomb, fop, peacock, swell.

danger *noun.* Exposure to harm, loss, or injury ▶ endangerment, hazard, imperilment, jeopardy, menace, peril, pitfall, risk, sword of Damocles, threat. [*Compare* **trap.**]

dangerous *adjective.* Involving or likely to cause risk, loss, or injury ▶ adventurous, chancy, grave, hazardous, insidious, jeopardous, menacing, parlous, perilous, risky, threatening, treacherous, unsafe, venturesome, venturous. *Slang:* dicey, hairy.

dangle *verb.* —*See* **hang** (1).

dangling *adjective.* —*See* **hanging, loose** (1).

dangly *adjective.* —*See* **hanging.**

dank *adjective.* Slightly wet ▶ clammy, damp, dewy, moist. [*Compare* **sticky, wet.**]

dapper *adjective.* —*See* **neat.**

dapple *verb.* —*See* **speckle.**

dare *verb.* To call on another to do something bold ▶ challenge, defy. *Idiom:* throw down the gauntlet. —*See also* **defy** (1), **venture.**

dare *noun.* An act of taunting another to do something bold or rash ▶ challenge, gauntlet, provocation. [*Compare* **defiance.**]

daredevil *noun.* One who seeks adventure ▶ adventurer, quester, venturer.

daredevil *adjective.* —*See* **adventurous.**

daredevilry *or* **daredeviltry** *noun.* —*See* **daring.**

daring *noun.* Willingness to take risks ▶ adventuresomeness, adventurousness, audaciousness, audacity, boldness, daredevilry, daredeviltry, daringness, derring-do, fearlessness, venturesomeness, venturousness. [*Compare* **courage, temerity.**]

daring *adjective.* —*See* **adventurous.**

dark *adjective.* **1.** Deficient in brightness ▶ dim, dusky, ill-lit, murky, obscure, shadowy, shady, stygian. [*Compare* **shady.**] **2.** Having a dark color or complexion ▶ black, brown, brunet, dusky, swarthy, tawny. —*See also* **black** (2), **bleak** (2), **evil, fateful** (1), **gloomy.**

dark *noun.* Absence or deficiency of light ▶ darkness, dimness, duskiness, murk, murkiness, obscureness, obscurity. [*Compare* **shade.**] —*See also* **night.**

CORE SYNONYMS: *dark, dim, murky, dusky, obscure, shady, shadowy.* These adjectives indicate a deficiency in brightness or light, and, by extension, a deficiency in or lack of clarity. *Dark,* the most widely applicable, can refer to insufficiency of illumination for seeing (*a dark evening*), deepness of shade or color (*dark brown*), absence of cheer (*a dark, somber mood*), or lack of rectitude (*a dark past*). *Dim* suggests lack of clarity of outline: "*life and the memory of it cramped,/dim, on a piece of Bristol board*" (Elizabeth Bishop). It can also apply to a source of light to indicate insufficiency: "*storied Windows richly dight,/Casting a dim religious light*" (John Milton). *Murky* implies darkness, often extreme, such as that produced by smoke or fog: "*The path was altogether indiscernible in the murky darkness which surrounded them*" (Sir Walter Scott). *Dusky* suggests the dimness that is characteristic of diminishing light, as at twilight: "*The dusky night rides down the sky,/And ushers in the morn*" (Henry Fielding). Also, it often refers to deepness of shade of a color: "*A dusky blush rose to her cheek*" (Edith Wharton). *Obscure* usually means unclear to the mind or senses, but it can refer to physical darkness: *the obscure rooms of a shuttered mansion. Shady* refers literally to what is sheltered from light, especially sunlight (*a shady grove of pines*) or figuratively to what is of questionable honesty (*shady business deals*). *Shadowy* also implies obstructed light (*a shadowy path*) but may suggest shifting illumination and indistinctness: "[He] *retreated from the limelight to the shadowy fringe of music history*" (Charles Sherman). It can also refer to something that seems to lack substance and is mysterious or sinister: *a shadowy figure in a black cape.*

---

darken *verb.* —*See* **shade** (2).

darkness *noun.* The condition of not being able to see ▶ blindness, legal blindness, sightlessness, visual impairment. —*See also* **dark, ignorance** (1).

darling *noun.* **1.** A person who is much loved ▶ beloved, dear, honey, love, precious, sugar, sweet, sweetheart, truelove. *Informal:* babe, baby, honeybun, honeybunch, sweetie, sweetie-pie, sweetpea. ***Idiom:*** light of one's life. **2.** One liked or preferred above all others ▶ favorite, pet. ***Idiom:*** apple of one's eye.

darling *adjective.* Regarded with much love and tenderness ▶ beloved, dear, desired, loved, precious. —*See also* **delightful, favorite.**

darn *adjective.* —*See* **damned.**

dart *verb.* —*See* **fly** (2), **rush, throw.**

dash *verb.* —*See* **blast** (2), **rush, splash** (1), **throw.**

dash *noun.* —*See* **bit**[1] (1), **energy, point** (2), **run** (1), **shade** (2), **spirit** (1).

dashing *adjective.* —*See* **brave, fashionable, lively.**

dastard *noun.* —*See* **coward.**

dastardliness *noun.* —*See* **cowardice.**

dastardly *adjective.* —*See* **cowardly.**

data *noun.* —*See* **information.**

date *noun.* A commitment, as for a performance by an entertainer ▶ booking, engagement. *Slang:* gig. —*See also* **engagement** (1).

date *verb.* To be with another person socially on a regular basis ▶ go out (with), go with, see. *Informal:* take out. ***Idioms:*** go steady, go together.

dated *adjective.* —*See* **old-fashioned.**

daub *verb.* —*See* **smear.**

daub *noun.* —*See* **smear.**

daunt *verb.* —*See* **discourage, dismay.**

dauntless *adjective.* —*See* **brave.**

dauntlessness *noun.* —*See* **courage.**

dawdle *verb.* —*See* **delay** (2), **idle** (2), **putter.**

dawdler *noun.* —*See* **laggard.**

dawdling *noun.* —*See* **hesitation.**

dawn *noun.* The first appearance of daylight in the morning ▶ aurora, cockcrow, dawning, daybreak, first light, morn, morning, sunrise, sunup. ***Idioms:*** break of day, crack of dawn. —*See also* **birth** (2).

dawn *verb.* —*See* **begin.**

dawn on *or* **upon** *verb.* To come as a realization ▶ register, sink in, soak in. [*Compare* **discover, strike, understand.**]

dawning *noun.* —*See* **dawn.**

day *noun.* —*See* **age** (2), **life.**

daybreak *noun.* —*See* **dawn.**

daydream *noun.* —*See* **dream** (1).

daydream *verb.* —*See* **dream.**

daydreamer *noun.* —*See* **dreamer** (1).

daydreaming *noun.* —*See* **trance.**

daydreaming *adjective.* —*See* **dreamy.**

daze *verb.* **1.** To dull the senses, as with a heavy blow, a shock, or fatigue ▶ bedaze, bemuse, benumb, bewilder, stagger, stun, stupefy. *Chiefly Regional:* maze. *Slang:* zonk. [*Compare* **confuse.**] **2.** To confuse with bright light ▶ bedazzle, blind, dazzle. —*See also* **drug** (2).

daze *noun.* A stunned or bewildered condition ▶ bafflement, befuddlement, bewilderedness, bewilderment, confusion, discombobulation, disorientation, distraction, fog, haze, muddle, mystification, perplexity, puzzlement, stupefaction, stupor, trance.

✚ **CORE SYNONYMS:** *daze, bemuse, benumb, stun, stupefy.* These verbs mean to dull or paralyze the senses, as with a heavy blow, a shock, or fatigue: *dazed by the defeat; bemused by the senator's resignation; a boring performance that be-*

numbed the audience; stunned by his sudden death; a display that stupefied all onlookers.

---

dazed *adjective.* —*See* **dizzy** (1).

dazzle *verb.* To confuse with bright light ▶ bedazzle, blind, daze.

dazzle *noun.* An intense blinding light ▶ blaze, flare, glare. [*Compare* **brilliance, glitter.**]

dazzling *adjective.* —*See* **brilliant, glorious.**

deacon *noun.* —*See* **cleric.**

deactivate *verb.* —*See* **discharge.**

dead *adjective.* **1.** No longer alive ▶ asleep, deceased, defunct, departed, expired, extinct, gone, late, lifeless, perished. ***Idioms:*** at rest, dead and buried, dead as a doornail, pushing up daisies, six feet under. **2.** Lacking physical feeling or sensitivity ▶ asleep, benumbed, deadened, dull, inert, insensible, insensitive, lifeless, numb, stuporous, torpid, unfeeling, unresponsive. [*Compare* **unconscious.**] **3.** Completely lacking sensation or consciousness ▶ inanimate, insensate, insentient, lifeless. —*See also* **barren** (2), **tired** (1), **utter**[2].

dead *adverb.* —*See* **completely** (1), **directly** (1), **directly** (3).

✦ CORE SYNONYMS: *dead, deceased, departed, extinct, lifeless.* These adjectives all mean no longer alive or active. *Dead* applies in general to whatever once had—but no longer has—physical life (*a dead man; a dead leaf*), function (*a dead battery*), or force or currency (*a dead issue; a dead language*). *Deceased* and *departed* refer only to nonliving humans: *attended a memorial service for a recently deceased friend; looking at pictures of departed relatives. Extinct* can refer to what has no living successors (*extinct species such as the dodo*) or to what is extinguished or inactive (*an extinct volcano*). *Lifeless* applies to what no longer has physical life (*a lifeless body*), to what does not support life (*a lifeless planet*), or to what lacks animation, spirit, or brightness (*a lifeless performance; lifeless colors*).

---

deadbeat *noun.* —*See* **wastrel** (2).

dead duck *noun. Slang* One that is ruined or doomed ▶ *Slang:* dead meat, goner, toast.

deaden *verb.* To render less sensitive ▶ benumb, blunt, desensitize, dull, numb. ***Idioms:*** put to sleep, take the edge off. [*Compare* **drug.**] —*See also* **muffle.**

dead end *noun.* A course leading nowhere ▶ blind alley, cul-de-sac.

dead heat *noun.* An equality of scores, votes, or performances in a contest ▶ deadlock, draw, stalemate, standoff, tie.

deadliness *noun.* The quality or condition of causing death or disaster ▶ fatality, fatefulness, lethality, lethalness.

deadlock *noun.* An equality of scores, votes, or performances in a contest ▶ dead heat, draw, stalemate, standoff, tie.

deadly *adjective.* Causing or tending to cause death ▶ deathly, fatal, lethal, mortal, pestilent. [*Compare* **poisonous.**] —*See also* **boring, dull** (1), **ghastly** (2).

✦ CORE SYNONYMS: *deadly, fatal, mortal, lethal.* These adjectives apply to what causes or is likely to cause death. *Deadly* means capable of killing: *a deadly poison. Fatal* describes conditions, circumstances, or events that have caused or are destined to cause death or dire consequences: *a fatal illness. Mortal* describes a condition or action that produces death: *a mortal wound. Lethal* refers to a sure agent of death that may have been created solely for the purpose of killing: *execution by lethal injection.*

---

dead meat *noun. Slang* One that is ruined or doomed ▶ *Slang:* dead duck, goner, toast.

deadpan *adjective.* —*See* **expressionless.**

deafening *adjective.* —*See* **loud.**

deal *noun.* **1.** A business agreement involving goods or services ▶ auction, barter, bargain, exchange, sale, trade, transaction. **2.** *Informal* Something offered or bought at a low price ▶ bargain, find. *Informal:* buy. *Slang:* steal. —*See also* **agreement** (1), **quantity** (2).

deal *verb.* **1.** To have for sale ▶ carry, keep, offer, stock. [*Compare* **sell.**] **2.** To engage in the illicit sale of narcotics ▶ peddle. *Slang:* push. [*Compare* **sell.**] **3.** To mete out by means of some action ▶ administer, deliver, give. —*See also* **distribute, sell.**

deal with *verb.* **1.** To be concerned with something ▶ address, consider, take up, treat. ***Idiom:*** have to do with. **2.** To behave in a specified way toward someone ▶ cope with, handle, treat.

dealer *noun.* A person engaged in buying and selling ▶ businessperson, entrepreneur, merchandiser, merchant, trader, tradesman, trafficker. [*Compare* **seller.**] —*See also* **pusher.**

dear *adjective.* —*See* **costly, darling.**

dear *noun.* —*See* **darling** (1).

dearth *noun.* The condition of lacking something ▶ absence, lack, want. [*Compare* **need, shortage.**]

death *noun.* **1.** The act or fact of dying ▶ decease, demise, dissolution, end, expiration, expiry, extinction, passing, quietus, rest. *Slang:* curtains. **2.** A loss of life, or one who has lost life, usually as a result of accident, disaster, or war ▶ casualty, fatality, kill, loss. [*Compare* **victim.**]

deathless *adjective.* ▶ immortal, undying. [*Compare* **endless.**]

deathlike *adjective.* —*See* **ghastly** (2).

deathly *adjective.* —*See* **deadly, ghastly** (2).

debacle *noun.* —*See* **collapse** (2), **disaster.**

debar *verb.* —*See* **exclude, forbid.**

debark *verb.* To come ashore from a seacraft ▶ alight, disembark, land, light.

debase *verb.* To lower in character or quality ▶ abase, cheapen, degrade, demean, devalue, downgrade. [*Compare* **belittle, humble.**] —*See also* **contaminate, corrupt, disgrace, humble.**

✤ **CORE SYNONYMS:** *debase, degrade, abase, demean, humble.* These verbs mean to lower in character or quality. *Debase* implies reduction in quality or value: *"debasing the moral currency"* (George Eliot). *Degrade* implies reduction to a state of shame or disgrace: *"If I pitied you for crying . . . you should spurn such pity. . . . Rise, and don't degrade yourself into an abject reptile!"* (Emily Brontë). *Abase* refers principally to loss of rank or prestige: *"Meg pardoned him, and Mrs. March's grave face relaxed . . . when she heard him declare that he would . . . abase himself like a worm before the injured damsel"* (Louisa May Alcott). *Demean* suggests lowering in social position: *"It puts him where he can make the advances without demeaning himself"* (William Dean Howells). *Humble* can refer to lowering in rank or, more often, to reducing in pride: *dreamed of humbling his opponent.*

debased *adjective.* —*See* **corrupt** (1), **impure** (1), **impure** (2), **unscrupulous.**

debasement *noun.* —*See* **degradation** (1).

debatable *adjective.* In doubt or dispute ▶ arguable, contentious, contestable, contested, disputable, doubtful, exceptionable, indefinite, moot, mootable, problematic, problematical, questionable, suspect, uncertain, unconfirmed, unsettled. *Informal:* iffy.

debate *verb.* —*See* **argue** (2), **confer** (1), **discuss.**

debate *noun.* —*See* **argument, deliberation** (1).

debauch *verb.* —*See* **corrupt.**

debauchee *noun.* —*See* **wanton.**

debaucher *noun.* A man who seduces women ▶ Don Juan, Lothario, seducer. —*See also* **wanton.**

debauchery *noun.* —*See* **corruption** (1).

debilitate *verb.* —*See* **enervate.**

debilitated *adjective.* —*See* **weak** (1).

debilitation *noun.* The sapping away of strength or energy ▶ attenuation, depletion, devitalization, enervation, enfeeblement, impairment, impoverishment, incapacitation, weakening.

debility *noun.* —*See* **infirmity.**

debit *noun.* —*See* **debt** (1).

debonair *adjective.* Gracious and tactful in social manner ▶ smooth, suave, urbane. [*Compare* **courteous, cultured, sophisticated.**] —*See also* **lighthearted.**

debris *noun.* —*See* **garbage, ruin** (2).

debt *noun.* **1.** Something, such as money, owed by one person to another ▶ arrearage, arrears, claim, debit, due, indebtedness, liability, obligation, score. **2.** A condition of owing something to another ▶ arrearage, arrears, encumbrance, indebtedness, liability, obligation.

debunk *verb.* —*See* **discredit.**

debut *noun.* The instance or occasion of being presented for the first time to society ▶ coming-out, presentation.

debut *verb.* To make one's formal entry, as into society ▶ come out. ***Idiom:*** make one's bow.

decadence *noun.* —*See* **deterioration** (1).

decamp *verb.* —*See* **escape** (1).

decampment *noun.* —*See* **escape** (1).

decant *verb.* —*See* **pour.**

decay *verb.* To become or cause to become rotten or unsound ▶ blight, break down, corrupt, crumble, curdle, decompose, deteriorate, disintegrate, fester, molder, putrefy, rot, spoil, taint, turn. ***Idioms:*** go bad, go to pot, go to seed.

decay *noun.* The condition of being decayed ▶ blight, breakdown, decomposition, decrepitude, deterioration, disintegration, putrefaction, putrescence, putridness, rot, rottenness, spoilage.

✤ **CORE SYNONYMS:** *decay, rot, putrefy, spoil, crumble, molder, disintegrate, decompose.* These verbs mean to become or cause something to become rotten or unsound. *Decay* can denote partial deterioration short of complete destruction: *Brush and floss regularly to prevent teeth from decaying. Rot* is sometimes synonymous with *decay,* but often, like *putrefy,* stresses offensiveness to the sense of smell: *The food left on the counter began to rot. Arctic cold prevented the prehistoric animal from putrefying. Spoil* usually refers to the process by which perishable substances become unfit for use or consumption: *Put the fish in the refrigerator before they spoil. Crumble* implies physical breakdown into small fragments or particles: *The ancient church had crumbled to ruins.* To *molder* is to crumble to dust: *The shawl had moldered away in the trunk. Disintegrate* refers to complete breakdown into component parts: *The sandstone façade had disintegrated from exposure to the elements. Decompose,* largely restricted to the breakdown of substances into their chemical components, also connotes rotting and putrefying, both literally and figuratively: "*trivial personalities decomposing in the eternity of print*" (Virginia Woolf).

---

decayed *adjective.* —*See* **bad** (2), **shabby.**

decaying *adjective.* —*See* **shabby.**

decease *verb.* —*See* **die.**

decease *noun.* —*See* **death** (1).

deceased *adjective.* —*See* **dead** (1).

deceit *noun.* The act or practice of deceiving ▶ cunning, deceitfulness, deception, double-dealing, duplicity, fraud, guile, shiftiness, trickery. —*See also* **cheat** (1).

deceitful *adjective.* —*See* **dishonest.**

deceitfulness *noun.* —*See* **art, deceit, dishonesty** (1).

deceive *verb.* To cause to accept something false by trickery or misrepresentation ▶ beguile, betray, bluff, cheat, cozen, delude, double-cross, dupe, fool, hoodwink, humbug, mislead, string along, swindle, take in, trick. *Informal:* bamboozle, beat, burn, have, sucker. *Slang:* four-flush, punk, snow. ***Idioms:*** lead astray, play false, pull the wool over someone's eyes, put something over on, slip one over on, take for a ride. [*Compare* **flatter.**]

✚ **CORE SYNONYMS:** *deceive, betray, mislead, beguile, delude, dupe, hoodwink, bamboozle, double-cross.* These verbs mean to cause someone to accept something false by trickery or misrepresentation. *Deceive* involves the deliberate misrepresentation of the truth: "*We are inclined to believe those whom we do not know, because they have never deceived us*" (Samuel Johnson). *Betray* implies treachery: "*When you betray somebody else, you also betray yourself*" (Isaac Bashevis Singer). *Mislead* means to lead in the wrong direction or into error of thought or action: "*My manhood, long misled by wandering fires,/Followed false lights*" (John Dryden). *Beguile* suggests deceiving by means of charm or allure: *They beguiled unwary investors with tales of overnight fortunes.* To *delude* is to mislead the mind or judgment: *The government deluded the public about the dangers of low-level radiation. Dupe* implies playing upon another's susceptibilities or naiveté: *The shoppers were duped by false advertising. Hoodwink* refers to deluding by trickery: *It is difficult to hoodwink a smart lawyer. Bamboozle* means to delude by the use of such tactics as hoaxing or artful persuasion: "*Perhaps if I wanted to be understood or to understand I would bamboozle myself into belief, but I am a reporter*" (Graham Greene). *Double-cross* implies the betrayal of a confidence or the willful breaking of a pledge: *The thief double-crossed his accomplice.*

---

deceiver *noun.* —*See* **cheat** (2), **liar.**

decency *noun.* **1.** A sense of rightness ▶ conscience, grace, properness, propriety. **2.** Conformity to recognized standards, as of conduct or appearance ▶ correctness, decentness, decorousness, decorum, properness, propriety, respectability, respectableness, seemliness. —*See also* **chastity.**

decent *adjective.* —*See* **acceptable** (2), **appropriate, chaste, clean** (2), **good** (1), **sufficient.** *Informal* Proper in appearance ▶ modest, presentable, respectable, tasteful.

decentness *noun.* —*See* **decency** (2).

deception *noun.* —*See* **deceit, trick** (1).

deceptive *adjective.* —*See* **dishonest, fallacious** (2).

decide *verb.* To make up or cause to make up one's mind ▶ clinch, conclude, determine, resolve, settle. —*See also* **choose** (1), **judge.**

✚ **CORE SYNONYMS:** *decide, determine, settle, conclude, resolve.* These verbs mean to make up or cause to make up one's mind. *Decide* is the least specific: "*If two laws conflict with each other, the courts must decide on the operation of each*" (John Marshall). *Determine* often involves somewhat narrower issues: *A jury will determine the verdict. Settle* stresses finality of decision: "*The lama waved a hand to show that the matter was finally settled in his mind*" (Rudyard Kipling). *Conclude* suggests that a decision, opinion, or judgment has been arrived at after careful consideration: *She concluded that the criticism was unjust. Resolve* stresses the exercise of choice in making a firm decision: *I resolved to lose weight.*

---

decided *adjective.* Without any doubt ▶ clear, clear-cut, definite, distinct, pronounced, set, settled, unquestionable. —*See also* **definite** (1), **firm**[1] (3), **intent.**

decidedly *adverb.* —*See* **very.**

decidedness *noun.* —*See* **decision** (2).

deciding *adjective.* —*See* **decisive.**

decimate *verb.* —*See* **massacre.**

decimation *noun.* —*See* **destruction, massacre.**

decipher *verb.* To find the key to a code or cipher ▶ break, crack, decrypt, puzzle out, unlock, unscramble. —*See also* **explain** (1), **solve** (1).

decipherable *adjective.* —*See* **explainable.**

decipherment *noun.* —*See* **explanation.**

decision *noun.* **1.** A position reached after consideration ▶ conclusion, determination, resolution. [*Compare* **deduction.**] **2.** Unwavering firmness of character, action, or will ▶ assuredness, decidedness, decisiveness, determination, firmness, purpose, purposefulness, resoluteness, resolution, resolve, toughness, will, willpower. [*Compare* **courage, drive.**] —*See also* **choice, ruling.**

✚ CORE SYNONYMS: *decision, conclusion, determination.* These nouns denote a position, opinion, or judgment reached after consideration: *a decision unfavorable to the opposition; came to the conclusion not to proceed; satisfied with the panel's determination.*

decisive *adjective.* Determining or having the power to determine an outcome ▶ conclusive, crucial, deciding, definitive, determinative. —*See also* **certain** (2), **definite** (1), **definitive, firm**[1] (3).

✚ CORE SYNONYMS: *decisive, conclusive, crucial, definitive, determinative.* These adjectives mean determining or having the power to determine an outcome: *the decisive vote; a conclusive reason; crucial experiments; a definitive verdict; the determinative battle.*

◀ ANTONYM: *indecisive*

decisiveness *noun.* —*See* **decision** (2).

deck[1] *verb.* —*See* **drop** (3).

deck[2] *verb.* —*See* **adorn** (1), **dress up.**

declaim *verb.* —*See* **rant.**

declaimer *noun.* —*See* **speaker** (1).

declamation *noun.* —*See* **oratory, speech** (2).

declamatory *adjective.* —*See* **oratorical.**

declaration *noun.* —*See* **announcement, assertion, message.**

declare *verb.* —*See* **announce, assert, confirm** (1), **say.**

déclassé *or* **declassed** *adjective.* —*See* **lowly** (1).

declension *noun.* —*See* **deterioration** (1).

declination *noun.* A marked loss of strength or effectiveness ▶ decline, deterioration, failure. —*See also* **deterioration** (1).

decline *verb.* To be unwilling to accept, consider, or receive ▶ deny, disallow, disapprove, dismiss, pass (on), rebuff, refuse, reject, spurn, turn down, withhold. *Slang:* nix. ***Idiom:*** turn thumbs down on. [*Compare* **deprive, forbid.**] —*See also* **deteriorate, drop** (2), **fade, fall** (4).

decline *noun.* A marked loss of strength or effectiveness ▶ declination, deterioration, failure. —*See also* **deterioration** (1), **drop** (3), **fall** (3).

✚ CORE SYNONYMS: *decline, refuse, reject, spurn, rebuff.* These verbs all mean to be unwilling to accept, consider, or receive someone or something. To *decline* implies courtesy or politeness: *"I declined election to the National Institute of Arts and Letters . . . and now I must decline the Pulitzer Prize"* (Sinclair Lewis). *Refuse* usually implies determination and often brusqueness: *"The commander . . . refused to discuss questions of right"* (George Bancroft). *"I'll make him an offer he can't refuse"* (Mario Puzo). *Reject* suggests the discarding of someone or something as defective or useless; it implies categoric refusal: *"He again offered himself for enlistment and was again rejected"* (Arthur S.M. Hutchinson). To *spurn* is to reject scornfully or contemptuously: *"The more she spurns my love,/The more it grows"* (William Shakespeare). *Rebuff* pertains to blunt, often disdainful rejection: "*He had . . . gone too far in his advances, and had been rebuffed*" (Robert Louis Stevenson).

---

declivity *noun.* —*See* **drop** (3).
décolleté *adjective.* —*See* **low** (2).
decompose *verb.* —*See* **decay, disintegrate.**
decomposition *noun.* —*See* **decay.**
decontaminate *verb.* To render free of microorganisms ▶ disinfect, irradiate, sanitize, sterilize. [*Compare* **clean.**]
decorate *verb.* —*See* **adorn** (1).
decoration *noun.* An emblem of honor worn on one's clothing ▶ badge, medal, ribbon. —*See also* **adornment.**
decorous *adjective.* —*See* **appropriate.**
decorousness *noun.* —*See* **decency** (2).
decorticate *verb.* —*See* **skin.**
decorum *noun.* —*See* **decency** (2), **manners.**
decoy *noun.* Something that leads one into danger or entrapment ▶ bait, lure. [*Compare* **trap, trick.**]
decrease *verb.* To become or cause to become gradually less ▶ abate, diminish, drain, dwindle, ebb, lessen, lower, peter out, ratchet down, reduce, shrink, tail away, tail off, taper off, wane. [*Compare* **depreciate, fall, shorten, subside.**]
decrease *noun.* The act or process of decreasing ▶ abatement, curtailment, cut, cutback, decrement, diminishment, diminution, drain, reduction, shrinkage, slash, slowdown, taper, tapering (off), wane, waning. [*Compare* **fall, waning.**]

✚ **CORE SYNONYMS:** *decrease, lessen, reduce, dwindle, abate, diminish, subside.* These verbs mean to become or cause to become gradually less. *Decrease* and *lessen* refer to steady or gradual diminution: *Lack of success decreases confidence. His appetite lessens as his illness progresses. Reduce* emphasizes bringing down in size, degree, or intensity: *The workers reduced their wage demands. Dwindle* suggests decreasing bit by bit to a vanishing point: *Their savings dwindled away. Abate* stresses a decrease in amount or intensity and suggests a reduction of excess: *Toward evening the fire began to abate. Diminish* implies taking away or removal: *The warden's authority diminished after the revolt. Subside* implies a falling away to a more normal level: *The wild enthusiasm aroused by the team's victory did not subside for days.*

◀ **ANTONYM:** *increase*

---

decree *noun.* —*See* **ruling.**
decree *verb.* —*See* **dictate, judge.**
decrement *noun.* —*See* **decrease.**
decrepit *adjective.* —*See* **shabby, weak** (1).
decrepitude *noun.* —*See* **decay, infirmity.**
decriminalize *verb.* —*See* **legalize.**
decry *verb.* —*See* **belittle, deplore** (1), **disapprove.**
decrypt *verb.* —*See* **decipher.**
decumbent *adjective.* —*See* **flat** (1).
decussate *verb.* —*See* **cross** (2).
dedicate *verb.* —*See* **apply** (1), **devote.**
dedicated *adjective.* —*See* **faithful.**
deduce *verb.* —*See* **infer.**
deduct *verb.* To take away a quantity from another quantity ▶ abate, discount, rebate, remove, subtract, take away, take off, withdraw. *Informal:* knock off, shave off. —*See also* **infer.**
deduction *noun.* **1.** An amount deducted ▶ abatement, discount, rebate, reduction. **2.** A position arrived at by reasoning from premises ▶ conclusion, inference, judgment. [*Compare* **belief.**] —*See also* **logic.**
deed *noun.* —*See* **accomplishment, act** (1), **ownership.**
deed *verb.* —*See* **transfer** (1).
deem *verb.* —*See* **believe** (3), **regard.**
de-emphasize *verb. Informal* To make less emphatic or obvious ▶ play down, soft-pedal, tone down. [*Compare* **moderate.**]

deep *adjective.* **1.** Extending far downward or inward from a surface ▶ abysmal, bottomless, low, profound. **2.** Beyond the understanding of an average mind ▶ abstract, abstruse, difficult, esoteric, formidable, inscrutable, profound, recondite. *Slang:* heavy. [*Compare* **incomprehensible.**] **3.** Resulting from or affecting one's innermost feelings ▶ great, heartfelt, intense, powerful, profound, strong. *—See also* **colorful** (1), **low** (1).

deep *noun.* Something of immeasurable and vast extent ▶ abysm, abyss, chasm, deeps, depth, depths, gulf. *—See also* **ocean.**

deepen *verb. —See* **intensify.**

deep-fry *verb. —See* **cook.**

deepness *noun.* **1.** The extent or measurement downward from a surface ▶ depth, drop, drop-off. **2.** Intellectual penetration or range ▶ depth, profoundness, profundity, weightiness. [*Compare* **discernment, intelligence, wisdom.**]

deep-seated *or* **deep-rooted** *adjective. —See* **confirmed** (1).

deep-six *verb. —See* **discard.**

deep water *noun. —See* **predicament.**

deface *verb. —See* **deform.**

defamation *noun. —See* **libel.**

defamatory *adjective. —See* **libelous.**

defame *verb. —See* **malign.**

default *noun. —See* **failure** (2).

defeasance *noun. —See* **abolition.**

defeat *verb.* To win a victory over, as in battle or a competition ▶ beat, best, checkmate, conquer, master, outgun, outplay, overcome, prevail over, subdue, subjugate, surmount, triumph over, vanquish, worst. *Informal:* trim. *Slang:* ace, KO, lick. ***Idioms:*** carry (*or* win) the day, get (*or* have) the best of, get (*or* have) the better of, go someone one better. [*Compare* **annihilate, overwhelm.**] *—See also* **frustrate.**

defeat *noun.* The act of defeating or the condition of being defeated ▶ beating, blowout, checkmate, clobbering, drubbing, overthrow, rout, thrashing, trouncing, vanquishment, waterloo. *Informal:* massacre, trimming, whipping. *Slang:* creaming, dusting, licking, shellacking.

✦ **CORE SYNONYMS:** *defeat, conquer, vanquish, beat, subdue, subjugate, overcome.* These verbs mean to win a victory over an adversary, as in battle or a competition. *Defeat* is the most general: "*Whether we defeat the enemy in one battle, or by degrees, the consequences will be the same*" (Thomas Paine). *Conquer* suggests decisive and often widescale victory: "*The Franks . . . having conquered the Gauls, established the kingdom which has taken its name from them*" (Alexander Hamilton). *Vanquish* emphasizes total mastery: *Napoleon's forces were vanquished at Waterloo. Beat* is similar to *defeat,* though less formal and often more emphatic: "*To win battles . . . you beat the soul . . . of the enemy man*" (George S. Patton). *Subdue* suggests mastery and control achieved by overpowering: "*It cost* [the Romans] *two great wars, and three great battles, to subdue that little kingdom* [Macedonia]" (Adam Smith). *Subjugate* more strongly implies reducing an opponent to submission: "*The last foreigner to subjugate England was a Norman duke in the Middle Ages named William*" (Stanley Meisler). To *overcome* is to prevail over, often by persevering: *He overcame his injury after months of physical therapy.*

---

defect *noun.* Something that mars the appearance or causes inadequacy or failure ▶ blemish, bug, failing, fault, flaw, glitch, imperfection, shortcoming, wart, weakness. ***Idiom:*** fly in the ointment. [*Compare* **abnormality, deformity.**] *—See also* **shortage.**

defect *verb.* To abandon one's cause or party usually to join another ▶ apostatize, desert, disavow, forsake, quit, renegade, renounce, secede, tergiversate, turn. *Slang:* rat. ***Idioms:*** change sides, turn one's coat. [*Compare* **abandon, repudiate.**]

✦ **CORE SYNONYMS:** *defect, blemish, imperfection, fault, flaw.* These nouns denote something that mars the appearance or causes inadequacy or failure. *Defect* denotes a serious functional or structural shortcoming: *"Ill breeding . . . is not a single defect, it is the result of many"* (Henry Fielding). A *blemish* mars appearance or character: *"Industry in art is a necessity—not a virtue—and any evidence of the same, in the production, is a blemish"* (James McNeill Whistler). *Imperfection* and *fault* apply more comprehensively to any deficiency or shortcoming: *"A true critic ought to dwell rather upon excellencies than imperfections"* (Joseph Addison). *"Each of us would point out to the other her most serious faults, and thereby help her to remedy them"* (Anna Howard Shaw). *Flaw* refers to an often small but always fundamental weakness: *Experiments revealed a very basic flaw in the theory.*

---

defection *noun.* An instance of defecting from or abandoning a cause ▶ abandonment, apostasy, disavowal, recreance, recreancy, renouncement, secession, tergiversation. —*See also* **emigration.**

defective *adjective.* Having a defect or defects ▶ amiss, blemished, faulty, flawed, imperfect. [*Compare* **shabby, trick.**] —*See also* **deficient.**

defector *noun.* A person who has defected ▶ apostate, deserter, recreant, renegade, runagate, tergiversator, traitor, turncoat. *Informal:* rat.

defend *verb.* **1.** To keep safe from danger, attack, or harm ▶ cover, guard, hedge, preserve, protect, safeguard, secure, shield, ward. **2.** To support against arguments, attack, or criticism ▶ apologize, bolster, justify, maintain, uphold, vindicate. ***Idioms:*** make a case for, speak up for, stand up for, stick up for.

✦ **CORE SYNONYMS:** *defend, protect, guard, preserve, shield, safeguard.* These verbs mean to make or keep safe from danger, attack, or harm. *Defend* implies repelling an attack: *defending her territory; defended his reputation. Protect* often suggests providing a barrier to discomfort, injury, or attack: *bought a dog to protect the children; wore sunglasses to protect her eyes. Guard* suggests keeping watch: *guarded the house against intruders.* To *preserve* is to take measures to maintain something in safety: *ecologists working to preserve our natural resources. Shield* suggests protecting with a piece of defensive armor: *hid the newspaper to shield me from the bad news. Safeguard* stresses protection against potential danger: *The Bill of Rights safeguards our individual liberties.*

---

defendable *adjective.* Capable of being defended against armed attack ▶ defensible, tenable. [*Compare* **safe.**]

defendant *noun.* A person against whom an action is brought ▶ accused, respondent.

defender *noun.* —*See* **advocate.**

defense *noun.* The act or a means of defending ▶ barricade, guard, hedge, preservation, protection, safeguard, security, shield, ward. —*See also* **apology** (1).

defenseless *adjective.* —*See* **vulnerable.**

defenselessness *noun.* —*See* **exposure.**

defensible *adjective.* **1.** Capable of being defended against armed attack ▶ defendable, tenable. [*Compare* **safe.**] **2.** Capable of being justified ▶ excusable, justifiable, tenable. [*Compare* **logical, sound**[2].]

defensive *adjective.* —*See* **preventive** (2).

defer[1] *verb.* To put off until a later time ▶ adjourn, delay, hold off, hold up, postpone, put off, remit, shelve, stall, stay, suspend, table, waive. *Informal:*

wait. ***Idioms:*** put on the back burner, put on hold, keep (*or* put) on ice.

✚ **CORE SYNONYMS:** *defer, postpone, shelve, stay, suspend.* These verbs mean to put off until a later time: *deferred paying the bills; postponing our trip; shelved the issue; stay an execution; suspending train service.*

defer[2] *verb.* To conform to the will or judgment of another, especially out of respect or courtesy ▶ bow, submit, yield. ***Idioms:*** give ground, give way, stand aside, take a back seat. [*Compare* **humor.**] —*See also* **surrender** (1).

deference *noun.* —*See* **honor** (1), **obedience.**

deferential *adjective.* Marked by courteous submission or respect ▶ duteous, dutiful, obeisant, polite, respectful, submissive, yielding.

deferment *or* **deferral** *noun.* —*See* **delay** (1).

defiance *noun.* **1.** The act or an instance of defying ▶ challenge, disobedience, insubordination, insurgence, naughtiness, noncompliance, opposition, provocation, rebellion, resistance. **2.** An attitude or behavior that is intentionally provocative or contemptuous ▶ contempt, contumaciousness, contumacy, despite, disregard, recalcitrance, recalcitrancy, rebelliousness.

defiant *adjective.* Marked by defiance ▶ contumacious, disobedient, insubordinate, rebellious, recalcitrant.

deficiency *noun.* —*See* **deprivation, shortage.**

deficient *adjective.* Lacking an essential element ▶ defective, inadequate, incomplete, lacking, sketchy, wanting. —*See also* **insufficient.**

deficit *noun.* —*See* **shortage.**

defile *verb.* —*See* **corrupt, denigrate, dirty, violate** (3).

defilement *noun.* —*See* **contamination.**

define *verb.* —*See* **clarify** (1), **determine.**

definite *adjective.* **1.** Clearly, fully, and emphatically expressed ▶ categorical, clear, clear-cut, decided, decisive, emphatic, explicit, express, positive, precise, ringing, specific, straightforward, strong, strongly worded, unambiguous, unequivocal. [*Compare* **apparent, assertive, convincing, sharp.**] **2.** Having distinct limits ▶ determinate, fixed, limited, precise, specific, unambiguous. ***Idioms:*** cast (*or* fixed *or* set) in stone, set in concrete (*or* cement). **3.** Known positively ▶ absolute, certain, positive, sure, unimpeachable. ***Idioms:*** beyond a doubt (*or* the shadow of a doubt), for certain (*or* sure). —*See also* **decided.**

✚ **CORE SYNONYMS:** *definite, categorical, explicit, express, specific.* These adjectives mean clearly, fully, and emphatically expressed: *a definite answer; explicit statements; a categorical refusal; my express wishes; a specific purpose.*

◀ **ANTONYMS:** *ambiguous, indefinite*

definitely *adverb.* —*See* **absolutely.**

definitive *adjective.* Serving the function of deciding or settling with finality ▶ authoritative, conclusive, consummate, decisive, determinative, final, ultimate. [*Compare* **authentic, complete, perfect.**] —*See also* **decisive.**

definitude *noun.* —*See* **accuracy.**

deflate *verb.* —*See* **discredit, humble.**

deflect *verb.* —*See* **bend** (2), **repel, turn** (2).

deflection *noun.* An act of reflection ▶ glance, reflection, scattering. [*Compare* **bounce.**]

deform *verb.* To alter and spoil the natural form or appearance of ▶ blemish, contort, deface, dent, disfigure, distort, injure, mar, misshape, mutilate, pit, pock, ravage, scar, twist, warp. [*Compare* **damage.**]

✚ **CORE SYNONYMS:** *deform, distort, twist, contort, warp.* These verbs mean to alter and spoil the natural form or appearance of something. *Deform* refers to change that disfigures and often implies the loss of desirable qualities such as beauty: *erosion that deformed the landscape.*To *distort* is to change the physical shape of something, as by torsion or exaggeration of certain features, or to misconstrue the meaning of something: *"The human understanding is like a false mirror, which, receiving rays irregularly, distorts and discolors the nature of things"* (Francis Bacon). *Twist* applies to distortion of form or meaning: *twisted his mouth in pain; accused me of twisting her words. Contort* implies violent change that produces unnatural or grotesque effects: *contorted her face with rage. Warp* can refer to turning from a flat or straight form or from a true course or direction: *floorboards that had warped over the years; judgment warped by prejudice.*

---

deformity *noun.* A disfiguring abnormality of shape or form ▶ blemish, contortion, defacement, deformation, dent, disfigurement, distortion, malformation, pit, pock, scar, warping. [*Compare* **abnormality, defect.**]

defraud *verb.* —*See* **cheat** (1).

defrauder *noun.* —*See* **cheat** (2).

deft *adjective.* —*See* **dexterous.**

deftness *noun.* —*See* **agility, dexterity.**

defunct *adjective.* —*See* **dead** (1).

defy *verb.* **1.** To confront boldly and courageously ▶ beard, brave, buck, challenge, dare, face, front, oppose. ***Idioms:*** beard the lion, fly in the face of, snap one's fingers at, stand up to, thumb one's nose at. [*Compare* **confront, contest.**] **2.** To call on another to do something bold ▶ challenge, dare. ***Idiom:*** throw down the gauntlet. —*See also* **disobey.**

✚ **CORE SYNONYMS:** *defy, brave, challenge, dare, face.* These verbs mean to confront boldly and courageously: *an innovator defying tradition; braving all criticism; challenged the opposition to produce proof; daring him to deny the statement; faced her accusers in a court of law.*

---

degeneracy *noun.* —*See* **deterioration** (1).

degenerate *adjective.* —*See* **corrupt** (1).

degenerate *verb.* To undergo moral deterioration ▶ fall, sink, slip. —*See also* **deteriorate, fade.**

degeneration *noun.* —*See* **degradation** (1), **deterioration** (1).

degradation *noun.* **1.** A lowering in or deprivation of character or self-esteem ▶ abasement, debasement, degeneration, disgracing, dishonor, dishonoring, humiliation, mortification. [*Compare* **disgrace, shame.**] **2.** The act or an instance of demoting ▶ demotion, downgrade, reduction.

degrade *verb.* —*See* **debase, demote, disgrace, humble.**

degraded *adjective.* —*See* **unscrupulous.**

degrading *adjective.* —*See* **disgraceful.**

degree *noun.* **1.** One of the units in a course, as on an ascending or descending scale ▶ grade, interval, level, mark, peg, point, rank, rung, stage, step, unit. *Informal:* notch. **2.** Relative intensity or amount, as of a quality or attribute ▶ extent, level, magnitude, measure, proportion, range, scope. —*See also* **length.**

dehydrate *verb.* —*See* **dry, preserve** (1).

deific *adjective.* —*See* **divine** (1).

deification *noun.* —*See* **exaltation.**

deign *verb.* —*See* **condescend** (1).

deject *verb.* —*See* **depress.**

dejected *adjective.* —*See* **depressed** (1), **despondent.**

dejection *noun.* —*See* **depression** (2).

delay *verb.* **1.** To cause to be later or slower than expected or desired ▶ clog, detain, hang up, hinder, hold up, impede, keep (back), retard, set back, slacken, slow (down *or* up), stall. ***Idiom:*** make late. [*Compare* **restrain, stop.**] **2.** To go or move slowly so that progress is hindered ▶ dally, dawdle, dilly-dally, drag, lag, linger, loiter, procrastinate, stall, tarry, trail. ***Idioms:*** drag one's feet, mark time, take one's time. [*Compare* **remain, wait.**] —*See also* **defer**[1].

delay *noun.* **1.** The act of putting off or the condition of being put off ▶ adjournment, deferment, deferral, holdup, moratorium, postponement, procrastination, shelving, stay, suspension, tabling, waiver. ***Idiom:*** putting on ice. **2.** The condition or fact of being made late or slow ▶ detainment, holdup, lag, retardation.

delectable *adjective.* —*See* **delicious, delightful.**

delectation *noun.* —*See* **delight.**

delegate *noun.* —*See* **representative.**

delegate *verb.* —*See* **entrust** (1).

delete *verb.* —*See* **cancel** (1).

deleterious *adjective.* —*See* **harmful.**

deletion *noun.* —*See* **erasure.**

deliberate *adjective.* **1.** Done or said on purpose ▶ conscious, intended, intentional, premeditated, purposeful, voluntary, willful, witting. **2.** Arising from or marked by careful consideration ▶ advised, calculated, considered, studied, studious, thought out. [*Compare* **sane, wary.**] **3.** Careful and slow in acting, moving, or deciding ▶ cautious, circumspect, judicious, leisurely, measured, methodic, methodical, prudent, sober, unhurried. [*Compare* **lethargic, slow.**] —*See also* **calculated.**

deliberate *verb.* —*See* **confer** (1), **discuss, ponder, think** (1).

✤ **CORE SYNONYMS:** *deliberate, intentional, voluntary, willful.* These adjectives refer to that which is done or said on purpose. *Deliberate* stresses premeditation and full awareness of the character and consequences of one's acts: *taking deliberate and decisive action. Intentional* applies to something undertaken to further a plan or realize an aim: "*I will abstain from all intentional wrongdoing and harm*" (Hippocratic Oath). *Voluntary* implies the operation of unforced choice: "*Ignorance, when it is voluntary, is criminal*" (Samuel Johnson). *Willful* implies deliberate, headstrong persistence in a self-determined course of action: *a willful waste of time.*

---

deliberation *noun.* **1.** An exchange of views in an attempt to reach a decision ▶ conference, consideration, consultation, counsel, debate, discussion, parley. **2.** Careful thought ▶ advisement, deliberation, study. [*Compare* **attention, examination, scrutiny.**] —*See also* **thought.**

deliberative *adjective.* —*See* **thoughtful.**

delicacy *noun.* Something fine and delicious, especially a food ▶ dainty, morsel, sweetmeat, tidbit, treat. *Informal:* goody. [*Compare* **luxury.**] —*See also* **infirmity, subtlety, tact.**

delicate *adjective.* **1.** Appealing to refined taste ▶ choice, dainty, elegant, exquisite, fine, genteel, gentle. [*Compare* **cultured.**] **2.** Showing sensitivity and skill in dealing with others ▶ diplomatic, discreet, graceful, politic, sensitive, tactful. **3.** Requiring great tact or skill ▶ demanding, difficult, exacting, precarious, sensitive, ticklish, touch-and-go, touchy, tricky. **4.** So slight as to be difficult to notice or appreciate ▶ fine, finespun, nice, precise, refined, subtle. —*See also* **fine**[1] (2), **fragile, gentle** (2), **weak** (1).

✤ **CORE SYNONYMS:** *delicate, choice, dainty, elegant, exquisite, fine.* These adjectives mean appealing to refined taste: *a delicate flavor; choice exotic flowers; a dainty dish; elegant handwriting; an exquisite wine; the finest embroidery.*

---

delicateness *noun.* —*See* **infirmity.**

delicious *adjective.* Highly pleasing, especially to the sense of taste ▶ ambrosial, appetizing, delectable, flavorful, heavenly, luscious, mouthwatering, palatable, savory, scrumptious, tasteful, tasty, toothsome. *Slang:* yummy. *—See also* **delightful.**

✦ CORE SYNONYMS: *delicious, ambrosial, delectable, luscious, scrumptious, toothsome, yummy.* These adjectives mean very pleasing to the sense of taste: *a delicious pâté; ambrosial fruit salad; delectable raspberries; luscious chocolate bonbons; a scrumptious peach; a toothsome apple; yummy fudge.*

delight *noun.* A feeling of extreme gratification aroused by something good or desired ▶ bliss, delectation, ecstasy, elation, enchantment, enjoyment, glee, joy, pleasure. *—See also* **amusement, happiness, luxury.**

delight *verb.* **1.** To give great or keen pleasure to ▶ amuse, cheer, elate, enchant, excite, gladden, gratify, overjoy, please, pleasure, thrill, tickle. [*Compare* **charm.**] **2.** To feel or take joy or pleasure ▶ exult, pleasure, rejoice. [*Compare* **enjoy, luxuriate.**] *—See also* **adore** (2).

✦ CORE SYNONYMS: *delight, gladden, gratify, please, tickle.* These verbs mean to give pleasure to: *a gift that would delight any child; was pleased by their success; praise that gladdens the spirit; progress that gratified all concerned; compliments that tickle their vanity.*

delighted *adjective. —See* **willing.**

delightful *adjective.* Giving great pleasure or delight ▶ adorable, amusing, blissful, charming, cute, delectable, delicious, enchanting, heavenly, lovable, lovely, luscious, pleasing, pleasurable, sweet. *Informal:* darling. [*Compare* **attractive, pleasant.**]

delimit *or* **delimitate** *verb. —See* **determine.**

delineate *verb. —See* **draft** (1), **represent** (2).

delineation *noun. —See* **form** (1), **representation.**

delineative *adjective. —See* **descriptive.**

delinquency *noun. —See* **breach** (1), **failure** (2).

delinquent *noun. —See* **criminal.**

deliquesce *verb. —See* **melt.**

delirious *adjective. —See* **frantic.**

deliver *verb.* **1.** To mete out by means of some action ▶ administer, deal, give. **2.** To yield oneself unrestrainedly, as to an impulse ▶ abandon, relinquish, surrender. ***Idioms:*** give oneself up (*or* over). *—See also* **bear** (4), **give** (1), **rescue, say.**

deliverance *noun. —See* **rescue.**

deliverer *noun. —See* **rescuer.**

delivery *noun.* The act of delivering or the condition of being delivered ▶ consignment, conveyance, shipment, surrender, transfer, transmission, transmittal. *—See also* **birth** (1), **rescue.**

dell *noun. —See* **valley.**

delude *verb. —See* **deceive.**

deluge *noun. —See* **flood, rain.**

deluge *verb.* To affect as if by an outpouring of water ▶ flood, inundate, overwhelm, swamp. *—See also* **flood** (1).

delusion *noun. —See* **illusion, myth** (2).

delusive *or* **delusory** *adjective. —See* **fallacious** (2), **illusive.**

deluxe *adjective. —See* **luxurious.**

delve *verb. —See* **dig, explore.**

demand *verb.* **1.** To ask for urgently or insistently ▶ appeal for, call for, claim, exact, importune, insist on, order, require, requisition. ***Idiom:*** cry out for. [*Compare* **urge.**] **2.** To have as a need or prerequisite ▶ ask, beg, call for, entail, involve, necessitate, need, require, take, want. [*Compare* **lack.**] *—See also* **claim.**

demand *noun.* **1.** The act of demanding ▶ appeal, behest, call, claim, cry, exaction, order, requisition. **2.** Something asked for or needed ▶ desire, exigence, exigency, need, requirement, want.

✦ CORE SYNONYMS: *demand, claim, exact, require.* These verbs mean to ask for urgently or insistently: *demanding better working conditions; claiming repayment of a debt; exacted obedience from the child; tax payments required by law.*

---

demanding *adjective.* —*See* **delicate** (3), **difficult** (1), **fussy, severe** (1), **troublesome** (2).
demarcate *verb.* —*See* **determine.**
demarcation *noun.* —*See* **distinction** (1).
demean[1] *verb.* —*See* **act** (1).
demean[2] *verb.* —*See* **debase, humble.**
demeanor *noun.* —*See* **bearing** (1).
dement *verb.* —*See* **derange.**
demented *adjective.* —*See* **insane.**
dementia *noun.* —*See* **insanity.**
demise *noun.* —*See* **death** (1).
demise *verb.* —*See* **die.**
demit *verb.* To relinquish one's engagement in or occupation with ▶ leave, quit, resign, terminate. ***Idioms:*** hang it up, throw in the towel. [*Compare* **break.**] —*See also* **abandon** (1).
demobilize *verb.* —*See* **discharge.**
democratic *adjective.* —*See* **popular.**
demolish *verb.* —*See* **destroy** (1), **destroy** (2).
demolition *noun.* —*See* **destruction.**
demon *noun.* An intensely energetic, enthusiastic person ▶ dynamo, hustler. *Informal:* eager beaver, firebreather, go-getter, live wire. —*See also* **fiend.**
demonstrate *verb.* To demonstrate and clarify with examples ▶ evidence, exemplify, illustrate, instance. [*Compare* **explain, show.**] —*See also* **prove, show** (1).
demonstration *noun.* —*See* **confirmation** (2), **display.**
demoralize *verb.* —*See* **corrupt, discourage.**
demoralizing *adjective.* —*See* **unwholesome** (2).
demote *verb.* To lower in rank or grade ▶ break, bump, degrade, downgrade, reduce. *Slang:* bust.

✚ **CORE SYNONYMS:** *demote, break, bust, degrade, downgrade, reduce.* These verbs mean to lower in rank, grade, or status: *was demoted from captain to lieutenant; a noncommissioned officer broken to the ranks; a detective who was busted to uniformed traffic patrol for insubordination; a supervisor degraded to an assistant; a popular author downgraded by critical opinion to a genre writer; was reduced from a command post to a desk job.*

◀ **ANTONYM:** *promote*

---

demotion *noun.* The act or an instance of demoting ▶ degradation, downgrade, reduction.
demur *verb.* —*See* **object.**
demur *noun.* —*See* **objection.**
demure *adjective.* —*See* **shy[1].**
demureness *noun.* —*See* **shyness.**
demystify *verb.* —*See* **explain** (1).
den *noun.* **1.** A place used as an animal's dwelling ▶ burrow, hole, lair. [*Compare* **cave.**] **2.** A hiding place ▶ covert, hideaway, hide-out, lair. —*See also* **pit[1].**
denature *verb.* —*See* **convert.**
denial *noun.* **1.** A refusal to grant the truth of a statement or charge ▶ abnegation, contradiction, disaffirmance, disavowal, disaffirmation, disclaimer, negation, rejection, renunciation, repudiation, traversal. **2.** A turning down of a request ▶ disallowance, nonacceptance, refusal, rejection, turndown. [*Compare* **forbiddance.**]
denigrate *verb.* To attack the reputation or honor of ▶ befoul, besmear, besmirch, bespatter, blacken, blot, cloud, defile, dirty, smear, smudge, smut, soil, spatter, stain, sully, taint, tarnish, tear down. ***Idioms:*** drag through the mud (*or* dirt), give a black eye to, give someone a bad name, sling (*or* throw) mud on. [*Compare* **disgrace, libel, malign, slam.**] —*See also* **belittle.**
denigration *noun.* —*See* **belittlement, libel.**
denizen *noun.* —*See* **inhabitant.**
denominate *verb.* —*See* **call, name** (1).

denomination *noun.* —*See* **kind**[2], **name** (1), **religion.**

denotation *noun.* —*See* **meaning.**

denotative *or* **denotive** *adjective.* —*See* **designative.**

denote *verb.* —*See* **designate, mean**[1].

dénouement *noun.* —*See* **end** (1).

denounce *verb.* —*See* **accuse, deplore** (1), **disapprove.**

denouncement *noun.* —*See* **accusation.**

denouncer *noun.* One that accuses ▶ accuser, arraigner, indicter, recriminator.

dense *adjective.* —*See* **backward** (1), **stupid, thick** (2), **thick** (3).

density *noun.* —*See* **stupidity, thickness.**

dent *verb.* —*See* **deform.**

dent *noun.* —*See* **deformity, depression** (1), **impression** (1).

dentate *adjective.* —*See* **saw-toothed.**

denude *verb.* —*See* **bare.**

denuded *adjective.* —*See* **empty** (2).

denunciation *noun.* —*See* **accusation, criticism, disapproval, vituperation.**

denunciative *or* **denunciatory** *adjective.* —*See* **accusatorial.**

deny *verb.* To refuse to admit the truth, reality, value, or worth of ▶ abnegate, contradict, contravene, controvert, disaffirm, disavow, dismiss, dispute, gainsay, negate, negative, oppugn, renounce, traverse. [*Compare* **contest.**] —*See also* **decline, deprive, repudiate.**

✚ **CORE SYNONYMS:** *deny, contradict, contravene, disaffirm, gainsay, negate.* These verbs mean to refuse to admit the truth, reality, value, or worth of: *denied the rumor; contradicted the statement; contravene a conclusion; disaffirm a suggestion; trying to gainsay the evidence; negated the allegations.*

◀ **ANTONYM:** *affirm*

---

depart *verb.* —*See* **deviate, die, differ, disappear** (2), **go** (1).

departed *adjective.* —*See* **dead** (1).

departing *adjective.* —*See* **parting.**

department *noun.* —*See* **area** (1), **branch** (3), **class** (1).

departure *noun.* The act of leaving ▶ adieu, departing, egress, embarkation, embarkment, exit, exodus, farewell, going, goodbye, leave-taking, parting, retirement, valediction, withdrawal. —*See also* **deviation, difference, digression, disappearance.**

depend on *or* **upon** *verb.* **1.** To place trust or confidence in ▶ bank on (*or* upon), believe in, confide in, count on (*or* upon), reckon on (*or* upon), rely on (*or* upon), trust (in). ***Idiom:*** put faith in. **2.** To be determined by or contingent on something unknown, uncertain, or changeable ▶ hang on (upon), hinge on (*or* upon), rest on (*or* upon), revolve around, turn on (*or* upon). —*See also* **expect** (1).

✚ **CORE SYNONYMS:** *depend on, rely on, trust, reckon on.* These verbs share the meaning to place or have trust or confidence in someone or something. *Depend on* implies confidence in the help or support of another: *depends on friends for emotional support. Rely on* implies complete confidence: "*You are the only woman I can rely on to be interested in her*" (John Galsworthy). *Trust* stresses confidence arising from belief that is often based on inconclusive evidence: "*We must try to trust one another. Stay and cooperate*" (Jomo Kenyatta). *Reckon on* implies a sense of confident expectancy: "*He reckons on finding a woman as big a fool as himself*" (George Meredith).

---

dependable *adjective.* Capable of being depended on ▶ honest, reliable, responsible, solid, sound, stable, steadfast, steady, steady-going, trustworthy, trusty.

✚ **CORE SYNONYMS:** *dependable, reliable, responsible, trustworthy.* These adjectives mean capable of being depended on or worthy of reliance or trust: *a reliable source of information; a dependable worker; a responsible babysitter; a trustworthy report.*

---

dependence *noun.* The state or relation of being determined or controlled ▶ dependency, reliance. [*Compare* **authority, dominance, need, relation.**] —*See also* **addiction, trust.**

dependency *noun.* The state or relation of being determined or controlled ▶ dependence, reliance. [*Compare* **authority, dominance, need, relation.**] —*See also* **possession.**

dependent *adjective.* Subject to the authority or control of another ▶ subject, subordinate, subservient. [*Compare* **auxiliary.**] —*See also* **conditional.**

dependent *or* **dependant** *noun.* A person who relies on another for support ▶ charge, ward.

depict *verb.* —*See* **interpret** (2), **represent** (2).

depiction *noun.* —*See* **interpretation, representation.**

deplete *verb.* —*See* **dry up** (2), **exhaust** (1).

depletion *noun.* The act of consuming ▶ consumption, expenditure, usage, use, utilization. [*Compare* **use.**] —*See also* **debilitation.**

deplorable *adjective.* Worthy of severe disapproval ▶ condemnable, disgraceful, reprehensible, shameful, unfortunate, woeful, wretched. [*Compare* **disgraceful, offensive, miserable.**] —*See also* **sorrowful.**

deplore *verb.* **1.** To express strong disapproval of ▶ bemoan, bewail, censure, condemn, decry, denounce, reprehend, reprobate. [*Compare* **disapprove, condemn, hate.**] **2.** To feel or express sorrow for ▶ regret, repent, rue, sorrow (over). [*Compare* **feel, grieve.**]

✚ **CORE SYNONYMS:** *deplore, reprehend, censure, condemn, denounce.* These verbs mean to express strong disapproval of: *Deplore* and *reprehend* imply sharp disapproval: *"Somehow we had to master events, not simply deplore them"* (Henry A. Kissinger); *"reprehends students who have protested apartheid"* (New York Times). *Censure* refers to open and strong expression of criticism; often it implies a formal reprimand: *"No man can justly censure or condemn another, because indeed no man truly knows another"* (Thomas Browne). *Condemn* denotes the pronouncement of harshly adverse judgment: *"The wrongs which we seek to condemn and punish have been so calculated, so malignant and so devastating that civilization cannot tolerate their being ignored because it cannot survive their being repeated"* (Robert H. Jackson). *Denounce* implies public proclamation of condemnation or repudiation: *The press denounces the new taxation policies.*

---

deploy *verb.* —*See* **arrange** (1).

deployment *noun.* —*See* **arrangement** (1).

depone *verb.* —*See* **testify.**

deponent *noun.* One who testifies, especially in court ▶ attestant, attester, testifier, witness.

deport *verb.* —*See* **act** (1), **banish.**

deportation *noun.* —*See* **exile.**

deportee *noun.* —*See* **émigré.**

deportment *noun.* —*See* **behavior** (1).

depose *verb.* —*See* **overthrow, testify.**

deposit *verb.* —*See* **bank**[2], **pawn**[1], **position.**

deposit *noun.* **1.** A partial or initial payment ▶ down payment, installment, security. **2.** Matter that settles on a bottom or collects on a surface by a natural process ▶ accumulation, alluvium, dregs, lees, precipitate, precipitation, sediment. [*Compare* **coat.**]

deposition *noun.* A formal declaration of truth or fact given under oath ▶ affidavit, testimony, witness.

depository *noun.* A place where something is deposited for safekeeping ▶ archive, bank, cache, depot, lockbox, repository, safe, store, storehouse, strongbox, treasure house, treasury, vault, warehouse. [*Compare* **hoard.**]

depot *noun.* A stopping place along a route for picking up or dropping off passengers ▶ station, stop, terminal, terminus. —*See also* **base**[1] (1), **depository.**

deprave *verb.* —*See* **corrupt.**

depraved *adjective.* —*See* **corrupt** (1).

depravity *noun.* —*See* **corruption** (1), **corruption** (2).

deprecate *verb.* —*See* **belittle, disapprove.**

deprecation *noun.* —*See* **belittlement, disapproval.**

deprecatory *or* **deprecative** *adjective.* —*See* **disparaging.**

depreciate *verb.* To make less in price or value ▶ cheapen, depress, devaluate, devalue, downgrade, lessen, lower, mark down, reduce, write down. [*Compare* **decrease.**] —*See also* **belittle, deteriorate, fall** (4).

depreciation *noun.* A lowering of price or value ▶ cheapening, depression, devaluation, lessening, markdown, reduction, shrinkage, write-down. [*Compare* **decrease.**] —*See also* **belittlement, deterioration** (1), **fall** (3).

depreciative *or* **depreciatory** *adjective.* —*See* **disparaging.**

depredate *verb.* —*See* **sack**[2].

depress *verb.* To make sad or gloomy ▶ dampen, deject, dishearten, dispirit, oppress, sadden, weigh down. *Slang:* bum out. ***Idioms:*** get one down, give one the blues (*or* blahs), make one blue. [*Compare* **discourage.**] —*See also* **depreciate, lower**[2], **push** (1).

depressant *noun.* —*See* **drug** (2).

depressed *adjective.* **1.** In low spirits ▶ blue, brokenhearted, dejected, desolate, disconsolate, discouraged, dismayed, dispirited, down, downcast, downhearted, dull, dyspeptic, dysphoric, gloomy, heartbroken, heartsick, heavyhearted, low, melancholic, melancholy, sad, sorrowful, spiritless, tristful, unhappy, wistful. *Informal:* blah. ***Idioms:*** down at (*or* in) the mouth, down in the dumps. [*Compare* **anxious, despondent, glum, lonely.**] **2.** Economically and socially below standard ▶ backward, deprived, disadvantaged, impoverished, poor, underprivileged. [*Compare* **poor.**] —*See also* **hollow** (2).

✦ **CORE SYNONYMS:** *depressed, blue, dejected, dispirited, downcast, downhearted.* These adjectives mean affected or marked by low spirits: *depressed by the loss of his job; lonely and blue in a strange city; is dejected but trying to look cheerful; a dispirited and resigned expression on her face; looked downcast after his defeat; a downhearted patient who welcomed visitors.*

---

depressing *adjective.* —*See* **bleak** (2), **sorrowful.**

depression *noun.* **1.** An area sunk below its surroundings ▶ basin, cavity, concavity, dent, dip, hollow, indentation, pit, recess, sag, sink, sinkhole. [*Compare* **hole, impression.**] **2.** A feeling or spell of dismally low spirits ▶ blues, dejection, despondence, despondency, disconsolation, discouragement, disheartenment, doldrums, dolefulness, downheartedness, dumps, dysphoria, funk, gloom, glumness, heartsickness, heavyheartedness, lowness, melancholy, mopes, mournfulness, sadness, sorrow, sorrowfulness, unhappiness, wistfulness. *Informal:* blahs. **3.** A period of decreased business activity and high unemployment ▶ downturn, recession, slowdown, slump. —*See also* **depreciation.**

deprivation *or* **deprival** *noun.* The condition of being deprived of what one once had or ought to have ▶ deficiency, destitution, dispossession, divestiture, hardship, loss, penury, poverty, privation. [*Compare* **lack, need, poverty, seizure.**] —*See also* **misery.**

deprive *verb.* To take or keep something away from ▶ deny, dispossess, divest, rob, strip, withhold. [*Compare* **decline, seize.**]

deprived *adjective.* —*See* **depressed** (2), **empty** (2).

depth *noun.* **1.** The extent or measurement downward from a surface ▶ deepness, drop, drop-off. **2.** Intellectual penetration or range ▶ deepness, profoundness, profundity, weightiness. [*Compare* **discernment, intelligence, wisdom.**] —*See also* **deep, intensity.**

depths *noun.* —*See* **deep, intensity.**

deputation *noun.* A diplomatic office or headquarters in a foreign country ▶ embassy, legation, mission.

deputy *noun.* —*See* **assistant, representative.**

derailed *adjective.* —*See* **insane.**

derange *verb.* To make insane ▶ craze, dement, madden, unbalance, unhinge. ***Idioms:*** push off (*or* over) the deep end. —*See also* **disorder, upset.**

derangement *noun.* —*See* **disorder** (1), **insanity.**

derelict *adjective.* —*See* **abandoned** (1), **negligent.**

derelict *noun.* —*See* **pauper.**

dereliction *noun.* The act of forsaking ▶ abandonment, desertion. [*Compare* **defection.**] —*See also* **breach** (1), **failure** (2).

deride *verb.* —*See* **ridicule.**

de rigueur *adjective.* —*See* **appropriate.**

derision *noun.* Words or actions intended to evoke contemptuous laughter ▶ mockery, ridicule. [*Compare* **sarcasm, taunt.**] —*See also* **disgrace.**

derisive *adjective.* —*See* **disparaging, sarcastic.**

derivation *noun.* —*See* **ancestry, derivative, origin.**

derivational *adjective.* Stemming from an original source ▶ derivative, derived, secondary.

derivative *noun.* Something derived from another ▶ byproduct, derivation, descendant, offshoot, outgrowth, spin-off. [*Compare* **copy.**]

derivative *or* **derivate** *adjective.* Stemming from an original source ▶ derivational, derived, secondary. —*See also* **imitative** (1).

derive *verb.* **1.** To obtain from another source ▶ draw, extract, gain, get, receive, take. **2.** To arrive at through reasoning ▶ determine, educe, evolve, excogitate, work out. [*Compare* **decide, infer.**] —*See also* **descend, stem.**

derived *adjective.* Stemming from an original source ▶ derivational, derivative, secondary.

derogate *verb.* —*See* **belittle.**

derogation *noun.* —*See* **belittlement.**

derogatory *or* **derogative** *adjective.* —*See* **disparaging.**

derrière *noun.* —*See* **buttocks.**

derring-do *noun.* —*See* **daring.**

descend *verb.* To have hereditary derivation ▶ come, derive, issue, spring. ***Idiom:*** trace one's descent. —*See also* **condescend** (1), **deteriorate, drop** (2), **fall** (1).

descendant *noun.* —*See* **derivative, progeny.**

descending *or* **descendent** *adjective.* Moving or sloping down ▶ downward, drooping, falling, plummeting, plunging, sinking.

descent *noun.* A sudden drop to a lower condition or status ▶ comedown, dip, down, downfall, downgrade, plunge, slide, tumble. —*See also* **ancestry, drop** (3), **fall** (1), **fall** (3).

describe *verb.* To communicate the facts, details, or particulars of something ▶ detail, narrate, recite, recount, rehearse, relate, report, tell. [*Compare* **call, explain.**] —*See also* **represent** (2).

✚ **CORE SYNONYMS:** *describe, narrate, recite, recount, rehearse, relate, report.* These verbs mean to communicate the facts, details, or particulars of something: *described the accident; narrated their travel experiences; an explorer reciting her adventures; a mercenary recounting his exploits; parents rehearsing street* *safety with their children; related the day's events; reported what she had seen.*

---

description *noun.* —*See* **kind[2], representation, story** (1).

descriptive *adjective.* Serving to describe ▶ colorful, delineative, graphic, representative, vivid. [*Compare* **eloquent, expressive.**]

descry *verb.* —*See* **discern, notice, see** (1).

desecrate *verb.* —*See* **violate** (3).

desecration *noun.* —*See* **sacrilege.**

desegregate *verb.* To open to all people regardless of race ▶ integrate.

desensitize *verb.* —*See* **deaden.**

desert[1] *noun.* A desolate or unproductive region ▶ badlands, barren, barrens, dust bowl, tundra, waste, wasteland. [*Compare* **country, wilderness.**]

desert *adjective.* —*See* **barren** (2), **dry** (2).

desert[2] *verb.* —*See* **abandon** (1), **defect.**

deserted *adjective.* —*See* **abandoned** (1), **lonely** (1).

deserter *noun.* —*See* **defector.**

desertion *noun.* The act of forsaking ▶ abandonment, dereliction. [*Compare* **defection.**]

deserts *noun.* —*See* **due, punishment.**

deserve *verb.* —*See* **earn** (1).

deserved *adjective.* —*See* **just.**

deserving *adjective.* —*See* **admirable.**

desiccate *verb.* —*See* **dry, dry up** (2).

design *verb.* **1.** To form a strategy for ▶ blueprint, cast, chart, conceive, concoct, contrive, devise, formulate, frame, lay, originate, plan, predetermine, premeditate, project, scheme, strategize, work out. *Informal:* dope out. ***Idiom:*** lay plans. [*Compare* **invent, plot.**] **2.** To work out and arrange the parts and details of ▶ blueprint, draft, lay out, map (out), outline, plan, set out, sketch. [*Compare* **draft.**] —*See also* **compose** (1), **intend.**

design *noun.* An element or component in a decorative composition ▶ device, figure, motif, motive. —*See also* **approach** (1), **form** (1), **intention.**

designate *verb.* To make known or identify, as by signs ▶ denote, earmark, identify, indicate, mark, pinpoint, point out, signal, signify, specify. [*Compare* **mark, represent, show.**] —*See also* **appoint, appropriate, call, name** (1).

designation *noun.* —*See* **appointment, name** (1).

designative *or* **designatory** *adjective.* Serving to designate or indicate ▶ denotative, denotive, exhibitive, exhibitory, indicative, indicatory, significant. [*Compare* **symbolic.**]

designed *adjective.* —*See* **calculated.**

designing *adjective.* Coldly planning to achieve selfish aims ▶ calculating, conniving, manipulative, scheming. [*Compare* **artful.**] —*See also* **artful.**

designs *noun.* —*See* **plot** (2).

desirable *adjective.* Arousing erotic desire ▶ alluring, enticing, sexy. *Slang:* foxy, hot, sizzling. ***Idiom:*** to die for. [*Compare* **seductive, sensual.**] —*See also* **advisable, attractive.**

desire *verb.* To have a strong longing for ▶ ache, aspire, covet, dream, hanker, hope, long, pant, pine, want, wish, yearn. *Informal:* die for, hone. ***Idioms:*** be dying (*or* itching) to, give the world for, set one's heart on. [*Compare* **lust.**] —*See also* **choose** (2).

desire *noun.* **1.** A strong wanting of what promises enjoyment or pleasure ▶ appetence, appetency, appetite, craving, hankering, hunger, itch, longing, lust, thirst, wish, yearning, yen. **2.** Sexual hunger ▶ amativeness, appetite, concupiscence, eroticism, erotism, itch, libidinousness, libido, lust, lustfulness, passion, prurience, pruriency, urge. *Slang:* horniness. —*See also* **demand** (2), **dream** (3).

✚ **CORE SYNONYMS:** *desire, covet, want, wish, yearn.* These verbs mean to have a strong longing for: *desire peace; coveted the new convertible; wanted a* *drink of water; got all that I wished for; yearned for a better career.*

---

desired *adjective.* —*See* **darling.**

desirous *adjective.* Having desire for something ▶ desiring, hankering, hungry. [*Compare* **voracious.**]

desist *verb.* —*See* **abandon** (2), **stop** (1).

desolate *adjective.* —*See* **abandoned** (1), **barren** (2), **gloomy, lonely** (1), **lonely** (2).

desolate *verb.* —*See* **consume** (1).

despair *verb.* To lose all hope ▶ despond, give in, give up. ***Idioms:*** throw in the sponge (*or* towel). [*Compare* **abandon, surrender.**]

despair *noun.* Utter lack of hope ▶ desperateness, desperation, despond, despondence, despondency, discouragement, dismay, hopelessness. [*Compare* **depression.**]

despairing *adjective.* —*See* **despondent.**

desperado *noun.* —*See* **criminal.**

desperate *adjective.* —*See* **despondent, intense, urgent** (1).

desperation *or* **desperateness** *noun.* —*See* **despair.**

despicable *or* **despisable** *adjective.* —*See* **offensive** (1).

despisal *noun.* The feeling of despising ▶ abhorrence, contempt, despite, disdain, dislike, hatred, loathing, revulsion, scorn. [*Compare* **disrespect, enmity, hate.**]

despise *verb.* To regard with utter contempt ▶ abominate, contemn, disdain, dismiss, scorn, scout, sneer at, sniff at, spit on. ***Idioms:*** have no use for, look down on (*or* upon), look down one's nose at. [*Compare* **dislike, revile, snub.**] —*See also* **hate.**

✦ **CORE SYNONYMS:** *despise, contemn, disdain, scorn, scout.* These verbs mean to regard with utter contempt: *despises incompetence; contemned the dictator's cruel actions; disdained my suggestion; a storyteller who scorns sentimentality; scouted simplistic explanations for the mistakes.*

◀ **ANTONYM:** *esteem*

---

despite *noun.* —*See* **defiance** (2), **despisal, indignity.**

despiteful *adjective.* —*See* **malevolent.**

despitefulness *noun.* —*See* **malevolence.**

despoil *verb.* —*See* **sack**^{2}, **violate** (3).

despond *verb.* To lose all hope ▶ despair, give in, give up. ***Idioms:*** throw in the sponge (*or* towel). [*Compare* **abandon, surrender.**]

despond *noun.* —*See* **despair.**

despondence *or* **despondency** *noun.* —*See* **depression** (2), **despair.**

despondent *adjective.* Having lost all hope ▶ dejected, despairing, desperate, discouraged, forlorn, hopeless, wretched. [*Compare* **depressed, glum, miserable.**]

✦ **CORE SYNONYMS:** *despondent, despairing, forlorn, hopeless.* These adjectives mean having lost all hope: *despondent about the company's failure in the marketplace; took a despairing view of world politics and current affairs; a forlorn cause; a hopeless case.*

---

despot *noun.* —*See* **authoritarian, dictator.**

despotic *adjective.* —*See* **absolute, authoritarian.**

despotism *noun.* —*See* **absolutism** (2), **absolutism** (1), **tyranny.**

desquamate *verb.* —*See* **flake.**

destiny *noun.* —*See* **fate** (1), **fate** (2).

destitute *adjective.* —*See* **empty** (2), **poor.**

destitution *noun.* —*See* **deprivation, poverty.**

destroy *verb.* **1.** To cause the complete ruin or wreckage of ▶ annihilate, bankrupt, break down, cross up, crush, demolish, devastate, finish, ravage, ruin, shatter, sink, smash, spoil, torpedo, undo, wash up, wrack, wreck. *Slang:* total. ***Idioms:*** lay waste to, put the kibosh on. [*Compare* **annihilate, botch, damage.**] **2.** To pull down or break up so that reconstruction is impossible ▶ demolish, dismantle, dynamite, knock down, level, obliterate, pull down, pulverize, raze, tear down, wreck. —*See also* **break** (2), **kill**[1], **murder.**

✚ **CORE SYNONYMS:** *destroy, raze, demolish, ruin, wreck.* These verbs mean to cause the complete ruin or wreckage of something or someone. *Destroy, raze,* and *demolish* can all imply reduction to ruins or even complete obliteration: "*I saw the best minds of my generation destroyed by madness*" (Allen Ginsberg); "*raze what was left of the city from the surface of the earth*" (John Lothrop Motley); *demolished the opposition's argument. Ruin* usually implies irretrievable harm but not necessarily total destruction: "*You will ruin no more lives as you ruined mine*" (Arthur Conan Doyle). To *wreck* is to ruin in or as if in a violent collision: "*The Boers had just wrecked a British military train*" (Arnold Bennett). When *wreck* is used in referring to the ruination of a person or of his or her hopes or reputation, it implies irreparable shattering: "*Coleridge, poet and philosopher wrecked in a mist of opium*" (Matthew Arnold).

destroyer *noun.* —*See* **ruin** (1).

destruction *noun.* The act of destroying or state of being destroyed ▶ annihilation, bane, decimation, demolition, devastation, havoc, pulverization, ruin, ruination, undoing, wrack, wreck, wreckage. —*See also* **damage, ruin** (1).

destructive *adjective.* —*See* **harmful.**

desuetude *noun.* —*See* **obsoleteness.**

desultory *adjective.* —*See* **aimless, random.**

detach *verb.* To remove from association with ▶ abstract, disassociate, disconnect, disengage, dissociate, separate, uncouple, withdraw. —*See also* **divide.**

detached *adjective.* **1.** Lacking interest in one's surroundings or worldly affairs ▶ aloof, disconnected, disinterested, incurious, indifferent, remote, unconcerned, uninterested, uninvolved. **2.** Feeling or showing no strong emotional involvement ▶ disinterested, dispassionate, impersonal, indifferent, neutral. —*See also* **apathetic, calm, cool, fair**[1] (1), **solitary.**

detachment *noun.* **1.** The act or process of detaching ▶ abstraction, disassociation, disconnection, disengagement, dissociation, separation, uncoupling, withdrawal. **2.** Dissociation from one's surroundings or worldly affairs ▶ aloofness, disinterest, distance, indifference, remoteness, unconcern, uninvolvement. **3.** A unit of troops on special assignment ▶ brigade, corps, detail, patrol, squad. —*See also* **apathy, division** (1), **fairness, force** (3).

detail *noun.* A small, often specialized element of a whole ▶ fine print, item, minutia, nicety, particular, singularity, specialty, technicality, trivia. [*Compare* **nitty-gritty.**] —*See also* **circumstance** (2), **detachment** (3), **element** (2).

detail *verb.* To state specifically ▶ particularize, provide, specify, stipulate. [*Compare* **assert, designate, dictate.**] —*See also* **describe.**

✚ **CORE SYNONYMS:** *detail, item, particular.* These nouns denote a small, often specialized element of a whole: *discussed the details of their trip; a shopping list with many items; furnished the particulars of the accident.*

detailed *adjective.* Characterized by attention to detail ▶ all-inclusive, blow-by-blow, circumstantial, comprehensive, elaborate, exhaustive, full, in-depth, minute, particular, thorough. —*See also* **elaborate.**

detain *verb.* To keep in custody ▶ hold. —*See also* **delay** (1), **imprison.**

detainment *noun.* —*See* **delay** (2), **detention.**

detect *verb.* —*See* **discern, discover, notice, see** (1).

detectable *adjective.* —*See* **perceptible.**

detective *noun.* A person whose work is investigating crimes or obtaining hidden evidence or information ▶ investigator, plainclothesman, private eye, private investigator, sherlock, sleuth. *Informal:* eye. *Slang:* dick, gumshoe.

detention *noun.* The state of being detained by legal authority ▶ arrest, charge, confinement, custody, detainment, imprisonment, incarceration, internment, quarantine, ward.

deter *verb.* —*See* **dissuade.**

deteriorate *verb.* To become lower in quality, character, or condition ▶ atrophy, decline, degenerate, depreciate, descend, ebb, languish, retrograde, sink, wane, weaken, worsen. ***Idioms:*** go bad, go to pot, go downhill, go to seed, go to the dogs, hit the skids. [*Compare* **decrease, fall.**] —*See also* **decay, fade.**

deterioration *noun.* **1.** Descent to a lower level or condition ▶ atrophy, decadence, declension, declination, decline, degeneracy, degeneration, depreciation, retrogradation, wane, weakening, worsening. **2.** A marked loss of strength or effectiveness ▶ declination, decline, failure. —*See also* **damage, decay.**

determent *noun.* —*See* **prevention.**

determinant *noun.* That which produces an effect ▶ antecedent, cause, occasion, reason. [*Compare* **impact, origin, stimulus.**]

determinate *adjective.* —*See* **definite** (2).

determination *noun.* The act or process of ascertaining dimensions, quantity, or capacity ▶ measure, measurement, mensuration, quantification. [*Compare* **computation, estimation.**] —*See also* **answer** (2), **decision** (1), **decision** (2), **intention, ruling.**

determinative *adjective.* —*See* **decisive, definitive.**

determine *verb.* To fix the limits of ▶ bound, circumscribe, define, delimit, delimitate, demarcate, limit, mark (out *or* off), measure, restrict. —*See also* **decide, derive** (2), **dictate, discover, govern, judge.**

determined *adjective.* —*See* **ambitious, firm**[1] (3), **intent.**

deterrence *noun.* —*See* **prevention.**

deterrent *adjective.* —*See* **preventive.**

deterrent *noun.* —*See* **restraint.**

detest *verb.* —*See* **hate.**

detestable *adjective.* —*See* **offensive** (1).

detestation *noun.* —*See* **hate** (1), **hate** (2).

detonate *verb.* —*See* **explode** (1).

detonation *noun.* —*See* **blast** (2), **crack** (1).

detour *verb.* —*See* **skirt.**

detract from *verb.* —*See* **damage.**

detraction *noun.* —*See* **belittlement, libel.**

detractive *adjective.* —*See* **disparaging, libelous.**

detriment *noun.* —*See* **disadvantage, harm.**

detrimental *adjective.* —*See* **harmful.**

de trop *adjective.* —*See* **superfluous.**

devaluate *verb.* —*See* **depreciate.**

devaluation *noun.* —*See* **depreciation.**

devalue *verb.* —*See* **debase, depreciate.**

devastate *verb.* —*See* **consume** (1), **destroy** (1).

devastation *noun.* —*See* **destruction.**

develop *verb.* **1.** To come gradually to have ▶ acquire, form, grow, incur, manifest, sustain. **2.** To be disclosed gradually ▶ disentangle, evolve, unfold, unfurl, unravel. [*Compare* **reveal.**] —*See also* **change** (2), **contract** (2), **elaborate, gain** (1), **happen** (1), **increase, mature, produce** (1).

developed *adjective.* —*See* **mature.**

developer *noun.* A person instrumental in the growth of something, especially in its early stages ▶ builder, contributor, creator, innovator, pioneer, producer. [*Compare* **originator.**]

development *noun.* A progression from a simple form to a more complex one ▶ advancement, blossoming, evolution, evolvement, growth, maturing, maturation, progress, unfolding. —*See also* **buildup** (2), **change** (1), **event** (1), **improvement** (1), **progress, variation.**

✤ CORE SYNONYMS: *development, evolution, progress.* These nouns mean a progression from a simpler or lower to a more advanced, mature, or complex form or stage: *the development of an idea into reality; the evolution of a plant from a seed; attempts made to foster social progress.*

deviance *or* **deviancy** *noun.* —*See* **abnormality.**

deviant *adjective.* —*See* **abnormal, errant** (2).

deviant *noun.* One whose sexual behavior differs from the accepted norm ▶ deviate, pervert. *Slang:* freak.

deviate *verb.* To turn away from a prescribed course of action or conduct ▶ depart, digress, divagate, diverge, drift, stray, swerve, vary, veer. ***Idiom:*** go off on a tangent. —*See also* **differ, digress, turn** (2).

deviate *noun.* One whose sexual behavior differs from the accepted norm ▶ deviant, pervert. *Slang:* freak.

✤ CORE SYNONYMS: *deviate, depart, digress, diverge, stray, swerve, veer.* These verbs mean to turn away from a prescribed course of action or conduct: *deviated from the original plan; won't depart from family traditions; digressed from the main topic; opinions that diverged; strays from the truth; a gaze that never swerved; a conversation that veered away from sensitive issues.*

deviation *noun.* A departing from what is prescribed ▶ aberration, departure, divagation, divergence, divergency, diversion, variation. —*See also* **abnormality, digression.**

✤ CORE SYNONYMS: *deviation, aberration, divergence.* These nouns mean a departure from what is prescribed or expected: *tolerates no deviation from the rules; regretted the aberrations of my adolescence; the divergence of a radical sect from accepted doctrines.*

device *noun.* **1.** Something, as a machine, that is devised for a particular function ▶ apparatus, appliance, contraption, contrivance, equipment, instrument, machine, mechanism. [*Compare* **gadget, tool.**] **2.** An element or component in a decorative composition ▶ design, figure, motif, motive. —*See also* **invention** (2), **trick** (1).

devil *noun.* —*See* **fiend, rascal.**

devilish *adjective.* —*See* **fiendish, mischievous.**

devilment *noun.* —*See* **mischief.**

deviltry *or* **devilry** *noun.* —*See* **crime** (2), **mischief.**

devious *adjective.* —*See* **erratic, indirect** (1), **underhand.**

deviousness *noun.* —*See* **art, dishonesty** (2).

devise *verb.* —*See* **design** (1), **invent, leave**[1] (1).

devised *adjective.* —*See* **calculated.**

devitalization *noun.* —*See* **debilitation.**

devitalize *verb.* —*See* **enervate.**

devoid *adjective.* —*See* **empty** (2).

devoir *noun.* —*See* **duty** (1).

devote *verb.* To give over by or as if by vow to a higher purpose ▶ bless, consecrate, dedicate, enshrine, hallow, pledge, sacrifice. [*Compare* **sanctify.**] —*See also* **apply** (1).

✤ CORE SYNONYMS: *devote, dedicate, consecrate, pledge.* These verbs mean to give over by or as if by vow to a higher purpose. *Devote* implies faithfulness and loyalty: *Nurses devote themselves to the care of the sick. Dedicate* connotes a solemn, often formal commitment: "*To such a task we can dedicate our lives and our fortunes*" (Woodrow Wilson). *Consecrate* suggests sacred commitment: *His entire life is consecrated to science.* To *pledge* is to back a personal commitment by a solemn promise: "*I pledge you, I pledge myself, to a new deal for the American people*" (Franklin D. Roosevelt).

---

devoted *adjective.* —*See* **affectionate, divine** (2), **faithful, pious.**

devotee *noun.* One zealously devoted to a religion ▶ acolyte, adherent, believer, disciple, enthusiast, fanatic, sectary, votary, zealot. [*Compare* **follower.**] —*See also* **fan**[2].

devotion *noun.* A state of often extreme religious ardor ▶ adoration, devoutness, faith, faithfulness, pietism, piety, piousness, religionism, religiosity, religiousness, reverence, spirituality, zeal. [*Compare* **adoration.**] —*See also* **love** (1), **love** (2).

devotional *adjective.* —*See* **pious.**

devotions *noun.* —*See* **prayer**[1] (2).

devour *verb.* To be avidly interested in ▶ feast on, relish. *Slang:* eat up. —*See also* **consume** (1), **eat** (1).

devout *adjective.* —*See* **divine** (2), **pious, reverent.**

devoutness *noun.* —*See* **devotion.**

dexterity *noun.* Skillfulness in the use of the hands or body ▶ adroitness, cleverness, deftness, dexterousness, facility, grace, nimbleness, prowess, quickness, skill, sleight. [*Compare* **agility.**] —*See also* **agility.**

dexterous *adjective.* Exhibiting or possessing skill and ease in performance ▶ adroit, agile, artful, clean, clever, deft, facile, handy, neat, nimble, skillful, slick. [*Compare* **able, energetic, expert, fluent.**]

✚ **CORE SYNONYMS:** *dexterous, deft, adroit, handy, nimble.* These adjectives refer to skill and ease in performance. *Dexterous* implies physical or mental agility: *dexterous fingers. Deft* suggests quickness, sureness, neatness, and lightness of touch: *deft strokes; a deft turn of phrase. Adroit* implies ease and natural skill, especially in challenging situations: *an adroit skier; an adroit negotiator. Handy* suggests a more modest aptitude, principally in manual work: *handy with tools. Nimble* stresses quickness and lightness in physical or mental performance: *nimble feet; nimble wits.*

---

dexterousness *noun.* —*See* **agility, dexterity.**

diablerie *noun.* —*See* **crime** (2), **mischief.**

diabolic *or* **diabolical** *adjective.* —*See* **fiendish.**

diagnosis *noun.* —*See* **examination** (2).

diagonal *adjective.* —*See* **oblique.**

diagram *noun.* —*See* **draft** (1).
diagram *verb.* —*See* **draft** (1).

dial *noun.* The marked outer surface of an instrument ▶ face, gauge, indicator.
dial *verb.* —*See* **telephone.**

dialect *noun.* A variety of a language that differs from the standard form ▶ argot, cant, jargon, lingo, patois, vernacular. —*See also* **language** (1), **language** (2).

✚ **CORE SYNONYMS:** *dialect, vernacular, jargon, cant, argot, lingo, patois.* These nouns denote varieties of a language that differ from the standard form. *Dialect* usually applies to the vocabulary, grammar, and pronunciation characteristic of specific geographic localities or social classes. The *vernacular* is the informal everyday language spoken by a people. *Jargon* is specialized language understood only by a particular group, as one sharing an occupation or interest. *Cant* now usually refers to the specialized vocabulary of a group or trade and is often marked by the use of stock phrases. *Argot* applies especially to the language of the underworld. *Lingo* is often applied to language that is unfamiliar or difficult to understand. *Patois* is sometimes used as a synonym for *jargon* or *cant,* but it can also refer to a regional dialect that has no literary tradition.

---

dialogist *noun.* —*See* **conversationalist.**

dialogue *or* **dialog** *noun.* —*See* **conversation, discourse, script** (2).

diametric *or* **diametrical** *adjective.* —*See* **opposite.**

diamond *noun.* A small sparkling decoration ▶ glitter, rhinestone, sequin, spangle.

diaphanous *adjective.* —*See* **sheer².**

diary *noun.* —*See* **memoir.**

diaspora *noun.* —*See* **emigration.**

diatribe *noun.* —*See* **tirade.**

dibs *noun.* —*See* **claim** (1).

dice *verb.* —*See* **cut** (2).

dicey *adjective.* —*See* **dangerous.**

dick *noun.* —*See* **detective.**

dicker *verb.* —*See* **haggle.**

dictate *verb.* To set forth expressly and authoritatively ▶ decree, determine, direct, fix, impose, lay down, mandate, ordain, prescribe, rule. ***Idioms:*** call the shots (*or* tune), lay down the law, lay it on the line. [*Compare* **stipulate.**] —*See also* **administer** (1), **boss, command** (1).

dictate *noun.* —*See* **command** (1), **rule.**

✚ CORE SYNONYMS: *dictate, decree, impose, ordain, prescribe.* These verbs mean to set forth expressly and authoritatively: *victors dictating the terms of surrender; martial law decreed by the governor; impose obedience; a separation seemingly ordained by fate; taxes prescribed by law.*

---

dictated *adjective.* —*See* **required.**

dictation *noun.* —*See* **command** (1).

dictator *noun.* An absolute ruler, especially one who is harsh and oppressive ▶ autarchist, authoritarian, autocrat, Big Brother, despot, führer, man on horseback, oligarch, oppressor, strongman, totalitarian, tyrant, usurper. —*See also* **authoritarian.**

dictatorial *adjective.* Given to asserting one's will or authority over others ▶ authoritarian, bossy, dogmatic, domineering, imperious, inquisitorial, magisterial, masterful, megalomaniacal, overassertive, overbearing, overweening, peremptory. [*Compare* **aggressive, dominant, severe.**] —*See also* **absolute, authoritarian.**

✚ CORE SYNONYMS: *dictatorial, authoritarian, dogmatic, imperious, overbearing.* These adjectives mean asserting or tending to assert one's authority or to impose one's will on others. *Dictatorial* stresses the highhanded, peremptory manner characteristic of a dictator: *He ordered the staff about in his usual dictatorial manner. Authoritarian* implies the expectation of unquestioning obedience: *The authoritarian principal disciplined the unruly students. Dogmatic* suggests the imposing of one's will or opinion as though these were beyond challenge: "*When people are least sure, they are often most dogmatic*" (John Kenneth Galbraith). *Imperious* suggests the arrogant manner of one accustomed to commanding: *She dismissed my opinion with an imperious gesture. Overbearing* implies a tendency to be oppressively or rudely domineering: *The overbearing customer demanded to see the manager.*

---

dictatorship *noun.* —*See* **absolutism** (1), **absolutism** (2), **tyranny.**

diction *noun.* —*See* **wording.**

dictionary *noun.* An alphabetical list of words often defined or translated ▶ glossary, lexicon, vocabulary, wordbook.

dictum *noun.* —*See* **message, ruling.**

didactic *or* **didactical** *adjective.* —*See* **moral.** Inclined to teach or moralize excessively ▶ academic, expositive, expository, didactical, moralizing, preachy, prescriptive. [*Compare* **instructive, pedantic.**]

diddle¹ *verb.* —*See* **cheat** (1).

diddle[2] *verb.* —*See* **idle** (1).
diddler *noun.* —*See* **cheat** (2).
die *verb.* To cease living ► decease, demise, depart, drop, expire, go, pass away, pass (on), perish, succumb. *Informal:* pop off. *Slang:* check out, croak, kick in, kick off. ***Idioms:*** bite the dust, breathe one's last, buy the farm, cash in, give up the ghost, go to one's grave, kick the bucket, meet one's end (*or* Maker), pass on to the Great Beyond, turn up one's toes. —*See also* **disappear** (2), **fade away, subside.**
die for *verb.* —*See* **desire.**
die-hard *adjective.* —*See* **stubborn** (1), **ultraconservative.**
die-hard *noun.* —*See* **ultraconservative.**
die-hardism *noun.* —*See* **stubbornness.**
diet *noun.* —*See* **food.**
differ *verb.* To be unlike or dissimilar ► contrast, depart, deviate, disagree, diverge, vary. ***Idiom:*** be at variance. —*See also* **conflict.**

✚ CORE SYNONYMS: *differ, disagree, diverge, vary.* These verbs mean to be unlike or dissimilar: *Birds differ from mammals. Their testimony disagreed on several points. Our viewpoints diverge on the matter of foreign policy. People vary in intelligence.*

◄ ANTONYM: *agree*

---

difference *noun.* The condition of being unlike or dissimilar ► contrast, departure, disagreement, discrepancy, disparity, dissimilarity, dissimilitude, distinction, divarication, divergence, divergency, nonconformity, separateness, unlikeness, variance, variation. [*Compare* **abnormality, inequality.**] —*See also* **conflict, gap** (3).

✚ CORE SYNONYMS: *difference, dissimilarity, unlikeness, divergence, variation, distinction, discrepancy.* These nouns refer to the condition of being unlike or dissimilar: *Difference* is the most general: *differences in color and size; a difference of opinion. Dissimilarity* is difference between things otherwise alike or comparable: *a dissimilarity between the twins' personalities. Unlikeness* usually implies greater and more obvious difference: *unlikeness among their teaching styles. Divergence* suggests an increasing difference: *points of divergence between British and American English. Variation* occurs between things of the same class or species; often it refers to modification of something original, prescribed, or typical: *variations in temperature; a variation in shape. Distinction* often means a difference in detail determinable only by close inspection: *the distinction between "good" and "excellent."* A *discrepancy* is a difference between things that should correspond or match: *a discrepancy between his words and his actions.*

---

different *adjective.* Not like another in nature, quality, amount, or form ► contrary, contrasting, disparate, dissimilar, distinct, divergent, diverse, separate, unlike, variant, various. —*See also* **new.**
differentiate *verb.* —*See* **distinguish** (1), **distinguish** (2).
differentiation *noun.* —*See* **distinction** (1).
difficult *adjective.* **1.** Not easy to do, achieve, or master ► arduous, challenging, complicated, demanding, effortful, exacting, exigent, hard, laborious, serious, tall, tough, uphill. [*Compare* **burdensome.**] **2.** Causing difficulty, trouble, or discomfort ► incommodious, inconvenient, troublesome. [*Compare* **disturbing.**] —*See also* **complex** (1), **contrary, deep** (2), **delicate** (3), **troublesome** (2).

✚ CORE SYNONYMS: *difficult, hard, arduous.* These adjectives mean requiring great physical or mental effort to do, achieve, or master. *Difficult* and *hard* are general terms and are interchangeable in many instances; however, *difficult* is often preferable where the need for skill or ingenuity is implied: *"All poetry is difficult to read,/—The sense of it is, anyhow"* (Robert Browning). *"You write with ease to show your breeding,/But easy writing's curst hard reading"* (Richard Brinsley Sheridan). *Arduous* applies to burdensome labor or sustained physical or spiritual effort: *"knowledge at which* [Isaac] *Newton arrived through arduous and circuitous paths"* (Thomas Macaulay).

◀ **ANTONYM:** *easy*

---

difficultly *adverb.* —*See* **hard** (2).

difficulty *noun.* Something that obstructs progress and requires great effort to overcome ▶ asperity, complication, hardship, impediment, obstacle, obstruction, plight, problem, rigor, stumbling block, trial, trouble, vicissitude. ***Idioms:*** a hard (*or* tough) nut to crack, a hard (*or* tough) row to hoe, heavy sledding. [*Compare* **bar, distress.**] —*See also* **argument, conflict, predicament.**

✚ **CORE SYNONYMS:** *difficulty, hardship, obstacle, rigor, vicissitude.* These nouns denote something that requires great effort to overcome: *grappling with financial difficulties; a life of hardship; the obstacles faced in obtaining a mortgage; undergoing the rigors of prison; withstood the vicissitudes of an army career.*

---

diffidence *noun.* —*See* **shyness.**

diffident *adjective.* —*See* **shy**[1]**.**

diffuse *verb.* —*See* **spread** (2).

diffuse *adjective.* —*See* **digressive, wordy** (1).

diffuseness *noun.* —*See* **wordiness.**

diffusion *noun.* —*See* **distribution** (2), **wordiness.**

dig *verb.* To break, turn over, or remove (earth or sand, for example) with or as if with a tool ▶ bore, burrow, delve, excavate, gouge, grub, scoop, shovel, spade. —*See also* **enjoy, explore, plunge, push** (1), **till, uncover, understand** (1).

dig out *or* **up** *verb.* —*See* **discover.**

dig *noun.* An act of thrusting into or against, as to attract attention ▶ jab, jog, nudge, poke, prod, punch, stab. [*Compare* **push.**] —*See also* **crack** (3), **taunt.**

digest *verb.* —*See* **absorb** (2).

digest *noun.* —*See* **synopsis.**

digestion *noun.* —*See* **absorption** (1).

dignification *noun.* —*See* **exaltation.**

dignified *adjective.* —*See* **ceremonious, serious** (1).

dignify *verb.* To lend dignity or honor to by an act or favor ▶ enrich, favor, grace, honor. [*Compare* **honor.**] —*See also* **distinguish** (3), **exalt.**

dignitary *noun.* An important, influential person ▶ character, eminence, leader, lion, luminary, magnate, nabob, notability, notable, personage, worthy. *Informal:* bigfoot, big name, big-timer, heavyweight, high-up, somebody, someone, VIP. *Slang:* big gun, big shot, big wheel, bigwig, muckamuck.

dignity *noun.* —*See* **elegance, honor** (2), **seriousness** (1).

digress *verb.* To turn aside, especially from the main subject in writing or speaking ▶ deviate, divagate, diverge, drift, maunder, ramble, stray, veer, wander. ***Idioms:*** go off at (*or* on) a tangent, go off the subject. —*See also* **deviate.**

digression *noun.* An instance of digressing ▶ aside, departure, deviation, divagation, divergence, divergency, diversion, excursion, excursus, irrelevancy, parenthesis, rambling, straying, tangent, wandering.

digressive *adjective.* Marked by or given to digression ▶ diffuse, discursive, excursive, long-winded, meandering, parenthetic, parenthetical, rambling, tangential.

digs *noun.* —*See* **home** (1).

dilapidated *adjective.* —*See* **shabby.**

dilate *verb.* —*See* **broaden, elaborate.**

dilatory *adjective.* —*See* **slow** (1).

dilemma *noun.* —*See* **predicament.**

dilettante *noun.* —*See* **amateur.**

dilettantish *adjective.* —*See* **amateurish.**

diligence *noun.* Steady attention and effort, as to one's occupation ▶ application, assiduity, assiduousness, conscientiousness, industriousness, industry, perseverance, persistence, pertinacity, sedulousness, studiousness. *Informal:* stick-to-itiveness.

diligent *adjective.* Characterized by steady attention and effort ▶ assiduous, conscientious, dogged, industrious, painstaking, persistent, pertinacious, sedulous, studious, unflagging, unremitting.

✚ **CORE SYNONYMS:** *diligent, industrious, painstaking, assiduous, sedulous.* These adjectives suggest steady attention and effort that is undertaken to accomplish something. *Diligent* indicates constant and customary work or activity: *The diligent detective pieced the clues together. Industrious* implies steady application that is often habitual or the result of a natural inclination: *All of the weeds were pulled by the industrious gardener. Painstaking* suggests constant, careful effort, often toward the achievement of a specific goal: *Piecing together the broken vase was a painstaking task. Assiduous* emphasizes sustained application: *Her assiduous efforts to learn French paid off. Sedulous* adds to *assiduous* the sense of persistent, thoroughgoing endeavor: *"the sedulous pursuit of legal and moral principles"* (Ernest van den Haag).

---

dilly-dallier *noun.* —*See* **laggard.**

dilly-dally *verb.* —*See* **delay** (2), **hesitate.** To shift from one attitude, interest, condition, or emotion to another ▶ swing, vacillate, waver.

dilute *verb.* To lessen the strength of by or as if by admixture ▶ adulterate, attenuate, cut, thin, water (down), weaken.

dilute *adjective.* Lower than normal in strength or concentration due to admixture ▶ adulterated, cut, thin, washy, watered-down, waterish, watery, weak.

dim *adjective.* —*See* **backward** (1), **bleak** (2), **dark** (1), **dull** (2), **pale** (2), **unclear.**

dim *verb.* —*See* **drug** (2), **obscure.**

dimensions *noun.* —*See* **size** (1).

diminish *verb.* —*See* **decrease, subside.**

diminishment *noun.* —*See* **decrease, waning.**

diminution *noun.* —*See* **decrease.**

diminutive *adjective.* —*See* **tiny.**

dimness *noun.* —*See* **dark.**

dimwit *noun.* —*See* **dullard.**

dimwitted *adjective.* —*See* **backward** (1), **stupid.**

din *noun.* —*See* **noise** (1).

ding *verb.* —*See* **bang, ring**[2].

ding-a-ling *noun.* —*See* **crackpot.**

ding-dong *noun.* —*See* **fool.**

dingy *adjective.* —*See* **dirty, shabby.**

dint *noun.* —*See* **impression** (1).

dip *verb.* **1.** To plunge briefly in or into a liquid ▶ douse, duck, dunk, immerge, immerse, souse, submerge, submerse. [*Compare* **steep**[2], **wet.**] **2.** To take a substance, as liquid, from a container by plunging the hand or a utensil into it ▶ bail, dredge, lade, ladle, scoop (up), spoon. —*See also* **drop** (2), **steal.**

dip into *verb.* —*See* **browse** (1).

dip *noun.* —*See* **depression** (1), **descent, drip** (2), **fall** (3), **fool, plunge.**

✚ **CORE SYNONYMS:** *dip, douse, duck, dunk.* These verbs mean to immerse briefly into a liquid: *dipped her hand into the basin; doused his head in the shower; playmates ducking each other in the pool; dunked his cookies in milk.*

---

diplomacy *noun.* —*See* **tact.**

diplomatic *adjective.* —*See* **delicate** (2), **gracious** (2).

dippiness *noun.* —*See* **foolishness.**

dippy *adjective.* —*See* **foolish.**

dipsomaniac *or* **dipso** *noun.* —*See* **drunkard.**

dire *adjective.* Having or threatening severe negative consequences ▶ grave, grievous, serious, severe. [*Compare* **disastrous.**] —*See also* **fateful** (1), **fearful, urgent** (1).

direct *verb.* To mark a written communication with its destination ▶ address, superscribe. [*Compare* **ticket.**] —*See also* **administer** (1), **advise, aim** (1), **apply** (1), **command** (1), **conduct** (1), **dictate, guide, stage.**

direct *adjective.* **1.** Proceeding or lying in an uninterrupted line or course ▶ linear, straight, straightforward, through, undeviating, unswerving. **2.** Marked by the absence of any intervention ▶ firsthand, immediate, primary. **3.** Of unbroken descent or lineage ▶ genealogical, hereditary, lineal, ancestral. [*Compare* **direct.**] —*See also* **frank.**

direct *adverb.* —*See* **directly** (1), **directly** (3).

direction *noun.* The spatial path along which motion or orientation is referred ▶ course, heading, route, way. —*See also* **advice, command** (1), **government** (1), **management.**

directionless *adjective.* —*See* **aimless.**

directive *noun.* —*See* **command** (1).

directly *adverb.* **1.** In a direct line ▶ dead, direct, due, right, straight, straightaway, undeviatingly, unswervingly. **2.** Without intermediary ▶ firsthand, immediately. **3.** With precision or absolute conformity ▶ bang, dead, direct, exactly, fair, flush, just, plumb, precisely, right, smack, spot-on, square, squarely, straight. *Slang:* smack-dab. —*See also* **flatly, immediately** (1).

director *noun.* —*See* **boss, chief, executive, guide.**

directorial *adjective.* —*See* **administrative.**

directorship *noun.* —*See* **management.**

directory *noun.* —*See* **list**[1].

direful *adjective.* —*See* **fateful** (1), **fearful.**

dirt *noun.* —*See* **earth** (1), **filth, obscenity** (2).

dirt-cheap *adjective.* —*See* **cheap.**

dirtiness *noun.* The condition or state of being dirty ▶ filth, filthiness, foulness, griminess, grubbiness, muckiness, nastiness, smuttiness, squalor, uncleanliness, uncleanness. —*See also* **contamination, obscenity** (1).

dirty *adjective.* Covered with or stained by dirt or other impurities ▶ black, dingy, filthy, foul, grimy, grubby, miry, muddy, nasty, smutty, soiled, squalid, unclean, uncleanly, vile. *Slang:* grungy. [*Compare* **slimy, turbid.**] —*See also* **impure** (2), **obscene, rough** (2), **unfair.**

dirty *verb.* To make dirty ▶ bedaub, befoul, begrime, bemire, besmirch, besoil, bespatter, black, blacken, defile, foul, mire, muck up, mud, muddy, slush, smudge, smutch, soil, sully. [*Compare* **contaminate, smear, stain.**] —*See also* **denigrate.**

✚ **CORE SYNONYMS:** *dirty, filthy, foul, squalid, grimy.* These adjectives apply to what is covered with or stained by dirt or other impurities. *Dirty* is the most general: *dirty clothes; dirty sidewalks.* Something that is *filthy* is disgustingly dirty: *filthy rags. Foul* suggests gross offensiveness, particularly to the sense of smell: *a foul stench; a foul pond. Squalid* suggests dirtiness, wretchedness, and sordidness: *lived in a squalid apartment. Grimy* describes something ingrained or smudged with dirt or soot: *grimy hands.*

◀ **ANTONYM:** *clean*

---

disability *noun.* —*See* **disadvantage.**

disable *verb.* **1.** To render powerless or motionless, as by inflicting severe injury ▶ cripple, handicap, immobilize, impair, incapacitate, invalidate, knock out, paralyze. ***Idioms:*** put out of action (*or* commission). [*Compare* **enervate.**] **2.**

To make incapable, as of doing a job ▶ disqualify, unfit.

disabuse *verb.* To free from false hopes or ideas ▶ disenchant, disillusion, undeceive. ***Idioms:*** bring down to earth, burst someone's bubble, open someone's eyes. [*Compare* **disappoint, free.**]

disaccord *noun.* —*See* **conflict.**

disaccord *verb.* —*See* **conflict.**

disacknowledge *verb.* —*See* **repudiate.**

disadvantage *noun.* An unfavorable condition, circumstance, or characteristic ▶ detriment, disability, downside, drawback, flaw, handicap, inconvenience, liability, minus, problem, shortcoming. [*Compare* **weakness.**]

✚ CORE SYNONYMS: *disadvantage, detriment, drawback, handicap.* These nouns denote a condition, circumstance, or characteristic unfavorable to success: *Poor health is a disadvantage to athletes. To its detriment, the museum has no parking lot. Every job has its drawbacks. Illiteracy is a serious handicap in life.*

---

disadvantaged *adjective.* —*See* **depressed** (2).

disadvantageous *adjective.* —*See* **unfavorable** (1).

disaffect *verb.* —*See* **estrange.**

disaffection *noun.* —*See* **breach** (2).

disaffirm *verb.* —*See* **deny.**

disaffirmation *or* **disaffirmance** *noun.* —*See* **denial** (1).

disagree *verb.* —*See* **conflict, differ.**

disagreeability *noun.* —*See* **temper** (1).

disagreeable *adjective.* —*See* **argumentative, bitter** (3), **ill-tempered, objectionable, unpleasant.**

disagreement *noun.* —*See* **argument, conflict, difference, gap** (3), **objection.**

disallow *verb.* —*See* **decline, forbid.**

disallowed *adjective.* —*See* **forbidden.**

disallowance *noun.* A turning down of a request ▶ denial, nonacceptance, refusal, rejection, turndown. —*See also* **forbiddance.**

disappear *verb.* **1.** To pass out of sight either gradually or suddenly ▶ dissipate, dissolve, ebb, evanesce, evaporate, fade, fade out, melt (away), vanish, wane. [*Compare* **lift.**] **2.** To cease to exist ▶ cease, depart, die (away *or* out), end, expire, perish. [*Compare* **die.**]

✚ CORE SYNONYMS: *disappear, evanesce, evaporate, fade, vanish.* These verbs mean to pass out of sight or existence: *a skyscraper disappearing in the fog; time seeming to evanesce; courage evaporating; memories fading away; hope slowly vanishing.*

---

disappearance *noun.* The act or an example of passing out of sight ▶ departure, dissipation, dissolution, evanescence, evaporation, expiration, fade-out, fading, vanishment, waning.

disappoint *verb.* To cause unhappiness by failing to satisfy the hopes, desires, or expectations of ▶ discontent, discourage, disenchant, disgruntle, dishearten, disillusion, dissatisfy, dispirit, embitter, fail, frustrate, let down, sour. ***Idioms:*** dash someone's hopes, fall short, shatter someone's dream.

disappointing *adjective.* Disturbing because of failure to measure up to a standard or produce the desired results ▶ anticlimactic, discouraging, disheartening, inadequate, inferior, insufficient, sorry, underwhelming, unlucky, unsatisfactory, unsatisfying.

disappointment *noun.* **1.** Unhappiness caused by the failure of one's hopes, desires, or expectations ▶ discontent, discontentment, discouragement, disenchantment, disgruntlement, disheartenment, disillusion, disillusionment, dissatisfaction, frustration, nonfulfillment, regret, unfulfillment. **2.** Something that disappoints ▶ anticlimax, bust, fiasco, letdown, washout. *Informal:* dud, fizzle, flop, lemon, nonevent. [*Compare* **failure.**]

disapprobation *noun.* —*See* **disapproval.**

disapproval *noun.* Unfavorable opinion or judgment ▶ condemnation, denunciation, deprecation, disapprobation, disesteem, disfavor, displeasure, dissatisfaction, rejection, reproach, reproof. [*Compare* **dislike, objection, rebuke.**]

disapprove *verb.* To have or express an unfavorable opinion of ▶ decry, denounce, deprecate, discountenance, disesteem, disfavor, dislike, frown on (*or* upon), object to, reject, reprobate, sniff at. ***Idioms:*** hold no brief for, look askance at, not go for, take a dim view of, take exception to. [*Compare* **condemn, deplore, disapprove, hate.**] —*See also* **decline.**

disarrange *verb.* —*See* **disorder, tousle.**

disarrangement *noun.* —*See* **disorder** (1).

disarray *noun.* —*See* **disorder** (1).
disarray *verb.* —*See* **disorder.**

disassemble *verb.* To divide into component parts ▶ break down, dismantle, dismount, take apart (*or* down).

disassociate *verb.* —*See* **detach.**

disassociation *noun.* —*See* **detachment** (1), **division** (1).

disaster *noun.* An occurrence inflicting widespread destruction and distress ▶ calamity, cataclysm, catastrophe, debacle, fiasco, holocaust, mishap, tragedy. —*See also* **collapse** (2).

disastrous *adjective.* Causing ruin or great destruction ▶ calamitous, cataclysmic, catastrophic, fatal, fateful, ruinous. [*Compare* **harmful, unfortunate.**]

disavow *verb.* —*See* **defect, deny, repudiate.**

disavowal *noun.* —*See* **defection, denial** (1).

disband *verb.* —*See* **divide, scatter** (2).

disbelief *noun.* The refusal or reluctance to believe ▶ discredit, distrust, doubt, dubiety, incredulity, incredulousness, mistrust, rejection, skepticism, unbelief. —*See also* **atheism.**

disbelieve *verb.* To give no credence to ▶ discredit, distrust, doubt, mistrust, question, reject. ***Idioms:*** place (*or* put *or* take) no stock in. [*Compare* **repudiate.**] —*See also* **distrust, doubt.**

disbelieving *adjective.* —*See* **atheistic, incredulous.**

disburden *verb.* —*See* **rid.**

disburse *verb.* —*See* **distribute, spend** (1).

disbursement *noun.* —*See* **cost** (1), **distribution** (1).

disc *noun. See* **disk.**

discard *verb.* To let go or get rid of as being useless or defective, for example ▶ dispose of, dump, junk, scrap, shed, slough, throw away, throw out, toss. *Informal:* chuck (out), jettison, shuck (off). *Slang:* deep-six, ditch, eighty-six. [*Compare* **abandon.**]

discarnate *adjective.* —*See* **immaterial.**

discern *verb.* To perceive and fix the identity of, especially with difficulty ▶ ascertain, descry, detect, distinguish, find out, make out, pick out, recognize, spot. —*See also* **discover, distinguish** (1), **notice, see** (1).

discernible *adjective.* —*See* **perceptible, visible.**

discerning *adjective.* —*See* **critical** (2), **discriminating.**

discernment *noun.* Skill in perceiving, discriminating, or judging ▶ acumen, astuteness, clear-sightedness, discrimination, eye, insight, intelligence, judgment, keenness, nose, penetration, perception, perceptiveness, percipience, percipiency, perspicacity, sagaciousness, sagacity, sageness, sensitivity, sharpness, shrewdness, wit. —*See also* **distinction** (1).

discharge *verb.* To release from military duty ▶ deactivate, demobilize, muster out, release, separate. —*See also* **clear** (3), **dismiss** (1), **excuse** (1), **free** (1), **fulfill, ooze, perform** (1), **pour, rid, settle** (3).
discharge *noun.* —*See* **barrage, blast** (2), **dismissal, performance.**

disciple *noun.* —*See* **devotee, follower.**

disciplinary *adjective.* —*See* **punishing.**

discipline *noun.* An area of academic study that is part of a larger body of learning ▶ branch, field, specialty. [*Compare* **area.**] —*See also* **punishment.**

discipline *verb.* —*See* **educate, punish.**

disclaim *verb.* —*See* **repudiate.**

disclaimer *noun.* —*See* **denial** (1).

disclose *verb.* —*See* **air** (2), **communicate** (1), **reveal.**

disclosure *noun.* —*See* **revelation.**

discolor *verb.* —*See* **stain.**

discombobulate *verb.* —*See* **confuse** (1).

discombobulation *noun.* —*See* **daze.**

discomfit *verb.* —*See* **embarrass.**

discomfiture *noun.* —*See* **embarrassment.**

discomfort *noun.* **1.** The state or quality of being inconvenient ▶ incommodiousness, incommodity, inconvenience, trouble. [*Compare* **bother.**] **2.** Something that causes difficulty, trouble, or lack of ease ▶ discommodity, incommodity, inconvenience. [*Compare* **annoyance.**] —*See also* **embarrassment.**

discomfort *verb.* —*See* **embarrass, inconvenience.**

discommode *verb.* —*See* **inconvenience.**

discommodity *noun.* Something that causes difficulty, trouble, or lack of ease ▶ discomfort, incommodity, inconvenience. [*Compare* **annoyance, bother.**]

discompose *verb.* —*See* **agitate** (2).

discomposure *noun.* —*See* **embarrassment.**

disconcert *verb.* —*See* **dismay, embarrass, upset.**

disconcertment *noun.* —*See* **agitation** (2).

disconnect *verb.* —*See* **detach, divide.**

disconnected *adjective.* —*See* **detached** (1).

disconnection *noun.* —*See* **detachment** (1).

disconsolate *adjective.* —*See* **depressed** (1).

discontent *noun.* —*See* **disappointment** (1).

discontent *verb.* —*See* **disappoint.**

discontentment *noun.* —*See* **disappointment** (1).

discontinuation *or* **discontinuance** *noun.* —*See* **break, stop** (1), **stop** (2).

discontinue *verb.* To bring an activity or relationship to an end suddenly ▶ break off, cease, interrupt, suspend, terminate. —*See also* **abandon** (2), **drop** (4), **stop** (1), **stop** (2).

discontinuity *noun.* —*See* **break.**

discord *noun.* —*See* **conflict.**

discord *verb.* —*See* **conflict.**

discordance *noun.* —*See* **conflict.**

discordant *adjective.* —*See* **discrepant, incongruous, inharmonious** (1), **inharmonious** (2).

discount *verb.* —*See* **belittle, deduct, lend.**

discount *noun.* —*See* **deduction** (1).

discountenance *verb.* —*See* **disapprove, embarrass.**

discourage *verb.* To make less hopeful or enthusiastic ▶ daunt, demoralize, dishearten, dismay, dispirit, unnerve. ***Idiom:*** dampen the spirits of. [*Compare* **disillusion.**] —*See also* **disappoint, dissuade.**

✚ **CORE SYNONYMS:** *discourage, dishearten, dismay, dispirit.* These verbs mean to make less hopeful or enthusiastic: *researchers who were discouraged by the problem's magnitude; apathy that disheartened the instructor; bad weather that dismayed the campers; a failure that dispirited the team.*

◀ **ANTONYM:** *encourage*

---

discouraged *adjective.* —*See* **depressed** (1), **despondent.**

discouraging *adjective.* —*See* **bleak** (2), **disappointing, sorrowful.**

discourse *noun.* A formal discussion of a subject, either written or spoken ▶

dialogue, disquisition, dissertation, essay, expatiation, lecture, monograph, talk, thesis, tract, treatise. [*Compare* **tirade.**] —*See also* **conversation, speech** (1).

discourse *verb.* —*See* **converse**[1], **elaborate.**

discourser *noun.* —*See* **conversationalist.**

discourteous *adjective.* —*See* **disrespectful, offensive** (2), **rude** (2).

discourtesy *noun.* —*See* **impudence.**

discover *verb.* To obtain knowledge or awareness of something not known before ▶ ascertain, detect, determine, dig (up *or* out), discern, ferret out, find (out), hear, learn, observe, realize, turn up, unearth. ***Idiom:*** get wind of. [*Compare* **discern.**]

✦ **CORE SYNONYMS:** *discover, ascertain, determine, learn.* These verbs mean to gain knowledge or awareness of something not known before, as through observation or study: *discovered a star in a distant galaxy; ascertaining the facts; tried to determine the origins of the problem; learned the sad news from the radio.*

discovery *noun.* Something that has been discovered ▶ ascertainment, find, finding, result, strike. [*Compare* **deduction, invention, novelty.**]

discredit *verb.* To cause to be no longer believed or valued ▶ debunk, deflate, explode, puncture. *Informal:* shoot down. ***Idioms:*** knock holes in, knock the bottom out of, shoot full of holes. —*See also* **disbelieve, disgrace.**

discredit *noun.* —*See* **disbelief, disgrace.**

discreditable *adjective.* —*See* **disgraceful.**

discreet *adjective.* —*See* **conservative** (2), **delicate** (2).

discrepancy *noun.* —*See* **difference, gap** (3).

discrepant *adjective.* In sharp opposition ▶ conflicting, contradictory, contrary, contrasting, counter, discordant, incompatible, incongruent, incongruous, inconsistent, opposite. [*Compare* **different, opposite.**] —*See also* **incongruous.**

discrete *adjective.* —*See* **distinct, individual** (2).

discretely *adverb.* —*See* **separately.**

discreteness *noun.* —*See* **individuality.**

discretion *noun.* Unrestricted freedom to choose ▶ convenience, leisure, pleasure, will. —*See also* **choice, distinction** (1), **prudence, tact.**

discretionary *adjective.* —*See* **arbitrary, optional.**

discriminate *verb.* —*See* **distinguish** (1), **distinguish** (2).

discriminate *adjective.* —*See* **discriminating.**

discriminating *adjective.* Able to recognize small differences or draw fine distinctions ▶ astute, discerning, discriminate, discriminative, discriminatory, percipient, perspicacious, select, selective, subtle. [*Compare* **critical.**] —*See also* **critical** (2).

discrimination *noun.* **1.** The ability to distinguish, especially to recognize small differences or draw fine distinctions ▶ acuteness, astuteness, percipience, percipiency, perspicacity, refinement, selectiveness, selectivity, subtlety, taste. **2.** Lack of equality, as of opportunity, treatment, or status ▶ inequality, unfairness, unjustness. [*Compare* **bias.**] **3.** Irrational suspicion or hatred of a particular group, race, or religion ▶ bigotry, intolerance, prejudice. [*Compare* **hate.**] —*See also* **discernment, distinction** (1).

discriminative *adjective.* —*See* **discriminating.**

discriminatory *adjective.* —*See* **biased, discriminating, unfair.**

discursive *adjective.* —*See* **digressive.**

discuss *verb.* To speak together and exchange ideas and opinions about ▶ argue, bandy, consider, converse, debate, deliberate, moot, parley, reason, talk over, thrash out (*or* over), thresh out (*or* over), toss around. *Informal:* hash over, kick around, knock about (*or* around). *Slang:* rap. ***Idioms:*** go into a huddle, put heads together. [*Compare* **confer.**]

discussion *noun.* —*See* **communication** (1), **conference** (1), **conversation, deliberation** (1).

disdain *verb.* —*See* **despise.**

disdain *or* **disdainfulness** *noun.* —*See* **arrogance, despisal.**

disdainful *adjective.* Showing scorn and disrespect toward someone or something ▶ contemptuous, dismissive, disrespectful, haughty, intolerant, scornful, slighting, sneering, supercilious, superior. ***Idiom:*** on one's high horse. [*Compare* **disparaging, direspectful.**] —*See also* **arrogant.**

disease *noun.* A pathological condition of mind or body ▶ ailment, complaint, disorder, ill, illness, infection, infirmity, malady, pathology, sickness. [*Compare* **distress, infirmity.**] —*See also* **contaminant.**

disembark *verb.* To come ashore from a seacraft ▶ alight, debark, land, light.

disembarrass *verb.* —*See* **rid.**

disembodied *adjective.* —*See* **immaterial.**

disenchant *verb.* —*See* **disabuse, disappoint.**

disencumber *verb.* —*See* **rid.**

disengage *verb.* —*See* **detach, divide, extricate, undo.**

disengagement *noun.* —*See* **detachment** (1).

disentangle *verb.* —*See* **develop** (2), **extricate.**

disfavor *or* **disesteem** *noun.* —*See* **disapproval, disgrace.**

disfavor *or* **disesteem** *verb.* —*See* **disapprove.**

disfavorable *adjective.* —*See* **disgraceful.**

disfigure *verb.* —*See* **deform.**

disfigurement *noun.* —*See* **damage, deformity.**

disgorge *verb.* —*See* **erupt.**

disgrace *noun.* Loss of honor, respect, or admiration ▶ bad name, bad odor, derision, discredit, disesteem, disfavor, dishonor, disrepute, humiliation, ignominy, ill repute, obloquy, odium, opprobrium, reproach, scorn, shame. [*Compare* **degradation, infamy, reflection, stain.**]

disgrace *verb.* To bring disgrace on ▶ abase, besmirch, blot, debase, degrade, discredit, dishonor, humiliate, pillory, shame, stigmatize, sully, tarnish. ***Idioms:*** be a reproach to, cause to lose face, heap dishonor (*or* ignominy) on, put to shame. [*Compare* **denigrate, humble, ridicule.**]

disgraceful *adjective.* Meriting or causing shame or dishonor ▶ degrading, discreditable, disfavorable, dishonorable, disreputable, humiliating, ignominious, opprobrious, reproachable, shameful. —*See also* **deplorable.**

disgracefulness *noun.* —*See* **infamy.**

disgruntle *verb.* —*See* **disappoint.**

disgruntlement *noun.* —*See* **disappointment** (1).

disguise *verb.* To change or modify so as to prevent recognition of the true identity or character of ▶ camouflage, cloak, dissemble, dissimulate, mask, masquerade, veil.

disguise *noun.* Clothes or other personal effects, such as makeup, worn to conceal one's identity ▶ costume, guise, mask, masquerade, veil. *Informal:* getup. —*See also* **act** (2), **façade** (2).

✚ **CORE SYNONYMS:** *disguise, camouflage, veil, dissemble, dissimulate, mask.* These verbs mean to change or modify so as to prevent recognition of the true identity or character of: *disguised her interest with nonchalance; trying to camouflage their impatience; veiled his anxiety with a smile; dissembling ill will with false solicitude; couldn't dissimulate his* *vanity; ambition that is masked as altruism.*

disguised *adjective.* —*See* **hidden** (1).

disgust *verb.* To offend the senses or feelings of ▶ appall, nauseate, repel, repulse, revolt, sicken, turn off. *Slang:* gross out. ***Idiom:*** turn one's stomach. —*See also* **offend** (2).

disgust *noun.* Extreme aversion caused by something offensive ▶ abhorrence, loathing, nausea, queasiness, repugnance, revulsion. [*Compare* **hate.**]

✚ CORE SYNONYMS: *disgust, nauseate, repel, revolt, sicken.* These verbs mean to offend the senses or feelings of: *a stench that disgusted us; hypocrisy that nauseated me; repelled by your arrogance; brutality that revolts my sensibilities; a fetid odor that sickened the workers.*

disgusted *adjective.* Out of patience ▶ fed up, sick, tired, weary. ***Idiom:*** sick and tired. [*Compare* **angry.**]

disgusting *adjective.* —*See* **offensive** (1), **unpalatable.**

disharmonious *adjective.* —*See* **inharmonious** (2).

disharmony *noun.* —*See* **conflict.**

dishearten *verb.* —*See* **depress, disappoint, discourage, dismay.**

disheartening *adjective.* —*See* **disappointing, sorrowful.**

disheartenment *noun.* —*See* **depression** (2).

dishevel *verb.* —*See* **tousle.**

disheveled *adjective.* —*See* **messy** (1).

dishonest *adjective.* Given to or marked by deliberate concealment or misrepresentation of the truth ▶ ambidextrous, deceitful, deceiving, deceptive, disingenuous, double-dealing, double-faced, duplicitous, false-hearted, insincere, lying, mendacious, perfidious, two-faced, untrustworthy, untruthful. *Informal:* crooked. [*Compare* **hypocritical, underhand.**] —*See also* **corrupt** (2).

✚ CORE SYNONYMS: *dishonest, lying, untruthful, deceitful, mendacious.* These adjectives mean deliberately concealing or misrepresenting the truth. *Dishonest* is the least specific: *a dishonest business executive. Lying* conveys a blunt accusation of untruth: *a lying witness giving inconsistent testimony. Untruthful* is a softer term and suggests lack of veracity and divergence from fact: *made an untruthful statement. Deceitful* implies misleading by falsehood or by concealment of the truth: *deceitful advertising. Mendacious* is more formal than *lying* and suggests a chronic inclination toward untruth: *a mendacious and troublesome employee.*

dishonesty *noun.* **1.** Lack of integrity ▶ deceitfulness, duplicitousness, duplicity, improbity, inveracity, mendacity, untrustworthiness. *Informal:* crookedness. **2.** Lack of straightforwardness and honesty in action ▶ chicanery, craft, craftiness, deviousness, indirection, shadiness, shiftiness, slyness, sneakiness, trickery, trickiness, underhandedness, wiliness. *Informal:* crookedness. [*Compare* **deceit, hypocrisy, trick.**] —*See also* **corruption** (2).

dishonor *noun.* —*See* **degradation** (1), **disgrace, disrespect.**

dishonor *verb.* —*See* **disgrace.**

dishonorable *adjective.* —*See* **corrupt** (2), **disgraceful.**

dishonorableness *noun.* —*See* **infamy.**

disillusion *verb.* —*See* **disabuse, disappoint.**

disillusion *noun.* —*See* **disappointment** (1).

disinclination *noun.* An attitude or feeling of distaste or mild aversion ▶ dislike, disrelish, distaste, mislike. [*Compare* **disapproval, disgust, enmity, hate.**] —*See also* **indisposition.**

disincline *verb.* —*See* **dissuade.**

disinclined *adjective.* —*See* **indisposed.**

disinfect *verb.* To render free of microorganisms ▶ decontaminate, irradiate, sanitize, sterilize.

disinfectant *noun.* —*See* **purifier.**
disinfection *noun.* —*See* **purity.**
disinformation *noun.* —*See* **propaganda.**
disingenuous *adjective.* —*See* **dishonest, underhand.**
disingenuousness *noun.* —*See* **art, insincerity.**
disintegrate *verb.* To reduce or become reduced to pieces or fragments ▶ atomize, break apart (down *or* up), crumble, decompose, dissolve, fragment, fragmentize. ***Idioms:*** fall apart (*or* to pieces), turn to dust (*or* ashes). [*Compare* **break, destroy, divide.**] —*See also* **decay.**
disintegration *noun.* —*See* **decay.**
disinter *verb.* —*See* **uncover.**
disinterest *noun.* —*See* **apathy, detachment** (2), **fairness.**
disinterested *adjective.* Feeling or showing no strong emotional involvement ▶ detached, dispassionate, impersonal, indifferent, neutral. —*See also* **apathetic, detached** (1), **fair[1]** (1).
disinterestedness *noun.* —*See* **fairness.**
disinvolve *verb.* —*See* **extricate.**
disjoin *or* **disjoint** *verb.* —*See* **divide.**
disjunction *or* **disjuncture** *noun.* —*See* **division** (1).
disk *or* **disc** *noun.* —*See* **circle** (1).
dislike *verb.* To regard with distaste or mild aversion ▶ disrelish, mislike. ***Idioms:*** be averse to, be cool toward, have an aversion to (*or* distaste for), have no use for, not be crazy (*or* nuts *or* wild) about, not care for. [*Compare* **despise, hate.**] —*See also* **disapprove.**
dislike *noun.* An attitude or feeling of distaste or mild aversion ▶ disinclination, disrelish, distaste, mislike. [*Compare* **disapproval, disgust, enmity, hate.**] —*See also* **despisal.**
dislocate *verb.* —*See* **disturb, slip** (2).
dislocation *noun.* —*See* **displacement.**
disloyal *adjective.* —*See* **faithless.**
disloyalty *noun.* —*See* **faithlessness.**
dismal *adjective.* —*See* **bleak** (2), **gloomy, sorrowful.**
dismantle *verb.* To take something apart ▶ break down, disassemble, dismount, take down. —*See also* **destroy** (2).
dismay *verb.* To deprive of courage or the power to act as a result of fear, anxiety, or disgust ▶ alarm, appall, consternate, daunt, disconcert, dishearten, dispirit, shake, shock, unnerve. [*Compare* **distress, frighten.**] —*See also* **discourage.**
dismay *noun.* —*See* **despair, fear.**

✤ **CORE SYNONYMS:** *dismay, appall, daunt, dishearten, shake.* These verbs mean to deprive a person of courage or the power to act as a result of fear or anxiety. *Dismay* is the least specific: *Plummeting stock prices dismayed speculators. Appall* implies a sense of helplessness caused by an awareness of the enormity of something: *"for as this appalling ocean surrounds the verdant land"* (Herman Melville). *Daunt* suggests an abatement of courage: *"captains courageous, whom death could not daunt"* (Anonymous ballad). *Dishearten* implies a loss of hope or enthusiasm: *The employees were disheartened by the news of the upcoming layoffs.* To *shake* is to dismay profoundly: *"A little swift brutality shook him to the very soul"* (John Galsworthy).

---

dismayed *adjective.* —*See* **depressed** (1).
dismaying *adjective.* —*See* **fearful.**
dismember *verb.* —*See* **cripple.**
dismiss *verb.* **1.** To end the employment or service of ▶ cashier, discharge, drop, lay off, let go, release, terminate. *Informal:* ax, fire, pink-slip. *Slang:* boot, bounce, can, sack. ***Idioms:*** give someone his or her walking papers, give someone the ax (*or* gate *or* pink slip), let go, show someone the door. **2.** To direct or allow to leave ▶ banish, cast out, dispatch, drive out, excuse, expel, release, run out, send away. ***Idioms:*** send

about one's business, send packing, show someone the door. **3.** To rid one's mind of ▶ banish, cast out, dispel, reject, repudiate, shut out. *—See also* **decline, deny, despise, drop** (4), **eject** (1).

✦ **CORE SYNONYMS:** *dismiss, boot, bounce, can, cashier, discharge, drop, fire, sack.* These verbs mean to end the employment or service of: *was dismissed for insubordination; was booted for being late; afraid of being bounced for union activities; wasn't canned because his uncle owns the business; will be cashiered from the army; resort workers discharged at the end of the season; was dropped for incompetence; was fired unjustly; a reporter sacked for revealing a confidential source.*

---

dismissal *noun.* The act of dismissing or the condition of being dismissed from employment ▶ discharge, expulsion, removal, termination. *Informal:* ax, pink slip. *Slang:* boot, bounce, sack. *—See also* **ejection.**

dismissive *adjective. —See* **disdainful, disparaging.**

dismount *verb.* To take something apart ▶ break down, disassemble, dismantle, take down.

disobedience *noun. —See* **defiance** (1).

disobedient *adjective.* Refusing or failing to obey ▶ bad, ill-behaved, insubordinate, naughty, noncompliant, ungovernable, unmanageable. *—See also* **defiant.**

disobey *verb.* To refuse or fail to obey ▶ break, defy, disregard, flout, oppose, rebel, resist, transgress, violate. ***Idiom:*** pay no attention to. [*Compare* **defy.**]

disorder *noun.* **1.** A lack of order or regular arrangement ▶ chaos, clutter, confusedness, confusion, derangement, disarrangement, disarray, disorderedness, disorderliness, disorganization, imbroglio, jumble, mess, mix-up, muddle, muss, scramble, shambles, topsy-turviness, tumble. *Slang:* snafu. **2.** A lack of civil order or peace ▶ anarchy, brouhaha, chaos, commotion, confusion, disturbance, fracas, lawlessness, melee, misrule, mob rule, riot, ruckus, tumult, turmoil, unrest, uproar. *—See also* **agitation** (1), **disease.**

disorder *verb.* To put out of proper order ▶ clutter, derange, disarrange, disarray, disorganize, disrupt, disturb, jumble, mess up, mix up, muddle, scatter, tumble, unsettle, upset. *—See also* **confuse** (3), **disturb, tousle, upset.**

disordered *adjective. —See* **confused** (2), **insane.**

disorderedness *noun. —See* **disorder** (1).

disordering *noun. —See* **upset.**

disorderliness *noun.* The state of being messy or unkempt ▶ chaos, disorganization, messiness, sloppiness, slovenliness, topsy-turviness, untidiness. *—See also* **disorder** (1), **unruliness.**

disorderly *adjective.* Upsetting civil order or peace ▶ disruptive, lawless, obstreperous, riotous, rowdy, turbulent. *—See also* **confused** (2), **unruly.**

disorganization *noun. —See* **disorder** (1), **disorderliness, upset.**

disorganize *verb. —See* **disorder, tousle.**

disorient *verb. —See* **agitate** (2), **confuse** (1).

disorientation *noun. —See* **daze.**

disoriented *adjective. —See* **confused** (1), **lost** (1).

disown *verb. —See* **repudiate.**

disparage *verb. —See* **belittle.**

disparagement *noun. —See* **belittlement.**

disparaging *adjective.* Tending or intending to belittle ▶ belittling, deprecative, deprecatory, depreciative, depreciatory, derisive, derogative, derogatory, detractive, dismissive, low, mocking, pejorative, slighting, uncomplimentary. [*Compare* **disdainful, sarcastic.**]

disparate *adjective. —See* **different, various.**

disparity *noun.* —*See* **difference, gap** (3), **inequality** (1).

dispassion *noun.* —*See* **fairness.**

dispassionate *adjective.* —*See* **cold** (2), **fair**[1] (1).

dispassionately *adverb.* —*See* **fairly** (1).

dispassionateness *noun.* —*See* **fairness.**

dispatch *verb.* —*See* **consume** (1), **dismiss** (2), **kill**[1], **send** (1).

dispatch *noun.* —*See* **haste** (1), **item, letter.**

dispel *verb.* To cause to separate and go in various directions ▶ disperse, dissipate, scatter. [*Compare* **divide, separate.**] —*See also* **dismiss** (3).

dispensable *adjective.* —*See* **unnecessary.**

dispensation *noun.* —*See* **distribution** (1).

dispense *verb.* —*See* **administer** (2), **administer** (3), **distribute, excuse** (1).

dispersal *noun.* —*See* **distribution** (2).

disperse *verb.* To cause to separate and go in various directions ▶ dispel, dissipate, scatter. [*Compare* **divide, separate.**] —*See also* **lift** (2), **scatter** (2), **spread** (2).

dispersion *noun.* —*See* **distribution** (2).

dispirit *verb.* —*See* **depress, disappoint, discourage, dismay.**

dispirited *adjective.* —*See* **depressed** (1).

dispiriting *adjective.* —*See* **sorrowful.**

displace *verb.* **1.** To substitute for or fill the place of ▶ replace, supersede, supplant, surrogate. ***Idioms:*** fill someone's shoes, take over from, take the reins from. [*Compare* **substitute.**] **2.** To take the place of another against the other's will ▶ cut out, force out, supplant, usurp. [*Compare* **assume, occupy, seize.**] —*See also* **disturb.**

displacement *noun.* A change in normal place or position ▶ dislocation, dislodging, disturbance, move, movement, rearrangement, relocation, shift. [*Compare* **removal, upset.**]

display *verb.* To make a public and usually ostentatious show of ▶ brandish, disport, exhibit, expose, flash, flaunt, parade, promenade, show (off), showcase, sport, strut, wear. —*See also* **bear** (3), **express** (1), **reveal, show** (1).

display *noun.* An act of showing or displaying ▶ demonstration, exhibit, exhibition, exposition, manifestation, presentation, show. —*See also* **array.**

✚ **CORE SYNONYMS:** *display, expose, parade, flaunt.* These verbs mean to make a public and usually ostentatious show of something or someone. *Display* suggests holding up something for view in a vulgar or boorish way: *He displayed his new sports car in the driveway for all of the neighbors to see. Expose* can imply revelation of something better left concealed: *Your comment exposes your insecurity. Parade* usually suggests a pretentious or boastful presentation: *"He early discovered that, by parading his unhappiness before the multitude, he produced an immense sensation"* (Thomas Macaulay). *Flaunt* implies an unabashed, prideful, often arrogant display: *"Every great hostelry flaunted the flag of some foreign potentate"* (John Dos Passos).

---

displease *verb.* —*See* **offend** (1), **offend** (2).

displeasing *adjective.* —*See* **offensive** (2), **unpleasant.**

displeasure *noun.* —*See* **disapproval, offense.**

disport *verb.* —*See* **display, play** (1).

disport *noun.* —*See* **amusement.**

disposal *noun.* The act of getting rid of something useless or used up ▶ discarding, dispatching, disposition, dumping, elimination, jettison, junking, removal, riddance, scrapping, unloading. —*See also* **arrangement** (1).

dispose *verb.* —*See* **arrange** (1), **influence.**

dispose of *verb.* To get rid of by selling ▶ close out, dump, sell off, unload. —*See also* **discard, settle** (1).

disposed *adjective.* —*See* **inclined.**

disposition *noun.* A person's customary manner of emotional response ▶ bent, complexion, habit, humor, nature, temper, temperament. [*Compare* **mood.**] —*See also* **arrangement** (1), **character** (1), **inclination** (1).

dispossess *verb.* —*See* **deprive.**

dispossession *noun.* —*See* **deprivation.**

disproportion *or* **disproportionateness** *noun.* —*See* **inequality** (1).

disproportionately *adverb.* —*See* **unduly.**

disprove *verb.* —*See* **refute.**

disputable *adjective.* —*See* **debatable.**

disputatious *adjective.* —*See* **argumentative.**

dispute *verb.* —*See* **argue** (1), **argue** (2), **contest, deny.**

dispute *noun.* —*See* **argument, objection.**

disqualify *verb.* To make incapable, as of doing a job ▶ disable, unfit.

disquiet *verb.* —*See* **agitate** (2).

disquiet *noun.* —*See* **anxiety** (1), **restlessness.**

disquieting *adjective.* —*See* **disturbing.**

disquietude *noun.* —*See* **anxiety** (1), **restlessness.**

disquisition *noun.* —*See* **discourse.**

disregard *verb.* —*See* **blink at, disobey, neglect** (1), **neglect** (2), **snub.**

disregard *noun.* —*See* **defiance** (1), **neglect, thoughtlessness** (2).

disregardful *adjective.* —*See* **thoughtless.**

disrelish *verb.* To regard with distaste ▶ dislike, mislike. ***Idioms:*** be averse to, be cool toward, have an aversion to (*or* distaste for), have no use for, not be crazy (*or* nuts *or* wild) about, not care for. [*Compare* **despise, disapprove, hate.**]

disrelish *noun.* An attitude or feeling of distaste or mild aversion ▶ disinclination, dislike, distaste, mislike. [*Compare* **disapproval, disgust, enmity, hate.**]

disremember *verb. Informal* To fail to remember ▶ forget. ***Idioms:*** draw a blank, go blank, have a senior moment, have no recollection (*or* memory).

disreputable *adjective.* —*See* **disgraceful.**

disreputability *or* **disreputableness** *noun.* —*See* **infamy.**

disrepute *noun.* —*See* **disgrace.**

disrespect *noun.* Lack of proper respect ▶ affront, dishonor, impoliteness, irreverence, lese majesty, rudeness. [*Compare* **despisal, thoughtlessness.**] —*See also* **impudence.**

disrespectful *adjective.* Having or showing a lack of respect ▶ cheeky, contemptuous, discourteous, ill-bred, impertinent, impolite, impudent, insolent, insulting, irreverent, rude, sassy, scornful, unmannered, unmannerly. —*See also* **disdainful, rude** (2).

disrobe *verb.* To remove all the clothing from ▶ strip, unclothe, undress. —*See also* **bare.**

disrupt *verb.* To break up the order or progress of ▶ disturb, interfere, interrupt, intrude, mess up, muddle, obstruct, upset. —*See also* **disorder, disturb.**

disruption *noun.* —*See* **break, upset.**

disruptive *adjective.* —*See* **disorderly, disturbing.**

dissatisfaction *noun.* —*See* **disappointment** (1), **disapproval.**

dissatisfactory *adjective.* —*See* **bad** (1).

dissatisfy *verb.* —*See* **disappoint.**

dissect *verb.* —*See* **analyze.**

dissection *noun.* —*See* **analysis.**

dissemblance *noun.* —*See* **act** (2).

dissemble *verb.* —*See* **act** (2), **disguise.**

disseminate *verb.* —*See* **spread** (2).

dissemination *noun.* —*See* **distribution** (2).

dissension *noun.* —*See* **conflict, division** (2).

dissent *verb.* —*See* **conflict.**

dissent *noun.* —*See* **conflict, division** (2).

dissenter *noun.* —*See* **opponent, rebel** (2), **separatist.**

dissentience *noun.* —*See* **conflict.**

dissertation *noun.* A thorough, written presentation of an original point of view ▶ thesis. —*See also* **discourse.**

disserve *verb.* —*See* **damage.**

disservice *noun.* —*See* **injustice** (1).

dissever *verb.* —*See* **cut** (2), **divide.**

disseverance *or* **disseverment** *noun.* —*See* **division** (1).

dissidence *noun.* —*See* **conflict.**

dissident *noun.* —*See* **separatist.**

dissident *adjective.* —*See* **inharmonious** (1).

dissimilar *adjective.* —*See* **different.**

dissimilarity *or* **dissimilitude** *noun.* —*See* **difference.**

dissimulate *verb.* —*See* **act** (2), **disguise.**

dissimulation *noun.* —*See* **act** (2).

dissipate *verb.* To cause to separate and go in various directions ▶ dispel, disperse, scatter. [*Compare* **divide, separate.**] —*See also* **disappear** (1), **lift** (2), **waste.**

dissipated *adjective.* —*See* **abandoned** (2).

dissipation *noun.* —*See* **disappearance.**

dissipative *adjective.* —*See* **extravagant.**

dissociate *verb.* —*See* **detach.**

dissociation *noun.* —*See* **detachment** (1), **division** (1).

dissolute *adjective.* —*See* **abandoned** (2).

dissoluteness *noun.* —*See* **license** (2).

dissolution *noun.* —*See* **death** (1), **disappearance, license** (2).

dissolve *verb.* To make a film image disappear gradually ▶ fade out. —*See also* **disappear** (1), **disintegrate, melt.**

dissonance *noun.* —*See* **conflict.**

dissonant *adjective.* —*See* **incongruous, inharmonious** (1), **inharmonious** (2).

dissuade *verb.* To persuade a person not to do something ▶ deter, discourage, disincline, divert, put off. ***Idiom:*** talk out of. [*Compare* **discourage.**]

✚ **CORE SYNONYMS:** *dissuade, deter, discourage.* These verbs mean to persuade someone not to do something: *tried to dissuade her from suing; couldn't be deterred from leaving; discouraged me from accepting the offer.*

◀ **ANTONYM:** *persuade*

---

distance *noun.* **1.** An extent, measured or unmeasured, of linear space ▶ gap, interval, length, range, reach, space, span, stretch. *Informal:* piece, way. [*Compare* **extent, gap.**] **2.** The fact or condition of being far removed or apart ▶ farness, remoteness, separateness, separation. —*See also* **detachment** (2), **expanse** (1).

distance *verb.* —*See* **estrange.**

distant *adjective.* Far from others in space, time, or relationship ▶ far, faraway, far-flung, far-off, remote, removed. ***Idioms:*** at a distance (*or* remove). —*See also* **cool.**

distaste *noun.* An attitude or feeling of mild aversion ▶ disinclination, dislike, disrelish, mislike. [*Compare* **disapproval, disgust, enmity, hate.**]

distasteful *adjective.* —*See* **bitter** (3), **unpalatable.**

distend *verb.* —*See* **broaden, swell.**

distill *verb.* —*See* **drip.**

distinct *adjective.* Distinguished from others by nature or qualities ▶ discrete, individual, separate, several, various. [*Compare* **unique.**] —*See also* **apparent** (1), **decided, different, sharp** (2).

✚ **CORE SYNONYMS:** *distinct, discrete, separate, several.* These adjectives mean distinguished from others in nature or qualities: *12 distinct colors; a company with six discrete divisions; a problem consisting of two separate issues; performed several steps of the process.*

---

distinction *noun.* **1.** The act or an instance of distinguishing ▶ demarcation, differentiation, discernment, discretion, discrimination, separation. **2.** Recognition of achievement or superiority or a sign of this ▶ accolade, award, citation, commendation, honor, kudos, laurels, medal, prize, ribbon, trophy. [*Compare* **reward.**] —*See also* **difference, fame, virtue.**

distinctive *adjective.* —*See* **special.**

distinctiveness *noun.* —*See* **identity** (1), **individuality.**

distinctness *noun.* —*See* **clarity.**

distinguish *verb.* **1.** To recognize as being different ▶ differentiate, discern, discriminate, know, separate, single out, tell. **2.** To make noticeable or different ▶ characterize, differentiate, discriminate, identify, individualize, mark, set apart, signalize, single out, singularize. —*See also* **discern, notice. 3.** To cause to be eminent or recognized ▶ dignify, elevate, ennoble, exalt, glorify, honor, praise, signalize. [*Compare* **celebrate, exalt, honor.**]

distinguishable *adjective.* —*See* **perceptible.**

distinguished *adjective.* —*See* **famous, noticeable.**

distort *verb.* To give an inaccurate view of by representing falsely or misleadingly ▶ alter, belie, bend, color, cook, falsify, fudge, load, misrepresent, misstate, pervert, slant, stretch, twist, warp, wrench, wrest. ***Idiom:*** give a false coloring to. [*Compare* **bias, equivocate, lie^2.**] —*See also* **deform.**

distortion *noun.* —*See* **deformity, equivocation, lie^2.**

distract *verb.* —*See* **agitate** (2).

distracted *verb.* —*See* **absent-minded.**

distraction *noun.* —*See* **amusement, daze.**

distrait *adjective.* —*See* **absent-minded.**

distraught *adjective.* —*See* **anxious, insane.**

distress *verb.* To cause emotional suffering or painful sorrow to ▶ aggrieve, anguish, grieve, harrow, hurt, injure, pain, traumatize, trouble, vex, wound. [*Compare* **afflict, agitate, annoy, offend.**] —*See also* **worry.**

distress *noun.* A state of physical or mental suffering ▶ affliction, agony, anguish, grief, hurt, injury, misery, pain, sorrow, torment, torture, vexation, woe, wound, wretchedness. *Slang:* murder. [*Compare* **annoyance, difficulty.**] —*See also* **anxiety** (1), **emergency, harm.**

distressed *adjective.* —*See* **anxious.**

distressing *or* **distressful** *adjective.* —*See* **disturbing.**

distribute *verb.* To give out in portions or shares ▶ admeasure, allocate, allot, allow, apportion, assign, deal (out), disburse, dish (out), dispense, divide, dole out, give (out), hand out, issue, measure out, mete out, parcel out, portion (out), ration (out), share. *Slang:* divvy. [*Compare* **appropriate.**] —*See also* **classify, spread** (2).

CORE SYNONYMS: *distribute, divide, dispense, dole out, deal, ration.* These verbs mean to give out in portions or shares. *Distribute* is the least specific: *The government distributed land to settlers. Divide* implies giving out portions, often equal, on the basis of a plan or purpose: *The estate will be divided among the heirs. Dispense* stresses the careful determination of portions, often according to measurement or weight: *The pharmacist dispensed the medication. Dole out* implies careful, usually sparing measurement of portions. It can refer to the distribution of charity: *The city doled out surplus milk to the needy.* It can also suggest lack of generosity: *The professor doled out meager praise to the students. Deal* implies orderly, equitable distribution, often piece by piece: *I dealt five cards to each player. Ration* refers to equitable division in limited portions of scarce, often necessary, items: *The government rationed fuel during the war.*

---

distribution *noun.* **1.** The act of distributing or the condition of being distributed ▶ admeasurement, allocation, allotment, apportionment, assignment, disbursement, dispensation, division, dishing out, doling out, meting out, portioning out, rationing out, sharing. **2.** The passing out or spreading about of something over a wide area ▶ circulation, diffusion, dispersal, dispersion, dissemination, scattering. *—See also* **allotment, arrangement** (1).

district *noun.* *—See* **area** (2), **neighborhood** (1), **territory.**

distrust *noun.* Lack of trust ▶ cynicism, doubt, leeriness, mistrust, skepticism, suspicion, wariness. *—See also* **disbelief, doubt.**

distrust *verb.* To lack trust or confidence in ▶ disbelieve, doubt, misdoubt, mistrust, question, suspect. *—See also* **disbelieve, doubt.**

distrustful *adjective.* Lacking trust or confidence ▶ cynical, distrusting, doubting, leery, mistrustful, skeptical, suspicious, untrusting, wary. [*Compare* **incredulous.**] *—See also* **doubtful** (2).

distrustfully *adverb.* *—See* **skeptically.**

distrusting *adjective.* *—See* **distrustful.**

disturb *verb.* To alter the settled state or position of ▶ dislocate, disorder, displace, disrupt, move, shake, shift, upset. *—See also* **agitate** (2), **annoy, disorder, disrupt.**

disturbance *noun.* *—See* **agitation** (1), **disorder** (2), **displacement, insanity.**

disturbed *adjective.* *—See* **anxious.**

disturbing *adjective.* Troubling to the mind or emotions ▶ agitating, annoying, bothersome, burdensome, disquieting, disruptive, distressing, distressful, galling, intrusive, irksome, irritating, nettlesome, perturbing, plaguy, provoking, troublesome, troubling, troublous, unsettling, upsetting, vexatious, vexing, worrisome. [*Compare* **uncomfortable.**]

disunion *noun.* *—See* **division** (1), **division** (2).

disunite *verb.* *—See* **divide, estrange.**

disunity *noun.* *—See* **division** (2).

disuse *noun.* *—See* **obsoleteness.**

ditch *noun.* *—See* **furrow.**

ditch *verb.* *—See* **discard.**

dither *noun.* *—See* **agitation** (2).

dither *verb.* *—See* **hesitate.**

dithyrambic *adjective.* *—See* **passionate.**

ditsiness *noun.* *—See* **foolishness.**

ditsy *adjective.* *—See* **foolish.**

ditto *noun.* *—See* **copy** (1).

ditto *verb.* *—See* **copy.**

ditty *noun.* *—See* **song.**

ditz *noun.* *—See* **fool.**

divagate *verb.* *—See* **deviate, digress.**

divagation *noun.* *—See* **deviation, digression.**

divarication *noun.* *—See* **difference.**

dive *verb.* *—See* **fall** (1), **fall** (4), **plunge.**

dive into *verb.* *—See* **attack** (2).

dive *noun.* *Slang* A disreputable or rundown bar or restaurant ▶ *Slang:* dump, honky-tonk, joint, juke house, juke joint. ***Idiom:*** hole in the wall. *—See also* **fall** (1), **fall** (3).

diverge *verb.* *—See* **branch, conflict, deviate, differ, digress.**

divergence *or* **divergency** *noun.* *—See* **abnormality, deviation, difference, digression, division** (2).

divergent *adjective.* *—See* **abnormal, different.**

divers *adjective.* *—See* **several, various.**

diverse *adjective.* *—See* **different, various.**

diversification *or* **diverseness** *noun.* *—See* **variety.**

diversified *adjective.* Not limited to a single class ▶ general, indefinite. *—See also* **various.**

diversiform *adjective.* *—See* **irregular.**

diversify *verb.* *—See* **branch.**

diversion *noun.* *—See* **amusement, deviation, digression.**

diversity *noun.* —*See* **variety.**

divert *verb.* —*See* **amuse, dissuade, turn** (2).

diverting *adjective.* —*See* **pleasant.**

divest *verb.* —*See* **bare, deprive.**

divestiture *noun.* —*See* **deprivation.**

divide *verb.* To break up the unity of something; separate into parts, sections, or branches ▶ break, break apart (*or* up), detach, disband, disconnect, disengage, disjoin, disjoint, dissever, disunite, divorce, part, partition, section, segment, separate, split (up), uncouple. [*Compare* **break, cut, disintegrate, tear**[1].] —*See also* **branch, classify, distribute.**

divide *noun.* —*See* **gap** (1).

divination *noun.* —*See* **magic** (1), **prophecy.**

divine *adjective.* **1.** Of, from, like, or being a god or God ▶ celestial, deific, godlike, godly, heavenly, holy, supernal. **2.** In the service or worship of God or a god ▶ anointed, consecrated, devoted, devout, faithful, hallowed, holy, ordained, pious, religious, sacred, sacrosanct, sanctified. [*Compare* **holy.**] —*See also* **heavenly** (1), **marvelous.**

divine *noun.* —*See* **cleric.**

divine *verb.* —*See* **foresee, prophesy, solve** (1).

divineness *noun.* —*See* **holiness.**

diviner *noun.* —*See* **prophet.**

divine spark *noun.* —*See* **spirit** (2).

divinitory *adjective.* —*See* **prophetic.**

division *noun.* **1.** The act or an instance of separating one thing from another ▶ detachment, disassociation, disjunction, disjuncture, disseverance, disseverment, dissociation, disunion, divorce, divorcement, fission, fissure, parting, partition, segmentation, separation, severance, split. **2.** The condition of being divided, as in opinion ▶ dissension, dissent, disunion, disunity, divergence, divergency, schism. [*Compare* **breach, conflict.**] —*See also* **allotment, branch** (1), **branch** (3), **class** (1), **conference** (2), **distribution** (1), **force** (3), **part** (1).

divorce *noun.* —*See* **division** (1).

divorce *verb.* —*See* **divide, separate** (1).

divorcement *noun.* —*See* **division** (1).

divulge *verb.* —*See* **air** (2), **betray** (2), **communicate** (1).

divulgence *noun.* —*See* **revelation.**

divvy *verb.* —*See* **distribute.**

divvy *noun.* —*See* **allotment.**

dizziness *noun.* A sensation of whirling or falling ▶ giddiness, grogginess, lightheadedness, unsteadiness, vertiginousness, vertigo, wooziness.

dizzy *adjective.* **1.** Having a sensation of whirling or falling ▶ dazed, giddy, groggy, lightheaded, reeling, spinning, staggered, unsteady, vertiginous, woozy. **2.** Producing dizziness or vertigo ▶ dizzying, giddy, sickening, vertiginous. [*Compare* **steep.**] —*See also* **confused** (1), **giddy** (2).

dizzy *verb.* —*See* **confuse** (1).

dizzying *adjective.* Producing dizziness or vertigo ▶ dizzy, giddy, sickening, vertiginous. [*Compare* **steep.**]

do *verb.* **1.** To meet a need or requirement ▶ answer, serve, suffice, suit. **2.** To be responsible for or guilty of an error or crime ▶ carry out, commit, perpetrate. *Informal:* pull off. [*Compare* **perform.**] **3.** *Informal* To spend or complete time, as a prison term ▶ put in, serve. **4.** To work at, especially as a profession ▶ follow, practice, pursue. ***Idiom:*** hang out one's shingle. [*Compare* **labor.**] —*See also* **act** (1), **act** (3), **cheat** (1), **cover** (2), **fulfill, manage, perform** (1), **satisfy** (1), **stage.**

do for *verb.* To work and care for ▶ attend, minister to, serve, wait on (*or* upon). [*Compare* **help, tend**[2], **work.**]

do in *verb.* —*See* **murder, ruin, tire** (1).

do over *verb.* To do or perform an act again ▶ duplicate, play over, redo, repeat, replay. [*Compare* **copy.**]

do up *verb.* To cover and tie something, as with paper and string ▶ package, wrap.

do *noun.* —*See* **party.**

doable *adjective.* —*See* **possible.**

docent *noun.* —*See* **guide.**

docile *adjective.* Capable of being educated ▶ educable, teachable, trainable. —*See also* **gentle** (3), **obedient.**

docket *noun.* —*See* **program** (1).

docket *verb.* To enter on a schedule ▶ calendar, program, slate, schedule. —*See also* **list**[1]**.**

doctor *verb.* To alter something so as to give it a false character ▶ fake, falsify. —*See also* **administer** (3), **bias** (2), **contaminate, cure, fix** (1).

doctored *adjective.* —*See* **impure** (2).

doctrinaire *adjective.* —*See* **conventional, narrow** (1).

doctrinal *adjective.* —*See* **conventional.**

doctrine *noun.* A statement presented for acceptance or belief, as by a religious or political group ▶ article of faith, belief, canon, concept, convention, credo, creed, dogma, gospel, ideology, line, opinion, orthodoxy, policy, position, precept, principle, proposition, teaching, tenet, theory, thesis. [*Compare* **law.**]

✚ **CORE SYNONYMS:** *doctrine, dogma, tenet.* These nouns denote a statement presented for acceptance or belief, as by a religious or political group: *the legal doctrine of due process; church dogma; experimentation, one of the tenets of the physical sciences.*

---

document *verb.* —*See* **prove.**

documentation *noun.* —*See* **confirmation** (2).

dodder *verb.* —*See* **stagger** (1).

doddering *adjective.* Relating to the mental deterioration that often accompanies old age ▶ doting, senile. [*Compare* **old, infirm.**]

dodge *verb.* —*See* **avoid, evade** (1).

dodge *noun.* —*See* **business** (2), **trick** (1).

dodger *noun.* —*See* **cheat** (2).

doff *verb.* —*See* **remove** (3).

dog *verb.* —*See* **follow** (3).

dog days *noun.* The season occurring between spring and autumn ▶ summer, summertime.

dog-eat-dog *adjective.* —*See* **competitive.**

dogged *adjective.* —*See* **diligent, stubborn** (1).

doggedness *noun.* —*See* **stubbornness.**

doggone *adjective.* —*See* **damned.**

dogma *noun.* —*See* **doctrine.**

dogmatic *adjective.* —*See* **dictatorial, intolerant** (1), **narrow** (1).

doing *noun.* —*See* **act** (1).

doldrums *noun.* —*See* **boredom, depression** (2).

dole *noun.* —*See* **allotment, relief** (2).

dole out *verb.* —*See* **distribute.**

doleful *adjective.* —*See* **sorrowful.**

dolefulness *noun.* —*See* **depression** (2).

do-little *noun.* —*See* **wastrel** (2).

doll *noun.* —*See* **beauty, girl.**

doll up *verb.* —*See* **adorn** (1), **dress up.**

dollop *noun.* —*See* **bit**[1] (2).

dolorous *adjective.* —*See* **sorrowful.**

dolt *noun.* —*See* **dullard.**

doltish *adjective.* —*See* **stupid.**

doltishness *noun.* —*See* **stupidity.**

domain *noun.* —*See* **area** (1).

dome *noun.* —*See* **head** (1).

domestic *adjective.* **1.** Of or relating to the family or household ▶ familial, family, home, homely, homey, household, residential. **2.** Trained or bred to live with and be of use to people ▶ broken (in), domesticated, housebroken, house-trained, naturalized, pet, tame. **3.** Of, from, or within a country's own territory ▶ aboriginal, autochthonous, home, homegrown, indigenous, internal, national, native. [*Compare* **indigenous.**]

domesticate *verb.* To train to live with and be of use to people ▶ break in, domesticize, gentle, housebreak, housetrain, master, naturalize, tame.

domesticated *adjective.* —*See* **domestic** (2).

domesticize *verb.* —*See* **domesticate.**

domicile *noun.* —*See* **home** (1).

domicile *verb.* —*See* **live[1], lodge.**

dominance *noun.* The condition or fact of being dominant ▶ ascendance, ascendancy, authority, command, control, domination, dominion, hegemony, lead, paramountcy, power, predominance, preeminence, preponderance, preponderancy, prepotency, rule, supremacy, sway. [*Compare* **authority.**] —*See also* **domination.**

dominant *adjective.* **1.** Exercising controlling power or influence ▶ ascendant, chief, commanding, controlling, dominating, dominative, governing, key, leading, main, major, paramount, predominant, preeminent, preponderant, prepotent, prevailing, primary, prime, principal, regnant, reigning, ruling, supreme. [*Compare* **primary.**] **2.** Exercising authority ▶ authoritative, commanding, lordly, masterful. [*Compare* **administrative.**]

✚ **CORE SYNONYMS:** *dominant, predominant, preponderant, paramount, preeminent.* These adjectives mean surpassing all others in power, influence, or position. *Dominant* applies to what exercises principal control or authority or is unmistakably ascendant: *For decades, the Soviet Union was the dominant nation of eastern Europe. Predominant* often implies being uppermost at a particular time or for the time being: "*Egrets, gulls and small mammals are the predominant wildlife on the island these days*" (Dan McCoubrey). *Preponderant* implies superiority as the result of outweighing or outnumbering all others: "*No big modern war has been won without preponderant sea power*" (Samuel Eliot Morison). *Paramount* means first in importance, rank, or regard: "*My paramount object in this struggle is to save the Union*" (Abraham Lincoln). *Preeminent* suggests generally recognized supremacy: *He is the preeminent tenor of the modern era.*

---

dominate *verb.* **1.** To occupy the preeminent position in ▶ command, control, lead, predominate, preponderate, prevail, reign, rule. ***Idioms:*** be cock of the walk, have the ascendancy, lord it over, reign supreme. **2.** To rise above, especially so as to afford a view of ▶ command, dwarf, overbear, overlook, overshadow, tower above (*or* over). —*See also* **administer** (1), **boss, enslave.**

dominating *adjective.* —*See* **dominant** (1).

domination *noun.* The act of exercising controlling power or the condition of being so controlled ▶ command, control, dominance, dominion, mastery, reign, repression, rule, subjugation, suppression, sway. —*See also* **authority, dominance, oppression.**

dominative *adjective.* —*See* **dominant** (1).

domineer *verb.* —*See* **boss.**

domineering *adjective.* —*See* **dictatorial.**

dominion *noun.* —*See* **authority, dominance, domination, ownership.**

don *verb.* To put an article of clothing on one's person ▶ assume, get on, pull on, put on, slip into (*or* on). —*See also* **dress** (1).

donate *verb.* To present as a gift to a charity or cause ▶ award, bequeath, bestow, contribute, endow, give (away), grant, hand out, pledge, present, subscribe. [*Compare* **gift.**] —*See also* **contribute** (1).

donation *noun.* Something given to a charity or cause ▶ alms, award, benefaction, beneficence, bequest, charity, contribution, endowment, gift, grant, gratuity, handout, largess, offering, pledge, present, subscription. [*Compare* **gift, gratuity, relief.**]

donator *noun.* —*See* **donor.**

done *adjective.* Having no further relationship ▶ finished, through. *—See also* **complete** (3), **through** (2).

done for *adjective. —See* **through** (2).

done in *adjective. —See* **tired** (1).

Don Juan *noun.* A man who seduces women ▶ debaucher, Lothario, seducer. [*Compare* **flirt, lecher.**] *—See also* **gallant, philanderer.**

donnish *adjective. —See* **pedantic.**

donnybrook *noun. —See* **fight** (1).

donor *noun.* A person who gives to a charity or cause ▶ benefactor, benefactress, contributor, donator, fairy godmother, giver, grantor, humanitarian, patron, patroness, philanthropist, provider, subscriber, supplier. *Informal:* angel. [*Compare* **patron, sponsor.**]

do-nothing *adjective. —See* **lazy.**

do-nothing *noun. —See* **wastrel** (2).

do-nothingism *noun. —See* **laziness.**

doodad *or* **doohickey** *noun. —See* **gadget.**

doodle *verb. —See* **putter.**

doom *noun. —See* **fate** (2).

doom *verb. —See* **condemn.**

doomed *adjective. —See* **condemned.**

doomsayer *noun. —See* **pessimist** (2).

doormat *noun. —See* **weakling.**

dope *noun. —See* **drug** (2), **fool, information.**

dope *verb. —See* **drug** (1).

dope out *verb. —See* **design** (1), **solve** (1).

doped *adjective. —See* **drugged.**

dopey *adjective. —See* **foolish, lethargic, stupid.**

dopeyness *noun. —See* **foolishness.**

dork *noun. —See* **drip** (2), **fool.**

dormancy *noun. —See* **abeyance.**

dormant *adjective. —See* **latent.**

dose *verb. —See* **administer** (3), **drug** (1).

dot *noun. —See* **bit**[1] (1), **point** (2).

dot *verb. —See* **speckle.**

dotage *noun.* The condition of being senile ▶ anecdotage, anility, caducity, senility. [*Compare* **age.**]

dote on *verb.* **1.** To like or enjoy enthusiastically, often excessively ▶ adore, delight (in), love. *Slang:* eat up, groove on. **2.** To overindulge with affection or attention ▶ spoil. [*Compare* **baby, rave.**]

doting *adjective.* Relating to the mental deterioration that often accompanies old age ▶ doddering, senile. [*Compare* **old, infirm.**] *—See also* **affectionate.**

dotty *adjective. —See* **insane.**

double *adjective.* **1.** Consisting of two identical or similar related things, parts, or elements ▶ dual, matched, paired, twin. [*Compare* **equal.**] **2.** Composed of two parts or things ▶ biform, binary, dual, duple, duplex, duplicate, geminate, twofold, two-part, two-piece. *—See also* **dishonest.**

double *noun.* One exactly resembling another ▶ clone, duplicate, image, picture, portrait, second, spitting image, twin. *Slang:* ringer. [*Compare* **copy.**] *—See also* **mate, substitute.**

double *verb.* **1.** To make or become twice as great ▶ duplicate, geminate, redouble, twin. **2.** To turn sharply around ▶ about-face, double back, reverse. ***Idiom:*** turn on one's heels. *—See also* **fold.**

double-cross *verb. —See* **betray** (1), **deceive.**

double cross *or* **double-cross** *noun. —See* **betrayal.**

double-crosser *noun. —See* **betrayer.**

double-dealing *adjective. —See* **dishonest.**

double-dealing *noun. —See* **deceit.**

double-edged *adjective. —See* **ambiguous** (2).

double-entendre *noun. —See* **ambiguity.**

double-faced *adjective. —See* **dishonest.**

doublespeak *noun. —See* **gibberish.**

doublet *noun. —See* **couple.**

double talk *noun. —See* **babble, gibberish.**

doubt *noun.* A lack of conviction or certainty ▶ distrust, doubtfulness, dubiety, dubiousness, incertitude, misgiving, mistrust, qualm, query, question, reservation, skepticism, suspicion, uncertainty, wonder. *—See also* **disbelief, distrust.**

doubt *verb.* To be uncertain, disbelieving, or skeptical about ▶ disbelieve, distrust, misdoubt, mistrust, query, question, waver, wonder. ***Idiom:*** have one's doubts. *—See also* **disbelieve, distrust.**

✚ **CORE SYNONYMS:** *doubt, dubiety, uncertainty, skepticism, suspicion, mistrust.* These nouns refer to the condition of being unsure or lacking conviction about someone or something. *Doubt* and *dubiety* imply a questioning state of mind: "*Doubt is part of all religion*" (Isaac Bashevis Singer). *On this point there can be no dubiety. Uncertainty* merely denotes a lack of assurance or conviction: *I regarded my decision with growing uncertainty. Skepticism* generally suggests an instinctive or habitual tendency to question and demand proof: "*A wise skepticism is the first attribute of a good critic*" (James Russell Lowell). *Suspicion* is doubt as to the innocence, truth, integrity, honesty, or soundness of someone or something: *His furtiveness aroused my suspicions. Mistrust* denotes lack of trust or confidence, as in a person's motives, arising from suspicion: *The staff viewed the consultant's hasty recommendations with mistrust.*

---

doubter *noun. —See* **skeptic.**

doubtful *adjective.* **1.** Not likely ▶ dubious, improbable, problematic, questionable, unapt, unlikely. **2.** Experiencing doubt ▶ ambivalent, distrustful, doubting, dubious, hesitant, irresolute, skeptical, suspicious, tentative, uncertain, undecided, unsure, vacillating, wavering. ***Idiom:*** in doubt. [*Compare* **distrustful, wary.**] *—See also* **ambiguous** (1), **debatable, shady** (1).

doubtfully *adverb. —See* **skeptically.**

doubtfulness *noun. —See* **doubt.**

doubting *adjective. —See* **distrustful, doubtful** (2).

doubting Thomas *noun. —See* **skeptic.**

doubtless *adverb. —See* **absolutely.**

doubtless *adjective. —See* **sure** (1).

doubtlessly *adverb. —See* **absolutely.**

doubtlessness *noun. —See* **sureness.**

dough *noun. —See* **money** (1).

doughtiness *noun. —See* **courage.**

doughty *adjective. —See* **brave.**

doughy *adjective. —See* **pale** (1), **soft** (1).

dour *adjective. —See* **bleak** (1), **forbidding, glum.**

douse *verb. —See* **dip** (1), **extinguish, wet** (1).

doused *adjective. —See* **wet.**

dove *noun. —See* **innocent** (1).

dovetail *verb.* To be the proper size and shape for something ▶ interlock, fit. ***Idiom:*** fit like a glove. *—See also* **agree** (1).

dovish *adjective. —See* **peaceable.**

dowdy *adjective. —See* **old-fashioned.**

dowel *noun. —See* **anchor.**

down *adjective. —See* **depressed** (1), **sick** (1), **slow** (2).

down *noun. —See* **descent, hill.**

down *verb. —See* **drink** (1), **drop** (3), **gulp.**

down-and-out *adjective. —See* **poor.**

down-and-outer *noun. —See* **pauper.**

down-at-heel *or* **down-at-the-heel** *adjective. —See* **shabby.**

downbeat *adjective. —See* **bleak** (2).

downcast *adjective. —See* **depressed** (1).

downer *noun. —See* **killjoy.**

downfall *noun.* A disastrous defeat or ruin ▶ collapse, fall, waterloo. [*Compare* **defeat.**] *—See also* **descent, rain, ruin** (1).

downgrade *noun.* The act or an instance of demoting ▶ demotion, degradation, reduction. *—See also* **descent.**

downgrade *verb.* —*See* **belittle, debase, demote, depreciate.**
downhearted *adjective.* —*See* **depressed** (1).
downheartedness *noun.* —*See* **depression** (2).
down payment *noun.* A partial or intial payment ▶ deposit, installment, security.
downpour *noun.* —*See* **flood, rain.**
downright *adjective.* —*See* **frank, utter**[2].
downright *adverb.* —*See* **completely** (1).
downside *noun.* —*See* **depression, disadvantage.**
downswing *or* **downslide** *noun.* —*See* **fall** (3).
downtime *noun.* —*See* **rest**[1] (1).
down-to-earth *adjective.* —*See* **realistic** (1).
downtrend *noun.* —*See* **fall** (3).
downturn *noun.* A period of decreased business activity and high unemployment ▶ depression, recession, slowdown, slump. —*See also* **fall** (3).
downward *adjective.* —*See* **descending.**
doze *verb.* —*See* **nap.**
doze *noun.* —*See* **nap.**
dozy *adjective.* —*See* **sleepy.**
drab *adjective.* —*See* **dull** (1), **dull** (2).
drabness *noun.* —*See* **dullness.**
draconian *adjective.* —*See* **severe** (1).
draft *noun.* **1.** A preliminary plan or version, as of a written work ▶ blueprint, diagram, framework, layout, outline, rough, skeleton, sketch. **2.** Compulsory enrollment in military service ▶ conscription, impressment, induction, levy, selective service. —*See also* **breeze** (1), **drink** (2), **pull** (1), **pull** (2).
draft *verb.* **1.** To draw up a preliminary plan or version of ▶ adumbrate, block in (*or* out), delineate, diagram, lay out, map out, outline, plan, plot, rough in (*or* out), sketch. **2.** To enroll compulsorily in military service ▶ conscript, impress, induct, levy. **3.** To devise and set down ▶ compose, draw up, formulate, frame. —*See also* **compose** (1).
drag *verb.* **1.** To hang down and be pulled along behind ▶ draggle, trail, train. **2.** To advance slowly ▶ crawl, creep, inch, poke. ***Idiom:*** go at a snail's pace. [*Compare* **trudge.**] —*See also* **delay** (2), **pull** (1).
drag *noun.* —*See* **brake, burden**[1] (1), **pull** (1), **pull** (2), **restraint.**
dragging *adjective.* —*See* **long**[1] (2).
draggle *verb.* To hang down and be pulled along behind ▶ drag, trail, train. [*Compare* **pull.**]
dragoon *verb.* —*See* **coerce.**
drain *verb.* **1.** To remove a liquid by a steady, gradual process ▶ bleed, draw (off), drink up, evaporate, let out, milk, pump, strain, tap. **2.** To lessen or weaken severely, as by removing something essential ▶ deplete, exhaust, impoverish, sap, use up. —*See also* **decrease, dry, exhaust** (1), **pour, tire** (1).
drain *noun.* —*See* **burden**[1] (1), **decrease.**
drainage basin *noun.* The region drained by a river system ▶ basin, watershed.
drained *adjective.* —*See* **tired** (1).
draining *adjective.* Causing fatigue ▶ exhausting, fatiguing, tiring, wearing, wearying. [*Compare* **burdensome.**]
dram *noun.* —*See* **bit**[1] (1), **drop** (4).
dramatic *adjective.* **1.** Of or relating to drama or the theater ▶ dramaturgic, dramaturgical, histrionic, histrionical, theatric, theatrical, thespian. **2.** Suggesting drama or a stage performance, as in emotionality or suspense ▶ climactic, emotional, exaggerated, exciting, flamboyant, histrionic, histrionical, melodramatic, moving, sensational, spectacular, suspenseful, tense, theatric, theatrical, thrilling, vivid. [*Compare* **showy.**]
dramatics *noun.* The art and occupation of an actor ▶ acting, stage, theater, theatrics. —*See also* **theatrics** (2).
dramatize *verb.* —*See* **act** (3), **stage.**

dramaturgic *or* **dramaturgical** *adjective.* —*See* **dramatic** (1).
drape *verb.* —*See* **clothe, dress** (1), **sprawl.**
draw *verb.* —*See* **attract, derive** (1), **drain** (1), **evoke, infer, pour, pull** (1), **represent** (2), **return** (3).
draw back *verb.* —*See* **retreat.**
draw down *verb.* —*See* **exhaust** (1).
draw in *verb.* **1.** To pull back in ▶ retract, withdraw. **2.** To involve someone in an activity ▶ engage. [*Compare* **involve.**] —*See also* **drink** (3).
draw into *verb.* —*See* **involve** (1).
draw on *verb.* —*See* **use.**
draw out *verb.* —*See* **lengthen.**
draw up *verb.* To devise and set down ▶ compose, draft, formulate, frame. [*Compare* **compose.**]
draw *noun.* An equality of scores, votes, or performances in a contest ▶ dead heat, deadlock, stalemate, standoff, tie. —*See also* **advantage** (3), **attraction, lure** (1), **pull** (1), **pull** (2).
drawback *noun.* —*See* **disadvantage.**
drawing *noun.* —*See* **representation.**
drawn *adjective.* —*See* **haggard.**
drawn-out *adjective.* —*See* **long**[1] (2).
dread *verb.* To be afraid ▶ fear. ***Idioms:*** break out in a cold sweat, have butterflies (in one's stomach), have knots (*or* a knot) in one's stomach, have one's heart in one's mouth, sweat blood (*or* bullets).
dread *noun.* —*See* **fear.**
dreadful *adjective.* —*See* **fearful, ghastly** (1), **terrible.**
dreadfully *adverb.* —*See* **very.**
dream *noun.* **1.** An illusory mental image ▶ daydream, fancy, fantasy, fiction, figment, hallucination, illusion, phantasm, phantasma, phantasmagoria, phantasmagory, reverie, vision. **2.** A fantastic, impracticable plan or desire ▶ bubble, castle in the air, chimera, fantasy, illusion, pipe dream, rainbow. **3.** A fervent hope ▶ ambition, aspiration, desire, goal, hope, ideal, vision, wish. —*See also* **trance.**
dream *verb.* To experience dreams or daydreams ▶ daydream, fancy, fantasize, hallucinate, imagine, muse, stargaze, woolgather. [*Compare* **imagine.**] —*See also* **desire.**
dream up *verb.* —*See* **imagine, invent.**
dreamer *noun.* **1.** A person inclined to be imaginative or idealistic but impractical ▶ daydreamer, fantasist, idealist, romantic, stargazer, theorist, theorizer, utopian, visionary, wishful thinker. **2.** One who aspires ▶ aspirant, aspirer, hopeful, seeker. *Informal:* wannabe.
dreamlike *adjective.* —*See* **illusive.**
dreamy *adjective.* Given to daydreams or reverie ▶ daydreaming, fanciful, fantasizing, moony, musing, stargazing, starry-eyed, visionary, woolgathering. —*See also* **marvelous.**
dreariness *noun.* —*See* **dullness.**
dreary *or* **drear** *adjective.* —*See* **boring, gloomy.**
dredge *verb.* —*See* **dip** (2).
dregs *noun.* —*See* **deposit** (2), **garbage, riffraff.**
drench *verb.* —*See* **wet** (1).
drenched *adjective.* —*See* **wet.**
dress *verb.* **1.** To put clothes on ▶ apparel, attire, clothe, costume, don, drape, garb, garment, invest, outfit, robe. *Informal:* tog. [*Compare* **clothe.**] **2.** To apply therapeutic materials to a wound ▶ bandage, bind, plaster, swathe, truss. **3.** To add fertilizer to soil ▶ fertilize, manure, top-dress. —*See also* **adorn** (1), **line.**
dress down *verb.* —*See* **chastise.**
dress up *verb.* To dress in formal or special clothing ▶ array, attire, bedeck, deck (out), prank, preen, primp. *Informal:* trick out (*or* up). *Slang:* doll up.
dress *noun.* **1.** Articles worn to cover the body ▶ apparel, attire, clothes, clothing, garb, garments, habiliments, raiment. *Informal:* duds, togs. *Slang:* threads. **2.** A set or style of clothing ▶ costume, ensemble, garb, gear, guise, habiliments, outfit, toilette, turnout,

wardrobe. *Informal:* getup, rig. **3.** A one-piece skirted outer garment for women and children ▶ frock, gown, jumper, muumuu, pinafore, shift, smock.

dressy *adjective.* —*See* **formal.**

dribble *verb.* —*See* **drip, drool.**

dribble *noun.* The process or sound of dripping ▶ drip, drizzle, mizzle, trickle.

driblet *noun.* —*See* **drop** (1).

drift *verb.* To move along with or be carried away by the action of water ▶ float, wash. —*See also* **blow**[1] (2), **deviate, digress, glide** (1), **heap** (1), **rove.**

drift *noun.* —*See* **flow, heap** (1), **import, thrust.**

drifter *noun.* —*See* **hobo.**

drill *noun.* —*See* **practice.**

drill *verb.* To engage in activities in order to strengthen or condition ▶ exercise, practice, train, work out. —*See also* **cut** (1), **indoctrinate** (1), **instill.**

drink *verb.* **1.** To take into the mouth and swallow a liquid ▶ down, drink up, gulp, guzzle, imbibe, lap up, pull on, quaff, sip, slurp, sup, swill. *Informal:* swig, toss back (*or* down). *Slang:* belt. ***Idiom:*** wet one's whistle. **2.** To take alcoholic liquor, especially excessively or habitually ▶ guzzle, imbibe, tipple. *Informal:* nip. *Slang:* booze, chug, chugalug, lush, soak, tank up. ***Idioms:*** bend the elbow, hit the bottle **3.** To take in moisture or liquid ▶ absorb, draw in, imbibe, osmose, soak (up), sop up, sponge up, take up. **4.** To salute by raising and drinking from a glass ▶ compliment, honor, pledge, salute, toast.

drink in *verb.* —*See* **absorb** (2).

drink up *verb.* —*See* **drain** (1).

drink *noun.* **1.** Any liquid that is fit for drinking ▶ beverage, brew, drinkable, libation, liquor, potable, potation, potion, refreshment. **2.** An act of drinking or the amount swallowed ▶ draft, potation, pull, quaff, sip, sup, swallow, swill, taste, tot. *Informal:* swig. *Slang:* belt.

drinkable *noun.* —*See* **drink** (1).

drip *verb.* To fall or let fall in drops of liquid ▶ distill, dribble, drizzle, drop, tear, trickle, weep.

drip *noun.* **1.** The process or sound of dripping ▶ dribble, drizzle, mizzle, trickle. **2.** *Slang* An unpleasant, tiresome person ▶ bore, chump. *Slang:* dip, dork, dweeb, jerk, lamer, nerd, nimrod, pill, poop, schmo, schmuck, turkey, twerp, twit. [*Compare* **fool.**]

dripping *adjective.* —*See* **wet.**

drippy *adjective.* —*See* **sentimental.**

drive *verb.* **1.** To run and control a motor vehicle ▶ chauffeur, motor, pilot, steer, taxi, wheel. *Slang:* tool. **2.** To force to move or advance with or as if with blows or pressure ▶ butt, jolt, propel, push, ram, shove, slam, thrust. [*Compare* **beat, hit.**] **3.** To urge to move along ▶ chase, herd, hustle, push, run, wrangle. [*Compare* **maneuver, provoke.**] **4.** To force to work hard ▶ push, task, tax, work. ***Idiom:*** crack the whip. [*Compare* **force.**] —*See also* **advance** (1), **hunt, instill, labor, plunge, urge.**

drive away *verb.* —*See* **estrange.**

drive out *verb.* —*See* **dismiss** (2).

drive *noun.* **1.** An organized effort to accomplish a purpose ▶ campaign, crusade, movement, push. [*Compare* **cause.**] **2.** An aggressive readiness along with energy to undertake taxing efforts ▶ enterprise, initiative, hustle, punch. *Informal:* get-up-and-go, gumption, push. [*Compare* **enthusiasm.**] **3.** A trip in a motor vehicle ▶ jaunt, ride, run. *Informal:* spin, turn, whirl. —*See also* **attack, way** (2).

✤ **CORE SYNONYMS:** *drive, campaign, crusade, movement, push.* These nouns denote an organized, vigorous effort to accomplish a purpose: *a drive to sell bonds; a fund-raising campaign; a crusade for improved social services; a movement to slash costs for prescription drugs; a push to get the bill passed.*

---

drivel *verb.* —*See* **chatter** (1), **drool.**

drivel *noun.* Saliva running from the mouth ▶ drool, salivation, slaver, slobber. —*See also* **babble, chatter, nonsense.**

driven *adjective.* —*See* **ambitious.**

driver *noun.* A person who operates a motor vehicle ▶ chauffeur, motorist, operator.

driving *adjective.* —*See* **energetic.**

drizzle *noun.* The process or sound of dripping ▶ dribble, drip, mizzle, trickle. —*See also* **rain.**

drizzle *verb.* —*See* **drip, rain** (2).

droit *noun.* —*See* **right.**

droll *adjective.* —*See* **funny** (1).

drollery *or* **drollness** *noun.* —*See* **humor.**

drone[1] *noun.* —*See* **drudge** (1), **drudge** (2), **wastrel** (2).

drone[2] *verb.* —*See* **hum.**

drone *noun.* —*See* **hum.**

drool *noun.* Saliva running from the mouth ▶ drivel, salivation, slaver, slobber.

drool *verb.* To let saliva run from the mouth ▶ dribble, drivel, salivate, slaver, slobber.

drool over *verb. Informal* To make an excessive show of desire for or interest in ▶ *Informal:* ogle, slobber over. [*Compare* **adore, desire, lust, rave.**]

droop *verb.* —*See* **drop** (1), **slouch** (2), **tire** (2), **wilt.**

drooping *adjective.* —*See* **languid, limp.**

droopy *adjective.* —*See* **limp.**

drop *noun.* **1.** A quantity of liquid falling or resting in a spherical mass ▶ bead, driblet, droplet, glob, globule, tear, teardrop. **2.** The extent or measurement downward from a surface ▶ deepness, depth, drop-off. **3.** A downward slope or distance ▶ decline, declivity, descent, drop-off, fall, pitch. **4.** A small amount of liquor ▶ belt, dram, jigger, shot, sip, splash, taste, tot. *Informal:* nip, slug. *Slang:* snort. —*See also* **advantage** (3), **bit**[1] (1), **fall** (1), **fall** (3).

drop *verb.* **1.** To go from a more erect posture to a less erect posture ▶ droop, fall, sag, sink, slump. [*Compare* **slouch.**] **2.** To slope downward ▶ decline, descend, dip, fall, pitch, sink. **3.** To bring down, as from a shot or blow ▶ chop down, cut down, down, fell, flatten, floor, ground, hew, knock down, level, mow down, prostrate, strike down, throw. *Slang:* deck. ***Idiom:*** lay low. **4.** To cease consideration or treatment of ▶ abandon, discontinue, dismiss, end, forget, give over (*or* up), quit, relinquish, skip, stop, write off. ***Idioms:*** have done with, wash one's hands of. [*Compare* **abandon.**] **5.** To take or leave out ▶ eliminate, exclude, let go, omit, prune, remove. [*Compare* **discard, remove.**] —*See also* **collapse** (1), **die, dismiss** (1), **drip, fall** (1), **fall** (2), **fall** (4), **lower**[2].

drop by *or* **in** *verb.* —*See* **visit.**

drop off *verb.* —*See* **nap.**

droplet *noun.* —*See* **drop** (1).

drop-off *noun.* The extent or measurement downward from a surface ▶ deepness, depth, drop. —*See also* **fall** (3).

drossy *adjective.* —*See* **worthless.**

droughty *adjective.* —*See* **dry** (2).

drove *noun.* —*See* **crowd, flock.**

drown *verb.* —*See* **flood** (1).

drowsy *adjective.* —*See* **sleepy.**

drub *verb.* —*See* **beat** (1), **overwhelm** (1), **slam** (1).

drubbing *noun.* —*See* **defeat.**

drudge *noun.* **1.** A person who does tedious, menial, or unpleasant work ▶ drone, foot soldier, hack, menial, scullion, slave. *Slang:* grunt. **2.** One who works or toils tirelessly ▶ drone, grind, grub, plodder. *Informal:* workhorse.

drudge *verb.* —*See* **grind** (2).

drudgery *noun.* —*See* **labor.**

drug *noun.* **1.** A substance used in the treatment of disease ▶ medicament, medication, medicine, pharmaceutical, pill, prescription. [*Compare* **cure.**] **2.** A substance that affects the central nervous system and is often addictive ▶ depressant, hallucinogen, narcotic, opiate, psychotropic, sedative, stimulant. *Informal:* dope. [*Compare* **soporific.**]

drug *verb.* **1.** To administer especially a pain-killing drug to someone ▶ anesthetize, chloroform, dose, etherize, knock out, medicate, narcotize, opiate, physic, put under, sedate, tranquilize. *Informal:* dope (up). [*Compare* **deaden.**] **2.** To addle the mind, as with a narcotic or alcohol ▶ befuddle, besot, blur, cloud, daze, dim, dull, fog, fuddle, impair, stupefy. [*Compare* **confuse, daze.**]

drug abuse *noun.* —*See* **addiction.**

drugged *adjective.* Stupefied, intoxicated, or otherwise influenced by the taking of drugs ▶ *Informal:* doped. *Slang:* baked, buzzed, high, hopped-up, lit (up), potted, ripped, spaced-out, stoned, tripping, turned-on, wasted, wiped-out, wired, zonked. ***Idiom:*** under the influence.

drum *verb.* —*See* **beat** (5).

drunk *adjective.* Stupefied, excited, or muddled with alcoholic liquor ▶ besotted, bibulous, crapulent, crapulous, drunken, inebriate, inebriated, intoxicated, sodden, sottish, tipsy. *Informal:* cockeyed, stewed. *Slang:* blind, blotto, bombed, boozed, boozy, crocked, high, lit (up), loaded, looped, pickled, pie-eyed, pixilated, plastered, polluted, potted, sloshed, smashed, soused, sozzled, stinking, stinko, stoned, tanked, tight, zonked. ***Idioms:*** drunk as a skunk, half-seas over, high as a kite, in one's cups, three sheets in (*or* to) the wind.

drunk *noun.* —*See* **bender, drunkard.**

drunkard *noun.* A person who is habitually drunk ▶ alcoholic, dipsomaniac, drunk, inebriate, sot, tippler, toper. *Slang:* alky, boozehound, boozer, dipso, lush, rummy, soak, souse, sponge, stiff, wino.

drunken *adjective.* —*See* **drunk.**

drunkenness *noun.* The condition of being intoxicated with alcoholic liquor ▶ crapulence, inebriation, inebriety, insobriety, intoxication, tipsiness. [*Compare* **bender, binge.**]

druthers *noun.* —*See* **choice.**

dry *adjective.* **1.** Having little or no liquid or moisture ▶ anhydrous, bone-dry, dried up, moistureless, sere, waterless. **2.** Having little or no precipitation ▶ arid, desert, droughty, parched, rainless, scorched, thirsty. [*Compare* **barren.**] **3.** Needing or desiring drink ▶ parched, thirsty. —*See also* **bare** (1), **boring, cold** (2), **dull** (1), **harsh, sour.**

dry *verb.* To make or become free of moisture ▶ dehydrate, desiccate, drain, dry out, exsiccate, parch. —*See also* **harden** (2).

dry up *verb.* **1.** To make or become no longer fresh or shapely because of loss of moisture ▶ frizzle, mummify, pucker, sear, shrivel, wither, wizen. **2.** To make or become no longer active or productive ▶ deplete, desiccate, give out, play out, run out. [*Compare* **exhaust.**]

✚ **CORE SYNONYMS:** *dry, dehydrate, desiccate, parch.* These verbs mean to make or become free of moisture: *drying the dishes; added water to eggs that were dehydrated; a factory where coconut meat is shredded and desiccated; land parched by the sun.*

◀ **ANTONYM:** *moisten*

---

dryness *noun.* —*See* **dullness, temperance** (2).

dry run *noun.* —*See* **test** (1).

dual *adjective.* Consisting of two identical or similar related things, parts, or elements ▶ double, matched, paired, twin. [*Compare* **equal.**] —*See also* **double** (2).

dub *verb.* —*See* **name** (1).

dub *noun.* —*See* **blunderer.**

dubiety *noun.* —*See* **disbelief, doubt.**

dubious *adjective.* —*See* **ambiguous** (1), **doubtful** (1), **doubtful** (2), **incredulous, shady** (1).

dubiously *adverb.* —*See* **skeptically.**

dubiousness *noun.* —*See* **doubt.**

dubitable *adjective.* —*See* **ambiguous** (1).

duck *verb.* —*See* **avoid, cut** (4), **dip** (1), **evade** (1).

duck *noun.* —*See* **plunge.**

duck soup *noun.* —*See* **breeze** (2).

duct *noun.* —*See* **vessel** (2).

ductile *adjective.* —*See* **flexible** (3), **malleable.**

ductility *noun.* —*See* **flexibility** (1).

dud *noun.* —*See* **disappointment** (2), **failure** (1).

dudgeon *noun.* —*See* **offense.**

duds *noun.* —*See* **dress** (1).

due *adjective.* **1.** Owed as a debt ▶ collectible, mature, outstanding, owed, owing, payable, receivable, unpaid, unsatisfied, unsettled. **2.** Known to be about to arrive ▶ anticipated, expected, scheduled, slated. **3.** In the relatively near future ▶ approaching, coming, forthcoming, upcoming. ***Idioms:*** around the corner, on the horizon. [*Compare* **close, imminent.**] —*See also* **just.**

due *noun.* Something justly deserved ▶ comeuppance, compensation, deserts, guerdon, payment, recompense, reward, satisfaction, wages. *Informal:* lumps. ***Idioms:*** what is coming to one, what one has coming. —*See also* **debt** (1), **right.**

due *adverb.* —*See* **directly** (1).

duel *verb.* —*See* **contend.**

duel *noun.* —*See* **confrontation.**

due process *noun.* The state, action, or principle of treating all persons equally in accordance with the law ▶ equity, justice. [*Compare* **fairness.**]

dues *noun.* —*See* **toll**[1] (1).

duet *noun.* —*See* **couple.**

due to *preposition.* —*See* **because of.**

dugout *noun.* A hollow beneath the earth's surface ▶ cave, cavern, grotto, tunnel. [*Compare* **hole.**]

dulcet *adjective.* —*See* **melodious.**

dulcify *verb.* —*See* **pacify.**

dull *adjective.* **1.** Lacking liveliness, charm, or surprise ▶ arid, aseptic, colorless, deadly, drab, dry, earthbound, flat, flavorless, lackluster, leaden, lifeless, lusterless, matter-of-fact, pedestrian, plodding, prosaic, spiritless, sterile, stodgy, unimaginative, uninspired. *Informal:* blah. [*Compare* **insipid, ordinary.**] **2.** Lacking vividness or color ▶ dim, drab, flat, gray, lackluster, lusterless, mat, muddy, murky. [*Compare* **pale.**] **3.** Not physically sharp or keen ▶ blunt, edgeless, obtuse, unpointed, unsharpened. —*See also* **backward** (1), **blind** (3), **boring, dead** (2), **depressed** (1), **gloomy, slow** (2).

dull *verb.* To make or become less sharp-edged ▶ blunt, hebetate, round, turn. ***Idiom:*** take the edge off. —*See also* **deaden, drug** (2), **muffle, obscure.**

✚ **CORE SYNONYMS:** *dull, colorless, drab, humdrum, lackluster, pedestrian, stodgy, uninspired.* These adjectives mean lacking in liveliness, charm, or surprise: *a dull, uninteresting performance; a colorless and unimaginative person; a drab and boring job; a humdrum conversation; a lackluster life; a pedestrian movie plot; a stodgy dinner party; an uninspired lecture.*

◀ **ANTONYM:** *lively*

---

dullard *noun.* A mentally dull person ▶ blockhead, chump, clod, dolt, dummkopf, dummy, dunce, idiot, imbecile, moron, nincompoop, nitwit, numskull, simpleton, softhead, thickhead, woodenhead. *Informal:* bonehead, knucklehead, lamebrain, muttonhead. *Slang:* airhead, boob, cretin, dimwit, dumbbell, dumbo, fathead, half-wit, lunkhead, pinhead, simp. [*Compare* **drip, fool, oaf, square.**]

dullness *noun.* A lack of excitement, liveliness, or interest ▶ asepticism, blandness, colorlessness, drabness, dreariness, dryness, familiarity, flatness, flavorlessness, insipidity, insipidness, jejuneness, lifelessness, mediocrity, routinism, sluggishness, staleness, sterileness, sterility, stodginess, tameness, tediousness, tedium, vapidity, vapidness, weariness. [*Compare* **monotony.**] —*See also* **lethargy.**

dumb *adjective.* —*See* **mute, speechless, stupid, worthless.**

dumbbell *noun.* —*See* **dullard.**

dumbfound *verb.* —*See* **stagger** (2).

dumbfounded *adjective.* —*See* **confused** (1).

dumbness *noun.* —*See* **silence** (2), **stupidity.**

dumbo *noun.* —*See* **dullard.**

dumbstruck *adjective.* —*See* **speechless.**

dummy *or* **dummkopf** *noun.* —*See* **dullard.**

dump *verb.* —*See* **discard, dump, rid.**

dump *noun. Slang* A disreputable or run-down bar or restaurant ▶ *Slang:* dive, honky-tonk, joint, juke house, juke joint. ***Idiom:*** hole in the wall.

dumping *noun.* —*See* **disposal.**

dumps *noun.* —*See* **depression** (2).

dumpy *adjective.* —*See* **stocky.**

dun *verb.* —*See* **bill**[1].

dunce *noun.* —*See* **dullard.**

dunk *verb.* —*See* **dip** (1).

dunk *noun.* —*See* **plunge.**

duo *noun.* —*See* **couple.**

dupable *adjective.* —*See* **gullible.**

dupe *noun.* A person who is easily deceived or victimized ▶ butt, cat's-paw, fool, gull, lamb, pushover, tool, victim. *Informal:* sucker. *Slang:* fall guy, gudgeon, mark, monkey, patsy, pigeon, sap. —*See also* **pawn**[2].

dupe *verb.* —*See* **deceive.**

duplex *or* **duple** *adjective.* —*See* **double** (2).

duplicate *noun.* —*See* **copy** (1), **double, mate.**

duplicate *verb.* **1.** To make or become twice as great ▶ double, geminate, redouble, twin. **2.** To do or perform an act again ▶ do over, play over, redo, repeat, replay. —*See also* **copy.**

duplicate *adjective.* —*See* **double** (2).

duplicitous *adjective.* —*See* **dishonest, underhand.**

duplicity *noun.* —*See* **deceit, dishonesty** (1).

durability *noun.* —*See* **continuation** (1), **endurance.**

durable *adjective.* —*See* **continuing.**

duration *noun.* —*See* **continuation** (1), **life, period** (1).

duress *noun.* —*See* **force** (1).

dusk *noun.* —*See* **evening.**

duskiness *noun.* —*See* **dark.**

dusky *adjective.* —*See* **dark** (1), **dark** (2).

dust *noun.* The substance of the body, especially after decay or cremation ▶ ashes, clay, cremains, remains.

dust *verb.* —*See* **sprinkle.**

dust bowl *noun.* —*See* **desert**[1].

dusting *noun.* —*See* **coat** (2), **defeat.**

dusty *adjective.* —*See* **fine**[1] (1).

dutiful *or* **duteous** *adjective.* —*See* **deferential, obedient.**

dutifulness *noun.* —*See* **obedience.**

duty *noun.* **1.** An act or course of action that is demanded of one, as by position, custom, law, or religion ▶ burden, charge, commitment, devoir, imperative, liability, must, need, obligation, onus, requirement, responsibility. **2.** The condition of being put to use ▶ adoption, application, employment, service, use, utilization. [*Compare* **exercise.**] —*See also* **task** (1), **tax.**

dwarf *adjective.* —*See* **tiny.**

dwarf *verb.* —*See* **dominate** (2).

dweeb *noun.* —*See* **drip** (2), **fool.**

dwell *verb.* —*See* **brood, consist, live**[1].

dwell on *verb.* —*See* **belabor.**

dweller *noun.* —*See* **inhabitant.**

dwelling *noun.* —*See* **home** (1).

dwindle *verb.* —*See* **decrease.**

dyad *noun.* —*See* **couple.**

dye *noun.* —*See* **color** (2).

dye *verb.* —*See* **color** (1).

dyestuff *noun.* —*See* **color** (2).

dying *adjective.* —*See* **parting.**

dynamic *or* **dynamical** *adjective.* —*See* **energetic, forceful.**

dynamism *noun.* —*See* **energy.**

dynamite *verb.* —*See* **destroy** (2).
dynamite *adjective.* —*See* **excellent.**

dynamo *noun.* An intensely energetic, enthusiastic person ▶ demon, hustler. *Informal:* eager beaver, firebreather, go-getter, live wire.

dyspeptic *adjective.* —*See* **depressed** (1).

dysphoria *noun.* —*See* **depression** (2).

dysphoric *adjective.* —*See* **depressed** (1).

E

eager *adjective.* Intensely desirous or interested ▶ agog, ardent, athirst, avid, bursting, hot, impatient, keen, solicitous, thirsting, thirsty. *Informal:* raring. ***Idioms:*** champing at the bit, hot to trot, ready and willing. —*See also* **willing.**

eager beaver *noun. Informal* An intensely energetic, enthusiastic person ▶ demon, dynamo, hustler. *Informal:* firebreather, go-getter, live wire.

eagerness *noun.* —*See* **enthusiasm** (1).

ear *noun.* The sense by which sound is perceived ▶ audition, hearing.

earlier *adjective.* —*See* **advance, past.**
earlier *adverb.* **1.** At a time in the past ▶ already, before, beforehand, erenow, erstwhile, formerly, once, previously. ***Idioms:*** ahead of time, in advance. **2.** Up to this time ▶ before, heretofore, previously, yet.

earliest *adjective.* —*See* **first.**

early *adjective.* **1.** Of, existing, or occurring in a distant period ▶ ancient, antediluvian, prehistoric, primal, primeval, primitive, primordial. [*Compare* **first.**] **2.** Developing, occurring, or appearing before the expected time ▶ precocious, premature, untimely. —*See also* **beginning.**
early *adverb.* Before the expected time ▶ ahead, beforehand, betimes. ***Idioms:*** ahead of schedule, ahead of time, in advance, with time to spare.

earmark *verb.* To attach a ticket to ▶ flag, label, mark, tag, ticket. —*See also* **appropriate, designate.**
earmark *noun.* —*See* **ticket** (1).

earn *verb.* **1.** To acquire as a result of one's behavior or effort ▶ deserve, gain, get, merit, win. *Informal:* rate. **2.** To receive, as wages, for one's labor ▶ draw, gain, get, make, win. *Informal:* bring in, pull down, pull in, rake in. ***Idioms:*** bring home the bacon, earn one's keep. —*See also* **return** (3).

✢ **CORE SYNONYMS:** *earn, deserve, gain, merit, rate, win.* These verbs mean to acquire as a result of one's behavior or effort: *earns a large salary; deserves our congratulations; gained an advantage by hiring a tutor; a suggestion that merits consideration; an event that rates a mention in the news; a candidate who won wide support.*

earnest[1] *adjective.* —*See* **grave[2]** (1), **serious** (1).

earnest[2] *noun.* —*See* **pawn[1].**

earnestness *noun.* —*See* **seriousness** (1).

earnings *noun.* Something earned, won, or otherwise acquired ▶ gain, profit, return. [*Compare* **increase.**] —*See also* **wage.**

earshot *noun.* Range of audibility ▶ hearing, sound. [*Compare* **range.**]

earsplitting *adjective.* —*See* **loud.**

earth *noun.* **1.** The soft part of the land surface of the world ▶ clay, dirt, ground, humus, loam, mud, sod, soil, terrain, topsoil, turf. **2.** The celestial body where humans live ▶ globe, orb, planet, world. —*See also* **humankind.**

earthbound *adjective.* —*See* **dull** (1), **earthly.**

earthen *or* **earthlike** *adjective.* Consisting of or resembling soil ▶ earthlike, earthy, terrestrial. —*See also* **earthly.**

earthling *noun.* —*See* **human being.**

earthly *adjective.* Relating to or characteristic of the earth or of human life on earth ▶ earthbound, earthen, earthlike, earthy, mundane, secular, sublunary, tellurian, telluric, temporal, terrene, terrestrial, worldly. [*Compare* **physical, profane.**] —*See also* **conceivable.**

earthquake *noun.* A shaking of the earth ▶ quake, seism, temblor, tremor. *Informal:* shake.

earth-shaking *adjective.* —*See* **important.**

earthwork *noun.* —*See* **bulwark.**

earthy *adjective.* Consisting of or resembling soil ▶ earthen, earthlike, terrestrial. —*See also* **earthly, racy.**

ease *noun.* **1.** Freedom from constraint, formality, embarrassment, or awkwardness ▶ casualness, comfort, easiness, informality, naturalness, poise, spontaneity, unceremoniousness, unrestraint. [*Compare* **abandon.**] **2.** The ability to perform without apparent effort ▶ easiness, effortlessness, facileness, facility, readiness. [*Compare* **ability.**] —*See also* **prosperity** (2), **relief** (1), **rest**[1] (2).

ease *verb.* **1.** To reduce in tension, pressure, or rigidity ▶ let up, loose, loosen, relax, slack, slacken, untighten. **2.** To make less difficult ▶ expedite, facilitate, grease, help along. ***Idioms:*** clear (*or* prepare *or* smooth) the way for, grease the wheels (*or* skids) for, open the door for (*or* to). **3.** To maneuver gently and slowly into place ▶ glide, slide, slip. **4.** To advance carefully and gradually ▶ edge, sidle. [*Compare* **crawl, sneak.**] —*See also* **relieve** (1), **subside.**

ease off *verb.* —*See* **weaken.**

easeful *adjective.* —*See* **comfortable.**

easiness *noun.* —*See* **ease** (2), **ease** (1).

easy *adjective.* **1.** Posing no difficulty ▶ effortless, facile, simple, smooth. *Informal:* snap. ***Idioms:*** easy as ABC (*or* falling off a log *or* one-two-three *or* pie), like taking candy from a baby, nothing to it. [*Compare* **breeze.**] **2.** Requiring little effort or exertion ▶ light, moderate, undemanding. *Informal:* cushy, soft. —*See also* **comfortable, easygoing, fluent, gradual** (2), **gullible, prosperous, tolerant, wanton** (1).

✚ **CORE SYNONYMS:** *easy, simple, facile, effortless.* These adjectives mean posing little if any difficulty. *Easy* applies to tasks that require little effort: "*The diagnosis of disease is often easy, often difficult, and often impossible*" (Peter M. Latham). *Simple* implies a lack of complexity that facilitates understanding or performance: "*the faculty . . . of reducing his thought on any subject to the simplest and plainest terms possible*" (Baron Charnwood). *Facile* stresses readiness and fluency: *a facile speaker.* Often, though, the word implies glibness or insincerity, superficiality, or lack of care: *an explanation too facile for complex events. Effortless* refers to performance in which the application of great strength or skill makes the execution seem easy: *wrote effortless prose.*

---

easygoing *adjective.* Unconstrained by rigid standards or ceremony ▶ casual, easy, informal, mellow, natural, relaxed, spontaneous, unceremonious, unrestrained. *Informal:* laid-back. [*Compare* **loose, tolerant.**] —*See also* **calm.**

eat *verb.* **1.** To take food into the body as nourishment ▶ consume, devour, ingest, partake. *Informal:* put away, tuck into. *Slang:* chow down, polish off. [*Compare* **chew, gulp.**] **2.** To have or take a meal ▶ breakfast, dine, lunch, snack, sup. ***Idioms:*** break bread, have (*or* take) a bite. **3.** To include as part of one's diet by nature or preference ▶ exist on, feed on, live on, subsist on. **4.** To do away with completely and destructively ▶ consume, devour, swallow (up), waste. —*See also* **erode.**

eat up *verb. Slang* To be avidly interested in ▶ devour, feast on, relish. —*See also* **consume** (1), **exhaust** (1), **adore** (2).

✚ **CORE SYNONYMS:** *eat, consume, devour, ingest.* These verbs mean to take food into the body as nourishment by the mouth: *ate a hearty dinner; greedily consumed the turkey and cheese sandwich; hyenas devouring their prey; whales ingesting krill.*

---

eatable *adjective.* Fit to be eaten ▶ comestible, edible, esculent, palatable.

eats *noun.* —*See* **food.**

ebb *verb.* —*See* **decrease, deteriorate, disappear** (1), **languish, recede, subside.**

ebb *noun.* —*See* **waning.**

ebony *or* **ebon** *adjective.* —*See* **black** (1).

ebullient *adjective.* —*See* **lively.**

eccentric *adjective.* Deviating from what is conventional or customary ▶ antic, bizarre, cranky, curious, erratic, fantastic, freakish, grotesque, idiosyncratic, odd, outlandish, peculiar, quaint, queer, quirky, singular, strange, unconventional, unnatural, unorthodox, unusual, weird. *Slang:* kooky, screwball. [*Compare* **exotic, insane.**]

eccentric *noun.* —*See* **character** (5), **crackpot.**

✚ **CORE SYNONYMS:** *eccentric, strange, peculiar, odd, queer, quaint, outlandish, singular, curious, fantastic, bizarre, grotesque.* These adjectives describe what deviates from the usual or customary. *Eccentric* describes something that parts from a conventional or established norm or pattern: *His musical compositions were innovative but eccentric. Strange* refers especially to what is unfamiliar, unknown, or inexplicable: *All summer I traveled through strange lands. Peculiar* particularly describes what is distinct from all others: *Cloves have a peculiar aromatic odor.* Something that is *odd* or *queer* fails to accord with what is ordinary, usual, or expected; both terms can suggest strangeness or peculiarity: *I find it odd that his name is never mentioned. "Now, my suspicion is that the universe is not only queerer than we suppose, but queerer than we can suppose"* (J.B.S. Haldane). *Quaint* refers to pleasing or old-fashioned peculiarity: *"the quaint streets of New Orleans, that most foreign of American cities"* (Winston Churchill). *Outlandish* suggests alien or bizarre strangeness: *The partygoers wore outlandish costumes. Singular* describes what is unique or unparalleled; the term often suggests a quality that arouses curiosity or wonder: *Such poise is singular in one so young. Curious* suggests strangeness that excites interest: *Americans living abroad often acquire a curious hybrid accent. Fantastic* describes what seems to have slight relation to the real world because of its strangeness or extravagance: *fantastic imaginary beasts such as the unicorn. Bizarre* stresses oddness that is heightened by striking contrasts and incongruities and that shocks or fascinates: *a bizarre art nouveau façade. Grotesque* refers principally to deformity and distortion that approach the point of caricature or even absurdity: *statues of grotesque creatures.*

---

eccentricity *noun.* Peculiar behavior ▶ idiosyncrasy, peculiarity, quirk, quirkiness, singularity. [*Compare* **abnormality.**]

ecclesiastic *noun.* —*See* **cleric.**

ecclesiastical *adjective.* Of or relating to a church or to an established religion ▶ church, churchly, religious, spiritual. [*Compare* **clerical, divine, holy, ritual.**] —*See also* **clerical.**

echelon *noun.* —*See* **place** (1).

echinate *adjective.* —*See* **thorny** (1).

echo *noun.* **1.** Imitative reproduction, as of the style of another ▶ imitation, reflection, reflex, repetition, reproduction. [*Compare* **mimicry.**] **2.** Repetition of sound via reflection from a surface ▶ repercussion, reverberation. —*See also* **mimic, repetition.**

echo *verb.* To send back the sound of ▶ bounce back, rebound, reecho, reflect, repeat, resound, reverberate. —*See also* **mimic.**

✣ **CORE SYNONYMS:** *echo, reecho, reflect, resound, reverberate.* These verbs mean to send back the sound of: *a cry echoed by the canyon; a cathedral roof reechoing joyous hymns; caves that reflect the noise of footsteps; cliffs resounding the thunder of the ocean; blasting reverberated by quarry walls.*

echoic *adjective.* Imitating sounds ▶ imitative, mimetic, onomatopoeic, onomatopoetic.

echoism *noun.* The formation of words in imitation of sounds ▶ mimesis, onomatopoeia.

eclipse *verb.* —*See* **obscure.**

economical *adjective.* Careful in the use of material resources ▶ canny, chary, frugal, provident, prudent, saving, Scotch, sparing, thrifty. [*Compare* **stingy.**]

✣ **CORE SYNONYMS:** *economical, sparing, frugal, thrifty.* These adjectives mean exercising or reflecting care in the use of resources, such as money. *Economical* emphasizes prudence, skillful management, and the avoidance of waste: *an economical shopper; an economical use of energy. Sparing* stresses restraint, as in expenditure: *a quiet librarian who was sparing of words. Frugal* implies self-denial and abstention from luxury: *a frugal diet; a frugal monk. Thrifty* suggests industry, care, and diligence in conserving means: *grew up during the Depression and learned to be thrifty.*

economize *verb.* —*See* **scrimp.**

economy *noun.* Careful use of material resources ▶ frugality, providence, prudence, thrift, thriftiness. [*Compare* **conservation.**]

economy *adjective.* —*See* **cheap.**

ecosystem *or* **ecosphere** *noun.* —*See* **environment** (3).

ecstasy *noun.* —*See* **delight, heaven.**

ecumenical *adjective.* —*See* **universal** (1).

edacious *adjective.* —*See* **gluttonous, voracious.**

edacity *noun.* —*See* **voracity.**

eddy *verb.* To move or cause to move like a rapidly rotating current of liquid ▶ swirl, whirl. [*Compare* **turn.**]

eddy *noun.* —*See* **breeze** (1), **whirlpool.**

edge *noun.* A cutting quality ▶ bite, incisiveness, keenness, sharpness, sting. —*See also* **advantage** (3), **blade, border** (1), **outskirts, tone** (2).

edge *verb.* To advance carefully and gradually ▶ ease, sidle. [*Compare* **crawl, sneak.**] —*See also* **border, insinuate, sharpen.**

edginess *noun.* —*See* **restlessness.**

edging *noun.* —*See* **border** (1).

edgy *adjective.* Feeling or exhibiting nervous tension ▶ fidgety, jittery, jumpy, nervous, restive, restless, skittish, taut, tense, twitchy. *Slang:* antsy, hyper, uptight. ***Idioms:*** a bundle of nerves, all wound up, on edge. [*Compare* **anxious.**]

edible *adjective.* Fit to be eaten ▶ comestible, eatable, esculent, palatable.

edibles *noun.* —*See* **food.**

edict *noun.* —*See* **law** (1), **message, ruling.**

edification *noun.* The condition of being informed spiritually ▶ enlightenment, illumination. [*Compare* **education.**] —*See also* **education** (1).

edifice *noun.* Something built, especially for human use ▶ building, construction, erection, pile, structure.

edify *verb.* To indulge in moral reflection, usually pompously ▶ moralize, pontificate, preach, sermonize. [*Compare* **chastise.**] —*See also* **illuminate** (2).

edifying *adjective.* —*See* **cultural, educational** (2), **moral.**

edit *verb.* —*See* **censor** (1), **revise.**

edition *noun.* —*See* **book, publication** (2).

editor *noun.* —*See* **press.**

editorial *noun.* —*See* **comment.**

editorialist *noun.* —*See* **press.**

editorialize *verb.* —*See* **comment.**

educable *adjective.* Capable of being educated ▶ docile, teachable, trainable. [*Compare* **obedient.**]

educate *verb.* To impart knowledge and skill to ▶ coach, discipline, form, instruct, school, teach, train, tutor. [*Compare* **indoctrinate.**] —*See also* **inform** (1).

✚ **CORE SYNONYMS:** *educate, teach, instruct, train, school, discipline.* These verbs mean to impart knowledge or skill. *Educate* often implies formal instruction but especially stresses the development of innate capacities: "*We are educated by others . . . and this cultivation, mingling with our innate disposition, is the soil in which our desires, passions, and motives grow*" (Mary Shelley). *Teach* is the most widely applicable: *taught the child to draw; taught literature at the college. Instruct* usually suggests methodical teaching: *instructed the undergraduates in music theory. Train* suggests concentration on particular skills intended to fit a person for a desired role: *trained the vocational students to be computer technicians. School* often implies an arduous learning process: *schooled the youngster to play the viola. Discipline* usually refers to the teaching of control, especially self-control: *disciplined myself to exercise every day.*

educated *adjective.* Showing evidence of schooling, training, or experience ▶ enlightened, erudite, informed, knowledgeable, learned, lettered, literate, scholarly, schooled, trained, versed, well-read, wise. [*Compare* **familiar, pedantic, studious.**] —*See also* **cultured, informed.**

✚ **CORE SYNONYMS:** *educated, learned, scholarly, versed.* These adjectives mean showing evidence of schooling, training, or experience: *an educated population; a learned jurist; a scholarly treatise; a naturalist versed in animal behavior.*

education *noun.* **1.** The act, process, or art of imparting knowledge and skill ▶ edification, instruction, pedagogics, pedagogy, schooling, teaching, training, tuition, tutelage, tutoring. **2.** Known facts, ideas, and skills that have been imparted ▶ erudition, instruction, knowledge, learning, scholarship, science. **3.** Training in the proper forms of social and personal conduct ▶ breeding, upbringing. [*Compare* **courtesy, manners.**]

educational *adjective.* **1.** Of or relating to education ▶ academic, instructional, pedagogic, pedagogical, scholastic, teaching. **2.** Serving to educate or inform ▶ edifying, educative, enlightening, illuminative, informative, instructional, instructive. [*Compare* **cultural.**]

educative *adjective.* —*See* **educational** (2).

educator *noun.* One who educates ▶ coach, instructor, master, pedagogue, schoolmaster, schoolmistress, schoolteacher, teacher, trainer, tutor. [*Compare* **adviser.**]

educe *verb.* —*See* **derive** (2), **evoke.**

eerie *or* **eery** *adjective.* —*See* **weird.**

efface *verb.* —*See* **cancel** (1).

effacement *noun.* —*See* **erasure.**

effect *noun.* **1.** Something brought about by a cause ▶ aftermath, consequence, corollary, end product, event, fruit, harvest, issue, outcome, precipitate, ramification, result, resultant, sequel, sequence, sequent, upshot. [*Compare* **derivative.**] **2.** The power or capacity to produce a desired result ▶ effectiveness, effectuality, effectualness, efficaciousness, efficacy, efficiency, influence, potency. [*Compare* **ability.**] **3.** The condition of being in full force or operation ▶ actualization, being, force, realization. [*Compare* **exercise.**]

effect *verb.* To succeed in doing ▶ accomplish, achieve, bring about, bring off, carry out, carry through, effectuate, execute, put through. *Informal:* swing. [*Compare* **accomplish, fulfill, perform, succeed.**] —*See also* **cause, enforce, perform** (1).

✚ **CORE SYNONYMS:** *effect, consequence, result, outcome, upshot, sequel.* These nouns denote an occurrence, situation, or condition that is brought about by a cause. An *effect* is produced by the action of an agent or a cause and follows it in time: "*Every cause produces more than one effect*" (Herbert Spencer). A *consequence* has a less sharply definable relationship to its cause: "*Servitude is at once the consequence of his crime and the punishment of his guilt*" (John P. Curran). A *result* is viewed as the end product of the operation of the cause: "*Judging from the results I have seen . . . I cannot say . . . that I agree with you*" (William H. Mallock). An *outcome* more strongly implies finality and may suggest the operation of a cause over a relatively long period: *The trial's outcome might have changed if the defendant had testified.* An *upshot* is a decisive result, often of the nature of a climax: "*The upshot of the matter . . . was that she showed both of them the door*" (Robert Louis Stevenson). A *sequel* is a consequence that ensues after a lapse of time: "*Our dreams are the sequel of our waking knowledge*" (Ralph Waldo Emerson).

effective *adjective.* **1.** Producing or able to produce a desired effect ▶ constructive, effectual, efficacious, efficient, instrumental, productive. [*Compare* **able, beneficial.**] **2.** In effect ▶ operational, operative. ***Idioms:*** in force (*or* operation). [*Compare* **active.**] —*See also* **convincing, forceful.**

✚ **CORE SYNONYMS:** *effective, effectual, efficacious, efficient.* These adjectives mean producing or capable of producing a desired effect: *an effective reprimand; an effectual complaint; an efficacious remedy; the efficient cause of the economic recovery.*

◀ **ANTONYM:** *ineffective*

effectiveness *noun.* —*See* **effect** (2).

effects *noun.* One's portable property ▶ belongings, chattel, goods, lares and penates, movables, personal effects, personal property, possessions, property, things. *Informal:* stuff. [*Compare* **holdings.**]

effectual *adjective.* —*See* **effective** (1).

effectuality *or* **effectualness** *noun.* —*See* **effect** (2).

effectuate *verb.* —*See* **cause, effect, enforce.**

effectuation *noun.* —*See* **performance.**

effeminacy *noun.* The quality of being effeminate ▶ effeminateness, effeteness, femininity, unmanliness, womanishness. [*Compare* **androgyny.**]

effeminate *adjective.* Having qualities traditionally attributed to a woman ▶ epicene, feminine, sissified, sissyish, unmanly, womanish. [*Compare* **androgynous.**]

effeminateness *noun.* —*See* **effeminacy.**

effervesce *verb.* —*See* **boil, foam.**

effervescence *noun.* —*See* **foam.**

effervescent *adjective.* —*See* **lively.**

effete *adjective.* —*See* **pale** (2).

effeteness *noun.* —*See* **effeminacy.**

efficacious *adjective.* —*See* **convincing, effective** (1).

efficacy *or* **efficaciousness** *noun.* —*See* **effect** (2).

efficiency *noun.* The quality of being efficient ▶ productiveness, productivity. [*Compare* **ability, diligence.**] —*See also* **apartment, effect** (2).

efficient *adjective.* Acting effectively with minimal waste ▶ productive, streamlined, well-oiled. [*Compare* **diligent, methodical.**] —*See also* **effective** (1).

effloresce *verb.* —*See* **bloom**[1] (1).

efflorescence *noun.* —*See* **bloom[1]** (1).
efflux *noun.* —*See* **flow.**
effort *noun.* The use of energy to do something ▶ endeavor, exertion, pains, strain, striving, struggle, trouble, while. *Informal:* elbow grease. [*Compare* **diligence, labor, strength.**] —*See also* **accomplishment, attempt, task** (2).
effortful *adjective.* Not natural or spontaneous ▶ contrived, forced, labored, strained. [*Compare* **awkward, stiff.**] —*See also* **difficult** (1).
effortless *adjective.* —*See* **easy** (1), **fluent.**
effortlessness *noun.* —*See* **ease** (2).
effrontery *noun.* —*See* **impudence.**
effulgence *noun.* —*See* **brilliance** (1).
effulgent *adjective.* —*See* **bright.**
effuse *verb.* —*See* **pour.**
egghead *noun.* —*See* **mind** (2).
egg on *verb.* —*See* **provoke.**
ego *noun.* —*See* **egotism, pride.**
egocentric *adjective.* Holding the philosophical view that the self is the center and norm of existence ▶ egoistic, egoistical, individualistic, solipsistic. —*See also* **egotistic** (2).
egocentric *noun.* —*See* **egotist.**
egocentricity *or* **egocentrism** *noun.* —*See* **egotism.**
egoism *noun.* —*See* **egotism.**
egoist *noun.* —*See* **egotist.**
egoistic *or* **egoistical** *adjective.* Holding the philosophical view that the self is the center and norm of existence ▶ egocentric, individualistic, solipsistic. —*See also* **egotistic** (2), **egotistic** (1).
egomania *noun.* —*See* **egotism.**
egomaniac *noun.* —*See* **egotist.**
egomaniacal *adjective.* —*See* **egotistic** (2).
egotism *noun.* Exaggerated love for oneself or belief in one's own importance ▶ amour-propre, conceit, ego, egocentricity, egocentrism, egoism, egomania, megalomania, narcissism, pride, self-absorption, self-centeredness, self-importance, self-involvement, selfishness, vainglory, vainness, vanity. *Informal:* big head, bigheadedness, swelled head. *Slang:* ego trip. [*Compare* **pride, arrogance, pretentiousness.**]

✦ **CORE SYNONYMS:** *egotism, conceit, egoism, narcissism, vanity.* These nouns denote excessive high regard for oneself: *boasting that reveals conceit; imperturbable egoism; arrogance and egotism that were obvious from her actions; narcissism that shut out everyone else; wounded his vanity by looking in the mirror.*

◀ **ANTONYM:** *humility*

egotist *noun.* A conceited, self-centered person ▶ egocentric, egoist, egomaniac, narcissist. [*Compare* **braggart.**]
egotistic *or* **egotistical** *adjective.* **1.** Thinking too highly of oneself ▶ conceited, egoistic, egoistical, narcissistic, vain, vainglorious. *Informal:* bigheaded, stuck-up, swellheaded. ***Idioms:*** full of (*or* stuck on) oneself. [*Compare* **arrogant, boastful.**] **2.** Concerned only with oneself ▶ egocentric, egoistic, egoistical, egomaniacal, self-absorbed, self-centered, self-involved, selfish, self-seeking, self-serving. ***Idiom:*** wrapped up in oneself.
ego trip *noun.* —*See* **egotism.**
egregious *adjective.* Conspicuously bad or offensive ▶ flagrant, glaring, gross, rank. [*Compare* **offensive, outrageous, shameless.**]
egregiousness *noun.* The quality or state of being flagrant ▶ flagrancy, glaringness, grossness, rankness. [*Compare* **impudence, outrageousness.**]
egress *noun.* —*See* **departure.**
eighty-six *verb.* —*See* **discard.**
ejaculate *verb.* —*See* **exclaim.**
ejaculation *noun.* —*See* **shout.**
eject *verb.* **1.** To put out by force ▶ bump, cast out, dismiss, evict, expel, oust, throw out. *Informal:* chuck. *Slang:* boot (out), bounce, kick out. ***Idioms:*** give someone the boot (*or* heave-ho *or* old heave-ho), send packing, show someone the door, throw out on one's

ear. [*Compare* **dismiss.**] **2.** To catapult oneself from a disabled aircraft ▶ bail out, jump. —*See also* **erupt.**

✚ **CORE SYNONYMS:** *eject, expel, evict, dismiss, oust.* These verbs mean to put out by force. To *eject* is to throw or cast out from within: *The fire ejected yellow flames into the night sky. Expel* means to drive out or away, and it implies permanent removal: *The dean expelled the student for having cheated. Evict* most commonly refers to the expulsion of persons from property by legal process: *The apartment manager evicted the noisy tenants. Dismiss* refers to putting someone or something out of one's mind (*trying to dismiss his fears*) or, in law, to refusing to give an appeal or a complaint further consideration (*dismissed the case for lack of evidence*). *Oust* is applied chiefly to the removal of a person from a position lawfully or otherwise: *There were no grounds for ousting the prime minister.*

ejection *noun.* The act of ejecting or the state of being ejected ▶ dismissal, ejectment, eviction, expulsion, ouster, removal. *Slang:* boot, bounce. [*Compare* **dismissal, exile.**]

ejectment *noun.* —*See* **ejection.**

elaborate *adjective.* Rich in detail ▶ complicated, detailed, fancy, fussy, intricate, ornate. [*Compare* **busy, ornate.**] —*See also* **complex** (1), **detailed.**

elaborate *verb.* To express at greater length or in greater detail ▶ amplify (on *or* upon), develop, dilate (on *or* upon), discourse (on *or* upon), enlarge (on *or* upon), expand (on *or* upon), expatiate (on *or* upon), flesh out. ***Idioms:*** fill in the details, get down to brass tacks, go into detail, go on and on. [*Compare* **belabor, explain.**]

✚ **CORE SYNONYMS:** *elaborate, complicated, intricate, ornate.* These adjectives mean marked by richness or complexity of detail: *an elaborate lace pattern; the eye, a complicated organ; an intricate problem; an ornate candelabra.*

◀ **ANTONYM:** *simple*

élan *or* **élan vital** *noun.* —*See* **spirit** (1).

elapse *verb.* To move past in time ▶ go by, lapse, pass (away *or* by), slip (away *or* by), tick away.

elastic *adjective.* —*See* **adaptable, flexible** (1), **flexible** (3).

elasticity *noun.* The ability to recover quickly from depression or discouragement ▶ bounce, buoyancy, flexibility, resilience, resiliency. —*See also* **flexibility** (1).

elate *verb.* To raise the spirits of ▶ animate, buoy (up), elevate, exhilarate, flush, inspire, inspirit, lift, uplift. [*Compare* **delight, encourage.**] —*See also* **delight** (1).

elated *adjective.* Feeling great delight and joy ▶ animated, elate, elevated, euphoric, exalted, exhilarated, inspired, overjoyed, uplifted. *Slang:* high, up. ***Idioms:*** flying (*or* riding) high, on cloud nine, on top of the world. [*Compare* **exultant, thrilled.**]

elatedness *noun.* —*See* **elation.**

elation *noun.* High spirits ▶ animation, elatedness, euphoria, exaltation, exhilaration, inspiration, lift, uplift. [*Compare* **happiness, high, merriment.**] —*See also* **delight.**

elbow *verb.* —*See* **muscle, push** (1).

elbow grease *noun.* —*See* **effort.**

elbowroom *noun.* —*See* **license** (1).

elder *noun.* One who stands above another in rank ▶ better, senior, superior. *Informal:* higher-up. —*See also* **senior** (2), **chief.**

elder *adjective.* —*See* **old** (2).

elderliness *noun.* —*See* **age** (1).

elderly *adjective.* —*See* **old** (2).

elect *verb.* To select by vote for an office ▶ vote (in). —*See also* **appoint, choose** (1).

elect *adjective.* Singled out in preference ▶ choice, chosen, exclusive, select. [*Compare* **excellent, favorite.**]

elect *noun.* One that is selected ▶ choice, chosen, pick, select. [*Compare* **best.**]

election *noun.* —*See* **appointment, choice.**

elective *adjective.* —*See* **optional.**

elector *noun.* One who votes ▶ balloter, voter. ***Idiom:*** member of the electorate.

electrify *verb.* —*See* **enrapture, startle.**

eleemosynary *adjective.* Of or concerned with charity ▶ altruistic, benevolent, charitable, philanthropic.

elegance *or* **elegancy** *noun.* Refinement of manner, form, and style ▶ chic, courtliness, dignity, elegancy, grace, polish, quality, sophistication, style, taste, tastefulness, urbanity. *Informal:* class. [*Compare* **attraction, culture, proportion.**]

elegant *adjective.* Exhibiting refined, tasteful beauty of manner, form, or style ▶ chic, courtly, exquisite, graceful, refined, tasteful. *Informal:* classy. [*Compare* **cultured.**] —*See also* **delicate** (1), **gracious** (2), **grand.**

element *noun.* **1.** An irreducible constituent of a whole ▶ basic, essential, fundamental, rudiment. ***Idiom:*** part and parcel. [*Compare* **nitty-gritty.**] **2.** An individually considered portion of a whole ▶ article, detail, item, particular, point. —*See also* **part** (1).

elemental *adjective.* Of or being an irreducible element ▶ basic, elementary, essential, fundamental, primal, primitive, ultimate, underlying. —*See also* **constitutional.**

elementary *adjective.* —*See* **elemental.** Of or treating the most basic aspects ▶ basal, basic, beginning, rudimental, rudimentary. [*Compare* **constitutional.**]

elephantine *adjective.* —*See* **enormous, ponderous.**

elevate *verb.* **1.** To move something to a higher position ▶ boost, heave, hike (up), hitch up, hoist, jack (up), lift, pick up, raise, rear, take up, uphold, uplift, upraise, uprear. **2.** To increase markedly in level or intensity, especially of sound ▶ amplify, heighten, raise. *Slang:* crank up, pump up. [*Compare* **increase.**] —*See also* **distinguish** (3), **elate, exalt, promote** (1).

✣ **CORE SYNONYMS:** *elevate, lift, raise, hoist, heave, boost.* These verbs mean to move something from a lower to a higher level or position. *Elevate* is often a general term (*elevated his sprained ankle*), but it more often suggests exalting, ennobling, or raising morally or intellectually: *"A generous and elevated mind is distinguished by nothing more certainly than an eminent degree of curiosity"* (Samuel Johnson). *Lift* sometimes stresses the expenditure of effort: *a trunk too heavy to lift. Raise* often implies movement to an approximately vertical position: *raised my hand so I could ask a question. Hoist* is applied principally to the lifting of heavy objects, often by mechanical means: *hoist a sunken ship.* To *heave* is to lift or raise with great effort or force: *heaved the pack onto his back. Boost* suggests upward movement effected by or as if by pushing from below: *boosted the child into the saddle.*

---

elevated *adjective.* **1.** Being positioned above a given level ▶ boosted, raised, uplifted, upraised. ***Idiom:*** on high. [*Compare* **higher.**] **2.** Abnormally increased, especially in intensity ▶ heightened, high, raised, supernormal. ***Idioms:*** off the charts, on the high end, over the top. [*Compare* **excessive.**] **3.** Being on a high intellectual or moral level ▶ high-minded, moral, noble, sublime. **4.** Exceedingly dignified in form, tone, or style ▶ eloquent, exalted, grand, high, high-flown, lofty, soaring, vaulting. [*Compare* **grandiose.**] **5.** At the upper end of a degree of measure ▶ great, high, large. [*Compare* **exalted, extreme.**] —*See also* **elated, exalted, high** (1).

elevation *noun.* The distance of something from a given level ▶ altitude, height, loftiness, tallness. [*Compare* **ascent.**] —*See also* **advancement, exaltation.**

✚ **CORE SYNONYMS:** *elevation, altitude, height.* These nouns denote the distance of something above a point of reference such as the horizon: *a city at an elevation of 3,000 feet above sea level; flying at an altitude of 1 mile; grew to a height of 6 feet.*

---

elf *noun.* —*See* **fairy, urchin.**

elfish *adjective.* —*See* **mischievous.**

elicit *verb.* —*See* **evoke.**

eligibility *noun.* —*See* **qualification.**

eligible *adjective.* Satisfying certain requirements, as for selection ▶ equal, fit, fitted, qualified, suitable, suited, up to, worthy. [*Compare* **appropriate.**] —*See also* **single.**

eliminate *verb.* To get rid of, especially by banishment or execution ▶ eradicate, liquidate, purge, remove, wipe out. ***Idioms:*** do away with, put an end to. [*Compare* **annihilate, banish, kill, rid.**] —*See also* **drop** (5), **exclude.**

✚ **CORE SYNONYMS:** *eliminate, eradicate, liquidate, purge.* These verbs mean to get rid of someone or something, especially by using drastic methods such as banishment or execution: *eliminated all opposition; eradicate guerrilla activity; liquidating traitors; purged the army of dissidents.*

---

elimination *noun.* The act or process of eliminating ▶ clearance, eradication, exclusion, liquidation, purge, removal, riddance. [*Compare* **abolition, ejection.**] —*See also* **disposal.**

eliminative *or* **eliminatory** *adjective.* Of, relating to, or tending to eliminate ▶ cathartic, emetic, evacuant, evacuative, excretory, purgative, urinary.

elite *or* **élite** *noun.* —*See* **best** (1), **society** (1).

elite *or* **élite** *adjective.* —*See* **exclusive** (3), **noble.**

elitist *or* **élitist** *noun.* One who despises people or things regarded as inferior, especially because of social or intellectual pretension ▶ prig, snob. *Informal:* snoot.

elitist *or* **élitist** *adjective.* —*See* **snobbish.**

elixir *noun.* Something believed to cure all human disorders ▶ catholicon, cure-all, panacea. [*Compare* **cure.**] —*See also* **cure.**

ellipse *noun.* —*See* **oval.**

ellipsoid *noun.* —*See* **oval.**

ellipsoid *or* **ellipsoidal** *adjective.* —*See* **oval.**

elliptical *adjective.* —*See* **oval.**

elocution *noun.* —*See* **oratory.**

elocutionary *adjective.* —*See* **oratorical.**

elongate *verb.* —*See* **lengthen.**

elongated *or* **elongate** *adjective.* —*See* **long**[1] (1).

elongation *noun.* —*See* **extension** (1).

eloquence *noun.* Smooth or effective skill in communicating ▶ articulacy, articulateness, eloquentness, expression, expressiveness, expressivity, facility, fluency, fluidity, glibness, rhetoric, silver tongue, volubility. ***Idioms:*** gift of gab

eloquent *adjective.* Fluently persuasive and forceful ▶ articulate, silver-tongued, smooth-spoken, voluble, well-spoken. [*Compare* **convincing, fluent, glib.**] —*See also* **elevated** (4), **expressive, oratorical.**

eloquentness *noun.* —*See* **eloquence.**

elsewhere *adjective.* —*See* **absent.**

elucidate *verb.* —*See* **clarify** (1), **explain** (1).

elucidation *noun.* —*See* **explanation.**

elucidative *adjective.* —*See* **explanatory.**

elude *verb.* To fail to be fixed by the mind, memory, or senses of ▶ escape, evade. ***Idiom:*** slip away from. [*Compare* **forget.**] —*See also* **avoid, lose** (3).

elusive *adjective.* **1.** Inclined or intended to evade ▶ evasive, fugitive, slippery. [*Compare* **slick, underhand.**] **2.** Deliberately ambiguous or vague ▶ evasive, equivocal, indirect, misleading. [*Compare* **ambiguous.**]

emaciated *adjective.* —*See* **haggard.**

emanate *verb.* —*See* **stem.**

emancipate *verb.* —*See* **free** (1).

emancipated *adjective.* —*See* **free** (1), **loose** (2).

emancipation *noun.* —*See* **liberty, rescue.**

embark *verb.* —*See* **start** (1).

embarkation *noun.* —*See* **birth** (2), **departure.**

embarkment *noun.* —*See* **departure.**

embarrass *verb.* To cause a person to be self-consciously distressed ▶ abash, chagrin, confound, confuse, discomfit, discomfort, disconcert, discountenance, faze, mortify. ***Idiom:*** put on the spot. [*Compare* **baffle, shame.**] —*See also* **complicate.**

✚ **CORE SYNONYMS:** *embarrass, abash, chagrin, discomfit, disconcert, faze, mortify.* These verbs mean to cause someone to feel self-conscious and uneasy: *The parents were embarrassed by their child's tantrum. I felt abashed at the extravagant praise. I will be chagrined if my confident prediction fails. He was discomfited by the sudden personal question. She is disconcerted by sarcastic remarks. They refuse to be fazed by your objections. We were mortified by the public display of vulgarity.*

---

embarrassing *adjective.* —*See* **awkward** (3).

embarrassment *noun.* Self-conscious distress ▶ abashment, chagrin, confusion, discomfiture, discomfort, discomposure, mortification. [*Compare* **disgrace.**] —*See also* **excess** (1).

embassy *noun.* A diplomatic office or headquarters in a foreign country ▶ deputation, legation, mission.

embed *or* **imbed** *verb.* —*See* **fix** (2).

embellish *verb.* To endow with beauty and elegance ▶ beautify, enhance, grace, set off. —*See also* **adorn** (1).

embellishment *noun.* —*See* **adornment.**

embezzle *verb.* —*See* **steal.**

embitter *verb.* —*See* **disappoint.**

embittered *adjective.* —*See* **resentful.**

embitterment *noun.* —*See* **resentment.**

emblazon *verb.* —*See* **adorn** (1), **color** (1).

emblem *noun.* An object or expression associated with and serving to identify something else ▶ attribute, metaphor, signifier, symbol, token. [*Compare* **expression, sign, term.**] —*See also* **sign** (1).

emblematic *or* **emblematical** *adjective.* —*See* **symbolic.**

embodiment *noun.* A concrete entity typifying an abstraction ▶ allegory, exemplification, exteriorization, externalization, hypostasis, illustration, image, incarnation, incorporation, instantiation, manifestation, materialization, objectification, personalization, personification, prosopopeia, reification, substantiation, type, typification. [*Compare* **representation, symbol.**] —*See also* **example** (1).

embody *verb.* **1.** To represent (an abstraction, for example) in or as if in bodily form ▶ allegorize, body forth, concretize, exteriorize, externalize, hypostatize, incarnate, instantiate, manifest, materialize, objectify, personalize, personify, reify, substantiate. [*Compare* **realize.**] **2.** To make a part of a united whole ▶ combine, incorporate, integrate. [*Compare* **assemble, combine.**] —*See also* **contain** (1).

embolden *verb.* —*See* **encourage** (1).

embrace *verb.* **1.** To put one's arms around affectionately ▶ clasp, enfold, hold, hug, press, squeeze. *Slang:* clinch. ***Idioms:*** fold to one's bosom, give a bear hug, take in one's arms, wrap one's arms around. [*Compare* **grasp, snuggle.**] **2.** To receive something given or offered willingly and gladly ▶ accept, take (up), welcome. *—See also* **adopt, contain (1), surround.**

embrace *noun.* The act of embracing ▶ bear hug, clasp, hug, squeeze. *Slang:* clinch. [*Compare* **hold.**]

embracement *noun.* *—See* **acceptance (1).**

embrangle *verb.* *—See* **involve (1).**

embranglement *noun.* *—See* **entanglement.**

embroil *verb.* *—See* **complicate, involve (1).**

embroilment *noun.* *—See* **entanglement.**

embryo *noun.* *—See* **germ (2).**

emend *verb.* *—See* **correct (1), revise.**

emendate *verb.* *—See* **revise.**

emendation *noun.* *—See* **revision.**

emendatory *adjective.* *—See* **corrective.**

emerge *verb.* *—See* **appear (1), begin.**

emergence *noun.* *—See* **appearance (2).**

emergency *noun.* A situation requiring immediate assistance or remedial action ▶ crisis, distress, exigence, exigency, extremity, flash point, front burner, hot water, pinch, straits, trauma, trouble, urgency.

emergency *adjective.* *—See* **auxiliary (2).**

emergent *adjective.* *—See* **urgent (1).**

emigrant *noun.* One who emigrates ▶ migrant. [*Compare* **émigré, foreigner, settler.**]

emigrate *verb.* To leave one's native land and settle in another ▶ immigrate (to), migrate, resettle, transmigrate. [*Compare* **move, settle.**]

emigration *noun.* Departure from one's native land to settle in another ▶ defection, diaspora, exodus, expatriation, migration, transmigration. ***Idiom:*** brain drain. [*Compare* **immigration, exile.**]

émigré *noun.* One forced to emigrate, usually for political reasons ▶ deportee, displaced person, DP, exile, expatriate, expellee, refugee. *—See also* **foreigner.**

eminence *noun.* *—See* **dignitary, fame, hill.**

eminency *noun.* *—See* **fame.**

eminent *adjective.* *—See* **exalted, famous, noticeable.**

eminently *adverb.* *—See* **very.**

emir *noun.* *—See* **chief.**

emissary *noun.* *—See* **representative.**

emit *verb.* To discharge material, as vapor or fumes, usually suddenly and violently ▶ exhale, give, give forth, give off, give out, issue, let off, let out, release, send forth, throw off, vent. [*Compare* **erupt.**] *—See also* **shed[1] (1).**

emollient *noun.* *—See* **ointment.**

emolument *noun.* *—See* **wage.**

emotion *noun.* A subjective mental state, such as love or hate ▶ affect, affection, affectivity, feeling, passion, sentiment. [*Compare* **passion.**]

✚ **CORE SYNONYMS:** *emotion, feeling, passion, sentiment.* These nouns refer to complex and usually strong subjective human response. Although *emotion* and *feeling* are sometimes interchangeable, *emotion* often implies the presence of excitement or agitation: "*Poetry is not a turning loose of emotion, but an escape from emotion*" (T.S. Eliot). *Feeling* is the more general and neutral: "*Poetry is the spontaneous overflow of powerful feelings: it takes its origin from emotion recollected in tranquillity*" (William Wordsworth). *Passion* is intense, compelling emotion: "*They seemed like ungoverned children inflamed with the fiercest passions of men*" (Francis Parkman). *Sentiment* often applies to a thought or opinion arising from or influenced by emotion: *We expressed our sentiments about the government's policies.* The word can also refer to delicate, sensitive, or higher or more refined feelings: "*The mystic reverence, the religious allegiance, which are essential to a true monarchy, are imaginative sentiments that no legislature can manufacture in any people*" (Walter Bagehot).

---

emotional *adjective.* **1.** Relating to, arising from, or appealing to the emotions ▶ affectional, affective, emotive. **2.** Readily stirred by emotion ▶ feeling, sensitive. [*Compare* **passionate.**] —*See also* **dramatic** (2).

emotionless *adjective.* —*See* **cold** (2).

emotive *adjective.* Relating to, arising from, or appealing to the emotions ▶ affectional, affective, emotional.

empathetic *or* **empathic** *adjective.* —*See* **sympathetic.**

empathize *verb.* **1.** To understand or be sensitive to another's feelings or ideas ▶ sympathize, understand. ***Idioms:*** feel someone's pain, put oneself (*or* walk) in someone else's shoes. **2.** To associate or affiliate oneself closely with a person or group ▶ identify, relate, sympathize. [*Compare* **understand.**]

empathy *noun.* A very close understanding between persons ▶ sympathy, understanding. —*See also* **pity** (1).

emperor *noun.* —*See* **chief.**

emphasis *noun.* Special attention given to something considered important ▶ accent, accentuation, stress, weight. [*Compare* **importance, notice.**]

✦ **CORE SYNONYMS:** *emphasis, accent, stress.* These nouns mean special weight placed on something considered important: *an education with an emphasis on science; will study music with an accent on jazz; laid heavy stress on law and order.*

emphasize *verb.* To accord emphasis to ▶ accent, accentuate, feature, highlight, italicize, play up, point up, spotlight, stress, underline, underscore. ***Idioms:*** call attention to, lay stress on. [*Compare* **concentrate.**]

emphatic *adjective.* —*See* **assertive, definite** (1).

emphatically *adverb.* —*See* **flatly.**

emplace *verb.* —*See* **position.**

emplacement *noun.* —*See* **position** (1).

employ *verb.* **1.** To obtain the use or services of ▶ enlist, engage, hire, recruit, retain, sign (on *or* up), take on. ***Idioms:*** bring aboard, put on the payroll. [*Compare* **authorize.**] **2.** To make busy ▶ busy, engage, occupy. [*Compare* **absorb, involve.**] —*See also* **absorb** (1), **operate, use.**

employ *noun.* The state of being employed ▶ employment, hire, service.

employable *adjective.* —*See* **open** (4), **usable.**

employed *adjective.* Having a job ▶ hired, jobholding, placed, retained, wage-earning, working. ***Idioms:*** bringing home the bacon, gainfully employed, off the dole —*See also* **busy** (1).

employee *noun.* One who is employed by another ▶ help, hireling, jobholder, staffer, staff member, wage earner, worker. *Informal:* hire, hired hand, nine-to-fiver. [*Compare* **assistant, laborer.**]

employer *noun.* One that employs persons for wages ▶ hirer. [*Compare* **boss.**]

employment *noun.* **1.** The act of employing for wages ▶ engagement, hire, hiring, retention. **2.** The state of being employed ▶ employ, hire, service. —*See also* **business** (2), **duty** (2), **exercise** (1).

emporium *noun.* A retail establishment where merchandise is sold ▶ boutique, outlet, shop, store.

empower *verb.* To give the means, ability, or opportunity to do ▶ enable, permit. ***Idioms:*** clear the path (*or* road *or* way) for, smooth the way for. [*Compare* **ease, permit.**] —*See also* **authorize.**

emprise *noun.* —*See* **adventure.**

emptiness *noun.* **1.** A desolate sense of loss ▶ blankness, desolation, emptiness, hollowness, vacuum, void. **2.** Total lack of ideas, meaning, or substance ▶ bareness, barrenness, blankness, hollowness, inanity, meaninglessness, vacancy, vacuity, vacuousness. [*Compare* **futility, insipidity.**] —*See also* **nothingness** (2).

empty *adjective.* **1.** Containing nothing ▶ bare, barren, blank, clear, null, vacant, vacuous, void. ***Idiom:*** clean as a whistle. **2.** Deprived of a quality or aspect that is desirable ▶ bankrupt, barren, bereft, denuded, deprived, destitute, devoid, innocent, lacking, void, wanting. ***Idioms:*** crying out for, in want (*or* need) of. *—See also* **hollow** (1), **vacant, worthless.**

empty *verb.* To remove the contents of ▶ clean out, clear, empty out, evacuate, gut, strip, vacate, void. *—See also* **pour, rid.**

✚ **CORE SYNONYMS:** *empty, vacant, blank, void, vacuous, bare, barren.* These adjectives mean lacking contents that could or should be present. *Empty* applies to what is wholly lacking contents or substance: *an empty room; empty promises. Vacant* refers to what is without an occupant or incumbent, or to what is without intelligence or thought: *a vacant auditorium; a vacant stare. Blank* stresses the absence of something, especially on a surface, that would convey meaning or content: *blank pages. Void* applies to what is free from or completely destitute of discernible content: *gibberish void of all meaning. Vacuous* describes what is as devoid of substance as a vacuum is: *led a vacuous life.* Something that is *bare* lacks surface covering (*a bare head*) or detail (*the bare facts*); the word also denotes the condition of being stripped of contents or furnishings: *a bare closet. Barren* literally and figuratively stresses lack of productivity: *barren land; writing barren of insight.*

---

empty-headed *adjective.* *—See* **giddy** (2), **vacant.**

empyreal *adjective.* *—See* **heavenly** (2).

emulate *verb.* *—See* **compete, follow** (5).

emulation *noun.* A strong desire to achieve something ▶ ambition, ambitiousness, aspiration. [*Compare* **drive, enthusiasm, thirst.**] *—See also* **mimicry.**

emulative *adjective.* *—See* **imitative** (1).

emulator *noun.* *—See* **competitor.**

emulous *adjective.* *—See* **ambitious, competitive.**

enable *verb.* To give the means, ability, or opportunity to do ▶ empower, permit. ***Idioms:*** clear the path (*or* road *or* way) for, smooth the way for. [*Compare* **ease, permit.**] *—See also* **authorize.**

enact *verb.* *—See* **act** (3), **establish** (2), **stage.**

enactment *noun.* *—See* **interpretation, law** (2).

enamel *noun.* *—See* **finish.**

enamel *verb.* *—See* **finish** (2).

enamored *adjective.* *—See* **infatuated.**

enceinte *adjective.* *—See* **pregnant** (1).

enchant *verb.* *—See* **charm** (1), **charm** (2), **delight** (1).

enchanter *noun.* *—See* **wizard.**

enchanting *adjective.* *—See* **attractive, delightful.**

enchantment *noun.* *—See* **attraction, delight, spell²**.

enchantress *noun.* A woman who practices magic ▶ hag, lamia, sorceress, witch. [*Compare* **wizard.**] *—See also* **seductress.**

encircle *verb.* To form a circle around ▶ band, begird, belt, cincture, circle, circumnavigate, circumscribe, gird, girdle, girt, loop, orbit, ring, surround. [*Compare* **turn.**] *—See also* **surround.**

enclose *verb.* **1.** To confine within a limited area ▶ bar, box (in), cage, close (in), closet, confine, contain, coop (in *or* up), cordon (off), corral, fence (in), immure, impound, pen, shut (away *or* in *or* up), wall (in *or* off *or* up). [*Compare* **imprison, surround.**] **2.** To surround and advance upon ▶ besiege, close in, encompass, envelop, hedge, hem, picket. [*Compare* **besiege, surround.**]

✚ **CORE SYNONYMS:** *enclose, cage, coop up, fence, pen, wall in.* These verbs mean to surround and confine within a limited area: *cattle enclosed in feedlots; was* *caged in the office all afternoon; was cooped up in a studio apartment; a garden fenced in by shrubbery; ships penned up in the harbor; prisoners who were walled in.*

---

enclosure *noun.* —*See* **court** (1).

encomiastic *adjective.* —*See* **complimentary** (1).

encomium *noun.* —*See* **praise** (1).

encompass *verb.* —*See* **contain** (1), **enclose** (2), **surround.**

encounter *verb.* **1.** To find or meet by chance ▶ alight on (*or* upon), bump into, chance on (*or* upon), come across, come on (*or* upon), find, happen on (*or* upon), hit (on *or* upon), light on (*or* upon), meet, run across, run into, see, stumble on (*or* upon), tumble on. ***Idiom:*** meet up with. **2.** To meet face-to-face, especially defiantly ▶ confront, face, front, meet. ***Idiom:*** stand up to. [*Compare* **contest, defy.**] —*See also* **contend, experience.**

encounter *noun.* —*See* **battle, confrontation.**

encourage *verb.* **1.** To impart courage, inspiration, and resolution to ▶ animate, cheer (on), embolden, inspire, inspirit, motivate. [*Compare* **provoke, urge.**] **2.** To impart emotional, moral, or mental strength to ▶ buck up, cheer (up), fortify, hearten, nerve, perk up. [*Compare* **comfort, energize.**] **3.** To lend supportive approval to ▶ countenance, favor, smile on (*or* upon). [*Compare* **approve, support.**] —*See also* **promote** (2).

✦ CORE SYNONYMS: *encourage, animate, cheer, embolden, inspirit, motivate.* These verbs mean to impart courage, inspiration, and resolution to: *encouraged the athlete to compete; played music to animate the crowd; a visitor cheering the patient; was emboldened to sing for the guests; a pep talk that inspirited the weary team; praise that motivated us.*

---

encouragement *noun.* Something that gives courage or confidence ▶ boost, exhortation, inspiration, lift, motivation, stimulation. *Informal:* pep talk. ***Idiom:*** shot in the arm. —*See also* **patronage** (1), **stimulus.**

encouraging *adjective.* Inspiring confidence or hope ▶ cheering, heartening, hopeful, likely, promising. [*Compare* **favorable, optimistic.**]

encroach *verb.* —*See* **intrude.**

encroachment *noun.* —*See* **trespass** (2).

encumber *verb.* —*See* **burden**[1], **hinder.**

encumbrance *noun.* An excessive, unwelcome burden ▶ imposition, infliction, intrusion, obtrusion. [*Compare* **meddling.**] —*See also* **bar** (1), **burden**[1] (2), **debt** (2).

end *noun.* **1.** A concluding or terminating ▶ cessation, close, closing, closure, completion, conclusion, consummation, cutoff, dénouement, ending, end of the line, expiration, finis, finish, period, shutdown, stopping point, termination, terminus, wind-up, wrap-up. [*Compare* **stop.**] **2.** The last part ▶ close, closing, conclusion, ending, envoy, epilogue, finale, finish, last, termination, wind-up, wrap-up. **3.** Residual matter ▶ butt, fragment, heel, leftovers, odds and ends, ort, scrap, shard, stub. [*Compare* **balance.**] —*See also* **back, death** (1), **fate** (2), **intention, length, limits.**

end *verb.* —*See* **conclude, disappear** (2), **drop** (4), **lapse.**

endanger *verb.* To expose to danger or destruction ▶ compromise, hazard, imperil, jeopardize, menace, peril, risk, threaten. ***Idioms:*** lay open, put in jeopardy (*or* harm's way).

✦ CORE SYNONYMS: *endanger, compromise, imperil, jeopardize, risk.* These verbs mean to subject to danger, loss, or destruction: *driving that endangers lives;*

compromised his health by smoking; a forest imperiled by acid rain; strikes that jeopardized company profits; wouldn't risk her financial security.

---

endangerment *noun.* —*See* **danger, exposure.**

endeavor *noun.* Something undertaken, especially something requiring extensive planning and work ▶ enterprise, project, undertaking, venture. [*Compare* **task.**] —*See also* **accomplishment, attempt, effort.**

endeavor *verb.* —*See* **attempt.**

ended *adjective.* —*See* **complete** (3).

endemic *adjective.* —*See* **indigenous.**

ending *noun.* —*See* **end** (1), **end** (2).

endless *adjective.* **1.** Having no ends or limits ▶ boundless, illimitable, immeasurable, infinite, limitless, measureless, unbounded, unlimited. [*Compare* **incalculable.**] **2.** Enduring for all time ▶ amaranthine, ceaseless, eternal, eterne, everlasting, immortal, never-ending, perpetual, sempiternal, unending. [*Compare* **continuing, forever, unchanging.**] —*See also* **continual.**

✚ **CORE SYNONYMS:** *endless, boundless, eternal, illimitable, infinite, sempiternal.* These adjectives mean being having no limits or being without a beginning or end: *an endless universe; boundless ambition; eternal beauty; illimitable space; infinite wisdom; sempiternal truth.*

---

endlessly *adverb.* —*See* **forever.**

endlessness *noun.* The quality or state of having no end ▶ ceaselessness, eternality, eternalness, eternity, everlastingness, interminability, perpetuity. [*Compare* **infinity.**]

endmost *adjective.* —*See* **last**[1] (2).

end of the line *noun.* —*See* **end** (1).

endorse *verb.* —*See* **confirm** (3), **permit** (2), **sign, support** (1).

endorsement *noun.* An indication of commendation or approval ▶ backing, blessing, recommendation, support. *Informal:* plug. [*Compare* **patronage, reference.**] —*See also* **confirmation** (1), **permission.**

endow *verb.* —*See* **donate, gift.**

endowed *adjective.* —*See* **gifted.**

endowment *noun.* A quality, ability, or accomplishment that makes a person suitable for a particular position or task ▶ attainment, credential, qualification, skill. [*Compare* **qualification.**] —*See also* **donation.**

end product *noun.* —*See* **effect** (1).

endue *verb.* —*See* **gift.**

endurable *adjective.* —*See* **bearable.**

endurance *noun.* The quality or power of withstanding hardship or stress ▶ durability, fortitude, hardiness, stamina, staying power, sticking power, toughness. [*Compare* **courage, decision, strength.**] —*See also* **continuation** (1).

endure *verb.* **1.** To put up with or continue despite difficulties ▶ abide, accept, bear (with), brook, go on, hang on, keep on, live through, persevere, persist, sit through, soldier on, stand (for), stick out, stomach, suffer, support, sustain, swallow, take, tolerate, withstand. *Informal:* lump. *Slang:* sweat out, tough out. ***Idioms:*** hang in there, go the distance, keep going, keep it up, learn to live with (*or* accept), make one's peace with, never say die, resign oneself to, put up with. [*Compare* **deal with, survive.**] **2.** To be in existence or in a certain state for an indefinitely long time ▶ abide, bide, continue, go on, hold out, hold steady, keep, last, perdure, perseverate, persist, remain, stand, stay. —*See also* **bear up.**

✚ **CORE SYNONYMS:** *endure, bear, stand, abide, suffer, tolerate.* These verbs mean to put up with or withstand something, especially something difficult or painful. *Endure* specifies a continuing capacity to face pain or hardship: *"Human life is everywhere a state in which much is to be endured and little to be enjoyed"* (Samuel Johnson). *Bear* pertains broadly to the capacity to withstand: *"Those best can bear reproof who merit praise"* (Alexander Pope). *Stand* implies resoluteness of spirit: *Actors who can't stand criticism shouldn't perform in public. Abide* and *suffer* suggest the capacity to withstand patiently: *She couldn't abide fools. He suffered their insults in silence. Tolerate,* when applied to something other than pain, connotes reluctant acceptance: *"A decent . . . examination of the acts of government should be not only tolerated, but encouraged"* (William Henry Harrison).

enduring *adjective.* —*See* **continuing, patient, vintage.**

enemy *noun.* —*See* **opponent.**

energetic *adjective.* Possessing, exerting, or displaying energy ▶ active, brisk, driving, dynamic, dynamical, enterprising, forceful, fresh, kinetic, lively, sprightly, spry, strenuous, vigorous, zippy. *Informal:* peppy, snappy. ***Idioms:*** ready (*or* raring) to go. [*Compare* **lusty, strong.**]

✚ **CORE SYNONYMS:** *energetic, active, dynamic, vigorous, lively.* These adjectives mean having or displaying energy. *Energetic* suggests sustained enthusiastic activity: *an energetic competitor. Active* means moving, doing, or functioning: *an active toddler; an active imagination; saw active service in the army. Dynamic* connotes energy and forcefulness that often inspires others: *a dynamic leader. Vigorous* implies healthy strength and robustness: *a vigorous crusader against drunk driving. Lively* suggests animated alertness: *a lively interest in politics.*

energetically *adverb.* —*See* **hard** (1).

energize *verb.* To give or impart vitality and energy to ▶ exhilarate, invigorate, stimulate, vitalize. *Informal:* jazz up, jump-start, pep up. *Slang:* pump up. ***Idioms:*** get the lead out of, light a fire under, put zip into. [*Compare* **fire, inspire, provoke, refresh.**]

energizer *noun.* —*See* **tonic.**

energizing *adjective.* —*See* **invigorating.**

energy *noun.* Capacity for work or vigorous activity ▶ animation, dash, dynamism, force, liveliness, might, potency, power, punch, sprightliness, starch, steam, strength, verve, vibrancy, vigor, vigorousness, vim, vitality. *Informal:* get-up-and-go, go, jump, pep, peppiness, snap, zip. ***Idiom:*** vim and vigor. [*Compare* **spirit.**]

✚ **CORE SYNONYMS:** *energy, strength, power, might, force.* These nouns denote the capacity for work or vigorous activity. *Energy* connotes vitality and intensity: *"The same energy of character which renders a man a daring villain would have rendered him useful to society, had that society been well organized"* (Mary Wollstonecraft). *Strength* refers especially to physical, mental, or moral robustness or vigor: *"enough work to do, and strength enough to do the work"* (Rudyard Kipling). *Power* is the ability to do something and especially to produce an effect: *"I do not think the United States would come to an end if we lost our power to declare an Act of Congress void"* (Oliver Wendell Holmes, Jr.). *Might* often implies abundant or extraordinary power: *"He could defend the island against the whole might of the German Air Force"* (Winston S. Churchill). *Force* is the application of power or strength: *"the overthrow of our institutions by force and violence"* (Charles Evans Hughes).

enervate *verb.* To lessen or deplete the nerve, power, or vitality of ▶ attenuate, debilitate, devitalize, enfeeble, eviscerate, gut, sap, undermine, undo, unnerve, weaken. [*Compare* **deplete, tire.**]

enervated *adjective.* —*See* **lethargic, weak** (1).

enervation *noun.* —*See* **debilitation, lethargy.**

enfeeble *verb.* —*See* **enervate.**

enfeeblement *noun.* —*See* **debilitation.**

enfold *verb.* —*See* **embrace** (1), **wrap** (1), **wrap** (2).

enforce *verb.* To compel observance of ▶ carry out, effect, effectuate, execute, implement, invoke, prosecute. ***Idioms:*** put in force, put into action (*or* effect *or* operation).

enforcement *noun.* Carrying a law or judgment into effect ▶ execution, implementation. [*Compare* **effect, exercise.**]

engage *verb.* **1.** To involve someone in an activity ▶ draw in. [*Compare* **involve.**] **2.** To make busy ▶ busy, employ, occupy. [*Compare* **absorb, involve.**] **3.** To come or bring together and interlock ▶ mesh. [*Compare* **attach, fit[1].**] —*See also* **absorb** (1), **book, contend, employ** (1), **grip, participate, pledge** (1), **pledge** (2).

engaged *adjective.* Pledged to marry ▶ affianced, bespoken, betrothed, intended, pledged, plighted, promised. —*See also* **busy** (1), **concerned.**

engagement *noun.* **1.** An arrangement to appear at a certain time and place ▶ appointment, assignation, commitment, date, rendezvous, tryst. **2.** A commitment, as for a performance by an entertainer ▶ booking, date. *Slang:* gig. **3.** The act or condition of being pledged to marry ▶ betrothal, espousal, troth. **4.** The act or fact of participating ▶ involvement, partaking, participation, sharing. **5.** The act of employing for wages ▶ employment, hire, hiring, retention. —*See also* **absorption** (2), **battle, promise** (1).

✚ **CORE SYNONYMS:** *engagement, appointment, assignation, date, rendezvous, tryst.* These nouns denote an arrangement to appear at a certain time and place: *a business engagement; a dental appointment; a secret assignation; a date to play tennis; a rendezvous of agents at the border; a lovers' tryst.*

---

engaging *adjective.* —*See* **attractive.**

engender *verb.* —*See* **breed, produce** (1).

engineer *verb.* —*See* **conduct** (1), **maneuver** (2).

englut *verb.* —*See* **gulp.**

engorge *verb.* —*See* **gulp, satiate.**

engorgement *noun.* —*See* **satiation.**

engrave *verb.* **1.** To cut a design or inscription into a hard surface, especially for printing ▶ carve, chase, chisel, etch, grave, incise, inscribe. **2.** To produce a deep impression of ▶ etch, fix, grave, impress, imprint, inscribe, stamp. [*Compare* **impress.**]

engross *verb.* —*See* **absorb** (1), **write.**

engrossed *adjective.* —*See* **rapt.**

engrossment *noun.* —*See* **absorption** (2).

engulf *verb.* —*See* **flood** (1), **overwhelm** (2).

enhance *verb.* **1.** To endow with beauty and elegance ▶ beautify, embellish, grace, set off. [*Compare* **adorn.**] **2.** To look good on or with ▶ become, flatter, suit. ***Idiom:*** put in the best light. —*See also* **improve, intensify, supplement.**

enhancement *noun.* Something that is added to another for embellishment or completion ▶ accompaniment, add-on, bells and whistles, complement, enrichment, extra, supplement. [*Compare* **addition, attachment.**] —*See also* **improvement** (1).

enigma *noun.* —*See* **mystery.**

enigmatic *adjective.* —*See* **ambiguous** (1), **mysterious.**

enjoin *verb.* —*See* **command** (1), **forbid.**

enjoy *verb.* To receive pleasure from ▶ appreciate, care for, like, relish, savor. *Informal:* go for, go in for. *Slang:* be into, dig. ***Idioms:*** be big on, be crazy (*or* wild) about, be fond of, get a charge (*or* bang *or* kick) out of, get off on, have a thing about (*or* soft spot for), lap up. [*Compare* **like[1].**] —*See also* **command** (2).

enjoyable *adjective.* —*See* **good** (1), **pleasant.**

enjoyment *noun.* —*See* **amusement, delight.**

enkindle *verb.* —*See* **fire** (1), **light**[1] (1).

enlace *verb.* —*See* **weave.**

enlarge *verb.* —*See* **broaden, elaborate, gain** (1), **increase.**

enlargement *noun.* —*See* **buildup** (2), **increase** (1).

enlighten *verb.* —*See* **illuminate** (2), **inform** (1).

enlightened *adjective.* —*See* **educated, informed.**

enlightening *adjective.* —*See* **cultural, educational** (2).

enlightenment *noun.* The condition of being informed spiritually ▶ edification, illumination. [*Compare* **education.**] —*See also* **culture** (3).

enlist *verb.* —*See* **employ** (1), **join** (1), **mobilize.**

enliven *verb.* **1.** To make lively or animated ▶ animate, brighten, light (up), perk up. **2.** To make alive ▶ animate, quicken, vitalize, vivify. [*Compare* **elate, energize, provoke.**]

enlivening *adjective.* —*See* **invigorating.**

enmesh *verb.* —*See* **catch** (1).

enmeshment *noun.* —*See* **entanglement.**

enmity *noun.* Deep-seated hatred, as between longtime opponents or rivals ▶ animosity, animus, antagonism, antipathy, feud, hostility, ill feeling, ill will, rancor. ***Idioms:*** bad blood, blood feud, hard feelings, no love lost. [*Compare* **despisal, hate, resentment.**]

✚ **CORE SYNONYMS:** *enmity, hostility, antagonism, animosity, rancor, antipathy, animus.* These nouns refer to the feeling or expression of deep-seated ill will. *Enmity* is hatred such as might be felt for an enemy: *the wartime enmity of the two nations. Hostility* implies the clear expression of enmity: *"If we could read the secret history of our enemies, we should find . . . enough to disarm all hostility"* (Henry Wadsworth Longfellow). *Antagonism* is hostility that quickly results in active resistance, opposition, or contentiousness: *"the early struggles of famous authors, the notorious antagonism of publishers and editors to any new writer of exceptional promise"* (Edith Wharton). *Animosity* often triggers bitter resentment or punitive action: *overcame her animosity toward her parents. Rancor* suggests vengeful hatred and resentment: *filled with rancor after losing his job. Antipathy* is deep-seated aversion or repugnance: *an antipathy to social pretension. Animus* is distinctively personal, often based on one's prejudices or temperament: *an inexplicable animus against intellectuals.*

ennoble *verb.* —*See* **distinguish** (3), **exalt.**

ennobled *adjective.* —*See* **exalted.**

ennoblement *noun.* —*See* **exaltation.**

ennui *noun.* —*See* **boredom.**

enormity *noun.* —*See* **outrage, outrageousness.**

enormous *adjective.* Of extraordinary size and power ▶ astronomical, behemoth, Brobdingnagian, Bunyanesque, colossal, cyclopean, elephantine, gargantuan, giant, gigantesque, gigantic, herculean, heroic, huge, immense, jumbo, mammoth, massive, massy, mastodonic, mighty, monstrous, monumental, mountainous, prodigious, pythonic, stupendous, super-size, titanic, tremendous, vast. *Informal:* monster, walloping. *Slang:* humongous, whopping. [*Compare* **big, bulky, grand.**]

✚ **CORE SYNONYMS:** *enormous, immense, huge, gigantic, colossal, mammoth, tremendous, stupendous, gargantuan, vast.* These adjectives describe what is of extraordinary size and power. *Enormous* suggests a marked excess beyond the norm in size, amount, or degree: *an enormous boulder. Immense* refers to boundless or immeasurable size or extent: *immense pleasure. Huge* especially implies greatness of size or capacity: *a huge success. Gigantic* refers to size likened to that of a giant: *a gigantic redwood tree. Colossal* suggests a hugeness that elicits awe or taxes belief: *a colossal ancient temple. Mammoth* is applied to something of unwieldy hugeness: *"mammoth stone figures in . . . buckled eighteenth-century pumps, the very soles of which seem mountainously tall"* (Cynthia Ozick). *Tremendous* suggests awe-inspiring or fearsome size: *ate a tremendous meal. Stupendous* implies size that astounds or defies description: *"The whole thing was a stupendous, incomprehensible farce"* (W. Somerset Maugham). *Gargantuan* especially stresses greatness of capacity, as for food or pleasure: *a gargantuan appetite. Vast* refers to greatness of extent, size, area, or scope: *"Of creatures, how few vast as the whale"* (Herman Melville).

---

enormousness *noun.* The quality of being enormous ▶ hugeness, immenseness, immensity, monumentality, prodigiousness, stupendousness, tremendousness, vastness. [*Compare* **bulk, size.**]

enough *adjective.* —*See* **sufficient.**

enough *pronoun.* An adequate quantity ▶ adequacy, sufficiency.

enounce *verb.* —*See* **assert, pronounce.**

enquire *verb. See* **inquire.**

enquirer *noun. See* **inquirer.**

enquiring *adjective. See* **inquiring.**

enquiry *noun. See* **inquiry.**

enrage *verb.* —*See* **anger** (1).

enrapture *verb.* To have a powerful emotional effect on someone ▶ carry away, electrify, excite, ravish, thrill, transport. *Slang:* send. [*Compare* **charm, delight.**]

✣ **CORE SYNONYMS:** *enrapture, ravish, thrill, transport.* These verbs mean to have a powerful, agreeable, and often overwhelming emotional effect on someone: *concertgoers who were enraptured by the music; a painting that ravished the eye; thrilled by their success; transported with joy.*

---

enraptured *adjective.* —*See* **infatuated.**

enrich *verb.* **1.** To lend dignity or honor to by an act or favor ▶ favor, grace, dignify, honor. [*Compare* **distinguish, exalt, honor.**] **2.** To make fertile ▶ fecundate, fertilize, pollinate. [*Compare* **impregnate.**] —*See also* **improve, supplement.**

enrichment *noun.* —*See* **enhancement.**

enroll *verb.* —*See* **join** (1), **list[1].**

ensanguine *verb.* To cover with blood ▶ bloodstain, bloody, incarnadine.

ensconce *verb.* —*See* **establish** (1), **hide[1].**

ensemble *noun.* —*See* **dress** (2).

enshrine *verb.* —*See* **devote.**

enshroud *verb.* —*See* **conceal, wrap** (2).

ensign *noun.* —*See* **flag[1].**

enslave *verb.* To make subservient or subordinate ▶ dominate, enthrall, indenture, make tributary, subject, subjugate, subordinate, take captive. [*Compare* **defeat.**]

enslavement *noun.* —*See* **slavery.**

ensnare *verb.* —*See* **catch** (1).

ensnarement *noun.* —*See* **entanglement.**

ensnarl *verb.* —*See* **catch** (1), **entangle.**

ensue *verb.* To occur as a consequence ▶ attend, follow, result. [*Compare* **stem.**] —*See also* **follow** (1).

ensuing *adjective.* —*See* **following.**

ensure *verb.* —*See* **guarantee** (2).

entail *verb.* To have as a condition or a consequence ▶ carry, involve. —*See also* **demand** (2), **imply.**

entangle *verb.* To twist together so that separation is difficult ▶ ensnarl, foul, mat, snarl, tangle. [*Compare* **weave.**] —*See also* **catch** (1), **complicate.**

entanglement *noun.* The condition of being entangled or implicated ▶ embranglement, embroilment, enmeshment, ensnarement, implication, involvement. —*See also* **tangle.**

entente *noun.* —*See* **combination, treaty.**

enter *verb.* **1.** To come or go into a place ▶ come in, go in, penetrate. ***Idioms:*** gain admittance (*or* entrance *or* entry), make an entrance, set foot in, walk through the door **2.** To gain entry into a computer network or database ▶ access, log in (*or* on). gain access (*or* admittance *or* entry), get connected. —*See also* **join** (1), **list**[1], **penetrate, start** (1).

enter into *verb.* —*See* **participate.**

enterprise *noun.* Something undertaken, especially something requiring extensive planning and work ▶ endeavor, project, undertaking, venture. [*Compare* **task.**] —*See also* **adventure, business** (1), **company** (1), **drive** (2).

enterprising *adjective.* —*See* **adventurous, ambitious, energetic.**

entertain *verb.* To receive an idea and think about it in order to form an opinion about it ▶ consider, hear of, think about (of). —*See also* **amuse, bear** (2), **ponder.**

entertaining *adjective.* —*See* **pleasant.**

entertainment *noun.* —*See* **amusement.**

enthrall *verb.* —*See* **charm** (2), **enslave, grip.**

enthralling *adjective.* —*See* **seductive.**

enthrallment *noun.* —*See* **absorption** (2).

enthuse *verb.* —*See* **rave.**

enthusiasm *noun.* **1.** Passionate devotion to or interest in a cause or subject ▶ ardency, ardor, eagerness, excitation, excitement, fanaticism, fervor, fever, fire, passion, verve, vigor, zeal, zealousness. [*Compare* **passion.**] **2.** A subject or activity that inspires lively interest ▶ craze, fad, fancy, hobbyhorse, infatuation, mania, passion, rage. [*Compare* **fashion, obsession.**] —*See also* **optimism.**

enthusiast *noun.* —*See* **devotee, fan**[2]**.**

enthusiastic *adjective.* Showing or having enthusiasm ▶ ardent, exuberant, fanatic, fanatical, fervent, fervid, keen, mad, obsessive, rabid, warm, zealous. *Informal:* crazy, gaga, wild. *Slang:* cuckoo, gung ho, nuts. [*Compare* **extreme, passionate.**] —*See also* **optimistic.**

entice *verb.* —*See* **attract, seduce.**

enticement *noun.* —*See* **attraction, lure** (1).

enticer *noun.* —*See* **seducer** (1).

enticing *adjective.* —*See* **attractive, desirable, seductive.**

entire *adjective.* —*See* **complete** (1), **good** (2).

entirely *adverb.* —*See* **completely** (1).

entirety *noun.* —*See* **completeness, whole.**

entitle *verb.* —*See* **authorize, name** (1).

entitlement *noun.* —*See* **license** (1), **right.**

entity *noun.* —*See* **existence, system, thing** (1).

entomb *verb.* —*See* **bury.**

entombment *noun.* —*See* **burial.**

entourage *noun.* —*See* **retinue.**

entrails *noun.* —*See* **viscera.**

entrance[1] *noun.* The act of entering ▶ entry, incoming, ingress, ingression, penetration. —*See also* **admission.**

entrance[2] *verb.* —*See* **charm** (1), **charm** (2).

entrancing *adjective.* —*See* **seductive.**

entrap *verb.* —*See* **catch** (1).

entreat *verb.* —*See* **appeal** (1).

entreaty *noun.* —*See* **appeal.**

entrée *noun.* —*See* **admission.**

entrench *verb.* —*See* **fix** (2).

entrenched *adjective.* —*See* **confirmed** (1).

entrenchment *noun.* —*See* **trespass** (2).

entrepreneur *noun.* —*See* **dealer.**

entrust *verb.* **1.** To put in the charge of another for care, use, or performance ▶ commend, commit, confide, consign, delegate, give (over), hand over, relegate, remand, remit, trust, turn over. ***Idioms:*** give in trust (*or* charge), give (*or* put) into custody. **2.** To place a trust upon ▶ charge, trust. [*Compare* **authorize.**]

✦ **CORE SYNONYMS:** *entrust, confide, commit, consign, delegate.* These verbs mean to put something in the charge of another for care, use, or performance: *The task was too dangerous to be entrusted to a child. He confided her plans to her family. The troops were committed to the general's charge. The owner consigned the paintings to a dealer for sale. She delegated the assignments to the junior members of the staff.*

entry *noun.* An item inserted, as in a diary, register, or reference book ▶ heading, headword, insertion, item, lemma, minute, note, posting, record. —*See also* **admission, entrance[1].**

entwine *verb.* —*See* **weave, wind[2].**

enumerate *verb.* To name or specify one by one ▶ count off, inventory, itemize, list, numerate, tick off. —*See also* **count** (2).

enumeration *noun.* —*See* **count** (1).

enunciate *verb.* —*See* **assert, pronounce.**

enunciation *noun.* —*See* **voicing.**

envelop *verb.* —*See* **enclose** (2), **wrap** (1), **wrap** (2).

envelope *noun.* —*See* **wrapper.**

envenom *verb.* —*See* **poison.**

envious *adjective.* Resentfully or painfully desirous of another's advantages ▶ begrudging, covetous, grudging, invidious, jaundiced, jealous. ***Idiom:*** green with envy.

enviousness *noun.* —*See* **envy.**

environ *verb.* —*See* **surround.**

environment *noun.* **1.** A surrounding area ▶ environs, locale, locality, neighborhood, precincts, purlieu, surroundings, vicinity. [*Compare* **limits, outskirts.**] **2.** The surrounding conditions and circumstances affecting growth or development ▶ ambiance, atmosphere, climate, context, medium, milieu, mise en scène, surroundings, world. **3.** The ecological circumstances in which organisms live ▶ biome, biosphere, ecosphere, ecosystem, habitat, natural world, nature, world. [*Compare* **habitat, universe.**] —*See also* **conditions.**

environs *noun.* —*See* **environment** (1), **outskirts.**

envisage *verb.* —*See* **imagine.**

envision *verb.* —*See* **foresee, imagine.**

envoy[1] *noun.* —*See* **messenger, representative.**

envoy[2] *noun.* —*See* **end** (2).

envy *noun.* Resentful or painful desire for another's advantages ▶ covetousness, enviousness, green-eyed monster, jaundice, jealousy. [*Compare* **resentment.**]

envy *verb.* To feel envy toward or for ▶ begrudge, covet, grudge.

✦ **CORE SYNONYMS:** *envy, begrudge, covet.* These verbs mean to feel resentful or painful desire for another's advantages or possessions. *Envy,* the most general, combines discontent, resentment, and desire: *"When I peruse the conquered fame of heroes and the victories of mighty generals, I do not envy the generals"* (Walt Whitman). *Begrudge* stresses ill will and reluctance to acknowledge another's right or claim: *Why begrudge him his success? Covet* stresses a secret or culpable longing for something to which one has no right: *"We hate no people and covet no people's lands"* (Wendell L. Willkie).

enwrap *verb.* —*See* **wrap** (2).

eon *or* **aeon** *noun.* —*See* **ages.**

ephemeral *adjective.* —*See* **transitory.**

epicene *adjective.* —*See* **androgynous, effeminate.**

epicenism *noun.* The quality of being androgynous ▶ androgyny, gender-neutrality, sexlessness. [*Compare* **effeminacy, masculinity.**]

epicure *noun.* —*See* **sybarite.**

epicurean *adjective.* **1.** Characterized by or devoted to pleasure and luxury as a lifestyle ▶ hedonic, hedonistic, sybaritic, voluptuary, voluptuous. [*Compare*

luxurious, sensual.] **2.** Relating to, suggestive of, or appealing to sense gratification ▶ sensual, sensuous, sensualistic, voluptuous.

epicurean *noun.* —*See* **sybarite.**

epidemic *noun.* —*See* **eruption.**

epidemic *adjective.* —*See* **prevailing.**

epidermis *noun.* The tissue forming the external covering of the body ▶ integument, skin.

epigrammatic *or* **epigrammatical** *adjective.* —*See* **pithy.**

epilogue *noun.* —*See* **end** (2).

episcopal *adjective.* —*See* **clerical.**

episode *noun.* —*See* **circumstance** (1), **event** (1).

episodic *adjective.* Happening or appearing consistently or repeatedly ▶ recurrent, regular, repeating, repetitive. [*Compare* **periodic, pervasive, thematic.**] —*See also* **intermittent.**

epistle *noun.* —*See* **letter.**

epithet *noun.* —*See* **name** (1), **swearword.**

epitome *noun.* An ideally representative example of a type ▶ archetype, exemplar, mirror, model, paragon, pattern, prototype. [*Compare* **model.**] —*See also* **synopsis.**

epitomize *verb.* —*See* **represent** (1), **review** (1).

epizoic *adjective.* —*See* **parasitic.**

epoch *noun.* —*See* **age** (2).

equable *adjective.* —*See* **unchanging.**

equal *adjective.* Agreeing exactly in value, quantity, or effect ▶ coequal, equipollent, equivalent, even, identical, same, tantamount. ***Idioms:*** on a par, one and the same. [*Compare* **like**[2].] —*See also* **eligible, fair**[1] (1).

equal *noun.* —*See* **peer**[2].

equal *verb.* **1.** To be equal or alike ▶ amount, be equivalent, be tantamount, compare, constitute, correspond, match, measure up, parallel, touch. *Informal:* stack up. ***Idioms:*** be one and the same as, have all the earmarks of, keep pace with. [*Compare* **resemble.**] **2.** To do or make something equal to ▶ match, meet, tie.

equality *noun.* —*See* **equivalence.**

equalize *verb.* To make equal ▶ align, democratize, equate, even, level (off), square, symmetrize. ***Idiom:*** put in line. [*Compare* **conventionalize, even**[1].] —*See also* **balance** (1).

equanimity *noun.* —*See* **balance** (2).

equate *verb.* —*See* **equalize, liken.**

equation *noun.* —*See* **equivalence.**

equidistant *adjective.* —*See* **central.**

equilibrium *noun.* —*See* **balance** (1).

equip *verb.* —*See* **furnish.**

equipment *noun.* —*See* **device** (1), **outfit.**

equipoise *noun.* —*See* **balance** (1).

equipollent *adjective.* —*See* **equal.**

equitable *adjective.* —*See* **fair**[1] (1).

equitableness *noun.* —*See* **fairness.**

equitably *adverb.* —*See* **fairly** (1).

equity *noun.* The state, action, or principle of treating all persons equally in accordance with the law ▶ due process, justice. [*Compare* **fairness.**]

equivalence *noun.* The state of being equivalent ▶ coequality, equality, equation, equivalency, par, parity, sameness. [*Compare* **likeness, sameness.**]

equivalency *noun.* —*See* **equivalence.**

equivalent *adjective.* —*See* **equal, like**[2], **proportional** (1).

equivalent *noun.* One that has the same functions and characteristics as another ▶ counterpart, opposite number, vis-à-vis. —*See also* **peer**[2].

equivocal *adjective.* Deliberately ambiguous or vague ▶ elusive, evasive, indirect, misleading. —*See also* **ambiguous** (1), **ambiguous** (2), **shady** (1).

equivocality *or* **equivocalness** *noun.* —*See* **ambiguity, vagueness.**

equivocate *verb.* **1.** To use evasive or deliberately vague language ▶ euphemize, fence, hedge, shuffle, tergiversate, weasel. *Informal:* pussyfoot, waffle. ***Idioms:*** beat about (*or* around) the bush, give one the runaround, hem and haw, mince words. [*Compare*

evade.] **2.** To stray from truthfulness or sincerity ▶ palter, prevaricate, shuffle. ***Idioms:*** bend (*or* stretch) the truth. [*Compare* **distort, lie²**.]

equivocation *noun.* The use or an instance of equivocal language ▶ ambiguity, distortion, equivoque, euphemism, fence, hedge, misrepresentation, prevarication, shuffle, tergiversation, weasel word. *Informal:* waffle. ***Idiom:*** hemming and hawing. [*Compare* **lie²**.] —*See also* **ambiguity.**

era *noun.* —*See* **age** (2).

eradicate *verb.* —*See* **annihilate, eliminate.**

eradication *noun.* —*See* **annihilation, elimination.**

erase *verb.* —*See* **annihilate, cancel** (1).

erasure *noun.* The act of erasing or the condition of being erased ▶ cancellation, deletion, effacement, expunction, obliteration.

erect *adjective.* —*See* **rigid.**

erect *verb.* To raise upright ▶ pitch, put up, raise, rear, set up, upraise, uprear. —*See also* **build.**

erector *noun.* —*See* **builder.**

eristic *adjective.* —*See* **argumentative.**

erode *verb.* To reduce gradually, as by chemical reaction, weather, or friction ▶ abrade, bite (into), consume, corrode, eat (away *or* into), gnaw (away *or* down), grind (away *or* down), wear (away *or* down). [*Compare* **decay, disintegrate.**]

erogenous *adjective.* —*See* **erotic.**

erotic *adjective.* Concerning or arousing sexual love or desire ▶ amatory, amorous, aphrodisiac, erogenous, libidinal, lascivious, salacious, sensual, sensuous, sexual, sexy, sizzling, spicy, steamy, suggestive. *Slang:* hot. [*Compare* **lascivious, desirable, obscene.**]

eroticism *noun.* The quality of being erotic ▶ amorousness, lasciviousness, salaciousness, sensualism, sensuality, sensuousness, sexuality, sexiness, suggestiveness. *Slang:* sizzle. [*Compare* **obscenity, sensuality.**] —*See also* **desire** (2), **sensuality** (1).

erotism *noun.* —*See* **desire** (2).

err *verb.* To make an error or mistake ▶ blunder, lapse, miscue, mistake, slip (up), stumble, trip (up). *Informal:* fluff. *Slang:* goof (up), screw up. ***Idioms:*** get (*or* start) off on the wrong foot, go astray (*or* awry), take a wrong step. [*Compare* **blunder, botch.**] —*See also* **offend** (3).

errand *noun.* —*See* **mission** (1).

errant *adjective.* **1.** Traveling about, especially in search of adventure ▶ itinerant, rambling, roaming, roving, wandering. [*Compare* **nomadic.**] **2.** Straying from a proper course or standard ▶ aberrant, deviant, erring, stray. ***Idioms:*** far afield, wide of (*or* off) the mark. [*Compare* **abnormal, wrong.**] —*See also* **aimless.**

erratic *adjective.* Without a fixed or regular course ▶ devious, stray, uncontrolled, unfixed, unstable, wandering, wayward. —*See also* **capricious, eccentric, uneven.**

erratum *noun.* —*See* **error.**

erring *adjective.* —*See* **errant** (2).

erroneous *adjective.* Containing an error or errors ▶ corrupt, fallacious, false, faulty, inaccurate, incorrect, mistaken, off, unsound, untrue, wrong. ***Idioms:*** all wet, in error, off base, off (*or* wide of) the mark.

error *noun.* An unintentional deviation from what is correct, right, or true ▶ erratum, false step, inaccuracy, incorrectness, lapse, miscue, miss, misstep, mistake, omission, oversight, slip, slip-up, trip. [*Compare* **blunder, defect, mess.**] —*See also* **fallacy** (1).

errorless *adjective.* —*See* **accurate.**

ersatz *noun.* —*See* **copy** (2).

ersatz *adjective.* —*See* **artificial** (1), **counterfeit.**

erstwhile *adverb.* —*See* **earlier** (1).

erstwhile *adjective.* —*See* **late** (2).

eruct *verb.* —*See* **erupt.**

erudite *adjective.* —*See* **educated.**

erudition *noun.* —*See* **education** (2).

erupt *verb.* To send forth confined matter violently ▶ belch, disgorge, eject, eruct, expel, spew, vomit. [*Compare* **pour, spurt.**] —*See also* **break out.**

eruption *noun.* A sudden emergence or increase ▶ breakout, burst, epidemic, explosion, flare, flare-up, irruption, outbreak, outburst, paroxysm, plague, rash, surge. —*See also* **blast** (2), **outburst.**

escalate *verb.* —*See* **increase, intensify.**

escalation *noun.* —*See* **increase** (1).

escapade *noun.* —*See* **adventure.**

escape *verb.* **1.** To break loose and leave suddenly, as from confinement or a difficult situation ▶ abscond, bail out, break out, decamp, flee, fly, get away, run away. *Informal:* make off, skip (out). *Slang:* lam. *Chiefly Regional:* absquatulate. ***Idioms:*** cut and run, blow (*or* fly) the coop, get clear of, give someone the slip, make a getaway, make good one's escape, make oneself scarce, skip town, take flight, take it on the lam, wriggle off the hook. [*Compare* **evade.**] **2.** To fail to be fixed by the mind, memory, or senses of ▶ elude, evade. ***Idiom:*** slip away from. [*Compare* **forget.**] —*See also* **avoid.**

escape *noun.* **1.** The act or an instance of escaping, as from confinement or difficulty ▶ break, breakout, decampment, escapement, flight, getaway. *Slang:* lam. [*Compare* **rescue.**] **2.** The act, an instance, or a means of avoiding ▶ avoidance, bypass, circumvention, evasion. [*Compare* **prevention.**]

escaped *adjective.* Fleeing or having fled, as from confinement or the police ▶ fugitive, fleeing, runaway. ***Idioms:*** on the lam (*or* loose *or* run).

escapee *noun.* One who flees, as from confinement or the police ▶ fugitive, outlaw, refugee, runaway. [*Compare* **criminal.**]

escapement *noun.* —*See* **escape** (1).

eschew *verb.* —*See* **avoid.**

escort *noun.* —*See* **guide.**

escort *verb.* —*See* **accompany, guide.**

esculent *adjective.* Fit to be eaten ▶ comestible, eatable, edible, palatable.

esoteric *adjective.* —*See* **deep** (2), **mysterious, obscure** (1).

especial *adjective.* —*See* **exceptional, special.**

espial *noun.* —*See* **notice** (1).

espousal *noun.* The act or condition of being pledged to marry ▶ betrothal, engagement, troth. —*See also* **acceptance** (1), **wedding.**

espouse *verb.* —*See* **adopt, marry.**

esprit *or* **esprit de corps** *noun.* A strong sense of enthusiasm and dedication to a common goal that unites a group ▶ esprit de corps, group spirit, morale, team spirit. [*Compare* **confidence, mood.**] —*See also* **spirit** (1).

espy *verb.* —*See* **see** (1).

essay *noun.* A relatively brief discourse written especially as an exercise ▶ composition, paper, theme. —*See also* **attempt, discourse, test** (1).

essay *verb.* —*See* **attempt, test** (1).

essence *noun.* A basic trait or set of traits that define and establish the character of something ▶ being, essentiality, grain, nature, quiddity, quintessence, sine qua non, substance, texture. [*Compare* **element.**] —*See also* **fragrance, heart** (1).

essential *adjective.* **1.** Incapable of being dispensed with ▶ critical, indispensable, necessary, needed, needful, prerequisite, required, requisite. [*Compare* **required.**] **2.** Constituting or forming part of the essence of something ▶ basic, constitutional, constitutive, fundamental, integral, quintessential, vital. [*Compare* **primary.**] —*See also* **elemental.**

essential *noun.* —*See* **condition** (2), **element** (1).

✚ **CORE SYNONYMS:** *essential, indispensable, necessary, needful, requisite.* These adjectives apply to something that is incapable of being dispensed with: *funds essential to completing the* *project; foods indispensable to good nutrition; necessary tools and materials; provided them with all things needful; lacking the requisite qualifications.*

essentiality *noun.* —*See* **essence.**

essentially *adverb.* In regard to the essence of a matter ▶ basically, fundamentally, underlyingly. ***Idioms:*** at bottom (*or* heart *or* root), at the end of the day, in essence, when all is said and done.

establish *verb.* **1.** To place securely in a position or condition ▶ ensconce, fix, install, invest, seat, set (up), settle. **2.** To put in force or cause to be by legal authority ▶ constitute, enact, institute, legislate, legitimate, make, ordain, promulgate. [*Compare* **confirm, legalize.**] —*See also* **base[1], found, govern, prove.**

established *adjective.* —*See* **accepted, confirmed** (1).

establishment *noun.* —*See* **company** (1), **foundation.**

establishmentarian *adjective.* —*See* **conventional.**

estate *noun.* —*See* **conditions, holdings, land, villa.**

esteem *noun.* A feeling of deference, approval, and liking ▶ account, admiration, appreciation, consideration, estimation, favor, honor, regard, respect. [*Compare* **adoration, honor.**] —*See also* **acceptance** (2).

esteem *verb.* —*See* **regard, value.**

✦ **CORE SYNONYMS:** *esteem, regard, admiration, respect.* These nouns refer to a feeling of deference, approval, and liking. *Esteem* connotes considered appraisal: *"The near-unanimity of esteem he enjoyed during his lifetime has by no means been sustained since"* (Will Crutchfield). *Regard* is the most general: *"I once thought you had a kind of regard for her"* (George Borrow). *Admiration* is a feeling of keen approbation: *"Greatness is a spiritual condition worthy to excite love, interest, and admiration"* (Matthew Arnold). *Respect* implies appreciative, often deferential regard resulting from careful assessment: *"I have a great respect for any man who makes his own way in life"* (Winston Churchill).

estimable *adjective.* —*See* **admirable.**

estimate *verb.* **1.** To make a judgment as to the worth or value of ▶ appraise, assay, assess, calculate, evaluate, gauge, judge, rate, size up, valuate, value, weigh. ***Idiom:*** take the measure of. [*Compare* **regard, test.**] **2.** To calculate approximately ▶ approximate, place, put, reckon, set. *Informal:* guesstimate. [*Compare* **predict.**]

estimate *noun.* **1.** The act or result of evaluating or appraising ▶ appraisal, appraisement, assessment, estimation, evaluation, judgment, valuation. **2.** A rough or tentative calculation ▶ approximation, estimation. *Informal:* guesstimate. ***Idioms:*** ballpark figure, educated guess, rough measure. [*Compare* **guess.**] —*See also* **belief** (1).

✦ **CORE SYNONYMS:** *estimate, appraise, assess, assay, evaluate, rate.* These verbs mean to form a judgment as to the worth of value of something. *Estimate* usually implies a subjective and somewhat inexact judgment: *difficult to estimate the possible results in advance. Appraise* stresses expert judgment: *appraised the works of art. Assess* implies authoritative judgment in setting a monetary value on something as a basis for taxation: *assessing real estate for investors. Assay* refers to careful examination, especially to chemical analysis of an ore: *will assay the ingot.* In extended senses *appraise, assess,* and *assay* can refer to any critical analysis: *appraised his character; will assess the impact of higher taxes; assaying the idea's merit. Evaluate* implies considered judgment in ascertaining value: *evaluating a student's thesis for content and organization. Rate* involves determining the rank or grade of someone or something in relation to others: *rated the restaurant higher than any other in the city.*

estimation *noun.* —*See* **belief** (1), **esteem, estimate** (1), **estimate** (2).

estrange *verb.* To make distant, hostile, or unsympathetic ▶ alienate, antagonize, come between, disaffect, distance, disunite, drive away. *Slang:* turn off. ***Idioms:*** set at odds, turn against one. [*Compare* **divide.**]

✦ **CORE SYNONYMS:** *estrange, alienate, disaffect.* These verbs mean to make another person distant, hostile, or unsympathetic. *Estrange* and *alienate* are often used with reference to two persons whose harmonious relationship has been replaced by hostility or indifference: *Political disagreements led to quarrels that finally estranged the two friends. His persistent antagonism alienated his wife. Disaffect* usually implies discontent, ill will, and disloyalty within the membership of a group: *Colonists were disaffected by the royal governor's actions.*

estrangement *noun.* —*See* **breach** (2).

estuary *noun.* —*See* **inlet, river.**

etceteras *noun.* —*See* **odds and ends.**

etch *verb.* —*See* **engrave** (1), **engrave** (2).

eternal *adjective.* Existing unchanged forever ▶ ageless, timeless. [*Compare* **endless.**] —*See also* **continual, endless** (2).

eternality *or* **eternalness** *noun.* —*See* **endlessness.**

eternalize *verb.* To cause to last endlessly ▶ eternize, immortalize, perpetuate. ***Idioms:*** cast (*or* etch *or* fix *or* set) in stone. [*Compare* **honor, memorialize.**]

eternally *adverb.* —*See* **forever.**

eterne *adjective.* —*See* **endless** (2).

eternity *noun.* **1.** The totality of time without beginning or end ▶ infinity, perpetuity, sempiternity. [*Compare* **forever.**] **2.** A place or state beyond death ▶ afterworld, empyrean, far shore, great beyond, happy hunting ground, heaven, hereafter, nirvana, paradise, Valhalla. —*See also* **ages, endlessness, immortality.**

eternize *verb.* To cause to last endlessly ▶ eternalize, immortalize, perpetuate. ***Idioms:*** cast (*or* etch *or* fix *or* set) in stone. [*Compare* **honor, memorialize.**]

ether *noun.* The gaseous mixture enveloping the earth ▶ air, atmosphere.

ethereal *adjective.* —*See* **immaterial, sheer**[2]**.**

ethic *noun.* —*See* **ethics** (2).

ethical *adjective.* In accordance with principles of right or good conduct ▶ conscientious, humane, moral, principled, proper, right, righteous, rightful, right-minded, scrupulous, virtuous, upright. [*Compare* **frank, honest.**]

✦ **CORE SYNONYMS:** *ethical, moral, virtuous, righteous.* These adjectives mean in accordance with principles of right or good conduct. *Ethical* stresses idealistic standards of right and wrong: *"Ours is a world of nuclear giants and ethical infants"* (Omar N. Bradley). *Moral* applies to personal character and behavior, especially sexual conduct: *"Our moral sense dictates a clearcut preference for these societies which share with us an abiding respect for individual human rights"* (Jimmy Carter). *Virtuous* implies moral excellence and loftiness of character: *"The life of the nation is secure only while the nation is honest, truthful, and virtuous"* (Frederick Douglass). *Righteous* emphasizes moral uprightness; when it is applied to actions, reactions, or impulses, it often implies justifiable outrage: *"He was . . . stirred by righteous wrath"* (John Galsworthy).

ethicality *or* **ethicalness** *noun.* —*See* **ethics** (1).

ethics *noun.* **1.** The quality of being in accord with standards of conduct ▶ ethicality, ethicalness, morality, propriety, rectitude, righteousness, rightness. **2.** A set of principles of right conduct ▶ ethic, morality, morals, mores, principles, standards.

ethos *noun.* —*See* **culture** (2), **psychology.**

etiolate *verb.* —*See* **pale.**

etiquette *noun.* —*See* **ceremony** (2), **manners.**

eulogistic *adjective.* —*See* **complimentary** (1).

eulogize *verb.* —*See* **honor** (1).

eulogy *noun.* —*See* **praise** (1).

euphemism *noun.* —*See* **equivocation.**

euphemize *verb.* —*See* **equivocate** (1).

euphonious *or* **euphonic** *adjective.* —*See* **melodious.**

euphoria *noun.* —*See* **elation.**

euphoric *adjective.* —*See* **elated.**

evacuant *adjective.* —*See* **eliminative.**

evacuate *verb.* —*See* **empty, retreat.**

evacuation *noun.* —*See* **retreat.**

evacuative *adjective.* —*See* **eliminative.**

evade *verb.* **1.** To avoid fulfilling or answering completely ▶ dodge, duck, fence, hedge, sidestep, skirt. ***Idioms:*** weasel out of, wiggle (*or* wriggle *or* worm) one's way out of. [*Compare* **maneuver, equivocate, escape.**] **2.** To fail to be fixed by the mind, memory, or senses of ▶ elude, escape. ***Idiom:*** slip away from. [*Compare* **forget.**] —*See also* **avoid, lose** (3).

evaluate *verb.* —*See* **estimate** (1), **test** (1).

evaluation *noun.* —*See* **estimate** (1), **test** (1).

evanesce *verb.* —*See* **disappear** (1).

evanescence *noun.* —*See* **disappearance.**

evanescent *adjective.* —*See* **transitory.**

evangelism *noun.* —*See* **propaganda.**

evangelist *noun.* A person doing religious or charitable work in a foreign country ▶ apostle, missionary, missioner. [*Compare* **cleric, representative.**] —*See also* **propagandist.**

evangelize *verb.* To deliver a sermon, especially as a vocation ▶ preach, sermonize. [*Compare* **address, moralize.**]

evaporate *verb.* To turn into vapor, especially when heated ▶ boil away, burn off, fume, steam, sublimate, sublime, vaporize, volatilize. —*See also* **disappear** (1), **drain** (1).

evaporation *noun.* —*See* **disappearance.**

evasion *noun.* —*See* **escape** (2).

evasive *adjective.* **1.** Inclined or intended to evade ▶ elusive, fugitive, slippery. [*Compare* **slick, underhand.**] **2.** Deliberately ambiguous or vague ▶ elusive, equivocal, indirect, misleading. [*Compare* **ambiguous.**]

eve *noun.* —*See* **evening.**

even *adjective.* **1.** Having no irregularities, roughness, or indentations ▶ flat, flush, level, mirrorlike, planar, plane, smooth, straight, unruffled, unwrinkled. [*Compare* **glossy.**] **2.** On the same plane or line ▶ coplanar, flush, in line, level, square, uniplanar. **3.** Owing or being owed nothing ▶ quit, quits, square. *Informal:* even-steven. **4.** Neither favorable nor unfavorable ▶ balanced, fifty-fifty, nip and tuck. **5.** Being an exact amount or number ▶ exact. ***Idioms:*** on the button (*or* money *or* nose). —*See also* **calm, equal, fair[1]** (1), **gradual** (2), **unchanging.**

even *adverb.* **1.** To a more extreme degree ▶ ever more so, still, yet. **2.** Not just this but also ▶ a fortiori, indeed, moreover, yea. ***Idioms:*** all the more, not to mention, what is more. —*See also* **exactly.**

even *verb.* To make even, smooth, or level ▶ align, flat, flatten, flush, level, plane, relax, roll (out), smooth, steamroll, steamroller, straighten. —*See also* **balance** (1), **equalize.**

✚ **CORE SYNONYMS:** *even, flat, level, plane, smooth, flush.* These adjectives describe surfaces without irregularities, roughness, or indentations: *Even* refers to flat surfaces in which no part is higher or lower than another: *the even surface of the mirror. Flat* applies to surfaces without curves, protuberances, or indentations: *a flat rock. Level* implies being parallel with the line of the horizon: *acres of level farmland. Plane* is a mathematical term referring to a surface containing all the straight lines connecting any two points on it: *a plane figure. Smooth* describes a surface on which the absence of irregularities can be established by sight or touch: *smooth marble. Flush* applies to a surface that is on an exact level with an adjoining one: *a door that is flush with the wall.*

---

evenhanded *adjective.* —*See* **fair**[1] (1).

evenhandedly *adverb.* —*See* **fairly** (1).

evenhandedness *noun.* —*See* **fairness.**

evening *noun.* The period between afternoon and nighttime ▶ dusk, eve, eventide, gloaming, nightfall, sundown, sunset, twilight. ***Idiom:*** close of day.

event *noun.* **1.** Something significant that happens ▶ circumstance, development, episode, happening, incident, news, phenomenon, occasion, occurrence, thing. ***Idioms:*** something to write home about, turn of events. **2.** Something demonstrated to exist or known to have existed ▶ actuality, fact, phenomenon, reality. ***Idioms:*** hard (*or* cold *or* plain) fact. [*Compare* **information.**] —*See also* **circumstance** (1), **competition** (2), **effect** (1).

even-tempered *adjective.* —*See* **calm.**

eventide *noun.* —*See* **evening.**

eventual *adjective.* —*See* **future.**

eventuality *noun.* —*See* **possibility** (1).

eventually *adverb.* —*See* **ultimately** (1).

everlasting *adjective.* —*See* **continual, endless** (2).

everlastingly *adverb.* —*See* **forever.**

everlastingness *noun.* —*See* **endlessness, immortality.**

evermore *adverb.* —*See* **forever.**

everyday *adjective.* Of or suitable for ordinary days or routine occasions ▶ casual, daily, quotidian, workaday, workday. [*Compare* **ordinary.**] —*See also* **common** (1).

everyday *noun.* —*See* **usual.**

everything *noun.* —*See* **whole.**

evict *verb.* —*See* **eject** (1).

eviction *noun.* —*See* **ejection.**

evidence *noun.* —*See* **confirmation** (2), **sign** (1).

evidence *verb.* To demonstrate and clarify with examples ▶ demonstrate, exemplify, illustrate, instance. [*Compare* **explain.**] —*See also* **confirm** (1), **prove, show** (1).

evident *adjective.* —*See* **apparent** (1).

evidently *adverb.* —*See* **apparently.**

evil *adjective.* Morally objectionable ▶ bad, black, dark, immoral, iniquitous, peccant, reprobate, sinful, vicious, wicked, wrong. [*Compare* **corrupt, sordid.**] —*See also* **fateful** (1), **harmful, malevolent.**

evil *noun.* **1.** The quality or state of being morally bad or objectionable ▶ iniquity, peccancy, sin, vice, wickedness, wrong. [*Compare* **corruption, malevolence.**] **2.** Whatever is destructive or harmful ▶ bad, badness, ill, worse. [*Compare* **harm.**] —*See also* **crime** (2), **curse** (3).

evildoer *noun.* One that performs evil acts ▶ miscreant, scoundrel, sinner, villain, wrongdoer. *Informal:* baddie, bad guy. *Slang:* black hat. [*Compare* **criminal, fiend, rascal.**]

evildoing *noun.* —*See* **crime** (2).

evil eye *noun.* Something or someone believed to bring bad luck ▶ curse, hex, hoodoo, Jonah. *Informal:* jinx. [*Compare* **charm, magic.**]

evince *verb.* —*See* **show** (1).

eviscerate *verb.* —*See* **enervate.**

evocative *adjective.* Tending to bring a memory, mood, or image, for example, subtly or indirectly to mind ▶ allusive, connotative, impressionistic, reminiscent, suggestive. [*Compare* **designative, symbolic.**]

evoke *verb.* To bring out something latent, hidden, or unexpressed ▶ call forth (*or* up), conjure (up), draw (out), educe, elicit, invoke, rouse, summon (forth). [*Compare* **arouse, revive.**]

✚ **CORE SYNONYMS:** *evoke, educe, elicit.* These verbs mean to call forth or bring out something latent, hidden, or unexpressed: *evoke laughter; educed significance from the event; trying to elicit the truth.*

---

evolution *noun.* —*See* **change** (1), **development.**

evolve *verb.* —*See* **change** (2), **derive** (2), **develop** (2).

evolvement *noun.* —*See* **development.**

exacerbate *verb.* —*See* **intensify.**

exact *adjective.* **1.** Strictly distinguished from others ▶ precise, very. **2.** Being an exact amount or number ▶ even. ***Idioms:*** on the button (*or* money *or* nose), spot on. —*See also* **accurate, close** (2).

exact *verb.* To establish and apply as compulsory ▶ assess, impose, levy, put. —*See also* **demand** (1), **extort.**

exacting *adjective.* —*See* **delicate** (3), **difficult** (1), **fussy, severe** (1).

exaction *noun.* —*See* **demand** (1), **toll[1]** (1).

exactitude *noun.* —*See* **accuracy, veracity.**

exactly *adverb.* In an exact manner ▶ even, faithfully, just, literally, precisely, strictly, verbatim. ***Idioms:*** in all respects (*or* every respect), just so, letter for letter, to a T, to the letter, word for word. —*See also* **directly** (3).

exactment *noun.* —*See* **toll[1]** (1).

exactness *noun.* —*See* **accuracy, veracity.**

exaggerate *verb.* To make something seem greater than is actually the case ▶ aggrandize, hyperbolize, inflate, magnify, overcharge, overemphasize, overstate, puff (up). ***Idioms:*** blow out of proportion, lay it on thick, stretch the truth. [*Compare* **boast, distort.**] —*See also* **increase.**

✚ **CORE SYNONYMS:** *exaggerate, inflate, magnify, overstate.* These verbs mean to make something seem larger or greater than it actually is: *exaggerated the size of the fish I caught; inflated his own importance; magnifying her part in their success; overstated his income on the loan application.*

◀ **ANTONYM:** *minimize*

---

exaggerated *adjective.* Represented as greater than is actually the case ▶ far-fetched, hyperbolic, inflated, magnified, overblown, overdrawn, overstated. [*Compare* **astonishing, doubtful, imaginary, outrageous.**] —*See also* **dramatic** (2).

exaggeration *noun.* The act or an instance of exaggerating ▶ hyperbole, hyperbolism, overstatement, tall talk. *Informal:* fish story, tall tale. [*Compare* **lie[2]**.]

exalt *verb.* To raise to a high position or status ▶ aggrandize, apotheosize, dignify, elevate, ennoble, glorify, magnify, uplift. ***Idioms:*** put (*or* place) on a pedestal. —*See also* **distinguish** (3), **honor** (1), **praise** (3), **promote** (1).

exaltation *noun.* The act of raising to a high position or status or the condition of being so raised ▶ aggrandizement, apotheosis, beatification, canonization, deification, dignification, elevation, ennoblement, glorification, lionization. —*See also* **elation, praise** (2).

exalted *adjective.* Raised to or occupying a high position or rank ▶ august, elevated, ennobled, eminent, grand, high-ranking, illustrious, lofty, noble, venerable. [*Compare* **famous.**] —*See also* **elevated** (4).

exam *noun.* —*See* **examination** (2), **test** (2).

examination *noun.* **1.** The act of examining carefully or critically ▶ audit, analysis, check, checkup, inquest, inquisition, inquiry, inspection, investigation, perusal, probe, research, review, scrutiny, search, study, survey, view. *Informal:* going-over, once-over. **2.** A medical inquiry into a patient's state of health ▶ analysis, checkup, diagnosis, exam, probe. *Informal:* workup. —*See also* **test** (2).

✚ **CORE SYNONYMS:** *examination, inquiry, inquest, inquisition, investigation, probe, research.* These nouns denote the act of examining something or someone carefully or critically, especially in the quest for knowledge, data, or truth: *an examination of the legal facts in the case; filed an inquiry about the lost shipment; holding an inquest to determine the cause of his death; an inquisition into her political activities; a criminal investigation; a probe into alleged police corruption; scientific research.*

examine *verb.* **1.** To look at or study carefully or critically ▶ analyze, audit, check (out), con, go over, inspect, investigate, peruse, pore over, research, review, scrutinize, study, survey, traverse, view. *Informal:* case. *Slang:* scope out. ***Idioms:*** bone up on, give the once-over (*or* a going-over), go over with a fine-tooth comb, put under a microscope. [*Compare* **estimate, explore, study, test.**] **2.** To subject to a test of knowledge or skill ▶ catechize, quiz, test. —*See also* **ask** (1), **test** (1).

example *noun.* **1.** One that is representative of a group or class ▶ case, embodiment, exemplar, exemplification, exponent, illustration, instance, instantiation, representative, sample, specimen. **2.** An instance that warns or discourages prospective imitators ▶ caveat, cautionary tale, exemplar, lesson, object lesson, warning. [*Compare* **preventive, warning.**] —*See also* **model.**

✚ **CORE SYNONYMS:** *example, instance, case, illustration, sample, specimen.* These nouns refer to what is representative of or serves to explain a larger group or class. An *example* is a typically representative part that demonstrates the character of the whole: *"Of the despotism to which unrestrained military power leads we have plenty of examples from Alexander to Mao"* (Samuel Eliot Morison). An *instance* is an example that is cited to prove or to illustrate a point: *an instance of flagrant corruption.* A *case* is an action, an occurrence, or a condition that relates specifically to something being discussed, decided, or treated: *a typical case of child neglect.* An *illustration* clarifies or explains: *The glossary provided an illustration of each word in context.* A *sample* is an actual part of something larger, presented as evidence of the quality or nature of the whole: *The disciplinarian gave us a sample of her temper. Specimen* often denotes an individual, representative member of a group or class: *This poem is a fair specimen of her work.*

exasperate *verb.* —*See* **anger** (1), **annoy.**

exasperation *noun.* —*See* **annoyance** (1).

excavate *verb.* —*See* **dig.**

exceed *verb.* To go beyond the limits of ▶ overleap, overpass, overreach, overrun, overshoot, overstep, surpass, transcend, transgress. —*See also* **surpass.**

exceedingly *adverb.* —*See* **very.**

excel *verb.* —*See* **surpass.**

excellence *noun.* The quality of being exceptionally good of its kind ▶ fineness, incomparability, preeminence, superbness, superiority, transcendence, virtuosity. [*Compare* **distinction.**]

excellent *adjective.* Exceptionally good of its kind ▶ ace, banner, blue-ribbon, brag, capital, champion, dandy, fine, first-class, first-rate, prime, prize, quality, remarkable, splendid, superb, superior, terrific, tiptop, top, world-class.

Informal: A-OK, A-one, bang-up, bully, great, jim-dandy, smashing, swell, topflight, topnotch. *Slang:* awesome, bad, boss, cool, corking, crackerjack, dynamite, hot, killer, phat, primo, tops. ***Idioms:*** out of this world, to die for. [*Compare* **best, choice, exceptional, marvelous.**]

except *verb.* —*See* **exclude, object.**

exception *noun.* —*See* **abnormality, objection.**

exceptionable *adjective.* —*See* **debatable, objectionable.**

exceptional *adjective.* Beyond what is usual, normal, or customary ▶ especial, exquisite, extraordinary, magnificent, memorable, notable, noteworthy, outstanding, preeminent, rare, remarkable, singular, special, sublime, towering, uncommon, unprecedented, unusual. *Informal:* standout. *Slang:* awesome, out of sight. [*Compare* **best, excellent, noticeable, unique.**] —*See also* **choice** (1).

exceptionally *adverb.* —*See* **unusually, very.**

excess *noun.* **1.** A condition of going or being beyond what is needed, desired, or appropriate ▶ embarrassment, excessiveness, exorbitance, extravagance, extravagancy, extravagantness, inordinacy, inordinateness, overabundance, oversufficiency, plethora, superabundance, superfluity, superfluousness, surfeit. ***Idiom:*** fifth wheel. **2.** Immoderate indulgence, as in food or drink ▶ immoderacy, immoderateness, immoderation, intemperance, overindulgence, surfeit. —*See also* **surplus.**

excess *adjective.* —*See* **superfluous.**

excessive *adjective.* Exceeding a normal or reasonable limit ▶ exorbitant, extravagant, extreme, immoderate, intemperate, inordinate, overabundant, overmuch, unbridled, undue, unrestrained. ***Idioms:*** out of all bounds (*or* proportion), out of control. [*Compare* **flagrant, outrageous.**] —*See also* **wanton** (2).

✣ **CORE SYNONYMS:** *excessive, exorbitant, extravagant, immoderate, inordinate, extreme.* These adjectives mean exceeding a normal, usual, reasonable, or proper limit. *Excessive* describes a quantity, amount, or degree that is more than what is justifiable, tolerable, or desirable: *excessive drinking. Exorbitant* usually refers to a quantity or degree that far exceeds what is customary or fair: *exorbitant interest rates. Extravagant* sometimes specifies lavish or unwise expenditure (*extravagant gifts*); often it implies unbridled divergence from reason or sound judgment (*extravagant claims*). *Immoderate* denotes lack of due moderation: *immoderate enthusiasm. Inordinate* implies an overstepping of bounds imposed by authority or dictated by good sense: *inordinate demands. Extreme* suggests the utmost degree of excessiveness: *extreme danger.*

---

excessively *adverb.* —*See* **unduly.**

excessiveness *noun.* —*See* **excess** (1).

exchange *verb.* To give and receive mutually, as words ▶ bandy, interchange, swap, trade. ***Idiom:*** give as good as one gets. [*Compare* **reciprocate, retaliate.**] —*See also* **change** (3).

exchange *noun.* —*See* **change** (2), **communication** (1), **deal** (1).

excitation *noun.* —*See* **enthusiasm** (1).

excite *verb.* —*See* **delight** (1), **enrapture, provoke.**

excited *adjective.* —*See* **thrilled.**

excitement *noun.* —*See* **agitation** (3), **enthusiasm** (1).

exciting *adjective.* —*See* **dramatic** (2), **invigorating.**

exclaim *verb.* To speak suddenly or sharply, as from surprise or emotion ▶ blurt (out), burst out, cry (out), ejaculate, rap out. [*Compare* **shout.**]

exclamation *noun.* —*See* **shout.**

exclude *verb.* To keep from being admitted, included, or considered ▶ ban, bar, blackball, blacklist, boycott, count out, debar, eliminate, except, keep out, ostracize, reject, rule out, shut out, vote down. [*Compare* **banish, forbid, decline.**] —*See also* **drop** (5).

✚ **CORE SYNONYMS:** *exclude, blackball, blacklist, boycott, ostracize, reject.* These verbs mean to keep from being admitted, included, or considered: *excluded the sensitive findings from the report; blackballed by the fraternity; blacklisted because of her political beliefs; a threat to boycott the product; ostracized following the harassment charges; rejected the proposals from the neighborhood groups.*

◀ **ANTONYM:** *admit*

---

exclusion *noun.* —*See* **elimination, prevention.**

exclusive *adjective.* **1.** Not divided among or shared with others ▶ particular, prerogative, private, single, sole. [*Compare* **individual.**] **2.** Singled out in preference ▶ choice, chosen, elect, select. [*Compare* **excellent, favorite.**] **3.** Catering to, used by, or admitting only the wealthy or socially superior ▶ chic, chichi, classy, elite, fancy, hoity-toity, posh, selective, smart, sophisticated, swank, swanky, tony. *Informal:* ritzy. [*Compare* **snobbish.**] —*See also* **concentrated** (1), **preventive** (1).

exclusively *adverb.* —*See* **solely.**

excogitate *verb.* —*See* **derive** (2), **ponder.**

excogitation *noun.* —*See* **thought.**

excogitative *adjective.* —*See* **thoughtful.**

excoriate *verb.* —*See* **chafe, slam** (1).

excretory *adjective.* —*See* **eliminative.**

excruciate *verb.* —*See* **afflict.**

excruciating *adjective.* —*See* **tormenting.**

exculpate *verb.* —*See* **clear** (3).

exculpation *noun.* A freeing or clearing from accusation or guilt ▶ absolution, acquittal, exoneration, justification, remission, vindication. [*Compare* **forgiveness.**]

excursion *noun.* A usually short journey taken for pleasure ▶ jaunt, junket, outing, trip. [*Compare* **expedition, journey.**] —*See also* **digression.**

excursionist *noun.* —*See* **tourist.**

excursive *adjective.* —*See* **digressive.**

excursus *noun.* —*See* **digression.**

excusable *adjective.* Capable of being justified ▶ defensible, justifiable, tenable. [*Compare* **logical, sound²**.] —*See also* **pardonable.**

excuse *verb.* **1.** To free from an obligation or duty ▶ absolve, discharge, dispense, exempt, let off, release, remise, remit, relieve, spare. ***Idioms:*** let off the hook, make excuses for. **2.** To show to be just, right, or valid ▶ justify, rationalize, vindicate. ***Idiom:*** make a case for. —*See also* **dismiss** (2), **forgive.**

excuse *noun.* **1.** An explanation offered to justify an action or make it better understood ▶ justification, plea, pretext, rationale, rationalization. *Informal:* alibi. [*Compare* **account, pretense.**] **2.** A statement of acknowledgment expressing regret or asking pardon ▶ apology, mea culpa, regrets. [*Compare* **acknowledgment.**] —*See also* **forgiveness.**

exec *noun.* —*See* **executive.**

execrable *adjective.* —*See* **damned.**

execrate *verb.* —*See* **hate, revile.**

execration *noun.* —*See* **curse** (1), **hate** (2).

execute *verb.* —*See* **administer** (2), **effect, enforce, fulfill, interpret** (2), **kill¹**, **perform** (1).

execution *noun.* Carrying a law or judgment into effect ▶ enforcement, implementation. [*Compare* **effect, exercise.**] —*See also* **interpretation, performance.**

executive *noun.* A person having administrative or managerial authority in an organization ▶ administrant, administrator, CEO, chair, chairman (of the board), chairwoman, chief executive, director, functionary, manager, middle manager, officer, official, president. *Informal:* exec, higher-up. [*Compare* **boss.**]

executive *adjective.* —*See* **administrative.**

exegesis *noun.* —*See* **commentary, explanation.**

exegetic *adjective.* —*See* **explanatory.**

exemplar *noun.* —*See* **epitome, example** (1), **example** (2), **model.**

exemplary *adjective.* Beyond reproach ▶ blameless, faultless, good, lily-white, irreprehensible, irreproachable, unblamable. —*See also* **admirable, ideal.**

exemplification *noun.* —*See* **embodiment, example** (1).

exemplify *verb.* To demonstrate and clarify with examples ▶ demonstrate, evidence, illustrate, instance. [*Compare* **explain, show.**] —*See also* **represent** (1).

exempt *verb.* —*See* **excuse** (1).

exemption *noun.* Temporary immunity from penalties ▶ grace, immunity, reprieve, respite. [*Compare* **delay, forgiveness.**]

exercise *noun.* **1.** The act of putting into play ▶ administration, adoption, application, employment, exertion, implementation, operation, play, recourse, resort, usage, use, utilization. **2.** Energetic physical action ▶ activity, exertion, workout. —*See also* **practice.**

exercise *verb.* **1.** To bring to bear steadily or forcefully, as influence ▶ exert, ply, wield. ***Idiom:*** throw one's weight around. **2.** To engage in activities in order to strengthen or condition ▶ drill, practice, train, work out. —*See also* **fulfill, practice** (1), **use.**

exert *verb.* To bring to bear steadily or forcefully, as influence ▶ exercise, ply, wield. ***Idiom:*** throw one's weight around. —*See also* **apply** (1).

exertion *noun.* Energetic physical action ▶ activity, exercise, workout. —*See also* **effort, exercise** (1).

exfoliate *verb.* —*See* **flake.**

exhalation *noun.* —*See* **breath.**

exhale *verb.* —*See* **breathe** (1), **emit.**

exhaust *verb.* **1.** To use all of ▶ consume, deplete, drain, draw down, eat up, expend, finish, play out, run through, sap, spend, use up. *Informal:* polish off. [*Compare* **dry.**] **2.** To be depleted ▶ consume, go, spend. ***Idiom:*** go down the drain. —*See also* **tire** (1).

✚ **CORE SYNONYMS:** *exhaust, deplete, drain.* These verbs all mean to use all of something. *Exhaust* stresses reduction to a point of uselessness: *"The resources of civilization are not yet exhausted"* (William Ewart Gladstone). *Deplete* refers to using up gradually and only hints at harmful consequences: *The campers' food supply was quickly depleted. Drain* suggests gradual drawing off and harm: *War often drains a nation's economy.*

---

exhausted *adjective.* —*See* **tired** (1).

exhausting *adjective.* Causing fatigue ▶ draining, fatiguing, tiring, wearing, wearying. [*Compare* **burdensome.**]

exhaustion *noun.* The condition of being extremely tired ▶ burnout, fatigue, prostration, tiredness, weariness. [*Compare* **debilitation, lethargy.**]

exhaustive *adjective.* —*See* **detailed, thorough.**

exhaustively *adverb.* —*See* **completely** (2).

exhibit *verb.* —*See* **bear** (3), **display, show** (1).

exhibit *noun.* —*See* **display, exhibition.**

exhibition *noun.* A large public display, as of goods or works of art ▶ bazaar, exhibit, expo, exposition, fair, festival, installation, retrospective, salon, show. [*Compare* **market, display.**] —*See also* **display.**

exhibitionism *noun.* —*See* **theatricalism.**

exhibitory *or* **exhibitive** *adjective.* —*See* **designative.**

exhilarant *adjective.* —*See* **invigorating.**

exhilarate *verb.* —*See* **elate, energize.**

exhilarated *adjective.* —*See* **cheerful.**

exhilarating *adjective.* —*See* **invigorating.**

exhilaration *noun.* —*See* **elation.**

exhort *verb.* —*See* **urge.**

exhume *verb.* —*See* **uncover.**

exigency *or* **exigence** *noun.* A condition in which something necessary or desirable is required or wanted ▶ necessity, need. —*See also* **crisis, demand** (2), **emergency.**

exigent *adjective.* —*See* **difficult** (1), **urgent** (1).

exiguous *adjective.* —*See* **meager.**

exile *noun.* Enforced removal from one's native country by official decree ▶ banishment, deportation, expatriation, extradition, ostracism, proscription, transportation. —*See also* **émigré, outcast.**

exile *verb.* —*See* **banish.**

exist *verb.* To have reality or life ▶ be, breathe, live, subsist. ***Idioms:*** be around, draw breath, have one's being, walk the earth. [*Compare* **endure, survive.**] —*See also* **consist.**

exist on *verb.* To include as part of one's diet by nature or preference ▶ eat, feed on, live on, subsist on.

existence *noun.* The fact or state of existing or of being actual ▶ actuality, being, entity, reality, substantiality, substantiveness. [*Compare* **certainty, fact.**] —*See also* **life, living, thing** (1).

✚ **CORE SYNONYMS:** *existence, actuality, being.* These nouns denote the fact or state of existing or of being actual: *laws in existence for centuries; an idea progressing from possibility to actuality; a point of view gradually coming into being.*

◀ **ANTONYM:** *nonexistence*

existent *adjective.* Occurring or existing in act or fact ▶ actual, extant, real, true. [*Compare* **physical.**] —*See also* **alive, present**[1].

existent *noun.* —*See* **thing** (1).

existing *adjective.* —*See* **alive, present**[1].

exit *noun.* —*See* **departure.**

exit *verb.* —*See* **go** (1).

exodus *noun.* —*See* **departure, emigration.**

exonerate *verb.* —*See* **clear** (3).

exoneration *noun.* —*See* **exculpation.**

exorbitance *noun.* —*See* **excess** (1).

exorbitant *adjective.* —*See* **excessive, steep**[1] (2).

exotic *adjective.* Very strange or strikingly unusual ▶ bizarre, fanciful, fantastic, grotesque, outlandish, outré, strange, unorthodox. ***Idioms:*** from another planet (*or* outer space), off the wall. [*Compare* **eccentric, unusual.**] —*See also* **foreign** (1).

expand *verb.* —*See* **broaden, elaborate, gain** (1), **increase, spread** (1).

expandable *adjective.* —*See* **extensible.**

expanse *noun.* **1.** A wide and open area, as of land, sky, or water ▶ distance, expansion, extent, range, reach, space, spread, stretch, sweep, tract, vista. [*Compare* **view.**] **2.** The extent of something from side to side ▶ breadth, broadness, wideness, width. [*Compare* **distance.**]

expansible *or* **expansile** *adjective.* —*See* **extensible.**

expansion *noun.* The process of increasing in extent or inclusiveness ▶ broadening, fanning out, extension, proliferation, spread. [*Compare* **distribution.**] —*See also* **expanse** (1), **increase** (1).

expansive *adjective.* —*See* **broad** (1), **general** (2), **outgoing.**

expansively *adverb.* —*See* **considerably.**

expatiate *verb.* —*See* **elaborate.**

expatiation *noun.* —*See* **discourse.**

expatriate *verb.* —*See* **banish.**

expatriate *noun.* —*See* **émigré, foreigner.**

expatriation *noun.* —*See* **emigration, exile.**

expect *verb.* **1.** To look forward to confidently ▶ anticipate, await, bargain for (*or* on), bet (on), count on, depend on (*or* upon), look for, wager, wait (for). *Informal:* figure on. [*Compare* **foresee, intend.**] **2.** To oblige to do or not do by force of authority, propriety, or custom ▶ oblige, obligate, require, suppose. [*Compare* **must.**] —*See also* **suppose** (1).

✚ **CORE SYNONYMS:** *expect, anticipate, await.* These verbs relate to the idea of looking forward to something in the future with confidence. To *expect* is to look forward to the likely occurrence or appearance of someone or something: "*We should not expect something for nothing—but we all do and call it Hope*" (Edgar W. Howe). *Anticipate* sometimes refers to taking advance action, as to forestall or prevent the occurrence of something expected or to meet a wish or request before it is articulated: *The sentinels anticipated the attack and locked the gates.* The term can also refer to having a foretaste of something expected: *The governor anticipated trouble and called in the National Guard.* To *await* is to wait expectantly and with certainty: *I am eagerly awaiting your letter.*

---

expectance *or* **expectancy** *noun.* The condition of looking forward to something, especially with eagerness ▶ anticipation, expectation, high hopes, hopefulness. [*Compare* **desire.**]

expectant *adjective.* Having or marked by expectation ▶ anticipant, anticipative, anticipatory, awaiting, hopeful, hoping, looking forward to. ***Idioms:*** in suspense, on tenterhooks (*or* the edge of one's seat), on the lookout (*or* watch) for, with bated breath. [*Compare* **eager, optimistic.**] —*See also* **pregnant** (1).

expectation *noun.* **1.** The condition of looking forward to something, especially with eagerness ▶ anticipation, expectance, expectancy, high hopes, hopefulness. [*Compare* **desire.**] **2.** Something expected ▶ anticipation, likelihood, promise, prospect. [*Compare* **chance, theory.**]

expected *adjective.* —*See* **due** (2).

expecting *adjective.* —*See* **pregnant** (1).

expectorate *noun.* —*See* **spit.**

expectorate *verb.* To expel a small amount of saliva or mucus from the mouth ▶ hawk, spit. [*Compare* **drool.**]

expediency *noun.* —*See* **makeshift.**

expedient *adjective.* —*See* **advisable, convenient** (1).

expedient *noun.* —*See* **makeshift.**

expedite *verb.* —*See* **ease** (2), **speed.**

expedition *noun.* A journey undertaken with a specific objective ▶ grand tour, mission, odyssey, pilgrimage, quest, safari, sortie, tour, trek, voyage. —*See also* **haste** (1).

expeditious *adjective.* —*See* **fast** (1), **quick.**

expeditiousness *noun.* —*See* **haste** (1).

expel *verb.* —*See* **banish, dismiss** (2), **eject** (1), **erupt.**

expellee *noun.* —*See* **émigré.**

expend *verb.* —*See* **exhaust** (1), **spend** (1).

expenditure *noun.* The act of consuming ▶ consumption, depletion, usage, use, utilization. [*Compare* **use.**] —*See also* **cost** (1).

expense *noun.* The expenditure at which something is obtained ▶ cost, price, sacrifice, toll. *Informal:* damage. —*See also* **cost** (1).

expenses *noun.* —*See* **overhead.**

expensive *adjective.* —*See* **costly.**

experience *noun.* Personal knowledge derived from participation or observation ▶ acquaintance, conversance, familiarity. [*Compare* **awareness.**] —*See also* **adventure, circumstance** (1).

experience *verb.* To participate in or partake of personally ▶ encounter, feel, go through, have, know, meet (with), pass through, sample, see, suffer, taste (of), undergo. ***Idiom:*** run up against.

experienced *adjective.* Skilled or knowledgeable through long practice ▶ old, practiced, seasoned, tried, versed, veteran. ***Idiom:*** knowing the ropes. [*Compare* **dependable, veteran.**]

experiment *or* **experimentation** *noun.* —*See* **test** (1).

experimental *adjective.* —*See* **pilot.**

expert *noun.* A person with a high degree of knowledge or skill in a particular field ▶ ace, adept, authority, connoisseur, dab hand, master, maven, past master, professional, proficient, specialist, wizard, world-beater. *Informal:* pro, whiz. *Slang:* crackajack, crackerjack.

expert *adjective.* Having or demonstrating a high degree of knowledge or skill ▶ adept, crack, master, masterful, masterly, professional, proficient, skilled, skillful. *Informal:* pro. *Slang:* crackajack, crackerjack. [*Compare* **able.**]

✦ **CORE SYNONYMS:** *expert, proficient, adept, skilled, skillful.* These adjectives mean having or demonstrating a high degree of knowledge, ability, or skill, as in a profession or field of study. *Expert* applies to one with consummate skill and command: *an expert violinist who played the sonata flawlessly. Proficient* implies an advanced degree of competence acquired through training: *is proficient in Greek and Latin. Adept* suggests a natural aptitude improved by practice: *became adept at cutting the fabric without using a pattern. Skilled* implies sound, thorough competence and often mastery, as in an art, craft, or trade: *a skilled gymnast who won an Olympic medal. Skillful* adds to *skilled* the idea of natural dexterity in performance or achievement: *is skillful in the use of the hand loom.*

---

expertise *or* **expertness** *noun.* —*See* **ability** (1).

expiable *adjective.* —*See* **pardonable.**

expiate *verb.* —*See* **purify** (1).

expiation *noun.* The act of making amends ▶ atonement, penance, reconciliation, reparation. [*Compare* **compensation, purification.**]

expiatory *adjective.* —*See* **purgative.**

expiration *noun.* —*See* **breath, death** (1), **disappearance, end** (1).

expire *verb.* —*See* **breathe** (1), **die, disappear** (2), **lapse.**

explain *verb.* **1.** To make understandable ▶ construe, decipher, demystify, elucidate, explicate, expound, gloss, interpret, spell out. ***Idioms:*** make perfectly clear, put into plain English, walk someone through. [*Compare* **clarify.**] **2.** To offer reasons for or a cause of ▶ account for, justify, rationalize. [*Compare* **resolve.**] —*See also* **solve** (1).

explain away *verb.* —*See* **extenuate.**

✦ **CORE SYNONYMS:** *explain, elucidate, expound, explicate, interpret, construe.* These verbs mean to make the nature or meaning of something understandable. *Explain* is the most widely applicable: *The professor explained the obscure symbols.* To *elucidate* is to throw light on something complex: *"Man's whole life and environment have been laid open and elucidated"* (Thomas Carlyle). *Expound* and *explicate* imply detailed and usually learned and lengthy exploration or analysis: *"We must never forget that it is a* constitution *we are expounding"* (John Marshall). *"Ordinary language philosophers tried to explicate the standards of usage"* (Jerrold J. Katz). To *interpret* is to reveal the underlying meaning of something by the application of special knowledge or insight: *"If a poet interprets a poem of his own he limits its suggestibility"* (William Butler Yeats). *Construe* involves putting a particular construction or interpretation on something: *"I take the official oath today . . . with no purpose to construe the Constitution or laws by any hypercritical rules"* (Abraham Lincoln).

---

explainable *adjective.* Capable of being explained or accounted for ▶ accountable, construable, decipherable, explicable, illustratable, interpretable. [*Compare* **justifiable, understandable.**]

explanation *noun.* Something that serves to explain or clarify ▶ clarification, construction, decipherment, elucidation, exegesis, explication, exposition, gloss, illumination, illustration, interpretation, spin. —*See also* **account** (1), **answer** (2).

explanatory *or* **explanative** *adjective.* Serving to explain ▶ elucidative, exegetic, explicative, expositive, expository, hermeneutic, hermeneutical, illustrative, interpretative, interpretive. [*Compare* **educational.**]

expletive *noun.* —*See* **swearword.**

explicable *adjective.* —*See* **explainable.**

explicate *verb.* —*See* **explain** (1).

explication *noun.* —*See* **explanation.**

explicative *adjective.* —*See* **explanatory.**

explicit *adjective.* —*See* **definite** (1), **graphic** (1).

explicitness *noun.* —*See* **clarity.**

explode *verb.* **1.** To release or cause to release energy suddenly and violently, especially with a loud noise ▶ backfire, blast, blow (up), burst, detonate, fire, fulminate, go off, touch off. **2.** To come open or fly apart suddenly and violently, as from internal pressure ▶ blow (out), burst, pop. *Slang:* bust. **3.** To increase or expand suddenly, rapidly, or without control ▶ balloon, mushroom, snowball. [*Compare* **increase.**] —*See also* **anger** (2), **break out, discredit.**

exploit *verb.* —*See* **abuse** (1), **abuse** (2), **manipulate** (1), **use.**

exploit *noun.* —*See* **accomplishment.**

exploitable *adjective.* —*See* **gullible.**

exploration *noun.* The act or an instance of exploring or investigating ▶ investigation, probe, reconnaissance. [*Compare* **examination.**]

explore *verb.* To go into or through for the purpose of making discoveries or acquiring information ▶ delve, dig, fathom, inquire, investigate, look into, plumb, probe, reconnoiter, scout, sound. [*Compare* **examine, snoop.**]

explosion *noun.* —*See* **blast** (2), **crack** (1), **eruption, outburst.**

exponent *noun.* —*See* **example** (1).

expose *verb.* To lay open, as to something undesirable or injurious ▶ subject, leave open. [*Compare* **endanger.**] —*See also* **bare, betray** (2), **display, reveal.**

exposé *noun.* —*See* **revelation.**

exposed *adjective.* —*See* **bleak** (1), **open** (2).

exposition *noun.* —*See* **commentary, display, exhibition, explanation.**

expository *or* **expositive** *adjective.* —*See* **didactic, explanatory.**

expostulate *verb.* —*See* **object.**

expostulation *noun.* —*See* **objection.**

exposure *noun.* The condition of being laid open to something undesirable or injurious ▶ assailability, defenselessness, endangerment, liability, openness, pregnability, susceptibility, susceptibleness, unprotectedness, vulnerability, vulnerableness. —*See also* **nudity, publicity, revelation.**

expound *verb.* —*See* **explain** (1).

express *verb.* **1.** To give expression to, as by gestures, facial aspects, or bodily posture ▶ communicate, convey, display, manifest. ***Idioms:*** give a sign (*or* token), make clear (*or* known *or* plain). [*Compare* **show.**] **2.** To extract from by applying pressure ▶ crush, press, squeeze. —*See also* **air** (2), **phrase, represent** (2), **say, send** (1).

express *adjective.* —*See* **definite** (1), **fast** (1), **special.**

expression *noun.* **1.** The act or an instance of expressing in words ▶ airing, articulation, pronunciation, statement, utterance, ventilation, verbalization, vocalization, voice. [*Compare* **embodiment, message, wording.**] **2.** Something that takes the place of words in communicating a thought or feeling ▶

gesture, indication, mark, sign, token. [*Compare* **sign.**] **3.** A word or group of words forming a unit and conveying meaning ▶ collocation, idiom, locution, phrase. [*Compare* **proverb.**] **4.** A disposition of the facial features that conveys meaning, feeling, or mood ▶ aspect, cast, countenance, face, lineaments, look, visage. [*Compare* **appearance, bearing.**] —*See also* **eloquence, representation, term.**

expressionless *adjective.* Lacking expression ▶ affectless, blank, deadpan, inexpressive, pokerfaced, zombie-like. [*Compare* **dull, reserved, vacant.**]

expressive *adjective.* Effectively conveying meaning, feeling, or mood ▶ eloquent, meaning, meaningful, significant. [*Compare* **eloquent, pregnant.**]

✣ **CORE SYNONYMS:** *expressive, eloquent, meaningful, significant.* These adjectives mean effectively conveying a feeling, idea, or mood: *an expressive gesture; an eloquent speech; a meaningful look; a significant smile.*

expressiveness *or* **expressivity** *noun.* —*See* **eloquence.**

expressway *noun.* —*See* **way** (2).

expropriate *verb.* —*See* **seize** (1).

expropriation *noun.* —*See* **seizure** (2).

expulsion *noun.* —*See* **dismissal, ejection.**

expunction *noun.* —*See* **erasure.**

expunge *verb.* —*See* **annihilate, cancel** (1).

expurgate *verb.* —*See* **censor** (1).

exquisite *adjective.* —*See* **beautiful, delicate** (1), **elegant, exceptional.**

exsiccate *verb.* —*See* **dry.**

extant *adjective.* Occurring or existing in act or fact ▶ actual, existent, real, true. [*Compare* **physical.**] —*See also* **alive.**

extemporaneous *or* **extemporary** *or* **extempore** *adjective.* Spoken, performed, or composed with little or no preparation or forethought ▶ ad-lib, extemporary, extempore, impromptu, improvised, offhand, snap, spur-of-the-moment, unrehearsed. *Informal:* off-the-cuff. [*Compare* **spontaneous.**]

✣ **CORE SYNONYMS:** *extemporaneous, extemporary, extempore, impromptu, offhand, unrehearsed, ad-lib.* These adjectives mean spoken, performed, done, or composed with little or no preparation or forethought. *Extemporaneous, extemporary,* and *extempore* most often apply to discourse that is delivered without the assistance of a written text, though it may have been planned in advance: *an extemporaneous address; an extemporary lecture; an extempore skit. Impromptu* even more strongly suggests happening on the spur of the moment: *an impromptu dinner. Offhand* implies not only spontaneity but also a casual or even cavalier manner: *an offhand remark.* What is *unrehearsed* is said or done without rehearsal or practice though not necessarily without forethought: *a few unrehearsed comments.* Something that is *ad-lib* is spontaneous and improvised and therefore not part of a prepared script or score: *an ad-lib joke.*

extemporization *noun.* Something improvised ▶ ad-lib, impromptu, improvisation. [*Compare* **makeshift.**]

extemporize *verb.* —*See* **improvise** (1).

extend *verb.* **1.** To proceed on a certain course or for a certain distance ▶ carry, continue, go, reach, run, stretch. **2.** To put forward, especially an appendage ▶ outstretch, reach, stretch (out). —*See also* **broaden, go** (4), **increase, lengthen, offer** (1), **spread** (1).

extended *adjective.* —*See* **broad** (1), **general** (2), **long**[1] (1).

extensible *or* **extendible** *or* **extensile** *adjective.* Capable of being extended or expanded ▶ expandable, expansible, expansile, protractile, stretch, stretchable, stretchy. [*Compare* **malleable.**]

extension *noun.* **1.** The act of making something longer or the condition of being made longer ▶ drawing out, elongation, lengthening, prolongation, protraction, spinning out, stretching, stringing out. **2.** A part added to a main structure ▶ addition, add-on, annex, arm, wing. *—See also* **branch** (1), **expansion, extent, increase** (1), **range** (1).

extensive *adjective.* *—See* **big, broad** (1), **general** (2).

extensively *adverb.* *—See* **considerably.**

extent *noun.* The measure of how far or long something goes in space, time, or degree ▶ coverage, extension, length, reach, span, stretch. [*Compare* **depth, width.**] *—See also* **degree** (2), **expanse** (1), **range** (1), **size** (1).

extenuate *verb.* To conceal or make light of a fault or offense ▶ explain away, gloss over, gloze (over), palliate, sleek over, whitewash. [*Compare* **belittle, soft-pedal.**]

✤ **CORE SYNONYMS:** *extenuate, gloss, gloze, palliate, whitewash.* These verbs mean to cause a fault or offense to seem less grave or less reprehensible: *couldn't extenuate the malfeasance; glossing over an unethical transaction; glozing sins and iniquities; palliate a crime; whitewashed official complicity in political extortion.*

---

exteriorization *noun.* *—See* **embodiment.**

exteriorize *verb.* *—See* **embody** (1).

exterminate *verb.* *—See* **annihilate.**

extermination *noun.* *—See* **annihilation.**

external *adjective.* *—See* **apparent** (2).

externalization *noun.* *—See* **embodiment.**

externalize *verb.* *—See* **embody** (1).

externally *adverb.* *—See* **apparently.**

extinct *adjective.* *—See* **dead** (1).

extinction *noun.* *—See* **annihilation, death** (1).

extinguish *verb.* To cause to stop burning or giving light ▶ damp, douse, put out, quench, smother, snuff out. [*Compare* **choke.**] *—See also* **abolish, annihilate, suppress.**

extinguishment *noun.* *—See* **annihilation.**

extirpate *verb.* *—See* **annihilate.**

extirpation *noun.* *—See* **annihilation.**

extol *verb.* *—See* **honor** (1), **praise** (1), **praise** (3).

extolment *noun.* *—See* **praise** (2).

extort *verb.* To obtain by coercion or intimidation ▶ blackmail, exact, graft, squeeze, wrench, wrest, wring. *Slang:* shake down.

extortionate *adjective.* *—See* **steep[1]** (2).

extra *adjective.* Being what remains, especially after a part has been removed ▶ leftover, remaining, stray. ***Idiom:*** left behind. *—See also* **additional, superfluous.**

extra *adverb.* *—See* **very.**

extra *noun.* *—See* **enhancement, surplus.**

extract *verb.* *—See* **derive** (1), **glean, pull** (2).

extraction *noun.* *—See* **ancestry.**

extradite *verb.* *—See* **banish.**

extradition *noun.* *—See* **exile.**

extramundane *adjective.* *—See* **supernatural** (1).

extraneous *adjective.* Not part of the essential nature of a thing ▶ alien, foreign, extrinsic. [*Compare* **irrelevant.**] *—See also* **irrelevant.**

extraordinarily *adverb.* *—See* **unusually.**

extraordinary *adjective.* *—See* **exceptional.**

extrasensory *adjective.* *—See* **supernatural** (1).

extravagance *or* **extravagancy** *noun.* Excessive or imprudent expenditure ▶ extravagancy, lavishness, overgenerosity, prodigality, profligacy, profusion, profuseness, squander, waste, wastefulness. *—See also* **excess** (1), **luxury.**

extravagant *adjective.* Characterized by excessive or imprudent spending ▶ dissipative, improvident, lavish, prodigal, profligate, profuse, spendthrift, thriftless, uneconomical, unthrifty, wasteful. ***Idiom:*** penny-wise and pound foolish. [*Compare* **careless, negligent.**] —*See also* **excessive, profuse.**

extravagantly *adverb.* —*See* **unduly.**

extravagantness *noun.* —*See* **excess** (1).

extraverted *adjective. See* **extroverted.**

extreme *adjective.* **1.** Most distant or remote, as from a center ▶ farthermost, farthest, furthermost, furthest, outermost, outmost, ultimate, utmost, uttermost. [*Compare* **last.**] **2.** Holding especially political views that deviate drastically from prevailing beliefs ▶ extremist, fanatic, fanatical, fire-breathing, fire-eating, fundamentalist, hard-line, lunatic, militant, rabid, radical, raving, revolutionary, ultra, wild-eyed, zealous. *Slang:* far-out. [*Compare* **enthusiastic, rebellious, ultraconservative, ultraliberal.**] —*See also* **excessive, maximum.**

extreme *noun.* Either of the two points at the ends of a spectrum or range ▶ extremity, limit. [*Compare* **climax, low.**] —*See also* **length.**

extremely *adverb.* —*See* **unduly, very.**

extremist *noun.* One who holds extreme views or advocates extreme measures ▶ fanatic, fire-breather, fire-eater, fundamentalist, hard-liner, militant, radical, revolutionary, revolutionist, ultra, ultraist, zealot. [*Compare* **ultraconservative, ultraliberal.**]

extremist *adjective.* —*See* **extreme** (2).

extremity *noun.* Either of the two points at the ends of a spectrum or range ▶ extreme, limit. [*Compare* **climax, low.**] —*See also* **emergency, length.**

extricate *verb.* To free from an entanglement ▶ clear, disengage, disentangle, disinvolve, free, release, untangle. [*Compare* **undo.**]

✚ **CORE SYNONYMS:** *extricate, disengage, disentangle, untangle.* These verbs mean to free from an entanglement: *extricated herself from an embarrassing situation; trying to disengage his attention from the television; disentangled the oar from the water lilies; a trapped animal that untangled itself from a net.*

---

extrinsic *adjective.* Not part of the essential nature of a thing ▶ alien, extraneous, foreign. —*See also* **irrelevant.**

extroverted *or* **extraverted** *adjective.* —*See* **outgoing.**

exuberant *adjective.* —*See* **enthusiastic, lively, profuse.**

exude *verb.* —*See* **ooze.**

exult *verb.* **1.** To feel or express an uplifting joy over a success or victory ▶ crow, gloat, glory, jubilate, triumph. *Slang:* high-five. [*Compare* **boast, celebrate, rejoice.**] **2.** To feel or take joy or pleasure ▶ delight, pleasure, rejoice. [*Compare* **enjoy, luxuriate.**]

exultant *adjective.* Feeling or expressing an uplifting joy over a success or victory ▶ gloating, jubilant, triumphant. [*Compare* **boastful.**]

exultation *noun.* The act or condition of feeling an uplifting joy over a success or victory ▶ crowing, exultance, exultancy, gloating, jubilance, jubilation, triumph.

exuviate *verb.* —*See* **shed**[1] (2).

eye *noun.* **1.** An organ of vision ▶ eyeball, orb. *Slang:* peeper, saucer. ***Idiom:*** window of the soul. **2.** The most intensely active central part ▶ midst, thick. [*Compare* **center.**] —*See also* **detective, discernment, loop, viewpoint, vision** (1).

eye *verb.* —*See* **gaze, look** (1), **watch** (1).

eye-catching *adjective.* —*See* **noticeable.**

eyeless *adjective.* —*See* **blind** (1).

eyelet *noun.* —*See* **hole** (2), **loop.**

eye opener *noun.* —*See* **revelation.**

eyesight *noun.* —*See* **vision** (1).

eyes-only *adjective.* —*See* **unspeakable** (2).

eyesore *noun.* —*See* **mess** (2).

eyewitness *noun.* Someone who sees something occur ▶ audience, seer, viewer, witness.

F

fable *noun.* A narrative not based on fact ▶ fiction, novel, romance, story. —*See also* **lie**[2], **myth** (1), **yarn.**

fabled *adjective.* —*See* **mythical.**

fabric *noun.* —*See* **texture.**

fabricate *verb.* —*See* **act** (2), **counterfeit, invent, make.**

fabricated *adjective.* —*See* **mythical.**

fabrication *noun.* —*See* **counterfeit, lie**[2], **myth** (2).

fabricator *noun.* One who makes a fraudulent copy of something ▶ counterfeiter, faker, falsifier, forger. —*See also* **liar.**

fabulist *noun.* —*See* **liar.**

fabulous *adjective.* —*See* **astonishing, marvelous, mythical.**

façade *noun.* **1.** The forward outer surface of a building ▶ face, front, frontage, frontispiece, frontal. **2.** A deceptive outward appearance ▶ charade, cover, disguise, face, false colors, front, gloss, guise, make-believe, mask, masquerade, pose, pretense, pretext, semblance, show, veneer, window-dressing. *Slang:* put-on. [*Compare* **affectation, act, veil.**]

face *noun.* **1.** The front surface of the head ▶ countenance, features, lineaments, muzzle, physiognomy, visage. *Informal:* mug. *Slang:* kisser, map, pan, puss. **2.** A contorted facial expression showing pain, contempt, or disgust ▶ grimace, moue, pout. *Informal:* mug. [*Compare* **frown, glare, sneer.**] **3.** An outward appearance ▶ aspect, countenance, features, lineaments, look, surface. **4.** An outer surface, layer, or part of an object ▶ facet, side, surface. [*Compare* **back, bottom, front.**] **5.** The marked outer surface of an instrument ▶ dial, gauge, indicator. [*Compare* **front.**] **6.** Credit or respect in the eyes of others ▶ prestige, standing, status. [*Compare* **honor, pride, reputation.**] —*See also* **expression** (4), **façade** (1), **façade** (2), **impudence.**

face *verb.* **1.** To have the face or front turned toward ▶ front, give onto, look (on *or* upon *or* toward). [*Compare* **overlook.**] **2.** To cover with a different material ▶ clad, cover, sheathe, side, surface, veneer. [*Compare* **gloss**[1], **finish.**] **3.** To meet face-to-face, especially defiantly ▶ confront, encounter, front, meet. ***Idiom:*** stand up to. [*Compare* **contest.**] —*See also* **defy** (1).

face-lift *or* **face-lifting** *noun.* —*See* **renewal** (1).

face-off *noun.* —*See* **confrontation.**

facet *noun.* An outer surface, layer, or part of an object ▶ face, side, surface. [*Compare* **back, bottom, front.**] —*See also* **viewpoint.**

facetious *adjective.* —*See* **funny** (1).

facile *adjective.* —*See* **dexterous, easy** (1), **glib.**

facileness *noun.* —*See* **ease** (2).

facilitate *verb.* —*See* **ease** (2), **promote** (2).

facilitator *noun.* —*See* **go-between.**

facilities *noun.* —*See* **amenities** (1).

facility *noun.* —*See* **dexterity, ease** (2), **eloquence.**

facsimile *noun.* —*See* **copy** (1).

fact *noun.* Something demonstrated to exist or known to have existed ▶ actuality, event, phenomenon, reality. ***Idioms:*** hard (*or* cold *or* plain) fact. [*Compare* **information.**] —*See also* **certainty, circumstance** (2).

faction *noun.* —*See* **alliance, conflict.**

factitious *adjective.* —*See* **counterfeit.**

factor *noun.* —*See* **circumstance** (2), **part** (1), **representative.**

factory *noun.* A building or complex in which an industry is located ▶ mill, plant, works.

facts *noun.* —*See* **information.**

factual *adjective.* —*See* **accurate, realistic** (2).

facultative *adjective.* —*See* **optional.**

faculty *noun.* —*See* **ability** (2), **talent.**

fad *noun.* —*See* **enthusiasm** (2), **fashion.**

fade *verb.* To lose strength or power ▶ decline, degenerate, fail, flag, languish, sink, wane, waste away, weaken. *Informal:* fizzle (out), peter out. [*Compare* **decrease, deteriorate, subside, tire.**] —*See also* **disappear** (1), **fade away, pale.**

fade away *verb.* To grow weaker in sound ▶ die (away *or* out *or* down), fade (out), quiet (down). [*Compare* **silence.**] —*See also* **lift** (2).

fade out *verb.* To grow weaker in sound ▶ die (away *or* out *or* down), fade (away), quiet (down). [*Compare* **silence.**] —*See also* **disappear** (1).

faded *adjective.* —*See* **pale** (1), **shabby.**

fade-out *noun.* —*See* **disappearance.**

fail *verb.* **1.** To go wrong or be unsuccessful ▶ choke, fall through, founder, go amiss, go astray, go awry, go wrong, miscarry, misfire, miss, strike out, wash out. *Informal:* fall down, flop, flunk. *Slang:* bomb. ***Idioms:*** come a cropper, fall flat, fall short, lay an egg, miss fire, miss the mark. **2.** To prove deficient or insufficient ▶ give out, run out. ***Idioms:*** fall short, run dry, run short. [*Compare* **decrease.**] —*See also* **collapse** (2), **disappoint, fade, malfunction, neglect** (2).

failing *noun.* —*See* **defect, weakness.**

fail-safe *adjective.* —*See* **sure** (2).

failure *noun.* **1.** A person or enterprise that is unsuccessful ▶ bust, fiasco, loser, miscarriage, nonperformer, washout. *Informal:* clinker, clunker, dud, flop, lead balloon. *Slang:* bomb, turkey. [*Compare* **collapse.**] **2.** Nonperformance of what ought to be done ▶ default, delinquency, dereliction, neglect, nonfeasance, omission, shirking. [*Compare* **negligence.**] **3.** A cessation of proper functioning ▶ breakdown, collapse, malfunction, outage. **4.** A marked loss of strength or effectiveness ▶ declination, decline, deterioration. —*See also* **bankruptcy.**

fainéant *adjective.* —*See* **lazy.**

fainéant *noun.* —*See* **wastrel** (2).

faint *adjective.* So soft as to be barely audible ▶ feeble, weak. [*Compare* **soft.**] —*See also* **gentle** (2), **light**[2] (2), **pale** (2), **remote** (2), **unclear, weak** (1).

faint *noun.* A temporary loss of consciousness ▶ blackout, fainting spell, swoon, syncope.

faint *verb.* To suffer temporary lack of consciousness ▶ black out, keel over, pass out, swoon. ***Idioms:*** drop (*or* faint *or* fall) dead away, lose consciousness, see stars. [*Compare* **collapse.**]

✦ **CORE SYNONYMS:** *faint, blackout, swoon, syncope.* These nouns denote a temporary loss of consciousness: *fell in a dead faint at the sight of the body; suffers blackouts at high altitudes; sank to the ground in a swoon; was taken to the clinic in a state of syncope.*

---

faint-hearted *adjective.* —*See* **cowardly.**

faint-heartedness *noun.* —*See* **cowardice.**

fair[1] *adjective.* **1.** Free from bias in judgment ▶ balanced, detached, disinterested, dispassionate, equal, equitable, even, evenhanded, fair-minded, impartial, indifferent, just, nondiscriminatory, nonpartisan, objective, square, unbiased, unprejudiced. ***Idioms:*** fair and square, on the level. [*Compare* **broad-minded, honest, neutral.**] **2.** Having light hair ▶ blond, fair-haired, flaxen-haired, golden-haired, light-haired, towheaded. **3.** Having a light color or complexion ▶ alabaster, ivory, light, milky, pale. —*See also* **acceptable** (2), **average, beautiful, clear** (2), **favorable** (1), **sportsmanlike.**

fair *adverb.* In a fair, sporting manner ▶ cleanly, correctly, fairly, properly, sportingly. ***Idioms:*** fair and square, on the up and up. —*See also* **directly** (3).

✤ **CORE SYNONYMS:** *fair, just, equitable, impartial, unprejudiced, unbiased, objective, dispassionate.* These adjectives mean free from favoritism, self-interest, or preference in judgment. *Fair* is the most general: *a fair referee; a fair deal. Just* stresses conformity with what is legally or ethically right or proper: *"a just and lasting peace"* (Abraham Lincoln). *Equitable* implies justice dictated by reason, conscience, and a natural sense of what is fair: *an equitable distribution of gifts among the children. Impartial* emphasizes lack of favoritism: *"the cold neutrality of an impartial judge"* (Edmund Burke). *Unprejudiced* means without preconceived opinions or judgments: *an unprejudiced evaluation of the proposal. Unbiased* implies absence of a preference or partiality: *gave an unbiased account of her family problems. Objective* implies detachment that permits impersonal observation and judgment: *an objective jury. Dispassionate* means free from or unaffected by strong emotions: *a dispassionate reporter.*

---

fair² *noun.* —*See* **exhibition.**

fair-haired *adjective.* —*See* **fair¹** (2), **favorite.**

fairish *adjective.* —*See* **acceptable** (2).

fairly *adverb.* **1.** In a just or equitable manner ▶ dispassionately, equitably, evenhandedly, impartially, indifferently, justly, objectively, squarely. **2.** To some extent ▶ pretty, quite, rather. ***Idioms:*** in part, kind of, more or less, sort of, to a (*or* some) degree. [*Compare* **approximately, considerably, usually.**] —*See also* **fair¹, really.**

fair-minded *adjective.* —*See* **fair¹** (1).

fairness *or* **fair-mindedness** *noun.* The quality or state of being just and unbiased ▶ detachment, disinterest, disinterestedness, dispassion, dispassionateness, equitableness, evenhandedness, impartiality, impartialness, justice, justness, nonpartisanship, objectiveness, objectivity. [*Compare* **honesty.**]

fair-weather *adjective.* —*See* **undependable** (1).

fairy *noun.* A creature or spirit that has supernatural powers ▶ brownie, dryad, elf, goblin, hobgoblin, jinni, kelpie, leprechaun, naiad, nymph, pixie, pooka, puck, selkie, sprite, sylph.

fairy godmother *noun.* —*See* **donor.**

fairy tale *noun.* —*See* **myth** (1).

fairy-tale *adjective.* —*See* **mythical.**

faith *noun.* Mental acceptance of the actuality of something ▶ belief, credence, credit. —*See also* **devotion, religion, trust.**

faithful *adjective.* Adhering firmly to a person, cause, duty, or faith ▶ allegiant, committed, constant, dedicated, devoted, fast, firm, liege, loyal, staunch, steadfast, true, true-blue. [*Compare* **dependable, firm¹.**] —*See also* **accurate, authentic** (2), **close** (2), **divine** (2).

faithful *noun.* The steadfast believers in a faith or cause ▶ adherents, congregation, fold. [*Compare* **follower, assembly.**]

✤ **CORE SYNONYMS:** *faithful, loyal, true, constant, fast, steadfast, staunch.* These adjectives mean adhering firmly and devotedly to someone or something that elicits or demands one's fidelity. *Faithful* and *loyal* both suggest undeviating attachment, though *loyal* applies more often to political allegiance: *a faithful employee; a loyal citizen. True* implies steadiness, sincerity, and reliability: *"I would be true, for there are those who trust me"* (Howard Arnold Walter). *Constant* stresses uniformity and invariability: *"But I am constant as the northern star"* (William Shakespeare). *Fast* suggests loyalty that is not easily deflected: *fast friends. Steadfast* strongly implies fixed, unswerving loyalty: *is a steadfast ally. Staunch* even more strongly suggests unshakable attachment or allegiance: *"He lived and died a staunch loyalist"* (Harriet Beecher Stowe).

---

faithfully *adverb.* —*See* **exactly.**

faithfulness *noun.* —*See* **fidelity, veracity.**

faithless *adjective.* Not true to duty or obligation ▶ disloyal, false, falsehearted, perfidious, recreant, traitorous, treacherous, unfaithful, untrue. [*Compare* **undependable.**] —*See also* **atheistic.**

✚ **CORE SYNONYMS:** *faithless, unfaithful, false, disloyal, traitorous, treacherous, perfidious.* These adjectives mean not true to duty or obligation. *Faithless* and *unfaithful* imply failure to adhere to promises, obligations, or allegiances: *was faithless to her ideals; an unfaithful spouse. False* emphasizes deceitfulness: *"To thine own self be true,/And it must follow, as the night the day,/Thou canst not then be false to any man"* (William Shakespeare). One who is *disloyal* betrays an allegiance: *disloyal staff members who exposed the senator's indiscretions. Traitorous* most commonly refers to disloyalty to a government or nation: *a traitorous double agent. Treacherous* suggests a propensity for betraying trust or faith: *"She gave the treacherous impulse time to subside"* (Henry James). *Perfidious* suggests vileness of behavior and often deceitfulness: *a compelling narrative about a perfidious assassin.*

---

faithlessness *noun.* Betrayal, especially of a duty or obligation ▶ betrayal, disloyalty, false-heartedness, falseness, falsity, foul play, infidelity, perfidiousness, perfidy, traitorousness, treacherousness, treachery, treason, unfaithfulness. [*Compare* **deceit.**] —*See also* **atheism.**

fake *noun.* A person who practices deceit, especially under an assumed identity ▶ charlatan, faker, fraud, humbug, impostor, mountebank, phony, pretender, quack, sham. [*Compare* **cheat, hypocrite, liar.**] —*See also* **counterfeit.**

fake *verb.* To alter something so as to give it a false character ▶ doctor, falsify. —*See also* **act** (2), **counterfeit, improvise** (1).

fake *adjective.* —*See* **counterfeit.**

faker *noun.* One who makes a fraudulent copy of something ▶ counterfeiter, fabricator, falsifier, forger. —*See also* **fake.**

fall *verb.* **1.** To move downward in response to gravity ▶ descend, dive, drop, go down, nose-dive, pitch, plummet, plunge, sink, spill, tumble. ***Idioms:*** fall flat on one's face, go flying, take a fall (*or* header *or* plunge *or* spill *or* tumble). [*Compare* **recede, settle, stumble.**] **2.** To come to the ground from an upright position ▶ fall over (*or* down), keel over, tip over, topple, tumble. [*Compare* **buckle.**] **3.** To undergo capture, defeat, or ruin ▶ collapse, go down, go under, topple. [*Compare* **succumb, surrender.**] **4.** To become lower in value or price ▶ decline, depreciate, dive, drop (off), fall off, nose-dive, plummet, plunge, sag, sink, skid, slip, slump, tumble. ***Idioms:*** take a sudden downtrend (*or* downturn). [*Compare* **collapse, decrease, deteriorate, slip.**] **5.** To undergo moral deterioration ▶ degenerate, sink, slip. [*Compare* **deteriorate.**] —*See also* **drop** (1), **drop** (2), **happen** (1), **subside.**

fall apart *verb.* —*See* **break** (3), **disintegrate.**

fall back *verb.* —*See* **back** (1), **relapse, retreat.**

fall down *or* **flat** *verb.* —*See* **fail** (1).

fall off *verb.* —*See* **subside.**

fall on *or* **upon** *verb.* —*See* **attack** (1).

fall out *verb.* —*See* **argue** (1).

fall short *verb.* To prove deficient or insufficient ▶ give out, run out. ***Idioms:*** run dry, run short. [*Compare* **decrease.**] —*See also* **fail** (1).

fall through *verb.* —*See* **fail** (1).

fall *noun.* **1.** A sudden downward motion toward the ground ▶ descent, dive, drop, nosedive, pitch, plunge, spill, tumble. *Informal:* header. **2.** A disastrous defeat or ruin ▶ collapse, downfall, waterloo. [*Compare* **defeat.**] **3.** A usually swift downward trend, as in prices ▶ decline, depreciation, descent, dip, dive, downslide, downswing, downtrend, downturn, drop, drop-off, nosedive, plunge, skid, slide, slump, tumble. [*Compare* **decrease, depreciation, depression.**] —*See also* **drop** (3).

fallacious *adjective.* **1.** Containing errors in reasoning ▶ false, illogical, inconsistent, invalid, irrational, self-contradictory, sophistic, specious, spurious, unsound, untenable. [*Compare* **baseless, foolish, unreasonable.**] **2.** Tending to lead one into error ▶ deceptive, delusive, delusory, illusive, illusory, insidious, misleading. [*Compare* **dishonest, false.**] —*See also* **erroneous.**

fallacy *noun.* **1.** An erroneous or false idea ▶ error, falsehood, falsity, misapprehension, misconception, misinterpretation, misunderstanding, untruth. [*Compare* **error, illusion.**] **2.** Plausible but invalid reasoning ▶ casuistry, sophism, sophistry, speciousness, spuriousness.

fallback *noun.* —*See* **retreat.**

fallen *adjective.* —*See* **condemned.**

fall guy *noun.* —*See* **dupe, scapegoat.**

false *adjective.* Not true ▶ apocryphal, counterfactual, fictitious, specious, spurious, truthless, untrue, untruthful, wrong. [*Compare* **baseless, dishonest.**] —*See also* **counterfeit, erroneous, faithless, fallacious** (1).

false colors *noun.* —*See* **façade** (2).

false-hearted *adjective.* —*See* **dishonest, faithless.**

false-heartedness *noun.* —*See* **faithlessness.**

falsehood *noun.* —*See* **fallacy** (1), **lie**^{2}, **mendacity.**

false impression *noun.* —*See* **misunderstanding.**

falseness *noun.* —*See* **faithlessness.**

falsification *noun.* —*See* **counterfeit, mendacity.**

falsifier *noun.* One who makes a fraudulent copy of something ▶ counterfeiter, fabricator, faker, forger. —*See also* **liar.**

falsify *verb.* To alter something so as to give it a false character ▶ fake, doctor. —*See also* **counterfeit, distort, lie**^{2}.

falsity *noun.* —*See* **faithlessness, fallacy** (1), **insincerity, lie**^{2}.

falter *verb.* —*See* **hesitate, stagger** (1), **stammer.**

fame *noun.* Wide recognition for one's deeds ▶ celebrity, distinction, eminence, eminency, famousness, glory, illustriousness, luster, mark, notability, note, notoriety, popularity, preeminence, prestige, renown, prominence, prominency, reputation, repute. [*Compare* **distinction, esteem, honor, reputation.**]

famed *adjective.* —*See* **famous.**

familial *adjective.* —*See* **ancestral, domestic** (1).

familiar *adjective.* Having good knowledge of something ▶ acquainted, conversant, schooled, versant, versed. ***Idiom:*** up on. [*Compare* **accustomed, informed.**] —*See also* **common** (1), **confidential** (2), **impudent, intimate**^{1} (1).

familiar *noun.* —*See* **friend.**

familiarity *noun.* Personal knowledge derived from participation or observation ▶ acquaintance, conversance, experience. [*Compare* **awareness.**] —*See also* **dullness, friendship, impudence.**

familiarize *verb.* To make known socially ▶ acquaint, introduce, present. —*See also* **accustom.**

family *noun.* **1.** A group of people living together as a unit ▶ house, household, ménage. **2.** A group of people sharing common ancestry ▶ clan, house, kindred, lineage, stock, tribe. ***Idioms:*** kith and kin, flesh and blood. —*See also* **ancestry, class** (1), **kin.**

family *adjective.* —*See* **domestic** (1).

family tree *noun.* A written record of ancestry ▶ genealogy, pedigree. *—See also* **ancestry.**

famished *adjective. —See* **hungry** (1).

famous *adjective.* Widely known ▶ celebrated, distinguished, eminent, famed, glorious, great, illustrious, important, leading, legendary, notable, noted, notorious, popular, preeminent, prestigious, prominent, recognized, redoubtable, renowned, reputable, storied, well-known. ***Idiom:*** of note. [*Compare* **exalted.**]

✚ **CORE SYNONYMS:** *famous, celebrated, eminent, famed, illustrious, notable, noted, preeminent, renowned.* These adjectives mean widely known and esteemed: *a famous actor; a celebrated musician; an eminent scholar; a famed scientist; an illustrious judge; a notable historian; a noted author; a preeminent archaeologist; a renowned painter.*

◀ **ANTONYM:** *obscure*

---

famousness *noun. —See* **fame.**

fan[1] *verb. —See* **spread** (1).

fan[2] *noun.* An ardent devotee ▶ admirer, aficionado, bug, devotee, enthusiast, fanatic, fancier, follower, groupie, hound, junkie, lover, maniac, zealot. *Informal:* buff, fiend. *Slang:* freak, head, nut. [*Compare* **follower.**]

fanatic *noun. —See* **devotee, extremist, fan[2].**

fanatic *or* **fanatical** *adjective. —See* **enthusiastic, extreme** (2).

fanaticism *noun. —See* **enthusiasm** (1).

fancier *noun. —See* **fan[2].**

fanciful *adjective.* Showing invention or whimsy in design ▶ fantastic, imaginative, whimsical. [*Compare* **capricious, elaborate, ornate.**] *—See also* **dreamy, exotic, imaginary.**

fancy *noun.* An impulsive turn of mind ▶ caprice, conceit, freak, humor, impulse, megrim, notion, vagary, whim, whimsy. ***Idiom:*** bee in one's bonnet. [*Compare* **mood.**] *—See also* **dream** (1), **enthusiasm** (2), **imagination, liking, love** (2).

fancy *adjective. —See* **elaborate, exclusive** (3), **luxurious.**

fancy *verb. —See* **dream, guess, imagine, like[1].**

fancy-free *adjective. —See* **lighthearted, single.**

fanfaronade *noun. —See* **boast.**

fanny *noun. —See* **buttocks.**

fantasist *noun. —See* **dreamer** (1).

fantasize *verb. —See* **dream, imagine.**

fantastic *adjective.* Showing invention or whimsy in design ▶ fanciful, imaginative, whimsical. [*Compare* **elaborate, ornate.**] *—See also* **astonishing, capricious, eccentric, exotic, fictitious, imaginary, marvelous.**

fantastical *adjective. —See* **imaginary, marvelous.**

fantasy *noun. —See* **dream** (1), **dream** (2), **imagination, myth** (2).

fantasy *adjective. —See* **mythical.**

far *adverb. —See* **considerably.**

far *adjective. —See* **distant.**

faraway *adjective. —See* **absent-minded, distant.**

farce *noun. —See* **mockery** (2), **satire.**

farceur *noun. —See* **joker.**

farcical *adjective.* Causing or deserving laughter or derision ▶ laughable, ludicrous, ridiculous, risible. [*Compare* **foolish.**]

farcicality *noun. —See* **humor.**

fare *verb. —See* **journey, manage.**

fare *noun. —See* **food, toll[1]** (1).

farewell *noun. —See* **departure.**

farewell *adjective. —See* **parting.**

farewell *interjection. —See* **goodbye.**

far-fetched *adjective. —See* **exaggerated, incredible.**

far-flung *adjective.* Spread out over a large area ▶ broad, widespread. *—See also* **distant.**

farm *verb. —See* **grow.**

farness *noun.* The fact or condition of being far removed or apart ▶ distance, remoteness, separateness, separation.

far-off *adjective.* —*See* **distant.**
far-out *adjective.* —*See* **extreme** (2).
far-ranging *or* **far-reaching** *adjective.* —*See* **general** (2).
farsighted *adjective.* —*See* **visionary.**
farsightedness *noun.* —*See* **vision** (2).
farthest *or* **farthermost** *adjective.* —*See* **extreme** (1).
fascinate *verb.* —*See* **charm** (1), **grip.**
fascinating *adjective.* —*See* **attractive.**
fascination *noun.* —*See* **attraction, obsession.**
fascism *noun.* —*See* **tyranny.**
fashion *noun.* The current custom ▶ craze, fad, furor, mode, rage, style, trend, vogue. *Informal:* thing. ***Idioms:*** the in thing, the last word, the latest thing. [*Compare* **custom.**] —*See also* **style, way** (1).
fashion *verb.* —*See* **adapt, form** (1), **make.**

✦ **CORE SYNONYMS:** *fashion, style, mode, vogue.* These nouns refer to the prevailing or preferred manner of dress, adornment, behavior, or way of life at a given time. *Fashion,* the broadest term, usually refers to what accords with conventions adopted by polite society or by any culture or subculture: *a time when long hair was the fashion. Style* is sometimes used interchangeably with *fashion,* but like *mode* often stresses adherence to standards of elegance: *traveling in style; miniskirts that were the mode in the late sixties. Vogue* is applied to fashion that prevails widely and often suggests enthusiastic but short-lived acceptance: *a video game that was in vogue a few years ago.*

fashionable *adjective.* In accordance with current fashion ▶ à la mode, chic, dashing, de rigueur, fashion-forward, mod, modish, smart, stylish, swank, swanky. *Informal:* classy, in, sharp, snappy, swish, trendy, with-it. *Slang:* funky, hip, hot, snazzy. ***Idioms:*** all the rage, up to the minute. [*Compare* **contemporary, elegant, luxurious.**]

✦ **CORE SYNONYMS:** *fashionable, chic, dashing, in, modish, sharp, smart, stylish, swank, trendy.* These adjectives mean in accordance with the current fashion: *a fashionable restaurant; a chic dress; a dashing hat; the in place to go; modish jewelry; a sharp jacket; a smart hotel; stylish clothes; a swank apartment; a trendy neighborhood.*

fast *adjective.* **1.** Characterized by great speed ▶ blinding, breakneck, brisk, expeditious, express, fleet, hasty, high-speed, hurried, quick, rapid, speedy, swift. *Informal:* hell-for-leather, pedal-to-the-metal. ***Idioms:*** quick as a bunny (*or* wink). **2.** Retaining original color ▶ colorfast, indelible. —*See also* **abandoned** (2), **faithful, firm**[1] (2), **intimate**[1] (1), **quick, tight** (1), **wanton** (1).
fast *adverb.* In a rapid way ▶ apace, hastily, hurriedly, posthaste, quick, quickly, rapidly, swiftly. *Informal:* flat out, hell-for-leather, lickety-split, pedal-to-the-metal, pronto. ***Idioms:*** full tilt, in a flash, in nothing flat, like a bat out of hell, like a blue streak, like a flash, like a house on fire, like a shot, like a streak, like greased lightning, like the wind, like wildfire, with dispatch.

✦ **CORE SYNONYMS:** *fast, rapid, swift, fleet, speedy, quick, hasty, expeditious.* These adjectives refer to something characterized by great speed. *Fast* and *rapid* are often used interchangeably, though *fast* is more often applied to the person or thing in motion, and *rapid,* to the activity or movement involved: *a fast runner; rapid strides. Swift* suggests smoothness and sureness of movement (*a swift current*), and *fleet,* lightness of movement (*The cheetah is the fleetest of animals*). *Speedy* refers to velocity (*a speedy train*) or to promptness or hurry (*a speedy resolution to the problem*). *Quick* most often applies to what takes little time or to what is prompt: *a quick snack; your quick reaction. Hasty* implies hurried action (*a hasty visit*) and often a lack of care or thought (*regretted the hasty decision*). *Expeditious* suggests rapid efficiency: *sent the package by the most expeditious means.*

◀ **ANTONYM:** *slow*

---

fasten *verb.* To cause to remain firmly in position or place; make secure ▶ anchor, bind, bolt, buckle, catch, chain, clamp, clip, fix, hitch, knot, lash, lock, moor, nail, pin, rivet, screw, secure, strap, tack, tie (up). ***Idiom:*** make fast. [*Compare* **support.**] —*See also* **attach** (1), **fix** (2), **fix** (3).

fasten on *or* **upon** *verb.* —*See* **impose on.**

✚ **CORE SYNONYMS:** *fasten, anchor, fix, moor, secure.* These verbs mean to cause to remain firmly in position or place: *fastened our seat belts; anchored the television antenna to the roof; fixed the flagpole in concrete; will moor the rowboat at the dock; secured the bolt after closing the door.*

---

fastener *or* **fastening** *noun.* A device for locking or for checking motion ▶ bar, binder, binding, buckle, catch, clamp, clasp, clip, collar, harness, hasp, hook, latch, lock, mortise, pawl, snap, vise. [*Compare* **anchor, bond, cord, nail.**]

fastidious *adjective.* —*See* **careful** (2), **fussy.**

fastidiousness *noun.* —*See* **thoroughness.**

fastigium *noun.* —*See* **climax.**

fastness *noun.* —*See* **stability.**

fast one *noun.* —*See* **trick** (1).

fat *adjective.* **1.** Having too much flesh or a full figure ▶ chubby, corpulent, fatty, flabby, fleshy, full, gross, heavy, meaty, obese, overblown, overweight, paunchy, plump, plumpish, porcine, portly, potbellied, pudgy, roly-poly, rotund, round, stout, tubby, weighty, zaftig. *Slang:* porky. [*Compare* **bulky, stocky.**] **2.** Relatively great in extent from one surface to the opposite ▶ thick. [*Compare* **bulky.**] —*See also* **fatty, profitable.**

fat *noun.* Adipose tissue ▶ blubber, lard, suet, tallow. [*Compare* **oil.**] —*See also* **surplus.**

✚ **CORE SYNONYMS:** *fat, obese, corpulent, fleshy, portly, stout, pudgy, rotund, plump, chubby.* These adjectives mean having an abundance and often an excess of flesh. *Fat* implies excessive weight and generally has negative connotations: *was getting fat and decided to exercise. Obese* and *corpulent* imply gross overweight: "*a woman of robust frame . . . though stout, not obese*" (Charlotte Brontë). *The dancer was corpulent but surprisingly graceful. Fleshy* implies a not necessarily excessive abundance of flesh: *firm, fleshy arms. Portly* refers to bulk combined with a stately or imposing bearing: "*a portly, rubicund man of middle age*" (Winston Churchill). *Stout* denotes a thickset, bulky figure: *a painting of stout peasants. Pudgy* means short and fat: *pudgy fingers. Rotund* suggests roundness of figure, often in a squat person: "*this pink-faced rotund specimen of prosperity*" (George Eliot). *Plump* and *chubby* apply to a pleasing fullness of figure: *a plump little toddler; chubby cheeks.*

---

fatal *adjective.* So critically decisive as to affect the future ▶ fateful, momentous. [*Compare* **decisive.**] —*See also* **deadly, disastrous.**

fatality *noun.* **1.** A loss of life, or one who has lost life, usually as a result of accident, disaster, or war ▶ casualty, death, kill, loss, statistic. [*Compare* **victim.**] **2.** The quality or condition of causing death or disaster ▶ deadliness, fatefulness, lethality, lethalness.

fate *noun.* **1.** The supposed power that predetermines events ▶ destiny, fortune, kismet, luck, predestination, preordination. [*Compare* **chance.**] **2.** A personal outcome or end ▶ destiny, doom, end, fortune, lot, luck, portion. [*Compare* **misfortune, ruin.**]

fated *adjective.* Governed by fate ▶ destined, foreordained, ordained, predestined, predetermined, preordained. [*Compare* **certain.**] —*See also* **condemned.**

fateful *adjective.* **1.** Bringing or predicting misfortune ▶ bad, baleful, dark, dire, direful, evil, forbidding, foreboding, grave, ill, ill-boding, ill-omened, inauspicious, looming, lowering, malign, menacing, ominous, portentous, sinister, sullen, threatening, unfavorable, unlucky, unpropitious. [*Compare* **unfortunate.**] **2.** So critically decisive as to affect the future ▶ fatal, momentous. [*Compare* **decisive.**] —*See also* **disastrous.**

✤ **CORE SYNONYMS:** *fateful, sinister, baleful, malign.* These adjectives mean bringing or predicting misfortune: *Fateful* applies to that which is ominously prophetic or portentous: *The fortune teller said that the remaining card represented a fateful sign of change. Sinister* refers to impending or lurking danger and often connotes evil: *We heard a sinister laugh from behind the door. Baleful* intensifies the sense of menace; it suggests a deadly, virulent, or poisonous quality: *The guard's baleful glare frightened the children. Malign* applies to what manifests an evil disposition, nature, influence, or intent: "*The Devil . . . with jealous leer malign/Eyed them askance*" (John Milton).

---

fatefulness *adjective.* The quality or condition of causing death or disaster ▶ deadliness, fatality, lethality, lethalness.

fatheadedness *noun.* —*See* **stupidity.**

father *noun.* A male parent ▶ begetter, paterfamilias, patriarch, sire. *Informal:* dad, daddy, pa, papa, pappy, pop. *Slang:* old boy, old man. —*See also* **ancestor** (1), **original, originator.**

father *verb.* To be the biological father of ▶ beget, get, sire. —*See also* **breed.**

fatherly *or* **fatherlike** *adjective.* Like a father, especially in caring ▶ fatherlike, paternal, patriarchal. [*Compare* **benevolent.**]

fathom *verb.* —*See* **explore, know** (1), **understand** (1).

fathomable *adjective.* —*See* **understandable.**

fatidic *or* **fatidical** *adjective.* —*See* **prophetic.**

fatigue *noun.* —*See* **exhaustion.**

fatigue *verb.* —*See* **bore²**, **tire** (1).

fatigued *adjective.* —*See* **tired** (1).

fatiguing *adjective.* Causing fatigue ▶ draining, exhausting, tiring, wearing, wearying. [*Compare* **burdensome.**]

fatty *adjective.* Having the qualities of fat ▶ adipose, blubbery, fat, greasy, oily, oleaginous, unctuous. —*See also* **fat** (1).

fatuity *noun.* —*See* **foolishness.**

fatuous *adjective.* —*See* **foolish.**

fatuousness *noun.* —*See* **foolishness.**

faucet *noun.* A device that regulates the flow of a liquid ▶ cock, fixture, petcock, spigot, stopcock, tap.

fault *noun.* —*See* **blame, crack** (2), **defect, weakness.**

fault *verb.* —*See* **criticize** (1).

faultfinder *noun.* —*See* **critic** (2), **grouch.**

faultfinding *adjective.* —*See* **critical** (1).

faultless *adjective.* —*See* **exemplary, innocent** (2), **perfect.**

faulty *adjective.* Having a defect or defects ▶ amiss, blemished, defective, flawed, imperfect. [*Compare* **shabby, trick.**] —*See also* **erroneous.**

faux pas *noun.* —*See* **blunder.**

favor *noun.* **1.** A kindly act ▶ benefaction, beneficence, benevolence, benignity, courtesy, good deed, good turn, grace, indulgence, kindness, kindliness, kind office, philanthropy, service. [*Compare* **help.**] **2.** Preferential treatment or bias ▶ favoritism, partiality, partialness, preference. [*Compare* **bias, prejudice.**]

—*See also* **acceptance** (2), **advantage** (2), **esteem, remembrance** (1).

favor *verb.* **1.** To show partiality toward someone ▶ prefer. ***Idioms:*** be partial, play favorites. [*Compare* **advance, baby.**] **2.** To be favorably disposed toward ▶ approve, countenance, hold with. *Informal:* go for. ***Idioms:*** be in favor of, take kindly to, think highly (*or* well) of. [*Compare* **assent, value.**] **3.** To lend supportive approval to ▶ countenance, encourage, smile on (*or* upon). [*Compare* **support.**] —*See also* **like[1], oblige** (1), **resemble.**

favorable *adjective.* **1.** Indicative of future success or full of promise ▶ auspicious, benign, bright, brilliant, fair, fortunate, good, propitious. [*Compare* **encouraging.**] **2.** Giving assent ▶ affirmative, agreeable, approving, assenting, positive. **3.** Disposed to favor one over another ▶ partial, preferential. [*Compare* **biased.**] —*See also* **beneficial, opportune, pleasant.**

✚ CORE SYNONYMS: *favorable, propitious, auspicious, benign.* These adjectives describe what is indicative of a successful outcome. *Favorable* can refer to what contributes in a positive way to the attainment of a goal: *a favorable review. Propitious* implies a favorable tendency or inclination: *"Miracles are propitious accidents"* (George Santayana). *Auspicious* refers to what presages good fortune: *an auspicious beginning. Benign* applies to people or things that exert a beneficial influence: *"I lingered round them, under that benign sky . . . and wondered how anyone could ever imagine unquiet slumbers, for the sleepers in that quiet earth"* (Emily Brontë).

favored *adjective.* —*See* **favorite.**

favorite *noun.* **1.** One liked or preferred above all others ▶ darling, pet. ***Idiom:*** apple of one's eye. **2.** A leading contestant or sure winner ▶ front-runner, leader, number one, vanguard. *Informal:* shoo-in.

favorite *adjective.* Being a favorite ▶ darling, fair-haired, favored, pet, popular, preferred, well-liked. [*Compare* **select.**]

favoritism *noun.* Preferential treatment or bias ▶ favor, partiality, partialness, preference. [*Compare* **bias, prejudice.**]

fawn *verb.* To behave obsequiously or submissively ▶ bootlick, cringe, grovel, kowtow, slaver, toady, truckle. *Informal:* apple-polish, brownnose. *Slang:* suck up. ***Idioms:*** curry favor, dance attendance, kiss someone's feet, lick someone's boots. [*Compare* **flatter.**]

✚ CORE SYNONYMS: *fawn, apple-polish, bootlick, kowtow, slaver, toady, truckle.* These verbs mean to curry favor by behaving obsequiously and submissively: *fawned on her superior; students apple-polishing the teacher; bootlicked to get a promotion; lawyers kowtowing to a judge; slavered over his rich uncle; toadying to members of the club; nobles truckling to the king.*

fawner *noun.* —*See* **sycophant.**

faze *verb.* —*See* **embarrass.**

fealty *noun.* —*See* **fidelity.**

fear *noun.* A feeling of agitation in the face of danger or trouble ▶ affright, alarm, apprehension, consternation, dismay, dread, fearfulness, fright, funk, horror, panic, terror, trepidation. *Slang:* cold feet. ***Idiom:*** fear and trembling. [*Compare* **anxiety, cowardice.**]

fear *verb.* To be afraid ▶ dread. ***Idioms:*** break out in a cold sweat, have butterflies (in one's stomach), have knots (*or* a knot) in one's stomach, have one's heart in one's mouth, sweat blood (*or* bullets). [*Compare* **flinch.**]

✚ CORE SYNONYMS: *fear, fright, dread, terror, horror, panic, alarm, dismay, consternation, trepidation.* These nouns denote the agitation and anxiety caused by the presence or imminence of danger. *Fear* is the most general term: "*Fear is the parent of cruelty*" (J.A. Froude). *Fright* is sudden, usually momentary, great fear: *In my fright, I forgot to lock the door. Dread* is strong fear, especially of what one is powerless to avoid: *His dread of strangers kept him from socializing. Terror* is intense, overpowering fear: "*And now at the dead hour of the night, amid the dreadful silence of that old house, so strange a noise as this excited me to uncontrollable terror*" (Edgar Allan Poe). *Horror* is a combination of fear and aversion or repugnance: *Murder arouses widespread horror. Panic* is sudden frantic fear, often groundless: *The fire caused a panic among the horses. Alarm* is fright aroused by the first realization of danger: *I watched with alarm as the sky darkened. Dismay* robs one of courage or the power to act effectively: *The rumor of war caused universal dismay. Consternation* is often paralyzing, characterized by confusion and helplessness: *Consternation gripped the city as the invaders approached. Trepidation* is dread characteristically marked by trembling or hesitancy: "*They were . . . full of trepidation about things that were never likely to happen*" (John Morley).

---

fearful *adjective*. Causing or capable of causing fear ▶ alarming, appalling, dire, direful, dismaying, dreadful, fearsome, formidable, frightening, frightful, unnerving, redoubtable, scary, terrible. [*Compare* **horrible, ghastly, weird.**] —*See also* **afraid, terrible.**

fearfulness *noun*. —*See* **fear.**

fearless *adjective*. —*See* **brave.**

fearlessness *noun*. —*See* **courage, daring.**

fearsome *adjective*. —*See* **afraid, fearful.**

feasible *adjective*. —*See* **possible.**

feast *noun*. A large, elaborately prepared meal ▶ banquet, junket. *Informal:* feed, spread.

feast *verb*. To sustain a living organism with food ▶ feast, feed, regale. ***Idiom:*** wine and dine. [*Compare* **support.**] —*See also* **celebrate** (2).

feast on *verb*. To be avidly interested in ▶ devour, relish. *Slang:* eat up.

feat *noun*. A clever, dexterous act ▶ stunt, trick. ***Idiom:*** sleight of hand. —*See also* **accomplishment.**

feather *noun*. —*See* **kind²**.

featherbrained *adjective*. —*See* **giddy** (2).

feature *noun*. —*See* **item, quality** (1).

feature *verb*. —*See* **emphasize, imagine.**

features *noun*. —*See* **appearance** (1), **face** (1), **face** (3).

febrile *or* **febrific** *adjective*. —*See* **feverish.**

feckless *adjective*. —*See* **careless.**

fecund *adjective*. Capable of reproducing ▶ fertile, fruitful, productive, prolific. —*See also* **fertile** (1).

fecundate *verb*. To make fertile ▶ enrich, fertilize, pollinate. [*Compare* **impregnate.**]

fecundity *noun*. —*See* **fertility, invention** (1).

federate *verb*. —*See* **ally, associate** (1).

federation *noun*. —*See* **alliance, union** (1).

fed up *adjective*. Out of patience ▶ disgusted, sick, tired, weary. ***Idioms:*** sick and tired, sick to death. [*Compare* **angry.**]

fee *noun*. —*See* **toll¹** (1), **wage.**

feeble *adjective*. So soft as to be barely audible ▶ faint, weak. [*Compare* **soft.**] —*See also* **implausible, weak** (1).

feeble-minded *adjective*. —*See* **backward** (1).

feebleness *noun*. —*See* **infirmity.**

feed *verb*. To sustain a living organism with food ▶ feast, nourish, regale. ***Idiom:*** wine and dine. [*Compare* **support.**] —*See also* **promote** (2).

feed on *verb*. To include as part of one's diet by nature or preference ▶ eat, exist on, live on, subsist on. [*Compare* **eat.**]

feed *noun. Informal* A large, elaborately prepared meal ▶ banquet, feast, junket. *Informal:* spread.

feel *verb.* **1.** To experience or express compassion ▶ ache, commiserate, condole, sympathize. ***Idioms:*** be (*or* feel) sorry, have one's heart ache (*or* bleed) for someone, have one's heart go out to someone. [*Compare* **comfort, pity.**] **2.** To have a belief or impression about something ▶ believe, hold, sense, think. [*Compare* **believe, perceive, regard.**] **3.** To give the impression of being ▶ appear, look, seem, sound. ***Idioms:*** have all the earmarks of being, give the idea (*or* impression) of being, strike one as being. [*Compare* **resemble.**] *—See also* **experience, grope, perceive, touch.**

feel for *verb. —See* **pity.**

feel out *verb.* To test the attitude of someone ▶ probe, sound (out). ***Idioms:*** put out feelers, run something up the flagpole, send up a trial balloon.

feel *noun.* **1.** A particular sensation conveyed by means of physical contact ▶ feeling, touch. [*Compare* **contact, brush.**] **2.** The faculty or ability to perceive tactile stimulation ▶ feeling, tactility, touch. ***Idiom:*** sense of touch. [*Compare* **sensation.**] **3.** The proper method for doing, using, or handling something ▶ knack, trick. *Informal:* hang. *—See also* **air** (3), **touch** (1).

feeler *noun.* Something, such as a remark, used to determine another person's attitude ▶ probe. ***Idiom:*** trial balloon. [*Compare* **advances, introduction.**]

feeling *noun.* **1.** An intuitive awareness or sense of something ▶ foreboding, forewarning, gut reaction, hunch, idea, impression, inkling, intuition, notion, premonition, presentiment, suspicion. [*Compare* **hint, instinct, qualm.**] **2.** A particular sensation conveyed by means of physical contact ▶ feel, touch. [*Compare* **contact, brush.**] **3.** The faculty or ability to perceive tactile stimulation ▶ feel, tactility, touch. ***Idiom:*** sense of touch. [*Compare* **sensation.**] **4.** A general cast of mind with regard to something ▶ attitude, sentiment. [*Compare* **idea.**] **5.** The quality or condition of being emotionally and intuitively sensitive ▶ sensibility, sensitiveness, sensitivity. [*Compare* **pity, sympathy.**] *—See also* **air** (3), **belief** (1), **emotion, sensation** (1), **touch** (1).

feeling *adjective.* Readily stirred by emotion ▶ emotional, sensitive. [*Compare* **passionate.**] *—See also* **sympathetic.**

feign *verb.* To claim or allege insincerely or falsely ▶ pretend, pretext, profess, purport. *—See also* **act** (2).

feigned *adjective. —See* **artificial** (2).

feint *noun. —See* **trick** (1).

feisty *adjective. —See* **argumentative.**

felicitate *verb.* To pay a compliment to ▶ commend, compliment, congratulate, praise. ***Idioms:*** pay tribute to, raise a glass to, take off one's hat to. [*Compare* **honor.**]

felicitations *noun. —See* **compliment.**

felicitous *adjective. —See* **appropriate.**

felicity *noun. —See* **happiness.**

feline *adjective. —See* **stealthy.**

fell *verb. —See* **drop** (3).

fellow *noun.* A man referred to familiarly or as a member of one's group ▶ brother. *Informal:* boy, chap, guy, jack, lad. *Slang:* dude, hombre, homeboy. *—See also* **associate** (1), **associate** (2), **boyfriend, mate, peer^2.**

fellow citizen *noun.* A person who is from one's own country ▶ compatriot, countryman, countrywoman, kinsman, kinswoman.

fellowship *noun. —See* **company** (3), **friendship, union** (1).

felon *noun. —See* **criminal.**

felonious *adjective. —See* **criminal** (1).

felony *noun. —See* **crime** (1).

female *adjective.* Relating to or characteristic of women ▶ feminine, womanish, womanly.

femaleness *or* **feminineness** *noun.* The quality or condition of being feminine ▶ feminineness, femininity, womanliness.

feminine *adjective.* Relating to or characteristic of women ▶ female, womanish, womanly. —*See also* **effeminate.**

femininity *noun.* The quality or condition of being feminine ▶ femaleness, feminineness, womanliness. —*See also* **effeminacy.**

femme fatale *noun.* —*See* **seductress.**

fen *noun.* —*See* **swamp.**

fence *verb.* To separate with or as if with a wall ▶ screen, partition, wall. —*See also* **contend, enclose** (1), **equivocate** (1), **evade** (1).

fence *noun.* —*See* **equivocation.**

fend *verb.* —*See* **manage, repel.**

fender-bender *noun.* —*See* **crash** (2).

feral *adjective.* —*See* **wild** (2).

ferment *verb.* —*See* **boil.**

ferment *noun.* —*See* **agitation** (1), **catalyst.**

ferocious *adjective.* So intense as to cause extreme suffering ▶ cruel, fierce, savage, vicious. —*See also* **cruel.**

ferociousness *noun.* —*See* **intensity.**

ferocity *noun.* —*See* **cruelty, intensity.**

ferret *verb.* —*See* **seek** (1).

ferret out *verb.* —*See* **discover.**

fertile *adjective.* **1.** Characterized by great productivity ▶ fecund, fruitful, productive, prolific, rich. [*Compare* **inventive.**] **2.** Capable of reproducing ▶ fecund, fruitful, productive, prolific.

✚ **CORE SYNONYMS:** *fertile, fecund, fruitful, productive, prolific.* These adjectives mean characterized by great productivity: *fertile farmland; a fecund imagination; fruitful efforts; a productive meeting; a prolific writer.*

---

fertility *noun.* The quality or state of being fertile ▶ fecundity, fruitfulness, productiveness, productivity, prolificacy, prolificness, richness. [*Compare* **invention.**]

fertilize *verb.* **1.** To add fertilizer to ▶ dress, manure, top-dress. **2.** To make fertile ▶ enrich, fecundate, pollinate. [*Compare* **impregnate.**]

fervency *noun.* —*See* **passion.**

fervent *adjective.* —*See* **enthusiastic, passionate.**

fervid *adjective.* —*See* **enthusiastic, frantic, passionate.**

fervor *noun.* —*See* **enthusiasm** (1), **heat** (1), **passion.**

fess up *verb.* —*See* **acknowledge** (1).

fester *verb.* —*See* **decay.**

festering *noun.* —*See* **irritation.**

festinate *verb.* —*See* **rush.**

festival *noun.* —*See* **celebration** (1), **exhibition.**

festive *adjective.* —*See* **merry.**

festiveness *noun.* —*See* **merriment** (2).

festivity *noun.* —*See* **celebration** (1), **celebration** (3), **merriment** (2), **party.**

festoon *noun.* —*See* **adorn** (1).

fetch *verb.* —*See* **bring** (1), **bring** (2).

fetching *adjective.* —*See* **attractive, becoming.**

fete *noun.* —*See* **celebration** (1), **party.**

fetid *adjective.* —*See* **smelly.**

fetish *noun.* —*See* **charm, obsession.**

fetor *noun.* —*See* **stench.**

fetter *noun.* —*See* **bond** (1), **cord.**

fetter *verb.* —*See* **hamper**[1].

fettle *noun.* —*See* **shape.**

feud *noun.* —*See* **argument, enmity.**

feud *verb.* —*See* **argue** (1).

fever *noun.* —*See* **enthusiasm** (1).

fevered *adjective.* —*See* **frantic.**

feverish *adjective.* Having an above-normal body temperature ▶ febrific, febrile, hectic, hot, pyretic. [*Compare* **sick.**] —*See also* **frantic, passionate.**

few *adjective.* —*See* **several.**

few *pronoun.* —*See* **several.**

fey *adjective.* —*See* **magic.**

fiancé *or* **fiancée** *noun.* —*See* **intended.**

fiasco *noun.* —*See* **disappointment** (2), **disaster, failure** (1), **mess** (1).

fiat *noun.* —*See* **command** (1).

fib *noun.* —*See* **lie**[2].

fib *verb.* —*See* **lie**[2].

fibber *noun.* —*See* **liar.**

fiber *noun.* A very fine continuous strand ▶ fibril, filament, microfiber, thread. [*Compare* **cord.**] —*See also* **character** (2), **texture.**

fibril *noun.* A very fine continuous strand ▶ fiber, filament, microfiber, thread. [*Compare* **cord.**]

fibrous *adjective.* Containing or consisting of fibers ▶ sinewy, stringy, threadlike.

fickle *adjective.* —*See* **capricious.**

fiction *noun.* A narrative not based on fact ▶ fable, novel, romance, story. [*Compare* **yarn.**] —*See also* **dream** (1), **lie**[2], **myth** (2).

fictional *adjective.* —*See* **fictitious.**

fictitious *adjective.* Consisting or suggestive of fiction ▶ fantastic, fictional, fictive, invented, made-up. [*Compare* **imaginary.**] —*See also* **false.**

fictive *adjective.* —*See* **fictitious.**

fiddle *verb.* To touch or handle something out of restlessness ▶ fidget, fool, play, toy, trifle, twiddle. *Informal:* monkey. [*Compare* **handle.**] —*See also* **bias** (2), **putter, tinker.**

fiddle away *verb.* —*See* **idle** (2).

fiddle-faddle *noun.* —*See* **trifle.**

fidelity *noun.* Faithfulness or devotion to a person, cause, or obligation ▶ allegiance, constancy, faithfulness, fealty, loyalty, steadfastness. [*Compare* **attachment.**] —*See also* **veracity.**

✚ CORE SYNONYMS: *fidelity, allegiance, fealty, loyalty.* These nouns denote faithfulness or devotion to a person, cause, or obligation. *Fidelity* implies the unfailing fulfillment of one's duties and obligations and strict adherence to vows or promises: *fidelity to one's spouse. Allegiance* is faithfulness considered as a duty: "*I know no South, no North, no East, no West, to which I owe any allegiance . . . . The Union, Sir, is my country*" (Henry Clay). *Fealty,* once applied to the obligation of a tenant or vassal to a feudal lord, now suggests faithfulness that one has pledged to uphold: *swore fealty to the laws of that country. Loyalty* implies a steadfast and devoted attachment that is not easily turned aside: *loyalty to an oath; loyalty to one's family.*

---

fidget *verb.* —*See* **fiddle.**

fidgets *noun.* —*See* **jitters.**

fidgety *adjective.* —*See* **edgy.**

field *noun.* **1.** An area of open land ▶ clearing, meadow, pasture. [*Compare* **lot.**] **2.** An area of academic study that is part of a larger body of learning ▶ branch, discipline, specialty. —*See also* **area** (1).

field *verb.* —*See* **answer.**

fiend *noun.* A perversely mean, cruel, or wicked person ▶ archfiend, barbarian, beast, brute, demon, devil, ghoul, hun, monster, ogre, savage, villain. [*Compare* **evildoer, rascal.**] —*See also* **fan**[2].

fiendish *adjective.* Perversely mean, cruel, or wicked ▶ devilish, diabolic, diabolical, ghoulish, hellish, infernal, ogreish, satanic, villainous. [*Compare* **evil, fierce, malevolent.**]

fierce *adjective.* —*See* **cruel, intense.**

fiercely *adverb.* —*See* **hard** (1).

fierceness *noun.* —*See* **cruelty, intensity.**

fiery *adjective.* —*See* **burning, hot** (1), **passionate, spicy.**

fiesta *noun.* —*See* **celebration** (1).

fifty-fifty *adjective.* Neither favorable nor unfavorable ▶ balanced, even, nip and tuck.

fight *noun.* **1.** A physical conflict involving two or more people ▶ affray, brawl, donnybrook, fistfight, fisticuffs, fracas, fray, free-for-all, melee, riot, row, ruction, scrap, scuffle, tumult, tussle. *Slang:* rumble, slugfest. [*Compare* **attack, brush**[1], **combat, conflict.**] **2.** The power or will to fight ▶ bellicoseness, bellicosity, belligerence, belligerency, combativeness, contentiousness, pugnacity, pugnaciousness, truculence, truculency. [*Compare* **aggression.**] —*See also* **argument, competition** (2).

fight *verb.* To exchange blows with another person ▶ brawl. *Slang:* rumble. ***Idioms:*** duke it out, mix it up, slug it out, trade blows. [*Compare* **wrestle.**] —*See also* **argue** (1), **contend, oppose.**

fight off *verb.* —*See* **repel.**

✚ CORE SYNONYMS: *fight, brawl, donnybrook, fray, free-for-all, melee, row, scuffle.* These nouns denote a physical conflict involving two or more people: *an argument that escalated into a fight; a barroom brawl; a vicious legal donnybrook; eager for the fray; a free-for-all in the schoolyard; police plunging into the melee; an angry domestic row; a scuffle between the opposing teams.*

---

fighter *noun.* **1.** One who engages in a combat or struggle ▶ belligerent, combatant, soldier, warrior. [*Compare* **aggressor, soldier.**] **2.** A contestant in a boxing match ▶ boxer, prizefighter, pugilist. *Slang:* pug.

figment *noun.* —*See* **dream** (1), **myth** (2).

figurative *adjective.* —*See* **symbolic.**

figure *noun.* **1.** An element or component in a decorative composition ▶ design, device, motif, motive. **2.** An amount represented in numerals ▶ number, quantity. [*Compare* **total.**] —*See also* **celebrity, character** (7), **constitution, form** (1), **sculpture.**

figure *verb.* —*See* **believe** (3), **calculate.**

figure on *verb.* —*See* **expect** (1).

figure out *verb. Informal* To arrive at an answer to a mathematical problem ▶ solve, work out. [*Compare* **calculate, decipher.**] —*See also* **solve** (1).

✚ CORE SYNONYMS: *figure, design, device, motif.* These nouns denote an element or a component in a decorative composition: *a tapestry with a floral figure; a living room rug with a geometric design; a brooch with a fanciful and intricate device; a silk scarf with a heart motif.*

---

figures *noun.* Arithmetic calculations ▶ arithmetic, computation, numbers. [*Compare* **addition, calculation.**]

figurine *noun.* —*See* **sculpture.**

figuring *noun.* The act, process, or result of calculating ▶ calculation, cast, computation, reckoning.

filament *noun.* A very fine continuous strand ▶ fiber, fibril, microfiber, thread. [*Compare* **cord.**]

filch *verb.* —*See* **steal.**

file[1] *noun.* —*See* **line.**

file *verb.* —*See* **line, list**[1].

file[2] *verb.* —*See* **scrape** (1), **sharpen.**

fill *verb.* **1.** To make full; put as much into as can be held ▶ charge, cram, crowd, freight, heap, jam, load, mob, pack, pile, stuff, top off. *Informal:* jam-pack. **2.** To plug up or block something, such as a hole or conduit ▶ block, choke, clog, close, congest, cork, plug, seal, stop. —*See also* **charge** (1), **satisfy** (1).

fill in *verb.* —*See* **inform** (1), **perfect, substitute.**

fill out *verb.* —*See* **perfect.**

fill *noun.* —*See* **filler** (1).

filler *noun.* **1.** Material used to fill a space or container ▶ caulking, fill, packing, padding, stuffing, wadding. **2.** Written material used to fill space in a publication ▶ boilerplate. [*Compare* **item.**]

fillet *noun.* —*See* **band**[1].

fill-in *noun.* —*See* **substitute.**

fill-in *adjective.* —*See* **temporary** (1).

filling *noun.* —*See* **plug.**

filling *adjective.* Not readily digested because of richness ▶ heavy, rich.

fillip *noun.* —*See* **stimulus.**

film *noun.* A motion picture ▶ motion picture, movie, picture. *Slang:* flick. —*See also* **skin** (2).

filmy *adjective.* —*See* **sheer**[2], **unclear.**

filth *noun.* Foul or dirty matter ▶ dirt, grime, muck, mud. *Slang:* crap, crud, grunge. [*Compare* **slime.**] —*See also* **dirtiness, obscenity** (2).

filthiness *noun.* —*See* **dirtiness, obscenity** (1).

filthy *adjective.* —*See* **dirty, obscene, offensive** (1).

finagle *verb.* —*See* **maneuver** (2).

final *adjective.* Of or relating to a terminative condition, stage, or point ▶ last, latter, terminal, ultimate. [*Compare* **climactic.**] —*See also* **definitive, last[1]** (1).

finale *noun.* —*See* **end** (2).

finalize *verb.* —*See* **settle** (1).

finally *adverb.* In conclusion ▶ conclusively, last, lastly, ultimately. ***Idioms:*** at last, in the end. —*See also* **ultimately** (1).

finance *noun.* The management of money ▶ banking, investment, money management.

finance *verb.* To supply capital to or for ▶ back, capitalize, fund, grubstake, stake, subsidize, subvent, underwrite. *Informal:* bankroll. ***Idiom:*** put up money for. [*Compare* **patronize, support.**]

finances *noun.* The monetary resources of a government, organization, or individual ▶ capital, funds, money (or moneys). [*Compare* **capital, money, resources.**]

financial *adjective.* Of or relating to finances ▶ fiscal, monetary, pecuniary.

financier *noun.* One who is occupied with or expert in large-scale financial affairs ▶ capitalist. *Informal:* moneyman.

financing *noun.* —*See* **capital** (1), **patronage** (1).

find *verb.* To look for and discover ▶ locate, pinpoint, spot. *Informal:* scare up. [*Compare* **trace, uncover.**] —*See also* **encounter** (1), **infer.**

find out *verb.* —*See* **discern, discover.**

find *noun.* Something offered or bought at a low price ▶ bargain. *Informal:* buy, deal. *Slang:* steal. —*See also* **discovery, treasure.**

finding *noun.* —*See* **discovery, ruling.**

fine[1] *adjective.* **1.** Consisting of small particles ▶ dusty, powdery, pulverous, pulverulent. [*Compare* **minute[2].**] **2.** Able to make or detect effects of great subtlety or precision ▶ delicate, nice, sensitive, subtle. [*Compare* **accurate.**] —*See also* **choice** (1), **clear** (2), **delicate** (1), **delicate** (4), **excellent, good** (1), **pointed.**

fine[2] *noun.* A sum of money levied as punishment for an offense ▶ amercement, mulct, penalty. [*Compare* **punishment.**]

fine *verb.* To impose a fine on ▶ amerce, mulct, penalize. [*Compare* **punish.**]

fineness *noun.* —*See* **excellence, subtlety.**

fine print *noun.* —*See* **detail.**

finery *noun.* —*See* **attire.**

finespun *adjective.* —*See* **delicate** (4).

finesse *verb.* To outmaneuver an opponent ▶ trump. *Informal:* one-up. ***Idioms:*** play gotcha, pull (*or* put over) a fast one. [*Compare* **deceive, outwit.**] —*See also* **maneuver** (1), **maneuver** (2).

finest *noun.* —*See* **police officer.**

fine-tune *verb.* —*See* **adjust.**

finger *verb.* —*See* **accuse, place** (1), **touch.**

finger *noun.* —*See* **beam** (1).

finger-pointing *noun.* —*See* **accusation, criticism.**

finicky *or* **finical** *adjective.* —*See* **fussy.**

finis *noun.* —*See* **end** (1).

finish *verb.* **1.** To complete a race or competition in a specified position ▶ come in, place, run. **2.** To apply a coating or surface material to ▶ enamel, glaze, lacquer, paint, plaster, polish, polyurethane, shellac, stain, surface, varnish, wax. [*Compare* **cover, face, gloss[1], smear.**] —*See also* **conclude, destroy** (1), **exhaust** (1), **kill[1], murder.**

finish *noun.* A final coating or material applied to a surface ▶ enamel, glaze, lacquer, paint, plaster, polish, polyurethane, shellac, stain, surface, varnish, wax. [*Compare* **coat, face, gloss[1].**] —*See also* **end** (1), **end** (2).

finished *adjective.* **1.** Having no further relationship ▶ done, through. **2.** Proficient as a result of practice and study ▶ accomplished, polished, practiced. [*Compare* **able, expert.**] *—See also* **complete** (3), **through** (2).

fink *noun.* *—See* **informer.**

fink *verb.* *—See* **inform** (2).

fink out *verb.* *—See* **renege.**

fire *noun.* **1.** The visible signs of combustion ▶ blaze, conflagration, flame, flare-up. **2.** Liveliness and vivacity of imagination ▶ brilliance, brilliancy, genius, inspiration. [*Compare* **intelligence, invention.**] *—See also* **barrage, brilliance** (1), **enthusiasm** (1), **passion.**

fire *verb.* **1.** To arouse the emotions of; make ardent ▶ animate, arouse, enkindle, impassion, inflame, inspire, kindle, rouse, stir. [*Compare* **move.**] **2.** To discharge a gun or firearm ▶ blast (away), fire away (off), pop (off), shoot (away *or* off). ***Idioms:*** go bang-bang, open fire, take a shot (*or* potshot). *—See also* **dismiss** (1), **explode** (1), **light[1]** (1), **throw.**

fire and brimstone *noun.* *—See* **bombast, hell.**

firebrand *noun.* *—See* **agitator.**

fired up *adjective.* *—See* **thrilled.**

fireplace *noun.* An open space for holding a fire at the base of a chimney ▶ grate, hearth, ingle.

fireproof *adjective.* Resistant to catching fire ▶ fire-resistant, fire-retardant, flameproof, flame-resistant, flame-retardant, incombustible, noncombustible, nonflammable.

fireworks *noun.* *—See* **argument.**

firm[1] *adjective.* **1.** Unyielding to pressure or force ▶ hard, incompressible, solid. **2.** Not easily moved or shaken ▶ fast, secure, solid, sound, stable, steady, strong, sturdy, substantial, sure, unshakable. [*Compare* **fixed, motionless.**] **3.** Indicating or possessing determination or resolution ▶ constant, decided, decisive, determined, resolute, resolved, single-minded, steadfast, steady, stiff, tough, unbending, uncompromising, unflinching, unwavering, unyielding. [*Compare* **insistent, intent, stubborn.**] *—See also* **faithful, tight** (1), **unchanging.**

firm up *verb.* *—See* **harden** (2).

firm[2] *noun.* *—See* **company** (1).

firmament *noun.* The celestial regions as seen from the earth ▶ air, heavens, sky. ***Idiom:*** wild blue yonder.

firmness *noun.* *—See* **changelessness, decision** (2), **stability.**

first *adjective.* Preceding all others in time ▶ earliest, inaugural, initial, maiden, original, pioneer, premier, primary, prime, primordial. [*Compare* **beginning.**] *—See also* **best** (1), **primary** (1).

first-class *adjective.* *—See* **choice** (1), **excellent.**

firsthand *adjective.* Marked by the absence of any intervention ▶ direct, immediate, primary.

firsthand *adverb.* Without intermediary ▶ directly, immediately.

first-rate *adjective.* *—See* **choice** (1), **excellent.**

fiscal *adjective.* Of or relating to finances ▶ financial, monetary, pecuniary.

fish *verb.* **1.** To try to catch fish ▶ angle, cast, go fishing, troll, trawl. ***Idioms:*** cast one's hook (*or* net). **2.** To try to obtain something, usually by subtleness and cunning ▶ angle, hint. [*Compare* **coax.**]

fish for *verb.* *—See* **seek** (1).

fish story *noun.* *—See* **exaggeration, lie[2].**

fishwife *noun.* *—See* **scold.**

fishy *adjective.* *—See* **shady** (1).

fission *noun.* *—See* **division** (1).

fissure *noun.* *—See* **breach** (2), **crack** (2), **division** (1).

fissure *verb.* *—See* **crack** (1).

fistfight *or* **fisticuffs** *noun.* *—See* **fight** (1).

fit[1] *verb.* To be the proper size and shape for something ▶ dovetail, interlock. ***Idiom:*** fit like a glove. *—See also* **adapt, agree** (1), **furnish, prepare, suit** (1).

fit out *or* **up** *verb.* *—See* **furnish.**

fit *adjective.* —*See* **appropriate, convenient** (1), **eligible, healthy, just.**

fit² *noun.* —*See* **outburst, seizure** (1), **temper** (2).

fitful *adjective.* —*See* **intermittent.**

fitfully *adverb.* —*See* **intermittently.**

fitness *noun.* —*See* **qualification, shape.**

fitted *adjective.* —*See* **eligible.**

fitting *adjective.* —*See* **appropriate, just.**

fitting *noun.* Something attached as a permanent part of something else ▶ apparatus, fixture, installation. [*Compare* **attachment.**]

fix *verb.* **1.** To restore to proper condition or functioning ▶ doctor, fix up, mend, overhaul, patch (up), repair, revamp, right, service. ***Idioms:*** put right (*or* to rights), set right (*or* to rights). [*Compare* **cure, restore.**] **2.** To place or set deeply or securely ▶ embed, entrench, fasten, implant, infix, ingrain, lodge, plant, root. **3.** To ascribe the blame for a misdeed or error ▶ affix, ascribe, assign, attribute, blame, fasten, impute, lay, pin, place. [*Compare* **attribute.**] **4.** To prearrange the outcome of a contest unlawfully ▶ rig, tamper. ***Idiom:*** stack the deck. —*See also* **adjust, attach** (1), **avenge, bribe, catch** (3), **correct** (1), **dictate, engrave** (2), **establish** (1), **fasten, govern, limit, prepare, settle** (1), **settle** (2), **sterilize** (2).

fix up *verb.* —*See* **fix** (1), **harden** (2), **renew** (1).

fix *noun.* —*See* **bribe, predicament.**

fixate *verb.* To dominate the mind or thoughts of ▶ obsess, possess, preoccupy. [*Compare* **absorb, grip.**]

fixation *noun.* —*See* **obsession.**

fixed *adjective.* Firmly in position ▶ anchored, embedded, fastened, immobile, immovable, riveted, rooted, secured, stationary, steadfast, steady, unmovable, unmoving. ***Idioms:*** cast (*or* etched *or* set) in stone. [*Compare* **firm¹.**] —*See also* **definite** (2), **intent, motionless, unchanging.**

fixture *noun.* Something attached as a permanent part of something else ▶ apparatus, fitting, installation. [*Compare* **attachment.**] —*See also* **faucet.**

fizz *noun.* —*See* **foam, hiss** (1).

fizz *verb.* —*See* **foam, hiss** (1).

fizzle *verb.* —*See* **fade, hiss** (1).

fizzle *noun.* —*See* **disappointment** (2), **hiss** (1).

fizzy *adjective.* —*See* **foamy.**

fjord *noun.* —*See* **inlet.**

flabbergast *verb.* —*See* **stagger** (2).

flabby *adjective.* —*See* **fat** (1), **limp.**

flaccid *adjective.* —*See* **limp.**

flag¹ *noun.* A piece of fabric used as a symbol or emblem ▶ banderole, banner, banneret, colors, ensign, jack, oriflamme, pennant, pennon, standard, streamer. —*See also* **ticket** (1).

flag *verb.* To attach a ticket to ▶ earmark, label, mark, tag, ticket. —*See also* **gesture.**

flag² *verb.* —*See* **fade, tire** (2), **wilt.**

flagellate *verb.* —*See* **beat** (2).

flagitiousness *noun.* —*See* **corruption** (1).

flagrancy *noun.* The quality or state of being flagrant ▶ egregiousness, glaringness, grossness, rankness. [*Compare* **impudence, outrageousness.**]

flagrant *adjective.* Conspicuously bad or offensive ▶ egregious, glaring, gross, rank. [*Compare* **offensive, outrageous, shameless.**]

✤ **CORE SYNONYMS:** *flagrant, glaring, gross, egregious, rank.* These adjectives refer to what is conspicuously bad or offensive. *Flagrant* applies to what is so offensive that it cannot escape notice: *flagrant disregard for the law.* What is *glaring* is blatantly and painfully manifest: *a glaring error; glaring contradictions. Gross* suggests a magnitude of offense or failing that cannot be condoned or forgiven: *gross ineptitude; gross injustice.* What is *egregious* is outrageously bad: *an egregious lie. Rank* implies that the term it qualifies is as indicated to an extreme, violent, or gross degree: *rank stupidity; rank treachery.*

---

flail *verb.* **1.** To swing about or strike at wildly ▶ thrash, thresh, toss. [*Compare* **stagger, sway.**] **2.** To beat plants to separate the grain from the straw ▶ thrash, thresh. —*See also* **beat** (1).

flair *noun.* —*See* **talent.**

flak *noun.* —*See* **barrage, criticism.**

flake *noun.* A small, thin piece of something ▶ chip, leaf, paring, scale, slice, sliver, shaving. [*Compare* **bit[1], cut, end.**] —*See also* **character** (5).

flake *verb.* To come or fall off in small, thin pieces ▶ chip, desquamate, exfoliate, peel, scale, shed.

flamboyant *adjective.* —*See* **dramatic** (2), **ornate, showy.**

flame *noun.* The visible signs of combustion ▶ blaze, conflagration, fire, flare-up. —*See also* **lover.**

flame *verb.* —*See* **burn** (2).

flameproof *or* **flame-resistant** *or* **flame-retardant** *adjective.* —*See* **fireproof.**

flaming *adjective.* —*See* **burning, passionate.**

flammable *adjective.* Easily ignited ▶ combustible, ignitable, inflammable.

flank *noun.* One of two or more contrasted parts or places identified by its location with respect to a center ▶ hand, side.

flank *verb.* —*See* **adjoin.**

flap *verb.* **1.** To move the arms or wings up and down ▶ beat, flitter, flop, flutter, waggle, wave. **2.** To move or cause to move about while being fixed at one edge ▶ flutter, fly, wave. —*See also* **blow[1]** (2), **fly** (1).

flap *noun.* A flat, thin piece that usually hangs over something ▶ fly, skirt. —*See also* **agitation** (1).

flapping *adjective.* —*See* **loose** (1).

flare *verb.* —*See* **break out, burn** (2), **glare** (2).

flare up *verb.* —*See* **anger** (2).

flare *noun.* An intense blinding light ▶ blaze, dazzle, glare. —*See also* **eruption, flare-up.**

flare-up *noun.* The visible signs of combustion ▶ blaze, conflagration, fire, flame. —*See also* **blast** (2), **eruption, outburst.**

flash *noun.* **1.** A sudden burst of light ▶ blink, coruscation, flicker, glance, gleam, glimmer, glint, scintillation, spark, twinkle, wink. **2.** A very brief interval of time ▶ blink, crack, instant, minute, moment, second, trice, twinkle, twinkling, wink. *Informal:* jiff, jiffy, sec. —*See also* **item.**

flash *verb.* —*See* **display, glitter, rush.**

✚ **CORE SYNONYMS:** *flash, jiffy, moment, instant, minute, second.* These nouns denote a brief interval of time. *Flash* and *jiffy* usually combine with *in a; in a flash* suggests the almost imperceptible duration of a flash of light, while *in a jiffy* means in a short space of time: *She finished the job in a flash. "He was on his stool in a jiffy, driving away with his pen"* (Charles Dickens). A *moment* is an indeterminately short but significant period: *I'll be with you in a moment. Instant* is a period of time almost too brief to detect; it implies haste: *He hesitated for just an instant. Minute* is often interchangeable with *moment* and *second* with *instant: The alarm will ring any minute. I'll be back in a second.*

---

flash point *noun.* —*See* **emergency.**

flashy *adjective.* —*See* **gaudy.**

flat *adjective.* **1.** Lying down ▶ decumbent, horizontal, procumbent, prone, prostrate, reclining, recumbent, stretched out, supine. **2.** Lacking an appetizing flavor ▶ bland, flavorless, insipid, stale, tasteless, unsavory. —*See also* **dull** (1), **dull** (2), **even** (1), **unchanging, utter[2].**

flat *adverb.* —*See* **completely** (1).

flat *verb.* —*See* **even.**

flatfoot *noun.* —*See* **police officer.**

flatly *adverb.* In a direct, positive manner ▶ directly, emphatically, point-blank, positively. *Informal:* flat out. ***Idiom:*** in no uncertain terms.
flatness *noun.* —*See* **changelessness, dullness.**
flat out *adverb.* —*See* **fast, flatly.**
flat-out *adjective.* —*See* **utter**[2].
flatten *verb.* —*See* **drop** (3), **even.**
flatter *verb.* **1.** To compliment excessively and ingratiatingly ▶ adulate, blandish, butter up, honey. *Informal:* soft-soap, sweet-talk. [*Compare* **coax, deceive, fawn, seduce.**] **2.** To look good on or with ▶ become, enhance, suit. ***Idiom:*** put in the best light. [*Compare* **suit.**]
flatterer *noun.* —*See* **sycophant.**
flattering *adjective.* Purposefully contrived to gain favor ▶ blandishing, buttery, cajoling, fawning, honey-tongued, ingratiating, ingratiatory, insinuating, saccharine, smooth-tongued, soft-soaping, sugary, wheedling. *Informal:* brownnosing. —*See also* **becoming.**
flattery *noun.* Excessive, ingratiating praise ▶ adulation, blandishment, blarney, oil. *Informal:* apple-polishing, soft soap, sweet talk. ***Idiom:*** honeyed words.
flatulent *adjective.* —*See* **inflated.**
flaunt *verb.* —*See* **display.**
flavor *noun.* **1.** A distinctive property of a substance affecting the sense of taste ▶ relish, savor, smack, tang, taste, zest. **2.** A distinctive yet intangible quality felt to be characteristic of a given thing ▶ aroma, atmosphere, savor, smack. [*Compare* **quality.**] —*See also* **flavoring.**
flavor *verb.* To impart flavor to ▶ season, spice (up), zest.

✚ **CORE SYNONYMS:** *flavor, relish, savor, tang, taste.* These nouns denote a distinctive property of a substance affecting the sense of taste: *the pungent flavor of garlic; the zesty relish of the salsa; the savor of rich chocolate; the fresh tang of lemonade; the salty taste of anchovies.*

flavorful *adjective.* —*See* **delicious.**
flavoring *noun.* A substance that imparts taste ▶ condiment, flavor, seasoner, seasoning, spice. [*Compare* **zest.**]
flavorless *adjective.* —*See* **dull** (1), **flat** (2).
flavorlessness *noun.* —*See* **dullness.**
flaw *noun.* —*See* **defect, disadvantage.**
flaw *verb.* —*See* **damage.**
flawed *adjective.* Having a defect or defects ▶ amiss, blemished, defective, faulty, imperfect. [*Compare* **shabby, trick.**]
flawless *adjective.* —*See* **good** (2), **perfect.**
flaxen-haired *adjective.* —*See* **fair**[1] (2).
flay *verb.* —*See* **bare, beat** (2), **slam** (1).
fleck *noun.* —*See* **point** (2).
fleck *verb.* —*See* **speckle.**
fledgling *noun.* —*See* **beginner.**
flee *verb.* —*See* **escape** (1).
fleece *verb.* —*See* **cheat** (1).
fleecy *adjective.* —*See* **hairy.**
fleer *verb.* To smile or laugh scornfully or derisively ▶ sneer, snicker, snigger. ***Idiom:*** curl one's lip. [*Compare* **grimace, laugh, ridicule.**]
fleer *noun.* A facial expression or laugh conveying scorn or derision ▶ sneer, snicker, snigger. [*Compare* **smile.**] —*See also* **taunt.**
fleet[1] *noun.* A group of warships operating under one command ▶ armada, flotilla.
fleet[2] *adjective.* —*See* **fast** (1), **transitory.**
fleet *verb.* —*See* **rush.**
fleeting *adjective.* —*See* **quick, transitory.**
fleetness *noun.* —*See* **haste** (1).
flesh *noun.* —*See* **humankind.**
fleshless *adjective.* —*See* **thin** (1).
fleshliness *noun.* —*See* **sensuality** (1).
fleshly *adjective.* —*See* **bodily, sensual** (2).
fleshy *adjective.* —*See* **bodily, fat** (1), **sensual** (2).
flex *verb.* —*See* **bend** (2).

flexibility *noun.* **1.** The quality or state of being flexible ▶ bendability, bounce, ductility, elasticity, flexibleness, give, limberness, lissomeness, litheness, malleability, malleableness, plasticity, pliability, pliableness, pliancy, pliantness, resilience, resiliency, spring, springiness, suppleness, tractableness, tractability. **2.** The ability to recover quickly from depression or from discouragement ▶ bounce, buoyancy, elasticity, resilience, resiliency.

flexible *adjective.* **1.** Capable of withstanding stress without injury ▶ elastic, flexile, plastic, resilient, springy, supple. [*Compare* **extensible.**] **2.** Having or showing bodily flexibility ▶ limber, lissome, lithe, lithesome, supple. [*Compare* **limp.**] **3.** Easily altered or influenced ▶ ductile, elastic, flexile, impressionable, malleable, plastic, pliable, pliant, suggestible, supple. [*Compare* **obedient.**] —*See also* **adaptable, malleable.**

✚ CORE SYNONYMS: *flexible, elastic, resilient, supple.* These adjectives refer literally to what is capable of withstanding stress without injury and figuratively to what can undergo change or modification: *a flexible wire; flexible plans; an elastic rubber band; an elastic interpretation of the law; thin, resilient copper; a resilient temperament; supple suede; a supple mind.*

---

flexibleness *noun.* —*See* **flexibility** (1).

flexile *adjective.* —*See* **flexible** (1), **flexible** (3), **malleable.**

flexuous *adjective.* —*See* **malleable, winding.**

flexure *noun.* —*See* **bend.**

flick *noun. Slang* A motion picture ▶ film, motion picture, movie, picture. —*See also* **brush**[1].

flick *verb.* —*See* **brush**[1], **tap**[1] (1).

flicker *verb.* To move like a bird in flight ▶ flit, flitter, flutter. [*Compare* **flap.**] —*See also* **glitter, smolder.**

flicker *noun.* —*See* **flash** (1).

flier *noun.* **1.** A person who flies an airplane ▶ aviator, pilot. *Slang:* flyboy. **2.** An announcement distributed on paper to a large number of people ▶ circular, handbill, leaflet, notice.

flight *noun.* —*See* **escape** (1), **flock, journey.**

flighty *adjective.* —*See* **capricious, giddy** (2).

flimflam *noun.* —*See* **cheat** (1).

flimflam *verb.* —*See* **cheat** (1).

flimflammer *noun.* —*See* **cheat** (2).

flimsiness *noun.* —*See* **infirmity.**

flimsy *adjective.* —*See* **implausible, pale** (2), **weak** (1).

flinch *verb.* To draw away or pull back in fear ▶ blench, cower, cringe, quail, recoil, shrink, shy, start, wince. [*Compare* **fear.**]

flinch *noun.* —*See* **recoil.**

fling *verb.* —*See* **throw.**

fling *noun.* **1.** *Informal* A brief trial ▶ crack, go, stab, try. *Informal:* shot, whack, whirl. **2.** A usually brief romance entered into lightly or frivolously ▶ dalliance, flirtation. [*Compare* **love.**] —*See also* **binge, throw.**

flinty *adjective.* —*See* **forbidding.**

flip *verb.* To throw a coin in order to decide something ▶ toss. ***Idiom:*** call heads or tails.

flip through *verb.* —*See* **browse** (1).

flip *adjective.* —*See* **impudent.**

flip-flop *noun.* —*See* **reversal** (1).

flippancy *noun.* —*See* **impudence.**

flippant *adjective.* —*See* **impudent.**

flirt *verb.* **1.** To treat something lightly or flippantly ▶ dally, play, toy, trifle. **2.** To make amorous advances without serious intentions ▶ coquet, dally, toy, trifle. *Slang:* mash. ***Idioms:*** come on to, make advances, make a play for, make eyes at. [*Compare* **philander, seduce.**]

flirt *noun.* **1.** A woman who is given to flirting ▶ coquette, tease. *Informal:* vamp. [*Compare* **seductress.**] **2.** A man who is given to flirting ▶ wolf. *Slang:* masher. [*Compare* **philanderer, seducer.**]

✢ CORE SYNONYMS: *flirt, dally, play, toy, trifle.* These verbs mean to treat something or someone lightly, casually, or flippantly: *flirted with the idea of getting a job; dallying with music; can't play with life; toyed with the problem; a person not to be trifled with.*

flirtation *noun.* **1.** The practice of flirting ▶ coquetry, dalliance. **2.** A usually brief romance entered into lightly or frivolously ▶ dalliance, fling. [*Compare* **love.**]

flirtatious *or* **flirty** *adjective.* Given to flirting ▶ coquettish, coy.

flit *verb.* To move like a bird in flight ▶ flicker, flitter, flutter. [*Compare* **flap.**] —*See also* **fly** (1), **rush.**

flitter *verb.* To move like a bird in flight ▶ flicker, flit, flutter. —*See also* **flap** (1), **fly** (1).

float *verb.* **1.** To stay on top of the surface of water or stay in mid-air ▶ bob, be buoyed, be buoyant, have buoyancy, hover, stay afloat. **2.** To move along with or be carried away by the action of water ▶ drift, wash. —*See also* **blow**[1] (2), **fly** (2), **glide** (1), **lend.**

flock *noun.* A number of animals considered collectively ▶ bevy, drove, flight, gaggle, gang, herd, kennel, litter, pack, pride, rout, school, stable, swarm, troop. —*See also* **crowd.**

flock *verb.* —*See* **band**[2], **crowd.**

✢ CORE SYNONYMS: *flock, herd, drove, pack, gang, brood.* These nouns denote a number of animals, birds, or fish considered collectively, and some have human connotations. *Flock* is applied to a congregation of animals of one kind, especially sheep or goats herded by people, and to any congregation of wild or domesticated birds, especially when on the ground. It is also applicable to people who form the membership of a church or to people under someone's care or supervision. *Herd* is used of a number of animals, especially cattle, herded by people; or of wild animals such as antelope, elephants, and zebras; or of whales and seals. Applied to people, it is used disparagingly of a crowd or of the masses and suggests the gregarious aspect of crowd psychology. *Drove* is used of a herd or flock, as of cattle or geese, that is being moved or driven from one place to another; less often it refers to a crowd of people in movement. *Pack* is applicable to any body of animals, especially wolves, or of birds, especially grouse, and to a body of hounds trained to hunt as a unit. It also refers disparagingly to a band or group of persons. *Gang* refers to a herd, especially of buffalo or elk; to a pack of wolves or wild dogs; or to various associations of persons, especially when engaged in violent or criminal pursuits. *Brood* is applicable to offspring that are still under the care of a mother, especially the offspring of domestic or game birds or, less formally, of people.

flog *verb.* —*See* **beat** (2).

flogging *noun.* —*See* **beating.**

flood *noun.* An abundant or overwhelming flow of water ▶ alluvion, cataract, deluge, downpour, freshet, inundation, overflow, spate, torrent. [*Compare* **abundance, excess, flow.**] —*See also* **flow, outburst.**

flood *verb.* **1.** To flow over completely ▶ deluge, drown, engulf, flush, inundate, overflow, overwhelm, submerge, submerse. [*Compare* **dip, flow.**] **2.** To affect as if by an outpouring of water ▶ deluge, inundate, overwhelm, swamp. —*See also* **crowd, illuminate** (1).

floor *verb.* —*See* **drop** (3), **stagger** (2).

floozy *noun.* —*See* **slut.**

flop *verb.* To drop or sink heavily and noisily ▶ plop, plump, plunk. [*Compare* **fall.**] —*See also* **fail** (1), **flap** (1), **retire** (1), **slouch** (2).

flop *noun.* —*See* **disappointment** (2), **failure** (1).

floppy *adjective.* —*See* **limp.**

flora *noun.* The plants of an area or region ▶ plant life, vegetation, verdure.

florescence *noun.* —*See* **bloom¹** (1).

floret *noun.* —*See* **flower.**

florid *adjective.* —*See* **gaudy, ornate, ruddy.**

flotilla *noun.* A group of warships operating under one command ▶ armada, fleet.

flotsam *noun.* —*See* **garbage.**

flounce *verb.* —*See* **strut.**

flounder *verb.* To move about in an indolent or clumsy manner ▶ roll about, roll around, wallow, welter. —*See also* **blunder, muddle.**

flourish *verb.* **1.** To wield boldly and dramatically ▶ brandish, sweep, wave. [*Compare* **handle.**] **2.** To grow rapidly and luxuriantly ▶ bloom, blossom, thrive. [*Compare* **increase.**] **3.** To be in one's prime ▶ flower, shine. ***Idioms:*** cut a figure, have one's day in the sun, make a splash. —*See also* **prosper.**

✚ **CORE SYNONYMS:** *flourish, brandish, sweep, wave.* These verbs mean to wield boldly and dramatically: *flourished the newly signed contract; brandish a sword; swept the magic wand across the brim of the hat; waving a baton.*

flourishing *adjective.* Improving, growing, or succeeding steadily ▶ booming, boomy, prospering, prosperous, roaring, successful, thrifty, thriving. [*Compare* **profuse.**]

flout *verb.* —*See* **disobey.**

flow *noun.* Something suggestive of running water ▶ cascade, current, drift, efflux, flood, flux, gush, outflow, outpour, outpouring, rush, spate, stream, surge, tide. [*Compare* **brook¹, flood, spurt.**]

flow *verb.* **1.** To move freely as a liquid ▶ circulate, course, purl, ripple, run, stream, sweep. [*Compare* **swirl.**] **2.** To come forth or issue in abundance ▶ cascade, gush, pour, run, rush, stream, surge, well. [*Compare* **flood, spurt.**] —*See also* **pour, stem, teem¹.**

✚ **CORE SYNONYMS:** *flow, current, flood, flux, rush, stream, tide.* These nouns denote something suggestive of running water: *a flow of thought; the current of history; a flood of interesting ideas; a flux of words; a rush of heartfelt sympathy; a stream of complaints; a tide of immigration.*

flower *noun.* The showy reproductive structure of a plant ▶ bloom, blossom, floret, floweret, flower head, pompon, posy, spike, spray. [*Compare* **bouquet.**] —*See also* **best** (1), **bloom¹** (1), **society** (1).

flower *verb.* To be in one's prime ▶ flourish, shine. ***Idioms:*** cut a figure, have one's day in the sun, make a splash. —*See also* **bloom¹** (1).

flowery *adjective.* —*See* **oratorical, ornate.**

flowing *adjective.* —*See* **fluent.**

flub *verb.* —*See* **botch.**

fluctuant *adjective.* —*See* **changeable** (1).

fluctuate *verb.* —*See* **change** (2), **sway.**

fluctuation *noun.* —*See* **change** (1).

fluency *noun.* —*See* **eloquence.**

fluent *adjective.* Marked by facility of expression ▶ easy, effortless, flowing, fluid, graceful, smooth. [*Compare* **eloquent, glib.**]

fluff *noun.* —*See* **blunder.**

fluff *verb.* —*See* **err.**

fluffy *adjective.* Having little weight; not heavy ▶ airy, light, lightweight, weightless. ***Idioms:*** light as air (*or* a feather). [*Compare* **immaterial, sheer².**] —*See also* **trivial.**

fluid *adjective.* Changing easily, as in expression ▶ changeable, mobile, plastic. [*Compare* **unstable.**] —*See also* **changeable** (1), **fluent.**

fluidity *noun.* —*See* **eloquence.**

fluke *noun.* —*See* **chance** (1), **luck.**

fluky *adjective.* —*See* **accidental.**

flummox *verb.* —*See* **baffle.**

fluorescent *adjective.* —*See* **colorful** (1).

flunk *verb.* —*See* **fail** (1).

flurry *noun.* —*See* **agitation** (3).
flurry *verb.* —*See* **agitate** (2).

flush *verb.* —*See* **blush, elate, even, flood** (1).
flush *noun.* **1.** A fresh rosy complexion ▶ bloom, blush, color, glow. [*Compare* **color, complexion.**] **2.** A feeling of pervasive emotional warmth ▶ glow, tingle. —*See also* **bloom**[1] (1).
flush *adjective.* —*See* **even** (1), **even** (2), **rich** (1), **ruddy.**
flush *adverb.* —*See* **directly** (3).

flushed *adjective.* —*See* **ruddy.**

fluster *verb.* —*See* **agitate** (2).
fluster *noun.* —*See* **agitation** (2).

flutter *verb.* **1.** To move or cause to move about while being fixed at one edge ▶ flap, fly, wave. **2.** To move quickly and irregularly like a bird in flight ▶ flicker, flit, flitter. —*See also* **beat** (5), **blink, blow**[1] (2), **flap** (1), **fly** (1).
flutter *noun.* —*See* **agitation** (2), **blink.**

flux *noun.* —*See* **flow, transition.**
flux *verb.* —*See* **melt.**

fly *verb.* **1.** To move through the air with or as if with wings ▶ flap, flit, flitter, flutter, sail, wing. **2.** To move quickly or smoothly through the air ▶ dart, float, glide, sail, shoot, skim, soar. [*Compare* **float, plunge.**] **3.** To move or cause to move about while being fixed at one edge ▶ flap, flutter, wave. —*See also* **blow**[1] (2), **escape** (1), **rush.**

flyblown *adjective.* —*See* **bad** (2).

flying *adjective.* —*See* **quick.**

foam *noun.* A mass of bubbles in or on the surface of a liquid ▶ barm, effervescence, fizz, froth, head, lather, spume, suds, yeast.
foam *verb.* To form or cause to form foam ▶ bubble, cream, effervesce, fizz, froth, lather, spume, suds, yeast. —*See also* **anger** (2).

foamy *adjective.* Consisting of or resembling foam ▶ barmy, fizzy, frothy, lathery, spumous, spumy, sudsy, yeasty.

fob off *verb.* To offer or put into circulation an inferior or fraudulent item ▶ foist, palm off, pass off, put off. [*Compare* **dump.**]

focal *adjective.* —*See* **central.**

focalize *verb.* —*See* **concentrate.**

focus *noun.* —*See* **center** (1), **center** (3), **object** (2).
focus *verb.* —*See* **apply** (1), **concentrate.**

foe *noun.* —*See* **opponent.**

fog *noun.* —*See* **daze, haze.**
fog *verb.* —*See* **drug** (2), **obscure.**

foggy *adjective.* —*See* **unclear.**

fogy *noun.* —*See* **square.**

foible *noun.* —*See* **weakness.**

foil *verb.* —*See* **frustrate.**

foist *verb.* To offer or put into circulation an inferior or fraudulent item ▶ fob off, palm off, pass off, put off. [*Compare* **dump.**] —*See also* **insinuate.**
foist on *or* **upon** *verb.* —*See* **impose on.**

fold *verb.* To bend together or form a crease so that one part lies over another ▶ crease, crimp, crinkle, double, plait, pleat, ply, pucker, rimple, ruck, rumple, wrinkle. —*See also* **beat** (6), **collapse** (2), **succumb.**
fold down *verb.* —*See* **break** (3).
fold *noun.* **1.** A line or an arrangement made by the doubling of one part over another ▶ crease, crimp, crinkle, crumple, plait, pleat, plica, plication, pucker, rimple, ruck, rumple, wrinkle. **2.** The steadfast believers in a faith or cause ▶ adherents, congregation, faithful. [*Compare* **follower, assembly.**] —*See also* **bend, pen**[2].

folklore *noun.* —*See* **lore** (1).

folks *noun.* —*See* **kin.**

folk tale *noun.* —*See* **myth** (1).

folkways *noun.* —*See* **culture** (2), **lore** (1).

follow *verb.* **1.** To occur after in time ▶ come next, ensue, succeed, supervene. ***Idioms:*** follow on (*or* upon) the heels of. **2.** To occur as a consequence ▶ attend, ensue, result. [*Compare* **stem.**] **3.** To keep another under surveillance by moving along behind ▶ chase, dog, heel, shadow, tag, track, trail. *Informal:* bird-dog, tail. [*Compare* **hunt, pursue.**] **4.** To act in compliance or conformity with ▶ abide by, adhere to, carry out, comply with, conform to, heed, keep, live by, mind, obey, observe. ***Idioms:*** keep to the straight and narrow, toe the line (*or* mark), walk the line. **5.** To take as a model ▶ copy, emulate, imitate, model oneself (on *or* upon *or* after), pattern oneself (on *or* upon *or* after). ***Idioms:*** follow in the footsteps of, follow suit, follow the example of, take as a model. [*Compare* **imitate.**] **6.** To work at, especially as a profession ▶ do, practice, pursue. ***Idiom:*** hang out one's shingle. [*Compare* **labor.**] **7.** To pay regular and close attention to ▶ monitor, observe, stake out, survey, watch. ***Idioms:*** have one's (*or* keep an) eye on, keep tabs on, keep track of, ride herd on. —*See also* **understand** (1).

✣ **CORE SYNONYMS:** *follow, succeed, ensue, result, supervene.* These verbs mean to occur after something or someone or as a consequence. *Follow,* which has the widest application, can refer to coming after in time or order, as a consequence or result, or by the operation of logic: *Night follows day. He disregarded doctor's orders, and a relapse followed. Because she decries violence, it follows that she won't carry a gun.* To *succeed* is to come next after another, especially in planned order determined by considerations such as rank, inheritance, or election: *The heir apparent succeeded to the throne. Ensue* usually applies to what is a consequence or logical development: *After the government was toppled, chaos ensued. Result* implies that what follows is caused by what has preceded: *Failure to file an income tax return can result in a fine. Supervene,* in contrast, refers to something that is often unexpected and that has little relation to what has preceded: *"A bad harvest supervened"* (Charlotte Brontë).

follower *noun.* One who supports and adheres to another ▶ adherent, believer, cohort, disciple, henchman, partisan, satellite, supporter. [*Compare* **pawn²**, **student, subordinate, sycophant.**] —*See also* **fan²**.

following *adjective.* **1.** Occurring after another ▶ coming, ensuing, next, subsequent, succeeding, supervening. ***Idioms:*** coming after, in the wake of. [*Compare* **consecutive.**] **2.** Occurring as a result ▶ attending, consequent, consequential, ensuing, resulting. [*Compare* **logical.**]

following *noun.* The body of persons who admire a public personality, especially an entertainer ▶ audience, public. [*Compare* **fan²**.] —*See also* **retinue.**

folly *noun.* —*See* **foolishness.**

foment *verb.* —*See* **provoke.**

fomenter *noun.* —*See* **agitator.**

fond *adjective.* —*See* **affectionate.**

fondle *verb.* —*See* **caress.**

fondness *noun.* —*See* **love** (1), **taste** (1).

font *noun.* —*See* **origin.**

food *or* **foodstuff** *noun.* Material that is fit to be eaten ▶ aliment, bread, comestibles, cooking, diet, eatables, edibles, fare, meat, nourishment, nutriment, nutrition, pabulum, provender, provisions, rations, sustenance, viands, victuals. *Slang:* chow, eats, grub, munchies.

fool *noun.* A person who is deficient in judgment and good sense ▶ ass, buffoon, idiot, imbecile, jackass, mooncalf, moron, nincompoop, ninny, nitwit, simpleton. *Informal:* dope, gander, goose. *Slang:* boob, bozo, cretin, dingdong, dim bulb, dip, ditz, dork, dweeb, geek, goof, jerk, nerd, nimrod, schmo, schmuck, simp, turkey, twit. [*Compare* **drip, dullard, oaf, square.**] —*See also* **dupe.**

fool *verb.* —*See* **deceive, fiddle, putter, tinker.**

fool around *verb.* **1.** *Informal* To make

jokes; behave playfully ▶ jest, joke, quip. *Informal:* clown (around), horse around. ***Idioms:*** crack wise, play the fool. [*Compare* **play.**] **2.** *Informal* To be sexually unfaithful to another ▶ philander. *Informal:* cheat, mess around, play around. *Slang:* two-time. —*See also* **misbehave, neck, putter.**

fool away *verb.* —*See* **waste.**

foolery *noun.* —*See* **foolishness.**

foolhardiness *noun.* —*See* **temerity.**

foolhardy *adjective.* —*See* **rash[1].**

foolish *adjective.* Displaying a lack of forethought and good sense ▶ absurd, asinine, brainless, daft, fatuous, harebrained, idiotic, imbecilic, inane, insane, lunatic, ludicrous, mad, mindless, moronic, nonsensical, preposterous, ridiculous, senseless, silly, witless, zany. *Informal:* cockeyed, crazy, daffy, loony, loopy. *Slang:* balmy, dippy, ditsy, dopey, goofy, jerky, wacky. [*Compare* **giddy, laughable, stupid.**]

✤ CORE SYNONYMS: *foolish, absurd, fatuous, ludicrous, preposterous, ridiculous, silly.* These adjectives are applied to what is so devoid of wisdom or good sense as to be laughable: *a foolish expenditure of energy; an absurd idea that is bound to fail; made fatuous remarks; ludicrous criticism that was immediately dismissed; a preposterous excuse that no one believed; offered a ridiculous explanation for his tardiness; a silly argument.*

foolishness *noun.* Foolish behavior ▶ absurdity, daftness, fatuity, fatuousness, folly, foolery, idiocy, imbecility, inanity, insanity, ludicracy, lunacy, madness, nonsense, preposterousness, ridiculousness, senselessness, silliness, tomfoolery, zaniness. *Informal:* boobishness, craziness, daffiness, looniness, loopiness. *Slang:* balminess, dippiness, ditsiness, dopeyness, goofiness, jerkiness, wackiness. [*Compare* **nonsense.**]

foolproof *adjective.* —*See* **sure** (2).

foot *noun.* —*See* **base[1]** (2).

foot *verb.* —*See* **add, dance, walk.**

footfall *noun.* —*See* **walk** (2).

foothold *noun.* A place providing support for the foot in climbing ▶ footing, perch, purchase, toehold.

footing *noun.* A place providing support for the foot in climbing ▶ foothold, perch, purchase, toehold. —*See also* **base[1]** (2), **basis** (1), **basis** (3), **place** (1).

footloose *adjective.* —*See* **single.**

footpace *noun.* A very slow rate of speed ▶ crawl, creep, slow motion. ***Idiom:*** snail's pace.

footpath *noun.* —*See* **way** (2).

footprints *noun.* —*See* **track.**

footstep *noun.* —*See* **walk** (2).

footstool *or* **footrest** *noun.* A stool or cushion for resting the feet ▶ hassock, ottoman.

foozle *noun.* —*See* **blunder.**

foozler *noun.* —*See* **blunderer.**

fop *noun.* A man who is preoccupied with or vain about his clothes ▶ beau, coxcomb, dandy, peacock, swell.

for *conjunction.* —*See* **because.**

forage *verb.* —*See* **browse** (2), **scour[2].**

foray *noun.* An act of invading, especially by military forces ▶ incursion, inroad, invasion, raid. [*Compare* **attack.**]

foray *verb.* —*See* **invade** (1).

forbear *verb.* —*See* **refrain, stop** (2).

forbearance *noun.* —*See* **patience, tolerance.**

forbearing *adjective.* —*See* **patient, tolerant.**

forbid *verb.* To refuse to allow ▶ ban, bar, debar, disallow, enjoin, interdict, outlaw, prohibit, proscribe, taboo. [*Compare* **exclude, hinder, prevent.**]

✤ CORE SYNONYMS: *forbid, ban, enjoin, interdict, prohibit, proscribe.* These verbs mean to refuse to allow: *laws that forbid speeding; banned smoking; was enjoined from broadcasting; interdict trafficking in drugs; rules that prohibit loitering; proscribed the importation of certain fruits.*

◀ **ANTONYM:** *permit*

forbiddance *noun.* A refusal to allow ▶ ban, disallowance, inhibition, interdiction, prohibition, proscription, taboo. [*Compare* **refusal, prevention.**]

forbidden *adjective.* Not allowed ▶ banned, barred, debarred, disallowed, illicit, impermissible, interdicted, outlawed, prohibited, proscribed, taboo, verboten. [*Compare* **criminal.**]

forbidding *adjective.* So disagreeable as to discourage approach ▶ dour, flinty, grim, inhospitable, stern, unhospitable, uninviting. [*Compare* **cool, hostile, severe.**] —*See also* **bleak** (1), **fateful** (1).

force *noun.* **1.** Strength or energy that overcomes resistance ▶ coercion, compulsion, constraint, duress, might, power, pressure, strength, violence. **2.** The condition of being in full effect or operation ▶ actualization, being, effect, realization. [*Compare* **exercise.**] **3.** A group of people organized for a particular purpose ▶ body, corps, crew, detachment, division, gang, patrol, platoon, side, squad, squadron, team, unit. [*Compare* **alliance, assembly, band[2], union.**] —*See also* **cogency, energy, impact, influence.**

force *verb.* **1.** To cause a person or thing to act or move in spite of resistance ▶ coerce, compel, constrain, make, obligate, oblige, pressure. [*Compare* **drive, urge.**] **2.** To compel another to participate in or submit to a sexual act ▶ assault, molest, rape, ravish, violate. —*See also* **coerce.**

force out *verb.* To take the place of another against the other's will ▶ cut out, displace, supplant, usurp. [*Compare* **assume, occupy.**]

✚ **CORE SYNONYMS:** *force, compel, coerce, constrain, oblige, obligate.* These verbs mean to cause a person or thing to follow a prescribed or dictated course in spite of resistance. *Force,* the most general, usually implies the exertion of physical power or the operation of circumstances that permit no options: *Tear gas forced the fugitives out of their hiding place. Compel* applies especially to an act dictated by one in authority: *Say nothing unless you're compelled to. Coerce* invariably implies the use of strength or harsh measures in securing compliance: "*The man of genius rules . . . by persuading an efficient minority to coerce an indifferent and self-indulgent majority*" (James Fitzjames Stephen). *Constrain* suggests that one is bound to a course of action by physical or moral means or by the operation of compelling circumstances: "*I will never be by violence constrained to do anything*" (Elizabeth I). *Oblige* implies the operation of authority, necessity, or moral or ethical considerations: "*Work consists of whatever a body is obliged to do*" (Mark Twain). *Obligate* applies when compliance is enforced by a legal contract or by the dictates of one's conscience or sense of propriety: *I am obligated to repay the loan.*

forced *adjective.* **1.** Accomplished by force ▶ coercive, forcible, violent. *Informal:* strong-arm. **2.** Not natural or spontaneous ▶ contrived, effortful, labored, strained. [*Compare* **awkward, stiff.**]

forceful *adjective.* Full of or displaying force ▶ dynamic, dynamical, effective, forcible, hard-hitting, mighty, potent, powerful, strong, vigorous. [*Compare* **intense, severe.**] —*See also* **assertive, convincing, energetic.**

forcefully *adverb.* —*See* **hard** (1).

forcefulness *noun.* —*See* **cogency, intensity.**

forcible *adjective.* Accomplished by force ▶ coercive, forced, violent. *Informal:* strong-arm. —*See also* **convincing, forceful.**

forcibly *adverb.* With force and violence ▶ coercively, violently. ***Idioms:*** against one's will, by force, under duress. *—See also* **hard** (1).

ford *verb. —See* **cross** (1).

fore *noun. —See* **forefront, front.**

forearm *verb. —See* **gird.**

forebear *noun. —See* **ancestor** (1).

forebode *verb. —See* **prophesy, threaten** (1).

foreboding *noun. —See* **feeling** (1), **omen.**

foreboding *adjective. —See* **fateful** (1).

forecast *verb. —See* **foreshadow, predict.**

forecast *noun. —See* **prediction.**

foredoomed *adjective. —See* **condemned.**

forefather *noun. —See* **ancestor** (1).

forefront *noun.* The position of greatest advancement or importance ▶ avant-garde, cutting edge, fore, front, lead, vanguard.

foregoing *adjective.* Next before the present one ▶ last, latter, preceding, previous. *—See also* **past.**

forehanded *adjective. —See* **wary.**

forehandedness *noun. —See* **prudence.**

foreign *adjective.* **1.** From or characteristic of another place or part of the world ▶ alien, exotic, expatriate, immigrant, nonnative, nonresident, strange. [*Compare* **distant.**] **2.** Not part of the essential nature of a thing ▶ alien, extraneous, extrinsic. [*Compare* **irrelevant.**]

✚ **CORE SYNONYMS:** *foreign, alien, exotic, strange.* These adjectives mean from or characteristic of another place or part of the world: *a foreign accent; alien customs; exotic birds; moved to a strange city.*

---

foreigner *noun.* A person coming from another country or into a new community ▶ alien, émigré, expatriate, immigrant, newcomer, nonresident, outlander, outsider, stranger.

foreknow *verb. —See* **foresee.**

foreknowledge *noun. —See* **vision** (2).

foreman *or* **forewoman** *noun. —See* **boss.**

foremost *adjective. —See* **best** (1), **primary** (1).

foremother *noun. —See* **ancestor** (1).

forenoon *noun.* The time of day from sunrise to noon ▶ A.M., before lunch, before noon, morning. [*Compare* **dawn.**]

forepart *noun. —See* **front.**

foreperson *noun. —See* **boss.**

forerun *verb. —See* **foreshadow, precede, prevent.**

forerunner *noun.* One that foreshadows or prepares for something else ▶ harbinger, herald, pioneer, precursor, presager, trailblazer, vanguard. *—See also* **ancestor** (2), **omen, original.**

foresee *verb.* To know in advance ▶ anticipate, divine, envision, foreknow, see. [*Compare* **expect, predict.**]

foreshadow *verb.* To give an indication of something in advance ▶ adumbrate, augur, bode, betoken, forecast, forerun, foreshow, foretell, foretoken, portend, prefigure, presage, prognosticate. [*Compare* **mean, prophesy.**]

foresight *noun. —See* **prudence, vision** (2).

foresighted *adjective. —See* **visionary.**

foresightedness *noun. —See* **prudence.**

forest *noun.* A dense growth of trees and underbrush covering an area ▶ backwoods, timberland, woodland, woods. [*Compare* **country, wilderness.**]

forestall *verb. —See* **hinder, prevent.**

forestallment *noun. —See* **prevention.**

foretaste *noun.* A limited or anticipatory experience ▶ sample, sampling, taste. [*Compare* **glance.**]

foretell *verb. —See* **foreshadow, predict, prophesy.**

foreteller *noun. —See* **prophet.**

forethought *or* **forethoughtfulness** *noun.* —*See* **prudence.**

foretoken *verb.* —*See* **foreshadow.**

foretoken *noun.* —*See* **omen.**

forever *adverb.* For all time; without end ▶ always, endlessly, eternally, everlastingly, evermore, permanently, perpetually, unendingly. ***Idioms:*** for ever and a day, for ever and ever, for good, for keeps, in perpetuity, till kingdom come, till Doomsday (*or* Judgment Day), till the cows come home, world without end. —*See also* **continually.**

forever *noun.* —*See* **ages.**

forewarn *verb.* —*See* **threaten** (1), **warn.**

forewarning *noun.* —*See* **feeling** (1), **omen.**

foreword *noun.* —*See* **introduction.**

forfeit *verb.* —*See* **abandon** (1).

forfend *verb.* —*See* **prevent.**

forgather *verb.* —*See* **assemble.**

forge[1] *verb.* —*See* **beat** (3), **counterfeit, make.**

forge[2] *verb.* —*See* **trudge.**

forger *noun.* One who makes a fraudulent copy of something ▶ counterfeiter, fabricator, faker, falsifier.

forgery *noun.* —*See* **counterfeit.**

forget *verb.* To fail to remember ▶ *Informal:* disremember. ***Idioms:*** draw a blank, go blank, have a senior moment, have no recollection (*or* memory). —*See also* **drop** (4), **neglect** (2).

forgetful *adjective.* —*See* **absent-minded, careless.**

forgivable *adjective.* —*See* **pardonable.**

forgive *verb.* To grant forgiveness to or for ▶ condone, excuse, let pass, overlook, pardon, remit. ***Idioms:*** forgive and forget, let bygones be bygones. [*Compare* **clear, excuse.**]

✚ **CORE SYNONYMS:** *forgive, pardon, excuse, condone.* These verbs mean to refrain from imposing punishment on an offender or demanding satisfaction for an offense. The first three can be used as conventional ways of offering apology. More strictly, to *forgive* is to grant pardon without harboring resentment: *"Children begin by loving their parents; as they grow older they judge them; sometimes they forgive them"* (Oscar Wilde). *Pardon* more strongly implies release from the liability for or penalty entailed by an offense: *After the revolution all political prisoners were pardoned.* To *excuse* is to pass over a mistake or fault without demanding punishment or redress: *"There are some acts of injustice which no national interest can excuse"* (J.A. Froude). To *condone* is to overlook an offense, usually a serious one, and often suggests tacit forgiveness: *Failure to protest the policy may imply a willingness to condone it.*

---

forgiveness *noun.* The act or an instance of forgiving ▶ absolution, amnesty, condonation, excuse, pardon, remission. [*Compare* **exculpation, grace.**]

forgo *verb.* —*See* **abandon** (1).

fork *noun.* —*See* **branch** (1).

fork *verb.* —*See* **branch, till.**

fork out *or* **over** *or* **up** *verb.* —*See* **spend** (1).

forlorn *adjective.* —*See* **abandoned** (1), **despondent, lonely** (1), **lonely** (2), **pitiful.**

form *noun.* **1.** The characteristic surface arrangement of a thing ▶ cast, configuration, contour, delineation, design, figure, outline, pattern, profile, shape, silhouette, structure. [*Compare* **arrangement, outline.**] **2.** A document used in applying, as for a job ▶ application, paper, sheet. **3.** A hollow device for shaping a fluid or plastic substance ▶ cast, matrix, mold. —*See also* **behavior** (1), **ceremony** (2), **constitution, custom, kind**[2], **ritual, shape, usual, variation.**

form *verb.* **1.** To give form to by or as if by pressing and kneading ▶ model, mold, sculpt, shape. [*Compare* **work.**] **2.** To be the constituent parts of ▶ compose, make up. [*Compare* **contain.**] —*See also* **develop** (1), **educate, make.**

✦ CORE SYNONYMS: *form, figure, shape, configuration, contour, profile.* These nouns refer to the characterstic surface arrangement or external outline of a thing. *Form* is the outline and structure of a thing as opposed to its substance: *a brooch in the form of a lovers' knot. Figure* refers usually to form as established by bounding or enclosing lines: *The cube is a solid geometric figure. Shape* implies three-dimensional definition that indicates both outline and bulk or mass: *"He faced her, a hooded and cloaked shape"* (Joseph Conrad). *Configuration* stresses the pattern formed by the arrangement of parts within an outline: *The map shows the configuration of North America, with its mountains, rivers, and plains. Contour* refers especially to the outline of a three-dimensional figure: *I traced the contour of the stone with my finger. Profile* denotes the outline of something viewed against a background and especially the outline of the human face in side view: *The police took a photograph of the mugger's profile.*

formal *adjective.* Requiring elegant clothes and fine manners ▶ black-tie, dressy, full-dress, white-tie. —*See also* **authoritative** (1), **ceremonious, cool, ritual.**

formal *noun.* —*See* **dance.**

formalistic *adjective.* —*See* **pedantic.**

formality *noun.* —*See* **ceremony** (2), **ritual.**

format *noun.* —*See* **arrangement** (1), **method.**

formation *noun.* —*See* **arrangement** (1).

former *adjective.* —*See* **late** (2), **past.**

formerly *adverb.* —*See* **earlier** (1).

formidable *adjective.* —*See* **burdensome, deep** (2), **fearful.**

formless *adjective.* —*See* **shapeless.**

formula *noun.* A means or method of entering into or achieving something desirable ▶ key, route, secret. *Informal:* ticket. [*Compare* **trick.**] —*See also* **law** (3), **way** (1).

formulaic *adjective.* —*See* **ordinary.**

formulate *verb.* To devise and set down ▶ compose, draft, draw up, frame. [*Compare* **compose.**] —*See also* **design** (1), **invent, phrase.**

formulated *adjective.* —*See* **calculated.**

fornicator *noun.* —*See* **philanderer.**

forsake *verb.* —*See* **abandon** (1), **defect.**

forsaken *adjective.* —*See* **abandoned** (1).

forswear *verb.* —*See* **abandon** (1), **break** (5), **lie**[2], **retract** (1).

fort *noun.* A position or building that has been fortified to be defended by soldiers ▶ bastion, citadel, fortification, fortress, redoubt, stronghold. [*Compare* **base**[1].]

forte *noun.* Something at which a person excels ▶ long suit, métier, specialty, strength, strong point, strong suit. *Slang:* bag, thing.

✦ CORE SYNONYMS: *forte, métier, specialty, strength.* These nouns denote something at which a person is particularly skilled: *Writing fiction is her forte. The theater is his métier. The professor's specialty was the study of ancient languages. Listening to patients is one of the strengths of a good doctor.*

forth *adverb.* —*See* **forward.**

forthcoming *adjective.* In the relatively near future ▶ approaching, coming, due, upcoming. ***Idioms:*** around the corner, on the horizon. [*Compare* **close, imminent.**]

forthright *adjective.* —*See* **frank.**

forthwith *adverb.* —*See* **immediately** (1).

fortification *noun.* —*See* **fort.**

fortify *verb.* To make firmer in a particular conviction or habit ▶ confirm, harden, reinforce, strengthen. [*Compare*

back, establish.] —*See also* **encourage (2), gird.**

fortitude *noun.* —*See* **courage, endurance.**

fortitudinous *adjective.* —*See* **brave.**

fortress *noun.* —*See* **fort.**

fortuitous *adjective.* Characterized by luck or good fortune ▶ fortunate, happy, lucky, providential. [*Compare* **opportune.**] —*See also* **accidental, opportune.**

fortuitousness *noun.* —*See* **chance (2).**

fortuity *noun.* —*See* **chance (1), chance (2).**

fortunate *adjective.* Characterized by luck or good fortune ▶ fortuitous, happy, lucky, providential. —*See also* **favorable (1), opportune.**

fortunateness *noun.* —*See* **luck.**

fortune *noun.* A large sum of money ▶ mint. *Informal:* bundle, pile, pretty penny, tidy sum, wad. ***Idiom:*** king's ransom. —*See also* **chance (2), fate (1), fate (2), luck, resources, wealth.**

fortuneteller *noun.* —*See* **prophet.**

forum *noun.* —*See* **assembly, conference (1), court (2).**

forward *verb.* —*See* **advance (1), send (1).**

forward *adjective.* —*See* **progressive (1).**

forward *adverb.* Toward the front or beyond a position ▶ ahead, forth, frontward, out, onward. ***Idiom:*** in advance.

forward-looking *or* **forward-thinking** *adjective.* —*See* **progressive (1).**

forwardness *noun.* —*See* **impudence.**

fossil *noun.* —*See* **square, ultraconservative.**

foster *verb.* To take care of and educate a child ▶ bring up, parent, raise, rear. —*See also* **advance (1), nurture, promote (2).**

foul *adjective.* —*See* **bad (2), bleak (1), dirty, obscene, offensive (1), smelly.**

foul *verb.* —*See* **contaminate, dirty, entangle.**

foul up *verb.* —*See* **botch.**

foul *noun.* —*See* **collision.**

foulness *noun.* —*See* **contamination, dirtiness, obscenity (1).**

foul play *noun.* —*See* **contamination, faithlessness.**

foul-smelling *adjective.* —*See* **smelly.**

foul-tasting *adjective.* —*See* **unpalatable.**

foul-up *noun.* —*See* **mess (1).**

found *verb.* To bring into existence formally ▶ constitute, create, establish, institute, organize, originate, set up, start. [*Compare* **start.**] —*See also* **base[1].**

✦ **CORE SYNONYMS:** *found, create, establish, institute, organize.* These verbs mean to bring something into existence formally and set it in operation: *founded a colony; created a trust fund; establishing a business; instituted an annual benefit concert; organizing a field trip.*

---

foundation *noun.* The act of founding or establishing ▶ constitution, creation, establishment, institution, organization, origination, start-up. [*Compare* **beginning.**] —*See also* **base[1] (2), basis (1), basis (2).**

foundational *adjective.* —*See* **radical.**

founder[1] *verb.* —*See* **fail (1), sink (1).**

founder[2] *noun.* —*See* **originator.**

foundling *noun.* —*See* **orphan.**

fountain *or* **fount** *or* **fountainhead** *noun.* —*See* **origin.**

four-flush *verb.* —*See* **deceive.**

fourth estate *noun.* —*See* **press.**

foxiness *noun.* —*See* **art.**

foxy *adjective.* —*See* **artful, desirable.**

fracas *noun.* —*See* **argument, disorder (2), fight (1).**

fraction *noun.* —*See* **part (1).**

fractional *adjective.* —*See* **partial (1).**

fractious *adjective.* —*See* **ill-tempered, unruly.**

fractiousness *noun.* —*See* **unruliness.**

fracture *verb.* —*See* **break (1), crack (1).**

fracture *noun.* —*See* **crack (2).**

fragile *adjective.* Easily broken or damaged ▶ breakable, brittle, delicate, frangible, friable. —*See also* **weak** (1).

✚ **CORE SYNONYMS:** *fragile, breakable, frangible, delicate, brittle.* These adjectives mean easily broken or damaged. *Fragile* applies to objects that are not made of strong or sturdy material and that require great care when handled: *fragile porcelain plates. Breakable* and *frangible* mean capable of being broken but do not necessarily imply inherent weakness: *breakable toys; frangible artifacts. Delicate* refers to what is so soft, tender, or fine as to be susceptible to injury: *delicate fruit. Brittle* refers to inelasticity that makes something especially likely to fracture or snap when it is subjected to pressure: *brittle bones.*

fragility *or* **fragileness** *noun.* —*See* **infirmity.**

fragment *noun.* —*See* **bit**[1] (1), **end** (3).

fragment *verb.* —*See* **disintegrate.**

fragmentary *adjective.* —*See* **partial** (1).

fragmentize *verb.* —*See* **disintegrate.**

fragrance *noun.* A sweet or pleasant odor ▶ aroma, bouquet, essence, perfume, redolence, scent. [*Compare* **smell, stench.**]

✚ **CORE SYNONYMS:** *fragrance, aroma, bouquet, perfume, redolence, scent.* These nouns denote a pleasant or sweet odor: *the fragrance of lilacs; the aroma of sizzling bacon; the bouquet of a fine wine; the perfume of roses; the redolence of fresh coffee; the scent of newly mown hay.*

fragrant *adjective.* Having a pleasant odor ▶ aromatic, odoriferous, odorous, perfumy, redolent, savory, scent-laden, sweet-smelling. [*Compare* **smelly.**]

fraidy cat *noun.* —*See* **coward.**

frail *adjective.* —*See* **weak** (1).

frailness *noun.* —*See* **infirmity.**

frailty *noun.* —*See* **infirmity, weakness.**

frame *noun.* A structure that supports or encloses something ▶ case, casing, framing, framework, shell, skeleton, substructure. [*Compare* **form, stage, support.**] —*See also* **constitution.**

frame *verb.* —*See* **build, compose, design** (1), **make, phrase.**

frame of mind *noun.* —*See* **mood.**

frame of reference *noun.* —*See* **viewpoint.**

framework *noun.* —*See* **draft** (1), **frame.**

framing *noun.* —*See* **frame.**

franchise *noun.* —*See* **right.**

frangible *adjective.* —*See* **fragile.**

frank *adjective.* Honest and direct, especially in speech; not lying or dissembling ▶ aboveboard, candid, direct, downright, forthright, free, free-spoken, honest, ingenuous, open, outspoken, plain, plainspoken, straight, straightforward, straight-out, unreserved, upfront, vocal. *Informal:* straight-from-the-shoulder, straight-shooting. [*Compare* **artless, genuine, serious.**]

✚ **CORE SYNONYMS:** *frank, candid, outspoken, straightforward, open.* These adjectives mean honest and direct, especially in speech or in revealing one's thoughts. *Frank* implies forthrightness, sometimes to the point of bluntness: *"Be calm and frank, and confess at once all that weighs on your heart"* (Emily Brontë). *Candid* often suggests refusal to evade difficult or unpleasant issues: *"Save, save, oh save me from the candid friend!"* (George Canning). *Outspoken* usually implies bold lack of reserve: *The outspoken activist protested the budget cuts. Straightforward* denotes directness of manner and expression: *"George was a straightforward soul . . . . 'See here!' he said. 'Are you engaged to anybody?'"* (Booth Tarkington). *Open* suggests freedom from all trace of reserve or secretiveness: *"I will be open and sincere with you"* (Joseph Addison).

frankness *noun.* —*See* **honesty.**

frantic *adjective.* Characterized by hurried activity and confusion or agitation

▶ delirious, fervid, fevered, feverish, frenetic, frenzied, hectic, mad, wild. [*Compare* **anxious, busy.**]

frantically *adverb.* —*See* **hard** (1).

fraternity *noun.* —*See* **union** (1).

fraternize *verb.* —*See* **associate** (2).

fraud *noun.* —*See* **cheat** (1), **deceit, fake.**

fraudulent *adjective.* —*See* **counterfeit.**

fraught *adjective.* —*See* **full** (1).

fray[1] *noun.* —*See* **fight** (1).

fray[2] *or* **frazzle** *verb.* To wear away along the edges ▶ frazzle, tatter. [*Compare* **erode, shred.**]

freak *noun. Slang* One whose sexual behavior differs from the accepted norm ▶ deviant, deviate, pervert. —*See also* **crackpot, fan**[2], **fancy.** —*See also* **monster.**

freakish *adjective.* Resembling a freak ▶ freaky, grotesque, monstrous. —*See also* **capricious, eccentric, weird.**

freaky *adjective.* Resembling a freak ▶ freakish, grotesque, monstrous. [*Compare* **eccentric, weird.**]

freckle *verb.* —*See* **speckle.**

free *adjective.* **1.** Not imprisoned, enslaved, or controlled by another ▶ autonomous, emancipated, freed, independent, liberated, manumitted, released, self-governing, self-ruling, sovereign. [*Compare* **voluntary.**] **2.** Costing nothing ▶ complimentary, gratis, gratuitous. ***Idioms:*** as a freebie, for free, for nothing, on the house. —*See also* **clear** (3), **frank, generous** (1), **loose** (2), **loose** (3), **open** (3), **open** (4).

free *verb.* **1.** To set at liberty ▶ discharge, emancipate, liberate, loose, manumit, release. *Slang:* spring. ***Idiom:*** let loose. [*Compare* **rescue.**] **2.** To rid of obstructions ▶ clear, open, remove, unblock. [*Compare* **rid.**] —*See also* **extricate, open** (1).

freebie *noun.* **1.** *Slang* A free ticket entitling one to transportation or admission ▶ pass. *Informal:* comp. **2.** *Slang* Something bestowed voluntarily ▶ bequest, gift, present, presentation. [*Compare* **grant.**]

freedom *noun.* The condition of being politically free ▶ autonomy, independence, liberty, self-determination, self-government, self-rule, sovereignty. —*See also* **liberty, right.**

free-for-all *noun.* —*See* **fight** (1).

free hand *noun.* —*See* **license** (1).

freehanded *adjective.* —*See* **generous** (1).

freehandedness *noun.* —*See* **generosity.**

freeload *verb.* To take advantage of the generosity of others ▶ leech, live off. *Informal:* sponge. *Slang:* beg.]

freeloader *noun.* —*See* **parasite.**

freeloading *adjective.* —*See* **parasitic.**

freely *adverb.* Of one's own free will ▶ by choice, spontaneously, voluntarily, willfully, willingly. ***Idioms:*** of one's own accord, on one's own volition.

freeman *noun.* —*See* **citizen.**

free-spoken *adjective.* —*See* **frank.**

freethinker *noun.* —*See* **rebel** (2).

freeway *noun.* —*See* **way** (2).

freewill *adjective.* —*See* **unpaid.**

free will *noun.* The mental faculty by which one deliberately chooses or decides ▶ volition, will. [*Compare* **spirit.**] —*See also* **choice.**

freezing *adjective.* —*See* **cold** (1).

freight *noun.* —*See* **burden**[1] (2), **transportation.**

freight *verb.* —*See* **burden**[1], **fill** (1).

frenetic *adjective.* —*See* **frantic.**

frenzied *adjective.* —*See* **frantic.**

frenziedly *adverb.* —*See* **hard** (1).

frequent *adjective.* —*See* **common** (1).

frequent *verb.* To visit regularly ▶ hang around, haunt, repair to, resort to. *Slang:* hang out. ***Idiom:*** go regularly to.

frequently *adverb.* —*See* **usually.**

fresh *adjective.* **1.** Not polluted or altered by human intervention ▶ pristine, pure, uncontaminated, undeveloped, unpolluted, unspoiled, untouched. [*Compare* **pastoral.**] **2.** Not sour or salted ▶ fresh, uncured, unsalted. —*See* *also* **additional, clean** (1), **energetic, impudent, inexperienced, new, young.**

freshen *verb.* To expose to circulating air ▶ aerate, air, ventilate, wind. *—See also* **blow**[1] (1), **refresh, tidy** (2).

freshet *noun. —See* **flood.**

freshman *noun. —See* **beginner.**

freshness *noun. —See* **novelty** (1).

fret *verb. —See* **annoy, brood, chafe.**

fretful *adjective. —See* **ill-tempered.**

friable *adjective. —See* **fragile.**

fricassee *verb. —See* **cook.**

friction *noun. —See* **conflict.**

friend *noun.* A person whom one knows well, likes, and trusts ▶ alter ego, amigo, brother, chum, comrade, confidant, confidante, crony, familiar, intimate, mate, sister, soul mate. *Informal:* bud, buddy, pal. *Slang:* sidekick. [*Compare* **associate.**] *—See also* **patron.**

friendliness *noun. —See* **amiability.**

friendly *adjective. —See* **amiable, intimate**[1] (1), **receptive.**

friendship *noun.* The condition of being friends ▶ amity, camaraderie, chumminess, closeness, companionship, comradeship, familiarity, fellowship, intimacy. [*Compare* **company.**]

fright *noun. —See* **fear, mess** (2).

frighten *verb.* To fill with fear ▶ affright, horrify, intimidate, panic, petrify, scare, scarify, startle, terrify, terrorize, unnerve. *Informal:* spook. ***Idioms:*** chill one to the bone, frighten (*or* scare) to death, give one the creeps (*or* heebie-jeebies), make one's blood run cold, make one's flesh crawl (*or* creep), make one's hair stand on end, put the fear of God into one, scare out of one's wits, scare silly (*or* stiff), scare the daylights out of, take one's breath away. [*Compare* **agitate, dismay.**]

✚ **CORE SYNONYMS:** *frighten, scare, terrify, terrorize, startle, panic.* These verbs mean to cause a person to experience fear. *Frighten* and the less formal *scare* are the most widely applicable: *"The Count's mysterious warning frightened me at the time"* (Bram Stoker). *The angry dog scared the small child. Terrify* implies overwhelming, often paralyzing fear: *"It is the coming of death that terrifies me"* (Oscar Wilde). *Terrorize* implies intimidation and sometimes suggests deliberate coercion: *"The decent citizen was terrorized into paying public blackmail"* (Arthur Conan Doyle). *Startle* suggests a momentary shock that may cause a sudden, involuntary movement of the body: *The clap of thunder startled us. Panic* implies sudden frantic fear that often impairs self-control and rationality: *The realistic radio drama panicked the listeners who tuned in after it had begun.*

---

frightened *adjective. —See* **afraid.**

frightening *verb. —See* **fearful.**

frightful *adjective. —See* **fearful, terrible.**

frigid *adjective.* Deficient in or lacking sexual desire ▶ ardorless, cold, inhibited, passionless, undersexed, unresponsive. *—See also* **cold** (1), **cool.**

frigidity *or* **frigidness** *noun. —See* **cold.**

frill *noun. —See* **luxury.**

fringe *noun. —See* **border** (1), **outskirts.**

fringe *verb. —See* **border.**

frippery *noun. —See* **attire, trifle.**

frisk *verb.* To examine a person or someone's personal effects in order to find something lost or concealed ▶ inspect, pat down, search. *Slang:* shake down. ***Idiom:*** do a body search of. *—See also* **gambol.**

frisk *noun.* A thorough search of a place or persons ▶ search. *Slang:* shakedown.

frisky *adjective. —See* **lively, mischievous.**

fritter away *verb. —See* **waste.**

frivolity *noun. —See* **trifle.**

frivolous *adjective. —See* **giddy** (2), **trivial.**

frizzle *verb. —See* **dry** (1).

frock *noun. —See* **dress** (3).

frolic *noun.* —*See* **prank[1].**

frolic *verb.* —*See* **gambol, play** (1), **revel.**

frolicsome *adjective.* —*See* **mischievous.**

front *noun.* The forward part of something ▶ bow, fore, forepart, front end, front side, head. —*See also* **façade** (1), **façade** (2), **forefront.**

front *verb.* **1.** To have the face or front turned toward ▶ face, give onto, look (on *or* upon *or* toward). [*Compare* **overlook.**] **2.** To meet face-to-face, especially defiantly ▶ confront, encounter, face, meet. ***Idiom:*** stand up to. [*Compare* **contest, defy.**] —*See also* **defy** (1).

frontage *or* **frontal** *noun.* —*See* **façade** (1).

frontier *noun.* —*See* **border** (2).

frontispiece *noun.* —*See* **façade** (1).

front-runner *noun.* A leading contestant or sure winner ▶ favorite, leader, number one, vanguard. *Informal:* shoo-in.

frontward *adverb.* —*See* **forward.**

frostiness *noun.* —*See* **cold.**

frosty *adjective.* —*See* **cold** (1), **cool.**

froth *noun.* —*See* **foam, trifle.**

froth *verb.* —*See* **boil, foam.**

frothy *adjective.* —*See* **foamy, giddy** (2), **trivial.**

froward *adjective.* —*See* **contrary, unruly.**

frown *verb.* To wrinkle one's brow, as in thought, puzzlement, or displeasure ▶ glower, lower, scowl. ***Idioms:*** knit one's brow, look black, turn one's mouth down. [*Compare* **glare, grimace.**]

frown on *or* **upon** *verb.* —*See* **disapprove.**

frown *noun.* The act of wrinkling the brow, as in thought, puzzlement, or displeasure ▶ black look, glower, lower, scowl. [*Compare* **face, glare, sneer.**]

✣ **CORE SYNONYMS:** *frown, glower, lower, scowl.* These verbs mean to wrinkle one's brow, as in thought, puzzlement, or displeasure: *frowns when he is annoyed; glowered upon being interrupted; lowering at the noisy child; scowled at my suggestion.*

---

frowzy *adjective.* —*See* **messy** (1), **moldy.**

frozen *adjective.* —*See* **motionless.**

frozenness *noun.* —*See* **cold.**

frugal *adjective.* —*See* **cheap, economical.**

frugality *noun.* —*See* **economy.**

fruit *noun.* —*See* **effect** (1), **harvest, progeny.**

fruitage *noun.* —*See* **harvest.**

fruitful *adjective.* Capable of reproducing ▶ fertile, fecund, productive, prolific. —*See also* **beneficial, fertile** (1).

fruitfulness *noun.* —*See* **fertility.**

fruition *noun.* —*See* **fulfillment** (1).

fruitless *adjective.* —*See* **futile.**

fruitlessness *noun.* —*See* **futility, sterility** (2).

fruity *adjective.* —*See* **insane.**

frump *noun.* —*See* **killjoy.**

frumpy *adjective.* —*See* **old-fashioned.**

frustrate *verb.* To prevent from accomplishing a purpose ▶ baffle, balk, check, checkmate, defeat, foil, stymie, thwart. *Informal:* cross, stump. ***Idiom:*** cut the ground from under. [*Compare* **disappoint, discourage, hinder, prevent.**] —*See also* **disappoint.**

frustration *noun.* —*See* **disappointment** (1), **prevention.**

fry *verb.* —*See* **cook.**

fuddle *verb.* —*See* **confuse** (1), **drug** (2).

fuddy-duddy *noun.* —*See* **square.**

fudge *verb.* —*See* **distort, muddle.**

fugacious *adjective.* —*See* **transitory.**

fugitive *adjective.* **1.** Fleeing or having fled, as from confinement or the police ▶ escaped, fleeing, runaway. ***Idioms:*** on the lam (*or* loose *or* run). **2.** Inclined or intended to evade ▶ elusive, evasive, slippery. [*Compare* **slick, underhand.**] —*See also* **transitory.**

fugitive *noun.* One who flees, as from confinement or the police ▶ escapee, outlaw, refugee, runaway. [*Compare* **criminal.**]

führer *noun.* —*See* **dictator.**

fulfill *verb.* To carry out the functions, requirements, or terms of ▶ discharge, do, execute, exercise, implement, keep, perform. ***Idiom:*** live up to. [*Compare* **effect.**] —*See also* **accomplish, perform** (1), **satisfy** (1), **satisfy** (2).

fulfilled *adjective.* Having achieved satisfaction, as of one's goal ▶ content, gratified, happy, satisfied.

fulfillment *noun.* **1.** The condition of being fulfilled ▶ accomplishment, attainment, completion, consummation, culmination, fruition, materialization, realization. [*Compare* **performance.**] **2.** The condition of being satisfied ▶ contentedness, contentment, gratification, satisfaction. [*Compare* **happiness, satiation.**]

full *adjective.* **1.** Completely filled ▶ awash, brimful, brimming, bursting, charged, chockablock, chock-full, crammed, fraught, jammed, jam-packed, loaded, overflowing, packed, replete, running over, stuffed. **2.** Having the appetite satisfied or overwhelmed ▶ cloyed, engorged, glutted, gorged, replete, sated, satiated, surfeited. **3.** Of full measure; not narrow or restricted ▶ ample, baggy, capacious, voluminous, wide. [*Compare* **loose.**] **4.** No less than; at least ▶ good, round, whole. —*See also* **close** (2), **complete** (1), **detailed, fat** (1), **unconditional.**

full-blooded *adjective.* —*See* **ruddy, thoroughbred.**

full-blown *adjective.* —*See* **mature.**

full-dress *adjective.* —*See* **formal, thorough.**

full-fledged *or* **full-grown** *adjective.* —*See* **mature, utter**[2].

full-length *adjective.* —*See* **complete** (2).

fullness *noun.* —*See* **completeness, satiation.**

full-strength *adjective.* —*See* **straight.**

fully *adverb.* —*See* **completely** (1).

fulminate *verb.* —*See* **explode** (1).

fulminate against *verb.* —*See* **revile.**

fulmination *noun.* —*See* **blast** (2), **tirade.**

fulsome *adjective.* —*See* **unctuous.**

fumble *verb.* —*See* **botch, grope, muddle.**

fumble *noun.* —*See* **blunder.**

fume *noun.* —*See* **state** (2).

fume *verb.* —*See* **anger** (2), **evaporate.**

fun *noun.* —*See* **amusement, merriment** (2), **play.**

fun *adjective.* —*See* **pleasant.**

function *noun.* **1.** The proper activity of a person or thing ▶ job, purpose, role, task. [*Compare* **duty, position, task.**] **2.** One's duty or responsibility in a common effort ▶ part, piece, role, share. —*See also* **party.**

function *verb.* To act or operate in a specified way ▶ act, behave, go, operate, perform, run, take, work. [*Compare* **officiate, substitute.**]

functional *adjective.* —*See* **practical.**

functionary *noun.* —*See* **executive.**

functioning *noun.* —*See* **behavior** (2).

functioning *adjective.* —*See* **active.**

fund *verb.* —*See* **finance.**

fundament *noun.* —*See* **buttocks.**

fundamental *adjective.* —*See* **elemental, essential** (2), **radical.**

fundamental *noun.* —*See* **basis** (1), **element** (1), **law** (3).

fundamentalist *noun.* —*See* **extremist.**

fundamentalist *adjective.* —*See* **extreme** (2).

fundamentally *adverb.* —*See* **essentially.**

funding *noun.* —*See* **capital** (1).

funds *noun.* The monetary resources of a government, organization, or individual ▶ capital, finances, money (or moneys). [*Compare* **capital, money, resources.**]

funeral *noun.* A ceremony held in connection with a burial or cremation ▶ funeral service, last rites, memorial service, obsequies, requiem. [*Compare* **burial.**]

funereal *adjective.* —*See* **gloomy.**

funk *noun.* —*See* **coward, cowardice, depression** (2), **fear.**

funky *adjective.* —*See* **afraid, fashionable, moldy, racy.**

funniness *noun.* —*See* **humor.**

funny *adjective.* **1.** Causing laughter or amusement ▶ amusing, comedic, comic, comical, droll, facetious, hilarious, humorous, jocose, jocular, laughable, priceless, risible, sidesplitting, uproarious, witty, zany. *Informal:* hysterical, killing, rich. *Slang:* ripe. ***Idioms:*** a laugh and a half, a riot, too funny for words. [*Compare* **pleasant.**] **2.** Agreeably curious, especially in an old-fashioned or unusual way ▶ curious, odd, quaint. **3.** Causing puzzlement; perplexing ▶ curious, odd, peculiar, queer, strange, weird. [*Compare* **shady, unusual.**]

funny *noun.* —*See* **joke** (1).

funny business *noun.* —*See* **mischief.**

funnyman *noun.* —*See* **joker.**

fur *noun.* The skin of an animal, sometimes including fur, hair or feathers ▶ hide, leather, pelt.

furbish *verb.* —*See* **gloss[1], renew** (1).

furfur *noun.* —*See* **scurf.**

furious *adjective.* —*See* **angry, intense.**

furiously *adverb.* —*See* **hard** (1).

furlough *noun.* A regularly scheduled period spent away from work or duty, often in recreation ▶ holiday, leave, sabbatical, vacation. ***Idioms:*** time (*or* day) off. [*Compare* **break, trip.**] —*See also* **license** (3).

furnish *verb.* To supply what is needed for some activity or purpose ▶ accouter, appoint, equip, fit, fit out (*or* up), gear, outfit, rig, turn out. [*Compare* **adorn.**] —*See also* **give** (1), **offer** (2).

✚ **CORE SYNONYMS:** *furnish, appoint, accouter, equip, outfit.* These verbs mean to provide with what is necessary for an activity or a purpose: *furnished the team with new uniforms; a library that was appointed in leather; knights who were accoutered for battle; equip a car with snow tires; had to outfit the children for summer camp.*

---

furor *noun.* —*See* **anger, fashion.**

furrow *noun.* A long, narrow, and usually shallow depression in the ground ▶ channel, ditch, groove, rut, trench, trough. —*See also* **wrinkle** (1).

furry *adjective.* —*See* **hairy.**

further *adjective.* —*See* **additional.**

further *adverb.* —*See* **additionally.**

further *verb.* —*See* **advance** (1).

furtherance *noun.* —*See* **advance, patronage** (1).

furthermore *adverb.* —*See* **additionally.**

furthest *or* **furthermost** *adjective.* —*See* **extreme** (1).

furtive *adjective.* —*See* **stealthy.**

furtiveness *noun.* —*See* **stealth.**

fury *noun.* —*See* **anger, intensity, scold.**

fuse *verb.* —*See* **attach** (1), **melt, mix** (1).

fusillade *noun.* —*See* **barrage.**

fusillade *verb.* —*See* **barrage.**

fusion *noun.* —*See* **mixture.**

fuss *noun.* —*See* **agitation** (3), **argument, bother, complaint, objection.**

fuss *verb.* —*See* **brood, complain.**

fuss at *verb.* —*See* **nag.**

fussy *adjective.* Very difficult to please ▶ choosy, dainty, demanding, exacting, fastidious, finical, finicky, meticulous, nice, particular, persnickety, squeamish. *Informal:* picky. ***Idiom:*** hard to please. [*Compare* **careful, contrary, discriminating.**] —*See also* **busy** (3), **careful** (2), **elaborate.**

fustian *noun.* —*See* **bombast.**

fustian *adjective.* —*See* **oratorical.**

fusty *adjective.* —*See* **moldy, old-fashioned.**

futile *adjective.* Having no useful result ▶ barren, bootless, fruitless, pointless, profitless, unavailing, unprofitable, unsuccessful, useless, vain. ***Idioms:*** in vain, to no avail, to no effect. [*Compare* **hollow, ineffectual.**]

✚ **CORE SYNONYMS:** *futile, barren, bootless, fruitless, unavailing, useless, vain.* These adjectives mean having no useful result or effect: *a futile effort; a barren search; bootless entreaties; fruitless labors; an unavailing attempt; a useless discussion; vain regrets.*

◀ **ANTONYM:** *useful*

---

futility *noun.* The condition or quality of being useless or ineffective ▶ barrenness, bootlessness, fruitlessness, pointlessness, profitlessness, unprofitableness, uselessness, vainness, vanity. [*Compare* **failure, ineffectuality.**]

future *noun.* **1.** Time that is yet to be ▶ by-and-by, futurity, hereafter, tomorrow. ***Idiom:*** time to come. [*Compare* **approach, possibility.**] **2.** Chance of success or advancement ▶ outlook, prospects. [*Compare* **chance.**]

future *adjective.* Being or occurring in the time ahead ▶ approaching, coming, eventual, forthcoming, later, subsequent. ***Idioms:*** down the road, in the cards, just around the corner, to be, to come. [*Compare* **coming, momentary, potential.**]

futuristic *adjective.* —*See* **progressive** (1).

futurity *noun.* Time that is yet to be ▶ by-and-by, future, hereafter, tomorrow. ***Idiom:*** time to come. [*Compare* **approach, possibility.**]

fuzz *noun.* —*See* **police officer.**

fuzzy *adjective.* —*See* **hairy, unclear.**

G

gab *verb.* —*See* **chatter** (1).

gab *noun.* —*See* **chatter.**

gabble *verb.* —*See* **babble.**

gabble *noun.* —*See* **babble.**

gabby *adjective.* —*See* **talkative.**

gabfest *noun.* —*See* **conversation.**

gad *verb.* —*See* **rove.**

gadabout *noun.* —*See* **hobo.**

gadget *noun.* A small specialized mechanical device ▶ apparatus, contraption, contrivance, gimmick, jigger, thing. *Informal:* doodad, doohickey, thingamabob, thingamajig, whatchamacallit, whatsit, widget. *Slang:* gizmo. [*Compare* **device, novelty.**]

gaffe *noun.* —*See* **impropriety** (2).

gag *noun.* —*See* **joke** (1), **prank[1].**

gag *verb.* —*See* **choke, repress.**

gaga *adjective.* —*See* **enthusiastic, giddy** (2), **insane.**

gage *noun.* —*See* **pawn[1].**

gaggle *noun.* —*See* **crowd, flock.**

gaiety *noun.* —*See* **merriment** (1), **merriment** (2).

gain *verb.* **1.** To achieve an increase of ▶ augment, build up, develop, enlarge, expand. **2.** To reach a goal or objective ▶ arrive at, attain, come to, get to. *Informal:* hit on (*or* upon). —*See also* **accomplish, benefit, capture, derive** (1), **earn** (1), **earn** (2), **get** (1), **recover** (2), **return** (3).

gain on *verb.* —*See* **approach** (1).

gain *noun.* Something earned, won, or otherwise acquired ▶ earnings, profit, return. —*See also* **advantage** (2).

gainful *adjective.* —*See* **profitable.**

gainsay *verb.* —*See* **deny.**

gait *noun.* —*See* **walk** (2).

gal *noun.* —*See* **girl.**

gala *noun.* —*See* **party.**

gala *adjective.* —*See* **merry.**

galaxy *noun.* —*See* **assembly.**

gale *noun.* —*See* **storm.**

gall[1] *noun.* —*See* **impudence, resentment.**

gall[2] *verb.* —*See* **annoy, chafe.**

gallant *adjective.* Respectfully attentive, especially to women ▶ chivalric, chivalrous, gentlemanly, knightly. —*See also* **attentive, brave, gracious** (2).

gallant *noun.* A man amorously attentive to women ▶ amorist, Casanova, Don Juan, lady's man, Lothario, Romeo. [*Compare* **beau.**]

gallantry *noun.* Respectful attention, especially toward women ▶ chivalrousness, chivalry. [*Compare* **consideration, courtesy.**] —*See also* **courage.**

gallimaufry *noun.* —*See* **assortment.**

galling *adjective.* —*See* **bitter** (3), **disturbing.**

gallivant *verb.* —*See* **rove.**

gallop *verb.* —*See* **run** (1).

gallop *noun.* —*See* **run** (1).

galumph *verb.* —*See* **blunder.**

galvanize *verb.* —*See* **provoke.**

gamble *verb.* **1.** To make a bet ▶ bet, game, lay, play, wager. ***Idiom:*** put one's money on something. **2.** To place something at risk, as in a speculation or a game of chance ▶ bet, chance, lay (down), post, put, risk, stake, venture, wager. *Informal:* go. **3.** To take a risk in the hope of gaining advantage ▶ speculate, venture. ***Idioms:*** go for broke, go out on a limb, play fast and loose, stick one's neck out, take a flier, take a shot (*or* stab) in the dark, tempt fate (*or* fortune), trust to chance (*or* luck).

gamble *noun.* An undertaking depending on chance ▶ bet, long shot, plunge, risk, speculation, tossup, venture, wager. *Informal:* flier. *Slang:* crapshoot. ***Idioms:*** leap (*or* shot) in the dark, roll of the dice, toss of a coin. [*Compare* **attempt, try.**] —*See also* **risk.**

gambler *noun.* **1.** One who gambles ▶ cardsharp, crapshooter, bettor, gamester, player, sharper. *Slang:* high roller. **2.** One who speculates for quick profits ▶ adventurer, operator, speculator.

gambol *verb.* To leap and skip about playfully ▶ caper, cavort, dance, frisk, frolic, rollick, romp. [*Compare* **bound**[1].]

game *noun.* An object for children to play with ▶ game, toy. [*Compare* **amusement.**] —*See also* **competition** (2), **play.**

game *verb.* To make a bet ▶ bet, gamble, lay, play, wager. ***Idiom:*** put one's money on something. —*See also* **cheat** (1).

game *adjective.* —*See* **brave, willing.**

gameness *noun.* —*See* **courage.**

game plan *noun.* —*See* **approach** (1).

gamesome *adjective.* —*See* **mischievous.**

gamester *noun.* —*See* **gambler** (1).

gamin *or* **gamine** *noun.* —*See* **urchin.**

gamut *noun.* —*See* **series.**

gamy *adjective.* —*See* **moldy.**

gander *noun.* —*See* **fool, glance** (1).

gang *noun.* An organized group of criminals, hoodlums, or wrongdoers ▶ band, pack, ring. *Informal:* mob. —*See also* **circle** (3), **flock, force** (3).

gang *verb.* —*See* **band**[2].

gang up on *verb.* —*See* **attack** (1).

gangling *or* **gangly** *adjective.* Tall, thin, and awkwardly built ▶ lanky, rangy, scraggy, spindling, spindly. [*Compare* **thin.**]

gangsta *noun.* —*See* **thug.**

gangster *noun.* —*See* **criminal.**

gap *noun.* **1.** A space between objects or points ▶ chasm, divide, gulf, interspace, interstice, interval, separation. [*Compare* **hole.**] **2.** An interval during which continuity is suspended ▶ break, hiatus, interlude, interim, interregnum, lacuna, lull, void. [*Compare* **break.**] **3.** A marked lack of correspondence or agreement ▶ difference, disagreement, discrepancy, disparity, imbalance, incompatibility, incongruity, inconsistency. [*Compare* **difference.**] —*See also* **breach, distance** (1).

gap *verb.* **1.** To make a hole or other opening in ▶ breach, break (through), hole, perforate, pierce, puncture. **2.** To open wide ▶ gape, yawn. [*Compare* **open, widen.**]

gape *verb.* **1.** To open the mouth wide with a deep breath, as when tired or bored ▶ yawn. **2.** To open wide ▶ gap, yawn. [*Compare* **open, widen.**] —*See also* **gaze.**

gape *noun.* An intent fixed look ▶ gaze, stare. [*Compare* **look.**]

gaping *adjective.* Open wide ▶ abysmal, abyssal, cavernous, yawning. [*Compare* **broad, open.**]

garb *noun.* —*See* **dress** (1), **dress** (2).

garb *verb.* —*See* **dress** (1).

garbage *noun.* Items or material discarded or rejected as useless or worthless ▶ debris, dregs, flotsam, jetsam, litter, refuse, rubbish, trash, waste. *Informal:* gunk. ***Idiom:*** flotsam and jetsam. —*See also* **nonsense.**

garble *verb.* —*See* **confuse** (3).

garden *adjective.* —*See* **ordinary.**

garden *verb.* —*See* **grow.**

garden-variety *adjective.* —*See* **ordinary.**

gargantuan *adjective.* —*See* **enormous.**

garish *adjective.* —*See* **gaudy.**

garland *noun.* —*See* **bouquet.**

garment *verb.* —*See* **dress** (1).

garments *noun.* —*See* **dress** (1).

garner *verb.* —*See* **accumulate, gather, glean.**

garner *noun.* The amount or quantity produced ▶ output, production, yield.

garnish *verb.* —*See* **adorn** (1).

garniture *or* **garnishment** *noun.* —*See* **adornment.**

garrulous *adjective.* —*See* **talkative.**

gas *noun.* —*See* **boast, chatter, scream** (2).

gas *verb.* —*See* **chatter** (1).

gasconade *verb.* —*See* **boast.**

gasconade *noun.* —*See* **boast.**

gash *verb.* —*See* **cut** (1).

gash *noun.* —*See* **cut** (1).

gasp *verb.* To utter in a breathless or hoarse manner ▶ croak, heave, pant, rasp, snort, wheeze. [*Compare* **shout.**] —*See also* **pant.**

gassy *adjective.* —*See* **inflated.**

gate *noun.* The amount of money collected as admission, especially to a sporting event ▶ box office, take, receipts.

gatecrash *verb.* —*See* **intrude.**

gather *verb.* To collect ripe crops ▶ crop, garner, harvest, pick, pluck, reap. —*See also* **accumulate, assemble, glean, infer.**

gathering *noun.* —*See* **accumulation** (1), **assembly, junction, party.**

gauche *adjective.* —*See* **tactless, unskillful.**

gaudy *adjective.* Tastelessly showy ▶ chintzy, flashy, florid, garish, loud, meretricious, tawdry, tinsel, vulgar. *Informal:* glitzy, tacky. [*Compare* **ornate, showy.**]

✣ **CORE SYNONYMS:** *gaudy, flashy, florid, garish, loud, meretricious, tacky, tawdry.* These adjectives mean tastelessly showy: *a gaudy costume; a flashy ring; a florid polyester tie; garish colors; a loud sport shirt; a meretricious yet stylish book; tacky knickknacks; tawdry ornaments.*

---

gauge *noun.* The marked outer surface of an instrument ▶ dial, face, indicator. —*See also* **standard.**

gauge *verb.* To ascertain the dimensions, quantity, or capacity of ▶ measure, quantify, quantitate. ***Idioms:*** take the dimensions (*or* measure) of. —*See also* **estimate** (1).

gaunt *adjective.* —*See* **haggard, thin** (1).

gauzy *adjective.* —*See* **sheer**[2]**.**

gawk *noun.* —*See* **oaf.**

gawk *verb.* —*See* **gaze.**

gawky *adjective.* —*See* **awkward** (1).

gay *adjective.* Having a sexual orientation to persons of the same sex ▶ homophile, homosexual, lesbian. —*See also* **cheerful, colorful** (1).

gaze *verb.* To look intently and fixedly ▶ eye, gape, gawk, goggle, ogle, peer, stare. *Slang:* rubberneck. ***Idioms:*** gaze openmouthed, fix (*or* rivet) the eyes (on). [*Compare* **glare, look, watch, squint.**]

gaze *noun.* An intent fixed look ▶ gape, stare. [*Compare* **look.**]

✣ **CORE SYNONYMS:** *gaze, stare, gape, gawk, peer.* These verbs mean to look long and intently. *Gaze* is often indicative of wonder, fascination, awe, or admiration: *gazing at the stars. Stare* can indicate curiosity, boldness, insolence, or stupidity: *stared at them in disbelief. Gape* suggests a prolonged open-mouthed look reflecting amazement, awe, or lack of intelligence: *tourists gaping at the sights.* To *gawk* is to gape or stare stupidly: *Drivers gawked at the disabled truck.* To *peer* is to look narrowly, searchingly, and seemingly with difficulty: *peered at us through her glasses.*

---

gear *noun.* —*See* **dress** (2), **outfit.**
gear *verb.* —*See* **furnish.**
geek *noun.* —*See* **fool.**
gelatinize *verb.* —*See* **coagulate.**
gelatinous *adjective.* —*See* **viscous.**
geld *verb.* —*See* **sterilize** (2).
gelid *adjective.* —*See* **cold** (1).
gelidity *or* **gelidness** *noun.* —*See* **cold.**
gelt *noun.* —*See* **money** (1).
gem *noun.* —*See* **treasure.**
geminate *verb.* To make or become twice as great ▶ double, duplicate, redouble, twin.
geminate *adjective.* —*See* **double** (2).
gendarme *noun.* —*See* **police officer.**
gender-neutral *adjective.* —*See* **androgynous.**
gender-neutrality *noun.* The quality of being androgynous ▶ androgyny, epicenism, sexlessness. [*Compare* **effeminacy, masculinity.**]
genealogical *adjective.* Of unbroken descent or lineage ▶ direct, hereditary, lineal, natural. —*See also* **ancestral.**
genealogy *noun.* A written record of ancestry ▶ family tree, pedigree. —*See also* **ancestry.**
general *adjective.* **1.** Concerned with, applicable to, or affecting the whole ▶ blanket, common, generic, total, universal. **2.** Covering a wide scope ▶ all-around, all-inclusive, all-round, broad, broad-spectrum, comprehensive, expansive, extended, extensive, far-ranging, far-reaching, global, inclusive, large, overall, popular, sweeping, wide-ranging, wide-reaching, widespread. ***Idiom:*** across-the-board. **3.** Not limited to a single class ▶ diversified, indefinite. —*See also* **common** (1), **common** (2), **loose** (3), **popular, prevailing.**
general *noun.* —*See* **chief.**

✚ **CORE SYNONYMS:** *general, common, generic, universal.* These adjectives mean concerned with, applicable to, or affecting the whole: *the general welfare; a common enemy; generic likenesses; universal military conscription.*

◀ **ANTONYM:** *particular*

---

generally *adverb.* —*See* **usually.**
generate *verb.* —*See* **cause, produce** (1).
generation *noun.* —*See* **life, progeny, reproduction.**
generative *adjective.* —*See* **inventive.**
generic *adjective.* —*See* **general** (1).
generosity *noun.* The quality or state of being generous ▶ big-heartedness, bounteousness, bountifulness, bounty, freehandedness, generousness, great-heartedness, large-heartedness, largess, lavishness, liberality, magnanimity, magnanimousness, munificence, openhandedness, unselfishness, unsparingness. [*Compare* **benevolence, consideration.**]
generous *adjective.* **1.** Willing to give of oneself and one's possessions ▶ big, big-hearted, bountiful, free, freehanded, great-hearted, handsome, large-hearted, lavish, liberal, magnanimous, munificent, openhanded, princely, prodigal, ungrudging, unselfish, unsparing, unstinting, warm-hearted. [*Compare* **benevolent, humanitarian.**] **2.** Characterized by abundance; as much as one needs or desires ▶ abounding, abundant, ample, bounteous, bountiful, copious, heavy, plenitudinous, plenteous, plentiful, substantial, voluminous. [*Compare* **profuse.**] —*See also* **obliging.**

✚ **CORE SYNONYMS:** *generous, abundant, ample, copious, plenitudinous,* *plentiful.* These adjectives mean being fully as much as one needs or desires: *a generous serving of mashed potatoes; the artist's abundant talent; ample space; copious provisions; a plenitudinous crop of wheat; a plentiful supply of freshly picked strawberries.*

◀ ANTONYM: *scant*

---

generousness *noun.* —*See* **generosity.**
genesis *noun.* —*See* **birth** (2).
genial *adjective.* —*See* **amiable.**
geniality *or* **genialness** *noun.* —*See* **amiability.**
genius *noun.* Liveliness and vivacity of imagination ▶ brilliance, brilliancy, fire, inspiration. [*Compare* **intelligence, invention.**] —*See also* **mind** (2), **talent.**
genius *adjective.* —*See* **intelligent.**
genocide *noun.* —*See* **massacre.**
genre *noun.* —*See* **class** (1).
genteel *adjective.* —*See* **courteous** (1), **delicate** (1), **gracious** (2), **prudish.**
genteelness *noun.* —*See* **courtesy.**
gentility *noun.* —*See* **courtesy, society** (1).
gentle *adjective.* **1.** Of a sympathetic, considerate character ▶ compassionate, kindly, mild, sensitive, soft, softhearted, tender, tenderhearted. [*Compare* **attentive, sympathetic.**] **2.** Free from severity or violence, as in sound or movement ▶ balmy, delicate, faint, mild, moderate, slight, smooth, soothing, soft. **3.** Easily managed or handled ▶ docile, domesticated, meek, mild, tame, yielding. [*Compare* **cooperative, obedient, obliging.**] —*See also* **delicate** (1), **gradual** (2), **light**[2] (2).
gentle *verb.* To make an animal docile ▶ break, bust, master, tame. —*See also* **domesticate, pacify.**
gentlemanly *adjective.* —*See* **courteous** (1), **gallant.**
gentry *noun.* —*See* **society** (1).
genuflect *verb.* —*See* **bow**[1] (1).
genuflection *noun.* —*See* **bow**[1].
genuine *adjective.* Free from hypocrisy or pretense ▶ heartfelt, hearty, honest, natural, plain, real, sincere, true, unaffected, unfeigned. [*Compare* **artless, frank, honest, serious.**] —*See also* **authentic** (1), **pure.**
genuinely *adverb.* —*See* **really.**
genuineness *noun.* —*See* **veracity.**
genus *noun.* —*See* **kind**[2].
georgic *adjective.* —*See* **country.**
germ *noun.* **1.** A tiny organism usually producing disease ▶ bacterium, bug, microbe, microorganism, parasite, pathogen, virus. **2.** A source of further growth and development ▶ bud, embryo, kernel, nucleus, seed, spark. [*Compare* **origin.**]
germane *adjective.* —*See* **relevant.**
germaneness *noun.* —*See* **relevance.**
gestation *noun.* The condition of carrying a developing fetus within the uterus ▶ gravidity, gravidness, parturiency, pregnancy.
gesticulate *verb.* —*See* **gesture.**
gesticulation *noun.* —*See* **gesture.**
gesture *noun.* An expressive, meaningful bodily movement ▶ gesticulation, indication, motion, nod, sign, signal, wag, wave. *Informal:* high sign. ***Idioms:*** thumbs up (*or* down). —*See also* **expression** (2).
gesture *verb.* To make bodily motions so as to convey an idea or complement speech ▶ beckon, flag, gesticulate, motion, pantomime, sign, signal, signalize, wave. ***Idiom:*** give the high sign.

✦ CORE SYNONYMS: *gesture, gesticulation, sign, signal.* These nouns denote an expressive, meaningful bodily movement: *a gesture of approval; frantic gesticulations to get help; made a sign for silence; gave the signal to advance.*

---

get *verb.* **1.** To come into possession of ▶ acquire, attain, come by, gain, glean, obtain, procure, reap, receive, secure, take, win. *Informal:* land, pick up. *Slang:* bag. [*Compare* **obtain.**] **2.** To succeed in communicating with ▶ *Informal:* contact, reach. *Informal:* catch. **3.** To be the biological father of ▶ beget, father, sire.

—*See also* **annoy, avenge, become** (1), **bring** (2), **capture, contract** (2), **derive** (1), **earn** (1), **earn** (2), **learn** (1), **move** (1), **understand** (1).

get across *verb.* —*See* **communicate** (1).

get ahead *verb.* To gain success ▶ arrive, get on, rise, succeed. ***Idioms:*** go far, go places, make good, make it. —*See also* **rise** (3).

get along *verb.* To grow old ▶ age, get on. —*See also* **advance** (2), **manage, relate** (2).

get around *verb.* To become known far and wide ▶ circulate, go around, spread, travel. ***Idioms:*** go (*or* make) the rounds. —*See also* **avoid.**

get away *verb.* —*See* **escape** (1), **go** (1).

get behind *verb.* —*See* **support** (1).

get by *verb.* —*See* **manage.**

get in *verb.* —*See* **arrive** (1).

get off *verb.* —*See* **go** (1), **start** (1).

get on *verb.* **1.** To gain success ▶ arrive, get ahead, rise, succeed. ***Idioms:*** go far, go places, make good, make it. **2.** To grow old ▶ age, get along. —*See also* **don, relate** (2).

get out *verb.* To be made public ▶ break, come out, out, transpire. *Informal:* leak (out). [*Compare* **air, announce, appear.**] —*See also* **run** (2).

get through *verb.* —*See* **survive** (1).

get to *verb.* —*See* **accomplish, annoy, persuade.**

get together *verb.* —*See* **assemble.** To come together by arrangement ▶ connect, hook up, meet (up), rendezvous. —*See also* **agree** (2).

get up *verb.* —*See* **rise** (1), **stand** (1).

get *noun.* —*See* **progeny.**

getaway *noun.* —*See* **escape** (1).

gettable *adjective.* —*See* **available.**

get-together *noun.* —*See* **assembly, party, visit** (1).

getup *noun.* —*See* **disguise, dress** (2).

get-up-and-go *noun.* —*See* **drive** (2), **energy.**

gewgaw *noun.* —*See* **novelty** (3).

ghastly *adjective.* **1.** Shockingly repellent ▶ appalling, dreadful, grim, grisly, gruesome, hideous, horrible, horrid, loathsome, lurid, macabre, terrifying. [*Compare* **fearful, offensive.**] **2.** Gruesomely suggestive of ghosts or death ▶ cadaverous, deadly, deathlike, deathly, ghostlike, ghostly, morbid, spectral, wraithlike. [*Compare* **pale, phantasmagoric, weird.**] —*See also* **terrible.**

✚ **CORE SYNONYMS:** *ghastly, grim, gruesome, grisly, macabre, lurid.* These adjectives describe what is shockingly repellent in aspect or appearance. *Ghastly* applies to what inspires shock or horror because it suggests death: *ghastly wounds. Grim* refers to what repels because of its stern or fierce aspect or its harsh, relentless nature: *the grim task of burying the victims of the earthquake. Gruesome* and *grisly* describe what horrifies or revolts because of its appalling crudity or utter inhumanity: *a gruesome murder; grisly jokes about cadavers. Macabre* suggests the horror of death and decay: *macabre stories about a madman. Lurid* sometimes refers to an unnatural hue suggestive of death: *The ill patient's skin took on a lurid pallor.* More often, the term describes what shocks because of its terrible and ghastly nature: *lurid crimes.* At other times, it merely refers to glaring and usually unsavory sensationalism: *a lurid account of the accident.*

---

ghettoize *verb.* —*See* **isolate** (1).

ghost *noun.* An immaterial supernatural being, especially the spirit of a dead person ▶ apparition, bogey, bogeyman, bogle, eidolon, phantasm, phantasma, phantom, revenant, shade, shadow, soul, specter, spirit, visitant, wraith. *Informal:* spook. *Chiefly Regional:* haunt. [*Compare* **fairy.**] —*See also* **shade** (2).

ghostly *or* **ghostlike** *adjective.* —*See* **ghastly** (2).

ghoul *noun.* —*See* **fiend.**

ghoulish *adjective.* —*See* **fiendish.**

GI *noun.* —*See* **soldier** (2).

giant *noun.* One that is extraordinarily large and powerful ▶ behemoth, colossus, elephant, gargantua, Goliath, Hercules, hulk, jumbo, leviathan, mammoth, monster, ogre, titan, whale. *Slang:* whopper.

giant *adjective.* —*See* **enormous.**

gibber *verb.* —*See* **babble.**

gibberish *noun.* Highly technical, often deliberately deceptive language ▶ abracadabra, doublespeak, double talk, gobbledygook, Greek, hocus-pocus, jabberwocky, mumbo jumbo. [*Compare* **nonsense.**] —*See also* **babble.**

gibbet *verb.* To execute by suspending by the neck ▶ hang. *Informal:* string up. *Slang:* swing.

gibe *or* **jibe** *verb.* —*See* **ridicule.**

gibe *noun.* —*See* **taunt.**

giddiness *noun.* —*See* **dizziness.**

giddy *adjective.* **1.** Producing dizziness or vertigo ▶ dizzy, dizzying, sickening, vertiginous. [*Compare* **steep.**] **2.** Given to lighthearted silliness ▶ empty-headed, featherbrained, flighty, frivolous, frothy, harebrained, lighthearted, scatterbrained, silly. *Informal:* gaga. *Slang:* birdbrained, dizzy. [*Compare* **foolish, stupid.**] —*See also* **dizzy** (1).

✚ **CORE SYNONYMS:** *giddy, dizzy, vertiginous.* These adjectives mean producing dizziness or vertigo: *a giddy precipice; a dizzy pinnacle; a vertiginous height.*

---

gift *noun.* Something bestowed voluntarily ▶ bequest, present, presentation. *Slang:* freebie. [*Compare* **grant.**] —*See also* **donation, talent.**

gift *verb.* To present with a gift ▶ award, endow, endue, give, invest. [*Compare* **grant.**]

gifted *adjective.* Possessing great natural ability or talent ▶ born, endowed, natural, precocious, talented. *Informal:* whiz-bang. [*Compare* **able, expert.**]

gig *noun. Slang* A commitment, as for a performance by an entertainer ▶ booking, date, engagement. —*See also* **position** (3).

gigantic *adjective.* —*See* **enormous.**

giggle *verb.* —*See* **laugh.**

giggle *noun.* —*See* **laugh.**

gigolo *noun.* —*See* **lecher, wanton.**

gild *verb.* —*See* **adorn** (1), **color** (2), **sweeten.**

gilded *or* **gilt** *adjective.* —*See* **ornate.**

gimcrack *noun.* —*See* **novelty** (3).

gimmick *noun.* —*See* **gadget, novelty** (3), **trick** (1), **wrinkle** (2).

ginger *noun.* —*See* **spirit** (1).

gingerliness *noun.* —*See* **care** (1), **caution.**

gingerly *adjective.* —*See* **wary.**

gird *verb.* To prepare oneself for action ▶ arm, brace, forearm, fortify, ready, steel, strengthen. ***Idioms:*** clear the deck, gird (*or* gird up) one's loins, screw up one's courage. —*See also* **encircle.**

girder *noun.* —*See* **beam** (2).

girdle *noun.* —*See* **band**[1]**.**

girdle *verb.* —*See* **encircle.**

girl *noun. Informal* A woman referred to informally ▶ lass. *Informal:* chick, damsel, doll, gal, missy, sis, sister. *Slang:* homegirl, momma.

girlfriend *noun.* A woman who is a man's romantic partner ▶ girl, inamorata, lady friend. *Slang:* old lady. [*Compare* **darling, lover.**]

girt *verb.* —*See* **encircle.**

gist *noun.* —*See* **heart** (1), **thrust.**

give *verb.* **1.** To relinquish to the possession or control of another ▶ deliver, furnish, hand, hand in, hand over, provide, render, supply, transfer, turn over. **2.** To present as a gift to a charity or cause ▶ bestow, contribute, donate, hand out. **3.** To mete out by means of some action ▶ administer, deal, deliver. **4.** To let have as a favor, prerogative, or privilege ▶ accord, award, concede, grant, vouchsafe. [*Compare* **yield.**] —*See also* **administer** (3), **allot, apply** (1), **bend** (3), **buckle, communicate**

(2), **confer** (2), **distribute, entrust** (1), **gift, permit** (3), **produce** (1), **spend** (1).

give away *verb.* —*See* **betray** (2), **donate.**

give back *verb.* —*See* **reinstall.** —*See also* **return** (2).

give forth *verb.* —*See* **emit, produce** (1).

give in *verb.* To lose all hope ▶ despair, despond, give up. ***Idioms:*** throw in the sponge (*or* towel). [*Compare* **abandon.**] —*See also* **surrender** (1).

give off *verb.* —*See* **emit.**

give onto *verb.* To have the face or front turned toward ▶ face, front, look (on *or* upon *or* toward). [*Compare* **overlook.**]

give out *verb.* To prove deficient or insufficient ▶ fail, run out. ***Idioms:*** fall short, run dry, run short. [*Compare* **decrease.**] —*See also* **collapse** (1), **dry up** (2), **emit, malfunction, tire** (2).

give over *verb.* To yield oneself unrestrainedly, as to an impulse ▶ deliver, relinquish, surrender. ***Idioms:*** give oneself up (*or* over). —*See also* **drop** (4).

give up *verb.* **1.** To lose all hope ▶ despair, despond, give in. ***Idioms:*** throw in the sponge (*or* towel). [*Compare* **abandon.**] **2.** To yield oneself unrestrainedly, as to an impulse ▶ deliver, relinquish, surrender. ***Idioms:*** give oneself up (*or* over). —*See also* **break** (5), **drop** (4), **surrender** (1).

give *noun.* —*See* **flexibility** (1).

give-and-take *noun.* —*See* **compromise.**

given *adjective.* —*See* **inclined, presumptive.**

given *noun.* —*See* **assumption.**

giver *noun.* —*See* **donor.**

gizmo *noun.* —*See* **gadget.**

glacial *adjective.* —*See* **cold** (1), **cool, slow** (1).

glad *adjective.* —*See* **cheerful, merry, willing.**

gladden *verb.* —*See* **delight** (1).

gladly *adverb.* —*See* **yes.**

gladness *noun.* —*See* **happiness, merriment** (1).

gladsome *adjective.* —*See* **merry.**

glamorous *adjective.* —*See* **attractive.**

glamour *noun.* —*See* **attraction, glitter** (2).

glance *verb.* **1.** To strike a surface at such an angle as to be deflected ▶ carom, fly off, graze, ricochet, skim, skip. [*Compare* **bounce.**] **2.** To look briefly and quickly ▶ glimpse, peek, peep. ***Idioms:*** steal a glance (*or* look). [*Compare* **look.**] —*See also* **glitter.**

glance at *or* **over** *or* **through** *verb.* —*See* **browse** (1).

glance *noun.* **1.** A quick look ▶ glimpse, look, peek, peep, scan. *Informal:* gander, look-see. **2.** An act of reflection ▶ deflection, reflection, scattering. [*Compare* **bounce.**] —*See also* **flash** (1).

glare *verb.* **1.** To stare fixedly and angrily ▶ glower, lower, scowl. ***Idioms:*** give the evil eye, look daggers. [*Compare* **frown, gaze, sneer.**] **2.** To shine intensely and blindingly ▶ beat down, blaze, flare, pulse, throb, vibrate. [*Compare* **beam.**] **3.** To be obtrusively conspicuous ▶ stand out, stick out. ***Idioms:*** stare someone in the face, stick out like a sore thumb.

glare *noun.* **1.** A fixed angry stare ▶ glower, lower, scowl. [*Compare* **face, sneer.**] **2.** An intense blinding light ▶ blaze, dazzle, flare. **3.** Light that is reflected ▶ highlight, reflection. [*Compare* **flash.**]

glaring *adjective.* Conspicuously bad or offensive ▶ egregious, flagrant, gross, rank. [*Compare* **offensive, outrageous, shameless.**] —*See also* **apparent** (1), **brilliant.**

glaringness *noun.* The quality or state of being flagrant ▶ egregiousness, flagrancy, grossness, rankness. [*Compare* **impudence, outrageousness.**]

glary *adjective.* —*See* **brilliant.**

glassy *adjective.* Of or resembling glass ▶ glasslike, hyaline, vitrescent, vitreous.

[*Compare* **translucent.**] —*See also* **glossy.**

glaze *noun.* —*See* **finish, gloss[1].**

glaze *verb.* —*See* **finish** (2), **gloss[1].**

gleam *verb.* To shine brightly and steadily but without a flame ▶ glow, incandesce, luminesce. —*See also* **beam, glitter.**

gleam *noun.* —*See* **flash** (1).

gleaming *adjective.* —*See* **glossy.**

glean *verb.* To collect something bit by bit ▶ cherry-pick, cull, extract, garner, gather, harvest, pick up. [*Compare* **accumulate.**] —*See also* **get** (1).

✚ CORE SYNONYMS: *glean, garner, gather, harvest.* These verbs mean to collect something bit by bit: *glean information; garner compliments; gathering mushrooms; harvested rich rewards.*

---

glee *noun.* —*See* **delight, happiness, merriment** (1).

gleeful *adjective.* —*See* **cheerful.**

gleefulness *noun.* —*See* **merriment** (1).

glen *noun.* —*See* **valley.**

glib *adjective.* Marked by ease and fluency of speech that is often insincere or superficial ▶ facile, offhand, slick, smooth, smooth-talking, smooth-tongued. [*Compare* **eloquent, fluent, suave, talkative.**]

✚ CORE SYNONYMS: *glib, slick, smooth-talking, smooth-tongued.* These adjectives mean marked by ease and fluency of speech that is often insincere or superficial: *a glib denial; a slick commercial; a smooth-talking salesperson; a smooth-tongued hypocrite.*

---

glibness *noun.* —*See* **eloquence.**

glide *verb.* **1.** To move smoothly, continuously, and effortlessly ▶ coast, drift, float, glissade, skate, skim, slide, slip, slither, waft. **2.** To maneuver gently and slowly into place ▶ ease, slide, slip. —*See also* **fly** (2), **sneak.**

✚ CORE SYNONYMS: *glide, slide, slip, coast, slither.* These verbs mean to move smoothly and continuously over or as if over a slippery surface. *Glide* refers to smooth, free-flowing, seemingly effortless movement: *"four snakes gliding up and down a hollow"* (Ralph Waldo Emerson). *Slide* usually implies rapid easy movement without loss of contact with the surface: *coal that slid down a chute to the cellar. Slip* is most often applied to accidental sliding resulting in loss of balance or foothold: *The mail carrier slipped on a patch of ice. Coast* applies especially to downward movement resulting from the effects of gravity or momentum: *The driver let the truck coast down the incline. Slither* can mean to slip and slide, as on an uneven surface, often with friction and noise: *"The detached crystals slithered down the rock face"* (H.G. Wells). The word can also suggest the sinuous gliding motion of a reptile: *An iguana slithered across the dusty trail.*

---

glimmer *noun.* —*See* **flash** (1).

glimmer *verb.* —*See* **glitter.**

glimpse *noun.* —*See* **glance** (1).

glimpse *verb.* To look briefly and quickly ▶ glance, peek, peep. ***Idioms:*** steal a glance (*or* look). [*Compare* **look.**]

glint *noun.* —*See* **flash** (1), **glitter** (1).

glint *verb.* —*See* **glitter.**

glissade *verb.* —*See* **glide** (1).

glisten *verb.* —*See* **glitter.**

glisten *noun.* —*See* **glitter** (1).

glistening *adjective.* —*See* **glossy, sparkling.**

glister *verb.* —*See* **glitter.**

glister *noun.* —*See* **glitter** (1).

glitch *noun.* —*See* **defect.**

glitter *noun.* **1.** Sparkling, brilliant light ▶ glint, glisten, glister, scintillation, shimmer, sparkle, twinkle. [*Compare* **flash.**] **2.** Brilliant, showy splendor ▶ brilliance, brilliancy, glamorousness, glamour, gorgeousness, magnificence, pageantry, pomp, resplendence, resplendency, showiness, sparkle, sumptuousness. *Informal:* glitz, razzle-dazzle.

Slang: bling, bling bling. [*Compare* **array, glory.**] **3.** A small sparkling decoration ▶ diamond, rhinestone, sequin, spangle.

glitter *verb.* To emit light in sudden or intermittent bursts ▶ blink, coruscate, flash, flicker, glance, gleam, glimmer, glint, glisten, glister, scintillate, shimmer, spangle, sparkle, twinkle, wink. [*Compare* **beam.**]

✦ **CORE SYNONYMS:** *glitter, sparkle, flash, gleam, glance, glint, glisten, shimmer, glimmer, twinkle, scintillate.* These verbs mean to emit light in sudden or intermittent bursts. *Glitter* and *sparkle* suggest a rapid succession of little flashes of high brilliance (*jewels glittering in the display case, crystal glasses sparkling in the candlelight*). *Flash* refers to a sudden and brilliant but short-lived outburst of light: *A bolt of lightning flashed across the horizon. Gleam* implies transient or constant light that often appears against a dark background: "*The light gleams an instant, then it's night once more*" (Samuel Beckett). *Glance* refers most often to light reflected obliquely: *Moonlight glanced off the windows of the darkened building. Glint* applies to briefly gleaming or flashing light: *Rays of sun glinted among the autumn leaves.* To *glisten* is to shine with a sparkling luster: *The snow glistened in the dawn light. Shimmer* means to shine with a soft, tremulous light: "*Everything about her shimmered and glimmered softly, as if her dress had been woven out of candle-beams*" (Edith Wharton). *Glimmer* refers to faint, fleeting light: "*On the French coast, the light/Gleams, and is gone; the cliffs of England stand,/Glimmering and vast, out in the tranquil bay*" (Matthew Arnold). To *twinkle* is to shine with quick, intermittent flashes or gleams: "*a few stars, twinkling faintly in the deep blue of the night sky*" (Hugh Walpole). *Scintillate* is applied to what flashes as if emitting sparks in a continuous stream: "*ammonium chloride . . . depositing minute scintillating crystals on the windowpanes*" (Primo Levi).

glitz *noun.* —*See* **glitter** (2).

glitzy *adjective.* —*See* **gaudy.**

gloaming *noun.* —*See* **evening.**

gloat *verb.* —*See* **exult** (1), **pride.**

gloating *noun.* —*See* **exultation.**

gloating *adjective.* Feeling or expressing an uplifting joy over a success or victory ▶ exultant, jubilant, triumphant. [*Compare* **boastful.**]

glob *noun.* —*See* **drop** (1).

global *adjective.* —*See* **general** (2), **universal** (1).

globe *noun.* The celestial body where humans live ▶ earth, orb, planet, world. —*See also* **ball.**

globetrotter *noun.* —*See* **tourist.**

globular *or* **globoid** *adjective.* —*See* **round** (1).

globule *noun.* —*See* **drop** (1).

gloom *noun.* —*See* **dark, depression** (2).

gloom *verb.* —*See* **obscure, shade** (2).

gloomy *adjective.* Dark and depressing ▶ black, bleak, blue, cheerless, comfortless, dark, desolate, dismal, drear, dreary, dull, funereal, glum, joyless, murky, sepulchral, somber, stygian, tenebrific. —*See also* **bleak** (2), **depressed** (1), **glum, sorrowful.**

glorification *noun.* —*See* **exaltation, praise** (2).

glorify *verb.* —*See* **distinguish** (3), **exalt, honor** (1), **praise** (3).

glorious *adjective.* Marked by extraordinary beauty and splendor ▶ brilliant, dazzling, gorgeous, magnificent, proud, radiant, resplendent, shining, splendid, splendiferous, splendorous, wonderful, wondrous. [*Compare* **beautiful, grand, showy.**] —*See also* **famous, marvelous.**

glory *noun.* A height of achievement or acclaim ▶ brilliance, grandeur, grandiosity, grandness, greatness, magnificence, majesty, splendor. —*See also* **fame, praise** (2).

glory *verb.* —*See* **exult** (1).

gloss[1] *noun.* A surface shininess ▶ burnish, glaze, luster, polish, sheen, shine, sleekness, varnish. [*Compare* **finish.**] —*See also* **façade** (2).

gloss *verb.* To give a bright sheen or luster to ▶ buff, burnish, furbish, glaze, polish, shine, sleek, varnish. —*See also* **color** (2).

gloss over *verb.* —*See* **extenuate, neglect** (1).

gloss[2] *noun.* —*See* **explanation.**

gloss *verb.* —*See* **explain** (1).

glossary *noun.* An alphabetical list of words often defined or translated ▶ dictionary, lexicon, vocabulary, wordbook.

glossy *adjective.* Having a high, radiant sheen ▶ brilliant, burnished, glassy, glazed, gleaming, glistening, lustrous, polished, shining, shiny. [*Compare* **sleek, sparkling.**]

glow *verb.* To shine brightly and steadily but without a flame ▶ gleam, incandesce, luminesce. —*See also* **beam, blush.**

glow *noun.* **1.** A fresh rosy complexion ▶ bloom, blush, color, flush. [*Compare* **color, complexion.**] **2.** A feeling of pervasive emotional warmth ▶ flush, tingle. —*See also* **light[1]** (1).

glower *verb.* **1.** To wrinkle one's brow, as in thought, puzzlement, or displeasure ▶ frown, lower, scowl. ***Idioms:*** knit one's brow, look black, turn one's mouth down. [*Compare* **grimace.**] **2.** To stare fixedly and angrily ▶ glare, lower, scowl. ***Idioms:*** give the evil eye, look daggers. [*Compare* **gaze, sneer.**]

glower *noun.* A fixed angry stare ▶ glare, lower, scowl. [*Compare* **face, sneer.**] —*See also* **frown.**

glowing *adjective.* —*See* **bright, passionate, ruddy.**

gloze *verb.* —*See* **color** (2), **extenuate.**

gluey *adjective.* —*See* **sticky** (1).

glum *adjective.* Broodingly and sullenly unhappy ▶ dour, gloomy, low, moody, morose, sad, saturnine, sour, sulky, sullen, surly. [*Compare* **depressed, despondent, ill-tempered.**] —*See also* **gloomy.**

glumness *noun.* —*See* **depression** (2).

glut *verb.* —*See* **gulp, satiate.**

glut *noun.* —*See* **surplus.**

glutinous *adjective.* —*See* **sticky** (1), **viscous.**

glutinousness *noun.* —*See* **viscosity.**

glutton *noun.* A person who eats or consumes immoderate amounts of food and drink ▶ hog, overeater, pig. [*Compare* **sybarite.**]

gluttonous *adjective.* Wanting to eat or drink more than one can reasonably consume ▶ edacious, greedy, hoggish, piggish, ravenous, voracious. —*See also* **voracious.**

gnash *verb.* To rub together noisily ▶ crunch, grind. —*See also* **chew.**

gnaw *verb.* —*See* **chew, erode.**

gnawing *adjective.* —*See* **sharp** (3).

gnomic *adjective.* —*See* **pithy.**

go *verb.* **1.** To move away from a place ▶ depart, exit, get away, get off, go away, leave, pull out, quit, remove, retire, run (along *or* away), set forth (*or* off *or* out), withdraw. *Informal:* cut out, push off, shove off. *Slang:* blow, bug out (*or* off), split, take off, vamoose. ***Idioms:*** get going (*or* moving), hit the road, light out for the territory, make oneself scarce, make tracks, pull up stakes, take leave. **2.** To move along a particular course ▶ pass, proceed, push on, wend. ***Idioms:*** make (*or* wend) one's way. [*Compare* **advance, journey, rove.**] **3.** To act or operate in a specified way ▶ act, behave, work. **4.** To change or fluctuate within limits ▶ cover, extend, range, run, vary. **5.** To have a proper or suitable place ▶ belong, fit. **6.** To be depleted ▶ dry up, give out, run out. ***Idioms:*** go down the drain, go up in smoke. [*Compare* **disappear, exhaust, waste.**] **7.** *Informal* To make an offer of

▶ bid, offer. —*See also* **agree** (1), **bear** (5), **buckle, cover** (2), **die, extend** (1), **gamble** (2), **resort.**

go along *verb.* To agree to cooperate or participate ▶ *Informal:* play along.

go around *verb.* To become known far and wide ▶ circulate, get around, spread, travel. —*See also* **skirt, turn** (1).

go at *verb.* —*See* **attack** (1), **attack** (2).

go away *verb.* To come to an end ▶ pass, pass away. [*Compare* **disappear.**] —*See also* **go** (1).

go back *verb.* —*See* **return** (1).

go by *verb.* —*See* **elapse, visit.**

go down *verb.* To undergo capture, defeat, or ruin ▶ collapse, fall, go under, topple. [*Compare* **succumb, surrender.**] —*See also* **fall** (1), **sink** (1).

go for *verb.* **1.** To require a specified price ▶ cost, sell for. [*Compare* **demand.**] **2.** To be favorably disposed toward ▶ approve, countenance, favor, hold with. ***Idioms:*** be in favor of, take kindly to, think highly (*or* well) of. [*Compare* **assent, value.**] —*See also* **bring** (2), **enjoy.**

go in *verb.* —*See* **enter** (1).

go off *verb.* —*See* **explode** (1).

go on *verb.* —*See* **chatter** (1), **endure** (1), **endure** (2).

go out *verb.* To be with another person socially on a regular basis ▶ date, go with, see. *Informal:* take out. ***Idioms:*** go steady, go together.

go over *verb.* —*See* **examine** (1), **practice** (1), **review** (1), **succeed** (2), **visit.**

go through *verb.* —*See* **experience, practice** (1).

go under *verb.* To undergo capture, defeat, or ruin ▶ collapse, fall, go down, topple. [*Compare* **succumb, surrender.**] —*See also* **collapse** (2), **sink** (1).

go up *verb.* —*See* **ascend.**

go with *verb.* To be with another person socially on a regular basis ▶ date, go out (with), see. *Informal:* take out. ***Idioms:*** go steady, go together. —*See also* **choose** (1), **suit** (1).

go *noun.* —*See* **attempt, energy, turn** (1).

goad *noun.* —*See* **provocation** (1), **stimulus.**

goad *verb.* —*See* **provoke.**

go-ahead *adjective.* —*See* **assertive.**

go-ahead *noun.* —*See* **permission.**

goal *noun.* —*See* **dream** (3), **intention.**

goat *noun.* —*See* **lecher, scapegoat.**

gob[1] *noun.* —*See* **heap** (2), **lump**[1].

gob[2] *noun.* —*See* **mouth** (1).

gob[3] *noun.* —*See* **sailor.**

gobble *verb.* —*See* **gulp.**

gobbledygook *noun.* —*See* **babble, gibberish.**

go-between *noun.* One who acts as an intermediate agent between persons or groups ▶ broker, contact, dealer, facilitator, interceder, intercessor, intermediary, intermediate, intermediator, mediator, middleman, negotiant, negotiator, ombudsman, troubleshooter. [*Compare* **agent, judge.**]

go-by *noun.* —*See* **snub.**

goddess *noun.* —*See* **beauty.**

godforsaken *adjective.* —*See* **lonely** (1).

godless *adjective.* —*See* **atheistic.**

godlessness *noun.* —*See* **atheism.**

godlike *adjective.* —*See* **divine** (1).

godliness *noun.* —*See* **holiness.**

godly *adjective.* —*See* **divine** (1), **pious.**

God's country *noun.* —*See* **country.**

godsend *noun.* —*See* **luck.**

gofer *noun.* —*See* **assistant.**

go-getter *noun. Informal* An intensely energetic, enthusiastic person ▶ demon, dynamo, hustler. *Informal:* eager beaver, firebreather, live wire.

goggle *verb.* —*See* **gaze.**

going *noun.* —*See* **departure.**

going *adjective.* —*See* **active.**

going-over *noun.* —*See* **examination** (1).

goldbrick *verb.* —*See* **idle** (1).

golden ager *noun.* —*See* **senior** (2).

golden-haired *adjective.* —*See* **fair**[1] (2).

Goliath *noun.* —*See* **giant.**

gone *adjective.* —*See* **absent, dead** (1), **infatuated, lost** (2), **pregnant** (1).

goner *noun. Slang* One that is ruined or doomed ▶ dead duck, dead meat, toast. [*Compare* **through.**]

good *adjective.* **1.** Having pleasant desirable qualities ▶ bonny, dandy, decent, enjoyable, fine, jolly, nice, worthy. *Informal:* all-right. [*Compare* **acceptable, choice, excellent.**] **2.** In excellent condition ▶ entire, flawless, intact, perfect, sound, unblemished, unbroken, undamaged, unharmed, unhurt, unimpaired, uninjured, unmarred, whole. **3.** No less than; at least ▶ full, round, whole. —*See also* **able, authentic** (1), **beneficial, benevolent** (1), **big, convenient** (1), **exemplary, favorable** (1), **honest, pleasant.**

good *noun.* **1.** The quality or state of being morally sound ▶ goodness, morality, probity, rectitude, righteousness, rightfulness, rightness, uprightness, virtue, virtuousness. [*Compare* **ethic.**] **2.** A product or products bought and sold in commerce ▶ commodity, goods, inventory, line, merchandise, stock, ware, wares. [*Compare* **product.**] —*See also* **interest** (1).

goodbye *interjection.* Used upon taking leave ▶ farewell, fare-thee-well. *Informal:* adiós, auf Wiedersehen, au revoir, ciao, hasta mañana, later, see you, so long, take care. ***Idioms:*** go in peace (*or* with God), see (*or* catch) you later.

goodbye *noun.* —*See* **departure.**

goodbye *adjective.* —*See* **parting.**

good deed *noun.* —*See* **favor** (1).

good-for-nothing *noun.* —*See* **riffraff, wastrel** (2).

good-for-nothing *adjective.* —*See* **worthless.**

goodhearted *adjective.* —*See* **benevolent** (1).

goodish *adjective.* —*See* **acceptable** (2).

good-looking *adjective.* —*See* **beautiful.**

goodly *adjective.* —*See* **big.**

good name *noun.* —*See* **honor** (2).

good-natured *adjective.* —*See* **amiable.**

goodness *noun.* —*See* **good** (1).

good report *noun.* —*See* **honor** (2).

goods *noun.* —*See* **effects, good** (2).

good-tempered *adjective.* —*See* **amiable.**

good turn *noun.* —*See* **favor** (1).

goodwill *noun.* —*See* **benevolence.**

goody *noun.* —*See* **delicacy.**

gooey *adjective.* —*See* **sentimental, sticky** (1).

goof *noun.* —*See* **blunder, fool.**

goof *verb.* —*See* **idle** (1).

goof up *verb.* —*See* **botch, err.**

goofiness *noun.* —*See* **foolishness.**

goofy *adjective.* —*See* **foolish.**

goon *noun.* —*See* **oaf, thug.**

goose *noun.* —*See* **fool.**

gore *verb.* —*See* **cut** (1).

gorge *verb.* —*See* **gulp, satiate.**

gorge *noun.* —*See* **valley.**

gorgeous *adjective.* —*See* **beautiful, glorious.**

gorgeousness *noun.* —*See* **glitter** (2).

gorilla *noun.* —*See* **thug.**

gory *adjective.* —*See* **bloody, murderous.**

gospel *noun.* —*See* **doctrine.**

gossamer *adjective.* —*See* **sheer**^{2}.

gossip *noun.* **1.** Idle, often sensational and groundless talk about others ▶ gossipry, hearsay, prattle, report, rumor, scandal, slander, talebearing, talk, tattle, tittle-tattle, word. *Slang:* scuttlebutt. **2.** A person habitually engaged in idle talk about others ▶ bigmouth, blab, chatterbox, gossiper, gossipmonger, newsmonger, rumormonger, scandalmonger, snoop, tabby, talebearer, taleteller, tattle, tattler, tattletale, telltale, whisperer. *Slang:* yenta. [*Compare* **busybody.**]

gossip *verb.* To engage in or spread gossip ▶ blab, chatter, jabber, noise, prattle, rumor, talk, tattle, tittle-tattle, whisper. ***Idioms:*** dish the dirt, spread a story, tell tales, tell tales out of school.

CORE SYNONYMS: *gossip, blab, tattle.* These verbs mean to engage in or communicate idle, often sensational and groundless talk about others: *gossiping about the neighbors; can't keep a secret—he always blabs; is disliked for tattling on mischief-makers.*

---

gossiper *or* **gossipmonger** *noun.* —*See* **gossip** (2).

gossipry *noun.* —*See* **gossip** (1).

gossipy *adjective.* Inclined to gossip ▶ blabby, talebearing, taletelling.

gouge *verb.* —*See* **cheat** (1), **cut** (1), **dig.**

gouge *noun.* —*See* **cut** (1).

govern *verb.* To control the functioning or outcome of ▶ control, determine, establish, fix, guide, regulate. ***Idioms:*** call the shots, pull the strings. —*See also* **administer** (1).

governable *adjective.* Capable of being governed ▶ administrable, controllable, manageable, rulable. [*Compare* **loyal, obedient.**]

governance *noun.* —*See* **government** (1).

governing *adjective.* —*See* **dominant** (1).

government *noun.* **1.** The continuous exercise of authority over a political unit ▶ administration, command, control, direction, governance, rule. [*Compare* **authority.**] **2.** A group of people who govern a political unit ▶ administration, authorities, ministry, officials, regime, state. ***Idiom:*** powers that be. [*Compare* **state.**] —*See also* **management.**

governmental *adjective.* Of or relating to government ▶ bureaucratic, gubernatorial, legislative, official, political, regulatory. —*See also* **administrative.**

governor *noun.* —*See* **chief.**

gown *noun.* —*See* **dress** (3).

grab *verb.* —*See* **catch** (2), **grasp, grip, seize** (1).

grab *noun.* —*See* **catch** (1), **seizure** (2).

grab bag *noun.* —*See* **assortment.**

grabbiness *noun.* —*See* **greed.**

grabble *verb.* —*See* **grope.**

grabby *adjective.* —*See* **greedy.**

grace *noun.* **1.** Temporary immunity from penalties ▶ exemption, immunity, reprieve, respite. [*Compare* **delay.**] **2.** A short prayer said at meals ▶ benediction, blessing, thanks, thanksgiving. [*Compare* **prayer**[1]**.**] —*See also* **benevolence, decency** (1), **dexterity, elegance, favor** (1), **holiness, mercy.**

grace *verb.* **1.** To lend dignity or honor to by an act or favor ▶ enrich, favor, dignify, honor. [*Compare* **distinguish, exalt, honor.**] **2.** To endow with beauty and elegance ▶ beautify, embellish, enhance, set off. [*Compare* **adorn.**]

graceful *adjective.* —*See* **attractive, delicate** (2), **elegant, fluent.**

graceless *adjective.* —*See* **awkward** (1).

gracious *adjective.* **1.** Characterized by kindness and warm, unaffected courtesy ▶ affable, courteous, hospitable. [*Compare* **amiable, attentive, courteous.**] **2.** Characterized by elaborate, usually formal courtesy ▶ chivalrous, circumstantial, courtly, diplomatic, elegant, gallant, genteel, stately. [*Compare* **ceremonious.**]

graciousness *noun.* —*See* **amenities** (2).

gradation *noun.* —*See* **shade** (1).

gradational *adjective.* Proceeding steadily by degrees ▶ gradual, piecemeal, progressive, step-by-step. ***Idioms:*** one foot after another, one step at a time. [*Compare* **consecutive, methodical, slow.**]

grade *noun.* Degree of excellence ▶ caliber, class, quality. —*See also* **ascent** (2), **class** (2), **degree** (1), **inclination** (2).

grade *verb.* To evaluate and assign a grade to ▶ correct, mark, score. —*See also* **classify.**

gradient *noun.* —*See* **ascent** (2), **inclination** (2).

gradual *adjective.* **1.** Proceeding steadily by degrees ▶ gradational, piecemeal, progressive, step-by-step. ***Idioms:*** one foot after another, one step at a time. [*Compare* **consecutive, methodical,**

slow.] **2.** Not steep or abrupt ▶ easy, even, gentle, mild, moderate, steady.

gradually *adverb.* In a gradual manner ▶ by degrees, in stages, piecemeal, progressively. ***Idioms:*** bit by bit, inch by inch, slowly but surely, step by step.

graft *noun.* —*See* **bribe, plunder.**

graft *verb.* —*See* **extort.**

grain *noun.* A fertilized plant ovule capable of germinating ▶ kernel, pip, pit, seed. —*See also* **bit**[1] (1), **essence, texture.**

grainy *adjective.* —*See* **coarse** (2).

grand *adjective.* Impressive in size, proportion, or appearance ▶ august, awe-inspiring, awesome, baronial, elegant, grandiose, great, imperial, imposing, lordly, magnific, magnificent, majestic, marvelous, noble, palatial, princely, regal, royal, splendid, stately, sublime, superb. [*Compare* **big, excellent, luxurious.**] —*See also* **elevated** (4), **exalted, important.**

✚ CORE SYNONYMS: *grand, magnificent, imposing, stately, majestic, august, grandiose.* These adjectives mean impressively large in size, proportion, or appearance. Both *grand* and *magnificent* apply to what is physically or aesthetically impressive. *Grand* implies dignity, sweep, or eminence: *a grand hotel lobby with marble floors. Magnificent* suggests splendor, sumptuousness, and grandeur: *a magnificent cathedral. Imposing* describes what impresses by virtue of its size, bearing, or power: *mountain peaks of imposing height. Stately* refers principally to what is dignified and handsome: *a stately oak. Majestic* suggests lofty dignity or nobility: *the majestic Alps. August* describes what inspires solemn reverence or awe: *the august presence of royalty. Grandiose* often suggests pretentiousness, affectation, or pompousness: *grandiose ideas.*

---

grandeur *noun.* —*See* **glory.**

grandiloquence *noun.* —*See* **bombast.**

grandiloquent *adjective.* —*See* **oratorical.**

grandiose *adjective.* —*See* **grand, pompous.**

grandioseness *noun.* —*See* **pretentiousness.**

grandiosity *noun.* —*See* **glory, pretentiousness.**

grandness *noun.* —*See* **glory.**

grant *verb.* To let have as a favor, prerogative, or privilege ▶ accord, award, concede, give, vouchsafe. [*Compare* **yield.**] —*See also* **acknowledge** (1), **confer** (2), **donate, transfer** (1).

grant *noun.* **1.** Money or other resources granted for a particular purpose ▶ appropriation, budget, subsidy, subvention. **2.** Legal transfer of ownership or title ▶ alienation, assignment, conveyance, transfer, transferal. —*See also* **conferment, donation.**

grantor *noun.* —*See* **donor.**

granular *adjective.* —*See* **coarse** (2).

granulate *verb.* —*See* **crush** (2).

graph *verb.* —*See* **plot** (1).

graphic *adjective.* **1.** Depicted in sharp and accurate detail ▶ explicit, lifelike, lucid, photographic, pictorial, picturesque, realistic, uncompromising, vivid. [*Compare* **accurate, clear, detailed.**] **2.** Evoking strong mental images through distinctiveness ▶ colorful, picturesque, striking, vivid. [*Compare* **ghastly.**] **3.** Of or relating to representation by means of writing ▶ calligraphic, scriptural, written. **4.** Of or relating to representation by drawings or pictures ▶ hieroglyphic, illustrative, photographic, pictographic, pictorial, symbolic. —*See also* **descriptive.**

✚ CORE SYNONYMS: *graphic, lifelike, realistic, vivid.* These adjectives mean strikingly sharp and accurate in detail: *a graphic account of the battle; a lifelike portrait; a realistic description; a vivid recollection.*

---

grapnel *noun.* —*See* **anchor.**

grapple *verb.* —*See* **contend, grasp.**

grapple *noun.* —*See* **hold** (1).

grasp *verb.* To take firmly with the hand and maintain a hold on ▶ clasp, clench, clutch, fist, grab, grapple, grip, seize. ***Idioms:*** grab ahold (*or* hold) of. [*Compare* **handle.**] —*See also* **absorb** (2), **know** (1), **understand** (1).

grasp *noun.* **1.** Firm control or influence ▶ grip, handle, hold. [*Compare* **control, dominance.**] **2.** The ability or power to seize or attain ▶ capacity, compass, range, reach, scope. [*Compare* **influence.**] **3.** Intellectual hold ▶ apprehension, comprehension, grip, hold, understanding. [*Compare* **knowledge.**] —*See also* **hold** (1).

grasping *adjective.* —*See* **greedy.**

graspingness *noun.* —*See* **greed.**

grate[1] *verb.* —*See* **scrape** (1), **shred.**

grate[2] *noun.* An open space for holding a fire at the base of a chimney ▶ fireplace, hearth, ingle.

grateful *adjective.* Showing or feeling gratitude ▶ appreciative, thankful. —*See also* **obliged** (1), **pleasant.**

gratefulness *noun.* —*See* **appreciation.**

gratification *noun.* The condition of being satisfied ▶ contentendness, contentment, fulfillment, satisfaction. [*Compare* **happiness, satiation.**]

gratified *adjective.* Having achieved satisfaction, as of one's goal ▶ content, fufilled, happy, satisfied.

gratify *verb.* To comply with the wishes or ideas of another ▶ cater (to), humor, indulge. [*Compare* **defer.**] —*See also* **delight** (1), **satisfy** (2).

gratifying *adjective.* —*See* **pleasant.**

grating *adjective.* —*See* **harsh.**

gratis *adjective.* Costing nothing ▶ free, complimentary, gratuitous. ***Idioms:*** as a freebie, for free, for nothing, on the house.

gratitude *noun.* —*See* **appreciation.**

gratuitous *adjective.* Costing nothing ▶ complimentary, free, gratis. ***Idioms:*** as a freebie, for free, for nothing, on the house. —*See also* **wanton** (2).

gratuity *noun.* A material favor or gift, usually money, given in return for service ▶ baksheesh, cumshaw, largess, perquisite, tip. *Informal:* perk. [*Compare* **bribe, reward.**] —*See also* **donation.**

grave[1] *noun.* A burial place or receptacle for human remains ▶ burial chamber, burial plot, catacomb, cinerarium, crypt, gravesite, mausoleum, ossuary, sepulcher, sepulture, tomb, vault.

grave[2] *adjective.* **1.** Having great consequence or weight ▶ earnest, heavy, momentous, serious, severe, weighty. [*Compare* **important.**] **2.** Having or threatening severe negative consequences ▶ dire, grievous, serious, severe. [*Compare* **disastrous.**] —*See also* **dangerous, fateful** (1), **serious** (1).

grave[3] *verb.* —*See* **engrave** (1), **engrave** (2).

gravelly *adjective.* —*See* **coarse** (2), **hoarse.**

graveness *noun.* The condition of being grave and of involving serious consequences ▶ gravity, momentousness, seriousness, weightiness. —*See also* **seriousness** (1).

gravid *adjective.* —*See* **pregnant** (1).

gravitas *noun.* —*See* **seriousness** (1).

gravitate *verb.* —*See* **sink** (1).

gravitation *noun.* —*See* **attraction.**

gravity *noun.* The condition of being grave and of involving serious consequences ▶ graveness, gravity, heaviness, momentousness, seriousness, weightiness. [*Compare* **severity.**] —*See also* **seriousness** (1).

gray *adjective.* —*See* **dull** (2).

gray matter *noun. Informal* The seat of the faculty of intelligence and reason ▶ brain, mind. [*Compare* **imagination.**] —*See also* **intelligence.**

graze[1] *verb.* —*See* **brush**[1], **glance** (1).

graze *noun.* —*See* **brush**[1].

graze[2] *verb.* —*See* **browse** (2).

grease *noun.* —*See* **bribe, oil.**

grease *verb.* —*See* **ease** (2), **oil.**

greasy *adjective.* —*See* **fatty.**

great *adjective.* At the upper end of a degree of measure ▶ elevated, high, large. [*Compare* **exalted, extreme.**] —*See also* **big, deep** (3), **excellent, famous, grand, important, marvelous.**

greater *adjective.* Being at a rank or level above another ▶ higher, senior, superior, upper. —*See also* **best** (2).

great-hearted *adjective.* —*See* **generous** (1).

great-heartedness *noun.* —*See* **generosity.**

greatly *adverb.* —*See* **very.**

greatness *noun.* —*See* **glory, size** (2).

greed *noun.* Excessive desire for more than one needs or deserves ▶ acquisitiveness, avarice, avariciousness, avidity, covetousness, cupidity, graspingness, hoggishness, rapacity. *Informal:* grabbiness. [*Compare* **voracity.**]

greedy *adjective.* Having a strong urge to obtain or retain something, especially material wealth ▶ acquisitive, avaricious, avid, covetous, grasping, hungry. *Informal:* grabby. [*Compare* **egotistic, stingy.**] —*See also* **gluttonous, voracious.**

green *noun.* —*See* **common, money** (1).
green *adjective.* —*See* **inexperienced, sour, young.**

green-eyed *adjective.* Fearful of the loss of position or affection ▶ clinging, clutching, jealous, possessive. —*See also* **envious.**

greenhorn *noun.* —*See* **beginner.**

green light *noun.* —*See* **permission.**

greenness *noun.* —*See* **inexperience, youth** (1).

greet *verb.* **1.** To address in a friendly and respectful way ▶ hail, salute, welcome. **2.** To approach for the purpose of speech ▶ accost, hail, salute. [*Compare* **encounter, interrupt, welcome.**]

greeting *noun.* An expression, in words or gestures, marking a meeting of persons ▶ hail, salutation, salute, welcome. *Informal:* hello.

greetings *interjection.* —*See* **hello.**

gregarious *adjective.* —*See* **outgoing, social.**

griddle *verb.* —*See* **cook.**

gridlock *noun.* —*See* **stop** (2).

grief *noun.* Mental anguish or pain caused by loss or despair ▶ anguish, heartache, heartbreak, sorrow, torment. —*See also* **distress.**

✚ **CORE SYNONYMS:** *grief, sorrow, anguish, heartache, heartbreak.* These nouns denote mental anguish or pain caused by loss or despair. *Grief* is deep, acute personal sadness, as that arising from irreplaceable loss: *"Grief fills the room up of my absent child,/Lies in his bed, walks up and down with me"* (William Shakespeare). *Sorrow* connotes sadness caused by misfortune, affliction, or loss; it can also imply contrition: *"sorrow for his . . . children, who needed his protection, and whom he could not protect"* (James Baldwin). *Anguish* implies agonizing, excruciating mental pain: *"I pray that our heavenly Father may assuage the anguish of your bereavement"* (Abraham Lincoln). *Heartache* most often applies to sustained private sorrow: *The child's difficulties are a source of heartache to the parents. Heartbreak* is overwhelming grief: *"Better a little chiding than a great deal of heartbreak"* (Shakespeare).

◀ **ANTONYM:** *joy*

---

grievance *noun.* —*See* **complaint, objection.**

grieve *verb.* To feel, show, or express grief ▶ anguish, bemoan, bewail, lament, mourn, sorrow, suffer, ululate. [*Compare* **cry, regret.**] —*See also* **distress.**

✚ **CORE SYNONYMS:** *grieve, lament, mourn, sorrow.* These verbs mean to feel, show, or express grief, sadness, or regret: *grieved over our father's death; pundits who were lamenting about the decline in academic standards; mourns* *for lost hopes; sorrowed by the level of poverty.*

◀ **ANTONYM:** *rejoice*

---

grievous *adjective.* Having or threatening severe negative consequences ▶ dire, grave, serious, severe. [*Compare* **disastrous.**] —*See also* **sorrowful.**

grift *noun.* —*See* **cheat** (1).

grifter *noun.* —*See* **cheat** (2).

grigri *noun.* —*See* **charm.**

grill *verb.* —*See* **ask** (1), **cook.**

grim *adjective.* —*See* **bleak** (1), **cruel, forbidding, ghastly** (1), **stubborn** (1).

grimace *noun.* A contorted facial expression showing pain, contempt, or disgust ▶ face, moue, pout. *Informal:* mug. [*Compare* **frown, glare, sneer.**]

grimace *verb.* To contort one's face to indicate pain, contempt, or disgust ▶ mouth, mug. ***Idioms:*** make a face, make faces. [*Compare* **frown, glare, sneer.**]

grime *noun.* —*See* **filth.**

griminess *noun.* —*See* **dirtiness.**

grimness *noun.* —*See* **stubbornness.**

grimy *adjective.* —*See* **dirty.**

grin *verb.* —*See* **smile.**

grin *noun.* A facial expression marked by an upward curving of the lips ▶ simper, smile, smirk. [*Compare* **sneer.**]

grind *verb.* **1.** To rub together noisily ▶ crunch, gnash. **2.** To do tedious, difficult or menial work ▶ drudge, grub, plod, slave, slog, struggle. [*Compare* **labor.**] **3.** *Informal* To apply one's mind to the acquisition of knowledge, especially when pressed for time ▶ lucubrate, study. *Informal:* bone up, cram. ***Idioms:*** burn the midnight oil, hit the books. [*Compare* **examine.**] **4.** To treat arbitrarily or cruelly ▶ grind down, oppress, trample. [*Compare* **abuse, enslave, suppress.**] —*See also* **crush** (2), **erode, sharpen.**

grind *noun.* —*See* **drudge** (2), **labor, routine, task** (2).

grip *verb.* To compel the attention, interest, or imagination of ▶ arrest, attract, captivate, capture, catch up, engage, enthrall, fascinate, hold, interest, intrigue, mesmerize, rivet, spellbind, transfix. *Informal:* grab. *Slang:* turn on. ***Idioms:*** catch one's eye, make one's mouth water, tickle one's fancy. [*Compare* **absorb, amuse, charm, possess.**] —*See also* **grasp.**

grip *noun.* **1.** Firm control or influence ▶ grasp, handle, hold. [*Compare* **control, dominance, influence.**] **2.** Intellectual hold ▶ apprehension, comprehension, grasp, hold, understanding. [*Compare* **knowledge.**] —*See also* **hold** (1), **suitcase.**

gripe *verb.* —*See* **complain.**

gripe *noun.* —*See* **complaint.**

griper *noun.* —*See* **grouch.**

grisly *adjective.* —*See* **ghastly** (1).

grit *noun.* —*See* **courage.**

gritty *adjective.* —*See* **brave, coarse** (2).

grizzled *adjective.* —*See* **old** (2).

grogginess *adjective.* —*See* **dizziness.**

groggy *adjective.* —*See* **dizzy** (1).

groom *verb.* —*See* **tidy** (2).

groove *noun.* —*See* **cut** (1), **furrow, routine.**

groove on *verb. Slang* To like or enjoy enthusiastically, often excessively ▶ adore, delight (in), dote on (*or* upon), love. *Slang:* eat up.

groovy *adjective.* —*See* **marvelous.**

grope *verb.* To reach about or search blindly or uncertainly ▶ feel, fumble, grabble, poke, scrabble. [*Compare* **seek.**] —*See also* **neck.**

gross *adjective.* Conspicuously bad or offensive ▶ egregious, flagrant, glaring, rank. [*Compare* **offensive, outrageous, shameless.**] —*See also* **coarse** (1), **complete** (1), **fat** (1), **obscene, unpalatable.**

gross *noun.* —*See* **whole.**

gross *verb.* —*See* **return** (3).

gross out *verb.* —*See* **disgust.**

grossness *noun.* The quality or state of being flagrant ▶ egregiousness, flagrancy, glaringness, rankness. [*Compare* **impudence, outrageousness.**] —*See also* **obscenity** (1).

grotesque *adjective.* Resembling a freak ▶ freakish, freaky, monstrous. [*Compare* **weird.**] —*See also* **eccentric, exotic.**

grotesque *noun.* —*See* **monster.**

grotto *noun.* —*See* **cave.**

grouch *noun.* A person who habitually complains or grumbles ▶ complainer, crab, faultfinder, growler, grumbler, grump, murmurer, mutterer, whiner. *Informal:* crank, griper, grouser. *Slang:* bellyacher, sorehead, sourpuss. [*Compare* **killjoy.**] —*See also* **complaint.**

grouch *verb.* —*See* **complain.**

grouchy *adjective.* —*See* **ill-tempered.**

ground *noun.* —*See* **base**[1] (2), **basis** (1), **earth** (1).

ground *verb.* —*See* **base**[1], **drop** (3).

groundless *adjective.* —*See* **baseless.**

groundlessly *adverb.* Without basis or foundation in fact ▶ baselessly, unfoundedly, unwarrantedly.

grounds *noun.* —*See* **basis** (1), **cause** (2), **land, reason** (1).

groundwork *noun.* —*See* **base**[1] (2), **basis** (1).

group *noun.* A number of individuals making up or considered a unit ▶ array, band, batch, bevy, body, bunch, bundle, clump, cluster, clutch, huddle, collection, knot, lot, party, set. [*Compare* **accumulation, crowd, system.**] —*See also* **assembly, circle** (3), **class** (1), **complex** (1).

group *verb.* —*See* **assemble, band**[2], **classify.**

group *adjective.* —*See* **cooperative.**

groupie *noun.* —*See* **fan**[2].

grouping *noun.* —*See* **arrangement** (1).

grouse *verb.* —*See* **complain.**

grouse *noun.* —*See* **complaint.**

grouser *noun.* —*See* **grouch.**

grovel *verb.* —*See* **fawn.**

groveler *noun.* —*See* **sycophant.**

grow *verb.* To raise crops or animals ▶ breed, cultivate, farm, garden, propagate, raise, tend, ranch. [*Compare* **nurture, plant, till.**] —*See also* **become** (1), **develop** (1), **increase, mature.**

growl *verb.* —*See* **rumble** (1), **snap** (3).

growler *noun.* —*See* **grouch.**

grown *or* **grown-up** *adjective.* —*See* **mature.**

growth *noun.* —*See* **buildup** (2), **bump** (1), **development, increase** (1).

grub *verb.* —*See* **dig, grind** (2).

grub *noun.* —*See* **drudge** (2), **food.**

grubbiness *noun.* —*See* **dirtiness.**

grubby *adjective.* —*See* **dirty.**

grubstake *noun.* —*See* **capital** (1).

grubstake *verb.* —*See* **finance.**

grudge *verb.* To feel envy toward or for ▶ begrudge, covet, envy.

grudging *adjective.* —*See* **envious.**

grueling *adjective.* —*See* **burdensome.**

gruesome *adjective.* —*See* **ghastly** (1).

gruff *adjective.* —*See* **abrupt** (1), **hoarse.**

grumble *verb.* —*See* **complain, rumble** (1).

grumble *noun.* —*See* **complaint.**

grumbler *noun.* —*See* **grouch.**

grump *noun.* *Informal* An expression of dissatisfaction or a circumstance regarded as a cause for such expression ▶ complaint, grievance. *Informal:* gripe. *Slang:* beef, kick. ***Idiom:*** bone to pick. —*See also* **grouch.**

grump *verb.* —*See* **complain.**

grumpy *adjective.* —*See* **ill-tempered.**

grunge *noun.* —*See* **filth.**

grungy *adjective.* —*See* **dirty.**

grunt *verb.* —*See* **complain.**

grunt *noun.* —*See* **complaint, drudge** (1), **soldier** (2).

guarantee *noun.* An assumption of responsibility, as one given by a manufacturer, for the quality, worth, or durability of a product ▶ certification, guaranty, surety, warrant, warranty. —*See also* **promise** (1).

guarantee *verb.* **1.** To assume responsibility for the quality, worth, or durability of ▶ certify, guaranty, stand behind, warrant. [*Compare* **confirm.**] **2.** To render certain ▶ assure, ensure, insure, secure, warrant. *Informal:* cinch, clinch.

guarantor *noun.* —*See* **sponsor.**

guaranty *noun.* An assumption of responsibility, as one given by a manufacturer, for the quality, worth, or durability of a product ▶ certification, guarantee, surety, warrant, warranty. *—See also* **pawn[1], promise** (1), **sponsor.**

guaranty *verb.* *—See* **guarantee** (1).

guard *noun.* One assigned to provide protection or keep watch over someone or something ▶ guardian, lookout, monitor, picket, protection, protector, sentinel, sentry, ward, watch, watchdog, watchman. [*Compare* **watcher.**] *—See also* **defense.**

guard *verb.* *—See* **defend** (1).

guarded *adjective.* *—See* **conservative** (2), **reserved.**

guardian *noun.* One who is legally responsible for the care and management of the person or property of an incompetent or a minor ▶ caretaker, conservator, custodian, keeper. [*Compare* **representative.**] *—See also* **guard.**

guardianship *noun.* *—See* **care** (2).

gubernatorial *adjective.* *—See* **governmental.**

gudgeon *noun.* *—See* **dupe.**

guerdon *noun.* *—See* **due, reward.**

guerdon *verb.* To bestow a reward on ▶ award, honor, reward. [*Compare* **confer.**]

guess *verb.* To predict or assume without sufficient information ▶ conjecture, fancy, imagine, infer, speculate, suppose, surmise, suspect, think. [*Compare* **believe, infer, suppose.**]

guess *noun.* A judgment, estimate, or opinion arrived at by guessing ▶ conjecture, guesswork, speculation, supposition, surmise. *Informal:* guesstimate. ***Idiom:*** shot in the dark. [*Compare* **assumption, belief, estimate.**]

guesstimate *verb.* *—See* **estimate** (2).

guesstimate *noun.* *—See* **estimate** (2).

guesswork *noun.* *—See* **guess.**

guest *noun.* A person or persons visiting one ▶ caller, guest, visitant, visitor.

guffaw *noun.* *—See* **laugh.**

guffaw *verb.* *—See* **laugh.**

guidance *noun.* *—See* **advice, management.**

guide *noun.* Something or someone that shows the way ▶ cicerone, conductor, director, docent, escort, lead, leader, pilot, shepherd, usher. *—See also* **adviser.**

guide *verb.* To show the way to ▶ conduct, direct, escort, lead, marshal, pilot, route, shepherd, show, steer, usher. *—See also* **advise, govern, maneuver** (1).

✦ **CORE SYNONYMS:** *guide, lead, pilot, shepherd, steer, usher.* These verbs mean to show or conduct someone the way to a place, destination, or goal: *guided me to my seat; led the troops into battle; a teacher piloting students through the zoo; shepherding tourists to the bus; steered the applicant to the third floor; ushering a visitor out.*

---

guideline *noun.* *—See* **rule.**

guild *noun.* *—See* **union** (1).

guile *noun.* *—See* **art, deceit.**

guileful *adjective.* *—See* **artful, underhand.**

guileless *adjective.* *—See* **artless.**

guilt *noun.* *—See* **blame, penitence.**

guiltless *adjective.* *—See* **innocent** (2).

guilty *adjective.* *—See* **blameworthy.**

guise *noun.* *—See* **appearance** (1), **disguise, dress** (2), **façade** (2).

gulf *noun.* A body of water partly enclosed by land but having a wide outlet to the sea ▶ bight, gulf, sound. [*Compare* **channel, harbor, inlet.**] *—See also* **deep, gap** (1).

gull *noun.* *—See* **dupe.**

gull *verb.* *—See* **cheat** (1).

gullible *adjective.* Easily imposed on or tricked ▶ credulous, dupable, easy, exploitable, naive, simple, susceptible, susceptive, trusting. [*Compare* **artless.**]

gulp *verb.* To swallow food or drink greedily or rapidly in large amounts ▶ bolt, englut, engorge, glut, gobble, gorge, guzzle, ingurgitate, stuff oneself, swill. *Informal:* down, pig out, wolf (down). ***Idioms:*** eat like a pig (*or* hog), feed one's face, make a pig (*or* hog) of oneself, stuff one's face. [*Compare* **eat, swallow.**] *—See also* **drink** (1), **pant.**

gulp *noun.* An act of swallowing ▶ ingestion, swallow, swig.

gummy *adjective.* *—See* **sticky** (1).

gumption *noun.—See* **common sense, drive** (2).

gumshoe *noun.* *—See* **detective.**

gumshoe *verb.* *—See* **sneak.**

gum up *verb.* *—See* **botch.**

gun *verb.* To wound or kill with a firearm ▶ gun down, pick off, shoot. *Slang:* plug. ***Idioms:*** fill full of lead (or holes). [*Compare* **kill**[1], **murder.**]

gun for *verb.* *—See* **pursue** (1).

gung ho *adjective.* *—See* **enthusiastic.**

gunk *noun.* *—See* **garbage, slime.**

gunsel *noun.* *—See* **thug.**

gurgle *verb.* *—See* **burble.**

gurgle *noun.* *—See* **burble.**

guru *noun.* *—See* **adviser, sage.**

gush *verb.* *—See* **flow** (2), **rave.**

gush *noun.* *—See* **flow, outburst.**

gushy *adjective.* *—See* **sentimental.**

gust *noun.* *—See* **outburst, wind**[1].

gust *verb.* *—See* **blow**[1] (1).

gusto *noun.* Spirited enjoyment ▶ relish, zest. [*Compare* **enthusiasm.**]

gusty *adjective.* *—See* **airy** (3).

gut *adjective.* *—See* **empty, inner** (2).

gut *verb.* *—See* **enervate.**

gutless *adjective.* *—See* **cowardly.**

gutlessness *noun.* *—See* **cowardice.**

gut reaction *noun.* *—See* **feeling** (1).

guts *noun.* *—See* **courage, viscera.**

gutsiness *noun.* *—See* **courage.**

gutsy *adjective.* *—See* **brave, lusty.**

gutter *noun.* *—See* **pit**[1].

gutter *verb.* *—See* **smolder.**

gutty *adjective.* *—See* **brave.**

guy[1] *noun.* *—See* **cord.**

guy[2] *noun.* *—See* **fellow.**

guzzle *verb.* *—See* **drink** (1), **drink** (2), **gulp.**

gyrate *verb.* *—See* **turn** (1).

gyration *noun.* *—See* **revolution** (1).

gyre *noun.* *—See* **circle** (1).

H

habiliments *noun.* *—See* **dress** (1), **dress** (2).

habit *noun.* Clothing worn by members of a religious order ▶ robe, vestment. [*Compare* **dress.**] *—See also* **constitution, custom, disposition.**

habitable *adjective.* Fit to live in ▶ inhabitable, livable.

habitat *noun.* The natural environment specific to an animal or to a plant ▶ habitation, niche, range, territory. [*Compare* **haunt.**] *—See also* **environment** (3).

habitation *noun.* *—See* **habitat, home** (1).

habitual *adjective.* **1.** Subject to a habit or pattern of behavior ▶ accustomed, chronic, routine. **2.** Subject to a disease or habit for a long time ▶ chronic, confirmed, habituated, inveterate. [*Compare* **stubborn.**] *—See also* **common** (1).

habitually *adverb.* *—See* **usually.**

habitualness *noun.* *—See* **usualness.**

habituate *verb.* *—See* **accustom.**

habituated *adjective.* **1.** In the habit ▶ accustomed, used, wont. **2.** Subject to a disease or habit for a long time ▶ chronic, confirmed, habitual, inveterate. [*Compare* **stubborn.**]

habitude *noun.* *—See* **custom.**

habitus *noun.* *—See* **constitution.**

hack1 *verb.* *—See* **cut** (1).

hack2 *noun.* *—See* **drudge** (1).

hackneyed *adjective.* *—See* **trite.**

haft *noun.* A protrusion or extension designed to be grasped by the hand ▶ handgrip, handle, hilt. [*Compare* **hold, knob.**]

hag *noun.* A woman who practices magic ▶ enchantress, lamia, sorceress, witch. [*Compare* **wizard.**]*—See also* **witch** (2).

haggard *adjective.* Appearing worn and exhausted ▶ careworn, drawn, emaciated, gaunt, pinched, hollow-eyed, shrunken, skeletal, wan, wasted, worn. ***Idiom:*** skin and bones. [*Compare* **exhausted, thin.**]

haggle *verb.* To argue about the terms, as of a sale ▶ bargain, chaffer, dicker, higgle, huckster, negotiate, palter, wrangle. [*Compare* **argue.**]

ha-ha *noun.* —*See* **joke** (1).

hail[1] *noun.* —*See* **barrage.**

hail[2] *verb.* **1.** To approach for the purpose of speech ▶ accost, greet, salute. [*Compare* **encounter, interrupt, welcome.**] **2.** To address in a friendly and respectful way ▶ greet, salute, welcome. **3.** To have as one's home or place of origin ▶ come, originate. [*Compare* **descend, stem.**] —*See also* **honor** (1).

hail *noun.* An expression, in words or gestures, marking a meeting of persons ▶ greeting, salutation, salute, welcome. *Informal:* hello.

hair *noun.* —*See* **shade** (2).

hairless *adjective.* —*See* **bare** (3).

hairline *noun.* Something suggesting the continuousness of a filament ▶ strand, thread. [*Compare* **thread.**]

hair-raising *adjective.* —*See* **horrible.**

hairsplitting *noun.* —*See* **quibbling.**

hairy *adjective.* Covered with hair ▶ bristly, downy, fleecy, flocculent, furry, fuzzy, hirsute, pilose, pubescent, shaggy, tufted, woolly. —*See also* **dangerous.**

halcyon *adjective.* —*See* **still.**

hale *adjective.* —*See* **healthy.**

haleness *noun.* —*See* **health** (1).

halfhearted *adjective.* Lacking warmth, interest, enthusiasm, or involvement ▶ Laodicean, lukewarm, tepid, unenthusiastic. [*Compare* **apathetic, cold, cool.**]

half-pint *noun.* —*See* **squirt** (2).

half-truth *noun.* —*See* **lie[2].**

half-wit *noun.* —*See* **dullard.**

half-witted *adjective.* —*See* **backward** (1), **stupid.**

halloo *noun.* —*See* **shout.**

halloo *verb.* —*See* **shout.**

hallow *verb.* To make sacred by a religious rite ▶ bless, consecrate, sanctify. [*Compare* **exalt.**] —*See also* **devote, revere.**

hallowed *adjective.* —*See* **divine** (2), **holy.**

hallucinate *verb.* —*See* **dream.**

hallucination *noun.* An experience of things or events that are not real ▶ phantasmagoria, phantasmagory. *Slang:* trip. —*See also* **dream** (1), **illusion.**

hallucinatory *adjective.* —*See* **illusive.**

hallucinogen *noun.* —*See* **drug** (2).

halo *noun.* —*See* **circle** (1).

halt[1] *noun.* —*See* **stop** (1), **stop** (2).

halt *verb.* —*See* **stop** (1), **stop** (2).

halt[2] *verb.* —*See* **hesitate, stagger** (1).

halting *adjective.* —*See* **hesitant.**

hamlet *noun.* —*See* **village.**

hammer *verb.* —*See* **beat** (1), **beat** (3), **beat** (5).

hamper[1] *verb.* To restrict the activity or free movement of ▶ chain, fetter, hamstring, handcuff, hobble, leash, manacle, shackle, tie, trammel. *Informal:* hogtie. —*See also* **hinder.**

✣ **CORE SYNONYMS:** *hamper, fetter, handcuff, hobble, hogtie, manacle, shackle, trammel.* These verbs mean to restrict the activity or free movement of: *a swimmer hampered by clothing; prisoners fettered by chains; handcuffed by rigid regulations; hobbled by responsibilities; leadership that refused to be hogtied; imagination manacled by fear; shackled by custom; trammeled by debts.*

---

hamper[2] *noun.* **1.** A kind of basket normally used to contain clothes or food ▶ laundry basket, food basket, gift basket, pannier. [*Compare* **basket.**] **2.** A container made of interwoven material ▶ basket, creel, pannier. [*Compare* **container.**]

hamstring *verb.* —*See* **hamper[1].**

hand *noun.* **1.** Approval expressed by clapping ▶ applause, ovation, plaudit. ***Idiom:*** round of applause. **2.** One of two or more contrasted parts or places identified by its location with respect to a center ▶ flank, side. —*See also* **help, laborer, viewpoint.**

hand *verb.* —*See* **give** (1).

hand down *verb.* To deliver an indictment or verdict, for example ▶ render, return. —*See also* **leave**[1] (1).

hand in *verb.* —*See* **give** (1).

hand on *verb.* —*See* **leave**[1] (1).

hand out *verb.* —*See* **confer** (2), **distribute, donate.**

hand over *verb.* —*See* **abandon** (1), **entrust** (1), **give** (1).

handbag *noun.* —*See* **purse.**

handbill *noun.* An announcement distributed on paper to a large number of people ▶ circular, flier, leaflet, notice.

handcuff *verb.* —*See* **hamper**[1].

handcuffs *noun.* —*See* **bond** (1).

handful *pronoun.* —*See* **several.**

handicap *noun.* —*See* **advantage** (1), **disadvantage.**

handicap *verb.* —*See* **disable** (1).

handicraft *noun.* —*See* **business** (2).

handle *verb.* **1.** To manipulate with the hands ▶ manipulate, ply, wield. **2.** To behave in a specified way toward someone ▶ cope with, treat. —*See also* **act** (1), **conduct** (1), **operate, sell, touch.**

handle *noun.* **1.** A protrusion or extension designed to be grasped by the hand ▶ haft, handgrip, hilt. [*Compare* **hold, knob.**] **2.** Firm control or influence ▶ grasp, grip, hold. [*Compare* **control, dominance, influence.**] —*See also* **name** (1).

✚ **CORE SYNONYMS:** *handle, manipulate, wield, ply.* These verbs mean to manipulate or operate with or as with the hands. *Handle* applies widely and suggests competence: *The lumberjack handled the ax expertly. The therapist handled every problem with sensitivity. Manipulate* connotes skillful or artful management: *The pilot confidently manipulated the controls in the cockpit.* When *manipulate* refers to people or personal affairs, it often implies deviousness or fraud in gaining an end: *I realized I'd been manipulated into helping them. Wield* implies freedom, skill, ease, and effectiveness in handling physical or figurative implements: *Ready to make kindling, she wielded a hatchet. The mayor's speechwriter wields a persuasive pen.* It also connotes effectiveness in the exercise of intangibles such as authority or influence: *The dictator wielded enormous power. Ply* suggests industry and persistence: *The hungry child was plying his knife and fork with gusto.* The term also applies to the regular and diligent engagement in a task or pursuit: *She plies the banker's trade with great success.*

---

hand-me-down *adjective.* —*See* **used** (2).

handout *noun.* —*See* **donation, relief** (2).

handsome *adjective.* —*See* **beautiful, generous** (1).

handwriting *noun.* —*See* **script** (1).

handy *adjective.* —*See* **convenient** (2), **convenient** (1), **dexterous, practical.**

hang *verb.* **1.** To fasten or be fastened at one point with no support from below ▶ dangle, depend, sling, suspend, swing. [*Compare* **drape.**] **2.** To execute by suspending by the neck ▶ gibbet. *Informal:* string up. *Slang:* swing. **3.** To remain stationary over a place or object ▶ hover, poise. [*Compare* **float.**]

hang around *verb.* —*See* **associate** (2), **frequent, remain.**

hang on *verb.* —*See* **depend on** (2), **endure** (1).

hang out *verb.* —*See* **associate** (2), **frequent.**

hang over *verb.* —*See* **threaten** (2).

hang up *verb.* —*See* **delay** (1).

hang upon *verb.* —*See* **depend on** (2).

hang *noun. Informal* The proper method for doing, using, or handling something ▶ feel, knack, trick.

hanger-on *noun.* —*See* **parasite.**

hanging *adjective.* Hung or appearing to be hung from a support ▶ dangling, dangly, pendent, pendulous, pensile, suspended. *—See also* **loose** (1).

hangout *noun.* *—See* **haunt.**

hangover *noun.* Unpleasant physical and mental effects following overindulgence in alcohol ▶ crapulence, katzenjammer. *Informal:* head.

hang-up *noun. Informal* An exaggerated concern ▶ anxiety, complex, neurosis, phobia. [*Compare* **anxiety, obsession.**]

hanker *verb.* *—See* **desire.**

hanky-panky *noun.* *—See* **mischief.**

hap *noun.* *—See* **chance** (1), **chance** (2).

hap *verb.* To take place by chance ▶ befall, betide, chance, happen. *—See also* **happen** (1).

haphazard *adjective.* *—See* **random.**

hapless *adjective.* *—See* **unfortunate** (1).

haplessness *noun.* *—See* **misfortune.**

happen *verb.* **1.** To take place ▶ arrive, befall, betide, come, come about, come off, develop, fall, hap, occur, pass, transpire, turn out. ***Idiom:*** come to pass. **2.** To take place by chance ▶ befall, betide, chance, hap.

happen on *or* **upon** *verb.* *—See* **encounter** (1).

✦ **CORE SYNONYMS:** *happen, befall, betide, occur, transpire.* These verbs mean to take place or to come about: *saw an extraordinary thing happen; predicted that misery will befall humankind; woe that betides the poor soldier; was caught outdoors when the thunderstorm occurred; described the accident exactly as it transpired.*

---

happening *noun.* *—See* **circumstance** (1), **event** (1).

happenstance *or* **happenchance** *noun.* *—See* **chance** (1).

happiness *noun.* A condition of supreme well-being and good spirits ▶ beatitude, blessedness, bliss, cheer, cheerfulness, contentedness, contentment, delight, felicity, gladness, glee, joy, joyfulness. [*Compare* **delight, elation, satisfaction.**]

happy *adjective.* **1.** Having achieved satisfaction, as of one's goal ▶ content, fufilled, gratified, satisfied. **2.** Characterized by luck or good fortune ▶ fortuitous, fortunate, lucky, providential. [*Compare* **opportune.**] *—See also* **cheerful, merry, willing.**

happy-go-lucky *adjective.* *—See* **lighthearted.**

harangue *noun.* *—See* **tirade.**

harangue *verb.* *—See* **rant.**

harass *verb.* To attack or disturb persistently ▶ annoy, badger, bait, bedevil, beleaguer, beset, besiege, harrow, harry, heckle, hector, hound, importune, persecute, pester, plague, taunt, tease, torment, worry. *Informal:* hassle, needle, ride. *Slang:* rag. [*Compare* **insult, nag, ridicule.**]

✦ **CORE SYNONYMS:** *harass, harry, hound, badger, pester, plague.* These verbs mean to attack, disturb, or trouble persistently or incessantly. *Harass* and *harry* imply systematic persecution by besieging with repeated annoyances, threats, or demands: *The landlord harassed tenants who were behind in their rent. A rude customer had harried the storekeeper. Hound* suggests unrelenting pursuit to gain a desired end: *Reporters hounded the celebrity for an interview.* To *badger* is to nag or tease persistently: *The child badgered his parents for a new bicycle.* To *pester* is to inflict a succession of petty annoyances: *"How she would have pursued and pestered me with questions and surmises"* (Charlotte Brontë). *Plague* refers to a problem likened to an epidemic disease: *"As I have no estate, I am plagued with no tenants or stewards"* (Henry Fielding).

---

harassment *noun.* *—See* **annoyance** (1).

harbor *noun.* A protected area of water where ships can anchor or dock ▶ anchorage, cove, haven, lagoon, road, roadstead, port. [*Compare* **bay**[1], **channel, inlet.**] —*See also* **cover** (1).

harbor *verb.* To give refuge to ▶ haven, house, shelter, take in. [*Compare* **defend.**] —*See also* **bear** (2), **lodge.**

harbinger *noun.* —*See* **forerunner, omen.**

harborage *noun.* —*See* **refuge** (1).

hard *adjective.* **1.** Unyielding to pressure ▶ firm, incompressible, solid. **2.** Physically toughened so as to have great endurance ▶ hard-bitten, hard-handed, hardy, rugged, tempered, tough. ***Idioms:*** hard (*or* tough) as nails, hard (*or* tough) as tacks. [*Compare* **muscular.**] **3.** Containing alcohol ▶ alcoholic, intoxicating, intoxicative, spiked, spirituous, stiff, strong. **4.** Indulging in drink to an excessive degree ▶ heavy. *Informal:* two-fisted. —*See also* **bitter** (2), **bleak** (1), **callous, certain** (2), **difficult** (1), **realistic** (1), **resentful, severe** (2), **severe** (1).

hard *adverb.* **1.** With great force, energy, or intensity ▶ all out, boldly, con brio, energetically, fervently, fiercely, forcefully, forcibly, frantically, frenziedly, furiously, lustily, powerfully, rabidly, severely, stoutly, strenuously, urgently, warmly, vigorously, wholeheartedly, zealously. ***Idioms:*** hammer and tongs, like all get-out, like blazes, tooth and nail, with might and main, with no holds barred. [*Compare* **very.**] **2.** With effort ▶ arduously, assiduously, difficultly, drudgingly, gruelingly, heavily, laboriously, rigorously, wearisomely. —*See also* **close.**

hard-bitten *adjective.* —*See* **hard** (2).

hard-boiled *adjective.* —*See* **callous.**

harden *verb.* **1.** To make resistant to hardship, especially through continued exposure ▶ acclimate, acclimatize, caseharden, indurate, season, strengthen, toughen. [*Compare* **deaden, gird.**] **2.** To make or become physically hard ▶ cake, cement, concrete, congeal, dry, firm up, fix, indurate, ossify, petrify, set, solidify, stiffen, toughen. [*Compare* **coagulate, thicken.**] **3.** To make firmer in a particular conviction or habit ▶ confirm, fortify, reinforce, strengthen. [*Compare* **back, establish.**]

✚ **CORE SYNONYMS:** *harden, acclimate, acclimatize, season, toughen.* These verbs mean to make resistant to hardship, especially through continued exposure: *was hardened to frontier life; is acclimated to the tropical heat; was acclimatized by long hours to overwork; became seasoned to life in prison; toughened by experience.*

---

hardened *adjective.* —*See* **callous.**

hard-fisted *adjective.* —*See* **stingy.**

hard-handed *adjective.* —*See* **hard** (2).

hardheaded *adjective.* —*See* **realistic** (1), **stubborn** (1).

hardheadedness *noun.* —*See* **stubbornness.**

hardhearted *adjective.* —*See* **callous.**

hard-hitting *adjective.* —*See* **forceful.**

hardiness *noun.* —*See* **endurance.**

hardly *adverb.* By a very little; almost not ▶ barely, just, scarce, scarcely. ***Idioms:*** by a hair (*or* whisker), by the skin of one's teeth. [*Compare* **approximately, merely, only.**]

hardness *noun.* —*See* **severity, stability.**

hard-shell *adjective.* —*See* **confirmed** (1).

hardship *noun.* —*See* **deprivation, difficulty, misery.**

hardy *adjective.* —*See* **brave, hard** (2), **healthy, strong** (2).

harebrained *adjective.* —*See* **foolish, giddy** (2).

hark *verb.* To make an effort to hear something ▶ attend, hearken, heed, listen. ***Idioms:*** give (*or* lend) an ear. —*See also* **hear.**

hark back *verb.* To cause one to remember or think of ▶ recall, suggest. ***Idioms:*** bring to mind, put one in mind of, take one back, remind one of. [*Compare* **refer, remind.**]

harlot *noun.* A woman who engages in sex for payment ▶ bawd, call girl, courtesan, harlot, scarlet woman, strumpet, tart. *Slang:* hooker, moll, working girl. ***Idioms:*** lady of easy virtue, lady of the night, lady of pleasure. [*Compare* **prostitute, slut.**]

harm *noun.* The action or result of inflicting loss or pain ▶ damage, detriment, distress, hurt, impairment, injury, mischief, trauma. [*Compare* **distress, evil, offense.**]

harm *verb.* —*See* **damage.**

harmful *adjective.* Causing harm, injury, or destruction ▶ adverse, bad, baneful, corrosive, corruptive, damaging, deleterious, destructive, detrimental, evil, hurtful, ill, injurious, malefic, maleficent, malevolent, malign, mischievous, naughty, nocuous, noisome, noxious, pernicious, ruinous, toxic, unhealthy, unwholesome. [*Compare* **disastrous.**]

harmless *adjective.* Devoid of hurtful qualities ▶ benign, hurtless, innocent, innocuous, inoffensive, safe, unoffensive. —*See also* **innocent** (2).

harmonic *adjective.* —*See* **harmonious** (2).

harmonious *adjective.* **1.** Having components that are pleasingly combined ▶ balanced, concordant, congruous, symmetrical. [*Compare* **pleasant.**] **2.** Characterized by harmony of sound ▶ consonant, harmonic, in tune, musical, symphonic, symphonious, well-voiced. —*See also* **agreeable, melodious, unanimous.**

harmonization *noun.* —*See* **agreement** (2), **arrangement** (1).

harmonize *verb.* **1.** To bring into accord ▶ accommodate, attune, conform, coordinate, integrate, proportion, reconcile, tune. [*Compare* **balance, mix.**] **2.** To combine and adapt in order to attain a particular effect ▶ arrange, blend, coordinate, correlate, integrate, mesh, orchestrate, synthesize, unify. **3.** To occur at the same time ▶ coincide, concur, synchronize. —*See also* **agree** (1), **agree** (2), **relate** (2).

harmony *noun.* **1.** Pleasing agreement, as of musical sounds ▶ accord, blend, concert, concord, consonance, euphoniousness, euphony, symphony, tune, tunefulness. **2.** A relationship or an affinity between people or things in which many properties are shared ▶ sympathy, synch, synchronization, synchrony. **3.** Satisfying arrangement marked by even distribution of elements, as in a design ▶ balance, proportion, symmetry. —*See also* **agreement** (2).

harness *noun.* —*See* **fastener.**

harness *verb.* —*See* **restrain, use.**

harp on *noun.* —*See* **belabor.**

harpy *noun.* —*See* **scold.**

harridan *noun.* —*See* **scold.**

harrow *verb.* To subject another to extreme physical cruelty, as in punishing ▶ crucify, rack, torment, torture. ***Idioms:*** put on the rack (*or* wheel), put the screws to. [*Compare* **punish.**] —*See also* **distress, harass.**

harrowing *adjective.* —*See* **horrible, tormenting.**

harry *verb.* —*See* **harass, invade** (1).

harsh *adjective.* Disagreeable to the senses, especially the sense of hearing ▶ dry, grating, hoarse, jarring, rasping, raspy, raucous, rough, scratchy, shrill, squawky, strident. [*Compare* **vociferous, inharmonious.**] —*See also* **biting, bitter** (2), **bleak** (1), **rough** (1), **severe** (1).

harshness *noun.* —*See* **severity.**

harum-scarum *adjective.* —*See* **rash**[1].

haruspex *noun.* —*See* **prophet.**

harvest *noun.* The produce harvested from the land ▶ crop, fruit, fruitage, vintage, yield. —*See also* **effect** (1).

harvest *verb.* —*See* **gather, glean.**

hash *noun.* —*See* **mess** (1).

hash over *verb.* —*See* **discuss.**

hasp *noun.* —*See* **fastener.**

hassle *noun.* —*See* **annoyance** (2), **argument, bother.**

hassle *verb.* —*See* **argue** (1), **harass.**

hassock *noun.* A stool or cushion for resting the feet ▶ footrest, footstool, ottoman.

haste *noun.* **1.** Rapidness of movement or activity ▶ alacrity, celerity, dispatch, expedition, expeditiousness, fleetness, hurry, hustle, quickness, rapidity, rapidness, rush, speed, speediness, swiftness. **2.** Careless headlong action ▶ hastiness, hurriedness, precipitance, precipitancy, precipitateness, precipitation, rashness, rush.

haste *verb.* —*See* **rush.**

✤ **CORE SYNONYMS:** *haste, celerity, dispatch, expedition, hurry, speed.* These nouns denote rapidity or promptness of movement or activity: *left the room in haste; a legal system not known for celerity; advanced with all possible dispatch; cleaned up with remarkable expedition; worked without hurry; driving with excessive speed.*

---

hasten *verb.* —*See* **rush, speed.**

hastily *adverb.* —*See* **fast.**

hastiness *noun.* —*See* **haste** (2).

hasty *adjective.* —*See* **fast** (1), **quick, rash[1].**

hatch *verb.* —*See* **breed, invent, plot** (2).

hatchet man *noun.* —*See* **murderer.**

hate *verb.* To feel hostility toward or strong dislike for something ▶ abhor, abominate, detest, execrate, loathe. ***Idioms:*** bear antipathy (*or* malice *or* ill will) toward, be repelled (*or* repulsed *or* revolted) by, be sick of, can't stand, hold in contempt. [*Compare* **despise, dislike, revile.**]

hate *noun.* **1.** A strong feeling of hostility or dislike ▶ abhorrence, abomination, antipathy, aversion, contempt, detestation, hatred, horror, loathing, odium, rancor, repellence, repellency, repugnance, repugnancy, repulsion, revulsion. [*Compare* **aggression, despisal, enmity, resentment.**] **2.** An object of extreme dislike ▶ abhorrence, abomination, anathema, aversion, bête noire, bugbear, detestation, execration. *Informal:* horror. [*Compare* **annoyance.**]

hateful *adjective.* —*See* **malevolent, offensive** (1).

hatred *noun.* —*See* **despisal, hate** (1).

haughtiness *noun.* —*See* **arrogance, condescension.**

haughty *adjective.* —*See* **arrogant, disdainful.**

haul *verb.* —*See* **carry** (1), **pull** (1).

haul *noun.* —*See* **burden[1]** (2), **pull** (1).

hauling *noun.* —*See* **transportation.**

haunt *verb.* To come to mind continually ▶ obsess, torment, trouble, weigh on (*or* upon). —*See also* **frequent.**

haunt *noun.* A frequently visited place ▶ meeting place, rendezvous, resort. *Slang:* hangout, stamping ground, stomping ground. [*Compare* **habitat.**] —*See also* **ghost.**

hauteur *noun.* —*See* **arrogance.**

have *verb.* **1.** To be filled by ▶ contain, hold. [*Compare* **constitute.**] **2.** To admit to one's possession, presence, or awareness ▶ accept, receive, take. [*Compare* **absorb.**] **3.** To organize and carry out an activity ▶ give, hold, stage, throw. [*Compare* **conduct.**] —*See also* **bear** (3), **bear** (4), **carry** (2), **command** (2), **contain** (1), **deceive, experience, participate, permit** (1).

have at *verb.* —*See* **attack** (1).

haven *noun.* —*See* **cover** (1), **harbor.**

haven *verb.* To give refuge to ▶ harbor, house, shelter, take in. [*Compare* **defend.**]

have-not *noun.* —*See* **pauper.**

havoc *noun.* —*See* **destruction.**

hawk[1] *verb.* To travel about selling goods ▶ huckster, peddle, vend. [*Compare* **sell.**]

hawk[2] *verb.* To expel a small amount of saliva or mucus from the mouth ▶ expectorate, spit. [*Compare* **drool.**]

hawkish *adjective.* —*See* **aggressive, military** (1).

hayseed *noun.* —*See* **clodhopper.**

haywire *adjective.* —*See* **insane.**

hazard *noun.* —*See* **chance** (1), **chance** (2), **danger, risk.**
hazard *verb.* —*See* **endanger, gamble** (2), **venture.**
hazardous *adjective.* —*See* **dangerous.**
haze *noun.* A suspension in the air of tiny particles of water, dust, or smoke ▶ brume, fog, mist, pall, smaze, smog, smudge, steam, vapor. —*See also* **daze.**
hazing *noun.* —*See* **initiation.**
hazy *adjective.* Heavy, dark, or dense, especially with impurities ▶ murky, smoggy, turbid. [*Compare* **dirty.**] —*See also* **unclear.**
head *noun.* **1.** The uppermost part of the body ▶ crown, noddle, pate, poll. *Slang:* bean, block, conk, dome, noggin, noodle, nut. **2.** The seat of the faculty of intelligence and reason ▶ brain, mind. *Informal:* gray matter. [*Compare* **imagination.**] **3.** A term or terms in large type introducing a text ▶ header, heading, headline. —*See also* **boss, chief, crisis, foam, front, talent.**
head *adjective.* —*See* **primary** (1).
head *verb.* —*See* **administer** (1), **aim** (1), **bear** (5).
head off *verb.* To block the progress of and force to change direction ▶ cut off, intercept. —*See also* **prevent.**
headache *noun.* —*See* **annoyance** (2), **bother, burden**[1] (1).
header *noun.* —*See* **fall** (1).
heading *noun.* **1.** A term or terms in large type introducing a text ▶ head, header, headline. **2.** The compass direction in which a ship or aircraft moves ▶ bearing, course, vector. —*See also* **direction, entry.**
headline *noun.* A term or terms in large type introducing a text ▶ head, header, heading. —*See also* **news.**
headliner *noun.* —*See* **lead.**
headlong *adjective.* —*See* **rash**[1].
headman *noun.* —*See* **chief.**
headquarters *noun.* —*See* **base**[1] (1), **center** (1), **home** (1).
head start *noun.* —*See* **advantage** (1).
headstrong *adjective.* —*See* **stubborn** (1), **unruly.**
headway *noun.* —*See* **advance, progress.**
headword *noun.* —*See* **entry.**
headwork *noun.* —*See* **thought.**
heal *verb.* —*See* **cure.**
health *noun.* **1.** The condition of being physically or mentally sound ▶ haleness, healthiness, heartiness, soundness, wellness, wholeness. [*Compare* **condition.**] **2.** The act of drinking to someone ▶ pledge, toast.
healthful *adjective.* Promoting good health ▶ healthsome, healthy, hearty, hygienic, salubrious, salutary, wholesome. [*Compare* **beneficial, nutritious.**] —*See also* **healthy.**
healthiness *noun.* —*See* **health** (1).
healthsome *adjective.* —*See* **healthful.**
healthy *adjective.* Having good health ▶ able-bodied, all right, fit, flourishing, hale, hardy, healthful, hearty, normal, right, robust, rosy-cheeked, sound, thriving, vigorous, well, whole, wholesome. ***Idioms:*** fit as a fiddle, hale and hearty, in fine fettle, in fine (*or* good) health, in fine (*or* good) shape, in the pink. [*Compare* **lusty, muscular, strong.**] —*See also* **big, healthful.**

✦ **CORE SYNONYMS:** *healthy, sound, wholesome, hale, robust, well, hardy, vigorous.* These adjectives mean having good physical or mental health. *Healthy* stresses the absence of disease and often implies energy and strength: *The healthy athlete biked twenty miles every day. Sound* emphasizes freedom from injury, imperfection, or impairment: *"The man with the toothache thinks everyone happy whose teeth are sound"* (George Bernard Shaw). *Wholesome* suggests appealing healthiness and well-being: *"Exercise develops wholesome appetites"* (Louisa May Alcott). *Hale* stresses freedom from infirmity, especially in elderly persons, while *robust* emphasizes healthy strength and ruggedness: *"He is pretty well advanced in years, but hale, robust, and florid"* (Tobias Smollett). *Well* indicates absence of or recovery from sickness: *You should stay home from work if you're not well. Hardy* implies robust and sturdy good health: *The hardy mountaineers camped in the Alps. Vigorous* suggests healthy, active energy and strength: *"a vigorous old man, who spent half of his day on horseback"* (W.H. Hudson).

◀ **ANTONYM:** *unhealthy*

---

heap *noun.* **1.** A group of things gathered haphazardly ▶ agglomeration, bank, cumulus, drift, hill, mass, mess, mound, mountain, pile, shock, stack, tumble. [*Compare* **accumulation.**] **2.** *Informal* An indeterminately great amount or number ▶ bunch, lot, multiplicity, ream. *Informal:* billion, bushel, gazillion, gob, jillion, load, million, mountain, oodles, passel, peck, pile, scad, slew, ton, trillion, wad, zillion. —*See also* **abundance.**

heap *verb.* **1.** To collect or pile up or onto something ▶ bank, drift, hill, load, lump, mound, pile (up *or* together), stack. [*Compare* **load.**] **2.** To give in great abundance ▶ lavish, rain, shower. [*Compare* **confer, donate, give.**] —*See also* **fill** (1).

heap up *verb.* —*See* **accumulate.**

✚ **CORE SYNONYMS:** *heap, bank, mound, pile, stack.* These nouns denote a group of things gathered haphazardly: *a heap of old newspapers; a bank of thunderclouds; a mound of boulders; a pile of boxes; a stack of firewood.*

---

hear *verb.* To perceive by ear, usually attentively ▶ attend, auscultate, hark, heed, listen. ***Idioms:*** give (*or* lend) one's ear. —*See also* **discover, understand** (1).

hear of *verb.* To receive an idea and think about it in order to form an opinion about it ▶ consider, entertain, think about (of).

hearing *noun.* **1.** The sense by which sound is perceived ▶ audition, auditory system, ear. **2.** Range of audibility ▶ earshot, sound. [*Compare* **range.**] **3.** A chance to be heard ▶ audience, audition, listen. ***Idiom:*** one's day in court. **4.** The examination of evidence, charges, and claims in court ▶ court case, inquest, inquiry, trial. [*Compare* **examination.**]

hearken *or* **harken** *verb.* To make an effort to hear something ▶ attend, hark, heed, listen. ***Idioms:*** give (*or* lend) an ear.

hearsay *noun.* —*See* **gossip** (1).

heart *noun.* **1.** The most central or essential part ▶ center, core, essence, gist, kernel, marrow, meat, nub, nucleus, pith, quintessence, root, soul, spirit, stuff, substance. [*Compare* **subject.**] **2.** The circulatory organ of the body ▶ blood pump. *Slang:* ticker. **3.** The seat of a person's innermost emotions and feelings ▶ bosom, breast, soul. ***Idioms:*** bottom (*or* cockles) of one's heart, one's heart of hearts. —*See also* **center** (1), **center** (3), **courage, pity** (1).

✚ **CORE SYNONYMS:** *heart, core, gist, nucleus, pith, substance.* These nouns denote the most central or essential part of something: *The negotiator addressed issues at the heart of the matter. The core of the editorial had to do with taxes. The gist of the lawyer's argument was that the evidence was inconclusive. The nucleus of the report recommended two basic changes. The scholars analyzed the pith of the essay. The committee judged the substance of the tenants' complaints.*

---

heartache *or* **heartbreak** *noun.* —*See* **grief.**

heartbreaking *adjective.* —*See* **sorrowful.**

heartbroken *adjective.* —*See* **depressed** (1).

hearten *verb.* —*See* **encourage** (2).

heartening *adjective.* —*See* **encouraging.**

heartfelt *adjective.* —*See* **deep** (3), **genuine.**

hearth *noun.* An open space for holding a fire at the base of a chimney ▶ fireplace, grate, ingle.

heartiness *noun.* —*See* **health** (1).

heartless *adjective.* —*See* **callous.**

heart-rending *adjective.* —*See* **affecting, sorrowful.**

heartsick *adjective.* —*See* **depressed** (1).

heartsickness *noun.* —*See* **depression** (2).

heart-to-heart *noun.* —*See* **conversation.**

hearty *adjective.* —*See* **genuine, healthful, healthy.**

heat *noun.* **1.** Warmth or degree of warmth ▶ fervor, hotness, temperature, torridity, torridness, warmth. **2.** A stage of a competition ▶ round, stage. [*Compare* **competition, turn.**] —*See also* **passion, police officer, pressure.**

heat up *verb.* —*See* **provoke.**

heated *adjective.* —*See* **hot** (1), **passionate.**

heathen *noun.* One who does not believe in God ▶ atheist, infidel, nonbeliever, pagan.

heathen *adjective.* Without belief in God ▶ pagan. [*Compare* **atheistic.**]

heave *verb.* To move vigorously from side to side or up and down ▶ pitch, rock, roll, toss. [*Compare* **lurch.**] —*See also* **elevate** (1), **gasp, pant, throw, vomit.**

heave *noun.* —*See* **lift, throw.**

heaven *noun.* A supremely beautiful, blissful state or experience ▶ bliss, ecstasy, Eden, nirvana, paradise, rapture, transport. *Informal:* cloud nine, seventh heaven. [*Compare* **delight, happiness.**] —*See also* **eternity** (2).

heavenly *adjective.* **1.** Of or relating to heaven ▶ celestial, divine, paradisaic, paradisaical, paradisal, paradisiac, paradisiacal, supernal. **2.** Of or relating to the heavens ▶ astronomical, celestial, cosmic, empyreal, supernal. —*See also* **delicious, delightful, divine** (1).

heavens *noun.* The celestial regions as seen from the earth ▶ air, firmament, sky. ***Idiom:*** wild blue yonder.

heavily *adverb.* —*See* **hard** (2).

heaviness *noun.* The state or degree of being heavy ▶ heftiness, mass, massiveness, ponderosity, ponderousness, weight, weightiness. *Informal:* avoirdupois. [*Compare* **importance.**]

heavy *adjective.* **1.** Having relatively great weight ▶ heavyweight, hefty, leaden, massive, ponderous, weighty. **2.** Indulging in drink to an excessive degree ▶ hard. *Informal:* two-fisted. **3.** Not readily digested because of richness ▶ filling, rich. **4.** Bearing a heavy load ▶ heavy-laden, laden, loaded, weighed down. —*See also* **bulky** (1), **bulky** (2), **burdensome, deep** (2), **fat** (1), **generous** (2), **grave²** (1), **intense, ponderous, rough** (2), **severe** (2), **thick** (3), **viscous.**

heavy *noun.* *Slang* A mean, worthless character in a story or play ▶ bad guy, villain.

✣ **CORE SYNONYMS:** *heavy, weighty, hefty, massive, ponderous.* These adjectives mean having a relatively great weight. *Heavy* refers to what has great physical weight (*a heavy boulder*) and figuratively to what is burdensome or oppressive to the spirit (*heavy responsibilities*). *Weighty* literally denotes having considerable weight (*a weighty package*); figuratively, it describes what is onerous, serious, or important (*a weighty decision*). *Hefty* refers principally to physical heaviness or brawniness: *a hefty book; a tall, hefty wrestler. Massive* describes what is bulky, heavy, solid, and strong: *massive marble columns. Ponderous* refers to what has great mass and weight and usually implies unwieldiness: *ponderous prehistoric beasts.* Figuratively it describes what is complicated, involved, or lacking in grace: *a lengthy narrative with a ponderous plot.*

◀ **ANTONYM:** *light*

---

heavy-footed *adjective.* —*See* **ponderous.**

heavy-handed *adjective.* —*See* **ponderous, unskillful.**

heavy-hearted *adjective.* —*See* **depressed** (1).

heavy-heartedness *noun.* —*See* **depression** (2).

heavy-laden *adjective.* Burdened by a weighty load ▶ heavy, laden, loaded, weighed down.

heavyset *adjective.* —*See* **stocky.**

heavyweight *noun.* —*See* **dignitary.**

heavyweight *adjective.* —*See* **big-league, heavy** (1).

hebetude *noun.* —*See* **lethargy.**

hebetudinous *adjective.* —*See* **lethargic, stupid.**

hecatomb *noun.* —*See* **offering.**

heckle *verb.* —*See* **harass.**

hectic *adjective.* —*See* **busy** (2), **feverish, frantic.**

hector *noun.* —*See* **bully.**

hector *verb.* —*See* **harass, intimidate.**

hedge *verb.* —*See* **defend** (1), **defense, enclose** (2), **equivocate** (1), **evade** (1), **surround.**

hedge *noun.* —*See* **equivocation.**

hedonist *noun.* —*See* **sybarite.**

hedonistic *or* **hedonic** *adjective.* Characterized by or devoted to pleasure and luxury as a lifestyle ▶ epicurean, sybaritic, voluptuary, voluptuous. [*Compare* **luxurious, sensual.**]

heebie-jeebies *noun.* —*See* **jitters.**

heed *verb.* To make an effort to hear something ▶ attend, hark, hearken, listen. ***Idioms:*** give (*or* lend) an ear. —*See also* **follow** (4), **hear.**

heed *noun.* —*See* **care** (1), **notice** (1).

heedful *adjective.* —*See* **alert, careful** (1).

heedfulness *noun.* —*See* **attention, care** (1).

heedless *adjective.* —*See* **careless.**

heedlessness *noun.* A careless, often reckless disregard for consequences ▶ abandon, blitheness, carelessness, thoughtlessness. [*Compare* **temerity.**]

heehaw *noun.* —*See* **laugh.**

heehaw *verb.* —*See* **laugh.**

heel[1] *verb.* —*See* **follow** (3).

heel[2] *verb.* —*See* **incline.**

heel *noun.* —*See* **inclination** (2).

heel[3] *noun.* —*See* **end** (3).

heftiness *noun.* —*See* **heaviness.**

hefty *adjective.* —*See* **bulky** (1), **bulky** (2), **heavy** (1), **severe** (2).

hegemony *noun.* —*See* **dominance.**

height *noun.* The distance of something from a given level ▶ altitude, elevation, loftiness, tallness. [*Compare* **ascent.**] —*See also* **climax, intensity.**

heighten *verb.* —*See* **elevate** (2), **intensify.**

heightened *adjective.* —*See* **elevated** (2), **intense.**

heinous *adjective.* —*See* **outrageous.**

heinousness *noun.* —*See* **outrageousness.**

heist *verb.* —*See* **rob, steal.**

heist *noun.* —*See* **larceny.**

hell *noun.* A place or experience of excruciating pain or punishment ▶ fire and brimstone, hellfire, inferno, living hell, perdition, persecution, torment, torture. [*Compare* **distress, misery.**]

hell *verb.* —*See* **revel.**

hellbound *adjective.* —*See* **condemned.**

hellfire *noun.* —*See* **hell.**

hell-for-leather *adverb.* —*See* **fast.**

hell-for-leather *adjective.* —*See* **fast** (1).

hellhole *noun.* —*See* **pit**[1].

hellish *adjective.* —*See* **fiendish.**

hello *interjection.* Used as a greeting ▶ good day, greetings, salutations. *Informal:* aloha, hey, hey ho, hey there, hi, hi there, howdy, howdy do. *Slang:* yo, 'sup. ***Idioms:*** how do you do, what's up.

hello *noun. Informal* An expression, in words or gestures, marking a meeting of persons ▶ hail, greeting, salutation, salute, welcome.

helot *noun.* —*See* **slave.**

helotry *noun.* —*See* **slavery.**

help *verb.* To give support or assistance to ▶ abet, aid, assist, boost, help out, relieve, succor. ***Idioms:*** come to the aid of, do a service, give (*or* lend) a hand, give a leg up, see someone through. [*Compare* **comfort, serve, support.**] —*See also* **improve, oblige** (1), **profit** (2).

help along *verb.* —*See* **ease** (2).

help *noun.* The act or an instance of helping ▶ abetment, aid, assist, assistance, hand, relief, succor, support. —*See also* **assistant, employee.**

✚ **CORE SYNONYMS:** *help, aid, assist, succor.* These verbs mean to give support or assistance to someone or something. *Help* and *aid,* the most general, are frequently interchangeable: *a medication that helps* (or *aids*) *the digestion. Help,* however, sometimes conveys a stronger suggestion of effectual action: *I'll help you move the piano. Assist* usually implies making a secondary contribution or acting as a subordinate: *Apprentices assisted the chef in preparing the banquet. Succor* refers to going to the relief of one in want, difficulty, or distress: *"Mr. Harding thought . . . of the worn-out, aged men he had succored"* (Anthony Trollope).

helper *noun.* —*See* **assistant.**

helpful *adjective.* Tending to contribute to a result ▶ conducive, contributive, contributory, participatory. [*Compare* **auxiliary.**] —*See also* **beneficial, benevolent** (1), **obliging.**

helping *noun.* —*See* **serving.**

helping *adjective.* —*See* **auxiliary** (1).

helpless *adjective.* Lacking power or strength ▶ impotent, powerless, unable. —*See also* **ineffectual** (2), **vulnerable.**

helplessness *noun.* —*See* **ineffectuality.**

helplessly *adverb.* Without regard to desire or inclination ▶ inextricably, involuntarily, perforce, willy-nilly.

helpmate *or* **helpmeet** *noun.* —*See* **spouse.**

helter-skelter *adjective.* —*See* **confused** (2).

helter-skelter *noun.* —*See* **agitation** (1).

hem *verb.* —*See* **enclose** (2), **surround.**

hem *noun.* —*See* **border** (1).

henchman *noun.* —*See* **follower.**

henpeck *verb.* —*See* **nag.**

herald *noun.* —*See* **forerunner, messenger.**

herald *verb.* —*See* **announce, proclaim.**

herculean *adjective.* —*See* **enormous.**

herd *verb.* —*See* **drive** (3).

herd *noun.* —*See* **crowd, flock.**

hereafter *noun.* Time that is yet to be ▶ by-and-by, future, futurity, tomorrow. ***Idiom:*** time to come. [*Compare* **approach, possibility.**] —*See also* **eternity** (2).

hereditary *adjective.* Of unbroken descent or lineage ▶ direct, genealogical, lineal, natural. —*See also* **ancestral, innate.**

heretic *noun.* —*See* **separatist.**

heretofore *adverb.* —*See* **earlier** (2).

heritage *noun.* **1.** Something immaterial, as a style or philosophy, that is passed from one generation to another ▶ inheritance, legacy, tradition. [*Compare* **culture.**] **2.** Any special privilege accorded a firstborn ▶ birthright, inheritance, legacy, patrimony. [*Compare* **right.**]

✚ **CORE SYNONYMS:** *heritage, inheritance, legacy, tradition.* These nouns denote something immaterial, such as a style, philosophy, or custom, that is passed from one generation to another: *a heritage of moral uprightness; a rich inheritance of storytelling; a legacy of philosophical thought; the tradition of noblesse oblige.*

hermeneutic *or* **hermeneutical** *adjective.* —*See* **explanatory.**

hero *noun.* A person revered especially for noble courage ▶ champion, heroine, paladin. ***Idiom:*** knight in shining armor. [*Compare* **winner.**] —*See also* **celebrity.**

heroic *adjective.* —*See* **brave, enormous.**

heroine *noun.* A woman revered especially for noble courage ▶ champion, hero, paladin. ***Idiom:*** knight in shining armor. [*Compare* **winner.**] —*See also* **celebrity.**

heroism *noun.* —*See* **courage.**

hesitancy *noun.* —*See* **hesitation.**

hesitant *adjective.* Given to or exhibiting hesitation ▶ halting, hesitating, indecisive, irresolute, pendulous, shilly-shally, tentative, timid, vacillant, vacillatory, wavering. ***Idiom:*** hemming and hawing. [*Compare* **indisposed.**] —*See also* **doubtful** (2).

hesitate *verb.* To be irresolute in acting or doing ▶ dally, dilly-dally, dither, falter, halt, pause, shilly-shally, stagger, vacillate, waver, wobble. ***Idiom:*** hem and haw. [*Compare* **delay.**]

✚ **CORE SYNONYMS:** *hesitate, vacillate, waver, falter.* These verbs mean to be irresolute, uncertain, or indecisive. To *hesitate* is to hold back or pause because of doubt or uncertainty: *"A President either is constantly on top of events or, if he hesitates, events will soon be on top of him"* (Harry S. Truman). *Vacillate* implies going back and forth between alternative, usually conflicting courses: *She vacillated about whether to go or to stay.* *Waver* suggests having second thoughts about a decision: *After much wavering, he finally gave his permission.* To *falter* is to be unsteady in resolution or action: *He resolved to ask for a raise but faltered when his boss entered the room.*

---

hesitation *noun.* The act of hesitating or state of being hesitant ▶ dawdling, hesitancy, indecision, indecisiveness, irresoluteness, irresolution, pause, shilly-shally, tentativeness, timidity, timidness, to-and-fro, vacillation, wavering. ***Idiom:*** hemming and hawing. [*Compare* **delay.**]

heterogeneity *or* **heterogeneousness** *noun.* —*See* **variety.**

heterogeneous *adjective.* —*See* **various.**

hew *verb.* —*See* **drop** (3).

hex *noun.* Something or someone believed to bring bad luck ▶ curse, evil eye, hoodoo, Jonah. *Informal:* jinx. [*Compare* **charm, magic.**] —*See also* **curse** (1).

hex *verb.* **1.** To bring bad luck or evil to ▶ curse, hoodoo. *Informal:* jinx. [*Compare* **afflict.**] **2.** To invoke evil upon ▶ anathematize, curse, damn, imprecate. [*Compare* **charm.**]

hey *interjection.* —*See* **hello.**

heyday *noun.* —*See* **bloom**[1] (1).

hi *interjection.* —*See* **hello.**

hiatus *noun.* —*See* **gap** (2), **rest**[1] (1).

hick *adjective.* —*See* **country.**

hick *noun.* —*See* **clodhopper.**

hidden *adjective.* **1.** Difficult or impossible to see or distinguish ▶ buried, camouflaged, cloaked, concealed, covert, disguised, imperceptible, indiscernible, indistinguishable, invisible, masked, obscured, secret, shrouded, unapparent, unnoticeable, unseen, veiled. [*Compare* **imperceptible, secret.**] **2.** Concealed from view ▶ blind, secluded, screened, secret. ***Idioms:*** out of sight, out of view. —*See also* **ulterior** (1).

hide[1] *verb.* To put or keep out of sight ▶ bury, cache, conceal, ensconce, occult, secrete, squirrel away. *Slang:* plant, stash. [*Compare* **save.**] —*See also* **block, conceal.**

hide out *verb.* To shut oneself up in secrecy ▶ *Informal:* hole up. ***Idioms:*** go underground, lay (*or* lie) low.

✚ **CORE SYNONYMS:** *hide, conceal, secrete, cache, bury.* These verbs mean to keep from the sight or knowledge of others. *Hide* and *conceal* are the most general and are often used interchangeably: *I used a throw rug to hide* (or *conceal*) *the stain on the carpet. I smiled to hide* (or *conceal*) *my hurt feelings. Secrete* and *cache* involve concealment in a place unknown to others; *cache* often implies storage for later use: *The lioness secreted her cubs in the tall grass. The mountain climbers cached their provisions in a cave. Bury* implies covering over: *The pirates buried the treasure. The author buried the point of the article in a mass of details.*

---

hide[2] *noun.* The skin of an animal, sometimes including fur, hair or feathers ▶ fur, leather, pelt.
hide *verb.* —*See* **beat** (2).

hideaway *noun.* A hiding place ▶ covert, den, hide-out, lair.

hidebound *adjective.* —*See* **intolerant** (1).

hideous *adjective.* —*See* **ghastly** (1), **ugly.**

hideousness *noun.* —*See* **ugliness.**

hide-out *noun.* A hiding place ▶ covert, den, hideaway, lair.

hiding *noun.* —*See* **beating.**

hierarch *noun.* —*See* **chief.**

hierarchy *noun.* —*See* **class** (2).

hieroglyphic *adjective.* —*See* **graphic** (4).

higgle *verb.* —*See* **haggle.**

higgledy-piggledy *adjective.* —*See* **confused** (2).

high *adjective.* **1.** Being of or at a relatively great height or altitude ▶ aerial, airy, elevated, lofty, sky-high, soaring, tall, towering. ***Idiom:*** on high. **2.** At the upper end of a degree of measure ▶ elevated, great, large. [*Compare* **exalted, extreme.**] **3.** Elevated in pitch ▶ acute, high-pitched, piercing, piping, shrieky, shrill, shrilly, treble. —*See also* **costly, drugged, drunk, elated, elevated** (4), **elevated** (2), **intense.**
high *noun.* —*See* **thrill.**

high-and-mighty *adjective.* —*See* **arrogant.**

highball *verb.* —*See* **rush.**

highborn *adjective.* —*See* **noble.**

highbred *adjective.* —*See* **noble, thoroughbred.**

highbrow *adjective.* —*See* **cultured, intellectual.**
highbrow *noun.* —*See* **mind** (2).

higher *adjective.* Being at a rank or level above another ▶ greater, senior, superior, upper.

higher-up *noun. Informal* One who stands above another in rank ▶ better, elder, senior, superior. [*Compare* **chief.**]

highest *adjective.* Of, being, located at, or forming the top ▶ loftiest, top, topmost, upmost, uppermost. [*Compare* **climactic.**] —*See also* **best** (1).

highfalutin *or* **hifalutin** *adjective.* —*See* **pompous.**

high-flown *adjective.* —*See* **elevated** (4), **oratorical.**

highflying *adjective.* —*See* **ambitious.**

high-grade *adjective.* —*See* **choice** (1).

high-hat *verb.* To treat in a superciliously indulgent manner ▶ condescend, patronize. ***Idiom:*** speak (*or* talk) down to. [*Compare* **insult, snub.**]
high-hat *adjective.* —*See* **arrogant, snobbish.**

high jinks *or* **hijinks** *noun.* —*See* **mischief.**

highlight *verb.* —*See* **emphasize.**
highlight *noun.* Light that is reflected ▶ glare, reflection. [*Compare* **flash.**]

highly *adverb.* —*See* **very.**

high-minded *adjective.* —*See* **elevated** (3).

high-pitched *adjective.* —*See* **high** (3).

high-priced *adjective.* —*See* **costly.**

high-ranking *adjective.* —*See* **exalted.**

high sign *noun.* —*See* **alarm, gesture.**

high-sounding *adjective.* —*See* **oratorical.**

high-speed *adjective.* —*See* **fast** (1).

high-spirited *adjective.* —*See* **lively.**

hightail *verb.* —*See* **run** (2).
high-up *noun.* —*See* **dignitary.**
highway *noun.* —*See* **way** (2).
highwayman *noun.* —*See* **thief.**
hijack *verb.* —*See* **coerce, seize** (1).
hike *verb.* **1.** To travel about or journey on foot ▶ backpack, march, tramp, trek. [*Compare* **journey, rove, walk.**] **2.** To increase in amount ▶ boost, jack (up), jump, raise, up. —*See also* **elevate** (1).
hike *noun.* —*See* **increase** (1), **increase** (2), **walk** (1).
hilarious *adjective.* —*See* **funny** (1).
hilarity *noun.* —*See* **merriment** (1).
hill *noun.* A natural land elevation ▶ bump, butte, down, eminence, hummock, knoll, prominence, rise. [*Compare* **plateau.**] —*See also* **heap** (1).
hill *verb.* —*See* **heap** (1).
hillbilly *noun.* —*See* **clodhopper.**
hilt *noun.* A protrusion or extension designed to be grasped by the hand ▶ haft, handgrip, handle. [*Compare* **hold, knob.**]
hind *adjective.* —*See* **back.**
hind end *noun.* —*See* **back.**
hinder *verb.* To interfere with the progress of ▶ bog (down), dampen, encumber, forestall, hamper, hold back, impede, interfere with, obstruct, retard, stem. ***Idioms:*** be (*or* stand *or* get) in the way of, put a damper on. [*Compare* **frustrate, restrain, stop.**] —*See also* **delay** (1).

✚ CORE SYNONYMS: *hinder, hamper, impede, obstruct.* These verbs mean to interfere with the progress of someone or something. To *hinder* is to hold back and often implies stopping or prevention: *The travelers were hindered by storms.* To *hamper* is to hinder by or as if by fastening or entangling: *His clothes hampered his efforts to swim to safety.* To *impede* is to slow by making action or movement difficult: "*Our journey was impeded by a thousand obstacles*" (Mary Shelley). *Obstruct* implies the presence of obstacles: *Competing agendas obstructed our ability to negotiate effectively.*

hindmost *or* **hindermost** *adjective.* —*See* **back, last**[1] (2).
hindquarters *noun.* —*See* **buttocks.**
hindrance *noun.* —*See* **bar** (1).
hinge on *or* **upon** *verb.* —*See* **depend on** (2).
hint *noun.* **1.** A subtle quality underlying or felt to underlie a situation, action, or person ▶ glimmering, implication, inkling, suspicion, undercurrent, undertone. **2.** A brief or indirect suggestion ▶ allusion, clue, cue, innuendo, insinuation, intimation, suggestion, wink. —*See also* **shade** (2), **tip**[3].
hint *verb.* To convey an idea by indirect, subtle means ▶ allude to, hint at, imply, insinuate, intimate, suggest. ***Idiom:*** drop a hint.

✚ CORE SYNONYMS: *hint, suggest, imply, intimate, insinuate.* These verbs mean to convey thoughts or ideas by indirect, subtle means. *Hint* refers to an oblique or covert suggestion that often contains clues: *My imagination supplied the explanation you only hinted at.* *Suggest* refers to the calling of something to mind as the result of an association of ideas: "*his erect and careless attitude suggesting assurance and power*" (Joseph Conrad). To *imply* is to suggest a thought or an idea by letting it be inferred from something else, such as a statement, that is more explicit: *The effusive praise the professor heaped on one of the students seemed to imply disapproval of the rest.* *Intimate* applies to indirect, subtle expression that often reflects discretion, tact, or reserve: *She intimated that her neighbors were having marital problems.* To *insinuate* is to suggest something, usually something unpleasant, in a covert, sly, and underhanded manner: *The columnist insinuated that the candidate raised money unethically.*

hinterland *noun.* —*See* **country.**

hip *adjective.* —*See* **aware, fashionable.**

hire *verb.* To engage the temporary use of something for a fee ▶ charter, lease, rent (out). —*See also* **employ** (1), **lease** (1).

hire *noun.* **1.** The act of employing for wages ▶ employment, engagement, hiring, retention. **2.** The state of being employed ▶ employ, employment, service. —*See also* **employee, wage.**

hired *adjective.* —*See* **employed.**

hired hand *or* **hireling** *noun.* —*See* **employee.**

hirer *noun.* One that employs persons for wages ▶ employer.

hirsute *adjective.* —*See* **hairy.**

hiss *noun.* **1.** A sibilant sound ▶ fizz, fizzing, fizzle, fizzling, rustle, rustling, sibilant, sizzle, sizzling, swish, swishing, whiz, whizzing, whoosh, whooshing. **2.** One of various derisive sounds of disapproval ▶ boo, catcall, hoot. *Slang:* bird, Bronx cheer, raspberry, razz.

hiss *verb.* **1.** To make a sibilant sound ▶ fizz, fizzle, rustle, sibilate, sizzle, swish, whiz, whoosh. **2.** To make a derisive sound of disapproval ▶ boo, catcall, hoot. *Slang:* bird, Bronx cheer, raspberry, razz. ***Idioms:*** give (*or* blow) a Bronx cheer, give (*or* blow) a raspberry. —*See also* **burn** (2).

hissy fit *noun.* —*See* **temper** (2).

historic *adjective.* —*See* **important, vintage.**

history *noun.* **1.** A chronological record of past events ▶ annals, archive, chronicle, historical record. [*Compare* **antiquity.**] **2.** One's previous experiences ▶ background, career, credentials, curriculum vitae, life history, past, record, resumé, vita. [*Compare* **accomplishment, qualification.**] —*See also* **story** (1).

histrionic *or* **histrionical** *adjective.* —*See* **dramatic** (1), **dramatic** (2).

histrionics *noun.* —*See* **theatrics** (2).

hit *verb.* To deliver a sudden, sharp blow to ▶ bash, box, bust, catch, clout, jab, knock, pop, punch, slam, slog, slug, smash, smite, sock, strike, swat, swing at, thwack, whack, wham, whop. *Informal:* biff, bop, clip, wallop. *Slang:* belt, conk, nail, paste. ***Idioms:*** let fly at, let someone have it, sock it to someone, take a swing (*or* swipe) at. —*See also* **collide, encounter** (1), **kill**[1], **strike** (2).

hit back *verb.* —*See* **retaliate.**

hit on *verb.* —*See* **accomplish.**

hit *noun.* A dazzling, often sudden instance of success ▶ sleeper. *Informal:* knockout, smash, smash hit, ten-strike, winner, wow. *Slang:* boff, boffo, boffola. [*Compare* **accomplishment.**] —*See also* **blow**[2], **collision, murder, pull** (2).

hitch *verb.* —*See* **fasten, stagger** (1).

hitch up *verb.* —*See* **elevate** (1).

hitch *noun.* **1.** A prison term ▶ stretch, time. **2.** *Informal* A tricky or unsuspected condition ▶ catch, rub, snag. [*Compare* **bar, disadvantage, trick.**] —*See also* **bond** (2), **turn** (1).

hit man *noun.* —*See* **murderer.**

hit-or-miss *adjective.* —*See* **random.**

hive *verb.* —*See* **accumulate.**

hoard *noun.* A supply stored or hidden for possible future use ▶ backlog, cache, inventory, nest egg, provision, reserve, reservoir, stash, stock, stockpile, store, supply, treasure. [*Compare* **accumulation.**]

hoard *verb.* —*See* **save** (1).

hoarse *adjective.* Rough, raw, or grating in sound ▶ croaking, croaky, gravelly, gruff, husky, ragged, raw. —*See also* **harsh.**

hoary *adjective.* —*See* **old** (2).

hoax *verb.* —*See* **cheat** (1).

hoax *noun.* —*See* **cheat** (1).

hobble *verb.* —*See* **hamper**[1], **stagger** (1).

hobble *noun.* —*See* **bond** (1).

hobby *noun.* —*See* **amusement.**

hobbyhorse *noun.* —*See* **enthusiasm** (2).

hobnob *verb.* —*See* **associate** (2).

hobo *noun.* One who wanders without a permanent home or livelihood ▶ drifter, gadabout, gypsy, itinerant, migrant, nomad, peregrinator, peripatetic, roamer, rover, swagman, tramp, transient, vagabond, vagrant, wanderer. [*Compare* **pauper.**]

hock *verb.* —*See* **pawn**[1]**.**

hocus-pocus *noun.* —*See* **gibberish.**

hodgepodge *noun.* —*See* **assortment.**

hoggish *adjective.* —*See* **gluttonous.**

hogtie *verb.* —*See* **hamper**[1]**.**

hogwash *noun.* —*See* **nonsense.**

hoi polloi *noun.* —*See* **commonalty.**

hoist *verb.* —*See* **elevate** (1).

hoist *noun.* —*See* **lift.**

hoity-toity *adjective.* —*See* **exclusive** (3), **pompous.**

hokey *adjective.* —*See* **sentimental.**

hold *verb.* **1.** To have and maintain in one's possession ▶ hold back, keep (back), reserve, retain, stick with, withhold. **2.** To be filled by ▶ contain, have. [*Compare* **constitute.**] **3.** To have the room or capacity for ▶ accommodate, contain. **4.** To view in a certain way ▶ believe, feel, sense, think. [*Compare* **perceive, regard.**] **5.** To prove valid under scrutiny ▶ hold up, prove out, stand up. *Informal:* wash. —*See also* **assert, bear** (1), **believe** (3), **command** (2), **embrace** (1), **grip, have** (3), **imprison, restrain, occupy** (2), **support** (2).

hold back *verb.* —*See* **hinder, repress, restrain.**

hold down *verb.* —*See* **repress, restrain.**

hold in *verb.* —*See* **restrain.**

hold off *verb.* —*See* **defer**[1]**, refrain.**

hold out *verb.* —*See* **endure** (2), **offer** (1).

hold up *verb.* To prove valid under scrutiny ▶ prove out, stand up. *Informal:* wash. —*See also* **bear, defer**[1]**, delay** (1), **rob.**

hold with *verb.* To be favorably disposed toward ▶ approve, countenance, favor. *Informal:* go for. ***Idioms:*** be in favor of, take kindly to, think highly (*or* well) of. [*Compare* **assent, value.**]

hold *noun.* **1.** An act or means of holding something ▶ clasp, clench, clutch, grapple, grasp, grip. **2.** Intellectual hold ▶ apprehension, comprehension, grasp, grip, understanding. [*Compare* **knowledge.**]

✤ **CORE SYNONYMS:** *hold, keep, retain, withhold, reserve.* These verbs mean to have and maintain in one's possession or control. *Hold* and *keep* are the most general: *A movie must be compelling in order to hold my interest. We received a few offers but decided to keep the house. Retain* means to continue to hold, especially in the face of possible loss: *Though unhappy, he retained his sense of humor. Withhold* implies reluctance or refusal to give, grant, or allow: *The tenant withheld his rent until the owner fixed the boiler.* To *reserve* is to hold back for the future or for a special purpose: *The farmer reserved two acres for an orchard.*

---

holder *noun.* An object, such as a carton, can, or jar, in which material is held or carried ▶ container, receptacle, repository, vessel. [*Compare* **depository, package.**] —*See also* **owner.**

holdings *noun.* A thing or set of things, such as land and assets, legally possessed ▶ belongings, estate, possessions, property. [*Compare* **effects.**]

holdup *noun.* —*See* **delay** (1), **delay** (2), **larceny.**

hole *noun.* **1.** A space in an otherwise solid mass ▶ cavity, hollow, pocket, space, vacuity, void. [*Compare* **crack, cut.**] **2.** An open space allowing passage ▶ aperture, eyelet, mouth, opening, orifice, outlet, slot, tunnel, vent. [*Compare* **gap, prick.**] **3.** A place used as an animal's dwelling ▶ burrow, den, lair. [*Compare* **cave.**] —*See also* **hut, predicament.**

hole *verb.* —*See* **breach.**

hole up *verb. Informal* To shut oneself up in secrecy ▶ hide out. ***Idioms:*** go underground, lay (*or* lie) low.

holiday *noun.* A regularly scheduled period spent away from work or duty, often in recreation ▶ furlough, leave, sabbatical, vacation. ***Idioms:*** time (*or* day) off. [*Compare* **break, trip.**] *—See also* **celebration** (1).

holier-than-thou *adjective.* Piously or overly sure of one's own righteousness ▶ moralistic, self-righteous. [*Compare* **arrogant, hypocritical, moral.**]

holiness *noun.* The quality of being or acting in accordance with what is holy or sacred ▶ beatitude, blessedness, divineness, godliness, grace, hallowedness, inviolability, sacredness, sacrosanctity, saintliness, sanctity, venerability, venerableness. [*Compare* **devotion.**]

holler *verb.* *—See* **bawl, complain, shout.**

holler *noun.* *—See* **shout.**

hollow *adjective.* **1.** Lacking value, use, or substance ▶ empty, idle, otiose, vacant, vain. [*Compare* **futile.**] **2.** Curving inward ▶ carved out, cavernous, concave, depressed, indented, sunken.

hollow *noun.* *—See* **depression** (1), **hole** (1), **valley.**

✚ **CORE SYNONYMS:** *hollow, empty, idle, otiose, vain.* These adjectives mean lacking value, use, or substance: *hollow threats; empty pleasures; idle dreams; an otiose belief in alchemy; vain regrets.*

---

hollow-eyed *adjective.* *—See* **haggard.**

hollowness *noun.* A desolate sense of loss ▶ blankness, desolation, emptiness, vacuum, void. *—See also* **emptiness** (2).

holocaust *noun.* *—See* **disaster, massacre.**

holy *adjective.* Regarded with particular reverence or respect, especially by a religion ▶ blessed, consecrated, hallowed, inviolable, sacred, sacrosanct, sanctified, venerable, venerated, virtuous. *—See also* **divine** (1), **divine** (2), **pious.**

holy war *noun.* A goal served with great or uncompromising dedication ▶ cause, crusade, jihad. [*Compare* **drive.**]

homage *noun.* *—See* **honor** (1).

home *noun.* **1.** A building or shelter where one lives ▶ abode, domicile, dwelling, habitation, house, lodging, place, residence. *Informal:* address, headquarters, nest, pad. *Slang:* digs. **2.** The natural environment specific to an animal or plant ▶ habitat, habitation, niche, range, territory. **3.** An institution that provides care and shelter ▶ asylum, hospice, hospital, sanatorium, shelter. *—See also* **base[1]** (1).

home *adjective.* *—See* **domestic** (1), **domestic** (3).

home base *noun.* *—See* **base[1]** (1).

homegrown *adjective.* *—See* **domestic** (3), **indigenous.**

homeliness *noun.* *—See* **ugliness.**

homely *adjective.* *—See* **domestic** (1), **ordinary, rustic, ugly.**

homemade *adjective.* *—See* **rude** (1).

home office *noun.* *—See* **base[1]** (1).

homespun *adjective.* *—See* **rustic.**

homey *adjective.* *—See* **comfortable, domestic** (1).

homicidal *adjective.* *—See* **murderous.**

homicide *noun.* *—See* **murder, murderer.**

homily *noun.* *—See* **speech** (2).

hominoid *adjective.* *—See* **humanlike.**

homogenize *verb.* *—See* **conventionalize, mix** (1).

homophile *adjective.* Having a sexual orientation to members of one's own sex ▶ gay, homosexual, lesbian.

Homo sapiens *noun.* *—See* **human being, humankind.**

homosexual *adjective.* Having a sexual orientation to members of one's own sex ▶ gay, homophile, lesbian.

homesteader *noun.* *—See* **settler.**

honcho *noun.* *—See* **chief.**

hone[1] *verb.* *—See* **perfect, sharpen.**

hone in *verb.* *—See* **concentrate.**

hone² *verb.* —*See* **desire.**

honest *adjective.* Marked by uprightness in principle and action ▶ aboveboard, good, honorable, incorruptible, respectable, righteous, straight, true, truthful, upright, upstanding, veracious. *Informal:* straight-shooting. ***Idioms:*** on the up-and-up. [*Compare* **ethical, innocent, moral.**] —*See also* **dependable, frank, genuine.**

honesty *noun.* The quality of being honest ▶ candidness, frankness, honor, honorableness, incorruptibility, integrity, openness, plainspokenness, reliability, righteousness, sincerity, truth, trustworthiness, upstandingness. —*See also* **character** (2).

honey *noun.* —*See* **darling** (1).

honey *verb.* —*See* **coax, flatter** (1), **sweeten.**

honeyed *adjective.* Having or suggesting the taste of sugar ▶ saccharine, sugary, sweet.

honky-tonk *noun. Slang* A disreputable or run-down bar or restaurant ▶ *Slang:* dive, dump, joint, juke house, juke joint. ***Idiom:*** hole in the wall.

honor *noun.* **1.** Great respect or high public esteem accorded as a right or as due ▶ deference, homage, obeisance, reverence, veneration. [*Compare* **testimonial.**] **2.** A person's high standing among others ▶ dignity, good name, good report, prestige, reputation, repute, respect, status. [*Compare* **exaltation.**] —*See also* **character** (2), **distinction** (2), **esteem, honesty.**

honor *verb.* **1.** To pay tribute or homage to ▶ acclaim, celebrate, eulogize, exalt, extol, glorify, hail, laud, lionize, magnify, panegyrize, praise. ***Idiom:*** sing someone's praises. [*Compare* **revere.**] **2.** To lend dignity or honor to by an act or favor ▶ enrich, favor, grace, dignify. [*Compare* **exalt.**] **3.** To bestow a reward on ▶ award, guerdon, reward. [*Compare* **confer.**] —*See also* **distinguish** (3), **drink** (4), **value.**

✤ **CORE SYNONYMS:** *honor, homage, reverence, veneration, deference.* These nouns denote respect or high public esteem accorded to another as a right or as due. *Honor* is the most general term: *The hero tried to be worthy of the honor in which he was held. Homage* is often in the form of a ceremonial tribute that conveys allegiance: "*There is no country in which so absolute a homage is paid to wealth*" (Ralph Waldo Emerson). *Reverence* is a feeling of deep respect and devotion: "*Kill reverence and you've killed the hero in man*" (Ayn Rand). *Veneration* is both the feeling and the reverential expression of respect, love, and awe: *Her veneration for her mentor never wavered. Deference* is courteous, respectful regard for another that often implies yielding to him or her: *The funeral was arranged with deference to the family of the deceased.*

---

honorable *adjective.* —*See* **admirable, honest.**

honorableness *noun.* —*See* **honesty.**

honorarium *noun.* —*See* **reward.**

hoodlum *or* **hood** *noun.* —*See* **thug.**

hoodoo *noun.* Something or someone believed to bring bad luck ▶ curse, evil eye, hex, Jonah. *Informal:* jinx. [*Compare* **charm, magic.**]

hoodoo *verb.* To bring bad luck or evil to ▶ curse, hex. *Informal:* jinx. [*Compare* **afflict.**]

hoodwink *verb.* —*See* **deceive.**

hooey *noun.* —*See* **nonsense.**

hoof *verb.* —*See* **dance, walk.**

hoofer *noun. Slang* A person who dances, especially professionally ▶ chorine, chorus boy, chorus girl, dancer, terpsichorean.

hoo-hah *noun.* —*See* **agitation** (1), **sensation** (2).

hook *noun.* —*See* **bend, fastener.**

hook *verb.* —*See* **bend** (1), **catch** (1), **catch** (3), **steal.**

hook up *verb.* To come together by arrangement ▶ connect, get together, meet (up), rendezvous.
hooker *noun.* —*See* **harlot.**
hookup *noun.* —*See* **relation** (1).
hooky *noun.* —*See* **absence** (1).
hooligan *noun.* —*See* **thug.**
hoop *noun.* —*See* **basket** (3), **circle** (1).
hoopla *noun.* —*See* **publicity.**
hoosegow *noun.* —*See* **jail.**
hoot *noun.* —*See* **hiss** (2), **scream** (2).
hoot *verb.* —*See* **hiss** (2).
hop *verb. Informal* To go aboard a means of transport ▶ board, catch, take. —*See also* **bound[1].**
hop up *verb.* —*See* **intensify.**
hop *noun.* A bouncing movement ▶ bounce, bound, rebound. —*See also* **bound[1]** (2), **dance.**
hope *verb.* —*See* **desire.**
hope *noun.* —*See* **dream** (3).
hopeful *adjective.* —*See* **encouraging, expectant.**
hopeful *noun.* One who aspires ▶ aspirant, aspirer. *Informal:* wannabe. —*See also* **applicant, comer** (2).
hopefulness *noun.* The condition of looking forward to something, especially with eagerness ▶ anticipation, expectance, expectancy, expectation, high hopes. [*Compare* **desire.**] —*See also* **optimism.**
hopeless *adjective.* Offering no hope or expectation of improvement ▶ cureless, incurable, irremediable, irreparable, lost, remediless. [*Compare* **futile.**] —*See also* **despondent.**
hopelessness *noun.* —*See* **despair.**
hopped-up *adjective.* —*See* **drugged.**
hopping *adjective.* —*See* **busy** (2).
horde *noun.* —*See* **crowd.**
horizon *noun.* —*See* **ken.**
horizontal *adjective.* —*See* **flat** (1).
hornets' nest *noun.* —*See* **problem.**
horn in *verb.* —*See* **intrude, meddle.**
horniness *noun.* —*See* **desire** (2).
horrendous *adjective.* —*See* **terrible.**
horrible *adjective.* Causing great horror ▶ bloodcurdling, hair-raising, harrowing, horrid, horrific, horrifying, nightmarish, petrifying, terrific, terrifying. —*See also* **ghastly** (1), **terrible.**
horrid *adjective.* —*See* **ghastly** (1), **horrible, offensive** (1).
horrific *adjective.* —*See* **horrible.**
horrified *adjective.* —*See* **afraid.**
horrify *verb.* —*See* **frighten.**
horror *noun.* —*See* **fear, hate** (1), **hate** (2), **outrage.**
hors d'oeuvre *noun.* —*See* **appetizer.**
horse around *verb. Informal* To make jokes; behave playfully ▶ jest, joke, quip. *Informal:* clown (around), fool around. ***Idioms:*** crack wise, play the fool. —*See also* **misbehave, play** (1).
horseplay *noun.* —*See* **misbehavior.**
horse sense *noun.* —*See* **common sense.**
hospice *noun.* —*See* **home** (3).
hospitable *adjective.* Characterized by kindness and warm, unaffected courtesy ▶ affable, courteous, gracious. [*Compare* **amiable, attentive, courteous.**]
hospital *noun.* —*See* **home** (3).
hospitality *noun.* —*See* **consideration** (1).
host *noun.* —*See* **crowd.**
hostage *noun.* —*See* **pawn[1].**
hostile *adjective.* **1.** Feeling or showing unfriendliness ▶ inimical, unfriendly. [*Compare* **mean[2].**] **2.** Not encouraging life or growth ▶ adverse, inhospitable, unfavorable. [*Compare* **severe.**] —*See also* **aggressive, belligerent, contrary.**
hostilities *noun.* —*See* **battle.**
hostility *noun.* —*See* **aggression, enmity.**
hot *adjective.* **1.** Marked by much heat ▶ ardent, baking, blistering, boiling, broiling, burning, fiery, heated, red-hot, roasting, scalding, scorching, searing, sizzling, sultry, sweltering, torrid, tropical, white-hot. ***Idioms:*** hot enough to fry an egg on, piping hot. **2.** *Informal* Of great current interest ▶ live, red-hot. [*Compare* **fashionable, important.**] —*See also* **desirable, eager, erotic,**

fashionable, feverish, marvelous, spicy.

hotbed *noun.* —*See* **center** (1), **origin.**

hot-blooded *adjective.* —*See* **passionate.**

hotdog *noun. Slang* A person who behaves ostentatiously or performs dangerous stunts ▶ showoff, showboat. [*Compare* **braggart.**]

hot-dog *verb. Slang* To behave in an ostentatious manner or perform dangerous stunts ▶ show off, showboat. [*Compare* **boast, swagger.**]

hotfoot *verb.* —*See* **run** (2), **rush.**

hotheaded *adjective.* —*See* **argumentative, rash**[1]**.**

hotheadedness *noun.* —*See* **temper** (1).

hotness *noun.* —*See* **heat** (1).

hot pursuit *noun.* The following of another in an attempt to overtake and capture ▶ chase, hunt, pursuit.

hot spot *noun.* —*See* **predicament.**

hot water *noun.* —*See* **emergency, predicament.**

hound *verb.* —*See* **harass.**

hound *noun.* —*See* **fan**[2]**.**

house *noun.* A group of people living together as a unit ▶ family, household, ménage. —*See also* **company** (1), **family** (2), **home** (1).

house *verb.* To give refuge to ▶ harbor, haven, shelter, take in. [*Compare* **defend.**] —*See also* **live**[1]**, lodge.**

housebreak *verb.* —*See* **domesticate.**

housebreaker *noun.* —*See* **thief.**

housebroken *adjective.* —*See* **domestic** (2).

housecleaning *noun. Informal* A thorough or drastic reorganization ▶ overhaul, reengineering, reshuffling, shakeup. [*Compare* **renewal, revolution.**]

household *noun.* A group of people living together as a unit ▶ family, house, ménage.

household *adjective.* —*See* **domestic** (1).

house of correction *noun.* —*See* **jail.**

house-train *verb.* —*See* **domesticate.**

house-trained *adjective.* —*See* **domestic** (2).

housing *noun.* Dwellings in general ▶ lodging, shelter. ***Idiom:*** a roof over one's head. [*Compare* **home, hut.**]

hovel *noun.* —*See* **hut.**

hover *verb.* To remain stationary over a place or object ▶ hang, poise. —*See also* **float** (1), **threaten** (2).

however *adverb.* —*See* **still** (1).

howl *verb.* To utter or emit a long, mournful, plaintive sound ▶ bay, moan, ululate, wail, yowl. —*See also* **bawl, cry, laugh, shout.**

howl *noun.* A long, mournful cry ▶ bay, moan, ululation, wail, yowl. —*See also* **laugh, scream** (2), **shout.**

howler *noun.* —*See* **blunder.**

hub *noun.* —*See* **center** (1), **center** (3).

hubbub *noun.* —*See* **noise** (1).

hubris *noun.* —*See* **arrogance.**

huckster *verb.* To travel about selling goods ▶ hawk, peddle, vend. —*See also* **haggle.**

huddle *verb.* —*See* **confer** (1), **stoop.**

huddle *noun.* —*See* **group.**

hue *noun.* —*See* **color** (1), **shade** (1).

huff *noun.* —*See* **offense, temper** (2).

huff *verb.* —*See* **insult, pant.**

huffy *adjective.* —*See* **angry.**

hug *verb.* —*See* **embrace** (1).

hug *noun.* —*See* **embrace.**

huge *adjective.* —*See* **enormous.**

hugely *adverb.* —*See* **very.**

hugeness *noun.* —*See* **enormousness.**

huggermugger *noun.* —*See* **secrecy.**

huggermugger *adjective.* —*See* **secret** (1).

huggermugger *adverb.* —*See* **secretly.**

huggermuggery *noun.* —*See* **secrecy.**

hulk *noun.* —*See* **giant, oaf.**

hulk *verb.* —*See* **blunder.**

hulking *or* **hulky** *adjective.* —*See* **bulky** (2).

hull *noun.* —*See* **skin** (3).

hull *verb.* —*See* **skin.**

hullabaloo *noun.* —*See* **noise** (1), **vociferation.**

hum *verb.* To make a continuous low-pitched droning sound ▶ bombinate, bumble, burr, buzz, drone, purr, whir, whiz.

hum *noun.* A continuous low-pitched droning sound ▶ bumble, burr, buzz, buzzing, drone, humming, purr, purring, whir, whirring, whiz, whizzing.

human *adjective.* Of or characteristic of human beings or humankind ▶ anthropic, anthropical, anthropoid, mortal. —*See also* **humanitarian.**

human *noun.* —*See* **human being.**

human being *noun.* A member of the human race ▶ being, body, creature, earthling, Homo sapiens, human, individual, life, man, mortal, party, person, personage, self, soul, spirit.

humane *adjective.* —*See* **ethical, humanitarian.**

humanistic *adjective.* —*See* **broad-minded.**

humanitarian *adjective.* Concerned with human welfare and the remedying of social ills ▶ charitable, compassionate, human, humane, humanistic, merciful, philanthropic, public-spirited, social-minded. [*Compare* **benevolent, generous, liberal, selfless.**]

humanitarian *noun.* —*See* **donor.**

✚ **CORE SYNONYMS:** *humanitarian, humane, compassionate, merciful.* These adjectives mean concerned with human welfare, the remedying of social ills, and the alleviation of suffering: *released the prisoner for humanitarian reasons; a humane physician; compassionate toward impoverished people; is merciful to the repentant.*

---

humanity *noun.* —*See* **benevolence, humankind.**

humanize *verb.* To fit for companionship with others, especially in attitude or manners ▶ acculturate, civilize, socialize.

humanizing *adjective.* —*See* **cultural.**

humankind *noun.* Humans as a group ▶ earth, flesh, Homo sapiens, human beings, humanity, human race, man, mankind, men and women, mortals, universe, world. [*Compare* **public.**]

humanlike *or* **humanoid** *adjective.* Resembling a human being ▶ anthropoid, anthropomorphic, anthropomorphous, hominoid, manlike. [*Compare* **human.**]

human race *noun.* —*See* **humankind.**

humble *adjective.* **1.** Having or expressing feelings of humility ▶ lowly, meek, modest, unambitious. [*Compare* **deferential.**] **2.** Of little distinction ▶ lowly, mean, simple. [*Compare* **modest.**] —*See also* **lowly** (1).

humble *verb.* To lower the pride or dignity of ▶ abase, debase, deflate, degrade, demean, humiliate, lower, mortify, puncture. *Slang:* put down. ***Idioms:*** bring low, put in one's place, take (*or* bring) down a notch, take (*or* bring) down a peg. [*Compare* **belittle, disgrace, shame.**] —*See also* **debase.**

humbleness *noun.* —*See* **modesty** (1).

humbug *noun.* —*See* **cheat** (1), **fake.**

humbug *verb.* —*See* **deceive.**

humdrum *adjective.* —*See* **boring, dull** (1), **ordinary.**

humdrum *noun.* —*See* **monotony.**

humid *adjective.* —*See* **sticky** (2).

humiliate *verb.* —*See* **disgrace, humble.**

humiliating *adjective.* —*See* **disgraceful.**

humiliation *noun.* —*See* **degradation** (1), **disgrace.**

humility *noun.* —*See* **modesty** (1).

humming *adjective.* —*See* **active, busy** (2).

hummock *noun.* —*See* **hill.**

humor *noun.* The quality of being laughable or comical ▶ comedy, comicality, comicalness, drollery, drollness, farcicality, funniness, humorousness, jocoseness, jocosity, jocularity, ludicrousness, ridiculousness, wit, wittiness, zaniness. —*See also* **disposition, fancy, mood.**

humor *verb.* To comply with the wishes or ideas of another ▶ cater (to), gratify, indulge. [*Compare* **defer.**] —*See also* **baby.**

humorist *noun.* —*See* **joker.**

humorous *adjective.* —*See* **clever** (2), **funny** (1).

humorousness *noun.* —*See* **humor.**

hump *noun.* —*See* **bump** (1).

hump *verb.* —*See* **stoop.**

humus *noun.* —*See* **earth** (1).

hunch *noun.* —*See* **feeling** (1), **lump**[1].

hunch *verb.* —*See* **stoop.**

hunger *noun.* —*See* **appetite, desire** (1).

hunger *verb.* To have a greedy, obsessive desire ▶ crave, itch, lust, thirst. [*Compare* **desire.**]

hungry *adjective.* **1.** Desiring or craving food ▶ famished, ravenous, starving, voracious. *Informal:* starved. ***Idiom:*** hungry as a wolf. **2.** Having desire for something ▶ desiring, desirous, hankering. [*Compare* **voracious.**] —*See also* **greedy.**

hunk *noun.* —*See* **beauty, lump**[1].

hunker down *verb.* To sit on one's heels ▶ squat. —*See also* **stoop.**

hunt *verb.* To look for and pursue game in order to capture or kill it ▶ chase (down), drive, run (down), stalk. [*Compare* **track.**] —*See also* **pursue** (1).

hunt down *verb.* —*See* **trace** (1).

hunt for *verb.* —*See* **seek** (1).

hunt *noun.* The following of another in an attempt to overtake and capture ▶ chase, hot pursuit, pursuit. —*See also* **pursuit** (2).

hurdle *noun.* —*See* **bar** (1).

hurdle *verb.* To pass by or over successfully ▶ clear, negotiate, surmount. —*See also* **jump** (1).

hurl *verb.* —*See* **throw, vomit.**

hurl *noun.* —*See* **throw.**

hurried *adjective.* —*See* **abrupt** (2), **fast** (1), **quick.**

hurriedly *adverb.* —*See* **fast.**

hurriedness *noun.* —*See* **haste** (2).

hurry *verb.* —*See* **rush, speed.**

hurry *noun.* —*See* **haste** (1).

hurry-scurry *noun.* —*See* **agitation** (2).

hurry-up *adjective.* Designed to meet emergency needs as quickly as possible ▶ *Informal:* crash, rush.

hurt *verb.* **1.** To cause bodily damage to a living thing ▶ injure, traumatize, wing, wound. [*Compare* **cut, break.**] **2.** To cause pain, soreness, or discomfort; be painful ▶ ache, bite, burn, smart, sting, twinge. **3.** To cause pain, soreness, or discomfort to ▶ bother, inflame, irritate, pain, pang, twinge. [*Compare* **afflict.**] —*See also* **damage, distress, offend** (1).

hurt *noun.* —*See* **distress, harm.**

hurtful *adjective.* —*See* **harmful, offensive** (2), **painful.**

hurtle *verb.* —*See* **shoot** (3), **throw.**

hurtless *adjective.* —*See* **harmless.**

husband *noun.* —*See* **spouse.**

husband *verb.* To protect an asset from loss or destruction ▶ conserve, preserve, save. [*Compare* **defend.**]

husbandry *noun.* —*See* **conservation.**

hush *verb.* —*See* **censor** (2), **conceal, repress, silence.**

hush *noun.* —*See* **silence** (1), **stillness.**

hushed *adjective.* —*See* **silent** (1), **soft** (2).

hush-hush *adjective.* —*See* **confidential** (1), **secret** (1).

husk *noun.* —*See* **skin** (3).

husk *verb.* —*See* **skin.**

husky[1] *adjective.* —*See* **hoarse.**

husky[2] *adjective.* —*See* **bulky** (2), **muscular.**

hussy *noun.* —*See* **slut.**

hustle *verb.* —*See* **drive** (3), **rush, speed.**

hustle *noun.* —*See* **drive** (2), **haste** (1), **trick** (1).

hustler *noun.* An intensely energetic, enthusiastic person ▶ demon, dynamo. *Informal:* eager beaver, firebreather, go-getter, live wire. —*See also* **prostitute.**

hut *noun.* A small, usually roughly built shelter ▶ cabin, hole, hovel, lean-to, shack, shanty, shed.

hutch *noun.* —*See* **cage.**

hutzpah *noun. See* **chutzpah.**

hyaline *adjective.* Of or resembling glass ▶ glasslike, glassy, vitreous, vitrescent. [*Compare* **translucent.**] —*See also* **clear** (1).

hybrid *noun.* —*See* **combination.**

hygienic *adjective.* —*See* **healthful, sterile** (1).

hymeneal *adjective.* —*See* **marital.**

hymn *noun.* —*See* **song.**

hymn *verb.* —*See* **praise** (3).

hype *noun.* —*See* **publicity.**

hype *verb.* —*See* **promote** (3).

hyper *adjective.* —*See* **edgy.**

hyperbole *or* **hyperbolism** *noun.* —*See* **exaggeration.**

hyperbolic *adjective.* —*See* **exaggerated.**

hyperbolize *verb.* —*See* **exaggerate.**

hypercritic *noun.* —*See* **critic** (2).

hypercritical *adjective.* —*See* **critical** (1).

hypersensitive *adjective.* —*See* **oversensitive.**

hypersensitivity *adjective.* —*See* **oversensitivity.**

hypnotic *adjective.* —*See* **soporific.**

hypnotic *noun.* —*See* **soporific.**

hypnotic state *noun.* —*See* **trance.**

hypnotize *verb.* —*See* **charm** (2).

hypocrisy *noun.* A show or expression of feelings or beliefs one does not actually hold or possess ▶ lip service, pharisaism, phoniness, piety, sanctimoniousness, sanctimony, tartuffery, two-facedness. [*Compare* **arrogance, deceit, dishonesty, faithlessness.**]

hypocrite *noun.* A person who practices hypocrisy ▶ dissembler, pharisee, phony, poser, tartuffe. [*Compare* **liar.**]

hypocritical *adjective.* Of or practicing hypocrisy ▶ Janus-faced, Pecksniffian, pharisaic, phony, pious, sanctimonious, two-faced. [*Compare* **arrogant, dishonest, faithless, underhand.**]

hypogeal *or* **hypogean** *or* **hypogeous** *adjective.* —*See* **underground.**

hypostasis *noun.* —*See* **embodiment.**

hypostatize *verb.* —*See* **embody** (1).

hypothecate *verb.* —*See* **pawn**[1].

hypothesis *noun.* —*See* **theory** (2).

hypothesize *verb.* To formulate as a tentative explanation ▶ speculate, theorize. [*Compare* **suppose.**]

hypothesized *or* **hypothetical** *adjective.* —*See* **supposed, theoretical** (2), **untried.**

hysterical *adjective.* —*See* **funny** (1).

I

I-beam *noun.* —*See* **beam** (2).

ice *verb.* —*See* **kill**[1].

iciness *noun.* —*See* **cold.**

icky *adjective.* —*See* **unpalatable, unpleasant.**

iconoclast *noun.* —*See* **rebel** (2).

icy *adjective.* —*See* **cold** (1), **cool.**

idea *noun.* That which exists in the mind as the product of careful mental activity ▶ concept, conception, image, notion, perception, thought. [*Compare* **decision, thought, understanding.**] —*See also* **approach** (1), **belief** (1), **feeling** (1), **import.**

✚ **CORE SYNONYMS:** *idea, thought, notion, concept, conception.* These nouns refer to that which exists in the mind as the product of careful mental activity. *Idea* has the widest range: *"Human history is in essence a history of ideas"* (H.G. Wells). *Thought* is distinctively intellectual and stresses contemplation and reasoning: *"Language is the dress of thought"* (Samuel Johnson). *Notion* often refers to a vague, general, or even fanciful idea: *"She certainly has some notion of drawing"* (Rudyard Kipling). *Concept* and *conception* are applied to mental formulations on a broad scale: *You seem to have absolutely no concept of time. "Every succeeding scientific discovery makes greater nonsense of old-time conceptions of sovereignty"* (Anthony Eden).

---

ideal *adjective.* Conforming to an ultimate form of perfection or excellence ▶ archetypal, archetypical, exemplary, idealized, model, perfect, quintessential, supreme. [*Compare* **excellent, perfect.**] —*See also* **theoretical** (2).

ideal *noun.* —*See* **dream** (3), **model.**

idealist *noun.* —*See* **dreamer** (1).

idealistic *adjective.* Characterized by ideals that often conflict with practical considerations ▶ blue-sky, impractical, quixotic, romantic, starry-eyed, unrealistic, utopian, visionary. ***Idiom:*** having one's head in the clouds. [*Compare* **impossible, optimistic.**]

ideate *verb.* —*See* **think** (1).

ideation *noun.* —*See* **thought.**

identical *adjective.* —*See* **equal, same.**

identicalness *noun.* The quality or condition of being exactly the same as something else ▶ identity, oneness, sameness, selfsameness. [*Compare* **likeness.**]

identify *verb.* To associate or affiliate oneself closely with a person or group ▶ empathize, relate, sympathize. [*Compare* **understand.**] —*See also* **associate** (3), **designate, distinguish** (2), **liken, mark** (1), **place** (1).

identity *noun.* **1.** The set of behavioral or personal characteristics by which an individual is recognizable ▶ distinctiveness, individualism, individuality, peculiarity, selfhood, singularity, uniqueness. [*Compare* **character.**] **2.** The quality or condition of being exactly the same as something else ▶ identicalness, oneness, sameness, selfsameness. [*Compare* **likeness.**]

ideological *adjective.* —*See* **theoretical** (1).

ideology *noun.* —*See* **doctrine.**

idiocy *noun.* —*See* **foolishness, nonsense, stupidity.**

idiom *noun.* —*See* **expression** (3), **language** (2).

idiosyncrasy *noun.* —*See* **eccentricity.**

idiosyncratic *adjective.* —*See* **eccentric.**

idiot *noun.* —*See* **dullard, fool.**

idiotic *adjective.* —*See* **foolish, stupid.**

idle *adjective.* **1.** Marked by a lack of activity or use ▶ inactive, inert, inoperative, unemployed, unoccupied, unused, vacant. [*Compare* **empty, motionless, still.**] **2.** Having no job ▶ jobless, unemployed, unoccupied, workless. ***Idioms:*** out of a job (*or* employ *or* work). —*See also* **baseless, hollow** (1), **lazy.**

idle *verb.* **1.** To pass time without working or in avoiding work ▶ bum (around), laze (around), loaf (around), loiter, lounge (around), piddle (around), shirk, slack off. *Informal:* vegetate. *Slang:* diddle (around), goldbrick, goof (off). ***Idioms:*** kill (*or* waste) time, twiddle one's thumbs. [*Compare* **delay.**] **2.** To spend (time) idly or pleasantly ▶ dawdle (away), fiddle away, idle away, kill, trifle away, waste, while (away), wile (away). [*Compare* **spend.**] —*See also* **stop** (2).

✚ **CORE SYNONYMS:** *idle, inactive, inert.* These adjectives mean marked by a lack of activity or use. *Idle* refers to persons who are not doing anything or are not busy: *employees idle because of the strike.* It also refers to what is not in use or operation: *idle machinery. Inactive* simply indicates absence of activity: *retired but not inactive; an inactive factory. Inert* describes things powerless to move themselves or to produce a desired effect; applied to persons, it implies lethargy or sluggishness, especially of mind or spirit: "*The Honorable Mrs. Jamieson . . . was fat and inert, and very much at the mercy of her old servants*" (Elizabeth C. Gaskell).

◀ **ANTONYM:** *active*

---

idleness *noun.* —*See* **inaction, laziness, stop** (2).

idler *noun.* —*See* **wastrel** (2).

idol *noun.* —*See* **celebrity.**

idolization *noun.* The act of adoring, especially reverently ▶ adoration, reverence, veneration, worship. [*Compare* **devotion, honor, praise.**]

idolize *verb.* —*See* **drool, revere.**

idyllic *adjective.* Charmingly simple and carefree ▶ arcadian, pastoral. [*Compare* **country, fresh, still.**]

i.e. *adverb.* —*See* **namely.**

iffy *adjective.* —*See* **ambiguous** (1), **debatable.**

ignis fatuus *noun.* —*See* **illusion.**

ignite *verb.* —*See* **light**[1] (1).

ignoble *adjective.* —*See* **lowly** (1), **sordid.**

ignominious *adjective.* —*See* **disgraceful.**

ignominiousness *noun.* —*See* **infamy.**

ignominy *noun.* —*See* **disgrace.**

ignorance *noun.* **1.** The condition of being ignorant; lack of knowledge or learning ▶ backwardness, benightedness, darkness, illiteracy, illiterateness, nescience, unintelligence. [*Compare* **inexperience, stupidity.**] **2.** The condition of being uninformed or unaware ▶ innocence, nescience, obliviousness, unawareness, unconsciousness, unfamiliarity. [*Compare* **artlessness, misunderstanding.**]

ignorant *adjective.* **1.** Without education or knowledge ▶ clueless, illiterate, lowbrow, nescient, uncultivated, uneducated, uninstructed, unlearned, unlettered, unread, unscholarly, unschooled, unstudious, untaught, untutored. ***Idiom:*** in the dark. [*Compare* **artless, backward, inexperienced.**] **2.** Exhibiting lack of education or knowledge ▶ backward, benighted, primitive, unenlightened, uninformed. [*Compare* **dumb, stupid.**] **3.** Not aware or informed ▶ clueless, ill-informed, innocent, misguided, misinformed, oblivious, unacquainted, unaware, unconscious, unenlightened, unfamiliar, unilluminated, uninformed, unknowing, unwitting. ***Idioms:*** in the dark, without a clue. [*Compare* **blind, confused.**]

ignore *verb.* —*See* **blink at, neglect** (1), **neglect** (2), **snub.**

ilk *noun.* —*See* **kind**[2].

ill *adjective.* —*See* **fateful** (1), **harmful, sick** (1).

ill *noun.* Whatever is destructive or harmful ▶ bad, badness, evil, worse. [*Compare* **harm.**] —*See also* **curse** (3), **disease.**

ill-advised *adjective.* —*See* **unwise.**

ill-behaved *adjective.* —*See* **unruly.**

ill-boding *adjective.* —*See* **fateful** (1).

ill-bred *adjective.* —*See* **coarse** (1), **disrespectful, rude** (2).

ill-chosen *adjective.* —*See* **unfortunate** (2).

ill-considered *adjective.* —*See* **rash**[1], **unwise.**

illegal *adjective.* Prohibited by law ▶ illegitimate, illicit, lawless, outlawed, unlawful, wrongful. ***Idiom:*** against the law. [*Compare* **forbidden.**] —*See also* **criminal** (1).

illegality *noun.* The state or quality of being illegal ▶ illegitimacy, illicitness, lawlessness, unlawfulness. —*See also* **crime** (1).

illegitimacy *noun.* The state or quality of being illegal ▶ illegality, illicitness, lawlessness, unlawfulness.

illegitimate *adjective.* Born to parents who are not married to each other ▶ baseborn, bastard, misbegotten, natural, spurious, unlawful. ***Idiom:*** born out of wedlock. —*See also* **criminal** (1), **illegal.**

ill-fated *adjective.* —*See* **unfortunate** (1).

ill-favored *adjective.* —*See* **objectionable, ugly.**

illiberal *adjective.* —*See* **intolerant** (1).

illicit *adjective.* Contrary to accepted, especially moral conventions ▶ criminal, unlawful. —*See also* **criminal** (1), **forbidden, illegal.**

illicitness *noun.* The state or quality of being illegal ▶ illegality, illegitimacy, lawlessness, unlawfulness.

illimitable *adjective.* —*See* **endless** (1).

illiteracy *noun.* —*See* **ignorance** (1).

illiterate *adjective.* —*See* **ignorant** (1).

illiterateness *noun.* —*See* **ignorance** (1).

ill-mannered *adjective.* —*See* **rude** (2).

illness *noun.* —*See* **disease, sickness.**

illogical *adjective.* Not governed by or predicated on reason ▶ irrational, unreasonable, unreasoned. ***Idioms:*** out of bounds, without rhyme or reason. [*Compare* **foolish.**] —*See also* **fallacious** (1).

illogicality *or* **illogicalness** *noun.* The absence of reason ▶ irrationality, unreason, unreasonableness. [*Compare* **fallacy, foolishness.**]

ill-omened *adjective.* —*See* **fateful** (1).

ill repute *noun.* —*See* **disgrace.**

ill-starred *adjective.* —*See* **unfortunate** (1).

ill-suited *adjective.* —*See* **improper** (2).

ill-tempered *adjective.* Having or showing a bad temper ▶ bad-tempered, cantankerous, churlish, crabbed, cranky, cross, curmudgeonly, disagreeable, fractious, fretful, grouchy, grumpy, ill-humored, ill-natured, irascible, irritable, nasty, peevish, petulant, querulous, short-tempered, snappish, snappy, splenetic, surly, testy, ugly, waspish. *Informal:* crabby, mean. *Slang:* snarky. ***Idiom:*** out of sorts. [*Compare* **abrupt, argumentative, testy.**]

ill-timed *adjective.* Not occurring at a favorable time ▶ inconvenient, inopportune, untimely. [*Compare* **fateful.**] —*See also* **unseasonable.**

ill-treat *verb.* —*See* **abuse** (1).

ill-treatment *noun.* —*See* **abuse** (2).

illume *verb.* —*See* **illuminate** (1), **illuminate** (2).

illuminate *verb.* **1.** To cover or fill with light ▶ flood, illume, illumine, light (up), lighten. [*Compare* **beam.**] **2.** To enable one to understand, especially in a spiritual or intellectual sense ▶ edify, enlighten, illume, illumine. ***Idioms:*** make plain, remove the scales from someone's eyes, shed (*or* throw) light upon. [*Compare* **explain.**] —*See also* **clarify** (1), **clear** (1).

illumination *noun.* **1.** The act of physically illuminating or the condition of being filled with light ▶ light, lighting. [*Compare* **brilliance.**] **2.** The condition of being informed spiritually ▶ edification, enlightenment. [*Compare* **education.**] —*See also* **explanation, light[1]** (1).

illuminative *adjective.* —*See* **educational** (2).

illumine *verb.* —*See* **illuminate** (1), **illuminate** (2).

ill-usage *noun.* —*See* **abuse** (1).

ill-use *verb.* —*See* **abuse** (1).

illusion *noun.* A phenomenon that causes a misperception ▶ delusion, hallucination, ignis fatuus, mirage, phantasm, phantasma, phantasmagoria, phantasmagory, will-o'-the-wisp. —*See also* **dream** (1), **dream** (2), **magic** (2).

illusive *or* **illusory** *adjective.* Of, relating to, or in the nature of an illusion; lacking reality ▶ chimeric, chimerical, delusive, delusory, dreamlike, hallucinatory, phantasmagoric, phantasmal, phantasmic, unreal, visionary. [*Compare* **imaginary.**] —*See also* **fallacious** (2).

illustratable *adjective.* —*See* **explainable.**

illustrate *verb.* To demonstrate and clarify with examples ▶ demonstrate, evidence, exemplify, instance. [*Compare* **explain, show.**] —*See also* **clarify** (1), **represent** (1).

illustration *noun.* —*See* **embodiment, example** (1), **explanation, representation.**

illustrative *adjective.* —*See* **explanatory, graphic** (4).

illustrious *adjective.* —*See* **exalted, famous.**

illustriousness *noun.* —*See* **fame.**

ill will *noun.* —*See* **enmity, malevolence.**

image *noun.* **1.** An image caused by reflection ▶ likeness, reflection. **2.** The character projected or given by someone to the public ▶ appearance, impression. [*Compare* **façade.**] —*See also* **copy** (1), **double, embodiment, idea.**

image *verb.* To send back or form an image of ▶ mirror, reflect. —*See also* **imagine, mimic, represent** (2).

imaginable *adjective.* —*See* **conceivable.**

imaginary *adjective.* Existing only in the imagination ▶ chimeric, chimerical, conceptual, fanciful, fantastic, fantastical, invented, make-believe, notional, unreal, visionary. ***Idiom:*** pie in the sky. [*Compare* **fictitious, illusive, mythical.**]

imagination *noun.* The power of the mind to form images ▶ creativity, inventiveness, fancy, fantasy, imaginativeness, mind's eye. [*Compare* **invention.**] —*See also* **vision** (2).

✚ **CORE SYNONYMS:** *imagination, fancy, fantasy.* These nouns refer to the power of the mind to form images, especially of what is not present to the senses. *Imagination* is the most broadly applicable: "*In the world of words, the imagination is one of the forces of nature*" (Wallace Stevens). *Fancy* especially suggests mental invention that is whimsical, capricious, or playful and that is characteristically well removed from reality: "*All power of fancy over reason is a degree of insanity*" (Samuel Johnson). *Fantasy* is applied principally to elaborate or extravagant fancy as a product of the imagination given free rein: "*The poet is in command of his fantasy, while it is exactly the mark of the neurotic that he is possessed by his fantasy*" (Lionel Trilling).

---

imaginative *adjective.* Showing invention or whimsy in design ▶ fanciful, fantastic, whimsical. [*Compare* **capricious, elaborate, ornate.**] —*See also* **visionary.**

imaginativeness *noun.* —*See* **imagination.**

imagine *verb.* To form mental images of ▶ call up, conceive, conjure up, dream up, envisage, envision, fancy, fantasize, image, make up, picture, see, think, vision, visualize. *Informal:* feature. [*Compare* **invent.**] —*See also* **dream, guess, suppose** (1).

imbalance *noun.* —*See* **gap** (3), **inequality** (1).

imbecile *noun.* —*See* **dullard, fool.**

imbecilic *adjective.* —*See* **foolish, stupid.**

imbecility *noun.* —*See* **foolishness, stupidity.**

imbed *verb. See* **embed.**

imbibe *verb.* —*See* **absorb** (2), **drink** (1), **drink** (2), **drink** (3).

imbibing *adjective.* —*See* **absorbent.**

imbroglio *noun.* —*See* **disorder** (1), **tangle.**

imbue *verb.* —*See* **charge** (1), **color** (1).

imitate *verb.* To copy the manner or expression of another, especially in an exaggerated or mocking way ▶ ape, burlesque, caricature, impersonate, mimic, mock, parody, simulate, travesty. ***Idioms:*** do a takeoff on, do (*or* make) like. [*Compare* **act, impersonate.**] —*See also* **copy, follow** (5), **mimic.**

✚ **CORE SYNONYMS:** *imitate, mimic, ape, parody, simulate.* These verbs mean to copy the manner or expression of another, especially in an exaggerated or mocking way. To *imitate* is the most general: *The student made the class laugh by imitating the stern principal.* To *mimic* is to make a close imitation, often with an intent to ridicule: "*fresh carved cedar, mimicking a glade/Of palm and plaintain*" (John Keats). To *ape* is to follow another's lead slavishly but often with an absurd result: "*Those* [superior] *states of mind do not come from aping an* *alien culture*" (John Russell). To *parody* is either to imitate with comic effect or to attempt a serious imitation and fail: "*All these peculiarities* [of Samuel Johnson's literary style] *have been imitated by his admirers and parodied by his assailants*" (Thomas Macaulay). To *simulate* is to feign or falsely assume the appearance or character of something: "*I . . . lay there simulating death*" (W.H. Hudson).

imitation *noun.* —*See* **copy** (2), **echo** (1), **mimicry, satire.**

imitation *adjective.* —*See* **artificial** (1).

imitative *adjective.* **1.** Of or involving imitation ▶ apish, derivative, emulative, mimetic, slavish. [*Compare* **counterfeit.**] **2.** Imitating sounds ▶ echoic, mimetic, onomatopoeic, onomatopoetic.

imitator *noun.* —*See* **mimic.**

immaculacy *or* **immaculateness** *noun.* —*See* **purity.**

immaculate *adjective.* —*See* **clean** (1).

immanent *adjective.* —*See* **constitutional.**

immaterial *adjective.* Having no body, form, or substance ▶ bodiless, discarnate, disembodied, ethereal, impalpable, incorporeal, insubstantial, intangible, metaphysical, nonphysical, spiritual, unbodied, uncorporal, unsubstantial. [*Compare* **supernatural.**] —*See also* **irrelevant.**

✦ **CORE SYNONYMS:** *immaterial, incorporeal, insubstantial, metaphysical, spiritual.* These adjectives mean lacking material body, form, or substance: *immaterial apparitions; an incorporeal spirit; insubstantial victories; metaphysical forces; spiritual beings.*

immature *adjective.* —*See* **childish, inexperienced, young.**

immaturity *noun.* —*See* **inexperience.**

immeasurable *adjective.* —*See* **endless** (1), **incalculable.**

immeasurability *or* **immeasurableness** *noun.* —*See* **infinity** (1).

immediate *adjective.* **1.** Occurring at once ▶ instant, instantaneous. [*Compare* **fast, quick.**] **2.** Marked by the absence of any intervention ▶ direct, firsthand, primary. —*See also* **close** (1), **present**[1]**.**

immediately *adverb.* **1.** Without delay ▶ ASAP, directly, forthwith, instant, instantly, now, promptly, right away, right off, straightaway, straight off. *Informal:* lickety-split, PDQ, yesterday. *Slang:* pronto. ***Idioms:*** at once, before you can say Jack Sprat (*or* Jack Robinson), first off, in the blink of an eye, like a shot, on the double, this instant (*or* minute *or* second). [*Compare* **fast.**] **2.** Without intermediary ▶ directly, firsthand.

immemorial *adjective.* —*See* **old** (1).

immense *adjective.* —*See* **enormous.**

immensity *or* **immenseness** *noun.* —*See* **enormousness.**

immerge *verb.* —*See* **dip** (1).

immerse *verb.* —*See* **absorb** (1), **dip** (1).

immersed *adjective.* —*See* **rapt.**

immersion *noun.* —*See* **absorption** (2).

immigrant *noun.* One who immigrates ▶ migrant. [*Compare* **émigré, settler.**] —*See also* **foreigner.**

immigrant *adjective.* —*See* **foreign** (1).

immigrate *verb.* To leave one's native land and settle in another ▶ emigrate (from), migrate, resettle, transmigrate. [*Compare* **move, settle.**]

immigration *noun.* Settling in a country to which one is not native ▶ migration, transmigration. [*Compare* **emigration.**]

imminence *noun.* The act or fact of coming near ▶ approach, coming, convergence, nearness. [*Compare* **advance, appearance.**]

imminent *adjective.* About to occur at any moment ▶ at hand, approaching, brewing, impending, in store, looming, proximate. ***Idioms:*** around the corner, in the offing, in the wind, on the horizon. [*Compare* **close, coming.**]

immobile *adjective.* —*See* **fixed, motionless.**

immobilization *noun.* —*See* **stop** (2).
immobilize *verb.* —*See* **disable** (1), **stop** (2).
immoderate *adjective.* —*See* **excessive.**
immoderation *or* **immoderacy** *noun.* —*See* **excess** (2).
immodest *adjective.* —*See* **improper** (1).
immolate *verb.* To offer as a sacrifice ▶ offer up, sacrifice, victimize.
immolation *noun.* —*See* **offering.**
immoral *adjective.* —*See* **evil, impure** (1).
immorality *noun.* —*See* **corruption** (1), **crime** (2).
immortal *adjective.* Not being subject to death ▶ deathless, undying. —*See also* **endless** (2).
immortality *noun.* Endless life after death ▶ afterlife, deathlessness, eternal life, eternity, everlasting life, everlastingness, life eternal, life everlasting. [*Compare* **endlessness, eternity.**]
immortalize *verb.* To cause to last endlessly ▶ eternalize, eternize, perpetuate. ***Idioms:*** cast (*or* etch *or* fix *or* set) in stone. [*Compare* **honor, memorialize.**]
immovable *adjective.* —*See* **fixed.**
immune *adjective.* —*See* **resistant, safe** (2).
immunity *noun.* **1.** The capacity to withstand ▶ imperviousness, insusceptibility, resistance, unsusceptibility. [*Compare* **endurance, stability.**] **2.** Temporary immunity from penalties ▶ exemption, grace, reprieve, respite. [*Compare* **delay.**] —*See also* **safety.**
immure *verb.* —*See* **enclose** (1), **imprison.**
immutability *noun.* —*See* **changelessness.**
immutable *adjective.* Incapable of changing or being modified ▶ inalterable, inconvertible, inflexible, invariable, ironclad, rigid, unalterable, unchangeable, unmodifiable. [*Compare* **continuing, firm, fixed.**] —*See also* **unchanging.**
imp *noun.* —*See* **rascal, urchin.**
impact *noun.* The strong effect exerted by one person or thing on another ▶ bearing, force, impression, influence, repercussion, reverberation. [*Compare* **cause, effect, stimulus.**] —*See also* **collision.**
impact *verb.* —*See* **collide, influence.**
impair *verb.* —*See* **damage, disable** (1), **drug** (2).
impairment *noun.* —*See* **damage, debilitation, harm.**
impale *verb.* —*See* **cut** (1).
impalpable *adjective.* —*See* **immaterial, imperceptible** (1).
impart *verb.* —*See* **communicate** (1), **confer** (2).
impartial *adjective.* —*See* **fair**[1] (1), **neutral** (1).
impartially *adverb.* —*See* **fairly** (1).
impartiality *or* **impartialness** *noun.* —*See* **fairness.**
impassable *adjective.* Incapable of being negotiated or overcome ▶ insuperable, insurmountable, unconquerable. [*Compare* **impossible, invincible.**]
impasse *noun.* —*See* **predicament.**
impassible *adjective.* —*See* **cold** (2).
impassion *verb.* —*See* **fire** (1).
impassioned *adjective.* —*See* **passionate.**
impassive *adjective.* —*See* **apathetic, cold** (2), **vacant.**
impassivity *or* **impassiveness** *noun.* —*See* **apathy.**
impatient *adjective.* Being unable or unwilling to endure irritation or opposition, for example ▶ intolerant, unforbearing, unindulgent. [*Compare* **ill-tempered, intolerant.**] —*See also* **anxious, eager.**
impeach *verb.* —*See* **accuse.**
impeachment *noun.* —*See* **accusation.**
impeccable *adjective.* —*See* **perfect.**
impecuniosity *or* **impecuniousness** *noun.* —*See* **poverty.**
impecunious *adjective.* —*See* **poor.**
impede *verb.* —*See* **delay** (1), **hinder.**
impediment *noun.* —*See* **bar** (1), **difficulty.**

impel *verb.* —*See* **provoke.**
impelled *adjective.* —*See* **obliged** (2).
impend *verb.* —*See* **threaten** (2).
impending *adjective.* —*See* **imminent.**
impenetrability *noun.* —*See* **safety.**
impenetrable *adjective.* —*See* **incomprehensible, mysterious, safe** (2).
impenitent *adjective.* Devoid of remorse ▶ remorseless, unrepentant.
imperative *adjective.* —*See* **required, urgent** (1).
imperative *noun.* —*See* **command** (1), **duty** (1).
imperceptible *adjective.* **1.** Incapable of being apprehended by the mind or the senses ▶ impalpable, imponderable, inappreciable, indiscernible, indistinguishable, insensible, intangible, invisible, subtle, unnoticeable, unobservable. [*Compare* **ambiguous, remote, unclear.**] **2.** So small as not to be discernible ▶ infinitesimal, microscopic. [*Compare* **tiny.**] —*See also* **hidden** (1).
imperfect *adjective.* Having a defect or defects ▶ amiss, blemished, defective, faulty, flawed. [*Compare* **shabby, trick.**] —*See also* **rough** (4).
imperfection *noun.* —*See* **defect.**
imperial *adjective.* —*See* **authoritative** (1), **grand.**
imperil *verb.* —*See* **endanger.**
imperilment *noun.* —*See* **danger.**
imperious *adjective.* —*See* **dictatorial.**
impermanent *adjective.* —*See* **temporary** (2).
impermissible *adjective.* —*See* **forbidden.**
impersonal *adjective.* Feeling or showing no strong emotional involvement ▶ detached, disinterested, dispassionate, indifferent, neutral. —*See also* **cool.**
impersonate *verb.* To assume the character or appearance of ▶ attitudinize, masquerade, pass for, pose as, posture. ***Idiom:*** pass oneself off as. —*See also* **act** (3), **imitate.**
impersonation *noun.* —*See* **mimicry, satire.**
impersonator *noun.* —*See* **mimic.**
impertinence *noun.* —*See* **impudence.**
impertinent *adjective.* —*See* **disrespectful, impudent, irrelevant, offensive** (2).
imperturbability *or* **imperturbableness** *noun.* —*See* **balance** (2).
imperturbable *adjective.* —*See* **calm.**
impervious *adjective.* —*See* **resistant.**
imperviousness *noun.* The capacity to withstand ▶ immunity, insusceptibility, resistance, unsusceptibility. [*Compare* **endurance, stability.**]
impetuous *adjective.* —*See* **rash**[1].
impetus *noun.* —*See* **stimulus.**
impiety *noun.* —*See* **atheism, sacrilege.**
impinge *verb.* —*See* **adjoin.**
impingement *noun.* —*See* **trespass** (2).
impious *adjective.* Showing irreverence and contempt for something sacred ▶ blasphemous, profane, sacrilegious. —*See also* **atheistic.**
impish *adjective.* —*See* **mischievous.**
impishness *noun.* —*See* **mischief.**
implacability *or* **implacableness** *noun.* —*See* **stubbornness.**
implacable *adjective.* —*See* **stubborn** (1), **vindictive.**
implant *verb.* —*See* **fix** (2), **instill, introduce** (2).
implausible *adjective.* Not plausible or believable ▶ feeble, flimsy, improbable, inconceivable, incredible, insubstantial, lame, shaky, tenuous, thin, unbelievable, unconceivable, unconvincing, unlikely, unsubstantial, weak. ***Idiom:*** beyond belief. [*Compare* **doubtful, fallacious, impossible.**]
implement *verb.* —*See* **enforce, fulfill, use.**
implement *noun.* A device used to do work or perform a task ▶ instrument, tool, utensil. [*Compare* **agent, device, gadget.**]
implementation *noun.* Carrying a law or judgment into effect ▶ enforcement, execution. [*Compare* **effect.**] —*See also* **exercise** (1).

implicate *verb.* To cause to appear involved in or guilty of a crime or fault ▶ criminate, incriminate, inculpate. [*Compare* **accuse.**] —*See also* **imply, involve** (1).

implicating *adjective.* —*See* **insinuating.**

implication *noun.* —*See* **entanglement, hint** (1).

implicit *adjective.* **1.** Conveyed indirectly without words or speech ▶ hinted, implied, inferred, insinuated, suggested, tacit, unarticulated, understood, unexpressed, unsaid, unspoken, unstated, unuttered, unvocalized, wordless. ***Idiom:*** taken for granted. [*Compare* **constitutional, silent.**] **2.** Having no reservations ▶ absolute, unconditional, undoubting, unfaltering, unhesitating, unquestioning, unreserved, wholehearted. ***Idiom:*** without reservations. [*Compare* **definite, sure.**]

implied *adjective.* —*See* **implicit** (1).

imploration *noun.* —*See* **appeal.**

implore *verb.* —*See* **appeal** (1).

imply *verb.* To involve by logical necessity ▶ entail, implicate, involve, lead to, point to, suggest. [*Compare* **demand, mean, suppose.**] —*See also* **hint.**

impolite *adjective.* —*See* **disrespectful, offensive** (2), **rude** (2).

impoliteness *noun.* —*See* **disrespect.**

impolitic *adjective.* —*See* **tactless, unwise.**

imponderable *adjective.* —*See* **imperceptible** (1).

import *verb.* —*See* **count** (1), **mean**[1].

import *noun.* The general sense or significance, as of an action or statement ▶ amount, burden, drift, gist, idea, purport, substance, tenor. ***Idioms:*** sum and substance, sum total. [*Compare* **heart, thrust.**] —*See also* **importance, meaning.**

importance *noun.* The quality or state of being important ▶ concern, concernment, consequence, import, magnitude, moment, significance, significancy, weight, weightiness. [*Compare* **import, meaning.**]

✚ **CORE SYNONYMS:** *importance, consequence, moment, significance, import, weight.* These nouns refer to the quality or state of being important, influential, or worthy of note or esteem. *Importance* is the most general term: *the importance of a proper diet. Consequence* is especially applicable to persons or things of notable rank or position (*scholars of consequence*) and to what is important because of its possible outcome, result, or effect (*tax laws of consequence to investors*). *Moment* implies importance or consequence that is readily apparent: *making decisions of great moment. Significance* and *import* refer to the quality of something, often not obvious, that gives it special meaning or value: *an event of real significance; works of great social import. Weight* suggests a personal evaluation or judgment of importance: *"The popular faction at Rome . . . was led by men of weight"* (J.A. Froude).

◀ **ANTONYM:** *unimportant*

---

important *adjective.* Having great significance ▶ big, consequential, considerable, crucial, earth-shaking, grand, great, historic, key, large, material, meaningful, momentous, monumental, significant, substantial, world-shaking. *Informal:* bigtime. [*Compare* **big-league, critical, essential, primary.**] —*See also* **famous, influential.**

importunate *adjective.* Firm or obstinate, as in making a demand or maintaining a stand ▶ importune, insistent, persistent, urgent. [*Compare* **firm, stubborn.**]

importune *verb.* —*See* **demand** (1), **harass.**

importune *adjective.* Firm or obstinate, as in making a demand or maintaining a stand ▶ importunate, insistent, persistent, urgent. [*Compare* **firm, stubborn.**]

impose *verb.* To establish and apply as compulsory ▶ assess, exact, levy, put. [*Compare* **bill, demand.**] —*See also* **dictate, inflict.**

impose on *or* **upon** *verb.* To force another to accept a burden ▶ charge with, fasten on (*or* upon), foist on (*or* upon), inflict on (*or* upon), lay on (*or* upon), put on (*or* upon), saddle with, tax with, yoke with. *Informal:* stick with. ***Idioms:*** weigh (*or* weight) down with. —*See also* **abuse** (1), **inconvenience.**

imposing *adjective.* —*See* **grand.**

imposition *noun.* An excessive, unwelcome burden ▶ encumbrance, infliction, intrusion, obtrusion. [*Compare* **burden, meddling.**]

impossible *adjective.* Not capable of happening or being done ▶ blue-sky, impracticable, impractical, infeasible, unachievable, unattainable, unimaginable, unobtainable, unrealizable, unthinkable, unworkable. ***Idioms:*** beyond the bounds of possiblity (*or* reason), hardly possible, out of the question. [*Compare* **implausible, incredible, insuperable, foolish.**] —*See also* **contrary, unbearable.**

impost *noun.* —*See* **tax.**

impostor *noun.* —*See* **fake.**

imposture *noun.* —*See* **trick** (1).

impotence *noun.* —*See* **ineffectuality, sterility** (2).

impotent *adjective.* Lacking power or strength ▶ helpless, powerless, unable. —*See also* **barren** (1), **ineffectual** (2).

impound *verb.* —*See* **enclose** (1), **seize** (1).

impoundment *noun.* —*See* **seizure** (2).

impoverish *verb.* —*See* **ruin.**

impoverished *adjective.* —*See* **depressed** (2), **poor.**

impoverishment *noun.* —*See* **debilitation, poverty.**

impracticable *adjective.* —*See* **impossible, unworkable.**

impractical *adjective.* —*See* **idealistic, impossible, inefficient, theoretical** (1), **theoretical** (2), **unwise.**

imprecate *verb.* To invoke evil upon ▶ anathematize, curse, damn, hex. [*Compare* **charm.**]

imprecation *noun.* —*See* **curse** (1).

imprecise *adjective.* —*See* **indefinite** (1), **loose** (3).

imprecision *noun.* —*See* **vagueness.**

impregnability *noun.* —*See* **safety.**

impregnable *adjective.* —*See* **safe** (2).

impregnate *verb.* To make pregnant ▶ inseminate. *Slang:* knock up. ***Idioms:*** get (*or* put) in a family way, get with child. [*Compare* **fertilize.**] —*See also* **charge** (1).

impress[1] *verb.* —*See* **engrave** (2), **instill, move** (1), **strike** (2).

impress *noun.* —*See* **impression** (1).

impress[2] *verb.* To enroll compulsorily in military service ▶ conscript, draft, induct, levy.

impressible *adjective.* —*See* **sensitive** (1).

impression *noun.* **1.** The visible effect made on a surface by pressure ▶ dent, dint, impress, imprint, indent, indentation, mark, print, stamp. [*Compare* **depression.**] **2.** The character projected or given by someone to the public ▶ appearance, image. [*Compare* **façade.**] **3.** Something, such as a feeling or idea, associated with a specific person or thing ▶ association, connection, connotation, suggestion. —*See also* **feeling** (1), **impact, mimicry, sensation** (1).

✦ **CORE SYNONYMS:** *impression, impress, imprint, print, stamp.* These nouns denote a visible effect made on a surface by pressure: *an impression of a notary's seal on wax; the impress of bare feet in the sand; a medal with the imprint of a bald eagle; the print of automobile tires in the tar; a gold ingot with the refiner's stamp.*

---

impressionable *adjective.* —*See* **flexible** (3), **sensitive** (1).

impressionistic *adjective.* Tending to bring a memory, mood, or image, for example, subtly or indirectly to mind ▶

allusive, connotative, evocative, reminiscent, suggestive. [*Compare* **designative, symbolic.**]

impressive *adjective.* —*See* **affecting, noticeable.**

impressment *noun.* —*See* **draft** (2).

imprimatur *noun.* —*See* **permission.**

imprint *verb.* —*See* **engrave** (2).

imprint *noun.* —*See* **impression** (1), **mark** (1).

imprison *verb.* To put in or as if in prison ▶ confine, detain, hold, immure, incarcerate, intern, jail, lock (away *or* in *or* up), shut (away *or* in *or* up). *Informal:* put away. ***Idioms:*** clap in jail (*or* prison *or* irons), put behind bars, throw in the cooler (*or* slammer). [*Compare* **enclose, restrain.**]

imprisonment *noun.* —*See* **detention.**

improbable *adjective.* —*See* **doubtful** (1), **implausible.**

improbity *noun.* —*See* **corruption** (2), **dishonesty** (1).

impromptu *adjective.* —*See* **extemporaneous.**

impromptu *noun.* Something improvised ▶ ad-lib, extemporization, improvisation. [*Compare* **makeshift.**]

improper *adjective.* **1.** Not in keeping with conventional mores ▶ immodest, indecent, indecorous, indelicate, indiscreet, naughty, risqué, unbecoming, unbefitting, unjudicious, ungentlemanly, unladylike, unseemly, untoward. ***Idiom:*** out of line. [*Compare* **abandoned, foolish, rude, wrong.**] **2.** Not suited to circumstances ▶ ill-fitted, ill-suited, inappropriate, inapt, incongruous, incorrect, inept, infelicitous, malapropos, mismatched, unapt, unbecoming, unbefitting, unfit, unfitting, unseemly, unsuitable, unsuited. ***Idioms:*** out of line (*or* place). [*Compare* **deficient, inadequate.**] —*See also* **objectionable.**

✚ CORE SYNONYMS: *improper, unbecoming, unseemly, indelicate, indecent, indecorous.* These adjectives mean not in keeping with conventional mores or accepted standards of what is right or proper. *Improper* often refers to unethical conduct, a breach of etiquette, or morally offensive behavior: *improper business practices; improper behavior at the dinner table. Unbecoming* suggests what is beneath the standard implied by one's character or position: *language unbecoming to an officer.* What is *unseemly* or *indelicate* is in gross violation of good taste; *indelicate* especially suggests immodesty, coarseness, or tactlessness: *an unseemly use of profanity; an indelicate suggestion. Indecent* refers to what is morally offensive or harmful: *an earthy but not indecent story. Indecorous* implies violation of societal manners: *an indecorous remark about overeating.*

---

improperness *noun.* —*See* **impropriety** (1).

impropriety *noun.* **1.** The condition of being improper ▶ improperness, inappropriateness, incongruity, incorrectness, indecency, indecorousness, indiscretion, unbecomingness, unfitness, unseemliness, unsuitability, unsuitableness. [*Compare* **impudence.**] **2.** An improper act or statement ▶ gaffe, gaucherie, indecency, indecorum, indelicacy, indiscretion, solecism. [*Compare* **blunder, breach.**] —*See also* **corruption** (3).

improve *verb.* To advance to a more desirable state ▶ ameliorate, amend, better, enhance, enrich, help, meliorate, upgrade. [*Compare* **correct, renew.**] —*See also* **recover** (2).

✚ CORE SYNONYMS: *improve, better, help, ameliorate.* These verbs mean to advance to a more desirable, valuable, or excellent state. *Improve* and *better,* the most general terms, are often interchangeable: *You can improve* (or *better*) *your mind through study; I got a haircut to improve* (or *better*) *my appearance. Help* usually implies limited relief or change: *Gargling helps a sore throat.* To *ameliorate* is to improve circumstances that demand change: *Volunteers were able to ameliorate conditions in the refugee camp.*

---

improvement *noun.* **1.** The act of making better or the condition of being made better ▶ advancement, amelioration, amendment, betterment, development, enhancement, melioration, refinement, rehabilitation, upgrade. [*Compare* **change, revision.**] **2.** Steady improvement, as of an individual or a society ▶ amelioration, betterment, development, melioration, progress.

improvident *adjective.* —*See* **extravagant, rash[1].**

improvisation *noun.* Something improvised ▶ ad-lib, extemporization, impromptu. [*Compare* **makeshift.**]

improvise *verb.* **1.** To compose or recite without preparation ▶ ad-lib, extemporize, fake, make up. ***Idioms:*** make it up as one goes along, play by ear, speak off the cuff, think on one's feet, wing it. [*Compare* **invent.**] **2.** To make or provide from available materials ▶ cobble together, jerry-rig, jury-rig, rig up, slap together, throw together. ***Idiom:*** make do with. [*Compare* **invent.**]

improvised *adjective.* —*See* **extemporaneous.**

imprudent *adjective.* —*See* **unwise.**

impudence *noun.* The state or quality of being impudent or arrogantly self-confident ▶ assumption, audaciousness, audacity, blatancy, boldness, brashness, brazenness, cheek, cheekiness, chutzpah, discourtesy, disrespect, effrontery, face, familiarity, flippancy, forwardness, gall, impertinence, impudency, incivility, insolence, nerve, nerviness, overconfidence, pertness, presumptuousness, pushiness, rudeness, sassiness, sauciness, shamelessness. *Informal:* brass, brassiness, crust, sauce, uppishness, uppityness. [*Compare* **back talk, flagrancy.**]

impudent *adjective.* Rude and disrespectful; without shame ▶ assuming, assumptive, audacious, bald-faced, barefaced, blatant, bold, boldfaced, brash, brazen, brazenfaced, cheeky, contumelious, familiar, flippant, forward, impertinent, insolent, malapert, nervy, overconfident, pert, presuming, presumptuous, pushy, sassy, saucy, shameless, smart, snippy, unabashed, unblushing. *Informal:* brassy, flip, fresh, smart-alecky, snippety, uppish, uppity. *Slang:* snotty, wise. [*Compare* **disrespectful, flagrant, offensive, rude.**]

✚ **CORE SYNONYMS:** *impudent, shameless, brazen, barefaced, brash, unblushing.* These adjectives apply to that which rudely and disrespectfully defies social or moral proprieties and is marked by a bold lack of shame. *Impudent* suggests offensive boldness or effrontery: *an impudent student; an impudent misrepresentation. Shameless* implies a lack of modesty, sense of decency, or regard for others' rights or feelings: *a shameless liar; a shameless accusation. Brazen* suggests flagrant, insolent audacity: *a brazen impostor; brazen arrogance. Barefaced* specifies undisguised brazenness: *a barefaced hypocrite; a barefaced lie. Brash* stresses impetuousness, lack of tact, and often crass indifference to consequences or to considerations of decency: *a brash newcomer; brash demands. Unblushing* implies an inappropriate lack of shame or embarrassment: *an unblushing apologist; unblushing obsequiousness.*

---

impulse *noun.* —*See* **fancy, stimulus.**

impulsive *adjective.* —*See* **capricious, rash[1], spontaneous.**

impulsivity *noun.* —*See* **spontaneity.**

impure *adjective.* **1.** Not chaste or moral ▶ corrupted, debased, debauched, defiled, immoral, unchaste, unclean, uncleanly, unvirtuous. [*Compare* **evil, improper, obscene.**] **2.** Mixed with other substances ▶ adulterated, alloyed, blended, combined, contaminated, corrupted, cut, debased, diluted, dirty, doctored, infected, loaded, mixed, polluted, sophisticated, sullied, tainted, tampered with, vitiated. [*Compare* **dirty.**]

impurity *noun.* —*See* **contaminant, contamination, corruption** (1).

imputation *noun.* An implied criticism ▶ reflection, slur. [*Compare* **crack, libel.**] —*See also* **accusation.**

impute *verb.* —*See* **fix** (3).

in *adjective.* —*See* **fashionable.**

inability *noun.* Lack of ability or capacity ▶ incapability, incapacity, incompetence, incompetency, inefficiency, ineptitude, ineptness, powerlessness. [*Compare* **disadvantage, futility, ineffectuality.**]

inaccessible *adjective.* **1.** Unable to be reached ▶ inapproachable, unapproachable, unattainable, unavailable, unobtainable, unreachable. ***Idioms:*** beyond reach, out of reach, out of the way. [*Compare* **distant, remote.**] **2.** Not accessible or handy ▶ inconvenient, unhandy. ***Idioms:*** beyond reach, out of reach, out of the way. [*Compare* **awkward.**] —*See also* **cool.**

inaccuracy *noun.* —*See* **error.**

inaccurate *adjective.* —*See* **erroneous.**

inaction *noun.* A lack of action or activity ▶ idleness, inactivity, inertness, inoperativeness, lifelessness, sedentariness, stagnation, vegetation. [*Compare* **abeyance, laziness, stillness.**]

inactive *adjective.* —*See* **idle** (1), **latent.**

inactivity *noun.* —*See* **inaction.**

inadequacy *noun.* —*See* **ineffectuality, shortage.**

inadequate *adjective.* —*See* **bad** (1), **deficient, disappointing, ineffectual** (2), **inefficient, insufficient.**

inadmissible *adjective.* —*See* **objectionable.**

inadvertent *adjective.* —*See* **accidental, careless, unintentional.**

inadvisable *adjective.* —*See* **unwise.**

inalterable *adjective.* —*See* **immutable.**

inane *adjective.* —*See* **foolish, vacant.**

inanimate *adjective.* Completely lacking sensation or consciousness ▶ dead, insensate, insentient, lifeless. [*Compare* **dead.**]

inanity *noun.* —*See* **emptiness** (2), **foolishness.**

inapplicable *adjective.* —*See* **irrelevant.**

inapposite *adjective.* —*See* **irrelevant.**

inappreciable *adjective.* —*See* **imperceptible** (1).

inapproachable *adjective.* —*See* **inaccessible** (1).

inappropriate *adjective.* —*See* **improper** (2), **unfortunate** (2).

inappropriateness *noun.* —*See* **impropriety** (1).

inapt *adjective.* —*See* **improper** (2), **inefficient.**

inarguable *adjective.* —*See* **certain** (2).

inarticulate *adjective.* —*See* **mute, speechless.**

inasmuch as *conjunction.* —*See* **because.**

inattentive *adjective.* —*See* **absent-minded, careless.**

inaudible *adjective.* —*See* **silent** (1).

inaugural *noun.* —*See* **initiation.**

inaugural *adjective.* —*See* **beginning, first.**

inaugurate *verb.* —*See* **initiate, start** (1).

inauguration *noun.* —*See* **beginning, initiation.**

inauspicious *adjective.* —*See* **bleak** (2), **fateful** (1).

in-between *adjective.* —*See* **middle.**

inborn *adjective.* —*See* **constitutional, innate, instinctive.**

inbred *adjective.* —*See* **constitutional.**

incalculable *adjective.* Too great to be calculated ▶ boundless, countless, immeasurable, incomputable, inestimable, infinite, innumerable, measureless, uncountable, unfathomable. [*Compare* **endless.**]

✤ **CORE SYNONYMS:** *incalculable, countless, immeasurable, incomputable,* *inestimable, infinite, innumerable, measureless.* These adjectives apply to that which is too great to be calculated or reckoned: *incalculable riches; countless hours; an immeasurable distance; an incomputable amount; jewels of inestimable value; an infinite number of reasons; innumerable difficulties; measureless power.*

---

incandesce *verb.* To shine brightly and steadily but without a flame ▶ gleam, glow, luminesce. *—See also* **beam.**

incandescent *adjective.* *—See* **bright.**

incantation *noun.* *—See* **spell[2].**

incapability *noun.* *—See* **inability, ineffectuality.**

incapable *adjective.* *—See* **ineffectual** (2), **inefficient.**

incapacitate *verb.* *—See* **disable** (1).

incapacitation *noun.* *—See* **debilitation.**

incapacity *noun.* *—See* **inability.**

incarcerate *verb.* *—See* **imprison.**

incarceration *noun.* *—See* **detention.**

incarnate *verb.* *—See* **embody** (1).

incarnate *adjective.* *—See* **bodily.**

incarnation *noun.* *—See* **embodiment.**

incautious *adjective.* *—See* **rash[1].**

incautiousness *noun.* *—See* **temerity.**

incendiary *noun.* *—See* **agitator.**

incense *verb.* *—See* **anger** (1).

incentive *noun.* *—See* **stimulus.**

inception *noun.* *—See* **beginning, birth** (2).

inceptive *adjective.* *—See* **beginning.**

incertitude *noun.* *—See* **doubt.**

incessant *adjective.* *—See* **continual.**

inch *verb.* To advance slowly ▶ crawl, creep, drag, poke. ***Idiom:*** go at a snail's pace. [*Compare* **trudge.**]

inchoate *adjective.* *—See* **shapeless.**

incident *noun.* *—See* **circumstance** (1), **event** (1).

incidental *adjective.* Not part of the real or essential nature of a thing ▶ adscititious, adventitious, inessential, supervenient. [*Compare* **irrelevant, unnecessary.**] *—See also* **accidental.**

incidentals *noun.* *—See* **odds and ends.**

incinerate *verb.* *—See* **burn** (1).

incipience *or* **incipiency** *noun.* *—See* **beginning.**

incipient *adjective.* *—See* **beginning.**

incise *verb.* *—See* **cut** (1), **engrave** (1).

incision *noun.* *—See* **cut** (1).

incisive *adjective.* *—See* **critical** (2).

incisiveness *noun.* *—See* **edge.**

incite *verb.* *—See* **provoke.**

incitement *or* **incitation** *noun.* *—See* **provocation** (1).

inciter *noun.* *—See* **agitator.**

incivility *noun.* *—See* **impudence, indignity.**

inclement *adjective.* *—See* **bleak** (1).

inclination *noun.* **1.** A natural or habitual preference for something ▶ affinity, bent, bias, cast, disposition, leaning, partiality, penchant, predilection, predisposition, prejudice, proclivity, proneness, propensity, tendency, trend, urge, turn. [*Compare* **fancy, liking, love.**] **2.** Deviation from a particular direction ▶ cant, grade, gradient, heel, incline, lean, list, rake, slant, slope, tilt, tip. [*Compare* **bend, hill.**]

CORE SYNONYMS: *inclination, bias, leaning, partiality, penchant, predilection, prejudice, proclivity, propensity.* These nouns denote a natural or habitual preference for something: *an inclination to indulge in sweets; a pro-American bias; conservative leanings; a partiality for liberal-minded friends; a penchant for exotic foods; a predilection for classical composers; a prejudice in favor of the underprivileged; a proclivity for self-assertiveness; a propensity for exaggeration.*

---

incline *verb.* To depart or cause to depart from true vertical or horizontal ▶ cant, heel, lean, list, rake, slant, slope, tilt, tip. [*Compare* **bend, turn.**] *—See also* **influence, tend[1].**

incline *noun.* *—See* **inclination** (2).

✚ CORE SYNONYMS: *incline, lean, slant, slope, tilt, tip.* These verbs mean to depart or cause to depart from true vertical or horizontal: *inclined her head toward the speaker; leaned against the railing; rays of light slanting through the window; a driveway that slopes downhill; tilted his hat at a rakish angle; tipped her chair against the wall.*

inclined *adjective.* Having or showing a tendency or likelihood ▶ apt, disposed, given, liable, likely, predisposed, prone, tending, wont. —*See also* **oblique.**

inclined plane *noun.* —*See* **ascent** (2).

include *verb.* To construct as an integral part ▶ build in, incorporate, integrate. —*See also* **contain** (1).

inclusive *adjective.* —*See* **general** (2).

incombustible *adjective.* —*See* **fireproof.**

income *noun.* —*See* **living.**

incoming *noun.* —*See* **entrance[1].**

incommode *verb.* —*See* **inconvenience.**

incommodious *adjective.* Causing difficulty, trouble, or discomfort ▶ difficult, inconvenient, troublesome. [*Compare* **awkward, disturbing.**]

incommodiousness *noun.* The state or quality of being inconvenient ▶ discomfort, incommodity, inconvenience, trouble. [*Compare* **bother.**]

incommodity *noun.* **1.** The state or quality of being inconvenient ▶ discomfort, incommodiousness, inconvenience, trouble. [*Compare* **bother.**] **2.** Something that causes difficulty, trouble, or lack of ease ▶ discomfort, discommodity, inconvenience. [*Compare* **annoyance.**]

incommunicative *adjective.* —*See* **taciturn.**

incomparability *noun.* —*See* **excellence.**

incomparable *adjective.* —*See* **unique.**

incompatibility *noun.* —*See* **gap** (3).

incompatible *adjective.* —*See* **discrepant, incongruous, opposite.**

incompetence *or* **incompetency** *noun.* —*See* **inability.**

incompetent *adjective.* —*See* **inefficient.**

incomplete *adjective.* —*See* **deficient, partial** (1), **rough** (4).

incompliance *or* **incompliancy** *noun.* —*See* **stubbornness.**

incompliant *adjective.* —*See* **stubborn** (1).

incomprehensible *adjective.* Incapable of being grasped by the intellect or understanding ▶ impenetrable, inscrutable, uncomprehensible, unfathomable, unintelligible. [*Compare* **complex, deep, mysterious.**]

incompressible *adjective.* Unyielding to pressure ▶ firm, hard, solid.

incomputable *adjective.* —*See* **incalculable.**

inconceivable *adjective.* —*See* **implausible, incredible.**

inconclusive *adjective.* —*See* **ambiguous** (1).

incongruent *adjective.* —*See* **discrepant, incongruous.**

incongruity *noun.* —*See* **gap** (3), **impropriety** (1), **inequality** (1).

incongruous *adjective.* Made up of parts or qualities that are disparate or otherwise markedly lacking in consistency ▶ conflicting, discordant, discrepant, dissonant, incompatible, incongruent, inconsistent, inconsonant, irregular, jarring, mismatched. [*Compare* **inharmonious, opposite.**] —*See also* **discrepant, improper** (2).

inconsequence *noun.* —*See* **trifle.**

inconsequent *or* **inconsequential** *adjective.* —*See* **trivial.**

inconsiderable *adjective.* —*See* **trivial.**

inconsiderableness *noun.* —*See* **trifle.**

inconsiderate *adjective.* —*See* **thoughtless.**

inconsideration *or* **inconsiderateness** *noun.* —*See* **thoughtlessness** (2).

inconsistency *noun.* —*See* **gap** (3), **instability.**

inconsistent *adjective.* —*See* **capricious, discrepant, fallacious** (1), **incongruous, uneven.**

inconsonant *adjective.* —*See* **incongruous, inharmonious** (1).

inconspicuous *adjective.* Not readily noticed or seen ▶ obscure, unassuming, unconspicuous, undistinguished, unnoticeable, unobtrusive. ***Idioms:*** having (*or* keeping) a low profile. [*Compare* **hidden, modest, secluded.**]

inconstant *adjective.* —*See* **capricious, changeable** (1).

incontestable *adjective.* —*See* **certain** (2).

incontinence *noun.* —*See* **abandon** (1).

incontrovertible *adjective.* —*See* **certain** (2).

inconvenience *noun.* **1.** The state or quality of being inconvenient ▶ discomfort, incommodiousness, incommodity, trouble. [*Compare* **bother.**] **2.** Something that causes difficulty, trouble, or lack of ease ▶ discomfort, discommodity, incommodity. [*Compare* **annoyance.**] —*See also* **disadvantage.**

inconvenience *verb.* To cause inconvenience for ▶ discomfort, discommode, impose on (*or* upon), incommode, put out, trouble. [*Compare* **annoy.**]

inconvenient *adjective.* **1.** Not accessible or handy ▶ inaccessible, unhandy. ***Idioms:*** beyond reach, out of reach, out of the way. [*Compare* **awkward, remote.**] **2.** Causing difficulty, trouble, or discomfort ▶ difficult, incommodious, troublesome. [*Compare* **disturbing.**] **3.** Not occurring at a favorable time ▶ ill-timed, inopportune, mistimed, untimely. [*Compare* **fateful.**]

incorporate *verb.* **1.** To construct as an integral part ▶ build, include, integrate. **2.** To make a part of a united whole ▶ combine, embody, integrate. —*See also* **absorb** (2), **associate** (1).

incorporated *adjective.* —*See* **built-in.**

incorporation *noun.* —*See* **absorption** (1), **combination, embodiment.**

incorporeal *adjective.* —*See* **immaterial.**

incorrect *adjective.* —*See* **erroneous, improper** (2).

incorrectness *noun.* —*See* **error, impropriety** (1).

incorrigible *adjective.* —*See* **confirmed** (1).

incorruptibility *noun.* —*See* **honesty.**

incorruptible *adjective.* —*See* **honest.**

increase *verb.* To make or become greater or larger ▶ aggrandize, amplify, augment, blow up, boost, build, build up, burgeon, develop, enlarge, escalate, exaggerate, expand, extend, grow, magnify, mount, multiply, proliferate, ratchet up, rise, rocket, run up, skyrocket, snowball, soar, step up, surge, swell, upsurge, wax. *Informal:* beef up. [*Compare* **advance, broaden, elevate, raise.**] —*See also* **breed.**

increase *noun.* **1.** The act of increasing or rising ▶ aggrandizement, amplification, augment, augmentation, boost, buildup, burgeoning, enlargement, escalation, expansion, extension, growth, hike, jump, magnification, multiplication, proliferation, raise, rise, snowballing, soaring, swell, upsurge, upswing, upturn. [*Compare* **advancement, progress.**] **2.** The amount by which something is increased ▶ advance, boost, hike, increment, jump, raise, rise.

✦ **CORE SYNONYMS:** *increase, expand, enlarge, extend, augment, multiply.* These verbs mean to make or become greater or larger. *Increase* sometimes suggests steady growth: *The mayor's political influence rapidly increased. "No machines will increase the possibilities of life. They only increase the possibilities of idleness"* (John Ruskin). To *expand* is to increase in size, area, volume, bulk, or range: *He inhaled deeply, expanding his chest. "Work expands so as to fill the time available for its completion"* (C. Northcote Parkinson). *Enlarge* refers to expansion in size, extent, capacity, or scope: *The landowner enlarged her property by repeated purchases. My knowledge of literature has enlarged considerably since I joined a reading group.* To *extend* is to lengthen in space or time or to broaden in range: *The transit authority extended the subway line to the next town. The baseball season extends into October. Augment* usually applies to what is already developed or well under way: *She augmented her collection of books each month. His depression augments with each visit to the hospital.* To *multiply* is to increase in number, especially by propagation or procreation: *"As for my cats, they multiplied"* (Daniel Defoe). *"May thy days be multiplied!"* (Sir Walter Scott).

◀ **ANTONYM:** *decrease*

---

incredible *adjective.* Not to be believed ▶ far-fetched, inconceivable, unbelievable, unimaginable, unthinkable. ***Idioms:*** beyond belief, contrary to all reason. [*Compare* **doubtful, outrageous.**] —*See also* **astonishing, implausible.**

incredibly *adverb.* —*See* **unusually.**

incredulity *noun.* —*See* **disbelief.**

incredulous *adjective.* Refusing or reluctant to believe ▶ disbelieving, dubious, questioning, skeptical, unbelieving, unconvinced. [*Compare* **distrustful, doubtful.**]

incredulousness *noun.* —*See* **disbelief.**

increment *noun.* —*See* **increase** (2).

incriminate *verb.* To cause to appear involved in or guilty of a crime or fault ▶ criminate, implicate, inculpate. [*Compare* **accuse.**] —*See also* **accuse.**

incriminating *adjective.* —*See* **accusatorial, insinuating.**

incrimination *noun.* —*See* **accusation.**

incriminatory *adjective.* —*See* **accusatorial.**

inculcate *verb.* —*See* **indoctrinate** (1), **instill.**

inculpable *adjective.* —*See* **innocent** (2).

inculpate *verb.* To cause to appear involved in or guilty of a crime or fault ▶ criminate, implicate, incriminate. [*Compare* **accuse.**] —*See also* **accuse.**

inculpation *noun.* —*See* **accusation.**

inculpatory *adjective.* —*See* **accusatorial.**

incumbency *noun.* The holding of a position ▶ occupancy, occupation, tenure. [*Compare* **period.**]

incur *verb.* —*See* **assume, contract** (2), **develop** (1).

incurable *adjective.* —*See* **confirmed** (1), **hopeless.**

incuriosity *noun.* —*See* **apathy.**

incurious *adjective.* —*See* **apathetic, detached** (1).

incuriousness *noun.* —*See* **apathy.**

incursion *noun.* An act of invading, especially by military forces ▶ foray, inroad, invasion, raid. [*Compare* **attack.**]

indebted *adjective.* —*See* **obliged** (1).

indebtedness *noun.* —*See* **debt** (1), **debt** (2).

indecency *noun.* —*See* **impropriety** (1), **impropriety** (2).

indecent *adjective.* —*See* **improper** (1), **obscene.**

indecision *noun.* —*See* **hesitation.**

indecisive *adjective.* —*See* **ambiguous** (1), **hesitant.**

indecisiveness *noun.* —*See* **hesitation.**

indecorous *adjective.* —*See* **improper** (1).

indecorum *noun.* An improper act or statement ▶ impropriety, indecency, indelicacy. —*See also* **impropriety** (2).

indeed *adverb.* In point of fact ▶ actually, really. —*See also* **even** (2), **really, yes.**

indefatigable *adjective.* —*See* **tireless.**

indefectible *adjective.* —*See* **perfect.**

indefensible *adjective.* —*See* **inexcusable.**

indefinable *adjective.* —*See* **unspeakable** (1).

indefinite *adjective.* **1.** Lacking precise limits ▶ imprecise, indeterminate, inexact, undefined, undetermined. [*Compare* **endless, incalculable.**] **2.** Marked by lack of firm decision or commitment; of questionable outcome ▶ open, uncertain, undecided, undetermined, unresolved, unsettled, unspecified, unsure, vague. ***Idiom:*** up in the air. [*Compare* **ambiguous.**] **3.** Not limited to a single class ▶ diversified, general. *—See also* **debatable, unclear.**

indefiniteness *noun.* *—See* **vagueness.**

indelible *adjective.* Retaining original color ▶ colorfast, fast. *—See also* **confirmed** (1).

indelicacy *noun.* *—See* **impropriety** (2).

indelicate *adjective.* *—See* **coarse** (1), **improper** (1), **tactless.**

indemnification *noun.* *—See* **compensation.**

indemnify *verb.* *—See* **compensate.**

indemnity *noun.* *—See* **compensation.**

indent *noun.* *—See* **impression** (1).

indent *verb.* *—See* **cut** (1).

indentation *noun.* *—See* **depression** (1), **impression** (1).

indented *adjective.* *—See* **hollow** (2).

indenture *verb.* *—See* **enslave.**

independence *noun.* The capacity to manage one's own affairs, make one's own judgments, and provide for oneself ▶ autonomy, self-containment, self-determination, self-reliance, self-sufficiency. *—See also* **freedom.**

independent *adjective.* **1.** Free from the influence, guidance, or control of others ▶ autonomous, individualistic, self-contained, self-determined, self-directed, self-reliant, self-sufficient. **2.** Able to support oneself financially ▶ self-sufficient, self-supporting. *—See also* **free** (1).

independent *noun.* *—See* **rebel** (2).

independently *adverb.* *—See* **separately.**

in-depth *adjective.* *—See* **detailed.**

indiscreet *adjective.* *—See* **improper** (1), **unwise.**

indescribable *adjective.* *—See* **unspeakable** (1).

indeterminate *adjective.* *—See* **ambiguous** (1), **indefinite** (1).

index *noun.* *—See* **list**[1], **sign** (1).

indicate *verb.* **1.** To give grounds for believing in the existence or presence of ▶ argue, attest, bespeak, betoken, mark, point to, testify, witness. **2.** To lead to by logical inference ▶ imply, point to, suggest. *—See also* **designate, mean**[1], **show** (2).

✣ **CORE SYNONYMS:** *indicate, argue, attest, bespeak, betoken, testify, witness.* These verbs mean to give grounds for supposing or inferring the existence or presence of something: *a fever indicating illness; a shabby house that argues poverty; paintings that attest the artist's genius; disorder that bespeaks negligence; melting snows that betoken spring floods; a comment testifying ignorance; a stunned silence that witnessed his shock.*

---

indication *noun.* *—See* **expression** (2), **gesture, sign** (1).

indicative *adjective.* *—See* **designative.**

indicator *noun.* *—See* **sign** (1). The marked outer surface of an instrument ▶ dial, face, gauge.

indicatory *adjective.* *—See* **designative.**

indict *verb.* *—See* **accuse.**

indicter *or* **indictor** *noun.* One that accuses ▶ accuser, arraigner, denouncer, recriminator.

indictment *noun.* *—See* **accusation.**

indifference *noun.* *—See* **apathy, detachment** (2), **trifle.**

indifferent *adjective.* *—See* **apathetic, average, cold** (2), **detached** (1), **fair**[1] (1), **ordinary.**

indifferently *adverb.* *—See* **fairly** (1).

indigence *noun.* *—See* **poverty.**

indigenous *adjective.* Existing, born, or produced in a land or region ▶ aboriginal, autochthonal, autochthonic, autochthonous, endemic, homegrown, local, native, regional. ***Idiom:*** native to the soil. —*See also* **constitutional, domestic** (3).

✦ **CORE SYNONYMS:** *indigenous, native, endemic, autochthonous, aboriginal.* These adjectives mean existing, born, or produced in a specific land, region, or country. *Indigenous* specifies that something or someone is from a particular place rather than coming or being brought in from elsewhere: *an indigenous crop; the Ainu, a people indigenous to the northernmost islands of Japan. Native* implies birth or origin in the specified place: *a native New Yorker; the native North American sugar maple.* Something *endemic* is prevalent in or peculiar to a particular locality or people: *endemic disease. Autochthonous* applies to what is native and unchanged by outside sources: *autochthonous folk melodies. Aboriginal* describes what has existed from the beginning; it is often applied to the earliest known inhabitants of a place: *the aboriginal population; aboriginal nature.*

---

indigent *adjective.* —*See* **poor.**

indigent *noun.* —*See* **pauper.**

indigestible *adjective.* —*See* **bitter** (3).

indignant *adjective.* —*See* **angry.**

indignation *noun.* —*See* **anger.**

indignity *noun.* An act that offends a person's sense of pride or dignity ▶ affront, aspersion, contumely, despite, incivility, insult, offense, outrage, putdown, slight. ***Idioms:*** backhanded (*or* lefthanded) compliment, kick in the teeth, slap in the face. [*Compare* **injustice, outrage, snub, vituperation.**]

indirect *adjective.* **1.** Not proceeding straight to the point or object ▶ anfractuous, backhanded, circuitous, circular, circumlocutory, curving, devious, meandering, oblique, out-of-the-way, rambling, roundabout, tortuous, twisting, wandering, winding, zigzag. [*Compare* **digressive.**] **2.** Deliberately ambiguous or vague ▶ elusive, equivocal, evasive, misleading. [*Compare* **ambiguous.**] —*See also* **underhand.**

indirection *noun.* —*See* **dishonesty** (2).

indiscernible *adjective.* —*See* **hidden** (1), **imperceptible** (1).

indiscreet *adjective.* —*See* **unwise.**

indiscretion *noun.* —*See* **impropriety** (1), **impropriety** (2).

indiscriminate *adjective.* —*See* **random.**

indispensable *adjective.* —*See* **essential** (1).

indisposed *adjective.* Not inclined or willing to do or undertake ▶ against, averse, disinclined, loath, opposed, reluctant, resistant, unwilling. ***Idioms:*** not feeling like, not in the mood. [*Compare* **hesitant, wary.**] —*See also* **sick** (1).

indisposition *noun.* The state of not being disposed or inclined ▶ averseness, aversion, disinclination, opposition, reluctance, resistance, unwillingness. [*Compare* **objection.**] —*See also* **sickness.**

indisputable *adjective.* —*See* **certain** (2).

indistinct *adjective.* —*See* **unclear.**

indistinctive *adjective.* Without definite or distinctive characteristics ▶ bland, colorless, neutral. [*Compare* **boring.**]

indistinguishable *adjective.* —*See* **hidden** (1), **imperceptible** (1).

indite *verb.* —*See* **compose** (1), **write.**

individual *adjective.* **1.** Belonging to, relating to, or affecting a particular person ▶ intimate, personal, private. **2.** Being or related to a distinct entity ▶ discrete, lone, particular, separate, single, singular, sole. —*See also* **distinct, special.**

individual *noun.* —*See* **human being, thing** (1).

individualism *noun.* —*See* **identity** (1).

individualistic *adjective.* Holding the philosophical view that the self is the center and norm of existence ▶ egocentric, egoistic, egoistical, solipsistic. [*Compare* **egotistic.**] —*See also* **independent** (1).

individuality *noun.* The quality of being individual ▶ discreteness, distinctiveness, particularity, separateness, singularity. [*Compare* **novelty, uniqueness.**] —*See also* **identity** (1).

individualize *verb.* —*See* **distinguish** (2).

individually *adverb.* —*See* **separately.**

indocile *adjective.* —*See* **unruly.**

indocility *noun.* —*See* **unruliness.**

indoctrinate *verb.* **1.** To instruct by rote or discipline, as in a body of doctrine or belief ▶ catechize, drill, inculcate. ***Idioms:*** beat (*or* drum *or* pound) something into someone's head, put someone through his or her paces. [*Compare* **educate, practice.**] **2.** To teach to accept a system of thought uncritically ▶ brainwash, program, propagandize. [*Compare* **bias, influence.**]

indoctrination *noun.* —*See* **propaganda.**

indolence *noun.* —*See* **laziness.**

indolent *adjective.* —*See* **lazy.**

indomitable *adjective.* Incapable of being conquered or subjugated ▶ invincible, unbeatable, unconquerable, undefeatable. [*Compare* **insuperable, safe.**]

indubitability *noun.* —*See* **sureness.**

indubitable *adjective.* —*See* **authentic** (1), **certain** (2).

indubitably *adverb.* —*See* **absolutely, yes.**

induce *verb.* —*See* **cause, persuade, urge.**

inducement *noun.* —*See* **lure** (1), **stimulus.**

induct *verb.* To enroll compulsorily in military service ▶ conscript, draft, impress, levy. —*See also* **initiate.**

induction *noun.* —*See* **draft** (2), **initiation, introduction, logic.**

inductive *adjective.* —*See* **introductory.**

indulge *verb.* To comply with the wishes or ideas of another ▶ cater (to), gratify, humor. [*Compare* **defer.**] —*See also* **baby, luxuriate, oblige** (1), **participate, satisfy** (2).

indulgence *noun.* —*See* **favor** (1), **license** (2), **luxury, tolerance.**

indulgent *adjective.* —*See* **obliging, tolerant.**

indurate *verb.* —*See* **harden** (1), **harden** (2).

industrious *adjective.* —*See* **diligent.**

industriousness *noun.* —*See* **diligence.**

industry *noun.* —*See* **business** (1), **diligence.**

indwelling *adjective.* —*See* **constitutional.**

inebriate *adjective.* —*See* **drunk.**

inebriate *noun.* —*See* **drunkard.**

inebriated *adjective.* —*See* **drunk.**

inebriation *or* **inebriety** *noun.* —*See* **drunkenness.**

inedible *adjective.* —*See* **unpalatable.**

ineffable *adjective.* —*See* **unspeakable** (1).

ineffective *adjective.* —*See* **ineffectual** (1), **ineffectual** (2).

ineffectiveness *noun.* —*See* **ineffectuality.**

ineffectual *adjective.* **1.** Not having the desired effect ▶ counterproductive, inefficacious, inefficient, useless. ***Idioms:*** all wind, to no avail. **2.** Not capable of accomplishing anything ▶ helpless, impotent, inadequate, incapable, ineffective, inefficient, insufficient, lame, powerless, unable, useless, weak. ***Idiom:*** all gas and no motor. [*Compare* **inefficient, futile.**]

ineffectuality *noun.* The condition or state of being incapable of accomplishing anything ▶ helplessness, impotence, inadequacy, incapability, ineffectiveness, ineffectualness, inefficacy, insufficiency, powerlessness, uselessness. [*Compare* **futility, inability.**]

inefficacious *adjective.* —*See* **ineffectual** (1).

inefficacy *noun.* —*See* **ineffectuality.**

inefficiency *noun.* —*See* **inability.**

inefficient *adjective.* Lacking the qualities, as efficiency or skill, required to produce desired results ▶ bungling, impractical, inadequate, inapt, incapable, incompetent, inept, inexpert, unable, unequal, unfit, unqualified, unskilled, unskillful, unworkmanlike. [*Compare* **amateurish, improper.**] —*See also* **ineffectual** (1).

inelastic *adjective.* —*See* **rigid.**

inelegant *adjective.* —*See* **coarse** (1).

ineluctable *adjective.* —*See* **certain** (1).

inept *adjective.* —*See* **awkward** (1), **improper** (2), **inefficient, unfortunate** (2), **unskillful.**

ineptitude *noun.* —*See* **inability.**

inequality *noun.* **1.** The condition or fact of being unequal, as in age, rank, or degree ▶ disparity, disproportion, disproportionateness, imbalance, incongruity. [*Compare* **difference.**] **2.** Lack of equality, as of opportunity, treatment, or status ▶ discrimination, unfairness, unjustness. [*Compare* **bias.**] —*See also* **irregularity.**

inequitable *adjective.* —*See* **unfair.**

inequity *noun.* —*See* **injustice** (1), **injustice** (2).

ineradicable *adjective.* —*See* **confirmed** (1).

inert *adjective.* —*See* **dead** (2), **idle** (1), **lethargic.**

inertness *noun.* —*See* **inaction, lethargy.**

inescapable *adjective.* —*See* **certain** (1).

inessential *adjective.* Not part of the real or essential nature of a thing ▶ adscititious, adventitious, incidental, supervenient. [*Compare* **irrelevant.**] —*See also* **unnecessary.**

inestimable *adjective.* —*See* **costly, incalculable.**

inevitable *adjective.* —*See* **certain** (1).

inexact *adjective.* —*See* **indefinite** (1), **loose** (3).

inexcusable *adjective.* Impossible to excuse, pardon, or justify ▶ indefensible, inexpiable, irremissible, unforgivable, unjustifiable, unpardonable, unwarrantable. [*Compare* **evil, deplorable.**]

inexhaustibility *or* **inexhaustibleness** *noun.* —*See* **infinity** (1).

inexhaustible *adjective.* —*See* **tireless.**

inexorability *or* **inexorableness** *noun.* —*See* **stubbornness.**

inexorable *adjective.* —*See* **stubborn** (1).

inexpedient *adjective.* —*See* **unwise.**

inexpensive *adjective.* —*See* **cheap.**

inexperience *noun.* Lack of experience and the knowledge gained from it ▶ greenness, immaturity, inexpertness, newness, rawness. [*Compare* **artlessness, ignorance.**]

inexperienced *adjective.* Lacking experience and the knowledge gained from it ▶ fresh, green, immature, inexpert, new, raw, unconversant, uninitiate, uninitiated, unpracticed, unseasoned, untried, unversed. ***Idiom:*** wet behind the ears. [*Compare* **artless, ignorant.**]

inexpert *adjective.* —*See* **inefficient, inexperienced.**

inexpertness *noun.* —*See* **inexperience.**

inexpiable *adjective.* —*See* **inexcusable.**

inexplicable *adjective.* That cannot be explained ▶ unaccountable, unexplainable. [*Compare* **mysterious.**]

inexplicit *adjective.* —*See* **ambiguous** (2).

inexpressible *adjective.* —*See* **unspeakable** (1).

inexpressive *adjective.* —*See* **expressionless.**

inextricable *adjective.* —*See* **complex** (1).

infallible *adjective.* —*See* **sure** (2).

infamous *adjective.* —*See* **notorious, offensive** (1).

infamy *or* **infamousness** *noun.* The condition of being infamous ▶ disgracefulness, dishonorableness, disreputability, disreputableness, ignominiousness, shamefulness. [*Compare* **disgrace.**] —*See also* **notoriety.**

infant *noun.* —*See* **baby** (1).

infant *adjective.* —*See* **young.**

infantile *adjective.* —*See* **babyish, childish.**

infantine *adjective.* —*See* **babyish.**

infatuated *or* **infatuate** *adjective.* Affected with intense romantic attraction ▶ beguiled, besotted, captivated, charmed, enamored, enraptured, obsessed, smitten, spellbound, taken. *Slang:* gone. ***Idioms:*** crazy (*or* mad *or* nuts *or* wild) about, cuckoo over, hung up on.

infatuation *noun.* An extravagant, short-lived romantic attachment ▶ *Informal:* crush, thing. ***Idiom:*** passing fancy. [*Compare* **love.**] —*See also* **enthusiasm** (2), **obsession.**

infeasible *adjective.* —*See* **impossible.**

infect *verb.* —*See* **communicate** (2), **contaminate, corrupt, poison.**

infection *noun.* —*See* **contaminant, contamination, disease.**

infectious *adjective.* —*See* **contagious.**

infelicitous *adjective.* —*See* **improper** (2), **unfortunate** (2).

infer *verb.* To arrive at a conclusion from evidence or reasoning ▶ conclude, deduce, deduct, draw, find, gather, judge, reason, understand. [*Compare* **believe, derive, suppose.**] —*See also* **guess.**

inference *noun.* A position arrived at by reasoning from premises ▶ conclusion, deduction, judgment. [*Compare* **belief.**]

inferential *adjective.* —*See* **supposed.**

inferior *adjective.* —*See* **bad** (1), **disappointing, minor** (1).

inferior *noun.* —*See* **subordinate.**

infernal *adjective.* —*See* **damned, fiendish.**

inferred *adjective.* —*See* **implicit** (1).

infertile *adjective.* —*See* **barren** (1), **barren** (2).

infertility *noun.* —*See* **sterility** (2).

infidel *noun.* One who does not believe in God ▶ atheist, heathen, nonbeliever, pagan.

infidelity *noun.* —*See* **faithlessness.**

infiltrate *verb.* —*See* **insinuate.**

infinite *adjective.* —*See* **endless** (1), **incalculable.**

infiniteness *noun.* —*See* **infinity** (1).

infinitesimal *adjective.* So small as not to be discernible ▶ imperceptible, microscopic. [*Compare* **tiny.**]

infinity *noun.* **1.** The state or quality of being infinite ▶ boundlessness, immeasurability, immeasurableness, inexhaustibility, inexhaustibleness, infiniteness, infinitude, limitlessness, measurelessness, unboundedness, unlimitedness. [*Compare* **endlessness.**] **2.** The totality of time without beginning or end ▶ eternity, perpetuity, sempiternity. [*Compare* **forever.**]

infirm *adjective.* —*See* **insecure** (2), **weak** (1).

infirmity *noun.* The condition of being infirm or physically weak ▶ debility, decrepitude, delicacy, delicateness, feebleness, flimsiness, fragileness, fragility, frailness, frailty, insubstantiality, puniness, unsoundness, unsubstantiality, weakliness, weakness. [*Compare* **breakdown.**] —*See also* **disease, sickness, weakness.**

infix *verb.* —*See* **fix** (2).

inflame *verb.* —*See* **fire** (1), **hurt** (3), **provoke.**

inflamed *adjective.* —*See* **painful.**

inflammation *noun.* —*See* **irritation.**

inflate *verb.* —*See* **exaggerate, swell.**

inflated *adjective.* Filled up with or as if with something insubstantial ▶ flatulent, gassy, overblown, tumescent, tumid, turgid, windy. —*See also* **exaggerated, oratorical, swollen.**

inflection *noun.* —*See* **tone** (2).

inflexibility *or* **inflexibleness** *noun.* —*See* **stubbornness.**

inflexible *adjective.* —*See* **immutable, narrow** (1), **rigid, stubborn** (1).

inflict *verb.* To cause to undergo or bear (something unwelcome or damaging, for example) ▶ bring, impose, play, visit, wreak.

inflict on *or* **upon** *verb.* —*See* **impose on.**

infliction *noun.* An excessive, unwelcome burden ▶ encumbrance, imposition, intrusion, obtrusion. [*Compare*

burden, meddling.] —*See also* **punishment.**

influence *noun.* Power to sway or affect based on prestige, wealth, ability, or position ▶ force, leverage, power, sway, weight. *Informal:* clout, muscle. *Slang:* pull. —*See also* **effect** (2), **impact.**

influence *verb.* To have an impact on in a certain way ▶ act on, affect, dispose, impact, incline, lead (into), predispose, sway, work on. [*Compare* **bias, change, persuade.**] —*See also* **move** (1).

influential *adjective.* Having or exercising influence ▶ consequential, guiding, important, powerful, seminal, weighty. [*Compare* **dominant, famous, important, primary.**]

infold *verb.* —*See* **wrap** (2).

inform *verb.* **1.** To impart information to ▶ acquaint, advise, apprise, cue in, educate, enlighten, fill in, notify, tell. ***Idiom:*** break the news. [*Compare* **communicate, describe, reveal, say.**] **2.** To give incriminating information about others, especially to the authorities ▶ report, talk, tattle, tell, tip (off). *Slang:* finger, fink, rat (out), sing, snitch, squeal, stool. ***Idioms:*** blow the whistle, drop a dime on, name names, put the finger on. [*Compare* **accuse, betray, implicate.**]

informal *adjective.* —*See* **conversational, easygoing.**

informality *noun.* —*See* **ease** (1).

informant *noun.* —*See* **informer.**

information *noun.* That which is known about a specific subject or situation ▶ data, facts, intelligence, knowledge, lore. ▶ info, low-down. *Slang:* dope, poop. [*Compare* **education, knowledge.**] —*See also* **news.**

informative *adjective.* —*See* **educational** (2).

informed *adjective.* Provided with information; made aware ▶ acquainted, advised, educated, enlightened, instructed, knowing, knowledgeable, up on. ***Idioms:*** in the know, up to date. [*Compare* **aware, familiar.**] —*See also* **educated.**

informer *noun.* One who gives incriminating information about others ▶ informant, mole, source, talebearer, tattler, tattletale, telltale, whistleblower. *Informal:* rat, tipster. *Slang:* canary, finger, fink, nark, snitch, snitcher, squealer, stoolie, stool pigeon. [*Compare* **betrayer, gossip.**]

infraction *noun.* —*See* **breach** (1).

infrequent *adjective.* Rarely occurring or appearing ▶ occasional, rare, scarce, sporadic, uncommon, unusual. ***Idioms:*** few and far between, like a snowball in summer, once in a lifetime. [*Compare* **intermittent, unique.**]

infrequently *adverb.* At rare intervals ▶ inhabitually, little, occasionally, rarely, seldom, sporadically, uncommonly. ***Idioms:*** hardly (*or* scarcely) ever, once in a blue moon, once in a great while, when the spirit moves.

infringe *verb.* —*See* **violate** (1).

infringement *noun.* —*See* **breach** (1), **trespass** (2).

infuriate *verb.* —*See* **anger** (1).

infuriated *adjective.* —*See* **angry.**

infuse *verb.* —*See* **introduce** (2), **steep²**.

ingenerate *verb.* —*See* **cause.**

ingenious *adjective.* —*See* **clever** (1), **inventive.**

ingénue *noun.* —*See* **innocent** (2).

ingenuity *or* **ingeniousness** *noun.* —*See* **invention** (1).

ingenuous *adjective.* —*See* **artless, frank.**

ingest *verb.* To cause to pass from the mouth into the stomach ▶ swallow, take. [*Compare* **drink, gulp.**] —*See also* **eat** (1).

ingestion *noun.* An act of swallowing ▶ gulp, swallow, swig.

ingle *noun.* An open space for holding a fire at the base of a chimney ▶ fireplace, grate, hearth.

ingrain *verb.* —*See* **fix** (2), **instill.**

ingrained *adjective.* —*See* **confirmed** (1), **constitutional.**

ingratiating *adjective.* —*See* **flattering.**

ingredient *noun.* —*See* **part** (1).

ingress *noun.* —*See* **admission, entrance**[1]**.**

ingression *noun.* —*See* **admission, entrance**[1]**.**

in-group *noun.* —*See* **circle** (3).

ingurgitate *verb.* —*See* **gulp.**

inhabit *verb.* To live in a place, as does a people ▶ occupy, people, populate. [*Compare* **live, settle.**]

inhabitable *adjective.* Fit to live in ▶ habitable, livable.

inhabitant *noun.* One who resides in a place, especially on a permanent basis ▶ denizen, dweller, native, occupant, resident, tenant, townsman, townswoman, villager. *Informal:* local. [*Compare* **citizen.**]

inhalation *noun.* —*See* **breath.**

inhale *verb.* —*See* **breathe** (1).

inharmonic *or* **inharmonical** *adjective.* —*See* **inharmonious** (2).

inharmonious *adjective.* **1.** Devoid of harmony and accord ▶ conflicting, differing, disagreeing, discordant, dissident, dissonant, inconsonant, uncongenial, unharmonious. ***Idioms:*** at odds, at opposite poles, at sixes and sevens, at war, out of accord. [*Compare* **discrepant, incongruous.**] **2.** Characterized by unpleasant discordance of sound ▶ cacophonous, discordant, disharmonious, dissonant, inharmonic, tuneless, unharmonious, unmelodious, unmusical, untuneful. [*Compare* **harsh.**]

inharmony *noun.* —*See* **conflict.**

inhere *verb.* —*See* **consist.**

inherent *adjective.* —*See* **constitutional, instinctive.**

inherit *verb.* To receive from one who has died ▶ come into. ***Idioms:*** be (*or* fall) heir to.

inheritance *noun.* **1.** Any special privilege accorded a firstborn ▶ birthright, heritage, legacy, patrimony. [*Compare* **right.**] **2.** Something immaterial, as a style or philosophy, that is passed from one generation to another ▶ heritage, legacy, tradition.

inherited *adjective.* —*See* **ancestral, innate.**

inhibit *verb.* To check the freedom and spontaneity of ▶ constrain, constrict, cramp. —*See also* **restrain.**

inhibited *adjective.* —*See* **frigid, reserved.**

inhibition *noun.* —*See* **forbiddance, restraint.**

inhibitive *or* **inhibitory** *adjective.* —*See* **repressive.**

inhospitable *adjective.* Not encouraging life or growth ▶ adverse, hostile, unfavorable. [*Compare* **severe.**] —*See also* **forbidding.**

inhospitality *noun.* Lack of cordiality and hospitableness ▶ aloofness, coldness, inhospitableness, uncivility, uncongeniality, unfriendliness, ungraciousness, unreceptiveness, unwelcome, unwelcomeness.

inhuman *adjective.* —*See* **cruel, outrageous.**

inhumane *adjective.* —*See* **cruel.**

inhumanity *noun.* —*See* **cruelty, outrage.**

inhumation *noun.* —*See* **burial.**

inhume *verb.* —*See* **bury.**

inimical *adjective.* Feeling or showing unfriendliness ▶ hostile, unfriendly. [*Compare* **mean**[2]**.**] —*See also* **contrary.**

iniquitous *adjective.* —*See* **evil.**

iniquity *noun.* —*See* **crime** (2), **evil** (1), **injustice** (2).

initial *adjective.* —*See* **beginning, first.**

initiate *verb.* To admit formally into membership or office, as with ritual ▶ inaugurate, induct, install, instate, invest. [*Compare* **admit, indoctrinate.**] —*See also* **start** (1).

initiate *noun.* —*See* **beginner.**

initiation *noun.* The act or process of formally admitting a person to membership or office ▶ hazing, inaugural, inauguration, induction, installation, instatement, investiture. [*Compare* **admission.**] —*See also* **beginning.**

initiative *noun.* —*See* **drive** (2).
initiatory *adjective.* —*See* **beginning.**
inject *verb.* —*See* **introduce** (2).
injudicious *adjective.* —*See* **unwise.**
injunction *noun.* —*See* **command** (1).
injure *verb.* To cause bodily damage to a living thing ▶ hurt, traumatize, wing, wound. [*Compare* **cut, break.**] —*See also* **damage, deform, distress, offend** (1).
injurious *adjective.* —*See* **harmful, libelous.**
injury *noun.* —*See* **damage, harm, injustice** (1).
injustice *noun.* **1.** An unjust act ▶ crime, disservice, inequity, injury, malpractice, offense, outrage, raw deal, wrong. [*Compare* **breach, crime, indignity.**] **2.** Lack of justice ▶ inequity, iniquity, unfairness, unjustness, wrong. [*Compare* **favoritism, inequality, prejudice.**] —*See also* **oppression.**

✣ **CORE SYNONYMS:** *injustice, injury, wrong.* These nouns denote acts or conditions that cause people to suffer hardship or loss undeservedly. An *injustice* is a violation of a person's rights; the term can also refer to unfair treatment of another or others: "*Injustice anywhere is a threat to justice everywhere*" (Martin Luther King, Jr.). An *injury* is an injustice for which legal redress is available: *The court awarded the plaintiff compensation for the injury to his property. Wrong* is now more emphatic than *injustice* and in a legal sense refers to what violates the rights of an individual or adversely affects the public welfare: "*The age of chivalry is never past, so long as there is a wrong left unredressed on earth*" (Charles Kingsley).

inkhorn *adjective.* —*See* **pedantic.**
inkling *noun.* —*See* **feeling** (1), **hint** (1).
inky *adjective.* —*See* **black** (2).
inlet *noun.* A usually narrow stretch of water leading inland ▶ estuary, fjord, mouth. [*Compare* **bay**[1]**, channel, harbor.**]
inlying *adjective.* Located inside or farther in ▶ inner, inside, interior, internal. [*Compare* **central, secluded.**]
inmost *adjective.* —*See* **central.**
inn *noun.* —*See* **bar** (2).
innate *adjective.* Possessed at birth ▶ congenital, connate, connatural, hereditary, inborn, inherited, native. [*Compare* **essential.**] —*See also* **constitutional, instinctive.**

✣ **CORE SYNONYMS:** *innate, inborn, congenital, hereditary.* These adjectives mean existing in a person or thing from birth or origin. Something that is *innate* seems essential to the nature, character, or constitution: *innate common sense. Inborn* strongly implies that something has been present since birth: *inborn intelligence. Congenital* is applied principally to characteristics, especially defects, acquired during fetal development: *a congenital disease.* It is also used figuratively of characteristics or people with characteristics that are so deep-seated as to appear natural: *a congenital pessimism; a congenital liar. Hereditary* refers to what is transmitted by biological heredity (*a hereditary heart anomaly*) or by tradition: "*that ignorance and superstitiousness hereditary to all sailors*" (Herman Melville).

inner *adjective.* **1.** Located inside or farther in ▶ inlying, inside, interior, internal. [*Compare* **central, secluded.**] **2.** Arising from one's mental or spiritual being ▶ interior, internal, intimate, inward, visceral. *Slang:* gut. [*Compare* **constitutional, essential, personal.**]
innermost *adjective.* —*See* **central, confidential** (2).
innerving *adjective.* —*See* **invigorating.**
inning *noun.* —*See* **turn** (1).
innocence *noun.* The stage of life between birth and puberty ▶ childhood, early years, preadolescence, prepubescence. [*Compare* **youth.**] —*See also* **artlessness, chastity, ignorance** (2).

innocent *adjective.* **1.** Free from evil and corruption ▶ angelic, angelical, clean, lily-white, pure, sinless, unblemished, uncorrupted, undefiled, unstained, unsullied, untainted, virginal. ***Idiom:*** pure as the driven snow. [*Compare* **clean, ethical, inexperienced, moral.**] **2.** Free from guilt or blame ▶ blameless, faultless, guiltless, harmless, inculpable, irreproachable, lily-white, unblamable, unoffending. *Slang:* clean. ***Idioms:*** above suspicion, in the clear. [*Compare* **honest.**] —*See also* **artless, empty** (2), **harmless, ignorant** (3).

innocent *noun.* **1.** A pure, uncorrupted person ▶ angel, cherub, dove, lamb, virgin. **2.** A guileless, unsophisticated person ▶ babe, child, ingénue, naive. ***Idioms:*** babe in the woods, pure heart, simple soul. [*Compare* **fool.**] —*See also* **child** (1).

innocuous *adjective.* —*See* **harmless, insipid.**

innocuousness *noun.* —*See* **insipidity.**

innovate *verb.* —*See* **introduce** (1).

innovation *noun.* A new and unusual thing ▶ novelty. ***Idioms:*** the latest craze (*or* fashion *or* thing), the in thing, whole new ball of wax. —*See also* **invention** (2), **vision** (2).

innovative *adjective.* —*See* **inventive, new.**

innovativeness *noun.* —*See* **novelty** (1).

innovator *noun.* —*See* **developer.**

innuendo *noun.* —*See* **hint** (2).

innumerable *adjective.* —*See* **incalculable.**

inobservant *adjective.* —*See* **careless.**

inobtrusive *adjective.* —*See* **modest** (1).

inoffensive *adjective.* —*See* **clean** (2), **harmless, insipid.**

inoperative *adjective.* —*See* **idle** (1).

inoperativeness *noun.* —*See* **inaction.**

inopportune *adjective.* Not occurring at a favorable time ▶ ill-timed, inconvenient, untimely. [*Compare* **fateful.**] —*See also* **unseasonable.**

inordinacy *noun.* —*See* **excess** (1).

inordinate *adjective.* —*See* **excessive.**

inordinately *adverb.* —*See* **unduly.**

inordinateness *noun.* —*See* **excess** (1).

input *noun.* The right or chance to express an opinion or participate in a decision ▶ say, suffrage, voice, vote. *Informal:* say-so.

inquest *noun.* The examination of evidence, charges, and claims in court ▶ court case, hearing, inquiry, trial. —*See also* **examination** (1).

inquietude *noun.* —*See* **restlessness.**

inquire *or* **enquire** *verb.* —*See* **ask** (1), **explore.**

inquirer *or* **enquirer** *noun.* One who inquires ▶ cross-examiner, inquisitor, interrogator, interviewer, investigator, prober, querier, quester, questioner, researcher. [*Compare* **busybody.**]

inquiring *or* **enquiring** *adjective.* —*See* **curious** (2).

inquiry *or* **enquiry** *noun.* **1.** A request for data ▶ interrogation, query, question, questioning. [*Compare* **demand, problem.**] **2.** The examination of evidence, charges, and claims in court ▶ court case, hearing, inquest, trial. —*See also* **examination** (1).

inquisition *noun.* —*See* **examination** (1).

inquisitive *adjective.* —*See* **curious** (1), **curious** (2).

inquisitiveness *noun.* —*See* **curiosity** (2), **curiosity** (1).

inquisitor *noun.* —*See* **inquirer.**

inquisitorial *adjective.* —*See* **curious** (1), **dictatorial.**

inroad *noun.* An act of invading, especially by military forces ▶ foray, incursion, invasion, raid. [*Compare* **attack.**]

insalubrious *adjective.* —*See* **morbid, unwholesome** (1).

insane *adjective.* Afflicted with or exhibiting irrationality and mental unsoundness ▶ brainsick, certifiable, crazed, crazy, daft, demented, derailed, disordered, distraught, dotty, lunatic, mad, maniac, maniacal, mentally ill, moonstruck, non compos mentis, off, sick, touched, unsound, wrong. *Informal:* bonkers, cracked, daffy, gaga, haywire, loony, unhinged. *Slang:* bananas, bats, batty, buggy, cuckoo, fruity, loco, nuts, nutty, psycho, screwy, unbalanced, wacko, wacky, whack. ***Idioms:*** around the bend, bereft of reason, crazy as a loon, having a screw loose, mad as a hatter (*or* March hare), not all there, not playing with a full deck, nutty as a fruitcake, off one's nut (*or* rocker), off (*or* out of) one's head, off the wall, out of one's mind (*or* gourd *or* senses *or* tree *or* wits), sick (*or* soft) in the head, stark raving mad, of unsound mind. —*See also* **foolish.**

insaneness *noun.* —*See* **insanity.**

insanity *noun.* Serious mental illness impairing a person's capacity to function normally ▶ brainsickness, craziness, dementia, derangement, disturbance, insaneness, lunacy, madness, mania, mental illness, psychopathy, unbalance. —*See also* **foolishness.**

✚ CORE SYNONYMS: *insanity, lunacy, madness, mania, dementia.* These nouns denote conditions of serious mental illness or disorder. *Insanity* is a grave, often prolonged condition that prevents a person from being held legally responsible for his or her actions: *was judged not guilty for reasons of insanity. Lunacy* often denotes derangement relieved intermittently by periods of clear-mindedness: *yelled wildly in a moment of utter lunacy. Madness* often stresses the violent aspect of mental illness: *a story about obsession and madness. Mania* refers principally to the excited, or manic, phase of bipolar disorder: *prescribed drugs to control the patient's periods of mania. Dementia* implies mental deterioration brought on by an organic brain disorder: *underwent progressive stages of dementia.*

---

insatiable *adjective.* —*See* **voracious.**

insatiability *noun.* —*See* **voracity.**

inscribe *verb.* —*See* **engrave** (1), **engrave** (2), **list**[1], **sign, write.**

inscrutable *adjective.* —*See* **deep** (2), **incomprehensible, mysterious.**

insecure *adjective.* **1.** Inadequately protected ▶ ill-protected, unattended, undefended, unfortified, unguarded, unprotected, unsafe, unshielded. [*Compare* **open, vulnerable.**] **2.** Lacking stability ▶ infirm, precarious, rickety, shaky, teetering, tottering, tottery, unstable, unsteady, unsure, wavering, weak, wiggly, wobbly. [*Compare* **weak.**]

insecurity *or* **insecureness** *noun.* —*See* **instability.**

inseminate *verb.* To make pregnant ▶ impregnate. *Slang:* knock up. ***Idioms:*** get (*or* put) in a family way, get with child. [*Compare* **fertilize.**]

insensate *adjective.* Completely lacking sensation or consciousness ▶ dead, inanimate, insentient, lifeless. [*Compare* **dead.**] —*See also* **callous, foolish.**

insensibility *or* **insensibleness** *noun.* —*See* **apathy.**

insensible *adjective.* —*See* **blind** (3), **callous, cold** (2), **dead** (2), **imperceptible** (1), **unconscious.**

insensitive *adjective.* —*See* **callous, cold** (2), **dead** (2), **tactless, thoughtless.**

insensitivity *noun.* —*See* **thoughtlessness** (2).

insentient *adjective.* Completely lacking sensation or consciousness ▶ dead, inanimate, insensate, lifeless. [*Compare* **dead.**]

insert *verb.* —*See* **introduce** (2), **list**[1].

insertion *noun.* —*See* **entry.**

inside *adjective.* Located inside or farther in ▶ inlying, inner, interior, internal. [*Compare* **central, secluded.**] —*See also* **confidential** (1).

insides *noun.* —*See* **viscera.**

inside track *noun.* —*See* **advantage** (3).

insidious *adjective.* —*See* **dangerous, fallacious** (2).

insight *noun.* —*See* **discernment, instinct, wisdom** (1).

insightful *adjective.* —*See* **visionary.**

insignificance *noun.* —*See* **obscurity, trifle.**

insignificant *adjective.* —*See* **obscure** (2), **trivial.**

insincere *adjective.* —*See* **artificial** (2), **dishonest.**

insincerity *noun.* Lack of sincerity ▶ ambidexterity, artificiality, disingenuousness, falsity, phoniness, pretense. [*Compare* **dishonesty, hypocrisy.**]

insinuate *verb.* To introduce or insert by subtle and artful means ▶ edge, foist, infiltrate, wind, work, worm. [*Compare* **maneuver.**] —*See also* **hint.**

insinuating *adjective.* Provoking a change of outlook and especially gradual doubt and suspicion ▶ implicating, incriminating, insinuative, insinuatory, suggestive. —*See also* **flattering.**

insinuation *noun.* —*See* **hint** (2).

insinuative *or* **insinuatory** *adjective.* —*See* **insinuating.**

insipid *adjective.* Lacking vigor, intensity, or bite ▶ bland, innocuous, inoffensive, jejune, milk-and-water, namby-pamby, vapid, washy, watered down, waterish, watery, white-bread. *Informal:* wishy-washy. [*Compare* **dull, harmless, trite.**] —*See also* **flat** (2).

insipidity *or* **insipidness** *noun.* The state or quality of being insipid ▶ banality, blandness, innocuousness, jejuneness, vapidity, vapidness, washiness, wateriness. *Informal:* wishy-washiness. [*Compare* **emptiness.**] —*See also* **dullness.**

insist *verb.* To take and maintain a stand obstinately ▶ be resolute, carry on, persevere, persist. ***Idioms:*** make (*or* take) a stand, not take no for an answer, stand firm (*or* tall), stick to one's guns, hold (*or* stand) one's ground. [*Compare* **carry on, continue, endure.**] —*See also* **assert.**

insist on *or* **upon** *verb.* —*See* **demand** (1).

insistence *or* **insistency** *noun.* **1.** The state or quality of being insistent ▶ perseverance, persistence, persistency. [*Compare* **decision.**] **2.** Urgent solicitation ▶ persuasion, pressing, urging. [*Compare* **demand.**]

insistent *adjective.* Firm or obstinate, as in making a demand or maintaining a stand ▶ importunate, importune, persistent, urgent. [*Compare* **firm, stubborn.**] —*See also* **assertive.**

insobriety *noun.* —*See* **drunkenness.**

insolence *noun.* —*See* **arrogance, impudence.**

insolent *adjective.* —*See* **arrogant, disrespectful, impudent.**

insolvency *noun.* —*See* **bankruptcy.**

insolvent *noun.* —*See* **pauper.**

insolvent *adjective.* —*See* **poor.**

insouciant *adjective.* —*See* **careless.**

inspect *verb.* To examine a person or someone's personal effects in order to find something lost or concealed ▶ frisk, pat down, search. *Slang:* shake down. ***Idiom:*** do a body search of. —*See also* **examine** (1).

inspection *noun.* —*See* **examination** (1).

inspiration *noun.* **1.** Liveliness and vivacity of imagination ▶ brilliance, brilliancy, fire, genius. [*Compare* **intelligence, invention.**] **2.** A sudden exciting thought ▶ brainstorm, bright idea. *Informal:* brain wave. [*Compare* **idea.**] —*See also* **breath, elation, encouragement, vision** (2).

inspire *verb.* —*See* **breathe** (1), **cause, elate, encourage** (1), **fire** (1), **provoke.**

inspired *adjective.* —*See* **visionary.**

inspirit *verb.* —*See* **elate, encourage** (1).

inspissate *verb.* To make thick or thicker, especially through evaporation or condensation ▶ condense, reduce, thicken. [*Compare* **coagulate.**]

instability *noun.* The quality or condition of being erratic and undependable ▶ flightiness, inconsistency, inconstancy, insecureness, insecurity, irregularity, precariousness, shakiness, unpredictability, unreliability, unstableness, unsteadiness, unsureness. [*Compare* **change.**]

install *verb.* —*See* **establish** (1), **initiate, position.**

installation *noun.* Something attached as a permanent part of something else ▶ apparatus, fitting, fixture. [*Compare* **attachment.**] —*See also* **base[1]** (1), **exhibition, initiation.**

installment *noun.* A partial or intial payment ▶ deposit, down payment, security.

instance *noun.* —*See* **example** (1), **lawsuit.**

instance *verb.* To demonstrate and clarify with examples ▶ demonstrate, evidence, exemplify, illustrate. [*Compare* **explain, show.**] —*See also* **name** (2).

instant *noun.* —*See* **flash** (2), **occasion** (1).

instant *adjective.* Occurring at once ▶ immediate, instantaneous. ***Idioms:*** on-the-spot, split-second. [*Compare* **fast, quick.**] —*See also* **urgent** (1).

instant *adverb.* —*See* **immediately** (1).

instantaneous *adjective.* Occurring at once ▶ immediate, instant. ***Idioms:*** on-the-spot, split-second. [*Compare* **fast, quick.**]

instantiate *verb.* —*See* **embody** (1).

instantiation *noun.* —*See* **embodiment, example** (1).

instantly *adverb.* —*See* **immediately** (1).

instate *verb.* —*See* **initiate.**

instatement *noun.* —*See* **initiation.**

instigate *verb.* —*See* **provoke.**

instigation *noun.* —*See* **provocation** (1).

instigator *noun.* —*See* **agitator.**

instill *verb.* To fix (an idea, for example) in someone's mind by reemphasis and repetition ▶ beat into, drill, drive, implant, impress, inculcate, ingrain, pound. ***Idioms:*** drum (*or* hammer *or* knock) into someone's head. [*Compare* **indoctrinate, teach.**]

instinct *noun.* The power to discern the true nature of a person or situation ▶ clairvoyance, insight, intuitiveness, intuition, penetration, sense, sixth sense. [*Compare* **discernment, feeling, inclination.**] —*See also* **talent.**

instinctive *adjective.* Derived from or prompted by a natural tendency or impulse ▶ inborn, inherent, innate, instinctual, intuitive, unlearned, untaught, visceral. [*Compare* **constitutional.**] —*See also* **spontaneous.**

✦ CORE SYNONYMS: *instinctive, instinctual, intuitive, visceral.* These adjectives mean derived from or prompted by a natural tendency or impulse: *an instinctive fear of snakes; instinctual behavior; an intuitive perception; visceral revulsion.*

---

instinctual *adjective.* —*See* **instinctive.**

institute *verb.* —*See* **establish** (2), **found, start** (1).

institute *noun.* —*See* **law** (1).

institution *noun.* —*See* **foundation.**

institutionalize *verb.* To place officially in confinement ▶ commit, consign. *Informal:* send up. [*Compare* **imprison.**]

instruct *verb.* —*See* **command** (1), **educate.**

instructed *adjective.* —*See* **informed.**

instruction *noun.* —*See* **command** (1), **education** (1), **education** (2).

instructional *adjective.* —*See* **educational** (1), **educational** (2).

instructive *adjective.* —*See* **educational** (2).

instructor *noun.* —*See* **educator.**

instrument *noun.* A device used to do work or perform a task ▶ implement, tool, utensil. [*Compare* **gadget.**] —*See also* **agent, device** (1), **pawn[2].**

instrumental *adjective.* —*See* **effective** (1).

instrumentalist *noun.* —*See* **player** (2).

instrumentality *noun.* —*See* **agent.**

insubordinate *adjective.* —*See* **defiant, unruly.**

insubordination *noun.* —*See* **defiance** (1).

insubstantial *adjective.* —*See* **immaterial, implausible, meager, weak** (1).

insubstantiality *noun.* —*See* **infirmity.**

insufferable *adjective.* —*See* **unbearable.**

insufficiency *noun.* —*See* **ineffectuality, shortage.**

insufficient *adjective.* Not enough to meet a demand or requirement ▶ deficient, inadequate, scarce, short, shy, under, wanting. ***Idioms:*** at a premium, in short supply, on the short end. [*Compare* **deficient, inefficient, meager.**] —*See also* **disappointing, ineffectual** (2).

insular *adjective.* —*See* **narrow** (1), **remote** (1).

insulate *verb.* —*See* **isolate** (1).

insulation *noun.* —*See* **isolation.**

insult *verb.* To cause resentment or hurt by callous, rude behavior ▶ affront, huff, miff, offend, outrage, pique. *Informal:* badmouth, slam. *Slang:* dis, put down. ***Idioms:*** add insult to injury, call names, give offense, hurt someone's feelings, step on someone's toes. [*Compare* **revile, ridicule, snub.**] —*See also* **offend** (1).

insult *noun.* —*See* **indignity, taunt.**

insulting *adjective.* —*See* **disrespectful, offensive** (2).

insuperable *adjective.* Incapable of being negotiated or overcome ▶ impassable, insurmountable, unconquerable. [*Compare* **impossible, invincible.**]

insupportable *adjective.* —*See* **unbearable.**

insure *verb.* —*See* **guarantee** (2).

insurgence *noun.* —*See* **defiance** (1), **rebellion.**

insurgency *noun.* —*See* **rebellion.**

insurgent *adjective.* —*See* **rebellious.**

insurgent *noun.* —*See* **rebel** (1).

insurmountable *adjective.* Incapable of being negotiated or overcome ▶ impassable, insuperable, unconquerable. [*Compare* **impossible, invincible.**]

insurrection *noun.* —*See* **rebellion.**

insurrectionary *or* **insurrectionist** *noun.* —*See* **rebel** (1).

insusceptibility *noun.* The capacity to withstand ▶ immunity, imperviousness, resistance, unsusceptibility. [*Compare* **endurance, stability.**]

insusceptible *adjective.* —*See* **cold** (2), **resistant.**

intact *adjective.* —*See* **complete** (1), **good** (2).

intake *noun.* —*See* **absorption** (1).

intangible *adjective.* —*See* **immaterial, imperceptible** (1).

integral *adjective.* —*See* **built-in, complete** (1), **essential** (2).

integral *noun.* —*See* **system.**

integrate *verb.* **1.** To construct as an integral part ▶ build in, include, incorporate. **2.** To make a part of a united whole ▶ combine, embody, incorporate. **3.** To open to all people regardless of race ▶ desegregate. —*See also* **combine** (1), **harmonize** (2), **harmonize** (1).

integrity *noun.* —*See* **character** (2), **completeness, honesty, soundness.**

integument *noun.* The tissue forming the external covering of the body ▶ epidermis, skin.

intellect *noun.* —*See* **intelligence, mind** (2).

intellection *noun.* —*See* **thought.**

intellective *adjective.* —*See* **mental.**

intellectual *adjective.* Appealing to or engaging the intellect ▶ cerebral, mental, sophisticated, thoughtful. *Informal:* eggheaded, highbrow. *Slang:* pointy-headed. [*Compare* **complex, educated.**] —*See also* **intelligent, mental.**

intellectual *noun.* —*See* **mind** (2).

intelligence *noun.* The faculty of thinking, reasoning, and applying knowledge ▶ aptitude, brainpower, brains, brightness, cleverness, intellect, mentality, mind, quick-wittedness, sense, smartness, understanding, wit. *Informal:* eggheadedness, gray matter. *Slang:* smarts. ***Idioms:*** intellectual (*or* mental) grasp, mental aptitude (*or* capacity), power of the mind (*or* thought). [*Compare* **com-**

mon sense.] —*See also* **discernment, information, news, wisdom** (1).

✚ **CORE SYNONYMS:** *intelligence, mind, intellect, brain, wit.* These nouns denote the faculty of thinking, reasoning, and acquiring and applying knowledge. *Intelligence* implies solving problems, learning from experience, and reasoning abstractly: "*The world of the future will be an ever more demanding struggle against the limitations of our intelligence*" (Norbert Wiener). *Mind* refers broadly to the capacities for thought, perception, memory, and decision: "*No passion so effectually robs the mind of all its powers of acting and reasoning as fear*" (Edmund Burke). *Intellect* stresses knowing, thinking, and understanding: "*Opinion is ultimately determined by the feelings, and not by the intellect*" (Herbert Spencer). *Brains* suggests strength of intellect: *We racked our brains to find a solution. Wit* stresses quickness of intelligence or facility of comprehension: "*There is no such whetstone, to sharpen a good wit and encourage a will to learning, as is praise*" (Roger Ascham).

---

intelligent *adjective.* Having or showing intelligence, often of a high order ▶ bright, brilliant, genius, intellectual, knowing, knowledgeable, smart. *Informal:* brainy. [*Compare* **critical, shrewd, wise.**] —*See also* **clever** (1), **logical** (2).

✚ **CORE SYNONYMS:** *intelligent, bright, brilliant, knowing, smart, intellectual.* These adjectives mean having or showing intelligence, often of a high order. *Intelligent* usually implies the ability to cope with new problems and to use the power of reasoning and inference effectively: *The intelligent math students excelled in calculus. Bright* implies quickness or ease in learning: *The bright child learned the alphabet quickly. Brilliant* suggests unusually impressive mental acuteness: "*The dullard's envy of brilliant men is always assuaged by the suspicion that they will come to a bad end*" (Max Beerbohm). *Knowing* implies the possession of knowledge, information, or understanding: *Knowing collectors bought all the auctioned paintings. Smart* refers to quick intelligence and often a ready capability for taking care of one's own interests: *Smart lawyers can effectively manipulate juries. Intellectual* implies the capacity to grasp difficult or abstract concepts: *Dinner at the philosopher's house was noted for its intellectual conversations.*

---

intelligibility *noun.* —*See* **clarity.**

intelligible *adjective.* —*See* **understandable.**

intemperance *noun.* —*See* **excess** (2).

intemperate *adjective.* —*See* **excessive.**

intend *verb.* To have in mind as a goal or purpose ▶ aim, contemplate, design, mean, plan, project, propose, purpose, target. *Chiefly Regional:* mind. ***Idioms:*** be fixing to, have one's heart set on, set one's sights on. [*Compare* **aim, decide, expect.**] —*See also* **mean**[1].

intended *adjective.* —*See* **deliberate** (1), **engaged.**

intended *noun. Informal* A person to whom one is engaged to be married ▶ betrothed, bride-to-be, fiancé, fiancée, future husband, future wife, husband-to-be, prospective spouse, wife-to-be.

intense *adjective.* Extreme in activity, strength, or effect ▶ all-out, concentrated, desperate, fierce, furious, heavy, heightened, high, intensive, overpowering, overwhelming, strong, terrible, vehement, violent. [*Compare* **forceful, severe, sharp.**] —*See also* **deep** (3).

✚ **CORE SYNONYMS:** *intense, fierce, overpowering, vehement, violent.* These adjectives mean extreme in activity, strength, or effect: *intense fear; fierce pride; an overpowering stench; vehement dislike; violent rage.*

---

intensely *adverb.* —*See* **very.**

intensify *verb.* To make greater in intensity or severity ▶ aggravate, deepen, enhance, escalate, exacerbate, heighten, redouble, sharpen, step up. *Slang:* hop up. ***Idioms:*** add fuel to the fire (*or* flame). [*Compare* **emphasize, increase, support.**]

intensity *noun.* Concentrated power or force, as of effort, opinion, or emotion ▶ concentration, depth, depths, ferociousness, ferocity, fever pitch, fierceness, forcefulness, fury, height, pitch, severity, strain, vehemence, vehemency, violence. [*Compare* **force, passion, strength.**]

intensive *adjective.* —*See* **concentrated** (1), **intense.**

intensively *adverb.* —*See* **completely** (2).

intent *noun.* —*See* **intention, meaning, thrust.**

intent *adjective.* Committed to or unwavering in a course of action ▶ bent, decided, determined, fixed, resolute, resolved, set, single-minded, unhesitating. [*Compare* **firm[1], insistent, stubborn.**] —*See also* **alert, rapt.**

intention *noun.* What one intends to do or achieve ▶ aim, ambition, design, determination, end, goal, intent, mark, meaning, object, objective, point, projection, purpose, target, view, why. ***Idioms:*** end in view, why and wherefore. [*Compare* **approach, dream, mission.**]

✦ **CORE SYNONYMS:** *intention, intent, purpose, goal, end, aim, object, objective.* These nouns refer to what one intends or plans to do or achieve. *Intention* simply signifies a course of action that one proposes to follow: *It is my intention to take a vacation next month. Intent* more strongly implies deliberateness: *The executor complied with the testator's intent. Purpose* strengthens the idea of resolution or determination: *"His purpose was to discover how long these guests intended to stay"* (Joseph Conrad). *Goal* may suggest an idealistic or long-term purpose: *The college's goal was to raise ten million dollars for a new library. End* suggests a long-range goal: *The candidate wanted to win and pursued every means to achieve that end. Aim* stresses the direction one's efforts take in pursuit of an end: *The aim of most students is to graduate.* An *object* is an end that one tries to carry out: *The object of chess is to checkmate your opponent's king. Objective* often implies that the end or goal can be reached: *The report outlines the committee's objectives.*

intentional *adjective.* —*See* **calculated, deliberate** (1).

inter *verb.* —*See* **bury.**

interaction *noun.* —*See* **communication** (1).

interceder *or* **intercessor** *noun.* —*See* **go-between.**

intercept *verb.* To block the progress of and force to change direction ▶ cut off, head off.

interchange *verb.* To take turns ▶ alternate, rotate, shift. —*See also* **change** (3), **exchange.**

interchange *noun.* Occurrence in successive turns ▶ alternation, rotation, shift. —*See also* **change** (2).

intercommunication *noun.* A situation allowing exchange of ideas or messages ▶ communication, correspondence, contact, touch. [*Compare* **communication.**] —*See also* **communication** (1).

interconnection *noun.* —*See* **relation** (1).

intercourse *noun.* —*See* **communication** (1).

interdependence *noun.* —*See* **relation** (1).

interdependent *adjective.* —*See* **complementary.**

interdict *verb.* —*See* **forbid.**

interdict *noun.* A coercive measure intended to ensure compliance or conformity ▶ interdiction, penalty, sanction. [*Compare* **restriction, punishment.**]

interdiction *noun.* A coercive measure intended to ensure compliance or conformity ▶ interdict, penalty, sanction. [*Compare* **restriction, punishment.**] —*See also* **forbiddance.**

interdictive *adjective.* —*See* **preventive** (1).

interest *noun.* **1.** Something that contributes to or increases one's well-being ▶ advantage, benefit, good, interests, profit, use. [*Compare* **advantage.**] **2.** A right or legal share in something ▶ claim, portion, stake, title. [*Compare* **cut, right.**] **3.** Something that concerns or involves one personally ▶ affair, business, concern, lookout. —*See also* **curiosity** (1).

interest *verb.* —*See* **grip.**

interested *adjective.* —*See* **concerned, curious** (2).

interestedness *noun.* —*See* **curiosity** (1).

interface *noun.* —*See* **communication** (1).

interfere *verb.* —*See* **disrupt, meddle.**

interfere with *verb.* —*See* **hinder.**

interference *noun.* —*See* **meddling.**

interfering *adjective.* —*See* **curious** (1).

interim *noun.* —*See* **gap** (2).

interim *adjective.* —*See* **temporary** (2), **temporary** (1).

interior *adjective.* Located inside or farther in ▶ inlying, inner, inside, internal. [*Compare* **central, secluded.**] —*See also* **inner** (2).

interject *verb.* —*See* **introduce** (2).

interlace *verb.* —*See* **weave.**

interlard *verb.* —*See* **introduce** (2).

interlock *verb.* To be the proper size and shape for something ▶ dovetail, fit. ***Idiom:*** fit like a glove.

interlocution *noun.* —*See* **conversation.**

interlocutor *noun.* —*See* **conversationalist.**

interlope *verb.* —*See* **intrude, meddle.**

interloper *noun.* —*See* **busybody.**

interlude *noun.* —*See* **gap** (2).

intermeddle *verb.* —*See* **meddle.**

intermediary *noun.* —*See* **agent, go-between.**

intermediary *adjective.* —*See* **middle.**

intermediate *noun.* —*See* **go-between.**

intermediate *adjective.* —*See* **middle.**

intermediator *noun.* —*See* **go-between.**

interment *noun.* —*See* **burial.**

interminability *noun.* —*See* **endlessness.**

interminable *adjective.* —*See* **continual, long[1]** (2).

intermingle *verb.* —*See* **mix** (1).

intermission *noun.* —*See* **abeyance, rest[1]** (1).

intermittent *adjective.* Happening or appearing now and then ▶ episodic, fitful, irregular, occasional, periodic, periodical, sporadic. *Informal:* on-again, off-again. ***Idioms:*** here and there, on and off. [*Compare* **infrequent, random.**]

✚ **CORE SYNONYMS:** *intermittent, periodic, sporadic, occasional, fitful.* These adjectives all mean recurring or reappearing now and then. *Intermittent* describes something that stops and starts at intervals: *intermittent rain showers.* Something *periodic* occurs at regular or at least generally predictable intervals: *periodic feelings of anxiety. Sporadic* implies scattered, irregular, unpredictable, or isolated instances: *sporadic bombing raids.* What is *occasional* happens at random and irregularly: *occasional outbursts of temper.* Something *fitful* occurs in spells and often abruptly: *fitful bursts of energy.*

---

intermittently *adverb.* Once in a while; at times ▶ betimes, fitfully, occasionally, periodically, sometimes, sporadically. ***Idioms:*** ever and again (*or* anon), now and again (*or* then).

intermix *verb.* —*See* **mix** (1).

intern *verb.* —*See* **imprison.**

internal *adjective.* Located inside or farther in ▶ inlying, inner, inside, interior. [*Compare* **central, secluded.**] —*See also* **domestic** (3), **inner** (2).

internment *noun.* —*See* **detention.**

interpose *or* **interpolate** *verb.* —*See* **introduce** (2).

interpret *verb.* **1.** To understand in a particular way ▶ construe, read, take. ***Idioms:*** read between the lines, see in a special light, take to mean. [*Compare* **understand.**] **2.** To perform according to one's artistic conception ▶ depict, execute, play, present, render, represent. [*Compare* **act.**] —*See also* **explain** (1), **translate.**

interpretable *adjective.* —*See* **explainable.**

interpretation *noun.* A performer's distinctive personal version of a song, dance, piece of music, or role ▶ depiction, enactment, execution, performance, portrayal, presentation, reading, realization, rendering, rendition, representation. —*See also* **commentary, explanation, translation.**

interpretive *or* **interpretative** *adjective.* —*See* **explanatory.**

interregnum *noun.* —*See* **gap** (2).

interrelated *adjective.* —*See* **complementary.**

interrelationship *noun.* —*See* **relation** (1).

interrogate *verb.* —*See* **ask** (1).

interrogation *noun.* A request for data ▶ inquiry, query, question, questioning. [*Compare* **demand, problem.**]

interrogator *or* **interrogater** *noun.* —*See* **inquirer.**

interrupt *verb.* **1.** To stop suddenly, as a conversation, activity, or relationship ▶ break off, cease, discontinue, suspend, terminate. **2.** To interject remarks or questions into another's discourse ▶ barge in, break in, chime in, chip in, cut in. ***Idioms:*** break one's train of thought, talk out of turn. [*Compare* **intrude, meddle.**] **3.** To stop for an indefinite period ▶ pause, suspend. ***Idioms:*** put on hold (*or* on ice). [*Compare* **rest.**] —*See also* **disrupt.**

interruption *noun.* —*See* **break.**

intersect *verb.* —*See* **cross** (2).

interstice *or* **interspace** *noun.* —*See* **gap** (1).

intertwine *verb.* —*See* **weave.**

interval *noun.* —*See* **bit**[1] (3), **degree** (1), **distance** (1), **gap** (1).

intervention *noun.* —*See* **meddling.**

interview *noun.* —*See* **conversation.**

intestinal fortitude *noun.* —*See* **courage.**

intestines *noun.* —*See* **viscera.**

intimacy *noun.* —*See* **friendship.**

intimate[1] *adjective.* **1.** Very closely associated ▶ bosom, chummy, close, cozy, familiar, fast, friendly, inseparable, near. *Informal:* solid, thick. *Slang:* tight. ***Idioms:*** buddy-buddy with, hand in glove with. [*Compare* **faithful.**] **2.** Belonging to, relating to, or affecting a particular person ▶ individual, personal, private. —*See also* **confidential** (2), **inner** (2).

intimate *noun.* One in whom secrets are confided ▶ confessor, confidant, confidante, repository. —*See also* **friend.**

intimate[2] *verb.* —*See* **hint.**

intimation *noun.* —*See* **hint** (2), **shade** (2).

intimidate *verb.* To frighten into submission, compliance, or acquiescence ▶ bludgeon, browbeat, bulldoze, bully, bullyrag, cow, hector, lean on, menace, push around, threaten. *Informal:* strong-arm. ***Idioms:*** flex one's muscles, put the screws (*or* squeeze) on, threaten with bodily harm, turn the heat on, twist someone's arm. [*Compare* **coerce, harass.**] —*See also* **frighten.**

✚ **CORE SYNONYMS:** *intimidate, browbeat, bulldoze, cow, bully, bludgeon.* These verbs all mean to frighten into submission, compliance, or acquiescence. *Intimidate* implies the presence or operation of a fear-inspiring force:

"*It* [atomic energy] *may intimidate the human race into bringing order into its international affairs*" (Albert Einstein). *Browbeat* suggests the persistent application of highhanded, disdainful, or imperious tactics: *browbeating a witness. Bulldoze* connotes the leveling of all spirit of opposition: *was bulldozed into hiring an unacceptable candidate. Cow* implies bringing out an abject state of timorousness and often demoralization: *a dog that was cowed by abuse.* To *bully* is to intimidate through blustering, domineering, or threatening behavior: *workers who were bullied into accepting a poor contract. Bludgeon* suggests the use of grossly aggressive or combative methods: *had to be bludgeoned into fulfilling his duties.*

---

intimidation *noun.* An expression of the intent to hurt or punish another ▶ menace, threat.

intimidator *noun.* —*See* **bully.**

intolerable *adjective.* —*See* **outrageous, unbearable.**

intolerance *noun.* Irrational suspicion or hatred of a particular group, race, or religion ▶ bigotry, discrimination, prejudice. [*Compare* **hate.**]

intolerant *adjective.* **1.** Not tolerant of the beliefs or opinions of others ▶ bigoted, close-minded, dogmatic, hidebound, illiberal, judgmental, narrow-minded, opinionated, puritanical. [*Compare* **biased, narrow, stubborn.**] **2.** Being unable or unwilling to endure irritation or opposition, for example ▶ impatient, unforbearing, unindulgent. [*Compare* **ill-tempered, intolerant.**] —*See also* **disdainful.**

intonation *noun.* —*See* **tone** (2).

intone *verb.* —*See* **sing.**

intoxicate *verb.* —*See* **poison.**

intoxicated *adjective.* —*See* **drunk.**

intoxicating *adjective.* —*See* **hard** (3), **invigorating.**

intoxication *noun.* —*See* **drunkenness.**

intoxicative *adjective.* —*See* **hard** (3).

intractability *or* **intractableness** *noun.* —*See* **unruliness.**

intractable *adjective.* —*See* **unruly.**

intransigence *or* **intransigency** *noun.* —*See* **stubbornness.**

intransigent *adjective.* —*See* **stubborn** (1).

intrepid *adjective.* —*See* **brave.**

intrepidity *or* **intrepidness** *noun.* —*See* **courage.**

intricacy *noun.* —*See* **complexity.**

intricate *adjective.* —*See* **complex** (1), **elaborate.**

intrigue *noun.* —*See* **plot** (2).

intrigue *verb.* —*See* **grip, plot** (2).

intrigued *adjective.* —*See* **curious** (2).

intrinsic *adjective.* —*See* **constitutional.**

introduce *verb.* **1.** To bring into currency, use, fashion, or practice ▶ innovate, launch, originate, pioneer, popularize, put forward, usher in. ***Idiom:*** start the ball rolling. [*Compare* **found, start.**] **2.** To put or set into, between, or among another or other things ▶ implant, infuse, inject, insert, interject, interlard, interpolate, interpose, put in, stick in, throw in. [*Compare* **attach, fix.**] **3.** To begin something with preliminary or prefatory material ▶ lead, precede, preface, ring in, usher in. ***Idioms:*** pave the way, ring up the curtain. [*Compare* **start.**] **4.** To make known socially ▶ acquaint, familiarize, present. —*See also* **broach, proclaim.**

✚ **CORE SYNONYMS:** *introduce, insert, interject, interpolate, interpose.* These verbs mean to put or set a person or thing into, between, or among others: *introduce suspense into a novel; insert a letter into an envelope; interject a comment into a conversation; interpolated a transitional passage into the text; interposed himself between the scrapping boys.*

---

introduction *noun.* A short section of preliminary remarks ▶ foreword, induction, lead-in, overture, preamble, preface, prelude, prolegomenon, prologue. —*See also* **admission, beginning.**

introductory *adjective.* Serving to introduce or prepare for something ▶ inductive, prefatory, preliminary, preparatory. —*See also* **beginning.**

✤ CORE SYNONYMS: *introductory, prefatory, preliminary, preparatory.* These adjectives mean serving to introduce or prepare for something: *introductory remarks; an author's prefatory notes; a preliminary investigation; preparatory steps.*

---

intromission *noun.* —*See* **admission.**

intromit *verb.* —*See* **accept** (3).

introversion *noun.* —*See* **reserve** (1).

introverted *adjective.* —*See* **reserved, shy¹.**

intrude *verb.* To force or come in as an improper or unwanted element ▶ barge in, charge in, cut in, encroach, gatecrash, horn in, interlope, obtrude, trespass. [*Compare* **interrupt, meddle.**] —*See also* **disrupt.**

intrusion *noun.* An excessive, unwelcome burden ▶ encumbrance, imposition, infliction, obtrusion. [*Compare* **burden.**] —*See also* **meddling, trespass** (2).

intrusive *adjective.* —*See* **curious** (1), **disturbing.**

intuit *verb.* —*See* **perceive.**

intuition *noun.* —*See* **feeling** (1), **instinct.**

intuitive *adjective.* —*See* **instinctive, visionary.**

intuitiveness *noun.* —*See* **instinct.**

inundate *verb.* To affect as if by an outpouring of water ▶ deluge, flood, overwhelm, swamp. —*See also* **flood** (1).

inundation *noun.* —*See* **flood.**

inure *verb.* —*See* **accustom.**

inured *adjective.* —*See* **accustomed** (1).

invade *verb.* **1.** To enter so as to attack, plunder, destroy, or conquer ▶ foray, harry, maraud, overrun, raid. ***Idioms:*** enter by force, take by storm. [*Compare* **attack, sack.**] **2.** To enter forcibly or illegally ▶ break in, burglarize, trespass. [*Compare* **rob, steal.**] —*See also* **occupy** (2).

invalid *adjective.* —*See* **fallacious** (1).

invalidate *verb.* —*See* **abolish, disable** (1).

invalidation *noun.* —*See* **abolition.**

invaluable *adjective.* —*See* **costly.**

invariable *adjective.* —*See* **immutable, unchanging.**

invariant *adjective.* —*See* **unchanging.**

invasion *noun.* An act of invading, especially by military forces ▶ foray, incursion, inroad, raid. [*Compare* **attack.**]

invective *noun.* —*See* **vituperation.**

invective *adjective.* —*See* **abusive.**

inveigh *verb.* —*See* **object.**

inveigle *verb.* —*See* **seduce.**

inveiglement *noun.* —*See* **lure** (1).

inveigler *noun.* —*See* **seducer** (1).

invent *verb.* To use ingenuity in making, developing, or achieving ▶ coin, concoct, contrive, devise, dream up, fabricate, formulate, hatch, make up, mint, think up. *Informal:* cook up. ***Idiom:*** come up with. [*Compare* **design, introduce, produce, make.**] —*See also* **lie².**

invented *adjective.* —*See* **fictitious.**

invention *noun.* **1.** The power or ability to invent ▶ creativeness, creativity, fecundity, ingeniousness, ingenuity, inventiveness, originality, resourcefulness. [*Compare* **ability, brilliance, imagination.**] **2.** Something invented ▶ brainchild, concoction, contrivance, device, innovation, origination. [*Compare* **device, discovery, novelty.**] —*See also* **beginning, composition** (1), **lie², myth** (2).

inventive *adjective.* Characterized by or productive of new things or new ideas ▶ artistic, creative, generative, ingenious, innovative, original, resourceful, seminal. [*Compare* **fertile, visionary.**] —*See also* **clever** (1), **new.**

inventiveness *noun.* —*See* **invention** (1).

inventor *noun.* —*See* **originator.**

inventory *noun.* —*See* **good** (2), **hoard, list[1].**
inventory *verb.* —*See* **enumerate.**
inveracity *noun.* —*See* **lie[2], mendacity.**
inverse *noun.* —*See* **opposite.**
inverse *adjective.* —*See* **opposite.**
inversion *noun.* —*See* **reversal** (1).
invert *verb.* —*See* **overturn, reverse** (1).
inverted *adjective.* —*See* **upside-down.**
invest *verb.* —*See* **bank[2], besiege, dress** (1), **establish** (1), **gift, initiate, wrap** (2).
investigate *verb.* —*See* **examine** (1), **explore.**
investigation *noun.* The act or an instance of exploring or investigating ▶ exploration, probe, reconnaissance. —*See also* **examination** (1).
investigative *adjective.* —*See* **curious** (2).
investigator *noun.* —*See* **detective, inquirer.**
investiture *noun.* —*See* **initiation.**
investment *noun.* **1.** The management of money ▶ banking, finance, money management. **2.** A prolonged encirclement of an objective by hostile troops ▶ beleaguerment, besiegement, blockade, siege. [*Compare* **attack.**]
inveterate *adjective.* Subject to a disease or habit for a long time ▶ chronic, confirmed, habitual, habituated. [*Compare* **stubborn.**] —*See also* **confirmed** (1).
invidious *adjective.* —*See* **envious, libelous.**
invigorate *verb.* —*See* **energize.**
invigorating *adjective.* Producing or stimulating physical, mental, or emotional vigor ▶ animating, bracing, energizing, enlivening, exciting, exhilarant, exhilarating, innerving, intoxicating, quickening, refreshing, reinvigorating, renewing, restorative, roborant, rousing, stimulating, tonic, vitalizing, vivifying. [*Compare* **curative, pleasant.**]
invincible *adjective.* Incapable of being conquered or subjugated ▶ indomitable, unbeatable, unconquerable, undefeatable. [*Compare* **safe.**]
inviolability *noun.* The quality or condition of being safe from assault, trespass, or violation ▶ sacredness, sacrosanctity, sanctity. —*See also* **holiness.**
inviolable *adjective.* —*See* **holy, safe** (2).
invisible *adjective.* —*See* **hidden** (1), **imperceptible** (1).
invitation *noun.* A spoken or written request for someone to take part or be present ▶ call, bid, summons. *Informal:* invite. [*Compare* **request.**] —*See also* **lure** (1), **offer.**
invite *verb.* To request that someone take part in or be present at a particular occasion ▶ ask, bid, summon. ***Idioms:*** extend an invitation to, request the presence of. [*Compare* **appeal, request.**] —*See also* **court** (1).
invite *noun.* *Informal* A spoken or written request for someone to take part or be present ▶ call, bid, invitation, summons. [*Compare* **request.**]
inviting *adjective.* —*See* **seductive.**
invocation *noun.* The act of praying ▶ benediction, prayer, supplication. [*Compare* **appeal.**]
invoice *noun.* —*See* **account** (2), **list[1].**
invoice *verb.* —*See* **bill[1].**
invoke *verb.* To offer a reverent petition to God or a god ▶ pray, supplicate. [*Compare* **appeal.**] —*See also* **cite, enforce, evoke.**
involuntarily *adverb.* —*See* **helplessly, spontaneously** (1).
involuntary *adjective.* —*See* **spontaneous, unintentional.**
involute *adjective.* —*See* **complex** (1).
involve *verb.* **1.** To draw in so that extrication is difficult ▶ catch up, draw into, embrangle, embroil, implicate, mix up, suck, wrap up. [*Compare* **catch.**] **2.** To have as a condition or a consequence ▶ carry, entail. —*See also* **absorb** (1), **complicate, contain** (1), **demand** (2), **imply.**
involved *adjective.* —*See* **complex** (1), **concerned.**

involvement *noun.* The act or fact of participating ▶ engagement, partaking, participation, sharing. *—See also* **absorption** (2), **entanglement.**

invulnerability *noun.* *—See* **safety.**

invulnerable *adjective.* *—See* **safe** (2).

inward *adjective.* *—See* **confidential** (2), **inner** (2).

in-your-face *adjective.* *—See* **assertive.**

iota *noun.* *—See* **bit**[1] (1).

irascibility *or* **irascibleness** *noun.* *—See* **temper** (1).

irascible *adjective.* *—See* **ill-tempered, testy.**

irate *adjective.* *—See* **angry.**

irateness *noun.* *—See* **anger.**

ire *noun.* *—See* **anger.**

ireful *adjective.* *—See* **angry.**

irenic *adjective.* *—See* **peaceable.**

irk *verb.* *—See* **annoy.**

irksome *adjective.* *—See* **boring, disturbing.**

iron *adjective.* *—See* **lusty, stubborn** (1).

iron *verb.* *—See* **press** (2).

ironbound *adjective.* *—See* **rough** (1).

ironclad *adjective.* *—See* **immutable.**

ironic *or* **ironical** *adjective.* *—See* **sarcastic.**

irons *noun.* *—See* **bond** (1).

irony *noun.* *—See* **sarcasm.**

irradiant *adjective.* *—See* **bright.**

irradiate *verb.* To render free of microorganisms ▶ decontaminate, disinfect, sanitize, sterilize. *—See also* **shed**[1] (1).

irradicable *adjective.* *—See* **confirmed** (1).

irrational *adjective.* Not governed by or predicated on reason ▶ illogical, unreasonable, unreasoned. ***Idioms:*** out of bounds, without rhyme or reason. [*Compare* **foolish.**] *—See also* **fallacious** (1).

irrationality *noun.* The absence of reason ▶ illogicality, illogicalness, unreason, unreasonableness. [*Compare* **fallacy, foolishness.**]

irrefutable *adjective.* *—See* **certain** (2).

irregular *adjective.* Not straight, uniform, or symmetrical ▶ asymmetric, asymmetrical, crooked, diversiform, nonuniform, variform. [*Compare* **uneven, rough.**] *—See also* **abnormal, incongruous, intermittent.**

irregularity *noun.* Lack of smoothness or regularity ▶ abrasiveness, asymmetry, bumpiness, choppiness, coarseness, crookedness, inequality, jaggedness, pockedness, raggedness, roughness, unevenness, ununiformity. *—See also* **abnormality.**

irrelevancy *noun.* *—See* **digression.**

irrelevant *adjective.* Not relevant or pertinent to the subject; not applicable ▶ extraneous, extrinsic, immaterial, impertinent, inapplicable, inapposite, unconnected, ungermane, unrelated. ***Idioms:*** beside the point, neither here nor there, off the subject (*or* topic), out of place. [*Compare* **digressive, trivial.**]

✦ **CORE SYNONYMS:** *irrelevant, extraneous, immaterial, impertinent.* These adjectives mean not pertinent to the subject under consideration: *an irrelevant comment; a question extraneous to the discussion; an objection that is immaterial; mentioned several impertinent facts.*

◀ **ANTONYM:** *relevant*

---

irreligion *noun.* *—See* **atheism.**

irreligious *adjective.* *—See* **atheistic.**

irremediable *adjective.* *—See* **hopeless.**

irremissible *adjective.* *—See* **inexcusable.**

irreparable *adjective.* *—See* **hopeless.**

irreprehensible *adjective.* *—See* **exemplary.**

irreproachable *adjective.* *—See* **exemplary, innocent** (2).

irresistible *adjective.* *—See* **certain** (1).

irresolute *adjective.* *—See* **doubtful** (2), **hesitant.**

irresolution *or* **irresoluteness** *noun.* *—See* **hesitation.**

irresponsible *adjective.* *—See* **careless, undependable** (1).

irreverence *noun.* *—See* **disrespect.**

irreverent *adjective.* —*See* **disrespectful.**

irrevocable *adjective.* That cannot be revoked or undone ▶ irretrievable, irreversible, unalterable. ***Idiom:*** beyond recall. [*Compare* **immutable, unchangeable.**]

irritability *noun.* —*See* **temper** (1).

irritable *adjective.* —*See* **ill-tempered.**

irritant *noun.* —*See* **annoyance** (2).

irritate *verb.* —*See* **anger** (1), **annoy, chafe, hurt** (3).

irritated *adjective.* —*See* **angry.**

irritating *adjective.* —*See* **disturbing, painful.**

irritation *noun.* An instance of being irritated, as in a part of the body ▶ festering, inflammation, rankling, redness, sensitiveness, soreness, tenderness. [*Compare* **bump, disease, pain.**] —*See also* **annoyance** (1), **annoyance** (2).

isochronal *or* **isochronous** *adjective.* —*See* **periodic.**

isolate *verb.* **1.** To set apart or cut off from others ▶ alienate, close off, cut off, ghettoize, insulate, seclude, segregate, separate, sequester, sequestrate, set apart. [*Compare* **exclude.**] **2.** To put into solitude ▶ cloister, seclude, sequester, sequestrate. [*Compare* **enclose, imprison.**]

isolate *adjective.* —*See* **solitary.**

✚ **CORE SYNONYMS:** *isolate, insulate, seclude, segregate, sequester.* These verbs mean to set apart or cut off from others: *a mountain that isolated the village from larger towns; insulated herself from the chaos surrounding her; a celebrity who was secluded from public scrutiny; segregated the infectious patients in a special ward; sequestering a jury during its deliberations.*

---

isolated *adjective.* —*See* **remote** (1), **solitary.**

isolation *noun.* The act or process of isolating ▶ alienation, insulation, segregation, separation, sequestration. [*Compare* **breach.**] —*See also* **seclusion, solitude.**

issue *noun.* —*See* **effect** (1), **problem, progeny, publication** (1).

issue *verb.* —*See* **appear** (1), **descend, distribute, emit, pour, publish** (1), **stem.**

italicize *verb.* —*See* **emphasize.**

itch *noun.* —*See* **desire** (1), **desire** (2).

itch *verb.* To have a greedy, obsessive desire ▶ crave, hunger, lust, thirst. [*Compare* **desire.**]

item *noun.* A detail of news or information ▶ article, bit, bulletin, dispatch, feature, flash, news flash, notice, paragraph, piece, squib, story, write-up. [*Compare* **message, news, story.**] —*See also* **detail, element** (2), **entry, object** (1).

item *adverb.* —*See* **additionally.**

itemize *verb.* —*See* **enumerate.**

iterate *verb.* To happen again or repeatedly ▶ reappear, recur, reoccur, repeat. —*See also* **repeat** (1).

iteration *noun.* —*See* **repetition.**

iterative *adjective.* Characterized by repetition ▶ reiterative, repetitious, repetitive. [*Compare* **boring, superfluous, wordy.**]

itinerant *adjective.* Moving from one area to another in search of work ▶ migrant, migratory. —*See also* **errant** (1), **nomadic.**

iterant *noun.* —*See* **hobo.**

ivory *adjective.* —*See* **fair**[1] (3).

ivory-tower *adjective.* —*See* **theoretical** (1).

J

jab *verb.* —*See* **hit, penetrate, push** (1).

jab *noun.* —*See* **blow**[2], **dig.**

jabber *verb.* —*See* **babble, chatter** (1), **gossip, mutter.**

jabber *noun.* —*See* **babble, chatter.**

jabberwocky *noun.* —*See* **babble, gibberish.**

jack *noun.* —*See* **fellow, flag[1], money** (1).
jack *verb.* To increase in amount ▶ boost, hike, jack up, jump, raise, up. —*See also* **elevate** (1).
Jack *noun.* —*See* **sailor.**
jackass *noun.* —*See* **fool.**
jacket *noun.* —*See* **coat** (1), **wrapper.**
jacket *verb.* —*See* **clothe.**
Jack-tar *noun.* —*See* **sailor.**
jade *noun.* —*See* **slut.**
jade *verb.* —*See* **tire** (1).
jaded *adjective.* —*See* **tired** (1).
jag[1] *noun.* —*See* **bender, binge.**
jag[2] *noun.* —*See* **spike.**
jagged *adjective.* —*See* **rough** (1).
jaggedness *noun.* —*See* **irregularity.**
jail *noun.* A place for the confinement of persons in lawful detention ▶ brig, house of correction, keep, penitentiary, prison. *Informal:* lockup, pen. *Slang:* big house, calaboose, can, clink, cooler, coop, hoosegow, joint, jug, pokey, slammer, stir.
jail *verb.* —*See* **imprison.**
jailer *noun.* A guard or keeper of a prison ▶ turnkey, warden. *Slang:* screw. [*Compare* **guard, police officer.**]
jam *verb.* —*See* **crowd, fill** (1), **push** (1).
jam *noun.* —*See* **predicament, push, stop** (2).
jam-pack *verb.* —*See* **fill** (1).
Janus-faced *adjective.* —*See* **hypocritical.**
jape *noun.* —*See* **joke** (1).
jar *verb.* To cause to move to and fro with short, jerky movements ▶ jiggle, joggle, shake. [*Compare* **jerk.**] —*See also* **agitate** (2), **bump, conflict.**
jar *noun.* —*See* **collision.**
jargon *noun.* —*See* **babble, dialect, language** (2).
jarring *adjective.* —*See* **harsh, incongruous.**
jaundice *verb.* —*See* **bias** (1).
jaundice *noun.* —*See* **envy.**
jaundiced *adjective.* —*See* **envious.**
jaunt *noun.* A usually short journey taken for pleasure ▶ excursion, junket, outing, trip. [*Compare* **excursion, journey.**] —*See also* **drive** (3).
jaunt *verb.* —*See* **journey.**
jaunty *adjective.* —*See* **lively.**
jaw *verb.* —*See* **chatter** (1).
jaw *noun.* —*See* **conversation.**
jazz up *verb.* —*See* **energize.**
jealous *adjective.* Fearful of the loss of position or affection ▶ clinging, clutching, green-eyed, possessive. [*Compare* **envious.**] —*See also* **envious.**
jealousy *noun.* —*See* **envy.**
jeer *verb.* —*See* **ridicule.**
jeer *noun.* —*See* **taunt.**
jeering *adjective.* —*See* **sarcastic.**
jejune *adjective.* —*See* **insipid.**
jejuneness *noun.* —*See* **dullness, insipidity.**
jell *or* **jelly** *verb.* —*See* **coagulate.**
jellyfish *noun.* —*See* **weakling.**
jeopardize *verb.* —*See* **endanger.**
jeopardous *adjective.* —*See* **dangerous.**
jeopardy *noun.* —*See* **danger.**
jeremiad *noun.* —*See* **tirade.**
jerk *verb.* To move or cause to move with a sudden abrupt motion ▶ lurch, snap, twitch, wrench, yank. [*Compare* **move.**] —*See also* **bump, recoil.**
jerk *noun.* A sudden motion, such as a pull ▶ lurch, snap, tug, twitch, wrench, yank. [*Compare* **pull.**] —*See also* **drip** (2), **fool, tremor** (2).

✚ **CORE SYNONYMS:** *jerk, snap, twitch, wrench, yank.* These verbs mean to move with a sudden abrupt motion: *jerked the rope twice to pull it taut; snapped the lock shut; was twitching her mouth nervously; wrenched the stick out of his hand; yanks the door open.*

---

jerkiness *noun.* —*See* **foolishness.**
jerky *adjective.* —*See* **foolish, tremulous.**
jerry-rig *verb.* —*See* **improvise** (2).
jest *noun.* An object of amusement or laughter ▶ butt, joke, laughingstock, mockery. ***Idiom:*** figure of fun. [*Com-

pare **fool.**] *—See also* **crack** (3), **joke** (1), **play.**

jest *verb.* To make jokes; behave playfully ▶ joke (around), quip. *Informal:* clown (around), fool around, horse around. ***Idioms:*** crack wise, play the fool. [*Compare* **play.**] *—See also* **ridicule.**

jester *noun.* *—See* **joker.**

jet[1] *adjective.* *—See* **black** (1).

jet[2] *noun.* A sudden swift stream of ejected liquid ▶ spout, spray, spurt, squirt. [*Compare* **flow.**]

jet *verb.* To eject or be ejected in a sudden thin, swift stream ▶ spout, spray, spurt, squirt. [*Compare* **erupt, flow.**]

jetsam *noun.* *—See* **garbage.**

jet-setter *noun.* *—See* **tourist.**

jettison *verb.* *—See* **discard.**

jettison *noun.* *—See* **disposal.**

jetty *adjective.* *—See* **black** (1).

jibber-jabber *verb.* *—See* **babble.**

jibber-jabber *noun.* *—See* **babble.**

jibe[1] *verb.* *—See* **agree** (1).

jibe[2] *verb.* *See* **gibe.**

jiffy *or* **jiff** *noun.* *—See* **flash** (2).

jig *noun.* *—See* **trick** (1).

jigger *noun.* *—See* **drop** (4), **gadget.**

jiggle *verb.* To cause to move to and fro with short, jerky movements ▶ jar, joggle, shake. [*Compare* **jerk.**] *—See also* **bump.**

jihad *noun.* A goal served with great or uncompromising dedication ▶ cause, crusade, jihad. [*Compare* **drive.**]

jillion *noun.* *—See* **heap** (2).

jilted *adjective.* *—See* **abandoned** (1).

jim-jams *noun.* *—See* **jitters.**

jingle *noun.* *—See* **song.**

jinx *noun.* *Informal* Something or someone believed to bring bad luck ▶ curse, evil eye, hex, hoodoo, Jonah. [*Compare* **charm, magic.**]

jinx *verb.* *Informal* To bring bad luck or evil to ▶ curse, hex, hoodoo.

jitters *noun.* A state of nervous restlessness or agitation ▶ fidgets, jumps, shivers, trembles. *Informal:* all-overs, shakes. *Slang:* heebie-jeebies, jim-jams, whim-whams, willies.

jittery *adjective.* *—See* **edgy.**

jive *verb.* *—See* **joke** (2).

job *noun.* *—See* **business** (2), **function** (1), **position** (3), **task** (1), **task** (2).

jobbery *noun.* *—See* **corruption** (2).

jobholder *noun.* *—See* **employee.**

jobholding *adjective.* *—See* **employed.**

jobless *adjective.* Having no job ▶ idle, unemployed, unoccupied, workless. ***Idioms:*** out of a job (*or* employ *or* work).

jockey *verb.* *—See* **maneuver** (1), **maneuver** (2).

jocose *adjective.* *—See* **funny** (1).

jocosity *or* **jocoseness** *noun.* *—See* **humor, merriment** (1).

jocular *adjective.* *—See* **funny** (1).

jocularity *noun.* *—See* **humor, merriment** (1).

jocund *adjective.* *—See* **cheerful.**

jocundity *noun.* *—See* **merriment** (1).

jog *verb.* *—See* **push** (1), **run** (1).

jog *noun.* *—See* **dig, run** (1).

joggle *verb.* To cause to move to and fro with short, jerky movements ▶ jar, jiggle, shake. [*Compare* **jerk.**]

join *verb.* **1.** To become a member of ▶ enlist, enroll, enter, muster in, sign up. *Informal:* sign on. **2.** To come together from different directions ▶ close, converge, meet, unite. *—See also* **adjoin, associate** (1), **band**[2], **combine** (1), **cooperate, participate.**

join *noun.* *—See* **joint** (1).

joint *noun.* **1.** A point or position at which two or more things are joined ▶ connection, coupling, join, junction, juncture, seam, union. **2.** *Slang* A disreputable or run-down bar or restaurant ▶ *Slang:* dive, dump, honky-tonk, juke house, juke joint. ***Idiom:*** hole in the wall. *—See also* **jail.**

joint *adjective.* *—See* **common** (2), **cooperative.**

jointly *adverb.* In, into, or as a single body ▶ together. ***Idioms:*** as one, in one breath, in the same breath, in unison, with one accord, with one voice.

joist *noun.* —*See* **beam** (2).

joke *noun.* **1.** Words intended to excite laughter or amusement ▶ gag, jape, jest, one-liner, quip, sally, witticism. *Informal:* funny, knee-slapper, rib-tickler, zinger. *Slang:* ha-ha. [*Compare* **crack, taunt.**] **2.** An object of amusement or laughter ▶ butt, jest, laughingstock, mockery. ***Idiom:*** figure of fun. [*Compare* **fool.**] —*See also* **prank**[1], **scream** (2).

joke *verb.* **1.** To make jokes; behave playfully ▶ jest, joke around, quip. *Informal:* clown (around), fool around, horse around. ***Idioms:*** crack wise, play the fool. [*Compare* **play.**] **2.** To tease or mock good-humoredly ▶ banter, chaff, josh. *Informal:* fun, kid, rib, ride. *Slang:* jive, rag, razz. ***Idiom:*** pull (someone's) leg.

✚ **CORE SYNONYMS:** *joke, jest, witticism, quip, gag.* These nouns refer to something that is said or done in order to evoke laughter or amusement. *Joke* especially denotes an amusing story with a punch line at the end: *told jokes at the party. Jest* suggests frolicsome humor: *amusing jests that defused the tense situation.* A *witticism* is a witty, usually cleverly phrased remark: *a speech full of witticisms.* A *quip* is a clever, pointed, often sarcastic remark: *responded to the tough questions with quips. Gag* is principally applicable to a broadly comic remark or to comic byplay in a theatrical routine: *one of the most memorable gags in the history of vaudeville.*

joker *noun.* A person whose words or actions provoke or are intended to provoke amusement or laughter ▶ clown, comedian, comic, farceur, funnyman, humorist, jester, jokester, quipster, wag, wit, zany. *Informal:* card. [*Compare* **smart aleck.**]

jokester *noun.* —*See* **joker.**

jollification *noun.* —*See* **celebration** (3).

jollies *noun.* —*See* **amusement, thrill.**

jolliness *noun.* —*See* **merriment** (1).

jollity *noun.* —*See* **merriment** (1), **merriment** (2).

jolly *adjective.* —*See* **cheerful, good** (1).

jolt *verb.* —*See* **bump, drive** (2), **startle.**

jolt *noun.* —*See* **collision, shock**[1].

jongleur *noun.* —*See* **poet.**

josh *verb.* —*See* **joke** (2).

jostle *verb.* —*See* **push** (1).

jostle *noun.* —*See* **push.**

jot *noun.* —*See* **bit**[1] (1).

jounce *noun.* —*See* **bump.**

journal *noun.* —*See* **memoir.**

journalist *noun.* —*See* **press.**

journey *noun.* The act of traveling from one place to another ▶ circuit, crossing, cruise, flight, odyssey, passage, peregrination, progress, transit, travel, traversal, trip, voyage, wayfaring. [*Compare* **expedition, trip.**]

journey *verb.* To make or go on a journey ▶ fare, jaunt, pass, peregrinate, sightsee, tour, travel, trek, trip, voyage. ***Idioms:*** hit the road, see the country (*or* world). [*Compare* **hike, migrate, rove.**]

joust *noun.* Any competition or test of opposing wills likened to the sport in which knights fought with lances ▶ tilt, tournament, tourney. [*Compare* **battle, competition.**]

joust *verb.* —*See* **contend.**

jovial *adjective.* —*See* **cheerful.**

joviality *noun.* —*See* **merriment** (1).

joy *noun.* —*See* **delight, happiness.**

joyful *adjective.* —*See* **cheerful, merry.**

joyfulness *noun.* —*See* **happiness.**

joyless *adjective.* —*See* **gloomy, sorrowful.**

joyous *adjective.* —*See* **merry.**

jubilance *noun.* —*See* **exultation.**

jubilant *adjective.* Feeling or expressing an uplifting joy over a success or victory ▶ exultant, gloating, triumphant. [*Compare* **boastful.**]

jubilate *verb.* —*See* **exult** (1).

jubilation *noun.* —*See* **celebration** (3), **exultation.**

jubilee *noun.* —*See* **celebration** (1).

Judas *noun.* —*See* **betrayer.**

judge *verb.* To make a decision about (a controversy or dispute, for example) after deliberation, as in a court of law ▶ adjudge, adjudicate, arbitrate, decide, decree, determine, referee, rule, umpire. ***Idiom:*** sit in judgment. [*Compare* **hear.**] —*See also* **believe** (3), **criticize** (1), **estimate** (1), **infer.**

judge *noun.* **1.** A public official who decides cases brought before a court of law in order to administer justice ▶ jurist, jurisprudent, justice, justice of the peace, magistrate. [*Compare* **go-between.**] **2.** A person, usually appointed, who decides the issues of, decides the results of, or supervises the conduct of a competition or conflict ▶ arbiter, arbitrator, referee, umpire. *Informal:* ref, ump. —*See also* **critic** (1).

✦ **CORE SYNONYMS:** *judge, arbitrator, arbiter, referee, umpire.* These nouns denote a person who decides the issues or results, or supervises the conduct, of a competition or conflict. A *judge* is one capable of making rational, dispassionate, and wise decisions: *In this case, the jury members are the judges of the truth.* An *arbitrator* is either appointed or derives authority from the consent of the disputants: *An experienced arbitrator mediated the contract dispute.* An *arbiter* is one whose opinion or judgment is recognized as being unassailable or binding: *The critic considered himself an arbiter of fine literature.* A *referee* is an attorney appointed by a court to investigate and report on a case: *The referee handled many bankruptcy cases each month.* An *umpire* is a person appointed to settle an issue that arbitrators are unable to resolve: *The umpire studied complex tax cases.* In sports *referee* and *umpire* refer to officials who enforce the rules and settle points at issue.

---

judgment *noun.* A position arrived at by reasoning from premises ▶ conclusion, deduction, inference. —*See also* **belief** (1), **common sense, criticism, discernment, estimate** (1), **ruling.**

judgmental *adjective.* —*See* **arbitrary, critical** (1), **intolerant** (1).

judiciary *or* **judicature** *noun.* —*See* **court** (2).

judicious *adjective.* —*See* **deliberate** (3), **sensible.**

jug *noun.* —*See* **jail.**

juju *noun.* —*See* **charm.**

jumble *verb.* —*See* **confuse** (1), **confuse** (3), **disorder, shuffle.**

jumble *noun.* —*See* **assortment, disorder** (1).

jumbled *adjective.* —*See* **confused** (2).

jumbo *noun.* —*See* **giant.**

jumbo *adjective.* —*See* **enormous.**

jump *verb.* **1.** To move off the ground by a muscular effort of the legs and feet ▶ hurdle, leap, pounce, spring, vault. [*Compare* **plunge.**] **2.** To move suddenly and involuntarily ▶ bolt, start. [*Compare* **bump, jerk.**] **3.** To catapult oneself from a disabled aircraft ▶ bail out, eject. **4.** To increase in amount ▶ boost, hike, jack (up), raise, up. —*See also* **bound**[1], **promote** (1).

jump on *verb.* —*See* **chastise.**

jump up *verb.* —*See* **stand** (1).

jump *noun.* **1.** The act of jumping ▶ leap, pounce, spring, vault. [*Compare* **fall.**] **2.** A sudden and involuntary movement ▶ bolt, start, startle. [*Compare* **jerk, recoil.**] —*See also* **advancement, advantage** (3), **bound**[1] (2), **energy, increase** (1), **increase** (2).

jumper *noun.* —*See* **dress** (3).

jumpiness *noun.* —*See* **restlessness.**

jumps *noun.* —*See* **jitters.**

jump-start *verb.* —*See* **energize.**

jumpy *adjective.* —*See* **edgy.**

junction *noun.* The act or fact of coming together ▶ concentration, concourse, confluence, conflux, convergence, crossroads, gathering, meeting, terminal. [*Compare* **unification.**] —*See also* **joint** (1).

juncture *noun.* A point or position at which two or more things are joined ▶ connection, coupling, joint, junction, seam, union. —*See also* **crisis, occasion** (1).

jungle *noun.* —*See* **tangle, wilderness.**

junior *adjective.* —*See* **minor** (1).

junior *noun.* —*See* **subordinate.**

junk *verb.* —*See* **discard.**

junk *noun.* —*See* **odds and ends.**

junk *adjective.* —*See* **unwholesome** (1).

junket *noun.* **1.** A large, elaborately prepared meal ▶ banquet, feast, junket. *Informal:* feed, spread. **2.** A usually short journey taken for pleasure ▶ excursion, jaunt, outing, trip. [*Compare* **excursion, journey.**]

junkie *noun.* —*See* **fan**[2]**.**

junky *noun.* —*See* **shoddy.**

jurisdiction *noun.* —*See* **authority.**

jurist *or* **jurisprudent** *noun.* A public official who decides cases brought before a court of law in order to administer justice ▶ judge, justice, justice of the peace, magistrate. [*Compare* **go-between, judge.**] —*See also* **lawyer.**

jury-rig *verb.* —*See* **improvise** (2).

just *adjective.* Consistent with prevailing or accepted standards or circumstances ▶ appropriate, deserved, due, fit, fitting, merited, proper, right, rightful, suitable. [*Compare* **relevant.**] —*See also* **fair**[1] (1), **lawful, sound**[2]**.**

just *adverb.* **1.** By a very little; almost not ▶ barely, hardly, scarce, scarcely. ***Idioms:*** by a hair (*or* whisker), by the skin of one's teeth. [*Compare* **approximately, merely, only.**] **2.** Nothing more than ▶ but, merely, only, simply. [*Compare* **barely, solely.**] —*See also* **completely** (1), **directly** (3), **exactly, lately, solely.**

justice *noun.* **1.** The state, action, or principle of treating all persons equally in accordance with the law ▶ due process, equitableness, equity. [*Compare* **legality.**] **2.** A public official who decides cases brought before a court of law in order to administer justice ▶ judge, jurisprudent, jurist, justice of the peace, magistrate. [*Compare* **go-between, judge.**] —*See also* **cogency, fairness.**

justifiable *adjective.* Capable of being justified ▶ defensible, excusable, tenable. [*Compare* **logical, sound**[2]**.**]

justification *noun.* —*See* **account** (1), **apology** (1), **basis** (2), **cause** (2), **confirmation** (2), **exculpation, excuse** (1).

justify *verb.* **1.** To show to be just, right, or valid ▶ excuse, rationalize, vindicate. ***Idiom:*** make a case for. **2.** To be an appropriate occasion for ▶ call for, befit, occasion, warrant. [*Compare* **suit.**] **3.** To offer reasons for or a cause of ▶ account for, explain, rationalize. [*Compare* **clarify, resolve.**] —*See also* **clear** (3), **confirm** (1), **defend** (2), **prove.**

justly *adverb.* —*See* **fairly** (1).

justness *noun.* —*See* **fairness.**

jut *verb.* —*See* **bulge.**

jut *noun.* —*See* **projection.**

juvenescence *noun.* —*See* **youth** (1).

juvenile *adjective.* Not yet a legal adult ▶ minor, underage. —*See also* **childish, young.**

juvenile *noun.* One who is not yet legally of age ▶ child, minor, underage person. [*Compare* **child, youth.**] —*See also* **child** (1).

juvenile delinquent *noun.* —*See* **urchin.**

juvenility *noun.* —*See* **youth** (1).

juxtapose *verb.* —*See* **compare.**

juxtaposition *noun.* —*See* **contrast.**

K

kaleidoscopic *adjective.* —*See* **changeable** (1).

kaput *adjective.* —*See* **through** (2).

katzenjammer *noun.* Unpleasant physical and mental effects following overindulgence in alcohol ▶ crapulence, hangover. *Informal:* head. —*See also* **vociferation.**

keel *verb.* —*See* **lurch** (1).

keel over *verb.* To suffer temporary lack of consciousness ▶ black out, faint, pass out, swoon. ***Idioms:*** drop (*or* faint *or* fall) dead away, see stars. [*Compare* **collapse.**] —*See also* **fall** (2).

keen[1] *adjective.* —*See* **clever** (1), **critical** (2), **eager, enthusiastic, marvelous, pointed, sharp** (1).

keen[2] *verb.* —*See* **cry.**

keenness *noun.* —*See* **discernment, edge.**

keep *verb.* **1.** To have for sale ▶ carry, deal (in), offer, stock. [*Compare* **sell.**] **2.** To supply with the necessities of life ▶ maintain, provide for, support. ***Idioms:*** put a roof over someone's head, put food on the table, take care of. [*Compare* **nourish.**] **3.** To have or put in a customary place ▶ cache, put, store. **4.** To remain fresh and unspoiled ▶ last. **5.** To persevere in some condition, action, or belief ▶ keep to, maintain, retain, stay with, stick to, stick with, sustain. **6.** To mark a day or an event with ceremonies of respect, festivity, or rejoicing ▶ celebrate, commemorate, observe, solemnize. [*Compare* **sanctify.**] —*See also* **delay** (1), **endure** (2), **follow** (4), **fulfill, hold** (1), **refrain, restrain, save** (1).

keep back *verb.* —*See* **hold** (1), **repress, restrain.**

keep off *verb.* —*See* **repel.**

keep on *verb.* —*See* **endure** (1).

keep out *verb.* —*See* **exclude.**

keep up *verb.* To keep in a condition of good repair, efficiency, or use ▶ maintain, preserve, sustain.

keep *noun.* —*See* **jail, living.**

keeper *noun.* One who is legally responsible for the care and management of the person or property of an incompetent or a minor ▶ caretaker, conservator, custodian, guardian. [*Compare* **representative.**]

keeping *noun.* —*See* **agreement** (2), **care** (2), **celebration** (2).

keepsake *noun.* —*See* **remembrance** (1).

keg *noun.* —*See* **vat.**

ken *noun.* The extent of one's perception, understanding, knowledge, or vision ▶ horizon, purview, range, reach, scope. [*Compare* **awareness, area.**]

kennel *noun.* —*See* **cage, flock.**

kernel *noun.* A fertilized plant ovule capable of germinating ▶ grain, pip, pit, seed. —*See also* **germ** (2), **heart** (1).

key *noun.* A means or method of entering into or achieving something desirable ▶ formula, route, secret. *Informal:* ticket. [*Compare* **trick.**] —*See also* **answer** (2).

key *adjective.* —*See* **dominant** (1), **important, primary** (1).

keystone *noun.* —*See* **basis** (1).

kibitz *verb.* —*See* **meddle.**

kibitzer *noun.* —*See* **busybody.**

kick *verb.* —*See* **break** (5), **complain, object.**

kick around *verb.* —*See* **discuss.**

kick back *verb.* —*See* **rest[1]** (1).

kick in *verb.* —*See* **contribute** (1), **die.**

kick off *verb.* —*See* **die, start** (1).

kick out *verb.* —*See* **eject** (1).

kick *noun.* **1.** *Slang* A stimulating or intoxicating effect ▶ charge, potency. *Informal:* punch, sting, wallop. **2.** *Slang* A temporary concentration of interest ▶ *Slang:* trip. —*See also* **complaint, objection, thrill, wrinkle** (2).

kickback *noun.* —*See* **bribe.**

kicker *noun.* —*See* **wrinkle** (2).

kickoff *noun.* —*See* **beginning.**

kicks *noun.* —*See* **amusement.**

kid *noun.* —*See* **child** (1), **teenager.**

kid *verb.* —*See* **joke** (2).

kidlike *noun.* —*See* **babyish.**

kidnap *verb.* To seize and detain a person unlawfully ▶ abduct, snatch, spirit away, take hostage. [*Compare* **seize, steal.**]

kids *noun.* *Informal* Young people collectively ▶ young, youth.

kill[1] *verb.* To cause the death of ▶ carry off, cut down, cut off, destroy, dispatch, execute, finish (off), slay. *Slang:* hit, ice, rub out, waste, wipe out, zap. ***Idioms:*** put an end to, put to death, put to sleep, take the life of. [*Compare* **massacre.**] —*See also* **afflict, annihilate, censor** (2), **idle** (2), **murder.**

kill *noun.* A loss of life, or one who has lost life, usually as a result of accident, disaster, or war ▶ casualty, death, fatality, loss. [*Compare* **victim.**]

kill² *noun.* —*See* **brook¹.**

killer *noun.* —*See* **murderer.**

killing *noun.* —*See* **murder.**

killing *adjective.* —*See* **funny** (1).

killjoy *noun.* One who spoils the enthusiasm or fun of others ▶ frump, spoilsport. *Informal:* stick-in-the-mud, wet blanket. *Slang:* bummer, downer, party pooper, pill. ***Idiom:*** dog in the manger. [*Compare* **grouch, square.**]

kilter *noun.* —*See* **shape.**

kin *noun.* One's relatives collectively ▶ family, folks, kindred, kinfolk, kith and kin, people. [*Compare* **relative.**]

kin *adjective.* —*See* **kindred, like².**

kind¹ *adjective.* —*See* **benevolent** (1).

kind² *noun.* A class that is defined by the common attribute or attributes possessed by all its members ▶ brand, breed, cast, denomination, description, feather, form, genus, ilk, lot, manner, mold, nature, order, persuasion, sort, species, stamp, stripe, type, variety. [*Compare* **class.**]

kindhearted *adjective.* —*See* **benevolent** (1).

kindheartedness *noun.* —*See* **benevolence.**

kindle *verb.* —*See* **arouse, clear** (1), **fire** (1), **light¹** (1).

kindliness *noun.* —*See* **benevolence, favor** (1).

kindly *adjective.* —*See* **benevolent** (1), **gentle** (1).

kindness *noun.* —*See* **amiability, benevolence, consideration** (1), **favor** (1).

kind office *noun.* —*See* **favor** (1).

kindred *noun.* —*See* **family** (2), **kin.**

kindred *adjective.* Connected by or as if by kinship or common origin ▶ agnate, akin, allied, cognate, connate, connatural, consanguine, consanguineous, kin, related. [*Compare* **ancestral.**]

kinetic *adjective.* —*See* **energetic.**

kinfolk *or* **kinfolks** *noun.* —*See* **kin.**

king *noun.* —*See* **chief.**

kink *noun.* —*See* **curl.**

kink *verb.* —*See* **bend** (3).

kinsman *or* **kinswoman** *noun.* **1.** A person connected to another person by blood or marriage ▶ relation, relative. [*Compare* **ancestry, family, kin.**] **2.** A person who is from one's own country ▶ compatriot, countryman, countrywoman, fellow citizen, kinswoman.

kismet *noun.* —*See* **fate** (1).

kiss *verb.* To touch or caress with the lips, especially as a sign of passion or affection ▶ buss, osculate, smack. *Informal:* peck. *Slang:* lock lips, make out, smooch, suck face, swap spit. [*Compare* **neck.**] —*See also* **brush¹.**

kiss *noun.* The act or an instance of kissing ▶ buss, osculation, smack, smacker. *Informal:* peck. *Slang:* smooch. —*See also* **brush¹.**

kisser *noun.* —*See* **face** (1), **mouth** (1).

kit *noun.* —*See* **pack** (1), **suitcase.**

kith and kin *noun.* —*See* **kin.**

kitty *noun.* —*See* **bet.**

klutz *noun.* —*See* **blunderer, oaf.**

klutzy *adjective.* —*See* **awkward** (1).

knack *noun.* The proper method for doing, using, or handling something ▶ feel, trick. *Informal:* hang. —*See also* **ability** (1), **talent.**

knapsack *noun.* —*See* **pack** (1).

knave *noun.* —*See* **cheat** (2).

knead *verb.* To handle in a way so as to mix, form, and shape ▶ manipulate, squeeze, work. —*See also* **rub.**

kneel *verb.* —*See* **bow¹** (1).

knee-slapper *noun.* —*See* **joke** (1).

knell *verb.* —*See* **ring².**

knickknack *noun.* —*See* **novelty** (3).

knife *verb.* —*See* **betray** (1), **cut** (1).

knifelike *adjective.* —*See* **sharp** (3).

knightly *adjective.* —*See* **gallant.**

knob *noun.* —*See* **bump** (1), **projection.**

knock *verb.* —*See* **bang, collide, criticize** (1), **hit.**

knock about *or* **around** *verb.* —*See* **batter, discuss, manhandle.**

knock down *verb.* —*See* **destroy** (2), **drop** (3).

knock off *verb.* To interrupt regular activity for a short period ▶ break, recess. ***Idioms:*** take a break, take a breather, take five (*or* ten). [*Compare* **rest**[1].] —*See also* **abandon** (2), **copy, deduct, murder, rob.**

knock out *verb.* —*See* **disable** (1), **drug** (1), **stagger** (2), **tire** (1).

knock over *verb.* —*See* **overturn, stagger** (2).

knock together *verb.* —*See* **build.**

knock *noun.* The sound made by a light blow ▶ rap, rapping, tap, tapping. —*See also* **beat** (1), **collision, criticism.**

knockabout *adjective.* —*See* **rough** (3).

knocked-out *adjective.* —*See* **tired** (1).

knocked-up *adjective.* —*See* **pregnant** (1).

knockoff *noun.* —*See* **copy** (2).

knockout *noun.* —*See* **beauty, conquest, hit.**

knoll *noun.* —*See* **hill.**

knot *noun.* —*See* **bond** (2), **bump** (1), **bump** (2), **group, projection, tangle.**

knot *verb.* To make fast or firmly fixed, as by means of a cord or rope ▶ bind, fasten, secure, tie, tie up. —*See also* **complicate, fasten.**

knotty *adjective.* —*See* **complex** (1).

know *verb.* **1.** To perceive directly with the intellect ▶ apprehend, compass, comprehend, fathom, grasp. ***Idioms:*** be sure, be certain. [*Compare* **understand.**] **2.** To be acquainted with ▶ know of, know about. ***Idioms:*** be acquainted with, be aware of. **3.** To undergo an emotional reaction ▶ experience, feel, have, savor, taste. **4.** To perceive to be identical with something held in the memory ▶ recognize. —*See also* **distinguish** (1), **experience, place** (1).

knowable *adjective.* —*See* **understandable.**

know-how *noun.* —*See* **ability** (1).

knowing *adjective.* —*See* **intelligent.** Possessing deep knowledge and understanding ▶ sagacious, sage, sapient, wise. —*See also* **shrewd.**

know-it-all *noun.* —*See* **smart aleck.**

knowledge *noun.* The sum of what has been perceived, discovered, or inferred ▶ lore, understanding, wisdom. [*Compare* **actuality.**] —*See also* **education** (2), **information.**

knowledgeable *adjective.* —*See* **educated, informed, intelligent.**

knuckleheaded *adjective.* —*See* **stupid.**

KO *verb.* —*See* **defeat.**

kook *noun.* —*See* **crackpot.**

kooky *adjective.* —*See* **eccentric.**

kosher *adjective.* —*See* **acceptable** (1), **authentic** (1).

kowtow *verb.* —*See* **bow**[1] (1), **fawn.**

kowtow *noun.* —*See* **bow**[1].

kudos *noun.* —*See* **distinction** (2), **praise** (1).

Kultur *noun.* The total product of human creativity and intellect ▶ civilization, culture, society.

kvetch *verb.* —*See* **complain.**

kvetch *noun.* —*See* **complaint.**

L

label *noun.* —*See* **mark** (1), **ticket** (1).

label *verb.* To attach a ticket to ▶ earmark, flag, mark, tag, ticket. —*See also* **call, mark** (1).

labile *adjective.* —*See* **changeable** (1).

labor *noun.* Physical exertion that is usually difficult and exhausting ▶ drudgery, moil, toil, travail, work. *Informal:* grind, sweat. ***Idiom:*** sweat of one's brow. —*See also* **birth** (1).

labor *verb.* To exert oneself steadily, often to the point of exhaustion ▶ drive, moil, slave, strain, strive, sweat, toil, travail, tug, work. ***Idioms:*** bend over backward, break one's back (*or* neck), break (*or* bust) one's butt, bust a gut, knock oneself out, work one's butt off, work oneself ragged, work one's fingers to the bone. [*Compare* **grind.**] —*See also* **belabor.**

✦ **CORE SYNONYMS:** *labor, work, toil, drudgery, travail.* These nouns refer to physical exertion that is usually difficult and exhausting. *Labor* and *work* are the most general: "*Which of us . . . is to do the hard and dirty work for the rest—and for what pay?*" (John Ruskin); "*garner the fruits of their own labors*" (Roger Casement). *Toil* applies principally to strenuous, fatiguing labor: "*I have nothing to offer but blood, toil, tears and sweat*" (Winston S. Churchill). *Drudgery* suggests dull, wearisome, or monotonous work: "*the drudgery of penning definitions and marking quotations for transcription*" (Thomas Macaulay). *Travail* connotes arduous work involving pain or suffering: "*prisoners of the splendor and travail of the earth*" (Henry Beston).

labored *adjective.* Not natural or spontaneous ▶ contrived, effortful, forced, strained. [*Compare* **awkward, stiff.**] —*See also* **ponderous.**

laborer *noun.* One who labors ▶ day laborer, hand, menial, operative, roustabout, toiler, wage slave, worker, working girl, workingman, workingwoman, workman, workwoman. [*Compare* **employee.**]

laborious *adjective.* —*See* **burdensome, difficult** (1).

laboriously *adverb.* —*See* **hard** (2).

labyrinth *noun.* —*See* **tangle.**

labyrinthine *adjective.* —*See* **complex** (1).

lace *noun.* —*See* **cord, web.**

lacerate *verb.* —*See* **cut** (1), **slam** (1).

laceration *noun.* Marked tissue damage, especially when produced by physical injury ▶ lesion, trauma, traumatism, wound. [*Compare* **harm.**]

lachrymose *adjective.* —*See* **tearful.**

lacing *noun.* —*See* **cord, web.**

lack *verb.* To be without what is needed, required, or essential ▶ need, require, want. [*Compare* **demand.**]

lack *noun.* The condition of lacking something ▶ absence, dearth, want. [*Compare* **need.**] —*See also* **shortage.**

✦ **CORE SYNONYMS:** *lack, want, need.* These verbs mean to be without something, especially something that is necessary or desirable. *Lack* emphasizes the absence of something: *I lack the money to buy new shoes. The plant died because it lacked moisture. Want* and *need* stress the urgent necessity for filling a void or remedying an inadequacy: "*Her pens were uniformly bad and wanted fixing*" (Bret Harte). *The garden needs care.*

lackadaisical *adjective.* —*See* **languid.**

lackey *noun.* —*See* **sycophant.**

lacking *adjective.* —*See* **deficient, empty** (2).

lackluster *adjective.* —*See* **dull** (1), **dull** (2).

laconic *adjective.* —*See* **brief, taciturn.**

lacquer *noun.* —*See* **finish.**

lacquer *verb.* —*See* **finish** (2).

lacuna *noun.* —*See* **gap** (2).

lad *noun.* —*See* **fellow.**

laden *adjective.* Burdened by a weighty load ▶ heavy, heavy-laden, loaded, weighed down.

ladle *verb.* —*See* **dip** (2).

lady-killer *noun.* —*See* **philanderer.**

lady's man *noun.* —*See* **gallant, philanderer.**

lag *verb.* —*See* **delay** (2).

lag *noun.* —*See* **delay** (2), **laggard.**

laggard *adjective.* —*See* **slow** (1).

laggard *or* **lagger** *noun.* One that lags ▶ dawdler, dilly-dallier, lag, lingerer, loiterer, poke, procrastinator, snail, straggler, tarrier. *Informal:* slowpoke.

lagging *adjective.* —*See* **backward** (2).

laid-back *adjective.* —*See* **easygoing.**

laid up *adjective.* —*See* **sick** (1).

lair *noun.* **1.** A place used as an animal's dwelling ▶ burrow, den, hole. [*Compare* **cave.**] **2.** A hiding place ▶ covert, den, hideaway, hide-out.

lam *verb.* —*See* **escape** (1).

lam *noun.* —*See* **escape** (1).

lamb *noun.* —*See* **dupe, innocent** (1).

lambaste *verb.* —*See* **beat** (1), **chastise, slam** (1).

lambency *noun.* —*See* **light**[1] (1).

lambent *adjective.* —*See* **bright.**

lame *adjective.* —*See* **implausible, ineffectual** (2).

lamebrained *adjective.* —*See* **stupid.**

lament *verb.* —*See* **cry, grieve.**

lament *noun.* —*See* **cry** (1).

lamentable *adjective.* —*See* **pitiful, sorrowful.**

lamentation *noun.* —*See* **cry** (1).

lamia *noun.* A woman who practices magic ▶ enchantress, hag, sorceress, witch. [*Compare* **wizard.**]

lamina *noun.* —*See* **skin** (2).

lampoon *noun.* —*See* **satire.**

lampoon *verb.* —*See* **ridicule.**

lance *verb.* —*See* **cut** (1).

land *noun.* Usually extensive real estate ▶ acreage, acres, estate, grounds, lands, manor, property. —*See also* **state** (1).

land *verb.* **1.** To come ashore from a seacraft ▶ alight, debark, disembark, light. **2.** To come to rest on the ground ▶ alight, light, set down, settle, touch down. —*See also* **get** (1).

landscape *noun.* —*See* **view** (2).

lane *noun.* —*See* **way** (2).

language *noun.* **1.** A system of terms used by a people sharing a history and culture ▶ dialect, mother tongue, speech, tongue, vernacular. **2.** Specialized expressions indigenous to a particular field, subject, trade, or subculture ▶ argot, cant, dialect, idiom, jargon, lexicon, lingo, parlance, patois, terminology, vernacular, vocabulary.

languid *adjective.* Lacking energy and vitality ▶ drooping, flagging, lackadaisical, languorous, leaden, limp, listless, lymphatic, sleepy, spiritless, unspirited. [*Compare* **apathetic, lazy, slow, weak.**]

languidness *noun.* —*See* **lethargy.**

languish *verb.* To become downcast from longing or grief ▶ ebb, pine (away), shrivel, waste (away), wither. —*See also* **deteriorate, fade.**

languor *noun.* —*See* **lethargy.**

languorous *adjective.* —*See* **languid.**

lank *adjective.* —*See* **thin** (1).

lanky *adjective.* —*See* **gangling, thin** (1).

lap *verb.* **1.** To flow against or along ▶ bathe, lave, lip, wash. [*Compare* **flow.**] **2.** To make the sound of moving or disturbed water ▶ splash, swash, wash. [*Compare* **swish.**] —*See also* **burble.**

lap up *verb.* —*See* **drink** (1).

lap *noun.* —*See* **burble.**

lapse *verb.* To become void, especially through passage of time or an omission ▶ cease, end, expire, run out, terminate. —*See also* **elapse, err, relapse, subside.**

lapse *noun.* —*See* **error, relapse.**

lapsed *adjective.* —*See* **past.**

larcenist *or* **larcener** *noun.* —*See* **thief.**

larcenous *adjective.* —*See* **thievish.**

larceny *noun.* The crime of taking someone else's property without consent ▶ banditry, brigandage, burglary, holdup, looting, mugging, pilferage, purloining, robbery, steal, stealing, theft, thievery. *Slang:* heist, rip-off, stickup.

lard *noun.* Adipose tissue ▶ blubber, fat, suet, tallow. [*Compare* **oil.**]

lares and penates *noun.* —*See* **effects.**

large *adjective.* At the upper end of a degree of measure ▶ elevated, great, high. [*Compare* **exalted, extreme.**] —*See also* **big, general** (2), **important.**

large-hearted *adjective.* —*See* **generous** (1).

large-heartedness *noun.* —*See* **generosity.**

largely *adverb.* —*See* **considerably.**

largeness *noun.* —*See* **size** (2).

larger *adjective.* —*See* **best** (2).

large-scale *adjective.* —*See* **big.**

largess *noun.* —*See* **donation, generosity, gratuity.**

largest *adjective.* —*See* **best** (2).

largish *adjective.* —*See* **big.**

lark *noun.* —*See* **prank**[1]**.**

larkish *adjective.* —*See* **mischievous.**

lascivious *adjective.* Feeling or preoccupied with sexual love or desire ▶ amorous, concupiscent, lecherous, lewd, libidinous, lubricious, lustful, lusty, passionate, prurient, sexy. [*Compare* **obscene, wanton.**] —*See also* **erotic.**

lash *verb.* —*See* **beat** (2), **fasten, slam** (1).

lashing *noun.* —*See* **beating.**

lass *noun.* —*See* **girl.**

lassitude *noun.* —*See* **apathy, lethargy.**

last[1] *adjective.* **1.** Coming after all others ▶ closing, concluding, final, terminal, ultimate. **2.** Bringing up the rear ▶ aftermost, endmost, hindermost, hindmost, lattermost, rearmost, tail. [*Compare* **extreme.**] **3.** Next before the present one ▶ foregoing, latter, preceding, previous. [*Compare* **past.**] **4.** Of or relating to a terminative condition, stage, or point ▶ final, latter, terminal, ultimate. [*Compare* **climactic.**]

last *adverb.* In conclusion ▶ conclusively, finally, lastly, ultimately. ***Idioms:*** at last, in the end. [*Compare* **ultimately.**]

last *noun.* —*See* **end** (2).

✚ **CORE SYNONYMS:** *last, final, terminal, ultimate.* These adjectives mean coming after all others in chronology or sequence. *Last* applies to what comes at the end of a series: *the last day of the month.* Something *final* stresses the definitiveness and decisiveness of the conclusion: *"I believe that unarmed truth and unconditional love will have the final word in reality"* (Martin Luther King, Jr.). *Terminal* applies to what marks or forms a limit or boundary, as in space, time, or development: *The railroad chose as its terminal city a town with a large harbor. Ultimate* applies to what concludes a series, process, or progression, to what constitutes a final result or objective, and to what is most distant or remote, as in time: *the ultimate sonata of that opus; our ultimate goal; the ultimate effect.*

◀ **ANTONYM:** *first*

---

last[2] *verb.* To remain fresh and unspoiled ▶ keep. —*See also* **endure** (2), **survive** (1).

lasting *adjective.* —*See* **continuing.**

lastly *adverb.* In conclusion ▶ conclusively, finally, last, ultimately. ***Idioms:*** at last, in the end. [*Compare* **ultimately.**]

last rites *noun.* —*See* **funeral.**

latch *noun.* —*See* **fastener.**

late *adjective.* **1.** Coming or occurring after the correct, usual, or expected time; not on time ▶ behindhand, belated, delayed, overdue, slow, tardy. **2.** Having been such previously ▶ erstwhile, former, old, once, onetime, past, previous, quondam, sometime, whilom. —*See also* **dead** (1).

late *adverb.* Not on time ▶ behind, behindhand, belatedly, slow, tardily. ***Idiom:*** behind time.

✚ **CORE SYNONYMS:** *late, behindhand, overdue, tardy.* These adjectives mean not arriving, occurring, acting, or done at the scheduled, expected, or usual time: *late for the plane; behindhand with her car payments; an overdue bus; tardy in making his dental appointment.*

◀ **ANTONYM:** *prompt*

---

lately *adverb.* Not long ago ▶ freshly, just (now), lately, latterly, newly, recently. ***Idioms:*** of late, only a moment (*or* while) ago.

latency *noun.* —*See* **abeyance.**

lateness *noun.* The quality or condition of not being on time ▶ belatedness, slowness, tardiness, unpunctuality.

latent *adjective.* Present but not evident or active ▶ abeyant, dormant, hibernating, inactive, lurking, possible, potential, quiescent, sleeping, smoldering, torpid. [*Compare* **hidden, implicit.**]

✤ **CORE SYNONYMS:** *latent, dormant, quiescent.* These adjectives mean present or in existence but not evident or active. What is *latent* is present but not evident: *latent ability. Dormant* evokes the idea of sleep: *a dormant volcano. Quiescent* sometimes, but not always, suggests temporary inactivity: *"For a time, he* [the whale] *lay quiescent"* (Herman Melville).

later *adjective.* Following something else in time ▶ after, posterior, subsequent, ulterior. [*Compare* **following.**] —*See also* **future.**
later *adverb.* At a subsequent time ▶ after, afterward, afterwards, latterly, next, subsequently, ulteriorly. ***Idioms:*** after a while, by and by, later on.
later *interjection.* —*See* **goodbye.**

latest *adjective.* —*See* **contemporary** (2).

lather *noun.* Moisture accumulated on a surface through sweating or condensation ▶ condensation, perspiration, sweat, transudation. —*See also* **agitation** (2), **foam.**
lather *verb.* To excrete moisture through a porous skin or layer ▶ perspire, sweat, transude. —*See also* **beat** (1), **foam.**

lathery *adjective.* —*See* **foamy.**

latitude *noun.* —*See* **license** (1).

latter *adjective.* **1.** Of or relating to a terminative condition, stage, or point ▶ final, last, terminal, ultimate. [*Compare* **climactic.**] **2.** Next before the present one ▶ foregoing, last, preceding, previous. [*Compare* **past.**]

latter-day *adjective.* —*See* **contemporary** (2).

latterly *adverb.* —*See* **lately, later.**

lattermost *adjective.* —*See* **last**[1] (2).

lattice *noun.* —*See* **web.**

laud *verb.* —*See* **honor** (1), **praise** (1), **praise** (3).
laud *noun.* —*See* **praise** (1).

laudable *adjective.* —*See* **admirable.**

laudation *noun.* —*See* **praise** (1), **praise** (2).

laudatory *adjective.* —*See* **complimentary** (1).

laugh *verb.* To express amusement or mirth by smiling and emitting inarticulate sounds ▶ bray, cachinnate, cackle, chortle, chuckle, giggle, guffaw, roar, snicker, snigger, tee-hee, titter. *Informal:* break up, heehaw, yuk. *Slang:* howl. ***Idioms:*** be in stitches, die laughing, laugh one's head off, roll in the aisles, split one's sides.
laugh at *verb.* —*See* **ridicule.**
laugh *noun.* An act of laughing ▶ bray, cachinnation, cackle, chortle, chuckle, giggle, guffaw, laughter, roar, snicker, snigger, tee-hee, titter. *Informal:* heehaw, yuk. *Slang:* howl. —*See also* **scream** (2).

laughable *adjective.* Causing or deserving laughter or derision ▶ farcical, ludicrous, ridiculous, risible. [*Compare* **foolish.**] —*See also* **funny** (1).

laughingstock *noun.* An object of amusement or laughter ▶ butt, jest, joke, mockery. ***Idiom:*** figure of fun.

laughter *noun.* —*See* **laugh.**

launch *verb.* —*See* **introduce** (1), **start** (1), **throw.**
launch *noun.* —*See* **beginning, throw.**

launder *verb.* —*See* **clean** (1).

laurels *noun.* —*See* **distinction** (2).

lavation *noun.* —*See* **purification** (1).

lave *verb.* To flow against or along ▶ bathe, lap, lip, wash. [*Compare* **flow.**] —*See also* **clean** (1).

lavish *adjective.* —*See* **extravagant, generous** (1), **luxurious, profuse.**
lavish *verb.* To give in great abundance ▶ heap, rain, shower. [*Compare* **confer, donate, give.**]

lavishness *noun.* —*See* **extravagance, generosity.**

law *noun.* **1.** A principle governing affairs within or among political units ▶ bylaw, canon, charter, edict, institute, ordinance, precept, prescription, regulation, rule, tenet. [*Compare* **doctrine.**] **2.** The formal product of a legislative or judicial body ▶ act, assize, bill, enactment, legislation, lex, measure, statute. [*Compare* **command, ruling.**] **3.** A broad and basic rule or truth ▶ axiom, formula, fundamental, maxim, principle, theorem, truism, universal. —*See also* **police officer, rule.**

law *verb.* To institute or subject to legal proceedings ▶ litigate, prosecute, sue. ***Idioms:*** bring suit, haul (*or* drag) into court.

lawbreaker *noun.* —*See* **criminal.**

lawful *adjective.* Within, allowed by, or sanctioned by the law ▶ authorized, just, legal, legitimate, licit, permitted, rightful, valid, warranted. *Slang:* legit. [*Compare* **acceptable.**]

lawfulness *noun.* —*See* **legality.**

lawless *adjective.* —*See* **criminal** (1), **disorderly, illegal, unruly.**

lawlessness *noun.* The state or quality of being illegal ▶ illegality, illegitimacy, illicitness, unlawfulness. —*See also* **disorder** (2), **unruliness.**

lawn *noun.* —*See* **common.**

lawsuit *noun.* A legal proceeding to demand justice or enforce a right ▶ action, case, cause, instance, litigation, suit.

lawyer *noun.* A person who practices law ▶ attorney, counsel, counselor, jurist, pettifogger. *Slang:* ambulance chaser, legal eagle.

lax *adjective.* —*See* **loose** (1), **negligent, tolerant.**

laxity *or* **laxness** *noun.* —*See* **license** (2), **negligence.**

lay[1] *verb.* **1.** To arrange tableware upon a table in preparation for a meal ▶ set, spread. **2.** To make a bet ▶ bet, gamble, game, play, wager. ***Idiom:*** put one's money on something. —*See also* **aim** (1), **bury, cite, design** (1), **fix** (3), **gamble** (2), **position.**

lay away *verb.* —*See* **bank**[2], **save** (1).

lay down *verb.* —*See* **abandon** (1), **dictate.**

lay for *verb.* —*See* **lurk.**

lay into *verb.* —*See* **attack** (1), **beat** (2).

lay off *verb.* —*See* **abandon** (2), **dismiss** (1).

lay on *or* **upon** *verb.* —*See* **impose on.**

lay out *verb.* To plan the details or arrangements of ▶ arrange, prepare, schedule, work out. —*See also* **design** (2), **draft** (1), **plot** (1), **spend** (1).

lay[2] *adjective.* —*See* **profane** (2).

layabout *noun.* —*See* **wastrel** (2).

layer *noun.* —*See* **coat** (2).

layout *noun.* —*See* **approach** (1), **arrangement** (1), **draft** (1).

layperson *noun.* —*See* **amateur.**

laze *verb.* —*See* **idle** (1).

laziness *noun.* The quality or state of being lazy ▶ fainéance, fainéancy, idleness, indolence, otioseness, otiosity, shiftlessness, sloth, slothfulness, sluggardness, sluggishness. *Informal:* do-nothingism.

lazy *adjective.* Resistant to exertion and activity ▶ fainéant, idle, indolent, otiose, shiftless, slothful, sluggard, sluggish. *Informal:* do-nothing. ***Idiom:*** bone lazy.

✣ **CORE SYNONYMS:** *lazy, fainéant, idle, indolent, slothful.* These adjectives mean resistant to exertion, work, and activity: *too lazy to wash the dishes; fainéant aristocrats; an idle drifter; an indolent hanger-on; slothful employees.*

---

lazybones *noun.* —*See* **wastrel** (2).

leach *verb.* —*See* **ooze.**

lead *verb.* To go through life in a certain way ▶ conduct, live, pass, pursue, spend. —*See also* **administer** (1), **dominate** (1), **guide, influence, introduce** (3).

lead off *verb.* —*See* **start** (1).

lead to *verb.* —*See* **cause, imply.**

lead *noun.* The main performer in a theatrical production ▶ headliner, leading lady, leading man, prima donna, principal, protagonist, star, starlet.

—*See also* **dominance, forefront, guide, management, tip[3].**

lead balloon *noun.* —*See* **failure** (1).

leaden *adjective.* —*See* **dull** (1), **heavy** (1), **languid, ponderous.**

leadenness *noun.* —*See* **lethargy.**

leader *noun.* A leading contestant or sure winner ▶ favorite, front-runner, number one, vanguard. *Informal:* shoo-in. —*See also* **chief, dignitary, guide.**

leadership *noun.* The capacity to lead others ▶ command, lead. —*See also* **management.**

lead-in *noun.* —*See* **introduction.**

leading *adjective.* —*See* **best** (1), **big-league, dominant** (1), **famous, primary** (1).

leadoff *noun.* —*See* **beginning.**

leadoff *adjective.* —*See* **beginning.**

leaf *noun.* —*See* **flake.**

leaf *verb.* —*See* **browse** (1).

leafless *adjective.* —*See* **bare** (3).

leaflet *noun.* An announcement distributed on paper to a large number of people ▶ circular, flier, handbill, notice.

league *noun.* —*See* **alliance, class** (2), **conference** (2), **union** (1).

league *verb.* —*See* **ally, band[2].**

leak *verb. Informal* To be made public ▶ break, come out, get out, out, transpire. *Informal:* leak out. [*Compare* **air, announce, appear.**] —*See also* **betray** (2), **ooze.**

lean[1] *verb.* —*See* **incline, tend[1].**

lean *noun.* —*See* **inclination** (2).

lean[2] *adjective.* —*See* **brief, thin** (1), **tight** (3).

leaning *noun.* —*See* **inclination** (1).

leaning *adjective.* —*See* **oblique.**

lean-to *noun.* —*See* **hut.**

leap *verb.* —*See* **bound[1], jump** (1).

leap *noun.* The act of jumping ▶ jump, pounce, spring, vault. [*Compare* **fall.**] —*See also* **bound[1]** (2).

learn *verb.* **1.** To gain knowledge or mastery of by study ▶ acquire, get, master. *Informal:* pick up. **2.** To commit to memory ▶ con, memorize. ***Idioms:*** learn by heart (*or* rote). [*Compare* **remember.**] —*See also* **absorb** (2), **discover.**

learned *adjective.* —*See* **educated.**

learner *noun.* —*See* **beginner, student.**

learning *noun.* —*See* **education** (2).

lease *verb.* **1.** To give temporary use of in return for payment ▶ hire (out), let (out), rent (out), sublet. **2.** To engage the temporary use of something for a fee ▶ charter, hire, rent.

leash *verb.* —*See* **hamper[1].**

leash *noun.* —*See* **brake.**

least *adjective.* —*See* **minimal.**

leather *noun.* The skin of an animal, sometimes including fur, hair, or feathers ▶ fur, hide, pelt.

leave[1] *verb.* **1.** To give property to another after one's death ▶ bequeath, devise, hand down, hand on, pass (along *or* on), transmit, will. [*Compare* **donate, give.**] **2.** To relinquish one's engagement in or occupation with ▶ demit, quit, resign, terminate. ***Idioms:*** hang it up, throw in the sponge (*or* towel). [*Compare* **break.**] —*See also* **abandon** (1), **go** (1).

leave off *verb.* —*See* **abandon** (2), **break** (5), **stop** (1).

leave[2] *noun.* A regularly scheduled period spent away from work or duty, often in recreation ▶ furlough, holiday, sabbatical, vacation. ***Idioms:*** time (*or* day) off. [*Compare* **break, trip.**] —*See also* **permission.**

leaven *or* **leavening** *noun.* —*See* **catalyst.**

leave-taking *noun.* —*See* **departure.**

leavings *noun.* —*See* **balance** (4).

lecher *noun.* An immoral or licentious man ▶ gigolo, goat, roué, satyr. *Informal:* dirty old man. *Slang:* lech. [*Compare* **philanderer, wanton.**]

lecherous *adjective.* —*See* **lascivious.**

lecture *noun.* —*See* **discourse, rebuke, speech** (2).

lecture *verb.* To talk to an audience formally ▶ address, prelect, sermonize, speak. [*Compare* **converse.**] —*See also* **chastise.**

lecturer *noun.* —*See* **speaker** (1).

leech *noun.* —*See* **parasite.**

leech *verb.* To take advantage of the generosity of others ▶ live off. *Informal:* sponge. *Slang:* freeload. [*Compare* **beg.**]

leeriness *noun.* —*See* **distrust.**

leery *adjective.* —*See* **distrustful.**

lees *noun.* —*See* **deposit** (2).

leeway *noun.* —*See* **license** (1).

left *adjective.* —*See* **liberal.**

left-handed *adjective.* —*See* **underhand.**

leftist *noun.* —*See* **liberal.**

leftist *adjective.* —*See* **liberal.**

leftover *adjective.* Being what remains, especially after a part has been removed ▶ extra, remaining, residual, stray. ***Idiom:*** left behind. [*Compare* **superfluous.**]

leftover *noun.* —*See* **balance** (4), **surplus.**

leftovers *noun.* —*See* **balance** (4).

left-wing *adjective.* —*See* **liberal.**

left-winger *noun.* —*See* **liberal.**

legacy *noun.* **1.** Something immaterial, as a style or philosophy, that is passed from one generation to another ▶ heritage, inheritance, tradition. **2.** Any special privilege accorded a firstborn ▶ birthright, heritage, inheritance, patrimony. [*Compare* **right.**]

legal *adjective.* —*See* **lawful.**

legality *noun.* The state or quality of being within the law ▶ lawfulness, legitimacy, legitimateness, licitness, permissibility, rightfulness, soundness, validity. [*Compare* **justice.**]

legalize *verb.* To make lawful ▶ decriminalize, legitimate, legitimatize, legitimize, warrant. [*Compare* **authorize, confirm, permit.**]

legation *noun.* A diplomatic office or headquarters in a foreign country ▶ deputation, embassy, mission.

legend *noun.* —*See* **celebrity, lore** (1), **myth** (1).

legendary *adjective.* —*See* **famous, mythical.**

legerdemain *noun.* —*See* **magic** (2).

legibility *noun.* —*See* **clarity.**

legion *noun.* —*See* **crowd.**

legion *adjective.* —*See* **many.**

legionnaire *or* **legionary** *noun.* —*See* **soldier** (2).

legislate *verb.* —*See* **establish** (2).

legislation *noun.* —*See* **law** (2).

legislative *adjective.* —*See* **governmental.**

legit *adjective.* —*See* **authentic** (1), **lawful.**

legitimacy *or* **legitimateness** *noun.* —*See* **legality.**

legitimate *adjective.* —*See* **authentic** (1), **lawful.** Being so legitimately ▶ rightful, true.

legitimate *verb.* —*See* **establish** (2), **legalize.**

legitimize *or* **legitimatize** *verb.* —*See* **legalize.**

legman *noun.* —*See* **press.**

leisure *noun.* Unrestricted freedom to choose ▶ convenience, discretion, pleasure, will. —*See also* **rest**[1] (2).

leisurely *adjective.* —*See* **deliberate** (3).

lemma *noun.* —*See* **assumption, entry.**

lend *verb.* To supply money, especially on credit ▶ advance, discount, float, loan. ***Idiom:*** extend credit to.

length *noun.* The ultimate point to which an action, thought, discussion, or policy is carried ▶ degree, end, extreme, extremity, limit. —*See also* **distance** (1), **extent.**

lengthen *verb.* To make or become longer ▶ draw out, elongate, extend, prolong, prolongate, protract, spin (out), stretch (out), string out. [*Compare* **broaden, increase.**]

lengthening *noun.* —*See* **extension** (1).

lengthy *adjective.* —*See* **long**[1] (1), **long**[1] (2).

lenience *or* **leniency** *noun.* —*See* **mercy, tolerance.**

lenient *adjective.* —*See* **tolerant.**

lese majesty *noun.* Willful violation of allegiance to one's country ▶ sedition, seditiousness, traitorousness, treason.

[*Compare* **faithlessness.**] —*See also* **disrespect.**

lesion *noun.* Marked tissue damage, especially when produced by physical injury ▶ laceration, trauma, traumatism, wound. [*Compare* **harm.**]

lessen *verb.* —*See* **decrease, depreciate, relieve** (1).

lesser *adjective.* —*See* **minor** (1).

lesson *noun.* —*See* **example** (2), **moral.**

let *verb.* —*See* **lease** (1), **permit** (1), **permit** (2), **permit** (3).

let down *verb.* —*See* **disappoint, lower**[2].

let go *verb.* —*See* **dismiss** (1), **drop** (5).

let in *verb.* —*See* **accept** (3).

let off *verb.* —*See* **emit, excuse** (1).

let out *verb.* —*See* **betray** (2), **drain** (1), **emit, lease** (1).

let up *verb.* —*See* **ease** (1), **subside.**

letdown *noun.* —*See* **disappointment** (2).

lethal *adjective.* —*See* **deadly.**

lethality *or* **lethalness** *noun.* The quality or condition of causing death or disaster ▶ deadliness, fatality, fatefulness.

lethargic *adjective.* Lacking mental and physical alertness and activity ▶ enervated, hebetudinous, inert, slothful, sluggish, stupid, stuporous, torpid. *Slang:* dopey. [*Compare* **dull, languid.**] —*See also* **apathetic.**

lethargy *noun.* A deficiency in mental and physical alertness and activity ▶ dullness, enervation, hebetude, inertness, languidness, languor, lassitude, leadenness, listlessness, slothfulness, sluggishness, stupor, torpidity, torpor. [*Compare* **stupidity.**] —*See also* **apathy.**

✚ **CORE SYNONYMS:** *lethargy, lassitude, torpor, torpidity, stupor, languor.* These nouns refer to a deficiency in mental and physical alertness and activity. *Lethargy* is a state of sluggishness, drowsy dullness, or apathy: *The war roused the nation from its lethargy. Lassitude* implies weariness or diminished energy such as might result from physical or mental strain: *"His anger had evaporated; he felt nothing but utter lassitude"* (John Galsworthy). *Torpor* and *torpidity* suggest the suspension of activity characteristic of an animal in hibernation: *"My calmness was the torpor of despair"* (Charles Brockden Brown). *Nothing could dispel the torpidity of the indifferent audience. Stupor* is often produced by the effects of alcohol or narcotics; it suggests a benumbed or dazed state of mind: *"The huge height of the buildings . . . the hubbub and endless stir . . . struck me into a kind of stupor of surprise"* (Robert Louis Stevenson). *Languor* is the indolence typical of one who is satiated by a life of luxury or pleasure: *After the banquet, I was overcome by languor.*

---

letter *noun.* A written communication that is directed to another ▶ correspondence, dispatch, epistle, line, memo, memorandum, message, missive, note. —*See also* **character** (7).

✚ **CORE SYNONYMS:** *letter, epistle, memorandum, missive, note.* These nouns denote a written communication that is directed to another: *received a letter of complaint; the Epistles of the New Testament; a company memorandum about the vacation policy; a missive of condolence; a thank-you note.*

---

lettered *adjective.* —*See* **educated.**

lettuce *noun.* —*See* **money** (1).

letup *noun.* —*See* **waning.**

level *noun.* —*See* **class** (2), **degree** (1), **degree** (2), **place** (1).

level *adjective.* —*See* **even** (1), **even** (2).

level *verb.* —*See* **aim** (1), **balance** (1), **destroy** (2), **drop** (3), **equalize, even.**

levelheaded *adjective.* —*See* **sensible.**

levelheadedness *adjective.* —*See* **balance** (2).

leverage *noun.* —*See* **advantage** (3), **influence.**

leviathan *noun.* —*See* **giant.**

levity *noun.* —*See* **trifle.**

levy *verb.* **1.** To establish and apply as compulsory ▶ assess, exact, impose, put. **2.** To enroll compulsorily in military service ▶ conscript, draft, impress, induct.

levy *noun.* —*See* **draft** (2), **tax.**

lewd *adjective.* —*See* **lascivious, obscene.**

lewdness *noun.* —*See* **obscenity** (1).

lex *noun.* —*See* **law** (2).

lexeme *noun.* —*See* **term.**

lexical *adjective.* Relating to, consisting of, or having the nature of words ▶ linguistic, verbal, wordy.

lexicon *noun.* **1.** An alphabetical list of words often defined or translated ▶ dictionary, glossary, vocabulary, wordbook. **2.** All the words of a language ▶ vocabulary, word-hoard. —*See also* **language** (2).

liability *noun.* —*See* **debt** (1), **debt** (2), **disadvantage, duty** (1), **exposure, responsibility.**

liable *adjective.* **1.** Legally or officially obligated ▶ accountable, amenable, answerable, responsible. [*Compare* **obligated.**] **2.** Tending to incur ▶ open, prone, subject, susceptible, susceptive, vulnerable. [*Compare* **helpless.**] —*See also* **inclined.**

✚ **CORE SYNONYMS:** *liable, responsible, answerable, accountable, amenable.* These adjectives mean legally or officially obliged to answer, as for one's actions, to an authority that may impose a penalty for failure. *Liable* may refer to a legal obligation, as to pay damages or to perform jury duty: *Wage earners are liable to income tax. Responsible* often implies the satisfactory performance of duties or the trustworthy care for or disposition of possessions: "*I am responsible for the ship's safety*" (Robert Louis Stevenson). *Answerable* suggests a moral or legal responsibility subject to review by a higher authority: *The court held the parents answerable for their minor child's acts of vandalism. Accountable* especially emphasizes giving an account of one's discharge of a responsibility: "*The liberal philosophy holds that enduring governments must be accountable to someone beside themselves*" (Walter Lippmann). *Amenable* implies being subject to the control of an authority and therefore the absence of complete autonomy: "*There is no constitutional tribunal to which* [the king] *is amenable*" (Alexander Hamilton).

---

liaison *noun.* —*See* **love** (3).

liar *noun.* One who tells lies ▶ deceiver, dissimulator, fabricator, fabulist, false witness, falsifier, fibber, perjurer, prevaricator. *Informal:* storyteller. [*Compare* **hypocrite.**]

libation *noun.* —*See* **drink** (1).

libel *noun.* The expression of injurious, malicious statements about someone ▶ aspersion, badmouthing, calumniation, calumny, character assassination, defamation, denigration, detraction, mudslinging, obloquy, scandal, slander, smear, smear campaign, traducement, vilification. [*Compare* **belittlement, vituperation.**]

libel *verb.* —*See* **malign.**

libelous *adjective.* Damaging to the reputation ▶ calumnious, defamatory, detractive, injurious, invidious, scandalous, slanderous. [*Compare* **derogatory.**]

liberal *adjective.* Favoring civil liberties and social reform, especially as a political philosophy ▶ left, leftist, left-wing, liberalistic, neoliberal, progressive, reformist, reform-minded, Whiggish. [*Compare* **ultraliberal.**] —*See also* **broad-minded, generous** (1).

liberal *noun.* One with politically liberal views ▶ leftist, left-winger, liberalist, neoliberal, progressive, Whig. [*Compare* **ultraliberal.**]

liberality *noun.* —*See* **generosity.**

liberate *verb.* —*See* **free** (1).
liberated *adjective.* —*See* **loose** (2).
liberation *noun.* —*See* **liberty, rescue.**
liberator *noun.* —*See* **rescuer.**
libertine *noun.* —*See* **wanton.**
libertine *adjective.* —*See* **wanton** (1).
libertinism *noun.* —*See* **license** (2).
liberty *noun.* The state of not being in confinement or servitude ▶ emancipation, freedom, liberation, manumission. —*See also* **freedom, license** (1).
libidinous *or* **libidinal** *adjective.* —*See* **lascivious.**
libido *or* **libidinousness** *noun.* —*See* **desire** (2).
libretto *noun.* —*See* **script** (2).
license *noun.* **1.** Freedom from normal restraints, limitations, or regulations ▶ elbowroom, entitlement, free hand, latitude, leeway, liberty, margin, play, privilege, room, scope. [*Compare* **right.**] **2.** Excessive freedom; lack of restraint ▶ anarchy, dissoluteness, dissolution, indulgence, laxity, laxness, libertinism, licentiousness, profligacy, slackness. [*Compare* **abandon, excess.**] **3.** A document that gives permission to do something ▶ commission, furlough, passport, permit, ticket, visa, warrant. —*See also* **permission.**
license *verb.* —*See* **authorize, permit** (2).

✦ **CORE SYNONYMS:** *license, elbowroom, latitude, leeway, margin, play, room, scope.* These nouns denote freedom from normal restraints, limitations, or regulations: *had license to do as they pleased; needed elbowroom to negotiate effectively; no latitude allowed in conduct; allowed the chef leeway in choosing the menu; no margin for error; imagination given full play; room for improvement in the design; permitting their talents free scope.*

---

licentious *adjective.* —*See* **abandoned** (2).
licentiousness *noun.* —*See* **license** (2).
licit *adjective.* —*See* **lawful.**
licitness *noun.* —*See* **legality.**
lick *verb.* —*See* **beat** (2), **defeat.**
lick *noun.* —*See* **blow**[2]**.**
lickety-split *adverb.* —*See* **fast, immediately** (1).
licking *noun.* —*See* **beating, defeat.**
lid *noun.* Something that covers, especially to prevent contents from spilling ▶ cap, cover, covering, top. [*Compare* **plug.**] —*See also* **limit** (1).
lie[1] *verb.* **1.** To be or place oneself in a prostrate or recumbent position ▶ couch, lie down, recline, repose, stretch (out). **2.** To take repose, as by sleeping or lying quietly ▶ curl up, recline, repose, rest, stretch (out). [*Compare* **nap, sleep.**] —*See also* **consist.**
lie[2] *noun.* An untrue declaration ▶ baldfaced lie, barefaced lie, canard, cock-and-bull story, distortion, fable, fabrication, falsehood, falsity, fib, fiction, half-truth, invention, inveracity, mendacity, misrepresentation, misstatement, prevarication, story, tale, untruth, white lie. *Informal:* fish story, tall tale. *Slang:* whopper.
lie *verb.* To present false information with the intention of deceiving ▶ falsify, fib, forswear, invent, make up, perjure, prevaricate. ***Idioms:*** lie like a trooper, like through one's teeth, speak with a forked tongue. [*Compare* **act, distort.**]

✦ **CORE SYNONYMS:** *lie, falsify, fib, prevaricate.* These verbs mean to present false information with the intention of deceiving someone: *a witness who lied under oath; a scoundrel who falsified evidence; fibbed to escape being scolded; didn't prevaricate but answered honestly.*

---

liege *adjective.* —*See* **faithful.**
lieu *noun.* The function or position customarily occupied by another ▶ place, stead.
lieutenant *noun.* —*See* **assistant, representative.**
life *noun.* The period during which someone or something exists ▶ course,

day, days, duration, existence, generation, lifetime, span, term, time. [*Compare* **age.**] —*See also* **human being, spirit** (1).

life force *noun.* —*See* **spirit** (2).

lifeless *adjective.* —*See* **dead** (1). Completely lacking sensation or consciousness ▶ dead, inanimate, insensate, insentient. —*See also* **barren** (2), **dead** (2), **dull** (1), **vacant.**

lifelessness *noun.* —*See* **dullness, inaction.**

lifelike *adjective.* —*See* **graphic** (1), **realistic** (2).

lifesaver *noun.* —*See* **rescuer.**

lifestyle *noun.* —*See* **culture** (2).

lifetime *noun.* —*See* **life.**

lift *verb.* **1.** To rise up in flight ▶ lift off, take off. **2.** To disappear by or as if by rising ▶ disperse, dissipate, fade away, scatter, thin out, withdraw. [*Compare* **disappear.**] **3.** To take back or remove ▶ countermand, overturn, pull, quash, recall, repeal, rescind, reverse, revoke. [*Compare* **abolish, retract.**] —*See also* **elate, elevate** (1), **plagiarize, rise** (2), **steal.**

lift *noun.* An instance of lifting or being lifted ▶ boost, heave, hoist, uplift, upthrust. —*See also* **ascent** (1), **elation, encouragement, thrill.**

liftoff *noun.* The act of rising in flight ▶ takeoff.

ligament *or* **ligature** *noun.* —*See* **bond** (2).

light[1] *noun.* **1.** Electromagnetic radiation that makes vision possible ▶ glow, illumination, lambency, lucency, luminescence. [*Compare* **flash.**] **2.** The act of physically illuminating or the condition of being filled with light ▶ illumination, lighting. [*Compare* **brilliance.**] —*See also* **viewpoint.**

light *verb.* **1.** To begin or cause to begin burning ▶ enkindle, fire, ignite, kindle, touch off. *Slang:* torch. ***Idioms:*** burst into flame, catch fire (*or* on fire), set fire to, set afire (*or* on fire). [*Compare* **burn.**] **2.** To make lively or animated ▶ animate, brighten, enliven, light up, perk up. —*See also* **illuminate** (1).

light *adjective.* —*See* **fair[1]** (3).

light[2] *adjective.* **1.** Having little weight; not heavy ▶ airy, fluffy, lightweight, weightless. ***Idioms:*** light as air, light as a feather. [*Compare* **immaterial, sheer[2].**] **2.** Of small intensity ▶ faint, gentle, moderate, modest, slight, soft. [*Compare* **imperceptible.**] **3.** Requiring little effort or exertion ▶ easy, moderate, undemanding. *Informal:* cushy, soft. —*See also* **lighthearted, trivial, wanton** (1).

light *verb.* To come ashore from a seacraft ▶ alight, debark, disembark, land. —*See also* **land** (2).

light into *verb.* —*See* **attack** (1), **slam** (1).

light on *or* **upon** *verb.* —*See* **encounter** (1).

light out *verb.* —*See* **bear** (5).

lighten[1] *verb.* —*See* **clear** (1), **illuminate** (1).

lighten[2] *verb.* —*See* **relieve** (1).

light-fingered *adjective.* —*See* **thievish.**

light-haired *adjective.* —*See* **fair[1]** (2).

lightheaded *adjective.* —*See* **dizzy** (1).

lightheadedness *noun.* —*See* **dizziness.**

lighthearted *adjective.* Happy and free from worry or care ▶ airy, blithe, buoyant, carefree, debonair, fancy-free, happy-go-lucky, light, untroubled. ***Idioms:*** free and easy, free as a bird, without a care in the world. [*Compare* **careless, lively, merry.**] —*See also* **cheerful, giddy** (2).

lightheartedness *noun.* —*See* **merriment** (1).

lighting *noun.* The act of physically illuminating or the condition of being filled with light ▶ illumination, light. [*Compare* **brilliance.**]

lightness *noun.* —*See* **trifle.**

lights out *noun.* —*See* **night.**

lightweight *adjective.* Having little weight; not heavy ▶ airy, fluffy, light, weightless. ***Idioms:*** light as air, light as a feather. [*Compare* **immaterial, sheer[2].**] —*See also* **trivial.**

lightweight *noun.* —*See* **nonentity.**

like[1] *verb.* To find agreeable ▶ adore, fancy, favor, love, take to. ***Idioms:*** take a fancy (*or* liking *or* shine) to. [*Compare* **value.**] —*See also* **choose** (2), **enjoy.**

like[2] *adjective.* Possessing the same or almost the same characteristics ▶ akin, alike, analogous, comparable, corresponding, equivalent, kin, matching, parallel, resembling, similar, uniform. [*Compare* **equal.**]

likeable *adjective.* —*See* **amiable.**

likelihood *noun.* Something expected ▶ anticipation, expectation, promise, prospect. [*Compare* **theory.**] —*See also* **chance** (3).

likely *adjective.* —*See* **conceivable, encouraging, inclined, presumptive, probable.**

likely *adverb.* —*See* **probably.**

like-minded *adjective.* —*See* **unanimous.**

liken *verb.* To represent as similar ▶ analogize, assimilate, compare, equate, identify, match, parallel, relate. [*Compare* **associate.**]

likeness *noun.* **1.** The quality or state of being alike ▶ affinity, alikeness, analogy, comparison, correspondence, parallelism, resemblance, similarity, similitude, uniformity, uniformness. [*Compare* **agreement, sameness.**] **2.** An image caused by reflection ▶ image, reflection. [*Compare* **copy.**] —*See also* **copy** (1).

✚ CORE SYNONYMS: *likeness, similarity, similitude, resemblance, analogy, affinity.* These nouns denote the quality or state of being alike. *Likeness* implies close agreement: *The forgery was renowned for its likeness to the original. Similarity* and *similitude* suggest agreement only in some respects or to some degree: *They were drawn to each other by similarity of interests. "A striking similitude between the brother and sister now first arrested my attention"* (Edgar Allan Poe). *Resemblance* refers to similarity in external or superficial details: *"The child . . . bore a remarkable resemblance to her grandfather"* (Lytton Strachey). *Analogy* is similarity, as of properties or functions, between things that are otherwise not comparable: *The operation of a computer presents an interesting analogy to the working of the human brain. Affinity* is likeness deriving from kinship or from the possession of shared properties or sympathies: *Being an orphan, she felt an affinity with other parentless children.*

likewise *adverb.* —*See* **additionally.**

likewise *adjective.* In a similar manner ▶ similarly, so. ***Idioms:*** by the same token, in like fashion, in like manner, in the same way.

liking *noun.* A desire for a particular thing or activity ▶ fancy, mind, pleasure, soft spot, will. [*Compare* **inclination, taste.**] —*See also* **love** (1).

Lilliputian *adjective.* —*See* **tiny.**

lilt *noun.* —*See* **tone** (2).

lily-livered *adjective.* —*See* **cowardly.**

lily-white *adjective.* —*See* **exemplary, innocent** (1), **innocent** (2).

limber *adjective.* —*See* **flexible** (2).

limberness *noun.* —*See* **flexibility** (1).

limit *noun.* **1.** The greatest amount or number allowed ▶ brim, cap, ceiling, cutoff, lid, limitation, maximum. [*Compare* **allotment, maximum.**] **2.** Either of the two points at the ends of a spectrum or range ▶ extreme, extremity. [*Compare* **climax, low.**] —*See also* **border** (1), **length, limits, restraint.**

limit *verb.* To place a limit on ▶ bound, circumscribe, confine, fix, restrict, set. [*Compare* **restrain.**] —*See also* **determine.**

✚ CORE SYNONYMS: *limit, restrict, confine, circumscribe.* These verbs mean to establish or keep within specified limits. *Limit* refers principally to the establishment of a maximum beyond which a person or thing cannot or may not go: *The Constitution limits the President's term of office to four years.* To *restrict* is to keep within prescribed limits, as of choice or action: *The sale of alcoholic beverages is restricted to those over 21. Confine* suggests imprisonment, restraint, or impediment: *The children were confined to the nursery. Circumscribe* connotes an encircling or surrounding line that confines, especially narrowly: *"A man . . . should not circumscribe his activity by any inflexible fence of rigid rules"* (John Stuart Blackie).

---

limitation *noun.* —*See* **limit** (1), **provision, restraint, restriction.**

limited *adjective.* —*See* **definite** (2), **local, narrow** (1), **qualified, restricted.**

limitless *adjective.* —*See* **endless** (1).

limitlessness *noun.* —*See* **infinity** (1).

limits *noun.* The boundary surrounding a certain area ▶ bound, bounds, confines, end, limit, perimeter, periphery, precincts. [*Compare* **border, circumference, outskirts.**]

limn *verb.* —*See* **represent** (2).

limp *verb.* —*See* **muddle, stagger** (1).

limp *adjective.* Not firm or stiff ▶ drooping, droopy, flabby, flaccid, floppy, soft. [*Compare* **flexible, loose, malleable.**] —*See also* **languid.**

✚ **CORE SYNONYMS:** *limp, flabby, flaccid, floppy.* These adjectives mean lacking in stiffness or firmness: *a limp shirt collar; flabby, wrinkled flesh; flaccid cheeks; a floppy hat brim.*

◀ **ANTONYM:** *firm*

---

limpid *adjective.* —*See* **clear** (1).

limpidity *or* **limpidness** *noun.* —*See* **clarity.**

line *noun.* A group of people or things arranged in a row ▶ column, file, queue, rank, row, string, tier. [*Compare* **series.**] —*See also* **ancestry, approach** (1), **business** (2), **cord, doctrine, good** (2), **letter, stripe, wrinkle** (1).

line *verb.* To place in or form a line or lines ▶ align, dress, file, line up, queue (up), range. [*Compare* **arrange.**] —*See also* **streak.**

lineage *noun.* —*See* **ancestry, family** (2).

lineal *adjective.* Of unbroken descent or lineage ▶ direct, genealogical, hereditary, natural. [*Compare* **ancestral.**]

lineaments *noun.* —*See* **expression** (4), **face** (1), **face** (3).

linear *adjective.* —*See* **direct** (1).

lineup *noun.* A list of candidates proposed or endorsed by a political party ▶ ballot, slate, ticket. —*See also* **arrangement** (1), **program** (1).

linger *verb.* —*See* **delay** (2), **remain.**

lingerer *noun.* —*See* **laggard.**

lingering *adjective.* —*See* **chronic** (2).

lingo *noun.* —*See* **dialect, language** (2).

linguistic *adjective.* Relating to, consisting of, or having the nature of words ▶ lexical, verbal, wordy.

liniment *noun.* —*See* **ointment.**

link *noun.* —*See* **bond** (2), **relation** (1).

link *verb.* —*See* **associate** (1), **associate** (3), **combine** (1).

linkage *noun.* —*See* **relation** (1).

lintel *noun.* —*See* **beam** (2).

lion *noun.* —*See* **celebrity, dignitary.**

lionization *noun.* —*See* **exaltation.**

lip *noun. Informal* Insolent talk ▶ back talk, mouth. *Informal:* sass. [*Compare* **impudence.**] —*See also* **border** (1), **projection.**

lip *verb.* To flow against or along ▶ bathe, lap, lave, wash. [*Compare* **flow.**]

lip service *noun.* —*See* **hypocrisy.**

liquefy *verb.* —*See* **melt.**

liquidate *verb.* —*See* **annihilate, eliminate, murder, settle** (3).

liquidation *noun.* —*See* **annihilation, elimination, massacre, murder.**

liquor *noun.* —*See* **drink** (1).

lissome *adjective.* —*See* **flexible** (2).

lissomeness *noun.* —*See* **flexibility** (1).

list[1] *noun.* A series, as of names or words, printed or written down ▶ agenda, catalog, checklist, directory, index, inventory, invoice, listing, manifest, register, roll, roster, schedule, table.

list *verb.* To place on a list or in a record or book ▶ book, catalog, chronicle, docket, enroll, enter, file, inscribe, insert, log, minute, post, record, register, set down, tabulate, write down. [*Compare* **schedule.**] *—See also* **enumerate.**

list[2] *noun.* *—See* **inclination** (2).

list *verb.* *—See* **incline.**

listen *verb.* To make an effort to hear something ▶ attend, hark, hearken, heed. ***Idioms:*** give (*or* lend) an ear. *—See also* **hear.**

listen *noun.* A chance to be heard ▶ audience, audition, hearing.

listing *noun.* *—See* **list[1].**

listless *adjective.* *—See* **apathetic, languid.**

listlessness *noun.* *—See* **apathy, boredom, lethargy.**

lit *adjective.* *—See* **drugged, drunk.**

litany *noun.* *—See* **prayer[1]** (2).

literal *adjective.* Employing the very same words as another ▶ undeviating, unvarnished, verbal, verbatim, word-for-word. ***Idiom:*** to the letter. [*Compare* **accurate, close.**] *—See also* **pedantic.**

literally *adverb.* *—See* **exactly.**

literary *adjective.* *—See* **pedantic.**

literate *adjective.* *—See* **educated.**

lithe *or* **lithesome** *adjective.* *—See* **flexible** (2).

litheness *noun.* *—See* **flexibility** (1).

litigate *verb.* To institute or subject to legal proceedings ▶ law, prosecute, sue. ***Idioms:*** bring suit, haul (*or* drag) into court.

litigation *noun.* *—See* **lawsuit.**

litigious *adjective.* *—See* **argumentative.**

litter *noun.* The offspring, as of an animal or bird, for example, that are the result of one breeding season ▶ brood, young. [*Compare* **progeny.**] *—See also* **flock, garbage.**

little *adjective.* Below average in amount, length, size, or scope ▶ bantam, compact, petite, runty, short, small, smallish, undersized. [*Compare* **stocky, tiny.**] *—See also* **narrow** (1), **trivial.**

little *adverb.* *—See* **infrequently.**

little *noun.* *—See* **bit[1]** (1).

little-known *adjective.* *—See* **obscure** (2).

littlest *adjective.* *—See* **minimal.**

liturgical *adjective.* *—See* **ritual.**

liturgy *noun.* *—See* **ceremony** (1).

livable *adjective.* Fit to live in ▶ habitable, inhabitable.

live[1] *verb.* To have as one's domicile, usually for an extended period ▶ abide, domicile, dwell, house, occupy, reside, stay. [*Compare* **inhabit.**] *—See also* **exist, lead.**

live by *verb.* *—See* **follow** (4).

live off *verb.* To take advantage of the generosity of others ▶ leech. *Informal:* sponge. *Slang:* freeload. [*Compare* **beg.**]

live on *verb.* To include as part of one's diet by nature or preference ▶ eat, exist on, feed on, subsist on.

live through *verb.* *—See* **endure** (1).

live[2] *adjective. Informal* Of great current interest ▶ hot, red-hot. [*Compare* **fashionable, important.**] *—See also* **alive.**

livelihood *noun.* *—See* **living.**

liveliness *noun.* *—See* **energy, spirit** (1).

lively *adjective.* Very brisk, alert, and full of high spirits ▶ animated, bouncy, breezy, bubbly, chipper, coltish, dashing, ebullient, effervescent, exuberant, frisky, high-spirited, jaunty, perky, pert, sassy, sparkling, sparkly, spirited, vibrant, vivacious. *Informal:* corky, peppy, snappy. ***Idioms:*** bright-eyed and bushy-tailed, full of life. [*Compare* **enthusiastic, passionate.**] *—See also* **energetic.**

live wire *noun. Informal* An intensely energetic, enthusiastic person ▶ demon, dynamo, hustler. *Informal:* eager beaver, firebreather, go-getter.

livid *adjective.* *—See* **angry, pale** (1).

living *adjective.* *—See* **alive.**

living *noun.* The means needed to support life ▶ alimentation, alimony, bread, bread and butter, existence, income, keep, livelihood, maintenance, subsistence, support, sustenance, upkeep.

living hell *noun.* —*See* **hell.**

load *noun.* —*See* **burden**[1] (2), **heap** (2).

load *verb.* To put explosive material into a weapon ▶ charge, prime, ready. —*See also* **burden**[1], **contaminate, distort, fill** (1), **heap** (1).

loaded *adjective.* Burdened by a weighty load ▶ heavy, heavy-laden, laden, weighed down. —*See also* **drunk, impure** (2), **rich** (1).

loaf *verb.* —*See* **idle** (1).

loafer *noun.* —*See* **wastrel** (2).

loam *noun.* —*See* **earth** (1).

loan *verb.* —*See* **lend.**

loath *adjective.* —*See* **indisposed.**

loathe *verb.* —*See* **hate.**

loathing *noun.* —*See* **despisal, disgust, hate** (1).

loathsome *adjective.* —*See* **ghastly** (1), **offensive** (1).

loathsomeness *noun.* —*See* **ugliness.**

lob *verb.* —*See* **throw.**

lob *noun.* —*See* **throw.**

local *adjective.* Confined to a particular location or site ▶ bounded, limited, localized, on-site, regional. —*See also* **city, indigenous, narrow** (1).

local *noun.* —*See* **inhabitant.**

locale *noun.* —*See* **environment** (1), **locality, scene** (1).

locality *noun.* A particular geographic area ▶ area, locale, location, neighborhood, place, vicinity. [*Compare* **position, scene.**] —*See also* **area** (2), **environment** (1).

localized *adjective.* —*See* **local.**

locate *verb.* **1.** To look for and discover ▶ find, pinpoint, spot. *Informal:* scare up. [*Compare* **trace, uncover.**] **2.** To move to a place and reside there ▶ relocate, settle. ***Idioms:*** fix one's residence, make one's home, put down roots, take up residence. [*Compare* **emigrate, live**[1], **move.**] —*See also* **position.**

location *noun.* —*See* **bearing** (3), **locality, position** (1).

lock[1] *noun.* —*See* **fastener.**

lock *verb.* —*See* **fasten.**

lock away *or* **in** *or* **up** *verb.* —*See* **imprison.**

lock[2] *noun.* —*See* **curl.**

lockup *noun.* —*See* **jail.**

loco *adjective.* —*See* **insane.**

locus *noun.* —*See* **center** (1), **position** (1).

locution *noun.* —*See* **expression** (3), **term, wording.**

lodge *verb.* To stay in or provide with lodging, especially temporarily ▶ accommodate, bed (down), berth, bestow, billet, board, bunk, domicile, harbor, house, put up, quarter, room, sojourn, stay, visit. [*Compare* **live**[1].] —*See also* **catch** (3), **fix** (2).

lodging *noun.* Dwellings in general ▶ housing, shelter. ***Idiom:*** a roof over one's head. [*Compare* **hut.**] —*See also* **home** (1).

lodgings *noun.* Usually temporary living accommodations ▶ barracks, quarters, rooms. *Slang:* crash-pad. [*Compare* **apartment, home.**]

loftiest *adjective.* Of, being, located at, or forming the top ▶ highest, top, topmost, upmost, uppermost. [*Compare* **climactic.**]

loftiness *noun.* The distance of something from a given level ▶ altitude, height, loftiness, tallness. [*Compare* **ascent.**] —*See also* **arrogance, pretentiousness.**

lofty *adjective.* —*See* **arrogant, elevated** (4), **exalted, high** (1).

log *verb.* —*See* **list**[1].

log in *or* **on** *verb.* To gain entry into a computer network or database ▶ access, enter. ***Idioms:*** gain access (*or* admittance *or* entry), get connected.

logic *noun.* Exact, valid, and rational reasoning ▶ analysis, argument, deduction, induction, ratiocination, rationality, reason. —*See also* **sense.**

logical *adjective.* **1.** Able to reason validly ▶ analytic, analytical, ratiocinative, rational. [*Compare* **sensible.**] **2.** Consistent with reason and intellect ▶ consequent, deducible, intelligent, rational, reasonable. [*Compare* **sound²**.]

✚ **CORE SYNONYMS:** *logical, analytic, ratiocinative, rational.* These adjectives mean capable of or showing correct and valid reasoning: *a logical mind; an analytic thinker; the ratiocinative process; a rational being.*

◀ **ANTONYM:** *illogical*

loiter *verb.* —*See* **delay** (2), **idle** (1).

loiterer *noun.* —*See* **laggard.**

loll *verb.* To take on or move with an awkward, slovenly posture ▶ slouch, slump. [*Compare* **bow¹, stoop.**] —*See also* **slouch** (2), **sprawl.**

lone *adjective.* Alone in a given category ▶ one, only, particular, separate, single, singular, sole, solitary, unique. ***Idioms:*** all by one's lonesome, first and last, one and only. —*See also* **individual** (2), **single, solitary.**

loneliness *noun.* —*See* **solitude.**

lonely *or* **lonesome** *adjective.* **1.** Empty of people ▶ deserted, desolate, forlorn, godforsaken, uninhabited, unfrequented, unpeopled, unpopulated, vacant. **2.** Dejected due to the awareness of being alone ▶ desolate, forlorn, lorn. [*Compare* **depressed, miserable.**] —*See also* **remote** (1), **solitary.**

long¹ *adjective.* **1.** Having great physical length ▶ elongate, elongated, extended, lengthy, outstretched, prolonged, stretching. **2.** Extending tediously beyond a standard duration ▶ dragging, drawn-out, interminable, lengthy, long-drawn-out, overlong, prolonged, protracted, sustained, unending.

long *noun.* —*See* **ages.**

long² *verb.* —*See* **desire.**

longanimity *noun.* —*See* **patience.**

long-drawn-out *adjective.* —*See* **long¹** (2).

long green *noun.* —*See* **money** (1).

longhand *noun.* —*See* **script** (1).

longing *noun.* —*See* **desire** (1).

long-lasting *or* **long-lived** *or* **long-standing** *adjective.* —*See* **continuing.**

long-suffering *adjective.* —*See* **patient.**

long-suffering *noun.* —*See* **patience.**

long suit *noun.* —*See* **forte.**

long-winded *adjective.* —*See* **digressive, wordy** (1).

long-windedness *noun.* —*See* **wordiness.**

look *verb.* **1.** To direct the eyes on an object ▶ consider, contemplate, eye, view. ***Idioms:*** clap (*or* lay *or* set) one's eyes on. [*Compare* **gaze, glimpse, survey, watch.**] **2.** To give the impression of being ▶ appear, feel, seem, sound. ***Idioms:*** have all the earmarks of being, give the idea (*or* impression) of being, strike one as being. [*Compare* **resemble.**]

look after *verb.* —*See* **tend².**

look for *verb.* —*See* **expect** (1), **seek** (1).

look in *verb.* —*See* **visit.**

look into *verb.* —*See* **explore.**

look on *or* **toward** *verb.* To have the face or front turned toward ▶ face, front, give onto. [*Compare* **overlook.**]

look out *verb.* To be careful ▶ beware, mind, watch out. ***Idioms:*** be on guard, be on the lookout, keep an eye peeled, take care (*or* heed).

look over *verb.* To view broadly or from a height ▶ overlook, scan, survey. —*See also* **browse** (1).

look through *verb.* —*See* **browse** (1).

look up *verb.* —*See* **visit.**

look upon *verb.* To have the face or front turned toward ▶ face, front, give onto. [*Compare* **overlook.**] —*See also* **regard.**

look *noun.* An act of directing the eyes on an object ▶ contemplation, regard, sight, view. [*Compare* **gaze, watch.**] —*See also* **appearance** (1), **expression** (4), **face** (3), **glance** (1).

looker *noun.* —*See* **beauty.**

looker-on *noun.* —*See* **watcher** (1).

look-in *noun.* —*See* **visit** (1).

lookout *noun.* **1.** The act of carefully watching ▶ monitoring, stakeout, surveillance, vigil, vigilance, watch. ***Idiom:*** watch and ward. [*Compare* **watch.**] **2.** A high structure or place commanding a wide view ▶ crow's nest, cupola, observation post, observatory, outlook, overlook, post, vista, watchtower. **3.** Something that concerns or involves one personally ▶ affair, business, concern, interest. —*See also* **guard, view** (2).

looks *noun.* —*See* **appearance** (1).

loom *verb.* —*See* **appear** (1), **threaten** (2).

looming *adjective.* —*See* **fateful** (1), **imminent.**

loon *noun.* —*See* **crackpot.**

looniness *noun.* —*See* **foolishness.**

loony *adjective.* —*See* **foolish, insane.**

loony *noun.* —*See* **crackpot.**

loop *noun.* A length of line folded over and joined at the ends so as to form a curve or circle ▶ circuit, coil, eye, eyelet, noose, ring, ringlet. [*Compare* **circle.**] —*See also* **conference** (2).

loop *verb.* —*See* **bend** (1), **encircle.**

looped *adjective.* —*See* **drunk.**

loopiness *noun.* —*See* **foolishness.**

loopy *adjective.* —*See* **foolish.**

loose *adjective.* **1.** Not tautly bound, held, or fastened ▶ dangling, flapping, hanging, lax, relaxed, slack, unbound, unfastened. [*Compare* **limp.**] **2.** Able to move about at will without bounds or restraint ▶ emancipated, free, liberated, unbridled, unchained, unchecked, unconfined, unfettered, unhindered, unrestrained, untrammeled. ***Idioms:*** at large, at liberty, free as a bird, on the loose. [*Compare* **clear.**] **3.** Lacking literal exactness ▶ approximate, broad, free, general, imprecise, inexact, rough. —*See also* **wanton** (1).

loose *verb.* —*See* **ease** (1), **free** (1), **shoot** (3), **undo.**

✚ **CORE SYNONYMS:** *loose, lax, slack.* These adjectives mean not tautly bound, held, or fastened: *loose reins; a lax rope; slack sails.*

◀ **ANTONYM:** *tight*

---

loosen *verb.* —*See* **ease** (1), **undo.**

loot *noun.* —*See* **plunder.**

loot *verb.* —*See* **sack**².

looter *noun.* —*See* **thief.**

looting *noun.* —*See* **larceny.**

lop¹ *verb.* —*See* **cut** (3).

lop² *verb.* —*See* **slouch** (2).

lope *verb.* —*See* **run** (1).

lope *noun.* —*See* **run** (1).

loquacious *adjective.* —*See* **talkative.**

lord *noun.* —*See* **chief.**

lordliness *noun.* —*See* **arrogance.**

lordly *adjective.* Exercising authority ▶ authoritative, commanding, dominant, masterful. [*Compare* **administrative.**] —*See also* **arrogant, grand.**

lore *noun.* **1.** A body of traditional beliefs and notions accumulated about a particular subject ▶ folklore, folkways, legend, myth, mythology, mythos, old wives' tale, tradition, superstition. [*Compare* **proverb.**] **2.** The sum of what has been perceived, discovered, or inferred ▶ knowledge, understanding, wisdom. [*Compare* **actuality.**] —*See also* **information.**

lorn *adjective.* —*See* **abandoned** (1), **lonely** (2).

lose *verb.* **1.** To be unable to find ▶ mislay, misplace, miss. ***Idiom:*** have something go missing. **2.** To fail to take advantage of ▶ miss, pass up, relinquish, squander, waste. ***Idioms:*** let slip, let slip through one's fingers, lose out on. [*Compare* **neglect.**] **3.** To get away from a pursuer ▶ elude, evade, outrun, shake off, slip, throw off. *Slang:* shake. ***Idiom:*** give someone the slip.

loser *noun.* —*See* **failure** (1), **unfortunate.**

loss *noun.* **1.** The act or an instance of losing something ▶ losing, mislaying, misplacement, missing. **2.** A loss of life, or one who has lost life, usually as a result of accident, disaster, or war ▶

casualty, death, fatality, kill. [*Compare* **victim.**] **3.** A sad or tragic deprivation ▶ waste. —*See also* **deprivation.**

lost *adjective.* **1.** Unable to find the correct way or place to go ▶ adrift, astray, disoriented, stray. ***Idiom:*** wandering in the wilderness. **2.** No longer in one's possession ▶ gone, mislaid, misplaced, missing, vanished. ***Idiom:*** gone missing. [*Compare* **absent.**] —*See also* **absent-minded, condemned, confused** (1), **hopeless.**

lot *noun.* **1.** A piece of land ▶ acreage, parcel, patch, plat, plot, tract. [*Compare* **field.**] **2.** *Informal* An indefinite amount or extent ▶ deal, quantity. —*See also* **abundance, allotment, fate** (2), **group, heap** (2), **kind**[2].

Lothario *noun.* A man who seduces women ▶ debaucher, Don Juan, seducer. [*Compare* **flirt, lecher, philanderer.**] —*See also* **gallant.**

lotion *noun.* —*See* **ointment.**

lottery *noun.* —*See* **chance** (2).

loud *adjective.* Marked by extremely high volume and intensity of sound ▶ blaring, booming, clamorous, deafening, earsplitting, noisy, piercing, roaring, shrill, stentorian, strident, thunderous. —*See also* **gaudy.**

✤ **CORE SYNONYMS:** *loud, earsplitting, stentorian, strident.* These adjectives mean marked by or producing great volume and often disagreeable intensity of sound: *loud trumpets; earsplitting shrieks; spoke in stentorian tones; strident, screeching brakes.*

◀ **ANTONYM:** *soft*

---

loudmouthed *adjective.* —*See* **vociferous.**

lounge *verb.* —*See* **idle** (1), **rest**[1] (1), **sprawl.**

lounge *noun.* —*See* **bar** (2).

lounger *noun.* —*See* **wastrel** (2).

louse *noun.* —*See* **creep** (2).

louse up *verb.* —*See* **botch.**

lousy *adjective.* —*See* **offensive** (1), **shoddy, terrible.**

lout *noun.* —*See* **oaf.**

lovable *adjective.* —*See* **delightful.**

love *noun.* **1.** An intense attachment to a person or thing ▶ adoration, affection, attachment, devotion, fondness, heart, liking, love affair, loyalties, passion, romance, tenderness, worship. [*Compare* **inclination.**] **2.** The passionate affection and desire felt by lovers for each other ▶ amativeness, amorousness, ardor, devotion, fancy, passion, romance. [*Compare* **desire.**] **3.** An intimate sexual relationship between two people ▶ affair, amour, liaison, love affair, romance. —*See also* **darling** (1).

love *verb.* To feel deep devoted love for ▶ adore, worship. ***Idioms:*** be soft (*or* stuck *or* sweet) on, place (*or* put) on a pedestal, worship the ground someone walks on. —*See also* **adore** (2), **like**[1].

✤ **CORE SYNONYMS:** *love, affection, devotion, fondness.* These nouns denote feelings of warm personal attachment or strong attraction to another person. *Love* is the most intense: *marrying for love. Affection* is a less ardent and more unvarying feeling of tender regard: *parental affection. Devotion* is earnest, affectionate dedication and implies selflessness: *teachers admired for their devotion to children. Fondness* is strong liking or affection: *a fondness for small animals.*

---

love affair *noun.* —*See* **love** (3), **love** (1).

loved *adjective.* —*See* **darling.**

lovely *adjective.* —*See* **attractive, beautiful, pleasant.**

lovely *noun.* —*See* **beauty.**

lover *noun.* A romantic interest, especially a regular sexual partner ▶ heartthrob, paramour, partner, steady. *Informal:* flame, significant other. *Slang:* main squeeze, squeeze. [*Compare* **boyfriend, darling, girlfriend.**] —*See also* **fan**[2].

loving *adjective.* —*See* **affectionate, sympathetic.**

low *adjective.* **1.** Being a sound produced by a relatively small frequency of vibrations ▶ alto, bass, contralto, deep, low-pitched. **2.** Cut to reveal the wearer's neck, chest, and back ▶ décolleté, low-cut, low-neck, low-necked, plunging. —*See also* **cheap, deep** (1), **depressed** (1), **disparaging, minor** (1), **offensive** (1), **sick** (1), **soft** (2), **sordid.**

low *noun.* A very low or lowest level, position, or degree ▶ bottom, minimum, nadir, rock bottom.

lowborn *adjective.* —*See* **lowly** (1).

lowbrow *adjective.* —*See* **ignorant** (1).

low-cost *adjective.* —*See* **cheap.**

low-cut *adjective.* —*See* **low** (2).

low-down *adjective.* —*See* **sordid.**

low-down *noun.* —*See* **information.**

lower[1] *verb.* **1.** To wrinkle one's brow, as in thought, puzzlement, or displeasure ▶ frown, glower, scowl. ***Idioms:*** knit one's brow, look black, turn one's mouth down. [*Compare* **grimace.**] **2.** To stare fixedly and angrily ▶ glare, glower, scowl. ***Idioms:*** give the evil eye, look daggers. [*Compare* **gaze, sneer.**] —*See also* **threaten** (2).

lower *noun.* A fixed angry stare ▶ glare, glower, scowl. [*Compare* **face, sneer.**] —*See also* **frown.**

lower[2] *verb.* To cause to descend ▶ cast down, depress, drop, let down, sink, take down. —*See also* **condescend** (1), **cut** (3), **decrease, depreciate, humble.**

lower *adjective.* —*See* **minor** (1).

lowering *adjective.* —*See* **fateful** (1).

lowest *or* **lowermost** *adjective.* Opposite to or farthest from the top ▶ bottom, nethermost, undermost.

low-grade *adjective.* —*See* **bad** (1).

low-key *or* **low-keyed** *adjective.* —*See* **soft** (2).

lowland *noun.* —*See* **valley.**

lowlife *noun.* —*See* **creep** (2).

lowliness *noun.* —*See* **modesty** (1).

lowly *adjective.* **1.** Lacking high station or birth ▶ baseborn, common, déclassé, declassed, humble, ignoble, lowborn, low-ranking, mean, plebeian, unwashed, vulgar. [*Compare* **poor.**] **2.** Having or expressing feelings of humility ▶ humble, meek, modest, unambitious. [*Compare* **deferential.**] **3.** Of little distinction ▶ humble, mean, simple. [*Compare* **modest.**]

low-necked *or* **low-neck** *adjective.* —*See* **low** (2).

lowness *noun.* —*See* **depression** (2).

low-pitched *adjective.* —*See* **low** (1).

low-priced *adjective.* —*See* **cheap.**

low-quality *adjective.* —*See* **bad** (1).

low-ranking *adjective.* —*See* **lowly** (1).

loyal *adjective.* —*See* **faithful.**

loyalties *noun.* —*See* **love** (1).

loyalty *noun.* —*See* **fidelity.**

lube *noun.* —*See* **oil.**

lube *verb.* —*See* **oil.**

lubricant *noun.* —*See* **oil.**

lubricate *verb.* —*See* **oil.**

lubricious *adjective.* —*See* **lascivious, slick, underhand.**

lucency *noun.* —*See* **light**[1] (1).

lucent *adjective.* —*See* **bright.**

lucid *adjective.* Mentally healthy ▶ compos mentis, normal, rational, sane. ***Idioms:*** all there, in one's right mind, of sound mind. [*Compare* **healthy.**] —*See also* **clear** (1), **graphic** (1), **understandable.**

lucidity *or* **lucidness** *noun.* —*See* **clarity, sanity.**

luck *noun.* Success attained as a result of chance ▶ dumb luck, fluke, fortunateness, fortune, godsend, good fortune (*or* luck), luckiness. ***Idioms:*** gift from above (*or* heaven *or* on high), stroke of luck. —*See also* **chance** (2), **fate** (1), **fate** (2).

luckless *adjective.* —*See* **unfortunate** (1).

lucky *adjective.* Characterized by luck or good fortune ▶ fortuitous, fortunate, happy, providential. [*Compare* **opportune.**]

✣ **CORE SYNONYMS:** *lucky, fortunate, happy, providential.* These adjectives mean characterized by luck or good fortune: *a lucky guess; a fortunate omen; a happy outcome; a providential recovery.*

◀ ANTONYM: *unlucky*

---

lucrative *adjective.* —*See* **profitable.**

lucre *noun.* —*See* **money** (1).

lucubrate *verb.* To apply one's mind to the acquisition of knowledge, especially when pressed for time ▶ study. *Informal:* bone up, cram, grind. ***Idioms:*** burn the midnight oil, hit the books. [*Compare* **examine.**]

ludicracy *noun.* —*See* **foolishness.**

ludicrous *adjective.* Causing or deserving laughter or derision ▶ farcical, laughable, ridiculous, risible. —*See also* **foolish.**

ludicrousness *noun.* —*See* **humor.**

lug[1] *noun.* —*See* **oaf.**

lug[2] *verb.* —*See* **carry** (1), **pull** (1).

lugubrious *adjective.* —*See* **sorrowful.**

lukewarm *adjective.* Lacking warmth, interest, enthusiasm, or involvement ▶ halfhearted, Laodicean, tepid, unenthusiastic. [*Compare* **apathetic, cold, cool.**]

lull *verb.* —*See* **pacify.**

lull *noun.* —*See* **gap** (2), **stillness.**

lumber *verb.* —*See* **blunder.**

luminary *noun.* —*See* **celebrity, dignitary.**

luminesce *verb.* To shine brightly and steadily but without a flame ▶ gleam, glow, incandesce. [*Compare* **beam.**]

luminescence *noun.* —*See* **light**[1] (1).

luminosity *noun.* —*See* **brilliance** (1).

luminous *or* **luminescent** *adjective.* —*See* **bright.**

lummox *noun.* —*See* **oaf.**

lump[1] *noun.* An irregularly shaped mass of indefinite size ▶ cake, chunk, clod, clot, clump, gob, hunch, nugget, slab, wad. *Informal:* hunk. —*See also* **bump** (1), **bump** (2), **oaf.**

lump *verb.* —*See* **blunder, heap** (1).

lump[2] *verb.* —*See* **endure** (1).

lumpenproletariat *noun.* —*See* **riffraff.**

lumpish *adjective.* —*See* **awkward** (1), **bulky** (1).

lumps *noun.* —*See* **due.**

lumpy *adjective.* —*See* **bulky** (1).

lunacy *noun.* —*See* **foolishness, insanity.**

lunatic *adjective.* —*See* **extreme** (2), **foolish, insane.**

lunatic *noun.* —*See* **crackpot.**

lunge *verb.* —*See* **plunge.**

lunkheaded *adjective.* —*See* **stupid.**

lurch *verb.* **1.** To lean suddenly, unsteadily, and erratically from the vertical axis ▶ keel, pitch, roll, seesaw, yaw. [*Compare* **incline, sway, toss.**] **2.** To move or cause to move with a sudden abrupt motion ▶ jerk, snap, twitch, wrench, yank. [*Compare* **move.**] —*See also* **blunder, bump, stagger** (1).

lurch *noun.* —*See* **jerk.**

lure *noun.* **1.** Something that attracts, especially with the promise of pleasure or reward ▶ allurement, attraction, bait, carrot, come-on, draw, enticement, inducement, inveiglement, invitation, magnet, seduction, temptation. **2.** Something that leads one into danger or entrapment ▶ bait, decoy. [*Compare* **trap, trick.**] —*See also* **attraction.**

lure *verb.* —*See* **attract, seduce.**

lurer *noun.* —*See* **seducer** (1).

lurid *adjective.* —*See* **ghastly** (1), **pale** (1).

luring *adjective.* —*See* **seductive.**

lurk *verb.* To wait furtively in order to attack someone ▶ ambush, await, prowl, skulk. *Informal:* lay for. ***Idioms:*** lay wait for, lie in wait for. [*Compare* **ambush.**] —*See also* **sneak.**

luscious *adjective.* —*See* **delicious, delightful.**

lush[1] *adjective.* —*See* **luxurious, profuse, thick** (3).

lush[2] *noun.* —*See* **drunkard.**

lush *verb.* —*See* **drink** (2).

lust *noun.* —*See* **desire** (1), **desire** (2).

lust *verb.* To have a greedy, obsessive desire ▶ crave, hunger, itch, thirst.

luster *noun.* —*See* **fame, gloss[1].**

lusterless *adjective.* —*See* **dull** (1), **dull** (2).

lustful *adjective.* —*See* **lascivious.**

lustfulness *noun.* —*See* **desire** (2).

lustral *adjective.* —*See* **purgative.**

lustrate *verb.* —*See* **purify** (1).

lustration *noun.* —*See* **purification** (2).

lustrative *adjective.* —*See* **purgative.**

lustrous *adjective.* —*See* **bright, glossy.**

lusty *adjective.* Full of vigor ▶ able-bodied, gutsy, iron, red-blooded, robust, strapping, sturdy, vigorous, vital. [*Compare* **energetic, healthy.**] —*See also* **lascivious.**

luxuriance *noun.* —*See* **prosperity** (2).

luxuriant *adjective.* —*See* **luxurious, profuse, thick** (3).

luxuriate *verb.* To take extravagant pleasure ▶ bask, indulge, revel, roll, rollick, splurge, wallow. [*Compare* **enjoy.**]

luxurious *adjective.* Characterized by extravagant, ostentatious magnificence ▶ deluxe, fancy, lavish, lush, luxuriant, opulent, palatial, plush, plushy, rich, ritzy, sumptuous. [*Compare* **exclusive, glorious, sybaritic.**]

luxury *noun.* Something costly and unnecessary ▶ delight, extravagance, extravagancy, frill, indulgence, rarity, treat. —*See also* **prosperity** (2).

✚ **CORE SYNONYMS:** *luxury, extravagance, frill.* These nouns denote something desirable and costly that is unnecessary: *the real luxury of riding in a limousine; a simple wedding without any extravagances; caviar and other culinary frills.*

◀ **ANTONYM:** *necessity*

---

lying *adjective.* —*See* **dishonest.**

lying *noun.* —*See* **mendacity.**

lying-in *noun.* —*See* **birth** (1).

lymphatic *adjective.* —*See* **languid.**

lyric *or* **lyrical** *adjective.* Relating to the characteristics of poetry ▶ poetic, poetical. [*Compare* **melodious, rhythmical.**]

lyricism *noun.* A creation or experience having beauty suggestive of poetry ▶ poem, poetry.

lyrics *noun.* —*See* **song.**

M

macabre *adjective.* —*See* **ghastly** (1), **morbid.**

macerate *verb.* —*See* **steep[2].**

machinate *verb.* —*See* **plot** (2).

machination *noun.* —*See* **plot** (2).

machine *noun.* —*See* **device** (1), **system.**

machismo *noun.* —*See* **masculinity.**

macho *adjective.* —*See* **manly.**

mackintosh *noun.* —*See* **coat** (1).

macrocosm *noun.* —*See* **universe.**

mad *adjective.* —*See* **angry, enthusiastic, foolish, frantic, insane.**

madcap *adjective.* —*See* **rash[1].**

madden *verb.* —*See* **anger** (1), **derange.**

made-to-order *adjective.* —*See* **custom.**

made-up *adjective.* Being fictitious and not real, as a name ▶ assumed, pretended, pseudonymous. [*Compare* **false.**] —*See also* **fictitious.**

madness *noun.* —*See* **foolishness, insanity.**

maelstrom *noun.* —*See* **whirlpool.**

magic *noun.* **1.** The use of supernatural powers to influence or predict events ▶ augury, black art, black magic, conjuration, divination, hoodoo, incantation, necromancy, obeah, occultism, sorcery, sortilege, thaumaturgy, theurgy, voodoo, witchcraft, witchery, witching, wizardry. [*Compare* **charm, prediction.**] **2.** The use of skillful tricks and deceptions to produce entertainingly baffling effects ▶ conjuration, conjuring, illusion, legerdemain, prestidigitation, sleight of hand, trickery. —*See also* **spell[2].**

magic *or* **magical** *adjective* Having, brought about by, or relating to supernatural powers or magic ▶ bewitching, enchanted, fey, spellbinding, talismanic, thaumaturgic, thaumaturgical, theurgic, theurgical, witching, wizardly. [*Compare* **mysterious, supernatural.**] —*See also* **attractive.**

magician *noun.* —*See* **wizard.**

magisterial *adjective.* —*See* **dictatorial.**

magistrate *noun.* A public official who decides cases brought before a court of law in order to administer justice ▶ judge, jurist, jurisprudent, justice, justice of the peace. [*Compare* **go-between, judge.**]

magnanimity *noun.* —*See* **generosity.**

magnanimous *adjective.* —*See* **generous** (1).

magnanimousness *noun.* —*See* **generosity.**

magnate *noun.* —*See* **dignitary.**

magnet *noun.* —*See* **lure** (1).

magnetic *adjective.* —*See* **attractive.**

magnetism *noun.* —*See* **attraction.**

magnetize *verb.* —*See* **attract.**

magnific *adjective.* —*See* **grand.**

magnification *noun.* —*See* **increase** (1), **praise** (2).

magnificence *noun.* —*See* **glitter** (2), **glory.**

magnificent *adjective.* —*See* **exceptional, glorious, grand.**

magnified *adjective.* —*See* **exaggerated.**

magnify *verb.* —*See* **exaggerate, exalt, honor** (1), **increase, praise** (3).

magniloquence *noun.* —*See* **bombast.**

magniloquent *adjective.* —*See* **oratorical.**

magnitude *noun.* —*See* **bulk** (1), **degree** (2), **importance, size** (1), **size** (2).

magnum opus *noun.* An outstanding and ingenious work ▶ chef-d'oeuvre, masterpiece, masterwork. [*Compare* **accomplishment, composition, treasure.**]

maiden *adjective.* —*See* **first.**

mail *verb.* —*See* **send** (1).

maim *verb.* —*See* **batter, cripple.**

main *adjective.* —*See* **dominant** (1), **primary** (1).

main *noun.* —*See* **ocean.**

mainly *adverb.* —*See* **usually.**

mainspring *noun.* —*See* **cause** (2).

maintain *verb.* **1.** To keep in a condition of good repair, efficiency, or use ▶ keep up, preserve, sustain. **2.** To supply with the necessities of life ▶ keep, provide for, support. ***Idioms:*** put a roof over someone's head, put food on the table, take care of. [*Compare* **nourish.**] —*See also* **assert, defend** (2), **keep** (5).

maintenance *noun.* The work of keeping something in proper condition ▶ preservation, repairs, reparation, sustenance, upkeep. [*Compare* **care.**] —*See also* **conservation, living.**

majestic *adjective.* —*See* **grand.**

majesty *noun.* —*See* **chief, glory.**

major *adjective.* —*See* **big-league, dominant** (1), **primary** (1).

major-league *adjective.* —*See* **big-league.**

make *verb.* To create by forming, combining, or altering materials ▶ assemble, build, compose, configure, construct, fabricate, fashion, forge, form, frame, manufacture, mold, pattern, produce, put together, shape, structure. [*Compare* **arrange, design, invent.**] —*See also* **appoint, bear** (5), **cause, cover** (2), **earn** (2), **establish** (2), **force** (1), **prepare, produce** (1).

make off *verb.* —*See* **escape** (1).

make out *verb.* —*See* **discern, manage, neck, understand** (1).

make over *verb.* —*See* **revolutionize.** —*See also* **transfer** (1).

make up *verb.* **1.** To reestablish friendship between ▶ conciliate, reconcile, reunite. [*Compare* **pacify.**] **2.** To be the constituent parts of ▶ compose, form. [*Compare* **contain.**] —*See also* **balance** (2), **imagine, improvise** (1), **invent, lie**[2], **recover** (1).

make *noun.* —*See* **constitution.**

make-believe *noun.* —*See* **façade** (2).

make-believe *adjective.* —*See* **imaginary, mythical.**

make-do *noun.* —*See* **makeshift.**

make-do *adjective.* —*See* **temporary** (2).

maker *noun.* One that assembles or makes something ▶ artificer, artisan, assembler, craftsman, craftsperson, craftswoman, fabricator, manufacturer, modeler, producer. [*Compare* **builder.**] —*See also* **originator.**

makeshift *noun.* Something used temporarily or reluctantly when other means are not available ▶ expediency, expedient, make-do, resort, shift, stopgap. [*Compare* **substitute.**]

makeshift *adjective.* —*See* **temporary** (2).

✦ **CORE SYNONYMS:** *makeshift, expedient, resort, stopgap.* These nouns denote something used temporarily or reluctantly as a substitute when other means fail or are not available: *lacked a cane but used a stick as a makeshift; exhausted every expedient before filing suit; will use force only as a last resort; a crate serving as a stopgap for a chair.*

---

makeup *or* **make-up** *noun.* —*See* **character** (1), **constitution.**

makings *noun.* Indication of future success or development ▶ possibility, potential, promise, prospects. [*Compare* **material.**]

maladroit *adjective.* —*See* **awkward** (1), **tactless, unskillful.**

malady *noun.* —*See* **disease, sickness.**

malaise *noun.* —*See* **sickness.**

malapert *adjective.* —*See* **impudent.**

malapropism *noun.* —*See* **corruption** (3).

malapropos *adjective.* —*See* **improper** (2).

malarkey *noun.* —*See* **nonsense.**

malcontent *noun.* —*See* **agitator.**

male *adjective.* —*See* **manly.**

malediction *noun.* —*See* **curse** (1).

malefaction *noun.* —*See* **crime** (1).

malefactor *noun.* —*See* **criminal.**

maleficent *or* **malefic** *adjective.* —*See* **harmful.**

maleness *noun.* —*See* **masculinity.**

malevolence *noun.* A desire to harm others or to see others suffer ▶ despitefulness, ill will, malice, maliciousness, malignancy, malignity, meanness, nastiness, poisonousness, spite, spitefulness, venomousness, viciousness, vindictiveness. [*Compare* **cruelty, evil, hate.**]

malevolent *adjective.* Characterized by intense ill will or spite ▶ black, despiteful, evil, evil-minded, hateful, ill-natured, malicious, malign, malignant, mean, nasty, poisonous, rancorous, spiteful, venomous, vicious, vindictive, wicked. *Slang:* bitchy. [*Compare* **cruel, fiendish, ill-tempered.**] —*See also* **harmful.**

malfeasance *noun.* —*See* **breach** (1), **corruption** (2).

malformation *noun.* —*See* **deformity.**

malfunction *verb.* To become unusable or stop working properly ▶ act up, break (down), crash, fail, give out. *Slang:* bust, conk out, crap out, poop out. ***Idioms:*** get out of whack (*or* kilter), go haywire, go on the blink (*or* fritz). [*Compare* **collapse, fail.**]

malfunction *noun.* A cessation of proper functioning ▶ breakdown, collapse, failure, outage.

malice *or* **maliciousness** *noun.* —*See* **malevolence.**

malicious *adjective.* —*See* **malevolent.**

malign *verb.* To make harmful and often untrue statements about ▶ asperse, backbite, calumniate, defame, libel, slander, slur, tear down, traduce, vilify. *Informal:* badmouth. ***Idioms:*** cast aspersions on, give someone a bad name, speak evil of. [*Compare* **belittle, denigrate, slam.**]

malign *adjective.* —*See* **fateful** (1), **harmful, malevolent.**

✦ **CORE SYNONYMS:** *malign, defame, traduce, vilify, asperse, slander, calumniate, libel.* These verbs mean to make evil, harmful, often untrue statements about another. *Malign* stresses malicious intent: "*Have I not taken your part when you were maligned?*" (Thackeray). *Defame* suggests damage to reputation through misrepresentation: *The plaintiff had been defamed and had legitimate grounds for a lawsuit. Traduce* connotes the resulting humiliation or disgrace: "*My character was traduced by Captain Hawkins . . . even the ship's company cried out shame*" (Frederick Marryat). *Vilify* pertains to open, deliberate, vicious defamation: "*One who belongs to the most vilified and persecuted minority in history is not likely to be insensible to the freedoms guaranteed by our Constitution*" (Felix Frankfurter). To *asperse* is to spread unfavorable charges or insinuations against: "*Who could be so base as to asperse the character of a family so harmless as ours?*" (Oliver Goldsmith). *Slander* and *calumniate* apply to oral expression: *He slandered his political opponent. She calumniated and ridiculed her former employer. Libel* involves the communication of written or pictorial material: *The celebrity sued the tabloid that libeled her.*

---

malignancy *noun.* —*See* **malevolence.**

malignant *adjective.* —*See* **malevolent, poisonous.**

malignity *noun.* —*See* **malevolence.**

malleability *or* **malleableness** *noun.* —*See* **flexibility** (1).

malleable *adjective.* Capable of being shaped, bent, or drawn out, as by hammering or pressure ▶ bendable, ductile, flexible, flexile, flexuous, moldable, plastic, pliable, pliant, supple, tractable, workable. [*Compare* **changeable, extensible.**] —*See also* **adaptable, flexible** (3).

✚ **CORE SYNONYMS:** *malleable, ductile, plastic, pliable, pliant.* These adjectives mean capable of being shaped, bent, or drawn out: *malleable metals such as gold and silver; ductile copper; a plastic substance such as wax; soaked the leather to make it pliable; pliant molten glass.*

---

malodor *noun.* —*See* **stench.**

malodorous *adjective.* —*See* **smelly.**

malpractice *noun.* —*See* **injustice** (1).

maltreat *verb.* —*See* **abuse** (1).

maltreatment *noun.* —*See* **abuse** (2).

mammoth *noun.* —*See* **giant.**

mammoth *adjective.* —*See* **enormous.**

man *noun.* —*See* **human being, humankind, police officer.**

manacle *noun.* —*See* **bond** (1).

manacle *verb.* —*See* **hamper**[1]**.**

manage *verb.* To progress or perform adequately, especially in difficult circumstances ▶ do, fare, fend, get along, get by, muddle through, scrape by, shift, squeak by. *Informal:* make out. ***Idioms:*** make do, make shift, make the best of it. [*Compare* **endure.**] —*See also* **administer** (1), **conduct** (1), **operate.**

manageable *adjective.* Capable of being governed ▶ administrable, controllable, governable, rulable. [*Compare* **loyal, obedient.**]

management *noun.* The act or practice of directing or controlling ▶ administration, charge, conduct, direction, directorship, guidance, government, lead, leadership, oversight, stewardship, superintendence, supervision. [*Compare* **domination, duty.**] —*See also* **conservation.**

manager *noun.* —*See* **boss, executive.**

managerial *adjective.* —*See* **administrative.**

mandate *noun.* —*See* **authority, command** (1), **possession.**

mandate *verb.* —*See* **dictate.**

mandatory *adjective.* —*See* **required.**

maneuver *noun.* **1.** A method of deploying troops and equipment in combat ▶ battle plan, plan of attack, stratagem, strategy, tactic. **2.** An action calculated to achieve an end ▶ measure, move, procedure, step, tactic. —*See also* **trick** (1).

maneuver *verb.* **1.** To direct the course of carefully ▶ finesse, guide, jockey, navigate, pilot, steer. ***Idiom:*** back and fill. [*Compare* **drive, operate.**] **2.** To use stratagems in gaining an end ▶ angle for, engineer, finesse, jockey, worm. *Informal:* finagle, wangle. ***Idioms:*** pull strings (*or* wires). [*Compare* **plot.**] —*See also* **manipulate** (1), **move** (2).

manful *adjective.* —*See* **manly.**

mangle[1] *verb.* —*See* **batter, botch, cripple.**

mangle[2] *verb.* —*See* **press** (2).

mangy *adjective.* —*See* **shabby.**

manhandle *verb.* To be rough or brutal with ▶ knock about (*or* around), rough up, slap around. *Slang:* mess up. [*Compare* **abuse, beat, hit.**] —*See also* **batter.**

manhood *noun.* —*See* **masculinity.**

mania *noun.* —*See* **enthusiasm** (2), **insanity, obsession.**

maniac *noun.* —*See* **fan**[2]**.**

maniacal *or* **maniac** *adjective.* —*See* **insane.**

manifest *verb.* —*See* **develop** (1), **embody** (1), **express** (1), **show** (1).

manifest *noun.* —*See* **list**[1]**.**

manifest *adjective.* —*See* **apparent** (1).

manifestation *noun.* —*See* **appearance** (2), **array, display, embodiment, sign** (1).

manifesto *noun.* —*See* **message.**

manifold *adjective.* —*See* **complex** (2).

manipulate *verb.* **1.** To influence or manage shrewdly or deviously ▶ exploit, maneuver, play, use. ***Idioms:*** pull strings, wheel and deal. [*Compare* **plot, wangle.**] **2.** To use with or as if with the hands ▶ handle, ply, wield. **3.** To handle in a way so as to mix, form, and shape ▶ knead, squeeze, work. —*See also* **rub, touch.**

✚ **CORE SYNONYMS:** *manipulate, exploit, maneuver.* These verbs mean to influence, manage, use, or control to one's advantage by artful or indirect means: *manipulated me into helping him; exploits natural resources; maneuvered me out of one job and into another.*

---

manipulation *noun.* —*See* **touch** (1).

manipulative *adjective.* Coldly planning to achieve selfish aims ▶ calculating, conniving, designing, scheming. [*Compare* **artful.**]

mankind *noun.* —*See* **humankind.**

manlike *adjective.* —*See* **humanlike, manly.**

manliness *noun.* —*See* **masculinity.**

manly *adjective.* Having qualities traditionally attributed to a man ▶ macho, male, manful, manlike, mannish, masculine, virile.

manmade *adjective.* —*See* **artificial** (1).

manner *noun.* —*See* **bearing** (1), **behavior** (1), **custom, kind**[2]**, style, way** (1).

mannered *adjective.* Artificially genteel ▶ affected, artificial, precious. *Informal:* la-di-da. —*See also* **prudish.**

mannerism *noun.* —*See* **affectation.**

mannerliness *noun.* —*See* **courtesy.**

mannerly *adjective.* —*See* **courteous** (1).

manners *noun.* Socially correct behavior ▶ decorum, etiquette, good behavior, good form, mores, proprieties, propriety, p's and q's, refinement. [*Compare* **courtesy.**]

mannish *adjective.* —*See* **manly.**

mannishness *noun.* —*See* **masculinity.**

man on horseback *noun.* —*See* **dictator.**

manor *noun.* —*See* **land, villa.**

manslaughter *noun.* —*See* **murder.**

manslayer *noun.* —*See* **murderer.**

mantic *adjective.* —*See* **prophetic.**

mantle *verb.* —*See* **blush, clothe.**

mantle *noun.* —*See* **veil.**

manufacture *verb.* —*See* **make.**

manufacture *noun.* Something produced by human effort ▶ produce, product, production, work. [*Compare* **composition, good.**]

manufactured *adjective.* —*See* **artificial** (1).
manufacturer *noun.* —*See* **maker.**
manumission *noun.* —*See* **liberty.**
manumit *verb.* —*See* **free** (1).
manumitted *adjective.* —*See* **free** (1).
manuscript *noun.* —*See* **script** (2).
many *adjective.* Amounting to or consisting of a large, indefinite number ▶ legion, multitudinous, myriad, numerous. *Informal:* umpteen. ***Idiom:*** quite a few. [*Compare* **abundance, generous, heap, incalculable.**]
many-colored *or* **many-hued** *adjective.* —*See* **multicolored.**
many-sided *adjective.* —*See* **versatile.**
map *verb.* —*See* **arrange** (2), **design** (2), **plot** (1).
map out *verb.* —*See* **draft** (1).
map *noun.* —*See* **face** (1).
mar *verb.* —*See* **damage, deform.**
maraud *verb.* —*See* **invade** (1).
marbles *noun.* —*See* **sanity.**
march[1] *verb.* To travel about or journey on foot ▶ backpack, hike, tramp, trek. [*Compare* **journey, walk, rove.**] —*See also* **advance** (2).
march *noun.* —*See* **advance, walk** (1).
march[2] *or* **marchland** *noun.* —*See* **border** (2).
margin *noun.* —*See* **border** (1), **license** (1).
margin *verb.* —*See* **border.**
marinate *verb.* —*See* **steep**[2].
marine *adjective.* **1.** Of or relating to the seas or oceans ▶ briny, maritime, oceangoing, oceanic, pelagic, saltwater, salty, sea, seafaring, seagoing, seawater, thalassic. **2.** Of or relating to sea navigation ▶ maritime, nautical, naval, navigational.
mariner *noun.* —*See* **sailor.**
marital *adjective.* Of, relating to, or typical of marriage ▶ conjugal, connubial, hymeneal, married, matrimonial, nuptial, spousal, wedded.
maritime *adjective.* Of or relating to sea navigation ▶ marine, nautical, naval, navigational. —*See also* **marine** (1).
mark *noun.* **1.** A name or other device placed on an article to signify its ownership, manufacture, or origin ▶ brand, colophon, imprint, label, monogram, trademark. [*Compare* **symbol.**] **2.** One that is fired at, attacked, or abused ▶ butt, target. —*See also* **character** (7), **degree** (1), **dupe, expression** (2), **fame, impression** (1), **intention, notice** (1), **quality** (1), **sign** (1), **standard.**
mark *verb.* **1.** To set off by or as if by a mark indicating ownership or manufacture ▶ brand, identify, label, tag, trademark. **2.** To attach a ticket to ▶ earmark, flag, label, tag, ticket. **3.** To evaluate and assign a grade to ▶ correct, grade, score. **4.** To make a target of ▶ target. ***Idioms:*** draw (*or* get) a bead on, get in one's sights. —*See also* **designate, determine, distinguish** (2), **indicate** (1), **notice, show** (2).
mark down *verb.* —*See* **depreciate.**

✣ **CORE SYNONYMS:** *mark, brand, label, tag.* These verbs mean to set off by or as if by a mark indicating ownership or manufacture: *marked the parts as they left the assembly line; brands cattle; labeled the boxes with the company logo; tagged suitcases.*

---

markdown *noun.* —*See* **depreciation.**
marked *adjective.* —*See* **noticeable.**
market *verb.* —*See* **promote** (3), **sell.**
marketability *or* **marketableness** *noun.* Market appeal ▶ salability, salableness, sell.
marks *noun.* —*See* **track.**
maroon *verb.* —*See* **abandon** (1).
marooned *adjective.* —*See* **abandoned** (1).
marriage *noun.* The state of being married ▶ conjugality, coupling, connubiality, holy matrimony, matrimony, union, wedded bliss, wedlock. [*Compare* **union.**] —*See also* **wedding.**
marriageable *adjective.* —*See* **single.**
married *adjective.* —*See* **marital.**
marrow *noun.* —*See* **heart** (1).
marrowy *adjective.* —*See* **pithy.**

marry *verb.* To join or be joined in marriage ▶ espouse, mate, unite, wed. *Slang:* get hitched, get hooked. ***Idioms:*** join in matrimony, join together, lead to the altar, take the plunge, tie the knot. —*See also* **combine** (1).

marsh *noun.* —*See* **swamp.**

marshal *verb.* —*See* **arrange** (1), **guide, mobilize.**

marshal *noun.* —*See* **police officer.**

marshland *noun.* —*See* **swamp.**

martial *adjective.* —*See* **military** (1), **military** (2).

martinet *noun.* —*See* **authoritarian.**

martyr *noun.* —*See* **victim.**

marvel *noun.* One that evokes great surprise and admiration ▶ astonishment, miracle, phenomenon, prodigy, sensation, stunner, surprise, wonder, wonderment. ***Idioms:*** one for the books, eighth wonder of the world. [*Compare* **display.**] —*See also* **wonder** (1).

marvel *verb.* To have a feeling of great awe and rapt admiration ▶ admire, wonder. ***Idioms:*** be agog (*or* agape *or* awestruck). [*Compare* **gaze, stagger.**]

✚ **CORE SYNONYMS:** *marvel, miracle, phenomenon, prodigy, sensation, wonder.* These nouns denote one that evokes great surprise, admiration, or amazement: *a marvel of modern technology; a miracle of culinary art; a phenomenon of medical science; a musical prodigy; the theatrical sensation of the season; saw the wonders of Prague.*

---

marvelous *adjective.* Particularly excellent ▶ dandy, divine, fabulous, fantastic, fantastical, glorious, sensational, spectacular, splendid, superb, terrific, wonderful. *Informal:* dreamy, great, ripping, super, swell, tremendous. *Slang:* cool, groovy, hot, keen, neat, nifty, phat. ***Idiom:*** out of this world. [*Compare* **excellent, exceptional.**] —*See also* **astonishing, grand.**

mascot *noun.* —*See* **charm.**

masculine *adjective.* —*See* **manly.**

masculinity *adjective.* The quality of being masculine ▶ machismo, maleness, manhood, manliness, mannishness, virility.

mash *verb.* —*See* **crush** (1), **flirt** (2).

masher *noun. Slang* A man who is given to flirting ▶ flirt, wolf. [*Compare* **philanderer, seducer.**]

mask *noun.* —*See* **disguise, façade** (2).

mask *verb.* —*See* **conceal, disguise.**

masquerade *noun.* —*See* **act** (2), **cheat** (1), **dance, disguise, façade** (2).

masquerade *verb.* —*See* **disguise, impersonate.**

masquerader *noun.* —*See* **cheat** (2).

mass *noun.* The greatest part or portion ▶ bulk, preponderance, preponderancy, weight. [*Compare* **center.**] —*See also* **abundance, accumulation** (1), **bulk** (1), **crowd, heap** (1), **heaviness, object** (1).

mass *verb.* —*See* **accumulate.**

massacre *noun.* The savage killing of many victims ▶ bloodbath, bloodletting, bloodshed, butchering, butchery, carnage, decimation, genocide, holocaust, liquidation, mass murder, slaughter. [*Compare* **murder.**]

massacre *verb.* To kill savagely and indiscriminately ▶ annihilate, butcher, decimate, kill off, slaughter, wipe out. [*Compare* **kill.**] —*See also* **overwhelm** (1).

massage *verb.* —*See* **bias** (2), **rub.**

masses *noun.* —*See* **commonalty.**

massive *adjective.* —*See* **bulky** (1), **enormous, heavy** (1).

massiveness *noun.* —*See* **heaviness.**

massy *adjective.* —*See* **enormous.**

master *noun.* —*See* **chief, conqueror, educator, expert, original, owner.**

master *adjective.* —*See* **expert.**

master *verb.* —*See* **defeat, domesticate, gentle, learn** (1).

masterful *adjective.* Exercising authority ▶ authoritative, commanding, dominant, lordly. [*Compare* **administrative.**] —*See also* **dictatorial, expert.**

masterly *adjective.* —*See* **expert.**

mastermind *noun.* —*See* **mind** (2).

masterpiece *or* **masterwork** *noun.* An outstanding and ingenious work ▶ chef-d'oeuvre, magnum opus. [*Compare* **accomplishment, composition, treasure.**]

masterstroke *noun.* —*See* **accomplishment.**

mastery *noun.* —*See* **ability** (1), **authority, domination.**

masticate *verb.* —*See* **chew.**

mastodonic *adjective.* —*See* **enormous.**

mat[1] *verb.* —*See* **entangle.**

mat[2] *or* **matte** *adjective.* —*See* **dull** (2).

match *noun.* —*See* **competition** (2), **couple, mate, parallel, peer[2].**

match *verb.* To do or make something equal to ▶ equal, meet, tie. —*See also* **agree** (1), **equal** (1), **liken, oppose, resemble, suit** (1).

matched *adjective.* Consisting of two identical or similar related things, parts, or elements ▶ double, dual, paired, twin. [*Compare* **double, equal.**]

matchless *adjective.* —*See* **unique.**

matchlessness *noun.* —*See* **uniqueness.**

mate *noun.* One of a matched pair of things ▶ companion, complement, counterpart, double, duplicate, fellow, match, twin. —*See also* **associate** (2), **friend, spouse.**

mate *verb.* —*See* **marry.**

materfamilias *noun.* —*See* **mother.**

material *noun.* **1.** That from which things are or can be made ▶ matter, medium, stuff, substance. ***Idiom:*** grist for one's mill. **2.** A person considered to have qualities suitable for a particular activity ▶ stuff, timber. [*Compare* **comer, potential.**] —*See also* **outfit.**

material *adjective.* Of or preoccupied with that which is material rather than spiritual or intellectual ▶ materialistic, sensual. [*Compare* **earthly, greedy, superficial.**] —*See also* **important, physical, relevant.**

materialistic *adjective.* Of or preoccupied with that which is material rather than spiritual or intellectual ▶ material, sensual. [*Compare* **earthly, greedy, superficial.**]

materiality *noun.* That which occupies space and can be perceived by the senses ▶ matter, substance. [*Compare* **element, object, thing.**] —*See also* **relevance.**

materialization *noun.* —*See* **appearance** (2), **embodiment, fulfillment** (1).

materialize *verb.* To make real or actual ▶ actualize, bring about, make happen, realize. ***Idioms:*** bring to pass, carry (*or* put) into effect. [*Compare* **effect, produce.**] —*See also* **appear** (1), **embody** (1).

materiel *or* **matériel** *noun.* —*See* **outfit.**

matriarch *noun.* —*See* **mother.**

matrimonial *adjective.* —*See* **marital.**

matrimony *noun.* —*See* **marriage.**

matrix *noun.* A hollow device for shaping a fluid or plastic substance ▶ cast, form, mold.

matter *noun.* **1.** That which occupies space and can be perceived by the senses ▶ materiality, substance. [*Compare* **element, object, thing.**] **2.** Something to be done, considered, or dealt with ▶ affair, business, thing. [*Compare* **business, task.**] —*See also* **material** (1), **problem, subject.**

matter *verb.* —*See* **count** (1).

matter-of-fact *adjective.* —*See* **cold** (2), **dull** (1), **realistic** (1).

maturate *verb.* —*See* **mature.**

maturation *noun.* —*See* **development.**

mature *adjective.* Having reached full growth and development ▶ adult, advanced, big, developed, evolved, full-blown, full-fledged, full-grown, full-size, grown, grown-up, matured, older, ripe. ***Idioms:*** in full bloom, in one's prime, of age. [*Compare* **aged.**] —*See also* **due** (1), **old** (2).

mature *verb.* To bring or come to full development ▶ age, develop, grow (up), maturate, mellow, ripen. ***Idioms:*** come of age, reach adulthood. [*Compare* **age.**]

✤ **CORE SYNONYMS:** *mature, age, develop, ripen.* These verbs mean to bring or come to full development or maximum excellence: *maturing the wines in vats; aged the brandy for 100 years; developed the flavor slowly; fruits that were ripened on the vine.*

---

maturity *noun.* —*See* **age** (1).

maudlin *adjective.* —*See* **sentimental.**

maudlinism *noun.* —*See* **sentimentality.**

maul *verb.* —*See* **batter, beat** (1).

maunder *noun.* —*See* **digress.**

maunder *verb.* —*See* **mutter.**

mausoleum *noun.* —*See* **grave[1].**

maven *noun.* —*See* **expert.**

maverick *noun.* —*See* **rebel** (2).

maw *noun.* —*See* **mouth** (1).

mawkish *adjective.* —*See* **sentimental.**

mawkishness *noun.* —*See* **sentimentality.**

maxim *noun.* —*See* **law** (3), **moral, proverb.**

maximal *adjective.* —*See* **maximum.**

maximum *noun.* The greatest quantity or highest degree attainable ▶ outside, top, ultimate, utmost, uttermost. *Slang:* max. ***Idioms:*** daddy of them all, the last word, ne plus ultra. [*Compare* **climax.**] —*See also* **limit** (1).

maximum *adjective.* Greatest in quantity or highest in degree that can be attained ▶ extreme, greatest, highest, maximal, peak, top, topmost, transcendent, ultimate, unsurpassable, utmost, uttermost. *Slang:* max, tops. [*Compare* **best.**]

maybe *or* **mayhap** *adverb.* Possibly but not certainly ▶ conceivably, feasibly, perchance, perhaps, possibly. [*Compare* **probably.**]

maze *noun.* —*See* **tangle.**

maze *verb.* —*See* **daze** (1).

mea culpa *noun.* A statement of acknowledgment expressing regret or asking pardon ▶ apology, excuse, regrets. [*Compare* **acknowledgment.**]

meadow *noun.* ▶ clearing, field, pasture. [*Compare* **lot.**]

meager *adjective.* Conspicuously deficient in quantity, fullness, or extent ▶ exiguous, insubstantial, poor, puny, scant, scanty, scrimpy, skimpy, spare, sparse, spartan, stingy, thin. *Slang:* measly. ***Idioms:*** in short supply, scraping the bottom of the barrel. [*Compare* **insufficient, little, trivial.**] —*See also* **thin** (1).

mean[1] *verb.* To have or convey a particular idea ▶ connote, convey, denote, import, intend, indicate, signify, spell. ***Idioms:*** add up to, come down to. [*Compare* **communicate, imply, represent.**] —*See also* **intend.**

mean[2] *adjective.* Of little distinction ▶ humble, lowly, simple. [*Compare* **modest.**] —*See also* **bad** (1), **ill-tempered, lowly** (1), **malevolent, offensive** (1), **sordid, stingy, troublesome** (2).

mean[3] *noun.* —*See* **average.**

mean *adjective.* —*See* **middle.**

meander *verb.* —*See* **rove, wind[2].**

meandering *adjective.* —*See* **digressive, indirect** (1), **winding.**

meaning *noun.* Something that is conveyed or signified ▶ acceptation, connotation, denotation, import, intent, message, point, purport, sense, significance, significancy, signification, value. [*Compare* **feeling, idea, import, thrust.**] —*See also* **intention.**

meaning *adjective.* —*See* **expressive.**

✤ **CORE SYNONYMS:** *meaning, acceptation, import, sense, significance, signification.* These nouns refer to the idea conveyed by something, such as a word, action, gesture, or situation: *Synonyms are words with the same or nearly the same meaning. In one of its acceptations, "value" is a technical term in music. The import of his statement is ambiguous. The term "anthropometry" has only one sense. The significance of a green traffic light is widely understood. Linguists have* *determined the hieroglyphics' signification.*

---

meaningful *adjective.* —*See* **expressive, important, pregnant** (2).

meaningless *adjective.* —*See* **mindless.**

meaninglessness *noun.* —*See* **emptiness** (2).

meanness *noun.* —*See* **malevolence, temper** (1).

means *noun.* —*See* **agent, approach** (1), **resources.**

measly *adjective.* —*See* **meager, trivial.**

measure *verb.* To ascertain the dimensions, quantity, or capacity of ▶ gauge, quantify, quantitate. ***Idioms:*** take the dimensions (*or* measure) of. [*Compare* **estimate.**] —*See also* **determine.**

measure out *verb.* —*See* **distribute.**

measure up *verb.* —*See* **equal** (1).

measure *noun.* **1.** The act or process of ascertaining dimensions, quantity, or capacity ▶ determination, measurement, mensuration, quantification. [*Compare* **computation, estimation.**] **2.** An action calculated to achieve an end ▶ maneuver, move, procedure, step, tactic. —*See also* **allotment, degree** (2), **law** (2), **moderation, quantity** (2), **rhythm, size** (1), **standard.**

measured *adjective.* —*See* **deliberate** (3), **rhythmical.**

measureless *adjective.* —*See* **endless** (1), **incalculable.**

measurelessness *noun.* —*See* **infinity** (1).

measurement *noun.* The act or process of ascertaining dimensions, quantity, or capacity ▶ determination, measure, mensuration, quantification. [*Compare* **calculation, estimation.**]

measurements *noun.* —*See* **size** (1).

meat *noun.* —*See* **food, heart** (1).

meatball *or* **meathead** *noun.* —*See* **oaf.**

meaty *adjective.* —*See* **fat** (1), **pregnant** (2).

mechanical *adjective.* —*See* **perfunctory.**

mechanism *noun.* —*See* **agent, device** (1).

medal *noun.* —*See* **decoration, distinction** (2).

medalist *noun.* —*See* **winner.**

meddle *verb.* To intervene officiously or indiscreetly in the affairs of others ▶ butt in, horn in, interfere, interlope, intermeddle, obtrude. *Informal:* kibitz. ***Idioms:*** poke (*or* stick) one's nose in, stick one's oar in. [*Compare* **interrupt, snoop.**] —*See also* **tinker.**

✦ **CORE SYNONYMS:** *meddle, interfere, obtrude.* These verbs mean to intervene officiously or indiscreetly in the affairs of others. *Meddle* stresses unwanted, unwarranted, or unnecessary intrusion: *"wholly unacquainted with the world in which they are so fond of meddling"* (Edmund Burke). *Interfere* implies action that seriously hampers, hinders, or frustrates: *"Romantics of all ages can recall occasions when lust interfered with reason"* (Christine Gorman). To *obtrude* is to impose oneself or one's ideas on others with undue insistence or without invitation: *He managed to obtrude his schemes on the members of the council.*

---

meddler *noun.* —*See* **busybody.**

meddling *noun.* The act or an instance of interfering or intruding ▶ interference, interfering, interrupting, intervention, intruding, intrusion, obtrusion, prying, snooping.

meddling *or* **meddlesome** *adjective.* —*See* **curious** (1).

media *noun.* —*See* **press.**

median *noun.* —*See* **average, center** (2).

median *or* **medial** *adjective.* —*See* **central, middle.**

mediate *verb.* To intervene between disputants in order to bring about an agreement ▶ arbitrate, moderate. [*Compare* **confer, judge.**] —*See also* **conduct** (3).

mediation *noun.* —*See* **compromise.**

mediator *noun.* —*See* **go-between.**

medicament *noun.* —*See* **cure, drug** (1).

medicate *verb.* —*See* **administer** (3), **drug** (1).

medication *noun.* —*See* **cure, drug** (1).

medicinal *adjective.* —*See* **curative.**

medicine *noun.* —*See* **cure, drug** (1).

mediocre *adjective.* —*See* **average, bad** (1), **ordinary.**

mediocrity *noun.* —*See* **dullness.**

meditate *verb.* —*See* **ponder.**

meditation *noun.* —*See* **thought.**

meditative *adjective.* —*See* **thoughtful.**

medium *noun.* —*See* **agent, average, environment** (2), **material** (1).

medium *adjective.* —*See* **average.**

medley *noun.* —*See* **assortment.**

meek *adjective.* Having or expressing feelings of humility ▶ humble, lowly, modest, unambitious. [*Compare* **deferential.**] —*See also* **gentle** (3).

meekness *noun.* —*See* **modesty** (1).

meet[1] *verb.* **1.** To come together face-to-face, especially defiantly ▶ confront, encounter, face, front. ***Idiom:*** stand up to. [*Compare* **contest, defy.**] **2.** To come together by arrangement ▶ connect, hook up, meet up, get together, rendezvous. [*Compare* **assemble.**] **3.** To come together from different directions ▶ close, converge, join, unite. [*Compare* **combine.**] **4.** To do or make something equal to ▶ equal, match, tie. —*See also* **adjoin, contend, encounter** (1), **experience, satisfy** (1).

meet *noun.* —*See* **competition** (2).

meet[2] *adjective.* —*See* **convenient** (1).

meeting *noun.* —*See* **assembly, confrontation, convention, junction.**

megalomania *noun.* ▶ egoism, self-importance. *Informal:* big head. [*Compare* **egotism.**]

megalomaniacal *adjective.* —*See* **dictatorial.**

megalopolis *noun.* —*See* **city.**

megrim *noun.* —*See* **fancy.**

melancholic *adjective.* —*See* **depressed** (1).

melancholy *noun.* —*See* **depression** (2).

melancholy *adjective.* —*See* **depressed** (1), **sorrowful.**

mélange *noun.* —*See* **assortment.**

meld *verb.* —*See* **combine** (1).

melee *noun.* —*See* **disorder** (2), **fight** (1).

meliorate *verb.* —*See* **improve.**

melioration *noun.* —*See* **improvement** (1), **progress.**

mellifluous *adjective.* —*See* **melodious.**

mellow *adjective.* Brought to full flavor and richness by aging ▶ aged, ripe. [*Compare* **mature.**] —*See also* **calm, easygoing, resonant.**

mellow *verb.* —*See* **mature.**

mellow out *verb.* —*See* **rest**[1] (1).

melodious *or* **melodic** *adjective.* Having or producing a pleasing melody or sound ▶ dulcet, euphonic, euphonious, harmonious, mellifluous, melodic, musical, silvery, sweet-sounding, tuneful. [*Compare* **harmonious, pleasant.**]

melodrama *or* **melodramatics** *noun.* —*See* **theatrics** (2).

melodramatic *adjective.* —*See* **dramatic** (2).

melody *noun.* A pleasing succession or arrangement of sound ▶ air, aria, strain, theme, tune. [*Compare* **song.**]

melt *verb.* To change from a solid to a liquid ▶ deliquesce, dissolve, flux, fuse, liquefy, run, thaw. —*See also* **disappear** (1).

member *noun.* —*See* **part** (1).

membrane *noun.* —*See* **skin** (2).

memento *noun.* —*See* **remembrance** (1).

memo *noun.* —*See* **letter, note.**

memoir *noun.* A personal narrative or record of experiences ▶ autobiography, commentaries, diary, journal, reminiscences. [*Compare* **memory, story.**]

memorable *adjective.* —*See* **exceptional.**

memorandum *noun.* —*See* **letter, note.**

memorial *noun.* Something, as a structure or custom, serving to honor or keep alive a memory ▶ commemoration, monument, remembrance. [*Compare* **testimonial.**]

memorial *adjective.* Serving to honor or keep alive a memory ▶ commemorative, monumental.

memorialize *verb.* To honor or keep alive the memory of ▶ commemorate. [*Compare* **immortalize.**]

memorize *verb.* To commit to memory ▶ con, learn. ***Idioms:*** learn by heart (*or* rote). [*Compare* **learn, remember.**]

memory *noun.* **1.** The power of retaining and recalling past experience ▶ recall, recollection, remembrance, reminiscence, retention. ***Idiom:*** power of recall. **2.** An act or instance of remembering ▶ mental image, recollection, remembrance, reminiscence. [*Compare* **idea.**]

menace *noun.* An expression of the intent to hurt or punish another ▶ intimidation, threat. —*See also* **danger.**

menace *verb.* —*See* **endanger, intimidate, threaten** (2).

menacing *adjective.* —*See* **dangerous, fateful** (1).

ménage *noun.* A group of people living together as a unit ▶ family, house, household.

mend *verb.* —*See* **correct** (1), **fix** (1), **recover** (2).

mendacious *adjective.* —*See* **dishonest.**

mendacity *noun.* The practice of lying ▶ falsehood, falsification, inveracity, lying, perjury, prevarication, truthlessness, untruthfulness. [*Compare* **deceit.**] —*See also* **dishonesty** (1), **lie^2.**

mendicancy *or* **mendicity** *noun.* The condition of being a beggar ▶ beggary, mendicity. [*Compare* **poverty.**]

mendicant *noun.* —*See* **beggar** (1).

mendicant *adjective.* —*See* **poor.**

menial *adjective.* —*See* **servile.**

menial *noun.* —*See* **drudge** (1), **laborer.**

mensuration *noun.* The act or process of ascertaining dimensions, quantity, or capacity ▶ determination, measure, measurement, quantification. [*Compare* **computation, estimation.**]

mental *adjective.* Relating to or performed by the mind ▶ cerebral, intellective, intellectual, psychic, psychical, psychological, reasoning, thinking. [*Compare* **arbitrary.**] —*See also* **intellectual.**

mental illness *noun.* —*See* **insanity.**

mental image *noun.* An act or instance of remembering ▶ memory, recollection, remembrance, reminiscence. [*Compare* **idea.**]

mentality *noun.* —*See* **intelligence, psychology.**

mentally ill *adjective.* —*See* **insane.**

mention *verb.* —*See* **name** (2), **refer** (1).

mentor *noun.* —*See* **adviser.**

mentor *verb.* —*See* **advise.**

mephitic *or* **mephitical** *adjective.* —*See* **poisonous, smelly.**

mercenary *noun.* A freelance fighter ▶ adventurer, soldier of fortune. [*Compare* **fighter, soldier.**]

mercenary *adjective.* —*See* **corrupt** (2).

merchandise *noun.* —*See* **good** (2).

merchandise *verb.* —*See* **sell.**

merchandiser *noun.* —*See* **dealer.**

merchant *noun.* —*See* **dealer.**

merchant *verb.* —*See* **sell.**

merciful *adjective.* —*See* **humanitarian, tolerant.**

mercifulness *noun.* —*See* **mercy.**

merciless *adjective.* —*See* **callous, cruel.**

mercurial *adjective.* Given to changeable emotional states, especially of anger or gloom ▶ moody, temperamental. [*Compare* **testy.**] —*See also* **capricious.**

mercy *noun.* Kind, forgiving, or compassionate treatment of or disposition toward others ▶ charity, clemency, grace, lenience, leniency, lenity, mercifulness. [*Compare* **pity.**]

✦ **CORE SYNONYMS:** *mercy, leniency, lenity, clemency, charity.* These nouns mean humane and kind, sympathetic, or forgiving treatment of or disposition toward others. *Mercy* is compassionate forbearance: *"We hand folks over to God's mercy, and show none ourselves"* (George Eliot). *Leniency* and *lenity* imply mildness, gentleness, and often a tendency to reduce punishment: *"When you have gone too far to recede, do not sue* [appeal] *to me for leniency"* (Charles Dickens). *"His Majesty gave many marks of his great lenity, often . . . endeavoring to extenuate your crimes"* (Jonathan Swift). *Clemency* is mercy shown by someone with judicial authority: *The judge believed in clemency for youthful offenders. Charity* is goodwill and benevolence in judging others: *"But how shall we expect charity towards others, when we are uncharitable to ourselves?"* (Thomas Browne).

---

mere *adjective.* Just sufficient ▶ bare, scant, scanty. [*Compare* **insufficient, meager.**]

merely *adverb.* Nothing more than ▶ but, just, only, simply. [*Compare* **barely, solely.**]

meretricious *adjective.* —*See* **gaudy.**

merge *verb.* —*See* **mix** (1).

merger *noun.* —*See* **combination, mixture.**

meridian *noun.* —*See* **climax.**

merit *noun.* A level of superiority that is usually high ▶ caliber, quality, stature, value, virtue, worth. [*Compare* **advantage.**] —*See also* **use** (2), **virtue.**

merit *verb.* —*See* **earn** (1).

merited *adjective.* —*See* **just.**

meritless *adjective.* —*See* **baseless.**

meritorious *adjective.* —*See* **admirable.**

merriment *noun.* **1.** A state of joyful exuberance ▶ blitheness, gaiety, gladness, glee, gleefulness, hilarity, jocoseness, jocosity, jocularity, jocundity, jolliness, jollity, joviality, lightheartedness, merriness, mirth, mirthfulness. [*Compare* **elation.**] **2.** Joyful, exuberant activity ▶ celebration, conviviality, festiveness, festivity, fun, gaiety, jollity, merrymaking, revelry, revels. [*Compare* **blast, celebration, party.**]

merriness *noun.* —*See* **merriment** (1).

merry *adjective.* Providing joy and pleasure, especially in celebration ▶ celebratory, cheerful, cheery, convivial, festive, gala, glad, gladsome, happy, joyful, joyous, mirthful. [*Compare* **lighthearted.**] —*See also* **cheerful.**

merrymaking *noun.* —*See* **celebration** (3), **merriment** (2).

mesa *noun.* A natural, flat land elevation ▶ plateau, table. [*Compare* **hill.**]

mesh *noun.* —*See* **tangle, web.**

mesh *verb.* To come or bring together and interlock ▶ engage. [*Compare* **attach, fit[1].**] —*See also* **harmonize** (2).

mesmerize *verb.* —*See* **charm** (2), **grip.**

mess *noun.* **1.** A confused or ruinous state ▶ botch, fiasco, foul-up, mix-up, muddle, shambles. *Informal:* hash. *Slang:* screwup, snafu. [*Compare* **blunder.**] **2.** An unsightly object ▶ disaster, eyesore, monstrosity, ugliness. *Informal:* fright, sight, ugly. ***Idiom:*** something the cat dragged in. —*See also* **abundance, disorder** (1), **heap** (1), **predicament, serving.**

mess *verb.* —*See* **tinker, tousle.**

mess around *verb. Informal* To be sexually unfaithful to another ▶ philander. *Informal:* cheat, fool around, play around. *Slang:* two-time. —*See also* **putter, tinker.**

mess up *verb.* —*See* **botch, confuse** (3), **disorder, disrupt, manhandle.**

message *noun.* Something announced or communicated ▶ announcement, annunciation, brief, bulletin, communication, communiqué, declaration, dictum, edict, manifesto, notice, notification, proclamation, pronouncement, statement, word. —*See also* **letter, meaning.**

messenger *noun.* A person who carries messages or is sent on errands ▶ bearer, carrier, conveyer, courier, envoy, errand boy, errand girl, herald, runner. *Slang:* gofer. [*Compare* **agent, go-between, representative.**]

messiness *noun.* —*See* **disorderliness.**

messy *adjective.* **1.** Marked by a lack of cleanliness or neatness ▶ careless, disheveled, frowzy, mussy, slapdash, slipshod, sloppy, slovenly, unkempt, untidy. **2.** Lacking regular or logical order ▶ disorderly, unsystematic.

✚ **CORE SYNONYMS:** *messy, sloppy, slovenly, unkempt, slipshod.* These adjectives mean marked by lack of cleanliness or neatness. *Messy* indicates that which is disorderly: *a messy desk. Sloppy* evokes the idea of careless spilling, spotting, or splashing; it suggests slackness, untidiness, or diffuseness: *a sloppy kitchen; sloppy dress; "I do not see how the sloppiest reasoner can evade that"* (H.G. Wells). *Slovenly* implies habitual negligence and a lack of system or thoroughness: *a slovenly appearance; slovenly inaccuracies. Unkempt* stresses dishevelment resulting from a neglectful lack of proper maintenance: *"an unwashed brow, an unkempt head of hair"* (Sir Walter Scott). *Slipshod* suggests inattention to detail and a general absence of meticulousness: *"the new owners' camp . . . a slipshod and slovenly affair, tent half stretched, dishes unwashed"* (Jack London).

---

metamorphose *verb.* —*See* **convert, revolutionize.**

metamorphosis *noun.* —*See* **conversion** (1), **revolution** (2).

metanoia *noun.* A fundamental change in one's beliefs ▶ conversion, rebirth, regeneration. [*Compare* **revival.**]

metaphor *noun.* An object or expression associated with and serving to identify something else ▶ attribute, emblem, signifier, symbol, token. [*Compare* **expression, sign, term.**]

metaphorical *or* **metaphoric** *adjective.* —*See* **symbolic.**

metaphrase *noun.* —*See* **translation.**
metaphrase *verb.* —*See* **translate.**

metaphysical *adjective.* —*See* **immaterial, supernatural** (1).

mete *verb.* —*See* **distribute.**

meter *noun.* —*See* **rhythm.**

method *noun.* Systematic arrangement and design ▶ format, order, orderliness, organization, pattern, plan, process, scheme, system, systematization, systemization. [*Compare* **arrangement, form.**] —*See also* **routine, way** (1).

methodical *or* **methodic** *adjective.* Arranged or proceeding in a set, systematized pattern ▶ arranged, neat, ordered, orderly, organized, regular, regulated, structured, systematic, systematical. [*Compare* **neat, symmetrical.**] —*See also* **deliberate** (3).

✚ **CORE SYNONYMS:** *methodical, orderly, systematic.* These adjectives mean arranged or proceeding in a set, systematized pattern. *Methodical* stresses adherence to a logically and carefully planned succession of steps: *methodical instructions for assembly. Orderly* especially implies correct or customary procedure or proper or harmonious arrangement: *an orderly evacuation of the burning building; orderly and symmetrical rows. Systematic* emphasizes observance of a coordinated and orderly set of procedures constituting part of a complex but unitary whole: *systematic research into antigens to combat immune disorders.*

---

methodize *verb.* —*See* **arrange** (1).

meticulous *adjective.* —*See* **careful** (2), **fussy.**

meticulousness *noun.* —*See* **accuracy, thoroughness.**

métier *noun.* —*See* **business** (2), **forte.**

metrical *adjective.* —*See* **rhythmical.**

metropolis *noun.* —*See* **city.**

metropolitan *adjective.* —*See* **city.**

mettle *noun.* —*See* **courage.**

mettlesome *adjective.* —*See* **brave.**
mewl *verb.* —*See* **cry.**
miasmic *adjective.* —*See* **poisonous.**
microbe *or* **microorganism** *noun.* —*See* **germ** (1).
microscopic *adjective.* So small as not to be discernible ▶ imperceptible, infinitesimal. —*See also* **tiny.**
mid *adjective.* —*See* **central, middle.**
middle *adjective.* Being at neither one extreme nor the other ▶ between, central, in-between, intermediary, intermediate, mean, medial, median, mid, middle-of-the-road, midway. [*Compare* **neutral.**] —*See also* **central.**
middle *noun.* —*See* **center** (2).
middleman *noun.* —*See* **go-between.**
middlemost *adjective.* —*See* **central.**
middle-of-the-road *adjective.* —*See* **middle.**
middling *adjective.* —*See* **average, ordinary.**
midget *adjective.* —*See* **tiny.**
midmost *adjective.* —*See* **central.**
midpoint *noun.* —*See* **average, center** (2).
midst *noun.* The most intensely active central part ▶ eye, thick. [*Compare* **center.**] —*See also* **center** (2).
midway *adjective.* —*See* **middle.**
mien *noun.* —*See* **appearance** (1), **bearing** (1).
miff *verb.* —*See* **insult, offend** (1).
miff *noun.* —*See* **offense.**
might *noun.* —*See* **ability** (2), **authority, energy, force** (1), **strength.**
mighty *adjective.* Having great physical strength ▶ potent, powerful, strong. [*Compare* **energetic, muscular.**] —*See also* **enormous, forceful.**
mighty *adverb.* —*See* **very.**
migrant *noun.* One who migrates ▶ emigrant, immigrant, transmigrant. [*Compare* **émigré, foreigner, settler.**] —*See also* **hobo.**
migrant *adjective.* Moving from one area to another in search of work ▶ itinerant, migratory. —*See also* **migratory** (1).
migrate *verb.* **1.** To leave one's native land and settle in another ▶ emigrate (from), immigrate (to), resettle, transmigrate. [*Compare* **move, settle.**] **2.** To change habitat seasonally ▶ transmigrate.
migration *noun.* Settling in a country to which one is not native ▶ immigration, transmigration. —*See also* **emigration.**
migrational *adjective.* —*See* **migratory** (1).
migratory *adjective.* **1.** Moving from one habitat to another on a seasonal basis ▶ migrant, migrational, seasonal, transient, transmigratory. [*Compare* **mobile, nomadic.**] **2.** Moving from one area to another in search of work ▶ itinerant, migrant.
mild *adjective.* Free from extremes in temperature ▶ balmy, clement, moderate, temperate. [*Compare* **pleasant.**] —*See also* **gentle** (1), **gentle** (2), **gentle** (3), **gradual** (2).
mildewed *adjective.* —*See* **moldy.**
milieu *noun.* —*See* **environment** (2).
militance *noun.* —*See* **aggression.**
militant *adjective.* —*See* **aggressive, belligerent, extreme** (2).
militant *noun.* —*See* **extremist.**
militaristic *adjective.* —*See* **military** (1).
militarize *verb.* —*See* **mobilize.**
military *adjective.* **1.** Of or inclined toward war ▶ bellicose, chauvinistic, hawkish, jingoistic, martial, militaristic, warlike, warmongering. [*Compare* **aggressive.**] **2.** Relating to armed service ▶ barracks, enlisted, martial, regimental, soldierly. ***Idiom:*** in uniform.
militiaman *noun.* —*See* **soldier** (2).
milk *verb.* —*See* **drain** (1).
milksop *noun.* —*See* **baby** (2), **coward.**
milky *adjective.* —*See* **fair**[1] (3).
mill *noun.* A building or complex in which an industry is located ▶ factory, plant, works.
mill *verb.* —*See* **crush** (2).
million *noun.* —*See* **heap** (2).
millstone *noun.* —*See* **burden**[1] (1).

milquetoast *noun.* —*See* **baby** (2), **coward.**

mime *noun.* —*See* **mimic, mimicry.**

mimesis *noun.* The formation of words in imitation of sounds ▶ echoism, onomatopoeia.

mimetic *adjective.* Imitating sounds ▶ echoic, imitative, onomatopoeic, onomatopoetic. —*See also* **imitative** (1).

mimic *verb.* To copy another slavishly ▶ clone, echo, image, imitate, mirror, parrot, reflect, repeat. [*Compare* **copy.**] —*See also* **imitate, resemble.**

mimic *noun.* One who imitates ▶ ape, echo, imitator, impersonator, mime, parrot. *Informal:* copycat.

mimicry *noun.* The act, practice, or art of copying the manner or expression of another ▶ aping, copying, echoing, emulation, imitation, impersonation, impression, mime, mirroring, parroting. [*Compare* **mockery.**]

mincing *adjective.* —*See* **prudish.**

mind *noun.* **1.** The seat of the faculty of intelligence and reason ▶ brain, head. *Informal:* gray matter. [*Compare* **imagination.**] **2.** A person of great mental ability ▶ brain, genius, highbrow, intellect, intellectual, mastermind, thinker. *Informal:* egghead, whiz. *Slang:* brainiac, pointy-head. [*Compare* **expert, sage.**] —*See also* **belief** (1), **intelligence, liking, psychology, sanity.**

mind *verb.* To be careful ▶ beware, look out, watch out. ***Idioms:*** be on guard, be on the lookout, keep an eye peeled, take care (*or* heed). —*See also* **care, follow** (4), **notice, remember** (1), **tend**[2]**.**

mind-boggling *or* **mind-blowing** *adjective.* —*See* **astonishing.**

minded *adjective.* —*See* **willing.**

mindful *adjective.* —*See* **careful** (1).

mindfulness *noun.* —*See* **care** (1).

mindless *adjective.* Lacking rational direction or purpose ▶ brainless, meaningless, pointless, purposeless, senseless. ***Idiom:*** without rhyme or reason. [*Compare* **boring, perfunctory, vacant.**] —*See also* **careless, foolish, stupid.**

mindlessness *noun.* —*See* **stupidity.**

mindset *or* **mind-set** *noun.* —*See* **mood, posture** (2), **psychology.**

mind's eye *noun.* —*See* **imagination.**

mingle *verb.* To take part in social activities ▶ mix, socialize. —*See also* **mix** (1).

miniature *or* **mini** *adjective.* —*See* **tiny.**

minim *noun.* —*See* **bit**[1] (1).

minimal *adjective.* Comprising the least possible ▶ least, littlest, minimum, minutest, slightest, smallest, tiniest. [*Compare* **trivial.**]

minimization *noun.* —*See* **belittlement.**

minimize *verb.* —*See* **belittle.**

minimum *adjective.* —*See* **minimal.**

minimum *noun.* A very low or lowest level, position, or degree ▶ bottom, low, nadir, rock bottom.

minion *noun.* —*See* **sycophant.**

minister *noun.* —*See* **cleric, representative.**

minister to *verb.* To work and care for ▶ attend, do for, serve, wait on (*or* upon). [*Compare* **help, work.**] —*See also* **tend**[2]**.**

ministerial *adjective.* —*See* **administrative, clerical.**

ministry *noun.* —*See* **government** (2).

minor *adjective.* **1.** Below another in standing, importance, or status ▶ collateral, inferior, junior, lesser, little known, low, lower, minor-league, petty, secondary, second-class, slight, small, subaltern, subordinate, under. *Informal:* smalltime. *Slang:* bush-league. [*Compare* **auxiliary, trivial.**] **2.** Not yet a legal adult ▶ juvenile, underage.

minor *noun.* One who is not yet legally of age ▶ child, juvenile, underage person. [*Compare* **child, youth.**]

minor-league *adjective.* —*See* **minor** (1).

minstrel *noun.* —*See* **poet.**

mint *noun.* —*See* **fortune.**

mint *verb.* —*See* **invent.**

minus *noun.* —*See* **disadvantage.**

minuscule *adjective.* —*See* **tiny.**
minute[1] *noun.* —*See* **entry, flash** (2).
minute *verb.* —*See* **list**[1]**.**
minute[2] *adjective.* —*See* **detailed, tiny.**
minutia *noun.* —*See* **detail, trifle.**
minx *noun.* —*See* **urchin.**
miracle *noun.* An event inexplicable by the laws of nature ▶ wonder. ***Idiom:*** act of God. —*See also* **marvel.**
miraculous *adjective.* —*See* **astonishing, supernatural** (1).
mirage *noun.* —*See* **illusion.**
mire *noun.* —*See* **slime, swamp.**
mire *verb.* —*See* **dirty.**
mirror *noun.* —*See* **epitome, model.**
mirror *verb.* To send back or form an image of ▶ image, reflect. —*See also* **mimic.**
mirth *noun.* —*See* **merriment** (1).
mirthful *adjective.* —*See* **cheerful, merry.**
mirthfulness *noun.* —*See* **merriment** (1).
miry *adjective.* —*See* **dirty, slimy.**
misadventure *noun.* —*See* **accident.**
misanthrope *or* **misanthropist** *noun.* A person who expects only the worst from people ▶ cynic, pessimist. [*Compare* **skeptic.**]
misapplication *noun.* —*See* **abuse** (1).
misapply *verb.* —*See* **abuse** (2).
misapprehend *verb.* —*See* **misunderstand.**
misapprehension *noun.* —*See* **fallacy** (1), **misunderstanding.**
misappropriate *verb.* —*See* **abuse** (2).
misappropriation *noun.* —*See* **abuse** (1).
misbegotten *adjective.* —*See* **illegitimate.**
misbehave *verb.* To behave in a rowdy, improper, or unruly fashion ▶ act out, act up, be naughty, carry on. *Informal:* cut up, fool around, horse around. [*Compare* **offend.**]
misbehavior *noun.* Improper, often rude behavior ▶ bad manners, horseplay, misconduct, misdoing, naughtiness, wrongdoing. [*Compare* **crime, impropriety.**]
miscalculate *verb.* To count or calculate wrongly ▶ miscount, misestimate, misjudge, misreckon, overestimate, underestimate. [*Compare* **err, misunderstand.**]
miscalculation *noun.* A wrong calculation ▶ misestimate, misestimation, misjudgment, misreckoning, overestimation, underestimation. [*Compare* **error, misunderstanding.**]
miscarriage *noun.* —*See* **failure** (1).
miscarry *verb.* —*See* **fail** (1).
miscellanea *noun.* —*See* **odds and ends.**
miscellaneous *adjective.* —*See* **various.**
miscellaneousness *noun.* —*See* **variety.**
miscellany *noun.* —*See* **assortment.**
mischance *noun.* —*See* **accident.**
mischief *noun.* Annoying yet harmless, usually playful acts ▶ devilment, devilry, deviltry, diablerie, high jinks, impishness, mischief-making, mischievousness, playfulness, prankishness, pranks, rascality, roguery, roguishness, tomfoolery, tricks. *Informal:* shenanigans. *Slang:* funny business, hanky-panky, monkey business, monkeyshines. [*Compare* **prank**[1]**.**] —*See also* **harm, rascal.**
mischievous *adjective.* Full of mischief or high-spirited fun ▶ arch, devilish, elfish, frisky, frolicsome, gamesome, impish, larkish, playful, prankish, puckish, rascally, roguish, sportful, sportive, trickish, waggish. [*Compare* **lively.**] —*See also* **harmful.**
mischievousness *noun.* —*See* **mischief.**
misconceive *verb.* —*See* **misunderstand.**
misconception *noun.* —*See* **fallacy** (1), **misunderstanding.**
misconduct *noun.* —*See* **misbehavior.**
misconstrue *verb.* —*See* **misunderstand.**
miscount *verb.* —*See* **miscalculate.**
miscreant *adjective.* —*See* **corrupt** (1).

miscreant *noun.* —*See* **evildoer.**
miscue *noun.* —*See* **error.**
miscue *verb.* —*See* **err.**
misdeed *noun.* —*See* **crime** (1), **crime** (2).
misdemeanor *noun.* —*See* **crime** (1).
misdoing *noun.* —*See* **misbehavior.**
misdoubt *verb.* —*See* **distrust, doubt.**
mise en scène *noun.* —*See* **environment** (2), **scene** (2).
miser *noun.* A stingy person ▶ churl, niggard, pinchpenny, Scrooge, skinflint. *Informal:* penny pincher. *Slang:* cheapskate, piker, stiff, tightwad.
miserable *adjective.* Very uncomfortable or unhappy ▶ afflicted, agonized, anguished, suffering, woebegone, woeful, wretched. [*Compare* **depressed, despondent, glum.**] —*See also* **shoddy.**
miserable *noun.* —*See* **unfortunate.**
miserly *adjective.* —*See* **stingy.**
misery *noun.* A state of prolonged anguish and privation ▶ deprival, deprivation, hardship, misfortune, suffering, woe, wretchedness. [*Compare* **hell, poverty.**] —*See also* **curse** (3), **distress, pain.**
misestimate *verb.* To make a mistake in judging ▶ misjudge, mistake, prejudge. [*Compare* **misunderstand, suppose.**] —*See also* **miscalculate.**
misestimate *or* **misestimation** *noun.* —*See* **miscalculation.**
misfire *verb.* —*See* **fail** (1).
misfortune *noun.* Bad fortune ▶ adversity, bad luck, haplessness, hard luck, ill luck, unfortunateness, unluckiness, untowardness. [*Compare* **predicament.**] —*See also* **accident, misery.**
misgiving *noun.* —*See* **doubt, qualm.**
misguided *adjective.* —*See* **ignorant** (3).
mishandle *verb.* —*See* **abuse** (1), **abuse** (2), **botch.**
mishandling *noun.* —*See* **abuse** (1), **abuse** (2).
mishap *noun.* —*See* **accident, disaster.**
mishear *verb.* —*See* **misunderstand.**
mishmash *noun.* —*See* **assortment.**
misinformed *adjective.* —*See* **ignorant** (3).
misinterpret *verb.* —*See* **misunderstand.**
misinterpretation *noun.* —*See* **fallacy** (1), **misunderstanding.**
misjudge *verb.* To make a mistake in judging ▶ misestimate, mistake, prejudge. [*Compare* **misunderstand, suppose.**] —*See also* **miscalculate.**
misjudgment *noun.* —*See* **miscalculation.**
mislaid *adjective.* —*See* **lost** (2).
mislay *verb.* To be unable to find ▶ lose, misplace, miss. ***Idiom:*** have something go missing.
mislead *verb.* —*See* **deceive.**
misleading *adjective.* Deliberately ambiguous or vague ▶ elusive, equivocal, evasive, indirect. [*Compare* **ambiguous.**] —*See also* **fallacious** (2).
mislike *verb.* To regard with distaste ▶ dislike, disrelish. ***Idioms:*** be averse to, be cool toward, have an aversion to (*or* distaste for), have no use for, not be crazy (*or* nuts *or* wild) about, not care for. [*Compare* **despise, disapprove, hate.**]
mislike *noun.* An attitude or feeling of distaste or mild aversion ▶ disinclination, dislike, disrelish, distaste. [*Compare* **disapproval, disgust, enmity, hate.**]
mismanage *verb.* —*See* **botch.**
mismatch *verb.* —*See* **conflict.**
mismatched *adjective.* —*See* **improper** (2), **incongruous.**
misplace *verb.* To be unable to find ▶ lose, mislay, miss. ***Idiom:*** have something go missing.
misplaced *adjective.* —*See* **lost** (2).
misplacement *noun.* —*See* **loss** (1).
misread *verb.* —*See* **misunderstand.**
misreckon *verb.* —*See* **miscalculate.**
misreckoning *noun.* —*See* **miscalculation.**
misrepresent *verb.* —*See* **distort.**
misrepresentation *noun.* —*See* **equivocation, lie**[2]**.**

misrule *noun.* —*See* **disorder** (2).

miss *verb.* To be unable to find ▶ lose, mislay, misplace. ***Idiom:*** have something go missing. —*See also* **fail** (1), **lose** (2).

miss *noun.* —*See* **error.**

misshape *verb.* —*See* **deform.**

missing *adjective.* —*See* **absent, lost** (2).

mission *noun.* **1.** An assignment one is sent to carry out ▶ charge, commission, errand, operation, undertaking. [*Compare* **adventure, intention, task.**] **2.** A diplomatic office or headquarters in a foreign country ▶ deputation, embassy, legation. **3.** An inner urge to pursue an activity or perform a service ▶ calling, vocation. [*Compare* **dream, duty, fate.**] —*See also* **expedition.**

missionary *or* **missioner** *noun.* A person doing religious or charitable work in a foreign country ▶ apostle, evangelist. [*Compare* **cleric, representative.**] —*See also* **propagandist.**

missive *noun.* —*See* **letter.**

misstate *verb.* —*See* **distort.**

misstatement *noun.* —*See* **lie**^{2}.

misstep *noun.* —*See* **error.**

missy *noun.* —*See* **girl.**

mist *noun.* —*See* **haze, rain.**

mist *verb.* —*See* **obscure, rain** (2).

mistake *noun.* —*See* **error, misunderstanding.**

mistake *verb.* **1.** To take one thing mistakenly for another ▶ confound, confuse, mix up. **2.** To make a mistake in judging ▶ misestimate, misjudge, prejudge. [*Compare* **miscalculate, suppose.**] —*See also* **err, misunderstand.**

mistaken *adjective.* —*See* **erroneous.**

mistimed *adjective.* —*See* **unseasonable.**

mistreat *verb.* —*See* **abuse** (1), **abuse** (2).

mistreatment *noun.* —*See* **abuse** (2).

mistrust *noun.* —*See* **disbelief, distrust, doubt.**

mistrust *verb.* —*See* **disbelieve, distrust, doubt.**

mistrustful *adjective.* —*See* **distrustful.**

mistrustfully *adverb.* —*See* **skeptically.**

misty *adjective.* —*See* **rainy, sentimental, unclear.**

misunderstand *verb.* To understand incorrectly ▶ misapprehend, misconceive, misconstrue, mishear, misinterpret, misread, mistake. ***Idioms:*** get something wrong, get the wrong idea, miss the point. [*Compare* **confuse, miscalculate.**]

misunderstanding *noun.* A failure to understand correctly ▶ confusion, false impression, misapprehension, misconception, misinterpretation, mistake. [*Compare* **miscalculation.**] —*See also* **argument, fallacy** (1).

misusage *noun.* —*See* **abuse** (2), **corruption** (3).

misuse *noun.* —*See* **abuse** (1).

misuse *verb.* —*See* **abuse** (1), **abuse** (2).

mite *noun.* —*See* **bit**^{1} (1).

mitigate *verb.* —*See* **relieve** (1).

mitigation *noun.* —*See* **relief** (1).

mix *verb.* **1.** To combine into one mass or mixture ▶ admix, alloy, amalgamate, blend, coalesce, commingle, commix, fuse, homogenize, intermingle, intermix, merge, mingle, stir. [*Compare* **combine.**] **2.** To take part in social activities ▶ mingle, socialize. —*See also* **beat** (6).

mix up *verb.* To take one thing mistakenly for another ▶ confound, confuse, mistake. —*See also* **confuse** (1), **disorder, involve** (1).

mix *noun.* —*See* **mixture.**

✚ **CORE SYNONYMS:** *mix, blend, mingle, merge, amalgamate, coalesce, fuse.* These verbs mean to put into or come together in one mass so that constituent parts or elements are diffused or commingled. *Mix* is the least specific: *The cook mixed eggs, flour, and sugar. Greed and charity don't mix.* To *blend* is to mix intimately and harmoniously so that the components lose their original definition: *The clerk blended the hot choco-*

late with coffee. Snow-covered mountains blended into the clouds. Mingle implies combination without loss of individual characteristics: *"Respect was mingled with surprise"* (Sir Walter Scott). *"His companions mingled freely and joyously with the natives"* (Washington Irving). *Merge* and *amalgamate* imply resultant homogeneity: *Tradition and innovation are merged in this new composition. Twilight merged into night. "The four sentences of the original are amalgamated into two"* (William Minto). *Coalesce* implies a slow merging: *Indigenous peoples and immigrants coalesced into the present-day population. Fuse* emphasizes an enduring union, as that formed by heating metals: *"He diffuses a tone and spirit of unity, that blends, and (as it were) fuses, each into each"* (Samuel Taylor Coleridge).

---

mixed *adjective.* —*See* **impure** (2), **various.**

mixed bag *noun.* —*See* **assortment.**

mixed-up *adjective.* —*See* **confused** (2), **confused** (1).

mixture *noun.* Something produced by mixing ▶ admixture, alloy, amalgam, amalgamation, blend, commixture, composite, fusion, merger, mix. [*Compare* **combination, unification.**] —*See also* **assortment.**

✚ **CORE SYNONYMS:** *mixture, blend, amalgam, admixture, composite.* These nouns refer to a combination produced by mixing. *Mixture* has the widest application: *She routinely drank a mixture of tea and honey. "He showed a curious mixture of eagerness and terror"* (Francis Parkman). *Blend* and *amalgam* imply that the original components have lost their distinctness: *The novel is a fascinating blend of romance and realism. The comedian's act was an amalgam of incisive wit and unceasing good humor. Admixture* suggests that one of the components is dissimilar to the others: *a perfume containing an essential oil with a large admixture of alcohol.* A *composite* has components that may retain part of their identities: *a musical suite that is a composite of operatic themes.*

---

mix-up *noun.* —*See* **disorder** (1), **mess** (1).

mizzle *noun.* The process or sound of dripping ▶ dribble, drip, drizzle, trickle. —*See also* **rain.**

mizzle *verb.* —*See* **rain** (2).

moan *noun.* —*See* **howl.**

moan *verb.* —*See* **complain, howl.**

mob *noun. Informal* An organized group of criminals, hoodlums, or wrongdoers ▶ band, gang, pack, ring. —*See also* **commonalty, crowd.**

mob *verb.* —*See* **fill** (1).

mobile *adjective.* **1.** Capable of moving or being moved from place to place ▶ movable, moving, portable, transportable, traveling, unstationary. [*Compare* **loose, migrant.**] **2.** Changing easily, as in expression ▶ changeable, fluid, plastic. [*Compare* **changeable, unstable.**]

mobilization *noun.* —*See* **preparation.**

mobilize *verb.* To assemble, prepare, or put into operation, as for war or a similar emergency ▶ activate, call up, enlist, marshal, militarize, muster, organize, rally, ready. ***Idioms:*** call to action, call out the troops. [*Compare* **assemble, energize, provoke.**]

mobster *noun.* —*See* **criminal.**

mock *verb.* —*See* **imitate, ridicule.**

mock *adjective.* —*See* **artificial** (1).

mockery *noun.* **1.** Words or actions intended to evoke contemptuous laughter ▶ derision, ridicule. [*Compare* **sarcasm, taunt.**] **2.** A false, derisive, or impudent imitation of something ▶ caricature, farce, parody, sham, travesty. [*Compare* **counterfeit, satire.**] **3.** An object of amusement or laughter ▶ butt, jest, joke, laughingstock. ***Idiom:*** figure of fun. [*Compare* **fool.**]

mocking *adjective.* —*See* **disparaging, sarcastic.**

mod *adjective.* —*See* **fashionable.**

mode *noun.* —*See* **condition** (1), **fashion, style, way** (1).

model *noun.* One that is worthy of imitation or duplication ▶ beau ideal, example, exemplar, ideal, mirror, nonpareil, paradigm, paragon, pattern, precedent, role model, standard. ***Idioms:*** man among men, woman among women. [*Compare* **celebrity.**] —*See also* **epitome, original.**

model *verb.* —*See* **base**[1], **follow** (5), **form** (1), **pose** (1).

model *adjective.* —*See* **ideal, typical.**

✚ **CORE SYNONYMS:** *model, exemplar, ideal, example, standard, pattern.* These nouns refer to someone or something worthy of imitation or duplication. *Model* and *exemplar* connote that which perfectly or most appropriately represents something or someone, by being either very worthy or truly representative: *"Our fellow countryman is a model of a man"* (Charles Dickens). *"He is indeed the perfect exemplar of all nobleness"* (Jane Porter). *An ideal* is a sometimes unattainable standard of perfection: *"Religion is the vision of . . . something which is the ultimate ideal, and the hopeless quest"* (Alfred North Whitehead). An *example* can refer to something that is worthy of imitation but can also indicate something that serves as a deterrent or warning: *"Our Government is the potent, the omnipresent teacher. For good or for ill, it teaches the whole people by its example"* (Louis D. Brandeis). A *standard* is an established criterion or recognized level of excellence: *"It wouldn't be quite fair to test him by our standards"* (William Dean Howells). A *pattern* serves as a model, plan, or guide in the creation of something: *"I will be the pattern of all patience"* (William Shakespeare).

---

moderate *verb.* **1.** To make or become less severe or extreme ▶ mute, play down, qualify, soften, subdue, tame, temper, tone down. [*Compare* **decrease, relieve.**] **2.** To intervene between disputants in order to bring about an agreement ▶ arbitrate, mediate. [*Compare* **confer, judge.**] —*See also* **subside.**

moderate *adjective.* **1.** Free from extremes in temperature ▶ balmy, clement, mild, temperate. [*Compare* **pleasant.**] **2.** Requiring little effort or exertion ▶ easy, light, undemanding. *Informal:* cushy, soft. —*See also* **acceptable** (2), **conservative** (2), **gentle** (2), **gradual** (2), **light**[2] (2).

✚ **CORE SYNONYMS:** *moderate, qualify, temper.* These verbs mean to make or become less severe or extreme: *moderated the severity of his rebuke; qualified her criticism; admiration tempered with fear.*

◀ **ANTONYM:** *intensify*

---

moderateness *noun.* —*See* **moderation.**

moderation *noun.* Avoidance of extremes of opinion, feeling, or personal conduct ▶ abstemiousness, measure, moderateness, sobriety, temperance. [*Compare* **prudence, restraint.**] —*See also* **waning.**

modern *adjective.* —*See* **contemporary** (2).

modern *noun.* A person of the present age ▶ contemporary.

modernize *verb.* To make modern in appearance or style ▶ streamline, update. ***Idioms:*** bring into the 21st century, bring up to date. [*Compare* **improve, renew.**]

modest *adjective.* **1.** Not showy or obtrusive, as in appearance, style, or behavior ▶ inobtrusive, plain, quiet, restrained, simple, subdued, tasteful, unassuming, unobtrusive, unostentatious, unpretentious. [*Compare* **appropriate, inconspicuous, reserved.**] **2.** Having or expressing feelings of humility ▶ humble, lowly, meek, unambitious.

[*Compare* **deferential.**] —*See also* **acceptable** (2), **chaste, clean** (2), **conservative** (2), **decent, light**[2] (2), **shy**[1].

✤ CORE SYNONYMS: *modest, plain, simple, unostentatious, unpretentious.* These adjectives mean not showy, obtrusive, or ostentatious: *a modest cottage; a plain hairstyle; a simple dark suit; an unostentatious office; an unpretentious country church.*

---

modesty *noun.* **1.** Lack of vanity or self-importance ▶ humbleness, humility, lowliness, meekness, unassumingness, unpretentiousness. **2.** Lack of ostentation or pretension ▶ inobtrusiveness, plainness, quietness, restraint, simpleness, simplicity, tastefulness, unassumingness, unobtrusiveness, unostentatiousness, unpretentiousness. —*See also* **chastity, shyness.**

modicum *noun.* —*See* **bit**[1] (1).

modifiable *adjective.* —*See* **changeable** (1).

modification *noun.* —*See* **change** (1), **variation.**

modified *adjective.* —*See* **qualified.**

modify *verb.* —*See* **change** (1), **change** (2).

modish *adjective.* —*See* **fashionable.**

modulate *verb.* —*See* **adjust.**

modus operandi *noun.* —*See* **approach** (1), **way** (1).

moil *verb.* —*See* **labor.**

moil *noun.* —*See* **labor.**

moist *adjective.* Slightly wet ▶ clammy, damp, dank, dewy. [*Compare* **sticky, wet.**]

moisten *verb.* To make moist ▶ bathe, dampen, wash, wet.

moistureless *adjective.* —*See* **dry** (1).

mold *noun.* A hollow device for shaping a fluid or plastic substance ▶ cast, form, matrix. —*See also* **kind**[2].

mold *verb.* —*See* **form** (1), **make.**

moldable *adjective.* —*See* **malleable.**

molder *verb.* —*See* **decay.**

moldy *or* **moldering** *adjective.* Smelling of mildew or decay ▶ frowzy, funky, fusty, gamy, mildewed, musty, rancid, rank, rotten, stale. [*Compare* **airless, bad, smelly.**]

mole *noun.* —*See* **informer.**

molecule *noun.* —*See* **bit**[1] (1).

molest *verb.* To compel another to participate in or submit to a sexual act ▶ assault, force, rape, ravish, violate. —*See also* **annoy.**

moll *noun.* —*See* **harlot.**

mollify *verb.* —*See* **pacify.**

mollycoddle *noun.* —*See* **baby** (2).

mollycoddle *verb.* —*See* **baby.**

molt *verb.* —*See* **shed**[1] (2).

mom *or* **mommy** *noun.* —*See* **mother.**

moment *noun.* —*See* **flash** (2), **importance, occasion** (1), **opportunity.**

momentary *adjective.* —*See* **transitory.**

momentous *adjective.* So critically decisive as to affect the future ▶ fatal, fateful. [*Compare* **decisive.**] —*See also* **grave**[2] (1), **important.**

momentousness *noun.* The condition of being grave and of involving serious consequences ▶ graveness, gravity, heaviness, seriousness, weightiness. [*Compare* **severity.**]

momma *noun.* —*See* **girl, mother.**

monarch *noun.* —*See* **chief.**

Monday morning quarterback *noun.* —*See* **critic** (2).

monetary *adjective.* Of or relating to finances ▶ financial, fiscal, pecuniary.

money *noun.* **1.** Something, such as coins or printed bills, used as a medium of exchange ▶ bills, cash, coin, currency, greenbacks, lucre, notes. *Informal:* bucks, wampum. *Slang:* bread, cabbage, dough, gelt, green, jack, juice, lettuce, long green, mazuma, moola, roll, scratch, shekels. [*Compare* **wage.**] **2.** The monetary resources of a government, organization, or individual ▶ capital, finances, funds. [*Compare* **capital, resources.**] —*See also* **wealth.**

moneyed *adjective.* —*See* **rich** (1).

moneymaking *adjective.* —*See* **profitable.**

moneyman *noun.* One who is occupied with or expert in large-scale financial affairs ▶ capitalist, financier.

money management *noun.* The management of money ▶ banking, finance, investment.

moniker *or* **monicker** *noun.* —*See* **name** (1).

monition *noun.* —*See* **warning.**

monitor *verb.* To pay regular and close attention to ▶ follow, observe, stake out, survey, watch. ***Idioms:*** have one's (*or* keep an) eye on, keep tabs on, keep track of, ride herd on. —*See also* **police, supervise.**

monitor *noun.* —*See* **guard.**

monitory *adjective.* Giving warning ▶ admonishing, admonitory, cautionary, warning.

monk *noun.* —*See* **cleric.**

monkey *noun.* —*See* **dupe.**

monkey *verb.* —*See* **fiddle, tinker.**

monkey business *noun.* —*See* **mischief.**

monkeyshine *noun.* —*See* **prank**[1]**.**

monocracy *noun.* —*See* **absolutism** (2).

monocratic *adjective.* —*See* **absolute.**

monogram *noun.* —*See* **mark** (1).

monograph *noun.* —*See* **discourse.**

monopolize *verb.* —*See* **absorb** (1).

monopoly *noun.* Exclusive control or possession ▶ corner. [*Compare* **domination.**] —*See also* **alliance, company** (1).

monotonous *adjective.* —*See* **boring.**

monotony *or* **monotonousness** *or* **monotone** *noun.* A tiresome lack of variety ▶ humdrum, invariability, repetition, repititiousness, repetitiveness, sameness, tedium, tediousness. [*Compare* **boredom, dullness, routine.**]

monster *noun.* A person or animal that is abnormally formed ▶ freak, grotesque, monstrosity, mooncalf, mutant. ***Idiom:*** freak of nature. [*Compare* **deformity.**] —*See also* **fiend, giant.**

monster *adjective.* —*See* **enormous.**

monstrosity *noun.* —*See* **mess** (2), **monster.** —*See also* **outrage, ugliness.**

monstrous *adjective.* Resembling a freak ▶ freakish, freaky, grotesque. [*Compare* **eccentric, weird.**] —*See also* **enormous, outrageous, ugly.**

monstrousness *noun.* —*See* **outrageousness, ugliness.**

monument *noun.* Something, as a structure or custom, serving to honor or keep alive a memory ▶ commemoration, memorial, remembrance. [*Compare* **testimonial.**]

monumental *adjective.* Serving to honor or keep alive a memory ▶ commemorative, memorial. —*See also* **enormous, important.**

monumentality *noun.* —*See* **enormousness.**

mooch *verb.* —*See* **beg, steal.**

moocher *noun.* —*See* **beggar** (1).

mood *noun.* A temporary state of mind or feeling ▶ frame of mind, humor, mindset, spirits, state of mind, temper, vein. [*Compare* **disposition, posture.**] —*See also* **air** (3), **temper** (3).

✚ **CORE SYNONYMS:** *mood, humor, temper.* These nouns refer to a temporary state of mind or feeling. *Mood* is the most inclusive: "*I was in no mood to laugh and talk with strangers*" (Mary Shelley). *Humor* often implies a state of mind resulting from one's characteristic disposition or temperament: "*All which had been done . . . was the effect not of humor, but of system*" (Edmund Burke). *Temper* most often refers to irritability or intense anger: "*The nation was in such a temper that the smallest spark might raise a flame*" (Thomas Macaulay).

---

moody *adjective.* Given to changeable emotional states, especially of anger or gloom ▶ mercurial, temperamental. [*Compare* **capricious, testy.**] —*See also* **glum.**

moola *or* **moolah** *noun.* —*See* **money** (1).

mooncalf *noun.* —*See* **fool, monster.**

moonstruck *or* **moonstricken** *adjective.* —*See* **insane.**

moony *adjective.* —*See* **dreamy.**

moor[1] *verb.* —*See* **attach** (1), **fasten.**

moor[2] *noun.* —*See* **swamp.**

mooring *noun.* —*See* **anchor.**

moot *verb.* —*See* **argue** (2), **broach, discuss.**

moot *adjective.* —*See* **debatable, theoretical** (1).

mope *verb.* To be sullenly aloof or withdrawn, as in silent resentment or protest ▶ pet, pout, sulk. [*Compare* **brood.**] —*See also* **brood.**

mopes *noun.* —*See* **depression** (2).

moppet *noun.* —*See* **child** (1).

moral *adjective.* Teaching morality ▶ didactic, didactical, edifying, moralistic, moralizing, preachy. —*See also* **chaste, elevated** (3), **ethical.**

moral *noun.* The principle taught by a fable or parable ▶ axiom, lesson, maxim, principle. [*Compare* **idea, law, meaning.**]

morale *noun.* A strong sense of enthusiasm and dedication to a common goal that unites a group ▶ esprit, esprit de corps, group spirit, team spirit. [*Compare* **confidence, mood, spirit.**]

✚ **CORE SYNONYMS:** *morale, esprit, esprit de corps.* These nouns denote a strong sense of enthusiasm and dedication to a common goal that unites a group: *the high morale of the troops; the esprit of an orchestra; the esprit de corps of the swim team.*

moralistic *adjective.* Piously or overly sure of one's own righteousness ▶ holier-than-thou, self-righteous. [*Compare* **arrogant, hypocritical, moral.**] —*See also* **moral.**

morality *noun.* —*See* **chastity, ethics** (1), **ethics** (2), **good** (1).

moralize *verb.* To indulge in moral reflection, usually pompously ▶ edify, pontificate, preach, sermonize. [*Compare* **chastise.**]

moralizing *adjective.* —*See* **didactic, moral.**

morals *noun.* —*See* **ethics** (2).

morass *noun.* —*See* **swamp, tangle.**

moratorium *noun.* —*See* **delay** (1).

morbid *adjective.* Characterized by preoccupation with unwholesome feelings or thoughts ▶ insalubrious, macabre, sick, unhealthy, unwholesome. [*Compare* **abnormal.**] —*See also* **ghastly** (2).

mordacity *or* **mordancy** *noun.* —*See* **sarcasm.**

mordant *or* **mordacious** *adjective.* —*See* **biting.**

more *adjective.* —*See* **additional.**

more *adverb.* To a greater extent ▶ better. ***Idioms:*** more fully, to a greater degree. —*See also* **additionally.**

moreover *adverb.* —*See* **additionally, even** (2).

mores *noun.* —*See* **culture** (2), **ethics** (2), **manners.**

morn *noun.* —*See* **dawn.**

morning *noun.* The time of day from sunrise to noon ▶ A.M., before lunch, before noon, forenoon. —*See also* **dawn.**

moron *noun.* —*See* **dullard, fool.**

moronic *adjective.* —*See* **foolish, stupid.**

morose *adjective.* —*See* **glum.**

morph *verb.* —*See* **convert.**

morsel *noun.* —*See* **bit**[1] (1), **bit**[1] (2), **delicacy.**

mortal *adjective.* —*See* **bodily, conceivable, deadly, human.**

mortal *noun.* —*See* **human being.**

mortgage *verb.* —*See* **pawn**[1].

mortification *noun.* —*See* **degradation** (1), **embarrassment.**

mortify *verb.* To cause to feel embarrassment, dishonor, and often guilt ▶ brand, reproach, shame, stigmatize. [*Compare* **belittle, denigrate.**] —*See also* **embarrass, humble.**

mortise *noun.* —*See* **fastener.**

mosey *verb.* —*See* **stroll.**

mossback *noun.* —*See* **square, ultraconservative.**

mossbacked *adjective.* —*See* **ultraconservative.**

most *adjective.* —*See* **best** (2).

most *adverb.* —*See* **very.**

mostly *adverb.* —*See* **usually.**

mother *noun.* A female parent ▶ materfamilias, matriarch. *Informal:* ma, mama, mammy, mom, momma, mommy, mum, mummy. *Slang:* old lady. —*See also* **ancestor** (1), **origin.**

motif *noun.* An element or component in a decorative composition ▶ design, device, figure, motive.

motion *noun.* The act or process of moving ▶ action, activity, move, movement, moving, stir, stirring. [*Compare* **change.**] —*See also* **gesture, proposal** (1).

motion *verb.* —*See* **gesture.**

motionless *adjective.* Not moving ▶ at rest, fixed, frozen, halted, immobile, paralyzed, resting, rigid, static, stationary, still, stock-still, transfixed, unmoving. ***Idioms:*** at a dead calm, at a quiet stop, at a standstill, at a deadlock. [*Compare* **dormant, fixed, inactive.**]

motivate *verb.* —*See* **encourage** (1), **provoke.**

motivation *noun.* Something that encourages ▶ encouragement, inspiration, stimulation. —*See also* **cause** (2), **stimulus.**

motive *noun.* An element or component in a decorative composition ▶ design, device, figure, motif. —*See also* **cause** (2).

motivic *adjective.* Of, constituting, or relating to a theme or themes ▶ thematic, topical.

motley *adjective.* —*See* **multicolored, various.**

motor *verb.* —*See* **drive** (1).

motorist *noun.* A person who operates a motor vehicle ▶ chauffeur, driver, operator.

mottle *verb.* —*See* **speckle.**

mottled *adjective.* —*See* **multicolored.**

motto *noun.* —*See* **cry** (2), **proverb.**

moue *noun.* A contorted facial expression showing pain, contempt, or disgust ▶ face, pout. *Informal:* mug. [*Compare* **frown, glare, sneer.**]

mound *noun.* —*See* **heap** (1).

mound *verb.* —*See* **heap** (1).

mount *verb.* —*See* **ascend, increase, rise** (2), **rise** (3), **stage.**

mountain *noun.* —*See* **abundance, heap** (1), **heap** (2).

mountainous *adjective.* —*See* **enormous.**

mountebank *noun.* —*See* **fake.**

mounting *noun.* —*See* **ascent** (1).

mourn *verb.* —*See* **grieve.**

mournful *adjective.* —*See* **sorrowful.**

mournfulness *noun.* —*See* **depression** (2).

mouse *noun. Slang* A bruise surrounding the eye ▶ black eye. *Slang:* shiner. [*Compare* **bruise.**] —*See also* **coward.**

mouse *verb.* —*See* **sneak.**

mouth *noun.* **1.** The opening in the body through which food is ingested ▶ chops, maw. *Slang:* gob, hole, jaws, kisser, pie hole, puss, smacker, trap, yap. **2.** Insolent talk ▶ back talk. *Informal:* lip, sass. [*Compare* **impudence.**] —*See also* **hole** (2), **inlet, speaker** (2).

mouth *verb.* To contort one's face to indicate pain, contempt, or disgust ▶ grimace, mug. ***Idioms:*** make a face, make faces. [*Compare* **frown, glare, sneer.**] —*See also* **rant.**

mouthful *noun.* —*See* **bit**[1] (2).

mouthpiece *noun.* —*See* **speaker** (2).

mouth-watering *adjective.* —*See* **delicious.**

movable *adjective.* —*See* **mobile** (1).

movables *noun.* —*See* **effects.**

move *verb.* **1.** To stir the emotions of ▶ affect, get (to), impress, influence, strike, touch. ***Idioms:*** hit (*or* touch) a soft spot, touch a chord, tug at one's heartstrings. [*Compare* **disturb, encourage.**] **2.** To go or cause to go from one place to another ▶ maneuver, remove, shift, transfer, travel. [*Compare* go, journey.] **3.** To change one's residence or place of business, for example ▶ relocate, remove, transfer. ***Idiom:*** pull up stakes. [*Compare* **emigrate, settle.**] **4.** To move or cause to move slightly ▶ budge, shift, stir. —*See also* **advance** (2), **disturb, persuade, propose, provoke.**

move apart *verb.* —*See* **scatter** (2).

move *noun.* —*See* **motion. 1.** The act of moving from one place to another ▶ relocation, remotion, removal. ***Idioms:*** change of address (*or* residence). [*Compare* **departure.**] **2.** An action calculated to achieve an end ▶ maneuver, measure, procedure, step, tactic. —*See also* **displacement, transition.**

✚ **CORE SYNONYMS:** *move, affect, influence, impress, touch, strike.* These verbs mean to stir the emotions of a person or group. *Move* suggests a profound emotional effect: *The account of her experiences moved us to tears.* To *affect* is to act upon a person's emotions: *Adverse criticism of the book didn't affect the author. Influence* implies some control over the thinking, actions, and emotions of another: *"Humanity is profoundly influenced by what you do"* (Pope John Paul II). To *impress* is to produce a marked, often enduring effect: *"The Tibetan landscape particularly impressed him"* (Doris Kerns Quinn). *Touch* usually means to arouse a tender response: *"The tributes* [to the two deceased musicians] *were fitting and touching"* (Daniel Cariaga). *Strike* implies keenness or force of mental response: *I was struck by the sudden change in his appearance.*

---

movement *noun.* —*See* **displacement, drive** (1), **motion, plot** (1).

moves *noun.* —*See* **advances.**

movie *noun.* A motion picture ▶ film, motion picture, picture. *Slang:* flick.

moving *adjective.* —*See* **affecting, dramatic** (2), **mobile** (1).

mow *verb.* —*See* **cut** (3).

moxie *noun.* —*See* **courage.**

Mrs. Grundy *noun.* —*See* **prude.**

much *noun.* —*See* **abundance.**

much *adverb.* —*See* **considerably.**

muchness *noun.* —*See* **plenty.**

mucilaginous *adjective.* —*See* **sticky** (1), **viscous.**

muck *noun.* —*See* **filth, slime.**

muck up *verb.* —*See* **botch, dirty.**

muckamuck *noun.* —*See* **dignitary.**

muckiness *noun.* —*See* **dirtiness.**

mucky *adjective.* —*See* **slimy.**

mud *verb.* —*See* **dirty.**

mud *noun.* —*See* **filth.**

muddle *verb.* To proceed or perform in an unsteady, faltering manner ▶ blunder, bumble, bungle, flounder, fudge, fumble, limp, shuffle, stagger, stumble. —*See also* **botch, confuse** (1), **confuse** (3), **disorder, disrupt.**

muddle through *verb.* —*See* **manage.**

muddle *noun.* —*See* **daze, disorder** (1), **mess** (1).

muddled *adjective.* —*See* **confused** (2).

muddle-headed *adjective.* —*See* **confused** (1).

muddy *adjective.* —*See* **dirty, dull** (2), **murky** (1).

muddy *verb.* —*See* **confuse** (3), **dirty.**

mudslinger *noun.* —*See* **critic** (2).

mudslinging *noun.* —*See* **libel.**

muff *verb.* —*See* **botch.**

muff *noun.* —*See* **blunder.**

muffle *verb.* To decrease or dull the sound of ▶ damp (down), dampen, deaden, dull, mute, stifle. [*Compare* **decrease, silence, soften.**] —*See also* **repress.**

muffler *noun.* —*See* **wrap.**

mug *noun. Informal* A contorted facial expression showing pain, contempt, or disgust ▶ face, grimace, moue, pout. [*Compare* **frown, glare, sneer.**] —*See also* **face** (1), **thug.**

mug *verb.* To contort one's face to indicate pain, contempt, or disgust ▶ grimace, mouth. ***Idioms:*** make a face, make faces. [*Compare* **frown, glare, sneer.**] *—See also* **rob.**

muggy *adjective.* *—See* **sticky** (2).

mulct *noun.* A sum of money levied as punishment for an offense ▶ amercement, fine, penalty. [*Compare* **punishment.**]

mulct *verb.* To impose a fine on ▶ amerce, fine, penalize. [*Compare* **punish.**] *—See also* **cheat** (1).

mule *noun. Slang* A person who engages in smuggling ▶ bootlegger, contrabandist, runner, smuggler.

mulish *adjective.* *—See* **stubborn** (1).

mulishness *noun.* *—See* **stubbornness.**

mull *verb.* *—See* **ponder.**

multicolored *adjective.* Having many different colors ▶ colorful, many-colored, many-hued, motley, mottled, pied, polychromatic, polychrome, polychromic, polychromous, varicolored, variegated, versicolor, versicolored. ***Idiom:*** of all the colors in the rainbow. [*Compare* **bright, colorful.**]

multifaceted *adjective.* *—See* **versatile.**

multifarious *adjective.* *—See* **various.**

multifariousness *noun.* *—See* **variety.**

multiform *adjective.* *—See* **various.**

multiformity *noun.* *—See* **variety.**

multinational *noun.* *—See* **company** (1).

multiple *or* **multiplex** *adjective.* *—See* **complex** (2).

multiplication *noun.* *—See* **buildup** (2), **increase** (1), **reproduction.**

multiplicity *noun.* *—See* **heap** (2), **variety.**

multiply *verb.* *—See* **breed, increase.**

multipurpose *or* **multitalented** *adjective.* *—See* **versatile.**

multitude *noun.* *—See* **commonalty, crowd.**

multitudinous *adjective.* *—See* **many.**

mum *adjective.* *—See* **speechless.**

mumble *verb.* *—See* **mutter.**

mumble *noun.* *—See* **murmur.**

mumbo jumbo *noun.* *—See* **gibberish.**

mummery *noun.* *—See* **ritual.**

mummify *verb.* *—See* **dry** (1).

mummy *noun.* *—See* **body** (2).

munch *verb.* *—See* **chew.**

mundane *adjective.* *—See* **earthly, ordinary.**

municipal *adjective.* *—See* **city.**

municipality *noun.* *—See* **city.**

munificence *noun.* *—See* **generosity.**

munificent *adjective.* *—See* **generous** (1).

murder *noun.* The crime of murdering someone ▶ assassination, blood, homicide, killing, liquidation, manslaughter, slaying. *Slang:* hit, rubout, wipeout.

murder *verb.* To take the life of a person or persons unlawfully ▶ assassinate, destroy, finish (off), kill, liquidate, slay. *Informal:* put away. *Slang:* bump off, do in, ice, snuff, knock off, off, pop off, rub out, snuff out, take out, waste, wipe out, zap. ***Idiom:*** do away with. [*Compare* **massacre.**] *—See also* **overwhelm** (1).

murderer *noun.* One who murders another ▶ assassin, butcher, cutthroat, exterminator, homicide, killer, liquidator, manslayer, massacrer, murderess, slaughterer, slayer, triggerman. *Slang:* axman, hatchet man, hired gun, hit man.

murderous *adjective.* Marked by or giving rise to murder or bloodshed ▶ bloodthirsty, bloody, bloody-minded, cutthroat, death-dealing, homicidal, gory, killing, man-killing, sanguinary, sanguineous, slaughterous. [*Compare* **deadly, fierce.**]

murk *or* **murkiness** *noun.* *—See* **dark.**

murky *adjective.* **1.** Darkened or clouded with sediment ▶ clouded, cloudy, muddy, roiled, roily, sedimentary, turbid, unsettled. **2.** Heavy, dark, or dense, especially with impurities ▶ hazy, smoggy, turbid. [*Compare* **dirty.**] *—See also* **dark** (1), **dull** (2), **unclear.**

murmur *noun.* A low, indistinct, and often continuous sound ▶ mumble, rustle, sigh, sough, susurration, susurrus, whisper. [*Compare* **hum.**] *—See also* **burble, complaint.**

murmur *verb.* To make a low, continuous, and indistinct sound ▶ rustle, sigh, sough, whisper. [*Compare* **hum.**] *—See also* **burble, complain, mutter.**

murmurer *noun.* *—See* **grouch.**

muscle *noun.* *—See* **authority, brawn, influence, strength.**

muscle *verb.* *Informal* To force one's way into a place or situation ▶ bulldoze, elbow, push, shoulder, shove. [*Compare* **push.**]

muscular *adjective.* Characterized by marked muscular development ▶ athletic, beefy, brawny, burly, husky, rugged, robust, sinewy, strapping, studly, sturdy. *Slang:* buff, built. [*Compare* **healthy, rugged, strong.**]

✤ CORE SYNONYMS: *muscular, athletic, brawny, burly, sinewy.* These adjectives mean strong and powerfully built: *a muscular build; an athletic swimmer; brawny arms; a burly lumberjack; a lean and sinewy frame.*

---

muscularity *noun.* *—See* **brawn.**

muse[1] *verb.* *—See* **dream, ponder.**

muse *noun.* *—See* **trance.**

muse[2] *noun.* *—See* **poet.**

mush *verb.* *—See* **crush** (1).

mush *or* **mushiness** *noun.* *—See* **sentimentality.**

mushroom *verb.* To increase or expand suddenly, rapidly, or without control ▶ balloon, explode, snowball. [*Compare* **increase.**]

mushy *adjective.* *—See* **sentimental, soft** (1).

musical *adjective.* *—See* **harmonious** (2), **melodious.**

musician *noun.* *—See* **player** (2).

musing *noun.* *—See* **thought.**

muskeg *noun.* *—See* **swamp.**

muss *verb.* *—See* **tousle.**

muss *noun.* *—See* **disorder** (1).

mussy *adjective.* *—See* **messy** (1).

must *verb.* To be required to do ▶ be compelled, be obliged, need, ought, should. ***Idioms:*** have got to, have to.

must *noun.* *—See* **condition** (2), **duty** (1).

muster *verb.* *—See* **assemble, mobilize.**

muster in *verb.* *—See* **join** (1).

muster out *verb.* *—See* **discharge.**

muster *noun.* *—See* **assembly.**

musty *adjective.* *—See* **moldy, trite.**

mutable *adjective.* *—See* **changeable** (1).

mutant *noun.* *—See* **monster.**

mutate *verb.* *—See* **change** (1), **change** (2), **convert.**

mutation *noun.* *—See* **change** (1), **conversion** (1).

mute *adjective.* Lacking the power or faculty of speech ▶ aphonic, dumb, inarticulate, silent, speechless, tongueless, tongue-tied, voiceless, wordless. *—See also* **speechless.**

mute *verb.* *—See* **moderate** (1), **muffle.**

muteness *noun.* *—See* **silence** (2).

mutilate *verb.* *—See* **batter, cripple, deform.**

mutineer *noun.* *—See* **rebel** (1).

mutinous *adjective.* *—See* **rebellious.**

mutiny *noun.* *—See* **rebellion.**

mutiny *verb.* To vehemently defy and break allegiance with ▶ rebel, revolt, rise (up). [*Compare* **defect, defy.**]

mutter *verb.* To speak or utter indistinctly, as by lowering the voice or partially closing the mouth ▶ jabber, maunder, mumble, murmur, whisper. ***Idioms:*** speak under one's breath, talk to one's self. *—See also* **complain.**

mutter *noun.* *—See* **complaint.**

mutterer *noun.* *—See* **grouch.**

muttonheaded *adjective.* *—See* **stupid.**

mutual *adjective.* Directed and received by each toward the other ▶ exchanged, give-and-take, reciprocal, reciprocative, requited, shared, two-sided. [*Compare* **cooperative.**] *—See also* **common** (2), **complementary.**

muumuu *noun.* *—See* **dress** (3).

muzzle *verb.* *—See* **repress.**

muzzle *noun.* *—See* **face** (1).

myriad *adjective.* *—See* **many.**

mysterious *adjective.* Difficult to explain or understand ▶ arcane, baffling, cabalistic, confounding, cryptic, enigmatic, esoteric, impenetrable, inexplicable, inscrutable, mystic, mystical, mystifying, occult, perplexing, puzzling, unaccountable. [*Compare* **funny, obscure, secret, weird.**]

✚ **CORE SYNONYMS:** *mysterious, esoteric, arcane, occult, inscrutable.* These adjectives mean difficult to explain or understand. Something that is *mysterious* arouses wonder and inquisitiveness: *"The sea lies all about us . . . . In its mysterious past it encompasses all the dim origins of life"* (Rachel Carson). What is *esoteric* is mysterious because only a select group knows and understands it: *a compilation of esoteric philosophical essays. Arcane* applies to what is hidden from general knowledge: *arcane economic theories. Occult* suggests knowledge reputedly gained only by secret, magical, or supernatural means: *an occult rite.* Something that is *inscrutable* cannot be fathomed by means of investigation or scrutiny: *"It is not for me to attempt to fathom the inscrutable workings of Providence"* (Earl of Birkenhead).

---

mystery *noun.* Anything that arouses curiosity or perplexes because it is unexplained, inexplicable, or secret ▶ brainteaser, conundrum, curiousity, enigma, perplexity, puzzle, puzzler, question mark, riddle, stickler, weirdness.

mystical *or* **mystic** *adjective.* —*See* **mysterious, supernatural** (1).

mystification *noun.* —*See* **daze.**

mystify *verb.* —*See* **baffle, confuse** (1).

mystifying *adjective.* —*See* **mysterious.**

myth *noun.* **1.** A traditional story or tale that has no proven factual basis ▶ fable, fairy tale, folk tale, just-so story, legend, parable. [*Compare* **fiction, story, yarn.**] **2.** A fiction or half-truth, especially one that forms part of an ideology ▶ creation, delusion, fabrication, fantasy, fiction, figment, invention. [*Compare* **lie**[2].] —*See also* **lore** (1).

mythical *or* **mythic** *adjective.* Having the nature of a fable; not real ▶ apocryphal, fabled, fabricated, fabulous, fairy-tale, fantasy, legendary, make-believe, mythologic, mythological. [*Compare* **fanciful, fictitious, imaginary.**]

mythological *or* **mythologic** *adjective.* —*See* **mythical.**

mythology *or* **mythos** *noun.* —*See* **lore** (1).

N

nab *verb.* —*See* **arrest, catch** (2).

nabob *noun.* —*See* **dignitary.**

nadir *noun.* A very low or lowest level, position, or degree ▶ bottom, low, minimum, rock bottom.

nag *verb.* To scold or find fault with constantly ▶ carp at, fuss at, niggle, peck at, pick at. *Informal:* henpeck. [*Compare* **annoy, harass, quibble.**] —*See also* **complain.**

nag *noun.* —*See* **scold.**

nagging *adjective.* —*See* **critical** (1), **painful.**

nail *verb.* —*See* **capture, fasten, hit.**

nail *noun.* A bolt or shaft hammered or drilled in place, used to support or hold together ▶ bolt, peg, pin, rivet, screw, spike, stud, tack. [*Compare* **anchor, cord, fastener.**]

naive *adjective.* —*See* **artless, gullible, superficial.**

naive *noun.* —*See* **innocent** (2).

naiveté *noun.* —*See* **artlessness.**

naked *adjective.* —*See* **bare** (3), **nude.**

nakedness *noun.* —*See* **nudity.**

namby-pamby *adjective.* —*See* **insipid, sentimental.**

namby-pamby *noun.* —*See* **baby** (2).

name *noun.* **1.** The word or words by which one is called and identified ▶ appellation, appellative, cognomen, compellation, denomination, designation, epithet, namesake, nickname, pet name, sobriquet, style, tag, title. *Slang:* handle, moniker. **2.** Public estimation of someone ▶ character, report, reputation, repute. *Informal:* rep. [*Compare* **image, place.**] —*See also* **celebrity.**

name *verb.* **1.** To give a name or title to ▶ baptize, call, christen, denominate, designate, dub, entitle, nickname, style, term, title. ***Idiom:*** give a handle to. [*Compare* **call.**] **2.** To refer to by name ▶ cite, instance, mention, point to, refer to, single out, specify. —*See also* **appoint, call.**

nameless *adjective.* Not known or not widely known by name ▶ obscure, unheard-of, unknown. —*See also* **anonymous.**

namelessness *noun.* —*See* **obscurity.**

namely *adverb.* That is to say ▶ i.e., particularly, scilicet, specifically, videlicet, viz. ***Idioms:*** by way of explanation, in other words, strictly speaking, that is, to wit.

namesake *noun.* —*See* **name** (1).

nap *noun.* A brief sleep ▶ catnap, doze, power nap, siesta, snooze. *Informal:* forty winks. [*Compare* **rest, sleep.**]

nap *verb.* To sleep for a brief period ▶ catnap, doze (off), drop off, nod (off), snooze. ***Idioms:*** catch (*or* grab *or* take) forty winks, get some shuteye. [*Compare* **rest, sleep.**]

narc *noun.* —*See* **police officer.**

narcissism *or* **narcism** *noun.* —*See* **egotism.**

narcissist *noun.* —*See* **egotist.**

narcissistic *adjective.* —*See* **egotistic** (1).

narcotic *noun.* —*See* **drug** (2), **soporific.**

narcotic *adjective.* —*See* **soporific.**

narcotize *verb.* —*See* **drug** (1).

nark *noun.* —*See* **informer.**

narrate *verb.* —*See* **describe.**

narrative *or* **narration** *noun.* —*See* **story** (1).

narrow *adjective.* **1.** Restricted in scope, outlook, or understanding ▶ confined, doctrinaire, dogmatic, inflexible, insular, limited, little, local, narrow-minded, parochial, petty, provincial, small, small-minded, small-town. **2.** Having the restricted outlook often characteristic of geographic isolation ▶ insular, limited, local, narrow-minded, parochial, provincial, small-town. —*See also* **remote** (2), **tight** (4).

narrow *verb.* —*See* **constrict** (1).

narrow-minded *adjective.* —*See* **intolerant** (1), **narrow** (1).

nascence *or* **nascency** *noun.* —*See* **birth** (2).

nastiness *noun.* —*See* **dirtiness, malevolence, obscenity** (1).

nasty *adjective.* So objectionable as to elicit despisal or deserve condemnation ▶ abhorrent, abominable, antipathetic, contemptible, despicable, despisable, detestable, disgusting, filthy, foul, infamous, loathsome, lousy, low, mean, nefarious, obnoxious, odious, repugnant, rotten, shabby, vile, wretched. —*See also* **bleak** (1), **dirty, ill-tempered, malevolent, obscene, offensive** (1).

nation *noun.* —*See* **state** (1).

national *adjective.* —*See* **domestic** (3), **popular.**

national *noun.* —*See* **citizen.**

nationalize *verb.* To place under government or group ownership or control ▶ communalize, socialize.

native *adjective.* —*See* **constitutional, crude, domestic** (3), **indigenous, innate, wild** (1).

native *noun.* —*See* **inhabitant.**

nativity *noun.* —*See* **birth** (1).

natter *verb.* —*See* **chatter** (1).

natty *adjective.* —*See* **neat.**

natural *adjective.* **1.** Produced by nature; not artificial or manmade ▶ additive-free, chemical-free, organic, unadulterated, unprocessed, unsynthetic. ***Idiom:*** pure as the driven snow. [*Compare* **authentic, pure.**] **2.** Of unbroken descent or lineage ▶ direct, genealogical, hereditary, lineal. [*Compare* **ancestral.**] —*See also* **artless, constitutional,**

easygoing, genuine, gifted, illegitimate, realistic (2), rustic, spontaneous, wild (1).

naturalistic *adjective.* —*See* **realistic** (2).

naturalize *verb.* —*See* **domesticate.**

naturalized *adjective.* —*See* **domestic** (2).

naturally *adverb.* —*See* **usually, yes.**

naturalness *noun.* —*See* **artlessness, ease** (1).

nature *noun.* —*See* **character** (1), **disposition, environment** (3), **essence, kind**[2], **universe.**

naughtiness *noun.* —*See* **defiance** (1), **misbehavior.**

naughty *adjective.* —*See* **harmful, improper** (1), **unruly.**

nausea *noun.* —*See* **disgust.**

nauseate *verb.* —*See* **disgust.**

nauseating *adjective.* —*See* **offensive** (1), **unpalatable.**

nautical *or* **naval** *adjective.* ▶ marine, maritime, navigational. [*Compare* **marine.**]

✚ **CORE SYNONYMS:** *nautical, marine, maritime, naval, navigational.* These adjectives mean of or relating to the sea, ships, shipping, sailors, or navigation: *nautical charts; marine insurance; maritime law; a naval officer; navigational hazards.*

---

nave *noun.* —*See* **center** (3).

navel *noun.* —*See* **center** (2).

navigable *adjective.* —*See* **passable.**

navigate *verb.* —*See* **maneuver** (1).

navigator *noun.* —*See* **sailor.**

nay *adverb.* —*See* **no.**

nay *noun.* A negative vote or voter ▶ no. —*See also* **no** (1).

near *adverb.* —*See* **close.**

near *adjective.* —*See* **close** (1), **intimate**[1] (1).

near *verb.* —*See* **approach** (1).

nearby *adjective.* —*See* **close** (1), **convenient** (2).

nearby *adverb.* —*See* **close.**

nearly *adverb.* —*See* **approximately.**

nearness *noun.* The act or fact of coming near ▶ approach, coming, convergence, imminence. [*Compare* **advance, appearance.**]

neat *adjective.* In good order or clean condition ▶ dapper, natty, orderly, prim, shipshape, snug, spick-and-span, spruce, taut, tidy, trig, trim, well-groomed, well-kept, well-ordered. ***Idioms:*** in apple pie order, in good order, neat as a pin. [*Compare* **clean, methodical.**] —*See also* **dexterous, marvelous, methodical, straight.**

✚ **CORE SYNONYMS:** *neat, tidy, trim, shipshape, spick-and-span.* These adjectives mean in good order or clean condition: *Neat* is the most general: *a neat room; neat hair. Tidy* emphasizes precise arrangement and order: *"When she saw me come in tidy and well dressed, she even smiled"* (Charlotte Brontë). *Trim* stresses especially smart appearance: *"A trim little sailboat was dancing out at her moorings"* (Herman Melville). *Shipshape* evokes meticulous order: *"We'll try to make this barn a little more shipshape"* (Rudyard Kipling). *Spick-and-span* suggests the immaculate freshness of something new: *"young men in spick-and-span uniforms"* (Edith Wharton).

---

neaten *verb.* —*See* **tidy** (1), **tidy** (2).

neb *noun.* —*See* **point** (1).

nebbish *noun.* —*See* **nonentity.**

nebulous *adjective.* —*See* **ambiguous** (2).

nebulousness *noun.* —*See* **vagueness.**

necessary *adjective.* —*See* **certain** (1), **essential** (1), **required.**

necessary *noun.* —*See* **condition** (2).

necessitate *verb.* —*See* **demand** (2).

necessitous *adjective.* —*See* **poor.**

necessity *noun.* A condition in which something necessary or desirable is required or wanted ▶ exigence, exigency, need. —*See also* **cause** (2), **condition** (2).

neck *verb. Informal* To engage in kissing, caressing, and other amorous behavior ▶ *Informal:* fool around, pet, spoon. *Slang:* grope, make out. ***Idioms:*** bill and coo, play kissy-face (*or* sucky-face), play post office. [*Compare* **caress, kiss, snuggle.**]

neck *noun.* —*See* **channel.**

neck of the woods *noun.* —*See* **area** (2).

necromancer *noun.* —*See* **wizard.**

need *noun.* A condition in which something necessary or desirable is required or wanted ▶ exigence, exigency, necessity. —*See also* **condition** (2), **demand** (2), **duty** (1), **poverty.**

need *verb.* To be without what is needed, required, or essential ▶ lack, require, want. [*Compare* **demand.**] —*See also* **demand** (2), **must.**

needful *adjective.* —*See* **essential** (1).

neediness *noun.* —*See* **poverty.**

needle *noun.* —*See* **spike.**

needle *verb.* —*See* **harass.**

needless *adjective.* —*See* **unnecessary.**

needy *adjective.* —*See* **poor.**

ne'er-do-well *noun.* —*See* **wastrel** (2).

nefarious *adjective.* —*See* **offensive** (1).

negate *verb.* —*See* **abolish, cancel** (2), **deny.**

negation *noun.* —*See* **abolition, denial** (1).

negative *adjective.* —*See* **unfavorable** (1).

negative *verb.* —*See* **deny, veto.**

neglect *verb.* **1.** To fail to care for or give proper attention to ▶ be lax about, disregard, gloss over, ignore, let slide, let slip, pass over, slight. ***Idioms:*** lose sight (*or* track) of, lie down on the job, turn a blind eye to. **2.** To fail to do or carry out ▶ disregard, fail (to do something), forget, ignore, omit, overlook, shirk. ***Idioms:*** leave undone, let slide, let slip, pass over. —*See also* **snub.**

neglect *noun.* An act or instance of neglecting ▶ disregard, negligence, omission, oversight, slight. [*Compare* **error, negligence.**] —*See also* **failure** (2).

neglectful *adjective.* —*See* **negligent.**

negligence *noun.* The state or quality of being negligent ▶ carelessness, forgetfulness, heedlessness, inattentiveness, laxity, laxness, remissness, slackness, sloppiness, thoughtlessness. [*Compare* **abandon, apathy, failure.**] —*See also* **breach** (1), **neglect.**

negligent *adjective.* Guilty of neglect; lacking due care or concern ▶ derelict, lax, neglectful, remiss, slack, slipshod, sloppy, unconcerned. [*Compare* **careless.**]

✚ **CORE SYNONYMS:** *negligent, derelict, lax, neglectful, remiss, slack.* These adjectives mean guilty of a lack of due care or concern: *an accident caused by a negligent driver; was derelict in his civic responsibilities; lax in attending classes; neglectful of her own financial security; remiss of you not to pay your bill; slack in maintaining discipline.*

---

negligibility *or* **negligibleness** *noun.* —*See* **trifle.**

negligible *adjective.* —*See* **remote** (2), **trivial.**

negotiable *adjective.* —*See* **passable.**

negotiant *noun.* —*See* **go-between.**

negotiate *verb.* To pass by or over successfully ▶ clear, hurdle, surmount. —*See also* **confer** (1), **haggle, settle** (2).

negotiation *noun.* The act or process of dealing with another to reach an agreement ▶ parley, talk. [*Compare* **conversation.**]

negotiator *noun.* —*See* **go-between.**

neighbor *verb.* —*See* **adjoin.**

neighborhood *noun.* **1.** An area in a city or town with distinctive characteristics ▶ area, community, district, quarter, quarters, ward. *Slang:* 'hood. **2.** *Informal* Approximate size or amount ▶ range, vicinity. *Slang:* ballpark. —*See also* **area** (2), **environment** (1), **locality.**

neighboring *adjective.* —*See* **adjoining, close** (1).

neighborly *adjective.* —*See* **amiable, attentive.**
nemesis *noun.* —*See* **opponent.**
neonate *noun.* —*See* **baby** (1).
neophyte *noun.* An entrant who has not yet taken the final vows of a religious order ▶ novice, novitiate, postulant. —*See also* **beginner.**
nerd *noun.* —*See* **drip** (2), **fool.**
nerve *noun.* —*See* **courage, impudence.**
nerve *verb.* —*See* **encourage** (2).
nerviness *noun.* —*See* **impudence.**
nervous *adjective.* —*See* **anxious, edgy.**
nervousness *noun.* —*See* **anxiety** (1), **restlessness.**
nervy *adjective.* —*See* **brave, impudent.**
nescience *noun.* —*See* **ignorance** (1), **ignorance** (2).
nescient *adjective.* —*See* **ignorant** (1).
nest *noun.* —*See* **home** (1).
nest egg *noun.* —*See* **hoard.**
nestle *verb.* —*See* **snuggle.**
net[1] *noun.* —*See* **basket** (3), **web.**
net *verb.* —*See* **capture, catch** (1).
net[2] *verb.* —*See* **return** (3).
nethermost *adjective.* —*See* **bottom.**
netting *noun.* —*See* **web.**
nettle *verb.* —*See* **annoy.**
nettlesome *adjective.* Full of irritating difficulties or controversies ▶ prickly, spiny, thorny. [*Compare* **complex, delicate, disturbing, troublesome.**] —*See also* **disturbing.**
network *noun.* —*See* **complex** (1), **web.**
neurosis *noun.* An exaggerated concern ▶ anxiety, complex, phobia. *Informal:* hang-up. [*Compare* **anxiety, obsession.**]
neuter *adjective.* —*See* **neutral** (1).
neuter *verb.* —*See* **sterilize** (2).
neutral *adjective.* **1.** Not inclining toward or actively taking either side in a matter under dispute ▶ impartial, neuter, nonaligned, nonpartisan, unbiased, uncommitted, uninvolved, unprejudiced. ***Idiom:*** on the fence. [*Compare* **fair, receptive.**] **2.** Without definite or distinctive characteristics ▶ bland, colorless, indistinctive. [*Compare* **boring.**] —*See also* **cold** (2).
neutralize *verb.* —*See* **cancel** (2).
never-ending *adjective.* —*See* **continual, endless** (2).
nevertheless *adverb.* —*See* **still** (1).
new *adjective.* Not the same as what was previously known or done ▶ brand-new, different, fresh, innovative, inventive, newfangled, novel, original, unfamiliar, unprecedented. [*Compare* **contemporary, progressive.**] —*See also* **additional, inexperienced, present**[1]**.**

✚ **CORE SYNONYMS:** *new, fresh, novel, newfangled, original.* These adjectives describe what has existed for only a short time, has only lately come into use, or has only recently arrived at a state or position, as of prominence. *New* is the most general: *a new movie; a new friend. "It is time for a new generation of leadership, to cope with new problems and new opportunities"* (John F. Kennedy). Something *fresh* has qualities of newness such as briskness, brightness, or purity: *fresh footprints in the snow; fresh hope of discovering a vaccine. Novel* applies to the new and strikingly unusual: *"His sermons were considered bold in thought and novel in language"* (Edith Wharton). *Newfangled* suggests that something is needlessly novel: *"the newfangled doctrine of utility"* (John Galt). Something that is *original* is novel and the first of its kind: *"The science of pure mathematics, in its modern development, may claim to be the most original creation of the human spirit"* (Alfred North Whitehead).

---

newborn *noun.* —*See* **baby** (1).
newcomer *noun.* One that arrives ▶ arrival, comer, visitor. [*Compare* **addition, company.**] —*See also* **beginner, foreigner.**
newfangled *adjective.* —*See* **new.**
newfangledness *noun.* —*See* **novelty** (1).
newly *adverb.* —*See* **lately.**

newness *noun.* —*See* **inexperience, novelty** (1).

news *noun.* New information, especially about recent events and happenings ▶ advice, headline, information, intelligence, report, tidings, word. *Informal:* scoop. [*Compare* **notice.**] —*See also* **event** (1).

✚ **CORE SYNONYMS:** *news, advice, intelligence, tidings, word.* These nouns denote new information about recent events and happenings: *just heard the good news; sent advice that the loan was approved; a source of intelligence about the war; tidings of victory; received word of his death.*

---

newscaster *noun.* —*See* **press.**

news flash *noun.* —*See* **item.**

newshound *noun.* —*See* **press.**

newsmonger *noun.* —*See* **gossip** (2).

newspaperman *or* **newspaperwoman** *or* **newsperson** *noun.* —*See* **press.**

next *adjective.* —*See* **adjoining, following** (1).

next *adverb.* —*See* **later.**

nexus *noun.* —*See* **bond** (2).

nib *noun.* —*See* **point** (1).

nibble *verb.* —*See* **browse** (2), **chew.**

nice *adjective.* —*See* **appropriate, delicate** (4), **fine**[1] (2), **fussy, good** (1), **pleasant.**

nicety *noun.* —*See* **detail, ritual, shade** (1).

niche *noun.* The proper or designated location ▶ place. —*See also* **crack** (2), **environment** (3), **habitat.**

nick *verb.* —*See* **cheat** (1), **cut** (1).

nick *noun.* —*See* **cut** (1), **prick.**

nickname *noun.* —*See* **name** (1).

nickname *verb.* —*See* **name** (1).

nictitate *verb.* —*See* **blink.**

nictitation *noun.* —*See* **blink.**

nifty *adjective.* —*See* **marvelous.**

niggard *noun.* —*See* **miser.**

niggard *adjective.* —*See* **stingy.**

niggardly *adjective.* —*See* **stingy.**

niggle *verb.* —*See* **nag, quibble.**

niggler *noun.* —*See* **critic** (2).

niggling *adjective.* —*See* **trivial.**

niggling *noun.* —*See* **quibbling.**

nigh *adverb.* —*See* **close.**

nigh *adjective.* —*See* **close** (1).

night *noun.* The period of time between sunset and sunrise ▶ after dark, after dinner, bedtime, dark, lights out, nighttime, P.M. ***Idioms:*** dark of night, hours of darkness, wee hours (of the night), witching hours. [*Compare* **evening.**]

night *adjective.* Of or occurring during the night ▶ nightly, nocturnal.

nightclub *noun.* —*See* **bar** (2).

nightfall *noun.* —*See* **evening.**

nightly *adjective.* Of or occurring during the night ▶ night, nocturnal.

nightmarish *adjective.* —*See* **horrible.**

nighttime *noun.* —*See* **night.**

nihility *noun.* —*See* **nothingness** (1).

nil *noun.* —*See* **nothing.**

nimble *adjective.* —*See* **dexterous.**

nimbleness *noun.* —*See* **agility, dexterity.**

nimrod *noun.* —*See* **drip** (2).

nincompoop *noun.* —*See* **dullard, fool.**

ninny *noun.* —*See* **fool.**

nip[1] *verb.* To try to bite something quickly or eagerly ▶ snap, snatch, strike. —*See also* **blast** (2), **steal.**

nip *noun.* —*See* **cold.**

nip[2] *noun.* —*See* **drop** (4).

nip *verb.* —*See* **bit**[1] (1), **drink** (2).

nip and tuck *adjective.* **1.** Almost even ▶ tight. ***Idiom:*** neck and neck. **2.** Neither favorable nor unfavorable ▶ balanced, even, fifty-fifty.

nippy *adjective.* —*See* **cold** (1).

nitpick *verb.* —*See* **quibble.**

nitpicker *noun.* —*See* **critic** (2).

nitpicking *noun.* —*See* **quibbling.**

nitty-gritty *noun. Informal* Practical or basic details ▶ brass tacks, details, nuts and bolts, practicalities, specifics. [*Compare* **detail, heart, element.**]

nitwit *noun.* —*See* **dullard, fool.**

nix *noun.* —*See* **nothing.**

nix *adverb.* —*See* **no.**

nix *verb.* —*See* **decline, veto.**

no *adverb.* Not so ▶ nay, not. *Informal:*

nope, noway. *Slang:* negative, nix. ***Idioms:*** by no means, absolutely not, not at all, not on your life, nothing doing.

no *noun.* **1.** A negative response ▶ nay, naysay, refusal, rejection, thumbs-down. *Slang:* no go. [*Compare* **refusal.**] **2.** A negative vote or voter ▶ nay.

no-account *adjective.* —*See* **worthless.**

nobility *noun.* Noble rank or status by birth ▶ birth, blood, blue blood, high blood, noble blood, noblesse, royalty. [*Compare* **ancestry, status.**] —*See also* **society** (1).

noble *adjective.* Of high birth or social position ▶ aristocratic, blue-blooded, elite, gentle, highborn, highbred, imperial, patrician, regal, royal, thoroughbred, titled, upper-class, wellborn. *Informal:* upper-crust. —*See also* **elevated** (3), **exalted, grand.**

noblesse *noun.* —*See* **nobility.**

nobody *pronoun.* No person ▶ none, not anybody, not one, no one. ***Idioms:*** no one at all, not a soul.

nobody *noun.* —*See* **nonentity.**

nocturnal *adjective.* Of or occurring during the night ▶ night, nightly.

nod *verb.* —*See* **assent, bow**[1] (1), **nap.**

nod *noun.* —*See* **acceptance** (1), **bow**[1], **gesture, permission.**

nodding *adjective.* —*See* **sleepy.**

noddle *noun.* —*See* **head** (1).

node *or* **nodule** *noun.* —*See* **bump** (1).

noggin *noun.* —*See* **head** (1).

no-good *adjective.* —*See* **worthless.**

no-good *noun.* —*See* **wastrel** (2).

noise *noun.* **1.** Sounds or a sound, especially when loud, confused, or disagreeable ▶ babel, cacophony, caterwaul, clamor, clangor, din, hubbub, hullabaloo, pandemonium, racket, row, rumpus, tumult, uproar. ***Idiom:*** hue and cry. [*Compare* **disorder, sensation.**] **2.** Vibrations detected by the ear ▶ sonance, sound. [*Compare* **tone.**]

noise *verb.* —*See* **announce, gossip.**

✚ **CORE SYNONYMS:** *noise, din, racket, uproar, pandemonium, hullabaloo, hubbub, clamor, babel.* These nouns refer to loud, confused, or disagreeable sound or sounds. *Noise* is the least specific: *nearly deafened by the noise in the subway.* A *din* is a jumble of loud, usually discordant sounds: *the din of the automobile factory. Racket* is loud, distressing noise: *the racket made by the delivery trucks rolling along cobblestone streets. Uproar, pandemonium,* and *hullabaloo* imply disorderly tumult together with loud, bewildering sound: "*The evening uproar of the howling monkeys burst out*" (W.H. Hudson); "*a pandemonium of dancing and whooping, drumming and feasting*" (Francis Parkman); *a tremendous hullabaloo in the agitated crowd. Hubbub* emphasizes turbulent activity and concomitant din: *the hubbub of bettors, speculators, tipsters, and touts. Clamor* is loud, usually sustained noise, as of a public outcry of dissatisfaction: "*not in the clamor of the crowded street*" (Henry Wadsworth Longfellow); *a debate that was interrupted by a clamor of opposition. Babel* stresses confusion of vocal sounds arising from simultaneous utterance and random mixture of languages: *guests chattering in a babel of tongues at the diplomatic reception.*

---

noiseless *adjective.* —*See* **silent** (1).

noiselessness *noun.* —*See* **silence** (1).

noisome *adjective.* —*See* **harmful, smelly.**

noisy *adjective.* —*See* **loud.**

nomad *noun.* —*See* **hobo.**

nomadic *adjective.* Leading the life of a person without a fixed domicile; moving from place to place ▶ drifting, itinerant, peripatetic, roaming, roving, traveling, vagabond, vagrant, wayfaring, wandering. [*Compare* **migratory, mobile.**]

nominate *verb.* —*See* **appoint.**

nomination *noun.* —*See* **appointment, proposal** (1).

nonaligned *adjective.* —*See* **neutral** (1).

nonappearance *noun.* —*See* **absence** (1).
nonassertive *adjective.* —*See* **shy**[1].
nonattendance *noun.* —*See* **absence** (1).
nonattendant *adjective.* —*See* **absent.**
nonbeing *noun.* —*See* **nothingness** (1).
nonbeliever *noun.* —*See* **skeptic.**
nonchalance *noun.* —*See* **apathy, balance** (2).
nonchalant *adjective.* —*See* **calm, careless.**
noncombustible *adjective.* —*See* **fireproof.**
noncommittal *adjective.* —*See* **reserved.**
noncompliance *noun.* —*See* **defiance** (1).
noncompliant *adjective.* —*See* **unruly.**
non compos mentis *adjective.* —*See* **insane.**
nonconformist *noun.* —*See* **rebel** (2), **separatist.**
nonconformity *noun.* —*See* **difference.**
nondescript *adjective.* —*See* **ordinary.**
nondiscriminatory *adjective.* —*See* **fair**[1] (1).
none *pronoun.* —*See* **nobody.**
nonentity *noun.* A totally insignificant person ▶ cipher, lightweight, menial, nebbish, no-account, nobody, nonperson, nothing, obscurity, scrub, small fry, whippersnapper. *Informal:* pip-squeak, squirt, zero. *Slang:* punk, shrimp, small fish, twerp, zilch. ***Idioms:*** small potatoes, small fish in a big pond. [*Compare* **drip, fool, squirt.**] —*See also* **nothingness** (1).
nonessential *adjective.* —*See* **unnecessary.**
nonesuch *noun.* A person or thing so excellent as to have no equal or match ▶ nonpareil, paragon, phoenix. [*Compare* **best, celebrity, model.**]
nonetheless *adverb.* —*See* **still** (1).
nonevent *noun.* —*See* **disappointment** (2).
nonexistence *noun.* —*See* **nothingness** (1).
nonexistent *adjective.* —*See* **absent.**
nonfeasance *noun.* —*See* **breach** (1), **failure** (2).
nonflammable *adjective.* —*See* **fireproof.**
nonnative *adjective.* —*See* **foreign** (1).
no-nonsense *adjective.* —*See* **practical, serious** (1).
nonpareil *adjective.* —*See* **unique.**
nonpareil *noun.* A person or thing so excellent as to have no equal or match ▶ nonesuch, paragon, phoenix. [*Compare* **best, celebrity, model.**] —*See also* **model.**
nonpartisan *adjective.* —*See* **fair**[1] (1), **neutral** (1).
nonpartisanship *noun.* —*See* **fairness.**
nonperformer *noun.* —*See* **failure** (1).
nonphysical *adjective.* —*See* **immaterial.**
nonplus *verb.* —*See* **baffle.**
nonprofessional *noun.* —*See* **amateur.**
nonprofessional *adjective.* —*See* **amateurish.**
nonresident *noun.* —*See* **foreigner.**
nonresident *adjective.* —*See* **foreign** (1).
nonresistant *adjective.* —*See* **passive.**
nonsense *noun.* Something that does not have or make sense ▶ balderdash, blather, bunkum, claptrap, drivel, foolishness, garbage, hogwash, idiocy, piffle, poppycock, rigmarole, rot, rubbish, senselessness, silliness, tomfoolery, trash, twaddle. *Informal:* tommyrot. *Slang:* applesauce, baloney, bilge, bull, bunk, crap, hooey, malarkey. [*Compare* **emptiness, gibberish.**] —*See also* **babble, foolishness, trifle.**
nonsensical *adjective.* —*See* **foolish.**
nonstop *adjective.* —*See* **continual.**
nonstop *adverb.* —*See* **continually.**
nonuniform *adjective.* —*See* **irregular.**
nonviolent *adjective.* —*See* **peaceable.**
noodle *noun.* —*See* **head** (1).
no one *pronoun.* —*See* **nobody.**

noose *noun.* —*See* **cord, loop, trap** (1).

nope *adverb.* —*See* **no.**

norm *noun.* —*See* **average, standard, usual.**

normal *adjective.* Mentally healthy ▶ compos mentis, lucid, rational, sane. ***Idioms:*** all there, in one's right mind, of sound mind. [*Compare* **healthy.**] —*See also* **common** (1), **conventional, healthy.**

normalcy *or* **normality** *noun.* —*See* **usualness.**

normalize *verb.* —*See* **conventionalize.**

normally *adverb.* —*See* **usually.**

nose *noun.* **1.** The human organ of smell ▶ proboscis. *Informal:* beak, snoot. *Slang:* honker, nozzle, schnoz, schnozzle, smeller, sniffer, snout. **2.** The sense by which odors are perceived ▶ olfaction, scent, smell. —*See also* **discernment.**

nose *verb. Informal* To look into or inquire about curiously, inquisitively, or in a meddlesome fashion ▶ poke, pry, snoop. *Informal:* sniff about (*or* around). ***Idiom:*** stick one's nose into. [*Compare* **meddle.**] —*See also* **smell** (1).

nose out *verb.* —*See* **trace** (1).

nosedive *noun.* —*See* **fall** (1), **fall** (3).

nose-dive *verb.* —*See* **fall** (1), **fall** (4).

nosegay *noun.* —*See* **bouquet.**

nosey *adjective. See* **nosy.**

nosh *noun.* —*See* **refreshment.**

nosiness *noun.* —*See* **curiosity** (2).

nostrum *noun.* —*See* **cure.**

nosy *or* **nosey** *adjective.* —*See* **curious** (1).

not *adverb.* —*See* **no.**

notability *noun.* —*See* **dignitary, fame.**

notable *adjective.* —*See* **exceptional, famous.**

notable *noun.* —*See* **celebrity, dignitary.**

notably *adverb.* —*See* **very.**

notation *noun.* —*See* **note.**

notch *noun. Informal* One of the units in a course, as on an ascending or descending scale ▶ degree, grade, level, peg, point, rung, stage, step. —*See also* **cut** (1), **degree** (1), **prick.**

notch *verb. Informal* To gain a point or points in a game or contest ▶ post, score, tally. ***Idioms:*** make a goal (*or* point). —*See also* **cut** (1).

notched *adjective.* —*See* **saw-toothed.**

note *noun.* A brief record written as an aid to the memory ▶ jotting, memorandum, notation, reminder. *Informal:* memo. —*See also* **comment, commentary, entry, fame, letter, notice** (1), **sign** (1).

note *verb.* —*See* **comment, notice, refer** (1).

noted *adjective.* —*See* **famous.**

noteworthy *adjective.* —*See* **exceptional.**

nothing *noun.* No thing; not anything ▶ naught, nil, null. *Informal:* zero. *Slang:* diddly-squat, goose egg, nix, squat, zilch. —*See also* **nonentity, nothingness** (1).

nothing *adjective.* —*See* **worthless.**

nothingness *noun.* **1.** The condition of not existing ▶ nihility, nonbeing, nonentity, nonexistence, nonsubsistence, nothing, nullity. **2.** Empty, unfilled space ▶ barrenness, blankness, emptiness, vacancy, vacuity, vacuum, void. [*Compare* **deep.**]

notice *noun.* **1.** The act of noting, observing, or taking into account ▶ attention, cognizance, espial, heed, looking, mark, note, observance, observation, regard, remark, seeing, viewing, watching, witnessing. **2.** An announcement distributed on paper to a large number of people ▶ circular, flier, handbill, leaflet. **3.** A report giving information ▶ advisory, bulletin. [*Compare* **report, warning.**] —*See also* **commentary, item, message, sign** (2).

notice *verb.* To perceive with a special effort of the senses or the mind ▶ descry, detect, discern, distinguish, mark, mind, note, observe, recognize, remark, see. [*Compare* **discover, see.**]

✦ **CORE SYNONYMS:** *notice, note, remark, observe.* These verbs mean to perceive with a special effort of the senses or the mind. *Notice, note,* and *remark* suggest close, detailed observation, and *note* in particular implies making a careful, systematic mental recording: *I notice that you're out of sorts. Be careful to note that we turn left at the museum. "Their assemblies afforded me daily opportunities of remarking characters and manners"* (Samuel Johnson). *Observe* emphasizes careful, closely directed attention: *"I saw the pots . . . and observed that they did not crack at all"* (Daniel Defoe).

noticeable *adjective.* Readily attracting notice ▶ arresting, bold, commanding, conspicuous, distinguished, eminent, eye-catching, impressive, marked, observable, outstanding, pointed, prominent, pronounced, remarkable, salient, signal, striking, undisguised. ***Idiom:*** sticking out like a sore thumb. [*Compare* **exceptional, obvious.**] —*See also* **apparent** (1), **perceptible.**

✦ **CORE SYNONYMS:** *noticeable, observable, marked, conspicuous, prominent, outstanding, salient, remarkable, arresting, striking.* These adjectives mean readily attracting notice. *Noticeable* and *observable* both refer to something that can be readily noticed or observed: *"His long, feminine eyelashes were very noticeable"* (Joseph Conrad). *The prowler's movements were observable from the window.* What is *marked* is emphatically evident: *a marked limp; a marked success. Conspicuous* applies to what is immediately apparent and noteworthy: *a conspicuous stain. "Conspicuous consumption of valuable goods is a means of reputability to the gentleman of leisure"* (Thorstein Veblen). *Prominent* and *outstanding* connote a standing out, especially among others of a kind: *the most prominent mountain in the range; the century's outstanding figures.* What is *salient* is so prominent and consequential that it seems to leap out and claim the attention: *"Defenders of the pit bull always seem to miss the salient point that it is the ferocity of the bite, not the number of bites, that has made the dog so feared today"* (Sports Illustrated). *Remarkable* describes what elicits comment because it is unusual or extraordinary: *"This story of Mongolian conquests is surely the most remarkable in all history"* (H.G. Wells). *Arresting* applies to what attracts and holds the attention: *one of Ellington's most arresting compositions. Striking* describes something that seizes the attention and produces a vivid impression on the sight or the mind: *The child bears a striking resemblance to his uncle.*

notification *noun.* —*See* **announcement, message.**

notify *verb.* —*See* **inform** (1).

notion *noun.* —*See* **belief** (1), **fancy, feeling** (1), **idea.**

notional *adjective.* —*See* **imaginary, theoretical** (2).

notoriety *noun.* Unfavorable, usually unsavory renown ▶ disrepute, ill fame, ill repute, infamousness, infamy, notoriousness. —*See also* **fame.**

notorious *adjective.* Known widely and unfavorably ▶ common, disreputable, ill-famed, ill-reputed, infamous. [*Compare* **evil, shady.**] —*See also* **famous.**

notoriousness *noun.* —*See* **notoriety.**

nourish *verb.* To sustain a living organism with food ▶ feast, feed, regale. ***Idiom:*** wine and dine. [*Compare* **support.**] —*See also* **bear** (2), **nurture, promote** (2).

nourishing *adjective.* —*See* **nutritious.**

nourishment *noun.* —*See* **food.**

novel *adjective.* —*See* **new, unusual.**

novel *noun.* A narrative not based on fact ▶ fiction, fable, romance, story. [*Compare* **yarn.**]

novelty *noun.* **1.** The quality of being novel ▶ freshness, imaginativeness, innovativeness, newfangledness, newness, originality, rareness, rarity, recentness, strangeness, uncommonness, uniqueness, unusualness. **2.** A new and unusual thing ▶ innovation. ***Idioms:*** the latest craze (*or* fashion *or* thing), the in thing, whole new ball of wax. **3.** A small showy article ▶ bauble, bibelot, bric-a-brac, curio, gewgaw, gimcrack, gimmick, knickknack, toy, trifle, trinket, whatnot. *Slang:* chachka. [*Compare* **gadget, remembrance.**]

novice *or* **novitiate** *noun.* An entrant who has not yet taken the final vows of a religious order ▶ neophyte, postulant. —*See also* **beginner.**

now *adverb.* **1.** At this moment ▶ actually, at present, currently. ***Idioms:*** even (*or* just *or* right) now, at this instant (*or* moment *or* time), here and now. [*Compare* **soon.**] **2.** At the present; these days ▶ nowadays, today. ***Idioms:*** in our time, in this day and age. —*See also* **immediately** (1).

now *noun.* The current time ▶ nowadays, present, today. ***Idioms:*** modern times, the here and now, the present age (*or* day *or* time).

now *adjective.* —*See* **present**[1].

nowadays *adverb.* At the present; these days ▶ now, today. ***Idioms:*** in our time, in this day and age.

nowadays *noun.* —*See* **now.**

noway *adverb.* —*See* **no.**

noxious *adjective.* —*See* **harmful, poisonous.**

nozzle *noun.* —*See* **nose** (1).

nuance *noun.* —*See* **shade** (1).

nub *noun.* —*See* **bump** (1), **heart** (1).

nuclear *adjective.* —*See* **central.**

nucleus *noun.* —*See* **center** (3), **germ** (2), **heart** (1).

nude *adjective.* Not wearing any clothes ▶ au naturel, bare, disrobed, exposed, naked, stripped, unclad, unclothed, undraped, undressed. ***Idioms:*** buck naked, in one's birthday suit, in the altogether (*or* buff *or* raw), naked as a jaybird, stark naked, without a stitch. —*See also* **bare** (3).

nudeness *noun.* —*See* **nudity.**

nudge *verb.* —*See* **push** (1).

nudge *noun.* —*See* **dig.**

nudity *noun.* The state of being without clothes ▶ bareness, exposure, nakedness, nudeness, undress.

nugatory *adjective.* —*See* **trivial.**

nugget *noun.* —*See* **lump**[1].

nuisance *noun.* —*See* **annoyance** (2).

null *noun.* —*See* **nothing.**

null *adjective.* —*See* **empty** (1).

nullification *noun.* —*See* **abolition.**

nullify *verb.* —*See* **abolish, cancel** (2).

nullity *noun.* —*See* **nothingness** (1).

numb *adjective.* —*See* **dead** (2).

numb *verb.* —*See* **deaden, paralyze.**

number *noun.* An amount represented in numerals ▶ figure, quantity. [*Compare* **total.**] —*See also* **bit**[1] (4), **quantity** (2), **song.**

number *verb.* —*See* **amount, count** (2).

number one *noun.* A leading contestant or sure winner ▶ favorite, front-runner, leader, vanguard. *Informal:* shoo-in.

number one *adjective.* —*See* **primary** (1).

numbers *noun.* Arithmetic calculations ▶ arithmetic, computation, figures. [*Compare* **addition, calculation.**]

numerate *verb.* —*See* **count** (2), **enumerate.**

numeration *noun.* —*See* **count** (1).

numerical *adjective.* —*See* **consecutive.**

numerous *adjective.* —*See* **many.**

numinous *adjective.* —*See* **supernatural** (1).

numskull *noun.* —*See* **dullard.**

nuptial *adjective.* —*See* **marital.**

nuptials *noun.* —*See* **wedding.**

nurse *verb.* —*See* **bear** (2), **nurture.**

nursling *noun.* —*See* **baby** (1).

nurture *verb.* To help grow or develop ▶ cultivate, foster, nourish, nurse, provide for, sustain, tend. [*Compare* **grow, rear**[2], **tend**[2].] —*See also* **promote** (2).

✦ **CORE SYNONYMS:** *nurture, cultivate, foster, nurse.* These verbs mean to promote and sustain the growth and development of someone or something: *nurturing hopes; cultivating tolerance; foster friendly relations; nursed the fledgling business.*

nut *noun.* —*See* **crackpot, fan[2], head** (1).
nutrient *adjective.* —*See* **nutritious.**
nutrition *or* **nutriment** *noun.* —*See* **food.**
nutritious *or* **nutritional** *or* **nutritive** *adjective.* Providing nourishment ▶ alimentary, nourishing, nutrient. [*Compare* **healthful.**]
nuts *adjective.* —*See* **enthusiastic, insane.**
nutty *adjective.* —*See* **insane.**
nuzzle *verb.* —*See* **snuggle.**

O

oaf *noun.* A large, ungainly, and dull-witted person ▶ ape, bear, gawk, hulk, lout, lump, ox. *Informal:* lummox. *Slang:* goon, klutz, lug, meatball, meathead, palooka, schlep, schlub. [*Compare* **blunderer, dullard, fool.**]
oath *noun.* —*See* **curse** (1), **promise** (1), **swearword.**
obduracy *or* **obdurateness** *noun.* —*See* **stubbornness.**
obdurate *adjective.* —*See* **callous, stubborn** (1).
obeah *noun.* —*See* **charm, magic** (1).
obedience *noun.* The quality, state, or act of willingly carrying out the wishes of others ▶ acquiescence, amenability, amenableness, complaisance, compliance, compliancy, deference, dutifulness, observance, submission, submissiveness, tractability, tractableness. [*Compare* **loyalty.**]
obedient *adjective.* Willing to carry out the wishes of others ▶ acquiescent, amenable, biddable, complaisant, compliant, conformable, docile, duteous, dutiful, pliant, submissive, supple, tractable. [*Compare* **deferential, loyal, passive.**]
obeisance *noun.* —*See* **bow[1], honor** (1).
obeisant *adjective.* —*See* **deferential.**
obese *adjective.* —*See* **fat** (1).
obey *verb.* —*See* **follow** (4).
obfuscate *verb.* —*See* **complicate, obscure.**
obiter dictum *noun.* —*See* **comment.**
object *noun.* **1.** Something having material existence ▶ article, body, item, mass, something, thing. *Informal:* thingamabob, thingamajig, thingy. [*Compare* **gadget.**] **2.** A focus of attention, thought, or action ▶ butt, focus, receiver, recipient, subject, target. —*See also* **intention, thing** (1).
object *verb.* To express opposition, often by argument ▶ challenge, demur, except, expostulate, inveigh, oppose, protest, remonstrate, speak up. *Informal:* kick, squawk. [*Compare* **argue, complain, contest, quibble.**] —*See also* **care.**
object to *verb.* —*See* **disapprove.**

✦ **CORE SYNONYMS:** *object, protest, demur, remonstrate, expostulate.* These verbs mean to express opposition to something, usually by presenting arguments against it. *Object* implies the expression of disapproval or distaste: "*Freedom of the press in Britain is freedom to print such of the proprietor's prejudices as the advertisers don't object to*" (Hannen Swaffer). *Protest* suggests strong opposition, usually forthrightly expressed: *The citizens protested against the tax hike.* To *demur* is to raise an objection that may delay decision or action: *We proposed a revote, but the president demurred. Remonstrate* implies the presentation of objections, complaints, or reproof: "*The people of Connecticut . . . remonstrated against the bill*" (George Bancroft). To *expostulate* is to express objection in the form of earnest reasoning: *The teacher expostulated with them on the foolhardiness of their behavior.*

---

objectification *noun.* —*See* **embodiment.**

objectify *verb.* —*See* **embody** (1).

objection *noun.* An expression of opposition ▶ argument, challenge, complaint, demur, demurral, disagreement, dispute, exception, expostulation, fuss, grievance, problem, protest, protestation, remonstrance, remonstration. *Slang:* kick.

objectionable *adjective.* Arousing disapproval ▶ disagreeable, exceptionable, ill-favored, improper, inadmissible, unacceptable, undesirable, unsuitable, unwanted, unwelcome. [*Compare* **deplorable, offensive.**]

objective *adjective.* —*See* **fair**[1] (1), **physical, real** (1), **realistic** (1).

objective *noun.* —*See* **intention.**

objectively *adverb.* —*See* **fairly** (1).

objectivity *noun.* —*See* **fairness.**

object lesson *noun.* —*See* **example** (2).

objurgate *verb.* —*See* **chastise.**

oblation *noun.* —*See* **offering.**

obligate *verb.* To oblige to do or not do by force of authority, propriety, or custom ▶ expect, oblige, require, suppose. [*Compare* **must.**] —*See also* **commit** (2), **force** (1).

obligated *adjective.* —*See* **obliged** (1), **obliged** (2).

obligation *noun.* —*See* **debt** (1), **debt** (2), **duty** (1).

obligatory *adjective.* —*See* **required.**

oblige *verb.* **1.** To perform a service or a courteous act for ▶ accommodate, aid, assist, favor, help, indulge, serve. **2.** To cause to do or not do by force of authority, propriety, or custom ▶ expect, obligate, require, suppose. [*Compare* **must.**] —*See also* **commit** (2), **force** (1).

✚ **CORE SYNONYMS:** *oblige, accommodate, favor, indulge.* These verbs mean to perform a service or a courteous act for: *obliged me by keeping the matter quiet; accommodating her by lending her money; favor an audience with an encore; indulged the twins by allowing them to stay up late.*

---

obliged *adjective.* **1.** Owing something, such as gratitude, to another ▶ beholden, grateful, indebted, obligated, thankful. ***Idiom:*** in someone's debt. **2.** Being legally or morally required to do something ▶ bound, committed, compelled, constrained, impelled, obligated, pledged, required, sworn. ***Idioms:*** duty (*or* honor) bound, under contract, under oath, under obligation. [*Compare* **liable.**]

obliging *adjective.* Ready to do favors for another ▶ accommodating, agreeable, complaisant, considerate, generous, helpful, indulgent. [*Compare* **amiable, obedient, willing.**]

oblique *adjective.* At an angle ▶ angled, askew, aslant, beveled, bias, biased, canted, diagonal, inclined, leaning, listing, pitched, raked, skewed, slanted, slanting, sloped, sloping, tilted. [*Compare* **transverse.**] —*See also* **indirect** (1).

obliterate *verb.* —*See* **annihilate, cancel** (1), **destroy** (2).

obliteration *noun.* —*See* **annihilation, erasure.**

oblivion *noun.* —*See* **obscurity.**

oblivious *adjective.* —*See* **absent-minded, ignorant** (3).

obliviousness *noun.* —*See* **ignorance** (2).

oblong *adjective.* —*See* **oval.**

obloquy *noun.* —*See* **disgrace, libel, vituperation.**

obnoxious *adjective.* —*See* **offensive** (1).

obscene *adjective.* Offensive to accepted standards of decency ▶ barnyard, bawdy, broad, coarse, dirty, filthy, foul, gross, indecent, lewd, nasty, profane, ribald, scatologic, scatological, scurrilous, smutty, vulgar. *Slang:* raunchy. [*Compare* **erotic, racy.**] —*See also* **outrageous.**

obscenity *noun.* **1.** The quality or state of being obscene ▶ bawdiness, coarseness, dirtiness, filthiness, foulness, grossness, indecentness, lewdness, nastiness, profaneness, profanity, scurrility, scurrilousness, smuttiness, vulgarity, vulgarness. *Slang:* raunch, raunchiness. **2.** Something that is offensive to accepted standards of decency ▶ bawdry, dirt, filth, pornography, profanity, ribaldry, scatology, sleaze, smut, vulgarity. *Slang:* porn, raunch. [*Compare* **impropriety.**] —*See also* **swearword.**

obscure *adjective.* **1.** Not widely understood ▶ abstruse, arcane, cabalistic, esoteric, occult, recondite. [*Compare* **mysterious.**] **2.** Not widely known ▶ insignificant, little-known, undistinguished, unheard-of, unknown. [*Compare* **anonymous, remote.**] —*See also* **ambiguous** (1), **ambiguous** (2), **dark** (1), **inconspicuous, unclear.**

obscure *verb.* To make dim or unclear ▶ adumbrate, becloud, bedim, befog, blear, blur, cloud, dim, dull, eclipse, fog, gloom, mist, obfuscate, overcast, overshadow, shadow. [*Compare* **shade.**] —*See also* **block, conceal.**

obscured *adjective.* —*See* **hidden** (1), **ulterior** (1).

obscurity *noun.* The quality or state of being little known ▶ anonymity, insignificance, namelessness, oblivion, obscureness, unimportance. —*See also* **dark, vagueness.**

obsequies *noun.* —*See* **funeral.**

obsequious *adjective.* —*See* **servile.**

observable *adjective.* —*See* **apparent** (1), **noticeable, perceptible, visible.**

observance *noun.* The act of observing, often for an extended time ▶ observation, scrutiny, watch, watching. —*See also* **celebration** (2), **ceremony** (1), **custom, notice** (1), **obedience.**

observant *adjective.* —*See* **alert, careful** (1).

observation *noun.* The act of observing, often for an extended time ▶ observance, scrutiny, watch, watching. —*See also* **comment, notice** (1).

observatory *noun.* —*See* **lookout** (2).

observe *verb.* **1.** To mark a day or an event with ceremonies of respect, festivity, or rejoicing ▶ celebrate, commemorate, keep, solemnize. [*Compare* **sanctify.**] **2.** To pay regular and close attention to ▶ follow, monitor, stake out, survey, watch. ***Idioms:*** have one's (*or* keep an) eye on, keep tabs on, keep track of, ride herd on. —*See also* **comment, discover, follow** (4), **notice, watch** (1).

observer *noun.* —*See* **watcher** (1).

obsess *verb.* **1.** To come to mind continually ▶ haunt, torment, trouble, weigh on (*or* upon). **2.** To dominate the mind or thoughts of ▶ fixate, possess, preoccupy. [*Compare* **absorb, grip.**]

obsessed *adjective.* —*See* **infatuated.**

obsession *noun.* An irrational preoccupation ▶ compulsion, fascination, fetish, fixation, infatuation, mania. *Informal:* thing. ***Idiom:*** bee in one's bonnet. [*Compare* **complex, enthusiasm.**]

obsessive *adjective.* —*See* **enthusiastic, voracious.**

obsessiveness *noun.* —*See* **voracity.**

obsolescent *adjective.* —*See* **obsolete.**

obsolete *adjective.* No longer in use ▶ obsolescent, outdated, outmoded, out-of-date, superannuated, superseded. ***Idioms:*** in mothballs, on the shelf. [*Compare* **old-fashioned.**]

obsoleteness *noun.* The quality or state of being obsolete ▶ desuetude, disuse, obsoletism, outdatedness, outmodedness.

obstacle *noun.* —*See* **bar** (1), **difficulty.**

obstinacy *noun.* —*See* **stubbornness, unruliness.**

obstinate *adjective.* Difficult to alleviate or cure ▶ persistent, pertinacious, stubborn. —*See also* **stubborn** (1), **unruly** (1).

obstinateness *noun.* —*See* **stubbornness, unruliness.**

obstreperous *adjective.* —*See* **disorderly, unruly, vociferous.**

obstreperousness *noun.* —*See* **unruliness.**

obstruct *verb.* To block or fill with obstacles ▶ bar, barricade, block, blockade, choke, clog, dam. ***Idioms:*** close (*or* cut) off, put obstacles in the way (*or* path) of, stand in the way (*or* path) of. —*See also* **block, disrupt, hinder.**

✚ **CORE SYNONYMS:** *obstruct, block, dam, bar.* These verbs mean to block or fill with obstacles. *Obstruct* is the most general: *A building obstructed our view of the mountains. Block* refers to complete obstruction that prevents progress, passage, or action: *"Do not block the way of inquiry"* (Charles S. Peirce). *Dam* suggests obstruction of the flow, progress, or release of something: *She dammed the brook to form a pool. He dammed up his emotions.* To *bar* is to prevent entry or exit or prohibit a course of action: *The legislature passed laws that bar price fixing.*

obstruction *noun.* —*See* **bar** (1), **difficulty.**

obtain *verb.* —*See* **get** (1).

obtainable *adjective.* —*See* **available.**

obtrude *verb.* —*See* **intrude, meddle.**

obtrusion *noun.* An excessive, unwelcome burden ▶ encumbrance, imposition, infliction, intrusion. [*Compare* **burden.**] —*See also* **meddling, trespass** (2).

obtrusive *adjective.* —*See* **curious** (1).

obtuse *adjective.* —*See* **blind** (3), **dull** (3), **stupid.**

obtuseness *noun.* —*See* **stupidity.**

obviate *verb.* —*See* **prevent.**

obviation *noun.* —*See* **prevention.**

obvious *adjective.* Easily seen through due to a lack of subtlety ▶ blatant, broad, clear, overt, patent, plain, transparent, undisguised, unmistakable, unsubtle. ***Idiom:*** sticking out like a sore thumb. —*See also* **apparent** (1).

occasion *noun.* **1.** The general point at which an event occurs ▶ instant, juncture, moment, point, stage, time. ***Idiom:*** point in time. [*Compare* **period.**] **2.** That which produces an effect ▶ antecedent, cause, determinant, reason. [*Compare* **impact, origin, stimulus.**] —*See also* **cause** (2), **circumstance** (1), **event** (1), **opportunity, party.**

occasion *verb.* —*See* **cause, justify** (2).

occasional *adjective.* —*See* **infrequent, intermittent.**

occasionally *adverb.* —*See* **infrequently, intermittently.**

occult *adjective.* —*See* **mysterious, obscure** (1).

occult *verb.* —*See* **hide**[1]**.**

occupancy *noun.* The holding of something, such as a position ▶ incumbency, occupation, tenure. [*Compare* **period.**]

occupant *noun.* —*See* **inhabitant.**

occupation *noun.* The holding of something, such as a position ▶ incumbency, occupancy, tenure. [*Compare* **period.**] —*See also* **business** (2).

occupied *adjective.* —*See* **busy** (1).

occupy *verb.* **1.** To live in a place, as does a people ▶ inhabit, people, populate. [*Compare* **live, settle.**] **2.** To seize or maintain control over by conquest ▶ capture, colonize, conquer, hold, invade, overrun, seize, subjugate, take over. ***Idiom:*** take possession of. [*Compare* **control.**] **3.** To make busy ▶ busy, employ, engage. —*See also* **absorb** (1), **live**[1]**.**

occur *verb.* —*See* **happen** (1).

occur to *verb.* —*See* **strike** (2).

occurrence *noun.* The condition or fact of being present ▶ attendance, presence. [*Compare* **existence.**] —*See also* **circumstance** (1), **event** (1).

ocean *noun.* A body of salt water covering a large part of the earth's surface ▶ brine, briny, deep, high seas, main, sea.

oceanic *adjective.* —*See* **marine** (1).

ocular *adjective.* Serving, resulting from, or relating to the sense of sight ▶ optic, optical, seeing, visual.

odd *adjective.* Agreeably curious, especially in an old-fashioned or unusual way ▶ curious, funny, quaint. —*See also* **accidental, eccentric, funny** (3).

oddball *noun.* —*See* **character** (5).

oddity *noun.* —*See* **abnormality, character** (5).

oddly *adverb.* —*See* **unusually.**

oddments *noun.* —*See* **odds and ends.**

odds *noun.* —*See* **advantage** (1), **chance** (3).

odds and ends *noun.* Articles too small or numerous to be specified ▶ bits and pieces, etceteras, incidentals, junk, miscellanea, oddments, sundries, things. [*Compare* **assortment.**] —*See also* **end** (3).

odious *adjective.* —*See* **offensive** (1).

odiousness *noun.* —*See* **ugliness.**

odium *noun.* —*See* **disgrace, hate** (1).

odor *noun.* The quality of something that may be perceived by smelling ▶ aroma, scent, smell. [*Compare* **fragrance, stench.**] —*See also* **track.**

odorous *or* **odoriferous** *adjective.* —*See* **fragrant, smelly.**

odyssey *noun.* —*See* **adventure, expedition, journey.**

off *adjective.* —*See* **absent, erroneous, insane, slow** (2).

off *verb.* —*See* **murder.**

offbeat *adjective.* —*See* **unusual.**

off-color *adjective.* —*See* **racy, sick** (1).

offend *verb.* **1.** To cause anger, resentment, or hurt feelings in ▶ affront, anger, annoy, chagrin, displease, hurt, injure, insult, miff, outrage, pique, provoke, put out, scandalize, upset, wound, wrong. [*Compare* **anger, annoy, stagger.**] **2.** To be very disagreeable or displeasing to ▶ disgust, displease, put off, repel, repulse, upset. *Slang:* turn off. ***Idioms:*** give offense to, not sit right (*or* well) with. **3.** To violate a rule or law ▶ err, sin, transgress, trespass. ***Idioms:*** break the law (*or* rules), go astray. —*See also* **insult.**

✚ **CORE SYNONYMS:** *offend, insult, affront, outrage.* These verbs mean to cause someone to feel anger, resentment, humiliation, or hurt. To *offend* is to cause displeasure, wounded feelings, or repugnance in another: *"He often offended men who might have been useful friends"* (John Lothrop Motley). *Insult* implies gross insensitivity, insolence, or contemptuous rudeness: *"I . . . refused to stay any longer in the room with him, because he had insulted me"* (Anthony Trollope). To *affront* is to insult openly, usually intentionally: *"He continued to belabor the poor woman in a studied effort to affront his hated chieftain"* (Edgar Rice Burroughs). *Outrage* implies the flagrant violation of a person's integrity, pride, or sense of right and decency: *"Agnes . . . was outraged by what seemed to her Rose's callousness"* (Mrs. Humphry Ward).

---

offender *noun.* —*See* **criminal.**

offense *noun.* Extreme displeasure caused by an insult or slight ▶ bad feelings, displeasure, dudgeon, huff, hurt, miff, pique, resentment, ruffled feathers, umbrage. [*Compare* **anger.**] —*See also* **attack, crime** (1), **crime** (2), **indignity, injustice** (1).

offensive *adjective.* **1.** So unpleasant or objectionable as to cause scorn or disgust ▶ abhorrent, abominable, antipathetic, atrocious, contemptible, despicable, despisable, detestable, disgusting, filthy, foul, hateful, horrid, infamous, loathsome, lousy, low, mean, nasty, nauseating, nefarious, obnoxious, odious, repellent, repugnant, repulsive, revolting, rotten, shabby, sickening, stomach-churning, ugly, unwholesome, vile, wretched. [*Compare* **bad, deplorable, disgraceful, obscene.**] **2.** Causing displeasure, anger, or hurt feelings ▶ discourteous, displeasing, hurtful, impertinent, impolite, insulting, rude, uncivil.

[*Compare* **impudent, objectionable.**] —*See also* **unpleasant.**

offensive *noun.* —*See* **attack.**

✚ **CORE SYNONYMS:** *offensive, hateful, detestable, odious, repellent.* These often interchangeable adjectives describe a person or thing that is so unpleasant or objectionable as to cause scorn or disgust. *Offensive* applies to what offends or excites displeasure: *an offensive suggestion. Hateful* refers to what evokes hatred or deep animosity: *"No vice is universally as hateful as ingratitude"* (Joseph Priestley). *Detestable* applies to what arouses abhorrence or scorn: *detestable crimes against humanity.* Something *odious* is the object of disgust, aversion, or intense displeasure: *"a kind of slimy stuff . . . of a most nauseous, odious smell"* (Daniel Defoe). Something *repellent* arouses repugnance or disgust: *repellent criminal behavior.*

---

offer *verb.* **1.** To put before another for acceptance ▶ advance, extend, hold out, present, proffer, put forward, put up, render, submit, tender, turn in, volunteer. ***Idioms:*** come forward with, hand to on a silver plate (*or* platter), lay before, lay at someone's feet. [*Compare* **donate.**] **2.** To make something readily available ▶ afford, furnish, make available, present, provide, render, supply. ***Idioms:*** place (*or* put) at one's disposal. [*Compare* **allow.**] **3.** To have for sale ▶ carry, deal (in), keep, stock. [*Compare* **sell.**] **4.** To make an offer of ▶ bid. *Informal:* go. —*See also* **propose.** *verb* **1.** To offer as a sacrifice ▶ immolate, sacrifice, victimize.

offer *noun.* An act of offering or the thing offered ▶ bid, invitation, presentation, proffer, tender. [*Compare* **proposal.**] —*See also* **attempt.**

✚ **CORE SYNONYMS:** *offer, proffer, tender, present.* These verbs mean to put before another for acceptance or rejection. *Offer* is the basic general term in this group: *offered us some tea; a store that offered sizable discounts. Proffer* implies voluntary action motivated especially by courtesy or generosity: *"Mr. van der Luyden . . . proffered to Newland low-voiced congratulations"* (Edith Wharton). To *tender* is to offer formally: *tendered her respects; tendered my resignation. Present* suggests formality and often a measure of ceremony: *"A footman entered, and presented . . . some mail on a silver tray"* (Winston Churchill).

---

offering *noun.* Something, especially a slain animal or group of animals, presented to a deity as an act of worship ▶ hecatomb, immolation, oblation, sacrifice, victim. —*See also* **donation.**

offhand *adjective.* —*See* **extemporaneous, glib.**

office *noun.* —*See* **branch** (3), **ceremony** (1), **position** (3), **task** (1).

officer *noun.* —*See* **executive, police officer.**

official *adjective.* —*See* **authoritative** (1), **ceremonious, governmental.**

official *noun.* —*See* **executive.**

officiate *verb.* To peform assigned or official duties ▶ act as, function as, serve as.

officious *adjective.* —*See* **curious** (1).

offish *adjective.* —*See* **cool.**

offset *noun.* —*See* **compensation.**

offset *verb.* —*See* **balance** (2), **cancel** (2).

offshoot *noun.* —*See* **branch** (1), **derivative, shoot.**

offspring *noun.* —*See* **progeny.**

off-the-cuff *adjective.* —*See* **extemporaneous.**

often *adverb.* —*See* **usually.**

ogle *verb. Informal* To make an excessive show of desire for or interest in ▶ *Informal:* drool over, slobber over. [*Compare* **adore, desire, flirt, lust, rave.**] —*See also* **gaze.**

ogre *noun.* —*See* **fiend.**

ogreish *adjective.* —*See* **fiendish.**

oil *noun.* A substance that is generally slippery, combustible, and not water-soluble ▶ crude, grease, lube, lubricant, petroleum, unction. [*Compare* **fat, ointment, slime.**] —*See also* **flattery.**

oil *verb.* To apply oil to something ▶ anoint, grease, lube, lubricate. [*Compare* **smear.**]

oily *adjective.* —*See* **fatty, slick, unctuous.**

ointment *noun.* A substance used on the skin to soothe or heal ▶ balm, cream, emollient, liniment, lotion, salve, unction, unguent.

OK *or* **okay** *noun.* —*See* **acceptance** (1), **permission.**

OK *or* **okay** *verb.* —*See* **permit** (2).

OK *or* **okay** *adverb.* —*See* **yes.**

OK *or* **okay** *adjective.* —*See* **acceptable** (2).

old *adjective.* **1.** Belonging to, existing, or occurring in times long past ▶ age-old, ancient, antediluvian, antiquated, antique, archaic, bygone, of yore, olden, old-time, timeworn, venerable. ***Idioms:*** old as Methuselah (*or* the hills *or* time). [*Compare* **early, shabby.**] **2.** Far along in life or time ▶ advanced, aged, aging, elder, elderly, grizzled, hoary, mature, older, senescent, senior. ***Idioms:*** getting along (*or* on) in years, long in the tooth, no spring chicken, over the hill. [*Compare* **senile.**] —*See also* **continuing, experienced, late** (2), **old-fashioned.**

old *noun.* —*See* **past.**

✚ **CORE SYNONYMS:** *old, ancient, archaic, antediluvian, antique, antiquated.* These adjectives describe what belongs to or dates from an earlier time or period. *Old* is the most general term: *old lace; an old saying. Ancient* pertains to the distant past: "*the hills,/Rock-ribbed, and ancient as the sun*" (William Cullen Bryant). *Archaic* implies a very remote, often primitive period: *an archaic Greek bronze of the seventh century* BC. *Antediluvian* applies to what is extremely outdated: "*a branch of one of your antediluvian families*" (William Congreve). *Antique* is applied to what is especially appreciated or valued because of its age: *antique furniture; an antique vase. Antiquated* describes what is out of date, no longer fashionable, or discredited: "*No idea is so antiquated that it was not once modern. No idea is so modern that it will not someday be antiquated*" (Ellen Glasgow).

---

old age *noun.* —*See* **age** (1).

old boy *noun.* —*See* **father.**

olden *adjective.* —*See* **old** (1).

older *adjective.* —*See* **old** (2).

old-fashioned *adjective.* Of a style or method formerly in vogue ▶ antiquated, antique, archaic, dated, dowdy, frumpish, frumpy, fusty, old, old-time, out, outdated, outmoded, out-of-date, passé, unfashionable. ***Idioms:*** old hat, old school. [*Compare* **obsolete, trite, vintage.**]

old hand *noun.* One who has had long experience in a given activity or capacity ▶ past master, vet, veteran. *Informal:* old-timer. [*Compare* **expert.**]

old lady *noun.* —*See* **girlfriend, mother.**

old-line *adjective.* —*See* **confirmed** (1), **ultraconservative.**

old maid *noun.* —*See* **prude.**

old man *noun.* —*See* **boyfriend, father.**

oldster *noun.* —*See* **senior** (2).

old-time *adjective.* —*See* **old-fashioned, old** (1).

old-timer *noun. Informal* One who has had long experience in a given activity or capacity ▶ old hand, past master, vet, veteran. [*Compare* **expert.**] —*See also* **senior** (2).

oleaginous *adjective.* —*See* **fatty, unctuous.**

olfaction *noun.* The sense by which odors are perceived ▶ nose, scent, smell.

oligarch *noun.* —*See* **dictator.**

olio *noun.* —*See* **assortment.**

omen *noun.* A phenomenon that serves as a sign or warning of some future good or evil ▶ augury, foreboding, forerunner, foreshadowing, foretoken, forewarning, harbinger, portent, prefigurement, presage, prognostic, prognostication, sign, thundercloud, warning. ***Idioms:*** writing (*or* handwriting) on the wall. [*Compare* **prediction, sign, threat.**]

ominous *adjective.* —*See* **fateful** (1).

omission *noun.* —*See* **error, failure** (2), **neglect.**

omit *verb.* —*See* **drop** (5), **neglect** (2).

omnipotence *noun.* —*See* **authority.**

omnipresent *adjective.* Ever present in all places ▶ ubiquitous, universal. [*Compare* **rampant.**]

omnivorous *adjective.* —*See* **voracious.**

omnivorousness *noun.* —*See* **voracity.**

omphalos *noun.* —*See* **center** (2).

once *adverb.* —*See* **earlier** (1).

once *adjective.* —*See* **late** (2).

once again *adverb.* —*See* **anew.**

once-over *noun.* —*See* **examination** (1).

one *adjective.* —*See* **lone.**

one-dimensional *adjective.* —*See* **superficial.**

one-liner *noun.* —*See* **joke** (1).

oneness *noun.* **1.** The condition of being one ▶ singleness, singularity, unity. **2.** An identity or coincidence of interests, purposes, or sympathies among the members of a group ▶ concord, solidarity, union, unity. [*Compare* **alliance, union.**] **3.** The quality or condition of being exactly the same as something else ▶ identicalness, identity, sameness, selfsameness. [*Compare* **likeness.**] —*See also* **completeness, uniqueness.**

onerous *adjective.* —*See* **burdensome.**

one-sided *adjective.* —*See* **biased.**

one-sidedness *noun.* —*See* **bias.**

onetime *adjective.* —*See* **late** (2).

one-up *verb. Informal* To outmaneuver an opponent ▶ finesse, trump. ***Idioms:*** play gotcha, pull (*or* put over) a fast one. [*Compare* **deceive, maneuver, outwit.**] —*See also* **surpass.**

ongoing *adjective.* —*See* **continual.**

onlooker *noun.* —*See* **watcher** (1).

only *adjective.* —*See* **lone, unique.**

only *adverb.* Nothing more than ▶ but, just, merely, simply. [*Compare* **barely.**] —*See also* **solely.**

onomatopoeia *noun.* The formation of words in imitation of sounds ▶ echoism, mimesis.

onomatopoetic *or* **onomatopoeic** *adjective.* Imitating sounds ▶ echoic, imitative, mimetic.

onrush *noun.* —*See* **attack.**

onset *noun.* —*See* **attack, birth** (2).

onslaught *noun.* —*See* **attack, charge** (1), **tirade.**

onus *noun.* —*See* **blame, burden**[1] (1), **duty** (1), **stain.**

onward *adverb.* —*See* **forward.**

onyx *adjective.* —*See* **black** (1).

oodles *noun.* —*See* **heap** (2).

oomph *noun.* —*See* **spirit** (1).

ooze *verb.* To flow or leak out or emit something slowly ▶ bleed, discharge, exude, leach, leak, percolate, seep, sweat, transpire, transude, weep. [*Compare* **drip, flow.**]

ooze *noun.* —*See* **slime.**

oozy *adjective.* —*See* **slimy.**

open *adjective.* **1.** Not closed, sealed, or fastened ▶ agape, ajar, cracked, unbuttoned, unbuckled, unclosed, undone, unlaced, unlocked, untied, unzipped, wide. [*Compare* **loose, yawning.**] **2.** Not covered ▶ exposed, revealed, spread, unconcealed, uncovered, unfurled, unprotected, unrolled, unsheltered. [*Compare* **apparent, perceptible.**] **3.** Not restricted or confined to few ▶ free, nonexclusive, open-door, public, unrestricted. [*Compare* **common.**] **4.** Available for use or occupation ▶ accessible, employable, free, operable, operative, practicable, unfilled, uninhabited, unoccupied, unreserved, usable, utilizable, vacant, vacated. [*Compare* **available, empty.**] —*See also* clear (3), frank, indefinite (2), liable (2), receptive.

open *verb.* **1.** To become or cause to become open ▶ crack, free, release, throw wide, unbutton, unbuckle, unclose, undo, unfasten, unlace, unlock, untie, unzip. [*Compare* **reveal, undo.**] **2.** To rid of obstructions ▶ clear, free, remove, unblock. [*Compare* **rid.**] —*See also* **spread** (1), **start** (1).

open-door *adjective.* —*See* **open** (3).

open-eyed *adjective.* —*See* **alert.**

openhanded *adjective.* —*See* **generous** (1).

openhandedness *noun.* —*See* **generosity.**

opening *noun.* —*See* **beginning, birth** (2), **hole** (2), **opportunity.**

opening *adjective.* —*See* **beginning.**

open-minded *adjective.* —*See* **broad-minded, receptive.**

open-mindedness *noun.* —*See* **openness.**

openness *noun.* Ready acceptance of new suggestions, ideas, or opinions ▶ amenability, amenableness, open-mindedness, receptiveness, receptivity, responsiveness. [*Compare* **acceptance.**] —*See also* **exposure, honesty.**

operable *adjective.* —*See* **open** (4).

operate *verb.* To control or direct the functioning of ▶ employ, handle, manage, run, use, utilize, wield, work. [*Compare* **administer, drive, govern, maneuver.**] —*See also* **conduct** (1), **function.**

operating *adjective.* —*See* **active.**

operation *noun.* —*See* **behavior** (2), **exercise** (1), **mission** (1).

operational *adjective.* In effect ▶ effective, operative. ***Idioms:*** in force (*or* operation). —*See also* **usable.**

operative *adjective.* In effect ▶ effective, operational. ***Idioms:*** in force (*or* operation). —*See also* **active, open** (4).

operative *noun.* —*See* **laborer, spy.**

operator *noun.* **1.** A person who operates a motor vehicle ▶ chauffeur, driver, motorist. **2.** One who speculates for quick profits ▶ adventurer, gambler, speculator.

opiate *noun.* —*See* **drug** (2), **soporific.**

opiate *adjective.* —*See* **soporific.**

opiate *verb.* —*See* **drug** (1).

opine *verb.* —*See* **believe** (3), **comment.**

opinion *noun.* —*See* **belief** (1), **doctrine, ruling.**

opinionated *adjective.* —*See* **biased, intolerant** (1).

opponent *noun.* One that opposes the purposes or interests of another ▶ adversary, antagonist, archenemy, dissenter, enemy, foe, nemesis, opposer, opposition, oppositionist, resister. —*See also* **competitor.**

✚ **CORE SYNONYMS:** *enemy, foe, opponent.* These nouns denote one who is hostile to or opposes the purposes or interests of another: *betrayed by enemies; a foe of fascism; a political opponent.*

---

opportune *adjective.* Suited for a particular purpose or occurring at a suitable time ▶ auspicious, favorable, fortuitous, fortunate, propitious, prosperous, seasonable, timely, well-timed. [*Compare* **appropriate, convenient.**]

opportunity *noun.* A favorable or advantageous combination of circumstances ▶ break, chance, main chance, moment, occasion, opening, option. *Informal:* shot. ***Idioms:*** big moment, chance of a lifetime, day in the sun. [*Compare* **turn.**]

✚ **CORE SYNONYMS:** *opportunity, occasion, opening, chance, break.* These nouns refer to a favorable or advantageous circumstance or combination of circumstances. *Opportunity* is an auspicious state of affairs or a suitable time: *"If you prepare yourself . . . you will be able to grasp opportunity for broader experience when it appears"* (Eleanor Roosevelt). *Occasion* suggests the proper time for action: *an auspicious occasion; an occasion for celebration.* An *opening* is an opportunity affording a good possibility of success: *waited patiently for her opening, then exposed the report's inconsistency. Chance* often implies an opportunity that arises through luck or accident: *a chance for us to chat; no chance of losing.* A *break* is an often sudden piece of luck, especially good luck: *got his first big break in Hollywood.*

---

oppose *verb.* To place in opposition or be in opposition to ▶ combat, counter, fight, match, pit, play off, resist, stand against, withstand. ***Idioms:*** bump heads with, meet head-on, mount (*or* offer) resistance, put up a fight, set (*or* be) at odds, set (*or* be) at someone's throat, stand in the way of, stand up to. [*Compare* **contend, hinder.**] —*See also* **balance** (2), **conflict, contest, defy** (1), **disobey, object.**

✚ **CORE SYNONYMS:** *oppose, fight, combat, resist, withstand.* These verbs mean to place someone or something in opposition to another. *Oppose* has the widest application: *The community opposed the building of a nuclear power plant. "The idea is inconsistent with our constitutional theory and has been stubbornly opposed . . . since the early days of the Republic"* (E.B. White). *Fight* and *combat* suggest vigor and aggressiveness: *"All my life I have fought against prejudice and intolerance"* (Harry S. Truman). *"We are not afraid . . . to tolerate any error so long as reason is left free to combat it"* (Thomas Jefferson). To *resist* is to strive to fend off or offset the actions, effects, or force of: *"Pardon was freely extended to all who had resisted the invasion"* (John R. Green). *Withstand* often implies successful resistance: *"Neither the southern provinces, nor Sicily, could have withstood his power"* (Henry Hallam).

---

opposed *adjective.* —*See* **indisposed, opposing.**

opposer *noun.* —*See* **opponent.**

opposing *adjective.* Acting against or in opposition ▶ adversarial, adverse, antagonistic, antipathetic, conflicting, countervailing, opposed, oppositional, resistant, unfavorable. ***Idioms:*** at odds, in opposition to. [*Compare* **contrary, hostile.**] —*See also* **opposite.**

opposite *adjective.* Diametrically opposed ▶ antipodal, antipodean, antithetical, antonymic, antonymous, contradictory, contrary, contrasting, converse, counter, diametric, diametrical, incompatible, inverse, irreconcilable, opposing, polar, reverse. —*See also* **discrepant.**

opposite *noun.* That which is diametrically opposed to another ▶ antipode, antipodes, antithesis, antonym, contradiction, contradictory, contrapositive, contrary, converse, counter, inverse, reverse.

✚ **CORE SYNONYMS:** *opposite, contrary, antithetical, contradictory.* These adjectives mean marked by a natural or innate and irreconcilable opposition. Two things that are altogether different are *opposite: Antonyms are words of opposite meaning. "It is said that opposite characters make a union happiest"* (Charles Reade). *Contrary* stresses extreme divergence: *Democrats and Republicans often hold contrary opinions. Antithetical* emphasizes diametrical opposition: *engaged in practices entirely antithetical to their professed beliefs. Contradictory* implies denial or inconsistency: *"contradictory attributes of unjust justice and loving vindictiveness"* (John Morley).

---

opposite number *noun.* One that has the same functions and characteristics as another ▶ counterpart, equivalent, vis-à-vis.

opposition *noun.* **1.** The act or condition of conflict ▶ antagonism, antithesis, aversion, combat, contradiction, contradistinction, contraposition, contrariety, contrariness, polarity. [*Com-

pare **conflict, enmity.**] **2.** The act of resisting ▶ renitence, renitency, resistance. **3.** A clandestine organization of freedom fighters in an oppressed land ▶ resistance, underground. *—See also* **indisposition, opponent.**

oppositional *adjective.* *—See* **opposing.**

oppositionist *noun.* *—See* **opponent.**

oppress *verb.* To treat arbitrarily or cruelly ▶ grind (down), trample. [*Compare* **enslave, suppress.**] *—See also* **abuse** (1), **burden[1], depress.**

oppression *noun.* Cruel exercise of power ▶ domination, injustice, persecution, repression, subjugation. [*Compare* **cruelty, slavery.**] *—See also* **tyranny.**

oppressive *adjective.* *—See* **burdensome.**

oppressor *noun.* *—See* **dictator.**

opprobrious *adjective.* *—See* **abusive, disgraceful.**

opprobrium *noun.* *—See* **disgrace, rebuke.**

oppugn *verb.* *—See* **deny.**

opt *verb.* *—See* **choose** (1).

optic *or* **optical** *adjective.* Serving, resulting from, or relating to the sense of sight ▶ ocular, seeing, visual.

optics *noun.* *—See* **vision** (1).

optimal *adjective.* *—See* **best** (1).

optimism *noun.* A tendency to expect a favorable outcome or to dwell on hopeful aspects ▶ assurance, cheerfulness, enthusiasm, hopefulness, sanguineness, sanguinity. [*Compare* **sureness.**]

optimist *noun.* One who expects a favorable outcome or dwells on hopeful aspects ▶ Pangloss, Pollyanna, positivist. [*Compare* **dreamer.**]

optimistic *adjective.* Expecting or suggesting a favorable outcome ▶ assured, cheerful, confident, enthusiastic, Panglossian, positive, roseate, rose-colored, rosy, sanguine, upbeat. ***Idioms:*** looking on the bright side, looking through rose-colored glasses. [*Compare* **encouraging, idealistic.**]

optimum *adjective.* *—See* **best** (1).

option *noun.* *—See* **choice, opportunity.**

optional *adjective.* Not compulsory or automatic ▶ discretionary, elective, facultative, noncompulsory, nonobligatory, permissible, possible. [*Compare* **voluntary.**]

opulence *noun.* *—See* **wealth.**

opulent *adjective.* *—See* **luxurious, profuse.**

opus *noun.* *—See* **composition** (1), **publication** (2).

oracle *noun.* *—See* **prophecy, prophet.**

oracular *adjective.* *—See* **prophetic.**

oral *adjective.* Expressed or produced in speech or by the voice ▶ articulate, phonetic, phonic, pronounced, spoken, unwritten, uttered, verbal, vocal, voiced, word-of-mouth.

orate *verb.* *—See* **rant.**

oration *noun.* *—See* **speech** (2).

orator *noun.* *—See* **speaker** (1).

oratorical *adjective.* Characterized by elevated language, such as that used in public speaking ▶ aureate, bombastic, declamatory, elocutionary, eloquent, flowery, fustian, grandiloquent, high-flown, high-sounding, inflated, magniloquent, orotund, overblown, rhetorical, sonorous.

oratory *noun.* The art of public speaking ▶ declamation, elocution, rhetoric, speech. [*Compare* **bombast, eloquence.**]

orb *noun.* **1.** The celestial body where humans live ▶ earth, globe, planet, world. **2.** An organ of vision ▶ eye, eyeball. *Slang:* peeper, saucer. ***Idiom:*** window of the soul. *—See also* **ball.**

orbicular *adjective.* *—See* **round** (1).

orbit *noun.* *—See* **area** (1), **circle** (2), **range** (1), **revolution** (1).

orbit *verb.* *—See* **encircle, turn** (1).

orchestrate *verb.* *—See* **compose** (1), **harmonize** (2).

ordain *verb.* *—See* **dictate, establish** (2).

ordained *adjective.* *—See* **divine** (2).

ordeal *noun.* *—See* **trial** (1).

order *noun.* —*See* **arrangement** (1), **class** (1), **class** (2), **command** (1), **demand** (1), **kind**[2], **method, series, shape, union** (1).

order *verb.* —*See* **arrange** (1), **boss, command** (1), **demand** (1).

orderliness *noun.* —*See* **method.**

orderly *adjective.* —*See* **methodical, neat.**

orders of the day *noun.* —*See* **program** (1).

ordinance *noun.* —*See* **ceremony** (1), **law** (1).

ordinarily *adverb.* —*See* **usually.**

ordinariness *noun.* —*See* **usualness.**

ordinary *adjective.* Being of no special quality or type ▶ average, bland, boring, common, commonplace, cut-and-dried, formulaic, garden, garden-variety, homely, humdrum, indifferent, mediocre, middling, mundane, nondescript, plain, routine, run-of-the-mill, so-so, standard, stock, undistinguished, unexceptional, unremarkable, white-bread. *Informal:* ho-hum. ***Idioms:*** fair-to-middling, no great shakes. [*Compare* **acceptable, humble, modest.**] —*See also* **common** (1).

ordinary *noun.* —*See* **usual.**

organ *noun.* —*See* **agent, branch** (3), **publication** (2).

organic *adjective.* —*See* **natural** (1).

organization *noun.* —*See* **alliance, arrangement** (1), **foundation, method, system, union** (1).

organizational *adjective.* —*See* **administrative.**

organize *verb.* —*See* **arrange** (1), **arrange** (2), **found, mobilize.**

organized *adjective.* —*See* **methodical.**

orgy *noun.* —*See* **binge.**

orientation *noun.* —*See* **bearing** (3).

orifice *noun.* —*See* **hole** (2).

oriflamme *noun.* —*See* **flag**[1].

origin *noun.* A point of origination ▶ beginning, birthplace, cradle, derivation, font, fount, fountain, fountainhead, hotbed, mother, parent, provenance, provenience, rise, root, rootstock, source, spring, well, wellspring. [*Compare* **germ.**] —*See also* **ancestry, birth** (2).

✚ **CORE SYNONYMS:** *origin, source, root.* These nouns signify the point at which something originates. *Origin* is the point at which something comes into existence: *The origins of some words are unknown.* When *origin* refers to people, it means parentage or ancestry: *"He came . . . of mixed French and Scottish origin"* (Charlotte Brontë). *Source* signifies the point at which something springs into being or from which it derives or is obtained: *"The mysterious . . . is the source of all true art and science"* (Albert Einstein). *Root* often denotes what is considered the fundamental cause of or basic reason for something: *"Lack of money is the root of all evil"* (George Bernard Shaw).

---

original *adjective.* Not derived from something else ▶ archetypal, archetypical, primary, prime, primitive, pristine, prototypic, prototypical, seminal. [*Compare* **elemental.**] —*See also* **authentic** (1), **first, inventive, new, radical.**

original *noun.* A first form from which varieties arise or imitations are made ▶ archetype, father, forerunner, master, model, paradigm, pattern, protoplast, prototype, standard. —*See also* **character** (5), **rebel** (2).

originality *noun.* —*See* **invention** (1), **novelty** (1).

originate *verb.* To have as one's home or place of origin ▶ hail, come. [*Compare* **descend.**] —*See also* **begin, design** (1), **found, introduce** (1), **produce** (1), **stem.**

origination *noun.* —*See* **beginning, foundation, invention** (2).

originator *noun.* One that creates, founds, or originates ▶ architect, author, begetter, creator, father, framer, founder, initiator, inventor, maker, parent, patriarch, prime mover. [*Compare* **developer.**]

orison *noun.* —*See* **prayer**[1] (2).

ornament *noun.* —*See* **adornment.**

ornament *verb.* —*See* **adorn** (1).

ornamentation *noun.* —*See* **adornment.**

ornate *adjective.* Elaborately and heavily ornamented ► baroque, decorated, flamboyant, florid, flowery, gilded, gilt, jeweled, ornamented, ostentatious, resplendent, rococo. [*Compare* **gaudy, showy.**] —*See also* **elaborate.**

orneriness *noun.* —*See* **temper** (1).

ornery *adjective.* —*See* **contrary.**

orotund *adjective.* —*See* **oratorical, resonant.**

orotundity *noun.* —*See* **bombast.**

orphan *noun.* A child or young animal without parents ► foundling, ragamuffin, stray, waif.

ort *noun.* —*See* **bit**[1] (1), **end** (3).

orthodox *adjective.* —*See* **accepted, conservative** (1), **conventional.**

orthodox *noun.* —*See* **conservative.**

orthodoxy *noun.* —*See* **doctrine.**

oscillate *verb.* —*See* **sway.**

osculate *verb.* —*See* **kiss.**

osculation *noun.* —*See* **kiss.**

osmose *verb.* —*See* **drink** (3).

osmosis *noun.* —*See* **absorption** (1).

ossify *verb.* —*See* **harden** (2).

ossuary *noun.* —*See* **grave**[1].

ostensible *or* **ostensive** *adjective.* —*See* **apparent** (2).

ostensibly *or* **ostensively** *adverb.* —*See* **apparently.**

ostentation *noun.* —*See* **pretentiousness.**

ostentatious *adjective.* —*See* **ornate, showy.**

ostracism *noun.* —*See* **exile.**

ostracize *verb.* —*See* **banish, exclude.**

other *adjective.* —*See* **additional.**

otherworldly *adjective.* —*See* **supernatural** (1), **weird.**

otiose *adjective.* —*See* **hollow** (1), **lazy.**

otiosity *or* **otioseness** *noun.* —*See* **laziness.**

ottoman *noun.* A stool or cushion for resting the feet ► footrest, footstool, hassock.

ought *verb.* —*See* **must.**

ounce *noun.* —*See* **bit**[1] (1).

oust *verb.* —*See* **eject** (1).

ouster *noun.* —*See* **ejection.**

out *verb.* To be made public ► break, come out, get out, transpire. *Informal:* leak (out). [*Compare* **air, announce, appear.**]

out *adjective.* —*See* **absent, old-fashioned, unconscious.**

out *adverb.* —*See* **forward.**

outage *noun.* A cessation or suspension of proper functioning ► breakdown, collapse, failure, malfunction. [*Compare* **collapse.**]

out-and-out *adjective.* —*See* **utter**[2].

outback *noun.* —*See* **wilderness.**

outbreak *noun.* —*See* **eruption, outburst.**

outburst *noun.* A sudden violent expression, as of emotion ► access, blowup, burst, dambreak, damburst, eruption, explosion, fit, flare-up, flood, gush, gust, outbreak, outpouring, paroxysm, torrent. —*See also* **eruption.**

outcast *noun.* Someone excluded from society ► exile, outsider, pariah, persona non grata, reject, untouchable. [*Compare* **fugitive.**]

outcast *adjective.* —*See* **abandoned** (1).

outcome *noun.* —*See* **effect** (1).

outcry *noun.* —*See* **shout, vociferation.**

outdated *adjective.* —*See* **obsolete, old-fashioned.**

outdo *verb.* —*See* **surpass.**

outdoors *noun.* —*See* **wilderness.**

outermost *adjective.* —*See* **extreme** (1).

outfit *noun.* Things needed for a task, journey, or other purpose ► accouterments, apparatus, equipment, gear, material, materiel, paraphernalia, rig, tackle, turnout. —*See also* **company** (1), **dress** (2).

outfit *verb.* —*See* **dress** (1), **furnish.**

✤ CORE SYNONYMS: *outfit, apparatus, equipment, gear, materiel, paraphernalia.* These nouns denote the materials needed for a task, journey, or other purpose: *an explorer's outfit; laboratory apparatus; hiking equipment; skiing gear; naval materiel; a beekeeper's paraphernalia.*

outflow *noun.* —*See* **flow.**

outfox *verb.* —*See* **outwit.**

outgoing *adjective.* Disposed to be open, sociable, and talkative ▶ communicable, communicative, expansive, extroverted, gregarious, unreserved. [*Compare* **amiable, friendly, social.**]

outgrowth *noun.* —*See* **bump** (1), **derivative.**

outgun *verb.* —*See* **defeat.**

outing *noun.* A usually short journey taken for pleasure ▶ excursion, jaunt, junket, trip. [*Compare* **excursion, journey.**]

outlander *noun.* —*See* **foreigner.**

outlandish *adjective.* —*See* **eccentric, exotic.**

outlast *verb.* To live, exist, or remain longer than ▶ outlive, outwear, survive. [*Compare* **survive.**]

outlaw *verb.* —*See* **forbid.**

outlaw *noun.* One who flees, as from confinement or the police ▶ escapee, fugitive, refugee, runaway. —*See also* **criminal.**

outlawed *adjective.* —*See* **illegal.**

outlay *noun.* —*See* **cost** (1), **overhead.**

outlay *verb.* —*See* **spend** (1).

outlet *noun.* **1.** A socket connected to a power supply ▶ plug, electric socket, socket, terminal, wall socket. **2.** A retail establishment where merchandise is sold ▶ boutique, emporium, shop, store. —*See also* **hole** (2).

outline *noun.* —*See* **draft** (1), **form** (1), **synopsis.**

outline *verb.* —*See* **design** (2), **draft** (1).

outlive *verb.* To live, exist, or remain longer than ▶ outlast, outwear, survive. [*Compare* **survive.**]

outlook *noun.* Chance of success or advancement ▶ future, prospects. [*Compare* **chance.**] —*See also* **lookout** (2), **posture** (2), **prediction, view** (2), **viewpoint.**

outlying *adjective.* —*See* **remote** (1).

outmaneuver *verb.* —*See* **outwit.**

outmatch *verb.* —*See* **surpass.**

outmoded *adjective.* —*See* **obsolete, old-fashioned.**

outmost *adjective.* —*See* **extreme** (1).

out-of-date *adjective.* —*See* **obsolete, old-fashioned.**

out of sight *adjective.* —*See* **exceptional.**

out-of-the-way *adjective.* —*See* **indirect** (1), **remote** (1).

outpace *verb.* —*See* **pass** (2).

outplay *verb.* —*See* **defeat.**

outpour *noun.* —*See* **flow.**

outpouring *noun.* —*See* **flow, outburst.**

output *noun.* The amount or quantity produced ▶ garner, production, yield. —*See also* **composition** (1).

outrage *noun.* A monstrous offense or evil ▶ atrocity, barbarity, enormity, horror, inhumanity, monstrosity. [*Compare* **crime.**] —*See also* **anger, indignity, injustice** (1).

outrage *verb.* —*See* **insult, offend** (1).

outrageous *adjective.* Exceeding the bounds of morality, decency, or reason ▶ appalling, atrocious, heinous, inhuman, intolerable, monstrous, obscene, preposterous, reprehensible, ridiculous, scandalous, shocking, unconscionable, ungodly, unreasonable, unspeakable, wanton. ***Idioms:*** beyond the pale, out of bounds, out of sight. [*Compare* **eccentric, excessive, flagrant, offensive, shameful.**]

outrageousness *noun.* The quality or state of being outrageous ▶ atrociousness, atrocity, enormity, heinousness, monstrousness, scandalousness. [*Compare* **flagrancy.**]

outré *adjective.* —*See* **exotic.**

outright *adjective.* —*See* **utter**[2]**.**

outrun *verb.* —*See* **lose** (3), **pass** (2), **surpass.**

outset *noun.* —*See* **birth** (2).

outshine *verb.* —*See* **surpass.**

outside *noun.* —*See* **maximum.**

outside *adjective.* —*See* **remote** (2).

outsider *noun.* —*See* **foreigner, outcast.**

outsize *adjective.* —*See* **big.**

outskirts *noun.* The periphery of a city or town ▶ city limits, edge, environs, exurbs, fringe, skirts, suburbs, town line. [*Compare* **border, limits.**]

outsmart *verb.* —*See* **outwit.**

outspoken *adjective.* —*See* **frank.**

outstanding *adjective.* —*See* **due** (1), **exceptional, noticeable.**

outstretch *verb.* To put forward, especially an appendage ▶ extend, reach, stretch (out). —*See also* **spread** (1).

outstretched *adjective.* —*See* **long**[1] (1).

outstrip *verb.* —*See* **pass** (2), **surpass.**

outthink *verb.* —*See* **outwit.**

outward *adjective.* —*See* **apparent** (2).

outwardly *adverb.* —*See* **apparently.**

outwear *verb.* To live, exist, or remain longer than ▶ outlast, outlive, survive. [*Compare* **survive.**]

outweigh *verb.* —*See* **cancel** (2).

outwit *verb.* To get the better of by cleverness or cunning ▶ outfox, outguess, outmaneuver, outsmart, outthink, overreach, second-guess, take in. ***Idioms:*** get the better of, put one over on. [*Compare* **baffle, confuse, deceive.**]

oval *adjective.* Resembling an egg in shape ▶ egg-shaped, ellipsoidal, elliptical, oblong, ovate, oviform, ovoid, ovoidal.

oval *noun.* An egg-shaped form or figure ▶ egg-shape, ellipse, ellipsoid, ovoid.

ovate *adjective.* —*See* **oval.**

ovation *noun.* Approval expressed by clapping ▶ applause, hand, plaudit. ***Idiom:*** round of applause. —*See also* **testimonial** (2).

over *noun.* —*See* **complete** (3).

overabundance *noun.* —*See* **excess** (1).

overabundant *adjective.* —*See* **excessive.**

over again *adverb.* —*See* **anew.**

overage *noun.* —*See* **surplus.**

overall *adjective.* —*See* **general** (2).

overambitious *adjective.* —*See* **ambitious.**

overbear *verb.* —*See* **dominate** (2).

overbearing *adjective.* —*See* **arrogant, dictatorial.**

overbearingness *noun.* —*See* **arrogance.**

overblown *adjective.* —*See* **exaggerated, fat** (1), **inflated, oratorical.**

overcast *verb.* —*See* **obscure, shade** (2).

overcharge *verb.* —*See* **cheat** (1), **exaggerate.**

overcoat *noun.* —*See* **coat** (1).

overcome *verb.* —*See* **defeat, overwhelm** (1), **overwhelm** (2).

overcome *adjective.* —*See* **anxious.**

overconfidence *noun.* —*See* **impudence.**

overconfident *adjective.* —*See* **impudent.**

overcritical *adjective.* —*See* **critical** (1).

overcrowded *adjective.* Filled beyond capacity ▶ choked, congested, overflowing, overpopulated, swarming, teeming. [*Compare* **full, tight.**]

overdo *verb.* To do, use, or stress something to excess ▶ overindulge, overreach, overwork, stretch, strain. ***Idioms:*** bite off more than one can chew, carry too far (*or* to extremes), do to death, go overboard (*or* too far *or* to extremes), kill oneself, knock oneself out. [*Compare* **exaggerate, exceed.**]

overdrawn *adjective.* —*See* **exaggerated.**

overdue *adjective.* —*See* **late** (1).

overeater *noun.* A person who eats or consumes immoderate amounts of food and drink ▶ glutton, hog, pig. [*Compare* **sybarite.**]

overemphasize *verb.* —*See* **belabor, exaggerate.**

overestimate *verb.* —*See* **miscalculate.**

overflow *verb.* —*See* **flood** (1), **teem**[1].

overflow *noun.* —*See* **flood, surplus.**

overflowing *adjective.* —*See* **full** (1), **overcrowded.**

overgenerosity *noun.* —*See* **extravagance.**

overgrown *adjective.* —*See* **thick** (3).

overhang *verb.* —*See* **bulge, threaten** (2).

overhang *noun.* —*See* **projection.**

overhaul *verb.* To reorganize thoroughly or drastically ▶ reconfigure, reengineer, reshuffle, shake up. ***Idioms:*** clean house, make a clean sweep. [*Compare* **renew, restore.**] —*See also* **fix** (1), **pass** (2).

overhaul *noun.* A thorough or drastic reorganization ▶ reengineering, reshuffling, shakeup. *Informal:* housecleaning. ***Idiom:*** clean sweep. [*Compare* **renewal, revolution.**]

overhead *noun.* The expenses associated with running an enterprise ▶ budget, costs, expenses, operating costs, operating expenses, outlay.

overindulge *verb.* —*See* **baby, overdo.**

overindulgence *noun.* —*See* **excess** (2).

overjoy *verb.* —*See* **delight** (1).

overjoyed *adjective.* —*See* **elated.**

overlay *verb.* —*See* **color** (2), **cover** (1).

overlay *noun.* —*See* **coat** (2).

overleap *verb.* —*See* **exceed.**

overlong *adjective.* —*See* **long**[1] (2).

overlook *verb.* To view broadly or from a height ▶ look over, scan, survey. [*Compare* **look.**] —*See also* **blink at, dominate** (2), **forgive, neglect** (2), **supervise.**

overlook *noun.* —*See* **lookout** (2).

overlord *noun.* —*See* **chief.**

overly *adverb.* —*See* **unduly.**

overmuch *adjective.* —*See* **excessive.**

overmuch *adverb.* —*See* **unduly.**

overmuch *noun.* —*See* **surplus.**

overpass *verb.* —*See* **exceed.**

overpopulated *adjective.* —*See* **overcrowded.**

overpower *verb.* —*See* **overwhelm** (1), **overwhelm** (2).

overpowering *adjective.* —*See* **intense, smelly.**

overpriced *adjective.* —*See* **steep**[1] (2).

overreach *verb.* —*See* **exceed, outwit, overdo.**

overrefined *adjective.* —*See* **prudish.**

overripe *adjective.* —*See* **bad** (2).

overrun *verb.* —*See* **exceed, invade** (1), **occupy** (2).

overrun *noun.* —*See* **surplus.**

oversee *verb.* —*See* **supervise.**

overseer *noun.* —*See* **boss.**

oversensitive *adjective.* Quick to take offense or become angry or upset ▶ hypersensitive, sensitive, thin-skinned, ticklish, touchy. [*Compare* **ill-tempered.**]

oversensitivity *adjective.* Quickness to take offense ▶ hypersensitivity, sensitivity, ticklishness, touchiness. ***Idiom:*** thin skin. [*Compare* **temper.**]

overshadow *verb.* —*See* **dominate** (2), **obscure, shade** (2).

overshoot *verb.* —*See* **exceed.**

oversight *noun.* —*See* **error, management, neglect.**

oversize *or* **oversized** *adjective.* —*See* **bulky** (1).

overspread *verb.* —*See* **cover** (1).

overstate *verb.* —*See* **exaggerate.**

overstated *adjective.* —*See* **exaggerated.**

overstatement *noun.* —*See* **exaggeration.**

overstep *verb.* —*See* **exceed, violate** (1).

overstock *noun.* —*See* **surplus.**

oversufficiency *noun.* —*See* **excess** (1).

oversupply *noun.* —*See* **surplus.**

overt *adjective.* —*See* **obvious.**

overtake *verb.* To come up even with another ▶ catch (up), pull alongside, pull even. [*Compare* **approach, equalize.**] —*See also* **pass** (2).

overthrow *verb.* To bring about the downfall of ▶ bring down, depose, overturn, subvert, topple, tumble, unhorse, upset. [*Compare* **defeat.**] —*See also* **overturn.**

overthrow *noun.* —*See* **defeat, upset.**

✚ CORE SYNONYMS: *overthrow, overturn, subvert, topple, upset.* These verbs mean to cause the downfall, destruction, abolition, or undoing of: *overthrow an empire; overturn existing institutions; subverting civil order; toppled the government; upset all our plans.*

overture *noun.* —*See* **advances, introduction.**

overturn *verb.* To turn or cause to turn from a vertical or horizontal position ▶ capsize, invert, knock over, overthrow, tip over, topple, turn over, upend, upset, upturn. —*See also* **lift** (3), **overthrow.**

overturn *noun.* —*See* **upset.**

overturned *adjective.* —*See* **upside-down.**

overused *adjective.* —*See* **trite.**

overview *noun.* A general or comprehensive view or treatment ▶ survey. [*Compare* **synopsis.**]

overweening *adjective.* —*See* **arrogant, dictatorial.**

overweight *adjective.* —*See* **fat** (1).

overwhelm *verb.* **1.** To render totally ineffective by decisive defeat ▶ crush, drub, overcome, overpower, rout, smash, steamroller, thrash, trounce. *Informal:* clobber, massacre, wallop, whip. *Slang:* cream, murder, shellac, skunk, smear. ***Idioms:*** clean someone's clock, eat someone alive, eat someone's lunch, kick someone's butt, take to the cleaners. [*Compare* **annihilate, defeat.**] **2.** To affect deeply or completely, as with emotion ▶ crush, engulf, overcome, overpower, pierce, prostrate. [*Compare* **daze, stagger.**] **3.** To affect as if by an outpouring of water ▶ deluge, flood, inundate, swamp. —*See also* **break** (2), **flood** (1).

overwhelming *adjective.* —*See* **astonishing, intense.**

overwork *verb.* —*See* **overdo.**

overworked *adjective.* —*See* **trite.**

overwrought *adjective.* —*See* **anxious.**

oviform *adjective.* —*See* **oval.**

ovoid *noun.* —*See* **oval.**

ovoid *or* **ovoidal** *adjective.* —*See* **oval.**

owed *or* **owing** *adjective.* —*See* **due** (1).

owing to *preposition.* —*See* **because of.**

own *verb.* —*See* **acknowledge** (1), **command** (2).

owner *noun.* A person who has legal title to property ▶ holder, landlady, landlord, master, possessor, proprietor, titleholder.

ownership *noun.* The fact of possessing or the legal right to possess something ▶ deed, dominion, possession, proprietorship, title.

ox *noun.* —*See* **oaf.**

P

pa *noun.* —*See* **father.**

pabulum *noun.* —*See* **food.**

pace *noun.* Rate of motion or performance ▶ speed, tempo, velocity. *Informal:* clip. —*See also* **walk** (2).

pace *verb.* —*See* **walk.**

pacific *or* **pacifical** *adjective.* —*See* **peaceable, still.**

pacifist *or* **pacifistic** *adjective.* —*See* **peaceable.**

pacify *verb.* To ease the anger or agitation of ▶ allay, appease, assuage, becalm, calm (down), conciliate, dulcify, gentle, lull, mollify, placate, propitiate, quiet, settle, soften, soothe, still, sweeten, tranquilize. ***Idiom:*** pour oil on troubled water. [*Compare* **moderate, satiate.**]

✚ CORE SYNONYMS: *pacify, mollify, conciliate, appease, placate.* These verbs refer to easing another's anger, belligerence, discontent, or agitation. To *pacify* is to restore calm to or establish peace in: "*The explanation . . . was merely an invention framed to pacify his guests*" (Charlotte Brontë). *An army was required in order to pacify the islands. Mollify* stresses the soothing of hostile feelings: *The therapist mollified the angry teenager by speaking gently. Conciliate* implies winning over, often by reasoning and with mutual concessions: "*A wise government knows how to enforce with temper or to conciliate with dignity*" (George Grenville). *Appease* and *placate* suggest satisfying claims or demands or tempering antagonism, often by granting concessions: *I appeased my friend's anger with a compliment. A sincere apology placated the indignant customer.*

pack *noun.* **1.** A container carried on the back or around the waist ▶ backpack, belly pack, daypack, fanny pack, haversack, kit, knapsack, rucksack, waist pack. **2.** An organized group of criminals, hoodlums, or wrongdoers ▶ band, gang, ring. *Informal:* mob. —*See also* **abundance, crowd, flock.**

pack *verb.* —*See* **carry** (1), **carry** (2), **fill** (1).

package *verb.* To cover and tie something, as with paper and string ▶ do up, wrap.

package *noun.* Something wrapped or enclosed, as for transporting ▶ box, bundle, carton, crate, mailer, packet, parcel, tin. [*Compare* **container.**]

packaging *noun.* —*See* **wrapper.**

packed *adjective.* —*See* **full** (1), **thick** (2).

packet *noun.* —*See* **package.**

packing *noun.* —*See* **filler** (1).

pact *noun.* —*See* **agreement** (1), **treaty.**

pad *noun.* —*See* **home** (1).

padding *noun.* —*See* **filler** (1).

paddock *noun.* —*See* **pen**[2].

padre *noun.* —*See* **cleric.**

paean *noun.* —*See* **praise** (1).

pagan *noun.* One who does not believe in God ▶ atheist, heathen, infidel, nonbeliever. —*See also* **sybarite.**

pagan *adjective.* Without belief in God ▶ heathen. [*Compare* **atheistic.**]

pageant *noun.* —*See* **array.**

pageantry *noun.* —*See* **celebration** (3), **glitter** (2).

pain *noun.* A sensation of physical discomfort occurring as the result of disease or injury ▶ ache, burn, cramp, crick, gripes, pang, prick, prickle, shoot, smart, soreness, spasm, stab, sting, stitch, throe, twinge. *Informal:* misery. [*Compare* **harm.**] —*See also* **annoyance** (2), **burden**[1] (1), **distress.**

pain *verb.* —*See* **afflict, distress, hurt** (3).

✦ **CORE SYNONYMS:** *pain, ache, pang, smart, stitch, throe, twinge.* These nouns denote a sensation of severe physical discomfort: *abdominal pain; aches in my leg; the pangs of a cramped muscle; aspirin that alleviated the smart; a stitch in my side; the throes of dying; a twinge of arthritis.*

painful *adjective.* Marked by, causing, or experiencing physical pain ▶ aching, achy, afflictive, hurtful, inflamed, irritating, nagging, raw, smarting, sore, stabbing, stinging, tender. [*Compare* **grievous, tormenting, uncomfortable.**] —*See also* **bitter** (3).

pains *noun.* —*See* **effort, thoroughness.**

painstaking *adjective.* —*See* **careful** (2), **diligent.**

painstaking *noun.* —*See* **thoroughness.**

paint *noun.* —*See* **color** (2), **finish.**

paint *verb.* —*See* **finish** (2).

pair *noun.* —*See* **couple.**

paired *adjective.* Consisting of two identical or similar related things, parts, or elements ▶ double, dual, matched, twin. [*Compare* **equal.**]

pal *noun.* —*See* **associate** (2), **friend.**

pal *verb.* —*See* **associate** (2).

paladin *noun.* A person revered especially for noble courage ▶ champion, hero, heroine. ***Idiom:*** knight in shining armor. [*Compare* **winner.**]

palatable *adjective.* Fit to be eaten ▶ comestible, eatable, edible, esculent. —*See also* **acceptable** (2), **delicious.**

palatial *adjective.* —*See* **grand, luxurious.**

palaver *noun.* —*See* **chatter.**

palaver *verb.* —*See* **chatter** (1).

pale *adjective.* **1.** Lacking color ▶ ashen, ashy, bloodless, cadaverous, colorless, doughy, etiolated, faded, livid, lurid, pallid, pastel, pasty, sallow, wan, washed out, waxen, waxy, whey-faced. ***Idioms:*** green about the gills, white as a sheet. [*Compare* **dull, haggard, sick.**] **2.** Being weak in quality or substance ▶ anemic, bloodless, dim, effete, faint, flimsy, pallid, sickly, thin, waterish, watery, weak. [*Compare* **insipid, weak.**] —*See also* **fair[1]** (3).

pale *verb.* To lose normal coloration; turn pale ▶ blanch, bleach, etiolate, fade, peak, sallow, wan, wash out, whiten.

palinode *noun.* —*See* **retraction.**

palliate *verb.* —*See* **extenuate, relieve** (1).

palliation *noun.* —*See* **relief** (1).

pallid *adjective.* —*See* **pale** (1), **pale** (2).

palmist *noun.* —*See* **prophet.**

palm off *verb.* To offer or put into circulation an inferior or fraudulent item ▶ foist, fob off, pass off, put off. [*Compare* **dump.**]

palpability *noun.* —*See* **tangibility.**

palpable *adjective.* Discernible by touch ▶ tactile, tangible, touchable. —*See also* **perceptible, physical.**

palpate *verb.* —*See* **touch.**

palpation *noun.* —*See* **touch** (1).

palpitate *verb.* —*See* **beat** (5).

palpitation *noun.* —*See* **beat** (3).

palter *verb.* —*See* **equivocate** (2), **haggle.**

paltriness *noun.* —*See* **trifle.**

paltry *adjective.* —*See* **shoddy, trivial.**

pamper *verb.* —*See* **baby.**

pamphleteer *noun.* —*See* **propagandist.**

pan *noun.* —*See* **criticism, face** (1).

pan *verb.* —*See* **criticize** (1).

pan out *verb.* —*See* **succeed** (2).

panacea *noun.* Something believed to cure all human disorders ▶ catholicon, cure-all, elixir. [*Compare* **cure.**]

pan-broil *verb.* —*See* **cook.**

pandemic *adjective.* —*See* **prevailing, universal** (1).

pandemonium *noun.* —*See* **noise** (1).

panegyric *noun.* —*See* **praise** (1).

panegyrize *verb.* —*See* **honor** (1).

panel *noun.* —*See* **conference** (1).

pan-fry *verb.* —*See* **cook.**

pang *noun.* —*See* **pain.**

pang *verb.* —*See* **hurt** (3).

Panglossian *adjective.* —*See* **optimistic.**

panhandle *verb.* —*See* **beg.**

panhandler *noun.* —*See* **beggar** (1).

panic *noun.* —*See* **fear, scream** (2).

panic *verb.* —*See* **frighten.**

panicky *or* **panic-stricken** *adjective.* —*See* **afraid.**

panicmonger *noun.* One who needlessly alarms others ▶ alarmist, Chicken Little, scaremonger. ***Idiom:*** one who cries wolf. [*Compare* **pessimist.**]

panoply *noun.* —*See* **array.**

panorama *noun.* —*See* **view** (2).

pant *verb.* To breathe hard ▶ blow, gasp, gulp, heave, huff, puff, wheeze. ***Idioms:*** suck air (*or* wind). [*Compare* **breathe.**] —*See also* **desire, gasp.**

pantomime *verb.* —*See* **gesture.**

pantywaist *noun.* —*See* **weakling.**

papa *noun.* —*See* **father.**

paper *noun.* **1.** Something that is the result of creative effort ▶ composition, essay, theme. **2.** A document used in applying, as for a job ▶ application, form, sheet. —*See also* **publication** (2).

papoose *noun.* —*See* **baby** (1).

pappy[1] *adjective.* —*See* **soft** (1).

pappy[2] *noun.* —*See* **father.**

par *noun.* —*See* **average, equivalence.**

parable *noun.* —*See* **myth** (1).
parade *noun.* A formal military inspection ▶ review. —*See also* **array.**
parade *verb.* —*See* **display.**
paradigm *noun.* —*See* **model, original.**
paradigmatic *adjective.* —*See* **typical.**
paradise *noun.* —*See* **eternity** (2), **heaven.**
paradisiac *or* **paradisaic** *or* **paradisal** *adjective.* —*See* **heavenly** (1).
paragon *noun.* A person or thing so excellent as to have no equal or match ▶ nonesuch, nonpareil, phoenix. [*Compare* **best, celebrity.**] —*See also* **epitome, model.**
paragraph *noun.* —*See* **item.**
parallel *adjective.* Lying in the same plane and not intersecting ▶ collateral. ***Idiom:*** side by side. —*See also* **concurrent, like**[2]**.**
parallel *noun.* Something closely analogous to something else ▶ analogue, analogy, congener, correlate, correlative, correspondent, counterpart, match. [*Compare* **copy, likeness.**]
parallel *verb.* —*See* **equal** (1), **liken.**
parallelism *noun.* —*See* **likeness** (1).
paralyze *verb.* To render helpless, as by emotion ▶ benumb, numb, petrify, stun, stupefy, wither. ***Idioms:*** strike dumb (*or* speechless). [*Compare* **daze, stagger.**] —*See also* **disable** (1).
paralyzed *adjective.* —*See* **motionless.**
paramount *adjective.* —*See* **dominant** (1), **primary** (1).
paramountcy *noun.* —*See* **dominance.**
paramour *noun.* —*See* **lover, philanderer.**
paranormal *adjective.* —*See* **supernatural** (1).
parapet *noun.* —*See* **bulwark.**
paraphernalia *noun.* —*See* **outfit.**
paraphrase *noun.* A restating of something in other, especially simpler, words ▶ rendering, rendition, restatement, translation, version. [*Compare* **summary, synopsis.**]
paraphrase *verb.* To express the meaning of in other, especially simpler, words ▶ rehash, render, rephrase, restate, reword, translate. [*Compare* **review.**]
parasite *noun.* One who depends on another for support without reciprocating ▶ bloodsucker, hanger-on, leech, sponge, sponger. *Slang:* freeloader. [*Compare* **beggar, sycophant.**] —*See also* **germ** (1).
parasitic *or* **parasitical** *adjective.* Of or characteristic of a parasite ▶ bloodsucking, epizoic. *Slang:* freeloading.
parboil *verb.* —*See* **cook.**
parcel *noun.* —*See* **lot** (1), **package.**
parcel out *verb.* —*See* **distribute.**
parch *verb.* —*See* **dry.**
parched *adjective.* Needing or desiring drink ▶ dry, thirsty. —*See also* **dry** (2).
pardon *verb.* —*See* **forgive, purify** (1).
pardon *noun.* —*See* **forgiveness.**
pardonable *adjective.* Admitting of forgiveness or pardon ▶ condonable, excusable, expiable, forgivable, remissible, understandable, venial. [*Compare* **acceptable, justifiable.**]
pardoning *noun.* —*See* **purification** (2).
pare *verb.* To reduce in complexity or scope ▶ boil down, simplify, streamline. ***Idioms:*** reduce to the basics (*or* essentials *or* bare bones). [*Compare* **explain.**] —*See also* **cut** (3), **skin.**
parent *noun.* —*See* **ancestor** (1), **origin, originator.**
parent *verb.* To take care of and educate a child ▶ bring up, foster, raise, rear. [*Compare* **nurture.**] —*See also* **breed.**
parentage *noun.* —*See* **ancestry.**
parenthesis *noun.* —*See* **digression.**
parenthetic *or* **parenthetical** *adjective.* —*See* **digressive.**
pariah *noun.* —*See* **outcast.**
parity *noun.* —*See* **equivalence.**
park *noun.* Public land kept for a special purpose ▶ preserve, reserve, reservation, sanctuary. —*See also* **common.**
parka *noun.* —*See* **coat** (1).
parlance *noun.* —*See* **language** (2), **wording.**

parley *noun.* The act or process of dealing with another to reach an agreement ▶ negotiation, talk. [*Compare* **conversation.**] —*See also* **conference** (1), **deliberation** (1).

parley *verb.* —*See* **confer** (1), **discuss.**

parlous *adjective.* —*See* **dangerous.**

parochial *adjective.* —*See* **narrow** (1).

parody *noun.* —*See* **mockery** (2), **satire.**

parody *verb.* —*See* **imitate.**

paroxysm *noun.* A condition of anguished struggle and disorder ▶ convulsion, throes. —*See also* **eruption, outburst, seizure** (1), **tremor** (2).

parrot *noun.* —*See* **mimic.**

parrot *verb.* —*See* **mimic.**

parry *verb.* —*See* **repel.**

parsimonious *adjective.* —*See* **stingy.**

parson *noun.* —*See* **cleric.**

part *noun.* **1.** A separate unit that belongs or contributes to a whole ▶ building block, component, constituent, division, element, factor, fraction, ingredient, member, percentage, piece, portion, section, sector, segment, subdivision. [*Compare* **bit[1], cut, element.**] **2.** One's duty or responsibility in a common effort ▶ function, piece, role, share. [*Compare* **function.**] **3.** A particular subdivision of a written work ▶ chapter, passage, section, segment. **4.** A person that is portrayed in a fictional or dramatic work ▶ character, persona, personage, role. —*See also* **allotment, viewpoint.**

part *verb.* —*See* **branch, divide, separate** (1).

part *adjective.* —*See* **partial** (1).

✚ **CORE SYNONYMS:** *part, component, constituent, element, factor, ingredient.* These nouns denote one of the separate units that belong or contribute to a whole: *protein, an important part of a balanced diet; jealousy, a component of his character; melody and harmony, two of the constituents of a musical composition; the grammatical elements of a sentence; ambition as a key factor in her success; humor, an effective ingredient of a speech.*

---

partake *verb.* —*See* **contribute** (2), **eat** (1), **participate.**

partial *adjective.* **1.** Not total ▶ fractional, fragmentary, incomplete, part, unfinished. [*Compare* **rough.**] **2.** Disposed to favor one over another ▶ favorable, preferential. —*See also* **biased.**

partiality *noun.* Preferential treatment or bias ▶ favor, favoritism, partialness, preference. [*Compare* **prejudice.**] —*See also* **bias, inclination** (1), **taste** (1).

partialness *noun.* Preferential treatment or bias ▶ favor, favoritism, partiality, preference. [*Compare* **bias, prejudice.**]

participant *noun.* One who participates ▶ actor, partaker, participator, party, player, sharer. [*Compare* **associate.**]

participate *verb.* To involve oneself in an activity ▶ carry on, engage, enter into, have, indulge, join (in), partake. ***Idioms:*** have a hand in, take part. [*Compare* **contribute.**] —*See also* **contribute** (2).

participation *noun.* The act or fact of participating ▶ engagement, involvement, partaking, sharing.

participatory *adjective.* Tending to contribute to a result ▶ conducive, contributive, contributory, helpful. [*Compare* **auxiliary.**]

particle *noun.* —*See* **bit[1]** (1).

particular *adjective.* —*See* **detailed, exclusive** (1), **fussy, individual** (2), **lone, special.**

particular *noun.* —*See* **circumstance** (2), **detail, element** (2).

particularity *noun.* —*See* **individuality.**

particularize *verb.* To state specifically ▶ detail, provide, specify, stipulate. [*Compare* **assert, describe, dictate.**]

particularly *adverb.* —*See* **namely, very.**

parting *noun.* —*See* **departure, division** (1).

parting *adjective.* Of, done, given, or said on departing ▶ departing, dying, farewell, goodbye, leaving, valedictory. [*Compare* **last.**]

partisan *noun.* —*See* **follower.**

partisan *adjective.* —*See* **biased.**

partisanship *noun.* —*See* **bias.**

partition *noun.* A solid structure that separates one area from another ▶ barrier, screen, wall. [*Compare* **border.**] —*See also* **division** (1).

partition *verb.* To separate with or as if with a wall ▶ fence, screen, wall. —*See also* **divide.**

partner *noun.* —*See* **associate** (1), **lover, spouse.**

partnership *noun.* —*See* **association** (1), **company** (1).

parturiency *noun.* The condition of carrying a developing fetus within the uterus ▶ gestation, gravidity, gravidness, pregnancy.

parturient *adjective.* —*See* **pregnant** (1).

parturition *noun.* —*See* **birth** (1).

party *noun.* A social gathering, especially for pleasure ▶ affair, celebration, festivity, fete, function, gala, gathering, get-together, occasion, social, soiree, tea. *Informal:* do. *Slang:* bash. [*Compare* **blast, celebration, dance.**] —*See also* **alliance, band**[2]**, group, human being, participant.**

party *verb.* —*See* **celebrate** (2), **revel.**

party pooper *noun.* —*See* **killjoy.**

pass *verb.* **1.** To move along a particular course ▶ go, proceed, push on, wend. ***Idioms:*** make (*or* wend) one's way. [*Compare* **advance, rove.**] **2.** To catch up with and move past ▶ outpace, outrun, outstrip, overhaul, overtake. [*Compare* **overtake.**] **3.** To use time in a particular way ▶ put in, spend. [*Compare* **idle.**] **4.** To come to one as by lot or inheritance ▶ devolve, fall. **5.** To come to an end ▶ go away, pass away. **6.** To be accepted or approved ▶ adopt, affiliate, carry, clear. *Informal:* sign off. —*See also* **communicate** (1), **communicate** (2), **confirm** (3), **cross** (1), **decline, die, elapse, happen** (1), **journey, lead, leave**[1] (1), **plunge, surpass.**

pass away *verb.* To come to an end ▶ go away, pass. —*See also* **die.**

pass for *verb.* —*See* **impersonate.**

pass off *verb.* To offer or put into circulation an inferior or fraudulent item ▶ foist, fob off, palm off, put off. [*Compare* **dump.**]

pass on *verb.* —*See* **conduct** (3), **die.**

pass out *verb.* To suffer temporary lack of consciousness ▶ black out, faint, keel over, swoon. ***Idioms:*** drop (*or* faint *or* fall) dead away, see stars. [*Compare* **collapse.**]

pass over *verb.* —*See* **blink at, neglect** (2).

pass through *verb.* —*See* **experience.**

pass up *verb.* —*See* **lose** (2).

pass *noun.* A free ticket entitling one to transportation or admission ▶ *Informal:* comp. *Slang:* freebie. —*See also* **crisis, way** (2).

passable *adjective.* Capable of being passed, traversed, or crossed ▶ navigable, negotiable, penetrable, surmountable, traversable. [*Compare* **clear.**] —*See also* **acceptable** (2).

passage *noun.* A particular subdivision of a written work ▶ chapter, part, section, segment. —*See also* **confirmation** (1), **journey, transition, way** (2).

passageway *noun.* —*See* **way** (2).

passé *adjective.* —*See* **old-fashioned.**

passel *noun.* —*See* **heap** (2).

passing *adjective.* —*See* **transitory.**

passing *noun.* —*See* **death** (1).

passion *noun.* Powerful, intense emotion ▶ ardor, fervency, fervor, fire, heat, warmth, zeal. *Slang:* sizzle. [*Compare* **intensity.**] —*See also* **desire** (2), **emotion, enthusiasm** (1), **enthusiasm** (2), **love** (1), **love** (2), **temper** (2).

✦ **CORE SYNONYMS:** *passion, fervor, fire, zeal, ardor.* These nouns denote powerful, intense emotion. *Passion* is a deep, overwhelming emotion: "*There is* *not a passion so strongly rooted in the human heart as envy"* (Richard Brinsley Sheridan). The term may signify sexual desire or anger: *"He flew into a violent passion and abused me mercilessly"* (H.G. Wells). *Fervor* is great warmth and intensity of feeling: *"The union of the mathematician with the poet, fervor with measure, passion with correctness, this surely is the ideal"* (William James). *Fire* is burning passion: *"In our youth our hearts were touched with fire"* (Oliver Wendell Holmes, Jr.). *Zeal* is strong, enthusiastic devotion to a cause, ideal, or goal and tireless diligence in its furtherance: *"Laurie* [resolved], *with a glow of philanthropic zeal, to found and endow an institution for . . . women with artistic tendencies"* (Louisa May Alcott). *Ardor* is fiery intensity of feeling: *"the furious ardor of my zeal repressed"* (Charles Churchill).

---

passionate *adjective.* Fired with intense feeling ▶ ardent, blazing, burning, dithyrambic, fervent, fervid, feverish, fiery, flaming, glowing, heated, hot-blooded, impassioned, perfervid, red-hot, scorching, torrid. [*Compare* **enthusiastic, lively.**] *—See also* **lascivious.**

passionless *adjective. —See* **cold** (2), **frigid.**

passive *adjective.* Submitting without objection or resistance ▶ acquiescent, nonresistant, resigned, submissive, yielding. [*Compare* **obedient.**]

passport *noun. —See* **license** (3).

past *adjective.* Just gone by or elapsed ▶ ago, antecedent, anterior, bygone, bypast, earlier, foregoing, former, lapsed, precedent, preceding, previous, prior. [*Compare* **last, old.**] *—See also* **late** (2).

past *noun.* The time before the present ▶ auld lang syne, old, yesterday, yesteryear, yore. ***Idioms:*** bygone days, days gone by, days of yore, long ago, the good old days, the old (*or* olden) days, water under the bridge. [*Compare* **antiquity.**] *—See also* **history** (2).

paste *verb. —See* **hit.**

paste *noun. —See* **blow**[2]**.**

pastel *adjective. —See* **pale** (1).

pastime *noun. —See* **amusement.**

past master *noun.* One who has had long experience in a given activity or capacity ▶ old hand, vet, veteran. *Informal:* old-timer. *—See also* **expert.**

pastor *noun. —See* **cleric.**

pastoral *adjective.* Charmingly simple and carefree ▶ arcadian, idyllic. [*Compare* **fresh, still.**] *—See also* **clerical, country.**

pasture *noun.* An area of open land ▶ clearing, field, meadow. [*Compare* **lot.**]

pasty *adjective. —See* **pale** (1).

pat *verb. —See* **caress, tap**[1] (1).

pat down *verb.* To examine a person or someone's personal effects in order to find something lost or concealed ▶ frisk, inspect, search. *Slang:* shake down. ***Idiom:*** do a body search of.

patch *verb. —See* **fix** (1).

patch *noun. —See* **lot** (1).

patchwork *noun. —See* **assortment.**

patchy *adjective. —See* **uneven.**

pate *noun. —See* **head** (1).

patent *adjective. —See* **apparent** (1), **obvious.**

paterfamilias *noun. —See* **father.**

paternal *adjective.* Like a father, especially in caring ▶ fatherlike, fatherly, patriarchal. [*Compare* **benevolent.**]

path *noun. —See* **way** (1), **way** (2).

pathetic *adjective. —See* **pitiful, terrible.**

pathogen *noun. —See* **germ** (1).

pathology *noun. —See* **disease.**

patience *noun.* The capacity of enduring hardship or inconvenience without complaint ▶ acceptance, forbearance, longanimity, long-suffering, resignation, stoicism, sufferance, tolerance. [*Compare* **endurance, tolerance.**]

✦ **CORE SYNONYMS:** *patience, long-suffering, resignation, forbearance.* These nouns denote the capacity to endure hardship, difficulty, or inconvenience without complaint. *Patience* emphasizes calmness, self-control, and the willingness or ability to tolerate delay: *Our patience will achieve more than our force* (Edmund Burke). *Long-suffering* is long and patient endurance, as of wrong or provocation: *The general, a man not known for docility and long-suffering, flew into a rage. Resignation* implies acceptance of or submission to something trying, as out of despair or necessity: *I undertook the job with an air of resignation. Forbearance* denotes restraint, as in retaliating, demanding what is due, or voicing disapproval: *"It is the mutual duty of all to practice Christian forbearance, love, and charity towards each other"* (Patrick Henry).

◀ **ANTONYM:** *impatience*

---

patient *adjective.* Enduring or capable of enduring hardship or inconvenience without complaint ▶ accepting, enduring, forbearing, long-suffering, resigned, stoic, tolerant. [*Compare* **passive.**]

patio *noun.* —*See* **court** (1).

patois *noun.* —*See* **dialect, language** (2).

patriarch *noun.* —*See* **father, originator.**

patriarchal *adjective.* Relating to or like a father, especially in caring ▶ fatherlike, fatherly, paternal. [*Compare* **benevolent.**]

patrician *adjective.* —*See* **noble.**

patriciate *noun.* —*See* **society** (1).

patrimonial *adjective.* —*See* **ancestral.**

patrimony *noun.* Any special privilege accorded a firstborn ▶ birthright, heritage, inheritance, legacy. [*Compare* **right.**]

patrol *verb.* —*See* **police.**

patrol *noun.* —*See* **detachment** (3), **force** (3).

patrolman *or* **patrolwoman** *noun.* —*See* **police officer.**

patron *noun.* One who supports or champions an activity, cause, or institution ▶ backer, benefactor, benefactress, contributor, friend, philanthropist, sponsor, supporter. *Informal:* angel. [*Compare* **advocate, follower.**] —*See also* **consumer, donor.**

patronage *noun.* **1.** Aid or support given by a patron ▶ advocacy, aegis, auspices, backing, championship, encouragement, financing, furtherance, patronization, promotion, sponsorship. [*Compare* **donation, help.**] **2.** The commercial transactions of customers with a supplier ▶ business, custom, trade, traffic. [*Compare* **business, deal.**] **3.** Customers or patrons collectively ▶ clientage, clientele, constituency, custom, trade. **4.** The political appointments or jobs that are at the disposal of those in power ▶ pork, spoils.

patroness *noun.* —*See* **donor.**

patronization *noun.* —*See* **condescension, patronage** (1).

patronize *verb.* **1.** To act as a patron to ▶ back, sponsor, support. [*Compare* **donate, finance, support.**] **2.** To treat in a superciliously indulgent manner ▶ condescend. *Informal:* high-hat. ***Idioms:*** lord it over, speak (*or* talk) down to. [*Compare* **insult, snub.**]

patsy *noun.* —*See* **dupe, scapegoat.**

patter *verb.* —*See* **chatter** (1).

patter *noun.* —*See* **chatter.**

pattern *noun.* —*See* **epitome, form** (1), **method, model, original, usual.**

pattern *verb.* —*See* **follow** (5), **make.**

paucity *noun.* —*See* **shortage.**

paunchy *adjective.* —*See* **fat** (1).

pauper *noun.* An impoverished person ▶ bankrupt, beggar, bum, derelict, down-and-out, down-and-outer, have-not, indigent, insolvent, tramp, vagabond. *Slang:* bag lady, skell. [*Compare* **beggar, hobo.**]

pauperism *noun.* —*See* **poverty.**

pauperize *verb.* —*See* **ruin.**

pause *verb.* To stop for an indefinite period ▶ interrupt, suspend. ***Idiom:*** put on hold. [*Compare* **rest.**] *—See also* **hesitate, remain.**

pause *noun.* *—See* **break, hesitation.**

pave *verb.* *—See* **cover** (1).

pawl *noun.* *—See* **fastener.**

pawn[1] *noun.* Something given to guarantee the repayment of a loan or the fulfillment of an obligation ▶ bail, bond, collateral, earnest, gage, guaranty, hostage, pledge, recognizance, security, token, warrant, warranty. [*Compare* **guarantee, promise.**]

pawn *verb.* To give or deposit as a pawn ▶ bond, collateralize, deposit, hypothecate, mortgage, pledge. *Slang:* hock.

pawn[2] *noun.* A person who is used or controlled by others ▶ cat's-paw, dupe, instrument, puppet, stooge, tool. [*Compare* **dupe.**]

pay *verb.* *—See* **compensate, return** (3), **settle** (3), **spend** (1).

pay back *verb.* *—See* **avenge.**

pay off *verb.* *—See* **avenge, bribe.**

pay *noun.* *—See* **wage.**

payable *adjective.* *—See* **due** (1).

payment *noun.* *—See* **compensation, cost** (1), **due, punishment, wage.**

payoff *noun.* *—See* **bribe, climax.**

payola *noun.* *—See* **bribe.**

PDQ *adverb.* *—See* **immediately** (1).

peace *noun.* *—See* **calm, stillness, truce.**

peaceable *adjective.* Inclined or disposed to peace; not quarrelsome or unruly ▶ conciliatory, dovish, irenic, nonviolent, pacific, pacifical, pacifist, pacifistic, peaceful. [*Compare* **amiable.**]

peaceful *adjective.* *—See* **calm, peaceable, still.**

peacefulness *noun.* *—See* **calm, stillness.**

peace officer *noun.* *—See* **police officer.**

peacock *verb.* *—See* **strut.**

peacock *noun.* A man who is vain about his clothes ▶ beau, coxcomb, dandy, fop, swell.

peak[1] *noun.* *—See* **bill**[2] (2), **climax.**

peak *verb.* *—See* **climax.**

peak *adjective.* Of or constituting a climax ▶ climactic, crowning, culminating. [*Compare* **last.**] *—See also* **maximum.**

peak[2] *verb.* *—See* **pale.**

peaked *adjective.* *—See* **sick** (1).

peal *verb.* *—See* **ring**[2]**.**

peanuts *noun.* *Informal* A small or trifling amount of money ▶ pocket money, small change. *Slang:* chicken feed, two bits.

pearl *noun.* *—See* **treasure.**

peasant *noun.* *—See* **clodhopper.**

peccancy *noun.* *—See* **crime** (2), **evil** (1).

peccant *adjective.* *—See* **evil.**

peck[1] *verb.* *—See* **kiss.**

peck at *verb.* *—See* **nag.**

peck *noun.* *—See* **kiss.**

peck[2] *noun.* *—See* **abundance, heap** (2).

Pecksniffian *adjective.* *—See* **hypocritical.**

peculiar *adjective.* *—See* **eccentric, funny** (3), **special.**

peculiarity *noun.* *—See* **eccentricity, identity** (1), **quality** (1).

peculiarly *adverb.* *—See* **unusually.**

pecuniary *adjective.* Of or relating to finances ▶ financial, fiscal, monetary.

pedagogic *or* **pedagogical** *adjective.* *—See* **educational** (1), **pedantic.**

pedagogue *noun.* *—See* **educator.**

pedagogy *or* **pedagogics** *noun.* *—See* **education** (1).

pedantic *adjective.* Characterized by a narrow concern for book learning and formal rules ▶ academic, bookish, donnish, formalistic, inkhorn, literal, literary, pedagogic, pedantical, purist, scholastic. [*Compare* **educated.**]

✚ **CORE SYNONYMS:** *pedantic, academic, bookish, donnish, scholastic.* These adjectives mean marked by a narrow, often tiresome focus on or display of learning and especially its trivial aspects: *a pedantic writing style; an academic insistence on precision; a* *bookish vocabulary; donnish refinement of speech; scholastic and excessively subtle reasoning.*

---

peddle *verb.* **1.** To travel about selling goods ▶ hawk, huckster, vend. **2.** To engage in the illicit sale of narcotics ▶ deal. *Slang:* push. *—See also* **sell.**

peddler *noun.* *—See* **pusher, seller.**

pedestal *noun.* *—See* **base**[1] (2).

pedestrian *adjective.* *—See* **dull** (1).

pedigree *noun.* A written record of ancestry ▶ family tree, genealogy. *—See also* **ancestry.**

pedigreed *adjective.* *—See* **thoroughbred.**

peek *verb.* To look briefly and quickly ▶ glance, glimpse, peep. ***Idioms:*** steal a glance (*or* look). [*Compare* **look.**]

peek *noun.* *—See* **glance** (1).

peel *noun.* *—See* **skin** (3).

peel *verb.* *—See* **bare, flake, skin.**

peep *verb.* To look briefly and quickly ▶ glance, glimpse, peek. ***Idioms:*** steal a glance (*or* look). [*Compare* **look.**]

peep *noun.* *—See* **glance** (1).

peer[1] *verb.* *—See* **gaze.**

peer[2] *noun.* One that is very similar to another in rank or position ▶ coequal, colleague, compeer, equal, equivalent, fellow, match, rival. [*Compare* **associate, parallel.**]

peerless *adjective.* *—See* **unique.**

peerlessness *noun.* *—See* **uniqueness.**

peeve *verb.* *—See* **annoy.**

peeve *noun.* *—See* **annoyance** (2).

peevish *adjective.* *—See* **ill-tempered.**

peevishness *noun.* *—See* **temper** (1).

peewee *adjective.* *—See* **tiny.**

peg *noun.* *—See* **degree** (1), **nail, plug, throw.**

peg *verb.* *—See* **throw.**

pejorative *adjective.* *—See* **disparaging.**

pelagic *adjective.* *—See* **marine** (1).

pelf *noun.* *—See* **wealth.**

pellucid *adjective.* *—See* **clear** (1).

pellucidity *or* **pellucidness** *noun.* *—See* **clarity.**

pelt[1] *noun.* The skin of an animal, sometimes including fur, hair or feathers ▶ fur, hide, leather.

pelt[2] *verb.* *—See* **barrage, beat** (1), **rush, throw.**

pen[1] *verb.* *—See* **compose** (1), **publish** (2), **write.**

pen[2] *noun.* An enclosure for livestock ▶ corral, fold, paddock, sty, yard. [*Compare* **cage.**] *—See also* **jail.**

pen *verb.* *—See* **enclose** (1).

penal *adjective.* *—See* **punishing.**

penalize *verb.* To impose a fine on ▶ amerce, fine, mulct. *—See also* **punish.**

penalty *noun.* **1.** A coercive measure intended to ensure compliance or conformity ▶ interdict, interdiction, sanction. [*Compare* **forbiddance, restriction.**] **2.** A sum of money levied as punishment for an offense ▶ amercement, fine, mulct. *—See also* **punishment.**

penance *noun.* The act of making amends ▶ atonement, expiation, reconciliation, reparation. [*Compare* **compensation, purification.**] *—See also* **punishment.**

penchant *noun.* *—See* **inclination** (1).

pendent *adjective.* *—See* **hanging.**

pendulous *adjective.* *—See* **hanging, hesitant.**

penetrable *adjective.* *—See* **passable.**

penetrate *verb.* To pass into or through by overcoming resistance ▶ break (through), enter, jab, perforate, pierce, poke, punch, puncture. [*Compare* **cut.**] *—See also* **enter** (1).

penetrating *adjective.* Having the quality or tendency to pervade or permeate ▶ permeating, pervading, pervasive, suffusive. [*Compare* **general, prevailing, recurrent.**] *—See also* **bitter** (2), **critical** (2).

penetration *noun.* *—See* **discernment, entrance**[1], **instinct.**

penitence *or* **penitency** *noun.* A feeling of regret for one's sins or misdeeds ▶ attrition, compunction, contriteness, contrition, guilt, regret, remorse, remorsefulness, repentance, rue, self-reproach, shame.

✚ CORE SYNONYMS: *penitence, compunction, contrition, remorse, repentance.* These nouns denote a feeling of regret for one's sins or misdeeds: *showed no penitence; ended the relationship without compunction; pangs of contrition; tears of remorse; sincere repentance.*

---

penitent *adjective.* —*See* **sorry.**
penitentiary *noun.* —*See* **jail.**
penmanship *noun.* —*See* **script** (1).
pennant *noun.* —*See* **flag[1].**
penniless *adjective.* —*See* **poor.**
pennilessness *noun.* —*See* **poverty.**
pennon *noun.* —*See* **flag[1].**
penny pincher *noun.* —*See* **miser.**
penny-pinching *adjective.* —*See* **stingy.**
pensile *adjective.* —*See* **hanging.**
pension *verb.* To withdraw or remove from business or active life ▶ retire, step down, superannuate. ***Idioms:*** call it quits, hang up one's spurs, put out to pasture, turn in one's badge. [*Compare* **dismiss, quit.**]
pensive *adjective.* —*See* **thoughtful.**
penumbra *noun.* Comparative darkness that results from the blocking of light rays ▶ shade, shadiness, shadow, umbra. [*Compare* **dark, twilight.**]
penurious *adjective.* —*See* **poor, stingy.**
penuriousness *noun.* —*See* **poverty.**
penury *noun.* —*See* **deprivation, poverty.**
people *noun.* —*See* **kin, public** (1).
people *verb.* To live in a place, as does a people ▶ inhabit, occupy, populate. [*Compare* **live, settle.**]
pep *noun.* —*See* **energy, spirit** (1).
pep up *verb.* —*See* **energize.**
pepper *verb.* —*See* **barrage, speckle, sprinkle.**
peppery *adjective.* —*See* **spicy, testy.**
peppiness *noun.* —*See* **energy, spirit** (1).
peppy *adjective.* —*See* **energetic, lively.**
pep talk *noun.* —*See* **encouragement.**
perambulate *verb.* —*See* **stroll.**
perambulation *noun.* —*See* **walk** (1).
perceivable *adjective.* —*See* **perceptible.**
perceive *verb.* To be intuitively aware of ▶ apprehend, feel, intuit, sense. ***Idioms:*** feel in one's bones, get vibrations. [*Compare* **understand.**] —*See also* **see** (1).
percentage *noun.* —*See* **part** (1).
perceptibility *noun.* —*See* **visibility.**
perceptible *adjective.* Capable of being perceived by the senses or the mind ▶ appreciable, cognizable, detectable, discernible, distinguishable, noticeable, observable, palpable, perceivable, ponderable, recognizable, sensible. [*Compare* **apparent, physical, understandable.**]

✚ CORE SYNONYMS: *perceptible, palpable, appreciable, noticeable, discernible.* These adjectives apply to what is capable of being perceived by the senses or the mind. *Perceptible* is the least specific: *She noticed a perceptible pause in the flow of his speech. Palpable* applies both to what is perceptible by means of the sense of touch and to what is readily perceived by the mind: "*The advantages Mr. Falkland possessed . . . are palpable*" (William Godwin). What is *appreciable* is capable of being estimated or measured: *The firm was accused of dumping appreciable amounts of noxious waste into the harbor. Noticeable* means easily observed: *There are noticeable shadows under your eyes. Discernible* means distinguishable, especially by the faculty of vision or the intellect: *The mediator found no discernible progress in the contract negotiations.*

---

perception *noun.* —*See* **awareness, discernment, idea, sensation** (1).
perceptive *adjective.* —*See* **critical** (2), **visionary.**
perceptiveness *noun.* —*See* **discernment.**

perch *verb.* —*See* **balance** (3).
perch *noun.* A place providing support for the foot in climbing ▶ foothold, footing, purchase, toehold.
perchance *adverb.* —*See* **maybe.**
percipience *or* **percipiency** *noun.* —*See* **discernment, discrimination** (1).
percipient *adjective.* —*See* **discriminating.**
percolate *verb.* —*See* **boil, ooze.**
percussion *noun.* —*See* **collision.**
perdition *noun.* —*See* **hell.**
perdurable *adjective.* —*See* **continuing.**
perdure *verb.* —*See* **endure** (2).
peregrinate *verb.* —*See* **journey, rove.**
peregrination *noun.* —*See* **journey.**
peregrinator *noun.* —*See* **hobo.**
peremptory *adjective.* —*See* **dictatorial.**
perennial *adjective.* —*See* **continual, continuing.**
perfect *adjective.* Free from flaws or blemishes ▶ absolute, clean, clear, consummate, faultless, flawless, impeccable, indefectible, regular, unblemished, unflawed, unmarked. ***Idiom:*** in mint condition. —*See also* **complete** (1), **good** (2), **ideal, pure, utter**[2]**.**
perfect *verb.* To bring to perfection or completion ▶ complement, complete, fill in (*or* out), hone, polish, refine, round off (*or* out), smooth. ***Idiom:*** smooth off the rough edges. [*Compare* **climax, complete, satisfy.**]

✚ **CORE SYNONYMS:** *perfect, consummate, faultless, flawless, impeccable.* These adjectives mean completely free from flaws or blemishes: *a perfect diamond; a consummate performer; faultless logic; a flawless instrumental technique; speaks impeccable Russian.*

perfection *noun.* —*See* **soundness.**
perfectly *adverb.* —*See* **completely** (1).
perfervid *adjective.* —*See* **passionate.**
perfidious *adjective.* —*See* **dishonest, faithless.**
perfidy *or* **perfidiousness** *noun.* Willful betrayal of fidelity, confidence, or trust ▶ treacherousness, treachery, treason. —*See also* **faithlessness.**
perforate *verb.* —*See* **breach, penetrate.**
perforation *noun.* —*See* **prick.**
perforce *adverb.* —*See* **helplessly.**
perform *verb.* **1.** To begin and carry through to completion ▶ accomplish, achieve, discharge, do, effect, execute, fulfill, prosecute, transact. *Informal:* pull off. [*Compare* **accomplish, effect.**] **2.** To make music ▶ concertize, play, render. —*See also* **act** (3), **fulfill, function, stage.**

✚ **CORE SYNONYMS:** *perform, execute, accomplish, achieve, effect, fulfill, discharge.* These verbs mean to begin and carry through to completion. To *perform* is to carry out an action, undertaking, or procedure, often with great skill or care. *The ship's captain performed the wedding ceremony. Laser experiments are performed regularly in the laboratory. Execute* implies performing a task or putting something into effect in accordance with a plan or design: "*To execute laws is a royal office; to execute orders is not to be a king*" (Edmund Burke). *Accomplish* connotes the successful completion of something, often of something that requires tenacity or talent: "*Make one brave push and see what can be accomplished in a week*" (Robert Louis Stevenson). To *achieve* is to accomplish something, often something significant, especially despite difficulty: "*Some are born great . . . Some achieve greatness . . . And some have greatness thrust upon them*" (William Shakespeare). *Effect* suggests the power of an agent to bring about a desired result: *The prescribed antibiotics didn't effect a complete cure.* To *fulfill* is to live up to expectations or satisfy demands, wishes, or requirements: *All their desires could not be fulfilled.* To *discharge* an obligation or duty is to perform all the steps necessary for its fulfillment: *"I have found it impossible . . . to discharge my duties as King as I would wish to do"* (Edward VIII).

---

performance *noun.* The act of beginning and carrying through to completion ▶ discharge, effectuation, execution, prosecution, transaction. [*Compare* **accomplishment, fulfillment.**] —*See also* **act** (1), **behavior** (2), **interpretation.**

performer *noun.* —*See* **player** (2).

perfume *noun.* —*See* **fragrance.**

perfume *verb.* To fill with a pleasant odor ▶ aromatize, scent.

perfumy *adjective.* —*See* **fragrant.**

perfunctory *adjective.* Done routinely and impersonally ▶ automatic, cursory, mechanical, routine. [*Compare* **apathetic, careless.**]

perhaps *adverb.* —*See* **maybe.**

periapt *noun.* —*See* **charm.**

peril *noun.* —*See* **danger.**

peril *verb.* —*See* **endanger.**

perilous *adjective.* —*See* **dangerous.**

perimeter *noun.* —*See* **border** (1), **circumference, limits.**

period *noun.* **1.** A specific length of time characterized by the occurrence of certain conditions or events ▶ duration, season, session, space, span, stretch, term, time. [*Compare* **bit**[1].] **2.** An interval regarded as a distinct evolutionary or developmental unit ▶ phase, stage. [*Compare* **degree.**] —*See also* **age** (2), **end** (1).

periodic *or* **periodical** *adjective.* Happening or appearing at regular intervals ▶ cyclic, cyclical, isochronal, isochronous. ***Idiom:*** like clockwork. [*Compare* **recurrent.**] —*See also* **intermittent.**

periodically *adverb.* —*See* **intermittently.**

peripatetic *adjective.* —*See* **nomadic.**

peripatetic *noun.* —*See* **hobo.**

periphery *noun.* —*See* **border** (1), **circumference, limits.**

periphrastic *adjective.* —*See* **wordy** (1).

perish *verb.* —*See* **die, disappear** (2).

perjure *verb.* —*See* **lie**[2].

perjurer *noun.* —*See* **liar.**

perjury *noun.* —*See* **mendacity.**

perk *noun.* —*See* **gratuity.**

perk up *verb.* To make lively or animated ▶ animate, brighten, enliven, light (up). —*See also* **encourage** (2), **recover** (2).

perky *adjective.* —*See* **lively.**

permanence *noun.* —*See* **changelessness, continuation** (1).

permanent *adjective.* —*See* **continuing, unchanging.**

permanently *adverb.* —*See* **forever.**

permeable *adjective.* —*See* **absorbent.**

permeate *verb.* —*See* **charge** (1).

permissibility *noun.* —*See* **legality.**

permissible *adjective.* —*See* **acceptable** (1), **optional.**

permission *noun.* The approving of an action, especially when done by one in authority ▶ allowance, approbation, approval, assent, authority, authorization, consent, endorsement, imprimatur, leave, license, nod, permit, rubber stamp, sanction, thumbs-up. *Informal:* go-ahead, green light, OK. ***Idiom:*** seal of approval. [*Compare* **acceptance, admission.**]

✚ **CORE SYNONYMS:** *permission, authorization, consent, leave, license, sanction.* These nouns denote the approving of an action, especially when granted by one in authority: *was refused permission to smoke; seeking authorization to begin construction; gave their consent to the marriage; will ask leave to respond to the speaker; was given license to depart; gave sanction to the project.*

◀ **ANTONYM:** *prohibition*

---

permissive *adjective.* —*See* **tolerant.**

permissiveness *noun.* —*See* **tolerance.**

permit *verb.* **1.** To neither forbid nor prevent ▶ allow, have, let, suffer, tolerate. **2.** To give one's consent to ▶ allow, approbate, approve, authorize, consent, endorse, let, license, sanction. *Informal:* green-light, OK. [*Compare* **assent, grant, legalize.**] **3.** To afford an opportunity for ▶ admit, allow, give, let. **4.** To give the means, ability, or opportunity to do ▶ empower, enable. ***Idioms:*** clear the path (*or* road *or* way) for, smooth the way for. [*Compare* **ease, permit.**]

permit *noun.* —*See* **license** (3), **permission.**

permitted *adjective.* —*See* **lawful.**

permutable *adjective.* —*See* **changeable** (1).

permutation *noun.* —*See* **change** (1), **variation.**

pernicious *adjective.* —*See* **harmful, poisonous.**

perorate *verb.* —*See* **rant.**

perp *noun.* —*See* **criminal.**

perpendicular *adjective.* —*See* **vertical.**

perpetrate *verb.* To be responsible for or guilty of an error or crime ▶ carry out, commit, do. *Informal:* pull off. [*Compare* **perform.**]

perpetrator *noun.* —*See* **criminal.**

perpetual *adjective.* —*See* **continual, endless** (2).

perpetually *adverb.* —*See* **forever.**

perpetuate *verb.* To cause to last endlessly ▶ eternalize, eternize, immortalize. ***Idioms:*** cast (*or* etch *or* fix *or* set) in stone. [*Compare* **honor, memorialize.**]

perpetuity *noun.* The totality of time without beginning or end ▶ eternity, infinity, sempiternity. [*Compare* **forever.**] —*See also* **endlessness.**

perplex *verb.* —*See* **baffle, complicate, confuse** (1).

perplexed *adjective.* —*See* **confused** (1).

perplexing *adjective.* —*See* **ambiguous** (1).

perplexity *noun.* —*See* **complexity, daze, mystery.**

perquisite *noun.* —*See* **gratuity, right.**

persecute *verb.* —*See* **abuse** (1), **harass.**

persecution *noun.* —*See* **hell, oppression.**

perseverance *noun.* The state or quality of being insistent ▶ insistence, insistency, persistence, persistency. [*Compare* **decision.**] —*See also* **diligence.**

perseverate *verb.* —*See* **endure** (2).

persevere *verb.* —*See* **endure** (1), **insist, survive** (1).

persist *verb.* —*See* **endure** (1), **endure** (2), **insist, survive** (1).

persistence *or* **persistency** *noun.* The state or quality of being insistent ▶ insistence, insistency, perseverance. [*Compare* **decision.**] —*See also* **continuation** (1), **diligence.**

persistent *adjective.* **1.** Firm or obstinate, as in making a demand or maintaining a stand ▶ importunate, importune, insistent, urgent. [*Compare* **firm, stubborn.**] **2.** Difficult to alleviate or cure ▶ obstinate, pertinacious, stubborn. —*See also* **chronic** (2), **continual, continuing, diligent.**

persnickety *adjective.* —*See* **fussy.**

person *noun.* —*See* **human being.**

persona *noun.* A person portrayed in fiction or drama ▶ character, part, personage, role.

personage *noun.* A person portrayed in fiction or drama ▶ character, part, persona, role. —*See also* **celebrity, dignitary, human being.**

personal *adjective.* **1.** Belonging to, relating to, or affecting a particular person ▶ individual, intimate, private. **2.** Belonging or confined to a particular person or group as opposed to the public or the government ▶ closed-door, private, privy. [*Compare* **secret.**] —*See also* **arbitrary, bodily, confidential** (2).

personal effects *noun.* —*See* **effects.**

personality *noun.* —*See* **celebrity, character** (1).

personalization *noun.* —*See* **embodiment.**

personalize *verb.* —*See* **embody** (1).

personal property *noun.* —*See* **effects.**

persona non grata *noun.* —*See* **outcast.**

personification *noun.* —*See* **embodiment.**

personify *verb.* —*See* **embody** (1), **represent** (1).

perspective *noun.* —*See* **posture** (2), **view** (2), **viewpoint.**

perspicacious *adjective.* —*See* **discriminating, shrewd.**

perspicacity *noun.* —*See* **discernment, discrimination** (1).

perspicuity *or* **perspicuousness** *noun.* —*See* **clarity.**

perspiration *noun.* Moisture accumulated on a surface through sweating or condensation ▶ condensation, lather, sweat, transudation.

perspire *verb.* To excrete moisture through a porous skin or layer ▶ lather, sweat, transude.

perspiring *adjective.* Relating to, producing, or covered with sweat ▶ sudoriferous, sweaty, sweating. [*Compare* **damp, sticky.**]

persuade *verb.* To succeed in causing a person to act or think in a certain way ▶ argue into, bring around (*or* round), coax, convince, get to, induce, move, prevail on (*or* upon), sell (on), talk into. [*Compare* **coax, influence.**] —*See also* **convince.**

✚ **CORE SYNONYMS:** *persuade, induce, prevail on, convince.* These verbs mean to succeed in causing a person to act or think in a certain way. *Persuade* means to win someone over, as by reasoning or personal forcefulness: *Nothing can persuade me to change my mind.* To *induce* is to lead, as to a course of action, by means of influence or persuasion: "*Pray what could induce him to commit so rash an action?*" (Oliver Goldsmith). One *prevails on* (or *upon*) somebody who resists: "*He had prevailed upon the king to spare them*" (Daniel Defoe). To *convince* is to persuade by the use of argument or evidence: *The sales clerk convinced me that the car was worth the price.*

---

persuasion *noun.* Urgent solicitation ▶ insistence, insistency, pressing, urging. [*Compare* **demand.**] —*See also* **belief** (1), **kind**[2], **religion.**

persuasive *adjective.* —*See* **convincing.**

persuasiveness *noun.* —*See* **cogency.**

pert *adjective.* —*See* **impudent, lively.**

pertain *verb.* —*See* **apply** (2).

pertinacious *adjective.* Difficult to alleviate or cure ▶ obstinate, persistent, stubborn. —*See also* **diligent, stubborn** (1).

pertinacity *or* **pertinaciousness** *noun.* —*See* **diligence, stubbornness.**

pertinence *noun.* —*See* **relevance.**

pertinent *adjective.* —*See* **relevant.**

pertness *noun.* —*See* **impudence, spirit** (1).

perturb *verb.* —*See* **agitate** (2).

perturbation *noun.* —*See* **agitation** (2).

perturbing *adjective.* —*See* **disturbing.**

perusal *noun.* —*See* **examination** (1).

peruse *verb.* —*See* **examine** (1).

pervade *verb.* —*See* **charge** (1).

pervasive *adjective.* Having the quality or tendency to pervade or permeate ▶ penetrating, permeating, pervading, suffusive. [*Compare* **general, prevailing, recurrent.**]

perverse *adjective.* —*See* **contrary, corrupt** (1), **stubborn** (1).

perversion *noun.* —*See* **abuse** (1), **corruption** (1).

perversity *or* **perverseness** *noun.* —*See* **stubbornness.**

pervert *verb.* —*See* **abuse** (2), **corrupt, distort.**

pervert *noun.* One whose sexual behavior differs from the accepted norm ▶ deviant, deviate. *Slang:* freak.

perverted *adjective.* —*See* **corrupt** (1).

pesky *adjective.* —*See* **troublesome** (2).

pessimist *noun.* **1.** A person who expects only the worst from people ▶ cynic, misanthrope, misanthropist. [*Compare* **skeptic.**] **2.** A prophet of misfortune or disaster ▶ apocalypticist, Cassandra, crapehanger, croaker, doomsayer, worrywart.

pessimistic *adjective.* —*See* **bleak** (2).

pest *noun.* —*See* **annoyance** (2).

pester *verb.* —*See* **annoy, harass.**

pestering *noun.* —*See* **annoyance** (1).

pestilence *noun.* —*See* **contaminant.**

pestilent *or* **pestilential** *adjective.* —*See* **contagious, deadly, poisonous.**

pestle *verb.* —*See* **crush** (2).

pet[1] *noun.* One liked or preferred above all others ▶ darling, favorite. ***Idiom:*** apple of one's eye.

pet *adjective.* —*See* **domestic** (2), **favorite.**

pet *verb.* —*See* **caress, neck.**

pet[2] *verb.* To be sullenly aloof or withdrawn, as in silent resentment or protest ▶ mope, pout, sulk. [*Compare* **brood.**]

petcock *noun.* —*See* **faucet.**

peter out *verb.* —*See* **decrease, fade.**

petite *adjective.* —*See* **little.**

petition *verb.* **1.** To bring an appeal or request to the attention of ▶ address, appeal, apply, approach. [*Compare* **request.**] **2.** To ask for employment, acceptance, or admission ▶ apply, put in. —*See also* **appeal** (1).

petition *noun.* —*See* **appeal.**

petitioner *noun.* One that asks a higher authority for something, as a favor or redress ▶ appealer, appellant, suitor. —*See also* **applicant.**

pet name *noun.* —*See* **name** (1).

petrified *adjective.* —*See* **afraid.**

petrify *verb.* —*See* **frighten, harden** (2), **paralyze.**

petroleum *noun.* —*See* **oil.**

pettifog *verb.* —*See* **quibble.**

pettifogger *noun.* —*See* **critic** (2), **lawyer.**

pettifoggery *noun.* —*See* **quibbling.**

pettiness *noun.* —*See* **trifle.**

petty *adjective.* —*See* **minor** (1), **narrow** (1), **stingy, trivial.**

petulance *noun.* —*See* **temper** (1).

petulant *adjective.* —*See* **ill-tempered.**

phantasm *or* **phantasma** *noun.* —*See* **dream** (1), **ghost, illusion.**

phantasmagoria *or* **phantasmagory** *noun.* An experience of things or events that are not real ▶ hallucination. *Slang:* trip. —*See also* **dream** (1), **illusion.**

phantasmagoric *adjective.* —*See* **illusive.**

phantasmal *or* **phantasmic** *adjective.* —*See* **illusive.**

phantom *noun.* —*See* **ghost.**

pharisaic *adjective.* —*See* **hypocritical.**

pharisaism *noun.* —*See* **hypocrisy.**

pharisee *noun.* —*See* **hypocrite.**

pharmaceutical *noun.* —*See* **drug** (1).

phase *noun.* An interval regarded as a distinct evolutionary or developmental unit ▶ period, stage. [*Compare* **degree.**] —*See also* **viewpoint.**

phenomenal *adjective.* —*See* **astonishing, physical.**

phenomenon *noun.* Something demonstrated to exist or known to have existed ▶ actuality, event, fact, reality. ***Idioms:*** hard (*or* cold *or* plain) fact. [*Compare* **information.**] —*See also* **event** (1), **marvel.**

phenomenonally *adverb.* —*See* **unusually.**

philander *verb.* To be sexually unfaithful to another ▶ *Informal:* cheat, fool around, mess around, play around. *Slang:* two-time.

philanderer *noun.* A man who philanders ▶ adulterer, Casanova, cheater, Don Juan, fornicator, lady's man, paramour, womanizer. *Slang:* lady-killer, wolf. ***Idioms:*** man on the make, skirt chaser. [*Compare* **flirt, seducer, wanton.**]

philanthropic *adjective.* Of or concerned with charity ▶ altruistic, benevolent, charitable, eleemosynary. —*See also* **humanitarian.**

philanthropist *noun.* —*See* **donor, patron.**

philanthropy *noun.* —*See* **benevolence, favor** (1).

philippic *noun.* —*See* **tirade.**

Philistine *noun.* —*See* **boor.**
philistine *adjective.* —*See* **coarse** (1).
philosopher *noun.* A person who seeks truth by thinking ▶ reasoner, theorist, thinker.
philosophizing *noun.* —*See* **theory** (1).
philosophy *noun.* —*See* **posture** (2).
phlegm *noun.* —*See* **apathy, spit.**
phlegmatic *adjective.* —*See* **apathetic, cold** (2).
phobia *noun.* An exaggerated concern ▶ anxiety, complex, neurosis. *Informal:* hang-up. [*Compare* **anxiety, obsession.**]
phoenix *noun.* A person or thing so excellent as to have no equal or match ▶ nonesuch, nonpareil, paragon. [*Compare* **best, celebrity, model.**]
phonate *verb.* —*See* **pronounce.**
phone *verb.* —*See* **telephone.**
phoniness *noun.* —*See* **hypocrisy, insincerity.**
phony *adjective.* —*See* **artificial** (2), **counterfeit, hypocritical.**
phony *noun.* —*See* **counterfeit, fake, hypocrite.**
photocopy *noun.* —*See* **copy** (1).
photocopy *verb.* —*See* **copy.**
photographic *adjective.* —*See* **graphic** (1), **graphic** (4).
phrase *noun.* —*See* **expression** (3), **wording.**
phrase *verb.* To convey in language or words of a particular form ▶ couch, express, formulate, frame, put, word. ***Idiom:*** put into words. [*Compare* **say.**]
phraseology *or* **phrasing** *noun.* —*See* **wording.**
phylactery *noun.* —*See* **charm.**
physic *noun.* —*See* **cure.**
physic *verb.* —*See* **drug** (1).
physical *adjective.* Composed of or relating to things that occupy space and can be perceived by the senses ▶ concrete, corporeal, material, objective, palpable, phenomenal, sensible, solid, substantial, tangible. [*Compare* **perceptible, real.**] —*See also* **bodily, sensual** (2).
physicality *noun.* —*See* **sensuality** (1), **tangibility.**
physiognomy *noun.* —*See* **face** (1).
physique *noun.* —*See* **brawn, constitution.**
picayune *adjective.* —*See* **trivial.**
picayune *noun.* —*See* **trifle.**
pick *verb.* —*See* **choose** (1), **gather, pull** (2).
pick at *or* **pick on** *verb.* —*See* **nag.**
pick off *verb.* To wound or kill with a firearm ▶ gun (down), shoot. *Slang:* plug. ***Idioms:*** fill full of lead (*or* holes). [*Compare* **kill**[1], **murder.**]
pick out *verb.* —*See* **discern.**
pick up *verb.* —*See* **arrest, continue, contract** (2), **elevate** (1), **get** (1), **glean, learn** (1).
pick *noun.* —*See* **best** (1), **choice, elect.**
picket *noun.* —*See* **guard.**
picket *verb.* To cease working in support of demands made upon an employer ▶ strike, walk out. ***Idioms:*** go (*or* go out) on strike, stage a strike (*or* sickout *or* walkout), stop work. —*See also* **enclose** (2).
pickings *noun.* —*See* **balance** (4).
pickle *noun.* —*See* **predicament.**
pickle *verb.* —*See* **preserve** (1), **steep**[2].
pickled *adjective.* —*See* **drunk.**
pick-me-up *noun.* —*See* **tonic.**
pickpocket *noun.* —*See* **thief.**
pickup *noun.* —*See* **arrest.**
picky *adjective.* —*See* **fussy.**
pictographic *adjective.* —*See* **graphic** (4).
pictorial *adjective.* —*See* **graphic** (4), **graphic** (1).
picture *noun.* —*See* **double, view** (2).
picture *verb.* —*See* **imagine, represent** (2).
picturesque *adjective.* Evoking strong mental images through distinctiveness ▶ colorful, graphic, striking, vivid. —*See also* **graphic** (1).
piddle *verb.* —*See* **idle** (1).
piddling *adjective.* —*See* **trivial.**

piece *noun.* One's duty or responsibility in a common effort ▶ function, part, role, share. —*See also* **bit**[1] (2), **composition** (1), **cut** (2), **distance** (1), **item, part** (1), **song.**

piecemeal *adjective.* Proceeding steadily by degrees ▶ gradational, gradual, progressive, step-by-step. ***Idioms:*** one foot after another, one step at a time. [*Compare* **consecutive, methodical, slow.**]

piecemeal *adverb.* —*See* **gradually.**

pie-eyed *adjective.* —*See* **drunk.**

pie hole *noun.* —*See* **mouth** (1).

pier *noun.* —*See* **column.**

pierce *verb.* —*See* **breach, cut** (1), **overwhelm** (2), **penetrate.**

piercing *adjective.* —*See* **high** (3), **loud, sharp** (3).

pietism *noun.* —*See* **devotion.**

pietistic *or* **pietistical** *adjective.* —*See* **pious.**

piety *noun.* —*See* **devotion, hypocrisy.**

piffle *noun.* —*See* **nonsense.**

pig *noun.* A person who eats or consumes immoderate amounts of food and drink ▶ glutton, hog, overeater. [*Compare* **sybarite.**]

pig out *verb.* —*See* **gulp.**

pigeon *noun.* —*See* **dupe.**

pigeonhole *verb.* —*See* **classify.**

piggish *adjective.* —*See* **gluttonous.**

pigheaded *adjective.* —*See* **stubborn** (1).

pigheadedness *noun.* —*See* **stubbornness.**

pigment *noun.* —*See* **color** (2).

pigment *verb.* —*See* **color** (1).

pilaster *noun.* —*See* **column.**

pile *noun.* Something built, especially for human use ▶ building, construction, edifice, erection, structure. —*See also* **abundance, fortune, heap** (1), **heap** (2).

pile *verb.* —*See* **crowd, fill** (1), **heap** (1).

pile up *verb.* —*See* **accumulate, crash.**

pileup *noun.* —*See* **crash** (2).

pilfer *verb.* —*See* **steal.**

pilferage *noun.* —*See* **larceny.**

pilferer *noun.* —*See* **thief.**

pilgrimage *noun.* —*See* **expedition.**

pill *noun.* —*See* **drip** (2), **drug** (1), **killjoy.**

pillage *verb.* —*See* **sack**[2].

pillage *noun.* —*See* **plunder.**

pillar *noun.* —*See* **column.**

pillory *verb.* —*See* **disgrace.**

pillow talk *noun.* —*See* **conversation.**

pilose *adjective.* —*See* **hairy.**

pilot *noun.* A person who flies an airplane ▶ aviator, flier. *Slang:* flyboy. —*See also* **guide.**

pilot *verb.* —*See* **drive** (1), **guide, maneuver** (1).

pilot *adjective.* Serving as a tentative model for future experiment or development ▶ experimental, probationary, probative, test, trial. [*Compare* **introductory.**]

pin *noun.* —*See* **nail.**

pin *verb.* —*See* **fasten, fix** (3).

pinafore *noun.* —*See* **dress** (3).

pinch *verb.* —*See* **arrest, scrimp, squeeze** (1), **steal.**

pinch *noun.* —*See* **arrest, bit**[1] (1), **emergency, predicament.**

pinchbeck *noun.* —*See* **copy** (2).

pinch-hit *verb.* —*See* **substitute.**

pinch hitter *noun.* —*See* **substitute.**

pinching *adjective.* —*See* **stingy.**

pinchpenny *noun.* —*See* **miser.**

pine *verb.* —*See* **desire, languish.**

pinheaded *adjective.* —*See* **stupid.**

pinheadedness *noun.* —*See* **stupidity.**

pink-slip *verb.* —*See* **dismiss** (1).

pinnacle *noun.* —*See* **climax.**

pinpoint *verb.* To look for and discover ▶ find, locate, spot. *Informal:* scare up. [*Compare* **trace, uncover.**] —*See also* **designate, place** (1).

pinpoint *noun.* —*See* **point** (2).

pintsize *or* **pintsized** *adjective.* —*See* **tiny.**

pioneer *noun.* —*See* **developer, forerunner, settler.**

pioneer *verb.* —*See* **introduce** (1).

pioneer *adjective.* —*See* **first.**

pious *adjective.* Deeply concerned with God and the beliefs and practice of religion ▶ devoted, devotional, devout, godly, holy, pietistic, pietistical, prayerful, religious, saintlike, saintly, zealous. [*Compare* **faithful, righteous, spiritual.**] —*See also* **divine** (2), **hypocritical, reverent.**

piousness *noun.* —*See* **devotion.**

pip *noun.* A fertilized plant ovule capable of germinating ▶ grain, kernel, pit, seed.

pipe dream *noun.* —*See* **dream** (2).

piping *adjective.* —*See* **high** (3).

pip-squeak *noun.* —*See* **nonentity, squirt** (2).

piquant *adjective.* —*See* **spicy.**

pique *noun.* —*See* **offense.**

pique *verb.* —*See* **insult, offend** (1), **pride, provoke.**

pirate *noun.* One who reproduces another's work without permission ▶ cribber, plagiarist, plagiarizer. [*Compare* **forger.**]

pirate *verb.* —*See* **plagiarize.**

pit[1] *noun.* A place known for its great filth or corruption ▶ cesspit, cesspool, cloaca, den, gutter, hellhole, septic tank, sewer, sink, sump. *Slang:* armpit. —*See also* **deformity, depression** (1), **trap** (1).

pit *verb.* —*See* **deform, oppose.**

pit[2] *noun.* A fertilized plant ovule capable of germinating ▶ grain, kernel, pip, seed.

pitch *verb.* To move vigorously from side to side or up and down ▶ heave, rock, roll, toss. —*See also* **drop** (2), **erect, fall** (1), **lurch** (1), **promote** (3), **throw.**

pitch into *verb.* —*See* **attack** (1).

pitch *noun.* —*See* **climax, drop** (3), **fall** (1), **intensity, publicity, throw, tone** (2).

pitch-black *or* **pitch-dark** *or* **pitchy** *adjective.* —*See* **black** (1).

piteous *adjective.* —*See* **pitiful.**

pitfall *noun.* —*See* **danger, trap** (1).

pith *noun.* —*See* **heart** (1).

pithy *adjective.* Precisely meaningful and tersely cogent ▶ aphoristic, compact, epigrammatic, epigrammatical, gnomic, marrowy, pointed, proverbial, pungent, sententious, succinct. *Informal:* brass-tacks. ***Idioms:*** down to brass tacks (*or* the nitty-gritty), short and sweet, to the point. [*Compare* **brief, critical.**] —*See also* **pregnant** (2).

pitiable *adjective.* —*See* **pitiful.**

pitiful *adjective.* Arousing or deserving pity ▶ forlorn, lamentable, pathetic, piteous, pitiable, poor, rueful, ruthful, sorry. [*Compare* **affecting, deplorable.**] —*See also* **terrible.**

✚ **CORE SYNONYMS:** *pitiful, pitiable, pathetic, piteous, lamentable.* These adjectives describe what inspires or deserves pity. *Pitiful* and *pitiable* apply to what is touchingly sad: "*She told a most pitiful story*" (Samuel Butler). "*The emperor had been in a state of pitiable vacillation*" (William Hickling Prescott). Something *pathetic* elicits sympathetic sadness and compassion: "*a most earnest . . . entreaty, addressed to you in the most pathetic tones of the voice so dear to you*" (Charles Dickens). Sometimes these three terms connote contemptuous pity, as for what is hopelessly inept or inadequate: "*To be guided by second-hand conjecture is pitiful*" (Jane Austen). "*That cold accretion called the world, which, so terrible in the mass, is so unformidable, even pitiable, in its units*" (Thomas Hardy). *The state government took over schools with pathetic academic standards. Piteous* applies to what cries out for pity: "*They . . . made piteous lamentation to us to save them*" (Daniel Defoe). *Lamentable* suggests the evocation of pity mixed with sorrow: "*Tell thou the lamentable tale of me,/And send the hearers weeping to their beds*" (William Shakespeare).

---

pitiless *adjective.* —*See* **callous, cruel.**

pity *noun.* **1.** Sympathetic, sad concern for someone in misfortune ▶ commiseration, compassion, condolence, empathy, heart, softheartedness, sympathy. [*Compare* **mercy.**] **2.** A great disappointment or regrettable fact ▶ crime, shame. *Slang:* bummer. ***Idiom:*** a crying shame.

pity *verb.* To feel pity for someone ▶ ache for, bleed for, commiserate with, feel for, sympathize with. ***Idioms:*** feel sorry for, have pity on, take pity on. [*Compare* **comfort, feel.**]

✚ **CORE SYNONYMS:** *pity, compassion, commiseration, sympathy, condolence, empathy.* These nouns signify sympathetic, sad concern aroused by the misfortune, affliction, or suffering of another. *Pity* often implies a feeling of sorrow that inclines one to help or to show mercy: *He felt pity for the outcast. Compassion* denotes deep awareness of the suffering of another and the wish to relieve it: "*Compassion is not weakness, and concern for the unfortunate is not socialism*" (Hubert H. Humphrey). *Commiseration* signifies the expression of pity or sorrow: *My advisors expressed their commiseration over the failure of the experiment. Sympathy* denotes the act of or capacity for sharing in the sorrows or troubles of another: "*They had little sympathy to spare for their unfortunate enemies*" (William Hickling Prescott). *Condolence* is a formal, conventional expression of pity, usually to relatives upon a death: *The minister extended her condolences to the bereaved family. Empathy* is an identification with and understanding of another's situation, feelings, and motives: *Having changed schools several times as a child, I feel empathy for the transfer students.*

---

pitying *adjective.* —*See* **sympathetic.**

pivot *verb.* To turn in place, as on a fixed point ▶ slue, swing, swivel, wheel. —*See also* **turn** (1).

pivot *noun.* —*See* **center** (3).

pivotal *adjective.* —*See* **primary** (1).

pixilated *adjective.* —*See* **drunk.**

placard *noun.* —*See* **sign** (2).

placate *verb.* —*See* **pacify.**

place *noun.* **1.** Positioning of one individual vis-à-vis others ▶ condition, echelon, footing, level, position, rank, situation, standing, station, status. [*Compare* **class.**] **2.** The function or position customarily occupied by another ▶ lieu, stead. **3.** The proper or designated location ▶ niche. —*See also* **home** (1), **locality, position** (1), **position** (3).

place *verb.* **1.** To establish the identity of ▶ identify, know, pinpoint, recognize. *Slang:* finger. ***Idiom:*** put one's finger on. [*Compare* **discern.**] **2.** To complete a race or competition in a specified position ▶ come in, finish, run. —*See also* **classify, estimate** (2), **fix** (3), **position.**

placement *noun.* —*See* **arrangement** (1), **position** (1).

placid *adjective.* —*See* **calm, still.**

placidity *or* **placidness** *noun.* —*See* **calm, stillness.**

plagiarist *or* **plagiarizer** *noun.* One who reproduces another's work without permission ▶ cribber, pirate. [*Compare* **forger.**]

plagiarize *verb.* To reproduce another's work without permission ▶ appropriate, borrow, crib, pirate, poach. *Informal:* lift. [*Compare* **adopt, copy, counterfeit.**]

plague *noun.* —*See* **annoyance** (2), **curse** (3), **eruption.**

plague *verb.* —*See* **afflict, harass.**

plaguy *adjective.* —*See* **disturbing.**

plain *adjective.* —*See* **apparent** (1), **bare** (1), **frank, genuine, modest** (1), **obvious, ordinary, pure, straight, ugly, utter²**.

plainclothesman *noun.* —*See* **detective.**

plain-Jane *adjective.* —*See* **bare** (1).

plainness *noun.* —*See* **clarity, modesty** (2), **ugliness.**

plainspoken *adjective.* —*See* **frank.**

plainspokenness *noun.* —*See* **honesty.**

plaint *noun.* —*See* **cry** (1).

plaintiff *noun.* One that makes a formal complaint, especially in court ▶ accuser, claimant, complainant.
plaintive *adjective.* —*See* **sorrowful.**
plait *verb.* —*See* **fold, weave.**
plait *noun.* —*See* **fold** (1).
plan *noun.* —*See* **approach** (1), **method.**
plan *verb.* To set the time for an event or occasion ▶ schedule, set, time. —*See also* **arrange** (2), **design** (1), **design** (2), **draft** (1), **intend, plot** (1).
planar *adjective.* —*See* **even** (1).
plane *adjective.* —*See* **even** (1).
plane *verb.* —*See* **even.**
planet *noun.* The celestial body where humans live ▶ earth, globe, orb, world.
planetary *adjective.* —*See* **universal** (1).
plangent *adjective.* —*See* **resonant.**
plans *noun.* Steps taken in preparation for an undertaking ▶ accommodations, arrangements, preparations, provisions.
plant *verb.* To put seeds or young plants in soil ▶ broadcast, pot, root, scatter, seed, set (out), sow, transplant. [*Compare* **grow, till.**] —*See also* **fix** (2), **hide**[1].
plant *noun.* A building or complex in which an industry is located ▶ factory, mill, works.
plant life *noun.* The plants of an area or region ▶ flora, vegetation, verdure.
plaster *noun.* —*See* **finish.**
plaster *verb.* —*See* **dress** (2), **finish** (2), **smear.**
plastered *adjective.* —*See* **drunk.**
plastic *adjective.* Changing easily, as in expression ▶ changeable, fluid, mobile. [*Compare* **changeable, unstable.**] —*See also* **flexible** (1), **flexible** (3), **malleable.**
plasticity *noun.* —*See* **flexibility** (1).
plat *noun.* —*See* **lot** (1).
plate *verb.* —*See* **cover** (1).
plateau *noun.* A natural, flat land elevation ▶ mesa, table. [*Compare* **hill.**]
platform *noun.* A temporary framework with a floor, used by laborers ▶ scaffold, scaffolding, stage, staging.
platitude *noun.* —*See* **cliché.**
platitudinal *or* **platitudinous** *adjective.* —*See* **trite.**
platoon *noun.* —*See* **force** (3).
plaudit *noun.* Approval expressed by clapping ▶ applause, hand, ovation. ***Idiom:*** round of applause. —*See also* **praise** (1).
plausibility *noun.* —*See* **verisimilitude.**
plausible *or* **plausibleness** *adjective.* —*See* **believable.**
play *verb.* **1.** To occupy oneself with amusement or diversion ▶ disport, frolic, recreate, sport. *Informal:* horse around. [*Compare* **gambol, idle, joke.**] **2.** To make a bet ▶ bet, gamble, game, lay, wager. ***Idiom:*** put one's money on something. **3.** To treat lightly or flippantly ▶ dally, flirt, toy, trifle. **4.** To make music ▶ concertize, perform, render. **5.** To be performed ▶ run, show. —*See also* **act** (3), **compete, fiddle, inflict, interpret** (2), **manipulate** (1).
play around *verb. Informal* To be sexually unfaithful to another ▶ philander. *Informal:* cheat, fool around, mess around. *Slang:* two-time. —*See also* **putter.**
play down *verb. Informal* To make less emphatic or obvious ▶ de-emphasize, soft-pedal, tone down. —*See also* **moderate** (1).
play off *verb.* To place in opposition or be in opposition to ▶ match, pit.
play out *verb.* —*See* **conclude, dry up** (2), **exhaust** (1), **unwind.**
play over *verb.* To do or perform an act again ▶ duplicate, do over, redo, repeat, replay. [*Compare* **copy.**]
play up *verb.* —*See* **emphasize.**
play *noun.* Actions that are taken as a joke ▶ fun, game, jest, sport. ***Idioms:*** fun and games, in fun. —*See also* **amusement, exercise** (1), **license** (1), **script** (2).
play-act *verb.* —*See* **act** (3), **act** (2).
play-acting *noun.* —*See* **theatrics** (2).
playbill *noun.* —*See* **program** (2).
player *noun.* **1.** A theatrical performer ▶ actor, actress, thespian, trouper. [*Com-

pare **fake, lead, mimic.**] **2.** One who plays a musical instrument ▶ bandsman, instrumentalist, musician, performer, virtuosa, virtuoso. [*Compare* **vocalist.**] —*See also* **gambler** (1), **participant.**

playful *adjective.* —*See* **mischievous.**

plaything *noun.* An object for children to play with ▶ game, toy. [*Compare* **amusement.**]

plaza *noun.* —*See* **common.**

plea *noun.* —*See* **apology** (1), **appeal, excuse** (1).

pleach *verb.* —*See* **weave.**

plead *verb.* —*See* **appeal** (1), **argue** (2).

pleasant *adjective.* Giving or affording pleasure, enjoyment, or entertainment ▶ agreeable, amusing, congenial, diverting, enjoyable, entertaining, favorable, feel-good, fun, good, grateful, gratifying, lovely, nice, pleasing, pleasurable, satisfying, welcome. ***Idiom:*** not half bad. [*Compare* **attractive, delightful, invigorating.**] —*See also* **amiable.**

pleasantness *noun.* —*See* **amiability.**

pleasantry *noun.* —*See* **amenities** (2).

please *verb.* —*See* **choose** (2), **delight** (1), **satisfy** (1).

pleased *adjective.* —*See* **willing.**

pleasing *or* **pleasurable** *adjective.* —*See* **delightful, pleasant.**

pleasure *noun.* Unrestricted freedom to choose ▶ convenience, discretion, leisure, will. [*Compare* **license.**] —*See also* **amusement, delight, liking.**

pleasure *verb.* To feel or take joy or pleasure ▶ delight, exult, rejoice. [*Compare* **enjoy, luxuriate.**] —*See also* **delight** (1).

pleat *noun.* —*See* **fold** (1).

pleat *verb.* —*See* **fold.**

plebeian *adjective.* —*See* **coarse** (1), **lowly** (1).

plebeians *or* **plebs** *noun.* —*See* **commonalty.**

pledge *noun.* The act of drinking to someone ▶ health, toast. —*See also* **donation, pawn[1], promise** (1).

pledge *verb.* **1.** To guarantee by a solemn promise ▶ betroth, covenant, engage, plight, promise, swear, troth, vow. ***Idioms:*** cross one's heart and hope to die, give one's word of honor. [*Compare* **confirm, contract, guarantee.**] **2.** To assume an obligation ▶ commit, contract, engage, promise, undertake. —*See also* **commit** (2), **devote, donate, drink** (4), **pawn[1].**

✦ **CORE SYNONYMS:** *pledge, promise, swear, vow.* These verbs mean to guarantee solemnly that one will follow a particular course of action: *pledged to uphold the law; promises to write soon; swore to get revenge; vowed to fight to the finish.*

---

plenitude *or* **plenteousness** *noun.* —*See* **plenty.**

plenitudinous *or* **plenteous** *or* **plentiful** *adjective.* —*See* **generous** (2).

plenty *noun.* Prosperity and a sufficiency of life's necessities ▶ abundance, ampleness, bounteousness, bountifulness, copiousness, cornucopia, horn of plenty, muchness, plenitude, plenteousness, plentifulness. —*See also* **abundance.**

pleonasm *noun.* —*See* **wordiness.**

pleonastic *adjective.* —*See* **wordy** (1).

plethora *noun.* —*See* **abundance, excess** (1).

pliability *or* **pliableness** *noun.* —*See* **flexibility** (1).

pliable *adjective.* —*See* **adaptable, flexible** (3), **malleable.**

pliancy *or* **pliantness** *noun.* —*See* **flexibility** (1).

pliant *adjective.* —*See* **adaptable, flexible** (3), **malleable, obedient.**

plica *or* **plication** *noun.* —*See* **fold** (1).

plight[1] *noun.* —*See* **difficulty, predicament.**

plight[2] *verb.* —*See* **pledge** (1).

plight *noun.* —*See* **promise** (1).

plighted *adjective.* —*See* **engaged.**

plod *verb.* —*See* **grind** (2), **trudge.**

plodder *noun.* —*See* **drudge** (2).

plodding *adjective.* —*See* **dull** (1), **ponderous, slow** (1).

plop *verb.* To drop or sink heavily and noisily ▶ flop, plump, plunk. [*Compare* **fall.**]

plot *noun.* **1.** The series of events and relationships forming the basis of a composition ▶ action, movement, scenario, story, story line. **2.** A secret plan to achieve an evil or illegal end ▶ cabal, collusion, connivance, conspiracy, designs, intrigue, machination, scheme. [*Compare* **trick.**] —*See also* **lot** (1).

plot *verb.* **1.** To show graphically the direction or location of, as by using coordinates ▶ chart, graph, lay out, map (out), plan. **2.** To work out a secret plan to achieve an evil or illegal end ▶ cabal, collude, connive, conspire, hatch, intrigue, machinate, scheme. [*Compare* **design.**] —*See also* **draft** (1).

plow *verb.* —*See* **till.**

ploy *noun.* —*See* **trick** (1).

pluck *verb.* —*See* **gather, pull** (2).

pluck *or* **pluckiness** *noun.* —*See* **courage.**

plucky *adjective.* —*See* **brave.**

plug *noun.* Something used to fill a hole, space, or container ▶ bung, choke, cork, filling, peg, spigot, spile, stop, stopper, stopple, tap, wad. [*Compare* **cover.**] —*See also* **endorsement, outlet** (1), **publicity.**

plug *verb. Slang* To wound or kill with a firearm ▶ gun (down), pick off, shoot. ***Idioms:*** fill full of lead (*or* holes). [*Compare* **kill**[1], **murder.**] —*See also* **fill** (2), **promote** (3).

plug-ugly *noun.* —*See* **thug.**

plum *noun.* A person or thing worth catching ▶ prize. *Informal:* catch. *Slang:* brass ring. —*See also* **reward, treasure.**

plumb *adjective.* —*See* **vertical.**

plumb *adverb.* —*See* **directly** (3).

plumb *verb.* —*See* **explore.**

plume *verb.* —*See* **pride.**

plummet *verb.* —*See* **fall** (1), **fall** (4).

plump[1] *or* **plumpish** *adjective.* —*See* **fat** (1).

plump[2] *verb.* To drop or sink heavily and noisily ▶ flop, plop, plunk. [*Compare* **fall.**]

plump for *verb.* —*See* **support** (1).

plunder *noun.* Goods or property seized unlawfully ▶ booty, graft, loot, pillage, prize, spoils. *Slang:* boodle, swag.

plunder *verb.* —*See* **sack**[2].

plunge *verb.* To penetrate into a substance or place with force ▶ dig, dive, drive, lunge, pass, ram, run, sink, stab, stick, strike, thrust. [*Compare* **cut.**] —*See also* **fall** (1), **fall** (4).

plunge into *verb.* —*See* **attack** (2).

plunge *noun.* The act of swimming ▶ dip, duck, dunk, swim. —*See also* **descent, fall** (1), **fall** (3), **gamble.**

plunging *adjective.* —*See* **descending, low** (2).

plunk *verb.* To drop or sink heavily and noisily ▶ flop, plop, plump. [*Compare* **fall.**] —*See also* **thud.**

plush *or* **plushy** *adjective.* —*See* **luxurious.**

ply[1] *verb.* —*See* **fold.**

ply[2] *verb.* **1.** To use with or as if with the hands ▶ handle, manipulate, wield. **2.** To bring to bear steadily or forcefully, as influence ▶ exercise, exert, wield. ***Idiom:*** throw one's weight around.

pneuma *noun.* —*See* **spirit** (2).

pneumatic *adjective.* Of or relating to air ▶ aerial, airy, atmospheric.

poach[1] *verb.* —*See* **cook.**

poach[2] *noun.* —*See* **plagiarize.**

pock *verb.* —*See* **deform.**

pock *noun.* —*See* **deformity, welt.**

pocket *noun.* —*See* **hole** (1).

pocketbook *noun.* —*See* **purse.**

pocket money *noun.* —*See* **peanuts.**

podium *noun.* —*See* **stage** (1).

poem *noun.* **1.** A poetic work ▶ poesy, poetry, rhyme, song, verse. **2.** A creation or experience having beauty suggestive of poetry ▶ lyricism, poetry.

poet *noun.* One who writes poetry ▶ bard, jongleur, minstrel, muse, poetess, rhymer, rhymester, troubadour, versifier.

poetic *or* **poetical** *adjective.* Relating to the characteristics of poetry ▶ lyric, lyrical, poetical. [*Compare* **melodious, rhythmical.**]

poetry *noun.* A creation or experience having beauty suggestive of poetry ▶ lyricism, poem. —*See also* **poem** (1).

poignant *adjective.* —*See* **affecting.**

point *noun.* **1.** A sharp or tapered end ▶ acicula, acumination, apex, cusp, mucro, mucronation, neb, nib, tip. [*Compare* **spike.**] **2.** A very small mark ▶ dash, dot, fleck, pinpoint, speck, speckle, spot. [*Compare* **impression.**] —*See also* **degree** (1), **element** (2), **intention, meaning, occasion** (1), **position** (1), **reason** (1), **subject, use** (2).

point *verb.* —*See* **aim** (1).

point out *verb.* —*See* **designate, refer** (1).

point to *verb.* —*See* **imply, indicate** (1), **name** (2).

point up *verb.* —*See* **emphasize.**

point-blank *adverb.* —*See* **flatly.**

pointed *adjective.* Having an end that tapers to a point ▶ acicular, aciculate, aciculated, acuminate, acute, barbed, cultrate, cuspate, cuspated, cuspidate, cuspidated, fine, keen, mucronate, pointy, pronged, spiked, spined, sharp, tined. [*Compare* **sharp, thorny.**] —*See also* **noticeable, pithy.**

pointer *noun.* —*See* **advice, tip**[3]**.**

pointless *adjective.* —*See* **aimless, futile, mindless.**

pointlessness *noun.* —*See* **futility.**

point of view *noun.* —*See* **viewpoint.**

pointy *adjective.* —*See* **pointed.**

poise *verb.* To remain stationary over a place or object ▶ hang, hover. —*See also* **balance** (1), **balance** (3).

poise *noun.* —*See* **balance** (1), **balance** (2), **bearing** (1), **ease** (1).

poised *adjective.* —*See* **calm, confident.**

poison *noun.* Anything that is injurious, destructive, or fatal ▶ bane, canker, contagion, toxicant, toxin, venom, virus. —*See also* **contaminant.**

poison *verb.* To harm with poison ▶ canker, envenom, infect, intoxicate. [*Compare* **hurt.**] —*See also* **contaminate, corrupt.**

poison *adjective.* —*See* **poisonous.**

poisonous *adjective.* Capable of injuring or killing by poison ▶ malignant, mephitic, mephitical, miasmic, noxious, pernicious, pestiferous, pestilent, pestilential, poison, toxic, toxicant, venomous, virulent. [*Compare* **deadly, harmful.**] —*See also* **malevolent, unwholesome** (2).

✚ **CORE SYNONYMS:** *poisonous, mephitic, pestilent, pestilential, toxic, venomous, virulent.* These adjectives mean having or likened to the destructive or fatal effect of a poison: *a poisonous snake; a mephitic vapor; a pestilent agitator; pestilential jungle mists; toxic fumes; venomous jealousy; a virulent form of cancer.*

---

poisonousness *noun.* —*See* **malevolence.**

poke[1] *verb.* **1.** To look into or inquire about curiously, inquisitively, or in a meddlesome fashion ▶ pry, snoop. *Informal:* nose (around), sniff about (*or* around). ***Idiom:*** stick one's nose into. [*Compare* **meddle.**] **2.** To advance slowly ▶ crawl, creep, drag, inch. ***Idiom:*** go at a snail's pace. [*Compare* **trudge.**] —*See also* **delay** (2), **grope, penetrate, push** (1).

poke *noun.* —*See* **dig, laggard.**

poke[2] *noun.* —*See* **bag.**

pokerfaced *adjective.* —*See* **expressionless.**

pokey *noun.* —*See* **jail.**

poky *adjective.* —*See* **slow** (1).

polar *adjective.* —*See* **cold** (1), **opposite.**

polarity *noun.* —*See* **opposition** (1).

pole *noun.* —*See* **stick** (2).

polemic *noun.* —*See* **argument.**

polemic *or* **polemical** *adjective.* —*See* **argumentative.**

police *verb.* To maintain or keep in order with or as if with police ▶ monitor, patrol, regulate, secure. ***Idioms:*** keep the peace, keep watch, pound a beat. [*Compare* **defend.**] —*See also* **tidy** (1).

policeman *or* **policewoman** *noun.* —*See* **police officer.**

police officer *noun.* A member of a law-enforcement agency ▶ bluecoat, constable, finest, marshal, officer, patrolman, patrolwoman, peace officer, policeman, policewoman, sheriff, trooper. *Informal:* cop, law. *Slang:* bull, copper, flatfoot, fuzz, gendarme, heat, man, narc. [*Compare* **detective.**]

policy *noun.* —*See* **doctrine.**

polish *verb.* To improve by making minor changes or additions ▶ remodel, retouch, touch up. [*Compare* **fix, renew.**] —*See also* **finish** (2), **gloss[1], perfect.**

polish off *verb.* —*See* **consume** (1), **eat** (1), **exhaust** (1).

polish *noun.* —*See* **elegance, finish, gloss[1].**

polished *adjective.* Proficient as a result of practice and study ▶ accomplished, finished, practiced. [*Compare* **able, expert.**] —*See also* **cultured, glossy.**

polite *adjective.* —*See* **attentive, courteous** (1), **deferential.**

politeness *noun.* —*See* **amenities** (2), **courtesy.**

politesse *noun.* —*See* **courtesy.**

politic *adjective.* —*See* **advisable, delicate** (2).

political *adjective.* —*See* **governmental.**

polity *noun.* —*See* **state** (1).

poll *noun.* A gathering of information or opinion from a variety of sources or individuals ▶ count, poll, survey. —*See also* **head** (1).

poll *verb.* To cast a vote ▶ ballot, vote. ***Idioms:*** exercise one's civic duty, go to the polls.

pollinate *verb.* To make fertile ▶ enrich, fecundate, fertilize. [*Compare* **impregnate, pregnant.**]

pollutant *noun.* —*See* **contaminant.**

pollute *verb.* —*See* **contaminate, corrupt, violate** (3).

polluted *adjective.* —*See* **impure** (2), **drunk.**

pollution *noun.* —*See* **contaminant, contamination.**

Pollyanna *noun.* One who expects a favorable outcome or dwells on hopeful aspects ▶ optimist, Pangloss, positivist. [*Compare* **dreamer.**]

poltroon *noun.* —*See* **coward.**

polychromatic *or* **polychrome** *adjective.* —*See* **multicolored.**

polysyllabic *adjective.* Having many syllables ▶ sesquipedal, sesquipedalian.

polyurethane *noun.* —*See* **finish.**

polyurethane *verb.* —*See* **finish** (2).

pomp *noun.* —*See* **array, glitter** (2).

pomposity *or* **pompousness** *noun.* —*See* **arrogance, pretentiousness.**

pompous *adjective.* Characterized by an exaggerated show of dignity or self-importance ▶ grandiose, hoity-toity, pontifical, pretentious, puffed-up, puffy, self-important. *Informal:* highfalutin. [*Compare* **arrogant, boastful, snobbish.**]

ponder *verb.* To think or think about carefully and at length ▶ chew on (*or* over), cogitate, consider, contemplate, deliberate, entertain, excogitate, meditate, mull, muse, reflect, revolve, ruminate, study, think, think out, think over, think through, turn over, weigh. ***Idioms:*** cudgel one's brains, put on one's thinking cap, rack one's brain. [*Compare* **brood, think.**]

ponderable *adjective.* —*See* **perceptible.**

pondering *noun.* —*See* **thought.**

ponderosity *or* **ponderousness** *noun.* —*See* **heaviness.**

ponderous *adjective.* Lacking fluency or grace ▶ elephantine, ham-handed, heavy, heavy-footed, heavy-handed, labored, leaden, lumbering, plodding. [*Compare* **awkward.**] —*See also* **bulky** (1), **heavy** (1).

pontifical *adjective.* —*See* **pompous.**

pontificate *verb.* To indulge in moral reflection, usually pompously ▶ edify, moralize, preach, sermonize. [*Compare* **chastise.**]

pony *noun.* —*See* **translation.**

pool *noun.* —*See* **alliance, bet.**

poop[1] *verb.* —*See* **tire** (1).

poop out *verb.* —*See* **malfunction, tire** (2).

poop[2] *noun.* —*See* **drip** (2).

pooped *adjective.* —*See* **tired** (1).

poor *adjective.* Having little or no money or wealth ▶ bankrupt, beggarly, busted, destitute, down-and-out, impecunious, impoverished, indigent, insolvent, mendicant, necessitous, needy, penniless, penurious, poverty-stricken. *Informal:* broke, strapped. ***Idioms:*** flat stone broke, hard up, on one's uppers, on the skids, on welfare. [*Compare* **unfortunate.**] —*See also* **bad** (1), **depressed** (2), **meager, pitiful, shoddy.**

✚ CORE SYNONYMS: *poor, indigent, needy, impecunious, penniless, impoverished, poverty-stricken, destitute.* These adjectives mean having little or no money or wealth. *Poor* is the most general: *"Resolve not to be poor: whatever you have, spend less. Poverty is a great enemy to human happiness"* (Samuel Johnson). *Indigent* and *needy* refer to one in need or want: *indigent people living on the street; distributed food to needy families. Impecunious* and *penniless* mean having little or no money: *"Certainly an impecunious Subaltern was not a catch"* (Rudyard Kipling). *Poor investments left him penniless.* A person or place that is *impoverished* has been reduced to poverty: *an impoverished, third-world country. Poverty-stricken* means suffering from poverty and miserably poor: *refugees living in poverty-stricken camps. Destitute* means lacking any means of subsistence: *tenants left destitute by the fire.*

poorly *adjective.* —*See* **sick** (1).

poorness *noun.* —*See* **poverty.**

pop[1] *verb.* **1.** To come open or fly apart suddenly and violently, as from internal pressure ▶ blow (out), burst, explode. *Slang:* bust. **2.** To discharge a gun or firearm ▶ blast (away), fire (away *or* off), pop off, shoot (away *or* off). ***Idioms:*** go bang-bang, open fire, take a shot (*or* potshot). —*See also* **crack** (2), **hit.**

pop in *verb.* —*See* **visit.**

pop off *verb.* —*See* **die.**

pop *noun.* —*See* **crack** (1).

pop[2] *noun.* —*See* **father.**

poppycock *noun.* —*See* **nonsense.**

populace *noun.* —*See* **commonalty.**

popular *adjective.* Of, representing, or carried on by people at large ▶ civic, civil, communal, democratic, general, national, public, social, societal. [*Compare* **common.**] —*See also* **acceptable** (2), **famous, favorite, general** (2), **prevailing.**

popularize *verb.* —*See* **introduce** (1), **promote** (3).

popularity *noun.* —*See* **fame.**

populate *verb.* To live in a place, as does a people ▶ inhabit, occupy, people. [*Compare* **live, settle.**]

porcine *adjective.* —*See* **fat** (1).

pork *noun.* The political appointments or jobs that are at the disposal of those in power ▶ patronage, spoils.

porky *adjective.* —*See* **fat** (1).

pornography *noun.* —*See* **obscenity** (2).

port *noun.* —*See* **cover** (1), **harbor.**

portable *adjective.* —*See* **mobile** (1).

portend *verb.* —*See* **foreshadow, predict, threaten** (1).

portent *noun.* —*See* **omen.**

portentous *adjective.* —*See* **fateful** (1).

portion *noun.* **1.** A right or legal share in something ▶ claim, interest, stake, title. [*Compare* **right.**] **2.** That which is inevitably destined ▶ destiny, fate, fortune, kismet, lot, predestination. —*See also* **allotment, cut** (2), **fate** (2), **part** (1), **quantity** (2), **serving.**

portion *verb.* —*See* **distribute.**

portly *adjective.* —*See* **fat** (1).
portrait *noun.* —*See* **double.**
portray *verb.* —*See* **act** (3), **represent** (2).
portrayal *noun.* —*See* **interpretation, representation.**
pose *verb.* **1.** To assume a particular position, as for a portrait ▶ attitudinize, model, posture, sit. ***Idioms:*** strike an attitude (*or* a pose). **2.** To seek an answer to a question ▶ ask, put, raise. [*Compare* **say.**] —*See also* **act** (2), **propose.**
pose as *verb.* —*See* **impersonate.**
pose *noun.* The way in which one is placed or arranged ▶ arrangement, attitude, position, posture. —*See also* **affectation, façade** (2), **posture** (1).
poser *noun.* —*See* **hypocrite.**
posh *adjective.* —*See* **exclusive** (3).
posit *verb.* —*See* **suppose** (1).
position *noun.* **1.** The place where a person or thing is located ▶ emplacement, location, locus, place, placement, point, site, situation, spot. **2.** The way in which one is placed or arranged ▶ arrangement, attitude, pose, posture. **3.** A post of employment ▶ appointment, berth, billet, job, office, place, situation, slot, spot, work. *Slang:* gig. [*Compare* **business.**] —*See also* **bearing** (3), **belief** (1), **doctrine, place** (1), **posture** (2), **viewpoint.**
position *verb.* To put in a certain position or location ▶ base, deposit, emplace, install, lay, locate, place, put, set, site, situate, spot, stick. [*Compare* **station.**]
positioning *noun.* —*See* **arrangement** (1).
positive *adjective.* —*See* **certain** (2), **definite** (1), **definite** (3), **favorable** (2), **optimistic, sure** (1), **utter^2.**
positively *adverb.* —*See* **absolutely, flatly, really.**
positivity *or* **positiveness** *noun.* —*See* **sureness.**
possess *verb.* To dominate the mind or thoughts of ▶ fixate, obsess, preoccupy. [*Compare* **absorb, grip.**] —*See also* **bear** (3), **carry** (2), **command** (2).
possessed *adjective.* —*See* **calm.**
possession *noun.* An area subject to rule by an outside power ▶ colony, dependency, mandate, protectorate, province, satellite, settlement, territory. —*See also* **ownership.**
possessions *noun.* —*See* **effects, holdings.**
possessive *adjective.* Fearful of the loss of position or affection ▶ clinging, clutching, green-eyed, jealous. [*Compare* **envious.**]
possessor *noun.* —*See* **owner.**
possibility *noun.* **1.** Something that may occur or be done ▶ contingency, eventuality, potential, potentiality. [*Compare* **expectation.**] **2.** Indication of future success or development ▶ makings, potential, promise, prospects. [*Compare* **material.**] —*See also* **chance** (3).
possible *adjective.* Capable of occurring or being done ▶ achievable, attainable, doable, feasible, performable, practicable, viable, workable. ***Idiom:*** within reach. —*See also* **conceivable, latent, optional, probable.**

✦ **CORE SYNONYMS:** *possible, workable, practicable, feasible, viable.* These adjectives mean capable of occurring or being done. *Possible* indicates that something may happen, exist, be true, or be realizable: *"I made out a list of questions and possible answers"* (Mary Roberts Rinehart). *Workable* is used of something that can be put into effective operation: *If the scheme is workable, how will you implement it?* Something that is *practicable* is capable of being effected, done, or put into practice: *"As soon as it was practicable, he would conclude his business"* (George Eliot). *Feasible* refers to what can be accomplished, brought about, or carried out: *Making cars by hand is possible but not economically feasible. Viable* implies having the capacity for continuing effectiveness or success: *"How viable are the ancient legends as vehicles for modern literary themes?"* (Richard Kain).

◂ **ANTONYM:** *impossible*

possibly *adverb.* —*See* **maybe.**

post[1] *verb.* To gain a point or points in a game or contest ▶ score, tally. *Informal:* notch. ***Idioms:*** make a goal (*or* point).

post[2] *noun.* —*See* **base**[1] **(1), column, lookout (2).**

post *verb.* To appoint and send to a particular place ▶ assign, set, station. [*Compare* **position.**] —*See also* **gamble (2).**

post[3] *verb.* —*See* **list**[1]**, send (1).**

poster *noun.* —*See* **sign (2).**

posterior *adjective.* Following something else in time ▶ after, later, subsequent, ulterior. [*Compare* **following.**] —*See also* **back.**

posterior *noun.* —*See* **buttocks.**

posterity *noun.* —*See* **progeny.**

posthaste *adverb.* —*See* **fast.**

posting *noun.* —*See* **entry.**

postpone *verb.* —*See* **defer**[1]**.**

postponement *noun.* —*See* **delay (1).**

postulant *noun.* An entrant who has not yet taken the final vows of a religious order ▶ neophyte, novice, novitiate.

postulate *verb.* —*See* **claim, suppose (1).**

postulate *or* **postulation** *noun.* —*See* **assumption.**

postulated *adjective.* —*See* **theoretical (2).**

posture *noun.* **1.** A way of holding or carrying one's body ▶ attitude, carriage, pose, stance. [*Compare* **bearing.**] **2.** A frame of mind affecting one's thoughts or behavior ▶ attitude, mindset, outlook, perspective, philosophy, position, stance. [*Compare* **mood, viewpoint.**] **3.** The way in which one is placed or arranged ▶ arrangement, attitude, pose, position.

posture *verb.* —*See* **impersonate, pose (1).**

✚ **CORE SYNONYMS:** *posture, attitude, carriage, pose, stance.* These nouns denote a way of holding or carrying one's body: *a model's erect posture; an attitude of prayer; the monarch's dignified carriage; an activist who struck a defiant pose; an athlete's alert stance.*

posy *noun.* —*See* **bouquet, flower.**

pot *noun.* —*See* **bet.**

pot *verb.* —*See* **plant, preserve (1).**

potable *noun.* —*See* **drink (1).**

potation *noun.* —*See* **drink (1), drink (2).**

potbellied *adjective.* —*See* **fat (1).**

potency *noun.* —*See* **effect (2), energy, kick, strength.**

potent *adjective.* **1.** Having a high concentration of the distinguishing ingredient ▶ concentrated, stiff, strong. [*Compare* **straight.**] **2.** Having great physical strength ▶ mighty, powerful, strong. [*Compare* **energetic, muscular.**] —*See also* **forceful.**

potentate *noun.* —*See* **chief.**

potential *noun.* Indication of future success or development ▶ makings, possibility, promise, prospects. [*Compare* **material.**] —*See also* **possibility (1).**

potential *adjective.* —*See* **latent, probable.**

potentiality *noun.* —*See* **possibility (1).**

pother *noun.* —*See* **bother.**

potion *noun.* —*See* **drink (1).**

potpourri *noun.* —*See* **assortment.**

potted *adjective.* —*See* **drugged, drunk.**

pouch *verb.* —*See* **bulge.**

pouch *noun.* —*See* **bag.**

pounce *verb.* —*See* **jump (1).**

pounce *noun.* The act of jumping ▶ jump, leap, spring, vault. [*Compare* **fall.**]

pound[1] *verb.* —*See* **beat (1), beat (3), beat (5), crush (2), instill.**

pound *noun.* —*See* **beat (1), blow**[2]**.**

pound[2] *noun.* —*See* **cage.**

pour *verb.* To cause a liquid to flow in a steady stream ▶ decant, discharge, drain, draw (off), effuse, empty, flow, issue, run. —*See also* **crowd, flow** (2), **rain** (2).

pour *noun.* —*See* **rain.**

pout *verb.* To be sullenly aloof or withdrawn, as in silent resentment or protest ▶ mope, pet, sulk. [*Compare* **brood.**]

pout *noun.* A contorted facial expression showing pain, contempt, or disgust ▶ face, grimace, moue. *Informal:* mug. [*Compare* **frown, glare, sneer.**]

poverty *noun.* The condition of being extremely poor ▶ beggary, destitution, impecuniosity, impecuniousness, impoverishment, indigence, need, neediness, pauperism, pennilessness, penuriousness, penury, poorness, privation, straits, want. [*Compare* **bankruptcy, beggary.**] —*See also* **deprivation, shortage.**

poverty-stricken *adjective.* —*See* **poor.**

powder *verb.* —*See* **crush** (2), **sprinkle.**

powdery *adjective.* —*See* **fine**[1] (1).

power *noun.* —*See* **authority, dominance, energy, force** (1), **influence, strength.**

powerful *adjective.* Having great physical strength ▶ mighty, potent, strong. [*Compare* **energetic, muscular.**] —*See also* **deep** (3), **forceful, influential, severe** (2).

powerfully *adverb.* —*See* **hard** (1).

powerfulness *noun.* —*See* **strength.**

powerless *adjective.* Lacking power or strength ▶ helpless, impotent, unable. —*See also* **ineffectual** (2).

powerlessness *noun.* —*See* **inability, ineffectuality.**

powwow *noun.* —*See* **conference** (1).

powwow *verb.* —*See* **confer** (1).

practicable *adjective.* —*See* **advisable, open** (4), **possible, practical.**

practical *adjective.* Serving or capable of serving a useful purpose ▶ functional, handy, no-nonsense, practicable, serviceable, useful, utilitarian. [*Compare* **beneficial, usable.**] —*See also* **realistic** (1).

practicality *noun.* —*See* **use** (2).

practical joke *noun.* —*See* **prank**[1].

practically *adverb.* —*See* **approximately.**

practice *verb.* **1.** To do or perform repeatedly so as to master ▶ exercise, go over (*or* through), rehearse, run through, walk through. [*Compare* **indoctrinate.**] **2.** To work at, especially as a profession ▶ do, follow, pursue. ***Idiom:*** hang out one's shingle. [*Compare* **labor.**] **3.** To engage in activities in order to strengthen or condition ▶ drill, exercise, train, work out. —*See also* **use.**

practice *noun.* Repetition of an action so as to develop or maintain one's skill ▶ conditioning, drill, exercise, regimen, rehearsal, routine, study, training, workout. —*See also* **business** (2), **custom.**

✦ **CORE SYNONYMS:** *practice, exercise, rehearse.* These verbs mean to do repeatedly so as to master: *practice the shot put; exercising one's wits; rehearsed the play for 14 days.*

---

practiced *adjective.* Proficient as a result of practice and study ▶ accomplished, finished, polished. [*Compare* **able, expert.**] —*See also* **experienced.**

praetorian *adjective.* —*See* **corrupt** (2).

pragmatic *or* **pragmatical** *adjective.* —*See* **realistic** (1).

praise *noun.* **1.** An expression of warm approval ▶ acclaim, acclamation, accolade, applause, approbation, celebration, cheer, commendation, compliment, encomium, eulogy, kudos, laud, laudation, paean, panegyric, plaudit. [*Compare* **applause, exaltation.**] **2.** The honoring of a deity, as in worship ▶ exaltation, extolment, glory, glorification, laudation, magnification, prostration. [*Compare* **adoration, honor.**] —*See also* **compliment.**

praise *verb.* **1.** To express warm approval of ▶ acclaim, accolade, applaud, cheer, commend, compliment, extol, laud. **2.** To pay a compliment to ▶ commend, compliment, congratulate, felicitate. ***Idioms:*** pay tribute to, raise a glass to, take off one's hat to. **3.** To honor a deity in religious worship ▶ exalt, extol, glorify, hymn, laud, magnify. [*Compare* **revere.**] —*See also* **distinguish** (3), **honor** (1).

✦ **CORE SYNONYMS:** *praise, acclaim, commend, extol, laud.* These verbs mean to express approval or admiration. To *praise* is to voice approbation, commendation, or esteem: "*She was enthusiastically praising the beauties of Gothic architecture*" (Francis Marion Crawford). *Acclaim* usually implies hearty approbation warmly and publicly expressed: *The film was highly acclaimed by many critics. Commend* suggests moderate or restrained approval, as that accorded by a superior: *The judge commended the jury for their hard work. Extol* suggests exaltation or glorification: "*that sign of old age, extolling the past at the expense of the present*" (Sydney Smith). *Laud* connotes respectful or lofty, often inordinate praise: "*aspirations which are lauded up to the skies*" (Charles Kingsley).

praiseworthy *adjective.* —*See* **admirable.**

prance *verb.* —*See* **strut.**

prank¹ *noun.* A mischievous act ▶ antic, caper, frolic, gag, joke, lark, practical joke, trick. *Informal:* shenanigan. *Slang:* monkeyshine, put-on. [*Compare* **mischief.**]

prank² *verb.* —*See* **dress up.**

prankish *adjective.* —*See* **mischievous.**

prankishness *or* **pranks** *noun.* —*See* **mischief.**

prankster *noun.* —*See* **rascal.**

prate *verb.* —*See* **babble, chatter** (1).
prate *noun.* —*See* **babble, chatter.**

prattle *verb.* —*See* **babble, chatter** (1), **gossip.**
prattle *noun.* —*See* **babble, chatter, gossip** (1).

praxis *noun.* —*See* **custom.**

pray *verb.* To offer a reverent petition to God or a god ▶ invoke, supplicate. —*See also* **appeal** (1).

prayer¹ *noun.* **1.** The act of praying ▶ benediction, invocation, supplication. **2.** A formula of words used in praying ▶ collect, devotions, litany, orison, rogations. [*Compare* **grace.**] —*See also* **appeal.**

prayer² *noun.* One who humbly entreats ▶ beggar, petitioner, suitor, suppliant, supplicant.

prayerful *adjective.* —*See* **pious.**

preach *verb.* **1.** To deliver a sermon, especially as a vocation ▶ evangelize, sermonize. [*Compare* **address.**] **2.** To indulge in moral reflection, usually pompously ▶ edify, moralize, pontificate, sermonize. [*Compare* **chastise.**]

preacher *noun.* —*See* **cleric.**

preachy *adjective.* —*See* **didactic, moral.**

preadolescence *noun.* The stage of life between birth and puberty ▶ childhood, early years, innocence, prepubescence. [*Compare* **youth.**]

preadolescent *noun.* —*See* **child** (1).

preamble *noun.* —*See* **introduction.**

prearrangement *noun.* —*See* **preparation.**

precarious *adjective.* —*See* **delicate** (3), **insecure** (2).

precariousness *noun.* —*See* **instability.**

precaution *noun.* —*See* **caution, prudence.**

precautionary *adjective.* —*See* **preservative, preventive** (2).

precede *verb.* To come, exist, or occur before in time ▶ antecede, antedate, forerun, predate, preexist. —*See also* **introduce** (3).

precedence *noun.* The act, condition, or right of preceding or coming before ▶ antecedence, precedency, precession, priority, right of way.

precedent *noun.* —*See* **custom, model.**
precedent *adjective.* —*See* **advance, past.**

preceding *adjective.* Next before the present one ▶ foregoing, last, latter, previous. —*See also* **advance, past.**

precept *noun.* —*See* **doctrine, law** (1).

precession *noun.* —*See* **precedence.**

precincts *noun.* —*See* **environment** (1), **limits.**

precious *adjective.* —*See* **costly, darling.**

precious *noun.* —*See* **darling** (1).

precipitance *or* **precipitancy** *noun.* —*See* **haste** (2).

precipitant *adjective.* —*See* **abrupt** (2), **rash**[1].

precipitate *verb.* To put down, especially in layers, by a natural process ▶ deposit. —*See also* **cause, rain** (2).

precipitate *adjective.* —*See* **abrupt** (2), **rash**[1].

precipitate *noun.* —*See* **deposit** (2), **effect** (1).

precipitateness *noun.* —*See* **haste** (2).

precipitation *noun.* —*See* **deposit** (2), **haste** (2), **rain.**

precipitous *adjective.* —*See* **steep**[1] (1).

precise *adjective.* Strictly distinguished from others ▶ exact, very. —*See also* **accurate, definite** (1), **definite** (2), **delicate** (4).

precisely *adverb.* —*See* **directly** (3), **exactly.**

precision *or* **preciseness** *noun.* —*See* **accuracy, clarity.**

preclude *verb.* —*See* **prevent.**

preclusion *noun.* —*See* **prevention.**

preclusive *adjective.* —*See* **preventive** (1).

precocious *adjective.* Developing, occurring, or appearing before the expected time ▶ early, premature, untimely. —*See also* **gifted, progressive** (1).

preconception *noun.* —*See* **bias.**

precondition *noun.* —*See* **condition** (2), **provision.**

precursor *noun.* —*See* **ancestor** (2), **forerunner.**

predate *verb.* —*See* **precede.**

predecessor *noun.* —*See* **ancestor** (2).

predestination *noun.* —*See* **fate** (1).

predetermine *verb.* —*See* **design** (1).

predetermined *adjective.* —*See* **calculated.**

predicament *noun.* A difficult, often embarrassing situation or condition ▶ box, corner, deep water, difficulty, dilemma, Dutch, fix, hole, hot spot, hot water, impasse, jam, mess, pinch, plight, quagmire, quandary, scrape, soup, straits, tightrope, trouble. *Informal:* bind, pickle, spot. ***Idiom:*** pretty kettle of fish. [*Compare* **crisis, difficulty, entanglement.**]

✚ **CORE SYNONYMS:** *predicament, plight, quandary, jam, fix, pickle.* These nouns refer to a situation from which it is difficult to free oneself. A *predicament* is a problematic situation about which one does not know what to do: "*Werner finds himself suddenly in a most awkward predicament*" (Thomas Carlyle). A *plight* is a bad or unfortunate situation: *The report examined the plight of homeless people.* A *quandary* is a state of perplexity, especially about what course of action to take: "*Having captured our men, we were in a quandary how to keep them*" (Theodore Roosevelt). *Jam* and *fix* are less formal terms that refer to predicaments from which it is difficult to escape: *kids who were in a jam with the authorities;* "*If we get left on this wreck we are in a fix*" (Mark Twain). An informal term, a *pickle* is an embarrassing or troublesome predicament: "*I could see no way out of the pickle I was in*" (Robert Louis Stevenson).

---

predicate *verb.* —*See* **base**[1].

predict *verb.* To tell about or make known in advance, especially by means of special knowledge ▶ call, forecast, foretell, portend, presage, prognosticate, project. [*Compare* **foresee, foreshadow, prophesy.**]

✚ **CORE SYNONYMS:** *predict, call, forecast, foretell, prognosticate.* These verbs mean to tell about or make known something in advance of its occurrence, especially by means of special knowledge or inference: *predict an eclipse; couldn't call the outcome of the game; forecasting the weather; foretold events that would happen; prognosticating a rebellion.*

---

prediction *noun.* The act of predicting ▶ forecast, outlook, prescience, prevision, prognosis, prognostication, projection. [*Compare* **omen, prophecy.**]

predictive *adjective.* Of or relating to prediction ▶ prescient, previsionary, prognostic, prognosticative. [*Compare* **prophetic.**]

predilection *noun.* —*See* **inclination** (1).

predispose *verb.* —*See* **influence.**

predisposed *adjective.* —*See* **inclined.**

predisposition *noun.* —*See* **inclination** (1).

predominance *noun.* —*See* **dominance.**

predominant *adjective.* —*See* **dominant** (1), **prevailing.**

predominate *verb.* —*See* **dominate** (1).

preeminence *noun.* —*See* **dominance, excellence, fame.**

preeminent *adjective.* —*See* **best** (1), **dominant** (1), **exceptional, famous.**

preempt *verb.* —*See* **seize** (1).

preemption *noun.* —*See* **seizure** (2).

preen *verb.* —*See* **dress up, pride.**

preexist *verb.* —*See* **precede.**

preface *noun.* —*See* **introduction.**

preface *verb.* —*See* **introduce** (3).

prefatory *adjective.* —*See* **introductory.**

prefer *verb.* To show partiality toward someone ▶ favor. ***Idioms:*** be partial, play favorites. [*Compare* **advance, baby.**] —*See also* **choose** (2).

preferable *adjective.* Of greater excellence than another ▶ better, superior.

preference *noun.* Preferential treatment or bias ▶ favor, favoritism, partiality, partialness. [*Compare* **bias, prejudice.**] —*See also* **choice, taste** (1).

preferential *adjective.* Disposed to favor one over another ▶ favorable, partial. [*Compare* **biased.**] —*See also* **unfair.**

preferment *noun.* —*See* **advancement.**

preferred *adjective.* —*See* **favorite.**

prefigure *verb.* —*See* **foreshadow.**

prefigurement *noun.* —*See* **omen.**

pregnability *noun.* —*See* **exposure.**

pregnable *adjective.* —*See* **vulnerable.**

pregnancy *noun.* The condition of carrying a developing fetus within the uterus ▶ gestation, gravidity, gravidness, parturiency.

pregnant *adjective.* **1.** Carrying a developing fetus within the uterus ▶ big, enceinte, expectant, expecting, gestating, gravid, parturient. *Slang:* gone, knocked-up, preggers, preggo. ***Idioms:*** having a bun in the oven, in a family way, with child. **2.** Conveying hidden or unexpressed meaning ▶ consequential, meaningful, meaty, pithy, significant, suggestive, weighty. [*Compare* **important.**]

prehistoric *adjective.* —*See* **early** (1).

prehistory *noun.* —*See* **antiquity.**

prejudge *verb.* To make a mistake in judging ▶ misestimate, misjudge, mistake. [*Compare* **misunderstand, suppose.**]

prejudice *noun.* Irrational suspicion or hatred of a particular group, race, or religion ▶ bigotry, discrimination, intolerance. [*Compare* **hate.**] —*See also* **bias, inclination** (1).

prejudice *verb.* —*See* **bias** (1), **damage.**

prejudiced *or* **prejudicial** *adjective.* —*See* **biased.**

prelate *noun.* —*See* **cleric.**

prelect *verb.* To talk to an audience formally ▶ lecture, sermonize, speak. [*Compare* **converse.**]

prelection *noun.* —*See* **speech** (2).

preliminary *adjective.* —*See* **introductory, rough** (4).

prelude *noun.* —*See* **introduction.**

premature *adjective.* Developing, occurring, or appearing before the expected time ▶ early, precocious, untimely.

premeditate *verb.* —*See* **design** (1).

premeditated *adjective.* —*See* **calculated, deliberate** (1).

premier *adjective.* —*See* **first, primary** (1).

premise *noun.* —*See* **assumption.**

premise *verb.* —*See* **suppose** (1).

premium *noun.* —*See* **reward.**

premium *adjective.* —*See* **choice** (1).

premonition *noun.* —*See* **feeling** (1).

preoccupation *noun.* —*See* **absorption** (2), **attention.**

preoccupied *adjective.* —*See* **absent-minded, rapt.**

preoccupy *verb.* To dominate the mind or thoughts of ▶ fixate, obsess, possess. [*Compare* **grip.**] —*See also* **absorb** (1).

pre-owned *adjective.* —*See* **used** (2).

prep *verb.* —*See* **prepare.**

preparation *noun.* The condition of being made ready beforehand ▶ mobilization, prearrangement, preparedness, readiness. ***Idiom:*** made ready.

preparations *noun.* Steps taken in preparation for an undertaking ▶ accommodations, arrangements, plans, provisions.

preparatory *adjective.* —*See* **introductory.**

prepare *verb.* To cause to be ready, as for use, consumption, or a special purpose ▶ cure, fit, fix, make, prime, ready. *Informal:* prep. —*See also* **arrange** (2).

prepared *adjective.* In a state of preparedness ▶ ready, set. *Informal:* go. *Slang:* together. ***Idioms:*** all set, in working order, on deck, ready (*or* raring) to go.

preparedness *noun.* —*See* **preparation.**

preponderance *or* **preponderancy** *noun.* The greatest part or portion ▶ bulk, mass, weight. [*Compare* **center.**] —*See also* **dominance.**

preponderant *adjective.* —*See* **dominant** (1).

preponderate *verb.* —*See* **dominate** (1).

prepossess *verb.* —*See* **bias** (1).

prepossessed *adjective.* —*See* **biased.**

prepossession *noun.* —*See* **absorption** (2), **bias.**

preposterous *adjective.* —*See* **foolish, outrageous.**

preposterousness *noun.* —*See* **foolishness.**

prepotency *noun.* —*See* **dominance.**

prepotent *adjective.* —*See* **dominant** (1).

prepubescence *noun.* The stage of life between birth and puberty ▶ childhood, early years, innocence, preadolescence. [*Compare* **youth.**]

prerequisite *noun.* —*See* **condition** (2), **provision, right.**

prerequisite *adjective.* —*See* **essential** (1).

prerogative *noun.* —*See* **authority, right.**

prerogative *adjective.* —*See* **exclusive** (1).

presage *noun.* —*See* **omen.**

presage *verb.* —*See* **foreshadow, predict.**

presager *noun.* —*See* **forerunner.**

prescience *noun.* —*See* **prediction, vision** (2).

prescient *adjective.* —*See* **predictive, visionary.**

prescribe *verb.* —*See* **administer** (3), **dictate.**

prescribed *adjective.* —*See* **required.**

prescript *noun.* —*See* **rule.**

prescription *noun.* —*See* **drug** (1), **law** (1).

prescriptive *adjective.* —*See* **didactic.**

presence *noun.* The condition or fact of being present ▶ attendance, occurrence. [*Compare* **existence.**] —*See also* **bearing** (1).

present[1] *noun.* —*See* **now.**

present *adjective.* In existence now ▶ contemporary, current, existent, existing, immediate, new, now, present-day. —*See also* **contemporary** (2).

present *verb.* —*See* **donate.**

present² *verb.* To make known socially ▶ acquaint, familiarize, introduce. —*See also* **cite, confer** (2), **interpret** (2), **offer** (1), **offer** (2), **stage.**

present *noun.* Something bestowed voluntarily ▶ bequest, gift, presentation. *Slang:* freebie. [*Compare* **grant.**] —*See also* **donation.**

presentable *adjective.* —*See* **decent.**

presentation *noun.* **1.** Something bestowed voluntarily ▶ bequest, gift, present. *Slang:* freebie. [*Compare* **grant.**] **2.** The instance or occasion of being presented for the first time to society ▶ coming-out, debut. —*See also* **conferment, display, interpretation, offer.**

present-day *adjective.* —*See* **present¹.**

presentiment *noun.* —*See* **feeling** (1).

preservation *noun.* —*See* **conservation, defense, maintenance.**

preservative *adjective.* Tending to or capable of preserving ▶ conservational, conservative, curatorial, precautionary, protective.

preserve *verb.* **1.** To prepare food for storage and future use ▶ brine, can, conserve, cure, dehydrate, dry, freeze, jerk, keep, kipper, pickle, pot, put up, refrigerate, salt, season, smoke, souse. **2.** To protect an asset from loss or destruction ▶ conserve, husband, save. [*Compare* **defend.**] **3.** To keep in a condition of good repair, efficiency, or use ▶ keep up, maintain, sustain. —*See also* **defend** (1).

preserve *noun.* Public land kept for a special purpose ▶ park, reservation, reserve, sanctuary. [*Compare* **common.**]

press *verb.* **1.** To extract from by applying pressure ▶ crush, express, squeeze. **2.** To smooth by applying heat or pressure ▶ calender, iron, mangle, roll. [*Compare* **even.**] —*See also* **advance** (2), **crowd, embrace** (1), **push** (1), **rub, touch, urge.**

press *noun.* A person or group of persons whose occupation is journalism ▶ anchor, anchorman, anchorperson, anchorwoman, columnist, commentator, correspondent, editor, editorialist, fourth estate, journalist, mass media, media, newscaster, newshound, newsman, newspaperman, newspaperwoman, newsperson, newswoman, reporter, stringer. *Informal:* legman. —*See also* **crowd, push.**

pressing *adjective.* —*See* **urgent** (1).

pressing *noun.* Urgent solicitation ▶ insistence, insistency, persuasion, urging. [*Compare* **demand.**]

pressure *noun.* An oppressive condition of distress ▶ strain, stress, tautness, tenseness, tension. *Informal:* heat. [*Compare* **anxiety.**] —*See also* **force** (1).

pressure *verb.* —*See* **force** (1).

prestidigitation *noun.* —*See* **magic** (2).

prestidigitator *noun.* —*See* **wizard.**

prestige *noun.* —*See* **face** (6), **fame, honor** (2).

prestigious *adjective.* —*See* **famous.**

presumable *adjective.* —*See* **presumptive.**

presume *verb.* To take advantage of unfairly ▶ abuse, exploit, impose, use. —*See also* **suppose** (1), **venture.**

presuming *adjective.* —*See* **impudent.**

presumption *noun.* —*See* **arrogance, assumption.**

presumptive *adjective.* Based on probability or presumption ▶ assumptive, given, likely, presumable, probable, prospective, supposable. ***Idiom:*** taken for granted. [*Compare* **due, supposed.**]

presumptuous *adjective.* —*See* **impudent.**

presumptuousness *noun.* —*See* **impudence.**

presuppose *verb.* —*See* **suppose** (1).

presupposition *noun.* —*See* **assumption.**

preteen *noun.* —*See* **child** (1).

pretend *verb.* To claim or allege insincerely or falsely ▶ feign, pretext, profess, purport. —*See also* **act** (2), **venture.**

pretend *adjective.* —*See* **artificial** (1).

pretended *adjective.* Being fictitious and not real, as a name ▶ assumed, made-up, pseudonymous. [*Compare* **false, fictitious.**] —*See also* **artificial** (2).

pretender *noun.* —*See* **fake.**

pretense *noun.* A professed but feigned reason or excuse ▶ pretension, pretext. [*Compare* **excuse.**] —*See also* **act** (2), **affectation, claim** (1), **façade** (2), **insincerity.**

pretension *noun.* A professed but feigned reason or excuse ▶ pretense, pretext. [*Compare* **excuse.**] —*See also* **claim** (1), **pretentiousness.**

pretentious *adjective.* —*See* **pompous, showy.**

pretentiousness *noun.* Boastful self-importance or display ▶ grandioseness, grandiosity, loftiness, ostentation, pomposity, pompousness, pretension. [*Compare* **arrogance, egotism.**]

preternatural *adjective.* Greatly exceeding or departing from the normal course of nature ▶ supernatural, unnatural. —*See also* **abnormal, supernatural** (1).

preternaturalness *noun.* —*See* **abnormality.**

pretext *noun.* A professed but feigned reason or excuse ▶ pretense, pretension. —*See also* **excuse** (1), **façade** (2).

pretext *verb.* To claim or allege insincerely or falsely ▶ feign, pretend, profess, purport.

pretty *adjective.* —*See* **attractive, beautiful.**

pretty *adverb.* —*See* **fairly** (2).

pretty penny *noun.* —*See* **fortune.**

prevail *verb.* —*See* **dominate** (1).

prevail on *or* **upon** *verb.* —*See* **persuade.**

prevail over *verb.* —*See* **defeat.**

prevailing *adjective.* Most generally existing or encountered at a given time ▶ current, epidemic, general, pandemic, popular, predominant, prevalent, rampant, regnant, reigning, rife, ruling, widespread. [*Compare* **common, pervasive.**] —*See also* **dominant** (1).

✚ **CORE SYNONYMS:** *prevailing, prevalent, current.* These adjectives denote what exists or is encountered generally at a given time. *Prevailing* applies to what is most frequent or common at a certain time or in a certain place: *took a poll to find the prevailing opinion. Prevalent* suggests widespread existence or occurrence but does not imply predominance: *a belief that was prevalent in the Middle Ages. Current* often stresses the present time and is frequently applied to what is subject to periodic change: *current psychoanalytic theories.*

---

prevalence *noun.* —*See* **usualness.**

prevalent *adjective.* —*See* **prevailing.**

prevaricate *verb.* —*See* **equivocate** (2), **lie²**.

prevarication *noun.* —*See* **equivocation, lie², mendacity.**

prevaricator *noun.* —*See* **liar.**

prevent *verb.* To prohibit from occurring by advance planning or action ▶ anticipate, avert, forerun, forestall, forfend, head off, obviate, preclude, prohibit, rule out, stave off, ward (off). ***Idioms:*** nip in the bud. [*Compare* **forbid, frustrate, stop.**]

✚ **CORE SYNONYMS:** *prevent, preclude, avert, obviate, forestall.* These verbs mean to stop or hinder something from happening, especially by advance planning or action. *Prevent* implies anticipatory counteraction: "*The surest way to prevent war is not to fear it*" (John Randolph). To *preclude* is to exclude the possibility of an event or action: "*a tranquillity which . . . his wife's presence would have precluded*" (John Henry Newman). To *avert* is to ward off something about to happen: *The pilot's quick thinking averted an accident. Obviate* implies that something, such as a difficulty, has been anticipated and disposed of effectively: "*the objections . . . having*

. . . *been obviated in the preceding chapter*" (Joseph Butler). *Forestall* usually suggests anticipatory measures taken to counteract, neutralize, or nullify the effects of something: *We installed an alarm system to forestall break-ins.*

---

prevention *noun.* The act of preventing ▶ determent, deterrence, exclusion, forestallment, frustration, obviation, preclusion, prohibition. [*Compare* **forbiddance, stop.**]

preventive *or* **preventative** *adjective.* **1.** Intended to prevent ▶ deterrent, exclusive, interdictive, preclusive, prohibitive, proscriptive. **2.** Defending against disease ▶ defensive, precautionary, prophylactic, protective.

previous *adjective.* Next before the present one ▶ foregoing, last, latter, preceding. —*See also* **advance, late** (2), **past.**

previously *adverb.* —*See* **earlier** (1), **earlier** (2).

prevision *noun.* —*See* **prediction.**

previsionary *adjective.* —*See* **predictive.**

prey *noun.* —*See* **victim.**

price *noun.* The expenditure at which something is obtained ▶ cost, price, sacrifice, toll. *Informal:* damage. —*See also* **cost** (1).

priceless *adjective.* —*See* **costly, funny** (1).

pricey *adjective.* —*See* **costly.**

prick *noun.* A small mark or hole made by a sharp, pointed object ▶ nick, notch, perforation, puncture, stab. [*Compare* **cut, scrape.**] —*See also* **pain, spike.**

prick *verb.* —*See* **cut** (1), **provoke.**

prickle *noun.* —*See* **pain, spike.**

prickliness *noun.* —*See* **temper** (1).

prickly *adjective.* Full of irritating difficulties or controversies ▶ nettlesome, spiny, thorny. [*Compare* **complex, delicate, disturbing, troublesome.**] —*See also* **thorny** (1).

pricky *adjective.* —*See* **thorny** (1).

pride *noun.* A sense of one's own dignity or worth ▶ amour-propre, ego, proudness, self-contentment, self-esteem, self-regard, self-respect, self-satisfaction. —*See also* **arrogance, egotism, flock.**

pride *verb.* To be proud of oneself, as for an accomplishment or achievement ▶ gloat, pique, plume, preen.

prideful *adjective.* —*See* **arrogant, proud.**

pridefulness *noun.* —*See* **arrogance.**

prier *or* **pryer** *noun.* A person who snoops ▶ pry, snoop, snooper. [*Compare* **busybody.**]

priest *noun.* —*See* **cleric.**

priestly *adjective.* —*See* **clerical.**

prig *noun.* One who despises people or things regarded as inferior, especially because of social or intellectual pretension ▶ elitist, snob. *Informal:* snoot. —*See also* **prude.**

priggish *adjective.* —*See* **arrogant, prudish.**

prim *adjective.* —*See* **neat, prudish.**

prima donna *noun.* —*See* **lead.**

primal *adjective.* —*See* **early** (1), **elemental.**

primary *adjective.* **1.** Most important, influential, or significant ▶ capital, cardinal, central, chief, crucial, first, foremost, head, key, leading, main, major, number one, paramount, pivotal, premier, prime, principal, staple, top, vital. [*Compare* **elemental, essential, important.**] **2.** Marked by the absence of any intervention ▶ direct, firsthand, immediate. —*See also* **dominant** (1), **first, original, radical.**

✦ **CORE SYNONYMS:** *primary, chief, principal, main, leading, foremost, prime.* These adjectives refer to what is first in importance, influence, or significance. *Primary* stresses first in the sense of origin, sequence, or development: *primary school.* It can also mean first in the sense of "fundamental": *the primary function of this machine. Chief* applies to a person of the highest authority: *a chief magistrate.* Used figuratively, *chief* implies maximum importance or value: *my chief joy. Principal* applies to someone or something of the first order in power or significance: *their principal source of entertainment. Main* applies to what exceeds others in extent, size, or importance: *the main building on the campus. Leading* suggests personal magnetism, a record of achievement, or capacity for influencing others: *one of the leading physicians of the city. Foremost* emphasizes the sense of having forged ahead of others: *the foremost research scientist of the day. Prime* applies to what is first in comparison with others and to what is of the best quality: *a theory of prime significance; a prime Burgundy.*

---

prime *adjective.* —*See* **choice** (1), **dominant** (1), **excellent, first, original, primary** (1).
prime *noun.* —*See* **bloom[1]** (1).
prime *verb.* —*See* **prepare.** To put explosive material into a weapon ▶ charge, load, ready.

primeval *adjective.* —*See* **early** (1).

primitive *adjective.* —*See* **early** (1), **elemental, ignorant** (2), **original, radical, rude** (1), **uncivilized.**

primogenitor *noun.* —*See* **ancestor** (1).

primordial *adjective.* —*See* **early** (1), **first.**

primp *verb.* —*See* **dress up.**

prince *noun.* —*See* **chief.**

princely *adjective.* —*See* **generous** (1), **grand.**

principal *adjective.* —*See* **dominant** (1), **primary** (1).
principal *noun.* —*See* **capital** (1), **lead.**

principle *noun.* —*See* **character** (2), **doctrine, law** (3), **moral.**

principled *adjective.* —*See* **ethical.**

principles *noun.* —*See* **ethics** (2).

print *noun.* —*See* **impression** (1), **track.**
print *verb.* —*See* **publish** (1).

printing *noun.* The entire number of copies of a publication printed from a single typesetting ▶ impression. —*See also* **publication** (1).

prior *adjective.* —*See* **advance, past.**

priority *noun.* —*See* **precedence.**

prison *noun.* —*See* **jail.**

priss *noun.* —*See* **prude.**

prissy *adjective.* —*See* **prudish.**

pristine *adjective.* —*See* **fresh** (1), **original.**

privacy *noun.* —*See* **solitude.**

private *adjective.* **1.** Belonging to, relating to, or affecting a particular person ▶ individual, intimate, personal. **2.** Belonging or confined to a particular person or group as opposed to the public or the government ▶ closed-door, personal, privy. [*Compare* **secret.**] —*See also* **confidential** (1), **exclusive** (1).

privation *noun.* —*See* **deprivation, poverty.**

privilege *noun.* —*See* **license** (1), **right.**

privileged *adjective.* —*See* **confidential** (3).

privy *adjective.* Belonging or confined to a particular person or group as opposed to the public or the government ▶ closed-door, personal, private. [*Compare* **secret.**] —*See also* **confidential** (1).

prize[1] *noun.* **1.** A memento received as a symbol of excellence or victory ▶ accolade, cup, award, trophy. [*Compare* **medal.**] **2.** A person or thing worth catching ▶ *Informal:* catch. ▶ plum. *Slang:* brass ring. —*See also* **best** (1), **distinction** (2), **reward, treasure.**
prize *verb.* —*See* **value.**
prize *adjective.* —*See* **excellent.**

prize[2] *noun.* —*See* **plunder.**

prizefighter *noun.* A contestant in a boxing match ▶ boxer, fighter, pugilist. [*Compare* **fighter.**]

prizewinner *noun.* —*See* **winner.**

pro *noun.* —*See* **expert, prostitute.**
pro *adjective.* —*See* **expert.**

probability *noun.* —*See* **chance** (3).

probable *adjective.* Having a good chance of happening or being true ▶ contingent, likely, possible, potential. ***Idiom:*** in the cards. [*Compare* **believable, inclined, liable.**] *—See also* **presumptive.**

probably *adverb.* More likely than not ▶ believably, likely, presumably, reasonably, seemingly. ***Idioms:*** all things being equal, in all likelihood (*or* probability). [*Compare* **maybe.**]

probationary *or* **probative** *adjective.* *—See* **pilot.**

probe *noun.* **1.** The act or an instance of exploring or investigating ▶ exploration, investigation, reconnaissance. **2.** Something, as a remark, used to determine another person's attitude ▶ feeler. ***Idiom:*** trial balloon. [*Compare* **advances, introduction.**] *—See also* **examination** (1), **examination** (2).

probe *verb.* To test the attitude of ▶ feel out, sound (out). ***Idioms:*** put out feelers, run something up the flagpole, send up a trial balloon. *—See also* **explore.**

prober *noun.* *—See* **inquirer.**

probing *adjective.* *—See* **critical** (2).

probity *noun.* *—See* **character** (2), **good** (1).

problem *noun.* A situation that presents difficulty, uncertainty, or perplexity ▶ case, hornets' nest, issue, matter, question. *Informal:* bind, can of worms, tight spot. [*Compare* **predicament.**] *—See also* **difficulty, disadvantage, qualm.**

problematic *adjective.* *—See* **ambiguous** (1), **debatable, doubtful** (1).

pro bono *adjective.* *—See* **unpaid.**

proboscis *noun.* *—See* **nose** (1).

procedure *noun.* An action calculated to achieve an end ▶ maneuver, measure, move, step, tactic. *—See also* **approach** (1).

proceed *verb.* To move along a particular course ▶ go, pass, push on, wend. ***Idioms:*** make (*or* wend) one's way. [*Compare* **hike, journey, rove.**] *—See also* **advance** (2), **continue, stem.**

process *noun.* *—See* **approach** (1), **method.**

procession *noun.* *—See* **advance, series.**

proclaim *verb.* To make known the presence or arrival of ▶ announce, herald, introduce, usher in. *—See also* **announce, show** (1).

proclamation *noun.* *—See* **announcement, message.**

proclivity *noun.* *—See* **inclination** (1).

procrastinate *verb.* *—See* **delay** (2).

procrastination *noun.* *—See* **delay** (1).

procrastinator *noun.* *—See* **laggard.**

procreant *adjective.* Of or relating to reproduction ▶ generative, procreative, reproductive.

procreate *verb.* *—See* **breed.**

procreation *noun.* *—See* **reproduction.**

procreative *adjective.* Of or relating to reproduction ▶ generative, procreant, reproductive.

procumbent *adjective.* *—See* **flat** (1).

procurable *adjective.* *—See* **available.**

procure *verb.* *—See* **get** (1).

prod *verb.* *—See* **provoke, push** (1).

prod *noun.* *—See* **dig, provocation** (1), **stimulus.**

prodigal *adjective.* *—See* **extravagant, generous** (1), **profuse.**

prodigal *noun.* *—See* **wastrel** (1).

prodigality *noun.* *—See* **extravagance.**

prodigious *adjective.* *—See* **astonishing, enormous.**

prodigiousness *noun.* *—See* **enormousness.**

prodigy *noun.* *—See* **marvel.**

produce *verb.* **1.** To bring into existence ▶ bear, bring forth, create, develop, engender, generate, give, give forth, make, originate, provide, spawn, yield. ***Idioms:*** give birth (*or* rise) to. [*Compare* **breed, give, offer.**] **2.** To bring (a product or idea, for example) into being ▶ develop, generate. *—See also* **cite, compose** (1), **make, return** (3), **stage.**

produce *noun.* Something produced by human effort ▶ product, production, manufacture, work. [*Compare* **composition, good.**]

✤ CORE SYNONYMS: *produce, bear, yield.* These verbs mean to bring forth as a product: *a mine that produces gold; a seed that finally bore fruit; a plant that yields a medicinal oil.*

---

producer *noun.* —*See* **developer, maker.**

product *noun.* Something produced by human effort ▶ produce, production, manufacture, work. [*Compare* **composition, good.**]

production *noun.* **1.** Something produced by human effort ▶ produce, product, manufacture, work. [*Compare* **good.**] **2.** The amount or quantity produced ▶ garner, output, yield. —*See also* **composition** (1).

productive *adjective.* **1.** Capable of reproducing ▶ fertile, fecund, fruitful, prolific. **2.** Acting effectively with minimal waste ▶ efficient, streamlined, well-oiled. [*Compare* **diligent, methodical.**] —*See also* **effective** (1), **fertile** (1).

productivity *or* **productiveness** *noun.* The quality of being efficient ▶ efficiency. [*Compare* **ability, diligence.**] —*See also* **fertility.**

profanation *noun.* —*See* **sacrilege.**

profane *adjective.* **1.** Showing irreverence and contempt for something sacred ▶ blasphemous, impious, sacrilegious. **2.** Not religious in subject matter, form, or use ▶ civil, lay, nonecclesiastical, nonreligious, nonspiritual, secular, temporal, worldly. [*Compare* **earthly.**] —*See also* **obscene.**

profane *verb.* —*See* **violate** (3).

profaneness *noun.* —*See* **obscenity** (1).

profanity *noun.* —*See* **obscenity** (1), **obscenity** (2), **swearword.**

profess *verb.* To claim or allege insincerely or falsely ▶ feign, pretend, pretext, purport. —*See also* **assert.**

profession *noun.* —*See* **assertion, business** (2), **religion.**

professional *adjective.* —*See* **expert.**

professional *noun.* —*See* **expert.**

proffer *verb.* —*See* **offer** (1), **propose.**

proffer *noun.* —*See* **offer.**

proficiency *noun.* —*See* **ability** (1).

proficient *adjective.* —*See* **expert.**

proficient *noun.* —*See* **expert.**

profile *noun.* —*See* **form** (1).

profit *noun.* Something earned, won, or otherwise acquired ▶ earnings, gain, return. [*Compare* **increase.**] —*See also* **advantage** (2), **interest** (1), **use** (2).

profit *verb.* **1.** To make a large profit ▶ batten, cash in. *Slang:* clean up. ***Idioms:*** make a killing, make out like a bandit. **2.** To be an advantage to ▶ advantage, avail, benefit, help, serve. ***Idioms:*** do someone good, serve someone well, stand someone in good stead. —*See also* **benefit.**

profitable *adjective.* Affording profit ▶ advantageous, bankable, fat, gainful, lucrative, moneymaking, remunerative, rewarding. —*See also* **beneficial.**

profitless *adjective.* —*See* **futile.**

profitlessness *noun.* —*See* **futility.**

profligacy *noun.* —*See* **extravagance, license** (2).

profligate *adjective.* —*See* **abandoned** (2), **extravagant.**

profligate *noun.* —*See* **wanton, wastrel** (1).

profound *adjective.* —*See* **deep** (1), **deep** (2), **deep** (3).

profoundness *noun.* Intellectual penetration or range ▶ deepness, depth, profundity, weightiness. [*Compare* **discernment, intelligence, wisdom.**]

profundity *noun.* Intellectual penetration or range ▶ deepness, depth, profoundness, weightiness. [*Compare* **discernment, intelligence.**] —*See also* **wisdom** (1).

profuse *adjective.* Given to or marked by unrestrained abundance ▶ extravagant, exuberant, lavish, lush, luxuriant, opulent, prodigal, riotous, superabundant. [*Compare* **generous.**] —*See also* **extravagant, thick** (3).

✚ **CORE SYNONYMS:** *profuse, exuberant, lavish, lush, luxuriant, prodigal, riotous.* These adjectives mean given to or marked by unrestrained abundance: *profuse apologies; an exuberant growth of moss; lavish praise; lush vegetation; luxuriant hair; a prodigal party giver; an artist's riotous use of color.*

◀ **ANTONYM:** *spare*

profuseness *noun.* —*See* **extravagance.**

profusion *noun.* —*See* **abundance, extravagance.**

progenitor *noun.* —*See* **ancestor** (1), **ancestor** (2).

progeny *noun.* A person or group descended directly from the same parents or ancestors ▶ brood, child, children, descendant, fruit, generation, get, issue, offspring, posterity, scion, seed, spawn. [*Compare* **ancestry, family.**]

prognosis *noun.* —*See* **prediction.**

prognostic *adjective.* —*See* **predictive.**

prognostic *noun.* —*See* **omen.**

prognosticate *verb.* —*See* **foreshadow, predict.**

prognostication *noun.* —*See* **omen, prediction.**

prognosticative *adjective.* —*See* **predictive.**

prognosticator *noun.* —*See* **prophet.**

program *noun.* **1.** An organized list, as of procedures, activities, or events ▶ agenda, calendar, catalog, docket, lineup, orders of the day, schedule, timetable. [*Compare* **approach, list[1].**] **2.** A document that complements a public performance, presentation, or offering ▶ bill, card, catalog, playbill, prospectus, syllabus. **3.** A show that is aired on television or radio ▶ airing, broadcast.

program *verb.* To enter on a schedule ▶ calendar, docket, schedule, slate. [*Compare* **list[1], post[3].**] —*See also* **indoctrinate** (2).

progress *noun.* Steady improvement, as of an individual or society ▶ advancement, amelioration, betterment, development, headway, improvement, melioration. [*Compare* **improvement.**] —*See also* **advance, development, journey.**

progress *verb.* —*See* **advance** (2), **rise** (3).

progression *noun.* —*See* **advance, series, transition.**

progressive *adjective.* **1.** Ahead of current trends or customs ▶ advanced, avant-garde, forward, forward-looking, forward-thinking, futuristic, precocious, revolutionary. ***Idiom:*** ahead of the times. [*Compare* **inventive, new.**] **2.** Proceeding steadily by degrees ▶ gradational, gradual, piecemeal, step-by-step. ***Idioms:*** one foot after another, one step at a time. [*Compare* **consecutive, methodical, slow.**] —*See also* **broad-minded, liberal.**

progressive *noun.* —*See* **liberal.**

prohibit *verb.* —*See* **forbid, prevent.**

prohibited *adjective.* —*See* **forbidden.**

prohibition *noun.* —*See* **forbiddance, prevention.**

prohibitive *adjective.* —*See* **preventive** (1).

project *noun.* Something undertaken, especially something requiring extensive planning and work ▶ endeavor, enterprise, undertaking, venture. —*See also* **approach** (1), **task** (1).

project *verb.* —*See* **bulge, design** (1), **intend, predict, shed[1]** (1), **shoot** (3).

projection *noun.* A part that protrudes or extends outward ▶ bulb, bulge, jut, knob, knot, lip, overhang, protrusion, protuberance, salient. [*Compare* **bump.**] —*See also* **intention, prediction.**

prolegomenon *noun.* —*See* **introduction.**

proletariat *noun.* —*See* **commonalty.**

proliferate *verb.* —*See* **breed, increase.**

proliferation *noun.* —*See* **buildup** (2), **expansion, increase** (1), **reproduction.**

prolific *adjective.* Capable of reproducing ▶ fertile, fecund, fruitful, productive. —*See also* **fertile** (1).

prolificacy *or* **prolificness** *noun.* —*See* **fertility.**

prolix *adjective.* —*See* **wordy** (1).

prolixity *noun.* —*See* **wordiness.**

prologue *noun.* —*See* **introduction.**

prolong *or* **prolongate** *verb.* —*See* **lengthen.**

prolongation *noun.* —*See* **extension** (1).

prolonged *adjective.* —*See* **chronic** (2), **long**[1] (1), **long**[1] (2).

prom *noun.* —*See* **dance.**

promenade *noun.* —*See* **dance, walk** (1).

promenade *verb.* —*See* **display, stroll.**

prominence *noun.* —*See* **fame, hill.**

prominency *noun.* —*See* **fame.**

prominent *adjective.* —*See* **famous, noticeable.**

promiscuous *adjective.* —*See* **wanton** (1).

promise *noun.* **1.** A declaration that one will or will not do a certain thing ▶ assurance, commitment, covenant, engagement, guarantee, guaranty, oath, pledge, plight, solemn word, vow, warrant, word, word of honor. [*Compare* **pawn**[1].] **2.** Indication of future success or development ▶ makings, possibility, potential, prospects. [*Compare* **material.**] **3.** Something expected ▶ anticipation, expectation, likelihood, prospect. [*Compare* **chance, theory.**]

promise *verb.* —*See* **pledge** (2), **pledge** (1).

promised *adjective.* —*See* **engaged.**

promising *adjective.* Showing great promise ▶ coming, up-and-coming. ***Idiom:*** on the way up. —*See also* **encouraging.**

promote *verb.* **1.** To raise in rank ▶ advance, elevate, exalt, jump, raise, up, upgrade. ***Idioms:*** kick upstairs, move up. **2.** To help bring about ▶ abet, cultivate, encourage, facilitate, feed, foster, nourish, nurture. [*Compare* **support.**] **3.** To attempt to sell or popularize by advertising or publicity ▶ advertise, ballyhoo, boost, build up, cry up, market, popularize, publicize, puff (up), purvey, sell, talk up, tout. *Informal:* pitch, plug. *Slang:* hype, push. ***Idioms:*** beat the drum for, make a plug for. [*Compare* **emphasize.**] —*See also* **advance** (1).

promotion *noun.* —*See* **advancement, advertising, patronage** (1), **publicity.**

prompt *adjective.* Occurring, acting, or performed exactly at the time appointed ▶ punctual, timely.

prompt *verb.* —*See* **cause, provoke.**

promptly *adverb.* —*See* **immediately** (1), **soon.**

promulgate *verb.* —*See* **announce, establish** (2).

promulgation *noun.* —*See* **announcement.**

prone *adjective.* —*See* **flat** (1), **inclined, liable** (2).

proneness *noun.* —*See* **inclination** (1).

prong *noun.* —*See* **spike.**

pronounce *verb.* To produce or make speech sounds ▶ articulate, enounce, enunciate, phonate, say, sound, utter, vocalize, voice. [*Compare* **say.**]

pronounced *adjective.* —*See* **apparent** (1), **decided, noticeable, oral.**

pronouncement *noun.* —*See* **message, ruling.**

pronto *adverb.* —*See* **fast, immediately** (1), **soon.**

pronunciation *noun.* —*See* **expression** (1), **voicing.**

proof *noun.* —*See* **confirmation** (2), **reason** (1), **test** (1).

proof *adjective.* —*See* **resistant.**

prop *noun.* —*See* **support.**

prop *verb.* —*See* **support** (2).

propaganda *noun.* The systematic widespread promotion of a particular doctrine or idea ▶ brainwashing, disinformation, evangelism, indoctrination, propagandism, proselytism. [*Compare* **advertising, publicity.**]

propagandist *noun.* One who disseminates or engages in propaganda ▶ brainwasher, disseminator, evangelist, indoctrinator, missionary, missioner, pamphleteer, proselytizer. [*Compare* **advocate.**]

propagandize *verb.* —*See* **indoctrinate** (2).

propagate *verb.* —*See* **announce, breed, grow.**

propagation *noun.* —*See* **reproduction.**

propel *verb.* —*See* **advance** (1), **drive** (2), **provoke, shoot** (3).

propensity *noun.* —*See* **inclination** (1).

proper *adjective.* —*See* **appropriate, convenient** (1), **ethical, just, prudish.**

properly *adverb.* —*See* **fair**[1]**.**

properness *noun.* —*See* **decency** (2), **decency** (1).

property *noun.* —*See* **effects, holdings, land, quality** (1).

prophecy *noun.* Something that is foretold by or as if by supernatural means ▶ augury, divination, oracle, soothsaying, vaticination, vision. [*Compare* **omen, prediction.**]

prophesier *noun.* —*See* **prophet.**

prophesy *verb.* To tell about or make known by or as if by supernatural means ▶ augur, divine, forebode, foretell, soothsay, vaticinate. [*Compare* **foreshadow, predict.**]

✦ **CORE SYNONYMS:** *prophesy, augur, divine, foretell, prophesy, vaticinate.* These verbs mean to tell about something beforehand by or as if by supernatural means: *prophesying a stock-market boom; augured a scandal; divined the enemy's victory; foretelling the future; atrocities vaticinated by the antifascists.*

---

prophet *noun.* A person who foretells future events by or as if by supernatural means ▶ augur, auspex, clairvoyant, diviner, foreteller, fortuneteller, haruspex, oracle, palmist, prognosticator, prophesier, prophetess, seer, sibyl, soothsayer, vaticinator.

prophetic *or* **prophetical** *adjective.* Of or relating to the foretelling of events by or as if by supernatural means ▶ augural, divinitory, fatidic, fatidical, mantic, oracular, sibylline, vatic, vatical, vaticinal, visionary. [*Compare* **predictive.**]

prophylactic *adjective.* —*See* **preventive** (2).

propitiate *verb.* —*See* **pacify.**

propitious *adjective.* —*See* **beneficial, favorable** (1), **opportune.**

proponent *noun.* —*See* **advocate.**

proportion *noun.* Satisfying arrangement marked by even distribution of elements, as in a design ▶ balance, harmony, symmetry. [*Compare* **agreement.**] —*See also* **degree** (2).

proportion *verb.* —*See* **harmonize** (1).

✦ **CORE SYNONYMS:** *proportion, harmony, symmetry, balance.* These nouns mean an aesthetic or satisfying arrangement marked by proper distribution of elements, as in design. *Proportion* is the agreeable relation of parts within a whole: *a house with rooms of gracious proportion. Harmony* is the pleasing interaction or appropriate combination of elements: *the harmony of your facial features. Symmetry* and *balance* both imply an arrangement of parts on either side of a dividing line, but *symmetry* frequently emphasizes mirror-image correspondence of parts, while *balance* often suggests dissimilar parts that offset each other harmoniously: *flowers planted in perfect symmetry around the pool; "In all perfectly beautiful objects, there is found the opposition of one part to another, and a reciprocal balance"* (John Ruskin).

---

proportional *or* **proportionate** *adjective.* **1.** Properly or correspondingly related in size, amount, or scale ▶ commensurable, commensurate, corresponding, equivalent. ***Idiom:*** in proportion. [*Compare* **equal.**] **2.** Characterized by or displaying symmetry, especially correspondence in scale or measure ▶ balanced, regular, symmetric, symmetrical. [*Compare* **even, parallel.**]

proportions *noun.* —*See* **size** (1).

proposal *noun.* **1.** Something that is put forward for consideration ▶ motion, nomination, proposition, submission, suggestion. **2.** Something offered ▶ bid, offer, proffer, tender. —*See also* **theory** (2).

propose *verb.* To state for consideration or debate ▶ advance, move, offer, pose, proffer, propound, put forward, set forth, submit, suggest, throw out. [*Compare* **broach, name, offer, refer.**] —*See also* **intend.**

✦ CORE SYNONYMS: *propose, pose, propound, submit.* These verbs mean to state for consideration or debate: *proposes a solution; posed many questions; propound a theory; submits a plan.*

---

proposition *noun.* —*See* **advances, doctrine, proposal** (1).

propound *verb.* —*See* **propose.**

proprieties *noun.* —*See* **amenities** (2).

proprietor *noun.* —*See* **owner.**

proprietorship *noun.* —*See* **ownership.**

propriety *noun.* —*See* **decency** (1), **decency** (2), **ethics** (1), **manners.**

prosaic *adjective.* —*See* **dull** (1), **realistic** (1).

proscenium *noun.* —*See* **stage** (1).

proscribe *verb.* —*See* **condemn, forbid.**

proscription *noun.* —*See* **exile, forbiddance.**

proscriptive *adjective.* —*See* **preventive** (1).

prosecute *verb.* To institute or subject to legal proceedings ▶ law, litigate, sue. ***Idioms:*** bring suit, haul (*or* drag) into court. —*See also* **enforce, perform** (1).

prosecution *noun.* —*See* **performance, pursuit** (2).

proselytism *noun.* —*See* **propaganda.**

proselytizer *noun.* —*See* **propagandist.**

prosopopeia *noun.* —*See* **embodiment.**

prospect *noun.* Something expected ▶ anticipation, expectation, likelihood, promise. [*Compare* **chance, theory.**] —*See also* **view** (2).

prospect *adjective.* —*See* **comer** (2).

prospective *adjective.* —*See* **presumptive.**

prospects *noun.* **1.** Chance of success or advancement ▶ outlook, future. **2.** Indication of future success or development ▶ makings, possibility, potential, promise. [*Compare* **material.**] —*See also* **chance** (3).

prospectus *noun.* —*See* **program** (2).

prosper *verb.* To do or fare well ▶ batten, boom, flourish, go, thrive. *Slang:* score. ***Idioms:*** do right for oneself, get (*or* go) somewhere, go great guns, go strong. [*Compare* **succeed.**]

prospering *adjective.* —*See* **flourishing.**

prosperity *noun.* **1.** A state of health, happiness, and prospering ▶ weal, welfare, well-being. [*Compare* **condition, happiness.**] **2.** Steady good fortune or financial security ▶ comfort, ease, luxuriance, luxury, prosperousness, wealth. *Informal:* easy street. ***Idioms:*** comfortable (*or* easy) circumstances, the good life. [*Compare* **success, wealth.**]

prosperous *adjective.* Enjoying steady good fortune or financial security ▶ comfortable, easy, successful, well-heeled, well-off, well-to-do. *Informal:* well-fixed. ***Idioms:*** comfortably off, in clover, on easy street, on top of the world. [*Compare* **rich.**] —*See also* **flourishing, opportune.**

prosperousness *noun.* —*See* **prosperity** (2).

prostitute *noun.* A person who engages in sex for payment ▶ sex worker, streetwalker, whore. *Slang:* hustler, pro. [*Compare* **harlot, slut.**]

prostrate *verb.* —*See* **drop** (3), **overwhelm** (2).

prostrate *adjective.* —*See* **flat** (1).

prostration *noun.* —*See* **exhaustion, praise** (2).
protagonist *noun.* —*See* **lead.**
protean *adjective.* —*See* **versatile.**
protect *verb.* —*See* **defend** (1).
protection *noun.* —*See* **bribe, care** (2), **conservation, cover** (1), **defense, guard.**
protective *adjective.* —*See* **preservative, preventive** (2).
protector *noun.* —*See* **guard.**
protectorate *noun.* —*See* **possession.**
pro tem *adjective.* —*See* **temporary** (1).
protest *verb.* —*See* **object.**
protest *or* **protestation** *noun.* —*See* **objection.**
protocol *noun.* —*See* **ceremony** (2).
protohistory *noun.* —*See* **antiquity.**
protoplast *noun.* —*See* **original.**
prototypal *adjective.* —*See* **typical.**
prototype *noun.* —*See* **ancestor** (2), **epitome, original.**
prototypical *or* **prototypic** *adjective.* —*See* **original, typical.**
protract *verb.* —*See* **lengthen.**
protracted *adjective.* —*See* **chronic** (2), **long**[1] (2).
protractile *adjective.* —*See* **extensible.**
protraction *noun.* —*See* **extension** (1).
protrude *verb.* —*See* **bulge.**
protrusion *noun.* —*See* **projection.**
protuberance *noun.* —*See* **bump** (1), **projection.**
protuberate *verb.* —*See* **bulge.**
proud *adjective.* Properly valuing oneself, one's honor, or one's dignity ▶ prideful, self-content, self-regarding, self-respecting, self-satisfied. —*See also* **arrogant, glorious.**
proudness *noun.* —*See* **arrogance, pride.**
prove *verb.* To establish as true or genuine through evidence ▶ authenticate, bear out, circumstantiate, confirm, corroborate, demonstrate, document, establish, evidence, justify, show, substantiate, sustain, validate, verify. ***Idiom:*** go to show. [*Compare* **back, confirm, defend, show.**] —*See also* **test** (1).
prove out *verb.* To prove valid under scrutiny ▶ hold up, stand up. *Informal:* wash. ***Idioms:*** hold water, pass muster, ring true.
provenance *noun.* —*See* **origin.**
provender *noun.* —*See* **food.**
provenience *noun.* —*See* **origin.**
proverb *noun.* A usually pithy and familiar statement generally accepted as wise or true ▶ adage, aphorism, apothegm, axiom, byword, maxim, motto, saw, saying. [*Compare* **doctrine, expression, lore.**]

✦ **CORE SYNONYMS:** *proverb, saying, maxim, adage, saw, motto, aphorism.* These nouns refer to concise verbal expressions setting forth wisdom or a truth. *Proverb* refers to an old and popular expression that illustrates something such as a basic truth or a practical precept: *"Slow and steady wins the race" is a proverb to live by.* A *saying* is an often repeated and familiar expression: *a collection of philosophical sayings. Maxim* denotes particularly an expression of a general truth or a rule of conduct: *"For a wise man, he seemed to me . . . to be governed too much by general maxims"* (Edmund Burke). *Adage* applies to a saying that has gained credit through long use: *a gift that gave no credence to the adage, "Good things come in small packages." Saw* often refers to a familiar saying that has become trite through frequent repetition: *old saws that gave little comfort to the losing team.* A *motto* expresses the aims, character, or guiding principles of a person, group, or institution: *"Exuberance over taste" is my motto. Aphorism,* denoting a concise expression of a truth or principle, implies depth of content and stylistic distinction: *Few writers have coined more aphorisms than Benjamin Franklin.*

---

proverbial *adjective.* —*See* **pithy.**
provide *verb.* —*See* **give** (1), **offer** (2), **produce** (1).

provide for *verb.* **1.** To supply with the necessities of life ▶ keep, maintain, support. ***Idioms:*** put a roof over someone's head, put food on the table, take care of. [*Compare* **nourish.**] **2.** To state specifically ▶ detail, particularize, specify, stipulate. [*Compare* **assert, describe, designate, dictate.**] *—See also* **nurture.**

providence *noun.* *—See* **economy, prudence.**

provident *adjective.* *—See* **economical.**

providential *adjective.* Characterized by luck or good fortune ▶ fortuitous, fortunate, happy, lucky. [*Compare* **opportune.**]

provider *noun.* *—See* **donor.**

province *noun.* *—See* **area** (1), **possession.**

provincial *adjective.* *—See* **country, narrow** (1).

provision *noun.* A restricting or modifying element ▶ condition, limitation, qualification, precondition, prerequisite, proviso, reservation, specification, stipulation, term. *Informal:* string. [*Compare* **restriction.**] *—See also* **hoard.**

provisional *adjective.* *—See* **conditional, temporary** (1), **temporary** (2).

provisions *noun.* Steps taken in preparation for an undertaking ▶ arrangements, accommodations, plans, preparations. *—See also* **food.**

proviso *noun.* *—See* **provision.**

provisory *adjective.* *—See* **conditional.**

provocation *noun.* **1.** Something that causes others to feel angry or resentful ▶ goad, incitation, incitement, instigation, prod, stimulus, trigger. **2.** An act of taunting another to do something bold or rash ▶ challenge, dare, gauntlet. *—See also* **annoyance** (1), **defiance** (1).

provocative *adjective.* *—See* **racy.**

provoke *verb.* To stir to action or feeling ▶ egg on, excite, foment, galvanize, goad, heat up, impel, incent, incentivize, incite, inflame, inspire, instigate, motivate, move, pique, prick, prod, prompt, propel, set off, spark, spur, stimulate, touch off, trigger, work up. [*Compare* **arouse, energize, move, urge.**] *—See also* **anger** (1), **annoy, cause, court** (1), **offend** (1).

✚ CORE SYNONYMS: *provoke, incite, excite, stimulate.* These verbs mean to stir someone to action or feeling. *Provoke* often merely states the consequences produced: *"Let my presumption not provoke thy wrath"* (William Shakespeare). *"A situation which in the country would have provoked meetings"* (John Galsworthy). To *incite* is to provoke and urge on: *Members of the opposition incited the insurrection. Excite* implies a strong or emotional reaction: *The movie will fail; the plot excites little interest or curiosity. Stimulate* suggests renewed vigor of action as if by spurring or goading: *"Our vigilance was stimulated by our finding traces of a large . . . encampment"* (Francis Parkman).

---

provoker *noun.* *—See* **aggressor.**

provoking *adjective.* *—See* **disturbing.**

prowess *noun.* *—See* **courage, dexterity.**

prowl *verb.* *—See* **lurk, sneak.**

prowler *noun.* One who behaves in a stealthy, furtive way ▶ skulker, sneak, sneaker, weasel. [*Compare* **creep, betrayer.**]

proximate *adjective.* *—See* **close** (1), **imminent.**

proxy *noun.* *—See* **representative, substitute.**

prude *noun.* One excessively concerned with being proper, modest, or righteous ▶ bluenose, Mrs. Grundy, prig, priss, puritan, schoolmarm, Victorian. *Informal:* old maid. [*Compare* **square.**]

prudence *noun.* The exercise of good judgment or common sense in practical matters ▶ caution, circumspection, discretion, forehandedness, foresight, foresightedness, forethought, forethoughtfulness, precaution, providence. [*Com-*

pare **care, caution, common sense.**] —*See also* **economy.**

✦ CORE SYNONYMS: *prudence, discretion, foresight, forethought, circumspection.* These nouns refer to the exercise of good judgment, common sense, and caution in the conduct of practical matters. *Prudence* is the most comprehensive: *"She had been forced into prudence in her youth, she learned romance as she grew older"* (Jane Austen). *Discretion* suggests wise self-restraint, as in resisting a rash impulse: *"The better part of valor is discretion"* (William Shakespeare). *Foresight* implies the ability to foresee and make provision for what may happen: *She had the foresight to make backups of her computer files. Forethought* suggests advance consideration of future eventualities: *The empty refrigerator indicated a lack of forethought. Circumspection* implies discretion, as out of concern for moral or social repercussions: *"The necessity of the times, more than ever, calls for our utmost circumspection"* (Samuel Adams).

---

prudent *adjective.* —*See* **deliberate** (3), **economical, sensible, wary.**

prudish *adjective.* Marked by excessive concern for modesty or propriety ▶ bluenosed, genteel, mannered, mincing, overnice, overrefined, priggish, prim, prissy, proper, puritanical, schoolmarmish, strait-laced, stuffy, Victorian. *Informal:* old-maidish. ***Idiom:*** prim and proper. [*Compare* **ceremonious, fussy, stiff.**]

prune *verb.* —*See* **cut** (3), **drop** (5).

pruner *noun.* —*See* **shears.**

prurience *or* **pruriency** *noun.* —*See* **desire** (2).

prurient *adjective.* —*See* **lascivious.**

pry *verb.* To look into or inquire about curiously, inquisitively, or in a meddlesome fashion ▶ poke, snoop. *Informal:* nose (around), sniff about (*or* around). ***Idiom:*** stick one's nose into. [*Compare* **meddle.**]

pry *noun.* A person who snoops ▶ prier, snoop, snooper. [*Compare* **busybody.**]

prying *adjective.* —*See* **curious** (1).

prying *noun.* —*See* **curiosity** (2).

p's and q's *noun.* —*See* **manners.**

pseudonymous *adjective.* Being fictitious and not real, as a name ▶ assumed, made-up, pretended. [*Compare* **false, fictitious.**]

psyche *noun.* —*See* **psychology, spirit** (2).

psyched *adjective.* —*See* **thrilled.**

psychic *adjective.* —*See* **mental.**

psycho *adjective.* —*See* **insane.**

psychological *adjective.* —*See* **mental.**

psychology *noun.* The thought processes characteristic of an individual or group ▶ ethos, mentality, mind, mindset, psyche. ***Idiom:*** what makes someone tick. [*Compare* **character, identity.**]

psychopathy *noun.* —*See* **insanity.**

psychotropic *noun.* —*See* **drug** (2).

pub *noun.* —*See* **bar** (2).

puberty *or* **pubescence** *noun.* —*See* **youth** (1).

public *adjective.* —*See* **common** (2), **open** (3), **popular.**

public *noun.* **1.** Persons as an organized body ▶ bloc, community, people, society. [*Compare* **circle.**] **2.** The body of persons who admire a public personality, especially an entertainer ▶ audience, following. [*Compare* **fan²**.] —*See also* **commonalty.**

public assistance *noun.* —*See* **relief** (2).

publication *noun.* **1.** The act or process of publishing printed matter ▶ circulation, issue, printing, publishing, release. **2.** An issue of printed material offered for sale or distribution ▶ edition, opus, organ, paper, title, volume, work. [*Compare* **advisory, book.**] —*See also* **announcement.**

public house *noun.* —*See* **bar** (2).

publicity *noun.* Information disseminated through various media to attract public notice ▶ advertisement, advertising, ballyhoo, buildup, exposure, promotion, puff, puffery. *Informal:* hoopla, pitch, plug. *Slang:* hype. [*Compare* **propaganda.**] —*See also* **advertising.**

publicize *verb.* —*See* **promote** (3).

publish *verb.* **1.** To present for circulation, exhibit, or sale ▶ bring out, issue, print, put out, release, run off. [*Compare* **spread.**] **2.** To be the author of a published work or works ▶ author, compose, pen, write. [*Compare* **compose, write.**] —*See also* **announce.**

publishing *noun.* —*See* **publication** (1).

pucker *noun.* —*See* **fold** (1).

pucker *verb.* —*See* **dry** (1), **fold.**

puckish *adjective.* —*See* **mischievous.**

pudgy *adjective.* —*See* **fat** (1).

puerile *adjective.* —*See* **childish, young.**

puff *noun.* —*See* **breeze** (1), **publicity, pull** (2).

puff *verb.* —*See* **blow[1]** (1), **boast, exaggerate, pant, promote** (3), **swell.**

puffed-up *or* **puffy** *adjective.* —*See* **pompous.**

puffery *noun.* —*See* **publicity.**

pugilist *noun.* A contestant in a boxing match ▶ boxer, fighter, prizefighter. [*Compare* **fighter.**]

pugnacious *adjective.* —*See* **aggressive.**

pugnacity *or* **pugnaciousness** *noun.* —*See* **aggression, fight** (2).

puke *verb.* —*See* **vomit.**

pulchritudinous *adjective.* —*See* **beautiful.**

pule *verb.* —*See* **cry.**

pull *verb.* **1.** To exert force so as to move something toward the source of the force ▶ drag, draw, haul, lug, tow, tug, yank. [*Compare* **trail.**] **2.** To remove from a fixed position ▶ extract, pick, pluck, rend, tear, wrench, wrest, yank. [*Compare* **remove.**] —*See also* **attract, lift** (3).

pull back *verb.* —*See* **retreat.**

pull down *verb.* —*See* **destroy** (2), **earn** (2).

pull in *verb.* —*See* **arrive** (1), **earn** (2), **restrain.**

pull off *verb. Informal* To be responsible for or guilty of an error or crime ▶ carry out, commit, do, perpetrate. —*See also* **perform** (1).

pull on *verb.* —*See* **don, drink** (1).

pull out *verb.* To withdraw from an association or federation ▶ break off, secede, splinter (off), withdraw. *Informal:* split (away). [*Compare* **quit.**] —*See also* **go** (1), **retreat.**

pull through *verb.* —*See* **survive** (1).

pull *noun.* **1.** The act of drawing or pulling a load ▶ draft, drag, draw, haul, tow, traction, yank. [*Compare* **jerk.**] **2.** An inhalation, as of a cigar, pipe, or cigarette ▶ draft, drag, draw, puff. *Slang:* hit. —*See also* **attraction, drink** (2), **influence.**

✚ **CORE SYNONYMS:** *pull, drag, draw, haul, tow, tug.* These verbs mean to exert force so as to move something toward the source of the force: *pull a sled up a hill; drag furniture across the floor; drew up a chair; hauls wood from the forest; a car that tows a trailer; tugged at the oars.*

◀ **ANTONYM:** *push*

---

pullback *noun.* —*See* **retreat.**

pullout *noun.* —*See* **retreat.**

pullulate *verb.* —*See* **teem[1].**

pulp *verb.* —*See* **crush** (1).

pulpit *noun.* —*See* **stage** (1).

pulpy *or* **pulpous** *adjective.* —*See* **soft** (1).

pulsate *verb.* —*See* **beat** (5).

pulsation *noun.* —*See* **beat** (3).

pulse *noun.* —*See* **beat** (3).

pulse *verb.* —*See* **beat** (5), **glare** (2).

pulverize *verb.* —*See* **crush** (2), **destroy** (2).

pulverous *or* **pulverulent** *adjective.* —*See* **fine[1]** (1).

pummel *verb.* —*See* **beat** (1).

pump *verb.* —*See* **ask** (1), **drain** (1).
pump up *verb.* —*See* **elevate** (2), **energize.**

punch *verb.* —*See* **breach, cut** (1), **hit, penetrate.**
punch *noun.* —*See* **blow**[2], **dig, drive** (2), **energy, kick.**

punch-drunk *adjective.* —*See* **confused** (1).

punctilious *adjective.* —*See* **careful** (2), **ceremonious.**

punctiliousness *noun.* —*See* **ceremony** (2), **thoroughness.**

punctual *adjective.* Occurring, acting, or performed exactly at the time appointed ▶ prompt, timely. ***Idioms:*** on the dot (*or* nose), on schedule, on time.

puncture *verb.* —*See* **breach, cut** (1), **discredit, humble, penetrate.**
puncture *noun.* —*See* **prick.**

pundit *noun.* —*See* **critic** (1), **sage.**

pungent *adjective.* —*See* **biting, bitter** (1), **pithy, spicy.**

puniness *noun.* —*See* **infirmity.**

punish *verb.* To subject one to a penalty for a wrong ▶ castigate, chastise, correct, discipline, penalize, sentence. [*Compare* **chastise, condemn, fine**[2].]

✚ **CORE SYNONYMS:** *punish, correct, chastise, discipline, castigate, penalize.* These verbs mean to subject a person to something negative for an offense, sin, or fault. *Punish* is the least specific: *The principal punished the students who were caught cheating.* To *correct* is to punish so that the offender will mend his or her ways: *Regulations formerly permitted prison wardens to correct unruly inmates. Chastise* implies either corporal punishment or a verbal rebuke as a means of effecting improvement in behavior: *I chastised the bully by giving him a thrashing. The sarcastic child was roundly chastised for insolence. Discipline* stresses punishment inflicted by an authority in order to control or to eliminate unacceptable conduct: *The worker was disciplined for insubordination. Castigate* means to censure or criticize severely, often in public: *The judge castigated the attorney for badgering the witness. Penalize* usually implies the forfeiture of money or of a privilege or gain because rules or regulations have been broken: *Those who file their income-tax returns late will be penalized.*

punishing *adjective.* Inflicting or aiming to inflict punishment ▶ correctional, disciplinary, penal, punitive, punitory. —*See also* **bitter** (2).

punishment *noun.* Something, such as loss, pain, or confinement, imposed for wrongdoing ▶ castigation, chastisement, correction, deserts, discipline, infliction, payment, penalty, penance, rap, retribution, sentence. [*Compare* **fine, ruling.**]

punitive *or* **punitory** *adjective.* —*See* **punishing.**

punk *noun.* —*See* **nonentity, squirt** (2), **thug.**
punk *verb.* —*See* **deceive.**

puny *adjective.* —*See* **meager, weak** (1).

pup *noun.* —*See* **squirt** (2).

pupil *noun.* —*See* **student.**

puppet *noun.* —*See* **pawn**[2].

puppy *noun.* —*See* **squirt** (2).

purblind *adjective.* —*See* **blind** (3).

purchase *verb.* —*See* **buy.**
purchase *noun.* **1.** Something that is bought or is capable of being bought ▶ buy. [*Compare* **effects, good.**] **2.** A place providing support for the foot in climbing ▶ foothold, footing, perch, toehold.

purchaser *noun.* —*See* **consumer.**

pure *adjective.* Free from extraneous elements ▶ absolute, clear, genuine, perfect, plain, sheer, simple, unadulterated, undiluted, unmixed. [*Compare* **perfect.**] —*See also* **chaste, fresh** (1), **innocent** (1), **straight, utter**[2].

✚ **CORE SYNONYMS:** *pure, absolute, sheer, simple, unadulterated.* These adjectives mean free of extraneous elements: *pure gold; absolute oxygen; sheer* *alcohol; a simple substance; unadulterated coffee.*

---

pureblood *or* **pureblooded** *or* **purebred** *adjective.* —*See* **thoroughbred.**

purely *adverb.* —*See* **completely** (1).

pureness *noun.* —*See* **purity.**

purgation *noun.* —*See* **purification** (2).

purgative *noun.* —*See* **purifier.**

purgative *or* **purgatorial** *adjective* Serving to purify of sin ▶ expiatory, lustral, lustrative, purificatory. —*See also* **eliminative.**

purge *verb.* —*See* **clear** (3), **eliminate, purify** (1).

purge *noun.* —*See* **elimination.**

purification *noun.* **1.** The act or process of removing physical impurities ▶ catharsis, clarification, cleaning, cleansing, lavation, refinement. **2.** A freeing from sin, guilt, or defilement ▶ ablution, catharsis, lustration, pardoning, purgation, redemption. [*Compare* **atonement.**]

purificatory *adjective.* —*See* **purgative.**

purifier *noun.* Something that purifies or cleans ▶ antiseptic, cathartic, clarifier, cleaner, cleanser, disinfectant, purgative, refiner, refinery.

purify *verb.* **1.** To free from sin, guilt, or defilement ▶ atone, cleanse, expiate, lustrate, pardon, purge, redeem. **2.** To remove impurities from ▶ clarify, clean, cleanse, refine. [*Compare* **clean.**]

purist *adjective.* —*See* **pedantic.**

puritan *noun.* —*See* **prude.**

puritan *adjective.* —*See* **ascetic.**

puritanical *adjective.* —*See* **ascetic, intolerant** (1), **prudish.**

purity *noun.* The condition of being clean and free of contaminants ▶ clarity, cleanliness, cleanness, disinfection, immaculacy, immaculateness, pureness, taintlessness. [*Compare* **sterility.**] —*See also* **chastity.**

purl *verb.* —*See* **burble, flow** (1).

purlieu *noun.* —*See* **environment** (1).

purloin *verb.* —*See* **steal.**

purloiner *noun.* —*See* **thief.**

purport *noun.* —*See* **import, meaning, thrust.**

purport *verb.* To claim or allege insincerely or falsely ▶ feign, pretend, pretext, profess.

purported *adjective.* —*See* **supposed.**

purpose *noun.* —*See* **decision** (2), **function** (1), **intention.**

purpose *verb.* —*See* **intend.**

purposeful *adjective.* —*See* **deliberate** (1).

purposefulness *noun.* —*See* **decision** (2).

purposeless *adjective.* —*See* **aimless, mindless.**

purr *verb.* —*See* **hum.**

purr *noun.* —*See* **hum.**

purring *adjective.* —*See* **active.**

purse *noun.* A closeable container for carrying money and personal items ▶ bag, clutch, handbag, pocketbook, reticule.

pursuance *noun.* —*See* **pursuit** (2).

pursue *verb.* **1.** To follow another with the intent of overtaking and capturing ▶ chase (down), gun for, hunt, run after. ***Idioms:*** be (*or* go) in pursuit, give chase. [*Compare* **follow, seek.**] **2.** To work at, especially as a profession ▶ do, follow, practice. ***Idiom:*** hang out one's shingle. [*Compare* **labor.**] —*See also* **court** (2), **lead.**

pursuing *noun.* —*See* **pursuit** (2).

pursuit *noun.* **1.** The following of another in an attempt to overtake and capture ▶ chase, hot pursuit, hunt. **2.** An attempt to accomplish or attain ▶ hunt, prosecution, pursuance, pursuing, quest, search. [*Compare* **expedition, exploration.**] —*See also* **business** (2).

purvey *verb.* —*See* **promote** (3).

purview *noun.* —*See* **ken, range** (1).

push *verb.* **1.** To apply pressure on, against, or with ▶ bear (down), butt, crowd, crush, depress, dig, elbow, jab, jam, jog, jostle, nudge, poke, press, prod, ram, shoulder, shove, thrust. **2.** *Slang* To engage in the illicit sale of narcotics ▶ deal, peddle. [*Compare*

sell.] **3.** To force to work hard ▶ drive, task, tax, work. ***Idiom:*** crack the whip. [*Compare* **force.**] —*See also* **advance** (1), **advance** (2), **drive** (2), **drive** (3), **muscle, promote** (3).

push off *verb.* —*See* **go** (1).

push on *verb.* To move along a particular course ▶ go, pass, proceed, wend. ***Idioms:*** make (*or* wend) one's way. [*Compare* **advance, journey, rove.**]

push *noun.* An act or instance of pushing ▶ butt, jam, jostle, press, shove, thrust. [*Compare* **dig.**] —*See also* **drive** (1), **drive** (2), **stimulus.**

pusher *noun. Slang* A person who sells narcotics illegally ▶ dealer, peddler, trafficker. *Slang:* connection.

pushiness *noun.* —*See* **impudence.**

pushover *noun.* —*See* **breeze** (2), **dupe, weakling.**

pushy *adjective.* —*See* **impudent.**

pusillanimity *noun.* —*See* **cowardice.**

pusillanimous *adjective.* —*See* **cowardly.**

puss *noun.* —*See* **face** (1), **mouth** (1).

pussyfoot *verb.* —*See* **equivocate** (1), **sneak.**

put *verb.* **1.** To establish and apply as compulsory ▶ assess, exact, impose, levy. **2.** To seek an answer to a question ▶ ask, pose, raise. [*Compare* **say.**] **3.** To have or put in a customary place ▶ cache, keep, store. —*See also* **air** (2), **estimate** (2), **gamble** (2), **phrase, position, translate.**

put away *verb.* —*See* **consume** (1), **eat** (1), **imprison, murder.**

put by *verb.* —*See* **save** (1).

put down *verb.* —*See* **belittle, criticize** (1), **humble, suppress.**

put forth *verb.* —*See* **broach.**

put forward *verb.* —*See* **offer** (1), **propose.**

put in *verb.* **1.** To ask for employment, acceptance, or admission ▶ apply, petition. **2.** To spend or complete time, as a prison term ▶ serve. *Informal:* do. **3.** To use time in a particular way ▶ pass, spend. [*Compare* **idle.**] —*See also* **introduce** (2).

put off *verb.* To offer or put into circulation an inferior or fraudulent item ▶ foist, fob off, palm off, pass off. [*Compare* **dump.**] —*See also* **defer**[1], **dissuade, offend** (2).

put on *verb.* —*See* **act** (2), **don, impose on, stage.**

put out *verb.* —*See* **annoy, extinguish, inconvenience, offend** (1), **publish** (1).

put through *verb.* —*See* **effect.**

put together *verb.* —*See* **make.**

put up *verb.* —*See* **build, erect, lodge, offer** (1), **preserve** (1).

putative *adjective.* —*See* **supposed.**

putdown *noun.* —*See* **indignity, snub.**

put-on *noun.* —*See* **façade** (2), **prank**[1].

putrefaction *or* **putrescence** *noun.* —*See* **decay.**

putrefy *verb.* —*See* **decay.**

putrid *or* **putrescent** *adjective.* —*See* **bad** (2).

putridness *noun.* —*See* **decay.**

putter *verb.* To waste time by engaging in aimless activity ▶ dawdle (about), doodle, fiddle (around), fool. *Informal:* fool around, mess around, play around. *Slang:* screw around (*or* off). [*Compare* **delay, idle.**]

puzzle *verb.* —*See* **confuse** (1).

puzzle out *verb.* —*See* **decipher.**

puzzle *noun.* —*See* **mystery.**

puzzled *adjective.* —*See* **confused** (1).

puzzlement *noun.* —*See* **daze.**

puzzler *noun.* —*See* **mystery.**

puzzling *adjective.* —*See* **mysterious.**

pygmy *adjective.* —*See* **tiny.**

pyretic *adjective.* —*See* **feverish.**

pythonic *adjective.* —*See* **enormous.**

Q

quack *noun.* —*See* **fake.**

quad *or* **quadrangle** *noun.* —*See* **court** (1).

quaff *verb.* —*See* **drink** (1).

quaff *noun.* —*See* **drink** (2).

quag *noun.* —*See* **swamp.**

quaggy *adjective.* —*See* **soft** (1).

quagmire *noun.* —*See* **predicament, swamp.**

quail *verb.* —*See* **flinch.**

quaint *adjective.* Agreeably curious, especially in an old-fashioned or unusual way ▶ curious, funny, odd. —*See also* **eccentric.**

quake *verb.* —*See* **shake** (1), **sway.**

quake *noun.* A shaking of the earth ▶ earthquake, seism, temblor, tremor. *Informal:* shake. —*See also* **tremor** (2).

quaking *or* **quaky** *adjective.* —*See* **tremulous.**

qualification *noun.* **1.** The quality or state of being eligible ▶ correctness, eligibility, fitness, suitability, suitableness, worthiness. **2.** A quality that makes a person suitable for a particular position or task ▶ attainment, credential, endowment, skill. **3.** The act or process of ascertaining dimensions, quantity, or capacity ▶ determination, measure, measurement, mensuration. [*Compare* **computation, estimation.**] —*See also* **provision.**

qualified *adjective.* Not total, unlimited, or wholehearted ▶ conditioned, limited, modified, reserved, restricted. —*See also* **eligible.**

qualify *verb.* —*See* **authorize, moderate** (1).

quality *noun.* **1.** A distinctive element ▶ attribute, character, characteristic, feature, mark, peculiarity, property, savor, trait. [*Compare* **essence.**] **2.** Degree of excellence ▶ caliber, class, grade. [*Compare* **degree.**] —*See also* **elegance, merit, society** (1).

quality *adjective.* —*See* **excellent.**

✤ **CORE SYNONYMS:** *quality, property, attribute, character, trait.* These nouns signify an element that distinguishes or identifies someone or something: *explained the qualities of noble gases; tested the resilient property of rubber; knew the attributes of a fine wine; liked the rural character of the ranch; had positive traits such as kindness and generosity.*

---

qualm *noun.* A feeling of uncertainty about the fitness or correctness of an action ▶ compunction, concern, misgiving, reservation, scruple, worry. *Informal:* problem, trouble. —*See also* **doubt.**

✤ **CORE SYNONYMS:** *qualm, scruple, compunction, misgiving.* These nouns denote a feeling of uncertainty about the fitness or correctness of an action. *Qualm* is a disturbing feeling of uneasiness and self-doubt: *"an ignorant ruffianly gaucho, who . . . would . . . fight, steal, and do other naughty things without a qualm"* (W.H. Hudson). *Scruple* is an uneasy feeling arising from conscience or principle about a course of action: *"My father's old-fashioned notions boggled a little at first to this arrangement . . . but his scruples were in the end overruled"* (John Galt). *Compunction* implies a prick or twinge of conscience aroused by wrongdoing or the prospect of wrongdoing: *stole the money without compunction. Misgiving* suggests often sudden apprehension: *had misgivings about quitting his job.*

---

quandary *noun.* —*See* **predicament.**

quantify *or* **quantitate** *verb.* To ascertain the dimensions, quantity, or capacity of ▶ gauge, measure. ***Idioms:*** take the dimensions (*or* measure) of. [*Compare* **estimate.**]

quantity *noun.* **1.** An amount represented in numerals ▶ figure, number. [*Compare* **total.**] **2.** An indefinite amount or extent ▶ bunch, deal, measure, number, portion. **3.** A measurable whole ▶ amount, body, budget, bulk, corpus, quantum. [*Compare* **hoard.**]

quantum *noun.* —*See* **allotment, quantity** (3).

quarantine *noun.* —*See* **detention.**

quarrel *noun.* —*See* **argument.**

quarrel *verb.* —*See* **argue** (1).

quarrelsome *adjective.* —*See* **aggressive, argumentative.**

quarry *noun.* —*See* **victim.**

quarter *noun.* **1.** One of four equal parts of something ▶ one-fourth, quartern. **2.** A coin equal to one-fourth of the dollar of the United States and Canada ▶ two bits, quarter-dollar. —*See also* **area** (2), **neighborhood** (1).

quarter *verb.* —*See* **cut** (2), **lodge.**

quarterback *verb.* —*See* **conduct** (1).

quartern *noun.* One of four equal parts of something ▶ one-fourth, quarter.

quarters *noun.* Usually temporary living accommodations ▶ barracks, lodgings, rooms. *Slang:* crash-pad. [*Compare* **apartment, home.**] —*See also* **neighborhood** (1).

quash *verb.* —*See* **lift** (3), **suppress.**

quaver *verb.* —*See* **shake** (1), **tremor** (2).

queasiness *noun.* —*See* **disgust.**

queasy *adjective.* —*See* **sick** (1).

queen *noun.* —*See* **chief.**

queer *adjective.* —*See* **eccentric, funny** (3).

quell *verb.* —*See* **relieve** (1), **suppress.**

quench *verb.* —*See* **extinguish, repress, suppress.**

querier *noun.* —*See* **inquirer.**

querulous *adjective.* —*See* **ill-tempered.**

query *noun.* A request for data ▶ inquiry, interrogation, question, questioning. [*Compare* **demand, problem.**] —*See also* **doubt.**

query *verb.* —*See* **ask** (1), **doubt.**

quest *noun.* —*See* **expedition, pursuit** (2).

quest *verb.* To try to find something ▶ cast about, hunt, look, search, seek.

quester *noun.* One who seeks adventure ▶ adventurer, daredevil, venturer. [*Compare* **builder.**] —*See also* **inquirer.**

question *noun.* A request for data ▶ inquiry, interrogation, query, questioning. [*Compare* **demand, problem.**] —*See also* **doubt, problem.**

question *verb.* —*See* **ask** (1), **disbelieve, distrust, doubt.**

questionable *adjective.* —*See* **ambiguous** (1), **debatable, doubtful** (1), **shady** (1).

questioner *noun.* —*See* **inquirer.**

questioning *adjective.* —*See* **curious** (2), **incredulous.**

questioning *noun.* A request for data ▶ inquiry, interrogation, query, question. [*Compare* **demand, problem.**]

questioningly *adverb.* —*See* **skeptically.**

queue *noun.* —*See* **line.**

queue *verb.* —*See* **line.**

quibble *verb.* To raise unnecessary or trivial objections ▶ carp, cavil, niggle, nitpick, pettifog, squabble. ***Idioms:*** pick apart (*or* to pieces). [*Compare* **complain, nag, object.**] —*See also* **argue** (1).

✚ **CORE SYNONYMS:** *quibble, carp, cavil, niggle, nitpick, pettifog.* These verbs mean to raise petty or frivolous objections or complaints: *quibbling about minor details; a critic who constantly carped; caviling about the price of coffee; an editor who niggled about commas; tried to stop nitpicking all the time; pettifogging about trivialities.*

---

quibbler *noun.* —*See* **critic** (2).

quibbling *noun.* The act of making trivial objections or distinctions ▶ caviling, hairsplitting, niggling, nitpicking, pettifoggery, trichoschistism.

quick *adjective.* Accomplished or experienced in very little time ▶ brief, expeditious, fast, fleeting, flying, hasty, hurried, rapid, short, speedy, swift. [*Compare* **instant, little, transitory.**] —*See also* **clever** (1), **fast** (1).

quick *noun.* —*See* **center** (3).

quick *adverb.* —*See* **fast.**

quicken *verb.* To make alive ▶ animate, enliven, vitalize, vivify. [*Compare* **elate, energize, provoke.**] —*See also* **speed.**

quickening *adjective.* —*See* **invigorating.**

quickly *adverb.* —*See* **fast, soon.**
quickness *noun.* —*See* **agility, dexterity, haste** (1).
quick-tempered *adjective.* —*See* **testy.**
quick-witted *adjective.* —*See* **clever** (1).
quiddity *noun.* —*See* **essence.**
quidnunc *noun.* —*See* **busybody.**
quiescence *noun.* —*See* **abeyance.**
quiescent *adjective.* —*See* **latent.**
quiet *adjective.* —*See* **modest** (1), **silent** (1), **soft** (2), **still, taciturn.**
quiet *noun.* —*See* **silence** (1), **stillness.**
quiet *verb.* —*See* **pacify, silence.**
quiet down *verb.* —*See* **fade away.**
quieten *verb.* —*See* **silence.**
quietness *noun.* —*See* **modesty** (2), **silence** (1), **stillness.**
quietude *noun.* —*See* **calm.**
quietus *noun.* —*See* **death** (1).
quill *noun.* —*See* **spike.**
quintessence *noun.* —*See* **essence, heart** (1).
quintessential *adjective.* —*See* **essential** (2), **ideal, typical.**
quip *noun.* —*See* **crack** (3), **joke** (1).
quip *verb.* To make jokes; behave playfully ▶ jest, joke (around). *Informal:* clown (around), fool around, horse around. ***Idioms:*** crack wise, play the fool. [*Compare* **play.**]
quipster *noun.* —*See* **joker.**
quirk *or* **quirkiness** *noun.* —*See* **eccentricity.**
quirky *adjective.* —*See* **eccentric.**
quit *verb.* To relinquish one's engagement in or occupation with ▶ demit, leave, resign, terminate. ***Idioms:*** hang it up, throw in the towel. [*Compare* **break, retire.**] —*See also* **abandon** (1), **abandon** (2), **act** (1), **defect, drop** (4), **go** (1), **stop** (1).
quit *adjective.* Owing or being owed nothing ▶ even, quits, square. *Informal:* even-steven.
quitclaim *noun.* —*See* **abandonment** (1).
quitclaim *verb.* —*See* **abandon** (1).
quite *adverb.* —*See* **completely** (1), **considerably, fairly** (2).
quits *adjective.* Owing or being owed nothing ▶ even, quit, square. *Informal:* even-steven.
quittance *noun.* —*See* **compensation.**
quiver *verb.* —*See* **shake** (1).
quiver *noun.* —*See* **tremor** (2).
quivering *or* **quivery** *adjective.* —*See* **tremulous.**
quixotic *adjective.* —*See* **idealistic.**
quiz *verb.* To subject to a test of knowledge or skill ▶ catechize, examine, quiz. —*See also* **ask** (1).
quiz *noun.* —*See* **test** (2).
quondam *adjective.* —*See* **late** (2).
quota *noun.* —*See* **allotment.**
quote-unquote *adjective.* —*See* **supposed.**
quotidian *adjective.* —*See* **everyday.**

R

rabble *noun.* —*See* **riffraff.**
rabble-rouser *noun.* —*See* **agitator.**
rabid *adjective.* —*See* **angry, enthusiastic, extreme** (2).
race[1] *noun.* —*See* **ancestry.**
race[2] *noun.* —*See* **competition** (1).
race *verb.* —*See* **compete, rush.**
racism *noun.* Discrimination based on race ▶ discrimination, intolerance, prejudice. [*Compare* **hate.**]
racist *adjective.* ▶ bigoted, discriminatory, prejudiced. [*Compare* **intolerant.**]
rack *verb.* To subject another to extreme physical cruelty, as in punishing ▶ crucify, harrow, torment, torture. ***Idioms:*** put on the rack (*or* wheel), put the screws to. [*Compare* **punish.**] —*See also* **afflict.**
racket *noun.* —*See* **business** (2), **noise** (1).
racy *adjective.* Bordering on indelicacy or impropriety ▶ blue, earthy, off-color, provocative, risqué, salty, scabrous, spicy, suggestive. *Slang:* funky. [*Compare* **erotic, obscene, rude.**] —*See also* **spicy.**
raddle *verb.* —*See* **weave.**

radiance *noun.* —*See* **brilliance** (1).

radiant *adjective.* —*See* **bright, glorious.**

radiate *verb.* —*See* **beam, branch, shed**[1] (1), **spread** (2).

radical *adjective.* Arising from or going to the root or source ▶ basal, basic, foundational, fundamental, original, primary, primitive, underlying. [*Compare* **deep, elemental, first, original.**] —*See also* **extreme** (2).

radical *noun.* —*See* **extremist, theme** (1).

rafter *noun.* —*See* **beam** (2).

rag *verb.* —*See* **harass, joke** (2).

ragamuffin *noun.* A person wearing ragged or tattered clothing ▶ tatterdemalion. [*Compare* **hobo.**] —*See also* **orphan.**

rage *noun.* —*See* **anger, enthusiasm** (2), **fashion.**

rage *verb.* —*See* **anger** (2).

ragged *adjective.* —*See* **hoarse, rough** (1), **shabby.**

raggedness *noun.* —*See* **irregularity.**

raggedy *adjective.* —*See* **shabby.**

raging *adjective.* —*See* **rough** (2).

rags *noun.* Torn and ragged clothing ▶ shreds, tatters.

ragtag and bobtail *noun.* —*See* **riffraff.**

raid *noun.* An act of invading, especially by military forces ▶ foray, incursion, inroad, invasion. [*Compare* **attack.**] —*See also* **charge** (1).

raid *verb.* —*See* **ambush, invade** (1).

rail[1] *noun.* A string of railroad cars led by a locomotive ▶ railroad train, railway, train. *Informal:* choo-choo, choo-choo train.

rail[2] *verb.* —*See* **revile.**

railing *noun.* —*See* **vituperation.**

raillery *noun.* —*See* **ribbing.**

railway *noun.* A string of railroad cars led by a locomotive ▶ rail, railroad train, train. *Informal:* choo-choo, choo-choo train.

raiment *noun.* —*See* **dress** (1).

rain *verb.* **1.** To give in great abundance ▶ heap, lavish, shower. [*Compare* **confer, donate, give.**] **2.** To fall in drops of water from clouds ▶ drizzle, mist, mizzle, pour, precipitate, shower, spatter, spit, sprinkle, teem. ***Idioms:*** come down in buckets (*or* sheets *or* torrents), rain cats and dogs. [*Compare* **splash, storm.**]

rain *noun.* Water condensed from atmospheric vapor and falling in drops ▶ cloudburst, deluge, downfall, downpour, drizzle, mist, mizzle, pour, precipitation, rainfall, shower, spit, sprinkle, torrent. [*Compare* **storm.**] —*See also* **barrage.**

raincoat *noun.* —*See* **coat** (1).

rainfall *noun.* —*See* **rain.**

rainless *adjective.* —*See* **dry** (2).

rainy *adjective.* Characterized by rain or drizzle ▶ damp, drizzly, misty, soft, wet. [*Compare* **stormy.**]

raise *verb.* **1.** To increase in amount ▶ boost, hike, jack (up), jump, up. [*Compare* **increase.**] **2.** To take care of and educate a child ▶ bring up, rear. **3.** To seek an answer to a question ▶ ask, pose, put. [*Compare* **say.**] —*See also* **arouse, broach, build, elevate** (1), **elevate** (2), **erect, grow, promote** (1).

raise *noun.* —*See* **advancement, increase** (1), **increase** (2).

raised *adjective.* —*See* **elevated** (1), **elevated** (2), **erect.**

rake[1] *noun.* —*See* **wanton.**

rake[2] *verb.* —*See* **incline.**

rake *noun.* —*See* **inclination** (2).

rake[3] *verb.* —*See* **till.**

rakehell *noun.* —*See* **wanton.**

rakish *adjective.* —*See* **abandoned** (2).

rally *verb.* —*See* **mobilize, recover** (2).

rally *noun.* The process or period of a return to health ▶ convalescence, recovery, recuperation. —*See also* **assembly.**

rallying cry *noun.* —*See* **cry** (2).

ram *verb.* —*See* **drive** (2), **plunge, push** (1).

ramble *verb.* —*See* **digress, rove, stroll.**

ramble on *verb.* —*See* **chatter** (1).

ramble *noun.* —*See* **walk** (1).

rambling *adjective.* —*See* **aimless, digressive, errant** (1), **indirect** (1).

ramification *noun.* —*See* **branch** (1), **effect** (1).

ramify *verb.* —*See* **branch.**

rampage *noun.* —*See* **binge.**

rampant *adjective.* —*See* **erect, prevailing.**

rampart *noun.* —*See* **bulwark.**

ramshackle *adjective.* —*See* **shabby.**

ranch *verb.* —*See* **grow.**

rancid *adjective.* —*See* **bad** (2), **moldy.**

rancor *noun.* —*See* **enmity, hate** (1), **resentment.**

rancorous *adjective.* —*See* **resentful.**

rancorousness *noun.* —*See* **resentment.**

random *adjective.* Having no particular pattern, purpose, organization, or structure ▶ chance, desultory, haphazard, hit-or-miss, indiscriminate, spot, unplanned, unpredictable. [*Compare* **confused, spontaneous.**]

✦ **CORE SYNONYMS:** *random, chance, haphazard, desultory.* These adjectives apply to what is determined not by deliberation but by accident. *Random* implies the absence of a specific pattern or objective: *took a random guess. Chance* stresses lack of premeditation: *a chance meeting with a friend. Haphazard* implies a carelessness or a willful leaving to chance: *a haphazard plan of action. Desultory* suggests a shifting about from one thing to another that reflects a lack of method: *a desultory conversation.*

R and R *noun.* —*See* **rest**[1] (2).

range *noun.* **1.** An area or set of parameters within which something or someone exists, acts, or has influence ▶ ambit, circle, compass, extension, extent, orbit, purview, reach, realm, scope, spectrum, sphere, sweep, swing, territory. [*Compare* **area, beat, limit.**] **2.** The ability or power to seize or attain ▶ capacity, compass, grasp, reach, scope. [*Compare* **influence.**] **3.** Approximate size or amount ▶ *Informal:* neighborhood. *Slang:* ballpark. ▶ vicinity. —*See also* **class** (2), **degree** (2), **distance** (1), **expanse** (1), **habitat, ken, series.**

range *verb.* —*See* **arrange** (1), **classify, go** (4), **line, rove.**

✦ **CORE SYNONYMS:** *range, ambit, compass, orbit, purview, reach, scope, sweep.* These nouns denote an area within which something or someone exists, acts, or has influence: *the range of a nuclear missile; the ambit of municipal legislation; information within the compass of the article; countries within the political orbit of a world power; regulations under the government's purview; outside the reach of the law; issues within the scope of an investigation; outside the sweep of federal authority.*

---

rangy *adjective.* —*See* **gangling.**

rank[1] *noun.* —*See* **class** (2), **degree** (1), **line, place** (1).

rank *verb.* —*See* **classify.**

rank[2] *adjective.* Conspicuously bad or offensive ▶ egregious, flagrant, glaring, gross. [*Compare* **offensive, outrageous, shameless.**] —*See also* **moldy, thick** (3).

rank and file *noun.* —*See* **commonalty.**

ranking *noun.* —*See* **arrangement** (1).

rankle *verb.* —*See* **annoy.**

rankness *noun.* The quality or state of being flagrant ▶ egregiousness, flagrancy, glaringness, grossness. [*Compare* **impudence, outrageousness.**]

ransack *verb.* —*See* **sack**[2], **scour**[2].

rant *verb.* To speak in a loud, pompous, or prolonged manner ▶ declaim, harangue, mouth (off), orate, perorate, rave. [*Compare* **revile.**] —*See also* **babble.**

rant *noun.* —*See* **bombast.**

rap[1] *verb.* —*See* **bang, chastise, criticize** (1), **tap**[1] (1).

rap out *verb.* —*See* **exclaim.**

rap *noun.* The sound that is made by a light blow ▶ knock, knocking, rapping, tap, tapping. [*Compare* **beat.**] —*See also* **beat** (1), **blame, punishment, rebuke.**

rap² *noun. Slang* An exchanging of views ▶ conference, discussion, ventilation. —*See also* **conversation.**

rap *verb.* —*See* **discuss.**

rapacious *adjective.* —*See* **voracious.**

rapaciousness *noun.* —*See* **voracity.**

rapacity *noun.* —*See* **greed, voracity.**

rape *verb.* To compel another to participate in or submit to a sexual act ▶ assault, force, molest, ravish, violate. —*See also* **sack².**

rapid *adjective.* —*See* **fast** (1), **quick.**

rapidity *noun.* —*See* **haste** (1).

rapidly *adverb.* —*See* **fast.**

rapidness *noun.* —*See* **haste** (1).

rapport *noun.* —*See* **agreement** (2).

rapprochement *noun.* A reestablishment of friendship or harmony ▶ conciliation, reconcilement, reconciliation, settlement. [*Compare* **agreement, atonement, compromise.**]

rap session *noun.* —*See* **conference** (1).

rapt *adjective.* Having one's thoughts fully occupied ▶ absorbed, engrossed, immersed, intent, involved, preoccupied, riveted. ***Idioms:*** wrapped (*or* caught) up in. [*Compare* **busy.**]

rapture *noun.* —*See* **heaven.**

rare *adjective.* Marked by great diffusion of component particles ▶ attenuate, attenuated, rarefied, thin. —*See also* **exceptional, infrequent.**

rarefied *adjective.* Marked by great diffusion of component particles ▶ attenuate, attenuated, rare, thin.

rarefy *verb.* To become diffuse ▶ attenuate, thin.

rarely *adverb.* —*See* **infrequently.**

raring *adjective.* —*See* **eager.**

rarity *noun.* —*See* **luxury, novelty** (1).

rascal *noun.* One who causes minor trouble or damage ▶ devil, imp, mischief, mischief-maker, prankster, rogue, scamp, scoundrel. *Informal:* cutup, scalawag. [*Compare* **agitator, evildoer, urchin.**]

rascality *noun.* —*See* **mischief.**

rascally *adjective.* —*See* **mischievous.**

rash¹ *adjective.* Characterized by unthinking boldness and haste ▶ brash, foolhardy, harum-scarum, hasty, headlong, hotheaded, ill-considered, impetuous, improvident, impulsive, incautious, madcap, precipitant, precipitate, reckless, slapdash, temerarious, unconsidered. [*Compare* **abrupt, callous, spontaneous, unwise.**]

CORE SYNONYMS: *rash, reckless, precipitate, foolhardy, temerarious, impetuous, hasty, headlong.* These adjectives describe unthinking boldness, haste, or lack of deliberation. *Rash* implies haste, impetuousness, and insufficient consideration: "*Take calculated risks. That is quite different from being rash*" (George S. Patton). *Reckless* suggests wild carelessness and disregard for consequences: "*conceiving measures to protect the fur-bearing animals from reckless slaughter*" (Getrude Atherton). *Precipitate* connotes headlong haste without due deliberation: "*destroyed in a precipitate burning of his papers a few days before his death*" (James Boswell). *Foolhardy* implies injudicious or imprudent boldness: *a foolhardy attempt to wrest the gun from the mugger. Temerarious* suggests reckless presumption: "*this temerarious foeman who dared intervene between himself* [the elephant] *and his intended victim*" (Edgar Rice Burroughs). *Impetuous* suggests forceful impulsiveness or impatience: "[a race driver who was] *flamboyant, impetuous, disdainful of death*" (Jim Murray). *Hasty* and *headlong* both stress hurried, often reckless action: "*Hasty marriage seldom proveth well*" (William Shakespeare). "*In his headlong flight down the circular staircase, . . .* [he] *had pitched forward violently, struck his head against the door* *to the east veranda, and probably broken his neck*" (Mary Roberts Rinehart).

---

rash² *noun.* —*See* **eruption.**
rashness *noun.* —*See* **haste** (2), **temerity.**
rasp *verb.* —*See* **gasp, scrape** (1).
raspberry *noun.* —*See* **hiss** (2).
raspberry *verb.* —*See* **hiss** (2).
rasping *adjective.* —*See* **harsh.**
raspy *or* **rasping** *adjective.* —*See* **harsh.**
rat *noun.* —*See* **betrayer, creep** (2), **defector, informer.**
rat *verb.* —*See* **betray** (1), **defect, inform** (2).
rat-a-tat-tat *noun.* —*See* **crack** (1).
rate *verb.* —*See* **classify, earn** (1), **estimate** (1).
rate *noun.* —*See* **toll¹** (1).
rather *adverb.* —*See* **fairly** (2).
ratification *noun.* —*See* **confirmation** (1).
ratify *verb.* —*See* **confirm** (3).
ratiocinate *verb.* —*See* **think** (1).
ratiocination *noun.* —*See* **logic.**
ratiocinative *adjective.* —*See* **logical** (1).
ration *noun.* —*See* **allotment.**
ration *verb.* —*See* **distribute.**
rational *adjective.* Mentally healthy ▶ compos mentis, lucid, normal, sane. ***Idioms:*** all there, in one's right mind, of sound mind. [*Compare* **healthy.**] —*See also* **logical** (1), **logical** (2), **sensible.**
rationale *noun.* —*See* **account** (1), **excuse** (1).
rationality *noun.* —*See* **logic, sanity, sense.**
rationalization *noun.* —*See* **account** (1), **excuse** (1).
rationalize *verb.* **1.** To show to be just, right, or valid ▶ excuse, justify, vindicate. ***Idiom:*** make a case for. **2.** To offer reasons for or a cause of ▶ account for, explain, justify. [*Compare* **clarify, resolve.**]
rationalness *noun.* —*See* **sense.**
rations *noun.* —*See* **food.**
rattle *verb.* To make or cause to make a succession of short, sharp sounds ▶ brattle, chatter, clack, clank, clatter. [*Compare* **knock, shake.**] —*See also* **agitate** (2), **bump, chatter** (1).
ratty *adjective.* —*See* **shabby.**
raucous *adjective.* —*See* **harsh.**
raunch *noun.* —*See* **obscenity.**
raunchiness *noun.* —*See* **obscenity** (1).
raunchy *adjective.* —*See* **obscene.**
ravage *verb.* —*See* **batter, consume** (1), **deform, destroy** (1), **sack².**
rave *verb.* To express great enthusiasm ▶ carry on, enthuse, gush, rhapsodize. *Informal:* boom. ***Idiom:*** wax poetic. [*Compare* **adore, drool.**] —*See also* **babble, rant.**
ravel *verb.* —*See* **complicate.**
ravenous *adjective.* —*See* **gluttonous, hungry** (1), **voracious.**
ravenousness *noun.* —*See* **voracity.**
ravish *verb.* To compel another to participate in or submit to a sexual act ▶ assault, force, molest, rape, violate. —*See also* **enrapture.**
ravishing *adjective.* —*See* **beautiful.**
raw *adjective.* Not cooked ▶ uncooked. —*See also* **bleak** (1), **crude, hoarse, inexperienced, painful, rude** (1).
rawboned *adjective.* —*See* **thin** (1).
raw deal *noun.* —*See* **injustice** (1).
rawness *noun.* —*See* **inexperience.**
ray *noun.* —*See* **beam** (1).
raze *verb.* —*See* **destroy** (2).
razz *noun.* —*See* **hiss** (2).
razz *verb.* —*See* **hiss** (2), **joke** (2).
razzle-dazzle *noun.* —*See* **glitter** (2).
reach *verb.* **1.** To put forward, especially an appendage ▶ extend, outstretch, stretch (out). **2.** To succeed in communicating with ▶ contact. *Informal:* catch, get. ***Idioms:*** catch up with, get hold of, get in touch with, get through to, get to, make contact with. [*Compare* **find, relate.**] —*See also* **accomplish, amount, arrive** (1), **extend** (1).
reach *noun.* The ability or power to seize or attain ▶ capacity, compass, grasp, range, scope. [*Compare* **influ-**

ence.] —*See also* **distance** (1), **expanse** (1), **extent, ken, range** (1).

react *verb.* To act in return to something, as a stimulus ▶ counter, respond. ***Idiom:*** act in response. [*Compare* **retaliate.**]

reactant *noun.* —*See* **catalyst.**

reaction *noun.* An action elicited by a stimulus ▶ response, retroaction. [*Compare* **retaliation.**] —*See also* **behavior** (2).

reactionary *adjective.* Clinging to obsolete ideas ▶ backward, unprogressive. —*See also* **ultraconservative.**

reactionary *noun.* —*See* **ultraconservative.**

reactivate *verb.* —*See* **revive** (1).

reactivation *noun.* —*See* **revival** (1).

read *verb.* To understand in a particular way ▶ construe, interpret, take. ***Idioms:*** read between the lines, see in a special light, take to mean. —*See also* **show** (2), **understand** (1).

readiness *noun.* —*See* **ease** (2), **preparation.**

reading *noun.* —*See* **interpretation.**

ready *adjective.* In a state of preparedness ▶ prepared, set. *Informal:* go. *Slang:* together. ***Idioms:*** all set, in working order, on deck, ready (*or* raring) to go. —*See also* **convenient** (2), **willing.**

ready *verb.* —*See* **gird, mobilize, prepare.**

real *adjective.* **1.** Having physical or verifiable existence ▶ concrete, objective, solid, substantial, substantive, tangible. [*Compare* **physical.**] **2.** Occurring or existing in act or fact ▶ actual, extant, existent, true. [*Compare* **physical.**] —*See also* **authentic** (1), **genuine.**

realistic *adjective.* **1.** Having or indicating an awareness of how things really are or what should be done ▶ down-to-earth, hard, hardheaded, matter-of-fact, objective, practical, pragmatic, pragmatical, prosaic, sober, straight, tough-minded, unromantic. [*Compare* **appropriate, frank, genuine.**] **2.** Accurately representing what is depicted or described ▶ factual, lifelike, natural, naturalistic, true, true-life, true-to-life, truthful. [*Compare* **accurate.**] —*See also* **graphic** (1).

reality *noun.* Something demonstrated to exist or known to have existed ▶ actuality, event, fact, phenomenon. ***Idioms:*** hard (*or* cold *or* plain) fact. [*Compare* **information.**] —*See also* **certainty, existence.**

realization *noun.* —*See* **fulfillment** (1), **accomplishment.** The condition of being in full force or operation ▶ actualization, being, effect, force. [*Compare* **exercise.**] —*See also* **interpretation.**

realize *verb.* To make real or actual ▶ actualize, bring about, make happen, materialize. ***Idioms:*** bring to pass, carry (*or* put) into effect. [*Compare* **effect, produce.**] —*See also* **accomplish, bring** (2), **discover, return** (3).

really *adverb.* In truth or fact ▶ actually, fairly, genuinely, indeed, positively, truly, truthfully, verily, veritably. ***Idioms:*** as a matter of fact, beyond (*or* without) a doubt, beyond a reasonable (*or* shadow of a) doubt, for fair (*or* real *or* sure *or* true), in point of fact. [*Compare* **absolutely, completely, considerably, unusually, very.**]

realm *noun.* —*See* **area** (1), **range** (1).

realness *noun.* —*See* **veracity.**

ream *noun.* —*See* **heap** (2).

ream *verb.* —*See* **cut** (1).

reanimate *verb.* —*See* **revive** (1).

reap *verb.* —*See* **cut** (3), **gather, get** (1), **return** (3).

reappear *verb.* To happen again or repeatedly ▶ iterate, recur, reoccur, repeat.

reappearance *noun.* —*See* **repetition.**

reappoint *verb.* —*See* **reinstall.**

rear¹ *noun.* The part or area farthest from the front ▶ back, rearward. —*See also* **back, buttocks.**

rear *adjective.* —*See* **back.**

rear² *verb.* To take care of and educate a child ▶ bring up, foster, parent, raise.

[*Compare* **nurture.**] —*See also* **build, elevate** (1), **erect.**

rear-end *verb.* —*See* **crash.**

rear-guard *adjective.* —*See* **ultraconservative.**

rearmost *adjective.* —*See* **last**[1] (2).

rearrange *verb.* —*See* **shuffle.**

rearrangement *noun.* —*See* **displacement.**

rearward *adverb.* —*See* **backward.**

rearward *adjective.* —*See* **back, backward** (3).

reason *noun.* **1.** A fact or circumstance that gives logical support to an assertion, claim, or proposal ▶ argument, case, grounds, point, proof, wherefore, why. ***Idiom:*** why and wherefore. [*Compare* **account, explanation.**] **2.** That which produces an effect ▶ antecedent, cause, determinant, occasion. [*Compare* **impact, origin, stimulus.**] —*See also* **account** (1), **basis** (2), **cause** (2), **common sense, logic, sanity, sense.**

reason *verb.* —*See* **discuss, infer, think** (1).

reasonable *adjective.* —*See* **acceptable** (2), **believable, conservative** (2), **logical** (2), **sensible.**

reasoning *noun.* —*See* **theory** (1).

reasoner *noun.* A person who seeks truth by thinking ▶ philosopher, theorist, thinker.

reassume *verb.* —*See* **resume.**

reassurance *noun.* A consoling in time of grief or pain ▶ comfort, consolation, solace, succor. [*Compare* **help, pity.**]

reassure *verb.* —*See* **comfort.**

reawaken *verb.* —*See* **revive** (1).

rebate *noun.* —*See* **deduction** (1).

rebate *verb.* —*See* **decrease, deduct.**

rebel *verb.* To vehemently defy and break allegiance with ▶ mutiny, revolt, rise (up). [*Compare* **defect, defy.**] —*See also* **disobey.**

rebel *noun.* **1.** A person who rebels ▶ insurgent, insurrectionary, insurrectionist, mutineer, revolutionary, revolutionist, subversive, transgressor. [*Compare* **separatist.**] **2.** Someone with unconventional opinions or approaches ▶ avant-gardist, dissenter, freethinker, iconoclast, independent, maverick, nonconformist, original, rule-breaker, visionary.

rebellion *noun.* Organized opposition intended to change or overthrow existing authority ▶ insurgence, insurgency, insurrection, mutiny, revolt, revolution, sedition, uprising. [*Compare* **competition, battle.**] —*See also* **defiance** (1).

rebellious *adjective.* Participating in open revolt against a government or ruling authority ▶ insurgent, insurrectionary, mutinous, revolutionary, seditionary, subversive. —*See also* **defiant.**

rebelliousness *noun.* —*See* **defiance** (2).

rebirth *noun.* A fundamental change in one's beliefs ▶ conversion, metanoia, regeneration. —*See also* **revival** (1).

rebound *verb.* **1.** To spring back or up after colliding with something ▶ bounce (back), bound, hop. **2.** To jerk backward, as a gun upon firing ▶ recoil. **3.** To reverse direction after striking something ▶ bounce, reflect, snap back, spring back. [*Compare* **bend, glance.**] —*See also* **echo.**

rebound *noun.* A bouncing movement ▶ bounce, bound, hop.

rebuff *noun.* —*See* **snub.**

rebuff *verb.* —*See* **decline, repel, snub.**

rebuild *verb.* —*See* **restore** (2).

rebuke *verb.* —*See* **chastise.**

rebuke *noun.* Words expressive of strong disapproval ▶ admonishment, admonition, berating, chiding, dressing-down, lecture, opprobrium, remonstrance, reprimand, reproach, reproof, reproval, scolding, slap, upbraiding. *Informal:* tongue-lashing. *Slang:* chewing-out, rap, slam. ***Idiom:*** trip to the woodshed. [*Compare* **criticism, snub, vituperation.**]

rebut *verb.* —*See* **refute.**

recalcitrance *or* **recalcitrancy** *noun.* —*See* **defiance** (2), **unruliness.**

recalcitrant *adjective.* —*See* **defiant, unruly.**

recall *verb.* To cause one to remember or think of ▶ hark back, suggest. ***Idioms:*** bring to mind, put one in mind of, take one back, remind one of. [*Compare* **refer, remind.**] —*See also* **lift** (3), **remember** (1), **retract** (1).

recall *noun.* —*See* **memory** (1), **repeal.**

recant *verb.* —*See* **retract** (1).

recantation *noun.* —*See* **retraction.**

recap *verb.* —*See* **repeat** (1), **review** (1).

recap *noun.* —*See* **summary.**

recapitulate *verb.* —*See* **repeat** (1), **review** (1).

recapitulation *noun.* —*See* **summary.**

recede *verb.* To move back or away from a point, limit, or mark ▶ ebb, retract, retreat, retrocede, retrograde, retrogress, step back. [*Compare* **back, wane, withdraw.**]

✦ CORE SYNONYMS: *recede, ebb, retract, retreat, retrograde.* To move back or away from a point, limit, or mark: *a hairline that had receded; waters that ebb at low tide; a turtle that retracted into its shell; an army that retreated to avoid defeat; academic standards that have retrograded.*

---

receipts *noun.* The amount of money collected as admission ▶ box office, gate, take.

receivable *adjective.* —*See* **due** (1).

receive *verb.* To admit to one's possession, presence, or awareness ▶ accept, have, take. [*Compare* **absorb.**] —*See also* **accept** (3), **derive** (1), **get** (1).

received *adjective.* —*See* **accepted, conventional.**

receiver *noun.* —*See* **object** (2).

recension *noun.* —*See* **revision.**

recent *adjective.* —*See* **contemporary** (2).

recently *adverb.* —*See* **lately.**

receptacle *noun.* An object, such as a carton, can, or jar, in which material is held or carried ▶ container, holder, repository, vessel. [*Compare* **depository, package.**]

receptive *adjective.* Ready and willing to receive favorably, as new ideas ▶ acceptant, amenable, friendly, open, open-minded, responsive. [*Compare* **alert, attentive, fair, neutral.**]

receptivity *or* **receptiveness** *noun.* —*See* **openness.**

recess *noun.* —*See* **depression** (1), **rest**[1] (1).

recess *verb.* To interrupt regular activity for a short period ▶ break. *Informal:* knock off. ***Idioms:*** take a break, take a breather, take five (*or* ten). [*Compare* **rest**[1].]

recession *noun.* A period of decreased business activity and high unemployment ▶ depression, downturn, slowdown, slump.

recidivism *noun.* —*See* **relapse.**

recipient *noun.* —*See* **object** (2).

reciprocal *adjective.* —*See* **complementary, mutual.**

reciprocate *verb.* To give or take mutually ▶ requite, return. ***Idiom:*** respond in kind. [*Compare* **exchange, respond.**] —*See also* **retaliate.**

✦ CORE SYNONYMS: *reciprocate, requite, return.* These verbs mean to give or take mutually: *doesn't reciprocate favors; consideration requited with disregard; return a compliment.*

---

reciprocation *noun.* —*See* **change** (2), **retaliation.**

reciprocative *adjective.* —*See* **mutual.**

reciprocity *noun.* —*See* **change** (2).

recite *verb.* —*See* **describe.**

reckless *adjective.* —*See* **careless, rash**[1], **wanton** (2).

recklessness *noun.* —*See* **temerity.**

reckon *verb.* —*See* **calculate, count** (2), **estimate** (2), **regard, suppose** (1).

reckon on *or* **upon** *verb.* —*See* **depend on** (1).

reckoning *noun.* The act, process, or result of calculating ▶ calculation, cast, computation, figuring. —*See also* **account** (2), **count** (1).

reclaim *verb.* —*See* **rescue, restore** (2).

re-claim *verb.* —*See* **resume.**

recline *verb.* To take repose, as by sleeping or lying quietly ▶ curl up, lie (down), repose, rest, stretch (out). [*Compare* **nap, sleep.**] —*See also* **lie**[1] (1).

reclining *adjective.* —*See* **flat** (1).

reclusion *noun.* —*See* **seclusion.**

reclusive *or* **recluse** *adjective.* —*See* **solitary.**

recognition *noun.* —*See* **acceptance** (2), **acknowledgment** (1).

recognizable *adjective.* —*See* **perceptible.**

recognizance *noun.* —*See* **pawn**[1].

recognize *verb.* To express recognition of ▶ acknowledge, admit. [*Compare* **confirm.**] —*See also* **discern, notice, place** (1).

recognized *adjective.* —*See* **accepted, famous.**

recoil *verb.* —*See* **flinch.**

recoil *noun.* An act of drawing back in an involuntary or instinctive fashion ▶ cringe, flinch, jerk (back), shrink, wince. [*Compare* **start.**]

recollect *verb.* —*See* **remember** (1).

recollection *noun.* An act or instance of remembering ▶ memory, mental image, remembrance, reminiscence. [*Compare* **idea.**] —*See also* **memory** (1).

recommend *verb.* —*See* **advise, support** (1).

recommendable *adjective.* —*See* **advisable.**

recommendation *noun.* A statement attesting to personal qualifications, character, and dependability ▶ character, reference, testimonial. [*Compare* **endorsement.**] —*See also* **advice, endorsement.**

recommendatory *adjective.* —*See* **advisory.**

recompense *verb.* —*See* **compensate.**

recompense *noun.* —*See* **compensation, due, wage.**

reconcile *verb.* **1.** To reestablish friendship between ▶ conciliate, make up, reunite. [*Compare* **pacify.**] **2.** To bring oneself to accept ▶ resign. ***Idiom:*** get used to. **3.** To make or become suitable to a particular situation or use ▶ acclimate, acclimatize, accommodate, adapt, adjust, conform, fashion, fit, square, suit, tailor. —*See also* **harmonize** (1), **settle** (2).

reconcilement *noun.* A reestablishment of friendship or harmony ▶ conciliation, rapprochement, reconciliation, settlement. [*Compare* **agreement, atonement, compromise.**]

reconciliation *noun.* **1.** A reestablishment of friendship or harmony ▶ conciliation, rapprochement, reconcilement, settlement. [*Compare* **agreement, atonement, compromise.**] **2.** The act of making amends ▶ atonement, expiation, penance, reparation. [*Compare* **compensation, purification.**]

recondite *adjective.* —*See* **ambiguous** (1), **deep** (2), **obscure** (1).

recondition *verb.* —*See* **renew** (1), **restore** (2).

reconfigure *verb.* —*See* **overhaul, shuffle.**

reconnaissance *noun.* The act or an instance of exploring or investigating ▶ exploration, investigation, probe. [*Compare* **examination.**]

reconnoiter *verb.* —*See* **explore.**

reconsider *verb.* To consider again, especially with the possibility of change ▶ reevaluate, reexamine, rethink, reweigh, review. [*Compare* **consider, doubt.**]

reconstruct *verb.* —*See* **restore** (2).

record *verb.* —*See* **list**[1], **show** (2).

record *noun.* —*See* **entry, history** (2), **story** (1), **trace.**

recount *verb.* —*See* **describe.**

recoup *verb.* —*See* **compensate, recover** (1).

recoup *noun.* The act of getting back or regaining ▶ recovery, repossession, retrieval.

recoupment *noun.* —*See* **compensation.**

recourse *noun.* That to which one turns for help when in desperation ▶ refuge, resort, resource. [*Compare* **help, support.**] —*See also* **exercise** (1).

recover *verb.* **1.** To get back ▶ make up, recoup, regain, repossess, retrieve. **2.** To regain one's health ▶ bounce back, come around (*or* round), convalesce, gain, get better, get well, improve, mend, perk up, rally, recuperate. ***Idiom:*** be on the mend. [*Compare* **revive.**] —*See also* **rescue.**

✦ **CORE SYNONYMS:** *recover, regain, recoup, retrieve.* These verbs mean to get back something lost or taken away. *Recover* is the least specific: *The police recovered the stolen car. "In a few days Mr. Barnstaple had recovered strength of body and mind"* (H.G. Wells). *Regain* suggests success in recovering something that has been taken from one: *"hopeful to regain/Thy Love"* (John Milton). To *recoup* is to get back the equivalent of something lost: *earned enough profit to recoup her expenses. Retrieve* pertains to the effortful recovery of something (*retrieved the ball*) or to the making good of something gone awry: *"By a brilliant coup he has retrieved . . . a rather serious loss"* (Samuel Butler).

---

recovery *noun.* **1.** The act of getting back or regaining ▶ recoup, repossession, retrieval. **2.** The process or period of a return to health ▶ convalescence, rally, recuperation. **3.** A return to former prosperity or status ▶ comeback, reestablishment, restoration. [*Compare* **renewal, revival.**]

recreance *or* **recreancy** *noun.* —*See* **defection.**

recreant *adjective.* —*See* **cowardly, faithless.**

recreant *noun.* —*See* **coward, defector.**

recreate *verb.* —*See* **amuse, play** (1).

re-create *verb.* —*See* **renew** (1).

recreation *noun.* —*See* **amusement.**

recriminate *verb.* —*See* **accuse.**

recrimination *noun.* —*See* **accusation.**

recriminator *noun.* One that accuses ▶ accuser, arraigner, denouncer, indicter.

recrudesce *verb.* —*See* **return** (1).

recruit *verb.* —*See* **employ** (1).

rectify *verb.* —*See* **correct** (1), **settle** (2).

rectitude *noun.* —*See* **ethics** (1), **good** (1).

rector *noun.* —*See* **cleric.**

recumbent *adjective.* —*See* **flat** (1).

recuperate *verb.* —*See* **recover** (2).

recuperation *noun.* The process or period of a return to health ▶ convalescence, rally, recovery.

recur *verb.* To happen again or repeatedly ▶ iterate, reappear, reoccur, repeat. —*See also* **return** (1).

recurrence *noun.* —*See* **repetition.**

recurrent *adjective.* Happening or appearing consistently or repeatedly ▶ episodic, regular, repeating, repetitive. [*Compare* **periodic, pervasive, thematic.**]

redaction *noun.* —*See* **revision.**

red-blooded *adjective.* —*See* **lusty.**

redden *verb.* —*See* **blush.**

redecorate *verb.* —*See* **renew** (1).

redeem *verb.* —*See* **cancel** (2), **purify** (1), **rescue.**

redeemer *noun.* —*See* **rescuer.**

redemption *noun.* —*See* **purification** (2).

red-hot *adjective. Informal* Of great current interest ▶ hot, live. [*Compare* **fashionable, important.**] —*See also* **hot** (1), **passionate.**

redo *verb.* To do or perform an act again ▶ do over, duplicate, play over, repeat, replay. [*Compare* **copy.**]

redolence *noun.* —*See* **fragrance.**

redolent *adjective.* —*See* **fragrant, spicy.**

redouble *verb.* To make or become twice as great ▶ double, duplicate, geminate, twin. —*See also* **intensify.**

redoubt *noun.* —*See* **fort.**

redoubtable *adjective.* —*See* **famous, fearful.**

red-pencil *verb.* —*See* **censor** (1).

redraft *verb.* —*See* **revise.**

redraft *noun.* —*See* **revision.**

redress *verb.* —*See* **avenge, compensate, correct** (1).

redress *noun.* —*See* **compensation.**

red tape *noun.* —*See* **bother.**

reduce *verb.* **1.** To lose body weight, as by dieting ▶ slim (down), thin (down), trim down. ***Idioms:*** get the weight off, lose weight, shed some pounds. **2.** To make thick or thicker, especially through the process of evaporation or condensation ▶ condense, inspissate, thicken. [*Compare* **coagulate.**] —*See also* **analyze, decrease, demote, depreciate, shorten.**

reduction *noun.* The act or an instance of demoting ▶ demotion, degradation, downgrade. —*See also* **analysis, decrease, deduction** (1), **depreciation.**

redundancy *or* **redundance** *noun.* —*See* **wordiness.**

redundant *adjective.* —*See* **superfluous, wordy** (1).

reduplication *noun.* —*See* **copy** (1).

reecho *verb.* —*See* **echo.**

reek *verb.* To have or give off a foul odor ▶ smell, stink. ***Idiom:*** stink to high heaven.

reek *noun.* —*See* **stench.**

reeking *or* **reeky** *adjective.* —*See* **smelly.**

reel *verb.* To have the sensation of turning in circles ▶ spin, swim, swirl, whirl. ***Idiom:*** go round and round. —*See also* **stagger** (1), **turn** (1).

reeling *adjective.* —*See* **dizzy** (1).

reengineer *verb.* —*See* **overhaul.**

reengineering *noun.* A thorough or drastic reorganization ▶ overhaul, reshuffling, shakeup. *Informal:* housecleaning. [*Compare* **renewal, revolution.**]

reestablish *verb.* To bring back into existence or use ▶ reinstate, reintroduce, renew, restore, return, revive. [*Compare* **restore.**]

reestablishment *noun.* A return to former prosperity or status ▶ comeback, recovery, restoration. [*Compare* **renewal, revival.**]

reevaluate *verb.* —*See* **reconsider.**

ref *noun.* —*See* **judge** (2).

refer *verb.* **1.** To make reference to something ▶ advert, allude (to), bring up, mention, note, point to (*or* out), touch (on *or* upon). ***Idioms:*** call (*or* direct) attention to. [*Compare* **cite, designate, propose, recall.**] **2.** To direct a person elsewhere for help or information ▶ send, transfer, turn over. —*See also* **apply** (2), **attribute, resort.**

refer to *verb.* —*See* **name** (2).

✚ **CORE SYNONYMS:** *refer, advert, mention, note.* These verbs mean to make reference to something. *The article referred to the mayor's indiscretion. In therapy, he adverted to childhood experiences. She often mentions her friends from college. Please note that your grade will depend on your attendance in class.*

---

referee *noun.* —*See* **judge** (2).

referee *verb.* —*See* **judge.**

reference *noun.* **1.** The act of referring ▶ citation, naming, pointing out, referral, signification, signifying. [*Compare* **meaning, sign.**] **2.** An object referred to ▶ referent, signified. [*Compare* **meaning.**] **3.** A statement attesting to personal qualifications, character, and dependability ▶ character, recommendation, testimonial. [*Compare* **endorsement.**]

referent *noun.* An object referred to ▶ reference, signified. [*Compare* **meaning.**]

referral *noun.* —*See* **reference** (1).

refine *verb.* To remove impurities from ▶ clarify, clean, cleanse, purify. [*Compare* **clean.**] —*See also* **perfect.**

refined *adjective.* Exhibiting refined, tasteful beauty of manner, form, or style

► exquisite, graceful. —*See also* **cultured, delicate** (4).

refinement *noun.* —*See* **culture** (3), **discrimination** (1), **elegance, improvement** (1), **manners, purification** (1).

refinery *or* **refiner** *noun.* —*See* **purifier.**

refining *adjective.* —*See* **cultural.**

reflect *verb.* **1.** To send back or form an image of ► image, mirror. [*Compare* **represent.**] **2.** To reverse direction after striking something ► bound (back), rebound, snap back, spring back. [*Compare* **bend, glance.**] —*See also* **bend** (2), **comment, echo, mimic, ponder, think** (1).

reflection *noun.* **1.** An image caused by reflection ► image, likeness. [*Compare* **copy.**] **2.** Light that is reflected ► glare, highlight. [*Compare* **flash.**] **3.** An act of reflection ► deflection, glance, scattering. [*Compare* **bounce.**] **4.** An implied criticism ► imputation, slur. [*Compare* **crack, libel.**] —*See also* **comment, echo** (1), **thought.**

reflective *adjective.* —*See* **thoughtful.**

reflex *adjective.* —*See* **spontaneous.**

reflex *noun.* —*See* **echo** (1).

reflexive *adjective.* —*See* **spontaneous.**

reform *verb.* —*See* **correct** (1).

reformative *or* **reformatory** *adjective.* —*See* **corrective.**

refract *verb.* —*See* **bend** (2).

refractoriness *noun.* —*See* **unruliness.**

refractory *adjective.* —*See* **unruly.**

refrain *verb.* To hold oneself back ► abstain, forbear, hold off, keep, withhold. *Informal:* sit out. [*Compare* **avoid, hesitate.**]

refrain from *verb.* —*See* **avoid.**

✚ **CORE SYNONYMS:** *refrain, abstain, forbear.* These verbs mean to hold oneself back from doing or saying something: *refrained from commenting; abstained from smoking; can't forbear criticizing them.*

---

refresh *verb.* To impart renewed energy and strength to a person ► freshen, reinvigorate, rejuvenate, renew, restore, revitalize, revivify. [*Compare* **energize.**] —*See also* **renew** (1).

refreshing *adjective.* —*See* **invigorating.**

refreshment *noun.* A light meal ► collation, snack. *Informal:* bite, nosh. *Slang:* munchies. [*Compare* **appetizer.**] —*See also* **drink** (1).

refuge *noun.* **1.** Protection or shelter, as from danger or hardship ► asylum, harborage, safety, sanctuary, shelter. ***Idiom:*** safe haven. [*Compare* **defense.**] **2.** That to which one turns for help when in desperation ► recourse, resort, resource. [*Compare* **help, support.**] —*See also* **cover** (1).

refugee *noun.* One who flees, as from confinement or the police ► escapee, fugitive, outlaw, runaway. [*Compare* **criminal.**] —*See also* **émigré.**

refulgent *adjective.* —*See* **bright.**

refund *verb.* To give back, especially money ► reimburse, repay, restitute. [*Compare* **compensate, return.**]

refund *noun.* A quantity of money that is returned ► reimbursement, repayment. [*Compare* **deduction, return.**]

refurbish *verb.* —*See* **renew** (1).

refurbishment *noun.* —*See* **renewal** (1).

refusal *noun.* A turning down of a request ► denial, disallowance, nonacceptance, rejection, turndown. [*Compare* **forbiddance.**] —*See also* **no** (1).

refuse[1] *verb.* —*See* **decline.**

refuse[2] *noun.* —*See* **garbage.**

refute *verb.* To prove or show to be false ► belie, confute, disprove, rebut. [*Compare* **cancel, discredit, repudiate.**]

regain *verb.* —*See* **recover** (1).

regal *adjective.* —*See* **grand, noble.**

regale *verb.* To sustain with food ► feast, feed, nourish. ***Idiom:*** wine and dine. [*Compare* **support.**] —*See also* **amuse.**

regalia *noun.* —*See* **attire.**

regard *verb.* To look upon in a particular way ► account, consider, deem, esteem, look upon, reckon, see, think of, view.

[*Compare* **believe.**] —*See also* **value, watch** (1).

regard *noun.* An act of directing the eyes on an object ▶ contemplation, look, sight, view. [*Compare* **gaze, watch.**] —*See also* **acceptance** (2), **care** (1), **consideration** (1), **curiosity** (1), **esteem, notice** (1), **viewpoint.**

✤ CORE SYNONYMS: *regard, consider, deem, account, reckon.* These verbs refer to looking upon something in a particular way. *Regard* often implies a personal attitude: *I regard your apology as genuine. Consider* suggests objective reflection and reasoning: *He considers success to be of little importance. Deem* is more subjective, emphasizing judgment rather than contemplation: *The faculty deemed the essay to be acceptable. Account* and *reckon* in this sense are literary and imply calculated judgment: "*I account no man to be a philosopher who attempts to do more*" (John Henry Newman). "*I cannot reckon you as an admirer*" (Nathaniel Hawthorne).

---

regardful *adjective.* —*See* **alert, attentive, careful** (1).

regardfulness *noun.* —*See* **attention.**

regards *noun.* Friendly greetings or acknoweldgment ▶ best, greetings, respects. [*Compare* **hello.**]

regenerate *verb.* —*See* **revive** (2).

regeneration *noun.* A fundamental change in one's beliefs ▶ conversion, metanoia, rebirth. [*Compare* **revival.**]

regime *noun.* —*See* **government** (2).

regimen *noun.* —*See* **practice, treatment.**

regiment *verb.* —*See* **arrange** (1).

region *noun.* —*See* **area** (2), **territory.**

regional *adjective.* Relating to a particular territory ▶ sectional, territorial. —*See also* **indigenous, local.**

register *noun.* To come as a realization ▶ dawn on (*or* upon), sink in, soak in. [*Compare* **discover, strike, understand.**] —*See also* **list**[1].

register *verb.* —*See* **list**[1], **show** (2).

regnant *adjective.* —*See* **dominant** (1), **prevailing.**

regress *verb.* —*See* **relapse.**

regression *noun.* —*See* **relapse.**

regret *verb.* To feel or express sorrow for ▶ deplore, repent, rue, sorrow (over). [*Compare* **feel, grieve.**]

regret *noun.* —*See* **disappointment** (1), **penitence.**

regretful *adjective.* —*See* **sorry.**

regrets *noun.* A statement of acknowledgment expressing regret or asking pardon ▶ apology, excuse, mea culpa. [*Compare* **acknowledgment.**]

regrettable *adjective.* —*See* **sorrowful.**

regular *adjective.* **1.** Characterized by or displaying symmetry, especially correspondence in scale or measure ▶ balanced, proportional, proportionate, symmetric, symmetrical. [*Compare* **even, parallel.**] **2.** Happening or appearing consistently or repeatedly ▶ episodic, recurrent, repeating, repetitive. [*Compare* **periodic, pervasive, thematic.**] —*See also* **common** (1), **conventional, methodical, perfect, unchanging.**

regularity *noun.* —*See* **changelessness, usualness.**

regularize *verb.* —*See* **conventionalize.**

regularly *adverb.* —*See* **usually.**

regulate *verb.* —*See* **adjust, arrange** (1), **govern, police.**

regulated *adjective.* —*See* **restricted.**

regulation *noun.* —*See* **law** (1), **rule.**

regulatory *adjective.* —*See* **governmental.**

rehab *noun.* —*See* **treatment.**

rehabilitate *verb.* —*See* **cure, restore** (2).

rehabilitation *noun.* —*See* **improvement** (1), **treatment.**

rehash *verb.* —*See* **paraphrase.**

rehearsal *noun.* —*See* **practice.**

rehearse *verb.* —*See* **describe, practice** (1).

reification *noun.* —*See* **embodiment.**

reify *verb.* —*See* **embody** (1).

reign *noun.* —*See* **domination.**
reign *verb.* —*See* **administer** (1), **dominate** (1).
reigning *adjective.* —*See* **dominant** (1), **prevailing.**
reimbursable *adjective.* Affording compensation ► compensative, compensatory, remunerative.
reimburse *verb.* To give back, especially money ► refund, repay, restitute. [*Compare* **compensate, return.**] —*See also* **compensate.**
reimbursement *noun.* A quantity of money that is returned ► refund, repayment. [*Compare* **deduction, return.**] —*See also* **compensation.**
rein *verb.* —*See* **restrain.**
rein *noun.* —*See* **brake.**
reinforce *verb.* To make firmer in a particular conviction or habit ► confirm, fortify, harden, strengthen. [*Compare* **back, establish.**] —*See also* **supplement, support** (2).
reinforcement *noun.* —*See* **support.**
reinstall *verb.* To put someone in the possession of a prior position or office ► give back, reappoint, reinstate, replace, restore, return.
reinstate *verb.* To bring back into existence or use ► reestablish, reintroduce, renew, restore, return, revive. —*See also* **reinstall.** —*See also* **restore** (2).
reintroduce *verb.* To bring back into existence or use ► reestablish, reinstate, renew, restore, return, revive. [*Compare* **restore.**]
reinvigorate *verb.* —*See* **refresh.**
reinvigorating *adjective.* —*See* **invigorating.**
reiterate *verb.* —*See* **repeat** (1).
reiteration *noun.* —*See* **repetition.**
reiterative *adjective.* Characterized by repetition ► iterative, repetitious, repetitive. [*Compare* **boring, superfluous, wordy.**]
reject *verb.* —*See* **decline, disapprove, disbelieve, dismiss** (3), **exclude, repudiate.**
reject *noun.* —*See* **outcast.**
rejected *adjective.* —*See* **abandoned** (1), **unwelcome.**
rejection *noun.* A turning down of a request ► denial, disallowance, nonacceptance, refusal, turndown. [*Compare* **forbiddance.**] —*See also* **denial** (1), **disapproval, disbelief, no** (1).
rejoice *verb.* To feel or take joy or pleasure ► delight, exult, pleasure. [*Compare* **enjoy, luxuriate.**] —*See also* **celebrate** (2).
rejoicing *noun.* —*See* **celebration** (3).
rejoin *verb.* —*See* **answer.**
rejoinder *noun.* —*See* **answer** (1).
rejuvenate *verb.* —*See* **refresh, renew** (1), **restore** (2).
rejuvenation *noun.* —*See* **renewal** (1).
rekindle *verb.* —*See* **revive** (1).
relapse *verb.* To slip from a higher or better condition to a former, usually lower or poorer one ► backslide, fall back, lapse, regress, retrogress, revert. [*Compare* **deteriorate.**]
relapse *noun.* A slipping from a higher or better condition to a former, usually lower or poorer one ► backslide, backsliding, lapse, recidivation, recidivism, regression, retrogradation, retrogression. [*Compare* **deterioration, reverse.**]
relate *verb.* **1.** To associate or affiliate oneself closely with a person or group ► empathize, identify, sympathize. [*Compare* **understand.**] **2.** To interact with another or others in a harmonious fashion ► communicate, connect, get along (on), harmonize. *Informal:* cotton (to). *Slang:* click. ***Idioms:*** be in synch, be on the same wavelength, hit it off, make a good fit (*or* match). [*Compare* **agree.**] —*See also* **apply** (2), **associate** (1), **describe, liken.**
related *adjective.* —*See* **kindred.**
relation *noun.* **1.** A logical or natural association between two or more things ► connection, correlation, interconnection, interdependence, interrelationship, link, linkage, relationship, tie-in. *Informal:* hookup. [*Compare* **bond, rel-**

evance.] **2.** A person connected to another person by blood or marriage ▶ kinsman, kinswoman, relative. [*Compare* **ancestry, family, kin.**]

relationship *noun.* —*See* **relation** (1).

relative *adjective.* Estimated by comparison ▶ comparable, comparative. —*See also* **conditional.**

relative *noun.* A person connected to another person by blood or marriage ▶ kinsman, kinswoman, relation. [*Compare* **ancestry, family, kin.**]

relax *verb.* —*See* **ease** (1), **even, rest**[1] (1).

relaxation *noun.* —*See* **rest**[1] (2).

relaxed *adjective.* —*See* **easygoing, loose** (1).

release *verb.* —*See* **discharge, dismiss** (1), **dismiss** (2), **emit, excuse** (1), **extricate, free** (1), **open** (1), **publish** (1), **rid, undo.**

release *noun.* —*See* **publication** (1), **rescue.**

relegate *verb.* —*See* **entrust** (1).

relent *verb.* —*See* **weaken.**

relentless *adjective.* —*See* **bitter** (2), **continual, stubborn** (1).

relentlessness *noun.* —*See* **stubbornness.**

relevance *or* **relevancy** *noun.* The relationship of something to the matter at hand ▶ applicability, application, appositeness, bearing, germaneness, materiality, pertinence, pertinency, relevancy. [*Compare* **importance, influence, interest.**]

relevant *adjective.* Related to or affecting the matter at hand ▶ applicable, apposite, apropos, germane, material, pertinent. ***Idiom:*** to the point. [*Compare* **influential, important.**]

✚ CORE SYNONYMS: *relevant, pertinent, germane, material, apposite, apropos.* These adjectives describe what relates to and has a direct bearing on the matter at hand. Something *relevant* is connected with a subject or issue: *performed experiments relevant to her research. Pertinent* suggests a logical, precise relevance: *assigned pertinent articles for the class to read. Germane* implies close kinship and appropriateness: *"He asks questions that are germane and central to the issue"* (Marlin Fitzwater). Something *material* is not only relevant but also crucial to a matter: *reiterated the material facts of the lawsuit. Apposite* implies a striking appropriateness and pertinence: *used apposite verbal images in the paper.* Something *apropos* is both to the point and opportune: *an apropos comment that concisely answered my question.*

◀ ANTONYM: *irrelevant*

---

reliability *noun.* —*See* **honesty, veracity.**

reliable *adjective.* —*See* **dependable.**

reliance *noun.* The state or relation of being determined or controlled ▶ dependence, dependency. [*Compare* **authority, dominance, need, relation.**] —*See also* **trust.**

relic *noun.* —*See* **remembrance** (1), **trace.**

relics *noun.* —*See* **body** (2).

relief *noun.* **1.** Reduction of pain or distress, or a cause of that reduction ▶ alleviation, assuagement, ease, mitigation, palliation, succor. [*Compare* **comfort, decrease, waning.**] **2.** Assistance, especially money, food, and other necessities, given to the needy or dispossessed ▶ aid, handout, public assistance, welfare. *Informal:* dole. [*Compare* **donation.**] —*See also* **help, sculpture, substitute.**

relieve *verb.* **1.** To make less severe or more bearable ▶ allay, alleviate, assuage, ease, lessen, lighten, mitigate, palliate, quell. [*Compare* **comfort, help.**] **2.** To free from a specific duty by acting as a substitute ▶ spell, take over. [*Compare* **substitute.**] —*See also* **excuse** (1), **help, rid.**

✚ CORE SYNONYMS: *relieve, allay, alleviate, assuage, lighten, mitigate, palliate.*

These verbs mean to make something less severe or more bearable. To *relieve* is to make more endurable something causing discomfort or distress: *"that misery which he strives in vain to relieve"* (Henry David Thoreau). *Allay* suggests at least temporary relief from what is burdensome or painful: *"This music crept by me upon the waters,/Allaying both their fury and my passion/With its sweet air"* (William Shakespeare). *Alleviate* connotes temporary lessening of distress without removal of its cause: *"No arguments shall be wanting on my part that can alleviate so severe a misfortune"* (Jane Austen). To *assuage* is to soothe or make milder: *The hardened criminal assuaged his guilt by confessing to the crime. Lighten* signifies to make less heavy or oppressive: *The senator proposed innovative legislation that would lighten the taxpayer's burden. Mitigate* and *palliate* connote moderating the force or intensity of something that causes suffering: *"I . . . prayed to the Lord to mitigate a calamity"* (John Galt). *"Men turn to him in the hour of distress, as of all statesmen the most fitted to palliate it"* (William E.H. Lecky).

---

reliever *noun.* —*See* **assistant.**

religion *noun.* A system of religious belief, worship, or ritual ▶ confession, creed, cult, denomination, faith, persuasion, profession, sect. [*Compare* **devotion, doctrine.**]

religiosity *or* **religionism** *noun.* —*See* **devotion.**

religious *adjective.* Of or relating to a church or to an established religion ▶ church, churchly, ecclesiastical, spiritual. [*Compare* **clerical, divine, holy, ritual.**] —*See also* **divine** (2), **pious.**

religiousness *noun.* —*See* **devotion.**

relinquish *verb.* To yield oneself unrestrainedly, as to an impulse ▶ abandon, deliver, surrender. ***Idioms:*** give oneself up (*or* over). —*See also* **abandon** (1), **drop** (4), **lose** (2).

relinquished *adjective.* —*See* **abandoned** (1).

relinquishment *noun.* —*See* **abandonment** (1).

relish *noun.* Spirited enjoyment ▶ gusto, zest. [*Compare* **enthusiasm.**] —*See also* **flavor** (1), **taste** (1).

relish *verb.* To be avidly interested in ▶ devour, feast on. *Slang:* eat up. —*See also* **enjoy.**

relocate *verb.* **1.** To change one's residence or place of business, for example ▶ move, remove, transfer. ***Idiom:*** pull up stakes. [*Compare* **emigrate, go.**] **2.** To move to a place and reside there ▶ locate, settle. ***Idioms:*** fix one's residence, make one's home, put down roots, take up residence. [*Compare* **live**[1]**.**]

relocation *noun.* The act of moving from one place to another ▶ move, remotion, removal. ***Idioms:*** change of address (*or* residence). [*Compare* **departure.**] —*See also* **displacement.**

reluctance *noun.* —*See* **indisposition.**

reluctant *adjective.* —*See* **indisposed.**

rely on *or* **upon** *verb.* —*See* **depend on** (1).

remain *verb.* To continue to be in a place ▶ abide, bide, linger, pause, stay, tarry, wait. *Informal:* hang around, stick around. ***Idioms:*** cool one's heels (*or* jets), stay put. [*Compare* **delay.**] —*See also* **endure** (2).

✦ **CORE SYNONYMS:** *remain, stay, wait, abide, tarry, linger.* These verbs mean to continue to be in a given place. *Remain* often implies continuing or being left after others have gone: *I remained at the end of the meeting to talk to the speaker. Stay* often suggests that the person involved is a guest or visitor: *"Must you go? Can't you stay?"* (Charles J. Vaughan). *Wait* suggests remaining in readiness, anticipation, or expectation: *"Your father is waiting for me to take a walk with him"* (Booth Tarkington). *Abide* implies continuing for a lengthy period: *"Abide with me"* (Henry Francis Lyte). *Tarry* and *linger* both imply a delayed departure, but *linger* more strongly suggests reluctance to leave: *"She was not anxious but puzzled that her husband tarried"* (Eden Phillpotts). *"I alone sit lingering here"* (Henry Vaughan).

---

remainder *noun.* —*See* **balance** (4), **trace.**

remaining *adjective.* Being what remains, especially after a part has been removed ▶ extra, leftover, stray. ***Idiom:*** left behind. [*Compare* **superfluous.**]

remains *noun.* The substance of the body, especially after decay or cremation ▶ ashes, clay, cremains, dust. —*See also* **balance** (4), **body** (2), **ruin** (2), **trace.**

remand *verb.* —*See* **entrust** (1).

remark *verb.* —*See* **comment, notice.**

remark *noun.* —*See* **comment, notice** (1).

remarkable *adjective.* —*See* **excellent, exceptional, noticeable.**

remarkably *adverb.* —*See* **unusually.**

remedial *adjective.* —*See* **corrective, curative.**

remedy *noun.* —*See* **cure.**

remedy *verb.* —*See* **correct** (1), **cure.**

remember *verb.* **1.** To renew an image or thought in the mind ▶ bethink, mind, recall, recollect, remind oneself, reminisce, retain, retrieve, revive. ***Idiom:*** bring to mind. [*Compare* **imagine, memorize, think.**] **2.** To care enough to keep someone in mind ▶ cherish, think about, think of.

✚ **CORE SYNONYMS:** *remember, recall, recollect, reminisce.* These verbs mean to bring an image or a thought back to the mind: *can't even seem to remember his name; recalling her kindness; recollected the events leading to the traffic accident; reminisced about playing varsity soccer in college.*

◀ **ANTONYM:** *forget*

---

remembrance *noun.* **1.** Something that causes one to remember ▶ favor, forget-me-not, keepsake, memento, relic, reminder, souvenir, token, trophy. [*Compare* **memorial, novelty.**] **2.** An act or instance of remembering ▶ memory, mental image, recollection, reminiscence. [*Compare* **idea.**] **3.** Something, as a structure or custom, that honors or keeps alive a memory ▶ commemoration, memorial, monument. [*Compare* **testimonial.**] —*See also* **memory** (1).

remind *noun.* To cause to remember ▶ bring back to. ***Idiom:*** make think of. [*Compare* **recall, suggest.**]

reminder *noun.* —*See* **note, remembrance** (1).

reminisce *verb.* —*See* **remember** (1).

reminiscence *noun.* An act or instance of remembering ▶ memory, mental image, recollection, remembrance. [*Compare* **idea.**] —*See also* **memory** (1).

reminiscences *noun.* —*See* **memoir.**

reminiscent *adjective.* Tending to bring a memory, mood, or image, for example, subtly or indirectly to mind ▶ allusive, connotative, evocative, impressionistic, suggestive. [*Compare* **designative, symbolic.**]

remise *verb.* —*See* **excuse** (1).

remiss *adjective.* —*See* **negligent.**

remissible *adjective.* —*See* **pardonable.**

remission *noun.* —*See* **abeyance, exculpation, forgiveness, waning.**

remissness *noun.* —*See* **negligence.**

remit *verb.* —*See* **abandon** (2), **compensate, defer[1], entrust** (1), **excuse** (1), **forgive, subside.**

remnant *noun.* —*See* **balance** (4), **trace.**

remodel *verb.* —*See* **adapt.**

remonstrance *noun.* —*See* **objection, rebuke.**

remonstrate *verb.* —*See* **object.**

remonstration *noun.* —*See* **objection.**

remorse *noun.* —*See* **penitence.**

remorseful *adjective.* —*See* **sorry.**

remorsefulness *noun.* —*See* **penitence.**

remorseless *adjective.* Devoid of remorse ▶ impenitent, unrepentant. —*See also* **callous, stubborn** (1).

remorselessness *noun.* —*See* **stubbornness.**

remote *adjective.* **1.** Far from centers of human population ▶ back, insular, isolated, lonely, lonesome, outlying, out-of-the-way, removed, secluded, solitary. *Slang:* backwater. ***Idioms:*** centrally isolated, in the middle of nowhere, off the beaten path (*or* track). [*Compare* **inaccessible, lonely, obscure.**] **2.** Small in degree, especially of probability ▶ faint, narrow, negligible, outside, slender, slight, slim. [*Compare* **doubtful, tiny.**] —*See also* **cool, detached** (1), **distant.**

remoteness *noun.* The fact or condition of being far removed or apart ▶ distance, farness, separateness, separation. —*See also* **detachment** (2).

removal *noun.* The act of moving from one place to another ▶ move, relocation, remotion. ***Idioms:*** change of address (*or* residence). [*Compare* **departure.**] —*See also* **disposal, ejection, elimination, retreat.**

remove *verb.* **1.** To move something from a position occupied ▶ carry (off *or* away), pick out, pluck out, rip out, take, take away, take off, take out, tear out, uproot, withdraw. ***Idioms:*** pluck (*or* pull) out by the roots. [*Compare* **carry, drop, pull.**] **2.** To change one's residence or place of business, for example ▶ move, relocate, transfer. ***Idiom:*** pull up stakes. [*Compare* **emigrate, go.**] **3.** To take from one's own person ▶ cast off, doff, pull off, slip off, slough off, take off. ***Idioms:*** slip (*or* step) out of. [*Compare* **bare.**] **4.** To rid of obstructions ▶ clear, free, open, unblock. [*Compare* **rid.**] —*See also* **deduct, eliminate, go** (1), **move** (2), **retreat.**

removed *adjective.* —*See* **distant, remote** (1), **solitary.**

remunerate *verb.* —*See* **compensate.**

remuneration *noun.* —*See* **compensation, wage.**

remunerative *adjective.* Affording compensation ▶ compensative, compensatory, reimbursable. —*See also* **profitable.**

renaissance *or* **renascence** *noun.* —*See* **revival** (1).

rend *verb.* —*See* **pull** (2), **tear**[1].

render *verb.* **1.** To make music ▶ concertize, perform, play. **2.** To deliver an indictment or verdict, for example ▶ hand down, return. —*See also* **abandon** (1), **give** (1), **interpret** (2), **offer** (1), **offer** (2), **paraphrase, represent** (2), **translate.**

rendering *noun.* —*See* **interpretation, paraphrase, representation, translation.**

rendezvous *noun.* —*See* **engagement** (1), **haunt.**

rendezvous *verb.* To come together by arrangement ▶ connect, hook up, get together, meet (up).

rendition *noun.* —*See* **interpretation, paraphrase.**

renege *verb.* To abandon a former position or commitment ▶ back down (*or* away *or* out), backpedal, blink, retreat, skip out, walk out. *Slang:* cop out, fink out. ***Idioms:*** beat a (hasty) retreat, cut and run. [*Compare* **abandon, escape, retreat, surrender.**]

renegade *noun.* —*See* **defector.**

renegade *verb.* —*See* **defect.**

renew *verb.* **1.** To make new or as if new again ▶ do over, fix up, furbish, recondition, re-create, redecorate, redo, refresh, refurbish, regenerate, rejuvenate, renovate, restore, revamp, smarten up, spruce up. ***Idioms:*** give a facelift to, give a new look to. [*Compare* **fix**[1], **modernize, overhaul, restore, streamline.**] **2.** To bring back into existence or use ▶ reestablish, reinstate, reintroduce, restore, return, revive. [*Compare* **restore.**] —*See also* **continue, refresh, revive** (1).

renewal *noun.* **1.** The act of making new or as if new again ▶ face-lift, facelifting, furbishment, reconditioning, redecorating, refurbishment, regeneration, rejuvenation, renovation, restoration, revampment. **2.** A continuing after interruption ▶ continuation, resumption, resurgence, revival. *—See also* **comeback, revival** (1).

renewing *adjective.* *—See* **invigorating.**

renounce *verb.* *—See* **abandon** (1), **break** (5), **defect, deny, repudiate.**

renouncement *noun.* *—See* **defection.**

renovate *verb.* *—See* **renew** (1), **restore** (2), **revive** (1).

renovation *noun.* *—See* **renewal** (1).

renown *noun.* Wide recognition for one's deeds ▶ celebrity, fame, famousness, notoriety, popularity, reputation, repute. *—See also* **fame.**

renowned *adjective.* *—See* **famous.**

rent[1] *verb.* To engage the temporary use of something for a fee ▶ charter, hire, lease. *—See also* **lease** (1).

rent[2] *noun.* A hole made by tearing ▶ rip, run, tear. [*Compare* **crack.**] *—See also* **breach** (2).

renunciation *noun.* *—See* **abandonment** (1), **denial** (1).

reoccupy *verb.* *—See* **resume.**

reoccur *verb.* To happen again or repeatedly ▶ iterate, reappear, recur, repeat. *—See also* **return** (1).

reoccurrence *noun.* *—See* **repetition.**

reopen *verb.* *—See* **continue.**

reorder *verb.* *—See* **shuffle.**

rep *noun. Informal* Public estimation of someone ▶ character, name, report, reputation, repute. [*Compare* **image, place.**]

repair[1] *verb.* *—See* **correct** (1), **fix** (1).

repair *noun.* *—See* **shape.**

repair[2] *verb.* *—See* **frequent, resort.**

repairs *noun.* *—See* **maintenance.**

reparation *noun.* The act of making amends ▶ atonement, expiation, penance, reconciliation. [*Compare* **compensation, purification.**] *—See also* **compensation, maintenance.**

reparative *adjective.* *—See* **corrective.**

repartee *noun.* *—See* **answer** (1).

repay *verb.* To give back, especially money ▶ refund, reimburse, restitute. [*Compare* **compensate, return.**] *—See also* **avenge, compensate, return** (3).

repayment *noun.* A quantity of money that is returned ▶ refund, reimbursement. [*Compare* **deduction, return.**] *—See also* **compensation.**

repeal *verb.* *—See* **lift** (3).

repeal *noun.* The act of reversing or annulling ▶ recall, rescindment, rescission, retraction, reversal, revocation. [*Compare* **abolition.**]

repeat *verb.* **1.** To state again ▶ iterate, recapitulate, reiterate, restate, retell, reutter. *Informal:* recap. [*Compare* **say, tell.**] **2.** To do or perform an act again ▶ do over, duplicate, play over, redo, replay. [*Compare* **copy.**] **3.** To happen again or repeatedly ▶ iterate, reappear, recur, reoccur. *—See also* **echo, mimic.**

repeat *noun.* *—See* **repetition.**

✚ **CORE SYNONYMS:** *repeat, iterate, reiterate, restate.* These verbs mean to state again: *repeated the warning; iterate a demand; reiterated the question; restated the obvious.*

---

repel *verb.* To turn aside or drive away ▶ beat off, check, deflect, fend (off), fight off, keep off, parry, rebuff, repulse, resist, stave off, ward off, withstand. [*Compare* **suppress.**] *—See also* **disgust, offend** (2).

repellence *or* **repellency** *noun.* *—See* **hate** (1).

repellent *adjective.* *—See* **offensive** (1), **resistant.**

repent *verb.* To feel or express sorrow for ▶ deplore, regret, rue, sorrow (over). [*Compare* **feel, grieve.**]

repentance *noun.* *—See* **penitence.**

repentant *adjective.* *—See* **sorry.**

repercussion *noun.* Repetition of sound via reflection from a surface ▶ echo, reverberation. *—See also* **impact.**

repetition *noun.* The act or process of repeating ▶ echo, iteration, reappearance, recurrence, reiteration, reoccurrence, repeat, restatement, return. [*Compare* **reproduction.**] —*See also* **echo** (1), **monotony.**

repetitious *adjective.* Characterized by repetition ▶ iterative, reiterative, repetitive. [*Compare* **superfluous, wordy.**]

repetitive *adjective.* **1.** Characterized by repetition ▶ iterative, reiterative, repetitious. [*Compare* **boring, superfluous, wordy.**] **2.** Happening or appearing consistently or repeatedly ▶ episodic, recurrent, regular, repeating. [*Compare* **periodic, pervasive, thematic.**]

rephrase *verb.* —*See* **paraphrase.**

repine *verb.* —*See* **complain.**

replace *verb.* To substitute for or fill the place of ▶ displace, supersede, supplant, surrogate. ***Idioms:*** fill someone's shoes, take over from, take the reins from. [*Compare* **substitute.**] —*See also* **reinstall.** —*See also* **return** (2).

✚ **CORE SYNONYMS:** *replace, supplant, supersede.* These verbs mean to substitute for or fill the place of another. To *replace* is to be or to furnish an equivalent or substitute, especially for one that has been lost, depleted, worn out, or discharged: "*A conspiracy was carefully engineered to replace the Directory by three Consuls*" (H.G. Wells). *Supplant* often suggests the use of intrigue or underhanded tactics to take another's place: "*The rivaling poor Jones, and supplanting him in her affections, added another spur to his pursuit*" (Henry Fielding). To *supersede* is to replace one person or thing by another held to be more valuable or useful, or less antiquated: "*In our island the Latin appears never to have superseded the old Gaelic speech*" (Thomas Macaulay).

---

replacement *noun.* —*See* **substitute.**

replay *verb.* To do or perform an act again ▶ do over, duplicate, play over, redo, repeat. [*Compare* **copy.**]

replete *adjective.* —*See* **full** (1), **full** (2).

repletion *noun.* —*See* **satiation.**

replica *noun.* —*See* **copy** (1).

replicate *verb.* —*See* **copy.**

replication *noun.* —*See* **copy** (1).

reply *verb.* —*See* **answer.**

reply *noun.* —*See* **answer** (1).

report *noun.* Public estimation of someone ▶ character, name, reputation, repute. *Informal:* rep. [*Compare* **image, place.**] —*See also* **crack** (1), **gossip** (1), **news, story** (1).

report *verb.* —*See* **communicate** (1), **describe, inform** (2).

repose *noun.* —*See* **calm, rest**[1] (2).

repose *verb.* To take repose, as by sleeping or lying quietly ▶ curl up, lie (down), recline, rest (1), stretch (out). [*Compare* **nap, sleep.**] —*See also* **consist, lie**[1] (1).

repository *noun.* **1.** A person in whom secrets are confided ▶ confessor, confidant, confidante, intimate. **2.** An object, such as a carton, a can, or a jar, in which material is held or carried ▶ container, holder, receptacle, vessel. [*Compare* **package.**] —*See also* **depository.**

repossess *verb.* —*See* **recover** (1), **resume.**

repossession *noun.* The act of getting back or regaining ▶ recoup, recovery, retrieval.

reprehend *verb.* —*See* **deplore** (1).

reprehensible *adjective.* —*See* **blameworthy, deplorable, outrageous.**

reprehension *noun.* —*See* **criticism.**

represent *verb.* **1.** To serve as an example, image, or symbol of ▶ epitomize, exemplify, illustrate, personify, stand for, symbolize, typify. [*Compare* **designate, embody, equal, mean.**] **2.** To present a lifelike image of ▶ characterize, delineate, depict, describe, draw, express, illustrate, image, limn, picture, portray, render, show. [*Compare* **act, interpret.**] **3.** To serve as an official delegate of ▶ act (as *or* for), answer for, speak for, stand for. ***Idioms:*** be spokesperson (*or* representative) for, be the voice of. [*Compare* **substitute.**] —*See also* **act** (3), **interpret** (2).

✦ **CORE SYNONYMS:** *represent, delineate, depict, limn, picture, portray.* These verbs mean to render or present a lifelike image of: *a statue representing a king; cave paintings that delineate hunters; a cartoon depicting a sea monster; the personality of a great leader limned in words; a landscape pictured in soft colors; a book portraying life in the Middle Ages.*

representation *noun.* The act or process of describing in lifelike imagery ▶ characterization, delineation, depiction, description, drawing, expression, illustration, portrayal, rendering. —*See also* **interpretation.**

representational *adjective.* —*See* **symbolic.**

representative *noun.* One who represents the interests of another ▶ advocate, ambassador, consul, delegate, deputy, emissary, envoy, factor, lieutenant, minister, proxy, steward. [*Compare* **agent, speaker, substitute.**] —*See also* **example** (1).

representative *adjective.* —*See* **descriptive, symbolic, typical.**

repress *verb.* To hold something requiring an outlet in check ▶ bottle up, burke, choke (back), gag, hold back, hold down, hold in, hush (up), keep back (*or* in), muffle, muzzle, quench, smother, squelch, stifle, strangle, subdue, suppress, throttle. *Informal:* sit on (*or* upon). ***Idioms:*** hold (*or* keep) in check. [*Compare* **censor, hinder, restrain, suppress.**]

repression *noun.* Forceful subjugation, as against an uprising ▶ clampdown, crackdown, lockdown, suppression. [*Compare* **restraint.**] —*See also* **domination, oppression.**

repressive *adjective.* Serving to restrain forcefully ▶ inhibitive, inhibitory, restraining, restrictive, stifling, suppressive. [*Compare* **absolute, authoritarian.**]

reprieve *noun.* ▶ exemption, grace, immunity, respite. [*Compare* **delay.**]

reprimand *verb.* —*See* **chastise.**

reprimand *noun.* —*See* **rebuke.**

reprint *noun.* —*See* **copy** (2).

reprint *verb.* —*See* **copy.**

reprisal *noun.* —*See* **retaliation.**

reproach *verb.* To cause to feel embarrassment, dishonor, and often guilt ▶ brand, mortify, shame, stigmatize. ***Idioms:*** put to shame, put to the blush. [*Compare* **belittle, denigrate, embarrass, humble.**] —*See also* **chastise.**

reproach *noun.* —*See* **disapproval, disgrace, rebuke.**

reproachable *adjective.* —*See* **disgraceful.**

reproachful *adjective.* —*See* **critical** (1).

reprobate *adjective.* —*See* **condemned, evil, wanton** (1).

reprobate *verb.* —*See* **deplore** (1), **disapprove.**

reprobate *noun.* —*See* **wanton.**

reprobation *noun.* —*See* **criticism.**

reproduce *verb.* —*See* **breed, copy.**

reproduction *noun.* The process by which an organism produces others of its kind ▶ breeding, generation, multiplication, procreation, proliferation, propagation, spawning. —*See also* **copy** (1), **echo** (1).

reproductive *adjective.* Of or relating to reproduction ▶ generative, procreant, procreative.

reproof *noun.* —*See* **disapproval, rebuke.**

reproval *noun.* —*See* **rebuke.**

reprove *verb.* —*See* **chastise, criticize** (1).

reptile *noun.* —*See* **creep** (2).

repudiate *verb.* To refuse to recognize or acknowledge ▶ deny, disacknowledge, disavow, disclaim, disown, reject, renounce. ***Idioms:*** turn one's back on, turn up one's nose at. [*Compare* **deny,**

disbelieve, retract.] —*See also* **dismiss** (3).

repudiation *noun.* —*See* **denial** (1).

repugnance *noun.* —*See* **disgust, hate** (1).

repugnancy *noun.* —*See* **hate** (1).

repugnant *adjective.* —*See* **offensive** (1).

repulse *verb.* —*See* **disgust, offend** (2), **repel.**

repulsion *noun.* —*See* **hate** (1).

repulsive *adjective.* —*See* **offensive** (1), **unpalatable.**

repulsiveness *noun.* —*See* **ugliness.**

reputable *adjective.* —*See* **admirable, famous.**

reputation *or* **repute** *noun.* Public estimation of someone ▶ character, name, report, repute. *Informal:* rep. [*Compare* **image, place.**] —*See also* **fame, honor** (2).

reputed *adjective.* —*See* **supposed.**

request *verb.* —*See* **appeal** (1).

requiem *noun.* —*See* **funeral.**

require *verb.* **1.** To be without what is needed, required, or essential ▶ lack, need, want. [*Compare* **demand.**] **2.** To oblige to do or not do by force of authority, propriety, or custom ▶ expect, oblige, obligate, suppose. [*Compare* **must.**] —*See also* **demand** (1), **demand** (2).

required *adjective.* Imposed on one by authority, command, or convention ▶ compulsory, dictated, imperative, mandatory, necessary, obligatory, prescribed, requisite. —*See also* **essential** (1), **obliged** (2).

requirement *noun.* —*See* **condition** (2), **demand** (2), **duty** (1).

requisite *adjective.* —*See* **essential** (1), **required.**

requisite *noun.* —*See* **condition** (2).

requisition *noun.* —*See* **appeal, demand** (1).

requisition *verb.* —*See* **demand** (1).

requital *noun.* —*See* **compensation, retaliation.**

requite *verb.* To give or take mutually ▶ reciprocate, return. ***Idiom:*** respond in kind. —*See also* **avenge, compensate, retaliate.**

requited *adjective.* —*See* **mutual.**

rescind *verb.* —*See* **lift** (3).

rescission *noun.* —*See* **repeal.**

rescue *verb.* To set free, as from danger or confinement ▶ bail out, deliver, reclaim, recover, redeem, salvage, save. ***Idioms:*** save by the bell, save someone's bacon (*or* neck), come to the rescue of. [*Compare* **free, help.**]

rescue *noun.* Extrication from danger or confinement ▶ deliverance, delivery, emancipation, freeing, liberation, release, salvage, salvation, saving. [*Compare* **freedom.**]

✦ **CORE SYNONYMS:** *rescue, save, reclaim, redeem, deliver.* These verbs mean to set free a person or thing from danger, evil, confinement, or servitude. *Rescue* and *save* are the most general, although *rescue* often implies saving from immediate harm or danger by direct action: *The curator rescued a rare manuscript from a fire. The smallpox vaccine has saved many lives. Reclaim* can mean to bring a person back, as from error to virtue or to right or proper conduct: *"To reclaim me from this course of life was the sole cause of his journey to London"* (Henry Fielding). To *redeem* is to free someone from captivity or the consequences of sin or error; the term can imply the expenditure of money or effort: *The price for redeeming the hostages was extortionate. Deliver* applies to liberating people from something such as misery, peril, error, or evil: *"consigned to a state of wretchedness from which no human efforts will deliver them"* (George Washington).

---

rescuer *noun.* One who frees someone from danger or confinement ▶ angel, deliverer, liberator, lifesaver, redeemer, savior. [*Compare* **guard, patron.**]

research *noun.* —*See* **examination** (1).

research *verb.* —*See* **examine** (1).
researcher *noun.* —*See* **inquirer.**
resemblance *noun.* —*See* **likeness** (1).
resemble *verb.* To be similar especially in appearance ▶ be like, look like, match, mimic, take after. *Chiefly Regional:* favor. ***Idioms:*** be a dead ringer for, be like as two peas in a pod, be the spitting (*or* spit and) image of. [*Compare* **agree, appear, equal.**]
resentful *adjective.* Bitingly hostile ▶ acrimonious, bitter, embittered, hard, rancorous, virulent. [*Compare* **angry, hostile.**]
resentfulness *noun.* —*See* **resentment.**
resentment *noun.* The quality or state of feeling bitter ▶ acrimony, bitterness, embitterment, gall, rancor, rancorousness, resentfulness, virulence, virulency. [*Compare* **enmity, hate.**] —*See also* **anger, offense.**
reservation *noun.* Public land kept for a special purpose ▶ park, preserve, reserve, sanctuary. [*Compare* **common.**] —*See also* **doubt, provision, qualm.**
reserve *verb.* —*See* **book, hold** (1).
reserve *noun.* **1.** The keeping of one's thoughts and emotions to oneself ▶ constraint, control, guardedness, introversion, remoteness, reservedness, restraint, reticence, self-control, self-restraint, taciturnity, uncommunicativeness, unresponsiveness. [*Compare* **balance, inhospitality, silence.**] **2.** Public land kept for a special purpose ▶ park, preserve, reservation, sanctuary. [*Compare* **common.**] —*See also* **hoard.**
reserve *adjective.* —*See* **auxiliary** (2).
reserved *adjective.* Tending to keep one's thoughts and emotions to oneself ▶ constrained, controlled, guarded, inhibited, introverted, noncommittal, remote, restrained, self-controlled, self-restrained, unresponsive. —*See also* **cool, qualified, taciturn.**
reservoir *noun.* —*See* **hoard.**
resettle *verb.* To leave one's native land and settle in another ▶ emigrate (from), immigrate (to), migrate, transmigrate. [*Compare* **move, settle.**]
reshape *verb.* —*See* **convert.**
reshuffle *verb.* —*See* **overhaul.**
reshuffling *noun.* A thorough or drastic reorganization ▶ overhaul, reengineering, shakeup. *Informal:* housecleaning. [*Compare* **renewal, revolution.**]
reside *verb.* —*See* **consist, live[1].**
residence *noun.* —*See* **home** (1).
resident *noun.* —*See* **inhabitant.**
residential *adjective.* —*See* **domestic** (1).
residual *adjective.* Being what remains, especially after a part has been removed ▶ extra, leftover, remaining, stray. ***Idiom:*** left behind. [*Compare* **superfluous.**]
residue *noun.* —*See* **balance** (4).
resign *verb.* **1.** To bring oneself to accept ▶ reconcile. ***Idiom:*** get used to. **2.** To relinquish one's engagement in or occupation with ▶ demit, leave, quit, terminate. ***Idioms:*** hang it up, throw in the sponge (*or* towel). [*Compare* **break.**] —*See also* **abandon** (1).
resignation *noun.* —*See* **abandonment** (1), **patience.**
resigned *adjective.* —*See* **passive, patient.**
resilience *or* **resiliency** *noun.* The ability to recover quickly from depression or discouragement ▶ bounce, buoyancy, elasticity, flexibility, resiliency. —*See also* **flexibility** (1).
resilient *adjective.* —*See* **flexible** (1).
resist *verb.* To take a stand against ▶ buck, challenge, contest, dispute, oppose, traverse. —*See also* **disobey, oppose, repel.**
resistance *noun.* **1.** The capacity to withstand ▶ immunity, imperviousness, insusceptibility, unsusceptibility. [*Compare* **endurance, stability.**] **2.** A clandestine organization of freedom fighters in an oppressed land ▶ opposition, underground. —*See also* **defiance** (1), **indisposition.**

resistant *adjective.* Having the capacity to withstand ▶ immune, impervious, insusceptible, proof, repellent, resisting, resistive, unsusceptible. [*Compare* **defiant, stable, strong, stubborn.**] —*See also* **indisposed, opposing.**

resister *noun.* —*See* **opponent.**

resisting *or* **resistive** *adjective.* —*See* **resistant.**

resolute *adjective.* —*See* **firm**[1] (3), **intent.**

resoluteness *noun.* —*See* **decision** (2).

resolution *noun.* —*See* **answer** (2), **decision** (1), **decision** (2), **ruling.**

resolve *verb.* —*See* **analyze, decide, settle** (2), **solve** (1).

resolve *noun.* —*See* **decision** (2).

resonance *noun.* —*See* **tone** (2).

resonant *adjective.* Having or producing a full, deep, or rich sound ▶ mellow, orotund, plangent, resounding, ringing, rotund, round, sonorous, vibrant. [*Compare* **loud.**]

resort *verb.* To look to when in need ▶ apply, go, refer, repair, run, turn. ***Idioms:*** fall back on (*or* upon), have recourse to. —*See also* **frequent.**

resort *noun.* That to which one turns for help when in desperation ▶ recourse, refuge, resource. [*Compare* **help, support.**] —*See also* **exercise** (1), **haunt, makeshift.**

✚ CORE SYNONYMS: *resort, apply, go, refer, turn.* These verbs mean to look to or fall back on someone or something when in need: *resorted to corporal punishment; apply to a bank for a loan; goes to her friends for comfort; referred to his notes to refresh his memory; turns to his parents for support.*

---

resound *verb.* —*See* **echo, rumble** (1).

resounding *adjective.* —*See* **resonant.**

resource *noun.* That to which one turns for help when in desperation ▶ recourse, refuge, resort. [*Compare* **help, support.**]

resourceful *adjective.* —*See* **clever** (1), **inventive.**

resourcefulness *noun.* —*See* **invention** (1).

resources *noun.* Things, such as money, property, or goods, having economic value ▶ assets, capital, fortune, means, wealth, wherewithal. [*Compare* **funds, money.**] —*See also* **amenities** (1), **capital** (1).

respect *verb.* —*See* **value.**

respect *noun.* The particular angle from which something is considered ▶ angle, aspect, facet, frame of reference, hand, light, phase, regard, side. —*See also* **esteem, honor** (2).

respectability *or* **respectableness** *noun.* —*See* **decency** (2).

respectable *adjective.* —*See* **acceptable** (2), **admirable, appropriate, big, decent, honest.**

respectful *adjective.* —*See* **attentive, deferential.**

respects *noun.* —*See* **regards.**

respiration *noun.* —*See* **breath.**

respire *verb.* —*See* **breathe** (1).

respite *noun.* Temporary immunity from penalties ▶ exemption, grace, immunity, reprieve. [*Compare* **delay.**] —*See also* **rest**[1] (1).

resplendence *or* **resplendency** *noun.* —*See* **glitter** (2).

resplendent *adjective.* —*See* **glorious, ornate, sparkling.**

respond *verb.* To act in return to something, as a stimulus ▶ counter, react. ***Idiom:*** act in response. [*Compare* **retaliate.**] —*See also* **answer.**

respondent *noun.* A person against whom an action is brought ▶ accused, defendant.

response *noun.* An action elicited by a stimulus ▶ reaction, retroaction. [*Compare* **retaliation.**] —*See also* **answer** (1).

responsibility *noun.* The state of being responsible ▶ accountability, amenability, amenableness, answerability, liability. [*Compare* **blame, burden**[1].] —*See also* **duty** (1).

responsible *adjective.* —*See* **dependable, liable** (1).

responsive *adjective.* Easily approached ▶ accessible, approachable, welcoming. [*Compare* **convenient.**] —*See also* **receptive, sensitive** (1).

responsiveness *noun.* —*See* **openness.**

rest[1] *noun.* **1.** A pause or interval, as from work or duty ▶ break, breathing spell, downtime, hiatus, intermission, recess, respite, time-out. *Informal:* breather. [*Compare* **abeyance, gap, stop.**] **2.** Freedom from labor, responsibility, or strain ▶ ease, leisure, relaxation, repose, time-out. *Informal:* R and R. [*Compare* **calm, inaction, sleep.**] —*See also* **death** (1).

rest *verb.* **1.** To take repose by ceasing work or other effort for an interval of time ▶ chill out, kick back, lounge, mellow out, relax, sit back, unbend, unwind. ***Idioms:*** lead (*or* live) the life of Riley, put one's feet up, take a load off one's feet, take it easy. **2.** To take repose, as by sleeping or lying quietly ▶ curl up, lie (down), recline, repose, stretch (out). [*Compare* **nap, sleep.**] **3.** To be in a certain position; have a location ▶ be located, be situated, sit, stand. —*See also* **base**[1]**, consist.**

rest on *or* **upon** *verb.* —*See* **depend on** (2).

✣ CORE SYNONYMS: *rest, break, intermission, recess, respite.* These nouns denote a pause or interval, as from work, duty, or action: *needed a rest after a long morning at work; took an hourlong break for dinner; a concert with a 15-minute intermission; the legislature's summer recess; toiling without respite.*

---

rest[2] *noun.* —*See* **balance** (4).

restart *verb.* —*See* **continue.**

restate *verb.* —*See* **paraphrase, repeat** (1).

restatement *noun.* —*See* **paraphrase, repetition.**

restful *adjective.* —*See* **comfortable.**

restitute *verb.* To give back, especially money ▶ reimburse, refund, repay. [*Compare* **compensate, return.**] —*See also* **restore** (2), **return** (2).

restitution *noun.* —*See* **compensation.**

restive *adjective.* —*See* **edgy.**

restiveness *noun.* —*See* **restlessness.**

restless *adjective.* Affording no quiet, repose, or rest ▶ uneasy, unquiet, unsettled. [*Compare* **wakeful.**] —*See also* **busy** (2), **edgy.**

restlessness *noun.* An uneasy or nervous state ▶ disquiet, disquietude, edginess, inquietude, jumpiness, nervousness, restiveness, skittishness, tenseness, twitchiness, unease, uneasiness, unrest. [*Compare* **agitation, anxiety, excitement.**]

restoration *noun.* A return to former prosperity or status ▶ comeback, reestablishment, renewal. —*See also* **renewal** (1), **revival** (1).

restorative *adjective.* —*See* **curative, invigorating.**

restorative *noun.* —*See* **cure, tonic.**

restore *verb.* **1.** To bring back into existence or use ▶ reestablish, reinstate, reintroduce, renew, return, revive. **2.** To bring back to a previous normal condition ▶ rebuild, reclaim, recondition, reconstruct, rehabilitate, reinstate, rejuvenate, renovate, restitute. —*See also* **refresh, reinstall.** —*See also* **renew** (1), **return** (2), **revive** (2).

restrain *verb.* To control, restrict, or arrest ▶ bit, bottle (up), brake, bridle, check, constrain, curb, harness, hold, hold back, hold down, hold in, inhibit, keep, keep back, pull in, rein (back, in, *or* up). ***Idioms:*** hold in leash, keep in check, keep under control, keep within bounds, put a lid on. [*Compare* **hinder, limit, repress, stop.**]

✣ CORE SYNONYMS: *restrain, curb, check, bridle, inhibit.* These verbs mean to restrict, arrest, or keep under control. *Restrain* implies restriction or limitation, as on one's freedom of action: *"a wise and frugal government, which shall restrain men from injuring one another"*

(Thomas Jefferson). To *curb* is to restrain as if with reins: *"You might curb your magnanimity"* (John Keats). *Check* implies arresting or stopping, often suddenly or forcibly: *"a light to guide, a rod/To check the erring"* (William Wordsworth). To *bridle* is often to hold in or govern one's emotions or passions: *I tried with all my might to bridle my resentment. Inhibit* usually connotes a check on one's actions, thoughts, or emotions: *A fear of strangers inhibited his ability to travel.*

---

restrained *adjective.* —*See* **conservative** (2), **modest** (1), **reserved, restricted.**

restraint *noun.* Something that limits or holds back ▶ check, circumscription, constraint, control, cramp, curb, deterrent, drag, inhibition, limit, limitation, restriction, stay, stricture. —*See also* **bond** (1), **brake, modesty** (2), **reserve** (1), **restriction.**

restrict *verb.* —*See* **determine, limit.**

restricted *adjective.* Kept within certain limits ▶ bridled, checked, circumscribed, confined, controlled, held back, limited, regulated, reined in, restrained. [*Compare* **local.**] —*See also* **confidential** (3), **qualified.**

restriction *noun.* The act of limiting or condition of being limited ▶ circumscription, confinement, constraint, limitation, restraint, stranglehold, throttlehold. [*Compare* **provision.**] —*See also* **restraint.**

restrictive *adjective.* —*See* **repressive, tight** (4).

restyle *verb.* —*See* **revise.**

result *verb.* To occur as a consequence ▶ attend, ensue, follow. [*Compare* **stem.**]

result in *verb.* —*See* **cause.**

result *noun.* —*See* **answer** (2), **discovery, effect** (1).

resultant *noun.* —*See* **effect** (1).

resume *verb.* To occupy or take again ▶ reassume, re-claim, reoccupy, repossess, retake, take back. —*See also* **continue.**

resumé *verb.* —*See* **history** (2).

resumption *noun.* A continuing after interruption ▶ continuation, renewal, resurgence, revival.

resurgence *noun.* A continuing after interruption ▶ continuation, renewal, resumption, revival. —*See also* **revival** (1).

resurrect *verb.* —*See* **revive** (1).

resurrection *noun.* —*See* **revival** (1).

resuscitate *verb.* —*See* **revive** (1), **revive** (2).

resuscitation *noun.* —*See* **revival** (1).

retail *verb.* —*See* **sell.**

retailer *noun.* —*See* **seller.**

retain *verb.* —*See* **employ** (1), **hold** (1), **keep** (5), **remember** (1).

retained *adjective.* —*See* **employed.**

retake *verb.* —*See* **resume.**

retaliate *verb.* To return like for like, especially to return an unfriendly or hostile action with a similar one ▶ counter, counterattack, hit back, reciprocate, requite, retort, strike back. [*Compare* **avenge, exchange.**]

retaliation *noun.* The act of retaliating ▶ counteraction, counterattack, counterblow, reciprocation, reprisal, requital, retribution, revenge, tit for tat, vengeance. ***Idioms:*** an eye for an eye, a tooth for a tooth, like for like, measure for measure.

retard *verb.* —*See* **delay** (1), **hinder.**

retardation *noun.* —*See* **delay** (2).

retch *verb.* —*See* **vomit.**

retell *verb.* —*See* **repeat** (1).

retention *noun.* The act of employing for wages ▶ employment, engagement, hire, hiring. —*See also* **memory** (1).

retentive *adjective.* —*See* **absorbent.**

rethink *verb.* —*See* **reconsider.**

reticence *noun.* Reserve in speech, behavior, or dress ▶ demureness, diffidence, modesty, self-effacement. —*See also* **reserve** (1).

reticent *adjective.* —*See* **cool, taciturn.**

retinue *noun.* A group of attendants or followers ▶ entourage, following, suite, train. [*Compare* **circle, follower, public.**]

retire *verb.* **1.** To go to bed ▶ bed (down). *Informal:* turn in. *Slang:* crash, flop. ***Idioms:*** call it a night, go beddy-bye (*or* night-night), hit the hay (*or* sack). [*Compare* **sleep.**] **2.** To withdraw or remove from business or active life ▶ pension (off), step down, superannuate. ***Idioms:*** call it quits, hang up one's spurs, put out to pasture, turn in one's badge. [*Compare* **dismiss, quit.**] —*See also* **go** (1), **retreat.**

retirement *noun.* —*See* **departure, retreat, seclusion, solitude.**

retiring *adjective.* —*See* **shy[1].**

retiringness *noun.* —*See* **shyness.**

retort

retort *verb.* —*See* **answer, retaliate.**

retort *noun.* —*See* **answer** (1).

retouch *verb.* To improve by making minor changes or additions ▶ polish, remodel, touch up. [*Compare* **fix, renew.**]

retract *verb.* **1.** To disavow something previously written or said irrevocably and usually formally ▶ abjure, countermand, forswear, recall, recant, take back, unsay, withdraw. [*Compare* **lift.**] **2.** To pull back in ▶ draw in, withdraw. —*See also* **recede.**

retraction *noun.* A formal statement of disavowal ▶ abjuration, countermand, palinode, recantation, retractation, withdrawal. —*See also* **repeal.**

retreat *noun.* The moving back of a military force in the face of enemy attack or after a defeat ▶ evacuation, fallback, pullback, pullout, removal, retirement, withdrawal. [*Compare* **escape.**] —*See also* **cover** (1), **solitude.**

retreat *verb.* To move back in the face of enemy attack or after a defeat ▶ draw back, evacuate, fall back, pull back, pull out, remove, retire, turn back, withdraw. ***Idioms:*** beat a retreat, give ground (*or* way). [*Compare* **escape.**] —*See also* **back** (1), **recede, renege.**

retribution *noun.* —*See* **punishment, retaliation.**

retrieval *noun.* The act of getting back or regaining ▶ recoup, recovery, repossession.

retrieve *verb.* —*See* **recover** (1), **remember** (1), **revive** (1).

retroaction *noun.* An action elicited by a stimulus ▶ reaction, response. [*Compare* **retaliation.**]

retrocede *verb.* —*See* **back** (1), **recede.**

retrogradation *noun.* —*See* **deterioration** (1), **relapse.**

retrograde *adjective.* —*See* **backward** (3).

retrograde *verb.* —*See* **back** (1), **deteriorate, recede.**

retrogress *verb.* —*See* **back** (1), **recede, relapse.**

retrogression *noun.* —*See* **relapse.**

retrogressive *adjective.* —*See* **backward** (3).

retrospective *noun.* —*See* **exhibition.**

return *verb.* **1.** To come back to a former condition or place ▶ come back, go back, recrudesce, recur, reoccur, revert, revisit, turn back. [*Compare* **relapse.**] **2.** To send, put, or carry back to a former location ▶ give back, replace, restitute, restore, take back. [*Compare* **refund.**] **3.** To make as income or profit ▶ bring in, clear, draw, earn, gain, gross, net, pay, produce, realize, reap, repay, yield. ***Idioms:*** *Informal* rake in. [*Compare* **earn.**] **4.** To bring back into existence or use ▶ reestablish, reinstate, reintroduce, renew, restore, revive. [*Compare* **restore.**] **5.** To give or take mutually ▶ reciprocate, requite. ***Idiom:*** respond in kind. [*Compare* **exchange, respond.**] **6.** To deliver an indictment or verdict, for example ▶ hand down, render. —*See also* **answer, reinstall.**

return *noun.* Something earned, won, or otherwise acquired ▶ earnings, gain, profit. [*Compare* **increase.**] —*See also* **answer** (1), **repetition.**

reunite *verb.* To reestablish friendship between ▶ conciliate, make up, reconcile. [*Compare* **pacify.**]

reutter *verb.* —*See* **repeat** (1).

revamp *verb.* —*See* **fix** (1), **renew** (1), **revise.**

revampment *noun.* —*See* **renewal** (1).

reveal *verb.* To make visible or known ▶ bare, disclose, display, expose, show, unclothe, uncover, unmask, unveil. ***Idioms:*** bring to light (*or* view), lay open (*or* bare), make plain (*or* public). [*Compare* **announce, display.**] —*See also* **betray** (2), **communicate** (1), **show** (1).

revel *verb.* To behave riotously ▶ carouse, frolic, party, riot, roister, romp. *Informal:* hell (around). ***Idioms:*** blow off steam, cut loose, kick over the traces, kick up one's heels, let go, let loose, make merry, make whoopee, paint the town red, raise Cain (*or* the devil *or* hell), whoop it up. —*See also* **celebrate** (2), **luxuriate.**

revel *noun.* —*See* **celebration** (1).

revelation *noun.* Something disclosed, especially something not previously known or realized ▶ apocalypse, disclosure, divulgence, exposé, exposure. *Informal:* eye opener. [*Compare* **acknowledgment, news.**]

revelry *noun.* —*See* **celebration** (3), **merriment** (2).

revels *noun.* —*See* **celebration** (1), **merriment** (2).

revenant *noun.* —*See* **ghost.**

revenge *noun.* The quality or condition of being vindictive ▶ spite, spitefulness, vengefulness, vindictiveness. [*Compare* **resentment.**] —*See also* **retaliation.**

revengeful *adjective.* —*See* **vindictive.**

reverberate *verb.* —*See* **echo.**

reverberation *noun.* Repetition of sound via reflection from a surface ▶ echo, repercussion. —*See also* **blast** (1), **impact.**

revere *verb.* To regard with deep respect, deference, and esteem ▶ adore, hallow, idolize, reverence, venerate, worship. [*Compare* **distinguish, praise, honor, value.**]

✚ **CORE SYNONYMS:** *revere, worship, venerate, adore, idolize.* These verbs mean to regard with deep respect, deference, and esteem. *Revere* suggests awe coupled with profound honor: *"At least one third of the population . . . reveres every sort of holy man"* (Rudyard Kipling). *Worship* implies reverent love and homage rendered to God or a god: *The ancient Egyptians worshiped a number of gods.* In a more general sense *worship* connotes an often uncritical devotion: *"She had worshiped intellect"* (Charles Kingsley). *Venerate* connotes reverence accorded by virtue, especially of dignity or age: *"I venerate the memory of my grandfather"* (Horace Walpole). To *adore* is to worship with deep, often rapturous love: *The students adored their caring teacher. Idolize* implies worship like that accorded an object of religious devotion: *He idolizes his wife.*

---

reverence *noun.* The act of adoring, especially reverently ▶ adoration, idolization, veneration, worship. [*Compare* **devotion, honor, praise.**] —*See also* **devotion, honor** (1).

reverence *verb.* —*See* **revere.**

reverend *noun.* —*See* **cleric.**

reverent *or* **reverential** *adjective.* Feeling or showing reverence ▶ devout, pious, venerational, worshipful. [*Compare* **deferential.**]

reverie *noun.* —*See* **dream** (1), **trance.**

reversal *noun.* **1.** The act of changing or being changed from one position, direction, or course to the opposite ▶ about-face, change of heart, flip-flop, inversion, transposition, turnabout, turnaround, U-turn. **2.** A change from better to worse ▶ backset, reverse, setback. [*Compare* **misfortune, relapse.**] —*See also* **accident, repeal.**

reverse *adjective.* —*See* **opposite.**

reverse *noun.* A change from better to worse ▶ backset, reversal, setback. [*Compare* **misfortune, relapse.**] —*See also* **opposite.**

reverse *verb.* **1.** To change to the opposite position, direction, or course ▶ flip-flop, invert, transpose, turn (about, around, over, *or* round). **2.** To turn sharply around ▶ about-face, double (back). ***Idioms:*** turn on one's heels. —*See also* **back** (1), **lift** (3).

✤ **CORE SYNONYMS:** *reverse, invert, transpose.* These verbs mean to change to the opposite position, direction, or course. *Reverse* implies a complete turning about to a contrary position: *reversed the placement of the sofa and chairs.* To *invert* is basically to turn something upside down or inside out, but the term may imply placing something in a reverse order: *inverted the glass; invert subject and verb to form an interrogative. Transpose* applies to altering position in a sequence by reversing or changing the order: *often misspells* receive *by transposing the* e *and the* i.

---

reversible *adjective.* —*See* **changeable** (1).

reversion *noun.* —*See* **relapse.**

revert *verb.* —*See* **relapse, return** (1).

review *verb.* **1.** To give a recapitulation of the salient facts of ▶ abstract, epitomize, go over, recapitulate, run down, run through, summarize, sum up, synopsize, wrap up. *Informal:* recap. [*Compare* **paraphrase.**] **2.** To write a critical report on ▶ criticize, critique. [*Compare* **comment, estimate.**] —*See also* **examine** (1), **reconsider.**

review *noun.* A formal military inspection ▶ parade. —*See also* **commentary, examination** (1).

reviewer *noun.* —*See* **critic** (1).

revile *verb.* To attack with harsh, often insulting language ▶ abuse, assail, blaspheme, execrate, fulminate against, rail (at), spit on, vilify, vituperate (against). ***Idioms:*** call names, vent one's spleen at. [*Compare* **chastise, despise, dislike, hate.**]

✤ **CORE SYNONYMS:** *revile, vituperate, rail.* These verbs mean to attack with harsh, often insulting language. *Revile* and *vituperate* stress the use of disparaging or abusive language: *critics who reviled the novel as unsophisticated pulp. "The incensed priests . . . continued to raise their voices, vituperating each other in bad Latin"* (Sir Walter Scott). *Rail* suggests bitter, harsh, or denunciatory language: *"Why rail at fate? The mischief is your own"* (John Greenleaf Whittier).

---

revilement *or* **reviling** *noun.* —*See* **vituperation.**

revisal *noun.* —*See* **revision.**

revise *verb.* To prepare a new version of ▶ amend, edit, emend, emendate, redraft, restyle, revamp, rework, rewrite, work over. [*Compare* **change.**] —*See also* **correct** (1).

revision *noun.* The act or process of revising ▶ amendment, emendation, recension, redaction, redraft, revisal, rewrite. [*Compare* **improvement.**]

revisit *verb.* —*See* **return** (1).

revitalization *noun.* —*See* **revival** (1).

revitalize *verb.* —*See* **refresh, revive** (1).

revival *noun.* **1.** The act of reviving or condition of being revived ▶ reactivation, rebirth, renaissance, renascence, renewal, restoration, resurgence, resurrection, resuscitation, revitalization, revivification. [*Compare* **comeback, renewal.**] **2.** A continuing after interruption ▶ continuation, renewal, resumption, resurgence. —*See also* **comeback.**

revive *verb.* **1.** To rouse from a state of inactivity or quiescence ▶ reactivate, reanimate, reawaken, rekindle, renew, renovate, resurrect, resuscitate, retrieve, revitalize, revivify. [*Compare* **refresh.**] **2.** To cause to come back to life or consciousness ▶ bring around (*or* round), regenerate, restore, resuscitate, revivify.

[*Compare* **cure, evoke, recover.**] **3.** To bring back into existence or use ▶ reestablish, reinstate, reintroduce, renew, restore, return. [*Compare* **restore.**] —*See also* **remember** (1).

✦ **CORE SYNONYMS:** *revive, rekindle, resuscitate, revivify.* These verbs mean to rouse from a state of inactivity or quiescence: *rains that revive lawns; rekindled an old romance after twenty years apart; resuscitating old hopes; a celebration that revivified our spirits.*

---

revivification *noun.* —*See* **revival** (1).
revivify *verb.* —*See* **refresh, revive** (1), **revive** (2).
revocation *noun.* —*See* **repeal.**
revoke *verb.* —*See* **lift** (3).
revolt *verb.* To vehemently defy and break allegiance with ▶ mutiny, rebel, rise (up). [*Compare* **defect, defy.**] —*See also* **disgust.**
revolt *noun.* —*See* **rebellion.**
revolting *adjective.* —*See* **offensive** (1).
revolution *noun.* **1.** A circular movement around a point or about an axis ▶ circle, circuit, circulation, circumvolution, gyration, orbit, rotation, spin, swirl, turn, twirl, wheel, whirl. **2.** A momentous or sweeping change ▶ cataclysm, convulsion, metamorphosis, transformation, upheaval. [*Compare* **change, shakeup.**] —*See also* **rebellion.**
revolutionary *adjective.* —*See* **extreme** (2), **progressive** (1), **rebellious.**
revolutionary *or* **revolutionist** *noun.* —*See* **extremist, rebel** (1).
revolutionize *verb.* To bring about a radical change in ▶ make over, metamorphose, remake, transform. ***Idioms:*** stand on its ear (*or* head), turn inside-out (*or* topsy-turvy *or* upside-down). [*Compare* **change, overhaul.**]
revolve *verb.* —*See* **ponder, turn** (1).
revolve around *verb.* —*See* **depend on** (2).
revulsion *noun.* —*See* **despisal, disgust, hate** (1).
reward *noun.* Something that is given in return for a service or accomplishment ▶ accolade, award, bonus, bounty, guerdon, honorarium, plum, premium, prize. ***Idioms:*** token of appreciation, token of esteem. [*Compare* **distinction, gratuity, trophy.**] —*See also* **compensation, due.**
reward *verb.* To bestow a reward on ▶ award, guerdon, honor. [*Compare* **confer.**] —*See also* **compensate.**
rewarding *adjective.* —*See* **profitable.**
reword *verb.* —*See* **paraphrase.**
rework *verb.* —*See* **revise.**
rewrite *verb.* —*See* **revise.**
rewrite *noun.* —*See* **revision.**
rhapsodize *verb.* —*See* **drool, rave.**
rhetoric *noun.* —*See* **eloquence, oratory.**
rhetorical *adjective.* —*See* **oratorical.**
rhetorician *noun.* —*See* **speaker** (1).
rhinestone *noun.* A small sparkling decoration ▶ diamond, glitter, sequin, spangle.
rhubarb *noun.* —*See* **argument.**
rhyme *noun.* —*See* **poem** (1).
rhymer *or* **rhymester** *noun.* —*See* **poet.**
rhythm *noun.* The patterned, recurring alternation of contrasting elements, such as stressed and unstressed notes in music ▶ beat, cadence, cadency, measure, meter, swing. [*Compare* **beat.**]
rhythmical *or* **rhythmic** *adjective.* Marked by a regular rhythm ▶ cadenced, measured, metrical. [*Compare* **poetic.**]
rib *verb.* —*See* **joke** (2).
ribald *adjective.* —*See* **obscene.**
ribaldry *noun.* —*See* **obscenity** (2).
riband *noun.* —*See* **band**[1].
ribbing *noun. Informal* Good-natured teasing ▶ badinage, banter, chaff, joking, kidding, raillery, taunt, teasing. [*Compare* **taunt.**]
ribbon *noun.* —*See* **band**[1], **decoration, distinction** (2).
rib-tickler *noun.* —*See* **joke** (1).
rich *adjective.* **1.** Possessing a large amount of money, land, or other mate-

rial possessions ▶ affluent, flush, moneyed, wealthy. *Slang:* loaded. ***Idioms:*** having money to burn, in the money, made of money, rolling in money (*or* dough). [*Compare* **luxurious, prosperous.**] **2.** Not readily digested because of richness ▶ filling, heavy. *—See also* **colorful** (1), **costly, fertile** (1), **funny** (1), **luxurious.**

✚ **CORE SYNONYMS:** *rich, affluent, flush, loaded, moneyed, wealthy.* These adjectives mean having an abundant supply of money, property, or possessions of value: *a rich business executive; an affluent banker; a speculator flush with cash; not merely rich but loaded; moneyed heirs; wealthy multinational corporations.*

◀ **ANTONYM:** *poor*

riches *noun.* —*See* **wealth.**

richness *noun.* —*See* **fertility.**

ricketiness *noun.* —*See* **unsteadiness.**

rickety *adjective.* —*See* **insecure** (2).

ricochet *verb.* —*See* **glance** (1), **bounce.**

rid *verb.* To relieve a burden ▶ clear, disburden, discharge, disembarrass, disencumber, dump, empty, release, relieve, shake off, throw off, unburden, unlade, unload. *Slang:* shake. [*Compare* **clear, eliminate.**]

riddance *noun.* —*See* **disposal, elimination.**

riddle *noun.* —*See* **mystery.**

ride *verb.* —*See* **harass, joke** (2).

ride out *verb.* —*See* **survive** (1).

ride *noun.* —*See* **drive** (3).

ridicule *noun.* Words or actions intended to evoke contemptuous laughter ▶ derision, mockery. [*Compare* **sarcasm, taunt.**]

ridicule *verb.* To subject to ridicule ▶ deride, gibe (at), jeer (at), jest (at), lampoon, laugh at, mock (at), pillory, scoff (at), scout (at), sneer at, taunt, twit. ***Idioms:*** make a laughingstock out of, make fun (*or* sport) of, poke fun at, thumb one's nose at. [*Compare* **belittle, denigrate, disgrace.**]

✚ **CORE SYNONYMS:** *ridicule, mock, taunt, twit, deride.* These verbs refer to making another the object of contemptuous laughter. *Ridicule* implies purposeful disparagement: *"My father discouraged me by ridiculing my performances"* (Benjamin Franklin). To *mock* is to poke fun at someone, often by mimicking and caricaturing speech or actions: *"Seldom he smiles, and smiles in such a sort/As if he mock'd himself, and scorn'd his spirit"* (William Shakespeare). *Taunt* suggests mocking, insulting, or scornful reproach: *"taunting him with want of courage to leap into the great pit"* (Daniel Defoe). To *twit* is to taunt by calling attention to something embarrassing: *"The schoolmaster was twitted about the lady who threw him over"* (J.M. Barrie). *Deride* implies scorn and contempt: *"Was all the world in a conspiracy to deride his failure?"* (Edith Wharton).

ridiculous *adjective.* Causing or deserving laughter or derision ▶ farcical, laughable, ludicrous, risible. *—See also* **foolish, outrageous.**

ridiculousness *noun.* —*See* **foolishness, humor.**

rife *adjective.* —*See* **prevailing.**

riffle *verb.* —*See* **browse** (1), **shuffle.**

riffraff *noun.* A person or group of persons regarded as worthless or contemptible ▶ dregs, good-for-nothing, lumpenproletariat, rabble, ragtag and bobtail, trash, vermin. *Slang:* scum. ***Idioms:*** scum of the earth, tag and rag, the great unwashed. [*Compare* **commonalty, nonentity.**]

rift *noun.* —*See* **breach** (2), **crack** (2).

rift *verb.* —*See* **break** (1), **crack** (1).

rig *verb.* To prearrange the outcome of a contest ▶ fix, tamper. ***Idiom:*** stack the deck. *—See also* **furnish.**

rig up *verb.* —*See* **improvise** (2).

rig *noun.* —*See* **dress** (2), **outfit.**

rigamarole *noun. See* **rigmarole.**

right *adjective.* Conforming to accepted standards ▶ becoming, befitting, comely, comme il faut, correct, decent, decorous, de rigueur, nice, proper, respectable, seemly. —*See also* **accurate, appropriate, conservative** (1), **ethical, healthy, just.**

right *noun.* A benefit granted to a person by law, nature, or custom ▶ birthright, civil liberty, droit, due, entitlement, franchise, freedom, perquisite, prerogative, privilege. [*Compare* **authority, claim, permission.**]

right *adverb.* —*See* **directly** (1), **directly** (3), **yes.**

right *verb.* —*See* **correct** (1), **fix** (1).

✚ **CORE SYNONYMS:** *right, privilege, prerogative, perquisite, birthright.* These nouns apply to a benefit granted to a person by law, nature, or custom. *Right* refers to a legally, morally, or traditionally just claim: "*I'm a champion for the Rights of Woman*" (Maria Edgeworth). "*An unconditional right to say what one pleases about public affairs is what I consider to be the minimum guarantee of the First Amendment*" (Hugo L. Black). *Privilege* usually suggests a right not enjoyed by everyone: *Use of the company jet was a privilege reserved for the top executives. Prerogative* denotes an exclusive right or privilege, as one based on custom, law, or office: *It is my prerogative to change my mind.* A *perquisite* is a privilege or advantage accorded to one by virtue of one's position or the needs of one's employment: "*The wardrobe of her niece was the perquisite of her* [maid]" (Tobias Smollett). A *birthright* is a right to which one is entitled by birth: *Many view gainful employment as a birthright.*

right away *adverb.* —*See* **immediately** (1).

righteous *adjective.* —*See* **ethical, honest.**

righteousness *noun.* —*See* **ethics** (1), **good** (1), **honesty.**

rightful *adjective.* **1.** In accordance with principles of right or good conduct ▶ ethical, moral, principled, proper, right, righteous, right-minded, virtuous. **2.** Being so legitimately ▶ legitimate, true. —*See also* **just, lawful.**

rightfulness *noun.* —*See* **good** (1), **legality.**

rightist *noun.* —*See* **conservative.**

rightist *adjective.* —*See* **conservative** (1).

right-minded *adjective.* —*See* **ethical.**

rightness *noun.* —*See* **accuracy, ethics** (1), **good** (1).

right off *adverb.* —*See* **immediately** (1).

right of way *noun.* —*See* **precedence.**

right on *adverb.* —*See* **yes.**

right-wing *adjective.* —*See* **conservative** (1).

right-winger *noun.* —*See* **conservative.**

rigid *adjective.* Not changing shape or bending ▶ inelastic, inflexible, stiff, unbending, unyielding. [*Compare* **firm**[1], **taut.**] —*See also* **immutable, motionless, severe** (1), **stubborn** (1).

✚ **CORE SYNONYMS:** *rigid, inflexible, stiff, inelastic.* These adjectives describe what is very firm and does not easily bend or give way. *Rigid* and *inflexible* apply to what cannot be bent without damage or deformation (*a table of rigid plastic; an inflexible knife blade*); figuratively they describe what does not relent or yield: "*under the dictates of a rigid disciplinarian*" (Thomas B. Aldrich). "*In religion the law is written, and inflexible, never to do evil*" (Oliver Goldsmith). *Stiff* refers to what can be flexed only with difficulty (*a brush with stiff bristles*); with reference to persons it often suggests a lack of ease, cold formality, or fixity, as of purpose: "*stiff in opinions*" (John Dryden). *Inelastic* refers largely to what will not stretch and spring back without marked physical change: *inelastic construction materials.*

◄ **ANTONYM:** *flexible*

rigidity *or* **rigidness** *noun.* —*See* **severity, stubbornness.**

rigmarole *or* **rigamarole** *noun.* —*See* **bother, nonsense.**

rigor *noun.* —*See* **difficulty, severity.**

rigorous *adjective.* —*See* **accurate, bitter** (2), **burdensome, close** (2), **severe** (1).

rigorousness *noun.* —*See* **severity.**

rile *verb.* —*See* **anger** (1), **annoy.**

rim *noun.* —*See* **border** (1).

rim *verb.* —*See* **border.**

rimple *noun.* —*See* **fold** (1).

rimple *verb.* —*See* **fold, wrinkle.**

rind *noun.* —*See* **skin** (3).

ring[1] *noun.* An organized group of criminals, hoodlums, or wrongdoers ▶ band, gang, pack. *Informal:* mob. —*See also* **alliance, circle** (1), **loop.**

ring *verb.* —*See* **encircle, surround.**

ring in *verb.* —*See* **introduce** (3).

ring[2] *verb.* To give forth or cause to give forth a clear resonant sound ▶ bell, bong, chime, ding, knell, peal, sound, strike, toll. —*See also* **telephone.**

ring *noun.* A telephone communication ▶ buzz, call.

ringer *noun.* —*See* **double, substitute.**

ringing *adjective.* —*See* **definite** (1), **resonant.**

ringleader *noun.* —*See* **chief.**

ringlet *noun.* —*See* **loop.**

rinky-dink *adjective.* —*See* **trivial.**

rinse *verb.* —*See* **clean** (1).

riot *noun.* —*See* **binge, disorder** (2), **fight** (1), **scream** (2).

riot *verb.* —*See* **revel.**

riot away *verb.* —*See* **waste.**

riotous *adjective.* —*See* **disorderly, profuse.**

rip *verb.* —*See* **rush, tear**[1].

rip into *verb.* —*See* **slam** (1).

rip off *verb.* —*See* **cheat** (1), **steal.**

rip up *verb.* —*See* **shred.**

rip *noun.* A hole that is made by tearing ▶ rent, run, tear. [*Compare* **crack.**]

rip[2] *noun.* —*See* **wanton.**

ripe *adjective.* Brought to full flavor and richness by aging ▶ aged, mellow. [*Compare* **mature.**] —*See also* **mature.**

ripen *verb.* —*See* **mature.**

rip-off *noun.* —*See* **larceny.**

riposte *noun.* —*See* **answer** (1).

riposte *verb.* —*See* **answer.**

ripped *adjective.* —*See* **drugged.**

ripping *adjective.* —*See* **marvelous.**

ripple *verb.* —*See* **burble, flow** (1), **wave** (1).

ripple *noun.* —*See* **burble, wave.**

rippled *adjective.* —*See* **wavy.**

rise *verb.* **1.** To leave one's bed ▶ arise, get up, roll out. *Informal:* turn out. *Slang:* hit the deck. ***Idioms:*** jump (*or* leap *or* pile *or* spring) out of bed, rise and shine. [*Compare* **wake**[1].] **2.** To move from a lower to a higher position ▶ arise, ascend, climb, lift, mount, soar, tower. [*Compare* **ascend, soar.**] **3.** To attain a higher status, rank, or condition ▶ advance, ascend, climb, get ahead, mount, progress. ***Idiom:*** go up the ladder. [*Compare* **advance.**] **4.** To gain success ▶ arrive, get ahead, get on, succeed. ***Idioms:*** go far, go places, make good, make it. **5.** To refuse allegiance to and oppose by force a government or authority ▶ mutiny, rebel, revolt, rise up. [*Compare* **defect, defy.**] —*See also* **blow**[1] (1), **increase, stand** (1), **stem.**

rise *noun.* —*See* **advancement, ascent** (1), **ascent** (2), **hill, increase** (1), **increase** (2), **origin.**

✤ **CORE SYNONYMS:** *rise, ascend, climb, soar, tower, mount.* These verbs mean to move upward from a lower to a higher position. *Rise* has the widest range of application: *We rose at dawn. The sun rises early in the summer. Prices rise and fall. Ascend* frequently suggests a gradual step-by-step rise: *The plane took off and ascended steadily until it was out of sight. Climb* connotes steady, often effortful progress, as against gravity: *"You climb up through the little grades and then get to the top"* (John Updike). *Soar* implies effortless ascent to a great height: *A lone condor soared above the Andean peaks.* To *tower* is to attain a height or prominence exceeding one's surroundings: *"the tall Lombardy poplar . . . towering high above all other trees"* (W.H. Hudson). *Mount* connotes a progressive climb to a higher level: *Our expenses mounted fearfully.*

◀ **ANTONYM:** *descend*

---

risible *adjective.* Causing or deserving laughter or derision ▶ farcical, laughable, ludicrous, ridiculous. [*Compare* **foolish.**] —*See also* **funny** (1).

rising *noun.* —*See* **ascent** (1).

rising star *noun.* —*See* **comer** (2).

risk *noun.* A possibility of danger or harm ▶ chance, gamble, hazard. *Informal:* shaky ground, thin ice. —*See also* **danger, gamble.**

risk *verb.* —*See* **endanger, gamble** (2), **venture.**

risk capital *noun.* —*See* **capital** (1).

risky *adjective.* —*See* **dangerous.**

risqué *adjective.* —*See* **improper** (1), **racy.**

rite *noun.* —*See* **ceremony** (1).

ritual *noun.* A conventional social gesture or act without intrinsic purpose ▶ ceremony, form, formality, mummery, nicety. [*Compare* **custom, manners.**] —*See also* **ceremony** (1).

ritual *adjective.* Of or characterized by ceremony ▶ ceremonial, ceremonious, formal, liturgical, ritualistic. [*Compare* **ceremonious, spiritual.**]

ritualistic *adjective.* —*See* **ritual.**

ritzy *adjective.* —*See* **exclusive** (3), **luxurious.**

rival *noun.* —*See* **competitor, peer**[2].

rival *verb.* To attempt to equal or surpass, as in quality or amount ▶ approach, approximate, border on (*or* upon), challenge, verge on. —*See also* **compete.**

rivalrous *adjective.* —*See* **competitive.**

rivalry *noun.* —*See* **competition** (1).

rive *verb.* —*See* **break** (1), **tear**[1].

river *noun.* A relatively large natural flow of water ▶ estuary, stream, tributary, watercourse, waterway. [*Compare* **brook**[1].]

rivet *noun.* —*See* **nail.**

rivet *verb.* —*See* **fasten, grip.**

riveted *adjective.* —*See* **rapt.**

road *noun.* —*See* **way** (2).

roam *verb.* —*See* **rove.**

roamer *noun.* —*See* **hobo.**

roaming *adjective.* —*See* **errant** (1).

roar *verb.* —*See* **blast** (1), **burn** (2), **laugh, shout.**

roar *noun.* A loud, deep, prolonged sound ▶ bawl, bellow, bluster, clamor, roll, rumble. —*See also* **blast** (1), **laugh, shout.**

roaring *adjective.* —*See* **flourishing, loud.**

roast *verb.* —*See* **burn** (3), **cook, slam** (1).

roasting *adjective.* —*See* **hot** (1).

rob *verb.* To take property or possessions from someone unlawfully and usually forcibly ▶ burglarize, hold up, mug, stick up. *Slang:* heist, knock off. [*Compare* **sack, steal.**] —*See also* **deprive.**

robber *noun.* —*See* **thief.**

robbery *noun.* —*See* **larceny.**

robe *noun.* Clothing worn by members of a religious order ▶ habit, vestment.

robe *verb.* —*See* **clothe.**

roborant *adjective.* —*See* **invigorating.**

roborant *noun.* —*See* **tonic.**

robust *adjective.* —*See* **healthy, lusty, muscular.**

rock *verb.* To move vigorously from side to side or up and down ▶ heave, pitch, roll, toss. [*Compare* **lurch.**] —*See also* **agitate** (1), **agitate** (2), **sway.**

rock bottom *noun.* A very low or lowest level, position, or degree ▶ bottom, low, minimum, nadir.

rocket *verb.* —*See* **rush, soar.**

rococo *adjective.* —*See* **ornate.**

rod *noun.* A straight, rigid piece of metal or other solid material ▶ bar, bloom, shaft, stem. [*Compare* **stick.**]
rogations *noun.* —*See* **prayer**[1] (2).
roger *adverb.* —*See* **yes.**
rogue *noun.* —*See* **rascal.**
roguery *noun.* —*See* **mischief.**
roguish *adjective.* —*See* **mischievous.**
roguishness *noun.* —*See* **mischief.**
roiled *or* **roily** *adjective.* —*See* **murky** (1), **rough** (2).
roister *verb.* —*See* **revel.**
role *noun.* **1.** One's duty or responsibility in a common effort ▶ function, part, piece, share. **2.** A person portrayed in fiction or drama ▶ character, part, persona, personage. —*See also* **function** (1).
role model *noun.* —*See* **model.**
roll *verb.* To move vigorously from side to side or up and down ▶ heave, pitch, rock, toss. [*Compare* **lurch.**] —*See also* **lurch** (1), **luxuriate, press** (2), **rumble** (1), **teem**[1], **throw, wrap** (1).
roll about *or* **around** *verb.* To move about in an indolent or clumsy manner ▶ flounder, wallow, welter.
roll out *verb.* —*See* **even, rise** (1).
roll up *verb.* —*See* **accumulate.**
roll *noun.* —*See* **list**[1], **roar, throw.**
rollick *verb.* —*See* **gambol, luxuriate.**
roly-poly *adjective.* —*See* **fat** (1).
romance *noun.* A narrative not based on fact ▶ fable, fiction, novel, story. [*Compare* **yarn.**] —*See also* **love** (1), **love** (2), **love** (3).
romance *verb.* —*See* **court** (2).
romantic *adjective.* —*See* **idealistic, sentimental.**
romantic *noun.* —*See* **dreamer** (1).
Romeo *noun.* —*See* **gallant.**
romp *verb.* —*See* **breeze, gambol, revel.**
romp *noun.* —*See* **runaway** (1).
roof *noun.* —*See* **climax.**
rook *noun.* —*See* **cheat** (2).
rook *verb.* —*See* **cheat** (1).
rookie *noun.* —*See* **beginner.**
room *noun.* —*See* **license** (1).
room *verb.* —*See* **lodge.**
roomy *adjective.* Having plenty of room ▶ ample, capacious, commodious, spacious. [*Compare* **big, broad.**]

✚ **CORE SYNONYMS:** *roomy, ample, capacious, commodious, spacious.* These adjectives mean having plenty of room: *roomy pockets; an ample kitchen; a capacious purse; a commodious harbor; a spacious apartment.*

---

roost *verb.* —*See* **balance** (3).
root[1] *noun.* —*See* **basis** (1), **center** (3), **heart** (1), **origin, theme** (1).
root *verb.* —*See* **annihilate, base**[1], **fix** (2), **plant.**
root[2] *verb.* To express approval audibly, as by clapping ▶ applaud, cheer, clap. ***Idioms:*** give a big hand (*or* welcome), give an ovation, give someone a hand, put one's hands together.
rooted *adjective.* —*See* **confirmed** (1), **fixed.**
roots *noun.* —*See* **ancestry.**
rootstock *noun.* —*See* **origin.**
rope *noun.* —*See* **cord.**
roseate *or* **rose-colored** *adjective.* —*See* **optimistic.**
roster *noun.* —*See* **list**[1].
rostrum *noun.* —*See* **stage** (1).
rosy *adjective.* —*See* **optimistic, ruddy.**
rot *verb.* —*See* **decay.**
rot *noun.* —*See* **decay, nonsense.**
rotate *verb.* To take turns ▶ alternate, interchange, shift. —*See also* **turn** (1).
rotation *noun.* Occurrence in successive turns ▶ alternation, interchange, shift. —*See also* **revolution** (1).
rote *noun.* —*See* **routine.**
rotten *adjective.* —*See* **bad** (2), **corrupt** (1), **moldy, offensive** (1), **shoddy, terrible, worthless.**
rottenness *noun.* —*See* **decay.**
rotund *adjective.* —*See* **fat** (1), **resonant.**
roué *noun.* —*See* **lecher.**
rough *adjective.* **1.** Having a surface that is not smooth ▶ abrasive, bumpy, coarse, cragged, craggy, harsh, ironbound, jagged, ragged, rugged, scab-

rous, scraggy, scratchy, uneven. **2.** Violently disturbed or agitated, as by storms ▶ blustery, dirty, heavy, raging, roiled, roily, rugged, stormy, tempestuous, tumultuous, turbulent, ugly, violent, wild. [*Compare* **intense.**] **3.** Marked by vigorous physical exertion ▶ arduous, knockabout, rough-and-tumble, rugged, strenuous, tough. [*Compare* **burdensome, difficult.**] **4.** Not perfected, elaborated, or completed ▶ crude, imperfect, incomplete, preliminary, sketchy, tentative, unfinished, unperfected, unpolished. —*See also* **bitter** (2), **burdensome, coarse** (1), **coarse** (2), **crude, harsh, loose** (3), **rude** (1), **wild** (1).

rough in *or* **out** *verb.* —*See* **draft** (1).

rough up *verb.* —*See* **batter, manhandle.**

rough *noun.* —*See* **draft** (1).

✚ CORE SYNONYMS: *rough, harsh, jagged, rugged, scabrous, uneven.* These adjectives mean having a surface that is not smooth. *Rough* describes something that to the sight or touch has inequalities, as projections or ridges: *rough bark; rough, chapped hands.* Something *harsh* is unpleasantly rough, discordant, or grating: *harsh, scratchy burlap. Jagged* refers to an edge or surface with irregular projections and indentations: *a jagged piece of glass. Rugged* can apply to land surfaces characterized by irregular, often steep rises and slopes: *rugged countryside. Scabrous* means rough and scaly to the touch: *granular, scabrous skin. Uneven* describes lines or surfaces of which some parts are not level with others: *uneven ground; uneven handwriting.*

rough-and-tumble *adjective.* —*See* **rough** (3).

roughly *adverb.* —*See* **approximately.**

roughneck *noun.* —*See* **thug.**

roughness *noun.* —*See* **irregularity.**

round *adjective.* **1.** Having the shape of a curve everywhere equidistant from a fixed point ▶ annular, circular, globoid, globular, orbicular, spheric, spherical. **2.** No less than; at least ▶ full, good, whole. —*See also* **complete** (1), **fat** (1), **resonant.**

round *noun.* A stage of a competition ▶ heat, stage. [*Compare* **competition, turn.**] —*See also* **beat** (2), **bend, circle** (1), **circle** (2), **series.**

round *verb.* —*See* **bend** (1), **dull.**

round off *verb.* —*See* **perfect.**

round up *verb.* —*See* **assemble.**

roundabout *adjective.* —*See* **indirect** (1).

rounded *adjective.* —*See* **bent.**

rounder *noun.* —*See* **wanton.**

roundlet *noun.* —*See* **circle** (1).

rounds *noun.* —*See* **routine.**

roundtable *noun.* —*See* **conference** (1).

round-the-clock *adjective.* —*See* **continual.**

rouse *verb.* —*See* **arouse, evoke, fire** (1), **wake**[1]**.**

rousing *adjective.* —*See* **invigorating.**

roustabout *noun.* —*See* **laborer.**

rout *noun.* —*See* **crowd, defeat, flock, runaway** (1).

rout *verb.* —*See* **overwhelm** (1).

route *noun.* A means or method of entering into or achieving something desirable ▶ formula, key, secret. *Informal:* ticket. [*Compare* **ticket.**] —*See also* **beat** (2), **direction, way** (2).

route *verb.* —*See* **guide, send** (1).

routine *noun.* A course of action to be followed regularly ▶ method, rote, rounds, rut, track, treadmill. *Informal:* grind. *Slang:* groove. —*See also* **bit**[1] (4), **custom, practice, usual.**

routine *adjective.* Subject to a habit or pattern of behavior ▶ accustomed, chronic, habitual. —*See also* **common** (1), **ordinary, perfunctory.**

routinely *adverb.* —*See* **usually.**

routineness *noun.* —*See* **usualness.**

routinism *noun.* —*See* **dullness.**

rove *verb.* To move about at random, especially over a wide area ▶ drift, gad, gallivant, meander, peregrinate, ramble, range, roam, stray, traipse, tramp, wander. [*Compare* **hike, journey, walk.**]

✚ **CORE SYNONYMS:** *rove, roam, wander, ramble, range, meander, stray, gallivant, gad.* These verbs mean to move about at random or without destination or purpose, especially over a wide area. *Rove* and *roam* emphasize freedom of movement, often over a wide area: "*For ten long years I roved about, living first in one capital, then another*" (Charlotte Brontë). "*Herds of horses and cattle roamed at will over the plain*" (George W. Cable). *Wander* and *ramble* stress the absence of a fixed course or goal: *wandered down the hall lost in thought.* "*They would go off together, rambling along the river*" (John Galsworthy). *Range* suggests wandering in all directions: "*a large hunting party known to be ranging the prairie*" (Francis Parkman). *Meander* suggests leisurely wandering over an irregular or winding course: "*He meandered to and fro . . . observing the manners and customs of Hillport society*" (Arnold Bennett). *Stray* refers to deviation from a proper course: "*I ask pardon, I am straying from the question*" (Oliver Goldsmith). *Gallivant* refers to wandering in search of pleasure: *gallivanted all over the city during our visit. Gad* suggests restlessness: *gadded about unaccompanied in foreign places.*

rover *noun.* —*See* **hobo.**

roving *adjective.* —*See* **errant** (1).

row[1] *noun.* —*See* **line.**

row[2] *noun.* —*See* **argument, fight** (1), **noise** (1).

row *verb.* —*See* **argue** (1).

rowdy *noun.* —*See* **thug.**

rowdy *adjective.* —*See* **disorderly.**

royal *adjective.* —*See* **grand, noble.**

royalty *noun.* —*See* **nobility.**

rub *verb.* To move over or along with pressure ▶ knead, manipulate, massage, press, rub down, stroke, work (over). [*Compare* **brush[1], touch.**] —*See also* **cancel** (1), **chafe.**

rub against *or* **along** *verb.* —*See* **brush[1].**

rub away *or* **off** *verb.* To remove an outer layer or something adherent from an object by friction ▶ scour, scrape, scrub. [*Compare* **chafe, scrape.**]

rub out *verb.* —*See* **annihilate, murder.**

rub *noun. Informal* A tricky or unsuspected condition ▶ catch, hitch, snag. [*Compare* **bar, disadvantage, trick.**] —*See also* **brush[1].**

rubber stamp *noun.* —*See* **permission.**

rubbish *noun.* —*See* **garbage, nonsense.**

rubble *noun.* —*See* **ruin** (2).

rube *noun.* —*See* **clodhopper.**

rubicund *adjective.* —*See* **ruddy.**

rubric *noun.* —*See* **rule.**

ruck[1] *noun.* —*See* **commonalty, crowd.**

ruck[2] *verb.* —*See* **fold.**

ruck *noun.* —*See* **fold** (1).

ruckus *noun.* —*See* **disorder** (2).

rudderless *adjective.* —*See* **aimless.**

ruddy *adjective.* Of a healthy reddish color ▶ blooming, blushing, florid, flush, flushed, full-blooded, glowing, red, rosy, rubicund, sanguine.

rude *adjective.* **1.** Lacking expert, careful craftsmanship ▶ crude, homemade, primitive, raw, rough, rough-hewn, unpolished. [*Compare* **shoddy.**] **2.** Lacking good manners ▶ discourteous, disrespectful, foul-mouthed, ill-bred, ill-mannered, impolite, rugged, uncivil, ungracious, unmannered, unmannerly, unpolished. [*Compare* **disrespectful, tactless, thoughtless.**] **3.** Characterized by unpleasant discordance of sound ▶ cacophonous, discordant, disharmonious, dissonant, inharmonic, inharmonious, unharmonious, unmusical. —*See also* **coarse** (1), **crude, disrespectful, offensive** (2), **uncivilized.**

✚ **CORE SYNONYMS:** *rude, crude, primitive, raw, rough.* These adjectives mean lacking expert or careful craftmanship: *a rude hut in the middle of the forest; a crude drawing; primitive kitchen facilities; a raw wooden canoe; a rough sketch.*

---

rudeness *noun.* —*See* **disrespect, impudence.**

rudiment *noun.* —*See* **basis** (1), **element** (1).

rudimentary *adjective.* —*See* **elementary.**

rue *verb.* To feel or express sorrow for ▶ deplore, regret, repent, sorrow (over). [*Compare* **feel, grieve.**]

rue *noun.* —*See* **penitence.**

rueful *adjective.* —*See* **pitiful, sorrowful, sorry.**

ruffian *noun.* —*See* **thug.**

ruffle *verb.* —*See* **agitate** (2), **annoy.**

ruffled feathers *noun.* —*See* **offense.**

rugged *adjective.* —*See* **hard** (2), **muscular, rough** (1), **rough** (2), **rough** (3).

ruin *noun.* **1.** Something that causes total loss or severe impairment ▶ bane, destroyer, destruction, downfall, ruination, undoing, wrecker. [*Compare* **breakdown, curse.**] **2.** The remains of something destroyed, disintegrated, or decayed ▶ debris, remains, rubble, wrack, wreck, wreckage. [*Compare* **trace.**] —*See also* **bankruptcy, destruction.**

ruin *verb.* To reduce to financial insolvency ▶ bankrupt, break, bust, do in, impoverish, pauperize. *Slang:* clean out. —*See also* **break** (2), **destroy** (1).

ruination *noun.* —*See* **bankruptcy, destruction, ruin** (1).

ruinous *adjective.* —*See* **disastrous, harmful, shabby.**

rulable *adjective.* Capable of being governed ▶ administrable, controllable, governable, manageable. [*Compare* **loyal, obedient.**]

rule *noun.* A code or set of codes governing action or procedure, for example ▶ dictate, guideline, law, prescript, regulation, rubric. [*Compare* **standard.**] —*See also* **authority, dominance, domination, government** (1), **law** (1), **usual.**

rule *verb.* —*See* **administer** (1), **boss, dominate** (1), **judge.**

rule out *verb.* —*See* **dictate, exclude, prevent.**

ruler *noun.* —*See* **chief.**

ruling *adjective.* —*See* **dominant** (1), **prevailing.**

ruling *noun.* An authoritative or official decision, especially one made by a court ▶ adjudication, decision, dictum, decree, determination, edict, finding, judgment, opinion, pronouncement, resolution, sentence, verdict. [*Compare* **command, law.**]

rumble *verb.* **1.** To make a continuous deep reverberating sound ▶ boom, growl, grumble, resound, roll. **2.** *Slang* To exchange blows with another person ▶ fight. ***Idioms:*** duke it out, mix it up, slug it out. [*Compare* **wrestle.**] —*See also* **blast** (1).

rumble *noun.* —*See* **blast** (1), **fight** (1), **roar.**

ruminate *verb.* —*See* **chew, ponder.**

rumination *noun.* —*See* **thought.**

ruminative *adjective.* —*See* **thoughtful.**

rummage *verb.* —*See* **scour**[2]**.**

rummy *noun.* —*See* **drunkard.**

rumor *noun.* —*See* **gossip** (1).

rumor *verb.* —*See* **gossip.**

rumormonger *noun.* —*See* **gossip** (2).

rump *noun.* —*See* **buttocks.**

rumple *verb.* —*See* **fold, tousle.**

rumple *noun.* —*See* **fold** (1).

rumpus *noun.* —*See* **noise** (1), **vociferation.**

run *verb.* **1.** To move on foot at a pace faster than a walk ▶ canter, gallop, jog, lope, scamper, scurry, scuttle, shin, sprint, trot. [*Compare* **bound**[1]**, rush.**] **2.** To leave hastily ▶ bolt, get out. *Informal:* clear out, get, hotfoot, skedaddle. *Slang:* hightail, scram, take off, vamoose. ***Idioms:*** beat it, hightail it, hotfoot it, make tracks, take a powder. **3.** To move or proceed away from a place ▶ depart, exit, get away, get off, go, go away, leave, pull out, quit, retire, run along, withdraw. *Informal:* cut out, push off, shove off. *Slang:* blow, split, take off. **4.** To complete a race or competition in a specified position ▶ come in, finish, place. **5.** To be performed ▶ play, show. —*See also* **administer** (1), **associate** (2), **amount, conduct** (1), **drive** (3), **extend** (1), **flow** (1), **flow** (2), **function, go** (4), **hunt, melt, operate, plunge, pour, resort, rush, smuggle, tear**[1].

run across *verb.* —*See* **encounter** (1).

run after *verb.* —*See* **court** (2), **pursue** (1).

run along *or* **away** *verb.* —*See* **go** (1).

run away *verb.* —*See* **escape** (1).

run down *verb.* —*See* **belittle, review** (1), **trace** (1).

run in *verb.* —*See* **arrest, visit.**

run into *verb.* —*See* **collide, encounter** (1).

run off *verb.* —*See* **publish** (1).

run on *verb.* —*See* **chatter** (1).

run out *verb.* To prove deficient or insufficient ▶ fail, give out. ***Idioms:*** fall short, run dry, run short. [*Compare* **decrease.**] —*See also* **dismiss** (2), **dry up** (2), **lapse.**

run through *verb.* —*See* **browse** (1), **exhaust** (1), **practice** (1), **review** (1).

run up *verb.* —*See* **increase.**

run *noun.* **1.** A pace faster than a walk ▶ canter, dash, gallop, jog, lope, sprint, trot. [*Compare* **hike, walk.**] **2.** A length of torn or unraveled stitches in knitted fabric ▶ rent, rip, tear. —*See also* **brook**[1], **cage, drive** (3), **series.**

runagate *noun.* —*See* **defector.**

runaway *noun.* **1.** An easy victory ▶ cakewalk, rout, walkaway, walkover. *Slang:* romp. ***Idiom:*** clean sweep. [*Compare* **breeze, defeat.**] **2.** One who flees, as from confinement or the police ▶ escapee, fugitive, outlaw, refugee. [*Compare* **criminal.**]

runaway *adjective.* **1.** Fleeing or having fled, as from confinement or the police ▶ escaped, fugitive, fleeing. ***Idioms:*** on the lam (*or* loose *or* run). **2.** Out of control ▶ amuck, unbridled, uncontrolled. ***Idioms:*** out of hand, running wild. [*Compare* **abandoned, loose.**]

rundown *noun.* —*See* **summary.**

rundown *adjective.* —*See* **shabby, tired** (1), **weak** (1).

rung *noun.* —*See* **degree** (1).

run-in *noun.* —*See* **argument.**

runner *noun.* A person who engages in smuggling ▶ bootlegger, contrabandist, smuggler. *Slang:* mule. —*See also* **messenger, shoot.**

running *adjective.* —*See* **active.**

run-of-the-mill *adjective.* —*See* **ordinary.**

run-through *noun.* —*See* **summary.**

runt *noun.* —*See* **squirt** (2).

runty *adjective.* —*See* **little.**

rupture *noun.* An opening, especially in a solid structure ▶ breach, break, gap, hole, perforation. —*See also* **breach** (2).

rupture *verb.* —*See* **crack** (1).

rural *adjective.* —*See* **country.**

ruse *noun.* —*See* **trick** (1).

rush *verb.* To move swiftly ▶ bolt, bucket, bustle, dart, dash, festinate, flash, fleet, flit, fly, haste, hasten, hurry, hustle, pelt, race, rocket, run, sail, sally, scoot, scour, shoot, speed, sprint, tear, trot, whirl, whisk, whiz, wing, zing, zip, zoom. *Informal:* rip. *Slang:* barrel, highball. ***Idioms:*** get a move on, get cracking, go like lightning, go like the wind, hotfoot it, make haste, make time, make tracks, run like the wind, shake a leg, step (*or* jump) on it. [*Compare* **run.**] —*See also* **attack** (1), **flow** (2).

rush *noun.* —*See* **charge** (1), **flow, haste** (2), **haste** (1).

rush *adjective.* Designed to meet emergency needs as quickly as possible ▶ *Informal:* crash, hurry-up.

rustic *adjective.* Of a charmingly plain and unsophisticated nature ▶ artless, homely, homespun, natural, simple, unadorned, unpolished. [*Compare* **coarse.**] —*See also* **country.**

rustic *noun.* —*See* **clodhopper.**

rustle *noun.* —*See* **hiss** (1), **murmur.**

rustle *verb.* To make a low, continuous, and indistinct sound ▶ murmur, sigh, sough, whisper. [*Compare* **burble, hum.**] —*See also* **hiss** (1).

rut *noun.* —*See* **furrow, routine.**

ruthful *adjective.* —*See* **pitiful.**

ruthless *adjective.* —*See* **cruel, unscrupulous.**

S

sabbatical *noun.* A regularly scheduled period spent away from work or duty, often in recreation ▶ furlough, holiday, leave, vacation. ***Idioms:*** time (*or* day) off. [*Compare* **break, trip.**]

saber-rattling *noun.* —*See* **aggression.**

sable *adjective.* —*See* **black** (1).

sabotage *noun.* Treacherous action to defeat or do harm to an endeavor ▶ subversion, undermining. [*Compare* **defeat, destruction.**]

sabotage *verb.* To damage, destroy, or defeat by sabotage ▶ subvert, undermine. [*Compare* **destroy, disorder.**]

sabulous *adjective.* —*See* **coarse** (2).

saccharine *adjective.* Having or suggesting the taste of sugar ▶ honeyed, sugary, sweet. —*See also* **flattering.**

sacerdotal *adjective.* —*See* **clerical.**

sachem *noun.* —*See* **chief.**

sack[1] *noun.* —*See* **bag, dismissal.**

sack *verb.* —*See* **dismiss** (1).

sack out *verb. Slang* To be asleep ▶ sleep, slumber. ***Idioms:*** be in the land of Nod, catch some shuteye, catch (*or* cop) some z's, saw logs (*or* wood), sleep like a log (*or* baby *or* rock *or* top), sleep tight. [*Compare* **nap, rest.**]

sack[2] *verb.* To rob of goods by force, especially in time of war ▶ depredate, despoil, loot, pillage, plunder, ransack, rape, ravage, strip. [*Compare* **attack, invade.**]

sacrarium *noun.* A sacred or holy place ▶ sanctorium, sanctuary, sanctum, shrine.

sacred *adjective.* —*See* **divine** (2), **holy, unspeakable** (2).

sacredness *noun.* —*See* **holiness.**

sacrifice *noun.* The expenditure at which something is obtained ▶ cost, expense, price, toll. *Informal:* damage. —*See also* **abandonment** (1), **offering.**

sacrifice *verb.* To offer as a sacrifice ▶ immolate, offer up, victimize. —*See also* **abandon** (1), **devote.**

sacrilege *noun.* An act of disrespect or impiety toward something regarded as sacred ▶ blasphemy, desecration, impiety, profanation, violation.

sacrilegious *adjective.* Showing irreverence and contempt for something sacred ▶ blasphemous, impious, profane.

sacrosanct *adjective.* —*See* **divine** (2), **holy.**

sacrosanctity *noun.* —*See* **holiness.**

sad *adjective.* —*See* **depressed** (1), **sorrowful.**

sadden *verb.* —*See* **depress.**

saddle *verb.* —*See* **burden**[1].

saddle with *verb.* —*See* **impose on.**

sadism *noun.* —*See* **cruelty.**

sadistic *adjective.* —*See* **cruel.**

sadness *noun.* —*See* **depression** (2).

safari *noun.* —*See* **expedition.**

safe *adjective.* **1.** Free from danger, injury, or the threat of harm ▶ unharmed, unhurt, uninjured, unscathed. ***Idioms:*** out of danger, out of harm's way, safe and sound. [*Compare* **good, healthy.**] **2.** Affording protection ▶ defended, guarded, immune, impenetrable, impregnable, invulnerable, secure, unassailable, unconquerable. [*Compare* **invincible.**] —*See also* **harmless.**

safe *noun.* —*See* **depository.**

safeguard *noun.* —*See* **care** (2), **defense.**

safeguard *verb.* —*See* **defend** (1).

safe house *noun.* —*See* **cover** (1).

safekeeping *noun.* —*See* **care** (2).

safeness *noun.* —*See* **safety.**

safety *noun.* The quality or state of being safe ▶ assurance, immunity, impenetrability, impregnability, invulnerability, safeness, security, unassailability, unconquerability. [*Compare* **defense.**] —*See also* **refuge** (1).

sag *verb.* —*See* **bend** (3), **drop** (1), **fall** (4), **slouch** (2), **wilt.**

sag *noun.* —*See* **depression** (1).

saga *verb.* —*See* **story** (1).

sagacious *adjective.* Possessing deep knowledge and understanding ▶ knowing, sage, sapient, wise. —*See also* **sensible, shrewd.**

sagacity *or* **sagaciousness** *noun.* —*See* **discernment, wisdom** (1).

sagamore *noun.* —*See* **chief.**

sage *noun.* A person noted for wisdom, knowledge, and judgment ▶ guru, pundit, savant, scholar, wise man, wise woman. [*Compare* **expert, mind.**]

sage *adjective.* Possessing deep knowledge and understanding ▶ knowing, sagacious, sapient, wise. —*See also* **sensible.**

sageness *noun.* —*See* **discernment, wisdom** (1).

sail *verb.* —*See* **blow[1]** (2), **breeze, fly** (1), **fly** (2), **rush.**

sail into *verb.* —*See* **attack** (1).

sailor *noun.* A person engaged in sailing or working on a ship ▶ boatman, Jack, Jack-tar, mariner, navigator, sea dog, seafarer, seaman. *Informal:* salt, tar. *Slang:* gob.

saintliness *noun.* —*See* **holiness.**

saintly *adjective.* —*See* **pious.**

salaam *verb.* —*See* **bow[1]** (1).

salaam *noun.* —*See* **bow[1].**

salability *or* **salableness** *noun.* Market appeal ▶ marketability, sell.

salacious *adjective.* —*See* **erotic.**

salad days *noun.* —*See* **youth** (1).

salary *noun.* —*See* **wage.**

sale *noun.* —*See* **deal** (1).

salesclerk *or* **salesperson** *noun.* —*See* **seller.**

salesman *or* **saleswoman** *noun.* —*See* **seller.**

salient *adjective.* —*See* **noticeable.**

salient *noun.* —*See* **projection.**

saline *adjective.* Containing salt ▶ brackish, briny, salty.

saliva *noun.* —*See* **spit.**

salivate *verb.* —*See* **drool.**

salivation *noun.* Saliva running from the mouth ▶ drivel, drool, slaver, slobber.

sallow *adjective.* —*See* **pale** (1).

sallow *verb.* —*See* **pale.**

sally *verb.* —*See* **rush.**

sally *noun.* —*See* **joke** (1).

salmagundi *noun.* —*See* **assortment.**

salon *noun.* —*See* **exhibition.**

saloon *noun.* —*See* **bar** (2).

salt *noun.* —*See* **sailor.**

salt *verb.* —*See* **preserve** (1).

salt away *verb.* —*See* **bank[2], save** (1).

salty *adjective.* Containing salt ▶ brackish, briny, saline. —*See also* **marine** (1), **racy.**

salutary *or* **salubrious** *adjective.* —*See* **beneficial, healthful.**

salutation *noun.* An expression, in words or gestures, marking a meeting of persons ▶ hail, greeting, salute, welcome. *Informal:* hello.

salutations *interjection.* —*See* **hello.**

salute *verb.* **1.** To address in a friendly and respectful way ▶ greet, hail, welcome. **2.** To approach for the purpose of speech ▶ accost, greet, hail. [*Compare* **encounter, interrupt, welcome.**] —*See also* **drink** (4).

salute *noun.* An expression, in words or gestures, marking a meeting of persons ▶ hail, greeting, salutation, welcome. *Informal:* hello. —*See also* **testimonial** (2).

salvage *noun.* —*See* **rescue.**

salvage *verb.* —*See* **rescue.**

salvation *noun.* —*See* **rescue.**

salve *noun.* —*See* **ointment.**

salve *verb.* —*See* **cure.**

salvo *noun.* —*See* **barrage, testimonial** (2).

same *adjective.* Being the one and not another; not different in nature or identity ▶ identical, selfsame, very. [*Com-

pare **like**[2].] *—See also* **equal, unchanging.**

sameness *noun.* The quality or condition of being exactly the same as something else ▶ identicalness, identity, oneness, selfsameness. [*Compare* **likeness.**] *—See also* **changelessness, equivalence, monotony.**

sample *noun.* A limited or anticipatory experience ▶ foretaste, sampling, taste. [*Compare* **glance.**] *—See also* **example** (1).

sample *verb.* *—See* **experience.**

sanctified *adjective.* *—See* **divine** (2), **holy.**

sanctify *verb.* To make sacred by a religious rite ▶ bless, consecrate, hallow. [*Compare* **exalt.**]

sanctimonious *adjective.* *—See* **hypocritical.**

sanctimony *or* **sanctimoniousness** *noun.* *—See* **hypocrisy.**

sanction *noun.* A coercive measure intended to ensure compliance or conformity ▶ interdict, interdiction, penalty. [*Compare* **forbiddance, restraint, punishment.**] *—See also* **confirmation** (1), **permission.**

sanction *verb.* *—See* **confirm** (3), **permit** (2).

sanctioned *adjective.* *—See* **accepted, authoritative** (1).

sanctity *noun.* *—See* **holiness.**

sanctuary *noun.* **1.** A sacred or holy place ▶ sacrarium, sanctorium, sanctum, shrine. **2.** Public land kept for a special purpose ▶ park, preserve, reserve, reservation. [*Compare* **common.**] *—See also* **cover** (1), **refuge** (1).

sandy *adjective.* *—See* **coarse** (2).

sane *adjective.* Mentally healthy ▶ compos mentis, lucid, normal, rational. ***Idioms:*** all there, in one's right mind, of sound mind. [*Compare* **healthy.**] *—See also* **sensible.**

saneness *noun.* *—See* **sanity.**

sang-froid *noun.* *—See* **balance** (2).

sanguinary *adjective.* *—See* **murderous.**

sanguine *adjective.* *—See* **optimistic, ruddy.**

sanguineous *adjective.* *—See* **murderous.**

sanguinity *or* **sanguineness** *noun.* *—See* **optimism.**

sanitary *adjective.* *—See* **sterile** (1).

sanitize *verb.* To render free of microorganisms ▶ decontaminate, disinfect, irradiate, sterilize. [*Compare* **clean.**] *—See also* **censor** (1).

sanitized *adjective.* *—See* **sterile** (1).

sanity *noun.* A healthy mental state ▶ lucidity, lucidness, mind, rationality, reason, saneness, sense (*or* senses), soundness, wits. *Slang:* marbles.

sap[1] *noun.* *—See* **dupe.**

sap[2] *verb.* *—See* **enervate, exhaust** (1).

sapience *noun.* *—See* **wisdom** (1).

sapient *adjective.* Possessing deep knowledge and understanding ▶ knowing, sagacious, sage, wise. *—See also* **sensible.**

sappiness *noun.* *—See* **sentimentality.**

sappy *adjective.* *—See* **sentimental.**

sarcasm *noun.* The use of irony to ridicule or express contempt ▶ acerbity, acidity, acridity, bitterness, causticity, corrosiveness, cynicism, irony, mordacity, mordancy, trenchancy. [*Compare* **mockery, ridicule.**]

sarcastic *adjective.* Contemptuous or ironic in manner or wit ▶ cynical, derisive, ironic, ironical, jeering, mocking, sardonic, satiric, satirical, scoffing, sneering, snide, wry. [*Compare* **biting.**]

✦ **CORE SYNONYMS:** *sarcastic, ironic, satirical, sardonic.* These adjectives mean contemptuous or ironic in manner or wit. *Sarcastic* suggests sharp taunting and ridicule that wounds: "*a deserved reputation for sarcastic, acerbic and uninhibited polemics*" (Burke Marshall). *Ironic* implies a subtler form of mockery in which an intended meaning is conveyed obliquely: "*a man of eccentric charm, ironic humor, and—above all—profound literary genius*" (Jonathan

Kirsch). *Satirical* implies exposure, especially of vice or folly, to ridicule: *"on the surface a satirical look at commercial radio, but also a study of the misuse of telecommunications"* (Richard Harrington). *Sardonic* is associated with scorn, derision, mockery, and often cynicism: *"He was proud, sardonic, harsh to inferiority of every description"* (Charlotte Brontë).

sardonic *adjective.* —*See* **sarcastic.**
sash *noun.* —*See* **band[1].**
sashay *verb.* —*See* **strut.**
sass *verb. Informal* To utter an impertinent rejoinder ▶ talk back, talk up. *Informal:* sauce. ***Idioms:*** give someone lip (*or* mouth *or* sass).
sass *noun. Informal* Insolent talk ▶ back talk, mouth. *Informal:* lip. [*Compare* **impudence, taunt.**]
sassiness *noun.* —*See* **impudence.**
sassy *adjective.* —*See* **impudent, lively.**
satanic *adjective.* —*See* **fiendish.**
satchel *noun.* —*See* **suitcase.**
sate *verb.* —*See* **satiate.**
satellite *noun.* —*See* **follower, possession.**
satiate *verb.* To satisfy to the full or to excess ▶ cloy, engorge, glut, gorge, sate, surfeit. [*Compare* **pacify, relieve, satisfy.**]
satiation *or* **satiety** *noun.* The condition of being full to or beyond satisfaction ▶ engorgement, fullness, repletion, surfeit. [*Compare* **fulfillment.**]
satiny *adjective.* Smooth and lustrous as if polished ▶ silken, silky, sleek. [*Compare* **even, glossy, slick.**]
satire *noun.* An artistic work that exposes folly by the use of humor, irony, or comic imitation ▶ burlesque, caricature, farce, imitation, impersonation, lampoon, parody, spoof. *Informal:* send-up, takeoff.

✚ **CORE SYNONYMS:** *satire, caricature, burlesque, parody, lampoon.* These nouns denote artistic forms that expose folly by the use of humor, irony, or comic imitation. *Satire* is a written work that usually involves ridiculing follies and vices: *She employs satire in her poetry.* A *caricature* grossly exaggerates a distinctive or striking feature with intent to ridicule: *He drew a caricature of the politician. Burlesque,* which usually denotes a dramatic work, suggests outlandish mimicry and broad comedy to provoke laughter: *We went to see a burlesque at the theater. Parody* employs the manner and style of a well-known work or writer for a ludicrous effect: *She wrote a parody of a famous novel.* A *lampoon* is a malicious but broadly humorous satire: *The lampoon was written by a standup comic.*

satirical *or* **satiric** *adjective.* —*See* **sarcastic.**
satisfaction *noun.* The condition of being satisfied ▶ contententdness, contentment, fulfillment, gratification. [*Compare* **happiness, satiation.**] —*See also* **compensation, due.**
satisfactory *adjective.* —*See* **acceptable** (2), **convincing, sufficient.**
satisfied *adjective.* Having achieved satisfaction, as of one's goal ▶ content, fulfilled, gratified, happy.
satisfy *verb.* **1.** To be suitable or sufficient to fulfill a need, demand, or purpose ▶ answer, do, fill, fulfill, meet, please, serve, suffice, suit. ***Idioms:*** fill the bill, pass muster. **2.** To grant or have what is demanded by a need or desire ▶ appease, content, fulfill, gratify, indulge. [*Compare* **delight, pacify, relieve, satiate.**] —*See also* **convince, settle** (3).

✚ **CORE SYNONYMS:** *satisfy, answer, fill, fulfill, meet.* These verbs mean to be suitable or sufficient to fulfill a need, demand, or purpose: *satisfied all requirements; answered our needs; fills a purpose; fulfilled their aspirations; met her obligations.*

satisfying *adjective.* —*See* **pleasant.**
saturate *verb.* —*See* **charge** (1), **wet** (1).

saturated *adjective.* —*See* **wet.**

saturnine *adjective.* —*See* **glum.**

satyr *noun.* —*See* **lecher.**

sauce *noun.* —*See* **impudence.**

sauce *verb. Informal* To utter an impertinent rejoinder ▶ talk back, talk up. *Informal:* sass. ***Idiom:*** give someone lip.

saucebox *noun.* —*See* **smart aleck.**

sauciness *noun.* —*See* **impudence.**

saucy *adjective.* —*See* **impudent.**

saunter *verb.* —*See* **stroll.**

saunter *noun.* —*See* **walk** (1).

sauté *verb.* —*See* **cook.**

savage *adjective.* —*See* **cruel, uncivilized, wild** (2).

savage *noun.* —*See* **fiend.**

savagery *noun.* —*See* **cruelty.**

savant *noun.* —*See* **sage.**

save *verb.* **1.** To keep or accumulate for future use ▶ hoard, keep, lay aside (*or* away *or* by), lay in (*or* up), put by, salt away, save up, set aside, set by, squirrel away, stockpile, store (up), stow, treasure, warehouse. *Informal:* sock away. *Slang:* stash. [*Compare* **accumulate, bank[2], hide[1].**] **2.** To protect an asset from loss or destruction ▶ conserve, husband, preserve. [*Compare* **defend.**] —*See also* **rescue, scrimp.**

saving *adjective.* —*See* **economical.**

savior *noun.* —*See* **rescuer.**

savoir-faire *noun.* —*See* **tact.**

savor *noun.* A distinctive yet intangible quality ▶ aroma, atmosphere, flavor, smack. —*See also* **flavor** (1), **quality** (1).

savor *verb.* **1.** To have a particular flavor or suggestion of something ▶ smack, smell, suggest, taste. [*Compare* **hint.**] **2.** To undergo an emotional reaction ▶ experience, feel, have, know, taste. —*See also* **enjoy.**

savory *adjective.* —*See* **delicious, fragrant, spicy.**

savvy *adjective.* —*See* **shrewd.**

savvy *noun.* —*See* **ability** (1).

savvy *verb.* —*See* **understand** (1).

saw *noun.* —*See* **cliché, proverb.**

saw-toothed *adjective.* Having a notched edge like a saw ▶ dentate, notched, serrate, serrated, toothed. [*Compare* **rough.**]

say *verb.* To put into words ▶ articulate, communicate, convey, declare, deliver, express, state, talk, tell, utter, vent, verbalize, vocalize, voice. ***Idioms:*** give tongue (*or* vent *or* voice) to. [*Compare* **air, believe, describe, speak.**] —*See also* **assert, pronounce.**

say *noun.* The right or chance to express an opinion or participate in a decision ▶ input, suffrage, voice, vote. *Informal:* say-so.

saying *noun.* Something said ▶ statement, utterance, word. [*Compare* **language, speech.**] —*See also* **proverb, voicing.**

say-so *noun. Informal* The right or chance to express an opinion or participate in a decision ▶ input, say, suffrage, voice, vote. —*See also* **authority.**

scabrous *adjective.* —*See* **racy, rough** (1).

scad *noun.* —*See* **heap** (2).

scaffolding *or* **scaffold** *noun.* A temporary framework with a floor, used by laborers ▶ platform, stage, staging. [*Compare* **base[1].**]

scalawag *noun.* —*See* **rascal.**

scalding *adjective.* —*See* **hot** (1).

scale[1] *noun.* Scaly pieces of dry shedded skin ▶ dander, dandruff, furfur, scurf. [*Compare* **flake.**] —*See also* **flake.**

scale *verb.* —*See* **flake, skin.**

scale[2] *verb.* —*See* **ascend.**

scale *noun.* —*See* **series.**

scalp *verb.* —*See* **cheat** (1).

scam *verb.* —*See* **cheat** (1).

scam *noun.* —*See* **cheat** (1).

scammer *noun.* —*See* **cheat** (2).

scamp *noun.* —*See* **rascal, urchin.**

scamper *verb.* —*See* **run** (1).

scan *verb.* To view broadly or from a height ▶ look over, overlook, survey. [*Compare* **look.**] —*See also* **browse** (1).

scan *noun.* —*See* **glance** (1).

scandal *noun.* —*See* **gossip** (1), **libel.**

scandalize *verb.* —*See* **offend** (1).

scandalmonger *noun.* —*See* **gossip** (2).

scandalous *adjective.* —*See* **libelous, outrageous.**

scandalousness *noun.* —*See* **outrageousness.**

scant *adjective.* Just sufficient ▶ bare, mere, scanty. [*Compare* **insufficient.**] —*See also* **meager.**

scantiness *or* **scantness** *noun.* —*See* **shortage.**

scanty *adjective.* Just sufficient ▶ bare, mere, scant. [*Compare* **insufficient.**] —*See also* **meager.**

scapegoat *noun.* One who is made an object of blame ▶ goat, whipping boy. *Slang:* fall guy, patsy. [*Compare* **dupe, victim.**]

scapegoat *verb.* —*See* **criticize** (1).

scar *verb.* —*See* **deform.**

scar *noun.* —*See* **deformity.**

scarce *adjective.* —*See* **infrequent, insufficient.**

scarce *or* **scarcely** *adverb.* By a very little; almost not ▶ barely, hardly, just, scarcely. ***Idioms:*** by a hair (*or* whisker), by the skin of one's teeth. [*Compare* **approximately, merely, only.**]

scarcity *or* **scarceness** *noun.* —*See* **shortage.**

scare *verb.* —*See* **frighten.**

scare up *verb.* To look for and discover ▶ find, locate, pinpoint, spot. [*Compare* **trace, uncover.**]

scared *adjective.* —*See* **afraid.**

scaredy-cat *noun.* —*See* **coward.**

scaremonger *noun.* One who needlessly alarms others ▶ alarmist, Chicken Little, panicmonger. ***Idiom:*** one who cries wolf. [*Compare* **pessimist.**]

scarf *noun.* A long piece of cloth worn about the head, neck, or shoulders ▶ ascot, cravat, fichu, headscarf, kerchief, muffler, rebozo. [*Compare* **wrap.**]

scarify[1] *verb.* —*See* **cut** (1), **slam** (1).

scarify[2] *verb.* —*See* **frighten.**

scarlet woman *noun.* —*See* **harlot.**

scary *adjective.* —*See* **fearful.**

scathe *verb.* —*See* **slam** (1).

scathing *adjective.* —*See* **biting.**

scatological *or* **scatologic** *adjective.* —*See* **obscene.**

scatology *noun.* —*See* **obscenity** (2).

scatter *verb.* **1.** To cause to separate and go in various directions ▶ dispel, disperse, dissipate. [*Compare* **divide, separate.**] **2.** To move apart and go in various directions ▶ break up, disband, disperse, move apart, separate, split up. [*Compare* **branch, divide.**] —*See also* **disorder, lift** (2), **plant, spread** (2).

✦ **CORE SYNONYMS:** *scatter, disperse, dissipate, dispel.* These verbs mean to cause a mass or aggregate to separate and go in various directions. *Scatter* refers to loose or haphazard distribution of components: "*the scattered driftwood, bleached and dry*" (Celia Laighton Thaxter). *Disperse* implies the complete breaking up of the mass or aggregate: "*only a few industrious Scots perhaps, who indeed are dispersed over the face of the whole earth*" (George Chapman). *Dissipate* suggests a reduction to nothing: "*The main of life is composed . . . of meteorous pleasures which dance before us and are dissipated*" (Samuel Johnson). *Dispel* suggests driving away or off by or as if by scattering: "*But he . . . with high words . . . gently raised/Their fainting courage, and dispelled their fears*" (John Milton).

---

scatterbrained *adjective.* —*See* **absent-minded, giddy** (2).

scattergood *noun.* —*See* **wastrel** (1).

scattering *noun.* An act of reflection ▶ deflection, glance, reflection. [*Compare* **bounce.**] —*See also* **distribution** (2).

scenario *noun.* —*See* **plot** (1), **script** (2).

scene *noun.* **1.** The place where an action or event occurs ▶ backdrop, locale, setting, site, stage. [*Compare* **environment, locality.**] **2.** The properties, objects, and accessories arranged for a dramatic presentation ▶ backdrop, background, mise en scène, props, scenery, set, setting, staging. [*Compare*

stage.] *—See also* **agitation** (1), **area** (1), **conditions, view** (2).

scenery *noun.* *—See* **scene** (2), **view** (2).

scent *noun.* **1.** The quality of something that may be perceived by the olfactory sense ▶ aroma, odor, smell. [*Compare* **fragrance, stench.**] **2.** The sense by which odors are perceived ▶ nose, olfaction, smell. *—See also* **fragrance, tip**[3], **track.**

scent *verb.* To fill with a pleasant odor ▶ aromatize, perfume. *—See also* **smell** (1).

schedule *noun.* *—See* **list**[1], **program** (1).

schedule *verb.* **1.** To enter on a schedule ▶ calendar, docket, program, slate. [*Compare* **list**[1].] **2.** To set the time for an event or occasion ▶ plan, set, time. *—See also* **arrange** (2).

scheduled *adjective.* *—See* **due** (2).

schema *noun.* *—See* **approach** (1).

scheme *noun.* *—See* **approach** (1), **method, plot** (2).

scheme *verb.* *—See* **design** (1), **plot** (2).

schemed *adjective.* *—See* **calculated.**

scheming *adjective.* Coldly planning to achieve selfish aims ▶ calculating, conniving, designing, manipulative. *—See also* **artful.**

schism *noun.* *—See* **breach** (2), **conflict, division** (2).

schismatic *noun.* *—See* **separatist.**

schlep *verb.* *—See* **carry** (1), **trudge.**

schlep *noun.* *—See* **oaf.**

schlocky *adjective.* *—See* **shoddy.**

schmaltz *or* **schmaltziness** *noun.* *—See* **sentimentality.**

schmaltzy *adjective.* *—See* **sentimental.**

schmuck *or* **schmo** *noun.* *—See* **drip** (2), **fool.**

schnoz *or* **schnozzle** *noun.* *—See* **nose** (1).

scholar *noun.* *—See* **sage, student.**

scholarly *adjective.* Devoted to study or reading ▶ bookish, studious. [*Compare* **intellectual.**] *—See also* **educated.**

scholarship *noun.* *—See* **education** (2).

scholastic *adjective.* *—See* **educational** (1), **pedantic.**

school *verb.* *—See* **educate.**

school *noun.* *—See* **class** (2), **flock.**

schooling *noun.* *—See* **education** (1).

schoolmaster *or* **schoolmistress** *noun.* *—See* **educator.**

schoolteacher *noun.* *—See* **educator.**

science *noun.* *—See* **education** (2).

scilicet *adverb.* *—See* **namely.**

scintillate *verb.* *—See* **glitter.**

scintillating *adjective.* *—See* **clever** (2), **sparkling.**

scintillation *noun.* *—See* **flash** (1), **glitter** (1).

scion *noun.* *—See* **progeny.**

scissors *noun.* *—See* **shears.**

scoff *verb.* *—See* **ridicule.**

scoff *noun.* *—See* **taunt.**

scoffing *adjective.* *—See* **sarcastic.**

scofflaw *noun.* *—See* **criminal.**

scold *verb.* *—See* **chastise.**

scold *noun.* A person, traditionally a woman, who persistently nags or criticizes ▶ fishwife, fury, harpy, harridan, nag, shrew, termagant, virago, vixen. *Informal:* battle-ax. [*Compare* **critic, grouch.**]

scolding *noun.* *—See* **rebuke.**

scoop *noun.* *—See* **news.**

scoop *verb.* *—See* **dig, dip** (2).

scoot *verb.* *—See* **rush.**

scope *noun.* The ability or power to seize or attain ▶ capacity, compass, grasp, range, reach. [*Compare* **influence.**] *—See also* **degree** (2), **ken, license** (1), **range** (1).

scope out *verb.* *—See* **examine** (1).

scorch *verb.* *—See* **blast** (2), **burn** (1), **slam** (1).

scorch *noun.* *—See* **burn.**

scorched *adjective.* *—See* **dry** (2).

scorching *adjective.* *—See* **biting, hot** (1), **passionate.**

score *noun.* *—See* **count** (1), **cut** (1), **debt** (1).

score *verb.* **1.** To gain a point or points in a game or contest ▶ post, tally.

Informal: notch. ***Idioms:*** make a goal (*or* point). **2.** To evaluate and assign a grade to ▶ correct, grade, mark. —*See also* **accomplish, buy, compose** (1), **count** (2), **prosper, slam** (1).

scores *noun.* —*See* **crowd.**

scorn *noun.* —*See* **despisal, disgrace.**

scorn *verb.* —*See* **despise.**

scornful *adjective.* —*See* **disdainful, disrespectful.**

Scotch *adjective.* —*See* **economical.**

scoundrel *noun.* —*See* **evildoer, rascal.**

scour[1] *verb.* To remove an outer layer or something adherent from an object by friction ▶ rub away, rub off, scrape, scrub. [*Compare* **chafe, scrape.**]

scour[2] *verb.* To search through or over thoroughly ▶ comb, forage, ransack, rummage, search. *Slang:* shake down. ***Idioms:*** beat the bushes, leave no stone unturned, look (*or* search) high and low, look (*or* search) up and down, turn inside out, turn upside down. [*Compare* **examine, explore, seek.**] —*See also* **rush.**

scourge *noun.* —*See* **curse** (3).

scourge *verb.* —*See* **afflict, beat** (2), **slam** (1).

scout[1] *verb.* —*See* **explore.**

scout[2] *verb.* —*See* **despise, ridicule.**

scowl *verb.* **1.** To wrinkle one's brow, as in thought, puzzlement, or displeasure ▶ frown, glower, lower. ***Idioms:*** knit one's brow, look black, turn one's mouth down. [*Compare* **grimace.**] **2.** To stare fixedly and angrily ▶ glare, glower, lower. ***Idioms:*** give the evil eye, look daggers. [*Compare* **gaze, sneer.**]

scowl *noun.* A fixed angry stare ▶ glare, glower, lower. [*Compare* **face, sneer.**] —*See also* **frown.**

scrabble *verb.* —*See* **grope.**

scraggy *adjective.* —*See* **rough** (1).

scram *verb.* —*See* **run** (2).

scramble *verb.* —*See* **ascend, confuse** (3), **shuffle.**

scramble *noun.* —*See* **disorder** (1).

scrap[1] *noun.* —*See* **bit[1]** (1), **bit[1]** (2), **end** (3).

scrap *verb. Slang* To decide not to continue ▶ call off, cancel. *Slang:* scratch, scrub. [*Compare* **defer, drop.**] —*See also* **discard.**

scrap[2] *noun.* —*See* **fight** (1).

scrape *verb.* **1.** To bring or come into abrasive contact, often with a harsh sound ▶ abrade, file, grate, rasp, scratch. [*Compare* **chafe.**] **2.** To remove an outer layer or something adherent from an object by friction ▶ rub away, rub off, scour, scrub. [*Compare* **chafe.**] —*See also* **scrimp.**

scrape *noun.* A mark or shallow cut made by contact with an object ▶ abrasion, scratch, scuff, striation. [*Compare* **cut, furrow, impression.**] —*See also* **predicament.**

scrappy *adjective.* —*See* **aggressive, argumentative.**

scratch *verb. Slang* To decide not to continue ▶ call off, cancel. *Slang:* scrap, scrub. [*Compare* **defer, drop.**] —*See also* **cancel** (1), **scrape** (1).

scratch *noun.* A mark or shallow cut made by contact with an object ▶ abrasion, scrape, scuff, striation. [*Compare* **cut, furrow, impression.**] —*See also* **money** (1).

scratchy *adjective.* —*See* **harsh, rough** (1).

scrawny *adjective.* —*See* **thin** (1).

screak *noun.* A long, loud, piercing cry, as in fright ▶ scream, screech, shriek. [*Compare* **howl.**]

screak *verb.* To utter a long, loud, piercing cry, as of fright ▶ scream, screech, shriek, shrill. [*Compare* **howl.**]

scream *verb.* To utter a long, loud, piercing cry, as in fright ▶ screak, screech, shriek, shrill. [*Compare* **howl.**] —*See also* **shout.**

scream *noun.* **1.** A long, loud, piercing cry, as of fright ▶ screak, screech, shriek. [*Compare* **howl.**] **2.** *Informal* Something or someone uproariously funny or absurd ▶ absurdity. *Informal:* hoot, joke, laugh. *Slang:* gas, howl, panic, riot. ***Idiom:*** a laugh a minute. [*Compare* **foolishness.**] *—See also* **shout.**

screech *noun.* A long, loud, piercing cry, as of fright ▶ screak, scream, shriek. [*Compare* **howl.**] *—See also* **shout.**

screech *verb.* To utter a long, loud, piercing cry, as in fright ▶ screak, scream, shriek, shrill. [*Compare* **howl.**] *—See also* **shout.**

screed *noun. —See* **tirade.**

screen *verb.* **1.** To shelter, especially from light ▶ shade, shadow. **2.** To separate with or as if with a wall ▶ fence, partition, wall. *—See also* **block, censor** (1), **conceal.**

screen *noun.* A solid structure that separates one area from another ▶ barrier, partition, wall. [*Compare* **border.**] *—See also* **cover** (1), **veil.**

screened *adjective.* Concealed from view ▶ blind, hidden, secluded, secret. ***Idioms:*** out of sight, out of view. [*Compare* **hidden.**]

screenplay *noun. —See* **script** (2).

screw *verb. —See* **fasten.**

screw around *or* **off** *verb. —See* **putter.**

screw up *verb. —See* **botch, err.**

screw *noun. —See* **nail.**

screwball *noun. —See* **crackpot.**

screwball *adjective. —See* **eccentric.**

screwup *noun. —See* **blunderer, mess** (1).

screwy *adjective. —See* **insane.**

scribble *verb. —See* **write.**

scrimp *verb.* To be frugal or sparing ▶ conserve, economize, pinch, save, scrape, skimp, spare, stint. ***Idioms:*** pinch pennies, tighten one's belt.

scrimpy *adjective. —See* **meager.**

script *noun.* **1.** Writing done with the hand ▶ calligraphy, cursive, handwriting, longhand, penmanship. **2.** The text of a play, movie, opera, or similar work ▶ book, dialogue, libretto, manuscript, play, screenplay, scenario.

scriptural *adjective.* Of or relating to representation by means of writing ▶ calligraphic, graphic, written.

Scrooge *noun. —See* **miser.**

scrounge *verb. —See* **beg.**

scrub *verb.* **1.** To remove an outer layer or something adherent from an object by friction ▶ rub away, rub off, scour, scrape. [*Compare* **chafe, scrape.**] **2.** *Slang* To decide not to continue ▶ call off, cancel. *Slang:* scrap, scratch. [*Compare* **defer, drop.**]

scrub *noun. —See* **nonentity, squirt** (2).

scrubby *adjective. —See* **shabby.**

scruffy *adjective. —See* **shabby.**

scrumptious *adjective. —See* **delicious.**

scrunch *verb. —See* **squeeze** (1), **stoop.**

scruple *noun. —See* **bit**[1] (1), **qualm.**

scrupulous *adjective. —See* **careful** (2), **ethical.**

scrupulousness *noun. —See* **thoroughness.**

scrutinize *verb. —See* **examine** (1), **watch** (1).

scrutiny *noun.* The act of observing, often for an extended time ▶ observance, observation, watch, watching. *—See also* **examination** (1).

scuff *verb. —See* **batter, trudge.**

scuff *noun.* A mark or shallow cut made by contact with an object ▶ abrasion, scrape, scratch, striation. [*Compare* **cut, furrow, impression.**]

scuffle *verb. —See* **contend, trudge.**

scuffle *noun. —See* **fight** (1).

scullion *noun. —See* **drudge** (1).

sculpt *verb. —See* **form** (1).

sculpture *noun.* A work of art created by shaping a solid material ▶ bust, carving, cast, figure, figurine, relief, statue, statuette. [*Compare* **form.**]

scum *noun. —See* **riffraff.**

scurf *noun.* Scaly pieces of dry shedded skin ▶ dander, dandruff, furfur, scale. [*Compare* **flake.**]

scurrility *or* **scurrilousness** *noun. —See* **obscenity** (1), **vituperation.**

scurrilous *adjective. —See* **abusive, obscene.**

scurry *or* **scuttle** *verb. —See* **run** (1).

scuttlebutt *noun. —See* **gossip** (1).

scythe *verb.* —*See* **cut** (3).

sea *noun.* —*See* **ocean.**

sea *adjective.* —*See* **marine** (1).

seafarer *or* **seadog** *noun.* —*See* **sailor.**

seal *verb.* To move a door, for example, in order to cover an opening ▶ close, clench, shut, slam. —*See also* **fill** (2).

seam *noun.* —*See* **joint** (1).

seaman *noun.* —*See* **sailor.**

seamy *adjective.* —*See* **sordid.**

sear *verb.* —*See* **burn** (1), **cook, dry** (1).

sear *noun.* —*See* **burn.**

search *verb.* To examine a person or someone's personal effects in order to find something lost or concealed ▶ frisk, inspect, pat down. *Slang:* shake down. ***Idiom:*** do a body search of. —*See also* **scour²**.

search for *verb.* —*See* **seek** (1).

search *noun.* A thorough search of a place or persons ▶ body search, frisk, patdown. *Slang:* shakedown. —*See also* **examination** (1), **pursuit** (2).

searing *adjective.* —*See* **biting, hot** (1).

season *noun.* —*See* **period** (1).

season *verb.* To impart flavor to ▶ flavor, spice (up), zest. —*See also* **harden** (1).

seasonable *adjective.* —*See* **opportune.**

seasonal *adjective.* —*See* **migratory** (1).

seasoned *adjective.* —*See* **experienced, spicy.**

seasoning *or* **seasoner** *noun.* —*See* **flavoring.**

seat *noun.* —*See* **base¹** (2), **buttocks, center** (1).

seat *verb.* —*See* **establish** (1).

sec *noun.* —*See* **flash** (2).

secede *verb.* To sever one's association with an alliance or federation ▶ break away, pull out, splinter (off), withdraw. *Informal:* split (away). [*Compare* **quit.**] —*See also* **defect.**

secession *noun.* —*See* **defection.**

seclude *verb.* To put into solitude ▶ cloister, isolate, sequester, sequestrate. [*Compare* **enclose, imprison.**] —*See also* **isolate** (1).

secluded *adjective.* Concealed from view ▶ blind, hidden, screened, secret. ***Idioms:*** out of sight, out of view. [*Compare* **hidden.**] —*See also* **remote** (1).

seclusion *noun.* The act of secluding or the state of being secluded ▶ isolation, reclusion, retirement, separateness, sequestration. —*See also* **solitude.**

second¹ *noun.* —*See* **flash** (2).

second² *noun.* —*See* **assistant, double.**

secondary *adjective.* Stemming from an original source ▶ derivational, derivative, derived. —*See also* **auxiliary** (2), **minor** (1).

secondary *noun.* —*See* **subordinate.**

second-class *adjective.* —*See* **bad** (1), **minor** (1).

second fiddle *noun.* —*See* **subordinate.**

secondhand *adjective.* —*See* **used** (2).

second-rate *adjective.* —*See* **bad** (1).

secrecy *noun.* The habit, practice, or policy of keeping secrets ▶ clandestineness, clandestinity, concealment, covertness, huggermugger, huggermuggery, secretiveness, secretness. [*Compare* **stealth.**]

secret *adjective.* **1.** Operating in a way so as to ensure concealment and confidentiality ▶ backstairs, clandestine, cloak-and-dagger, covert, huggermugger, sub-rosa, undercover. *Informal:* hush-hush. [*Compare* **artful, ulterior.**] **2.** Concealed from view ▶ blind, hidden, screened, secluded. ***Idioms:*** out of sight, out of view. [*Compare* **hidden.**] —*See also* **confidential** (1), **hidden** (1).

secret *noun.* A means or method of entering into or achieving something desirable ▶ formula, key, route. *Informal:* ticket. [*Compare* **trick.**]

✦ **CORE SYNONYMS:** *secret, stealthy, covert, clandestine, furtive, surreptitious, underhand.* These adjectives mean operating or designed so as to ensure concealment and confidentiality. *Secret* is the most general: *a desk with a secret compartment; secret business negotia-*

tions. Stealthy suggests quiet, cautious deceptiveness intended to escape notice: *heard stealthy footsteps on the stairs. Covert* describes something that is concealed or disguised: *protested covert actions undertaken by the CIA. Clandestine* implies stealth and secrecy for the concealment of an often illegal or improper purpose: *clandestine intelligence operations. Furtive* suggests the slyness, shiftiness, and evasiveness of a thief: *a menacing and furtive look to his eye.* Something *surreptitious* is stealthy, furtive, and often unseemly or unethical: *the surreptitious mobilization of troops preparing for a sneak attack. Underhand* implies unfairness, deceit, or slyness as well as secrecy: *achieved success by underhand methods.*

---

secrete *verb.* —*See* **hide[1].**

secretive *adjective.* —*See* **stealthy.**

secretiveness *noun.* —*See* **secrecy, stealth.**

secretly *adverb.* In a secret way ▶ clandestinely, covertly, huggermugger, sub rosa. ***Idioms:*** behind closed doors, by stealth, on the q.t., on the sly, under cover (*or* wraps), under the radar.

secretness *noun.* —*See* **secrecy.**

sect *noun.* —*See* **religion.**

sectarian *noun.* —*See* **separatist.**

sectary *noun.* —*See* **devotee, separatist.**

section *noun.* A particular subdivision of a written work ▶ chapter, part, passage, segment. —*See also* **area** (2), **branch** (3), **part** (1).

section *verb.* —*See* **divide.**

sectional *adjective.* Relating to or restricted to a particular territory ▶ regional, territorial. [*Compare* **local.**]

sector *noun.* —*See* **area** (2), **part** (1).

secular *adjective.* —*See* **earthly, profane** (2).

secure *adjective.* —*See* **confident, firm[1]** (2), **safe** (2), **sure** (2), **tight** (1).

secure *verb.* To make fast or firmly fixed, as by means of a cord or rope ▶ bind, fasten, knot, tie, tie up. —*See also* **attach** (1), **capture, cause, defend** (1), **fasten, get** (1), **guarantee** (2), **police.**

security *noun.* A partial or initial payment ▶ deposit, down payment, installment. —*See also* **defense, pawn[1], safety, stability.**

sedate[1] *adjective.* —*See* **serious** (1).

sedate[2] *verb.* —*See* **drug** (1).

sedateness *noun.* —*See* **seriousness** (1).

sedative *adjective.* —*See* **soporific.**

sedative *noun.* —*See* **drug** (2), **soporific.**

sediment *noun.* —*See* **deposit** (2).

sedimentary *adjective.* —*See* **murky** (1).

sedition *noun.* Willful violation of allegiance to one's country ▶ lese majesty, seditiousness, traitorousness, treason. [*Compare* **faithlessness.**] —*See also* **rebellion.**

seditious *adjective.* Involving or constituting treason ▶ traitorous, treasonable, treasonous. [*Compare* **faithless.**]

seditiousness *noun.* Willful violation of allegiance to one's country ▶ lese majesty, sedition, traitorousness, treason. [*Compare* **faithlessness.**]

seduce *verb.* To beguile or lure into a wrong or foolish course of action, especially a sexual act ▶ allure, entice, inveigle, lure, tempt. ***Idiom:*** lead astray. [*Compare* **charm, corrupt, flirt, philander.**]

✚ **CORE SYNONYMS:** *seduce, lure, entice, inveigle, tempt.* These verbs mean to lead or attempt to lead into a wrong or foolish course. To *seduce* is to entice away and usually suggests the overcoming of moral resistance: "*The French King attempted by splendid offers to seduce him from the cause of the Republic*" (Thomas Macaulay). *Lure* suggests the use of something that attracts like bait: *Industry often lures scientists from universities by offering them huge salaries.* To *entice* is to draw on skillfully, as by arousing hopes or desires: *The* *teacher tried to entice the shy child into entering the classroom. Inveigle* implies winning over by coaxing, flattery, or artful talk: *He inveigled a friend into becoming his law partner. Tempt* implies an encouragement or an attraction to do something, especially something immoral, unwise, or contrary to one's better judgment: *I am tempted to tell him what I really think of him.*

---

seducer *noun.* **1.** A person who beguiles or seduces ▶ allurer, beguiler, charmer, enticer, inveigler, lurer, tempter. **2.** A man who seduces women ▶ debaucher, Don Juan, Lothario. [*Compare* **flirt, lecher, philanderer.**]

seduction *noun.* —*See* **lure** (1).

seductive *adjective.* Tending to seduce ▶ alluring, beguiling, bewitching, come-hither, enthralling, enticing, entrancing, inviting, luring, sexy, siren, tantalizing, tempting, witching. [*Compare* **attractive, beautiful.**]

seductress *noun.* A woman who seduces or exploits men ▶ enchantress, femme fatale, siren, temptress. *Informal:* vamp, witch. [*Compare* **flirt.**]

sedulous *adjective.* —*See* **diligent.**

sedulousness *noun.* —*See* **diligence.**

see *verb.* **1.** To perceive with the eyes ▶ behold, catch, descry, detect, discern, espy, perceive, spot, spy. ***Idioms:*** cast one's eyes on, catch sight of, get a load of, get a look at, lay (*or* clap) eyes on. [*Compare* **glimpse, look.**] **2.** To be with another person socially on a regular basis ▶ date, go out (with), go with. *Informal:* take out. ***Idioms:*** go steady, go together. —*See also* **encounter** (1), **experience, foresee, imagine, notice, regard, understand** (1), **visit, watch** (1).

see through *verb.* —*See* **conclude.**

see to *verb.* —*See* **tend**[2].

✚ **CORE SYNONYMS:** *see, behold, descry, espy, perceive, discern.* These verbs refer to being or becoming visually aware of something. *See,* the most general, can mean merely to use the faculty of sight but more often implies recognition, understanding, or appreciation: *"If I have seen further (than . . . Descartes) it is by standing upon the shoulders of Giants"* (Isaac Newton). *Behold* implies gazing at or looking intently upon what is seen: *"My heart leaps up when I behold/A rainbow in the sky"* (William Wordsworth). *Descry* and *espy* both stress acuteness of sight that permits the detection of something distant or obscure: *"the lighthouse, which can be descried from a distance"* (Michael Strauss). *"espied the misspelled Latin word in* [the] *letter"* (Los Angeles Times). *Perceive* and *discern* both imply not only visual recognition but also mental comprehension; *perceive* is especially associated with insight, and *discern,* with the ability to distinguish, discriminate, and make judgments: *"I plainly perceive* [that] *some objections remain"* (Edmund Burke). *"Your sense of humor would discern the hollowness beneath all the pomp and ceremony"* (Edna Ferber).

---

seeable *adjective.* —*See* **visible.**

seed *noun.* A fertilized plant ovule capable of germinating ▶ grain, kernel, pip, pit. —*See also* **ancestry, germ** (2), **progeny.**

seed *verb.* —*See* **plant.**

seedtime *noun.* The season of the year during which the weather becomes warmer and plants revive ▶ spring, springtide, springtime.

seedy *adjective.* —*See* **shabby.**

seeing *noun.* —*See* **vision** (1).

seeing *adjective.* Serving, resulting from, or relating to the sense of sight ▶ ocular, optic, optical, visual.

seek *verb.* **1.** To try to find something ▶ cast about (*or* around), ferret (around), fish for, hunt for, look for, search for, sniff about (*or* around). [*Compare* **pursue, scour**[2].] **2.** To strive toward a goal ▶ aspire, seek. ***Idioms:*** go (*or* grab) for the brass ring, keep one's eyes on the prize, set one's sights on. *—See also* **appeal** (1), **attempt.**

seeker *noun.* One who aspires ▶ aspirant, aspirer, dreamer, hopeful. *Informal:* wannabe. *—See also* **applicant.**

seem *verb.* To give the impression of being ▶ appear, feel, look, sound. ***Idioms:*** have all the earmarks of being, give the idea (*or* impression) of being, strike one as being. [*Compare* **resemble.**]

seeming *adjective.* *—See* **apparent** (2).

seemingly *adverb.* *—See* **apparently.**

seemliness *noun.* *—See* **decency** (2).

seemly *adjective.* *—See* **appropriate.**

seep *verb.* *—See* **ooze.**

seer *noun.* Someone who sees something occur ▶ audience, eyewitness, viewer, witness. *—See also* **prophet.**

seesaw *verb.* *—See* **lurch** (1).

seethe *verb.* *—See* **anger** (2), **boil.**

see-through *adjective.* *—See* **clear** (1).

segment *noun.* A particular subdivision of a written work ▶ chapter, part, passage, section. *—See also* **part** (1).

segment *verb.* *—See* **divide.**

segmentation *noun.* *—See* **division** (1).

segregate *verb.* *—See* **isolate** (1).

segregation *noun.* *—See* **isolation.**

seism *noun.* A shaking of the earth ▶ earthquake, quake, temblor, tremor. *Informal:* shake.

seize *verb.* **1.** To lay claim to or take possession of ▶ appropriate, arrogate, assume, commandeer, confiscate, expropriate, grab, hijack, impound, preempt, take (over), snatch, usurp. ***Idiom:*** help oneself to. [*Compare* **steal.**] **2.** To have a sudden overwhelming effect on ▶ catch, strike, take. [*Compare* **move.**] *—See also* **arrest, catch** (2), **grasp, occupy** (2).

✚ **CORE SYNONYMS:** *seize, appropriate, arrogate, commandeer, confiscate, preempt, usurp.* These verbs mean to lay claim to or take possession of something: *seized hidden contraband; appropriated the family car; arrogated the chair at the head of the table; commandeered a plane for the escape; confiscating stolen property; preempted the glory for themselves; usurped the throne.*

---

seizure *noun.* **1.** A sudden and often acute manifestation of a disease ▶ apoplexy, attack, convulsion, fit, paroxysm. *Informal:* spell. **2.** The act of taking possession of something ▶ appropriation, arrogation, assumption, commandeering, confiscation, expropriation, grab, hijacking, impoundment, preemption, seizing, snatch, takeover, taking, usurpation. [*Compare* **larceny.**] *—See also* **arrest, catch** (1).

seldom *adverb.* *—See* **infrequently.**

select *verb.* *—See* **choose** (1).

select *adjective.* Singled out in preference ▶ choice, chosen, elect, exclusive. [*Compare* **excellent, favorite.**] *—See also* **choice** (1), **discriminating.**

select *noun.* *—See* **elect.**

selection *noun.* *—See* **choice.**

selective *adjective.* *—See* **discriminating, exclusive** (3).

selective service *noun.* *—See* **draft** (2).

selectivity *or* **selectiveness** *noun.* *—See* **discrimination** (1).

self *noun.* *—See* **human being.**

self-absorbed *adjective.* *—See* **egotistic** (2).

self-absorption *noun.* *—See* **egotism.**

self-assurance *noun.* *—See* **confidence.**

self-assured *adjective.* *—See* **confident.**

self-centered *adjective.* *—See* **egotistic** (2).

self-centeredness *noun.* *—See* **egotism.**

self-confidence *noun.* *—See* **confidence.**

self-confident *adjective.* *—See* **confident.**

self-conscious *adjective.* *—See* **awkward** (3).

self-contained *adjective.* *—See* **independent** (1).

self-containment *noun.* —*See* **independence.**

self-content *adjective.* —*See* **proud.**

self-contentment *noun.* —*See* **pride.**

self-contradictory *adjective.* —*See* **fallacious** (1).

self-control *noun.* —*See* **reserve** (1).

self-controlled *adjective.* —*See* **reserved.**

self-denial *noun.* —*See* **temperance** (1).

self-denying *adjective.* —*See* **ascetic, selfless.**

self-determination *noun.* —*See* **freedom, independence.**

self-determined *or* **self-directed** *adjective.* —*See* **independent** (1).

self-effacement *noun.* —*See* **shyness.**

self-effacing *adjective.* —*See* **shy[1].**

self-esteem *noun.* —*See* **pride.**

self-evident *adjective.* —*See* **apparent** (1).

self-forgetful *or* **self-forgetting** *adjective.* —*See* **selfless.**

self-governing *adjective.* —*See* **free** (1).

self-government *noun.* —*See* **freedom.**

selfhood *noun.* —*See* **identity** (1).

self-importance *noun.* —*See* **arrogance, egotism.**

self-important *adjective.* —*See* **arrogant, pompous.**

self-involved *adjective.* —*See* **egotistic** (2).

self-involvement *noun.* —*See* **egotism.**

selfish *adjective.* —*See* **egotistic** (2).

selfishness *noun.* —*See* **egotism.**

selfless *adjective.* Without concern for oneself ▶ self-denying, self-forgetful, self-forgetting, self-sacrificing, unselfish. [*Compare* **benevolent, generous, humanitarian.**]

self-possessed *adjective.* —*See* **confident.**

self-possession *noun.* —*See* **balance** (2), **confidence.**

self-regard *noun.* —*See* **pride.**

self-reliance *noun.* —*See* **independence.**

self-reliant *adjective.* —*See* **independent** (1).

self-reproach *noun.* —*See* **penitence.**

self-respect *noun.* —*See* **pride.**

self-respecting *adjective.* —*See* **proud.**

self-restrained *adjective.* —*See* **reserved.**

self-restraint *noun.* —*See* **reserve** (1).

self-righteous *adjective.* Piously or overly sure of one's own righteousness ▶ holier-than-thou, moralistic. [*Compare* **arrogant, hypocritical, moral.**]

self-rule *noun.* —*See* **freedom.**

self-ruling *adjective.* —*See* **free** (1).

self-sacrificing *adjective.* —*See* **selfless.**

selfsame *adjective.* —*See* **same.**

selfsameness *noun.* The quality or condition of being exactly the same as something else ▶ identicalness, identity, oneness, sameness. [*Compare* **likeness.**]

self-satisfaction *noun.* —*See* **arrogance, pride.**

self-satisfied *noun.* —*See* **arrogant, proud.**

self-seeking *adjective.* —*See* **egotistic** (2).

self-serving *adjective.* —*See* **egotistic** (2).

self-sufficiency *noun.* —*See* **independence.**

self-sufficient *adjective.* Able to support oneself financially ▶ independent, self-supporting. —*See also* **independent** (1).

self-supporting *adjective.* Able to support oneself financially ▶ independent, self-sufficient.

sell *verb.* To offer for sale ▶ deal (in), handle, market, merchandise, merchant, peddle, retail, trade (in), vend. ***Idioms:*** put up for sale, put on the block. [*Compare* **carry, offer.**] —*See also* **convince, persuade, promote** (3).

sell for *verb.* To require a specified price ▶ cost, go for. ***Idiom:*** set someone back. [*Compare* **demand.**] *—See also* **bring** (2).

sell off *or* **out** *verb.* To get rid of by selling ▶ close out, dispose of, dump, unload.

sell *noun. Slang* Market appeal ▶ marketability, marketableness, salability, salableness.

seller *noun.* One who sells ▶ barker, clerk, crier, hawker, peddler, retailer, salesclerk, salesman, salesperson, saleswoman, vendor. [*Compare* **dealer.**]

sellout *noun. —See* **betrayal.**

semblance *noun. —See* **appearance** (1), **façade** (2), **shade** (2).

seminal *adjective. —See* **influential, inventive, original.**

seminar *noun. —See* **conference** (1).

sempiternal *adjective. —See* **endless** (2).

sempiternity *noun.* The totality of time without beginning or end ▶ eternity, infinity, perpetuity. [*Compare* **forever.**]

send *verb.* **1.** To cause something to be conveyed to a destination ▶ address, consign, dispatch, express, forward, mail, post, route, ship, transmit. [*Compare* **convey, pass.**] **2.** To direct or allow to leave ▶ dismiss, send away. ***Idioms:*** send about one's business, send packing, show someone the door. **3.** To direct a person elsewhere for help or information ▶ refer, transfer, turn over. *—See also* **enrapture.**

send away *verb. —See* **dismiss** (2).

send for *verb. —See* **assemble.**

send forth *verb. —See* **emit, shed**[1] (1).

send up *verb. —See* **commit.**

✚ **CORE SYNONYMS:** *send, dispatch, forward, route, ship, transmit.* These verbs mean to cause to go or be taken to a destination: *sent the package by parcel post; dispatched a union representative to the factory; forwards the mail to their new address; routed the soldiers through New York; shipped his books to his dormitory; transmits money by cable.*

send-up *noun. —See* **satire.**

senescence *or* **senectitude** *noun. —See* **age** (1).

senescent *adjective. —See* **old** (2).

senile *adjective.* Relating to the mental deterioration that often accompanies old age ▶ doddering, doting. [*Compare* **old, infirm.**]

senility *noun.* The condition of being senile ▶ anecdotage, anility, caducity, dotage. [*Compare* **age.**]

senior *adjective.* Being at a rank or level above another ▶ greater, higher, superior, upper. *—See also* **old** (2).

senior *noun.* **1.** One who stands above another in rank ▶ better, elder, superior. *Informal:* higher-up. [*Compare* **chief.**] **2.** An elderly person ▶ ancient, elder, golden ager, senior citizen. *Informal:* oldster, old-timer.

senior citizen *noun. —See* **senior** (2).

seniority *noun. —See* **age** (1).

sensation *noun.* **1.** The capacity for or an act of responding to a stimulus ▶ feeling, impression, perception, sense, sensibility, sensitiveness, sensitivity. [*Compare* **awareness, emotion.**] **2.** A condition of intense public interest or excitement ▶ ado, brouhaha, bustle, stir, uproar. *Informal:* to-do. *Slang:* hoohah. [*Compare* **agitation.**] *—See also* **marvel.**

sensational *adjective.* Of or relating to sensation or the senses ▶ sensitive, sensorial, sensory, sensual, sensuous. *—See also* **dramatic** (2), **marvelous.**

sense *noun.* What is sound or reasonable ▶ logic, rationality, rationalness, reason, reasonableness. *—See also* **awareness, common sense, intelligence, meaning, sanity, sensation** (1).

sense *verb.* To view in a certain way ▶ believe, hold, think. [*Compare* **believe, regard.**] *—See also* **perceive, understand** (1).

senseless *adjective. —See* **foolish, mindless, unconscious.**

senselessness *noun. —See* **foolishness, nonsense.**

sensibility *noun.* The quality or condition of being emotionally and intuitively sensitive ▶ feeling, sensibility, sensitiveness. [*Compare* **pity, sympathy.**] —*See also* **sensation** (1).

sensible *adjective.* Proceeding from or exhibiting good judgment and prudence ▶ balanced, commonsensible, commonsensical, judicious, levelheaded, prudent, rational, reasonable, sagacious, sage, sane, sapient, sober, sound, well-founded, well-grounded, wise. [*Compare* **advisable, logical.**] —*See also* **aware, perceptible, physical, sensitive** (1).

sensitive *adjective.* **1.** Able to receive and respond to external stimuli ▶ impressible, impressionable, responsive, sensible, sentient, susceptible, susceptive. [*Compare* **aware.**] **2.** Readily stirred by emotion ▶ emotional, feeling. [*Compare* **passionate.**] —*See also* **confidential** (3), **critical** (2), **delicate** (2), **delicate** (3), **fine**[1] (2), **gentle** (1), **oversensitive, sensational.**

sensitiveness *noun.* The quality or condition of being emotionally and intuitively sensitive ▶ feeling, sensibility, sensitivity. [*Compare* **pity, sympathy.**] —*See also* **sensation** (1).

sensitivity *noun.* The quality or condition of being emotionally and intuitively sensitive ▶ feeling, sensibility, sensitiveness. [*Compare* **pity, sympathy.**] —*See also* **discernment, oversensitivity, sensation** (1), **subtlety, tact.**

sensory *or* **sensorial** *adjective.* —*See* **sensational.**

sensual *adjective.* **1.** Relating to, suggestive of, or appealing to sense gratification ▶ epicurean, sensuous, sensualistic, voluptuous. [*Compare* **sybaritic.**] **2.** Relating to the desires and appetites of the body, especially sexual desire ▶ animal, carnal, fleshly, fleshy, physical, sexual, sexy, voluptuous. **3.** Of or preoccupied with material rather than spiritual or intellectual things ▶ material, materialistic. [*Compare* **earthly, greedy, superficial.**] —*See also* **erotic, sensational.**

sensualism *noun.* The quality or condition of being sensuous ▶ sensuality, sensuousness, voluptuousness. —*See also* **eroticism.**

sensualist *noun.* —*See* **sybarite.**

sensualistic *adjective.* Relating to, suggestive of, or appealing to sense gratification ▶ epicurean, sensual, sensuous, voluptuous. [*Compare* **sybaritic.**]

sensuality *noun.* **1.** The quality or condition of being sensual or being preoccupied with bodily desires ▶ animalism, animality, carnality, eroticism, fleshliness, physicality, sexiness, sexuality, suggestiveness, voluptuousness. [*Compare* **desire.**] **2.** The quality or condition of being sensuous ▶ sensuousness, sensualism, voluptuousness. —*See also* **eroticism.**

sensuous *adjective.* Relating to, suggestive of, or appealing to sense gratification ▶ epicurean, sensual, sensualistic, voluptuous. [*Compare* **sybaritic.**] —*See also* **erotic, sensational.**

✚ **CORE SYNONYMS:** *sensuous, sensual, voluptuous.* These adjectives mean of, given to, or furnishing gratification of the senses. *Sensuous* usually applies to the senses involved in aesthetic enjoyment, as of art or music: "*The sensuous joy from all things fair/His strenuous bent of soul repressed*" (John Greenleaf Whittier). *Sensual* more often applies to the physical senses or appetites, particularly those associated with sexual pleasure: "*Of music Dr. Johnson used to say that it was the only sensual pleasure without vice*" (William Seward). *Voluptuous* principally implies abandoning oneself to pleasures, especially sensual pleasures: "*Lucullus . . . returned to Rome to lounge away the remainder of his days in voluptuous magnificence*" (J.A. Froude).

---

sensuousness *noun.* The quality or condition of being sensuous ▶ sensualism, sensuality, voluptuousness. *—See also* **eroticism.**

sentence *noun.* *—See* **ruling.**

sentence *verb.* *—See* **condemn, punish.**

sentenced *adjective.* *—See* **condemned.**

sententious *adjective.* *—See* **pithy.**

sentient *adjective.* *—See* **aware, sensitive** (1).

sentiment *noun.* A general cast of mind with regard to something ▶ attitude, feeling. [*Compare* **idea.**] *—See also* **belief** (1), **emotion, sentimentality.**

sentimental *adjective.* Affectedly or extravagantly emotional ▶ bathetic, bleeding-heart, corny, gushy, maudlin, mawkish, misty, misty-eyed, namby-pamby, romantic, romanticized, slushy, sobby, soft, soppy, syrupy, treacly. *Informal:* gooey, mushy, schmaltzy, sloppy, soft-boiled, soupy. *Slang:* drippy, hokey, sappy, tear-jerking.

✚ CORE SYNONYMS: *sentimental, bathetic, maudlin, mawkish, romantic, slushy, soppy.* These adjectives mean affectedly or extravagantly emotional: *a sentimental card; a bathetic novel; maudlin expressions of sympathy; mawkish sentiment; a romantic adolescent; slushy poetry; a soppy letter.*

sentimentality *or* **sentimentalism** *noun.* The quality or condition of being affectedly or overly emotional ▶ bathos, corniness, maudlinism, mawkishness, romanticism, sentiment, treacle. *Informal:* mush, mushiness, sloppiness, schmaltz, schmaltziness. *Slang:* hokiness, sappiness.

sentry *or* **sentinel** *noun.* *—See* **guard.**

separate *verb.* **1.** To end an association by or as if by leaving one another ▶ break off, break up, divorce, part. *Informal:* split (up). ***Idioms:*** call it quits, come to a parting of the ways, part company. **2.** To set apart one kind or type from others ▶ sift, sort, winnow. ***Idiom:*** separate the sheep from the goats. *—See also* **classify, detach, discharge, distinguish** (1), **divide, isolate** (1), **scatter** (2), **slip** (2).

separate *adjective.* *—See* **different, distinct, individual** (2), **lone.**

separately *adverb.* As a separate unit ▶ apart, discretely, independently, individually, singly. ***Idioms:*** one at a time, one by one. [*Compare* **alone.**]

separateness *noun.* *—See* **difference, individuality, seclusion.**

separation *noun.* *—See* **detachment** (1), **distinction** (1), **division** (1), **gap** (1), **isolation.**

separatist *or* **separationist** *noun.* A person who dissents from the doctrine of an established church ▶ dissenter, dissident, heretic, nonconformist, schismatic, sectarian, sectary. [*Compare* **rebel.**]

sepulcher *noun.* *—See* **grave**[1]**.**

sepulcher *verb.* *—See* **bury.**

sepulture *noun.* *—See* **burial, grave**[1]**.**

sequel *noun.* *—See* **effect** (1).

sequence *noun.* *—See* **arrangement** (1), **effect** (1), **series.**

sequent *adjective.* *—See* **consecutive.**

sequent *noun.* *—See* **effect** (1).

sequential *adjective.* *—See* **consecutive.**

sequester *or* **sequestrate** *verb.* To put into solitude ▶ cloister, isolate, seclude. [*Compare* **enclose, imprison.**] *—See also* **isolate** (1).

sequestration *noun.* *—See* **isolation, seclusion.**

sequin *noun.* A small sparkling decoration ▶ diamond, glitter, rhinestone, spangle.

sere *adjective.* *—See* **dry** (1).

serendipitous *adjective.* *—See* **accidental.**

serendipity *noun.* *—See* **chance** (2).

serene *adjective.* *—See* **calm, still.**

serenity *noun.* *—See* **calm, stillness.**

serf *noun.* *—See* **slave.**

serfdom *noun.* *—See* **slavery.**

serial *or* **seriate** *adjective.* —*See* **consecutive.**

series *noun.* A number of things placed or occurring one after the other ▶ chain, concatenation, consecution, course, gamut, order, procession, progression, range, round, run, scale, sequence, string, succession, suite, train. *Informal:* streak. [*Compare* **group, line.**]

✦ **CORE SYNONYMS:** *series, succession, progression, sequence, chain, train, string.* These nouns denote a number of things placed or occurring one after the other. *Series* refers to like, related, or identical things arranged or occurring in order: *a series of days; a series of facts.* In a *succession* the elements follow each other, generally in order of time and without interruption: *a succession of failures.* A *progression* reveals a definite pattern of advance: *a geometric progression.* In a *sequence* elements are ordered in a way that indicates a causal, temporal, numerical, or logical relationship or a recurrent pattern: *a natural sequence of ideas.* In a *chain* the elements are closely linked or connected: *the chain of command; a chain of proof. Train* can apply to a procession or to a sequence of ideas or events: *a train of mourners; my train of thought.* A *string* consists of similar or uniform elements likened to objects threaded on a long cord: *a string of islands; a string of questions.*

serious *adjective.* **1.** Characterized by careful thought and a lack of frivolity or exaggeration ▶ businesslike, dignified, earnest, grave, no-nonsense, sedate, sober, sobersided, solemn, somber, staid. ***Idiom:*** in earnest. [*Compare* **ceremonious, forbidding, frank, severe.**] **2.** Having or threatening severe negative consequences ▶ dire, grave, grievous, severe. [*Compare* **disastrous, fateful.**] —*See also* **difficult** (1), **grave²** (1).

✦ **CORE SYNONYMS:** *serious, sober, grave, solemn, earnest, sedate, staid.* These adjectives mean characterized by careful thought and a lack of frivolity or exaggeration. *Serious* implies a concern with responsibility and work as opposed to play: *serious students of music. Sober* emphasizes circumspection and self-restraint: *"My sober mind was no longer intoxicated by the fumes of politics"* (Edward Gibbon). *Grave* suggests the dignity and somberness associated with weighty matters: *"a quiet, grave man, busied in charts, exact in sums, master of the art of tactics"* (Walter Bagehot). *Solemn* often adds to *grave* the suggestion of impressiveness: *the judge's solemn tone as she handed down her decision. Earnest* implies sincerity and intensity of purpose: *disputants who showed an earnest desire to reach an equitable solution. Sedate* implies a composed, dignified manner: *"One of those calm, quiet, sedate natures, to whom the temptations of turbulent nerves or vehement passions are things utterly incomprehensible"* (Harriet Beecher Stowe). *Staid* emphasizes dignity and an often strait-laced observance of propriety: *"a grave and staid God-fearing man"* (Tennyson).

seriousness *noun.* **1.** The quality of being dignified and serious, as in manner or bearing ▶ dignity, earnestness, graveness, gravitas, gravity, sedateness, sobersidedness, sobriety, solemnness, solemnity, somberness, staidness. [*Compare* **ceremony, severity.**] **2.** The condition of being grave and of involving serious consequences ▶ graveness, gravity, heaviness, momentousness, weightiness. [*Compare* **severity.**]

sermon *noun.* —*See* **speech** (2).

sermonize *verb.* **1.** To deliver a sermon, especially as a vocation ▶ evangelize, preach. [*Compare* **address.**] **2.** To indulge in moral reflection, usually pompously ▶ edify, moralize, pontificate, preach. [*Compare* **chastise.**] **3.** To talk to an audience formally ▶ lecture, prelect, speak. [*Compare* **converse.**]

serpentine *adjective.* —*See* **winding.**

serrated *or* **serrate** *adjective.* —*See* **saw-toothed.**

servant *noun.* —*See* **slave.**

serve *verb.* **1.** To work and care for ▶ attend, do for, minister to, wait on (*or* upon). [*Compare* **help, tend², work.**] **2.** To place food before someone ▶ wait on (*or* upon). [*Compare* **give, distribute.**] **3.** To spend or complete time, as a prison term ▶ put in. *Informal:* do. —*See also* **oblige** (1), **profit** (2), **satisfy** (1).

service *noun.* The state of being employed ▶ employ, employment, hire. —*See also* **ceremony** (1), **duty** (2), **favor** (1).

service *verb.* —*See* **fix** (1).

serviceable *adjective.* —*See* **practical, usable.**

serviceman *or* **servicewoman** *noun.* —*See* **soldier** (2).

services *noun.* —*See* **amenities** (1).

servile *adjective.* Excessively eager to serve or obey ▶ bootlicking, cringing, fawning, grovelling, menial, obsequious, slavish, subservient, sycophantic, toadying. [*Compare* **humble, lowly, unctuous.**]

servility *or* **servileness** *noun.* —*See* **slavery.**

serving *noun.* An individual quantity of food ▶ bowlful, helping, mess, plateful, portion. [*Compare* **allotment.**]

servitude *noun.* —*See* **slavery.**

sesquipedalian *or* **sesquipedal** *adjective.* Having many syllables ▶ polysyllabic.

session *noun.* —*See* **convention, period** (1).

set¹ *verb.* **1.** To arrange tableware upon a table in preparation for a meal ▶ lay, spread. **2.** To set the time for an event or occasion ▶ plan, schedule, time. [*Compare* **arrange.**] **3.** To appoint and send to a particular place ▶ assign, post, station. [*Compare* **position.**] —*See also* **adjust, aim** (1), **coagulate, estimate** (2), **harden** (2), **limit, position, settle** (2).

set about *verb.* —*See* **start** (1).

set apart *verb.* —*See* **appropriate, distinguish** (2), **isolate** (1).

set aside *verb.* —*See* **abolish, appropriate, save** (1).

set back *verb.* —*See* **delay** (1).

set by *verb.* —*See* **save** (1).

set down *verb.* —*See* **land** (2), **list¹.**

set forth *verb.* —*See* **go** (1), **propose.**

set in *verb.* To manifest strong winds and precipitation ▶ blow (up), squall, storm. [*Compare* **rain.**]

set off *verb.* To endow with beauty and elegance ▶ beautify, embellish, enhance, grace. [*Compare* **adorn.**] —*See also* **balance** (2), **cancel** (2), **cause, go** (1), **provoke.**

set out *verb.* —*See* **arrange** (2), **bear** (5), **design** (2), **go** (1), **plant, start** (1).

set to *verb.* —*See* **start** (1).

set up *verb.* —*See* **erect, establish** (1), **found, treat** (2).

set *adjective.* In a state of preparedness ▶ prepared, ready. *Informal:* go. *Slang:* together. ***Idioms:*** all set, in working order, on deck, ready (*or* raring) to go. —*See also* **confirmed** (1), **decided, intent, special, unchanging.**

set² *noun.* —*See* **circle** (3), **class** (1), **group, scene** (2).

setback *noun.* A change from better to worse ▶ backset, reverse, reversal. [*Compare* **misfortune, relapse.**] —*See also* **accident.**

setoff *noun.* —*See* **compensation.**

setting *noun.* —*See* **conditions, scene** (1), **scene** (2).

settle *verb.* **1.** To put into correct or conclusive form ▶ arrange, conclude, dispose of, finalize, fix. [*Compare* **conclude.**] **2.** To bring something into a state of agreement or accord ▶ arrange, conclude, fix, negotiate, reconcile, rectify, resolve, set, settle upon, smooth over, straighten out. [*Compare* **compromise, decide, judge.**] **3.** To set right by giving what is due ▶ clear, discharge, liquidate, pay (off *or* up), satisfy, square. [*Compare* **satisfy.**] **4.** To move to a place and reside there ▶ locate, relocate. ***Idioms:*** fix one's residence, make one's home, put down roots, take up residence. [*Compare* **emigrate, live[1], move.**] —*See also* **decide, establish** (1), **land** (2), **pacify, sink** (1).

settled *adjective.* —*See* **confirmed** (1), **decided.**

settlement *noun.* A reestablishment of friendship or harmony ▶ conciliation, rapprochement, reconcilement, reconciliation. [*Compare* **agreement, atonement, compromise.**] —*See also* **compensation, compromise, possession, village.**

settler *noun.* One who settles in a new region ▶ colonial, colonist, colonizer, homesteader, pioneer.

setup *noun.* —*See* **arrangement** (1).

seventh heaven *noun.* —*See* **heaven.**

sever *verb.* —*See* **cut** (2).

several *adjective.* Consisting of a number more than two or three but less than many ▶ certain, divers, few, some, sundry, various. —*See also* **distinct.**

several *pronoun.* A number more than two or three but less than many ▶ few, handful, small number, some, smattering, sprinkling. [*Compare* **couple.**]

severance *noun.* —*See* **division** (1).

severe *adjective.* **1.** Rigorous and unsparing in treating others ▶ demanding, draconian, exacting, hard, harsh, rigid, rigorous, stern, strict, stringent, tough, uncompromising, unyielding. [*Compare* **cruel, firm[1], forbidding, stubborn.**] **2.** Conveying great physical force ▶ hard, heavy, hefty, powerful. [*Compare* **forceful, intense.**] **3.** Having or threatening severe negative consequences ▶ dire, grave, grievous, serious. [*Compare* **disastrous, fateful.**] —*See also* **bare** (1), **bitter** (2), **bleak** (1), **burdensome, grave[2]** (1).

severity *noun.* The fact or condition of being rigorous and unsparing ▶ austerity, hardness, harshness, rigidity, rigidness, rigor, rigorousness, sternness, strictness, stringency, toughness. [*Compare* **cruelty, seriousness, stubbornness.**] —*See also* **intensity.**

sewer *noun.* —*See* **pit[1].**

sexiness *noun.* —*See* **eroticism, sensuality** (1).

sexism *noun.* Discrimination based on gender ▶ discrimination, intolerance, prejudice. [*Compare* **hate.**]

sexist *adjective.* ▶ bigoted, discriminatory, prejudiced. [*Compare* **intolerant.**]

sexless *adjective.* —*See* **androgynous.**

sexlessness *noun.* The quality of being androgynous ▶ androgyny, epicenism, gender-neutrality. [*Compare* **effeminacy, masculinity.**]

sexual *adjective.* Employed in reproduction ▶ reproductive. —*See also* **erotic, sensual** (2).

sexuality *noun.* —*See* **eroticism, sensuality** (1).

sexy *adjective.* —*See* **desirable, erotic, lascivious, seductive, sensual** (2).

shabby *adjective.* Showing signs of wear and tear or neglect ▶ bedraggled, broken-down, decayed, decaying, decrepit, deteriorated, dilapidated, dingy, down-at-heel, faded, frayed, mangy, ragged, raggedy, ramshackle, ruinous, rundown, scrubby, scruffy, seedy, shoddy, sleazy, tatterdemalion, tattered, tatty, threadbare, tumbledown, worn, worn-out. *Informal:* tacky. *Slang:* ratty. ***Idioms:*** all the worse for wear, gone to pot (*or* seed), past cure (*or* hope). [*Compare* **miserable, shoddy, terrible.**] —*See also* **bad** (1), **offensive** (1).

shack *noun.* —*See* **hut.**

shackle *noun.* —*See* **bond** (1).

shackle *verb.* —*See* **hamper[1].**

shade *noun.* **1.** A slight variation between nearly identical entities ▶ gradation, hue, nicety, nuance, subtlety. **2.** A slight amount or indication ▶ breath, dash, ghost, hair, hint, intimation, semblance, shadow, soupçon, streak, suggestion, suspicion, taste, tinge, touch, trace, whiff, whisper. *Informal:* whisker. [*Compare* **bit**[1].] **3.** Comparative darkness that results from the blocking of light rays ▶ penumbra, shadiness, shadow, umbra. [*Compare* **dark, twilight.**] —*See also* **color** (1), **ghost.**

shade *verb.* **1.** To shelter, especially from light ▶ screen, shadow. **2.** To make dark or darker ▶ adumbrate, darken, gloom, overcast, overshadow, shadow. [*Compare* **obscure.**] **3.** To make a slight reduction in a price ▶ shave, trim. —*See also* **change** (1).

✦ **CORE SYNONYMS:** *shade, nuance, gradation.* These nouns denote a slight variation or differentiation between nearly identical entities: *subtle shades of meaning; sensitive to delicate nuances of style; gradations of feeling from infatuation to deep affection.*

---

shaded *adjective.* —*See* **shady** (2).

shadiness *noun.* Comparative darkness that results from the blocking of light rays ▶ penumbra, shade, shadow, umbra. [*Compare* **dark, twilight.**] —*See also* **dishonesty** (2).

shadow *noun.* **1.** Comparative darkness that results from the blocking of light rays ▶ penumbra, shade, shadiness, umbra. [*Compare* **dark, twilight.**] **2.** An agent assigned to observe and report on another ▶ watcher. *Informal:* tail. [*Compare* **detective.**] —*See also* **ghost, shade** (2).

shadow *verb.* To shelter, especially from light ▶ screen, shade. —*See also* **follow** (3), **obscure, shade** (2).

shadowy *adjective.* —*See* **dark** (1), **shady** (2), **unclear.**

shady *adjective.* **1.** Of doubtful honesty or character ▶ doubtful, dubious, equivocal, left-handed, questionable, suspect, suspicious, uncertain, untrustworthy. *Informal:* fishy. [*Compare* **dishonest, illegal, underhand.**] **2.** Full of or affording shade ▶ dappled, leafy, shaded, shadowy, umbrageous. [*Compare* **gloomy.**] —*See also* **dark** (1).

shaft *noun.* —*See* **beam** (1), **column, rod.**

shaggy *adjective.* —*See* **hairy.**

shake *verb.* **1.** To move to and fro in short, jerky movements ▶ quake, quaver, quiver, shiver, shudder, switch, tremble, twitter, vibrate. [*Compare* **bump.**] **2.** To cause to move to and fro with short, jerky movements ▶ jar, jiggle, joggle. [*Compare* **jerk.**] —*See also* **agitate** (1), **dismay, disturb, lose** (3), **rid, sway.**

shake down *verb. Slang* To examine a person or someone's personal effects in order to find something lost or concealed ▶ frisk, inspect, pat down, search. ***Idiom:*** do a body search of. —*See also* **extort.**

shake off *verb.* —*See* **lose** (3), **rid.**

shake up *verb.* —*See* **agitate** (2), **overhaul.**

shake *noun. Informal* A shaking of the earth ▶ earthquake, quake, seism, temblor, tremor, vibration. —*See also* **tremor** (2).

✦ **CORE SYNONYMS:** *shake, tremble, quake, quiver, shiver, shudder.* These verbs mean to move to and fro in short, jerky movements. *Shake* is the most general: *The floor shook when I walked heavily across the room. Tremble* implies quick, rather slight movement, as from excitement, weakness, or anger: *The speaker trembled as he denounced his opponents. Quake* refers to more violent movement, as that caused by shock or upheaval: *I was so scared that my legs began to quake. Quiver* suggests a slight, rapid, tremulous movement: "*Her lip quivered like that of a child about to cry*" (Booth Tarkington). *Shiver* involves rapid trembling, as of a person experiencing a chill: "*as I in hoary winter night stood shivering in the snow*" (Robert Southwell). *Shudder* applies chiefly to convulsive shaking caused by fear, horror, or revulsion: "*She starts like one that spies an adder/ . . . The fear whereof doth* *make him shake and shudder"* (William Shakespeare).

---

shakedown *noun. Slang* A thorough search of a place or persons ▶ frisk, search. —*See also* **test** (1).

shaken *adjective.* —*See* **anxious.**

shakes *noun.* —*See* **jitters.**

shakeup *noun.* A thorough or drastic reorganization ▶ overhaul, reengineering, reshuffling. *Informal:* housecleaning. [*Compare* **renewal, revolution.**]

shakiness *noun.* —*See* **instability.**

shaky *adjective.* —*See* **implausible, insecure** (2), **tremulous.**

shallow *adjective.* —*See* **superficial.**

sham *noun.* —*See* **act** (2), **counterfeit, fake, mockery** (2).

sham *adjective.* —*See* **counterfeit.**

sham *verb.* —*See* **act** (2).

shamble *verb.* —*See* **trudge.**

shambles *noun.* —*See* **disorder** (1), **mess** (1).

shame *noun.* A great disappointment or regrettable fact ▶ crime, pity. *Slang:* bummer. ***Idiom:*** a crying shame. —*See also* **disgrace, penitence.**

shame *verb.* To cause to feel embarrassment, dishonor, and often guilt ▶ brand, mortify, reproach, stigmatize. ***Idioms:*** put to shame, put to the blush. [*Compare* **belittle, denigrate, embarrass, humble.**] —*See also* **disgrace.**

shameful *adjective.* —*See* **deplorable, disgraceful.**

shamefulness *noun.* —*See* **infamy.**

shameless *adjective.* —*See* **impudent, unscrupulous.**

shamelessness *noun.* —*See* **impudence.**

shanty *noun.* —*See* **hut.**

shape *noun.* A state of sound readiness ▶ condition, fettle, fitness, form, kilter, order, repair, trim. —*See also* **constitution, form** (1).

shape *verb.* —*See* **adapt, form** (1), **make.**

shapeless *adjective.* Having no distinct shape ▶ amorphous, formless, inchoate, unformed, unshaped, unstructured.

✤ **CORE SYNONYMS:** *shapeless, amorphous, formless, unformed, unshaped.* These adjectives mean having no distinct shape: *a mass of shapeless slag; an amorphous cloud; an aggregate of formless particles; an unformed lump of clay; unshaped dough.*

---

shapely *adjective.* Having a full, voluptuous figure ▶ big-bosomed, bosomy, buxom, curvaceous, curvy, full-bosomed, full-figured, well-developed, well-endowed, zaftig. *Informal:* built. *Slang:* stacked.

shard *noun.* —*See* **bit**[1] (1), **end** (3).

share *noun.* One's duty or responsibility in a common effort ▶ function, part, piece, role. [*Compare* **function.**] —*See also* **allotment.**

share *verb.* To tell in confidence ▶ breathe, confide, unbosom, whisper. [*Compare* **communicate, reveal, say.**] —*See also* **contribute** (2), **distribute.**

shared *adjective.* —*See* **common** (2), **mutual.**

sharing *noun.* The act or fact of participating ▶ engagement, involvement, partaking, participation. —*See also* **distribution** (1).

sharp *adjective.* **1.** Having a fine edge, as for cutting ▶ honed, keen, keen-edged, knife-edged, razor-edged, razor-sharp, sharpened, whetted. **2.** Clearly defined; not ambiguous ▶ clear, distinct, unambiguous, unequivocal, unmistakable, well-defined. [*Compare* **apparent, definite.**] **3.** Marked by pain that is severe or intense ▶ acute, biting, gnawing, knifelike, piercing, shooting, stabbing, throbbing. [*Compare* **bitter, intense, severe.**] —*See also* **abrupt** (2), **artful, biting, clever** (1), **critical** (2), **fashionable, pointed, sour, spicy, steep**[1] (1).

✤ **CORE SYNONYMS:** *sharp, keen, acute.* These adjectives all apply literally to fine edges, points, or tips. Figuratively they indicate mental alertness and clarity of comprehension. *Sharp* suggests quickness and astuteness: *"a young man of sharp and active intellect"* (John Henry Newman). *Keen* implies clear-headedness and acuity: *a journalist with a keen mind and quick wits. Acute* suggests penetrating perception or discernment: *an acute observer of national politics.*

---

sharpen *verb.* To give a sharp edge to ▶ edge, file, grind, hone, strop, whet. ***Idioms:*** make sharp, put an edge on. *—See also* **intensify.**

sharper *noun. —See* **cheat** (2).

sharpness *noun. —See* **discernment, edge.**

sharp-tongued *adjective. —See* **abusive, biting.**

sharp-witted *adjective. —See* **clever** (1).

shatter *verb. —See* **break** (1), **break** (2), **destroy** (1).

shave *verb.* To make a slight reduction in a price ▶ shade, trim. *—See also* **brush[1], cut** (3).

shaving *noun. —See* **flake.**

shawl *noun. —See* **wrap.**

shawl *verb. —See* **clothe.**

shear *verb. —See* **cut** (3).

shears *noun.* An implement used for cutting or pruning ▶ clippers, cutters, loppers, nippers, pruner, scissors, snips, snippers.

sheath *or* **sheathing** *noun. —See* **skin** (2).

sheathe *verb. —See* **face** (2).

shed[1] *verb.* **1.** To send out heat, light, or energy ▶ cast (out), emit, irradiate, project, radiate, send forth, send out, throw (out). [*Compare* **beam, emit.**] **2.** To cast off by a natural process ▶ exuviate, molt, slough, throw off. *—See also* **discard, flake.**

shed[2] *noun. —See* **hut.**

sheen *noun. —See* **gloss[1].**

sheer[1] *verb. —See* **swerve.**

sheer[2] *adjective.* Thin, fine, and light ▶ airy, diaphanous, ethereal, filmy, gauzy, gossamer, gossamery, transparent, vaporous, vapory. *—See also* **pure, steep[1]** (1), **utter[2].**

✚ **CORE SYNONYMS:** *sheer, airy, diaphanous, ethereal, filmy, gauzy, gossamer, transparent, vaporous.* These adjectives mean so thin, fine, and light as to suggest air or a thin film: *sheer silk stockings; airy curtains blowing at the window; a diaphanous veil; ethereal mist; the filmy wings of a moth; gauzy clouds in the sky; a gown of gossamer fabric; transparent chiffon; vaporous shadows at dusk.*

---

sheet *noun.* A document used in applying, as for a job ▶ application, form, paper. *—See also* **coat** (2), **skin** (2).

sheik *noun. —See* **chief.**

shell *noun. —See* **frame, skin** (3).

shell *verb. —See* **barrage, skin.**

shell out *verb. —See* **spend** (1).

shellac *verb. —See* **finish** (2), **overwhelm** (1).

shellac *noun. —See* **finish.**

shellacking *noun. —See* **defeat.**

shelter *noun.* Dwellings in general ▶ housing, lodging. ***Idiom:*** a roof over one's head. [*Compare* **home, hut.**] *—See also* **cover** (1), **home** (3), **refuge** (1).

shelter *verb.* To give refuge to ▶ harbor, haven, house, take in. [*Compare* **defend.**]

shelve *verb. —See* **defer[1].**

shenanigan *noun. —See* **prank[1], trick** (1).

shenanigans *noun. —See* **mischief.**

shepherd *noun. —See* **guide.**

shepherd *verb. —See* **guide.**

sheriff *noun. —See* **police officer.**

sherlock *noun. —See* **detective.**

shield *noun. —See* **defense.**

shield *verb. —See* **defend** (1).

shift *verb.* **1.** To move or cause to move slightly ▶ budge, move, stir. **2.** To take turns ▶ alternate, interchange, rotate.

—*See also* **change** (3), **disturb, move** (2), **turn** (2).

shift *noun.* **1.** Occurrence in successive turns ▶ alternation, interchange, shift. **2.** An often sudden change or departure, as in a trend ▶ tack, turn, twist. [*Compare* **deviation.**] —*See also* **change** (1), **change** (2), **conversion** (1), **displacement, dress** (3), **makeshift, transition, turn** (1).

shiftiness *noun.* —*See* **deceit, dishonesty** (2).

shiftless *adjective.* —*See* **lazy.**

shiftlessness *noun.* —*See* **laziness.**

shifty *adjective.* —*See* **capricious, underhand.**

shill *noun.* —*See* **cheat** (2).

shilly-shally *verb.* —*See* **hesitate.**

shilly-shally *adjective.* —*See* **hesitant.**

shilly-shally *noun.* —*See* **hesitation.**

shimmer *verb.* —*See* **glitter.**

shimmer *noun.* —*See* **glitter** (1).

shin *verb.* —*See* **run** (1).

shindig *or* **shindy** *noun.* —*See* **blast** (3).

shine *verb.* To be in one's prime ▶ flourish, flower. ***Idioms:*** cut a figure, have one's day in the sun, make a splash. —*See also* **beam, gloss**[1].

shine *noun.* —*See* **gloss**[1].

shiner *noun. Slang* A bruise surrounding the eye ▶ black eye. *Informal:* mouse. [*Compare* **bruise.**]

shining *adjective.* —*See* **bright, glorious, glossy.**

shiny *adjective.* —*See* **bright, glossy.**

ship *noun.* A conveyance that travels over water ▶ bark, barque, boat, craft, vessel, watercraft.

ship *verb.* —*See* **send** (1).

shipment *noun.* —*See* **delivery.**

shipping *noun.* —*See* **transportation.**

shipshape *adjective.* —*See* **neat.**

shipwreck *verb.* To damage, disable, or destroy a seacraft ▶ run aground, sink, wreck. [*Compare* **sink.**]

shirk *verb.* —*See* **cut** (4), **idle** (1), **neglect** (2).

shirker *noun.* —*See* **wastrel** (2).

shirking *noun.* —*See* **failure** (2).

shiver[1] *verb.* —*See* **shake** (1).

shiver *noun.* —*See* **tremor** (2).

shiver[2] *verb.* —*See* **break** (1).

shivering *adjective.* —*See* **tremulous.**

shivers *noun.* —*See* **jitters.**

shivery *adjective.* —*See* **cold** (1), **tremulous.**

shock[1] *noun.* Something that stuns or jars the mind ▶ blow, bombshell, jolt, rude awakening, surprise, trauma, wake-up call. ***Idiom:*** bolt from the blue. —*See also* **collision.**

shock *verb.* —*See* **dismay, stagger** (2), **startle.**

shock[2] *noun.* —*See* **heap** (1).

shocking *adjective.* —*See* **outrageous, terrible.**

shoddy *adjective.* Of decidedly inferior quality ▶ base, cheap, junky, lousy, miserable, paltry, poor, rotten, sleazy, sorry, trashy, worthless. *Informal:* cheesy. *Slang:* crappy, crummy, schlocky, stinko. [*Compare* **bad, rude, terrible.**] —*See also* **shabby.**

shoo-in *noun. Informal* A leading contestant or sure winner ▶ favorite, front-runner, leader, number one, vanguard.

shoot *verb.* **1.** To wound or kill with a firearm ▶ gun (down), pick off. *Slang:* plug. ***Idioms:*** fill full of lead (*or* holes). [*Compare* **kill**[1], **murder.**] **2.** To discharge a gun or firearm ▶ blast (away), fire (away *or* off), pop (off), shoot away, shoot off. ***Idioms:*** go bang-bang, open fire, take a shot (*or* potshot). **3.** To launch with great force ▶ fire, hurtle, loose, project, propel. ***Idiom:*** let fly. —*See also* **fly** (2), **rush, throw.**

shoot down *verb.* —*See* **discredit.**

shoot for *or* **at** *verb.* —*See* **attempt.**

shoot up *verb.* —*See* **soar.**

shoot *noun.* A young stemlike growth arising from a plant ▶ bine, offshoot, runner, sprig, sprout, sucker, tendril. —*See also* **pain.**

shooting *adjective.* —*See* **sharp** (3).

shop *noun.* A retail establishment where merchandise is sold ▶ boutique, emporium, outlet, store.

shopper *noun.* —*See* **consumer.**

shopworn *adjective.* —*See* **trite.**

shore *noun.* —*See* **support.**

shore *verb.* —*See* **support** (2).

short *adjective.* —*See* **abrupt** (1), **brief, insufficient, little, quick, transitory.**

short *adverb.* Without adequate preparation ▶ aback, unawarely, unawares. *Idioms:* by surprise, off guard.

shortage *noun.* The condition or fact of being deficient ▶ defect, deficit, deficiency, inadequacy, insufficiency, lack, paucity, poverty, scantiness, scantness, scant supply, scarceness, scarcity, shortcoming, shortfall, underage. [*Compare* **absence, need.**]

shortchange *verb.* —*See* **cheat** (1).

shortcoming *noun.* —*See* **defect, disadvantage, shortage, weakness.**

shorten *verb.* To make short or shorter ▶ abbreviate, abridge, boil down, condense, curtail, reduce, shrink, truncate. [*Compare* **constrict, cut, decrease.**]

✚ CORE SYNONYMS: *shorten, abbreviate, abridge, curtail, truncate.* These verbs mean to make short or shorter: *vices that will shorten your life; abbreviated the speech; abridging the citizens' rights; curtailed their visit; truncated the conversation.*

◀ ANTONYM: *lengthen*

---

shortfall *noun.* —*See* **shortage.**

short fuse *noun.* —*See* **temper** (1).

short-handed *adjective.* Having fewer workers or participants than are needed ▶ short-staffed, undermanned, understaffed.

short-lived *adjective.* —*See* **transitory.**

short-range *adjective.* Designed or implemented so as to gain a temporary limited advantage ▶ tactical. —*See also* **temporary** (2).

short-spoken *adjective.* —*See* **abrupt** (1).

short-staffed *adjective.* Having fewer workers or participants than are needed ▶ short-handed, undermanned, understaffed.

short-tempered *adjective.* —*See* **ill-tempered, testy.**

short-term *adjective.* —*See* **temporary** (2).

shorty *noun.* —*See* **squirt** (2).

shot *noun. Informal* A brief trial ▶ crack, go, stab, try. *Informal:* fling, whack, whirl. —*See also* **attempt, drop** (4), **opportunity.**

should *verb.* —*See* **must.**

shoulder *verb.* —*See* **assume, bear** (1), **muscle, push** (1).

shout *verb.* To speak or say in a loud cry ▶ bawl, bellow, blare, bluster, call (out), clamor, cry (out), halloo, holler, howl, roar, scream, screech, shriek, squawk, vociferate, wail, whoop, yell. [*Compare* **exclaim, howl, yelp.**]

shout *noun.* A loud call or cry ▶ bellow, call, cry, ejaculation, exclamation, halloo, holler, howl, outcry, roar, scream, screech, shriek, squawk, wail, whoop, yell. [*Compare* **vociferation, yelp.**]

✚ CORE SYNONYMS: *shout, bawl, bellow, holler, howl, roar, whoop, yell.* These verbs mean to speak or say in a loud, strong cry: *fans shouting their approval; bawled out orders; bellows with rage; hollered a warning; howling with pain; a crowd roaring its disapproval; children whooping at play; troops yelling as they attacked.*

---

shove *verb.* —*See* **drive** (2), **muscle, push** (1).

shove off *verb.* —*See* **go** (1).

shove *noun.* —*See* **push.**

shovel *verb.* —*See* **dig.**

show *verb.* **1.** To make manifest or apparent ▶ demonstrate, display, evidence, evince, exhibit, manifest, proclaim, reveal. [*Compare* **clarify, explain.**] **2.** To give a precise indication of, as on a register or scale ▶ indicate, mark, read, record, register. **3.** To be performed ▶ play, run. —*See also* **ap-**

pear (1), **display, guide, prove, represent** (2), **reveal.**

show off *verb.* To behave in an ostentatious manner or perform dangerous stunts ▶ *Slang:* hot-dog, showboat. [*Compare* **boast, swagger.**] —*See also* **display.**

show up *verb.* —*See* **arrive** (1).

show *noun.* —*See* **act** (2), **array, display, exhibition, façade** (2).

showboat *noun.* A person who behaves in an ostentatious manner or performs dangerous stunts ▶ *Slang:* hotdog, showoff. [*Compare* **braggart.**]

showboat *verb.* To behave in an ostentatious manner or perform dangerous stunts ▶ *Slang:* hot-dog, show off. [*Compare* **boast, swagger.**]

showcase *verb.* —*See* **display.**

showdown *noun.* —*See* **confrontation.**

shower *noun.* —*See* **barrage, rain.**

shower *verb.* To give in great abundance ▶ heap, lavish, rain. [*Compare* **confer, donate, give.**] —*See also* **barrage, rain** (2).

showiness *noun.* —*See* **glitter** (2).

showoff *noun.* A person who behaves in an ostentatious manner or performs dangerous stunts ▶ *Slang:* hotdog, showboat. [*Compare* **braggart.**]

showy *adjective.* Marked by outward, often extravagant display ▶ flamboyant, ostentatious, pretentious, splashy, splurgy. [*Compare* **gaudy, ornate.**]

✢ CORE SYNONYMS: *showy, flamboyant, ostentatious, pretentious, splashy.* These adjectives mean marked by outward, often extravagant display: *a showy rhinestone bracelet; an entertainer's flamboyant personality; an ostentatious sable coat; a pretentious scholarly edition; a splashy advertising campaign.*

---

shred *noun.* —*See* **bit**[1] (1).

shred *verb.* To pull or cut into many pieces ▶ cut up, grate, rip up, slice up, tear up.

shreds *noun.* Torn and ragged clothing ▶ rags, tatters.

shrew *noun.* —*See* **scold.**

shrewd *adjective.* Having or showing a clever awareness and resourcefulness in practical matters ▶ astute, cagey, canny, knowing, perspicacious, sagacious, slick, smart, street-smart, wise. *Informal:* savvy. [*Compare* **sophisticated.**] —*See also* **artful, clever** (1).

✢ CORE SYNONYMS: *shrewd, sagacious, astute, perspicacious.* These adjectives mean having or showing a clever awareness, sound judgment, and resourcefulness, especially in practical matters. *Shrewd* suggests a sharp intelligence, hardheadness, and often an intuitive grasp of practical considerations: *"He was too shrewd to go along with them upon a road which could lead only to their overthrow"* (J.A. Froude). *Sagacious* connotes prudence, discernment, and farsightedness: *"He was observant and thoughtful, and given to asking sagacious questions"* (John Galt). *Astute* suggests shrewdness, especially with regard to one's own interests: *An astute tenant always reads the small print in a lease. Perspicacious* implies penetration and clear-sightedness: *She is much too perspicacious to be taken in by such a spurious argument.*

---

shrewdness *noun.* —*See* **art, discernment.**

shriek *noun.* A long, loud, piercing cry, as of fright ▶ screak, scream, screech. [*Compare* **howl.**] —*See also* **shout.**

shriek *verb.* To utter a long, loud, piercing cry, as in fright ▶ screak, scream, screech, shrill. [*Compare* **howl.**] —*See also* **shout.**

shrieky *adjective.* —*See* **high** (3).

shrill *adjective.* —*See* **harsh, high** (3), **loud.**

shrill *verb.* To utter a long, loud, piercing cry, as of fright ▶ screak, scream, screech, shriek. [*Compare* **howl.**]

shrilly *adjective.* —*See* **high** (3).

shrimp *noun.* —*See* **nonentity, squirt** (2).

shrine *noun.* A sacred or holy place ▶ sacrarium, sanctorium, sanctuary, sanctum.

shrink *verb.* —*See* **constrict** (1), **decrease, flinch, shorten.**

shrink *noun.* —*See* **recoil.**

shrinkage *noun.* —*See* **constriction, decrease, depreciation.**

shrivel *verb.* —*See* **blast** (2), **dry** (1), **languish.**

shroud *verb.* —*See* **block, conceal, wrap** (2).

shroud *noun.* A cloth or garment in which a corpse is buried ▶ cerecloth, cerement, cerements, grave clothes, winding sheet. —*See also* **veil.**

shrubbery *noun.* —*See* **brush**[2].

shrunken *adjective.* —*See* **haggard.**

shuck *verb.* —*See* **discard, skin.**

shudder *verb.* —*See* **shake** (1).

shudder *noun.* —*See* **tremor** (2).

shuddering *adjective.* —*See* **tremulous.**

shuffle *verb.* To mix together so as to change the order of arrangement ▶ jumble, rearrange, reconfigure, reorder, riffle, scramble. *Informal:* rejigger. —*See also* **equivocate** (1), **equivocate** (2), **muddle, trudge.**

shuffle *noun.* —*See* **equivocation.**

shun *verb.* —*See* **avoid, snub.**

shunt *verb.* —*See* **turn** (2).

shush *verb.* —*See* **silence.**

shut *verb.* To move a door, for example, in order to cover an opening ▶ close, clench, seal, slam.

shut away *or* **in** *or* **up** *verb.* —*See* **enclose** (1), **imprison.**

shut off *or* **out** *verb.* —*See* **block.**

shut out *verb.* —*See* **dismiss** (3), **exclude.**

shut up *verb.* To enclose so as to hinder or prohibit escape ▶ closet, confine, imprison. —*See also* **silence.**

shutdown *noun.* —*See* **end** (1).

shuteye *noun.* The natural recurring condition of suspended consciousness by which the body rests ▶ dreamland, slumber. *Slang:* z's. ***Idioms:*** land of Nod, the arms of Morpheus. [*Compare* **nap, rest.**]

shy[1] *adjective.* Awkward or unconfident in the presence of others ▶ backward, bashful, coy, demure, diffident, introverted, modest, nonassertive, retiring, self-effacing, timid, unassuming. [*Compare* **cool, reserved, taciturn.**] —*See also* **insufficient.**

shy *verb.* —*See* **flinch.**

✚ **CORE SYNONYMS:** *shy, bashful, diffident, modest, coy, demure.* These adjectives mean awkward, reticent, or unconfident in the presence of others. One who is *shy* draws back from others, either because of a withdrawn nature or out of timidity: "*The poor man was shy and hated society*" (George Bernard Shaw). *Bashful* generally suggests self-consciousness or awkwardness in the presence of others: "*I never laughed, being bashful./Lowering my head, I looked at the wall*" (Ezra Pound). *Diffident* implies lack of self-confidence: *He was too diffident to express his opinion. Modest* is associated with an unassertive nature and absence of vanity or pretension: *Despite her fame she remained a modest, unassuming person. Coy* usually implies feigned, often flirtatious shyness: "*yielded with coy submission*" (John Milton). *Demure* often denotes an affected shyness or modesty: *Her assistant nodded in agreement, flashing a demure smile.*

---

shy[2] *verb.* —*See* **throw.**

shy *noun.* —*See* **throw.**

shyness *noun.* An awkwardness or lack of self-confidence in the presence of others ▶ backwardness, bashfulness, coyness, demureness, diffidence, modesty, retiringness, self-effacement, timidity, timidness. [*Compare* **reserve.**]

sibilant *noun.* —*See* **hiss** (1).

sibilate *verb.* —*See* **hiss** (1).

sibyl *noun.* —*See* **prophet.**

sibylline *adjective.* —*See* **prophetic.**

sick *adjective.* **1.** Suffering from or appearing to suffer from an illness ▶ ailing, anemic, down, ill, indisposed, low, nauseated, nauseous, off-color, peaked, queasy, sickly, unhealthy, unwell. *Informal:* laid up. *Chiefly Regional:* poorly. ***Idioms:*** green around the gills, under the weather. [*Compare* **feverish, infirm, pale, weak.**] **2.** Out of patience ▶ disgusted, fed up, tired, weary. ***Idiom:*** sick and tired. [*Compare* **angry.**] —*See also* **insane, morbid.**

sicken *verb.* —*See* **contract** (2), **disgust.**

sickening *adjective.* Producing dizziness or vertigo ▶ dizzy, dizzying, giddy, vertiginous. [*Compare* **steep.**] —*See also* **offensive** (1), **unpalatable.**

sickle *verb.* —*See* **cut** (3).

sickly *adjective.* —*See* **pale** (2), **sick** (1).

sickness *noun.* The condition of being sick ▶ affliction, ailment, bug, complaint, failing health, ill health, illness, indisposition, infirmity, malady, malaise, poor health, unhealthiness. [*Compare* **distress.**] —*See also* **disease.**

side *noun.* **1.** An outer surface, layer, or part of an object ▶ face, facet, surface. [*Compare* **back, bottom, front.**] **2.** One of two or more contrasted parts or places identified by its location with respect to a center ▶ flank, hand. —*See also* **force** (3), **viewpoint.**

side *verb.* —*See* **face** (2).

side with *verb.* —*See* **support** (1).

sidekick *noun.* —*See* **associate** (2), **friend.**

sidesplitting *adjective.* —*See* **funny** (1).

sidestep *verb.* —*See* **evade** (1).

sideswipe *verb.* —*See* **crash.**

sideswipe *noun.* —*See* **crash** (2).

sidle *verb.* To advance carefully and gradually ▶ ease, edge. [*Compare* **crawl, sneak.**]

siege *noun.* A prolonged encirclement of an objective by hostile troops ▶ beleaguerment, besiegement, blockade, investment. [*Compare* **attack.**]

siege *verb.* —*See* **besiege.**

siesta *noun.* —*See* **nap.**

sift *verb.* To set apart one kind or type from others ▶ separate, sort, winnow. ***Idiom:*** separate the sheep from the goats.

sigh *verb.* To make a low, continuous, and indistinct sound ▶ murmur, rustle, sough, whisper. [*Compare* **burble, hum.**]

sigh *noun.* —*See* **murmur.**

sight *noun.* An act of directing the eyes on an object ▶ contemplation, look, regard, view. [*Compare* **gaze, watch.**] —*See also* **mess** (2), **view** (2), **vision** (1).

sightless *adjective.* —*See* **blind** (1).

sightlessness *noun.* The condition of not being able to see ▶ blindness, darkness, legal blindness, visual impairment.

sightly *adjective.* —*See* **beautiful.**

sightseer *noun.* —*See* **tourist.**

sign *noun.* **1.** Something visible or evident that gives grounds for believing in the existence or presence of something else ▶ badge, emblem, evidence, index, indication, indicator, mark, manifestation, note, signification, stamp, symbol, symptom, token, witness. [*Compare* **hint, symbol, trace, track.**] **2.** A usually public posting that conveys a message ▶ bill, billboard, notice, placard, poster. —*See also* **character** (7), **expression** (2), **gesture, omen.**

sign *verb.* To affix one's signature to ▶ autograph, endorse, inscribe, subscribe, undersign. ***Idioms:*** put one's John Hancock on, set one's hand to. —*See also* **employ** (1), **gesture.**

sign off *verb.* —*See* **pass** (6).

sign on *verb.* —*See* **join** (1).

sign over *verb.* —*See* **transfer** (1).

sign up *verb.* —*See* **join** (1).

✚ **CORE SYNONYMS:** *sign, symbol, emblem, badge, mark, token, symptom, note.* These nouns denote something visible or evident that gives grounds for believing in the existence or presence of something else. *Sign* is the most general: "*The exile of Gaveston was the sign of the barons' triumph*" (John R. Green). *Sym-*

bol and *emblem* often refer to something associated with and standing for, representing, or identifying something else: *"There was One whose suffering changed an instrument of torture, degradation and shame, into a symbol of glory, honor, and immortal life"* (Harriet Beecher Stowe); *"a bed of sweet-scented lillies, the emblem of France"* (Amy Steedman). *Badge* usually refers to something that is worn as an insignia of membership, is an emblem of achievement, or is a characteristic sign: *a sheriff's badge. "Sweet mercy is nobility's true badge"* (William Shakespeare). *Mark* can refer to a visible trace or impression (*a laundry mark*) or to an indication of a distinctive trait or characteristic: *Intolerance is the mark of a bigot. Token* usually refers to evidence or proof of something intangible: *sent flowers as a token of her affection. Symptom* suggests outward evidence of a process or condition, especially an adverse condition: *bad weather that showed no symptoms of improving anytime soon. Note* applies to the sign of a particular quality or feature: *"the eternal note of sadness"* (Matthew Arnold).

---

signal *noun.* —*See* **gesture.**

signal *adjective.* —*See* **noticeable.**

signal *verb.* —*See* **designate, gesture.**

signalize *verb.* —*See* **distinguish** (2), **distinguish** (3), **gesture.**

significance *or* **significancy** *noun.* —*See* **importance, meaning.**

significant *adjective.* —*See* **big, designative, expressive, important, pregnant** (2).

significantly *adverb.* —*See* **considerably.**

signification *noun.* —*See* **meaning, reference** (1), **sign** (1).

signifier *noun.* An object or expression associated with and serving to identify something else ▶ attribute, emblem, metaphor, symbol, token. [*Compare* **expression, sign, term.**]

signify *verb.* —*See* **count** (1), **designate, mean**[1]**.**

silence *noun.* **1.** The absence of sound or noise ▶ hush, noiselessness, quiet, quietness, soundlessness, still, stillness. [*Compare* **calm, stillness.**] **2.** The avoidance of speech ▶ dumbness, muteness, speechlessness, wordlessness. [*Compare* **reserve.**]

silence *verb.* To cause to become silent ▶ hush, quiet, quieten, shush, shut up, still. [*Compare* **repress, suppress.**] —*See also* **censor** (2).

silent *adjective.* **1.** Marked by, done with, or making no sound or noise ▶ hushed, inaudible, noiseless, quiet, soundless, still. **2.** Not voiced or expressed ▶ tacit, undeclared, unexpressed, unsaid, unspoken, unuttered, unvoiced, wordless. [*Compare* **implicit, ulterior.**] —*See also* **mute, speechless, taciturn.**

✣ **CORE SYNONYMS:** *silent, still, quiet, noiseless, soundless.* These adjectives mean marked by, done with, or making no sound or noise. *Silent* can suggest a profound hush: *"I like the silent church before the service begins"* (Ralph Waldo Emerson). *Still* implies lack of motion or disturbance and often connotes rest or tranquillity: *"But after tempest . . . /There came a day as still as heaven"* (Tennyson). *Quiet* suggests the absence of bustle, tumult, or agitation: *"life being very short, and the quiet hours of it few"* (John Ruskin). *Noiseless* and *soundless* imply the absence of disturbing sound: *"th' inaudible and noiseless foot of time"* (William Shakespeare); *"the soundless footsteps on the grass"* (John Galsworthy).

---

silhouette *noun.* —*See* **form** (1).

silky *or* **silken** *adjective.* Smooth and lustrous as if polished ▶ satiny, sleek. [*Compare* **even, glossy, slick.**]

silliness *noun.* —*See* **foolishness, nonsense.**

silly *adjective.* —*See* **foolish, giddy** (2).

silver-tongued *adjective.* —*See* **eloquent.**

similar *adjective.* —*See* **like²**.

similarity *noun.* —*See* **likeness** (1).

similarly *adjective.* In a similar manner ▶ likewise, so. ***Idioms:*** by the same token, in like fashion, in like manner, in the same way.

similitude *noun.* —*See* **likeness** (1).

simmer *verb.* —*See* **boil, cook.**

simmer down *verb.* —*See* **compose** (4).

simper *verb.* —*See* **smile.**

simper *noun.* A facial expression marked by an upward curving of the lips ▶ grin, smile, smirk. [*Compare* **sneer.**]

simple *adjective.* Of little distinction ▶ humble, lowly, mean. [*Compare* **modest.**] —*See also* **artless, backward** (1), **bare** (1), **easy** (1), **gullible, modest** (1), **pure, rustic.**

simple *noun.* —*See* **fool.**

simple-minded *adjective.* —*See* **backward** (1).

simpleness *noun.* —*See* **artlessness, modesty** (2).

simpleton *noun.* —*See* **dullard, fool.**

simplex *noun.* —*See* **theme** (1).

simplicity *noun.* —*See* **artlessness, clarity, modesty** (2), **stupidity.**

simplify *verb.* To reduce in complexity or scope ▶ boil down, pare (down), streamline. ***Idioms:*** reduce to the basics (*or* essentials *or* bare bones). [*Compare* **explain.**] —*See also* **clarify** (1).

simply *adverb.* Nothing more than ▶ but, just, merely, only. [*Compare* **barely, solely.**]

simulacrum *noun.* —*See* **copy** (1).

simulate *verb.* —*See* **act** (2), **copy, imitate.**

simulated *adjective.* —*See* **artificial** (1).

simulation *noun.* —*See* **act** (2), **affectation, copy** (2).

simultaneous *adjective.* —*See* **concurrent.**

simultaneously *adverb.* At the same time ▶ concurrently, synchronously, together. ***Idioms:*** all at once, all together.

sin *noun.* —*See* **crime** (2), **evil** (1).

sin *verb.* —*See* **offend** (3).

since *conjunction.* —*See* **because.**

sincere *adjective.* —*See* **genuine.**

sincerity *noun.* —*See* **honesty.**

sine qua non *noun.* —*See* **condition** (2), **essence.**

sinew *noun.* —*See* **strength.**

sinewy *adjective.* Containing or consisting of fibers ▶ fibrous, stringy, threadlike. —*See also* **muscular.**

sinful *adjective.* —*See* **evil.**

sing *verb.* To utter words or sounds in musical tones ▶ carol, chant, croon, intone, trill, vocalize, warble. *Slang:* belt (out). —*See also* **inform** (2).

singe *verb.* —*See* **burn** (1).

singe *noun.* —*See* **burn.**

singer *noun.* —*See* **vocalist.**

single *adjective.* Not married or involved in a committed relationship ▶ available, eligible, fancy-free, footloose, lone, marriageable, nubile, sole, spouseless, unattached, unmarried, unwed. ***Idioms:*** footloose and fancy-free, in the market. —*See also* **exclusive** (1), **individual** (2), **lone, solitary.**

single *verb.* —*See* **choose** (1).

single out *verb.* —*See* **distinguish** (1), **distinguish** (2), **name** (2).

single-handedly *adverb.* —*See* **alone.**

single-minded *adjective.* —*See* **firm¹** (3), **intent.**

singleness *noun.* The condition of being one ▶ oneness, singularity, unity. [*Compare* **completeness.**] —*See also* **solitude, uniqueness.**

singly *adverb.* —*See* **alone, separately.**

singular *adjective.* —*See* **eccentric, exceptional, individual** (2), **lone, unique.**

singularity *noun.* The condition of being one ▶ oneness, singleness, unity. [*Compare* **completeness.**] —*See also* **detail, eccentricity, identity** (1), **individuality, uniqueness.**

singularize *verb.* —*See* **distinguish** (2).
singularly *adverb.* —*See* **unusually.**
sinister *adjective.* —*See* **fateful** (1).
sink *verb.* **1.** To go beneath the surface or to the bottom of a liquid ▶ founder, go down, go under, gravitate, settle, submerge, submerse, subside. **2.** To undergo moral deterioration ▶ degenerate, fall, slip. [*Compare* **deteriorate.**] **3.** To damage, disable, or destroy a seacraft ▶ run aground, shipwreck, wreck. —*See also* **condescend** (1), **destroy** (1), **deteriorate, drop** (1), **drop** (2), **fade, fall** (1), **fall** (4), **lower**[2], **plunge.**
sink in *verb.* To come as a realization ▶ dawn on (*or* upon), register, soak in. [*Compare* **discover, strike, understand.**]
sink *noun.* —*See* **depression** (1), **pit**[1].
sinkhole *noun.* —*See* **depression** (1).
sinless *adjective.* —*See* **innocent** (1).
sinner *noun.* —*See* **evildoer.**
sinuate *verb.* —*See* **crawl** (1).
sinuous *adjective.* —*See* **winding.**
sip *verb.* —*See* **drink** (1).
sip *noun.* —*See* **drink** (2), **drop** (4).
sire *noun.* —*See* **father.**
sire *verb.* To be the biological father of ▶ beget, father, get. —*See also* **breed.**
siren *noun.* —*See* **seductress.**
siren *adjective.* —*See* **seductive.**
sis *noun.* —*See* **girl.**
sissified *adjective.* —*See* **effeminate.**
sissy *adjective.* —*See* **cowardly.**
sissy *noun.* —*See* **coward.**
sissyish *adjective.* —*See* **effeminate.**
sister *noun.* —*See* **friend, girl.**
sisterhood *noun.* —*See* **company** (3).
sit *verb.* **1.** To assume a position resting on the buttocks with the torso upright ▶ be seated, seat oneself, sit down. *Informal:* park oneself. ***Idioms:*** take a load off (one's feet), take a seat. [*Compare* **squat.**] **2.** To be in a certain position; have a location ▶ be located, be situated, rest, stand. —*See also* **pose** (1).
sit back *verb.* —*See* **rest**[1] (1).
sit on *or* **upon** *verb.* —*See* **repress.**
sit out *verb.* —*See* **refrain.**
sit through *verb.* —*See* **endure** (1).
site *noun.* —*See* **position** (1), **scene** (1).
site *verb.* —*See* **position.**
situate *verb.* —*See* **position.**
situation *noun.* —*See* **bearing** (3), **condition** (1), **place** (1), **position** (1), **position** (3).
sixth sense *noun.* —*See* **instinct.**
sizable *adjective.* —*See* **big.**
sizableness *noun.* —*See* **size** (2).
sizably *adverb.* —*See* **considerably.**
size *noun.* **1.** The amount of space occupied by something ▶ area, dimensions, extent, magnitude, measure, measurements, proportions, volume. [*Compare* **range.**] **2.** The quality or state of being large in amount, extent, or importance ▶ amplitude, bigness, greatness, largeness, magnitude, sizableness, voluminousness. [*Compare* **enormousness, heaviness.**] —*See also* **bulk** (1).
size *verb.* —*See* **classify.**
size up *verb.* —*See* **estimate** (1).
sizzle *verb.* —*See* **hiss** (1).
sizzle *noun.* —*See* **eroticism, hiss** (1), **passion.**
sizzling *adjective.* —*See* **desirable, erotic, hot** (1).
skate *verb.* —*See* **breeze, glide** (1).
skedaddle *verb.* —*See* **run** (2).
skein *noun.* —*See* **tangle.**
skeletal *adjective.* —*See* **haggard.**
skeleton *noun.* —*See* **draft** (1), **frame.**
skell *noun.* —*See* **pauper.**
skeptic *noun.* One who habitually or instinctively doubts or questions ▶ agnostic, doubter, doubting Thomas, nonbeliever, unbeliever.
skeptical *adjective.* —*See* **distrustful, doubtful** (2), **incredulous.**
skeptically *adverb.* With skepticism ▶ askance, distrustfully, distrustingly, doubtfully, doubtingly, dubiously, leerily, mistrustfully, questioningly, suspiciously, untrustingly. ***Idioms:*** with a grain of salt, with reservations.
skepticism *noun.* —*See* **disbelief, distrust, doubt.**

sketch *noun.* A short theatrical piece within a larger production ▶ act, skit. [*Compare* **satire.**] —*See also* **draft** (1), **synopsis.**

sketch *verb.*—*See* **design** (2), **draft** (1).

sketchy *adjective.* —*See* **deficient, rough** (4), **superficial.**

skew *verb.*—*See* **bias** (2), **swerve, tend[1].**

skid *noun.* —*See* **fall** (3).

skid *verb.* —*See* **fall** (4), **stumble.**

skill *noun.* A quality that makes a person suitable for a particular position or task ▶ attainment, credential, endowment, qualification.—*See also* **ability** (1), **dexterity.**

skilled *adjective.* —*See* **able, expert.**

skillful *adjective.* —*See* **able, dexterous, expert.**

skim *verb.* —*See* **browse** (1), **brush[1]**, **fly** (2), **glance** (1), **glide** (1).

skim *noun.* —*See* **brush[1].**

skimp *verb.* —*See* **scrimp.**

skimpy *adjective.* —*See* **meager.**

skin *noun.* **1.** The tissue forming the external covering of the body ▶ epidermis, integument. **2.** A thin outer covering of an object ▶ film, lamina, membrane, sheath, sheathing, sheet. [*Compare* **coat.**] **3.** The outer covering of a fruit or similar plant part ▶ hull, husk, peel, rind, shell, zest.

skin *verb.* To remove the skin of ▶ decorticate, hull, husk, pare, peel, scale, shell, shuck, strip. —*See also* **cheat** (1).

skin-deep *adjective.* —*See* **superficial.**

skinflint *noun.* —*See* **miser.**

skinny *adjective.* —*See* **thin** (1).

skip *verb. Informal* To fail to attend on purpose ▶ duck, shirk. ***Idiom:*** go AWOL. [*Compare* **cut** (4). —*See also* **bound[1]**, **drop** (4), **escape** (1), **glance** (1).

skip out *verb.* —*See* **renege.**

skip *noun.* —*See* **bound[1].**

skipper *noun.* ▶ captain, commander, shipmaster.

skirmish *noun.* —*See* **battle.**

skirt *verb.* To pass around but not through ▶ bypass, circumnavigate, circumvent, detour, go around. [*Compare* **avoid.**] —*See also* **evade** (1).

skirts *noun.* —*See* **outskirts.**

skit *noun.* A short theatrical piece within a larger production ▶ act, sketch. [*Compare* **satire.**]

skitter *verb.* —*See* **bound[1].**

skittish *adjective.* —*See* **edgy.**

skulk *verb.* —*See* **lurk, sneak.**

skull *noun.* The bony framework of the head ▶ braincase, brainpan, cranium. [*Compare* **head.**]

skunk *verb.* —*See* **overwhelm** (1).

skunk *noun.* —*See* **creep** (2).

sky *noun.* The celestial regions as seen from the earth ▶ air, firmament, heavens. ***Idiom:*** wild blue yonder.

sky *verb.* —*See* **soar.**

sky-high *adjective.* —*See* **high** (1), **steep[1]** (2).

skyrocket *verb.* —*See* **soar.**

slab *noun.* —*See* **cut** (2), **lump[1].**

slack *adjective.* —*See* **loose** (1), **negligent, slow** (2).

slack *verb.* To avoid the fulfillment of ▶ disregard, neglect, shirk. ***Idiom:*** let slide. —*See also* **ease** (1).

slack off *verb.* —*See* **idle** (1), **subside.**

slacken *verb.* —*See* **delay** (1), **ease** (1), **subside, weaken.**

slackening *noun.* —*See* **waning.**

slacker *noun.* —*See* **wastrel** (2).

slackness *noun.* —*See* **license** (2), **negligence.**

slam *verb.* **1.** *Slang* To criticize harshly and devastatingly ▶ blast, blister, drub, excoriate, flay, lacerate, lash, rip into, scarify, scathe, scorch, score, scourge, slap, slash, tear into, wither. *Informal:* bash, cut up, lambaste, light into, roast. *Slang:* trash. ***Idioms:*** burn someone's ears, crawl (*or* jump) all over someone, jump down someone's throat, let someone have it, pin someone's ears back, put someone on the griddle, put someone on the hot seat, rake over the coals, read the riot act to. [*Compare* **chastise, criticize, malign.**] **2.** To move a door, for example, in order to cover an opening ▶ close, clench, seal, shut. —*See also* **bang, collide, drive** (2), **hit.**

slam *noun.* A forceful movement causing a loud noise ▶ bang, crash, smash, wham. —*See also* **rebuke.**

slammer *noun.* —*See* **jail.**

slander *noun.* —*See* **gossip** (1), **libel.**

slander *verb.* —*See* **malign.**

slanderous *adjective.* —*See* **libelous.**

slant *verb.* —*See* **bias** (2), **distort, incline, swerve, tend**[1]**.**

slant *noun.* —*See* **ascent** (2), **bias, inclination** (2), **viewpoint.**

slanted *adjective.* —*See* **biased, oblique.**

slanting *adjective.* —*See* **oblique.**

slap *noun.* A sharp blow, especially with the open hand ▶ box, cuff, smack, smacker, spank, swat, whack. *Informal:* spat. [*Compare* **blow**[2]**.**] —*See also* **clash, rebuke.**

slap *verb.* To hit with a sharp blow, especially of the open hand ▶ box, clap, cuff, smack, spank, swat, whack. *Informal:* spat. [*Compare* **beat, hit.**] —*See also* **slam** (1).

slap around *verb.* —*See* **manhandle.**

slapdash *adjective.* —*See* **messy** (1), **rash**[1]**.**

slash *verb.* —*See* **cut** (1), **cut** (3), **slam** (1).

slash *noun.* —*See* **cut** (1), **decrease.**

slashing *adjective.* —*See* **biting.**

slate *noun.* A list of candidates proposed or endorsed by a political party ▶ ballot, lineup, ticket.

slate *verb.* To enter on a schedule ▶ calendar, docket, program, schedule. [*Compare* **list**[1]**, post**[3]**.**]

slated *adjective.* —*See* **due** (2).

slattern *noun.* —*See* **slut.**

slaughter *noun.* —*See* **massacre.**

slaughter *verb.* —*See* **massacre.**

slaughterer *noun.* —*See* **murderer.**

slaughterous *adjective.* —*See* **murderous.**

slave *noun.* One bound to serve another person or influence ▶ bondservant, chattel, helot, serf, servant, vassal. [*Compare* **subordinate.**] —*See also* **drudge** (1), **sycophant.**

slave *verb.* —*See* **grind** (2), **labor.**

slaver *verb.* —*See* **drool, fawn.**

slaver *noun.* Saliva running from the mouth ▶ drivel, drool, salivation, slobber.

slavery *noun.* A state of subjugation to an owner or master ▶ bondage, enslavement, helotry, involuntary servitude, serfdom, servileness, servility, servitude, thrall, thralldom, villeinage, yoke.

slavish *adjective.* —*See* **imitative** (1), **servile.**

slay *verb.* —*See* **kill**[1]**, murder.**

slayer *noun.* —*See* **murderer.**

sleaze *noun.* —*See* **obscenity** (2).

sleazy *adjective.* —*See* **shabby, shoddy.**

sled *or* **sledge** *verb.* To ride or be pulled on a sled in the snow ▶ coast, sleighride, slide. ***Idioms:*** go sledding (*or* coasting *or* sleigh-riding).

sleek *adjective.* **1.** Smooth and lustrous as if polished ▶ satiny, silken, silky. [*Compare* **even, glossy, slick.**] **2.** Having slender and graceful lines ▶ streamlined, trim. —*See also* **unctuous.**

sleek *verb.* —*See* **gloss**[1]**.**

sleek over *verb.* —*See* **extenuate.**

✣ **CORE SYNONYMS:** *sleek, satiny, silken, silky.* These adjectives mean having a surface that is smooth and lustrous as if polished: *sleek black fur; satiny gardenia petals; silken butterfly wings; silky skin.*

---

sleekness *noun.* —*See* **gloss**[1]**.**

sleep *noun.* The natural recurring condition of suspended consciousness by which the body rests ▶ dreamland, slumber. *Slang:* shuteye, z's. ***Idioms:*** land of Nod, the arms of Morpheus. [*Compare* **nap, rest.**]

sleep *verb.* To be asleep ▶ slumber. *Slang:* sack out. ***Idioms:*** be in the land of Nod, catch some shuteye, catch (*or* cop) some z's, saw logs (*or* wood), sleep like a log (*or* baby *or* rock *or* top), sleep tight. [*Compare* **nap, rest.**]

sleeper *noun.* —*See* **hit.**

sleeping *adjective.* In a state of sleep ▶ asleep, snoozing, unawake. *Slang:* conked out, sacked out, zonked. ***Idioms:*** catching (*or* copping) some z's, dead to the world, in dreamland, fast (*or* sound) asleep, in a sound (*or* wakeless) sleep, in the arms of Morpheus, in the land of Nod, out like a light, sawing logs (*or* wood). —*See also* **latent.**

sleepless *adjective.* Marked by an absence of sleep ▶ slumberless, wakeful. [*Compare* **wakeful.**]

sleepwalking *noun.* —*See* **trance.**

sleepy *adjective.* Ready for or needing sleep ▶ dozy, drowsy, nodding, slumberous, slumbery, somnolent, soporific. —*See also* **languid, soporific.**

sleight *noun.* —*See* **dexterity, trick** (1).

sleight of hand *noun.* —*See* **magic** (2).

slender *adjective.* —*See* **remote** (2), **thin** (1).

sleuth *noun.* —*See* **detective.**

slew *or* **slue** *noun.* —*See* **heap** (2).

slice *noun.* —*See* **bit**[1] (2), **cut** (1), **cut** (2), **flake.**

slice *verb.* —*See* **cut** (2).

slice up *verb.* —*See* **shred.**

slick *adjective.* So smooth and glassy as to offer insecure hold or footing ▶ lubricious, oily, slippery, slithery. ***Idiom:*** slippery as an eel. [*Compare* **sleek.**] —*See also* **dexterous, glib, shrewd.**

slick up *verb.* —*See* **tidy** (2).

slicker *noun.* —*See* **coat** (1).

slide *verb.* **1.** To ride or be pulled on a sled in the snow ▶ coast, sled, sledge, sleigh-ride. ***Idioms:*** go sledding (*or* coasting *or* sleigh-riding). **2.** To maneuver gently and slowly into place ▶ ease, glide, slip. [*Compare* **ease.**] —*See also* **crawl** (1), **glide** (1), **sneak, stumble.**

slide *noun.* —*See* **descent, fall** (3).

slight *adjective.* —*See* **gentle** (2), **light**[2] (2), **minor** (1), **remote** (2).

slight *verb.* —*See* **belittle, neglect** (1), **snub.**

slight *noun.* —*See* **indignity, neglect.**

slighting *adjective.* —*See* **disdainful, disparaging.**

slim *adjective.* —*See* **remote** (2), **thin** (1).

slim *verb.* To lose body weight, as by dieting ▶ reduce, slim down, thin, trim down. ***Idioms:*** get the weight off, lose weight, shed some pounds.

slime *noun.* A viscous, usually dirty substance ▶ mire, muck, ooze, slop, sludge, slush. *Informal:* goo, gunk. *Slang:* goop. [*Compare* **oil.**]

slimy *adjective.* Relating to or covered with slime ▶ miry, mucky, oozy, sludgy, slushy. *Informal:* gooey, gunky. *Slang:* goopy. [*Compare* **fatty.**]

sling *noun.* —*See* **throw.**

sling *verb.* —*See* **hang** (1), **throw.**

slink *verb.* —*See* **sneak.**

slinkiness *noun.* —*See* **stealth.**

slinky *adjective.* —*See* **stealthy.**

slip *verb.* **1.** To maneuver gently and slowly into place ▶ ease, glide, slide. [*Compare* **ease.**] **2.** To displace a bone from a socket or joint ▶ dislocate, separate, throw out. ***Idiom:*** throw out of joint. **3.** To undergo moral deterioration ▶ degenerate, fall, sink. [*Compare* **deteriorate.**] —*See also* **elapse, err, fall** (4), **glide** (1), **lose** (3), **sneak, stumble, undo.**

slip into *or* **on** *verb.* —*See* **don.**

slip up *verb.* —*See* **err.**

slip *noun.* A minor mistake ▶ lapse, slip-up. *Informal:* fluff. —*See also* **error.**

slippery *adjective.* Inclined or intended to evade ▶ elusive, evasive, fugitive. [*Compare* **underhand.**] —*See also* **slick.**

slipshod *adjective.* —*See* **messy** (1), **negligent.**

slip-up *noun.* A minor mistake ▶ lapse, slip. *Informal:* fluff. —*See also* **error.**

slit *noun.* —*See* **cut** (1).

slit *verb.* —*See* **cut** (1), **cut** (2).

slither *verb.* —*See* **crawl** (1), **glide** (1), **stumble.**

slithery *adjective.* —*See* **slick.**

sliver *noun.* —*See* **bit**[1] (2), **cut** (2), **flake.**

slob *noun.* —*See* **boor.**

slobber *noun.* Saliva running from the mouth ► drivel, drool, salivation, slaver.
slobber *verb.* —*See* **drool.**
slobber over *verb. Informal* To make an excessive show of desire for or interest in ► *Informal:* drool over, ogle. [*Compare* **adore, desire, lust, rave.**]
slog *verb.* —*See* **grind** (2), **hit, trudge.**
slog *noun.* —*See* **task** (2).
slogan *noun.* —*See* **cry** (2).
slop *noun.* —*See* **slime.**
slop *verb.* —*See* **splash** (1), **trudge.**
slope *verb.* —*See* **incline.**
slope *noun.* —*See* **ascent** (2), **inclination** (2).
sloppiness *noun.* —*See* **disorderliness, sentimentality.**
sloppy *adjective.* —*See* **messy** (1), **negligent, sentimental.**
slosh *verb.* —*See* **splash** (1).
sloshed *adjective.* —*See* **drunk.**
slot *noun.* —*See* **hole** (2), **position** (3).
sloth *noun.* —*See* **laziness, wastrel** (2).
slothful *adjective.* —*See* **lazy, lethargic.**
slothfulness *noun.* —*See* **laziness, lethargy.**
slouch *verb.* **1.** To take on or move with an awkward, slovenly posture ► loll, slump. [*Compare* **bow[1], stoop.**] **2.** To hang limply and loosely ► droop, flop, loll, lop, sag, wilt.
slouch *noun.* —*See* **wastrel** (2).
slough[1] *noun.* —*See* **swamp.**
slough[2] *verb.* —*See* **discard, shed[1]** (2).
slovenliness *noun.* —*See* **disorderliness.**
slovenly *adjective.* —*See* **messy** (1).
slow *adjective.* **1.** Proceeding at a rate less than usual or desired ► crawling, creeping, delaying, dilatory, glacial, laggard, laboring, plodding, procrastinating, slow-footed, slow-going, slow-paced, sluggish, snaillike, tardy. *Informal:* poky. ***Idiom:*** slow as molasses in January. [*Compare* **deliberate, languid, lethargic.**] **2.** Characterized by reduced economic activity ► down, dull, off, slack, sluggish, soft, stagnant. —*See also* **backward** (1), **late** (1).
slow *adverb.* —*See* **late.**
slow *verb.* —*See* **delay** (1).

✚ **CORE SYNONYMS:** *slow, dilatory, sluggish, laggard.* These adjectives mean proceeding at a rate less than usual or desired. *Slow* is the least specific: *a slow bus; a slow heartbeat; slow to anger. Dilatory* implies lack of promptness caused by delay, procrastination, or indifference: *paid a late fee because I was dilatory in paying the bill. Sluggish* suggests a lack of movement, activity, or progress: *was sluggish after eating the heavy lunch; sluggish growth. Laggard* implies hanging back or falling behind: "*the horses' laggard pace*" (Rudyard Kipling).

◄ **ANTONYM:** *fast*

---

slowdown *noun.* A period of decreased business activity and high unemployment ► depression, downturn, recession, slump. —*See also* **decrease.**
slow-going *or* **slow-footed** *adjective.* —*See* **slow** (1).
slow motion *noun.* A very slow rate of speed ► crawl, creep, footpace. ***Idiom:*** snail's pace.
slowness *noun.* The quality or condition of not being on time ► belatedness, lateness, tardiness, unpunctuality.
slow-paced *adjective.* —*See* **slow** (1).
slowpoke *noun.* —*See* **laggard.**
slow-witted *adjective.* —*See* **backward** (1).
sludge *noun.* —*See* **slime.**
sludgy *adjective.* —*See* **slimy.**
slue *or* **slew** *verb.* To turn in place, as on a fixed point ► pivot, swing, swivel, wheel. [*Compare* **turn.**] —*See also* **swerve.**
slug[1] *noun.* —*See* **drop** (4).
slug[2] *noun.* —*See* **wastrel** (2).
slug[3] *verb.* —*See* **hit.**
slug *noun.* —*See* **blow[2].**
slugabed *noun.* —*See* **wastrel** (2).
slugfest *noun.* —*See* **fight** (1).
sluggard *noun.* —*See* **wastrel** (2).

sluggard *adjective.* —*See* **lazy.**

sluggardness *noun.* —*See* **laziness.**

sluggish *adjective.* —*See* **lazy, lethargic, slow** (1), **slow** (2).

sluggishness *noun.* —*See* **dullness, laziness, lethargy.**

slumber *verb.* To be asleep ▶ sleep. *Slang:* sack out. ***Idioms:*** be in the land of Nod, catch some shuteye, catch (*or* cop) some z's, saw logs (*or* wood), sleep like a log (*or* baby *or* rock *or* top), sleep tight. [*Compare* **nap, rest.**]

slumber *noun.* The natural recurring condition of suspended consciousness by which the body rests ▶ dreamland, sleep. *Slang:* shuteye, z's. ***Idioms:*** land of Nod, the arms of Morpheus. [*Compare* **nap, rest.**]

slumberless *adjective.* Marked by an absence of sleep ▶ sleepless, wakeful. [*Compare* **wakeful.**]

slumberous *or* **slumbrous** *adjective.* —*See* **sleepy, soporific.**

slumbery *adjective.* —*See* **sleepy.**

slump *verb.* To take on or move with an awkward, slovenly posture ▶ loll, slouch. [*Compare* **bow**[1], **stoop.**] —*See also* **drop** (1), **fall** (4).

slump *noun.* A period of decreased business activity and high unemployment ▶ depression, downturn, recession, slowdown. —*See also* **fall** (3).

slur *verb.* —*See* **malign.**

slur *noun.* An implied criticism ▶ imputation, reflection. [*Compare* **crack, libel.**]

slurp *verb.* —*See* **drink** (1).

slush *noun.* —*See* **slime.**

slush *verb.* —*See* **dirty.**

slushy *adjective.* —*See* **sentimental, slimy.**

slut *noun.* A person, typically a woman, who is sexually promiscuous ▶ baggage, hussy, jade, slattern, tart, tramp, wanton, wench, whore. *Slang:* floozy. [*Compare* **harlot, prostitute.**]

sluttish *adjective.* —*See* **wanton** (1).

sly *adjective.* —*See* **artful, stealthy.**

slyness *noun.* —*See* **art, dishonesty** (2), **stealth.**

smack[1] *verb.* —*See* **bang, kiss, slap.**

smack *noun.* —*See* **beat** (1), **clash, kiss, slap.**

smack *adverb.* —*See* **directly** (3).

smack[2] *noun.* A distinctive yet intangible quality ▶ aroma, atmosphere, flavor, savor. [*Compare* **quality.**] —*See also* **flavor** (1).

smack *verb.* To have a particular flavor or suggestion of something ▶ savor, smell, suggest, taste. [*Compare* **hint.**]

smack-dab *adverb.* —*See* **directly** (3).

smacker *noun.* —*See* **kiss, mouth** (1), **slap.**

small *adjective.* —*See* **little, minor** (1), **narrow** (1), **soft** (2), **trivial.**

small change *noun.* —*See* **peanuts, trifle.**

smallest *adjective.* —*See* **minimal.**

small fry *noun.* —*See* **nonentity, squirt** (2).

smallish *adjective.* —*See* **little.**

small-minded *adjective.* —*See* **narrow** (1), **trivial.**

smallness *noun.* —*See* **trifle.**

small potatoes *noun.* —*See* **trifle.**

small talk *noun.* —*See* **chatter.**

smalltime *or* **small-time** *adjective.* —*See* **minor** (1).

small-town *adjective.* —*See* **narrow** (1).

smarmy *adjective.* —*See* **unctuous.**

smart *adjective.* —*See* **clever** (1), **clever** (2), **exclusive** (3), **fashionable, impudent, intelligent, shrewd.**

smart *verb.* —*See* **hurt** (2).

smart *noun.* —*See* **pain.**

smart aleck *noun.* *Informal* One who is obnoxiously self-assertive and arrogant ▶ *Informal:* know-it-all, saucebox, smarty, smarty-pants, wisenheimer. *Slang:* wiseacre, wisecracker, wise guy. [*Compare* **boaster, joker.**]

smart-alecky *adjective.* —*See* **impudent.**

smarten *verb.* —*See* **renew** (1).

smarting *adjective.* —*See* **painful.**

smarts *noun.* —*See* **intelligence.**

smarty *or* **smarty-pants** *noun.* —*See* **smart aleck.**

smash *verb.*—*See* **bang, beat** (1), **break** (1), **crash, crush** (1), **crush** (2), **destroy** (1), **hit, overwhelm** (1).

smash *noun.* A forceful movement causing a loud noise ▶ bang, crash, slam, wham. —*See also* **clash, collapse** (2), **collision, crash** (2), **hit.**

smashed *adjective.* —*See* **drunk.**

smash hit *noun.* —*See* **hit.**

smashup *noun.* —*See* **collapse** (2), **crash** (2).

smatterer *noun.* —*See* **amateur.**

smear *verb.* To spread with a greasy, sticky, or dirty substance ▶ bedaub, besmear, dab, daub, plaster, smirch, smudge. [*Compare* **dirty, finish, oil, stain.**] —*See also* **denigrate, overwhelm** (1).

smear *noun.* A discolored mark made by smearing or soiling ▶ blot, blotch, daub, smirch, smudge, smutch, splotch, spot, stain. —*See also* **libel.**

smell *verb.* **1.** To perceive with the olfactory sense ▶ nose, scent, sniff, snuff, whiff. ***Idioms:*** catch (*or* get) a whiff of. [*Compare* **breathe.**] **2.** To have or give off a foul odor ▶ reek, stink. ***Idiom:*** stink to high heaven. **3.** To have a particular flavor or suggestion of something ▶ savor, smack, suggest, taste. [*Compare* **hint.**]

smell out *verb.* To follow the traces of, as in hunting ▶ sniff out, trace, track (down), trail. ***Idiom:*** be hot on the trail of. [*Compare* **hunt.**]

smell *noun.* **1.** The sense by which odors are perceived ▶ nose, olfaction, scent. **2.** The quality of something that may be perceived by smelling ▶ aroma, odor, scent. [*Compare* **fragrance, stench.**] —*See also* **air** (3).

✣ **CORE SYNONYMS:** *smell, aroma, odor, scent.* These nouns denote a quality that can be perceived by the olfactory sense: *the smell of gasoline; the aroma of frying onions on the stove; antiseptic hospital odors; the scent of pine needles in the forest.*

---

smelly *adjective. Informal* Having an unpleasant odor ▶ fetid, foul, foul-smelling, malodorous, mephitic, mephitical, noisome, odoriferous, odorous, overpowering, reeking, reeky, stinking. [*Compare* **bad, fragrant, moldy, offensive.**]

smidgen *noun.* —*See* **bit**[1] (1).

smile *noun.* A facial expression marked by an upward curving of the lips ▶ grin, simper, smirk. [*Compare* **sneer.**]

smile *verb.* To curve the lips upward in expressing amusement, pleasure, or happiness ▶ beam, grin, simper, smirk. ***Idioms:*** break into a smile, crack (*or* flash *or* give) a smile.

smile on *or* **upon** *verb.* To lend supportive approval to ▶ countenance, encourage, favor. [*Compare* **approve, support.**]

smirch *verb.* —*See* **smear.**

smirk *verb.* —*See* **smile.**

smirk *noun.* A facial expression marked by an upward curving of the lips ▶ grin, simper, smile. [*Compare* **sneer.**]

smite *verb.* —*See* **afflict, hit.**

smitten *adjective.* —*See* **infatuated.**

smock *noun.* —*See* **dress** (3).

smog *noun.* —*See* **haze.**

smoggy *adjective.* Heavy, dark, or dense, especially with impurities ▶ hazy, murky, turbid. [*Compare* **dirty.**]

smoke *verb.* —*See* **smolder.**

smolder *verb.* To undergo partial or unsteady combustion ▶ flicker, gutter, smoke, sputter. [*Compare* **burn.**] —*See also* **boil.**

smooch *noun.* —*See* **kiss.**

smooch *verb.* —*See* **kiss.**

smooth *adjective.* Gracious and tactful in social manner ▶ debonair, suave, urbane. [*Compare* **courteous, cultured, sophisticated.**] —*See also* **easy** (1), **even** (1), **fluent, gentle** (2), **glib.**

smooth *verb.* —*See* **even, perfect.**

smooth over *verb.* —*See* **settle** (2).

smooth-spoken *adjective.* —*See* **eloquent.**
smooth-talking *or* **smooth-tongued** *adjective.* —*See* **glib.**
smother *verb.* —*See* **choke, extinguish, repress.**
smudge *verb.* —*See* **denigrate, dirty, smear.**
smudge *noun.* —*See* **haze, smear.**
smug *adjective.* —*See* **arrogant.**
smuggle *verb.* To bring in or take out secretly and illegally ▶ bootleg, run, sneak, spirit. ***Idiom:*** run contraband.
smuggler *noun.* A person who engages in smuggling ▶ bootlegger, contrabandist, runner. *Slang:* mule.
smut *noun.* —*See* **obscenity** (2).
smut *verb.* —*See* **denigrate, stain.**
smutch *verb.* —*See* **dirty.**
smutch *noun.* —*See* **smear.**
smuttiness *noun.* —*See* **dirtiness, obscenity** (1).
smutty *adjective.* —*See* **dirty, obscene.**
snack *noun.* —*See* **refreshment.**
snack *verb.* —*See* **eat** (2).
snaffle *noun.* —*See* **brake.**
snafu *noun.* —*See* **disorder** (1), **mess** (1).
snafu *verb.* —*See* **botch, confuse** (3).
snafu *adjective.* —*See* **confused** (2).
snag *noun. Informal* A tricky or unsuspected condition ▶ catch, hitch, rub. [*Compare* **disadvantage, trick.**] —*See also* **bar** (1), **spike.**
snag *verb.* —*See* **catch** (2), **catch** (3).
snail *noun.* —*See* **laggard.**
snake *verb.* —*See* **crawl** (1), **sneak, wind²**.
snake *noun.* —*See* **betrayer, creep** (2).
snaky *adjective.* —*See* **winding.**
snap *verb.* **1.** To make a light, sharp noise ▶ clack, click. [*Compare* **crackle.**] **2.** To try to bite something quickly or eagerly ▶ nip, snatch, strike. **3.** To speak abruptly and sharply ▶ bark, growl, snarl. ***Idioms:*** bite someone's head off, snap someone's head (*or* nose) off. [*Compare* **chastise, revile, say, shout.**] **4.** To move or cause to move with a sudden abrupt motion ▶ jerk, lurch, twitch, wrench, yank. [*Compare* **move.**] —*See also* **break** (3), **crack** (2).
snap back *verb.* To reverse direction after striking something ▶ bounce (back), rebound, reflect, spring back. [*Compare* **bend, glance.**]
snap *noun.* A light, sharp noise ▶ clack, click, crackle. —*See also* **breeze** (2), **crack** (1), **energy, fastener, jerk.**
snap *adjective.* —*See* **easy** (1), **extemporaneous.**
snappish *adjective.* —*See* **ill-tempered.**
snappy *adjective.* —*See* **energetic, fashionable, ill-tempered, lively.**
snare *noun.* —*See* **trap** (1).
snare *verb.* —*See* **catch** (1).
snarl¹ *verb.* —*See* **snap** (3).
snarl² *noun.* —*See* **tangle.**
snarl *verb.* —*See* **complicate, confuse** (3), **entangle.**
snatch *verb.* **1.** To try to bite something quickly or eagerly ▶ nip, snap, strike. **2.** To seize and detain a person unlawfully ▶ abduct, kidnap, spirit away, take hostage. —*See also* **catch** (2), **seize** (1), **steal.**
snatch *noun.* —*See* **catch** (1), **seizure** (2).
snazzy *adjective.* —*See* **fashionable.**
sneak *verb.* To move silently and furtively ▶ creep, glide, lurk, mouse, prowl, pussyfoot, skulk, slide, slink, slip, snake, steal. *Slang:* gumshoe. [*Compare* **lay¹**.] —*See also* **smuggle.**
sneak *or* **sneaker** *noun.* One who behaves in a stealthy, furtive way ▶ prowler, skulker, sneaker, weasel. [*Compare* **creep, betrayer.**]
sneakiness *noun.* —*See* **dishonesty** (2), **stealth.**
sneaking *adjective.* —*See* **stealthy.**
sneaky *adjective.* —*See* **stealthy, underhand.**
sneer *noun.* A facial expression or laugh conveying scorn or derision ▶ fleer, snicker, snigger. [*Compare* **face, grimace, laugh, smile.**]
sneer *verb.* To smile or laugh scornfully or derisively ▶ fleer, snicker, snigger.

Idiom: curl one's lip. [*Compare* **grimace, laugh, smile.**]

sneer at *verb.* —*See* **despise, ridicule.**

sneering *adjective.* —*See* **disdainful, sarcastic.**

snicker *verb.* To smile or laugh scornfully or derisively ▶ fleer, sneer, snigger. *Idiom:* curl one's lip. [*Compare* **grimace, smile.**] —*See also* **laugh.**

snicker *noun.* A facial expression or laugh conveying scorn or derision ▶ fleer, sneer, snigger. [*Compare* **smile.**] —*See also* **laugh.**

snide *adjective.* —*See* **sarcastic.**

sniff *verb.* To breathe audibly through the nose ▶ sniffle, snort, snuff, snuffle. —*See also* **smell** (1).

sniff about *or* **around** *verb. Informal* To look into or inquire about curiously, inquisitively, or in a meddlesome fashion ▶ poke, pry, snoop. *Informal:* nose (around). *Idioms:* stick one's nose into. [*Compare* **meddle.**] —*See also* **seek** (1).

sniff at *verb.* —*See* **despise, disapprove.**

sniff out *verb.* To follow the traces of, as in hunting ▶ smell out, trace, track, trail. *Idiom:* be hot on the trail of. [*Compare* **hunt.**]

sniffle *verb.* To breathe audibly through the nose ▶ sniff, snort, snuff, snuffle. —*See also* **cry.**

snigger *noun.* A facial expression or laugh conveying scorn or derision ▶ fleer, sneer, snicker. [*Compare* **smile.**] —*See also* **laugh.**

snigger *verb.* To smile or laugh scornfully or derisively ▶ fleer, sneer, snicker. *Idiom:* curl one's lip. [*Compare* **grimace, smile.**] —*See also* **laugh.**

snip *noun.* —*See* **bit**[1] (1), **cut** (2).

snip *verb.* —*See* **cut** (2), **cut** (3).

snippet *noun.* —*See* **bit**[1] (1), **cut** (2).

snippety *or* **snippy** *adjective.* —*See* **impudent.**

snit *noun.* —*See* **state** (2).

snitch *or* **snitcher** *verb.* —*See* **inform** (2), **steal.**

snitch *noun.* —*See* **informer.**

snivel *verb.* —*See* **complain, cry.**

snob *noun.* One who despises people or things regarded as inferior, especially because of social or intellectual pretension ▶ elitist, prig. *Informal:* snoot.

snobbery *noun.* —*See* **condescension.**

snobbish *or* **snobby** *adjective.* Characteristic of or resembling a snob ▶ elitist. *Informal:* high-hat, snooty, stuck-up, uppish, uppity. [*Compare* **arrogant, pompous.**]

snoop *verb.* To look into or inquire about curiously, inquisitively, or in a meddlesome fashion ▶ poke, pry. *Informal:* nose (around), sniff about (*or* around). *Idiom:* stick one's nose into. [*Compare* **meddle.**]

snoop *or* **snooper** *noun.* A person who snoops ▶ prier, pry. [*Compare* **busybody.**] —*See also* **gossip** (2).

snoopiness *noun.* —*See* **curiosity** (2).

snoopy *adjective.* —*See* **curious** (1).

snoot *noun. Informal* One who despises people or things regarded as inferior, especially because of social or intellectual pretension ▶ elitist, prig, snob. —*See also* **nose** (1).

snootiness *noun.* —*See* **condescension.**

snooty *adjective.* —*See* **arrogant, snobbish.**

snooze *verb.* —*See* **nap.**

snooze *noun.* —*See* **nap.**

snort *noun.* —*See* **drop** (4).

snort *verb.* To breathe audibly through the nose ▶ sniff, sniffle, snuff, snuffle. —*See also* **gasp.**

snotty *adjective.* —*See* **impudent.**

snout *noun.* —*See* **nose** (1).

snow *verb.* —*See* **deceive.**

snowball *verb.* To increase or expand suddenly, rapidly, or without control ▶ balloon, explode, mushroom. —*See also* **increase.**

snow job *noun.* —*See* **trick** (1).

snub *verb.* To slight someone deliberately ▶ cut, disregard, ignore, neglect, rebuff, shun, slight, spurn. *Informal:* cold-shoulder. *Idioms:* give someone the cold shoulder, give someone the go-by, turn one's back on, turn up one's nose at, close (*or* shut) the door on. [*Compare* **belittle, blackball, neglect.**]

snub *noun.* A deliberate slight or affront ▶ cut, putdown, rebuff, spurning. *Informal:* cold shoulder, go-by. [*Compare* **rebuke.**]

snuff *verb.* To breathe audibly through the nose ▶ sniff, sniffle, snort, snuffle. —*See also* **smell** (1).

snuff out *verb.* —*See* **annihilate, extinguish, murder.**

snuffle *verb.* To breathe audibly through the nose ▶ sniff, sniffle, snort, snuff.

snug *adjective.* —*See* **comfortable, neat, tight** (4).

snug *verb.* —*See* **snuggle.**

snuggle *verb.* To lie or press close together, usually with another person or thing ▶ cuddle, nestle, nuzzle, snug. [*Compare* **embrace, neck.**]

so *adjective.* In a similar manner ▶ likewise, similarly. ***Idioms:*** by the same token, in like fashion, in like manner, in the same way.

soak *verb.* —*See* **cheat** (1), **drink** (3), **drink** (2), **steep**[2], **wet** (1).

soak in *verb.* To come as a realization ▶ dawn on (*or* upon), register, sink in. [*Compare* **discover, strike, understand.**]

soak up *verb.* —*See* **absorb** (2).

soak *noun.* —*See* **drunkard.**

soaked *or* **soaking** *adjective.* —*See* **wet.**

soar *verb.* To rise steeply and abruptly ▶ rocket, sky, skyrocket. *Informal:* shoot up. —*See also* **fly** (2), **increase, rise** (2).

soaring *adjective.* —*See* **elevated** (4), **high** (1).

sob *verb.* —*See* **cry.**

sobbing *noun.* —*See* **cry** (1).

sobby *adjective.* —*See* **sentimental.**

sober *adjective.* —*See* **deliberate** (3), **realistic** (1), **sensible, serious** (1), **temperate** (2).

soberness *noun.* —*See* **temperance** (2).

sobersided *adjective.* —*See* **serious** (1).

sobersidedness *noun.* —*See* **seriousness** (1).

sobriety *noun.* —*See* **moderation, seriousness** (1), **temperance** (1), **temperance** (2).

sobriquet *noun.* —*See* **name** (1).

so-called *adjective.* —*See* **supposed.**

sociability *noun.* —*See* **amiability.**

sociable *adjective.* —*See* **amiable, social.**

sociableness *noun.* —*See* **amiability.**

social *adjective.* Enjoying company ▶ companionable, convivial, gregarious, sociable. [*Compare* **amiable, outgoing, talkative.**] —*See also* **popular.**

social *noun.* —*See* **party.**

✚ **CORE SYNONYMS:** *social, companionable, convivial, gregarious, sociable.* These adjectives refer to those who enjoy the company of others: *a friendly social gathering; a companionable pet; a cheery, convivial disposition; a gregarious person who avoids solitude; a sociable conversation.*

◀ **ANTONYM:** *antisocial*

---

socialize *verb.* **1.** To take part in social activities ▶ mingle, mix. **2.** To place under government or group ownership or control ▶ communalize, nationalize. **3.** To fit for companionship with others, especially in attitude or manners ▶ acculturate, civilize, humanize.

societal *adjective.* —*See* **popular.**

society *noun.* **1.** People of the highest social level ▶ aristocracy, blue blood, crème de la crème, elite, flower, gentility, gentry, high society, jet set, nobility, patriciate, quality, smart set, upper class, who's who. *Informal:* upper crust. **2.** The total product of human creativity and intellect ▶ civilization, culture, Kultur. —*See also* **company** (3), **culture** (2), **public** (1), **union** (1).

sock *verb.* —*See* **hit.**

sock *noun.* —*See* **blow**[2].

sock away *verb.* —*See* **bank**[2], **save** (1).

socket *noun.* —*See* **outlet** (1).

sock-hop *noun.* —*See* **dance.**

sod *noun.* —*See* **earth** (1).

sodden *adjective.* —*See* **drunk, wet.**

sodden *verb.* —*See* **wet** (1).

soft *adjective.* **1.** Yielding easily to pressure or weight ▶ doughy, mushy, pappy, pulpous, pulpy, quaggy, spongy, squashy, squishy, yielding. *Informal:* squooshy. **2.** Not irritating, strident, or loud ▶ hushed, low, low-key, low-keyed, muffled, muted, quiet, small, subdued, whispery. [*Compare* **faint, low.**] —*See also* **comfortable, gentle** (1), **gentle** (2), **light**^{2} (2), **limp, rainy, sentimental, slow** (2), **tolerant.**

soften *verb.* —*See* **moderate** (1), **pacify, weaken.**

softhead *noun.* —*See* **dullard, fool.**

softheaded *adjective.* —*See* **stupid.**

softheadedness *noun.* —*See* **stupidity.**

softhearted *adjective.* —*See* **gentle** (1), **sympathetic.**

soft-pedal *verb. Informal* To make less emphatic or obvious ▶ de-emphasize, play down, tone down. [*Compare* **moderate.**]

soft soap *noun.* —*See* **flattery.**

soft-soap *verb.* —*See* **coax, flatter** (1).

soft spot *noun.* —*See* **liking.**

softy *noun.* —*See* **baby** (2), **weakling.**

soggy *adjective.* —*See* **sticky** (2), **wet.**

soil *noun.* —*See* **earth** (1).

soil *verb.* —*See* **corrupt, denigrate, dirty.**

soiled *adjective.* —*See* **dirty.**

soiree *or* **soireé** *noun.* —*See* **party.**

sojourn *verb.* —*See* **lodge.**

sojourn *noun.* A remaining in a place as a guest or lodger ▶ stay, stop, stopover, visit.

sojourner *noun.* —*See* **tourist.**

solace *noun.* A consoling in time of grief or pain ▶ comfort, consolation, reassurance, succor. [*Compare* **help, pity.**]

solace *verb.* —*See* **comfort.**

soldier *noun.* **1.** One who engages in a combat or struggle ▶ belligerent, combatant, fighter, warrior. [*Compare* **aggressor.**] **2.** An enlisted person ▶ GI, legionnaire, legionary, military man, military woman, militiaman, serviceman, serviceperson, servicewoman, trooper. *Slang:* GI Jane, GI Joe, grunt. [*Compare* **mercenary.**]

soldier *verb.* —*See* **endure** (1).

soldierly *adjective.* —*See* **military** (2).

soldier of fortune *noun.* A freelance fighter ▶ adventurer, mercenary. [*Compare* **fighter, soldier.**]

sole *adjective.* —*See* **exclusive** (1), **individual** (2), **lone, single.**

solecism *noun.* —*See* **blunder, corruption** (3), **impropriety** (2).

solely *adverb.* To the exclusion of anyone or anything else ▶ alone, exclusively, just, only. [*Compare* **completely, merely.**] —*See also* **alone.**

solemn *adjective.* —*See* **ceremonious, serious** (1).

solemnity *noun.* —*See* **celebration** (2), **ceremony** (1), **seriousness** (1).

solemnization *noun.* —*See* **celebration** (2).

solemnize *verb.* To mark a day or an event with ceremonies of respect, festivity, or rejoicing ▶ celebrate, commemorate, keep, observe. [*Compare* **sanctify.**]

solemnness *noun.* —*See* **seriousness** (1).

solicit *verb.* —*See* **appeal** (1), **bill**^{1}, **court** (1).

solicitous *adjective.* —*See* **anxious, attentive, careful** (2), **eager.**

solicitude *noun.* —*See* **anxiety** (1), **consideration** (1).

solid *adjective.* Unyielding to pressure ▶ firm, hard, incompressible. —*See also* **dependable, firm**^{1} (2), **intimate**^{1} (1), **physical, real** (1), **sound**^{2}, **unanimous.**

solidarity *noun.* An identity or coincidence of interests, purposes, or sympathies among the members of a group ▶ concord, oneness, union, unity. [*Compare* **alliance, union.**]

solidify *verb.* —*See* **harden** (2).

solidity *noun.* The quality, condition, or degree of being thick ▶ compactness, density, thickness. —*See also* **stability.**

solipsistic *adjective.* Holding the philosophical view that the self is the center and norm of existence ▶ egocentric, egoistic, egoistical, individualistic. [*Compare* **egotistic.**]

solitarily *adverb.* —*See* **alone.**

solitariness *noun.* —*See* **solitude.**

solitary *adjective.* Set away from or lacking the company of all others ▶ alone, apart, cloistered, companionless, detached, friendless, isolate, isolated, lone, lonely, lonesome, recluse, reclusive, removed, sequestered, single, unaccompanied. ***Idiom:*** by one's lonesome. [*Compare* **abandoned, lonely.**] —*See also* **cool, lone, remote** (1).

✚ CORE SYNONYMS: *solitary, alone, lonely, lonesome.* These adjectives describe lack of companionship. *Solitary* often stresses physical isolation that is self-imposed: *I thoroughly enjoyed my solitary dinner. Alone* emphasizes being apart from others but does not necessarily imply unhappiness: "*I am never less alone, than when I am alone*" (James Howell). *Lonely* often connotes painful awareness of being alone: "'*No doubt they are dead,' she thought, and felt . . . sadder and . . . lonelier for the thought*" (Ouida). *Lonesome* emphasizes a plaintive desire for companionship: "*You must keep up your spirits, mother, and not be lonesome because I'm not at home*" (Charles Dickens).

solitude *noun.* The quality or state of being alone ▶ aloneness, isolation, loneliness, privacy, retirement, retreat, seclusion, singleness, solitariness. [*Compare* **calm, stillness.**]

✚ CORE SYNONYMS: *solitude, isolation, seclusion, retirement.* These nouns denote the quality or state of being alone. *Solitude* implies the absence of all others: "*The worst solitude is to be destitute of sincere friendship*" (Francis Bacon). "*I love tranquil solitude*" (Percy Bysshe Shelley). *Isolation* emphasizes total separation or detachment from others: "*the isolation of Crusoe, depicted by Defoe's genius*" (Winston Churchill). *Seclusion* suggests removal, though not necessarily complete inaccessibility; the term often connotes a withdrawal from social contact: *enjoyed my walk in the seclusion of the woods. Retirement* suggests a withdrawal or retreat from active life, as for serenity or privacy: "*an elegant sufficiency, content,/Retirement, rural quiet, friendship, books*" (James Thomson).

solemn word *noun.* —*See* **promise** (1).

solo *adverb.* —*See* **alone.**

solution *noun.* —*See* **answer** (2).

solve *verb.* **1.** To find a solution for ▶ answer, clear up, decipher, divine, explain, reason out, resolve, think out (*or* through), unravel, untangle. *Informal:* dope out, figure out. ***Idioms:*** get to the bottom of, hit on the answer (*or* solution), put two and two together. [*Compare* **analyze, decipher.**] **2.** To arrive at an answer to a mathematical problem ▶ work out. *Informal:* figure out. [*Compare* **calculate.**]

✚ CORE SYNONYMS: *solve, decipher, resolve, unravel.* These verbs mean to find a solution: *solve a riddle; can't decipher your handwriting; resolve a problem; unravel a mystery.*

somatic *adjective.* —*See* **bodily.**

somber *adjective.* —*See* **gloomy, serious** (1).

some *adjective.* —*See* **several.**

some *adverb.* —*See* **approximately.**

some *pronoun.* —*See* **several.**

somebody *or* **someone** *noun.* —*See* **dignitary.**

something *noun.* —*See* **object** (1), **thing** (1).

sometime *adjective.* —*See* **late** (2).

sometimes *adverb.* —*See* **intermittently.**

somnifacient *adjective.* —*See* **soporific.**
somnifacient *noun.* —*See* **soporific.**

somniferous *or* **somnific** *adjective.* —*See* **soporific.**

somnolent *adjective.* —*See* **sleepy, soporific.**

sonance *noun.* Vibrations detected by the ear ▶ noise, sound. [*Compare* **tone.**]

song *noun.* A brief composition written or adapted for singing ▶ ballad, carol, ditty, hymn, jingle, lyrics, number, piece, tune. [*Compare* **melody.**] —*See also* **poem** (1).

sonorous *adjective.* —*See* **oratorical, resonant.**

soon *adverb.* In the near future ▶ before long, by and by, imminently, presently, promptly, quickly, shortly, without delay. *Informal:* pronto. ***Idioms:*** before long, in a bit (*or* jiffy *or* minute *or* moment), in short order. [*Compare* **immediately.**]

soothe *verb.* —*See* **comfort, pacify.**

soothing *adjective.* —*See* **comfortable, gentle** (2).

soothsay *verb.* —*See* **prophesy.**

soothsayer *noun.* —*See* **prophet.**

soothsaying *noun.* —*See* **prophecy.**

sooty *adjective.* —*See* **black** (1).

sop *verb.* —*See* **wet** (1).
sop up *verb.* —*See* **drink** (3).
sop *noun.* —*See* **bribe.**

sophism *noun.* —*See* **fallacy** (1).

sophistic *adjective.* —*See* **fallacious** (1).

sophisticate *verb.* —*See* **contaminate.**

sophisticated *adjective.* Experienced in the ways of the world; lacking natural simplicity ▶ cosmopolitan, worldly, worldly-wise. [*Compare* **experienced, shrewd, suave.**] —*See also* **complex** (1), **cultured, exclusive** (3), **impure** (2), **intellectual.**

sophistication *noun.* —*See* **contamination, culture** (3), **elegance.**

sophistry *noun.* —*See* **fallacy** (2).

sophomoric *adjective.* —*See* **childish.**

soporific *adjective.* Inducing sleep or sedation ▶ hypnotic, narcotic, opiate, sedative, sleepy, slumberous, somnifacient, somniferous, somnific, somnolent, stupefacient, stupefying, tranquilizing. —*See also* **sleepy.**
soporific *noun.* Something that induces sleep or sedation ▶ hypnotic, narcotic, opiate, sedative, somnifacient, stupefacient, tranquilizer. [*Compare* **drug.**]

sopping *adjective.* —*See* **wet.**

soppy *adjective.* —*See* **sentimental, wet.**

sorcerer *noun.* —*See* **wizard.**

sorceress *noun.* A woman who practices magic ▶ enchantress, hag, lamia, witch. [*Compare* **wizard.**]

sorcery *noun.* —*See* **magic** (1).

sordid *adjective.* Having or proceeding from low moral standards ▶ base, ignoble, low, low-down, mean, seamy, squalid, vile. [*Compare* **corrupt, disgraceful.**]

✚ **CORE SYNONYMS:** *sordid, mean, low, base, ignoble.* These adjectives mean lacking in dignity or falling short of moral standards. *Sordid* suggests foul, repulsive degradation: *"It is through art . . . that we can shield ourselves from the sordid perils of actual existence"* (Oscar Wilde). *Mean* suggests pettiness or spite: *"Never ascribe to an opponent motives meaner than your own"* (J.M. Barrie). Something *low* violates standards of morality, ethics, or propriety: *low cunning; a low trick. Base* suggests a contemptible, mean-spirited, or selfish lack of human decency: *"that liberal obedience, without which your army would be a base rabble"* (Edmund Burke). *Ignoble* means lacking noble qualities, such as elevated moral character: *"For my part I think it a less evil that some criminals should escape than that the government should play an ignoble part"* (Oliver Wendell Holmes, Jr.).

sore *adjective.* —*See* **angry, painful.**
sorehead *noun.* —*See* **grouch.**
soreness *noun.* —*See* **irritation, pain.**
sorority *noun.* —*See* **union** (1).
sorrow *noun.* —*See* **curse** (3), **depression** (2), **distress, grief.**
sorrow *verb.* To feel or express sorrow for ▶ deplore, regret, repent, rue. [*Compare* **feel.**] —*See also* **grieve.**
sorrowful *adjective.* Causing or expressing sadness, sorrow, or regret ▶ blue, cheerless, deplorable, depressing, discouraging, disheartening, dismal, dispiriting, doleful, dolorous, gloomy, grievous, heartbreaking, heart-rending, joyless, lamentable, lugubrious, melancholy, mournful, plaintive, regrettable, rueful, sad, saddening, woebegone, woeful. [*Compare* **affecting, gloomy, pitiful.**] —*See also* **depressed** (1).

✚ **CORE SYNONYMS:** *sorrowful, sad, melancholy, doleful, woebegone.* These adjectives mean causing or expressing sadness, sorrow, or regret. *Sorrowful* applies to emotional pain as that resulting from loss: *sorrowful mourners at the funeral. Sad* is the most general term: *"Better by far you should forget and smile/Than that you should remember and be sad"* (Christina Rossetti). *Melancholy* can refer to lingering or habitual somberness or sadness: *a melancholy poet's gloomy introspection. Doleful* describes what is mournful or morose: *the doleful expression of a reprimanded child. Woebegone* suggests grief or wretchedness, especially as reflected in a person's appearance: *"His sorrow . . . made him look . . . haggard and . . . woebegone"* (George du Maurier).

sorry *adjective.* Feeling or expressing sympathy, pity, or regret ▶ apologetic, compunctious, contrite, penitent, penitential, regretful, remorseful, repentant, rueful. ***Idiom:*** down on one's knees. —*See also* **disappointing, pitiful, shoddy.**
sort *noun.* —*See* **kind².**
sort *verb.* To set apart one kind or type from others ▶ separate, sift, winnow. ***Idiom:*** separate the sheep from the goats. —*See also* **arrange** (1), **classify.**
sortie *noun.* —*See* **battle, expedition.**
sortilege *noun.* —*See* **magic** (1).
so-so *adjective.* —*See* **ordinary.**
sot *noun.* —*See* **drunkard.**
sottish *adjective.* —*See* **drunk.**
sough *noun.* —*See* **murmur.**
sough *verb.* To make a low, continuous, and indistinct sound ▶ murmur, rustle, sigh, whisper. [*Compare* **burble, hum.**]
soul *noun.* The seat of a person's innermost emotions and feelings ▶ bosom, breast, heart. ***Idioms:*** the bottom (*or* cockles) of one's heart, one's heart of hearts. —*See also* **ghost, heart** (1), **human being, spirit** (2).
soulless *adjective.* —*See* **callous.**
soul mate *noun.* —*See* **friend.**
sound¹ *noun.* **1.** Vibrations detected by the ear ▶ noise, sonance. [*Compare* **noise, tone.**] **2.** Range of audibility ▶ earshot, hearing. [*Compare* **range.**]
sound *verb.* To give the impression of being ▶ appear, feel, look, seem. ***Idioms:*** have all the earmarks of being, give the idea (*or* impression) of being, strike one as being. [*Compare* **resemble.**] —*See also* **explore, pronounce, ring².**
sound² *adjective.* Based on good judgment, reasoning, or evidence ▶ cogent, just, solid, tight, valid, well-considered, well-founded, well-grounded. [*Compare* **convincing, logical.**] —*See also* **dependable, firm¹** (2), **good** (2), **healthy, sensible.**

✚ **CORE SYNONYMS:** *sound, valid, cogent.* These adjectives describe assertions, arguments, conclusions, reasons, or intellectual processes that are based on good judgment, reasoning, or evidence. What is *sound* is free from logical flaws or is based on valid reasoning: *a sound theory; sound principles.* What is *valid* is based on or borne out by truth or fact or has legal force: *a valid excuse; a valid claim.* Something *cogent* is both sound and compelling: *cogent testimony; a cogent explanation.*

---

sound³ *verb.* To test the attitude of someone ▶ feel (out), probe, sound out. ***Idioms:*** put out feelers, run something up the flagpole, send up a trial balloon.

sound⁴ *noun.* A body of water partly enclosed by land but having a wide outlet to the sea ▶ bay, bight, gulf. [*Compare* **channel, harbor, inlet.**]

soundless *adjective.* —*See* **silent** (1).

soundlessness *noun.* —*See* **silence** (1).

soundness *noun.* The condition of being free from defects or flaws ▶ flawlessness, intactness, integrity, perfection, wholeness. ***Idiom:*** mint condition. —*See also* **health** (1), **legality, sanity, stability.**

soup *noun.* —*See* **predicament.**

soupçon *noun.* —*See* **shade** (2).

soupy *adjective.* —*See* **sentimental.**

sour *adjective.* Having a taste characteristic of that produced by acids ▶ acerbic, acetous, acid, acidic, acidulous, dry, green, sharp, tangy, tart, unripe, vinegary. [*Compare* **bitter** (1). —*See also* **glum.**

sour *verb.* —*See* **disappoint.**

✚ **CORE SYNONYMS:** *sour, acid, acidic, acidulous, dry, tart.* These adjectives mean having a taste characteristic of that produced by an acid: *sour cider; acid, unripe grapes; mildly acidic yogurt; an acidulous tomato; dry white wine; tart cherries.*

---

source *noun.* An acquaintance who is in a position to help ▶ connection, contact. —*See also* **informer, origin.**

sourpuss *noun.* —*See* **grouch.**

souse *verb.* —*See* **dip** (1), **steep²**, **wet** (1).

souse *noun.* —*See* **bender, drunkard.**

soused *adjective.* —*See* **drunk.**

souvenir *noun.* —*See* **remembrance** (1).

sovereign *adjective.* —*See* **free** (1).

sovereign *noun.* —*See* **chief.**

sovereignty *noun.* —*See* **authority, freedom.**

sow *verb.* —*See* **plant.**

sozzled *noun.* —*See* **drunk.**

space *noun.* —*See* **bit¹** (3), **distance** (1), **expanse** (1), **hole** (1), **period** (1).

spaced-out *adjective.* —*See* **absent-minded, drugged.**

spacious *adjective.* Having plenty of room ▶ ample, capacious, commodious, roomy. [*Compare* **big.**] —*See also* **broad** (1).

spade *verb.* —*See* **dig, till.**

span¹ *noun.* —*See* **distance** (1), **extent, life, period** (1).

span *verb.* —*See* **cross** (1).

span² *noun.* —*See* **couple.**

spangle *noun.* A small sparkling decoration ▶ diamond, glitter, rhinestone, sequin.

spangle *verb.* —*See* **glitter.**

spank *verb.* —*See* **slap.**

spank *noun.* —*See* **slap.**

spar *verb.* —*See* **argue** (1), **contend.**

spare *verb.* —*See* **excuse** (1), **scrimp.**

spare *adjective.* —*See* **bare** (1), **meager, superfluous, thin** (1), **tight** (3).

sparing *adjective.* —*See* **economical.**

spark¹ *noun.* —*See* **flash** (1), **germ** (2).

spark *verb.* To set in motion ▶ activate, actuate, start, turn on. [*Compare* **energize.**] —*See also* **provoke.**

spark² *verb.* —*See* **court** (2).

sparkle *verb.* —*See* **glitter.**

sparkle *noun.* —*See* **glitter** (1), **glitter** (2), **spirit** (1).

sparkling *adjective.* Full of bright shifting or flickering light ▶ coruscating, flashing, gleaming, glinting, glistening, glittering, resplendent, scintillating, shimmering, twinkling, twinkly. [*Compare* **bright, brilliant, glossy.**] —*See also* **clever** (2), **lively.**

sparkly *adjective.* —*See* **lively.**

sparse *adjective.* —*See* **meager.**

spartan *adjective.* —*See* **bare** (1), **meager, temperate** (2).

spasm *noun.* —*See* **pain, tremor** (2).

spasmodic *adjective.* —*See* **uneven.**

spat *noun.* —*See* **argument, slap.**

spat *verb.* —*See* **argue** (1), **slap.**

spate *noun.* —*See* **flood, flow.**

spatter *verb.* —*See* **denigrate, rain** (2), **splash** (1), **stain.**

spawn *verb.* —*See* **breed, produce** (1).

spawn *noun.* The offspring, as of an animal or bird, for example, that are the result of one breeding season ▶ brood, litter, young. —*See also* **progeny.**

spawning *noun.* —*See* **reproduction.**

spay *verb.* —*See* **sterilize** (2).

speak *verb.* **1.** To express oneself in speech ▶ talk, verbalize, vocalize. ***Idioms:*** bend someone's ear, open one's mouth (*or* lips), put in (*or* into) words, wag one's tongue. [*Compare* **babble, chatter, say.**] **2.** To direct speech to ▶ address, talk. **3.** To talk to an audience formally ▶ lecture, prelect, sermonize. —*See also* **converse**[1].

speak for *verb.* To serve as an official delegate of ▶ act (as *or* for), answer for, represent, stand for. ***Idioms:*** be spokesperson (*or* representative) for, be the voice of. [*Compare* **substitute.**]

speak up *verb.* —*See* **object.**

speaker *noun.* **1.** One who delivers a public speech ▶ declaimer, lecturer, orator, rhetorician, speechifier, speechmaker. **2.** A person who speaks on behalf of another or others ▶ mouth, spokesman, spokesperson, spokeswoman. *Informal:* mouthpiece. [*Compare* **representative.**]

spear *verb.* —*See* **cut** (1).

special *adjective.* Relating to, identifying, or setting apart an individual or group ▶ characteristic, distinctive, distinguishing, especial, express, individual, particular, peculiar, set, specific, typical, vintage. [*Compare* **definite, distinct.**] —*See also* **exceptional.**

specialist *noun.* —*See* **expert.**

specialty *noun.* An area of academic study that is part of a larger body of learning ▶ branch, discipline, field. [*Compare* **area.**] —*See also* **business** (2), **detail, forte.**

species *noun.* —*See* **kind**[2].

specific *adjective.* —*See* **definite** (1), **definite** (2), **special.**

specifically *adverb.* —*See* **namely.**

specification *noun.* —*See* **provision.**

specify *verb.* To state specifically ▶ detail, particularize, provide, stipulate. [*Compare* **assert, describe, dictate.**] —*See also* **designate, name** (2).

specimen *noun.* —*See* **example** (1).

specious *adjective.* —*See* **fallacious** (1), **false.**

speciousness *noun.* —*See* **fallacy** (2).

speck *noun.* —*See* **bit**[1] (1), **point** (2).

speck *verb.* —*See* **speckle.**

speckle *verb.* To mark with many small spots ▶ bespeckle, besprinkle, dapple, dot, fleck, freckle, mottle, pepper, speck, spot, sprinkle, stipple. [*Compare* **streak.**]

speckle *noun.* —*See* **point** (2).

spectacle *noun.* —*See* **array, view** (2).

spectacular *adjective.* —*See* **dramatic** (2), **marvelous.**

spectator *noun.* —*See* **watcher** (1).

specter *noun.* —*See* **ghost.**

spectral *adjective.* —*See* **ghastly** (2).

spectrum *noun.* —*See* **range** (1).

speculate *verb.* To formulate as a tentative explanation ▶ hypothesize, theorize. [*Compare* **suppose.**] —*See also* **gamble** (3), **guess, think** (1).

speculation *noun.* —*See* **assumption, gamble, guess, theory** (1), **thought.**

speculative *adjective.* —*See* **curious** (2), **theoretical** (1), **thoughtful.**

speculator *noun.* One who speculates for quick profits ▶ adventurer, gambler, operator.

speech *noun.* **1.** The faculty, act, or product of speaking ▶ discourse, talk, utterance, verbalization, vocalization. [*Compare* **babble, chatter, expression.**] **2.** A usually formal spoken communication to an audience ▶ address, allocution, declamation, homily, lecture, oration, prelection, sermon, talk. [*Compare* **discourse, tirade.**] —*See also* **conversation, language** (1), **oratory.**

speechifier *noun.* —*See* **speaker** (1).

speechless *adjective.* Temporarily unable or unwilling to speak, as from shock or fear ▶ dumb, dumbstruck, inarticulate, mum, mute, silent, tongue-tied, voiceless, wordless. —*See also* **mute.**

speechlessness *noun.* —*See* **silence** (2).

speechmaker *noun.* —*See* **speaker** (1).

speed *verb.* To increase the speed of ▶ accelerate, expedite, hasten, hurry, hustle, quicken, speed up, step up. —*See also* **rush.**

speed *noun.* Rate of motion or performance ▶ pace, tempo, velocity. *Informal:* clip. —*See also* **haste** (1).

✚ **CORE SYNONYMS:** *speed, hurry, hasten, quicken, accelerate.* These verbs mean to proceed or cause to proceed rapidly or more rapidly. *Speed* refers to swift motion or action: *The train sped through the countryside. Postal workers labored overtime to speed delivery of the holiday mail. Hurry* implies a markedly faster rate than usual, often with concomitant confusion or commotion: *Hurry, or you'll miss the plane! Don't let anyone hurry you into making a decision. Hasten* suggests urgency and often eager or rash swiftness: *My doctor hastened to reassure me that the tests were negative. His off-color jokes only hastened his dismissal. Quicken* and especially *accelerate* refer to increase in rate of activity, growth, or progress: *The skater's breathing quickened as he neared the end of his routine. The runner quickened her pace as she drew near the finish line. The economic expansion has continued but is no longer accelerating. Heat greatly accelerates the deterioration of perishable foods.*

speediness *noun.* —*See* **haste** (1).

speedy *adjective.* —*See* **fast** (1), **quick.**

spell[1] *verb.* —*See* **mean**[1].

spell out *verb.* —*See* **explain** (1).

spell[2] *noun.* A word or formula believed to have magic powers ▶ abracadabra, charm, enchantment, incantation, magic. [*Compare* **curse.**]

spell *verb.* —*See* **charm** (2).

spell[3] *noun.* —*See* **bit**[1] (3), **seizure** (1), **turn** (1).

spell *verb.* To free from a specific duty by acting as a substitute ▶ relieve, take over. [*Compare* **substitute.**]

spellbind *verb.* —*See* **charm** (2), **grip.**

spend *verb.* **1.** To give money as payment ▶ disburse, expend, give, lay out, outlay, pay (out). *Informal:* fork out (*or* over *or* up), shell out. [*Compare* **waste.**] **2.** To use time in a particular way ▶ pass, put in. [*Compare* **idle.**] **3.** To be depleted ▶ consume, exhaust, go. ***Idiom:*** go down the drain. —*See also* **exhaust** (1), **lead.**

✚ **CORE SYNONYMS:** *spend, disburse, expend.* These verbs mean to pay or give out money or an equivalent: *spent eight dollars for a movie ticket; disbursed funds from the account; expended all her energy teaching the class.*

◀ **ANTONYM:** *save*

spendthrift *noun.* —*See* **wastrel** (1).

spendthrift *adjective.* —*See* **extravagant.**

spent *adjective.* —*See* **tired** (1).

spew *verb.* —*See* **erupt, vomit.**

sphere *noun.* —*See* **ball, range** (1).

spherical *or* **spheric** *adjective.* —*See* **round** (1).

spheroid *noun.* —*See* **ball.**

spice *noun.* —*See* **flavoring.**

spice *verb.* To impart flavor to ▶ flavor, season.

spice up *verb.* —*See* **change** (1).

spick-and-span *adjective.* —*See* **clean** (1), **neat.**

spicy *adjective.* Having a sharp, penetrating flavor or aroma ▶ aromatic, fiery, hot, peppery, piquant, pungent, racy, redolent, savory, seasoned, sharp, zesty. [*Compare* **delicious.**] —*See also* **erotic, racy.**

spiel *verb.* —*See* **chatter** (1).

spigot *noun.* —*See* **faucet, plug.**

spike *noun.* A sharp protuberance or projection ▶ barb, jag, needle, prick, prickle, prong, quill, snag, spine, spinule, spur, sticker, thorn, tine, tooth. [*Compare* **point.**] —*See also* **nail.**

spiky *adjective.* —*See* **thorny** (1).

spile *noun.* —*See* **plug.**

spill *verb.* —*See* **betray** (2), **fall** (1), **spread** (2).

spill *noun.* —*See* **fall** (1).

spin *verb.* To have the sensation of turning in circles ▶ reel, swim, swirl, whirl. ***Idiom:*** go round and round. —*See also* **lengthen, turn** (1).

spin *noun.* —*See* **drive** (3), **explanation, revolution** (1).

spindling *or* **spindly** *adjective.* —*See* **gangling.**

spine *noun.* —*See* **courage, spike.**

spineless *adjective.* —*See* **cowardly.**

spinning *adjective.* —*See* **dizzy** (1).

spinoff *noun.* —*See* **derivative.**

spinule *noun.* —*See* **spike.**

spiny *adjective.* Full of irritating difficulties or controversies ▶ nettlesome, prickly, thorny. [*Compare* **complex, delicate, disturbing, troublesome.**] —*See also* **thorny** (1).

spiral *verb.* —*See* **wind**[2].

spiral *noun.* —*See* **curl.**

spiral *adjective.* —*See* **curly.**

spirit *noun.* **1.** A lively, emphatic, eager quality or manner ▶ animation, bounce, brio, dash, élan, esprit, life, liveliness, pertness, sparkle, verve, vigor, vim, vivaciousness, vivacity, zing, zip. *Informal:* ginger, pep, peppiness. *Slang:* oomph. [*Compare* **energy.**] **2.** The vital principle or animating force within living beings ▶ anima, breath, consciousness, divine spark, élan vital, life force, pneuma, psyche, soul, vital force, vitality. —*See also* **courage, ghost, heart** (1), **human being, temper** (3).

spirit *verb.* —*See* **smuggle.**

spirit away *verb.* To seize and detain a person unlawfully ▶ abduct, kidnap, snatch, take hostage. [*Compare* **seize, steal.**] —*See also* **steal.**

✣ **CORE SYNONYMS:** *spirit, dash, verve, vigor, vim.* These nouns denote a lively, emphatic, eager quality or manner: *a cheerleading cry that showed real spirit; played the piano with dash; painted with verve; intellectual vigor; arguing with their usual vim.*

---

spirited *adjective.* —*See* **brave, lively.**

spiritless *adjective.* —*See* **depressed** (1), **dull** (1), **languid.**

spirits *noun.* —*See* **mood.**

spiritual *adjective.* Of or relating to a church or to an established religion ▶ church, churchly, ecclesiastical, religious. [*Compare* **clerical, divine, holy, ritual.**] —*See also* **immaterial, supernatural** (1).

spirituality *noun.* —*See* **devotion.**

spirituous *adjective.* —*See* **hard** (3).

spit *noun.* Saliva or other liquid ejected from the mouth ▶ expectorate, mucus, phlegm, saliva, spittle, sputum. [*Compare* **drool.**] —*See also* **rain.**

spit *verb.* To expel a small amount of saliva or mucus from the mouth ▶ expectorate, hawk. [*Compare* **drool.**] —*See also* **rain** (2).

spit up *verb.* —*See* **vomit.**

spite *noun.* The quality or condition of being vindictive ▶ revenge, spitefulness, vengefulness, vindictiveness. [*Compare* **resentment.**] —*See also* **malevolence.**

spiteful *adjective.* —*See* **malevolent, vindictive.**

spitefulness *noun.* The quality or condition of being vindictive ▶ revenge, spite, vengefulness, vindictiveness. [*Compare* **resentment.**] —*See also* **malevolence.**

spitting image *noun.* —*See* **double.**

spittle *noun.* —*See* **spit.**

splash *verb.* **1.** To hurl or scatter liquid ▶ bespatter, dash, slop, slosh, spatter, splatter, spray, sprinkle, swash. [*Compare* **rain, squirt.**] **2.** To make the sound of moving or disturbed water ▶ lap, swash, wash. [*Compare* **burble, swish.**]

splash *noun.* —*See* **drop** (4).

splashy *adjective.* —*See* **showy.**

splatter *verb.* —*See* **splash** (1), **stain.**

splay *verb.* —*See* **spread** (1).

spleen *noun.* —*See* **temper** (1).

splendid *adjective.* —*See* **excellent, glorious, grand, marvelous.**

splendor *noun.* —*See* **glory.**

splendorous *or* **splendrous** *adjective.* —*See* **glorious.**

splenetic *adjective.* —*See* **ill-tempered.**

splice *verb.* —*See* **weave.**

splinter *verb.* To withdraw from an association or federation ▶ pull out, secede, splinter off, withdraw. *Informal:* split (away). [*Compare* **quit.**] —*See also* **break** (1).

split *verb. Informal* To withdraw from an association or federation ▶ pull out, secede, splinter (off), withdraw. *Informal:* split (away). [*Compare* **quit.**] —*See also* **branch, crack** (1), **cut** (2), **divide, go** (1), **separate** (1), **tear**[1].

split up *verb.* —*See* **scatter** (2).

split *noun.* —*See* **allotment, breach** (2), **crack** (2), **cut** (1), **division** (1).

splotch *noun.* —*See* **smear.**

splotch *verb.* —*See* **stain.**

splurge *noun.* —*See* **binge.**

splurge *verb.* —*See* **luxuriate, waste.**

splurgy *adjective.* —*See* **showy.**

splutter *verb.* To make a series of short, sharp noises ▶ crackle, crepitate, sputter. [*Compare* **crack, hiss, snap.**] —*See also* **stammer.**

spoil *verb.* To overindulge with affection or attention ▶ dote on. [*Compare* **rave.**] —*See also* **baby, botch, decay, destroy** (1).

spoilage *noun.* —*See* **decay.**

spoiled *adjective.* —*See* **bad** (2).

spoils *noun.* The political appointments or jobs that are at the disposal of those in power ▶ patronage, pork. —*See also* **plunder.**

spoilsport *noun.* —*See* **killjoy.**

spoken *adjective.* —*See* **oral.**

spokesman *or* **spokeswoman** *noun.* —*See* **speaker** (2).

sponge *noun.* —*See* **drunkard, parasite.**

sponge *verb.* To take advantage of the generosity of others ▶ leech, live off. *Slang:* freeload. [*Compare* **beg.**]

sponge up *verb.* —*See* **absorb** (2), **drink** (3).

spongy *adjective.* —*See* **absorbent, soft** (1).

sponsor *noun.* One who assumes financial responsibility for another ▶ backer, guarantor, guaranty, surety, underwriter. *Informal:* angel. [*Compare* **advocate, donor.**] —*See also* **patron.**

sponsor *verb.* To act as a patron to ▶ back, patronize, support. [*Compare* **donate, finance, support.**]

sponsorship *noun.* —*See* **patronage** (1).

spontaneity *noun.* The absence of forethought, prompting, or planning in action ▶ automaticity, impulsiveness, impulsivity, instinctiveness, involuntariness, reflexiveness, reflexivity. [*Compare* **improvisation, temerity.**] —*See also* **ease** (1).

spontaneous *adjective.* Acting or happening without apparent forethought, prompting, or planning ▶ automatic, impulsive, instinctive, involuntary, natural, reflex, reflexive, unplanned, unpremeditated, unprompted, unrehearsed. [*Compare* **extemporaneous, instinctive, rash**[1], **unintentional.**] —*See also* **easygoing, voluntary.**

✤ **CORE SYNONYMS:** *spontaneous, impulsive, instinctive, involuntary, automatic.* These adjectives mean acting, reacting, or happening without apparent forethought, prompting, or planning. *Spontaneous* applies to what arises naturally rather than resulting from external constraint or stimulus: "*The highest and best form of efficiency is the spontaneous cooperation of a free people*" (Woodrow Wilson). *Impulsive* refers to the operation of a sudden urge or feeling not governed by reason: *Buying a car was an impulsive act that he immediately regretted. Instinctive* implies behavior that is a natural consequence of membership in a species. The term also applies to what reflects or comes about as a result of a natural inclination or innate impulse: *Helping people in an emergency seems as instinctive as breathing. Involuntary* refers to what is not subject to the control of the will: "*People drew in their breath with involuntary surprise and suspense*" (Harriet Beecher Stowe). *Automatic* implies an unvarying mechanical response or reaction: *She accepted the subpoena with an automatic "thank you."*

---

spontaneously *adverb.* **1.** Without apparent forethought, prompting, or planning ▶ automatically, impulsively, instinctively, involuntarily, reflexively. **2.** Of one's own free will ▶ by choice, freely, voluntarily, willfully, willingly. ***Idioms:*** of one's own accord, on one's own volition.

spoof *noun.* —*See* **satire.**

spook *noun.* —*See* **ghost, spy.**

spook *verb.* —*See* **frighten.**

spooked *adjective.* —*See* **afraid.**

spooky *adjective.* —*See* **weird.**

spoon *verb.* —*See* **dip** (2), **neck.**

spoor *noun.* —*See* **track.**

sporadic *adjective.* —*See* **infrequent, intermittent.**

sporadically *adverb.* —*See* **infrequently, intermittently.**

sport *noun.* —*See* **amusement, play.**

sport *verb.* —*See* **display, play** (1).

sport coat *or* **sports coat** *or* **sport jacket** *or* **sports jacket** *noun.* —*See* **coat** (1).

sporting *adjective.* According to the rules ▶ clean, fair, sportsmanlike, sportsmanly.

sportingly *adverb.* —*See* **fair[1].**

sportive *adjective.* —*See* **mischievous.**

sportsmanlike *or* **sportsmanly** *adjective.* According to the rules ▶ clean, fair, sporting.

spot *noun.* —*See* **point** (2), **position** (1), **position** (3), **predicament, smear, stain.**

spot *verb.* To look for and discover ▶ find, locate, pinpoint. *Informal:* scare up. [*Compare* **trace, uncover.**] —*See also* **discern, position, see** (1), **speckle, stain.**

spot *adjective.* —*See* **random.**

spotless *adjective.* —*See* **clean** (1).

spotlight *verb.* —*See* **emphasize.**

spotty *adjective.* —*See* **uneven.**

spousal *adjective.* —*See* **marital.**

spousals *noun.* —*See* **wedding.**

spouse *noun.* A person who is married to another ▶ consort, helpmate, helpmeet, husband, mate, partner, wife. *Informal:* better half, hubby, missis, other half. *Slang:* old lady, old man. [*Compare* **lover.**]

spouseless *adjective.* —*See* **single.**

spout *verb.* To eject or be ejected in a sudden thin, swift stream ▶ jet, spray, spurt, squirt. [*Compare* **erupt, flow.**]

spout *noun.* A sudden swift stream of ejected liquid ▶ jet, spray, spurt, squirt. [*Compare* **flow.**]

sprain *verb.* To injure a bodily part by twisting ▶ strain, twist, turn, wrench. [*Compare* **hurt.**]

sprawl *verb.* To sit or lie with the limbs spread out awkwardly ▶ drape, loll, lounge, spread-eagle, straddle. [*Compare* **lie[1], slouch.**] —*See also* **spread** (2).

sprawl *noun.* —*See* **buildup** (2).

spray *noun.* A sudden swift stream of ejected liquid ▶ jet, spout, spurt, squirt. [*Compare* **flow.**]

spray *verb.* To eject or be ejected in a sudden thin, swift stream ▶ jet, spout, spurt, squirt. [*Compare* **erupt, flow.**] —*See also* **splash** (1).

spread *verb.* **1.** To move or arrange so as to cover a larger area ▶ expand, extend, fan (out), open (out *or* up), outstretch, splay, stretch, unfold, unfurl, unroll. **2.** To extend or distribute over a wide area ▶ circulate, diffuse, disperse, disseminate, distribute, radiate, scatter, spill, sprawl, straggle, strew. [*Compare* **distribute.**] **3.** To become known far and wide ▶ circulate, get around, go around, travel. ***Idioms:*** go (*or* make) the rounds. **4.** To arrange tableware upon a table in preparation for a meal ▶ lay, set. —*See also* **broaden, communicate** (2), **cover** (1).

spread *noun. Informal* A large, elaborately prepared meal ▶ banquet, feast, junket. *Informal:* feed. —*See also* **buildup** (2), **expanse** (1), **expansion.**

spread *adjective.* —*See* **open** (2).

spread-eagle *verb.* —*See* **sprawl.**

spree *noun.* —*See* **bender, binge.**

sprig *noun.* —*See* **shoot.**

sprightliness *noun.* —*See* **energy.**

sprightly *adjective.* —*See* **energetic.**

spring *verb.* —*See* **bound[1], descend, free** (1), **jump** (1), **stem.**

spring back *verb.* To reverse direction after striking something ▶ bounce (back), rebound, reflect, snap back. [*Compare* **bend, glance.**]

spring for *verb.* —*See* **treat** (2).

spring *noun.* **1.** The act of jumping ▶ jump, pounce, leap, vault. [*Compare* **fall.**] **2.** The season of the year during which the weather becomes warmer and plants revive ▶ seedtime, springtide, springtime. —*See also* **birth** (2), **bound[1]** (2), **cause** (2), **flexibility** (1), **origin, youth** (1).

springiness *noun.* —*See* **flexibility** (1).

springtime *noun.* The season of the year during which the weather becomes warmer and plants revive ▶ seedtime, spring, springtide. —*See also* **youth** (1).

springy *adjective.* —*See* **flexible** (1).

sprinkle *verb.* To scatter or release in drops or small particles ▶ besprinkle, dust, pepper, powder. [*Compare* **spread.**] —*See also* **rain** (2), **speckle, splash** (1).

sprinkle *noun.* —*See* **rain.**

sprint *verb.* —*See* **run** (1), **rush.**

sprint *noun.* —*See* **run** (1).

sprite *noun.* —*See* **fairy.**

sprout *noun.* —*See* **shoot.**

spruce *adjective.* —*See* **neat.**

spruce *verb.* —*See* **renew** (1), **tidy** (1), **tidy** (2).

spry *adjective.* —*See* **energetic.**

spryness *noun.* —*See* **agility.**

spume *noun.* —*See* **foam.**

spume *verb.* —*See* **foam.**

spumous *or* **spumy** *adjective.* —*See* **foamy.**

spunk *or* **spunkiness** *noun.* —*See* **courage.**

spunky *adjective.* —*See* **brave.**

spur *noun.* —*See* **spike, stimulus.**

spur *verb.* —*See* **provoke.**

spurious *adjective.* —*See* **counterfeit, fallacious** (1), **false, illegitimate.**

spuriousness *noun.* —*See* **fallacy** (2).

spurn *verb.* —*See* **decline, snub.**

spur-of-the-moment *adjective.* —*See* **extemporaneous.**

spurt *noun.* A sudden swift stream of ejected liquid ▶ jet, spout, spray, squirt. [*Compare* **flow.**]

spurt *verb.* To eject or be ejected in a sudden thin, swift stream ▶ jet, spout, spray, squirt. [*Compare* **erupt, flow.**]

sputter *verb.* To make a series of short, sharp noises ▶ crackle, crepitate, splutter. [*Compare* **crack, hiss, snap.**] —*See also* **smolder, stammer.**

sputum *noun.* —*See* **spit.**

spy *noun.* A person who secretly observes others to obtain information ▶ agent, asset, fifth columnist, operative, secret agent, undercover agent. *Informal:* spook.

spy *verb.* —*See* **see** (1).

squabble *verb.* —*See* **argue** (1), **quibble.**

squabble *noun.* —*See* **argument.**

squad *noun.* —*See* **detachment** (3), **force** (3).

squadron *noun.* —*See* **force** (3).

squalid *adjective.* Heavily soiled; very dirty or unclean ▶ filthy, foul, nasty, vile. —*See also* **dirty, sordid.**

squall[1] *verb.* —*See* **bawl, cry.**

squall[2] *noun.* —*See* **storm.**

squall *verb.* To manifest strong winds and precipitation ▶ blow (up), set in, storm. [*Compare* **rain.**]

squalor *noun.* —*See* **dirtiness.**

squander *verb.* —*See* **lose** (2), **waste.**

squander *noun.* —*See* **extravagance.**

square *noun. Slang* An old-fashioned person who is reluctant to change or innovate ▶ fogy, fossil, fuddy-duddy, mossback. *Informal:* stick-in-the-mud, stuffed shirt. [*Compare* **drip, dullard, fool.**] —*See also* **common.**

square *adjective.* Owing or being owed nothing ▶ even, quit, quits. *Informal:* even-steven. —*See also* **conventional, even** (2), **fair**[1] (1).

square *verb.* —*See* **agree** (1), **equalize, settle** (3).

square *adverb.* —*See* **directly** (3).

squarely *adverb.* —*See* **directly** (3), **fairly** (1).

squash *verb.* —*See* **crush** (1), **suppress.**

squashy *adjective.* —*See* **soft** (1).

squat *verb.* —*See* **stoop.**

squat *adjective.* —*See* **stocky.**

squawk *verb.* —*See* **complain, object, shout.**

squawk *noun.* —*See* **complaint, shout.**

squawky *adjective.* —*See* **harsh.**

squeal *verb.* To utter a shrill, short cry ▶ yap, yawp, yelp, yip. [*Compare* **cry, shout.**] —*See also* **inform** (2).

squeal *noun.* A shrill, short cry ▶ yap, yawp, yelp, yip.

squealer *noun.* —*See* **informer.**

squeamish *adjective.* —*See* **fussy.**

squeeze *verb.* **1.** To subject to compression ▶ compact, compress, constrict, constringe, pinch, scrunch. [*Compare* **crush, wrench.**] **2.** To extract from by applying pressure ▶ crush, express, press. **3.** To handle in a way so as to mix, form, and shape ▶ knead, manipulate, work. —*See also* **crowd, embrace** (1), **extort.**

squeeze *noun.* —*See* **constriction, embrace.**

squelch *verb.* —*See* **repress, suppress.**

squib *noun.* —*See* **item.**

squiggle *verb.* —*See* **crawl** (1).

squint *verb.* To peer with the eyes partly closed ▶ squinch. ***Idiom:*** screw up one's eyes. [*Compare* **gaze, glimpse.**] —*See also* **tend**[1].

squint-eyed *or* **squinty** *adjective.* Marked by or affected with a squint ▶ cross-eyed, strabismal, strabismic.

squirm *verb.* To twist agitatedly, as in pain, struggle, or embarrassment ▶ toss, twist, writhe. [*Compare* **shake.**] —*See also* **crawl** (1).

squirrel away *verb.* —*See* **hide**[1], **save** (1).

squirt *verb.* To eject or be ejected in a sudden thin, swift stream ▶ jet, spout, spray, spurt. [*Compare* **erupt, flow.**]

squirt *noun.* **1.** A sudden swift stream of ejected liquid ▶ jet, spout, spurt, spray. [*Compare* **flow.**] **2.** *Informal* A small or young person ▶ pup, puppy, scrub, small fry. *Informal:* pip-squeak, shorty *Slang:* half-pint, punk, runt, shrimp. —*See also* **nonentity.**

squishy *adjective.* —*See* **soft** (1).

stab *verb.* —*See* **cut** (1), **plunge.**

stab *noun.* —*See* **attempt, dig, pain, prick.**

stabbing *adjective.* —*See* **painful, sharp** (3).

stability *noun.* Reliability in withstanding pressure, force, or stress ▶ fastness, firmness, hardness, security, solidity, soundness, stableness, steadiness, strength, sturdiness, sureness. [*Compare* **balance.**]

stabilize *verb.* —*See* **balance** (1), **support** (2).

stable *adjective.* —*See* **dependable, firm**[1] (2).
stable *noun.* —*See* **crowd, flock.**
stableness *noun.* —*See* **stability.**
stack *noun.* —*See* **heap** (1).
stack *verb.* —*See* **heap** (1).
stack up *verb.* —*See* **equal** (1).
staff *noun.* —*See* **stick** (2).
staffer *noun.* —*See* **employee.**
stage *noun.* **1.** A raised platform on which theatrical performances or speeches are given ▶ boards, dais, podium, proscenium, pulpit, rostrum, soapbox. **2.** The art and occupation of an actor ▶ acting, dramatics, theater, theatrics. **3.** A temporary framework with a floor, used by laborers ▶ platform, scaffold, scaffolding, staging. [*Compare* **base**[1].] **4.** An interval regarded as a distinct evolutionary or developmental unit ▶ period, phase. [*Compare* **age.**] **5.** A stage of a competition ▶ heat, round. [*Compare* **competition, turn.**] —*See also* **degree** (1), **occasion** (1), **scene** (1).
stage *verb.* To produce on the stage ▶ act (out), direct, do, dramatize, enact, give, mount, perform, present, produce, put on. [*Compare* **conduct.**] —*See also* **have** (3).
stagger *verb.* **1.** To walk unsteadily ▶ careen, dodder, falter, halt, hitch, hobble, limp, lurch, reel, stumble, sway, teeter, totter, weave, wobble. [*Compare* **blunder, sway, trudge.**] **2.** To overwhelm with surprise, wonder, or bewilderment ▶ boggle, bowl over, dumbfound, flabbergast, floor, shock, stun. *Informal:* knock out (*or* over). ***Idioms:*** be thunderstruck at, strike dumb (*or* speechless), take someone's breath away. [*Compare* **startle, surprise.**] —*See also* **daze** (1), **hesitate, muddle.**
staggering *adjective.* —*See* **astonishing.**
staginess *noun.* —*See* **theatricalism.**
stagnant *adjective.* —*See* **airless** (2), **slow** (2).
stagnation *noun.* —*See* **inaction.**
staid *adjective.* —*See* **serious** (1).
staidness *noun.* —*See* **seriousness** (1).
stain *verb.* To mark or soil with foreign matter ▶ bespatter, bestain, blotch, discolor, smut, spatter, splatter, splotch, spot. [*Compare* **dirty, smear.**] —*See also* **color** (1), **corrupt, denigrate, finish** (2).
stain *noun.* A mark of discredit or disgrace ▶ black eye, blemish, blot, onus, spot, stigma, taint, tarnish. ***Idioms:*** a blot on one's name (*or* escutcheon). [*Compare* **disgrace, reflection.**] —*See also* **color** (2), **finish, smear.**

✚ CORE SYNONYMS: *stain, blot, stigma, taint.* These nouns denote a mark of discredit or disgrace, as on one's good name: *a stain on his honor; the blot of treason; the stigma of ignominious defeat; the taint of vice.*

---

stainless *adjective.* —*See* **clean** (1).
stake *noun.* A right or legal share in something ▶ claim, interest, portion, title. [*Compare* **cut, right.**] —*See also* **bet, capital** (1), **stick** (1).
stake *verb.* —*See* **finance, gamble** (2).
verb To pay regular and close attention to ▶ follow, monitor, observe, survey, watch. ***Idioms:*** have one's (*or* keep an) eye on, keep tabs on, keep track of, ride herd on.
stakeout *noun.* —*See* **lookout** (1).
stale *adjective.* —*See* **airless** (1), **flat** (2), **moldy, trite.**
stalemate *noun.* An equality of scores, votes, or performances in a contest ▶ dead heat, deadlock, draw, standoff, tie.
staleness *noun.* —*See* **dullness.**
stalk[1] *noun.* The main ascending part of a plant, which supports the other parts ▶ stem, stock, trunk. [*Compare* **shoot.**]
stalk[2] *verb.* —*See* **hunt.**
stall[1] *verb.* —*See* **stop** (1), **stop** (2).
stall *noun.* A small, often makeshift structure for the display and sale of goods ▶ booth, counter, stand. [*Compare* **store.**] —*See also* **cage.**

stall[2] *verb.*—*See* **defer**[1], **delay** (1), **delay** (2).
stalwart *adjective.* —*See* **strong** (2).
stamina *noun.* —*See* **endurance.**
stammer *verb.* To speak with involuntary repetitions or pauses; speak hesitatingly or clumsily ▶ falter, splutter, sputter, stumble, stutter. [*Compare* **babble, chatter, hesitate.**]
stammer *noun.* A way of speaking marked by involuntary repetitions and pauses ▶ stammering, stutter, stuttering.
stamp *verb.* To step on heavily and repeatedly so as to crush, injure, or destroy ▶ stomp, tramp, trample, tread, tromp. [*Compare* **crush.**] —*See also* **beat** (3), **engrave** (2), **trudge.**
stamp out *verb.* —*See* **annihilate.**
stamp *noun.* —*See* **appearance** (1), **impression** (1), **kind**[2], **sign** (1).
stamping ground *noun.* —*See* **haunt.**
stance *noun.*—*See* **posture** (1), **posture** (2).
stand *verb.* **1.** To adopt a standing posture ▶ arise, get up, jump up, rise, stand up, uprise. ***Idioms:*** get (*or* jump *or* leap *or* spring) to one's feet, take one's feet. **2.** To be in a certain position; have a location ▶ be located, be situated, rest, sit. —*See also* **endure** (1), **endure** (2), **treat** (2).
stand against *verb.* —*See* **oppose.**
stand behind *verb.* —*See* **guarantee** (1), **support** (1).
stand by *verb.* —*See* **support** (1).
stand for *verb.* To serve as an official delegate of ▶ act (as *or* for), answer for, represent, speak for. ***Idioms:*** be spokesperson (*or* representative) for, be the voice of. [*Compare* **substitute.**] —*See also* **represent** (1).
stand in *verb.* —*See* **substitute.**
stand out *verb.* To be obtrusively conspicuous ▶ glare, stick out. ***Idioms:*** stare someone in the face, stick out like a sore thumb. —*See also* **bulge.**
stand up *verb.* To prove valid under scrutiny ▶ hold up, prove out. *Informal:* wash. ***Idioms:*** hold water, pass muster, ring true. —*See also* **bear.**
stand *noun.* A small, often makeshift structure for the display and sale of goods ▶ booth, counter, stall. [*Compare* **store.**] —*See also* **base**[1] (2), **viewpoint.**
standard *noun.* A means by which individuals are compared and judged ▶ benchmark, criterion, gauge, mark, measure, norm, test, touchstone, yardstick. [*Compare* **condition, law, rule.**] —*See also* **flag**[1], **model, original.**
standard *adjective.* —*See* **authoritative** (1), **conventional, ordinary.**

✚ **CORE SYNONYMS:** *standard, benchmark, criterion, gauge, measure, touchstone, yardstick.* These nouns denote a point of reference against which individuals are compared and judged: *a book that is a standard of literary excellence; a painting that is a benchmark of quality; criteria for hiring an excellent teacher; behavior that is a gauge of self-control; donations from the public, a measure of the importance of the arts; the program's success, a touchstone of cooperation in the community; farm failures, a yardstick of federal banking policy.*

---

standardize *verb.* —*See* **conventionalize.**
standards *noun.* —*See* **ethics** (2).
standby *adjective.* —*See* **auxiliary** (2).
stand-in *noun.* —*See* **substitute.**
standing *noun.* —*See* **basis** (3), **face** (6), **place** (1).
standing *adjective.* —*See* **vertical.**
standoff *noun.* An equality of scores, votes, or performances in a contest ▶ dead heat, deadlock, draw, stalemate, tie.
standoffish *adjective.* —*See* **cool.**
standout *adjective.* —*See* **exceptional.**
standpat *adjective.* —*See* **ultraconservative.**
standpoint *noun.* —*See* **viewpoint.**
standstill *noun.* —*See* **stop** (2).
star *noun.* —*See* **celebrity, lead.**
starch *noun.* —*See* **energy.**

staple *adjective.* —*See* **primary** (1).

starchy *adjective.* Rigidly constrained or formal; lacking grace and spontaneity ▶ buckram, stiff, stilted, wooden. [*Compare* **cool, forced, prudish.**]

star-crossed *adjective.* —*See* **unfortunate** (1).

stare *verb.* —*See* **gaze.**

stare *noun.* An intent fixed look ▶ gape, gaze. [*Compare* **look.**]

stargaze *verb.* —*See* **dream.**

stargazer *noun.* —*See* **dreamer** (1).

stark *adjective.* —*See* **bare** (1), **bleak** (1), **utter**[2].

starry-eyed *adjective.* —*See* **dreamy, idealistic.**

start *verb.* **1.** To go about the initial step in doing something ▶ approach, begin, commence, embark on (*or* upon), enter (on *or* upon), get off, inaugurate, initiate, institute, launch, lead off, open, set about, set out, set to, take on, take up, undertake. *Informal:* kick off. ***Idioms:*** get cracking, get going, get the ball rolling, get the show on the road, take the plunge. [*Compare* **cause, introduce, produce.**] **2.** To set in motion ▶ activate, actuate, spark, turn on. [*Compare* **energize, provoke.**] **3.** To move suddenly and involuntarily ▶ bolt, jump. [*Compare* **bump, jerk.**] —*See also* **begin, flinch, found.**

start out *verb.* —*See* **bear** (5).

start *noun.* A sudden and involuntary movement ▶ bolt, jump, startle. [*Compare* **jerk, recoil.**] —*See also* **advantage** (1), **beginning, birth** (2).

✤ **CORE SYNONYMS:** *start, begin, commence, initiate, inaugurate.* These verbs mean to go about the initial step in doing something. *Start, begin,* and *commence* are equivalent in meaning, though *commence* is more formal, and *start* often stresses the point where inaction turns to action: *The play begins at eight o'clock. The festivities commenced with the national anthem. We will stay on the platform until the train starts. Initiate* applies to causing the first steps in a process: *I initiated a lawsuit against the driver who hit my car. Inaugurate* often connotes a formal beginning: "*The exhibition inaugurated a new era of cultural relations*" (Serge Schmemann).

---

starter *noun.* —*See* **appetizer.**

startle *verb.* To cause to experience a sudden momentary shock ▶ electrify, jolt, shock. ***Idioms:*** give someone a start, make someone jump, make someone's heart skip a beat (*or* stand still). [*Compare* **stagger.**] —*See also* **frighten, surprise.**

startle *noun.* A sudden and involuntary movement ▶ bolt, jump, start. [*Compare* **jerk, recoil.**]

start-up *or* **startup** *noun.* —*See* **foundation.**

starving *adjective.* —*See* **hungry** (1).

stash *verb.* —*See* **hide**[1], **save** (1).

stash *noun.* —*See* **hoard.**

stasis *noun.* —*See* **balance** (1).

state *noun.* **1.** An organized geopolitical unit ▶ body politic, country, land, nation, polity. **2.** *Informal* A condition of excited distress ▶ fume. *Informal:* snit, sweat, swivet. *Slang:* tizzy. [*Compare* **agitation, distress.**] —*See also* **condition** (1), **government** (2).

state *verb.* —*See* **air** (2), **assert, say.**

stately *adjective.* —*See* **ceremonious, gracious** (2), **grand.**

statement *noun.* Something said ▶ saying, utterance, word. [*Compare* **language, speech.**] —*See also* **account** (2), **assertion, expression** (1), **message, story** (1).

state of mind *noun.* —*See* **mood.**

static *adjective.* —*See* **motionless.**

station *noun.* A stopping place along a route for picking up or dropping off passengers ▶ depot, stop, terminal, terminus. —*See also* **base**[1] (1), **place** (1).

station *verb.* To appoint and send to a particular place ▶ assign, post, set. [*Compare* **position.**]

stationary *adjective.* —*See* **fixed, motionless.**

statue *or* **statuette** *noun.* —*See* **sculpture.**

statuesque *adjective.* —*See* **beautiful.**

stature *noun.* —*See* **merit.**

status *noun.* —*See* **basis** (3), **condition** (1), **face** (6), **honor** (2), **place** (1).

statute *noun.* —*See* **law** (2).

staunch *adjective.* —*See* **faithful.**

stave *noun.* —*See* **stick** (2).

stave off *verb.* —*See* **prevent, repel.**

stay[1] *verb.* —*See* **defer**[1], **endure** (2), **live**[1], **lodge, remain, stop** (2), **visit** (1).

stay with *verb.* —*See* **keep** (5).

stay *noun.* A remaining in a place as a guest or lodger ▶ sojourn, stop, stopover, visit. —*See also* **delay** (1), **restraint, stop** (1).

stay[2] *noun.* —*See* **support.**

staying power *noun.* —*See* **endurance.**

stead *noun.* The function or position customarily occupied by another ▶ lieu, place.

steadfast *adjective.* —*See* **dependable, faithful, firm**[1] (3), **fixed.**

steadfastness *noun.* —*See* **fidelity.**

steadiness *noun.* —*See* **balance** (2), **changelessness, stability.**

steady *adjective.* —*See* **dependable, firm**[1] (2), **firm**[1] (3), **fixed, gradual** (2), **unchanging.**

steady *verb.* —*See* **balance** (1), **support** (2).

steady *noun.* —*See* **lover.**

steady-going *adjective.* —*See* **dependable.**

steal *verb.* To take another's property without permission ▶ abscond with, carry off, crib, embezzle, filch, mooch, pilfer, purloin, snatch, spirit away, thieve. *Informal:* lift, swipe. *Slang:* boost, cop, dip, heist, hook, nip, pinch, rip off, snitch. ***Idioms:*** make (*or* walk) off with, run off (*or* away) with. [*Compare* **kidnap, rob, sack**[2], **seize.**] —*See also* **sneak.**

steal *noun. Slang* Something offered or bought at a low price ▶ bargain, find. *Informal:* buy, deal. —*See also* **larceny.**

✣ **CORE SYNONYMS:** *steal, purloin, filch, snitch, pilfer, cop, hook, swipe, lift, pinch.* These verbs mean to take another's property without permission, often surreptitiously. *Steal* is the most general: *stole a car; steals research from colleagues.* To *purloin* is to make off with something, often in a breach of trust: *purloined the key to his cousin's safe-deposit box. Filch* and *snitch* often suggest that what is stolen is of little value, while *pilfer* sometimes connotes theft of or in small quantities: *filched towels from the hotel; snitch a cookie; pilfered fruit from the farmer. Cop, hook,* and *swipe* frequently connote quick, furtive snatching or seizing: *copped a necklace from the counter; planning to hook a fur coat; swiped a magazine from the rack.* To *lift* is to take something surreptitiously and keep it for oneself: *a pickpocket who lifts wallets on the subway. Pinch* suggests stealing something by or as if by picking it up between the thumb and the fingers: *pinched a dollar from his mother's purse.*

---

stealer *noun.* —*See* **thief.**

stealth *noun.* The act of proceeding so as to escape observation ▶ furtiveness, secretiveness, slinkiness, slyness, sneakiness, stealthiness, surreptitiousness. [*Compare* **art, secrecy.**]

stealthy *adjective.* Moving or acting so as to escape observation ▶ catlike, feline, furtive, secretive, slinky, sly, sneaking, sneaky, surreptitious. [*Compare* **artful, secret, underhand.**]

steam *noun.* —*See* **energy, haze.**

steam *verb.* —*See* **anger** (2), **burn** (3), **evaporate.**

steamroller *verb.* —*See* **even, overwhelm** (1).

steamy *adjective.* —*See* **erotic.**

steel *verb.* —*See* **gird.**

steep¹ *adjective.* **1.** Having a sharp inclination; almost perpendicular ▶ abrupt, bold, precipitous, sharp, sheer, sudden. [*Compare* **vertical.**] **2.** Exceeding a normal limit, especially in price ▶ exorbitant, extortionate, overpriced, sky-high, stiff, stratospheric, unconscionable. [*Compare* **costly, excessive.**]

✣ **CORE SYNONYMS:** *steep, abrupt, precipitous, sheer.* These adjectives mean so sharply inclined as to be almost perpendicular: *steep cliffs; an abrupt drop-off; precipitous hills; a sheer descent.*

steep² *verb.* To cause something to become thoroughly wet or saturated by immersion in a liquid ▶ infuse, macerate, marinate, pickle, soak, souse, suffuse. [*Compare* **charge, dip, wet.**]

steer *verb.* —*See* **conduct** (1), **drive** (1), **guide, maneuver** (1).

steer *noun.* —*See* **tip³.**

stem *verb.* To have as a source ▶ arise, come, derive, emanate, flow, issue, originate, proceed, rise, spring, upspring. [*Compare* **appear, begin.**] —*See also* **hinder.**

stem *noun.* The main ascending part of a plant, which supports the other parts ▶ stalk, stock, trunk. [*Compare* **shoot.**] —*See also* **rod, theme** (1).

✣ **CORE SYNONYMS:** *stem, arise, derive, emanate, flow, issue, originate, proceed, rise, spring.* These verbs mean to have as a source: *customs that stem from the past; misery that arose from war; rights that derive from citizenship; disapproval that emanated from the teacher; happiness that flows from their friendship; prejudice that issues from fear; a proposal that originated in the Congress; a mistake that proceeded from carelessness; rebellion that rises in the provinces; new industries that spring up.*

stench *noun.* A strong, foul odor ▶ fetor, malodor, reek, stink. [*Compare* **fragrance, smell.**]

✣ **CORE SYNONYMS:** *stench, fetor, malodor, reek, stink.* These nouns denote a strong, foul odor: *the stench of burning rubber; the fetor of polluted waters; the malodor of diesel fumes; the reek of stale sweat; a stink of decayed flesh.*

stentorian *adjective.* —*See* **loud, vociferous.**

step *noun.* An action calculated to achieve an end ▶ maneuver, measure, move, procedure, tactic. —*See also* **degree** (1), **walk** (2).

step *verb.* —*See* **dance, walk.**

step back *verb.* —*See* **recede.**

step down *verb.* To withdraw or remove from business or active life ▶ pension (off), retire, superannuate. ***Idioms:*** call it quits, hang up one's spurs, put out to pasture, turn in one's badge. [*Compare* **dismiss, quit.**]

step up *verb.* —*See* **increase, intensify, speed.**

step-by-step *adjective.* Proceeding steadily by degrees ▶ gradational, gradual, piecemeal, progressive. ***Idioms:*** one foot after another, one step at a time. [*Compare* **consecutive, methodical, slow.**]

stereotype *noun.* —*See* **cliché.**

stereotype *verb.* —*See* **classify, conventionalize.**

stereotyped *adjective.* —*See* **conventional, trite.**

stereotypical *or* **stereotypic** *adjective.* —*See* **trite.**

sterile *adjective.* **1.** Free or freed from microorganisms ▶ antiseptic, aseptic, disinfected, germ-free, germless, hygienic, sanitary, sanitized, sterilized. [*Compare* **clean.**] **2.** Lacking originality ▶ uncreative, unimaginative, uninspired, uninventive, unoriginal. [*Compare* **boring, trite.**] —*See also* **barren** (1), **barren** (2), **dull** (1).

sterileness *noun.* —*See* **dullness.**

sterility *noun.* **1.** The state or condition of being free from microorganisms ▶ asepsis, germlessness, sanitization, sterilization. [*Compare* **purity.**] **2.** The state or condition of being unable to reproduce ▶ barrenness, fruitlessness, impotence, infertility, unfruitfulness. *—See also* **dullness.**

sterilization *noun.* The state or condition of being free from microorganisms ▶ asepsis, germlessness, sanitization, sterility.

sterilize *verb.* **1.** To render free of microorganisms ▶ decontaminate, disinfect, irradiate, sanitize. **2.** To render incapable of reproducing ▶ alter, castrate, fix, geld, neuter, spay, unsex.

sterilized *adjective. —See* **sterile** (1).

sterling *adjective. —See* **choice** (1).

stern[1] *adjective. —See* **forbidding, severe** (1).

stern[2] *noun. —See* **back.**

sternness *noun. —See* **severity.**

stew *verb. —See* **brood, cook.**

stew *noun. —See* **agitation** (2).

steward *noun. —See* **representative.**

stewardship *noun. —See* **management.**

stewed *adjective. —See* **drunk.**

stick *noun.* **1.** A short straight piece of wood ▶ baton, branch, lath, stake, switch, twig, wand. [*Compare* **rod.**] **2.** A fairly long, straight piece of solid material used especially as a support in walking ▶ cane, crook, pole, staff, stave, walking stick.

stick *verb. —See* **baffle, bond, catch** (3), **cheat** (1), **cut** (1), **plunge, position.**

stick around *verb. —See* **remain.**

stick in *verb. —See* **introduce** (2).

stick out *verb.* To be obtrusively conspicuous ▶ glare, stand out. ***Idioms:*** stare someone in the face, stick out like a sore thumb. *—See also* **bulge, endure** (1).

stick to *verb. —See* **keep** (5).

stick up *verb. —See* **rob.**

stick with *verb. —See* **hold** (1), **impose on, keep** (5).

sticker *noun. —See* **spike.**

sticking power *noun. —See* **endurance.**

stick-in-the-mud *noun. —See* **killjoy, square.**

stick-to-itiveness *noun. —See* **diligence.**

stickup *noun. —See* **larceny.**

sticky *adjective.* **1.** Having the property of adhering ▶ adhesive, gluey, glutinous, gooey, gummy, mucilaginous, tacky. [*Compare* **viscous.**] **2.** Damp and warm ▶ humid, muggy, soggy, sultry. [*Compare* **damp, hot, rainy, wet.**] **3.** *Informal* Hard to deal with or get out of ▶ rough, tight, tricky. [*Compare* **delicate.**]

sticky-fingered *adjective. —See* **thievish.**

stiff *adjective.* **1.** Rigidly constrained or formal; lacking grace and spontaneity ▶ buckram, starchy, stilted, wooden. [*Compare* **cool, forced, prudish.**] **2.** Having a high concentration of the distinguishing ingredient ▶ concentrated, potent, strong. [*Compare* **straight.**] *—See also* **firm**[1] (3), **rigid, steep**[1] (2).

stiff *noun. —See* **body** (2), **drunkard, hard** (3), **miser.**

stiffen *verb. —See* **coagulate, harden** (2), **tense.**

stiff-necked *adjective. —See* **stubborn** (1).

stifle *verb. —See* **censor** (2), **choke, muffle, repress.**

stifling *adjective. —See* **airless** (1), **repressive.**

stigma *noun. —See* **stain.**

stigmatize *verb.* To cause to feel embarrassment, dishonor, and often guilt ▶ brand, mortify, reproach, shame. ***Idioms:*** put to shame, put to the blush. [*Compare* **belittle, denigrate, embarrass, humble.**] *—See also* **disgrace.**

still *adjective.* Free from disturbance, agitation, or commotion ▶ calm, halcyon, pacific, peaceful, placid, quiet, serene, tranquil, untroubled. [*Compare* **calm, idyllic.**] *—See also* **airless** (2), **motionless, silent** (1).

still *noun. —See* **silence** (1).

still *adverb.* **1.** In spite of a preceding event or consideration ▶ all the same, anyway, however, nevertheless, nonetheless, yet. *Informal:* still and all. ***Idiom:*** be that as it may. **2.** To a more extreme degree ▶ even, ever more so, yet. *—See also* **additionally.**

still *verb.* *—See* **pacify, silence.**

✚ CORE SYNONYMS: *still, calm, peaceful, placid, serene, tranquil.* These adjectives denote absence of disturbance, agitation, or commotion: *lily pads that floated on the still waters; calm acceptance of the inevitable; a peaceful hike through the scenic hills; a soothing, placid temperament; spent a serene, restful weekend at the lake; hoped for a more tranquil life in the country.*

---

stillness *noun.* An absence of motion or disturbance ▶ calm, calmness, hush, lull, peace, peacefulness, placidity, placidness, quiet, quietness, serenity, tranquillity, untroubledness. *—See also* **silence** (1).

stilted *adjective.* Rigidly constrained or formal; lacking grace and spontaneity ▶ buckram, starchy, stiff, wooden. [*Compare* **cool, forced, prudish.**]

stimulant *noun.* *—See* **drug** (2), **stimulus, tonic.**

stimulate *verb.* *—See* **energize, provoke.**

stimulating *adjective.* *—See* **invigorating.**

stimulation *noun.* *—See* **encouragement, stimulus.**

stimulator *noun.* *—See* **stimulus.**

stimulus *noun.* Something that causes and encourages an action or response ▶ catalyst, encouragement, fillip, goad, impetus, impulse, incentive, inducement, motivation, prod, push, spur, stimulant, stimulation, stimulator. [*Compare* **cause, impact.**] *—See also* **provocation** (1).

sting *verb.* *—See* **cheat** (1), **cut** (1), **hurt** (2).

sting *noun.* *—See* **cheat** (1), **edge, kick, pain.**

stinging *adjective.* *—See* **biting, bitter** (2), **painful.**

stingy *adjective.* Ungenerously or pettily reluctant to spend money ▶ cheap, close, close-fisted, costive, hard-fisted, mean, miserly, niggard, niggardly, parsimonious, penny-pinching, penurious, petty, pinching, tight, tightfisted. [*Compare* **greedy.**] *—See also* **meager.**

stink *verb.* To have or give off a foul odor ▶ reek, smell. ***Idioms:*** stink (*or* smell) to high heaven.

stink *noun.* *—See* **complaint, stench.**

stinking *adjective.* *—See* **drunk, smelly.**

stinko *adjective.* *—See* **drunk, shoddy.**

stint *verb.* *—See* **scrimp.**

stint *noun.* *—See* **task** (1), **turn** (1).

stipend *noun.* *—See* **wage.**

stipple *verb.* *—See* **speckle.**

stipulate *verb.* To state specifically ▶ detail, particularize, provide, specify. [*Compare* **assert, describe, designate, dictate.**] *—See also* **contract** (1).

stipulation *noun.* *—See* **provision.**

stir[1] *verb.* To move or cause to move slightly ▶ budge, move, shift. *—See also* **arouse, beat** (6), **blow[1]** (1), **cause, fire** (1), **mix** (1), **wake[1].**

stir *noun.* *—See* **agitation** (1), **agitation** (3), **motion, sensation** (2).

stir[2] *noun.* *—See* **jail.**

stir-fry *verb.* *—See* **cook.**

stirring *adjective.* *—See* **affecting.**

stitch *noun.* *—See* **pain.**

stock *noun.* The main ascending part of a plant, which supports the other parts ▶ stalk, stem, trunk. [*Compare* **shoot.**] *—See also* **ancestry, family** (2), **good** (2), **hoard.**

stock *verb.* To have for sale ▶ carry, deal (in), keep, offer. [*Compare* **sell.**]

stock *adjective.* *—See* **ordinary, trite.**

stockpile *noun.* *—See* **hoard.**

stockpile *verb.* *—See* **save** (1).

stock-still *adjective.* *—See* **motionless.**

stocky *adjective.* Short, heavy, and solidly built ▶ blocky, chunky, compact, dumpy, heavyset, squat, stodgy, stubby, stumpy, thick, thickset. [*Compare* **bulky, fat.**]

stodginess *noun.* —*See* **dullness.**

stodgy *adjective.* —*See* **dull** (1), **stocky.**

stoic *adjective.* —*See* **patient.**

stoicism *noun.* —*See* **patience.**

stoked *adjective.* —*See* **thrilled.**

stole *noun.* —*See* **wrap.**

stolid *adjective.* —*See* **cold** (2).

stolidity *or* **stolidness** *noun.* —*See* **apathy.**

stomach *noun.* —*See* **appetite.**

stomach *verb.* —*See* **endure** (1).

stomp *verb.* To step on heavily and repeatedly so as to crush, injure, or destroy ▶ stamp, tramp, trample, tread, tromp. [*Compare* **crush.**] —*See also* **trudge.**

stomping ground *noun.* —*See* **haunt.**

stoned *adjective.* —*See* **drugged, drunk.**

stonyhearted *adjective.* —*See* **callous.**

stooge *noun.* —*See* **pawn**[2]**.**

stool *verb.* —*See* **inform** (2).

stoolie *or* **stool pigeon** *noun.* —*See* **informer.**

stoop *verb.* To bend or lower the body ▶ arch, bend (down), bow, crouch, huddle, hump, hunch, hunker (down), scrunch, squat. [*Compare* **bow**[1]**, slouch, sit.**] —*See also* **condescend** (1).

stop *verb.* **1.** To come to a cessation ▶ cease, check, desist, discontinue, halt, leave off, quit, stall, surcease. ***Idioms:*** come to a halt (*or* standstill *or* stop). [*Compare* **conclude.**] **2.** To prevent the occurrence or continuation of a movement, action, or operation ▶ arrest, belay, cease, check, discontinue, forbear, halt, idle, immobilize, stall, stay, surcease, tie up. ***Idioms:*** bring to a standstill (*or* screeching halt), call a halt to, cut short, put a stop to. [*Compare* **hinder, restrain, suspend.**] —*See also* **abandon** (2), **break** (5), **drop** (4), **fill** (2), **veto, visit.**

stop *noun.* **1.** The act of stopping ▶ cessation, check, cutoff, discontinuance, discontinuation, halt, idling, stay, stoppage, surcease. **2.** The condition of being stopped ▶ cease, cessation, discontinuance, discontinuation, gridlock, halt, idleness, immobilization, jam, standstill, stoppage, surcease, tie-up. [*Compare* **break.**] **3.** A stopping place along a route for picking up or dropping off passengers ▶ depot, station, terminal, terminus. **4.** A remaining in a place as a guest or lodger ▶ sojourn, stay, stopover, visit. —*See also* **bar** (1), **end** (1), **plug, visit** (1).

✚ **CORE SYNONYMS:** *stop, cease, desist, discontinue, halt, quit.* These verbs mean to bring or come to an end: *stop arguing; ceased crying; desist from complaining; discontinued the treatment; halting the convoy; quit laughing.*

◀ **ANTONYM:** *start*

---

stopcock *noun.* —*See* **faucet.**

stopgap *noun.* —*See* **makeshift.**

stopgap *adjective.* —*See* **temporary** (2).

stopover *noun.* A remaining in a place as a guest or lodger ▶ sojourn, stay, stop, visit.

stoppage *noun.* A cessation of normal activity, caused by an accident or strike, for example ▶ gridlock, immobilization, jam, tie-up. —*See also* **stop** (1), **stop** (2).

stopper *noun.* —*See* **plug.**

stopping point *noun.* —*See* **end** (1).

stopple *noun.* —*See* **plug.**

store *noun.* A retail establishment where merchandise is sold ▶ boutique, emporium, outlet, shop. —*See also* **depository, hoard.**

store *verb.* To have or put in a customary place ▶ cache, keep, put. —*See also* **save** (1).

storehouse *noun.* —*See* **depository.**

storied *adjective.* —*See* **famous.**

storm *noun.* An atmospheric disturbance characterized by strong winds and precipitation ▶ blizzard, blow, cyclone, electrical storm, gale, hurricane, ice storm, monsoon, rainstorm, snowstorm, squall, tempest, thunderstorm, typhoon. [*Compare* **rain.**] —*See also* **barrage.**

storm *verb.* To manifest strong winds and precipitation ▶ blow (up), set in, squall. [*Compare* **rain.**] —*See also* **anger** (2), **attack** (1).

stormy *adjective.* —*See* **agitated, rough** (2).

story *noun.* **1.** A recounting of past events ▶ account, chronicle, description, history, narration, narrative, record, report, saga, statement, version. **2.** A narrative not based on fact ▶ fable, fiction, novel, romance. —*See also* **item, lie**[2], **plot** (1), **yarn.**

story line *noun.* —*See* **plot** (1).

storyteller *noun.* —*See* **liar.**

stout *adjective.* —*See* **brave, bulky** (2), **fat** (1), **strong** (2).

stouthearted *adjective.* —*See* **brave.**

stoutheartedness *noun.* —*See* **courage.**

stow *verb.* —*See* **save** (1).

strabismal *or* **strabismic** *adjective.* Marked by or affected with a squint ▶ cross-eyed, squint-eyed, squinty.

straddle *verb.* To sit or stand with a leg on each side of ▶ bestride, stride. —*See also* **sprawl.**

straggle *verb.* —*See* **spread** (2).

straggler *noun.* —*See* **laggard.**

straight *adjective.* Not diluted or mixed with other substances ▶ full-strength, neat, plain, pure, unblended, undiluted, unmixed. [*Compare* **strong.**] —*See also* **conventional, direct** (1), **even** (1), **frank, honest, realistic** (1).

straight *adverb.* —*See* **directly** (1), **directly** (3).

straightaway *adverb.* —*See* **directly** (1), **immediately** (1).

straighten *verb.* —*See* **even, tidy** (1).

straighten out *verb.* —*See* **settle** (2).

straightforward *adjective.* —*See* **definite** (1), **direct** (1), **frank.**

straight-from-the-shoulder *adjective.* —*See* **frank.**

straight off *adverb.* —*See* **immediately** (1).

straight-out *adjective.* —*See* **frank.**

straight-shooting *adjective.* —*See* **frank, honest.**

strain[1] *verb.* To injure a bodily part by twisting ▶ sprain, turn, twist, wrench. [*Compare* **hurt.**] —*See also* **burden**[1], **drain** (1), **labor, overdo.**

strain *noun.* —*See* **burden**[1] (1), **effort, intensity, pressure.**

strain[2] *noun.* An inherent, contrasting, or unexpected quality, especially in a person's character ▶ streak, vein. [*Compare* **disposition, inclination.**] —*See also* **melody.**

strained *adjective.* Not natural or spontaneous ▶ contrived, effortful, forced, labored. [*Compare* **awkward, stiff.**]

strait *noun.* —*See* **channel.**

strait-laced *adjective.* —*See* **prudish.**

straits *noun.* —*See* **emergency, poverty, predicament.**

strand *noun.* Something suggesting the continuousness of a filament ▶ hairline, thread. [*Compare* **thread.**]

strange *adjective.* —*See* **eccentric, exotic, foreign** (1), **funny** (3), **weird.**

strangely *adverb.* —*See* **unusually.**

stranger *noun.* —*See* **foreigner.**

strangle *verb.* —*See* **choke, repress.**

strangulate *verb.* —*See* **choke.**

strap *noun.* —*See* **band**[1].

strap *verb.* —*See* **beat** (2), **fasten.**

strapped *adjective.* —*See* **poor.**

strapping *adjective.* —*See* **lusty, muscular.**

stratagem *noun.* A method of deploying troops and equipment in combat ▶ battle plan, maneuver, plan of attack, strategy, tactic. —*See also* **trick** (1).

strategize *verb.* —*See* **design** (1).

strategy *noun.* A method of deploying troops and equipment in combat ▶ battle plan, maneuver, plan of attack, stratagem, tactic. —*See also* **approach** (1).

stratify *verb.* —*See* **classify.**

stratospheric *adjective.* —*See* **steep**[1] (2).

stratum *noun.* —*See* **class** (2).

straw boss *noun.* —*See* **boss.**

stray *verb.* —*See* **deviate, digress, rove.**

stray *adjective.* Being what remains, especially after a part has been removed ▶ extra, leftover, remaining. ***Idiom:*** left behind. [*Compare* **superfluous.**] —*See also* **errant** (2), **erratic, lost** (1).

stray *noun.* —*See* **orphan.**

streak *noun.* An inherent, contrasting, or unexpected quality, especially in a person's character ▶ strain, vein. [*Compare* **disposition, inclination.**] —*See also* **series, shade** (2), **stripe.**

streak *verb.* To mark with a line or band, as of different color or texture ▶ band, bar, line, striate, stripe, variegate. [*Compare* **speckle.**]

✦ **CORE SYNONYMS:** *streak, strain, vein.* These nouns denote an inherent, contrasting or unexpected quality, especially in a person's character: *a streak of humor; a strain of melancholy; a vein of stubbornness.*

---

stream *noun.* —*See* **beam** (1), **flow, river.**

stream *verb.* —*See* **blow**[1] (2), **flow** (1), **flow** (2).

streamer *noun.* —*See* **flag**[1].

streamline *verb.* **1.** To make modern in appearance or style ▶ modernize, update. ***Idiom:*** bring up to date. [*Compare* **improve, renew.**] **2.** To reduce in complexity or scope ▶ boil down, pare (down), simplify. ***Idioms:*** reduce to the basics (*or* essentials *or* bare bones). [*Compare* **explain.**]

streamlined *adjective.* **1.** Acting effectively with minimal waste ▶ efficient, productive, well-oiled. [*Compare* **diligent, methodical.**] **2.** Having slender and graceful lines ▶ sleek, trim.

street *noun.* —*See* **way** (2).

street-smart *adjective.* —*See* **shrewd.**

streetwalker *noun.* —*See* **prostitute.**

strength *noun.* The state or quality of being physically strong ▶ brawn, might, muscle, potency, power, powerfulness, sinew, thews. [*Compare* **endurance.**] —*See also* **energy, force** (1), **forte, stability, virtue.**

strengthen *verb.* To make firmer in a particular conviction or habit ▶ confirm, fortify, harden, reinforce. [*Compare* **back, establish.**] —*See also* **gird, harden** (1), **supplement, support** (2).

strenuous *adjective.* —*See* **energetic, rough** (3).

strenuously *adverb.* —*See* **hard** (1).

stress *noun.* Special attention given to something considered important ▶ accent, accentuation, emphasis, weight. [*Compare* **importance, notice.**] —*See also* **anxiety** (1), **pressure.**

stress *verb.* —*See* **emphasize.**

stressor *noun.* A cause of distress or anxiety ▶ care, concern, trouble, worry. [*Compare* **anxiety, burden**[1].]

stretch *verb.* **1.** To put forward, especially an appendage ▶ extend, outstretch, reach, stretch out. **2.** To take repose, as by sleeping or lying quietly ▶ curl up, lie (down), recline, repose, rest. [*Compare* **nap, sleep.**] —*See also* **distort, extend** (1), **lengthen, lie**[1] (1), **overdo, spread** (1), **tense.**

stretch *noun.* A prison term ▶ hitch, time. —*See also* **distance** (1), **expanse** (1), **extent, period** (1), **turn** (1).

stretch *adjective.* —*See* **extensible.**

stretchable *adjective.* —*See* **extensible.**

stretching *noun.* —*See* **extension** (1).

stretching *adjective.* —*See* **long**[1] (1).

stretchy *adjective.* —*See* **extensible.**

strew *verb.* —*See* **spread** (2).

striate *verb.* —*See* **streak.**

striation *noun.* A mark or shallow cut made by contact with an object ▶ abrasion, scrape, scratch, scuff. [*Compare* **cut, furrow, impression.**] —*See also* **stripe.**

stricken *adjective.* —*See* **unfortunate** (1).

strict *adjective.* —*See* **close** (2), **severe** (1).
strictly *adverb.* —*See* **exactly.**
strictness *noun.* —*See* **severity.**
stricture *noun.* —*See* **restraint.**
stride *verb.* To sit or stand with a leg on each side of ▶ bestride, straddle. —*See also* **walk.**
stride *noun.* —*See* **advance, walk** (2).
strident *adjective.* —*See* **harsh, loud, vociferous.**
strife *noun.* —*See* **battle, competition** (1), **conflict.**
strike *verb.* **1.** To try to bite something quickly or eagerly ▶ nip, snap, snatch. **2.** To enter a person's mind ▶ come to, hit, impress, occur to. ***Idioms:*** come (*or* spring) to mind, cross (*or* enter) one's mind, dawn on. [*Compare* **register.**] **3.** To have a sudden overwhelming effect on ▶ catch, seize, take. **4.** To cease working in support of demands made upon an employer ▶ picket, walk out. ***Idioms:*** go (*or* go out on) strike, stage a strike (*or* sickout *or* walkout), stop work. —*See also* **afflict, attack** (1), **cancel** (1), **collide, hit, move** (1), **plunge, ring**[2].
strike back *verb.* —*See* **retaliate.**
strike down *verb.* —*See* **drop** (3).
strike out *verb.* —*See* **bear** (5), **fail** (1).
strike *noun.* A cessation of work by employees in support of demands made upon their employer ▶ job action, sickout, walkout, work stoppage, work to rule. —*See also* **attack, discovery.**
striking *adjective.* Evoking strong mental images through distinctiveness ▶ colorful, graphic, picturesque, vivid. —*See also* **noticeable.**
string *noun.* —*See* **cord, line, press, provision, series.**
string *verb.* To put objects onto a thread ▶ thread.
string out *verb.* —*See* **lengthen.**
string up *verb. Informal* To execute by suspending by the neck ▶ gibbet, hang. *Slang:* swing.
stringency *noun.* —*See* **severity.**
stringent *adjective.* —*See* **severe** (1).
stringy *adjective.* Containing or consisting of fibers ▶ fibrous, sinewy, threadlike.
strip[1] *verb.* —*See* **bare, deprive, empty, sack**[2], **skin.**
strip[2] *noun.* —*See* **band**[1], **stripe.**
stripe *noun.* A long narrow area that has a different color or marking from what surrounds it ▶ band, bar, line, streak, striation, strip. —*See also* **band**[1], **kind**[2].
stripe *verb.* —*See* **streak.**
strive *verb.* —*See* **attempt, contend, labor.**
striving *noun.* —*See* **competition** (1), **effort.**
stroke *noun.* —*See* **blow**[2], **touch** (1).
stroke *verb.* —*See* **caress, rub, touch.**
stroll *verb.* To walk at a leisurely pace ▶ amble, perambulate, promenade, ramble, saunter, toddle, wander. *Informal:* mosey. [*Compare* **hike, strut, walk.**]
stroll *noun.* —*See* **walk** (1).
strong *adjective.* **1.** Having great physical strength ▶ mighty, potent, powerful. [*Compare* **energetic, lusty, muscular.**] **2.** Capable of exerting considerable effort or of withstanding considerable stress or hardship ▶ hardy, stalwart, stout, sturdy, tough. **3.** Having a high concentration of the distinguishing ingredient ▶ concentrated, potent, stiff. [*Compare* **straight.**] —*See also* **deep** (3), **definite** (1), **firm**[1] (2), **forceful, hard** (3), **intense.**
strong-arm *adjective. Informal* Accomplished by force ▶ coercive, forced, forcible, violent.
strong-arm *verb.* —*See* **coerce, intimidate.**
stronghold *noun.* —*See* **fort.**
strongman *noun.* —*See* **dictator.**
strong point *or* **strong suit** *noun.* —*See* **forte.**
strop *noun.* —*See* **band**[1].
strop *verb.* —*See* **sharpen.**
structure *noun.* Something built, especially for human use ▶ building, con-

struction, edifice, erection, pile. —*See also* **form** (1).

structure *verb.* —*See* **make.**

struggle *verb.* —*See* **attempt, contend, grind** (2).

struggle *noun.* —*See* **battle, competition** (1), **effort.**

strumpet *noun.* —*See* **harlot.**

strut *verb.* To walk with pompous bearing ▶ flounce, peacock, prance, swagger, swank, swash. *Informal:* sashay. [*Compare* **hike, stroll, walk.**] —*See also* **display.**

stub *noun.* —*See* **end** (3).

stubborn *adjective.* **1.** Firmly, often unreasonably immovable in purpose or will ▶ adamant, adamantine, brassbound, bullheaded, die-hard, dogged, grim, hardheaded, headstrong, implacable, incompliant, inexorable, inflexible, intransigent, iron, mulish, obdurate, obstinate, pertinacious, perverse, pigheaded, relentless, remorseless, rigid, stiff-necked, tenacious, unbendable, unbending, uncompliant, uncompromising, unrelenting, unyielding, willful. ***Idioms:*** stubborn as a mule (*or* ox). **2.** Difficult to alleviate or cure ▶ obstinate, persistent, pertinacious.

✚ **CORE SYNONYMS:** *stubborn, inflexible, inexorable, adamant, obdurate, obstinate, headstrong, bullheaded, pigheaded, mulish, dogged, pertinacious.* These adjectives mean firmly, often unreasonably immovable in purpose or will. *Stubborn* pertains to innate, often perverse resoluteness or unyieldingness: *"She was very stubborn when her mind was made up"* (Samuel Butler). *Inflexible* implies unyielding adherence to fixed principles or purposes: *My boss is inflexible on many issues. Inexorable* implies lack of susceptibility to persuasion: *"Cynthia was inexorable—she would have none of him"* (Winston Churchill). It also describes things that are inevitable, relentless, and often severe in effect: *"Russia's final hour, it seemed, approached with inexorable certainty"* (W. Bruce Lincoln). *Adamant* implies imperviousness to pleas or appeals: *He is adamant about leaving right now. Obdurate* implies hard, callous resistance to tender feelings: *The child's misery would move even the most obdurate heart. Obstinate* implies unreasonable rigidity: *"Mr. Quincy labored hard with the governor to obtain his assent, but he was obstinate"* (Benjamin Franklin). One who is *headstrong* is stubbornly, often recklessly willful: *The headstrong teenager ignored school policy. Bullheaded* suggests foolish or irrational obstinacy, and *pigheaded,* stupid obstinacy: *Don't be bullheaded; see a doctor. "It's a pity pious folks are so apt to be pigheaded"* (Harriet Beecher Stowe). *Mulish* implies the obstinacy and intractability associated with a mule: *"Obstinate is no word for it, for she is mulish"* (Ouida). *Dogged* emphasizes stubborn perseverance: *dogged persistence; "two warring ideals in one dark body, whose dogged strength alone keeps it from being torn asunder"* (W.E.B. Du Bois). *Pertinacious* stresses a tenacity of purpose, opinion, or course of action that is sometimes viewed as vexatious: *The tax bill's vocal and pertinacious critics led to its defeat.*

---

stubbornness *noun.* The quality or state of being immovable in purpose or will ▶ bullheadedness, die-hardism, doggedness, grimness, hardheadedness, implacability, implacableness, incompliance, incompliancy, inexorability, inexorableness, inflexibility, inflexibleness, intransigence, intransigency, mulishness, obduracy, obdurateness, obstinacy, obstinateness, pertinaciousness, pertinacity, perverseness, perversity, pigheadedness, relentlessness, remorselessness, rigidity, rigidness, tenaciousness, tenacity, willfulness. [*Compare* **cruelty, decision, severity.**]

stubby *adjective.* —*See* **stocky.**

stuck *adjective.* —*See* **confused** (1).

stuck-up *adjective.* —*See* **egotistic** (1), **snobbish.**

stud *noun.* —*See* **beauty, column, nail.**

student *noun.* One who is being educated ▶ apprentice, learner, pupil, scholar, trainee. [*Compare* **follower.**]

studied *adjective.* —*See* **artificial** (2), **deliberate** (2).

studio *noun.* An artist's workspace ▶ atelier, workroom, workshop. —*See also* **apartment.**

studious *adjective.* Devoted to study or reading ▶ bookish, scholarly. [*Compare* **educated, intellectual, learned.**] —*See also* **deliberate** (2), **diligent.**

studiousness *noun.* —*See* **diligence.**

study *noun.* Careful consideration ▶ advisement, consideration, deliberation. [*Compare* **attention, scrutiny.**] —*See also* **examination** (1), **practice, trance.**

study *verb.* To apply one's mind to the acquisition of knowledge, especially when pressed for time ▶ lucubrate. *Informal:* bone up, cram, grind. ***Idioms:*** burn the midnight oil, hit the books. —*See also* **examine** (1), **ponder.**

stuff *noun.* A person considered to have qualities suitable for a particular activity ▶ material, timber. [*Compare* **comer, potential.**] —*See also* **effects, heart** (1), **material** (1).

stuff *verb.* —*See* **fill** (1).

stuffing *noun.* —*See* **filler** (1).

stuffy *adjective.* —*See* **airless** (1), **boring, prudish.**

stultify *verb.* —*See* **bore**[2].

stumble *verb.* To lose one's balance and fall or almost fall ▶ skid, slide, slip, slither, trip. ***Idioms:*** go flying, have one's feet go out from under one, lose one's footing, make a false step, take a skid (*or* slide). [*Compare* **fall.**] —*See also* **blunder, err, muddle, stagger** (1), **stammer.**

stumble on *or* **upon** *verb.* —*See* **encounter** (1).

stumble *noun.* —*See* **blunder.**

stumbling block *noun.* —*See* **difficulty.**

stump *verb.* —*See* **baffle, blunder, frustrate.**

stumpy *adjective.* —*See* **stocky.**

stun *verb.* —*See* **daze** (1), **paralyze, stagger** (2).

stunner *noun.* —*See* **beauty, marvel.**

stunning *adjective.* —*See* **astonishing, beautiful.**

stunt *noun.* A clever, dexterous act ▶ feat, trick. ***Idiom:*** sleight of hand. [*Compare* **accomplishment.**]

stupefacient *adjective.* —*See* **soporific.**

stupefacient *noun.* —*See* **soporific.**

stupefaction *noun.* —*See* **daze, wonder** (1).

stupefy *verb.* —*See* **daze** (1), **drug** (2), **paralyze.**

stupendous *adjective.* —*See* **astonishing, enormous.**

stupendousness *noun.* —*See* **enormousness.**

stupid *adjective.* Lacking in or showing a lack of intelligence ▶ birdbrained, blockheaded, brainless, cloddish, dense, doltish, dumb, hebetudinous, idiotic, imbecilic, mindless, moronic, obtuse, softheaded, thickheaded, thick-witted, unintelligent, witless. *Informal:* boneheaded, knuckleheaded, lamebrained, muttonheaded, thick. *Slang:* dimwitted, dopey, fatheaded, half-witted, lunkheaded, pinheaded. [*Compare* **backward, foolish, ignorant.**] —*See also* **lethargic, worthless.**

stupidity *noun.* The state of being stupid ▶ brainlessness, cloddishness, density, doltishness, dumbness, idiocy, imbecility, mindlessness, obtuseness, simplicity, softheadedness, stupidness, witlessness. *Informal:* boneheadedness. *Slang:* dimwittedness, dopiness, fatheadedness, pinheadedness. [*Compare* **foolishness, lethargy.**]

stupor *noun.* —*See* **daze, lethargy.**

stuporous *adjective.* —*See* **dead** (2), **lethargic.**

sturdiness *noun.* —*See* **stability.**

sturdy *adjective.* —*See* **bulky** (2), **firm**[1] (2), **lusty, muscular, strong** (2).

Sturm und Drang *noun.* —*See* **agitation** (1).

stutter *verb.* —*See* **stammer.**

stutter *noun.* A way of speaking marked by involuntary repetitions and pauses ▶ stammer, stammering, stuttering.

sty *noun.* —*See* **pen**[2].

style *noun.* A distinctive way of expressing oneself ▶ fashion, manner, mode, tone, vein. —*See also* **bearing** (1), **behavior** (1), **elegance, fashion, name** (1), **way** (1).

style *verb.* —*See* **call, name** (1).

stylish *adjective.* —*See* **fashionable.**

stylize *verb.* —*See* **conventionalize.**

stymie *verb.* —*See* **frustrate.**

suave *adjective.* Gracious and tactful in social manner ▶ debonair, smooth, urbane. [*Compare* **courteous, cultured, glib, sophisticated.**]

sub *noun.* —*See* **substitute.**

sub *verb.* —*See* **substitute.**

subaltern *adjective.* —*See* **minor** (1).

subaltern *noun.* —*See* **subordinate.**

subdivide *verb.* —*See* **analyze, branch.**

subdivision *noun.* —*See* **analysis, branch** (1), **part** (1).

subdue *verb.* —*See* **defeat, moderate** (1).

subdued *adjective.* —*See* **modest** (1), **soft** (2).

subject *noun.* What a speech, piece of writing, or artistic work is about ▶ argument, case, matter, point, subject matter, text, theme, topic. [*Compare* **heart, problem.**] —*See also* **area** (1), **citizen, object** (2).

subject *adjective.* Subject to the authority or control of another ▶ dependent, subordinate, subservient. [*Compare* **auxiliary.**] —*See also* **conditional, liable** (2).

subject *verb.* To lay open, as to something undesirable or injurious ▶ expose, leave open. [*Compare* **endanger.**] —*See also* **enslave.**

✚ **CORE SYNONYMS:** *subject, matter, topic, theme.* These nouns denote the principal idea or point of a speech, a piece of writing, or an artistic work. *Subject* is the most general: "*Well, honor is the subject of my story*" (William Shakespeare). *Matter* refers to the material that is the object of thought or discourse: "*This distinction seems to me to go to the root of the matter*" (William James). A *topic* is a subject of discussion, argument, or conversation: "*They would talk of . . . fashionable topics, such as pictures, taste, Shakespeare*" (Oliver Goldsmith). *Theme* refers especially to an idea, a point of view, or a perception that is developed and expanded on in a work of art: "*To produce a mighty book, you must choose a mighty theme*" (Herman Melville).

---

subjective *adjective.* —*See* **arbitrary.**

subject matter *noun.* —*See* **subject.**

subjoin *verb.* —*See* **attach** (2).

subjugate *verb.* —*See* **defeat, enslave, occupy** (2).

subjugation *noun.* —*See* **conquest, domination, oppression.**

subjugator *noun.* —*See* **conqueror.**

sublet *verb.* —*See* **lease** (1).

sublime *adjective.* —*See* **elevated** (3), **exceptional, grand.**

sublime *verb.* —*See* **evaporate.**

submerge *or* **submerse** *verb.* —*See* **dip** (1), **flood** (1), **sink** (1).

submission *noun.* The act of submitting or surrendering to the power of another ▶ capitulation, giving up, surrender. —*See also* **obedience, proposal** (1).

✚ **CORE SYNONYMS:** *submission, surrender, capitulation.* These nouns denote the act of giving up one's person, one's possessions, or people under one's command to the power or control of another. *Submission* stresses the subordination of the side that has yielded: "*Our cruel and unrelenting enemy leaves us only the choice of brave resistance, or* *the most abject submission"* (George Washington). *Surrender* is the most general: "*No terms except unconditional and immediate surrender can be accepted*" (Ulysses S. Grant). *Capitulation* implies surrender under specific prearranged conditions: *Lack of food and ammunition forced the capitulation of the rebels.*

---

submissive *adjective.* —*See* **deferential, obedient, passive.**

submissiveness *noun.* —*See* **obedience.**

submit *verb.* To conform to the will or judgment of another ▶ bow, defer, yield. [*Compare* **humor.**] —*See also* **offer** (1), **propose, succumb, surrender** (1).

subordinate *adjective.* Subject to the authority or control of another ▶ dependent, subject, subservient. [*Compare* **auxiliary.**] —*See also* **minor** (1).

subordinate *noun.* One belonging to a lower class or rank ▶ inferior, junior, secondary, subaltern, underling. *Informal:* second fiddle. [*Compare* **assistant, pawn[2], slave, sycophant.**]

subordinate *verb.* —*See* **enslave.**

suborn *verb.* —*See* **bribe, corrupt.**

subpar *adjective.* —*See* **bad** (1).

sub rosa *adverb.* —*See* **secretly.**

sub-rosa *adjective.* —*See* **secret** (1).

subscribe *verb.* —*See* **assent, contribute** (1), **donate, sign.**

subscriber *noun.* —*See* **donor.**

subscription *noun.* —*See* **donation.**

subsequent *adjective.* Following something else in time ▶ after, later, posterior, ulterior. —*See also* **following** (1), **future.**

subsequently *adverb.* —*See* **later.**

subservient *adjective.* Subject to the authority or control of another ▶ dependent, subject, subordinate. [*Compare* **auxiliary.**] —*See also* **servile.**

subside *verb.* To become less active or intense ▶ abate, bate, die (away, down, off, *or* out), diminish, ease (off *or* up), ebb, fall, fall off, lapse, let up, moderate, remit, slacken, slack off, wane, wind down. [*Compare* **fall, depreciate.**] —*See also* **decrease, sink** (1).

subsidence *noun.* —*See* **waning.**

subsidiary *adjective.* —*See* **auxiliary** (1).

subsidiary *noun.* —*See* **branch** (3).

subsidize *verb.* —*See* **finance.**

subsidy *noun.* Money or other resources granted for a particular purpose ▶ appropriation, budget, grant, subvention.

subsist *verb.* To have being or actuality ▶ be, exist. —*See also* **exist.**

subsist on *verb.* To include as part of one's diet by nature or preference ▶ eat, exist on, feed on, live on.

subsistence *noun.* —*See* **living.**

subsisting *adjective.* —*See* **alive.**

substance *noun.* —*See* **essence, heart** (1), **import, material** (1), **thrust.**

substance abuse *noun.* —*See* **addiction.**

substandard *adjective.* —*See* **bad** (1).

substantial *adjective.* —*See* **big, firm[1]** (2), **generous** (2), **important, physical, real** (1).

substantiality *noun.* —*See* **existence.**

substantially *adverb.* —*See* **considerably.**

substantiate *verb.* —*See* **back** (2), **confirm** (1), **embody** (1), **prove.**

substantiation *noun.* —*See* **confirmation** (2), **embodiment.**

substantive *adjective.* —*See* **real** (1).

substantiveness *noun.* —*See* **existence.**

substitute *noun.* One that can take the place of another ▶ alternate, cover, double, proxy, relief, replacement, stand-in, surrogate. *Informal:* fill-in, pinch hitter, ringer, sub. [*Compare* **auxiliary, counterpart.**]

substitute *verb.* To act as a substitute ▶ cover for, fill in, function as, serve as, stand in, supply. *Informal:* pinch-hit, sub. ***Idiom:*** take the place of. —*See also* **change** (3).

substitute *adjective.* —*See* **temporary** (1).

substitution *noun.* —*See* **change** (2).

substratum *noun.* —*See* **base**[1] (2).

substructure *noun.* —*See* **base**[1] (2), **frame.**

subsume *verb.* —*See* **contain** (1).

subterfuge *noun.* —*See* **trick** (1).

subterranean *or* **subterrestrial** *adjective.* —*See* **underground.**

subtle *adjective.* —*See* **delicate** (4), **discriminating, fine**[1] (2), **imperceptible** (1), **underhand.**

subtlety *noun.* The ability to make or detect effects of great precision ▶ delicacy, fineness, niceness, sensitivity, subtleness. —*See also* **discrimination** (1), **shade** (1).

subtract *verb.* —*See* **deduct.**

suburbs *noun.* —*See* **outskirts.**

subvent *verb.* —*See* **finance.**

subvention *noun.* Money or other resources granted for a particular purpose ▶ appropriation, budget, grant, subsidy.

subversion *noun.* Treacherous action to defeat or do harm to an endeavor ▶ sabotage, undermining. [*Compare* **defeat, destruction.**]

subversive *adjective.* —*See* **rebellious.**

subversive *noun.* —*See* **rebel** (1).

subvert *verb.* To damage, destroy, or defeat by sabotage ▶ sabotage, undermine. [*Compare* **destroy, disorder.**] —*See also* **corrupt, overthrow.**

succeed *verb.* **1.** To gain success ▶ arrive, get ahead, get on, rise. ***Idioms:*** go far, go places, make good, make it. **2.** To turn out well ▶ come off, go (over), pan out, work (out). *Slang:* click. ***Idiom:*** fall into place. [*Compare* **effect, manage.**] —*See also* **follow** (1).

succeeding *adjective.* —*See* **following** (1).

success *or* **successfulness** *noun.* —*See* **accomplishment.**

successful *adjective.* —*See* **flourishing, prosperous.**

succession *noun.* —*See* **series.**

successive *or* **successional** *adjective.* —*See* **consecutive.**

succinct *adjective.* —*See* **brief, pithy.**

succor *noun.* A consoling in time of grief or pain ▶ comfort, consolation, reassurance, solace. [*Compare* **pity.**] —*See also* **help, relief** (1).

succor *verb.* —*See* **comfort, help.**

succorer *noun.* —*See* **assistant.**

succumb *verb.* To give in from or as if from a gradual loss of strength ▶ bow, buckle, capitulate, fold, submit, surrender, yield. —*See also* **collapse** (1), **die.**

suck *verb.* —*See* **involve** (1).

suck up *verb.* —*See* **fawn.**

sucker *noun.* —*See* **dupe, shoot.**

sucker *verb.* —*See* **deceive.**

sudden *adjective.* —*See* **abrupt** (2), **steep**[1] (1).

sudoriferous *adjective.* Producing or covered with sweat ▶ perspiring, sweating, sweaty. [*Compare* **damp, sticky.**]

suds *noun.* —*See* **foam.**

suds *verb.* —*See* **foam.**

sudsy *adjective.* —*See* **foamy.**

sue *verb.* To institute or subject to legal proceedings ▶ law, litigate, prosecute. ***Idioms:*** bring suit, haul (*or* drag *or* hale) into court. —*See also* **appeal** (1).

suet *noun.* Adipose tissue ▶ blubber, fat, lard, tallow. [*Compare* **oil.**]

suffer *verb.* —*See* **endure** (1), **experience, grieve, permit** (1).

sufferable *adjective.* —*See* **bearable.**

sufferance *noun.* —*See* **patience.**

sufferer *noun.* —*See* **victim.**

suffering *noun.* —*See* **misery.**

suffering *adjective.* —*See* **miserable.**

suffice *verb.* —*See* **satisfy** (1).

sufficiency *noun.* An adequate quantity ▶ adequacy, enough.

sufficient *adjective.* Being what is needed without being in excess ▶ adequate, ample, comfortable, competent, decent, enough, satisfactory. —*See also* **acceptable** (2).

✚ **CORE SYNONYMS:** *sufficient, adequate, enough.* These adjectives mean being what is needed without being in excess: *has sufficient income to retire comfortably; bought an adequate supply of food; drew enough water to fill the tub.*

◀ ANTONYM: *insufficient*

---

suffocate *verb.* —*See* **choke.**

suffocating *adjective.* —*See* **airless** (1).

suffrage *noun.* The right or chance to express an opinion or participate in a decision ▶ input, say, voice, vote. *Informal:* say-so.

suffuse *verb.* —*See* **charge** (1), **steep**[2].

suffusive *adjective.* Having the quality or tendency to pervade or permeate ▶ penetrating, permeating, pervading, pervasive. [*Compare* **general, prevailing, recurrent.**]

sugar *verb.* —*See* **sweeten.**

sugar *noun.* —*See* **darling** (1).

sugarcoat *verb.* —*See* **color** (2), **sweeten.**

sugary *adjective.* Having or suggesting the taste of sugar ▶ honeyed, saccharine, sweet. —*See also* **flattering.**

suggest *verb.* **1.** To cause one to remember or think of ▶ hark back, recall. ***Idioms:*** bring to mind, put one in mind of, take one back, remind one of. [*Compare* **refer, remind.**] **2.** To have a particular flavor or suggestion of something ▶ savor, smack, smell, taste. —*See also* **hint, imply, propose.**

suggested *adjective.* —*See* **implicit** (1).

suggestible *adjective.* —*See* **flexible** (3).

suggestion *noun.* Something, such as a feeling or idea, associated with a specific person or thing ▶ association, connection, connotation, impression. —*See also* **advice, hint** (2), **proposal** (1), **shade** (2).

suggestive *adjective.* Tending to bring a memory, mood, or image, for example, subtly or indirectly to mind ▶ allusive, connotative, evocative, impressionistic, reminiscent. [*Compare* **designative, symbolic.**] —*See also* **erotic, insinuating, pregnant** (2), **racy.**

suggestiveness *noun.* —*See* **eroticism, sensuality** (1).

suit *verb.* **1.** To be suitable to or in keeping with ▶ become, befit, fit, go with, match. ***Idioms:*** be one's cup of tea, be right down one's alley, suit one to a T. [*Compare* **agree.**] **2.** To look good on or with ▶ become, enhance, flatter. ***Idiom:*** put in the best light. —*See also* **adapt, satisfy** (1).

suit *noun.* —*See* **lawsuit.**

suitability *or* **suitableness** *noun.* —*See* **qualification.**

suitable *adjective.* —*See* **convenient** (1), **eligible, just.**

suitcase *noun.* A container or piece of luggage for carrying clothing and other items ▶ bag, carryall, carryon, duffle (bag), flight bag, grip, kit, overnight bag, portmanteau, satchel, shoulder bag, valise.

suit coat *or* **suit jacket** *noun.* —*See* **coat** (1).

suite *noun.* —*See* **apartment, retinue, series.**

suited *adjective.* —*See* **eligible.**

suitor *noun.* **1.** One that asks a higher authority for something, as a favor or redress ▶ appealer, appellant, petitioner. **2.** One who humbly entreats ▶ beggar, petitioner, prayer, suppliant, supplicant. —*See also* **beau** (1).

sulk *verb.* To be sullenly aloof or withdrawn, as in silent resentment or protest ▶ mope, pet, pout. [*Compare* **brood.**]

sulky *adjective.* —*See* **glum.**

sullen *adjective.* —*See* **fateful** (1), **glum.**

sully *verb.* —*See* **denigrate, dirty, disgrace.**

sultry *adjective.* —*See* **hot** (1), **sticky** (2).

sum *noun.* —*See* **summary, system, total, whole.**

sum *verb.* —*See* **add.**

sum up *verb.* —*See* **amount, review** (1).

summarize *verb.* —*See* **review** (1).

summary *noun.* A review of the essential points or consequences of something ▶ recap, recapitulation, rundown, run-through, sum, summation, summing-up, wrap-up. [*Compare* **essence, story, synopsis.**]

summary *adjective.* —*See* **brief.**

summation *noun.* The act or process of adding ▶ addition, totalization. [*Compare* **calculation.**] —*See also* **summary, total.**

summer *or* **summertime** *noun.* The season occurring between spring and autumn ▶ dog days.

summing-up *noun.* —*See* **summary.**

summit *noun.* —*See* **climax, conference** (1).

summon *verb.* To request that someone take part in or be present at a particular occasion ▶ ask, bid, invite. ***Idioms:*** extend an invitation to, request the presence of. [*Compare* **appeal, request.**] —*See also* **assemble, command** (1), **evoke.**

summons *noun.* A spoken or written request for someone to take part or be present ▶ bid, call, invitation. *Informal:* invite. [*Compare* **request.**]

sump *noun.* —*See* **pit**[1]**.**

sumptuous *adjective.* —*See* **luxurious.**

sumptuousness *noun.* —*See* **glitter** (2).

sum total *noun.* —*See* **total.**

sunder *verb.* —*See* **break** (1).

sundown *noun.* —*See* **evening.**

sundries *noun.* —*See* **odds and ends.**

sundry *adjective.* —*See* **several, various.**

sunken *adjective.* —*See* **hollow** (2).

sunny *adjective.* —*See* **cheerful, clear** (2).

sunrise *noun.* —*See* **dawn.**

sunset *noun.* —*See* **evening.**

sunup *noun.* —*See* **dawn.**

sup *verb.* —*See* **drink** (1), **eat** (2).

sup *noun.* —*See* **drink** (2).

super *adjective.* —*See* **marvelous.**

super *adverb.* —*See* **unduly.**

superabundance *noun.* —*See* **excess** (1).

superabundant *adjective.* —*See* **profuse.**

superannuate *verb.* To withdraw or remove from business or active life ▶ pension (off), retire, step down. ***Idioms:*** call it quits, hang up one's spurs, put out to pasture, turn in one's badge. [*Compare* **dismiss, quit.**]

superannuated *adjective.* —*See* **obsolete.**

superb *adjective.* —*See* **excellent, grand, marvelous.**

superbness *noun.* —*See* **excellence.**

supercilious *adjective.* —*See* **arrogant, disdainful.**

superciliousness *noun.* —*See* **arrogance.**

supererogatory *or* **supererogative** *adjective.* —*See* **superfluous, wanton** (2).

superficial *adjective.* Lacking in intellectual depth or thoroughness ▶ cursory, naive, one-dimensional, shallow, sketchy, skin-deep, surface, uncritical. [*Compare* **trite.**] —*See also* **apparent** (2).

superficially *adverb.* —*See* **apparently.**

superfluity *noun.* —*See* **excess** (1), **surplus.**

superfluous *adjective.* Being more than is needed, desired, or appropriate ▶ de trop, excess, extra, leftover, redundant, spare, supererogatory, supernumerary, surplus. [*Compare* **excessive, remaining, unnecessary.**]

✚ **CORE SYNONYMS:** *superfluous, excess, extra, spare, supernumerary, surplus.* These adjectives mean being more than is needed, desired, or appropriate: *delete superfluous words; trying to lose excess weight; found some extra change on the dresser; sleeping in the spare room; supernumerary ornamentation; distributed surplus food to the needy.*

---

superfluousness *noun.* —*See* **excess** (1).

superhighway *noun.* —*See* **way** (2).

superhuman *adjective.* —*See* **supernatural** (1).
superintend *verb.* —*See* **supervise.**
superintendence *noun.* —*See* **care** (2), **management.**
superintendent *noun.* —*See* **boss.**
superior *adjective.* **1.** Of greater excellence than another ▶ better, preferable. **2.** Being at a rank or level above another ▶ greater, higher, senior, upper. —*See also* **arrogant, choice** (1), **disdainful, excellent.**
superior *noun.* One who stands above another in rank ▶ better, elder, senior. *Informal:* higher-up. [*Compare* **chief.**] —*See also* **boss.**
superiority *noun.* —*See* **advantage** (3), **arrogance, authority, excellence.**
superlative *adjective.* —*See* **best** (1).
supernal *adjective.* —*See* **divine** (1), **heavenly** (1), **heavenly** (2).
supernatural *adjective.* **1.** Of or relating to existence outside the natural world ▶ extramundane, extrasensory, metaphysical, miraculous, mystic, mystical, numinous, otherworldly, paranormal, preternatural, spiritual, superhuman, superphysical, supersensible, transcendental, unearthly, unworldly. [*Compare* **divine, heavenly, immaterial, weird.**] **2.** Greatly exceeding or departing from the normal course of nature ▶ preternatural, unnatural. [*Compare* **abnormal.**]
supernormal *adjective.* —*See* **elevated** (2).
supernumerary *adjective.* —*See* **superfluous.**
supernumerary *noun.* —*See* **surplus.**
superphysical *adjective.* —*See* **supernatural** (1).
superscribe *verb.* ▶ address, direct. [*Compare* **ticket.**]
supersede *verb.* To substitute for or fill the place of ▶ displace, replace, supplant, surrogate. ***Idioms:*** fill someone's shoes, take over from, take the reins from. [*Compare* **substitute.**]
superseded *adjective.* —*See* **obsolete.**
supersensible *adjective.* —*See* **supernatural** (1).
superstar *noun.* —*See* **celebrity.**
superstition *noun.* —*See* **lore** (1).
supervene *verb.* —*See* **follow** (1).
supervening *adjective.* —*See* **following** (1).
supervenient *adjective.* Not part of the real or essential nature of a thing ▶ adscititious, adventitious, incidental, inessential. [*Compare* **irrelevant, unnecessary.**]
supervise *verb.* To direct and watch over the work and performance of others ▶ boss, monitor, overlook, oversee, superintend, watch over. [*Compare* **arrange, conduct.**]

✚ **CORE SYNONYMS:** *supervise, boss, overlook, oversee, superintend.* These verbs mean to direct and watch over the work and performance of others: *supervised a team of investigators; bossed a construction crew; overlooks farm hands; overseeing plumbers and electricians; superintend a household staff.*

---

supervision *noun.* —*See* **care** (2), **management.**
supervisor *noun.* —*See* **boss.**
supervisory *adjective.* —*See* **administrative.**
supine *adjective.* —*See* **apathetic, cowardly, flat** (1).
supplant *verb.* **1.** To take the place of another against the other's will ▶ cut out, displace, force out, usurp. [*Compare* **assume, occupy, seize.**] **2.** To substitute for or fill the place of ▶ displace, replace, supersede, surrogate. ***Idioms:*** fill someone's shoes, take over from, take the reins from. [*Compare* **substitute.**]
supple *adjective.* —*See* **adaptable, flexible** (1), **flexible** (2), **flexible** (3), **malleable, obedient.**
supplement *verb.* To add to or make whole ▶ accompany, augment, complement, complete, enhance, enrich, rein-

force, strengthen. [*Compare* **increase, support.**]

supplement *noun.* —*See* **attachment, enhancement.**

supplemental *or* **supplementary** *adjective.* —*See* **additional, auxiliary** (2), **complementary.**

suppleness *noun.* —*See* **flexibility** (1).

supplicant *or* **suppliant** *noun.* One who humbly entreats ▶ beggar, petitioner, prayer, suitor.

supplicate *verb.* To offer a reverent petition to God or a god ▶ invoke, pray. —*See also* **appeal** (1).

supplication *noun.* The act of praying ▶ benediction, invocation, prayer. —*See also* **appeal.**

supplier *noun.* —*See* **donor.**

supply *verb.* —*See* **give** (1), **offer** (2), **substitute.**

supply *noun.* —*See* **hoard.**

support *verb.* **1.** To aid the cause of by approving or favoring ▶ advocate, back, champion, endorse, get behind, plump for, recommend, side with, stand behind, stand by, uphold. ***Idioms:*** align oneself with, go to bat for, throw one's weight behind. **2.** To make stronger or more resistant ▶ bolster, brace, bracket, buoy (up), buttress, hold (up), prop (up), reinforce, shore (up), stabilize, steady, strengthen, sustain, tighten, undergird, underpin, underprop, uphold. [*Compare* **balance, fasten.**] **3.** To supply with the necessities of life ▶ keep, maintain, provide for. ***Idioms:*** put a roof over someone's head, put food on the table, take care of. [*Compare* **nourish.**] **4.** To act as a patron to ▶ back, patronize, sponsor. [*Compare* **donate, finance.**] —*See also* **back** (2), **bear** (1), **endure** (1).

support *noun.* A means or device that keeps something erect, stable, or secure ▶ brace, bracket, buttress, crutch, prop, reinforcement, shore, stay, underpinning. —*See also* **endorsement, help, living.**

✢ **CORE SYNONYMS:** *support, uphold, back, advocate, champion.* These verbs mean to aid the cause of by approving or favoring. *Support* is the most general: "*the policy of Cromwell, who supported the growing power of France against the declining power of Spain*" (William E.H. Lecky). To *uphold* is to maintain or affirm in the face of a challenge or strong opposition: "*The Declaration of Right upheld the principle of hereditary monarchy*" (Edmund Burke). *Back* suggests material or moral support intended to contribute to or assure success: *The important medical research was backed by the federal government. Advocate* implies verbal support, often in the form of pleading or arguing: *Scientists advocate a reduction in saturated fats in the human diet.* To *champion* is to fight for one that is under attack or is unable to act in its own behalf: "*championed the government and defended the system of taxation*" (Samuel Chew).

---

supportable *adjective.* —*See* **bearable.**

supporter *noun.* —*See* **advocate, follower, patron.**

supportive *adjective.* —*See* **auxiliary** (1), **sympathetic.**

supposable *adjective.* —*See* **presumptive.**

suppose *verb.* **1.** To consider to be true without proof ▶ assume, imagine, posit, postulate, premise, presume, presuppose. *Informal:* expect, reckon. ***Idioms:*** take for granted (*or* as a given). [*Compare* **believe, infer.**] **2.** To oblige to do or not do by force of authority, propriety, or custom ▶ expect, oblige, obligate, require. [*Compare* **must.**] —*See also* **guess.**

✢ **CORE SYNONYMS:** *suppose, presume, presuppose, postulate, posit, assume.* These verbs signify to take something for granted or as being a fact without proof. To *suppose* often suggests that what is taken to be true is based on uncertain or tentative grounds: *Scientists suppose that dinosaurs lived in swamps.* To *presume* is to suppose that something is reasonable or possible in the absence of proof to the contrary: "*I presume you're tired after the long ride*" (Edith Wharton). *Presuppose* can mean to believe or suppose in advance: *It is unrealistic to presuppose a sophisticated knowledge of harmony in a beginning music student. Postulate* and *posit* denote the assertion of the existence, reality, necessity, or truth of something as the basis for reasoning or argument: "*We can see individuals, but we can't see providence; we have to postulate it*" (Aldous Huxley). To *assume* is to accept something as existing or being true without proof or on inconclusive grounds: "*We must never assume that which is incapable of proof*" (G.H. Lewes).

---

supposed *adjective.* Presumed to be true, real, or genuine, especially on inconclusive grounds ▶ alleged, conjectural, hypothetic, hypothetical, hypothesized, inferential, presumed, purported, putative, reputed, so-called, suppositional, suppositious, supposititious, suppositive. *Informal:* quote-unquote. [*Compare* **ambiguous, presumptive.**]

✚ **CORE SYNONYMS:** *supposed, conjectural, hypothetical, putative, reputed, suppositious, supposititious.* These adjectives mean presumed to be true, real, or genuine, especially on inconclusive grounds: *the supposed cause of inflation; conjectural criticism; the hypothetical site of a lost culture; a foundling's putative father; the reputed author of the article; suppositious reconstructions of dead languages; supposititious hypotheses.*

---

supposition *noun.* —*See* **assumption, guess.**

suppositional *or* **suppositive** *adjective.* —*See* **supposed.**

supposititious *or* **suppositious** *adjective.* —*See* **counterfeit, supposed.**

suppress *verb.* To overcome opposition or uprising with overwhelming force ▶ choke off, crush, extinguish, put down, quash, quell, quench, squash, squelch. ***Idiom:*** put the lid on. [*Compare* **abolish, defeat, frustrate.**] —*See also* **censor** (2), **repress.**

suppression *noun.* Forceful subjugation, as against an uprising ▶ clampdown, crackdown, lockdown, repression. [*Compare* **oppression, restraint.**] —*See also* **domination.**

suppressive *adjective.* —*See* **repressive.**

supremacy *noun.* —*See* **authority, dominance.**

supreme *adjective.* —*See* **authoritative** (1), **best** (1), **dominant** (1), **ideal.**

surcease *verb.* —*See* **stop** (1), **stop** (2).
surcease *noun.* —*See* **stop** (1), **stop** (2).

sure *adjective.* **1.** Having no doubt ▶ assured, certain, confident, convinced, doubtless, positive, undoubting. **2.** Certain not to fail, miss, or err ▶ certain, fail-safe, foolproof, infallible, secure, unerring, unfailing. *Informal:* sure-fire. *Slang:* idiot-proof. [*Compare* **dependable.**] —*See also* **certain** (1), **certain** (2), **definite** (3), **firm**[1] (2).

✚ **CORE SYNONYMS:** *sure, certain, confident, positive.* These adjectives mean having no doubt or impossible to doubt. *Sure* and *certain* are frequently used interchangeably; *sure,* however, is the more subjective term, whereas *certain* may possibly imply belief based on experience or evidence: "*Never teach a child anything of which you are not yourself sure*" (John Ruskin). "*In this world nothing is certain but death and taxes*" (Benjamin Franklin). *Confident* suggests assurance that is founded on faith or reliance in oneself or in others: *The senator is confident of reelection. Positive* suggests full, emphatic certainty: *The prosecutor presented positive proof of the defendant's guilt.*

sure-fire *adjective.* —*See* **sure** (2).

surely *adverb.* —*See* **absolutely.**

sureness *noun.* The fact or condition of being without doubt ▶ assurance, assuredness, certainty, certitude, confidence, conviction, doubtlessness, indubitability, positiveness, positivity, surety. [*Compare* **impudence.**] —*See also* **stability.**

✤ CORE SYNONYMS: *sureness, certainty, certitude, assurance, conviction.* These nouns mean freedom from doubt. *Sureness* is the most general: *The jury was swayed by the sureness of the recollection of the witness. Certainty* implies a thorough consideration of evidence: *"the emphasis of a certainty that is not impaired by any shade of doubt"* (Mark Twain). *Certitude* is based more on personal belief than on objective facts: *"Certitude is not the test of certainty"* (Oliver Wendell Holmes, Jr.). *Assurance* is a feeling of confidence resulting from subjective experience: *"There is no such thing as absolute certainty, but there is assurance sufficient for the purposes of human life"* (John Stuart Mill). *Conviction* arises from the vanquishing of doubt: *"His religion . . . was substantial and concrete, made up of good, hard convictions and opinions.* (Willa Cather).

sure thing *noun.* —*See* **certainty.**

surety *noun.* An assumption of responsibility, as one given by a manufacturer, for the quality, worth, or durability of a product ▶ certification, guarantee, guaranty, warrant, warranty. —*See also* **sponsor, sureness.**

surface *noun.* An outer surface, layer, or part of an object ▶ face, facet, side. [*Compare* **back, bottom, front.**] —*See also* **face** (3), **finish.**

surface *verb.* —*See* **face** (2), **finish** (2).

surface *adjective.* —*See* **superficial.**

surfeit *verb.* —*See* **satiate.**

surfeit *noun.* —*See* **excess** (1), **excess** (2), **satiation, surplus.**

surge *verb.* —*See* **flow** (2), **increase.**

surge *noun.* —*See* **eruption, flow.**

surly *adjective.* —*See* **glum, ill-tempered.**

surmise *verb.* —*See* **guess.**

surmise *noun.* —*See* **guess.**

surmised *adjective.* —*See* **untried.**

surmount *verb.* To pass by or over successfully ▶ clear, hurdle, negotiate. —*See also* **defeat.**

surmountable *adjective.* —*See* **passable.**

surpass *verb.* To be greater or better than ▶ best, better, exceed, excel, one-up, outdo, outmatch, outrun, outshine, outstrip, pass, top, transcend. *Informal:* beat. ***Idioms:*** go beyond, go one better. [*Compare* **dominate.**] —*See also* **exceed.**

✤ CORE SYNONYMS: *surpass, excel, exceed, transcend, outdo, outstrip.* These verbs mean to be greater or better than someone or something. To *surpass* another is to be superior in performance, quality, or degree: *an athlete surpassed by none. Excel* is to be preeminent (*excels at figure skating*) or to be at a level higher than another or others (*excelled her father as a lawyer*). *Exceed* can refer to being superior (*an invention that exceeds all others in ingenuity*), to being greater than another (*a salary exceeding 70 thousand dollars a year*), and to going beyond a proper limit (*exceed one's authority*). *Transcend* often implies the attainment of a level so high that comparison is hardly possible: *Great art transcends mere rules of composition.* To *outdo* is to excel in doing or performing: *won't be outdone in generosity. Outstrip* strongly suggests leaving another behind, as in a contest: *a case of the student outstripping the teacher.*

surplus *noun.* A thing, amount, or quantity beyond what is needed, desired, or appropriate ▶ excess, extra, fat, glut, leftover, overage, overflow, overmuch, overrun, overstock, oversupply, superfluity, supernumerary, surfeit, surplusage. ***Idiom:*** fifth wheel. [*Compare* **excess.**]

surplus *adjective.* —*See* **superfluous.**

surplusage *noun.* —*See* **surplus.**

surprise *verb.* To impress strongly by what is unexpected or unusual ▶ amaze, astonish, astound, awe, startle. ***Idioms:*** catch (*or* take) unawares, take aback, throw for a loop. [*Compare* **stagger, startle.**] —*See also* **ambush.**

surprise *noun.* —*See* **marvel, shock[1], wonder** (1).

surprisingly *adverb.* —*See* **unusually.**

surrender *verb.* **1.** To give up in favor of another ▶ acquiesce, blink, bow, capitulate, concede, give in, give up, submit, yield. ***Idiom:*** bend one's knee. **2.** To yield oneself unrestrainedly, as to an impulse ▶ abandon, deliver, relinquish. ***Idioms:*** give oneself up (*or* over). —*See also* **abandon** (1), **succumb.**

surrender *noun.* The act of submitting or surrendering to the power of another ▶ capitulation, giving up, submission. [*Compare* **obedience.**] —*See also* **abandonment** (1), **delivery.**

✚ **CORE SYNONYMS:** *surrender, yield, bow, submit, capitulate.* These verbs mean to give up something in favor of something else, especially when one can no longer oppose or resist. *Surrender* and *yield* have the widest application: *The enemy troops surrendered to the victors.* "*The child . . . soon yielded to the drowsiness*" (Charles Dickens). *Bow* suggests giving way in defeat or through courtesy: "*Bow and accept the end/Of a love*" (Robert Frost). *Submit* implies giving way out of necessity, as after futile or unsuccessful resistance: "*obliged to submit to those laws which are imposed upon us* (Abigail Adams). *Capitulate* implies surrender to pressure, force, compulsion, or inevitability: "*I will be conquered; I will not capitulate* [to illness]" (Samuel Johnson).

---

surreptitious *adjective.* —*See* **stealthy.**

surrogate *noun.* —*See* **substitute.**

surrogate *verb.* To substitute for or fill the place of ▶ displace, replace, supersede, supplant. ***Idioms:*** fill someone's shoes, take over from, take the reins from. [*Compare* **substitute.**]

surround *verb.* To shut in on all sides ▶ beset, circle, compass, embrace, encircle, encompass, environ, hedge (in), hem (in), ring. [*Compare* **enclose, wrap.**] —*See also* **encircle.**

✚ **CORE SYNONYMS:** *surround, circle, compass, encircle, encompass, ring.* These verbs mean to shut in on all sides: *Suburbs surround the city. A crown circled the king's head. Fog compassed the mountain peak. A belt encircled her waist. A lake encompassed the small island. Guests ringed the coffee table.*

---

surroundings *noun.* —*See* **conditions, environment** (1), **environment** (2).

surveillance *noun.* —*See* **lookout** (1).

survey *verb.* **1.** To pay regular and close attention to ▶ follow, monitor, observe, stake out, watch. ***Idioms:*** have one's (*or* keep an) eye on, keep tabs on, keep track of, ride herd on. **2.** To view broadly or from a height ▶ look over, overlook, scan. [*Compare* **look.**] —*See also* **examine** (1), **watch** (1).

survey *noun.* **1.** A gathering of information or opinion from a variety of sources or individuals ▶ canvass, count, poll. **2.** A general or comprehensive view or treatment ▶ overview. [*Compare* **synopsis.**] —*See also* **examination** (1).

survival *noun.* —*See* **continuation** (1).

survive *verb.* **1.** To exist in spite of adversity ▶ come through, get through, last, make it, outride, persevere, persist, pull through, ride out, weather. [*Compare* **endure.**] **2.** To live, exist, or remain longer than ▶ outlast, outlive, outwear.

susceptibility *noun.* —*See* **exposure.**
susceptible *or* **susceptive** *adjective.* —*See* **gullible, liable** (2), **sensitive** (1), **vulnerable.**
susceptibleness *noun.* —*See* **exposure.**
suspect *verb.* —*See* **distrust, guess.**
suspect *adjective.* —*See* **debatable, shady** (1).
suspend *verb.* **1.** To stop for an indefinite period ▶ interrupt, pause. ***Idiom:*** put on hold. [*Compare* **rest.**] **2.** To bring an activity or relationship to an end suddenly ▶ break off, cease, discontinue, interrupt, terminate. —*See also* **defer[1], hang** (1).
suspenseful *adjective.* —*See* **dramatic** (2).
suspension *noun.* —*See* **abeyance, break, delay** (1).
suspicion *noun.* —*See* **distrust, doubt, feeling** (1), **hint** (1), **shade** (2).
suspicious *adjective.* —*See* **distrustful, doubtful** (2), **shady** (1).
suspiciously *adverb.* —*See* **skeptically.**
sustain *verb.* To keep in a condition of good repair, efficiency, or use ▶ keep up, maintain, preserve. —*See also* **back** (2), **bear** (1), **confirm** (1), **develop** (1), **endure** (1), **keep** (5), **nurture, prove, support** (2).
sustained *adjective.* —*See* **long[1]** (2).
sustenance *noun.* —*See* **food, living, maintenance.**
susurration *or* **susurrus** *noun.* —*See* **murmur.**
suzerain *noun.* —*See* **chief.**
svelte *adjective.* —*See* **thin** (1).
swaddle *verb.* —*See* **wrap** (1).
swag *noun.* —*See* **plunder.**
swagger *verb.* —*See* **boast, strut.**
swagman *noun.* —*See* **hobo.**
swain *noun.* —*See* **beau** (1).
swale *noun.* —*See* **swamp, valley.**
swallow *verb.* To cause to pass from the mouth into the stomach ▶ ingest, take. [*Compare* **drink, eat, gulp.**] —*See also* **believe** (1), **endure** (1).
swallow up *verb.* —*See* **consume** (1).
swallow *noun.* An act of swallowing ▶ gulp, ingestion, swig. —*See also* **bit[1]** (2), **drink** (2).
swamp *or* **swampland** *noun.* A usually low-lying area of soft waterlogged ground and standing water ▶ bog, fen, marsh, marshland, mire, moor, morass, muskeg, quag, quagmire, slough, swale, wetland.
swamp *verb.* To affect as if by an outpouring of water ▶ deluge, flood, inundate, overwhelm.
swank *adjective.* —*See* **exclusive** (3), **fashionable.**
swank *verb.* —*See* **strut.**
swanky *adjective.* —*See* **exclusive** (3), **fashionable.**
swap *verb.* —*See* **change** (3), **exchange.**
swap *noun.* —*See* **change** (2).
swarm *noun.* —*See* **crowd, flock.**
swarm *verb.* —*See* **crowd, teem[1].**
swarming *adjective.* —*See* **busy** (2), **overcrowded.**
swarthy *adjective.* —*See* **dark** (2).
swash *verb.* To make the sound of moving or disturbed water ▶ lap, splash, wash. [*Compare* **burble, swish.**] —*See also* **splash** (1), **strut.**
swat *verb.* —*See* **hit, slap.**
swat *noun.* —*See* **blow[2], slap.**
swatch *noun.* —*See* **band[1].**
swath *noun.* —*See* **band[1].**
swathe *verb.* —*See* **dress** (2), **wrap** (1).
sway *verb.* To move back and forth or from side to side ▶ fluctuate, oscillate, quake, rock, shake, swing, switch, teeter, totter, tremble, undulate, vacillate, vibrate, wag, waggle, wave, waver, weave, wobble. [*Compare* **shake.**] —*See also* **influence, stagger** (1).
sway *noun.* —*See* **authority, dominance, domination, influence.**

✤ **CORE SYNONYMS:** *sway, swing, oscillate, rock, vibrate, fluctuate, undulate, waver.* These verbs mean to move back and forth or from side to side. *Sway* suggests the movement of something unsteady, light, or flexible: *"thousands of* *the little yellow blossoms all swaying to the light wind"* (W.H. Hudson). *Swing* usually applies to arclike movement of something attached at one extremity and free at the other: *The ship's lanterns swung violently in the raging storm. Oscillate* literally refers to a steady back-and-forth motion, as that of a pendulum; figuratively, it denotes vacillation, as between conflicting purposes: *"a king . . . oscillating between fear of Rome and desire of independence"* (Walter Besant). To *rock* is to swing gently or rhythmically or sway or tilt violently: *"The ruins of the ancient church seemed actually to rock and threaten to fall"* (Sir Walter Scott). *Vibrate* implies quick periodic oscillations; it can also suggest trembling, pulsating, or quivering: *"Music, when soft voices die,/Vibrates in the memory"* (Percy Bysshe Shelley). *Fluctuate* implies fairly constant alternating change: *"Prices fluctuated violently from the irregularity of the crops"* (Lesley B. Simpson). *Undulate* generally refers to smooth wavelike movement: *"gleaming seaweed that curls and undulates with the tide"* (Willa Cather). *Waver* typically suggests unsteady, uncertain movement: *A police officer stopped the driver who was wavering from lane to lane on the country road.*

---

swear *verb.* To use profane or obscene language ▶ blaspheme, curse, damn. *Informal:* cuss. *—See also* **assert, pledge** (1), **testify.**

swear at *verb.* To hurl strong deprecations, curses, or insults at ▶ *Informal:* cuss at (*or* out), mouth off at. [*Compare* **curse, insult, revile.**]

swear off *verb.* *—See* **abandon** (2), **break** (5).

swearword *noun.* A profane or obscene term ▶ blasphemy, curse, epithet, expletive, oath, obscenity, profanity. *Informal:* cuss. ***Idioms:*** bad (*or* dirty) word, four-letter word.

sweat *verb.* To excrete moisture through a porous skin or layer ▶ lather, perspire, transude. *—See also* **labor, ooze.**

sweat out *verb.* *—See* **endure** (1).

sweat *noun.* Moisture accumulated on a surface through sweating or condensation ▶ condensation, lather, perspiration, transudation. *—See also* **labor, state** (2), **task** (2).

sweaty *or* **sweating** *adjective.* Producing or covered with sweat ▶ perspiring, sudoriferous. [*Compare* **damp, sticky.**]

sweep *verb.* *—See* **blow**[1] (1), **flourish, flow** (1).

sweep *noun.* *—See* **expanse** (1), **range** (1).

sweeping *adjective.* *—See* **general** (2).

sweet *adjective.* **1.** Having or suggesting the taste of sugar ▶ honeyed, saccharine, sugary. **2.** Not sour or salted ▶ fresh, uncured, unsalted. *—See also* **amiable, attractive, delightful.**

sweet *noun.* *—See* **darling** (1).

sweeten *verb.* To make superficially more acceptable or appealing ▶ candy, gild, honey, sugar, sugarcoat. [*Compare* **moderate.**] *—See also* **pacify.**

sweetheart *noun.* *—See* **darling** (1).

sweetmeat *noun.* *—See* **delicacy.**

sweet-sounding *adjective.* *—See* **melodious.**

sweet talk *noun.* *—See* **flattery.**

sweet-talk *verb.* *—See* **coax, flatter** (1).

swell *verb.* To expand from or as if from internal pressure ▶ balloon, bloat, blow up, bulge, bulge out, distend, inflate, puff, puff out, puff up, tumefy, tumesce. [*Compare* **bulge.**] *—See also* **boast, increase.**

swell *noun.* A man who is vain about his clothes ▶ beau, coxcomb, dandy, fop, peacock. *—See also* **increase** (1), **wave.**

swell *adjective.* *—See* **excellent, marvelous.**

swelled head *noun.* *—See* **egotism.**

swellheaded *adjective.* *—See* **arrogant, egotistic** (1).

swelling *noun.* *—See* **bump** (2).

swelter *verb.* —*See* **burn** (3).
sweltering *adjective.* —*See* **hot** (1).
swerve *verb.* To turn aside sharply from a straight course ▶ angle, cut, sheer, skew, slant, slue, tack, veer, zag, zig, zigzag. [*Compare* **bend, glance.**] —*See also* **deviate.**
swift *adjective.* —*See* **fast** (1), **quick.**
swiftly *adverb.* —*See* **fast.**
swiftness *noun.* —*See* **agility, haste** (1).
swig *noun.* An act of swallowing ▶ gulp, ingestion, swallow. —*See also* **drink** (2).
swig *verb.* —*See* **drink** (1).
swill *verb.* —*See* **drink** (1), **gulp.**
swill *noun.* —*See* **drink** (2).
swim *verb.* To have the sensation of turning in circles ▶ reel, spin, swirl, whirl. ***Idiom:*** go round and round. —*See also* **teem**[1].
swim *noun.* —*See* **plunge.**
swindle *verb.* —*See* **cheat** (1), **deceive.**
swindle *noun.* —*See* **cheat** (1).
swindler *noun.* —*See* **cheat** (2).
swing *verb.* **1.** To turn in place, as on a fixed point ▶ pivot, slue, swivel, wheel. **2.** To shift from one attitude, interest, condition, or emotion to another ▶ dilly-dally, vacillate, waver. **3.** *Slang* To execute by suspending by the neck ▶ gibbet, hang. *Informal:* string up. —*See also* **effect, hang** (1), **sway, turn** (2).
swing at *verb.* —*See* **hit.**
swing *noun.* —*See* **blow**[2], **range** (1), **rhythm.**
swinger *noun.* —*See* **wanton.**
swipe *verb.* —*See* **steal.**
swipe *noun.* —*See* **blow**[2], **taunt.**
swirl *verb.* **1.** To move or cause to move like a rapidly rotating current of liquid ▶ eddy, whirl. **2.** To rotate rapidly ▶ spin, twirl, whirl. **3.** To have the sensation of turning in circles ▶ reel, spin, swim, whirl. ***Idiom:*** go round and round. —*See also* **turn** (1).
swirl *noun.* —*See* **curl, revolution** (1), **whirlpool.**
swish *verb.* —*See* **hiss** (1).
swish *adjective.* —*See* **fashionable.**
swish *noun.* —*See* **hiss** (1).
switch *verb.* **1.** To move to and fro vigorously and usually repeatedly ▶ wag, waggle, wave. **2.** To leave or discard for another ▶ change, shift. —*See also* **change** (3), **shake** (1), **turn** (2).
switch *noun.* —*See* **change** (2), **stick** (1).
swivel *verb.* To turn in place, as on a fixed point ▶ pivot, slue, swing, wheel. [*Compare* **turn.**]
swivet *noun.* —*See* **state** (2).
swollen *adjective.* Expanded from or as if from internal pressure ▶ bloated, blown up, bulging, distended, inflated, puffed (up *or* out), tumescent. [*Compare* **inflated.**] —*See also* **boastful.**
swoon *verb.* To suffer temporary lack of consciousness ▶ black out, faint, keel over, pass out. ***Idioms:*** drop (*or* faint *or* fall) dead away, see stars. [*Compare* **collapse.**]
swoon *noun.* A temporary lack of consciousness ▶ blackout, faint, fainting spell, syncope.
sword of Damocles *noun.* —*See* **danger.**
sybarite *noun.* A person devoted to pleasure and luxury ▶ epicure, epicurean, hedonist, pagan, pleasure-seeker, sensualist, voluptuary.
sybaritic *adjective.* Characterized by or devoted to pleasure and luxury as a lifestyle ▶ epicurean, hedonic, hedonistic, voluptuary, voluptuous. [*Compare* **luxurious, sensual.**]
sycophant *noun.* One who flatters another or behaves obsequiously in an attempt to win favor ▶ adulator, bootlicker, courtier, fawner, flatterer, groveler, lackey, minion, slave, toady, truckler, yes man. *Informal:* apple-polisher, brownnose, brownnoser. [*Compare* **follower, parasite, slave, subordinate.**]
sycophantic *adjective.* —*See* **servile.**
syllabus *noun.* —*See* **program** (2).
symbiotic *adjective.* —*See* **complementary.**

symbol *noun.* An object or expression associated with and serving to identify something else ▶ attribute, emblem, metaphor, signifier, token. [*Compare* **expression, term.**] —*See also* **character** (7), **sign** (1).

symbolic *adjective.* Serving as a symbol ▶ emblematic, emblematical, figurative, metaphoric, metaphorical, representational, representative, symbolical. [*Compare* **designative.**] —*See also* **graphic** (4).

symbolize *verb.* —*See* **represent** (1).

symmetrical *or* **symmetric** *adjective.* **1.** Characterized by or displaying symmetry, especially correspondence in scale or measure ▶ balanced, proportional, proportionate, regular. [*Compare* **even, parallel.**] **2.** Having components that are pleasingly combined ▶ balanced, concordant, congruous, harmonious.

symmetry *noun.* Satisfying arrangement marked by even distribution of elements, as in a design ▶ balance, harmony, proportion. [*Compare* **agreement.**]

sympathetic *adjective.* Feeling or expressing sympathy or pity ▶ bleeding-heart, comforting, commiserative, compassionate, concerned, condolatory, empathetic, empathic, feeling, loving, pitying, softhearted, supportive, tender, understanding, warm-hearted. [*Compare* **attentive, generous, gentle.**]

sympathize *verb.* **1.** To experience or express compassion ▶ ache, commiserate, condole, feel. ***Idioms:*** be (*or* feel) sorry, have one's heart bleed for someone, have one's heart go out to someone. [*Compare* **comfort, pity.**] **2.** To understand or be sensitive to another's feelings or ideas ▶ empathize, understand. ***Idioms:*** feel someone's pain, put oneself (*or* walk) in someone else's shoes. **3.** To associate or affiliate oneself closely with a person or group ▶ empathize, identify, relate. [*Compare* **understand.**]

sympathy *noun.* **1.** A very close understanding between persons ▶ empathy, understanding. **2.** A relationship or an affinity between people or things in which many properties are shared ▶ harmony, synch, synchronization, synchrony. [*Compare* **agreement.**] —*See also* **pity** (1).

symphonic *or* **symphonious** *adjective.* —*See* **harmonious** (2).

symphony *noun.* —*See* **harmony** (1).

symposium *noun.* —*See* **conference** (1).

symptom *noun.* —*See* **sign** (1).

synch *noun.* A relationship or an affinity between people or things in which many properties are shared ▶ harmony, sympathy, synchronization, synchrony. [*Compare* **agreement.**]

synchronize *verb.* To occur at the same time ▶ coincide, concur, harmonize.

synchronous *or* **synchronic** *adjective.* —*See* **concurrent, contemporary** (1).

synchronously *adverb.* At the same time ▶ concurrently, simultaneously, together. ***Idioms:*** all at once, all together.

synchrony *or* **synchronization** *noun.* A relationship or an affinity between people or things in which many properties are shared ▶ harmony, sympathy, synch. [*Compare* **agreement.**]

syncope *noun.* A temporary lack of consciousness ▶ blackout, faint, fainting spell, swoon.

syndicate *noun.* —*See* **alliance.**

syndrome *noun.* —*See* **complex** (1).

synergistic *or* **synergetic** *adjective.* —*See* **cooperative.**

synergy *noun.* —*See* **cooperation.**

synod *noun.* —*See* **convention.**

synopsis *noun.* A shortened version or summary ▶ abridgment, abstract, brief, condensation, digest, epitome, outline, sketch. [*Compare* **summary.**]

synopsize *verb.* —*See* **review** (1).

synthesize *verb.* —*See* **harmonize** (2).

synthetic *adjective.* —*See* **artificial** (1).

syrupy *adjective.* —*See* **viscous.**

system *noun.* An organized array of individual elements and parts forming and working as a unit ▶ arrangement, body, entity, integral, machine, organization, sum, totality, whole. —*See also* **complex** (1), **method, way** (1).

systematic *or* **systematical** *adjective.* —*See* **methodical.**

systematization *or* **systemization** *noun.* —*See* **method.**

systematize *verb.* —*See* **arrange** (1).

systemize *verb.* —*See* **arrange** (1).

T

tab *noun.* —*See* **account** (2), **cost** (1), **ticket** (1).

tabby *noun.* —*See* **gossip** (2).

table *noun.* **1.** A natural, flat land elevation ▶ mesa, plateau. [*Compare* **hill.**] **2.** An orderly columnar display of data ▶ chart, tabulation. —*See also* **list**[1].

table *verb.* —*See* **defer**[1].

tableau *noun.* —*See* **view** (2).

taboo *noun.* —*See* **forbiddance.**

taboo *adjective.* —*See* **forbidden.**

taboo *verb.* —*See* **forbid.**

tabulate *verb.* —*See* **list**[1].

tabulation *noun.* An orderly columnar display of data ▶ chart, table. [*Compare* **list**[1].]

tacit *adjective.* —*See* **implicit** (1), **silent** (2).

taciturn *adjective.* Habitually untalkative ▶ close, close-mouthed, incommunicable, incommunicative, laconic, quiet, reserved, reticent, silent, tightlipped, uncommunicable, uncommunicative, untalkative. [*Compare* **brief.**]

✚ **CORE SYNONYMS:** *taciturn, silent, reticent, reserved, laconic, uncommunicative, tightlipped.* These adjectives describe people who habitually do not talk much. *Taciturn* implies unsociableness and a tendency to speak only when it is absolutely necessary: *"At the Council board he was taciturn; and in the House of Lords he never opened his lips"* (Thomas Macaulay). *Silent* often implies a habitual disinclination to speak or to speak out: *"The coroner was a very silent man"* (Mary Roberts Rinehart). The term may also mean refraining from speech, as out of fear or confusion: *"The person in custody must, prior to interrogation, be clearly informed that he has the right to remain silent"* (Earl Warren). *Reticent* suggests a reluctance to share one's thoughts and feelings: *"She had been shy and reticent with me, and now . . . she was telling me aloud the secrets of her inmost heart"* (W.H. Hudson). *Reserved* suggests aloofness and reticence: *"a reserved man, whose inner life was intense and sufficient to him"* (Arnold Bennett). *Laconic* denotes terseness or conciseness in expression, but when applied to people it often implies an unwillingness to use words: *"Mountain dwellers and mountain lovers are a laconic tribe. They know the futility of words"* (Edna Ferber). *Uncommunicative* suggests a disposition to withhold opinions, feelings, or knowledge from others: *an uncommunicative witness.* *Tightlipped* strongly implies a steadfast unwillingness to divulge information being sought: *remained tightlipped when asked about her personal life.*

tack *noun.* An often sudden change or departure, as in a trend ▶ shift, turn, twist. [*Compare* **change, deviation.**] —*See also* **approach** (1), **nail.**

tack *verb.* —*See* **fasten, swerve.**

tackle *noun.* —*See* **outfit.**

tackle *verb.* —*See* **assume, attack** (2).

tacky *adjective.* —*See* **coarse** (1), **gaudy, shabby, sticky** (1).

tact *noun.* The ability to say and do the right thing at the right time ▶ address, delicacy, diplomacy, discretion, savoir-faire, sensitivity, tactfulness. [*Compare* **consideration, decency.**]

✚ **CORE SYNONYMS:** *tact, address, diplomacy, savoir-faire.* These nouns denote the ability to say and do the right thing at the right time with skill, sensitivity, and finesse. *Tact* implies propriety and the ability to speak or act unoffensively: "*He had . . . a tact that would preserve him from flagrant error in any society*" (Francis Parkman). *Address* suggests deftness and grace in social situations: "*With the charms of beauty she combined the address of an accomplished intriguer*" (Charles Merivale). *Diplomacy* implies adroit management of difficult situations: *Diffusing the confrontation between management and the union workers required delicate diplomacy. Savoir-faire* involves knowing the right or graceful thing to say or do: *The hosts of the party set the shy visitor at ease with their savoir-faire.*

---

tactful *adjective.* —*See* **delicate** (2).

tactfulness *noun.* —*See* **tact.**

tactic *noun.* **1.** An action calculated to achieve an end ▶ maneuver, measure, move, procedure, step. **2.** A method of deploying troops and equipment in combat ▶ battle plan, maneuver, plan of attack, stratagem, strategy. —*See also* **approach** (1).

tactile *adjective.* **1.** Discernible by touch ▶ palpable, tangible, touchable. **2.** Relating to the sense of touch ▶ tactual.

tactility *noun.* The faculty or ability to perceive tactile stimulation ▶ feel, feeling, touch. ***Idiom:*** sense of touch. [*Compare* **sensation.**] —*See also* **tangibility.**

taction *noun.* A coming together or touching ▶ contact, contingence, touch. [*Compare* **brush**[1]**, touch.**]

tactless *adjective.* Lacking sensitivity and skill in dealing with others ▶ brash, clumsy, gauche, impolitic, indelicate, insensitive, maladroit, undiplomatic, unpolitic, untactful. [*Compare* **abrupt, rude.**]

tactlessness *noun.* —*See* **thoughtlessness** (2).

tactual *adjective.* Relating to the sense of touch ▶ tactile.

tad *noun.* —*See* **bit**[1] (1).

tag *verb.* To attach a ticket to ▶ earmark, flag, label, mark, ticket. —*See also* **call, follow** (3), **mark** (1).

tag *noun.* —*See* **name** (1), **ticket** (1).

tag end *noun.* —*See* **back.**

tail *noun.* **1.** Something that follows or is drawn along behind ▶ trail, train, wake. [*Compare* **stream.**] **2.** *Informal* An agent assigned to observe and report on another ▶ shadow, watcher. [*Compare* **detective.**] —*See also* **back, buttocks.**

tail *adjective.* —*See* **last**[1] (2).

tail *verb.* —*See* **follow** (3).

tail away *or* **off** *verb.* —*See* **decrease.**

tail end *noun.* —*See* **back.**

tailor *verb.* —*See* **adapt, bias** (2).

tailored *adjective.* —*See* **custom.**

tailor-made *adjective.* —*See* **appropriate, convenient** (1), **custom.**

taint *verb.* —*See* **contaminate, corrupt, decay, denigrate.**

taint *noun.* —*See* **contaminant, stain.**

tainted *adjective.* —*See* **impure** (2).

taintlessness *noun.* —*See* **purity.**

take *verb.* **1.** To have a sudden overwhelming effect on ▶ catch, seize, strike. **2.** To cause to pass from the mouth into the stomach ▶ ingest, swallow. [*Compare* **drink, eat, gulp.**] **3.** To admit to one's possession, presence, or awareness ▶ accept, have, receive. [*Compare* **absorb.**] **4.** To receive something given or offered willingly and gladly ▶ accept, embrace, take up, welcome. **5.** To go aboard a means of transport ▶ board, catch. *Informal:* hop. **6.** To understand in a particular way ▶ construe, interpret, read. **7.** To take away a quantity from another quantity ▶ abate, deduct, discount, rebate, subtract, take off. *Informal:* knock off. —*See also* **attract, bring** (1), **capture, cheat** (1), **choose** (1), **contract** (2), **demand** (2), **derive** (1), **endure** (1), **function, get** (1), **remove** (1), **seize** (1), **understand** (1).

take after *verb.* —*See* **resemble.**

take apart *verb.* —*See* **disassemble.**

take away *verb.* To move something from a position occupied ▶ remove, take (off *or* out), withdraw. *—See also* **deduct.**

take back *verb.* *—See* **resume, retract** (1), **return** (2).

take down *verb.* *—See* **disassemble, lower**[2]**.**

take in *verb.* *—See* **accept** (3), **contain** (1), **deceive, outwit, understand** (1).

take off *verb.* To rise up in flight ▶ lift off. *—See also* **deduct, go** (1), **remove** (3), **remove** (1), **run** (2).

take on *verb.* *—See* **adopt, assume, contend, employ** (1), **start** (1).

take out *verb.* *Informal* To be with another person socially on a regular basis ▶ date, go out (with), go with, see. ***Idioms:*** go steady, go together. *—See also* **murder, remove** (1).

take over *verb.* To free from a specific duty by acting as a substitute ▶ relieve, spell. [*Compare* **substitute.**] *—See also* **assume, occupy** (2).

take to *verb.* *—See* **like**[1]**.**

take up *verb.* *—See* **absorb** (2), **adopt, continue, deal** (1), **drink** (3), **elevate** (1), **start** (1).

take *noun.* The amount of money collected as admission ▶ box office, gate, receipts. *—See also* **attempt.**

take-in *noun.* *—See* **trick** (1).

takeoff *noun.* The act of rising in flight ▶ liftoff. *—See also* **satire.**

taking *adjective.* *—See* **attractive, contagious.**

tale *noun.* *—See* **lie**[2]**, yarn.**

talebearer *noun.* *—See* **gossip** (2), **informer.**

talebearing *noun.* *—See* **gossip** (1).

talebearing *adjective.* Inclined to gossip ▶ blabby, gossipy, taletelling.

talent *noun.* An innate capability ▶ aptitude, aptness, bent, faculty, flair, genius, gift, head, instinct, knack, turn. [*Compare* **ability.**]

talented *adjective.* *—See* **gifted.**

taleteller *noun.* *—See* **gossip** (2).

taletelling *adjective.* Inclined to gossip ▶ blabby, gossipy, talebearing.

talisman *noun.* *—See* **charm.**

talismanic *adjective.* *—See* **magic.**

talk *verb.* **1.** To express oneself in speech ▶ speak, verbalize, vocalize. [*Compare* **babble, chatter.**] **2.** To direct speech to ▶ address, speak. *—See also* **confer** (1), **converse**[1]**, gossip, inform** (2), **say.**

talk back *verb.* To utter an impertinent rejoinder ▶ talk up. *Informal:* sass, sauce. ***Idiom:*** give someone lip.

talk down *verb.* *—See* **belittle.**

talk into *verb.* *—See* **persuade.**

talk over *verb.* *—See* **discuss.**

talk up *verb.* To utter an impertinent rejoinder ▶ talk back. *Informal:* sass, sauce. ***Idiom:*** give someone lip. *—See also* **promote** (3).

talk *noun.* The act or process of dealing with another to reach an agreement ▶ negotiation, parley. *—See also* **conversation, discourse, gossip** (1), **speech** (1), **speech** (2).

talkative *adjective.* Given to conversation ▶ chatty, conversational, garrulous, loquacious, talky, voluble. *Slang:* gabby. [*Compare* **wordy.**]

talker *noun.* *—See* **conversationalist.**

talkfest *noun.* *—See* **conversation.**

talky *adjective.* *—See* **talkative.**

tall *adjective.* *—See* **difficult** (1), **high** (1).

tallow *noun.* Adipose tissue ▶ blubber, fat, lard, suet. [*Compare* **oil.**]

tall tale *noun.* *—See* **exaggeration, lie**[2]**, yarn.**

tall talk *noun.* *—See* **exaggeration.**

tally *noun.* The total number of points made by a contestant, side, or team in a game or contest ▶ score. *—See also* **account** (2), **count** (1).

tally *verb.* To gain a point or points in a game or contest ▶ post, score. *Informal:* notch. ***Idioms:*** make a goal (*or* point). *—See also* **agree** (1), **count** (2).

tame *adjective.* *—See* **domestic** (2), **gentle** (3).

tame *verb.* *—See* **domesticate, gentle, moderate** (1).

tameness *noun.* —*See* **dullness.**

tamper *verb.* To prearrange the outcome of a contest ▶ fix, rig. ***Idiom:*** stack the deck. —*See also* **tinker.**

tang *noun.* —*See* **flavor** (1).

tangent *noun.* —*See* **digression.**

tangential *adjective.* —*See* **digressive.**

tangibility *noun.* The quality or condition of being tangible ▶ corporeality, palpability, physicality, tactility, tangibleness, touchableness. [*Compare* **matter.**]

tangible *adjective.* Discernible by touch ▶ palpable, tactile, touchable. —*See also* **physical, real** (1).

tangle *noun.* Something that is intricately or bewilderingly complex ▶ cat's cradle, entanglement, imbroglio, jungle, knot, labyrinth, maze, mesh, morass, skein, snarl, web. —*See also* **argument.**

tangle *verb.* —*See* **argue** (1), **catch** (1), **complicate, entangle.**

tangled *adjective.* —*See* **complex** (1).

tangy *adjective.* —*See* **sour.**

tank *noun.* —*See* **vat.**

tanked *adjective.* —*See* **drunk.**

tank up *verb.* —*See* **drink** (2).

tantalize *verb.* To excite by exposing something desirable while keeping it out of reach ▶ bait, tease. ***Idiom:*** make one's mouth water. [*Compare* **charm, flirt.**]

tantalizing *adjective.* —*See* **seductive.**

tantamount *adjective.* —*See* **equal.**

tantrum *noun.* —*See* **temper** (2).

tap[1] *verb.* **1.** To strike lightly or gently ▶ dab, flick, pat, rap. [*Compare* **brush[1], dig.**] **2.** To indicate time or rhythm ▶ beat, count. ***Idioms:*** keep time, mark time. —*See also* **appoint, beat** (5).

tap *noun.* The sound made by a light blow ▶ knock, rap, rapping, tapping. [*Compare* **beat.**]

tap[2] *verb.* To monitor telephone calls with a concealed device connected to the circuit ▶ bug, wiretap. —*See also* **drain** (1).

tap *noun.* —*See* **faucet, plug.**

tape *noun.* —*See* **band[1].**

taper *noun.* —*See* **decrease.**

taper *verb.* —*See* **decrease.**

tar *noun.* —*See* **sailor.**

tardily *adverb.* —*See* **late.**

tardiness *noun.* The quality or condition of not being on time ▶ belatedness, lateness, slowness, unpunctuality.

tardy *adjective.* —*See* **late** (1), **slow** (1).

target *noun.* One that is fired at, attacked, or abused ▶ butt, mark. —*See also* **intention, object** (2).

target *verb.* To make a target of ▶ mark. ***Idioms:*** draw (*or* get) a bead on, get in one's sights. —*See also* **intend.**

tariff *noun.* —*See* **tax, toll[1]** (1).

tarnish *verb.* —*See* **damage, denigrate, disgrace.**

tarnish *noun.* —*See* **stain.**

tarrier *noun.* —*See* **laggard.**

tarry *verb.* —*See* **delay** (2), **remain.**

tart[1] *adjective.* —*See* **sour.**

tart[2] *noun.* —*See* **harlot, slut.**

tartuffe *noun.* —*See* **hypocrite.**

tartuffery *noun.* —*See* **hypocrisy.**

task *noun.* **1.** A piece of work that has been assigned ▶ assignment, chore, duty, job, office, project, stint. **2.** A difficult or tedious undertaking ▶ chore, effort, grind, slog, sweat. *Informal:* job. [*Compare* **labor.**] —*See also* **function** (1).

task *verb.* To force to work hard ▶ drive, push, tax, work. ***Idiom:*** crack the whip. [*Compare* **force.**]

✚ **CORE SYNONYMS:** *task, job, chore, stint, assignment.* These nouns denote a piece of work that one must do. A *task* is a well-defined responsibility that is usually imposed by another and that may be burdensome: *I stayed at work late to finish the task at hand. Job* often suggests a specific short-term undertaking: *"did little jobs about the house with skill"* (W.H. Auden). *Chore* generally denotes a minor, routine, or odd job: *The farmer's morning chores included milking the cows. Stint* refers to a person's prescribed share of work: *Her stint* *as a lifeguard usually consumes three hours a day. Assignment* generally denotes a task allotted by a person in authority: *His homework assignment involved writing an essay.*

---

taskmaster *or* **taskmistress** *noun.* —*See* **boss.**

taste *verb.* **1.** To have a particular flavor or suggestion of something ▶ savor, smack, smell, suggest. [*Compare* **hint.**] **2.** To undergo an emotional reaction ▶ experience, feel, have, know, savor. —*See also* **experience.**

taste *noun.* **1.** A liking for something ▶ fondness, partiality, preference, relish, weakness. [*Compare* **inclination.**] **2.** A limited or anticipatory experience ▶ foretaste, sample, sampling. [*Compare* **glance.**] —*See also* **appetite, bit[1]** (2), **discrimination** (1), **drink** (2), **drop** (4), **elegance, flavor** (1), **shade** (2).

tasteful *adjective.* —*See* **decent, delicious, elegant, modest** (1).

tastefulness *noun.* —*See* **elegance, modesty** (2).

tasteless *adjective.* —*See* **coarse** (1), **flat** (2).

tasty *adjective.* —*See* **delicious.**

tatter *noun.* To wear away along the edges ▶ fray, frazzle. [*Compare* **erode, shred.**]

tatterdemalion *noun.* A person wearing ragged or tattered clothing ▶ ragamuffin. [*Compare* **hobo.**]

tatterdemalion *adjective.* —*See* **shabby.**

tattered *adjective.* —*See* **shabby.**

tatters *noun.* Torn and ragged clothing ▶ rags, shreds.

tattle *verb.* —*See* **chatter** (1), **gossip, inform** (2).

tattle *noun.* —*See* **chatter, gossip** (1), **gossip** (2).

tattler *or* **tattletale** *noun.* —*See* **gossip** (2), **informer.**

tatty *adjective.* —*See* **shabby.**

taunt *noun.* An instance of mockery or derision ▶ cut, fleer, gibe, insult, jeer, scoff, twit. *Informal:* swipe. *Slang:* dig. [*Compare* **indignity, libel.**] —*See also* **ribbing.**

taunt *verb.* —*See* **harass, ridicule.**

taut *adjective.* Stretched tightly ▶ strained, tense, tight. [*Compare* **rigid.**] —*See also* **edgy, neat, tight** (3).

✚ **CORE SYNONYMS:** *taut, tense, tight.* These adjectives mean not slack or loose on account of being pulled or drawn out fully: *taut sails; tense piano strings; a tight shirt.*

---

tauten *verb.* —*See* **tense.**

tautness *noun.* —*See* **pressure.**

tautological *adjective.* —*See* **wordy** (1).

tavern *noun.* —*See* **bar** (2).

tawdry *adjective.* —*See* **gaudy.**

tawny *adjective.* —*See* **dark** (2).

tax *noun.* A compulsory contribution, usually of money, that is required for the support of an authority ▶ assessment, customs, duty, impost, levy, tariff, tithe, tribute. [*Compare* **toll.**] —*See also* **burden[1]** (1), **toll[1]** (1).

tax *verb.* To force to work hard ▶ drive, push, task, work. ***Idiom:*** crack the whip. [*Compare* **force.**] —*See also* **accuse, burden[1], chastise.**

tax with *verb.* —*See* **impose on.**

taxi *verb.* —*See* **drive** (1).

taxing *adjective.* —*See* **burdensome.**

taxpayer *noun.* —*See* **citizen.**

tea *noun.* —*See* **party.**

teach *verb.* —*See* **educate.**

teachable *adjective.* Capable of being educated ▶ docile, educable, trainable. [*Compare* **obedient.**]

teacher *noun.* —*See* **educator.**

teaching *noun.* —*See* **doctrine, education** (1).

teaching *adjective.* —*See* **educational** (1).

team *noun.* —*See* **force** (3).

teamwork *noun.* —*See* **cooperation.**

tear[1] *verb.* To separate or pull apart by force ▶ rend, rip, rive, run, split. [*Compare* **cut, shred.**] —*See also* **pull** (2), **rush.**

tear down *verb.* —*See* **denigrate, destroy** (2), **malign.**

tear into *verb.* —*See* **attack** (1), **slam** (1).

tear up *verb.* —*See* **shred.**

tear *noun.* A hole made by tearing ▶ rent, rip, run. [*Compare* **crack.**] —*See also* **bender.**

✚ **CORE SYNONYMS:** *tear, rip, rend, split.* These verbs mean to separate or pull apart by force. *Tear* involves pulling something apart or into pieces: *"She tore the letter in shreds"* (Edith Wharton). *Rip* implies rough or forcible tearing: *Carpenters ripped up the old floorboards. Rend* usually refers to violent tearing or wrenching apart: *"Come as the winds come, when/Forests are rended"* (Sir Walter Scott). To *split* is to cut or break something into parts or layers, especially along its entire length or along a natural line of division: *"They* [wood stumps] *warmed me twice—once while I was splitting them, and again when they were on the fire"* (Henry David Thoreau).

---

tear² *noun.* —*See* **drop** (1).

tear *verb.* To fill with tears ▶ tear (up), water, well (up). [*Compare* **flow.**] —*See also* **drip.**

teardrop *noun.* —*See* **drop** (1).

tearful *adjective.* Filled with or shedding tears ▶ lachrymose, teary, weeping, weepy. ***Idioms:*** in tears, with tears in one's eyes. [*Compare* **depressed, sorrowful.**]

tear-jerking *adjective.* —*See* **sentimental.**

tears *noun.* —*See* **cry** (1).

teary *adjective.* —*See* **tearful.**

tease *verb.* To arouse hope or desire without affording satisfaction ▶ bait, tantalize. ***Idiom:*** make one's mouth water. [*Compare* **charm, flirt.**] —*See also* **harass.**

tease *noun.* A woman who is given to flirting ▶ coquette, flirt. *Informal:* vamp. [*Compare* **seductress.**] —*See also* **bully.**

technicality *noun.* —*See* **detail.**

technique *noun.* —*See* **ability** (1), **approach** (1).

tedious *adjective.* —*See* **boring.**

tedium *or* **tediousness** *noun.* —*See* **boredom, dullness, monotony.**

tee-hee *verb.* —*See* **laugh.**

tee-hee *noun.* —*See* **laugh.**

teem¹ *verb.* To be abundantly filled or richly supplied ▶ abound, bristle, crawl, flow, overflow, pullulate, roll, swarm, swim.

✚ **CORE SYNONYMS:** *teem, abound, crawl, overflow, swarm.* These verbs mean to be abundantly filled or richly supplied: *The street teemed with pedestrians. The garden abounds with flowers. The sidewalk was crawling with vendors. The house overflowed with guests. The parade route swarmed with spectators.*

---

teem² *verb.* —*See* **rain** (2).

teeming *adjective.* —*See* **busy** (2), **overcrowded.**

teen *noun.* —*See* **teenager.**

teenager *noun.* A young person, usually between the ages of 13 and 19 ▶ adolescent, teen, youth. *Informal:* kid, teener. *Slang:* teenybopper. [*Compare* **minor.**]

teeny *or* **teensy** *or* **teeny-weeny** *or* **teensy-weensy** *adjective.* —*See* **tiny.**

teenybopper *noun.* —*See* **teenager.**

tee off *verb.* —*See* **anger** (1).

teeter *verb.* —*See* **balance** (3), **stagger** (1), **sway.**

teetering *adjective.* —*See* **insecure** (2).

teetotalism *noun.* —*See* **temperance** (2).

telephone *verb.* To communicate with someone by telephone ▶ buzz, call (up), dial, phone, ring (up). ***Idioms:*** get someone on the horn, give someone a buzz (*or* call *or* ring).

tell *verb.* —*See* **betray** (2), **command** (1), **communicate** (1), **count** (2), **describe, distinguish** (1), **inform** (1), **say.**

tell off *verb.* —*See* **chastise.**

telling *adjective.* —*See* **convincing.**

telltale *noun.* —*See* **gossip** (2).

tellurian *or* **telluric** *adjective.* —*See* **earthly.**

temblor *noun.* A shaking of the earth ▶ earthquake, quake, seism, tremor. *Informal:* shake.

temerarious *adjective.* —*See* **rash**[1]**.**

temerity *noun.* Foolhardy boldness or disregard of danger ▶ brashness, foolhardiness, incautiousness, rashness, recklessness, temerariousness. [*Compare* **courage, daring.**]

temper *noun.* **1.** A tendency to become angry or irritable ▶ bile, biliousness, cantankerousness, crankiness, disagreeability, hotheadedness, irascibility, irascibleness, irritability, orneriness, peevishness, petulance, petulancy, prickliness, spleen, temperament, testiness, tetchiness, waspishness. *Informal:* dander, meanness. *Slang:* short fuse. ***Idiom:*** low boiling point. [*Compare* **oversensitivity.**] **2.** An angry outburst ▶ fit, huff, passion, tantrum. *Informal:* conniption, conniption fit, hissy, hissy fit. [*Compare* **state.**] **3.** A prevailing quality, as of thought, behavior, or attitude ▶ climate, mood, spirit, timbre, tone. —*See also* **disposition, mood.**

temper *verb.* —*See* **adjust, moderate** (1).

temperament *noun.* —*See* **character** (1)**, disposition, temper** (1).

temperamental *adjective.* Given to changeable emotional states, especially of anger or gloom ▶ mercurial, moody. [*Compare* **testy.**] —*See also* **capricious.**

temperance *noun.* **1.** Moderation or restraint of one's behavior or desires ▶ abstinence, continence, self-denial, sobriety. **2.** The practice of refraining from use of alcoholic liquors ▶ abstinence, dryness, soberness, sobriety, teetotalism. —*See also* **moderation.**

✤ **CORE SYNONYMS:** *temperance, sobriety, abstinence, self-denial, continence.* These nouns refer to the moderation or restraint of one's appetites or desires. *Temperance* refers to moderation and self-restraint and *sobriety* to gravity in bearing, manner, or treatment; both nouns denote moderation in or abstinence from the consumption of alcoholic liquor: *Teetotalers preach temperance for everyone. "[T]hose moments which would come between the subsidence of actual sobriety and the commencement of intoxication"* (Anthony Trollope). *Abstinence* implies the willful avoidance of pleasures, especially of food and drink, thought to be harmful or self-indulgent: *"I vainly reminded him of his protracted abstinence from food"* (Emily Brontë). *Self-denial* suggests resisting one's own desires for the achievement of a higher goal: *I practiced self-denial to provide for my family's needs. Continence* specifically refers to abstention from sexual activity: *The nun took a vow of continence.*

---

temperate *adjective.* **1.** Free from extremes in temperature ▶ balmy, clement, mild, moderate. [*Compare* **pleasant.**] **2.** Characterized by self-restraint in appetites and behavior ▶ abstemious, continent, sober, spartan, unindulgent. [*Compare* **ascetic.**] —*See also* **conservative** (2).

tempest *noun.* —*See* **agitation** (1)**, storm.**

tempestuous *adjective.* —*See* **agitated, rough** (2).

tempo *noun.* Rate of motion or performance ▶ pace, speed, velocity. *Informal:* clip.

temporal *adjective.* —*See* **earthly, profane** (2)**, transitory.**

temporary *adjective.* **1.** Temporarily assuming the duties of another ▶ acting, ad interim, interim, pro tem, provisional, substitute. *Informal:* fill-in. **2.** Intended, used, or present for a limited time ▶ ad hoc, impermanent, interim, make-do, makeshift, provisional, short-range, short-term, stopgap. —*See also* **transitory.**

✚ **CORE SYNONYMS:** *temporary, acting, ad interim, interim, provisional.* These adjectives mean temporarily assuming the duties of another: *a temporary chairperson; the acting dean; an ad interim admissions committee; an interim administration; a provisional mayor.*

◀ **ANTONYM:** *permanent*

tempt *verb.* —*See* **court** (1), **seduce.**

temptation *noun.* —*See* **lure** (1).

tempter *noun.* —*See* **seducer** (1).

tempting *adjective.* —*See* **attractive, seductive.**

temptress *noun.* —*See* **seductress.**

tenable *adjective.* **1.** Capable of being justified ▶ defensible, excusable, justifiable. [*Compare* **logical, sound[2].**] **2.** Capable of being defended against armed attack ▶ defendable, defensible. [*Compare* **safe.**]

tenacious *adjective.* —*See* **stubborn** (1), **tight** (1).

tenacity *or* **tenaciousness** *noun.* —*See* **stubbornness.**

tenant *noun.* —*See* **inhabitant.**

tend[1] *verb.* To have a tendency or inclination ▶ incline, lean, skew, slant, squint, trend. [*Compare* **inclined.**]

tend[2] *verb.* To have the care and supervision of ▶ attend, baby-sit, care for, look after, mind, minister to, see to, watch (over). ***Idioms:*** keep an eye on, look out for, take care (*or* charge) of, take under one's wing. [*Compare* **administer, serve, supervise.**] —*See also* **grow, nurture.**

✚ **CORE SYNONYMS:** *tend, attend, mind, minister to, watch.* These verbs mean to have the care or supervision of: *tended her plants; attends the sick; minded the unreliable furnace; ministered to flood victims; watched the house while the owners were away.*

tendency *noun.* —*See* **inclination** (1), **thrust.**

tendentious *adjective.* —*See* **biased.**

tendentiousness *noun.* —*See* **bias.**

tender[1] *adjective.* —*See* **affectionate, gentle** (1), **painful, sympathetic.**

tender[2] *noun.* —*See* **offer.**

tender *verb.* —*See* **offer** (1).

tenderfoot *noun.* —*See* **beginner.**

tenderhearted *adjective.* —*See* **gentle** (1).

tenderness *noun.* —*See* **consideration** (1), **irritation, love** (1).

tending *adjective.* —*See* **inclined.**

tendril *noun.* —*See* **shoot.**

tenebrific *adjective.* —*See* **gloomy.**

tenet *noun.* —*See* **doctrine, law** (1).

tenor *noun.* —*See* **import, thrust.**

tense *adjective.* Stretched tightly ▶ taut, tight. [*Compare* **rigid.**] —*See also* **dramatic** (2), **edgy.**

tense *verb.* To make or become tense ▶ brace, stiffen, stretch, tauten, tighten.

tenseness *noun.* —*See* **pressure, restlessness.**

tension *noun.* —*See* **pressure.**

ten-strike *noun.* —*See* **hit.**

tentative *adjective.* —*See* **conditional, doubtful** (2), **hesitant, rough** (4).

tentativeness *noun.* —*See* **hesitation.**

tenuous *adjective.* —*See* **implausible.**

tenure *noun.* The holding of a position ▶ incumbency, occupancy, occupation. [*Compare* **period.**]

tepid *adjective.* Lacking warmth, interest, enthusiasm, or involvement ▶ halfhearted, Laodicean, lukewarm, unenthusiastic. [*Compare* **apathetic, cold, cool.**]

tergiversate *verb.* —*See* **defect, equivocate** (1).

tergiversation *noun.* —*See* **ambiguity, defection, equivocation.**

tergiversator *noun.* —*See* **defector.**

term *noun.* A sound or combination of sounds that symbolizes and communicates a meaning ▶ expression, lexical item, lexeme, locution, vocable, word.

[*Compare* **speech.**] —*See also* **life, period** (1), **provision.**

term *verb.* —*See* **call, name** (1).

termagant *noun.* —*See* **scold.**

terminal *adjective.* Of or relating to a terminative condition, stage, or point ▶ final, last, latter, ultimate. [*Compare* **climactic.**] —*See also* **last**[1] (1).

terminal *noun.* A stopping place along a route for picking up or dropping off passengers ▶ depot, station, stop, terminus. —*See also* **junction, outlet** (1).

terminate *verb.* **1.** To bring an activity or relationship to an end suddenly ▶ break off, cease, discontinue, interrupt, suspend. **2.** To relinquish one's engagement in or occupation with ▶ demit, leave, quit, resign. ***Idioms:*** hang it up, throw in the towel. [*Compare* **break.**] —*See also* **conclude, dismiss** (1), **lapse.**

termination *noun.* —*See* **dismissal, end** (1), **end** (2).

terminology *noun.* —*See* **language** (2).

terminus *noun.* A stopping place along a route for picking up or dropping off passengers ▶ depot, station, stop, terminal. —*See also* **end** (1).

terms *noun.* —*See* **basis** (3).

terpsichorean *noun.* A person who dances, especially professionally ▶ chorine, chorus boy, chorus girl, dancer. *Slang:* hoofer.

terrain *noun.* The character, natural features, and configuration of land ▶ topography. ***Idiom:*** the lay of the land. —*See also* **area** (1), **earth** (1), **territory.**

terrene *adjective.* —*See* **earthly.**

terrestrial *adjective.* Consisting of or resembling soil ▶ earthen, earthlike, earthy. —*See also* **earthly.**

terrible *adjective.* Very bad ▶ abysmal, appalling, awful, dreadful, fearful, frightful, ghastly, horrendous, horrible, lousy, pathetic, pitiful, rotten, shocking, woebegone, wretched. *Slang:* crappy. ***Idiom:*** for the birds. [*Compare* **bad, deplorable, shoddy.**] —*See also* **fearful, intense.**

terrific *adjective.* —*See* **excellent, horrible, marvelous.**

terrified *adjective.* —*See* **afraid.**

terrify *verb.* —*See* **frighten.**

territorial *adjective.* Relating to or restricted to a particular territory ▶ regional, sectional. [*Compare* **local.**]

territory *noun.* A particular area used for or associated with a specific individual or activity ▶ belt, country, district, region, terrain, zone. *Slang:* turf. [*Compare* **environment.**] —*See also* **area** (1), **beat** (2), **habitat, possession, range** (1).

terror *noun.* —*See* **fear.**

terrorize *verb.* —*See* **frighten.**

terse *adjective.* —*See* **brief.**

test *noun.* **1.** A procedure that ascertains effectiveness, value, proper function, or other quality ▶ assay, dry run, essay, evaluation, experiment, experimentation, proof, shakedown, trial, tryout. [*Compare* **estimate.**] **2.** A set of questions or exercises designed to determine knowledge or skill ▶ catechism, catechization, exam, examination, quiz. [*Compare* **inquiry.**] —*See also* **standard.**

test *verb.* **1.** To subject to a test of effectiveness, value, function, or other quality ▶ appraise, assay, check, essay, evaluate, examine, prove, try (out). ***Idioms:*** bring to the test, feel the cloth, kick the tires, make trial of, put to the proof (*or* test). **2.** To subject to a test of knowledge or skill ▶ catechize, examine, quiz. [*Compare* **ask.**]

test *adjective.* —*See* **pilot.**

testament *noun.* —*See* **confirmation** (2).

testifier *noun.* One who testifies, especially in court ▶ attestant, attester, deponent, witness.

testify *verb.* To give evidence or testimony under oath ▶ attest, depone, depose, swear, witness. ***Idioms:*** bear witness, take the stand. —*See also* **certify, confirm** (1), **indicate** (1).

testimonial *noun.* **1.** A statement attesting to personal qualifications, character, and dependability ▶ character, recommendation, reference. [*Compare* **endorsement.**] **2.** A formal token of appreciation and admiration for a person's high achievements ▶ ovation, salute, salvo, tribute. [*Compare* **honor, memorial, toast[2].**] —*See also* **confirmation** (2).

testimony *noun.* A formal declaration of truth or fact given under oath ▶ affidavit, deposition, witness. —*See also* **confirmation** (2).

testiness *noun.* —*See* **temper** (1).

testy *adjective.* Easily moved to anger ▶ choleric, irascible, peppery, quick-tempered, short-tempered, tetchy, touchy. —*See also* **ill-tempered.**

tetchiness *noun.* —*See* **temper** (1).

tetchy *adjective.* —*See* **testy.**

tete-a-tete *noun.* —*See* **conversation.**

text *noun.* —*See* **subject.**

texture *noun.* A distinctive, complex underlying pattern or structure ▶ contexture, fabric, fiber, grain, warp and woof, weave, web. [*Compare* **character, form, quality.**] —*See also* **essence.**

thalassic *adjective.* —*See* **marine** (1).

thankful *adjective.* Showing or feeling gratitude ▶ appreciative, grateful. —*See also* **obliged** (1).

thankfulness *noun.* —*See* **appreciation.**

thankless *adjective.* **1.** Not showing or feeling gratitude ▶ unappreciative, ungrateful, unthankful, unthanking. **2.** Not apt to be appreciated ▶ unappreciated, ungrateful, unthankful.

thanks *noun.* A short prayer said at meals ▶ benediction, blessing, grace, thanksgiving. [*Compare* **prayer[1].**] —*See also* **appreciation.**

thanksgiving *noun.* A short prayer said at meals ▶ benediction, blessing, grace, thanks. [*Compare* **prayer[1].**]

thaumaturgic *or* **thaumaturgical** *adjective.* —*See* **magic.**

thaumaturgy *noun.* —*See* **magic** (1).

thaw *verb.* —*See* **melt.**

theater *noun.* The art and occupation of an actor ▶ acting, dramatics, stage, theatrics.

theatric *or* **theatrical** *adjective.* —*See* **dramatic** (1), **dramatic** (2).

theatricalism *or* **theatricality** *noun.* Showy mannerisms and behavior ▶ campiness, exhibitionism, staginess, theatricalness. [*Compare* **affectation, theatrics.**]

theatricals *noun.* —*See* **theatrics** (2).

theatricism *noun.* —*See* **affectation.**

theatrics *noun.* **1.** The art and occupation of an actor ▶ acting, dramatics, stage, theater. **2.** Overemotional, exaggerated behavior calculated for effect ▶ dramatics, histrionics, melodrama, melodramatics, play-acting, theatricals. [*Compare* **theatricalism.**]

theft *noun.* —*See* **larceny.**

thematic *adjective.* Of, constituting, or relating to a theme or themes ▶ motivic, topical.

theme *noun.* **1.** The main part of a word to which affixes are attached ▶ base, radical, root, simplex, stem. **2.** A relatively brief discourse written especially as an exercise ▶ composition, essay, paper. —*See also* **melody, subject.**

theorem *noun.* —*See* **law** (3), **theory** (2).

theoretical *or* **theoretic** *adjective.* **1.** Concerned primarily with theories rather than practical matters ▶ abstract, academic, armchair, conceptual, ideological, impractical, ivory-tower, moot, speculative. [*Compare* **idealistic.**] **2.** Existing only in concept and not in reality ▶ abstract, conceptual, hypothetic, hypothetical, hypothesized, ideal, impractical, notional, postulated, virtual. [*Compare* **imaginary, supposed.**] —*See also* **untried.**

✚ **CORE SYNONYMS:** *theoretical, abstract, academic, armchair, speculative.* These adjectives mean concerned primarily with theories rather than practical matters: *theoretical linguistics; abstract reasoning; a purely academic dis-*

cussion; armchair reasoning; speculative knowledge.

---

theoretics *noun.* —*See* **theory** (1).

theorist *or* **theoretic** *noun.* A person who seeks truth by thinking ▶ philosopher, reasoner, thinker. —*See also* **dreamer** (1).

theorization *noun.* —*See* **theory** (1).

theorize *verb.* To formulate as a tentative explanation ▶ hypothesize, speculate. [*Compare* **suppose.**]

theorizer *noun.* —*See* **dreamer** (1).

theory *noun.* **1.** Abstract reasoning, as opposed to experience ▶ conceptualization, conjecture, philosophizing, reasoning, speculating, speculation, theoretics, theorization, theorizing. [*Compare* **thought.**] **2.** A proposition maintained by argument or empirical evidence ▶ contention, hypothesis, proposal, theorem, thesis. [*Compare* **assumption, reason.**] —*See also* **doctrine.**

therapeutic *adjective.* —*See* **curative.**

therapy *or* **therapeutics** *noun.* —*See* **treatment.**

thesis *noun.* —*See* **discourse, doctrine, theory** (2).

thespian *noun.* A theatrical performer ▶ actor, actress, player, trouper. [*Compare* **fake, lead, mimic.**]

thespian *adjective.* —*See* **dramatic** (1).

theurgic *or* **theurgical** *adjective.* —*See* **magic.**

theurgy *noun.* —*See* **magic** (1).

thick *adjective.* **1.** Relatively great in extent from one surface to the opposite ▶ fat. [*Compare* **bulky.**] **2.** Having all parts near to each other ▶ close, compact, compressed, consolidated, crowded, dense, packed, tight. [*Compare* **full.**] **3.** Growing profusely ▶ dense, heavy, lush, luxuriant, overgrown, profuse, rank. —*See also* **intimate**[1] (1), **stocky, stupid, viscous.**

thick *noun.* The most intensely active central part ▶ eye, midst. [*Compare* **center.**]

thicken *verb.* To make thick or thicker, especially through evaporation or condensation ▶ condense, inspissate, reduce. [*Compare* **coagulate.**]

thicket *noun.* —*See* **brush**[2].

thickhead *noun.* —*See* **dullard.**

thickheaded *adjective.* —*See* **stupid.**

thickness *noun.* The condition or degree of being dense or close together ▶ closeness, compaction, compactness, denseness, density. —*See also* **viscosity.**

thickset *adjective.* —*See* **stocky.**

thick-witted *adjective.* —*See* **backward** (1), **stupid.**

thief *noun.* A person who steals ▶ bandit, brigand, burglar, highwayman, housebreaker, larcener, larcenist, looter, pickpocket, pilferer, purloiner, robber, stealer.

thieve *verb.* —*See* **steal.**

thievery *noun.* —*See* **larceny.**

thievish *or* **thieving** *adjective.* Given to committing theft ▶ larcenous, light-fingered, sticky-fingered.

thin *adjective.* **1.** Having little flesh or fat on the body ▶ angular, bony, fleshless, gaunt, gracile, lank, lanky, lean, meager, rawboned, scrawny, skinny, slender, slim, spare, stringy, svelte, twiggy, weedy, willowy. ***Idioms:*** all skin and bones, skinny as a rail (*or* post *or* beanpole). [*Compare* **gangling.**] **2.** Marked by great diffusion of component particles ▶ attenuate, attenuated, rare, rarefied. —*See also* **dilute, implausible, meager, pale** (2).

thin *verb.* **1.** To lose body weight, as by dieting ▶ slim (down), trim down. ***Idioms:*** get the weight off, lose weight, shed some pounds. **2.** To become diffuse ▶ attenuate, rarefy. —*See also* **dilute.**

thin out *verb.* —*See* **lift** (2).

✚ **CORE SYNONYMS:** *thin, lean, spare, skinny, scrawny, lank, lanky, rawboned, gaunt.* These adjectives mean having little flesh or fat on the body. *Thin* is the most general: *clothing that only thin* *models could wear. Lean* emphasizes absence of fat: *fattened the lean cattle for market. Spare* sometimes suggests trimness and good muscle tone: *"an old man, very tall and spare, with an ascetic aspect"* (William H. Mallock). *Skinny* and *scrawny* imply unattractive thinness, as with undernourishment: *The child has skinny legs with prominent knees. "He* [had] *a long, scrawny neck that rose out of a very low collar"* (Winston Churchill). *Lank* describes one who is thin and tall, and *lanky* one who is thin, tall, and ungraceful: *"He was . . . exceedingly lank, with narrow shoulders"* (Washington Irving). *The boy had developed into a lanky adolescent. Rawboned* suggests a thin, bony, gangling build: *a rawboned cowhand. Gaunt* implies boniness and a haggard appearance; it may suggest illness or hardship: *a white-haired pioneer, her face gaunt from overwork.*

---

thing *noun.* **1.** One that exists independently ▶ being, entity, existence, existent, individual, object, something. **2.** Something to be done, considered, or dealt with ▶ affair, business, matter. [*Compare* **business, problem, task.**] **3.** An extravagant, short-lived romantic attachment ▶ *Informal:* crush, infatuation. ***Idiom:*** passing fancy. [*Compare* **love, obsession.**] *—See also* **act** (1), **circumstance** (1), **event** (1), **fashion, forte, gadget, object** (1), **obsession.**

thingamabob *or* **thingamajig** *noun.* *—See* **gadget, object** (1).

things *noun.* *—See* **effects, odds and ends.**

think *verb.* **1.** To use the powers of the mind, as in conceiving ideas, drawing inferences, and making judgments ▶ cerebrate, cogitate, conceptualize, deliberate, ideate, ratiocinate, reason, reflect, speculate. ***Idioms:*** put on one's thinking cap, use one's head. [*Compare* **remember.**] **2.** To view in a certain way ▶ believe, feel, hold, sense. [*Compare* **perceive, regard.**] *—See also* **believe** (3), **guess, imagine, ponder.**

think about *or* **of** *verb.* **1.** To receive an idea and think about it in order to form an opinion about it ▶ consider, entertain, hear of. **2.** To care enough to keep someone in mind ▶ remember. *—See also* **regard.**

think out *or* **through** *verb.* *—See* **ponder, solve** (1).

think over *verb.* *—See* **ponder.**

think up *verb.* *—See* **invent.**

✦ **CORE SYNONYMS:** *think, cerebrate, cogitate, reason, reflect, speculate.* These verbs mean to use the powers of the mind, as in conceiving ideas, drawing inferences, and making judgments: *thought before answering; sat in front of the fire cerebrating; cogitates about business problems; reasons clearly; took time to reflect before deciding; speculates on what will happen.*

---

thinkable *adjective.* *—See* **conceivable.**

thinker *noun.* A person who seeks truth by thinking ▶ philosopher, reasoner, theorist. *—See also* **mind** (2).

thinking *adjective.* *—See* **thoughtful.**

thinking *noun.* *—See* **thought.**

third estate *noun.* *—See* **commonalty.**

thirst *verb.* To have a greedy, obsessive desire ▶ crave, hunger, itch, lust. [*Compare* **desire.**]

thirst *noun.* *—See* **appetite, desire** (1).

thirsting *adjective.* *—See* **eager.**

thirsty *adjective.* Needing or desiring drink ▶ dry, parched. ***Idioms:*** dry as a bone (*or* whistle). *—See also* **dry** (2), **eager.**

thistly *adjective.* *—See* **thorny** (1).

thong *noun.* *—See* **cord.**

thorn *noun.* *—See* **annoyance** (2), **spike.**

thorny *adjective.* **1.** Covered with sharp protuberances ▶ aculeate, barbed, brambly, briery, bristled, bristly, echinate, glochidiate, muricate, prickly, pricky, spiky, spiny, thistly. **2.** Full of irritating difficulties or controversies ▶

nettlesome, prickly, spiny. [*Compare* **complex, delicate, disturbing, troublesome.**] —*See also* **uncomfortable.**

thorough *adjective.* Covering all aspects with painstaking accuracy ▶ complete, exhaustive, full-dress, thoroughgoing, thoroughpaced. [*Compare* **diligent.**] —*See also* **detailed, utter².**

thoroughbred *adjective.* Of pure breeding stock ▶ full-blooded, highbred, pedigreed, pureblood, pureblooded, purebred. —*See also* **noble.**

thoroughfare *noun.* —*See* **way** (2).

thoroughgoing *adjective.* —*See* **thorough, utter².**

thoroughly *adverb.* —*See* **completely** (1), **completely** (2).

thoroughness *noun.* Attentiveness to detail ▶ care, carefulness, fastidiousness, meticulousness, pains, painstaking, punctiliousness, scrupulousness.

thoroughpaced *adjective.* —*See* **thorough.**

thought *noun.* The act or process of thinking ▶ brainstorming, brainwork, cerebration, cogitation, conceptualization, conceptualizing, contemplation, deliberation, excogitation, headwork, ideation, intellection, meditation, musing, pondering, reflection, rumination, speculation, thinking. [*Compare* **theory.**] —*See also* **idea.**

thoughtful *adjective.* Of, characterized by, or disposed to thought ▶ cogitative, contemplative, deliberative, excogitative, meditative, pensive, reflective, ruminative, speculative, thinking. ***Idiom:*** in a brown study. [*Compare* **dreamy, rapt, serious.**] —*See also* **attentive, intellectual.**

✚ **CORE SYNONYMS:** *thoughtful, pensive, contemplative, reflective, meditative.* These adjectives mean characterized by or disposed to thought, especially serious or deep thought. *Thoughtful* can refer to absorption in thought or to the habit of reflection and circumspection: *Thoughtful voters carefully considered the candidates. Pensive* often connotes a wistful, dreamy, or sad quality: *"while pensive poets painful vigils keep"* (Alexander Pope). *Contemplative* implies slow directed consideration, often with conscious intent of achieving better understanding or spiritual or aesthetic enrichment: *"The Contemplative Atheist is rare . . . And yet they seem to be more than they are"* (Francis Bacon). *Reflective* suggests careful analytical deliberation, as in reappraising past experience: *"Cromwell was of the active, not the reflective temper"* (John Morley). *Meditative* implies earnest sustained thought: *The scholar was reticent, aloof, and meditative.*

---

thoughtfulness *noun.* —*See* **consideration** (1).

thoughtless *adjective.* Devoid of consideration for others' feelings ▶ disregardful, inconsiderate, insensitive, unthinking, unthoughtful. [*Compare* **rude, tactless.**] —*See also* **careless.**

thoughtlessness *noun.* **1.** A careless, often reckless disregard for consequences ▶ abandon, blitheness, carelessness, heedlessness. [*Compare* **temerity.**] **2.** A lack of consideration for others' feelings ▶ disregard, inconsiderateness, inconsideration, insensitivity, tactlessness, unthoughtfulness. [*Compare* **disrespect.**]

thought out *adjective.* —*See* **deliberate** (2).

thrall *or* **thralldom** *or* **thraldom** *noun.* —*See* **slavery.**

thrash *verb.* **1.** To beat plants to separate the grain from the straw ▶ flail, thresh. **2.** To swing about or strike at wildly ▶ flail, thresh, toss. ***Idiom:*** toss and turn. [*Compare* **stagger, sway.**] —*See also* **beat** (1), **beat** (2), **overwhelm** (1).

thrash out *or* **over** *verb.* —*See* **discuss.**

thrashing *noun.* —*See* **beating, defeat.**

thread *noun.* **1.** A very fine continuous strand ▶ fiber, fibril, filament, microfiber. [*Compare* **cord.**] **2.** Something suggesting the continuousness of a filament ▶ hairline, strand.

thread *verb.* To put objects onto a thread ▶ string.

threadbare *adjective.* —*See* **shabby, trite.**

threadlike *adjective.* Containing or consisting of fibers ▶ fibrous, sinewy, stringy.

threads *noun.* —*See* **dress** (1).

threat *noun.* An expression of intent to hurt or punish another ▶ intimidation, menace. —*See also* **danger.**

threaten *verb.* **1.** To give warning signs of ▶ bode, forebode, forewarn, portend. [*Compare* **foreshadow.**] **2.** To be imminent ▶ brew, hang over, hover, impend, loom, lower, menace, overhang. ***Idiom:*** breathe down one's neck. [*Compare* **approach.**] —*See also* **endanger, intimidate.**

threatening *adjective.* —*See* **dangerous, fateful** (1).

three *or* **threesome** *noun.* —*See* **trio.**

thresh *verb.* **1.** To beat plants to separate the grain from the straw ▶ flail, thrash. **2.** To swing about or strike at wildly ▶ flail, thrash, toss. ***Idiom:*** toss and turn. [*Compare* **stagger, sway.**] —*See also* **beat** (1).

thresh out *or* **over** *verb.* —*See* **discuss.**

threshold *noun.* —*See* **border** (1).

thrift *or* **thriftiness** *noun.* —*See* **economy.**

thriftless *adjective.* —*See* **extravagant.**

thrifty *adjective.* —*See* **economical.**

thrill *noun.* A strong, pleasant feeling of excitement or stimulation ▶ lift. *Informal:* wallop. *Slang:* bang, boot, buzz, high, jollies, kick. ***Idiom:*** kick in the pants. —*See also* **tremor** (2).

thrill *verb.* —*See* **delight** (1), **enrapture.**

thrilled *adjective.* Feeling strong pleasure or excitement ▶ atingle, excited, fired up, worked up. *Informal:* psyched. *Slang:* stoked, turned-on, wired. ***Idiom:*** pleased as punch. [*Compare* **elated, passionate.**]

thrilling *adjective.* —*See* **dramatic** (2).

thrive *verb.* To grow rapidly ▶ bloom, blossom, flourish. [*Compare* **increase.**] —*See also* **prosper.**

thriving *adjective.* —*See* **flourishing, healthy.**

throb *verb.* —*See* **beat** (5), **glare** (2).

throb *noun.* —*See* **beat** (3).

throbbing *adjective.* —*See* **brilliant, sharp** (3).

throe *noun.* —*See* **pain.**

throes *noun.* A condition of agonizing struggle or trouble ▶ convulsion, paroxysm, spasm.

throng *noun.* —*See* **crowd.**

throng *verb.* —*See* **crowd.**

throttle *verb.* —*See* **choke, repress.**

through *adjective.* **1.** Having no further relationship ▶ done, finished. **2.** No longer effective, capable, or valuable ▶ done, done for, finished, washed-up. *Informal:* kaput. ***Idioms:*** at the end of one's line (*or* road), over the hill, past one's prime. [*Compare* **goner.**] —*See also* **complete** (3), **direct** (1).

through *preposition.* —*See* **because of.**

throw *verb.* To send through the air with a motion of the hand or arm ▶ bowl, cast, dart, dash, fling, heave, hurl, hurtle, launch, lob, pelt, pitch, roll, shoot, shy, sling, toss. *Informal:* chuck, fire, peg. —*See also* **baffle, confuse** (1), **drop** (3), **have** (3), **shed[1]** (1).

throw away *verb.* —*See* **discard, waste.**

throw in *verb.* —*See* **introduce** (2).

throw off *verb.* —*See* **emit, lose** (3), **rid, shed[1]** (2).

throw out *verb.* —*See* **discard, eject** (1), **propose, slip** (2).

throw over *verb.* —*See* **abandon** (1).

throw up *verb.* —*See* **vomit.**

throw *noun.* An act of throwing ▶ bowl, cast, fling, heave, hurl, launch, lob, peg, pitch, roll, shy, sling, toss. *Informal:* chuck.

✣ **CORE SYNONYMS:** *throw, cast, hurl, fling, pitch, toss.* These verbs mean to send something through the air with a motion of the hand or arm. *Throw* is the least specific: *throwing a ball; threw the life preserver to the struggling swimmer. Cast* usually refers to throwing something light: *cast her fishing line into the stream. Hurl* and *fling* mean to throw with great force: *"Him the Almighty Power/Hurl'd headlong flaming from th' Ethereal Sky"* (John Milton). *He flung the tarpaulin over the boat. Pitch* often means to throw with careful aim: *"a special basket in my study . . . into which I pitch letters, circulars, pamphlets and so forth"* (H.G. Wells). *Toss* usually means to throw lightly or casually: *"Campton tossed the card away"* (Edith Wharton).

thrust *noun.* The current of thought uniting all elements of a text or discourse ▶ aim, burden, drift, gist, intent, purport, substance, tendency, tenor. [*Compare* **heart, meaning.**] *—See also* **push.**
thrust *verb. —See* **drive** (2), **plunge, push** (1).
thruway *noun. —See* **way** (2).
thud *verb.* To make a dull sound by or as if by striking a surface with a heavy object ▶ clomp, clump, clunk, plunk, thump, whomp. [*Compare* **bang.**]
thud *noun. —See* **beat** (1).
thug *noun.* A person who treats others violently or roughly, especially for hire ▶ hoodlum, hooligan, mug, roughneck, rowdy, ruffian, tough. *Informal:* bruiser, toughie. *Slang:* gangsta, goon, gorilla, gunsel, hood, plug-ugly, punk. [*Compare* **criminal.**]
thumb *verb. —See* **browse** (1).
thumbs-down *noun. —See* **no** (1).
thumbs-up *noun. —See* **permission.**
thump *noun. —See* **beat** (1), **blow**[2].
thump *verb. —See* **bang, beat** (1), **beat** (5), **thud.**
thunder *noun. —See* **blast** (1).
thunder *verb. —See* **blast** (1).
thundercloud *noun.* An indication of impending danger or harm ▶ foreboding, forewarning, threat. *—See also* **omen.**
thunderous *adjective. —See* **loud.**
thwack *verb. —See* **bang, hit.**
thwack *noun. —See* **blow**[2].
thwart *verb. —See* **frustrate.**
thwart *adjective. —See* **transverse.**
tic *noun. —See* **tremor** (2).
tick *noun. —See* **beat** (3).
tick *verb. —See* **beat** (5).
tick away *verb. —See* **elapse.**
tick off *verb. —See* **anger** (1), **enumerate.**
ticker *noun. Slang* The circulatory organ of the body ▶ blood pump, heart.
ticket *noun.* **1.** An identifying or descriptive slip ▶ earmark, flag, label, tab, tag. **2.** A list of candidates proposed or endorsed by a political party ▶ ballot, lineup, slate. **3.** *Informal* A means or method of entering into or achieving something desirable ▶ formula, key, route, secret. [*Compare* **trick.**] **4.** A written or printed notification of a legal infraction ▶ citation. *—See also* **license** (3).
ticket *verb.* To attach a ticket to ▶ earmark, flag, label, mark, tag.
ticking *adjective. —See* **active.**
tickle *verb. —See* **delight** (1).
tickled *adjective. —See* **willing.**
ticklish *adjective. —See* **capricious, delicate** (3), **oversensitive.**
tidbit *noun. —See* **bit**[1] (2), **delicacy.**
tide *noun. —See* **flow.**
tidings *noun. —See* **news.**
tidy *verb.* **1.** To make or keep an area clean and orderly ▶ clean (up), clear (up), neaten (up), police, spruce (up), straighten (up). **2.** To make neat, trim, or presentable ▶ clean (up), freshen (up), groom, neaten (up), slick up, spruce (up), tidy up, trig (out), trim.
tidy *adjective. —See* **acceptable** (2), **big, neat.**
tidy sum *noun. —See* **fortune.**

tie *verb.* To do or make something equal to ▶ equal, match, meet. *—See also* **fasten, hamper[1].**

tie up *verb. —See* **absorb** (1), **fasten, stop** (2).

tie *noun.* An equality of scores, votes, or performances in a contest ▶ dead heat, deadlock, draw, stalemate, standoff. *—See also* **bond** (2).

tie beam *noun. —See* **beam** (2).

tie-in *noun. —See* **relation** (1).

tier *noun. —See* **class** (2), **line.**

tie-up *noun. —See* **stop** (2).

tiff *noun. —See* **argument.**

tiff *verb. —See* **argue** (1).

tight *adjective.* **1.** Persistently holding to something ▶ clinging, fast, firm, secure, tenacious. [*Compare* **fixed.**] **2.** Stretched tightly ▶ taut, tense. [*Compare* **rigid.**] **3.** Characterized by an economy of artistic expression ▶ lean, minimalist, spare, taut. [*Compare* **bare.**] **4.** Affording little room for movement ▶ close, confining, cramped, crowded, narrow, restrictive, snug. **5.** Difficult to deal with or get out of ▶ rough, tricky. *Informal:* sticky. [*Compare* **delicate.**] **6.** Almost even ▶ nip and tuck. ***Idiom:*** neck and neck. *—See also* **drunk, intimate[1]** (1), **sound[2], stingy, thick** (2).

tighten *verb. —See* **constrict** (1), **support** (2), **tense.**

tightfisted *adjective. —See* **stingy.**

tightlipped *adjective. —See* **taciturn.**

tightrope *noun. —See* **predicament.**

tightwad *noun. —See* **miser.**

till *verb.* To prepare soil for the planting and raising of crops ▶ cultivate, culture, dig, fork, harrow, hoe, plow, rake, spade, turn (over), work. [*Compare* **fertilize, grow, plant.**]

tilt *noun.* A competition or test of opposing wills suggesting the sport fought by mounted knights with lances ▶ joust, tournament, tourney. [*Compare* **battle, competition.**] *—See also* **inclination** (2).

tilt *verb. —See* **contend, incline.**

timber *noun.* A person considered to have qualities suitable for a particular activity ▶ material, stuff. [*Compare* **comer, potential.**] *—See also* **beam** (2).

timberland *noun.* A dense growth of trees and underbrush covering an area ▶ backwoods, forest, woodland, woods. [*Compare* **country, wilderness.**]

timbre *noun.* The distinct quality or character of a sound ▶ tonality, tone, tone color. *—See also* **temper** (3).

time *noun.* A prison or jail term ▶ hitch, stretch. *—See also* **age** (2), **bit[1]** (3), **life, occasion** (1), **period** (1), **turn** (1).

time *verb.* **1.** To set the time for an event or occasion ▶ plan, schedule, set. [*Compare* **arrange.**] **2.** To record the speed or duration of ▶ clock. [*Compare* **measure.**]

time-honored *adjective. —See* **accepted, conventional.**

time immemorial *noun. —See* **antiquity.**

timeless *adjective.* Existing unchanged forever ▶ ageless, eternal. [*Compare* **endless.**] *—See also* **continual, vintage.**

timely *adjective.* Occurring, acting, or performed exactly at the time appointed ▶ prompt, punctual. ***Idioms:*** on the dot (*or* nose), on schedule, on time. *—See also* **opportune.**

time-out *noun. —See* **rest[1]** (1), **rest[1]** (2).

timetable *noun. —See* **program** (1).

timeworn *adjective. —See* **old** (1), **trite.**

timid *adjective. —See* **afraid, hesitant, shy[1].**

timidity *or* **timidness** *noun. —See* **hesitation, shyness.**

timorous *adjective. —See* **afraid.**

tinct *noun. —See* **color** (1).

tincture *noun. —See* **color** (2).

tincture *verb. —See* **color** (1).

tine *noun. —See* **spike.**

tinge *noun. —See* **color** (1), **shade** (2).

tinge *verb. —See* **color** (1).

tingle *noun.* A feeling of pervasive emotional warmth ▶ flush, glow.

tinker *verb.* To handle something in an attempt to adjust or improve it ▶ fiddle, fool, meddle, mess (around), tamper. *Informal:* monkey. [*Compare* **adjust, fix.**] —*See also* **fiddle.**

tinsel *adjective.* —*See* **gaudy.**

tint *noun.* —*See* **color** (1).

tint *verb.* —*See* **color** (1).

tiny *adjective.* Extremely small ▶ diminutive, dwarf, Lilliputian, microscopic, midget, mini, miniature, minuscule, minute, pygmy, wee. *Informal:* peewee, pintsize, pintsized, teensy, teensy-weensy, teeny, teeny-weeny, weeny. [*Compare* **imperceptible, little.**]

✚ **CORE SYNONYMS:** *tiny, diminutive, miniature, minuscule, minute, wee.* These adjectives mean extremely small: *the tiny feet of a newborn baby; diminutive in stature; a miniature camera; a minuscule amount of rain; minute errors; felt a wee bit better.*

tip[1] *noun.* —*See* **point** (1).

tip *verb.* To put a topping on ▶ cap, crest, crown, top, top off. [*Compare* **cover.**]

tip[2] *verb.* —*See* **incline.**

tip over *verb.* —*See* **fall** (2), **overturn.**

tip *noun.* —*See* **inclination** (2).

tip[3] *noun.* An item of advance or inside information given as a guide to action ▶ clue, hint, lead, pointer, scent, steer. *Informal:* tip-off. [*Compare* **hint.**] —*See also* **advice, gratuity.**

tip *verb.* —*See* **inform** (2).

tip-off *noun.* —*See* **tip**[3].

tipple *verb.* —*See* **drink** (2).

tippler *noun.* —*See* **drunkard.**

tipsiness *noun.* —*See* **drunkenness.**

tipster *noun.* —*See* **informer.**

tipsy *adjective.* —*See* **drunk.**

tiptop *adjective.* —*See* **excellent.**

tirade *noun.* A long, violent, or blustering speech, usually of censure or denunciation ▶ berating, diatribe, fulmination, harangue, jeremiad, onslaught, philippic, screed, tongue-lashing, upbraiding. [*Compare* **vituperation.**]

tire *verb.* **1.** To make weary ▶ drain, exhaust, fatigue, frazzle, jade, tire out, wear down, wear out, weary. *Informal:* knock out, tucker (out). *Slang:* do in, poop (out). ***Idioms:*** run ragged, take it out of. [*Compare* **enervate.**] **2.** To grow weary ▶ burn out, droop, flag, give out, wear down, wear out, wilt. *Slang:* poop (out). [*Compare* **collapse, fade, labor.**] —*See also* **bore**[2].

✚ **CORE SYNONYMS:** *tire, weary, fatigue, exhaust, jade.* These verbs mean to make someone weary. *Tire* often suggests a state resulting from exertion, excess, dullness, or ennui: "*When a man is tired of London, he is tired of life*" (Samuel Johnson). *Weary* often implies dissatisfaction, as that resulting from what is irksome or boring: *found the long journey wearying; soon wearied of their constant bickering. Fatigue* implies great weariness, as that caused by stress or overwork: "*fatigued by an endless rotation of thought and wild alarms*" (Mary Wollstonecraft). To *exhaust* means to wear out completely, and it connotes total draining of physical or emotional strength: "*Like all people who try to exhaust a subject, he exhausted his listeners*" (Oscar Wilde). *Jade* refers principally to dullness that most often results from overindulgence: "*Contemplation of works of art without understanding them jades the faculties and enslaves the intelligence*" (John Ruskin).

tired *adjective.* **1.** Depleted of energy ▶ bleary, dead, drained, exhausted, fatigued, jaded, rundown, spent, tired-out, wearied, weariful, weary, worn-down, worn-out. *Informal:* beat, bushed, knocked-out, tuckered (out). *Slang:* done in, pooped (out), wiped, wiped-out. ***Idioms:*** all in, ready to drop. **2.** Out of patience ▶ disgusted, fed up, sick, weary. ***Idiom:*** sick and tired. [*Compare* **angry.**] —*See also* **trite.**

tiredness *noun.* —*See* **exhaustion.**

tired-out *adjective.* —*See* **tired** (1).

tireless *adjective.* Having or showing a capacity for protracted effort, regardless of difficulty or frustration ▶ indefatigable, inexhaustible, unfailing, unflagging, untiring, unwearied, unwearying, weariless. [*Compare* **firm, stubborn.**]

✚ **CORE SYNONYMS:** *tireless, indefatigable, unflagging, untiring, unwearied, weariless.* These adjectives mean having or showing a capacity for protracted effort, regardless of difficulty or frustration: *a tireless worker; an indefatigable advocate of human rights; unflagging pursuit of excellence; untiring energy; an unwearied researcher; a weariless defender of freedom of the press.*

tiresome *adjective.* —*See* **boring.**
tiring *adjective.* Causing fatigue ▶ draining, exhausting, fatiguing, wearing, wearying. [*Compare* **burdensome.**]
tissue *noun.* —*See* **complex** (1).
titan *noun.* —*See* **giant.**
titanic *adjective.* —*See* **enormous.**
tit for tat *noun.* —*See* **retaliation.**
tithe *noun.* —*See* **tax.**
title *noun.* A right or legal share in something ▶ claim, interest, portion, stake. [*Compare* **cut, right.**] —*See also* **claim** (1), **name** (1), **ownership, publication** (2).
title *verb.* —*See* **call, name** (1).
titleholder *noun.* —*See* **owner, winner.**
titter *verb.* —*See* **laugh.**
titter *noun.* —*See* **laugh.**
tittle *noun.* —*See* **bit**[1] (1).
tittle-tattle *noun.* —*See* **gossip** (1).
tittle-tattle *verb.* —*See* **gossip.**
tizzy *noun.* —*See* **state** (2).
toady *noun.* —*See* **sycophant.**
toady *verb.* —*See* **fawn.**
to-and-fro *noun.* —*See* **hesitation.**
toast[1] *verb.* —*See* **cook.**
toast *noun. Slang* One that is ruined or doomed ▶ dead duck, dead meat, goner. [*Compare* **through.**]
toast[2] *noun.* The act of drinking to someone ▶ health, pledge.
toast *verb.* —*See* **drink** (4).
today *noun.* —*See* **now.**
today *adverb.* At the present; these days ▶ now, nowadays. ***Idioms:*** in our time, in this day and age.
toddle *verb.* —*See* **stroll.**
toddler *noun.* —*See* **baby** (1).
to-do *noun.* —*See* **agitation** (1), **sensation** (2).
toehold *noun.* A place providing support for the foot in climbing ▶ foothold, footing, perch, purchase. —*See also* **advantage** (1).
tog *verb.* —*See* **dress** (1).
together *adverb.* **1.** In, into, or as a single body ▶ jointly. ***Idioms:*** all together, as one, in one breath, in the same breath, in unison, with one accord, with one voice. **2.** At the same time ▶ concurrently, simultaneously, synchronously. ***Idioms:*** all at once, all together.
together *adjective. Slang* In a state of preparedness ▶ prepared, ready, set. *Informal:* go. ***Idioms:*** all set, in working order, on deck, ready (*or* raring) to go.
togs *noun.* —*See* **dress** (1).
toil *verb.* —*See* **labor, trudge.**
toil *noun.* —*See* **labor.**
toiler *noun.* —*See* **laborer.**
toilette *noun.* —*See* **dress** (2).
token *noun.* An object or expression associated with and serving to identify something else ▶ attribute, emblem, metaphor, signifier, symbol. [*Compare* **term.**] —*See also* **expression** (2), **pawn**[1], **remembrance** (1), **sign** (1).
tolerable *adjective.* —*See* **acceptable** (2), **average, bearable.**
tolerance *noun.* Forbearing or lenient treatment ▶ charitableness, charity, forbearance, indulgence, lenience, leniency, lenity, permissiveness, toleration. [*Compare* **forgiveness.**] —*See also* **patience.**
tolerant *adjective.* Not strict or severe ▶ charitable, clement, easy, forbearing, indulgent, lax, lenient, merciful, permissive, soft. —*See also* **broad-minded, patient.**

tolerate *verb.* —*See* **endure** (1), **permit** (1).
toleration *noun.* —*See* **tolerance.**
toll[1] *noun.* **1.** A fixed amount of money charged for a privilege or service ▶ charge, dues, exaction, exactment, fare, fee, rate, tariff, tax. [*Compare* **cost.**] **2.** The expenditure at which something is obtained ▶ cost, expense, price, sacrifice. *Informal:* damage.
toll[2] *verb.* —*See* **ring**[2].
tomb *noun.* —*See* **grave**[1].
tome *noun.* —*See* **book.**
tomfoolery *noun.* —*See* **foolishness, mischief, nonsense.**
tommyrot *noun.* —*See* **nonsense.**
tomorrow *noun.* Time that is yet to be ▶ by-and-by, future, futurity, hereafter. ***Idiom:*** time to come. [*Compare* **approach, possibility.**]
ton *noun.* —*See* **heap** (2).
tonality *noun.* The distinct quality or character of a sound ▶ timbre, tone, tone color.
tone *noun.* **1.** The distinct quality or character of a sound ▶ timbre, tonality, tone color. **2.** An expressive vocal quality ▶ accent, edge, inflection, intonation, lilt, pitch, resonance, sonority, sonorousness. ***Idiom:*** tone of voice. —*See also* **air** (3), **color** (1), **style, temper** (3).
tone down *verb. Informal* To make less emphatic or obvious ▶ de-emphasize, play down, soft-pedal. [*Compare* **moderate.**] —*See also* **moderate** (1).
tongue *noun.* —*See* **language** (1).
tongue-lashing *noun.* —*See* **tirade.**
tongueless *or* **tongue-tied** *adjective.* —*See* **mute.**
tonic *noun.* An agent, such as a medicine or drink, that restores vigor or energy ▶ energizer, restorative, roborant, stimulant. *Informal:* bracer, pick-me-up. ***Idiom:*** shot in the arm. [*Compare* **cure, drug.**]
tonic *adjective.* —*See* **invigorating.**
tony *adjective.* —*See* **exclusive** (3).
too *adverb.* —*See* **additionally.**
tool *noun.* A device used to do work or perform a task ▶ implement, instrument, utensil. [*Compare* **agent, device, gadget.**] —*See also* **dupe, pawn**[2].
tool *verb.* —*See* **drive** (1).

✦ **CORE SYNONYMS:** *tool, instrument, implement, utensil.* These nouns refer to devices used to do work or perform a task. *Tool* applies broadly to a device that facilitates work; specifically it denotes a small manually operated device: *a box full of tools for bike repair. Instrument* refers especially to a relatively small precision tool used by trained professionals: *sterilized the scalpel and the other instruments. Implement* is the preferred term for tools used in agriculture and certain building trades: *rakes, hoes, and other implements. Utensil* often refers to an implement used in a household, especially in the kitchen: *cooking utensils hung by the stove.*

---

tooth *noun.* —*See* **spike.**
toothed *adjective.* —*See* **saw-toothed.**
toothsome *adjective.* —*See* **delicious.**
top *noun.* Something that covers, especially to prevent contents from spilling ▶ cap, cover, covering, lid. [*Compare* **plug.**] —*See also* **best** (1), **climax, maximum.**
top *adjective.* Of, being, located at, or forming the top ▶ highest, loftiest, topmost, upmost, uppermost. [*Compare* **climactic.**] —*See also* **best** (1), **excellent, maximum, primary** (1).
top *verb.* To put a topping on ▶ cap, crest, crown, tip, top off. [*Compare* **cover.**] —*See also* **climax, surpass.**
top off *verb.* —*See* **fill** (1).
top-drawer *adjective.* —*See* **choice** (1).
toper *noun.* —*See* **drunkard.**
topflight *adjective.* —*See* **excellent.**
topic *noun.* —*See* **subject.**
topical *adjective.* Of, constituting, or relating to a theme or themes ▶ motivic, thematic. —*See also* **contemporary** (2).
topmost *adjective.* Of, being, located at, or forming the top ▶ highest, loftiest,

top, upmost, uppermost. [*Compare* **climactic.**] —*See also* **maximum.**

topnotch *adjective.* —*See* **excellent.**

topography *noun.* The character, natural features, and configuration of land ▶ terrain. ***Idiom:*** the lay of the land.

topple *verb.* To undergo capture, defeat, or ruin ▶ collapse, fall, go down, go under. [*Compare* **succumb, surrender.**] —*See also* **fall** (2), **overthrow, overturn.**

top secret *noun.* —*See* **confidential** (3).

topsy-turviness *noun.* —*See* **disorder** (1), **disorderliness.**

topsy-turvy *adjective.* —*See* **confused** (2), **upside-down.**

torch *verb.* —*See* **burn** (1), **light[1]** (1).

torment *verb.* **1.** To subject another to extreme physical cruelty, as in punishing ▶ crucify, harrow, rack, torture. ***Idioms:*** put on the rack (*or* wheel), put the screws to. [*Compare* **punish.**] **2.** To come to mind continually ▶ haunt, obsess, trouble, weigh on (*or* upon). —*See also* **afflict, harass.**

torment *noun.* —*See* **annoyance** (2), **distress, grief, hell.**

tormenting *adjective.* Extraordinarily painful or distressing ▶ agonizing, anguishing, atrocious, excruciating, harrowing, torturous. [*Compare* **bitter, terrible, unbearable.**]

tormentor *noun.* —*See* **bully.**

torpedo *verb.* —*See* **destroy** (1).

torpid *adjective.* —*See* **dead** (2), **latent, lethargic.**

torpor *or* **torpidity** *noun.* —*See* **lethargy.**

torrent *noun.* —*See* **flood, outburst, rain.**

torrid *adjective.* —*See* **hot** (1), **passionate.**

torridity *or* **torridness** *noun.* —*See* **heat** (1).

tort *noun.* —*See* **crime** (1).

tortuous *adjective.* —*See* **complex** (1), **indirect** (1), **winding.**

torture *verb.* To subject another to extreme physical cruelty, as in punishing ▶ crucify, harrow, rack, torment. ***Idioms:*** put on the rack (*or* wheel), put the screws to. [*Compare* **punish.**] —*See also* **afflict.**

torture *noun.* —*See* **distress, hell.**

torturous *adjective.* —*See* **tormenting.**

Tory *noun.* —*See* **conservative.**

Tory *adjective.* —*See* **conservative** (1).

toss *verb.* **1.** To move vigorously from side to side or up and down ▶ heave, pitch, rock, roll. [*Compare* **lurch.**] **2.** To swing about or strike at wildly ▶ flail, thrash, thresh. ***Idiom:*** toss and turn. [*Compare* **stagger, sway.**] **3.** To twist agitatedly, as in pain, struggle, or embarrassment ▶ squirm, twist, writhe. [*Compare* **shake.**] **4.** To throw a coin in order to decide something ▶ flip. ***Idiom:*** call heads or tails. —*See also* **agitate** (2), **discard, throw.**

toss around *verb.* —*See* **discuss.**

toss back *or* **down** *verb.* —*See* **drink** (1).

toss *noun.* —*See* **throw.**

tot[1] *noun.* —*See* **baby** (1), **child** (1), **drink** (2), **drop** (4).

tot[2] *verb.* —*See* **add.**

total *noun.* A number or quantity obtained as a result of addition ▶ aggregate, amount, sum, summation, sum total, totality. [*Compare* **account, count.**] —*See also* **whole.**

total *adjective.* —*See* **complete** (1), **general** (1), **utter[2].**

total *verb.* —*See* **add, amount, crash, destroy** (1).

totalitarian *adjective.* —*See* **absolute, authoritarian.**

totalitarian *noun.* —*See* **authoritarian, dictator.**

totalitarianism *noun.* —*See* **absolutism** (1), **tyranny.**

totality *noun.* —*See* **completeness, system, total, whole.**

totalization *noun.* The act or process of adding ▶ addition, summation. [*Compare* **calculation.**]

totalize *verb.* —*See* **add.**

totally *adverb.* —*See* **completely** (1).

tote *verb.* —*See* **carry** (1).
tote *noun.* —*See* **bag.**

totter *verb.*—*See* **stagger** (1), **sway.**

tottering *or* **tottery** *adjective.* —*See* **insecure** (2).

touch *verb.* To bring especially the hands or fingers into contact with ▶ feel, finger, handle, manipulate, palpate, press, stroke. [*Compare* **caress, brush¹, rub.**] —*See also* **adjoin, equal** (1), **move** (1).
touch down *verb.* —*See* **land** (2).
touch off *verb.* —*See* **cause, explode** (1), **light¹** (1), **provoke.**
touch on *or* **upon** *verb.*—*See* **refer** (1).
touch up *verb.* To improve by making minor changes or additions ▶ polish, remodel, retouch. [*Compare* **fix, renew.**]
touch *noun.* **1.** An act of touching ▶ feel, feeling, manipulation, palpation, stroke. **2.** A coming together so as to be touching ▶ contact, contingence. **3.** The faculty or ability to perceive tactile stimulation ▶ feel, feeling, tactility. ***Idiom:*** sense of touch. [*Compare* **sensation.**] **4.** A particular sensation conveyed by means of physical contact ▶ feel, feeling. [*Compare* **contact, brush.**] **5.** A situation allowing exchange of ideas or messages ▶ communication, contact, correspondence, intercommunication. [*Compare* **communication.**] —*See also* **shade** (2).

✚ **CORE SYNONYMS:** *touch, feel, finger, handle, palpate.* These verbs mean to bring the hands or fingers into contact with so as to give or receive a physical sensation: *gently touched my hand; felt the runner's pulse; fingered the worry beads; handle a bolt of fabric; palpates the patient's abdomen.*

---

touchable *adjective.* Discernible by touch ▶ palpable, tactile, tangible.

touchableness *noun.* —*See* **tangibility.**

touch-and-go *adjective.* —*See* **delicate** (3).

touched *adjective.* —*See* **insane.**

touching *adjective.* —*See* **affecting.**

touchstone *noun.* —*See* **standard.**

touchy *adjective.* —*See* **delicate** (3), **oversensitive, testy.**

tough *adjective.* —*See* **bitter** (2), **burdensome, difficult** (1), **firm¹** (3), **hard** (2), **rough** (3), **severe** (1), **strong** (2).
tough *noun.* —*See* **thug.**
tough out *verb.* —*See* **endure** (1).

toughen *verb.*—*See* **harden** (1), **harden** (2).

toughie *noun.* —*See* **thug.**

tough-minded *adjective.* —*See* **realistic** (1).

toughness *noun.* —*See* **decision** (2), **endurance, severity.**

tour *noun.* —*See* **circle** (2), **expedition, turn** (1).
tour *verb.* —*See* **journey.**

tour de force *noun.* —*See* **accomplishment.**

tourist *noun.* One who travels for pleasure ▶ day-tripper, excursionist, globetrotter, jet-setter, sightseer, sojourner, traveler, vacationer, visitor.

tournament *or* **tourney** *noun.* Any competition or test of opposing wills likened to the sport in which knights fought with lances ▶ joust, tilt. [*Compare* **battle.**] —*See also* **competition** (2).

tousle *verb.* To put something into a state of disarray, such as the hair or clothes ▶ disarrange, dishevel, disorder, disorganize, mess (up), muss (up), rumple. [*Compare* **dirty.**]

tout *verb.* —*See* **promote** (3).

tow *verb.* —*See* **pull** (1).
tow *noun.* —*See* **pull** (1).

toward *adjective.* —*See* **beneficial.**

tower *verb.* —*See* **rise** (2).
tower above *verb.* —*See* **dominate** (2).

towering *adjective.* —*See* **exceptional, high** (1).

towheaded *adjective.* —*See* **fair¹** (2).

town *noun.* —*See* **city.**

townsman *or* **townswoman** *noun.* —*See* **inhabitant.**

toxic *adjective.* —*See* **harmful, poisonous.**

toxicant *adjective.* —*See* **poisonous.**
toxicant *noun.* —*See* **poison.**

toxin *noun.* —*See* **poison.**

toy *noun.* An object for children to play with ▶ game, plaything. [*Compare* **amusement.**] —*See also* **novelty** (3).
toy *verb.* To treat lightly or flippantly ▶ dally, flirt, play, trifle. —*See also* **fiddle, flirt** (2).

trace *noun.* A mark or remnant that indicates the former presence of something ▶ record, relic, remainder, remains, remnant, vestige. [*Compare* **sign.**] —*See also* **shade** (2), **track.**
trace *verb.* **1.** To pursue and locate ▶ hunt down, nose out, run down, track down. ***Idioms:*** run to earth (*or* ground). **2.** To follow the traces or scent of, as in hunting ▶ smell out, sniff out, track, trail. ***Idiom:*** be hot on the trail of. [*Compare* **hunt.**]

track *noun.* A visible sign or mark of the passage of someone or something ▶ footmarks, footprints, marks, odor, print, scent, spoor, trace, trail. [*Compare* **lead, sign.**] —*See also* **routine.**
track *verb.* To follow the traces or scent of, as in hunting ▶ smell out, sniff out, trace, trail. ***Idiom:*** be hot on the trail of. [*Compare* **hunt.**] —*See also* **cross** (1), **follow** (3).
track down *verb.* —*See* **trace** (1).

tract[1] *noun.* —*See* **area** (2), **expanse** (1), **lot** (1).

tract[2] *noun.* —*See* **discourse.**

tractability *or* **tractableness** *noun.* —*See* **flexibility** (1), **obedience.**

tractable *adjective.* —*See* **malleable, obedient.**

traction *noun.* —*See* **pull** (1).

trade *noun.* —*See* **business** (1), **business** (2), **change** (2), **deal** (1), **patronage** (2), **patronage** (3).
trade *verb.* —*See* **change** (3), **exchange, sell.**

trademark *noun.* —*See* **mark** (1).
trademark *verb.* —*See* **mark** (1).

tradeoff *noun.* —*See* **compromise.**

trader *or* **tradesman** *noun.* —*See* **dealer.**

trading *noun.* —*See* **business** (1).

tradition *noun.* Something immaterial, as a style or philosophy, that is passed from one generation to another ▶ heritage, inheritance, legacy. —*See also* **ceremony** (1), **culture** (2), **lore** (1).

traditional *adjective.* —*See* **accepted, conventional.**

traditionalist *noun.* —*See* **conservative.**
traditionalist *or* **traditionalistic** *adjective.* —*See* **conservative** (1).

traditionalize *verb.* —*See* **conventionalize.**

traduce *verb.* —*See* **malign.**

traducement *noun.* —*See* **libel.**

traffic *noun.* —*See* **business** (1), **patronage** (2).

trafficker *noun.* —*See* **dealer, pusher.**

tragedy *noun.* —*See* **disaster.**

trail *verb.* **1.** To hang down and be pulled along behind ▶ drag, draggle, train. [*Compare* **pull.**] **2.** To follow the traces of, as in hunting ▶ smell out, sniff out, trace, track. ***Idiom:*** be hot on the trail of. [*Compare* **hunt.**] **3.** To follow closely or persistently ▶ dog, heel, tag. —*See also* **delay** (2), **follow** (3), **trudge.**
trail *noun.* Something that follows or is drawn along behind ▶ tail, train, wake. [*Compare* **stream.**] —*See also* **track, way** (2).

trailblazer *noun.* —*See* **forerunner.**

train *noun.* **1.** A string of railroad cars led by a locomotive ▶ rail, railroad train, railway. *Informal:* choo-choo, choo-choo train. **2.** Something that follows or is drawn along behind ▶ tail, trail, wake. [*Compare* **stream.**] —*See also* **retinue, series.**
train *verb.* **1.** To hang down and be pulled along behind ▶ drag, draggle, trail. [*Compare* **pull.**] **2.** To engage in activities in order to strengthen or con-

dition ▶ drill, exercise, practice, work out. —*See also* **aim** (1), **educate.**

trainable *adjective.* Capable of being educated ▶ docile, educable, teachable. [*Compare* **obedient.**]

trained *adjective.* —*See* **educated.**

trainee *noun.* —*See* **student.**

trainer *noun.* —*See* **educator.**

training *noun.* —*See* **education** (1), **practice.**

traipse *verb.* —*See* **rove.**

trait *noun.* —*See* **quality** (1).

traitor *noun.* —*See* **betrayer, defector.**

traitorous *adjective.* Involving or constituting treason ▶ seditious, treasonable, treasonous. —*See also* **faithless.**

traitorousness *noun.* Willful violation of allegiance to one's country ▶ lese majesty, sedition, seditiousness, treason. —*See also* **faithlessness.**

trammel *noun.* —*See* **bond** (1).

trammel *verb.* —*See* **catch** (1), **hamper**[1].

tramp *verb.* **1.** To travel about or journey on foot ▶ hike, backpack, march, trek. [*Compare* **journey, walk.**] **2.** To step on heavily and repeatedly so as to crush, injure, or destroy ▶ stamp, stomp, trample, tread, tromp. [*Compare* **crush.**] —*See also* **rove, trudge.**

tramp *noun.* —*See* **hobo, pauper, slut, walk** (1).

trample *verb.* **1.** To step on heavily and repeatedly so as to crush, injure, or destroy ▶ stamp, stomp, tramp, tread, tromp. [*Compare* **crush, trudge.**] **2.** To treat arbitrarily or cruelly ▶ grind (down), oppress. [*Compare* **abuse, enslave, suppress.**]

trampy *verb.* —*See* **wanton** (1).

trance *noun.* The condition of being so lost in solitary thought that one is unaware of one's surroundings ▶ absent-mindedness, abstraction, bemusement, brown study, daydreaming, dream, half-conscious state, hypnotic state, muse, reverie, sleepwalking, study. —*See also* **daze.**

tranquil *adjective.* —*See* **calm, still.**

tranquilize *verb.* —*See* **drug** (1), **pacify.**

tranquilizer *noun.* —*See* **soporific.**

tranquillity *or* **tranquility** *noun.* —*See* **calm, stillness.**

transact *verb.* —*See* **perform** (1).

transaction *noun.* —*See* **deal** (1), **performance.**

transcend *verb.* —*See* **exceed, surpass.**

transcendence *noun.* —*See* **excellence.**

transcendent *adjective.* —*See* **maximum.**

transcendental *adjective.* —*See* **supernatural** (1).

transcribe *verb.* —*See* **translate.**

transfer *verb.* **1.** To change the ownership of property by means of a legal document ▶ assign, cede, convey, deed, grant, make over, sign over, transmit. **2.** To change one's residence or place of business, for example ▶ move, relocate, remove. ***Idiom:*** pull up stakes. [*Compare* **emigrate, go.**] **3.** To direct a person elsewhere for help or information ▶ refer, send, turn over. —*See also* **communicate** (2), **conduct** (3), **give** (1), **move** (2).

transfer *noun.* —*See* **delivery, grant.**

transferable *adjective.* —*See* **contagious.**

transferal *noun.* —*See* **grant.**

transfiguration *noun.* —*See* **conversion** (1).

transfigure *verb.* —*See* **convert.**

transfix *verb.* —*See* **cut** (1), **grip.**

transform *verb.* —*See* **convert, revolutionize.**

transformable *adjective.* —*See* **changeable** (1).

transformation *noun.* —*See* **conversion** (1), **revolution** (2).

transfuse *verb.* —*See* **charge** (1).

transgress *verb.* —*See* **disobey, exceed, offend** (3), **violate** (1).

transgression *noun.* —*See* **breach** (1), **trespass** (2).

transgressor *noun.* —*See* **criminal, rebel** (1).

transient *adjective.* —*See* **migratory** (1), **transitory.**
transient *noun.* —*See* **hobo.**

transit *noun.* —*See* **journey, transition, transportation.**
transit *verb.* —*See* **cross** (1).

transition *noun.* Passage from one form, state, or stage to another ▶ change, flux, move, passage, progression, shift, transit, turn. ***Idiom:*** change of course. [*Compare* **change, conversion.**]

transitory *adjective.* Lasting or existing only for a short time ▶ brief, ephemeral, evanescent, fleet, fleeting, fugacious, fugitive, momentary, passing, short, short-lived, temporal, temporary, transient. [*Compare* **temporary.**]

translate *verb.* To express in another language ▶ construe, interpret, metaphrase, put, render, transcribe, transliterate, transpose. [*Compare* **convert.**] —*See also* **convert, paraphrase.**

translation *noun.* The act or process of translating ▶ construe, crib, interpretation, metaphrase, pony, rendering, transliteration, trot. —*See also* **conversion** (1), **paraphrase.**

transliterate *verb.* —*See* **translate.**

transliteration *noun.* —*See* **translation.**

translucent *adjective.* —*See* **clear** (1).

transmigrant *noun.* One who emigrates ▶ emigrant, immigrant, migrant.

transmigrate *verb.* **1.** To leave one's native land and settle in another ▶ emigrate (from), immigrate (to), migrate, resettle. [*Compare* **move, settle.**] **2.** To change habitat seasonally ▶ migrate.

transmigration *noun.* Settling in a country to which one is not native ▶ immigration, migration. —*See also* **emigration.**

transmigratory *adjective.* —*See* **migratory** (1).

transmission *noun.* —*See* **delivery.**

transmit *verb.* —*See* **communicate** (1), **communicate** (2), **conduct** (3), **leave**[1] (1), **send** (1), **transfer** (1).

transmittable *adjective.* —*See* **contagious.**

transmogrification *noun.* —*See* **conversion** (1).

transmogrify *verb.* —*See* **convert.**

transmutable *adjective.* —*See* **changeable** (1).

transmutation *noun.* —*See* **conversion** (1).

transmute *verb.* —*See* **convert.**

transparent *adjective.* —*See* **clear** (1), **obvious, sheer**[2].

transpire *verb.* To be made public ▶ break, come out, get out, out. *Informal:* leak (out). [*Compare* **air, announce, appear.**] —*See also* **happen** (1), **ooze.**

transplant *verb.* —*See* **plant.**

transport *verb.* —*See* **banish, bring** (1), **carry** (1), **enrapture.**
transport *noun.* —*See* **heaven, transportation.**

transportable *adjective.* —*See* **mobile** (1).

transportation *noun.* The moving of persons or goods from one place to another ▶ carriage, carrying, conveyance, conveying, freight, hauling, shipping, transit, transport. —*See also* **exile.**

transpose *verb.* —*See* **change** (3), **convert, reverse** (1), **translate.**

transposition *noun.* —*See* **change** (2), **reversal** (1).

transubstantiate *verb.* —*See* **convert.**

transubstantiation *noun.* —*See* **conversion** (1).

transude *verb.* To excrete moisture through a porous skin or layer ▶ lather, perspire, sweat. —*See also* **ooze.**

transversal *adjective.* —*See* **transverse.**

transverse *adjective.* Situated or lying across ▶ across, crossing, crossways, crosswise, thwart, transversal, traverse. [*Compare* **oblique.**]

trap *noun.* **1.** A device or stratagem for catching or tricking a person or animal ▶ booby trap, deadfall, gin, noose, pit, pitfall, snare, springe, tripwire. [*Compare* **lure, trick.**] **2.** An attack or stratagem for capturing or tricking an unsuspecting person ▶ ambuscade, ambush. [*Compare* **deceit.**] —*See also* **mouth** (1).

trap *verb.* —*See* **catch** (1).

trash *noun.* —*See* **garbage, nonsense, riffraff.**

trash *verb. Slang* To injure or destroy property maliciously ▶ wreck, vandalize. [*Compare* **destroy.**] —*See also* **slam** (1).

trashy *adjective.* —*See* **shoddy.**

trauma *noun.* Marked tissue damage, especially when produced by physical injury ▶ laceration, lesion, traumatism, wound. —*See also* **emergency, harm, shock**[1]**.**

traumatize *verb.* To cause bodily damage to a living thing ▶ hurt, injure, wing, wound. [*Compare* **cut, break.**] —*See also* **distress.**

travail *noun.* —*See* **birth** (1), **labor.**

travail *verb.* —*See* **labor.**

travel *verb.* To become known far and wide ▶ circulate, get around, go around, spread. ***Idioms:*** go (*or* make) the rounds. —*See also* **journey, move** (2).

travel *noun.* —*See* **journey.**

traveler *noun.* —*See* **tourist.**

traveling *adjective.* —*See* **mobile** (1), **nomadic.**

traversable *adjective.* —*See* **passable.**

traversal *noun.* —*See* **denial** (1), **journey.**

traverse *verb.* —*See* **contest, cover** (2), **cross** (1), **deny, examine** (1).

traverse *adjective.* —*See* **transverse.**

travesty *noun.* —*See* **mockery** (2).

travesty *verb.* —*See* **imitate.**

trawl *verb.* —*See* **fish** (1).

treacherous *adjective.* —*See* **dangerous, faithless.**

treacherousness *noun.* —*See* **faithlessness.**

treachery *noun.* —*See* **betrayal, faithlessness.**

treacle *noun.* —*See* **sentimentality.**

tread *verb.* To step on heavily and repeatedly so as to crush, injure, or destroy ▶ stamp, stomp, tramp, trample, tromp. [*Compare* **crush, trudge.**] —*See also* **walk.**

tread *noun.* —*See* **walk** (2).

treadmill *noun.* —*See* **routine.**

treason *noun.* Willful violation of allegiance to one's country ▶ lese majesty, sedition, seditiousness, traitorousness. —*See also* **faithlessness.**

treasonous *or* **treasonable** *adjective.* Involving or constituting treason ▶ seditious, traitorous. [*Compare* **faithless.**]

treasure *noun.* Someone or something considered exceptionally precious ▶ find, gem, pearl, plum, prize. *Informal:* catch. ***Idioms:*** apple of one's eye, pride and joy. [*Compare* **masterpiece.**] —*See also* **hoard, wealth.**

treasure *verb.* —*See* **save** (1), **value.**

treasury *or* **treasure house** *noun.* —*See* **depository.**

treat *verb.* **1.** To behave in a specified way toward someone ▶ cope with, handle. **2.** To pay for the food, drink, or entertainment of another ▶ *Informal:* set up, stand. *Slang:* blow, spring for. ***Idioms:*** pick up the check (*or* tab), stand treat. [*Compare* **amuse.**] —*See also* **administer** (3), **deal** (1).

treat *noun.* —*See* **amusement, delicacy, luxury.**

treatise *noun.* —*See* **discourse.**

treatment *noun.* The systematic application of remedies to effect a cure ▶ care, doctoring, medical care, nursing, regimen, rehabilitation, therapeutics, therapy. *Informal:* rehab. [*Compare* **drug.**] —*See also* **cure.**

treaty *noun.* A formal agreement between two or more states or nations ▶ accord, agreement, concord, concordat, convention, entente, pact. [*Compare* **agreement, bargain, compromise, truce.**]

treble *adjective.* —*See* **high** (3).

trek *verb.* To travel about or journey on foot ▶ backpack, hike, march, tramp. [*Compare* **rove, walk.**] —*See also* **journey.**

trek *noun.* —*See* **expedition.**
tremble *verb.* —*See* **shake** (1), **sway.**
tremble *noun.* —*See* **tremor** (2).
trembles *noun.* —*See* **jitters.**
trembling *adjective.* —*See* **tremulous.**
trembling *noun.* —*See* **tremor** (2).
tremendous *adjective.* —*See* **enormous, marvelous.**
tremendousness *noun.* —*See* **enormousness.**
tremor *noun.* **1.** A shaking of the earth ▶ earthquake, quake, seism, temblor. *Informal:* shake. **2.** A nervous shaking of the body ▶ jerk, paroxysm, quake, quaver, quiver, shake, shaking, shiver, shudder, spasm, thrill, tic, tremble, trembling, twitch, vibrating, vibration. [*Compare* **shake.**]
tremulant *adjective.* —*See* **tremulous.**
tremulous *adjective.* Marked by or affected with tremors ▶ aquiver, jerky, quaking, quaky, quavering, quivering, quivery, shaky, shivering, shivery, shuddering, trembling, tremulant, twittery, vibrating. —*See also* **afraid.**
trench *noun.* —*See* **furrow.**
trenchancy *noun.* —*See* **sarcasm.**
trenchant *adjective.* —*See* **biting, brief, critical** (2).
trench coat *noun.* —*See* **coat** (1).
trend *noun.* —*See* **fashion, inclination** (1).
trend *verb.* —*See* **tend[1].**
trendy *adjective.* —*See* **fashionable.**
trepidation *noun.* —*See* **fear.**
trespass *verb.* To enter forcibly or illegally ▶ break in, burglarize, invade. [*Compare* **rob, steal.**] —*See also* **intrude, offend** (3).
trespass *noun.* **1.** The act of entering a building or room with the intent to commit theft ▶ break-in, breaking and entering, burglary, forced entry. [*Compare* **larceny.**] **2.** An advance beyond proper or legal limits ▶ encroachment, entrenchment, impingement, infringement, intrusion, obtrusion, overstepping, transgression. [*Compare* **invasion.**] —*See also* **breach** (1).
trestle *noun.* —*See* **beam** (2).
triad *noun.* —*See* **trio.**
trial *noun.* **1.** A state of pain or anguish that tests one's resiliency and character ▶ affliction, crucible, ordeal, tribulation, visitation. [*Compare* **difficulty.**] **2.** The examination of evidence, charges, and claims in court ▶ court case, hearing, inquest, inquiry. [*Compare* **examination.**] **3.** An operation employed to resolve an uncertainty ▶ experiment, experimentation, test. —*See also* **annoyance** (2), **attempt, burden[1]** (1), **competition** (2), **test** (1).
trial *adjective.* —*See* **pilot.**

✦ **CORE SYNONYMS:** *trial, affliction, crucible, ordeal, tribulation.* These nouns denote a state of pain or anguish that tests one's resiliency and character: *no consolation in their hour of trial; the affliction of a bereaved family; the crucible of revolution; the ordeal of being an innocent murder suspect; a time of relentless tribulation.*

---

tribe *noun.* —*See* **family** (2).
tribulation *noun.* —*See* **burden[1]** (1), **trial** (1).
tribunal *noun.* —*See* **court** (2).
tributary *noun.* —*See* **branch** (1), **brook[1], river.**
tribute *noun.* —*See* **compliment, tax, testimonial** (2).
trice *noun.* —*See* **flash** (2).
trick *noun.* **1.** An indirect, usually cunning means of gaining an end ▶ artifice, deception, device, dodge, feint, gimmick, hustle, imposture, jig, maneuver, ploy, ruse, sleight, stratagem, subterfuge, wile. *Informal:* con game, fast one, shenanigan, take-in. *Slang:* snow job. [*Compare* **move, plot, trap.**] **2.** The proper method for doing, using, or handling something ▶ feel, knack. *Informal:* hang. **3.** A clever, dexterous act ▶ feat, stunt. ***Idiom:*** sleight of hand. [*Compare* **accomplishment.**] —*See also* **prank[1], turn** (1), **wrinkle** (2).
trick *verb.* —*See* **deceive.**

trick out *or* **up** *verb.* —*See* **dress up.**

trick *adjective.* So weak or defective as to be liable to fail ▶ undependable, unreliable. [*Compare* **defective, weak.**]

✦ **CORE SYNONYMS:** *trick, wile, artifice, ruse, feint, stratagem, maneuver, dodge.* These nouns denote means for achieving an end by cunning, indirection, or deviousness. *Trick* implies willful deception: "*The . . . boys . . . had all sorts of tricks to prevent us from winning*" (W.H. Hudson). *Wile* suggests deceiving and entrapping a victim by playing on his or her weak points: "*He did not fail to see/His uncle's cunning wiles and treachery*" (William Morris). *Artifice* refers to something especially contrived to create a desired effect: "*Should the public forgive artifices used to avoid military service?*" (Godfrey Sperling). *Ruse* stresses the creation of a false impression: *Your pretended deafness was a ruse to enable you to learn our plans, wasn't it? Feint* denotes a deceptive act calculated to distract attention from one's real purpose: *One person bumped into me as a feint while the other stole my wallet. Stratagem* implies carefully planned deception used to achieve an objective: *The manager used ruthless stratagems to win the promotion. Maneuver* often applies to a single strategic move: "*To this day they always speak of that Reform Bill as if it had been a dishonest maneuver*" (The Standard). *Dodge* stresses shifty and ingenious deception: "'*It was all false, of course?' 'All, sir,' replied Mr. Weller, '. . . artful dodge'*" (Charles Dickens).

trickery *noun.* —*See* **deceit, dishonesty** (2).

trickiness *noun.* —*See* **dishonesty** (2).

trickle *verb.* —*See* **drip.**

trickle *noun.* The process or sound of dripping ▶ dribble, drip, drizzle, mizzle.

tricks *noun.* —*See* **mischief.**

trickster *noun.* —*See* **cheat** (2).

tricky *adjective.* —*See* **artful, delicate** (3).

tried *adjective.* —*See* **experienced.**

trifle *noun.* Something or things of little importance ▶ fiddle-faddle, frippery, frivolity, froth, inconsequence, inconsequentiality, inconsequentialness, inconsiderableness, indifference, insignificance, insignificancy, levity, lightness, minutia, negligibility, negligibleness, nonsense, paltriness, pettiness, picayune, small change, smallness, triviality, trivialness, unimportance. *Informal:* small potatoes. —*See also* **bit**[1] (1), **novelty** (3).

trifle *verb.* To treat lightly or flippantly ▶ dally, flirt, play, toy. —*See also* **fiddle, flirt** (2).

trifle away *verb.* —*See* **idle** (2), **waste.**

trifling *adjective.* —*See* **trivial.**

trig *adjective.* —*See* **neat.**

trig *verb.* —*See* **tidy** (2).

trigger *noun.* —*See* **provocation** (1).

trigger *verb.* —*See* **cause, provoke.**

triggerman *noun.* —*See* **murderer.**

trillion *noun.* —*See* **heap** (2).

trim *verb.* To make a slight reduction in prices ▶ shade, shave. —*See also* **adorn** (1), **beat** (2), **cheat** (1), **cut** (3), **defeat, tidy** (2).

trim down *verb.* To lose body weight, as by dieting ▶ reduce, slim (down), thin (down). ***Idioms:*** get the weight off, lose weight, shed some pounds.

trim *noun.* —*See* **adornment, shape.**

trim *adjective.* Having slender and graceful lines ▶ sleek, streamlined. —*See also* **neat.**

trimming *noun.* —*See* **adornment, beating, defeat.**

trine *or* **trinity** *noun.* —*See* **trio.**

trinket *noun.* —*See* **novelty** (3).

trio *noun.* A group of three individuals ▶ three, threesome, triad, trine, trinity, triple, triumvirate, triune, triunity, troika. [*Compare* **group.**]

trip *noun.* **1.** A usually short journey taken for pleasure ▶ excursion, jaunt, junket, outing. [*Compare* **expedition.**]

2. *Slang* A temporary concentration of interest ▶ *Slang:* kick. **3.** *Slang* An experience of things or events that are not real ▶ hallucination, phantasmagoria, phantasmagory. *—See also* **error, journey.**

trip *verb.* *—See* **bound[1], journey, stumble.**

trip up *verb.* *—See* **err.**

triple *noun.* *—See* **trio.**

tripping *adjective.* *—See* **drugged.**

tristful *adjective.* *—See* **depressed** (1).

trite *adjective.* Without freshness or appeal because of overuse ▶ banal, bromidic, clichéd, commonplace, corny, hackneyed, musty, overused, overworked, platitudinal, platitudinous, shopworn, stale, stereotyped, stereotypic, stereotypical, stock, threadbare, timeworn, tired, unimaginative, uninspired, unoriginal, warmed-over, well-worn, worn-out. [*Compare* **boring, dull.**]

triturate *verb.* *—See* **crush** (2).

triumph *verb.* *—See* **exult** (1).

triumph over *verb.* *—See* **defeat.**

triumph *noun.* *—See* **accomplishment, conquest, exultation.**

triumphal *adjective.* *—See* **victorious.**

triumphant *adjective.* Feeling or expressing an uplifting joy over a success or victory ▶ exultant, gloating, jubilant. [*Compare* **boastful.**] *—See also* **victorious.**

triumvirate *noun.* *—See* **trio.**

triune *or* **triunity** *noun.* *—See* **trio.**

trivia *noun.* *—See* **detail, trifle.**

trivial *adjective.* Of little importance or seriousness ▶ fluffy, frivolous, frothy, inconsequent, inconsequential, inconsiderable, insignificant, light, lightweight, little, negligible, niggling, nugatory, paltry, petty, picayune, piddling, small, small-minded, trifling, unimportant. *Slang:* measly, rinky-dink, two-bit. [*Compare* **superficial, worthless.**]

✚ **CORE SYNONYMS:** *trivial, trifling, paltry, petty, picayune.* These adjectives all apply to what is of little importance or seriousness. *Trivial* and *trifling* refer to what is so insignificant as to be utterly commonplace or unremarkable: *"I think all Christians . . . agree in the essential articles, and that their differences are trivial"* (Samuel Johnson). *"I regret the trifling narrow contracted education of the females of my own country"* (Abigail Adams). *Paltry* describes what falls so far short of what is required or desired that it arouses contempt: *"He . . . considered the prize too paltry for the lives it must cost"* (John Lothrop Motley). *Petty* can refer to what is of minor or secondary significance or size: *"Our knights are limited to petty enterprises"* (Sir Walter Scott). What is *picayune* is of negligible value or importance: *considered the violation a picayune infraction of the law.*

◀ **ANTONYM:** *important*

triviality *or* **trivialness** *noun.* *—See* **trifle.**

troika *noun.* *—See* **trio.**

troll *verb.* *—See* **fish** (1).

tromp *verb.* To step on heavily and repeatedly so as to crush, injure, or destroy ▶ stamp, stomp, tramp, trample, tread. [*Compare* **crush.**] *—See also* **trudge.**

troop *noun.* *—See* **assembly, band[2], crowd, flock.**

troop *verb.* *—See* **associate** (2), **crowd.**

trooper *noun.* *—See* **police officer, soldier** (2).

trophy *noun.* A memento received as a symbol of excellence or victory ▶ accolade, award, cup, prize. [*Compare* **medal, reward.**] *—See also* **distinction** (2), **remembrance** (1).

tropical *adjective.* *—See* **hot** (1).

trot *noun.* *—See* **run** (1), **translation.**

trot *verb.* *—See* **run** (1), **rush.**

troth *noun.* The act or condition of being pledged to marry ▶ betrothal, engagement, espousal.

troth *verb.* *—See* **pledge** (1).

troubadour *noun.* —*See* **poet.**

trouble *noun.* A cause of distress or anxiety ▶ care, concern, stressor, worry. [*Compare* **anxiety, burden[1].**] —*See also* **difficulty, effort, emergency, inconvenience, predicament, qualm.**

trouble *verb.* To come to mind continually ▶ haunt, obsess, torment, weigh on (*or* upon). —*See also* **distress, inconvenience, worry.**

troublemaker *noun.* —*See* **agitator.**

troubleshooter *noun.* —*See* **go-between.**

troublesome *adjective.* **1.** Causing difficulty, trouble, or discomfort ▶ difficult, incommodious, inconvenient. **2.** Hard to treat, manage, or cope with ▶ demanding, difficult, trying, wicked. *Informal:* pesky. *Slang:* mean. [*Compare* **fussy, unruly.**] —*See also* **disturbing.**

troubling *or* **troublous** *adjective.* —*See* **disturbing.**

trough *noun.* —*See* **furrow.**

trounce *verb.* —*See* **overwhelm** (1).

trouncing *noun.* —*See* **defeat.**

troupe *noun.* —*See* **band[2].**

trouper *noun.* A theatrical performer ▶ actor, actress, player, thespian. [*Compare* **fake, lead, mimic.**]

truancy *or* **truantry** *noun.* —*See* **absence** (1).

truant *verb.* —*See* **cut** (4).

truant *adjective.* —*See* **absent.**

truce *noun.* A temporary cessation of hostilities by mutual agreement ▶ armistice, cease-fire, peace, white flag. ***Idioms:*** cooling-off period, peace agreement, suspension of hostilities. [*Compare* **break.**]

truckle *verb.* —*See* **fawn.**

truckler *noun.* —*See* **sycophant.**

truculence *or* **truculency** *noun.* —*See* **aggression, cruelty, fight** (2).

truculent *adjective.* —*See* **aggressive, biting, cruel.**

trudge *verb.* To walk in a laborious way ▶ forge, plod, scuff, scuffle, shamble, shuffle, slog, slop, stamp, stomp, toil, trail, tramp, trample, wade. *Informal:* tromp. *Slang:* schlep. [*Compare* **crawl, trample, walk.**]

true *adjective.* **1.** Occurring or existing in act or fact ▶ actual, existent, extant, real. [*Compare* **physical.**] **2.** Marked by uprightness in principle and action ▶ good, honest, honorable, incorruptible, righteous, upright, upstanding. *Informal:* straight-shooting. ***Idiom:*** on the up-and-up. **3.** Being so legitimately ▶ legitimate, rightful. [*Compare* **lawful.**] —*See also* **accurate, authentic, faithful, genuine, honest, realistic** (2).

true-life *adjective.* —*See* **realistic** (2).

truelove *noun.* —*See* **darling** (1).

truism *noun.* —*See* **cliché, law** (3).

truly *adverb.* —*See* **really.**

trump *verb.* To outmaneuver an opponent ▶ finesse. *Informal:* one-up. ***Idioms:*** play gotcha, pull (*or* put over) a fast one. [*Compare* **deceive, maneuver, outwit.**]

trump *or* **trump card** *noun.* A key resource to be used at an opportune moment ▶ ace. *Informal:* clincher. ***Idiom:*** ace in the hole.

trumpet *verb.* —*See* **announce.**

truncate *verb.* —*See* **cut** (3), **shorten.**

trunk *noun.* **1.** The human body excluding the head and limbs ▶ body, midsection, torso. **2.** The main ascending part of a plant, which supports the other parts ▶ stalk, stem, stock. [*Compare* **shoot.**]

truss *verb.* —*See* **dress** (2).

trust *noun.* Absolute certainty that a person or thing will not fail ▶ belief, confidence, dependence, faith, reliance. —*See also* **alliance, care** (2).

trust *verb.* **1.** To have confidence in the truthfulness of ▶ believe, credit. ***Idioms:*** give credence to, have faith (*or* trust *or* confidence) in, take at one's word. **2.** To place a trust upon ▶ charge, entrust. [*Compare* **authorize.**] —*See also* **depend on** (1), **entrust** (1).

✦ **CORE SYNONYMS:** *trust, faith, confidence, reliance, dependence.* These nouns denote a feeling of certainty that a person or thing will not fail. *Trust* implies depth and assurance of feeling that is often based on inconclusive evidence: *The mayor vowed to justify the trust the electorate had placed in him. Faith* primarily connotes unquestioning, often emotionally charged belief: *"Often enough our faith beforehand in an uncertified result is the only thing that makes the result come true"* (William James). *Confidence* frequently implies stronger grounds for assurance: *"Confidence is a plant of slow growth in an aged bosom: youth is the season of credulity"* (William Pitt). *Reliance* generally connotes a confident and trustful commitment to another: *"What reliance could they place on the protection of a prince so recently their enemy?"* (William Hickling Prescott). *Dependence* most often suggests reliance on another to whom one is often subordinate: *"When I had once called him in, I could not subsist without Dependence on him"* (Richard Steele).

---

trusting *adjective.* —*See* **gullible.**

trustworthiness *noun.* —*See* **honesty.**

trustworthy *adjective.* —*See* **authentic** (2), **dependable.**

trusty *adjective.* —*See* **dependable.**

truth *noun.* —*See* **certainty, honesty, veracity.**

truthful *adjective.* —*See* **honest, realistic** (2).

truthfully *adverb.* —*See* **really.**

truthfulness *noun.* —*See* **veracity.**

truthless *adjective.* —*See* **false.**

truthlessness *noun.* —*See* **mendacity.**

try *verb.* —*See* **attempt, burden**[1], **test** (1).

try *noun.* —*See* **attempt.**

trying *adjective.* —*See* **burdensome, troublesome** (2).

tryout *noun.* —*See* **test** (1).

tryst *noun.* —*See* **engagement** (1).

tub *noun.* —*See* **vat.**

tubby *adjective.* —*See* **fat** (1).

tucker *verb.* —*See* **tire** (1).

tuckered *adjective.* —*See* **tired** (1).

tug *verb.* —*See* **labor, pull** (1).

tug *noun.* —*See* **jerk.**

tug of war *noun.* —*See* **competition** (1).

tuition *noun.* —*See* **education** (1).

tumble *verb.* To bring about the downfall of ▶ bring down, overthrow, overturn, subvert, topple, unhorse. —*See also* **disorder, fall** (1), **fall** (2), **fall** (4).

tumble on *verb.* —*See* **encounter** (1).

tumble *noun.* —*See* **descent, disorder** (1), **fall** (1), **fall** (3), **heap** (1).

tumbledown *adjective.* —*See* **shabby.**

tumesce *verb.* —*See* **swell.**

tumescent *adjective.* —*See* **inflated, swollen.**

tumid *adjective.* —*See* **inflated.**

tumult *noun.* —*See* **agitation** (1), **agitation** (2), **disorder** (2), **fight** (1), **noise** (1).

tumultuous *adjective.* —*See* **agitated, rough** (2).

tundra *noun.* —*See* **desert**[1].

tune *noun.* —*See* **agreement** (2), **harmony** (1), **melody, song.**

tune *verb.* —*See* **harmonize** (1).

tune up *verb.* —*See* **adjust.**

tuneful *adjective.* —*See* **melodious.**

tunnel *noun.* —*See* **cave, hole** (2).

turbid *adjective.* Heavy, dark, or dense, especially with impurities ▶ hazy, murky, smoggy. [*Compare* **dirty.**] —*See also* **confused** (1), **murky** (1).

turbulence *noun.* —*See* **agitation** (1).

turbulent *adjective.* —*See* **agitated, disorderly, rough** (2).

turf *noun.* —*See* **area** (1), **earth** (1), **territory.**

turgid *adjective.* —*See* **inflated.**

turgidity *noun.* —*See* **bombast.**

turkey *noun.* —*See* **drip** (2), **failure** (1), **fool.**

turmoil *noun.* —*See* **agitation** (1), **agitation** (2), **disorder** (2).

turn *verb.* **1.** To move in circles or around an axis ▶ circle, circumvolve, go around (*or* round), gyrate, orbit, pivot, reel, revolve, rotate, spin, swirl, twirl, wheel, whirl. [*Compare* **incline.**] **2.** To change the direction or course of ▶ avert, deflect, deviate, divert, redirect, shift, shunt, sidetrack, swing, switch, turn aside, veer. [*Compare* **swerve.**] **3.** To change to the opposite position, direction, or course ▶ invert, reverse, transpose, turn (about, around, over, *or* round). **4.** To injure a bodily part by twisting ▶ sprain, strain, twist, wrench. [*Compare* **hurt.**] —*See also* **aim** (1), **apply** (1), **bear** (5), **become** (1), **bend** (1), **bend** (2), **change** (1), **change** (2), **convince, decay, defect, dull, resort, upset.**

turn back *verb.* —*See* **retreat, return** (1).

turn down *verb.* —*See* **decline, veto.**

turn in *verb.* —*See* **betray** (1), **offer** (1), **retire** (1).

turn off *verb.* —*See* **disgust, estrange, offend** (2).

turn on *verb.* To set in motion ▶ activate, actuate, spark, start. [*Compare* **energize, provoke.**] —*See also* **depend on** (2), **grip.**

turn out *verb.* —*See* **furnish, happen** (1), **rise** (1).

turn over *verb.* To direct a person elsewhere for help or information ▶ refer, send, transfer. —*See also* **entrust** (1), **give** (1), **overturn, ponder, till.**

turn up *verb.* —*See* **appear** (1), **arrive** (1), **discover, uncover.**

turn *noun.* **1.** A limited, often assigned period of activity, duty, or opportunity ▶ bout, go, hitch, inning, shift, spell, stint, stretch, time, tour, trick, watch. *Informal:* crack, shot, whack. [*Compare* **opportunity, try.**] **2.** An often sudden change or departure, as in a trend ▶ shift, tack, twist. [*Compare* **change, deviation.**] —*See also* **bend, circle** (2), **drive** (3), **inclination** (1), **revolution** (1), **talent, transition, walk** (1).

✚ **CORE SYNONYMS:** *turn, circle, rotate, revolve, gyrate, spin, whirl, swirl.* These verbs mean to move or cause to move in a circle. *Turn* and *circle* are the most general: *The mechanic made sure the wheels turned properly. Seagulls circled above the ocean. Rotate* refers to movement around an object's own axis or center: *Earth rotates on its axis once each day. Revolve* involves orbital movement: *Earth revolves around the sun. Gyrate* suggests revolving in or as if in a spiral course: *The top gyrated on the counter and slowly came to a stop.* To *spin* is to rotate rapidly, often within a narrow compass: *"He . . . spun round, flung up his arms, and fell on his back, shot through"* (John Galsworthy). *Whirl* applies to rapid or forceful revolution or rotation: *During the blizzard, snowflakes whirled down from the sky. Swirl* can connote a graceful undulation, spiral, or whorl: *The baker swirled the icing around the cake.*

---

turnabout *or* **turnaround** *noun.* —*See* **reversal** (1).

turncoat *noun.* —*See* **defector.**

turndown *noun.* A turning down of a request ▶ denial, disallowance, nonacceptance, refusal, rejection. [*Compare* **forbiddance.**]

turned-on *adjective.* —*See* **drugged, thrilled.**

turning point *noun.* —*See* **crisis.**

turnkey *noun.* A guard or keeper of a prison ▶ jailer, warden. *Slang:* screw. [*Compare* **guard, police officer.**]

turnout *noun.* —*See* **dress** (2), **outfit.**

turnpike *noun.* —*See* **way** (2).

turpitude *noun.* —*See* **corruption** (1).

tush *noun.* —*See* **buttocks.**

tussle *verb.* —*See* **contend.**

tussle *noun.* —*See* **fight** (1).

tutelage *noun.* —*See* **care** (2), **education** (1).

tutor *noun.* —*See* **educator.**

tutor *verb.* —*See* **educate.**

tutoring *noun.* —*See* **education** (1).

twaddle *noun.* —*See* **babble, nonsense.**

tweak *verb.* —*See* **adjust.**

twelvemonth *noun.* A period of time of approximately 12 months, especially that period during which the earth completes a single revolution around the sun ▶ calendar year, season cycle, year.

24-7 *adverb.* —*See* **continually.**

twerp *noun.* —*See* **drip** (2), **nonentity.**

twiddle *verb.* —*See* **fiddle.**

twig *noun.* —*See* **stick** (1).

twiggy *adjective.* —*See* **thin** (1).

twilight *noun.* —*See* **evening.**

twill *verb.* —*See* **weave.**

twin *adjective.* Consisting of two identical or similar related things, parts, or elements ▶ double, dual, matched, paired. [*Compare* **equal.**]

twin *noun.* —*See* **double, mate.**

twin *verb.* To make or become twice as great ▶ double, duplicate, geminate, redouble.

twine *verb.* —*See* **weave, wind**[2]**.**

twinge *noun.* —*See* **pain.**

twinge *verb.* —*See* **hurt** (2), **hurt** (3).

twinkle *verb.* —*See* **blink, glitter.**

twinkle *noun.* —*See* **flash** (1), **flash** (2), **glitter** (1).

twinkling *noun.* —*See* **flash** (2), **sparkling.**

twirl *verb.* —*See* **turn** (1).

twirl *noun.* —*See* **revolution** (1).

twist *verb.* **1.** To injure a bodily part by twisting ▶ sprain, strain, turn, wrench. [*Compare* **hurt.**] **2.** To alter the position of by a sharp, forcible twisting or turning movement ▶ wrench, wrest, wring. **3.** To twist agitatedly, as in pain, struggle, or embarrassment ▶ squirm, toss, writhe. [*Compare* **shake.**] —*See also* **deform, distort, weave, wind**[2]**.**

twist *noun.* An often sudden change or departure, as in a trend ▶ shift, tack, turn. [*Compare* **change, deviation.**] —*See also* **curl, wrinkle** (2).

twisting *adjective.* —*See* **indirect** (1), **winding.**

twit *verb.* —*See* **ridicule.**

twit *noun.* —*See* **drip** (2), **fool, taunt.**

twitch *verb.* To move or cause to move with a sudden abrupt motion ▶ jerk, lurch, snap, wrench, yank. [*Compare* **move.**]

twitch *noun.* —*See* **jerk, tremor** (2).

twitchy *adjective.* —*See* **edgy.**

twitter *verb.* —*See* **shake** (1).

twitter *noun.* —*See* **agitation** (2).

twittery *adjective.* —*See* **tremulous.**

two *noun.* —*See* **couple.**

two bits *noun.* A coin equal to one-fourth of the dollar of the United States and Canada ▶ quarter, quarter-dollar. —*See also* **peanuts.**

two-edged *adjective.* —*See* **ambiguous** (2).

two-faced *adjective.* Of or practicing hypocrisy ▶ Janus-faced, Pecksniffian, phony. —*See also* **dishonest.**

two-facedness *noun.* —*See* **hypocrisy.**

two-fisted *adjective. Informal* Indulging in drink to an excessive degree ▶ hard, heavy.

twofold *adjective.* Twice as much or as large ▶ double. —*See also* **double** (2).

twosome *noun.* —*See* **couple.**

two-time *verb. Informal* To be sexually unfaithful to another ▶ philander. *Informal:* cheat, fool around, mess around, play around.

type *noun.* —*See* **embodiment, kind**[2]**.**

typical *or* **typic** *adjective.* Having the nature of, constituting, or serving as a type ▶ archetypal, archetypic, archetypical, classic, classical, model, paradigmatic, prototypal, prototypic, prototypical, quintessential, representative. [*Compare* **epitome, model.**] —*See also* **common** (1), **conventional, special.**

typically *adverb.* —*See* **usually.**

typification *noun.* —*See* **embodiment.**

typify *verb.* —*See* **represent** (1).

tyrannical *or* **tyrannic** *adjective.* —*See* **absolute, authoritarian.**

tyrannize *verb.* To treat arbitrarily or cruelly ▶ grind (down), oppress, trample. [*Compare* **abuse, enslave, suppress.**] —*See also* **boss.**

tyrannous *adjective.* —*See* **absolute.**

tyranny *noun.* Absolute power, especially when exercised unjustly or cruelly ▶ authoritarianism, autocracy, despotism, dictatorship, fascism, imperiousness, oppression, totalitarianism. ***Idiom:*** reign of terror. [*Compare* **oppression.**] —*See also* **absolutism** (2).

tyrant *noun.* —*See* **authoritarian, dictator.**

tyro *noun.* —*See* **beginner.**

U

ubiquitous *adjective.* Ever present in all places ▶ omnipresent, universal. [*Compare* **rampant.**]

ugliness *noun.* The quality or condition of being ugly ▶ frightfulness, hideousness, homeliness, loathsomeness, monstrosity, monstrousness, odiousness, plainness, repulsiveness, unattractiveness, uncomeliness, unloveliness, unsightliness, vileness. —*See also* **mess** (2).

ugly *adjective.* Displeasing to the eye ▶ hideous, homely, ill-favored, monstrous, plain, unattractive, uncomely, unlovely, unsightly. ***Idioms:*** not much for looks, not much to look at, short on looks, ugly as sin. —*See also* **ill-tempered, offensive** (1), **rough** (2).

ugly *noun.* —*See* **mess** (2).

✚ **CORE SYNONYMS:** *ugly, hideous, ill-favored, unsightly.* These adjectives mean displeasing or offensive to the eye: *ugly furniture; a hideous scar; an ill-favored countenance; an unsightly billboard.*

◀ **ANTONYM:** *beautiful*

---

uh-huh *adverb.* —*See* **yes.**

ulterior *adjective.* **1.** Lying beyond what is obvious or avowed ▶ buried, concealed, covert, hidden, obscured, undisclosed, unrevealed. ***Idioms:*** under cover (*or* wraps). [*Compare* **hidden, secret, silent.**] **2.** Following something else in time ▶ after, later, posterior, subsequent. [*Compare* **following.**]

ulteriorly *adverb.* —*See* **later.**

ultimate *adjective.* Of or relating to a terminative condition, stage, or point ▶ final, last, latter, terminal. [*Compare* **climactic.**] —*See also* **definitive, elemental, extreme** (1), **last[1]** (1), **maximum.**

ultimate *noun.* —*See* **maximum.**

ultimately *adverb.* **1.** After a considerable length of time, usually after a delay ▶ eventually, finally. ***Idioms:*** at last (*or* long last), at the end of the day, in due course, in good (*or* due) time, in the end (*or* long run), in the fullness of time, when all is said and done. **2.** In conclusion ▶ conclusively, finally, last, lastly. ***Idioms:*** at last, in the end.

ultra *adjective.* —*See* **extreme** (2).

ultra *noun.* —*See* **extremist.**

ultraconservative *adjective.* Extremely or stubbornly conservative ▶ archconservative, die-hard, fossilized, mossbacked, old-line, old-school, reactionary, rear-guard, standpat. [*Compare* **conservative, extreme, stubborn.**]

ultraconservative *noun.* One who is extremely or stubbornly conservative ▶ archconservative, die-hard, fossil, mossback, reactionary, standpatter. [*Compare* **extremist.**]

ultraist *noun.* —*See* **extremist.**

ultraliberal *adjective.* Extremely or stubbornly liberal ▶ archliberal, bleeding-heart, do-good, Jacobinical, radical. *Slang:* crunchy-granola, goo-goo, pink. [*Compare* **extreme, liberal, stubborn.**]

ultraliberal *noun.* One who is extremely or stubbornly liberal ▶ archliberal, bleeding-heart, do-gooder, Jacobin, radical, yippie. *Informal:* tree-hugger. *Slang:* pinko. [*Compare* **extremist.**]

ultramodern *adjective.* —*See* **contemporary** (2).

ululate *verb.* —*See* **grieve, howl.**

ululation *noun.* —*See* **howl.**

umbra *noun.* Comparative darkness that results from the blocking of light rays ▶

penumbra, shade, shadow, shadiness. [*Compare* **dark, twilight.**]

umbrage *noun.* —*See* **offense.**

umbrageous *adjective.* —*See* **shady** (2).

umpire *noun.* —*See* **judge** (2).

umpire *verb.* —*See* **judge.**

umpteen *adjective.* —*See* **many.**

unabashed *adjective.* —*See* **impudent.**

unabbreviated *adjective.* —*See* **complete** (2).

unable *adjective.* Lacking power or strength ▶ helpless, impotent, powerless. —*See also* **ineffectual** (2), **inefficient.**

unabridged *adjective.* —*See* **complete** (2).

unacceptable *adjective.* —*See* **objectionable, unbearable.**

unaccompanied *adjective.* —*See* **solitary.**

unaccountable *adjective.* That cannot be explained ▶ inexplicable, unexplainable. [*Compare* **mysterious.**]

unachievable *adjective.* —*See* **impossible.**

unacquainted *adjective.* —*See* **ignorant** (3).

unadorned *adjective.* —*See* **bare** (1), **rustic.**

unadulterated *adjective.* —*See* **natural** (1), **pure.**

unadvantageous *adjective.* —*See* **unfavorable** (1).

unaffected *adjective.* —*See* **artless, cold** (2), **genuine.**

unafraid *adjective.* —*See* **brave.**

unalterable *adjective.* That cannot be revoked or undone ▶ irretrievable, irreversible, irrrevocable. ***Idiom:*** beyond recall. [*Compare* **unchangeable.**] —*See also* **immutable.**

unambiguous *adjective.* —*See* **definite** (2), **definite** (1), **sharp** (2).

unambitious *adjective.* Having or expressing feelings of humility ▶ humble, lowly, meek, modest. [*Compare* **deferential.**]

unanimity *noun.* —*See* **agreement** (2).

unanimous *adjective.* Being in or characterized by complete agreement ▶ accordant, agreeing, assenting, concordant, consensual, consonant, harmonious, like-minded, solid, undivided, unified, universal. ***Idioms:*** as one, at one, of one mind, with one voice. [*Compare* **agreeable, common, cooperative.**]

unanimousness *noun.* —*See* **agreement** (2).

unanticipated *adjective.* —*See* **accidental.**

unapparent *adjective.* —*See* **hidden** (1).

unappeasable *adjective.* —*See* **voracious.**

unappetizing *adjective.* —*See* **unpalatable.**

unappreciated *adjective.* Not apt to be appreciated ▶ thankless, ungrateful, unthankful.

unappreciative *adjective.* —*See* **thankless** (1).

unapproachable *adjective.* —*See* **cool, inaccessible** (1).

unapt *adjective.* —*See* **doubtful** (1), **improper** (2).

unassailability *noun.* —*See* **safety.**

unassailable *adjective.* —*See* **certain** (2), **safe** (2).

unassuming *adjective.* —*See* **inconspicuous, modest** (1), **shy**[1].

unassumingness *noun.* —*See* **modesty** (1), **modesty** (2).

unattached *adjective.* —*See* **single.**

unattainable *adjective.* —*See* **impossible, inaccessible** (1).

unattractive *adjective.* —*See* **ugly.**

unattractiveness *noun.* —*See* **ugliness.**

unavailable *adjective.* —*See* **inaccessible** (1).

unavailing *adjective.* —*See* **futile.**

unavoidable *adjective.* —*See* **certain** (1).

unawake *adjective.* —*See* **sleeping.**

unaware *adjective.* —*See* **ignorant** (3).

unawareness *noun.* —*See* **ignorance** (2).

unawares *adverb.* Without adequate preparation ▶ aback, short, unawarely. ***Idioms:*** by surprise, off guard, with one's pants down.

unbalance *verb.* —*See* **derange.**

unbalance *noun.* —*See* **insanity.**

unbalanced *adjective.* —*See* **insane.**

unbarred *adjective.* —*See* **clear** (3).

unbearable *adjective.* So unpleasant or painful as not to be endured or tolerated ▶ impossible, insufferable, insupportable, intolerable, unacceptable, unendurable, unsufferable, unsupportable. [*Compare* **tormenting.**]

unbecoming *adjective.* —*See* **coarse** (1), **improper** (1), **improper** (2).

unbecomingness *noun.* —*See* **impropriety** (1).

unbefitting *adjective.* —*See* **improper** (1), **improper** (2).

unbelief *noun.* —*See* **atheism, disbelief.**

unbelievable *adjective.* —*See* **astonishing, implausible, incredible.**

unbeliever *noun.* —*See* **skeptic.**

unbelieving *adjective.* —*See* **incredulous.**

unbend *verb.* —*See* **rest**[1] (1).

unbendable *adjective.* —*See* **stubborn** (1).

unbending *adjective.* —*See* **firm**[1] (3), **rigid, stubborn** (1).

unbiased *adjective.* —*See* **fair**[1] (1), **neutral** (1).

unbind *verb.* —*See* **undo.**

unblamable *adjective.* —*See* **exemplary, innocent** (2).

unblemished *adjective.* —*See* **good** (2), **innocent** (1), **perfect.**

unblended *adjective.* —*See* **straight.**

unblock *verb.* To rid of obstructions ▶ clear, free, open, remove. [*Compare* **rid.**]

unblocked *adjective.* —*See* **clear** (3).

unblushing *adjective.* —*See* **impudent.**

unbodied *adjective.* —*See* **immaterial.**

unbosom *verb.* To tell in confidence ▶ breathe, confide, share, whisper. [*Compare* **communicate, reveal, say.**]

unbound *adjective.* —*See* **loose** (1).

unbounded *adjective.* —*See* **endless** (1), **utter**[2].

unboundedness *noun.* —*See* **infinity** (1).

unbridled *adjective.* Out of control ▶ amuck, runaway, uncontrolled. ***Idioms:*** out of hand, running wild. —*See also* **abandoned** (2), **excessive, loose** (2).

unbroken *adjective.* —*See* **continual, good** (2), **wild** (2).

unburden *verb.* —*See* **rid.**

uncalled-for *adjective.* —*See* **unnecessary, wanton** (2).

uncanny *adjective.* —*See* **weird.**

uncaring *adjective.* —*See* **callous.**

unceasing *adjective.* —*See* **continual.**

uncensored *adjective.* —*See* **complete** (2).

unceremonious *adjective.* —*See* **easygoing.**

unceremoniousness *noun.* —*See* **ease** (1).

uncertain *adjective.* —*See* **ambiguous** (1), **ambiguous** (2), **capricious, changeable** (1), **debatable, doubtful** (2), **indefinite** (2), **shady** (1).

uncertainty *noun.* —*See* **doubt, vagueness.**

unchained *adjective.* —*See* **loose** (2).

unchangeable *adjective.* —*See* **immutable.**

unchanging *adjective.* Having no change or variation; remaining unchanged ▶ changeless, consistent, constant, equable, even, firm, fixed, flat, immutable, invariable, invariant, permanent, regular, same, set, steady, unfailing, uniform, unvarying. ***Idioms:*** cast (*or* etched *or* fixed *or* set) in stone, steady as she goes. [*Compare* **continual, continuing, endless.**]

unchaste *adjective.* —*See* **impure** (1), **wanton** (1).

unchecked *adjective.* —*See* **loose** (2).

uncivil *adjective.* —*See* **offensive** (2), **rude** (2).

uncivility *noun.* —*See* **inhospitality.**

uncivilized *adjective.* Not civilized ▶ barbarian, barbaric, barbarous, brutish, primitive, rude, savage, uncultivated, uncultured, untamed, wild. *—See also* **coarse** (1).

unclad *adjective.* *—See* **nude.**

unclasp *verb.* *—See* **undo.**

unclean *or* **uncleanly** *adjective.* *—See* **dirty, impure** (1).

uncleanliness *or* **uncleanness** *noun.* *—See* **contamination, dirtiness.**

unclear *adjective.* Not clearly perceptible; difficult to see clearly ▶ blear, bleary, blurry, cloudy, dim, faint, filmy, foggy, fuzzy, hazy, indefinite, indistinct, misty, murky, obscure, shadowy, undistinct, vague. *—See also* **ambiguous** (1), **ambiguous** (2).

unclearness *noun.* *—See* **vagueness.**

unclose *verb.* *—See* **open** (1).

unclothe *verb.* To remove the clothing or covering from ▶ disrobe, strip, undress. *—See also* **reveal.**

unclouded *adjective.* *—See* **clear** (2).

uncoil *verb.* *—See* **unwind.**

uncomeliness *noun.* *—See* **ugliness.**

uncomely *adjective.* *—See* **ugly.**

uncomfortable *adjective.* Causing discomfort ▶ comfortless, thorny, uncomforting. *Informal:* uncomfy. [*Compare* **disturbing, painful, tormenting.**] *—See also* **awkward** (3).

uncomfy *adjective.* *—See* **uncomfortable.**

uncommitted *adjective.* *—See* **neutral** (1).

uncommon *adjective.* *—See* **exceptional, infrequent.**

uncommonly *adverb.* *—See* **infrequently, unusually.**

uncommonness *noun.* *—See* **uniqueness.**

uncommunicative *adjective.* *—See* **cool, taciturn.**

uncommunicativeness *noun.* *—See* **reserve** (1).

uncompassionate *adjective.* *—See* **callous.**

uncompelled *adjective.* *—See* **voluntary.**

uncompensated *adjective.* *—See* **unpaid.**

uncompliant *adjective.* *—See* **stubborn** (1).

uncomplimentary *adjective.* *—See* **disparaging.**

uncomprehending *adjective.* *—See* **blind** (3).

uncomprehensible *adjective.* *—See* **incomprehensible.**

uncompromising *adjective.* *—See* **firm**[1] (3), **graphic** (1), **severe** (1), **stubborn** (1).

unconceivable *adjective.* *—See* **implausible.**

unconcern *noun.* *—See* **apathy, detachment** (2).

unconcerned *adjective.* *—See* **apathetic, careless, detached** (1).

unconditional *adjective.* Without limitations or mitigating conditions ▶ absolute, full, unconditioned, unqualified, unreserved. [*Compare* **utter**[2].] *—See also* **implicit** (2).

unconditioned *adjective.* *—See* **unconditional.**

unconfined *adjective.* *—See* **loose** (2).

unconfirmed *adjective.* *—See* **debatable.**

uncongenial *adjective.* *—See* **inharmonious** (1), **unpleasant.**

uncongeniality *noun.* *—See* **inhospitality.**

unconnected *adjective.* *—See* **irrelevant.**

unconquerability *noun.* *—See* **safety.**

unconquerable *adjective.* **1.** Incapable of being conquered or subjugated ▶ indomitable, invincible, unbeatable, undefeatable. [*Compare* **insuperable.**] **2.** Incapable of being negotiated or overcome ▶ impassable, insuperable, insurmountable. [*Compare* **impossible.**] *—See also* **safe** (2).

unconscionable *adjective.* *—See* **outrageous, steep**[1] (2), **unscrupulous.**

unconscious *adjective.* Lacking consciousness ▶ cold, comatose, insensible, out, senseless. ***Idioms:*** blacked out, out like a light, out cold. [*Compare* **dead, inanimate.**] —*See also* **ignorant** (3).

unconsciousness *noun.* —*See* **ignorance** (2).

unconsidered *adjective.* —*See* **rash**[1].

unconspicuous *adjective.* —*See* **inconspicuous.**

unconstrained *adjective.* —*See* **abandoned** (2).

uncontaminated *adjective.* —*See* **fresh** (1).

uncontrollability *or* **uncontrollableness** *noun.* —*See* **unruliness.**

uncontrollable *adjective.* —*See* **unruly.**

uncontrolled *adjective.* Out of control ▶ amuck, runaway, unbridled. ***Idioms:*** out of hand, running wild. [*Compare* **loose.**] —*See also* **abandoned** (2), **erratic.**

unconventional *adjective.* —*See* **eccentric, unusual.**

unconventionally *adverb.* —*See* **unusually.**

unconversant *adjective.* —*See* **inexperienced.**

unconvinced *adjective.* —*See* **incredulous.**

unconvincing *adjective.* —*See* **implausible.**

uncooked *adjective.* Not cooked ▶ raw.

uncool *adjective.* —*See* **conventional.**

uncoordinated *adjective.* —*See* **awkward** (1).

uncorporal *adjective.* —*See* **immaterial.**

uncorrupted *adjective.* —*See* **innocent** (1).

uncountable *adjective.* —*See* **incalculable.**

uncouple *verb.* —*See* **detach, divide.**

uncoupling *noun.* —*See* **detachment** (1).

uncouth *adjective.* —*See* **coarse** (1).

uncover *verb.* To find by investigation ▶ dig (up *or* out), disinter, exhume, turn up, unearth. ***Idiom:*** bring to light. [*Compare* **discover.**] —*See also* **bare, betray** (2), **reveal.**

uncovered *adjective.* —*See* **open** (2).

uncreative *adjective.* —*See* **sterile** (2).

uncritical *adjective.* —*See* **superficial.**

unction *noun.* —*See* **oil, ointment.**

unctuous *adjective.* Affectedly, smugly, or self-servingly earnest ▶ fulsome, oily, oleaginous, sleek, smarmy. [*Compare* **flattering, glib, servile.**] —*See also* **fatty.**

✣ **CORE SYNONYMS:** *unctuous, fulsome, oily, oleaginous, smarmy.* These adjectives mean affectedly, smugly, or self-servingly earnest: *an unctuous toady; gave the dictator a fulsome introduction; oily praise; oleaginous hypocrisy; smarmy self-importance.*

---

uncultivated *adjective.* —*See* **coarse** (1), **ignorant** (1), **uncivilized, wild** (1).

uncultured *adjective.* —*See* **coarse** (1), **uncivilized.**

uncut *adjective.* —*See* **complete** (2).

undamaged *adjective.* —*See* **good** (2).

undaunted *adjective.* —*See* **brave.**

undauntedness *noun.* —*See* **courage.**

undeceive *verb.* —*See* **disabuse.**

undecided *adjective.* —*See* **doubtful** (2), **indefinite** (2).

undeclared *adjective.* —*See* **silent** (2).

undecorated *adjective.* —*See* **bare** (1).

undefended *adjective.* —*See* **insecure** (1).

undefiled *adjective.* —*See* **innocent** (1).

undemanding *adjective.* Requiring little effort or exertion ▶ easy, light, moderate. *Informal:* cushy, soft.

undemonstrated *adjective.* —*See* **untried.**

undemonstrative *adjective.* —*See* **cool.**

undeniable *adjective.* —*See* **certain** (2).

undependable *adjective.* **1.** Not to be depended on ▶ fair-weather, irresponsible, unreliable, untrustworthy. [*Compare* **capricious, changeable.**] **2.** So weak or defective as to be liable to fail ▶ trick, unreliable. [*Compare* **defective, weak.**]

under *adjective.* —*See* **insufficient, minor** (1).

underage¹ *noun.* —*See* **shortage.**
underage² *adjective.* Not yet a legal adult ▶ juvenile, minor.
underbrush *noun.* —*See* **brush².**
undercover *adjective.* —*See* **secret** (1).
undercurrent *noun.* —*See* **hint** (1).
underdeveloped *adjective.* —*See* **backward** (2).
underdog *noun.* —*See* **unfortunate.**
underestimate *verb.* —*See* **miscalculate.**
undergird *verb.* —*See* **base¹, support** (2).
undergo *verb.* —*See* **experience.**
underground *adjective.* Located or operating beneath the earth's surface ▶ belowground, buried, hypogeal, hypogean, hypogeous, subterranean, subterrestrial.
underground *noun.* A clandestine organization of freedom fighters in an oppressed land ▶ opposition, resistance.
underhand *or* **underhanded** *adjective.* Marked by or done in a deceptive or secret manner ▶ devious, disingenuous, duplicitous, guileful, indirect, left-handed, lubricious, shifty, sneaky, subtle, unscrupulous. [*Compare* **artful, secret, shady, stealthy.**]
underhandedness *noun.* —*See* **dishonesty** (2).
underline *verb.* —*See* **emphasize.**
underling *noun.* —*See* **subordinate.**
underlying *adjective.* —*See* **elemental, radical.**
undermanned *adjective.* Having fewer workers or participants than are needed ▶ short-handed, short-staffed, understaffed.
undermine *verb.* To damage, destroy, or defeat by sabotage ▶ sabotage, subvert. [*Compare* **destroy, disorder.**] —*See also* **enervate.**
undermining *noun.* Treacherous action to defeat or do harm to an endeavor ▶ sabotage, subversion. [*Compare* **defeat, destruction.**]
undermost *adjective.* —*See* **bottom.**
underneath *noun.* —*See* **bottom** (1).
underpin *verb.* —*See* **base¹, support** (2).
underpinning *noun.* —*See* **base¹** (2), **basis** (1), **support.**
underprivileged *adjective.* —*See* **depressed** (2).
underprivileged *noun.* —*See* **unfortunate.**
underprop *verb.* —*See* **support** (2).
underscore *verb.* —*See* **emphasize.**
undersexed *adjective.* —*See* **frigid.**
underside *noun.* —*See* **bottom** (1).
undersign *verb.* —*See* **sign.**
undersized *adjective.* —*See* **little.**
understaffed *adjective.* Having fewer workers or participants than are needed ▶ short-handed, short-staffed, undermanned.
understand *verb.* **1.** To perceive and recognize the meaning of ▶ accept, apprehend, catch (on), compass, comprehend, conceive, fathom, follow, get, grasp, make out, read, see, sense, take, take in. *Informal:* hear, savvy. *Slang:* dig. ***Idioms:*** get (*or* have) a handle on, get the picture. [*Compare* **know.**] **2.** To understand or be sensitive to another's feelings or ideas ▶ empathize, sympathize. ***Idioms:*** feel someone's pain, put oneself (*or* walk) in someone else's shoes. —*See also* **infer.**

✚ **CORE SYNONYMS:** *understand, comprehend, apprehend, grasp.* These verbs denote perception and recognition of the nature and meaning of something. Both *understand* and *comprehend* stress complete realization and knowledge: *"No one who has not had the responsibility can really understand what it is like to be President"* (Harry S. Truman). *"To comprehend is to know a thing as well as that thing can be known"* (John Donne). *Apprehend* denotes both mental and intuitive awareness: *"Intelligence is quickness to apprehend"* (Alfred North Whitehead). To *grasp* is to seize an idea firmly: *"We have grasped the mystery of* *the atom and rejected the Sermon on the Mount"* (Omar N. Bradley).

---

understandable *adjective.* Capable of being readily understood ▶ appreciable, apprehensible, coherent, comprehensible, fathomable, intelligible, knowable, lucid, unambiguous. *—See also* **pardonable.**

understanding *noun.* **1.** Intellectual hold ▶ apprehension, comprehension, grasp, grip, hold. [*Compare* **knowledge.**] **2.** A very close understanding between persons ▶ empathy, sympathy. **3.** The sum of what has been perceived, discovered, or inferred ▶ knowledge, lore, wisdom. [*Compare* **actuality.**] *—See also* **agreement** (1), **intelligence.**

understanding *adjective. —See* **sympathetic.**

understood *adjective. —See* **implicit** (1).

undersurface *noun. —See* **bottom** (1).

undertake *verb. —See* **assume, pledge** (2), **start** (1).

undertaking *noun.* Something undertaken, especially something requiring extensive planning and work ▶ endeavor, enterprise, project, venture. [*Compare* **task.**] *—See also* **attempt, mission** (1).

undertone *noun. —See* **color** (1), **hint** (1).

underwhelming *adjective. —See* **disappointing.**

underwrite *verb. —See* **finance.**

underwriter *noun. —See* **sponsor.**

undescribable *adjective. —See* **unspeakable** (1).

undesigned *adjective. —See* **unintentional.**

undesirable *adjective. —See* **objectionable, unwelcome.**

undesired *adjective. —See* **unwelcome.**

undetected *adjective.* Not found ▶ undiscovered, unexposed, unfound.

undetermined *adjective. —See* **indefinite** (1), **indefinite** (2).

undeveloped *adjective. —See* **backward** (2), **fresh** (1).

undeviating *adjective. —See* **direct** (1), **literal.**

undevised *adjective. —See* **unintentional.**

undiluted *adjective. —See* **pure, straight.**

undiplomatic *adjective. —See* **tactless.**

undirected *adjective. —See* **aimless.**

undisciplined *adjective. —See* **unruly.**

undisclosed *adjective. —See* **ulterior** (1).

undiscovered *adjective.* Not found ▶ undetected, unexposed, unfound.

undisputable *adjective. —See* **certain** (2).

undistinct *adjective. —See* **unclear.**

undistinguished *adjective. —See* **inconspicuous, obscure** (2), **ordinary.**

undivided *adjective. —See* **concentrated** (1), **unanimous.**

undo *verb.* To free from ties or fasteners ▶ disengage, loose, loosen, release, slip, unbind, unclasp, unfasten, unloose, unloosen, untie. *—See also* **cancel** (1), **destroy** (1), **enervate, open** (1).

undoing *noun. —See* **destruction, ruin** (1).

undomesticated *adjective. —See* **wild** (1), **wild** (2).

undoubted *adjective. —See* **authentic** (1).

undoubtedly *adverb. —See* **absolutely, yes.**

undoubting *adjective. —See* **implicit** (2), **sure** (1).

undress *verb. —See* **bare.**

undress *noun. —See* **nudity.**

undue *adjective. —See* **excessive.**

undulate *verb. —See* **crawl** (1), **sway, wave** (1).

unduly *adverb.* Too much ▶ disproportionately, excessively, extravagantly, extremely, inordinately, overly, overmuch. *Informal:* super.

undying *adjective.* Not being subject to death ▶ deathless, immortal. [*Compare* **endless.**] *—See also* **continual.**

unearth *verb.* —*See* **discover, uncover.**
unearthly *adjective.* —*See* **supernatural** (1), **weird.**
unease *or* **uneasiness** *noun.* —*See* **anxiety** (1), **restlessness.**
uneasy *adjective.* Affording no quiet, repose, or rest ▶ restless, unquiet, unsettled. [*Compare* **edgy, wakeful.**] —*See also* **anxious, awkward** (3).
uneatable *adjective.* —*See* **unpalatable.**
uneconomical *adjective.* —*See* **extravagant.**
unedited *adjective.* —*See* **complete** (2).
uneducated *adjective.* —*See* **ignorant** (1).
unemotional *adjective.* —*See* **cold** (2).
unemployable *adjective.* —*See* **unworkable.**
unemployed *adjective.* Having no job ▶ idle, jobless, unoccupied, workless. ***Idioms:*** out of a job (*or* employ *or* work). —*See also* **idle** (1).
unencouraging *adjective.* —*See* **bleak** (2).
unending *adjective.* —*See* **continual, endless** (2), **long**[1] (2).
unendingly *adverb.* —*See* **forever.**
unendurable *adjective.* —*See* **unbearable.**
unenlightened *adjective.* —*See* **ignorant** (2), **ignorant** (3).
unenthusiastic *adjective.* Lacking warmth, interest, enthusiasm, or involvement ▶ halfhearted, Laodicean, lukewarm, tepid. [*Compare* **apathetic, cold, cool.**]
unequal *adjective.* —*See* **inefficient, unfair.**
unequaled *adjective.* —*See* **unique.**
unequivocal *adjective.* —*See* **definite** (1), **sharp** (2), **utter**[2].
unerring *adjective.* —*See* **sure** (2).
unessential *adjective.* —*See* **unnecessary.**
unethical *adjective.* —*See* **unscrupulous.**
uneven *adjective.* Lacking consistency or regularity in quality or performance ▶ erratic, inconsistent, patchy, spasmodic, spotty, unsteady, variable. [*Compare* **intermittent.**] —*See also* **rough** (1), **unfair.**
unevenness *noun.* —*See* **irregularity.**
unexampled *adjective.* —*See* **unique.**
unexceptionable *adjective.* —*See* **acceptable** (1).
unexceptional *adjective.* —*See* **ordinary.**
unexpected *adjective.* —*See* **accidental.**
unexpectedly *adverb.* —*See* **unusually.**
unexplainable *adjective.* That cannot be explained ▶ inexplicable, unaccountable. [*Compare* **mysterious.**]
unexposed *adjective.* Not found ▶ undetected, undiscovered, unfound.
unexpressed *adjective.* —*See* **implicit** (1), **silent** (2).
unexpurgated *adjective.* —*See* **complete** (2).
unfailing *adjective.* —*See* **continual, sure** (2), **tireless, unchanging.**
unfair *adjective.* Not fair, right, or just ▶ dirty, discriminatory, inequitable, preferential, unequal, uneven, unjust, wrong. [*Compare* **biased, unscrupulous.**]
unfairness *noun.* Lack of equality, as of opportunity, treatment, or status ▶ discrimination, inequality, unjustness. [*Compare* **bias.**] —*See also* **injustice** (2).
unfaithful *adjective.* —*See* **faithless.**
unfaithfulness *noun.* —*See* **faithlessness.**
unfaltering *adjective.* —*See* **implicit** (2).
unfamiliar *adjective.* —*See* **ignorant** (3), **new.**
unfamiliarity *noun.* —*See* **ignorance** (2).
unfasten *verb.* —*See* **open** (1), **undo.**
unfastened *adjective.* —*See* **loose** (1).
unfathomable *adjective.* —*See* **incalculable, incomprehensible.**
unfavorable *adjective.* **1.** Tending to discourage, retard, or make more difficult ▶ adverse, antagonistic, disadvantageous, negative, unadvantageous, unsat-

isfactory, untoward. [*Compare* **inhospitable.**] **2.** Not encouraging life or growth ▶ adverse, hostile, inhospitable. [*Compare* **severe.**] —*See also* **fateful** (1), **opposing.**

unfeeling *adjective.* —*See* **callous, dead** (2).

unfeigned *adjective.* —*See* **genuine.**

unfettered *adjective.* —*See* **loose** (2).

unfinished *adjective.* —*See* **partial** (1), **rough** (4).

unfit *adjective.* —*See* **improper** (2), **inefficient.**

unfit *verb.* To make incapable, as of doing a job ▶ disable, disqualify.

unfitness *noun.* —*See* **impropriety** (1).

unflagging *adjective.* —*See* **diligent, tireless.**

unflappability *noun.* —*See* **balance** (2).

unflappable *adjective.* —*See* **calm.**

unflawed *adjective.* —*See* **perfect.**

unflinching *adjective.* —*See* **brave, firm**[1] (3).

unfold *verb.* —*See* **develop** (2), **spread** (1).

unfolding *noun.* —*See* **development.**

unforbearing *adjective.* Being unable or unwilling to endure irritation or opposition, for example ▶ impatient, intolerant, unindulgent. [*Compare* **ill-tempered, intolerant.**] —*See also* **vindictive.**

unforced *adjective.* —*See* **voluntary.**

unforgivable *adjective.* —*See* **inexcusable.**

unforgiving *adjective.* —*See* **vindictive.**

unformed *adjective.* —*See* **shapeless.**

unfortunate *adjective.* **1.** Involving or undergoing chance misfortune ▶ hapless, hexed, ill-fated, ill-starred, jinxed, luckless, star-crossed, stricken, unhappy, unlucky, untoward. **2.** Characterized by inappropriateness and gracelessness, especially in expression ▶ awkward, ill-chosen, inappropriate, inept, infelicitous, unhappy. [*Compare* **improper, inconvenient, unwise.**] —*See also* **deplorable.**

unfortunate *noun.* A person living under very unhappy circumstances ▶ loser, miserable, underdog, underprivileged, wretch.

✚ **CORE SYNONYMS:** *unfortunate, hapless, ill-fated, ill-starred, luckless, unlucky.* These adjectives mean involving or undergoing chance misfortune: *an unfortunate turn of events; a hapless victim; an ill-fated business venture; an ill-starred romance; a luckless suitor; an unlucky accident.*

◀ **ANTONYM:** *fortunate*

---

unfortunateness *noun.* —*See* **misfortune.**

unfound *adjective.* Not found ▶ undetected, undiscovered, unexposed.

unfounded *adjective.* —*See* **baseless.**

unfoundedly *adverb.* Without basis or foundation in fact ▶ baselessly, groundlessly, unwarrantedly.

unfrequented *adjective.* —*See* **lonely** (1).

unfriendliness *noun.* —*See* **inhospitality.**

unfriendly *adjective.* Feeling or showing unfriendliness ▶ hostile, inimical. [*Compare* **mean**[2].]

unfruitful *adjective.* —*See* **barren** (1), **barren** (2).

unfurl *verb.* —*See* **develop** (2), **spread** (1).

ungainly *adjective.* —*See* **awkward** (1), **awkward** (2).

ungodly *adjective.* —*See* **atheistic, outrageous.**

ungovernable *adjective.* —*See* **unruly.**

ungovernableness *noun.* —*See* **unruliness.**

ungoverned *adjective.* —*See* **abandoned** (2).

ungraceful *adjective.* —*See* **awkward** (1).

ungracious *adjective.* —*See* **rude** (2).

ungraciousness *noun.* —*See* **inhospitality.**

ungrateful *adjective.* Not apt to be appreciated ▶ thankless, unappreciated, unthankful. —*See also* **thankless** (1).

ungrudging *adjective.* —*See* **generous** (1).

unguarded *adjective.* —*See* **insecure** (1).

unguent *noun.* —*See* **ointment.**

unhandy *adjective.* Not accessible or handy ▶ inaccessible, unhandy. ***Idioms:*** beyond reach, out of reach, out of the way. [*Compare* **remote.**] —*See also* **awkward** (2).

unhappiness *noun.* —*See* **depression** (2).

unhappy *adjective.* —*See* **depressed** (1), **unfortunate** (1), **unfortunate** (2).

unharmed *adjective.* —*See* **good** (2), **safe** (1).

unharmonious *adjective.* —*See* **inharmonious** (1), **inharmonious** (2).

unhealthful *adjective.* —*See* **unwholesome** (1).

unhealthy *adjective.* —*See* **corrupt** (1), **harmful, morbid, sick** (1), **unwholesome** (1), **unwholesome** (2).

unheard-of *adjective.* —*See* **obscure** (2).

unheeding *adjective.* —*See* **careless.**

unhesitating *adjective.* —*See* **implicit** (2), **intent.**

unhindered *adjective.* —*See* **clear** (3), **loose** (2).

unhinge *verb.* —*See* **derange.**

unhinged *adjective.* —*See* **insane.**

unhorse *verb.* —*See* **overthrow.**

unhospitable *adjective.* —*See* **forbidding.**

unhurried *adjective.* —*See* **deliberate** (3).

unhurt *adjective.* —*See* **good** (2), **safe** (1).

unhygienic *adjective.* —*See* **unwholesome** (1).

unidentified *adjective.* —*See* **anonymous.**

unification *noun.* A bringing together into a whole ▶ coalition, consolidation, union, unity. —*See also* **combination.**

unified *adjective.* —*See* **unanimous.**

uniform *adjective.* —*See* **like**[2], **unchanging.**

uniformity *noun.* —*See* **changelessness, consistency, likeness** (1).

uniformness *noun.* —*See* **likeness** (1).

unify *verb.* —*See* **combine** (1), **harmonize** (2).

unimaginable *adjective.* —*See* **impossible, incredible.**

unimaginative *adjective.* —*See* **dull** (1), **sterile** (2), **trite.**

unimpaired *adjective.* —*See* **good** (2).

unimpeachable *adjective.* —*See* **definite** (3).

unimpeded *adjective.* —*See* **clear** (3).

unimportance *noun.* —*See* **obscurity, trifle.**

unimportant *adjective.* —*See* **trivial.**

unimpressionable *adjective.* —*See* **cold** (2).

unindulgent *adjective.* Being unable or unwilling to endure irritation or opposition, for example ▶ impatient, intolerant, unforbearing. [*Compare* **ill-tempered, intolerant.**]

uninformed *adjective.* —*See* **ignorant** (2), **ignorant** (3).

uninhabited *adjective.* —*See* **lonely** (1), **open** (4).

uninhibited *adjective.* —*See* **abandoned** (2).

uninitiate *adjective.* —*See* **inexperienced.**

uninitiate *noun.* —*See* **amateur.**

uninitiated *adjective.* —*See* **inexperienced.**

uninjured *adjective.* —*See* **good** (2), **safe** (1).

uninspired *adjective.* —*See* **dull** (1), **sterile** (2), **trite.**

uninstructed *adjective.* —*See* **ignorant** (1).

unintelligent *adjective.* —*See* **stupid.**

unintelligible *adjective.* —*See* **incomprehensible.**

unintended *adjective.* —*See* **accidental, unintentional.**

unintentional *adjective.* Not intended ▶ accidental, inadvertent, involuntary, undesigned, undevised, unintended, unmeant, unplanned, unthinking, unwitting.

uninterest *noun.* —*See* **apathy.**

uninterested *adjective.* —*See* **apathetic, detached** (1).

uninteresting *adjective.* —*See* **boring.**

uninterrupted *adjective.* —*See* **continual.**

uninventive *adjective.* —*See* **sterile** (2).

uninvited *adjective.* —*See* **unwelcome.**

uninviting *adjective.* —*See* **forbidding.**

uninvolved *adjective.* —*See* **detached** (1), **neutral** (1).

uninvolvment *noun.* —*See* **detachment** (2).

union *noun.* **1.** A group of people who are united in a relationship and having some interest, activity, or purpose in common ▶ association, club, confederation, congress, federation, fellowship, fraternity, guild, league, order, organization, society, sorority. [*Compare* **group.**] **2.** An identity or coincidence of interests, purposes, or sympathies among the members of a group ▶ concord, oneness, solidarity, unity. —*See also* **alliance, combination, joint** (1), **marriage, unification.**

uniplanar *adjective.* —*See* **even** (2).

unique *adjective.* Without equal or rival ▶ alone, incomparable, matchless, nonpareil, only, peerless, singular, unequaled, unexampled, unexcelled, unmatched, unparalleled, unrivaled, unsurpassed. ***Idioms:*** beyond compare, in a class by itself, second to none. [*Compare* **best, exceptional.**] —*See also* **lone, unusual.**

uniquely *adverb.* —*See* **unusually.**

uniqueness *noun.* The quality or condition of being unique ▶ matchlessness, oneness, peerlessness, singleness, singularity, uncommonness. [*Compare* **individuality.**] —*See also* **identity** (1), **novelty** (1).

unison *noun.* —*See* **agreement** (2).

unit *noun.* —*See* **band²**, **degree** (1), **force** (3).

unite *verb.* To come together from different directions ▶ close, converge, join, meet. —*See also* **band²**, **combine** (1), **cooperate, marry.**

united *adjective.* —*See* **cooperative.**

unity *noun.* **1.** The condition of being one ▶ oneness, singleness, singularity. [*Compare* **completeness.**] **2.** An identity or coincidence of interests, purposes, or sympathies among the members of a group ▶ concord, oneness, solidarity, union. [*Compare* **alliance, union.**] —*See also* **agreement** (2), **combination, unification.**

universal *adjective.* **1.** So pervasive and all-inclusive as to exist in or affect the whole world ▶ catholic, cosmic, cosmopolitan, ecumenical, global, pandemic, planetary, worldwide. **2.** Ever present in all places ▶ omnipresent, ubiquitous. [*Compare* **rampant.**] —*See also* **general** (1), **unanimous.**

universal *noun.* —*See* **law** (3).

universe *noun.* The totality of all existing things ▶ cosmos, creation, macrocosm, nature, wide world, world. ***Idiom:*** sum of all things. [*Compare* **environment.**] —*See also* **humankind.**

unjudicious *adjective.* —*See* **improper** (1).

unjust *adjective.* —*See* **unfair.**

unjustifiable *adjective.* —*See* **inexcusable.**

unjustness *noun.* Lack of equality, as of opportunity, treatment, or status ▶ discrimination, inequality, unfairness. [*Compare* **bias.**] —*See also* **injustice** (2).

unkempt *adjective.* —*See* **messy** (1).

unknowing *adjective.* —*See* **ignorant** (3).

unknown *adjective.* —*See* **anonymous, obscure** (2).

unlade *verb.* —*See* **rid.**

unlawful *adjective.* Contrary to accepted, especially moral conventions ▶ criminal, illicit. [*Compare* **forbidden.**]

—*See also* **criminal** (1), **illegal, illegitimate.**

unlawfulness *noun.* The state or quality of being illegal ▶ illegality, illegitimacy, illicitness, lawlessness.

unlearned *adjective.* —*See* **ignorant** (1), **instinctive.**

unlike *adjective.* —*See* **different.**

unlikely *adjective.* —*See* **doubtful** (1), **implausible.**

unlikeness *noun.* —*See* **difference.**

unlimited *adjective.* —*See* **endless** (1), **utter**[2].

unlimitedness *noun.* —*See* **infinity** (1).

unlit *adjective.* —*See* **black** (2).

unload *verb.* —*See* **rid, unload.**

unloose *or* **unloosen** *verb.* —*See* **undo.**

unloveliness *noun.* —*See* **ugliness.**

unlovely *adjective.* —*See* **ugly.**

unluckiness *noun.* —*See* **misfortune.**

unlucky *adjective.* —*See* **disappointing, fateful** (1), **unfortunate** (1).

unmanageability *noun.* —*See* **unruliness.**

unmanageable *adjective.* —*See* **awkward** (2), **unruly.**

unmanliness *noun.* —*See* **cowardice, effeminacy.**

unmanly *adjective.* —*See* **cowardly, effeminate.**

unmannered *or* **unmannerly** *adjective.* —*See* **disrespectful, rude.**

unmarked *adjective.* —*See* **perfect.**

unmarred *adjective.* —*See* **good** (2).

unmarried *adjective.* —*See* **single.**

unmask *verb.* —*See* **reveal.**

unmatched *adjective.* —*See* **unique.**

unmeant *adjective.* —*See* **unintentional.**

unmentionable *adjective.* —*See* **unspeakable** (2).

unmerciful *adjective.* —*See* **callous.**

unmindful *adjective.* —*See* **careless.**

unmistakable *adjective.* —*See* **obvious, sharp** (2).

unmitigated *adjective.* —*See* **utter**[2].

unmixed *adjective.* —*See* **pure, straight.**

unmovable *adjective.* —*See* **fixed.**

unmoved *adjective.* —*See* **cold** (2).

unmoving *adjective.* —*See* **fixed, motionless.**

unmusical *adjective.* —*See* **inharmonious** (2).

unnamed *adjective.* —*See* **anonymous.**

unnatural *adjective.* Greatly exceeding or departing from the normal course of nature ▶ preternatural, supernatural. [*Compare* **supernatural.**] —*See also* **abnormal, eccentric.**

unnaturalness *noun.* —*See* **abnormality.**

unnecessary *adjective.* Not necessary ▶ dispensable, inessential, needless, nonessential, uncalled-for, unessential, unneeded, unrequired. [*Compare* **extra, irrelevant.**]

unneeded *adjective.* —*See* **unnecessary.**

unnegotiable *adjective.* —*See* **unworkable.**

unnerve *verb.* —*See* **discourage, dismay, enervate, frighten.**

unnerving *adjective.* —*See* **fearful.**

unnoticeable *adjective.* —*See* **hidden** (1), **imperceptible** (1), **inconspicuous.**

unobjectionable *adjective.* —*See* **acceptable** (1).

unobservable *adjective.* —*See* **imperceptible** (1).

unobstructed *adjective.* —*See* **clear** (3).

unobtainable *adjective.* —*See* **impossible, inaccessible** (1).

unobtrusive *adjective.* —*See* **inconspicuous, modest** (1).

unoccupied *adjective.* Having no job ▶ idle, jobless, unemployed, workless. ***Idioms:*** out of a job (*or* employment *or* work). —*See also* **idle** (1), **open** (4).

unoffensive *adjective.* —*See* **harmless.**

unordinary *adjective.* —*See* **unusual.**

unoriginal *adjective.* —*See* **sterile** (2), **trite.**

unorthodox *adjective.* —*See* **eccentric, exotic.**

unostentatious *adjective.* —*See* **modest** (1).

unostentatiousness *noun.* —*See* **modesty** (2).

unpaid *adjective.* Contributing one's time without pay ▶ freewill, pro bono, uncompensated, unrecompensed, unremunerated, unsalaried, voluntary, volunteer. —*See also* **due** (1).

unpalatable *adjective.* So unpleasant in flavor as to be inedible ▶ disgusting, distasteful, foul-tasting, inedible, nauseating, repulsive, sickening, unappetizing, uneatable, unsavory, untasteful, untasty. *Informal:* icky. *Slang:* gross, yucky. [*Compare* **unpleasant.**] —*See also* **bitter** (3).

unparalleled *adjective.* —*See* **unique.**

unpardonable *adjective.* —*See* **inexcusable.**

unpeopled *adjective.* —*See* **lonely** (1).

unperceptive *adjective.* —*See* **blind** (3).

unperfected *adjective.* —*See* **rough** (4).

unpitying *adjective.* —*See* **callous.**

unplanned *adjective.* —*See* **accidental, random, spontaneous, unintentional.**

unpleasant *adjective.* Not pleasant or agreeable ▶ bad, disagreeable, displeasing, offensive, uncongenial, unsympathetic. *Informal:* icky. *Slang:* yucky. [*Compare* **offensive.**] —*See also* **bitter** (3).

unplugged *adjective.* —*See* **clear** (3).

unpolished *adjective.* —*See* **coarse** (1), **rough** (4), **rude** (1), **rude** (2), **rustic, unskillful.**

unpolitic *adjective.* —*See* **tactless.**

unpolluted *adjective.* —*See* **fresh** (1).

unpopulated *adjective.* —*See* **lonely** (1).

unpracticed *adjective.* —*See* **inexperienced, untried.**

unprecedented *adjective.* —*See* **exceptional, new.**

unpredictable *adjective.* —*See* **capricious, random.**

unprejudiced *adjective.* —*See* **fair**[1] (1), **neutral** (1).

unpremeditated *adjective.* —*See* **spontaneous.**

unpretentious *adjective.* —*See* **modest** (1).

unpretentiousness *noun.* —*See* **modesty** (1), **modesty** (2).

unprincipled *adjective.* —*See* **unscrupulous.**

unprocessed *adjective.* —*See* **crude, natural** (1).

unproductive *adjective.* —*See* **barren** (2).

unprofessional *adjective.* —*See* **amateurish.**

unprofitable *adjective.* —*See* **futile.**

unprofitableness *noun.* —*See* **futility.**

unprogressive *adjective.* Clinging to obsolete ideas ▶ backward, reactionary. [*Compare* **conservative.**]

unpromising *adjective.* —*See* **bleak** (2).

unpropitious *adjective.* —*See* **bleak** (2), **fateful** (1).

unprotected *adjective.* —*See* **insecure** (1), **open** (2), **vulnerable.**

unprotectedness *noun.* —*See* **exposure.**

unproved *adjective.* —*See* **baseless, untried.**

unqualified *adjective.* —*See* **inefficient, unconditional, utter**[2].

unquestionable *adjective.* —*See* **authentic** (1), **certain** (2), **decided.**

unquestionably *adverb.* —*See* **absolutely, yes.**

unquestioned *adjective.* —*See* **certain** (2).

unquestioning *adjective.* —*See* **implicit** (2).

unquiet *adjective.* Affording no quiet, repose, or rest ▶ restless, uneasy, unsettled. [*Compare* **edgy, wakeful.**]

unravel *verb.* —*See* **develop** (2), **solve** (1), **unwind.**

unreachable *adjective.* —*See* **inaccessible** (1).

unread *adjective.* —*See* **ignorant** (1).

unreal *adjective.* —*See* **illusive, imaginary.**

unrealistic *adjective.* —*See* **idealistic.**

unrealizable *adjective.* —*See* **impossible.**

unreasonable *adjective.* Not governed by or predicated on reason ▶ illogical, irrational, unreasoned. ***Idioms:*** out of bounds, without rhyme or reason. [*Compare* **fallacious, foolish.**] —*See also* **outrageous.**

unreasonableness *or* **unreason** *noun.* The absence of reason ▶ illogicality, illogicalness, irrationality. [*Compare* **fallacy, foolishness.**]

unreasoned *adjective.* Not governed by or predicated on reason ▶ illogical, irrational, unreasonable. ***Idioms:*** out of bounds, without rhyme or reason. [*Compare* **fallacious, foolish.**]

unreceptiveness *noun.* —*See* **inhospitality.**

unrecompensed *adjective.* —*See* **unpaid.**

unreel *verb.* —*See* **unwind.**

unrefined *adjective.* —*See* **coarse** (1), **crude.**

unrehearsed *adjective.* —*See* **extemporaneous, spontaneous.**

unrelated *adjective.* —*See* **irrelevant.**

unrelenting *adjective.* —*See* **stubborn** (1).

unreliable *adjective.* So weak or defective as to be liable to fail ▶ trick, undependable. [*Compare* **defective, weak.**] —*See also* **undependable** (1).

unrelieved *adjective.* —*See* **utter²**.

unremarkable *adjective.* —*See* **ordinary.**

unremitting *adjective.* —*See* **continual, diligent.**

unremunerated *adjective.* —*See* **unpaid.**

unrepentant *adjective.* Devoid of remorse ▶ impenitent, remorseless.

unrequired *adjective.* —*See* **unnecessary.**

unreserved *adjective.* —*See* **frank, implicit** (2), **open** (4), **outgoing, unconditional, utter²**.

unresolved *adjective.* —*See* **indefinite** (2).

unresponsive *adjective.* —*See* **apathetic, cold** (2), **dead** (2), **frigid.**

unresponsiveness *noun.* —*See* **apathy.**

unrest *noun.* —*See* **agitation** (1), **disorder** (2), **restlessness.**

unrestrained *adjective.* —*See* **abandoned** (2), **easygoing, excessive, loose** (2).

unrestraint *noun.* —*See* **abandon** (1), **ease** (1).

unrestricted *adjective.* —*See* **open** (3).

unrevealed *adjective.* —*See* **ulterior** (1).

unrivaled *or* **unrivalled** *adjective.* —*See* **unique.**

unroll *verb.* —*See* **spread** (1), **unwind.**

unromantic *adjective.* —*See* **realistic** (1).

unruffled *adjective.* —*See* **calm, even** (1).

unruliness *noun.* The quality or condition of being unruly ▶ disorderliness, fractiousness, indocility, intractability, intractableness, lawlessness, obstinacy, obstinateness, obstreperousness, recalcitrance, recalcitrancy, refractoriness, uncontrollability, uncontrollableness, ungovernableness, unmanageability, untowardness, wildness. [*Compare* **defiance, mischief.**]

unruly *adjective.* Not submitting to discipline or control ▶ bad, disorderly, fractious, froward, headstrong, ill-behaved, indocile, insubordinate, intractable, lawless, naughty, noncompliant, obstinate, obstreperous, recalcitrant, refractory, uncontrollable, undisciplined, ungovernable, unmanageable, untoward, wayward, wild. ***Idioms:*** out of control, out of line. [*Compare* **mischevous, rebellious.**]

✚ **CORE SYNONYMS:** *unruly, intractable, refractory, recalcitrant, headstrong, wayward.* These adjectives mean not submitting to discipline or control: *Unruly* is the most general: *unruly behavior in class. Intractable* and *refractory* refer to what is obstinate and difficult to manage or control: "*the intractable ferocity of his captive*" (Edgar Allan Poe).

"The idea of ecclesiastical authority . . . woke all the refractory nerves of opposition inherited from five generations of Puritans" (Harriet Beecher Stowe). One that is *recalcitrant* rebels against authority: *arrested the recalcitrant protestors. Headstrong* describes one obstinately bent on having his or her own way: *The headstrong senator ignored his constituency.* One who is *wayward* willfully and often perversely departs from what is desired, advised, expected, or required: *"a lively child, who had been spoilt and indulged, and therefore was sometimes wayward"* (Charlotte Brontë).

---

unsafe *adjective.* —*See* **dangerous, insecure** (1).

unsaid *adjective.* —*See* **implicit** (1), **silent** (2).

unsalaried *adjective.* —*See* **unpaid.**

unsalutary *adjective.* —*See* **unwholesome** (1).

unsatisfactory *adjective.* —*See* **bad** (1), **disappointing, unfavorable** (1).

unsatisfied *adjective.* —*See* **due** (1).

unsatisfying *adjective.* —*See* **disappointing.**

unsavory *adjective.* —*See* **flat** (2), **unpalatable.**

unsay *adjective.* —*See* **retract** (1).

unscathed *adjective.* —*See* **safe** (1).

unscholarly *or* **unschooled** *adjective.* —*See* **ignorant** (1).

unscientific *adjective.* —*See* **arbitrary.**

unscrupulous *adjective.* Lacking scruples or principles ▶ amoral, conscienceless, debased, degraded, ruthless, shameless, unconscionable, unethical, unprincipled. [*Compare* **dishonest, evil, sordid.**] —*See also* **underhand.**

unseasonable *adjective.* Not suitable for or characteristic of the season ▶ ill-timed, inopportune, mistimed, untimely. ***Idiom:*** out of season. [*Compare* **improper.**]

unseasoned *adjective.* —*See* **inexperienced.**

unseeing *adjective.* —*See* **blind** (1), **blind** (3).

unseemliness *noun.* —*See* **impropriety** (1).

unseemly *adjective.* —*See* **improper** (1), **improper** (2).

unseen *adjective.* —*See* **hidden** (1).

unselfish *adjective.* —*See* **generous** (1), **selfless.**

unselfishness *noun.* —*See* **generosity.**

unserviceable *adjective.* —*See* **unworkable.**

unsettle *verb.* —*See* **agitate** (2), **disorder, upset.**

unsettled *adjective.* Affording no quiet, repose, or rest ▶ restless, uneasy, unquiet. [*Compare* **edgy, wakeful.**] —*See also* **anxious, changeable** (1), **debatable, due** (1), **indefinite** (2).

unsettling *adjective.* —*See* **disturbing.**

unsex *verb.* —*See* **sterilize** (2).

unshakable *adjective.* —*See* **firm**[1] (2).

unshaped *adjective.* —*See* **shapeless.**

unshielded *adjective.* —*See* **insecure** (1).

unsightliness *noun.* —*See* **ugliness.**

unsightly *adjective.* —*See* **ugly.**

unsigned *adjective.* —*See* **anonymous.**

unskilled *adjective.* —*See* **amateurish, inefficient.**

unskillful *adjective.* Clumsily lacking in the ability to do or perform ▶ awkward, bumbling, bungling, clumsy, floundering, fumbling, gauche, ham-fisted, ham-handed, heavy-handed, inept, maladroit, unpolished. [*Compare* **awkward.**] —*See also* **amateurish, inefficient.**

unsleeping *adjective.* Not in a state of sleep or unable to sleep ▶ awake, wakeful, wide-awake. ***Idiom:*** tossing and turning. [*Compare* **restless.**]

unsoiled *adjective.* —*See* **clean** (1).

unsophisticated *adjective.* —*See* **artless.**

unsought *adjective.* —*See* **unwelcome.**

unsound *adjective.* —*See* **erroneous, fallacious** (1), **insane, unwise, weak** (1).

unsoundness *noun.* —*See* **infirmity.**

unsparing *adjective.* —*See* **generous** (1).

unsparingness *noun.* —*See* **generosity.**

unspeakable *adjective.* **1.** Beyond description ▶ incommunicable, indefinable, indescribable, ineffable, inexpressible, undescribable, unutterable. ***Idioms:*** beyond description (*or* words), defying description. [*Compare* **incredible.**] **2.** That may not be spoken of or uttered ▶ eyes-only, sacred, unmentionable, unutterable. [*Compare* **forbidden, holy, secret.**] —*See also* **outrageous.**

✚ **CORE SYNONYMS:** *unspeakable, indefinable, indescribable, ineffable, inexpressible, unutterable.* These adjectives refer to that which is beyond expression or description: *unspeakable misery; indefinable yearnings; indescribable beauty; ineffable ecstasy; inexpressible anguish; unutterable contempt.*

---

unspecified *adjective.* —*See* **indefinite** (2).

unspoiled *adjective.* —*See* **fresh** (1).

unspoken *adjective.* —*See* **implicit** (1), **silent** (2).

unstable *adjective.* —*See* **capricious, changeable** (1), **erratic, insecure** (2).

unstableness *noun.* —*See* **instability.**

unstained *adjective.* —*See* **innocent** (1).

unsteadiness *noun.* The quality or condition of being physically unsteady ▶ ricketiness, wiggling, wobbliness, wonkiness. —*See also* **dizziness, instability.**

unsteady *adjective.* —*See* **capricious, changeable** (1), **dizzy** (1), **insecure** (2), **uneven.**

unstinting *adjective.* —*See* **generous** (1).

unstudied *adjective.* —*See* **artless.**

unstudious *adjective.* —*See* **ignorant** (1).

unsubstantial *adjective.* —*See* **immaterial, implausible, weak** (1).

unsubstantiality *noun.* —*See* **infirmity.**

unsubtle *adjective.* —*See* **obvious.**

unsuccessful *adjective.* —*See* **futile.**

unsufferable *adjective.* —*See* **unbearable.**

unsuitability *or* **unsuitableness** *noun.* —*See* **impropriety** (1).

unsuitable *adjective.* —*See* **improper** (2), **objectionable.**

unsuited *adjective.* —*See* **improper** (2).

unsullied *adjective.* —*See* **clean** (1), **innocent** (1).

unsupportable *adjective.* —*See* **unbearable.**

unsure *adjective.* —*See* **ambiguous** (1), **doubtful** (2), **indefinite** (2), **insecure** (2).

unsureness *noun.* —*See* **instability.**

unsurpassable *adjective.* —*See* **maximum.**

unsurpassed *adjective.* —*See* **best** (1), **unique.**

unsusceptibility *noun.* The capacity to withstand ▶ immunity, imperviousness, insusceptibility, resistance. [*Compare* **endurance, stability.**]

unsusceptible *adjective.* —*See* **cold** (2), **resistant.**

unswerving *adjective.* —*See* **concentrated** (1), **direct** (1).

unsympathetic *adjective.* —*See* **callous, unpleasant.**

unsystematic *adjective.* —*See* **confused** (2).

untactful *adjective.* —*See* **tactless.**

untainted *adjective.* —*See* **innocent** (1).

untalkative *adjective.* —*See* **taciturn.**

untamed *adjective.* —*See* **uncivilized, wild** (2).

untangle *verb.* —*See* **extricate, solve** (1).

untasteful *adjective.* —*See* **unpalatable.**

untaught *adjective.* —*See* **ignorant** (1), **instinctive.**

untenable *adjective.* —*See* **fallacious** (1).

untested *adjective.* —*See* **untried.**

unthankful *adjective.* Not apt to be appreciated ▶ thankless, unappreciated, ungrateful. —*See also* **thankless** (1).
unthanking *adjective.* —*See* **thankless** (1).
unthinkable *adjective.* —*See* **impossible, incredible.**
unthinking *adjective.* —*See* **careless, thoughtless, unintentional.**
unthoughtful *adjective.* —*See* **thoughtless.**
unthoughtfulness *noun.* —*See* **thoughtlessness** (2).
unthrifty *adjective.* —*See* **extravagant.**
untidiness *noun.* —*See* **disorderliness.**
untidy *adjective.* —*See* **messy** (1).
untie *verb.* —*See* **open** (1), **undo.**
untighten *verb.* —*See* **ease** (1).
untimely *adjective.* **1.** Not occurring at a favorable time ▶ ill-timed, inconvenient, inopportune. **2.** Developing, occurring, or appearing before the expected time ▶ early, precocious, premature. —*See also* **unseasonable.**
untiring *adjective.* —*See* **tireless.**
untouchable *noun.* —*See* **outcast.**
untouched *adjective.* —*See* **callous, fresh** (1).
untoward *adjective.* —*See* **improper** (1), **unfavorable** (1), **unfortunate** (1), **unruly.**
untowardness *noun.* —*See* **misfortune, unruliness.**
untrammeled *adjective.* —*See* **loose** (2).
untried *adjective.* Not tested or proved ▶ conjectured, hypothesized, hypothetical, surmised, theoretical, theorized, undemonstrated, unestablished, unpracticed, unproved, untested. [*Compare* **new, pilot.**] —*See also* **inexperienced.**
untroubled *adjective.* —*See* **lighthearted, still.**
untroubledness *noun.* —*See* **stillness.**
untrue *adjective.* —*See* **erroneous, faithless, false.**
untrusting *adjective.* —*See* **distrustful.**
untrustworthiness *noun.* —*See* **dishonesty** (1).
untrustworthy *adjective.* —*See* **dishonest, shady** (1), **undependable** (1).
untruth *noun.* —*See* **fallacy** (1), **lie²**.
untruthful *adjective.* —*See* **dishonest, false.**
untruthfulness *noun.* —*See* **mendacity.**
untwine *verb.* —*See* **unwind.**
untwist *verb.* —*See* **unwind.**
unusable *adjective.* —*See* **unworkable.**
unused *adjective.* —*See* **idle** (1).
unusual *adjective.* Not usual or ordinary ▶ atypic, atypical, novel, unconventional, unique, unordinary, unwonted. *Slang:* offbeat. [*Compare* **abnormal, exotic.**] —*See also* **eccentric, exceptional, infrequent.**
unusually *adverb.* In a manner or to a degree that is unusual ▶ abnormally, atypically, bizarrely, curiously, exceptionally, extraordinarily, incredibly, oddly, peculiarly, phenomenally, remarkably, singularly, strangely, surprisingly, uncommonly, unconventionally, unexpectedly, uniquely. [*Compare* **absolutely, completely, considerably, really, very.**]
unutterable *adjective.* —*See* **unspeakable** (1), **unspeakable** (2).
unuttered *adjective.* —*See* **implicit** (1), **silent** (2).
unvarnished *adjective.* —*See* **bare** (1), **literal.**
unvarying *adjective.* —*See* **unchanging.**
unveil *verb.* —*See* **betray** (2), **reveal.**
unventilated *adjective.* —*See* **airless** (1).
unversed *adjective.* —*See* **inexperienced.**
unvoiced *adjective.* —*See* **silent** (2).
unwanted *adjective.* —*See* **objectionable, unwelcome.**
unwarranted *adjective.* —*See* **baseless, wanton** (2).

unwarrantedly *adverb.* Without basis or foundation in fact ▶ baselessly, groundlessly, unfoundedly.

unwashed *adjective.* —*See* **lowly** (1).

unwavering *adjective.* —*See* **firm**[1] (3).

unwearied *adjective.* —*See* **tireless.**

unwed *adjective.* —*See* **single.**

unwelcome *adjective.* Not welcome or wanted ▶ banished, excluded, rejected, undesirable, undesired, uninvited, unsought, unwanted, unwished-for. —*See also* **objectionable.**

unwelcome *or* **unwelcomeness** *noun.* —*See* **inhospitality.**

unwell *adjective.* —*See* **sick** (1).

unwholesome *adjective.* **1.** Not sustaining or promoting health ▶ insalubrious, junk, unhealthful, unhealthy, unhygienic, unsalutary. **2.** Morally detrimental ▶ contaminative, corruptive, demoralizing, poisonous, unhealthy. [*Compare* **evil.**] —*See also* **harmful, morbid, offensive** (1).

unwholesomeness *noun.* —*See* **contamination.**

unwieldy *adjective.* —*See* **awkward** (2).

unwilling *adjective.* —*See* **indisposed.**

unwillingness *noun.* —*See* **indisposition.**

unwind *verb.* To cause a line to become longer and less taut ▶ play out, uncoil, unravel, unreel, unroll, untwine, untwist. [*Compare* **extricate, undo.**] —*See also* **rest**[1] (1).

unwise *adjective.* Not wise ▶ contraindicated, ill-advised, ill-considered, impolitic, impractical, imprudent, inadvisable, indiscreet, inexpedient, injudicious, unsound. [*Compare* **foolish, rash, unruly.**]

unwished-for *adjective.* —*See* **unwelcome.**

unwitting *adjective.* —*See* **ignorant** (3), **unintentional.**

unwonted *adjective.* —*See* **unusual.**

unworkable *adjective.* Incapable of being used or availed of to advantage ▶ impracticable, unemployable, unnegotiable, unserviceable, unusable, useless. —*See also* **impossible.**

unworkmanlike *adjective.* —*See* **inefficient.**

unworldly *adjective.* —*See* **artless, supernatural** (1).

unwritten *adjective.* —*See* **oral.**

unyielding *adjective.* —*See* **firm**[1] (3), **rigid, severe** (1), **stubborn** (1).

up *adjective.* —*See* **elated.**

up *verb.* To increase in amount ▶ boost, hike, jack (up), jump, raise. —*See also* **promote** (1).

up-and-comer *noun.* —*See* **comer** (2).

up-and-coming *adjective.* Showing great promise ▶ coming, promising. ***Idiom:*** on the way up.

upbeat *adjective.* —*See* **optimistic.**

upbraid *verb.* —*See* **chastise.**

upbraiding *noun.* —*See* **tirade.**

upbringing *noun.* Training in the proper forms of social and personal conduct ▶ breeding, education. [*Compare* **courtesy, manners.**]

upchuck *verb.* —*See* **vomit.**

upcoming *adjective.* In the relatively near future ▶ approaching, coming, due, forthcoming. ***Idioms:*** around the corner, on the horizon. [*Compare* **close, imminent.**]

update *verb.* To make modern in appearance or style ▶ modernize, streamline. ***Idiom:*** bring up to date. [*Compare* **improve, renew.**]

upend *verb.* —*See* **overturn.**

upfront *adjective.* —*See* **frank.**

upgrade *verb.* —*See* **improve, promote** (1).

upgrade *noun.* —*See* **advancement, improvement** (1).

upheaval *noun.* —*See* **revolution** (2), **upset.**

uphill *adjective.* —*See* **difficult** (1).

uphold *verb.* —*See* **bear** (1), **defend** (2), **elevate** (1), **support** (1), **support** (2).

upkeep *noun.* —*See* **living, maintenance.**

uplift *verb.* —*See* **elate, elevate** (1), **exalt.**

uplift *noun.* —*See* **elation, lift.**

upmost *adjective.* Of, being, located at, or forming the top ▶ highest, loftiest, top, topmost, uppermost. [*Compare* **climactic.**]

up on *adjective.* —*See* **informed.**

upper *adjective.* Being at a rank or level above another ▶ greater, higher, senior, superior.

upper class *noun.* —*See* **society** (1).

upper-class *adjective.* —*See* **noble.**

upper crust *noun.* —*See* **society** (1).

upper-crust *adjective.* —*See* **noble.**

upper hand *noun.* —*See* **advantage** (3).

uppermost *adjective.* Of, being, located at, or forming the top ▶ highest, loftiest, top, topmost, upmost. [*Compare* **climactic.**]

uppity *or* **uppish** *adjective.* —*See* **impudent, snobbish.**

uppityness *or* **uppishness** *noun.* —*See* **impudence.**

upraise *or* **uprear** *verb.* —*See* **elevate** (1), **erect.**

upraised *adjective.* —*See* **elevated** (1), **erect.**

upright *adjective.* —*See* **erect, ethical, honest, vertical.**

uprightness *noun.* —*See* **character** (2), **good** (1).

uprise *verb.* —*See* **stand** (1).

uprising *noun.* —*See* **rebellion.**

uproar *noun.* —*See* **agitation** (1), **disorder** (2), **noise** (1), **sensation** (2), **vociferation.**

uproarious *adjective.* —*See* **funny** (1).

uproot *verb.* —*See* **annihilate.**

upset *verb.* To disturb the health or physiological functioning of ▶ derange, disconcert, disorder, turn, unsettle. [*Compare* **derange.**] —*See also* **agitate** (2), **disorder, disrupt, disturb, offend** (1), **offend** (2), **overthrow, overturn.**

upset *noun.* The act or an example of upsetting ▶ disordering, disorganization, disruption, overthrow, overturn, upheaval. [*Compare* **defeat, disturbance.**] —*See also* **agitation** (2).

upset *adjective.* —*See* **anxious, upside-down.**

upsetting *adjective.* —*See* **disturbing.**

upshot *noun.* —*See* **effect** (1).

upside-down *adjective.* Turned over completely ▶ capsized, inverted, overturned, topsy-turvy, upended, upset, upturned. ***Idiom:*** bottom-side up. —*See also* **confused** (2).

upspring *verb.* —*See* **stem.**

upstanding *adjective.* —*See* **erect, honest.**

upstandingness *noun.* —*See* **honesty.**

upsurge *verb.* —*See* **increase.**

upsurge *noun.* —*See* **increase** (1).

upswing *noun.* —*See* **increase** (1).

uptight *adjective.* —*See* **edgy.**

up to *adjective.* Having the necessary strength or ability ▶ equal. —*See also* **eligible.**

up-to-date *or* **up-to-the-minute** *adjective.* —*See* **contemporary** (2).

upturn *noun.* —*See* **increase** (1).

upturn *verb.* —*See* **overturn.**

upturned *adjective.* —*See* **upside-down.**

urban *adjective.* —*See* **city.**

urbane *adjective.* Gracious and tactful in social manner ▶ debonair, smooth, suave. [*Compare* **courteous, glib, sophisticated.**] —*See also* **cultured.**

urbanity *noun.* —*See* **amenities** (2), **elegance.**

urchin *noun.* A mischievous youngster ▶ brat, elf, gamin, gamine, imp, juvenile delinquent, minx, scamp, whelp. ***Idiom:*** holy terror. [*Compare* **child, rascal.**]

urge *verb.* To impel to action ▶ drive, exhort, induce, press. [*Compare* **provoke.**]

urge *noun.* —*See* **desire** (2), **inclination** (1).

urgency *noun.* —*See* **emergency.**

urgent *adjective.* **1.** Demanding immediate attention ▶ acute, burning, climacteric, compelling, critical, crucial, crying, desperate, dire, emergent, exigent, imperative, instant, pressing, vital. [*Compare* **essential, important, pri-**

mary.] **2.** Firm or obstinate, as in making a demand or maintaining a stand ▶ importunate, importune, insistent, persistent. [*Compare* **firm, stubborn.**]

✣ **CORE SYNONYMS:** *urgent, exigent, pressing, imperative.* These adjectives mean demanding immediate attention. *Urgent* often implies that a matter takes precedence over others: *"My business is too urgent to waste time on apologies"* (John Buchan). *Exigent* and *pressing* suggest an urgency that requires prompt action: *"When once disease was introduced into the rural districts, its effects appeared more horrible, more exigent, and more difficult to cure, than in towns"* (Mary Shelley). *"The danger now became too pressing to admit of longer delay"* (James Fenimore Cooper). *Imperative* implies a need or demand whose fulfillment cannot be evaded or deferred: *The necessity for preventing war has become imperative.*

urging *noun.* Urgent solicitation ▶ insistence, insistency, persuasion, pressing. [*Compare* **demand.**]

urinary *adjective.* —*See* **eliminative.**

usable *adjective.* In a condition to be used ▶ applicable, employable, operational, serviceable, utilizable. [*Compare* **active, practical.**] —*See also* **open** (4).

usage *noun.* The act of consuming ▶ consumption, depletion, expenditure, use, utilization. [*Compare* **use.**] —*See also* **custom, exercise** (1).

usance *noun.* —*See* **custom.**

use *verb.* To put into action or use ▶ actuate, adopt, apply, draw on, employ, exercise, exploit, harness, implement, practice, utilize, work. ***Idioms:*** avail oneself of, bring into play, bring to bear, make use of, put into practice, put to use. [*Compare* **exercise, handle.**] —*See also* **abuse** (1), **manipulate** (1), **operate.**

use up *verb.* —*See* **exhaust** (1).

use *noun.* **1.** The act of consuming ▶ consumption, depletion, expenditure, usage, utilization. **2.** The quality of being suitable or adaptable to an end ▶ account, advantage, avail, benefit, merit, point, practicality, profit, usefulness, utility. [*Compare* **purpose.**] —*See also* **custom, duty** (2), **exercise** (1), **interest** (1).

✣ **CORE SYNONYMS:** *use, employ, utilize.* These verbs mean to put into action or use. To *use* is to put into service or apply for a purpose: *uses a hearing aid; used the press secretary as spokesperson; using a stick to stir the paint. Employ* is often interchangeable with *use: She employed her education to maximum advantage.* It can also denote engaging or maintaining the services of another: *"When men are employed, they are best contented"* (Benjamin Franklin). *Utilize* is especially appropriate in the narrower sense of making something profitable or of finding new and practical uses for it: *Waterpower has been widely utilized to generate electricity.*

used *adjective.* **1.** In the habit ▶ accustomed, habituated, wont. **2.** Previously owned or made use of; not new ▶ hand-me-down, pre-owned, secondhand. [*Compare* **obsolete, old-fashioned.**]

useful *adjective.* —*See* **beneficial, convenient** (1), **practical.**

usefulness *noun.* —*See* **use** (2).

useless *adjective.* —*See* **futile, ineffectual** (1), **ineffectual** (2), **unworkable.**

uselessness *noun.* —*See* **futility, ineffectuality.**

user *noun.* —*See* **consumer.**

usher *noun.* —*See* **guide.**

usher *verb.* —*See* **guide.**

usher in *verb.* —*See* **introduce** (3), **proclaim.**

usual *adjective.* —*See* **common** (1), **conventional.**

usual *noun.* A regular or customary matter, condition, or course of events ▶

average, commonplace, everyday, form, norm, ordinary, pattern, routine, rule.

usually *adverb.* In an expected or customary manner ▶ commonly, consistently, customarily, frequently, generally, habitually, mainly, mostly, naturally, normally, often, ordinarily, regularly, routinely, typically. ***Idioms:*** as usual, by and large, on the whole, per usual. [*Compare* **approximately, fairly.**]

usualness *noun.* The quality or condition of being usual ▶ averageness, commonness, customariness, habitualness, normalcy, normality, ordinariness, prevalence, regularity, routineness.

usurp *verb.* To take the place of another against the other's will ▶ cut out, displace, force out, supplant. [*Compare* **assume, occupy.**] *—See also* **seize** (1).

usurpation *noun. —See* **seizure** (2).

usurper *noun. —See* **dictator.**

utensil *noun.* A device used to do work or perform a task ▶ implement, instrument, tool. [*Compare* **agent, device, gadget.**]

utilitarian *adjective. —See* **practical.**

utility *noun. —See* **use** (2).

utilizable *adjective. —See* **open** (4), **usable.**

utilization *noun. —See* **consumption, duty** (2), **exercise** (1).

utilize *verb. —See* **operate, use.**

utmost *adjective. —See* **extreme** (1), **maximum.**

utmost *noun. —See* **maximum.**

utopian *adjective. —See* **idealistic.**

utopian *noun. —See* **dreamer** (1).

utter[1] *verb. —See* **pronounce, say.**

utter[2] *adjective.* Completely such, without qualification or exception ▶ absolute, all-out, arrant, complete, consummate, crashing, damned, dead, downright, flat, full-fledged, out-and-out, outright, perfect, plain, pure, sheer, stark, thorough, thoroughgoing, total, unbounded, unequivocal, unlimited, unmitigated, unqualified, unrelieved, unreserved. *Informal:* flat out, positive. ***Idiom:*** out-and-out. [*Compare* **maximum.**]

utterance *noun.* Something said ▶ saying, statement, word. [*Compare* **language.**] *—See also* **expression** (1), **speech** (1), **voicing.**

uttered *adjective. —See* **oral.**

utterly *adverb. —See* **completely** (1).

uttermost *adjective. —See* **extreme** (1), **maximum.**

uttermost *noun. —See* **maximum.**

U-turn *noun. —See* **reversal** (1).

V

vacancy *noun. —See* **emptiness** (2), **nothingness** (2).

vacant *adjective.* Lacking intelligent thought or content ▶ blank, empty, empty-headed, impassive, inane, lifeless, unreasoning, vacuous. [*Compare* **absent-minded, foolish, stupid.**] *—See also* **empty** (1), **hollow** (1), **idle** (1), **lonely** (1), **open** (4).

vacate *verb. —See* **empty.**

vacation *noun.* A regularly scheduled period spent away from work or duty, often in recreation ▶ furlough, holiday, leave, sabbatical. ***Idioms:*** time (*or* day) off. [*Compare* **break, trip.**]

vacationer *noun. —See* **tourist.**

vaccinate *verb. —See* **administer** (3).

vacillant *adjective. —See* **hesitant.**

vacillate *verb.* To shift from one attitude, interest, condition, or emotion to another ▶ dilly-dally, swing, waver. *—See also* **change** (2), **hesitate, sway.**

vacillating *adjective. —See* **doubtful** (2).

vacillation *noun. —See* **hesitation.**

vacillatory *adjective. —See* **hesitant.**

vacuity *noun. —See* **emptiness** (2), **hole** (1), **nothingness** (2).

vacuous *adjective. —See* **empty** (1), **vacant.**

vacuousness *noun. —See* **emptiness** (2).

vacuum *noun. —See* **emptiness** (1), **nothingness** (2).

vagabond *noun.* —*See* **hobo, pauper.**
vagabond *adjective.* —*See* **nomadic.**
vagary *noun.* —*See* **fancy.**
vagrant *adjective.* —*See* **capricious, nomadic.**
vagrant *noun.* —*See* **hobo.**
vague *adjective.* —*See* **ambiguous** (2), **indefinite** (2), **unclear.**
vagueness *noun.* The quality or state of being imprecise or indefinite ▶ ambiguity, ambiguousness, cloudiness, equivocalness, fuzziness, imprecision, indefiniteness, indistinctness, inexactness, looseness, nebulousness, obscureness, obscurity, uncertainty, unclearness.
vain *adjective.* —*See* **egotistic** (1), **futile, hollow** (1).
vainglorious *adjective.* —*See* **egotistic** (1).
vainglory *noun.* —*See* **egotism.**
vainness *noun.* —*See* **egotism, futility.**
vale *noun.* —*See* **valley.**
valediction *noun.* —*See* **departure.**
valedictory *adjective.* —*See* **parting.**
valiance *or* **valiancy** *or* **valiantness** *noun.* —*See* **courage.**
valiant *adjective.* —*See* **brave.**
valid *adjective.* —*See* **authentic** (2), **believable, lawful, sound²**.
validate *verb.* —*See* **confirm** (1), **prove.**
validation *noun.* —*See* **confirmation** (2).
validity *noun.* —*See* **legality, veracity.**
valise *noun.* —*See* **suitcase.**
valley *noun.* An elongated lowland between mountains or hills ▶ canyon, dale, dell, glen, gorge, hollow, lowland, swale, vale.
valor *noun.* —*See* **courage.**
valorous *adjective.* —*See* **brave.**
valuable *adjective.* —*See* **beneficial, costly.**
valuate *verb.* —*See* **estimate** (1).
valuation *noun.* A measure of those qualities that determine merit, desirability, usefulness, or importance ▶ account, value, worth. [*Compare* **cost, importance.**] —*See also* **estimate** (1).
value *verb.* To have a high opinion of or regard for ▶ admire, appreciate, cherish, consider, esteem, honor, prize, regard, respect, treasure. ***Idioms:*** hold dear, look up to, think highly (*or* much *or* well) of, set store by. [*Compare* **revere, enjoy, like¹.**] —*See also* **estimate** (1).
value *noun.* A measure of those qualities that determine merit, desirability, usefulness, or importance ▶ account, valuation, worth. [*Compare* **cost, importance.**] —*See also* **meaning, merit.**

✚ **CORE SYNONYMS:** *value, appreciate, prize, esteem, treasure, cherish.* These verbs mean to have a highly favorable opinion of or regard for someone or something. *Value* implies high regard for the importance or worth of the object: *"In principle, the modern university values . . . the free exchange of ideas . . ."* (Eloise Salholz). *Appreciate* applies especially to high regard based on critical assessment, comparison, and judgment: *As immigrants, they appreciated their newfound freedom. Prize* often suggests pride of possession: *"the nonchalance prized by teen-agers"* (Elaine Louie). *Esteem* implies respect: *"If he had never esteemed my opinion before, he would have thought highly of me then"* (Jane Austen). *Treasure* and *cherish* stress solicitous care and affectionate regard: *We treasure our freedom. "They seek out the Salish Indian woman . . . to learn the traditions she cherishes"* (Tamara Jones).

---

valueless *adjective.* —*See* **worthless.**
vamoose *verb.* —*See* **go** (1), **run** (2).
vamp *noun. Informal* A woman who is given to flirting ▶ coquette, flirt, tease. —*See also* **seductress.**
vamp *verb.* —*See* **charm** (2).
vandalize *verb.* To injure or destroy property maliciously ▶ wreck. *Slang:* trash. [*Compare* **destroy.**]
vanguard *noun.* A leading contestant or sure winner ▶ favorite, front-runner,

leader, number one. *Informal:* shoo-in. —*See also* **forefront, forerunner.**

vanilla *adjective.* —*See* **bare** (1).

vanish *verb.* —*See* **disappear** (1).

vanished *adjective.* —*See* **lost** (2).

vanishment *noun.* —*See* **disappearance.**

vanity *noun.* —*See* **egotism, futility.**

vanquish *verb.* —*See* **defeat.**

vanquisher *noun.* —*See* **conqueror.**

vanquishing *adjective.* —*See* **victorious.**

vanquishment *noun.* —*See* **defeat.**

vantage *noun.* —*See* **advantage** (1), **advantage** (3), **viewpoint.**

vapid *adjective.* —*See* **insipid.**

vapidity *or* **vapidness** *noun.* —*See* **dullness, insipidity.**

vapor *noun.* —*See* **haze.**

vaporize *verb.* —*See* **evaporate.**

vaporous *or* **vapory** *adjective.* —*See* **sheer**[2].

variable *adjective.* —*See* **capricious, changeable** (1), **uneven.**

variance *noun.* —*See* **conflict, difference, variety.**

variant *noun.* —*See* **variation.**

variant *adjective.* —*See* **changeable** (1), **different.**

variation *noun.* One that is slightly different from others of the same kind or designation ▶ adaptation, alteration, alternative, development, form, modification, permutation, variant, variety, version. —*See also* **change** (1), **deviation, difference.**

varicolored *adjective.* —*See* **multicolored.**

varied *adjective.* —*See* **various.**

variegate *verb.* —*See* **streak.**

variegated *adjective.* —*See* **multicolored, various.**

variegation *noun.* —*See* **variety.**

variety *noun.* The quality of being made of many different elements, forms, kinds, or individuals ▶ disparateness, diverseness, diversification, diversity, heterogeneity, heterogeneousness, miscellaneousness, multifariousness, multiformity, multiplicity, variance, variegation, variousness. —*See also* **assortment, kind**[2], **variation.**

variform *adjective.* —*See* **irregular.**

various *adjective.* Consisting of a number of different kinds ▶ assorted, disparate, divers, diverse, diversified, heterogeneous, miscellaneous, mixed, motley, multifarious, multiform, sundry, varied, variegated. [*Compare* **complex.**] —*See also* **different, distinct, several, versatile.**

✦ **CORE SYNONYMS:** *various, miscellaneous, heterogeneous, mixed, varied, assorted.* These adjectives mean consisting of a number of different kinds. *Various* is the most general: *a news program that covers various topics. Miscellaneous* implies a varied, often haphazard combination: *is selling postcards and miscellaneous novelties. Heterogeneous* emphasizes diversity and dissimilarity: *a heterogeneous urban population. Mixed* suggests a combination of differing but not necessarily conflicting elements: *a mixed program of baroque and contemporary music. Varied* stresses absence of uniformity: "*The assembly was large and varied, containing clergy and laity, men and women*" (Nicholas P.S. Wisemen). *Assorted* often suggests the purposeful arrangement of different but complementary elements: *a pretty arrangement of assorted flowers.*

---

variousness *noun.* —*See* **variety.**

varnish *verb.* —*See* **color** (2), **finish** (2), **gloss**[1].

varnish *noun.* —*See* **finish, gloss**[1].

vary *verb.* —*See* **change** (1), **change** (2), **conflict, deviate, differ, go** (4).

varying *adjective.* —*See* **changeable** (1).

vassal *noun.* —*See* **slave.**

vast *adjective.* —*See* **enormous.**

vastly *adverb.* —*See* **very.**

vastness *noun.* —*See* **enormousness.**

vat *noun.* A large vessel used to hold or store liquids ▶ barrel, basin, cask, cistern, keg, tank, tub, vessel.

vatic *or* **vatical** *or* **vaticinal** *adjective.* —*See* **prophetic.**
vaticinate *verb.* —*See* **prophesy.**
vaticination *noun.* —*See* **prophecy.**
vaticinator *noun.* —*See* **prophet.**
vault[1] *noun.* —*See* **depository, grave**[1]**.**
vault[2] *verb.* —*See* **jump** (1).
vault *noun.* The act of jumping ▶ jump, pounce, leap, spring. [*Compare* **fall.**]
vaunt *verb.* —*See* **boast.**
vaunt *noun.* —*See* **boast.**
vaunter *noun.* —*See* **braggart.**
vector *noun.* The compass direction in which a ship or aircraft moves ▶ bearing, course, heading. [*Compare* **direction.**]
veer *verb.* —*See* **deviate, digress, swerve, turn** (2).
vegetate *verb.* —*See* **idle** (1).
vegetation *noun.* The plants of an area or region ▶ flora, plant life, verdure.
vehemence *or* **vehemency** *noun.* —*See* **intensity.**
vehement *adjective.* —*See* **intense.**
veil *noun.* A covering that obscures or hides something ▶ cloak, cover, mantle, screen, shroud. [*Compare* **cover, façade.**] —*See also* **disguise.**
veil *verb.* —*See* **conceal, disguise, wrap** (2).
vein *noun.* An inherent, contrasting or unexpected quality, especially in a person's character ▶ strain, streak. [*Compare* **disposition, inclination.**] —*See also* **mood, style, vessel** (2).
velocity *noun.* Rate of motion or performance ▶ pace, speed, tempo. *Informal:* clip.
venal *adjective.* —*See* **corrupt** (2).
venality *noun.* —*See* **corruption** (2).
vend *verb.* To travel about selling goods ▶ hawk, huckster, peddle. —*See also* **sell.**
vendor *or* **vender** *noun.* —*See* **seller.**
veneer *noun.* —*See* **façade** (2).
veneer *verb.* —*See* **color** (2), **face** (2).
venerability *noun.* —*See* **holiness.**
venerable *adjective.* —*See* **admirable, exalted, holy, old** (1).
venerate *verb.* —*See* **revere.**
veneration *noun.* The act of adoring, especially reverently ▶ adoration, idolization, reverence, worship. [*Compare* **devotion, praise.**] —*See also* **honor** (1).
venerational *adjective.* —*See* **reverent.**
vengeance *noun.* —*See* **retaliation.**
vengeful *adjective.* —*See* **vindictive.**
vengefulness *noun.* The quality or condition of being vindictive ▶ revenge, spite, spitefulness, vindictiveness. [*Compare* **resentment.**]
venial *adjective.* —*See* **pardonable.**
venom *noun.* —*See* **poison.**
venomous *adjective.* —*See* **biting, malevolent, poisonous.**
venomousness *noun.* —*See* **malevolence.**
vent *noun.* —*See* **hole** (2).
vent *verb.* —*See* **air** (2), **emit, say.**
ventilate *verb.* To expose to circulating air ▶ aerate, air, freshen, wind. —*See also* **air** (2).
ventilated *adjective.* —*See* **airy** (3).
ventilation *noun.* —*See* **expression** (1).
venture *verb.* To express at the risk of rebuff or criticism ▶ adventure, brave, chance, dare, hazard, presume, pretend, risk. ***Idioms:*** make bold (*or* so bold), take the liberty. —*See also* **gamble** (2), **gamble** (3).
venture *noun.* Something undertaken, especially something requiring extensive planning and work ▶ endeavor, enterprise, project, undertaking. [*Compare* **task.**] —*See also* **adventure, bet, gamble.**
venture capital *noun.* —*See* **capital** (1).
venturer *noun.* One who seeks adventure ▶ adventurer, daredevil, quester. [*Compare* **builder.**]
venturesome *or* **venturous** *adjective.* —*See* **adventurous, dangerous.**
venturesomeness *or* **venturousness** *noun.* —*See* **daring.**
veracious *adjective.* —*See* **accurate, honest.**

veracity *or* **veraciousness** *noun.* Correspondence with fact or truth ▶ accuracy, accurateness, authenticity, correctness, credibility, exactitude, exactness, faithfulness, fidelity, genuineness, realness, reliability, truth, truthfulness, validity, veridicality, verity. [*Compare* **certainty.**]

verbal *adjective.* Relating to, consisting of, or having the nature of words ▶ lexical, linguistic, wordy. *—See also* **literal, oral.**

verbalism *noun.* *—See* **wording.**

verbalization *noun.* *—See* **expression (1), speech (1).**

verbalize *verb.* To express oneself in speech ▶ speak, talk, vocalize. *—See also* **say.**

verbatim *adjective.* *—See* **literal.**

verbatim *adverb.* *—See* **exactly.**

verbiage *noun.* *—See* **wordiness.**

verbose *adjective.* *—See* **wordy (1).**

verbosity *or* **verboseness** *noun.* *—See* **wordiness.**

verboten *adjective.* *—See* **forbidden.**

verdict *noun.* *—See* **ruling.**

verdure *noun.* The plants of an area or region ▶ flora, plant life, vegetation.

verge *noun.* *—See* **border (1).**

verge *verb.* *—See* **adjoin, border.**

verge on *verb.* *—See* **rival.**

veridical *adjective.* *—See* **accurate.**

veridicality *noun.* *—See* **veracity.**

verification *noun.* *—See* **confirmation (1), confirmation (2).**

verify *verb.* *—See* **certify, confirm (1), prove.**

verily *adverb.* *—See* **really.**

verisimilitude *noun.* Appearance of truth or authenticity ▶ believability, color, credibility, credibleness, creditability, creditableness, plausibility, plausibleness. [*Compare* **truth, veracity.**]

veritable *adjective.* *—See* **authentic (1).**

veritably *adverb.* *—See* **really.**

verity *noun.* *—See* **veracity.**

vermin *noun.* *—See* **riffraff.**

vernacular *noun.* *—See* **dialect, language (1), language (2).**

versant *adjective.* Having good knowledge of something ▶ aquainted, conversant, familiar, schooled, versed. ***Idiom:*** up on. [*Compare* **accustomed, informed.**]

versatile *adjective.* Having many aspects, uses, or abilities ▶ all-around, all-purpose, all-round, many-sided, multifaceted, multipurpose, multitalented, protean, various. *—See also* **adaptable.**

✚ **CORE SYNONYMS:** *versatile, all-around, many-sided, multifaceted, multipurpose, multitalented.* These adjectives mean having many aspects, uses, or abilities: *a versatile writer; an all-around athlete; a many-sided subject; a multifaceted undertaking; a multipurpose wrench; a multitalented entertainer.*

---

verse *noun.* *—See* **poem (1).**

versed *adjective.* Having good knowledge of something ▶ acquainted, conversant, familiar, schooled, versant. ***Idiom:*** up on. [*Compare* **accustomed, informed.**] *—See also* **educated, experienced.**

versicolor *or* **versicolored** *adjective.* *—See* **multicolored.**

versifier *noun.* *—See* **poet.**

version *noun.* *—See* **paraphrase, story (1), variation.**

vertex *noun.* *—See* **climax.**

vertical *adjective.* At right angles to the horizon or to level ground ▶ on end, perpendicular, plumb, standing, upright. [*Compare* **erect, steep.**]

✚ **CORE SYNONYMS:** *vertical, upright, perpendicular, plumb.* These adjectives mean being at right angles to the horizon or to level ground. *Vertical* and *upright* are often used to signify contrast with what is horizontal: *wallpaper with vertical stripes; an upright column. Perpendicular* and *plumb* are generally used to specify an angle of precisely 90 degrees: *a perpendicular escarpment; careful to make the doorjambs plumb.*

◄ **ANTONYM:** *horizontal*

vertiginous *adjective.* Producing dizziness or vertigo ▶ dizzy, dizzying, giddy, sickening. *—See also* **dizzy** (1).

vertiginousness *noun. —See* **dizziness.**

vertigo *noun. —See* **dizziness.**

verve *noun. —See* **energy, enthusiasm** (1), **spirit** (1).

very *adverb.* To a high degree ▶ acutely, awfully, decidedly, dreadfully, eminently, exceedingly, exceptionally, extra, extremely, greatly, highly, hugely, intensely, most, notably, particularly, vastly. *Informal:* awful, mighty. [*Compare* **absolutely, completely, considerably, really, unusually.**]

very *adjective.* **1.** Strictly distinguished from others ▶ exact, precise. **2.** Considered apart from anything else ▶ mere. *—See also* **same.**

vessel *noun.* **1.** A conveyance that travels over water ▶ bark, barque, boat, craft, ship, watercraft. **2.** A tube that contains a body fluid ▶ artery, blood vessel, canal, capillary, duct, vein. **3.** An object, such as a carton, can, or jar, in which material is held or carried ▶ container, holder, receptacle, repository. [*Compare* **depository, package.**] *—See also* **vat.**

vest *verb. —See* **clothe.**

vested *adjective. —See* **confirmed** (1).

vestige *noun. —See* **trace.**

vestment *noun.* Clothing worn by members of a religious order ▶ habit, robe.

veteran *or* **vet** *noun.* One who has had long experience in a given activity or capacity ▶ old hand, past master, vet. *Informal:* old-timer. [*Compare* **expert.**]

veteran *adjective. —See* **experienced.**

veto *verb.* To prevent or forbid authoritatively ▶ blackball, block, negative, stop, turn down. *Slang:* nix. ***Idiom:*** turn thumbs down on. [*Compare* **abolish, decline, forbid, prevent, refuse**[1].]

vex *verb. —See* **annoy, complicate, distress.**

vexation *noun. —See* **annoyance** (1), **annoyance** (2), **distress.**

vexatious *or* **vexing** *adjective. —See* **disturbing.**

viable *adjective. —See* **possible.**

viands *noun. —See* **food.**

vibe *noun. —See* **air** (3).

vibrancy *noun. —See* **energy.**

vibrant *adjective. —See* **colorful** (1), **lively, resonant.**

vibrate *verb. —See* **glare** (2), **shake** (1), **sway.**

vibrating *adjective. —See* **tremulous.**

vibrating *noun. —See* **tremor** (2).

vibration *noun. —See* **air** (3), **tremor** (2).

vicar *noun. —See* **cleric.**

vice *noun. —See* **corruption** (1), **evil** (1).

vicinity *noun.* Approximate size or amount ▶ range. *Informal:* neighborhood. *Slang:* ballpark. *—See also* **environment** (1), **locality.**

vicious *adjective. —See* **cruel, evil, malevolent.**

viciousness *noun. —See* **malevolence.**

vicissitude *noun. —See* **change** (1), **difficulty.**

victim *noun.* One that is made to suffer injury, loss, or death ▶ casualty, martyr, prey, quarry, statistic, sufferer, wounded. [*Compare* **fatality, scapegoat, unfortunate.**] *—See also* **dupe, offering.**

victimization *noun. —See* **cheat** (1).

victimize *verb.* To offer as a sacrifice ▶ immolate, offer up, sacrifice. *—See also* **abuse** (1), **cheat** (1).

victimizer *noun. —See* **cheat** (2).

victor *noun. —See* **conqueror, winner.**

Victorian *adjective. —See* **prudish.**

Victorian *noun. —See* **prude.**

victorious *adjective.* Being the winner in a contest or struggle ▶ champion, conquering, triumphal, triumphant, vanquishing, winning.

victory *noun. —See* **conquest.**

victuals *noun. —See* **food.**

videlicet *adverb. —See* **namely.**

vie *verb. —See* **compete.**

view *noun.* **1.** An act of directing the eyes on an object ▶ contemplation, look, regard, sight. [*Compare* **gaze, watch.**] **2.** That which is or can be seen ▶ landscape, lookout, outlook, panorama, perspective, picture, prospect, scene, scenery, sight, spectacle, tableau, vista. ***Idiom:*** field of vision. —*See also* **belief** (1), **examination** (1), **intention, viewpoint.**

view *verb.* —*See* **examine** (1), **look** (1), **regard.**

viewable *adjective.* —*See* **visible.**

viewer *noun.* Someone who sees something occur ▶ audience, eyewitness, seer, witness.

viewpoint *noun.* The position from which something is observed or considered ▶ angle, aspect, eye, facet, frame of reference, hand, light, outlook, part, perspective, phase, point of view, position, regard, respect, side, slant, stand, standpoint, vantage, view. [*Compare* **belief, posture.**]

viga *noun.* —*See* **beam** (2).

vigil *noun.* —*See* **lookout** (1).

vigilance *noun.* —*See* **alertness, lookout** (1).

vigilant *adjective.* —*See* **alert.**

vigor *noun.* —*See* **energy, enthusiasm** (1), **spirit** (1).

vigorous *adjective.* —*See* **energetic, forceful, healthy, lusty.**

vigorously *adverb.* —*See* **hard** (1).

vigorousness *noun.* —*See* **energy.**

vile *adjective.* —*See* **dirty, offensive** (1), **sordid.**

vileness *noun.* —*See* **ugliness.**

vilification *noun.* —*See* **libel.**

vilify *verb.* —*See* **malign, revile.**

villa *noun.* A house in the country ▶ chalet, cottage, country home, country house, dacha, estate, manor. [*Compare* **home.**]

village *noun.* A small group of dwellings, usually in a rural area ▶ community, hamlet, settlement, small town. [*Compare* **city.**]

villager *noun.* —*See* **inhabitant.**

villain *noun.* A mean, worthless character in a story or play ▶ *Slang:* bad guy, heavy. —*See also* **evildoer, fiend.**

villainous *adjective.* —*See* **corrupt** (1), **fiendish.**

villainy *or* **villainousness** *noun.* —*See* **corruption** (1).

villeinage *noun.* —*See* **slavery.**

vim *noun.* —*See* **energy, spirit** (1).

vincible *adjective.* —*See* **vulnerable.**

vinculum *noun.* —*See* **bond** (2).

vindicate *verb.* To show to be just, right, or valid ▶ excuse, justify, rationalize. ***Idiom:*** make a case for. —*See also* **avenge, claim, clear** (3), **defend** (2).

vindication *noun.* —*See* **apology** (1), **exculpation.**

vindictive *adjective.* Disposed to seek revenge ▶ avenging, implacable, revengeful, spiteful, unforbearing, unforgiving, vengeful. [*Compare* **resentful.**] —*See also* **malevolent.**

vindictiveness *noun.* The quality or condition of being vindictive ▶ revenge, spite, spitefulness, vengefulness. [*Compare* **resentment.**] —*See also* **malevolence.**

vintage *adjective.* Characterized by enduring excellence, appeal, and importance ▶ ageless, antique, classic, classical, enduring, historic, timeless. [*Compare* **old.**] —*See also* **special.**

vintage *noun.* —*See* **harvest.**

violate *verb.* **1.** To fail to fulfill a promise or conform to a regulation ▶ breach, break, contravene, infringe, overstep, transgress. **2.** To compel another to participate in or submit to a sexual act ▶ assault, force, molest, rape, ravish. **3.** To spoil or mar the sanctity of ▶ defile, desecrate, despoil, pollute, profane. [*Compare* **debase, dirty, disgrace.**] —*See also* **disobey.**

violation *noun.* —*See* **breach** (1), **sacrilege.**

violence *noun.* —*See* **force** (1), **intensity.**

violent *adjective.* Accomplished by force ▶ coercive, forced, forcible. *Informal:*

strong-arm. —*See also* **intense, rough** (2).

violently *adverb.* With force and violence ▶ coercively, forcibly. ***Idioms:*** against one's will, by force, under duress.

VIP *noun.* —*See* **dignitary.**

virago *noun.* —*See* **scold.**

virgin *adjective.* —*See* **chaste, crude.**

virgin *noun.* —*See* **innocent** (1).

virginal *adjective.* —*See* **chaste, innocent** (1).

virginity *noun.* —*See* **chastity.**

virile *adjective.* —*See* **manly.**

virility *noun.* —*See* **masculinity.**

virtual *adjective.* —*See* **theoretical** (2).

virtue *noun.* A particularly good or beneficial quality ▶ asset, beauty, distinction, merit, strength. [*Compare* **advantage, excellence, quality.**] —*See also* **chastity, good** (1), **merit.**

virtuoso *or* **virtuosa** *noun.* —*See* **player** (2).

virtuous *adjective.* —*See* **chaste, ethical, holy.**

virtuousness *noun.* —*See* **chastity, good** (1).

virulence *or* **virulency** *noun.* —*See* **resentment.**

virulent *adjective.* —*See* **contagious, poisonous, resentful.**

virus *noun.* —*See* **germ** (1), **poison.**

visa *noun.* —*See* **license** (3).

visage *noun.* —*See* **appearance** (1), **expression** (4), **face** (1).

vis-à-vis *noun.* One that has the same functions and characteristics as another ▶ counterpart, equivalent, opposite number.

viscera *noun.* Internal organs of the abdomen ▶ bowels, entrails, intestines. *Informal:* guts, insides.

visceral *adjective.* —*See* **inner** (2), **instinctive.**

viscid *adjective.* —*See* **viscous.**

viscidity *noun.* —*See* **viscosity.**

viscose *adjective.* —*See* **viscous.**

viscosity *noun.* The physical property of being viscous ▶ glutinousness, sliminess, stickiness, thickness, viscidity.

viscous *adjective.* Having a heavy, gluey quality ▶ gelatinous, glutinous, heavy, mucilaginous, syrupy, thick, viscid, viscose. [*Compare* **slimy, sticky.**]

vise *noun.* —*See* **fastener.**

visibility *noun.* The quality or degree of being visible or providing a clear view ▶ clarity, clearness, observability, perceptibility, visuality, visualness. ***Idiom:*** range of vision.

visible *adjective.* Capable of being seen ▶ discernible, observable, seeable, viewable, visual. ***Idioms:*** in sight (*or* view), on display (*or* view). [*Compare* **noticeable, perceptible.**] —*See also* **apparent** (1).

vision *noun.* **1.** The faculty of seeing ▶ eye, eyesight, optics, seeing, sight. [*Compare* **view.**] **2.** Discernment or perception which is unusually competent or creative ▶ farsightedness, foreknowledge, foresight, imagination, innovation, inspiration, prescience. ***Idioms:*** breadth (*or* depth) of view. [*Compare* **brilliance, discernment, instinct, invention.**] —*See also* **beauty, dream** (1), **dream** (3), **prophecy.**

vision *verb.* —*See* **imagine.**

visionary *adjective.* Characterized by foresight or vision ▶ farsighted, foresighted, imaginative, inspired, insightful, intuitive, perceptive, prescient. [*Compare* **intelligent, inventive.**] —*See also* **dreamy, idealistic, illusive, imaginary, prophetic.**

visionary *noun.* —*See* **dreamer** (1).

visit *verb.* To go to or seek out the company of someone in order to socialize ▶ call, come around, come by (*or* over), drop by (*or* in), go by (*or* over), look in (*or* up), pop in, run in, see, stop by (*or* in). ***Idiom:*** pay a visit (*or* a call). —*See also* **converse**[1], **inflict, lodge.**

visit *noun.* **1.** An act or an instance of going or coming to see another ▶ call, get-together, look-in, social call, stay, stop, visitation. **2.** A remaining in a place as a guest or lodger ▶ sojourn, stay, stop, stopover.

visitant *noun.* A person or persons visiting one ▶ caller, company, guest, visitor. —*See also* **ghost.**

visitation *noun.* —*See* **trial** (1), **visit** (1).

visitor *noun.* **1.** A person or persons visiting one ▶ caller, company, guest, visitant. **2.** One that arrives ▶ arrival, comer, newcomer. [*Compare* **addition, company.**] —*See also* **tourist.**

visor *noun.* —*See* **bill²** (2).

vista *noun.* —*See* **expanse** (1), **lookout** (2), **view** (2).

visual *adjective.* Serving, resulting from, or relating to the sense of sight ▶ ocular, optic, optical, seeing. —*See also* **visible.**

visuality *noun.* —*See* **visibility.**

visualize *verb.* —*See* **imagine.**

vital *adjective.* —*See* **alive, essential** (2), **lusty, primary** (1), **urgent** (1).

vital force *noun.* —*See* **spirit** (2).

vitality *noun.* —*See* **energy, spirit** (2).

vitalize *verb.* To make alive ▶ animate, enliven, quicken, vivify. [*Compare* **elate, provoke.**] —*See also* **energize.**

vitalizing *adjective.* —*See* **invigorating.**

vitiate *verb.* —*See* **abolish, corrupt, damage.**

vitreous *or* **vitrescent** *adjective.* Of or resembling glass ▶ glasslike, glassy, hyaline. [*Compare* **translucent.**]

vitriolic *adjective.* —*See* **biting.**

vituperate *verb.* —*See* **revile.**

vituperation *noun.* Sustained, harshly abusive language ▶ abuse, billingsgate, condemnation, contumely, denunciation, invective, obloquy, railing, revilement, reviling, scurrility, scurrilousness. [*Compare* **belittlement, curse, libel, tirade.**]

vituperative *adjective.* —*See* **abusive.**

vivacious *adjective.* —*See* **lively, spirit** (1).

vivacity *or* **vivaciousness** *noun.* —*See* **spirit** (1).

vivid *adjective.* Evoking strong mental images through distinctiveness ▶ colorful, graphic, picturesque, striking. —*See also* **colorful** (1), **descriptive, dramatic** (2), **graphic** (1).

vivify *verb.* To make alive ▶ animate, enliven, quicken, vitalize. [*Compare* **elate, energize, provoke.**]

vivifying *adjective.* —*See* **invigorating.**

vixen *noun.* —*See* **scold.**

viz. *adverb.* —*See* **namely.**

vocable *noun.* —*See* **term.**

vocabulary *noun.* **1.** All the words of a language ▶ lexicon, word-hoard. **2.** An alphabetical list of words often defined or translated ▶ dictionary, glossary, lexicon, wordbook.

vocal *adjective.* Characterized by, containing, or functioning as a vowel or vowels ▶ sonorant, vocalic, vowel. —*See also* **frank, oral.**

vocalism *noun.* —*See* **voicing.**

vocalist *noun.* A person who sings ▶ singer, songster, songstress, voice. *Slang:* crooner, songbird. [*Compare* **player.**]

vocalization *noun.* —*See* **expression** (1), **speech** (1), **voicing.**

vocalize *verb.* To express oneself in speech ▶ speak, talk, verbalize. —*See also* **pronounce, say, sing.**

vocation *noun.* An inner urge to pursue an activity or perform a service ▶ calling, mission. [*Compare* **dream, duty, fate.**] —*See also* **business** (2).

vociferate *verb.* —*See* **shout.**

vociferation *noun.* Loud and insistent utterances or noisemaking, usually expressing disapproval ▶ brouhaha, clamor, hullabaloo, katzenjammer, outcry, rumpus, uproar. ***Idiom:*** hue and cry. [*Compare* **noise.**]

vociferous *or* **vociferant** *adjective.* Offensively loud and insistent ▶ blatant, boisterous, clamorous, obstreperous, stentorian, strident. *Informal:* loudmouthed. [*Compare* **harsh, loud.**]

✦ **CORE SYNONYMS:** *vociferous, blatant, boisterous, strident, clamorous.*

These adjectives mean conspicuously and usually offensively loud and insistent. *Vociferous* suggests a noisy outcry, as of vehement protest: *vociferous complaints. Blatant* connotes coarse or vulgar noisiness: *"Up rose a blatant Radical"* (Walter Bagehot). *Boisterous* implies unrestrained noise, tumult, and often rowdiness: *boisterous youths. Strident* stresses offensive harshness, shrillness, or discordance: *a legislator with a strident voice.* Something *clamorous* is both vociferous and sustained: *a clamorous uproar.*

---

vogue *noun.* —*See* **fashion.**

voice *noun.* The right or chance to express an opinion or participate in a decision ▶ input, say, suffrage, vote. *Informal:* say-so, two cents, two cents worth. —*See also* **expression** (1), **vocalist.**

voice *verb.* —*See* **air** (2), **pronounce, say.**

voiced *adjective.* —*See* **oral.**

voiceless *adjective.* —*See* **mute, speechless.**

voicing *noun.* The use of the vocal organs to produce sound or speech ▶ articulation, enunciation, pronunciation, saying, utterance, vocalism, vocalization. [*Compare* **speech.**]

void *adjective.* —*See* **empty** (1), **empty** (2).

void *noun.* —*See* **emptiness** (1), **gap** (2), **hole** (1), **nothingness** (2).

void *verb.* —*See* **abolish, empty.**

voidance *noun.* —*See* **abolition.**

volatile *adjective.* —*See* **capricious.**

volatilize *verb.* —*See* **evaporate.**

volition *noun.* The mental faculty by which one deliberately chooses or decides ▶ free will, will. [*Compare* **spirit.**] —*See also* **choice.**

volitional *adjective.* —*See* **voluntary.**

volley *noun.* —*See* **barrage.**

volubility *noun.* —*See* **eloquence.**

voluble *adjective.* —*See* **eloquent, talkative.**

volume *noun.* —*See* **book, bulk** (1), **publication** (2), **size** (1).

voluminous *adjective.* —*See* **bulky** (1), **full** (3), **generous** (2).

voluntarily *adverb.* Of one's own free will ▶ by choice, freely, spontaneously, willfully, willingly. ***Idioms:*** of one's own accord, on one's own (*or* own volition).

voluntary *adjective.* Of or relating to free exercise of the will ▶ spontaneous, uncompelled, unforced, volitional, willed, willful, willing. [*Compare* **free, independent.**] —*See also* **deliberate** (1), **unpaid.**

voluntary *noun.* Someone who offers his or her services freely ▶ volunteer.

volunteer *verb.* —*See* **offer** (1).

volunteer *adjective.* —*See* **unpaid.**

volunteer *noun.* Someone who offers his or her services freely ▶ voluntary.

voluptuary *noun.* —*See* **sybarite.**

voluptuary *adjective.* Characterized by or devoted to pleasure and luxury as a lifestyle ▶ epicurean, hedonic, hedonistic, sybaritic, voluptuous. [*Compare* **luxurious, sensual.**]

voluptuous *adjective.* **1.** Characterized by or devoted to pleasure and luxury as a lifestyle ▶ epicurean, hedonic, hedonistic, sybaritic, voluptuary. [*Compare* **luxurious.**] **2.** Relating to, suggestive of, or appealing to sense gratification ▶ epicurean, sensual, sensualistic, sensuous. —*See also* **sensual** (2).

voluptuousness *noun.* The quality or condition of being sensuous ▶ sensualism, sensuality, sensuousness. —*See also* **sensuality** (1).

vomit *verb.* To eject the contents of the stomach through the mouth ▶ heave, retch, spit up, throw up. *Informal:* puke. *Slang:* barf, boot, chuck, hurl, ralph, spew, upchuck, yack, yarf. ***Idioms:*** blow chunks, do the technicolor yawn, drive (*or* ride) the porcelain bus, hug the throne, worship the porcelain god. —*See also* **erupt.**

voodoo *verb.* —*See* **charm** (2). *noun.* —*See* **magic** (1).

voracious *adjective.* Having an insatiable appetite for an activity or pursuit ▶ avid, edacious, gluttonous, greedy, insatiable, obsessive, omnivorous, rapacious, ravenous, unappeasable, wolfish. [*Compare* **enthusiastic, greedy.**] —*See also* **gluttonous, hungry** (1).

✚ **CORE SYNONYMS:** *voracious, gluttonous, rapacious, ravenous.* These adjectives mean having an insatiable appetite for an activity or pursuit: *a voracious reader of history; a gluttonous consumer of fine foods; a rapacious acquirer of competing businesses; a politician ravenous for power.*

---

voracity *noun.* The quality or condition of being voracious ▶ avidity, avidness, edacity, insatiability, obsessiveness, omnivorousness, rapaciousness, rapacity, ravenousness, voraciousness. [*Compare* **appetite, enthusiasm, greed, lust.**]

vortex *noun.* —*See* **whirlpool.**

votary *noun.* —*See* **devotee.**

vote *verb.* **1.** To select by vote for an office ▶ elect, vote in. [*Compare* **choose.**] **2.** To cast a vote ▶ ballot, poll. ***Idioms:*** exercise one's civic duty, go to the polls. —*See also* **choose** (1).

vote down *verb.* —*See* **exclude.**

vote *noun.* The right or chance to express an opinion or participate in a decision ▶ input, say, suffrage, voice. *Informal:* say-so.

voter *noun.* One who votes ▶ balloter, elector. ***Idiom:*** member of the electorate.

vouch *verb.* To confirm formally as true, accurate, or genuine ▶ attest, certify, testify, vouch for, witness. ***Idiom:*** bear witness to. —*See also* **back** (2).

vouchsafe *verb.* To let have as a favor, prerogative, or privilege ▶ accord, award, concede, give, grant. [*Compare* **yield.**] —*See also* **condescend** (1).

vow *noun.* —*See* **promise** (1).

vow *verb.* —*See* **pledge** (1).

vowel *adjective.* Characterized by, containing, or functioning as a vowel or vowels ▶ sonorant, vocal, vocalic.

voyage *noun.* —*See* **expedition, journey.**

voyage *verb.* —*See* **journey.**

vulgar *adjective.* —*See* **coarse** (1), **gaudy, lowly** (1), **obscene.**

vulgarian *noun.* —*See* **boor.**

vulgarity *noun.* —*See* **obscenity** (1), **obscenity** (2).

vulgarness *noun.* —*See* **obscenity** (1).

vulnerability *or* **vulnerableness** *noun.* —*See* **exposure.**

vulnerable *adjective.* Susceptible to physical or emotional injury or attack ▶ assailable, attackable, defenseless, helpless, pregnable, susceptible, susceptive, unprotected, vincible. ***Idioms:*** like a sitting duck, open to attack. [*Compare* **insecure, open.**] —*See also* **liable** (2).

W

wackiness *or* **whackiness** *noun.* —*See* **foolishness.**

wacky *or* **whacky** *adjective.* —*See* **foolish, insane.**

wad *noun.* —*See* **fortune, heap** (2), **lump[1], plug.**

wadding *noun.* —*See* **filler** (1).

wade *verb.* —*See* **trudge.**

wade in *or* **into** *verb.* —*See* **attack** (2).

waffle *verb.* —*See* **equivocate** (1).

waffle *noun.* —*See* **equivocation.**

waft *verb.* —*See* **blow[1]** (2), **glide** (1).

waft *noun.* —*See* **wind[1].**

wag[1] *verb.* —*See* **sway.**

wag *noun.* —*See* **gesture.**

wag[2] *noun.* —*See* **joker.**

wage *noun.* Payment for work done ▶ compensation, earnings, emolument, fee, hire, pay, payment, recompense, remuneration, salary, stipend.

wage *verb.* To engage in (a war or campaign, for example) ▶ carry on, carry out, conduct. [*Compare* **oppose.**]

wage earner *noun.* —*See* **employee.**

wager *noun.* —*See* **bet, gamble.**

wager *verb.* To make a bet ▶ bet, gamble, game, lay, play. ***Idiom:*** put one's money on something. —*See also* **expect** (1), **gamble** (2).

wages *noun.* —*See* **due.**

wage slave *noun.* —*See* **laborer.**

waggish *adjective.* —*See* **mischievous.**

waggle *verb.* —*See* **crawl** (1), **flap** (1), **sway.**

waif *noun.* —*See* **orphan.**

wail *verb.* —*See* **bawl, cry, howl, shout.**

wail *noun.* —*See* **howl, shout.**

wailing *noun.* —*See* **cry** (1).

wait *verb.* —*See* **defer**[1], **expect** (1), **remain.**

wait on *or* **upon** *verb.* **1.** To work and care for ▶ attend, do for, minister to, serve. [*Compare* **cater, help, tend**[2], **work.**] **2.** To place food before someone ▶ cater, serve. [*Compare* **give, distribute.**]

waive *verb.* —*See* **abandon** (1), **defer**[1].

waiver *noun.* —*See* **abandonment** (1), **delay** (1).

wake[1] *verb.* To cease or cause to cease sleeping ▶ arouse, awake, awaken, get up, rouse, roust, stir, wake up, waken. [*Compare* **rise.**]

wake *noun.* A watch over the body of a dead person before burial ▶ watch.

wake[2] *noun.* Something that follows or is drawn along behind ▶ tail, trail, train. [*Compare* **stream.**]

wakeful *adjective.* **1.** Not in a state of sleep or unable to sleep ▶ awake, unsleeping, wide-awake. ***Idiom:*** tossing and turning. [*Compare* **restless.**] **2.** Marked by an absence of sleep ▶ sleepless, slumberless. —*See also* **alert.**

wakefulness *noun.* —*See* **alertness.**

waken *verb.* —*See* **arouse, wake**[1].

wale *noun.* —*See* **welt.**

walk *noun.* **1.** An act of walking ▶ amble, constitutional, hike, march, perambulation, promenade, ramble, saunter, stroll, tramp, turn, wander. **2.** A manner of walking ▶ footfall, footstep, gait, pace, step, stride, tread.

walk *verb.* To go on foot ▶ ambulate, foot, pace, step, stride, tread. *Slang:* hoof. ***Idioms:*** foot it, hoof it. [*Compare* **hike, rove, stroll, trudge.**]

walk out *verb.* To cease working in support of demands made upon an employer ▶ picket, strike. ***Idioms:*** go (*or* go out on) strike, stage a strike (*or* sickout *or* walkout), stop work. —*See also* **renege.**

walk through *verb.* —*See* **practice** (1).

walkaway *noun.* —*See* **breeze** (2), **runaway** (1).

walking stick *noun.* —*See* **stick** (2).

walk of life *noun.* —*See* **business** (2).

walkout *noun.* A cessation of work by employees in support of demands made upon their employer ▶ job action, sickout, strike, work stoppage, work to rule.

walkover *noun.* —*See* **breeze** (2), **runaway** (1).

wall *noun.* A solid structure that separates one area from another ▶ barrier, partition, screen. [*Compare* **border.**] —*See also* **bar** (1).

wall *verb.* To separate with or as if with a wall ▶ fence, partition, screen. —*See also* **enclose** (1).

wallop *verb.* —*See* **hit, overwhelm** (1).

wallop *noun.* —*See* **blow**[2], **kick, thrill.**

walloping *adjective.* —*See* **enormous.**

wallow *verb.* To move about in an indolent or clumsy manner ▶ flounder, roll about, roll around, welter. —*See also* **luxuriate.**

waltz *verb.* —*See* **breeze.**

wampum *noun.* —*See* **money** (1).

wan *adjective.* —*See* **haggard, pale** (1).

wan *verb.* —*See* **pale.**

wand *noun.* —*See* **stick** (1).

wander *verb.* —*See* **digress, rove, stroll.**

wander *noun.* —*See* **walk** (1).

wanderer *noun.* —*See* **hobo.**

wandering *adjective.* —*See* **aimless, errant** (1), **erratic, indirect** (1), **nomadic.**

wane *verb.* —*See* **decrease, deteriorate, disappear** (1), **fade, subside.**

wane *noun.* —*See* **decrease, deterioration** (1), **waning.**

wangle *verb.* —*See* **maneuver** (2).

waning *noun.* The process of becoming less active or intense ▶ abatement, diminishment, easing, ebb, falling off, lapsing, letup, moderation, remission, slackening, subsidence, wane. [*Compare* **decrease.**]

wannabe *noun. Informal* One who aspires ▶ aspirant, aspirer, dreamer, hopeful, seeker.

want *verb.* To be without what is needed, required, or essential ▶ lack, need, require. —*See also* **choose** (2), **demand** (2), **desire.**

want *noun.* The condition of lacking something ▶ absence, dearth, lack. [*Compare* **need, shortage.**] —*See also* **demand** (2), **poverty.**

wanting *adjective.* —*See* **deficient, empty** (2), **insufficient.**

wanton *adjective.* **1.** Sexually unrestrained ▶ easy, fast, libertine, light, loose, promiscuous, reprobate, sluttish, trampy, unchaste, whorish. **2.** Not required, necessary, or warranted by the circumstances of the case ▶ excessive, gratuitous, reckless, supererogative, supererogatory, uncalled-for, unwarranted. [*Compare* **careless, obscene.**] —*See also* **abandoned** (2), **outrageous.**

wanton *noun.* An immoral or licentious person ▶ debauchee, debaucher, gigolo, libertine, profligate, rake, rakehell, reprobate, rip, rounder. *Slang:* swinger. [*Compare* **lecher, philanderer.**] —*See also* **slut.**

wantonness *noun.* —*See* **abandon** (1).

war *noun.* —*See* **battle, competition** (1).

war *verb.* —*See* **contend.**

warble *verb.* —*See* **sing.**

war cry *noun.* —*See* **cry** (2).

ward *noun.* A person who relies on another for support ▶ charge, dependent. —*See also* **care** (2), **defense, detention, guard, neighborhood** (1).

ward *verb.* —*See* **defend** (1), **prevent.**

ward off *verb.* —*See* **repel.**

warden *noun.* A guard or keeper of a prison ▶ jailer, turnkey. *Slang:* screw. [*Compare* **guard, police officer.**]

wardrobe *noun.* —*See* **dress** (2).

ware *noun.* —*See* **good** (2).

warehouse *noun.* —*See* **depository.**

warehouse *verb.* —*See* **save** (1).

warfare *noun.* —*See* **battle, competition** (1), **conflict.**

wariness *noun.* —*See* **alertness, care** (1), **caution, distrust.**

warlike *adjective.* —*See* **aggressive, military** (1).

warlock *noun.* —*See* **wizard.**

warm *adjective.* —*See* **amiable, enthusiastic.**

warmed-over *adjective.* —*See* **trite.**

warm-hearted *adjective.* —*See* **amiable, generous** (1), **sympathetic.**

warmongering *noun.* —*See* **aggression.**

warmonger *adjective.* —*See* **aggressive, military** (1).

warmth *noun.* —*See* **amiability, heat** (1), **passion.**

warn *verb.* To notify someone of imminent danger or risk ▶ admonish, alarm, alert, caution, forewarn. ***Idioms:*** put on (*or* on one's) guard. [*Compare* **inform, threaten.**]

warning *noun.* Advice to beware, as of a person or thing ▶ alarum, admonishment, admonition, caution, caveat, monition. ***Idiom:*** shot across someone's bow. [*Compare* **advice.**] —*See also* **alarm, example** (2), **omen.**

warning *adjective.* Giving warning ▶ admonishing, admonitory, cautionary, monitory.

warp *verb.* —*See* **bend** (2), **bend** (3), **bias** (1), **corrupt, deform, distort.**

warp and woof *noun.* —*See* **texture.**

warped *adjective.* —*See* **bent.**

warrant *noun.* An assumption of responsibility, as one given by a manufacturer, for the quality, worth, or durability of a product ▶ certification, guarantee, guaranty, surety, warranty. —*See* *also* **basis** (2), **confirmation** (2), **license** (3), **pawn**[1], **promise** (1).

warrant *verb.* —*See* **confirm** (1), **guarantee** (1), **guarantee** (2), **justify** (2), **legalize.**

warranted *adjective.* —*See* **lawful.**

warranty *noun.* An assumption of responsibility, as one given by a manufacturer, for the quality, worth, or durability of a product ▶ certification, guarantee, guaranty, surety, warrant. —*See also* **pawn**[1].

warrior *noun.* One who engages in a combat or struggle ▶ belligerent, combatant, fighter, soldier. [*Compare* **aggressor, soldier.**]

wart *noun.* —*See* **welt, defect.**

wary *adjective.* Trying attentively to avoid danger, risk, or error ▶ careful, cautious, chary, circumspect, forehanded, gingerly, prudent. —*See also* **alert, distrustful.**

wash *verb.* **1.** To make moist ▶ bathe, dampen, moisten, wet. **2.** To flow against or along ▶ bathe, lap, lave, lip. [*Compare* **flow.**] **3.** To make the sound of moving or disturbed water ▶ lap, splash, swash. [*Compare* **burble, swish.**] **4.** To move along with or be carried away by the action of water ▶ drift, float. **5.** *Informal* To prove valid under scrutiny ▶ hold up, prove out, stand up. ***Idioms:*** hold water, pass muster, ring true. —*See also* **clean** (1), **color** (1).

wash out *verb.* —*See* **fail** (1), **pale.**

wash up *verb.* —*See* **destroy** (1).

wash *noun.* —*See* **color** (1).

washed out *adjective.* —*See* **pale** (1).

washed-up *adjective.* —*See* **through** (2).

washiness *noun.* —*See* **insipidity.**

washout *noun.* —*See* **disappointment** (2), **failure** (1).

washy *adjective.* —*See* **dilute, insipid.**

waspish *adjective.* —*See* **biting, ill-tempered.**

waspishness *noun.* —*See* **temper** (1).

waste *verb.* To use, consume, spend, or expend thoughtlessly or carelessly ▶ dissipate, fool away, fritter away, riot away, splurge, squander, throw away, trifle away. *Slang:* blow. [*Compare* **consume, give.**] —*See also* **consume** (1), **idle** (2), **kill**[1], **languish, lose** (2), **murder.**

waste away *verb.* —*See* **fade.**

waste *noun.* A sad or tragic deprivation ▶ loss. [*Compare* **deprivation.**] —*See also* **desert**[1], **extravagance, garbage.**

waste *adjective.* —*See* **barren** (2).

CORE SYNONYMS: *waste, blow, dissipate, fritter away, squander.* These verbs mean to use, consume, spend, or expend thoughtlessly or carelessly: *wasted my inheritance; blew a fortune at the casino; dissipated their energies in pointless argument; frittering away her entire allowance; squandered his talent on writing jingles.*

ANTONYM: *save*

---

wasted *adjective.* —*See* **drugged, haggard.**

wasteful *adjective.* —*See* **extravagant.**

wastefulness *noun.* —*See* **extravagance.**

wasteland *noun.* —*See* **desert**[1].

waster *noun.* —*See* **wastrel** (1).

wastrel *noun.* **1.** A person who spends money or resources wastefully ▶ prodigal, profligate, scattergood, spendthrift, waster. **2.** A self-indulgent person who spends time avoiding work or other useful activity ▶ bum, drone, fainéant, idler, loafer, ne'er-do-well, shirker, slacker, sluggard. *Informal:* do-little, do-nothing, good-for-nothing, layabout, lazybones, lounger, no-good, sloth, slug. *Slang:* couch potato, deadbeat, slouch, slugabed.

watch *verb.* **1.** To look at or on attentively or carefully ▶ eye, observe, regard, scrutinize, see, survey. [*Compare* **look.**] **2.** To pay regular and close attention to ▶ follow, monitor, observe, stake out, survey. ***Idioms:*** have one's (*or* keep an) eye on, keep tabs on, keep track of, ride herd on. —*See also* **tend²**.

watch out *verb.* To be careful ▶ beware, look out, mind. ***Idioms:*** be on guard, be on the lookout, keep an eye peeled, take care (*or* heed).

watch over *verb.* —*See* **supervise.**

watch *noun.* **1.** The act of observing, often for an extended time ▶ observance, observation, scrutiny, watching. [*Compare* **look.**] **2.** A watch over the body of a dead person before burial ▶ wake. —*See also* **guard, lookout** (1), **turn** (1).

watchdog *noun.* —*See* **guard.**

watcher *noun.* **1.** Someone who observes ▶ beholder, bystander, gaper, gawker, looker-on, observer, onlooker, spectator. *Slang:* rubbernecker. [*Compare* **guard.**] **2.** An agent assigned to observe and report on another ▶ shadow. *Informal:* tail. [*Compare* **detective.**]

watchful *adjective.* —*See* **alert, careful** (1).

watchfulness *noun.* —*See* **alertness, care** (1).

watching *noun.* The act of observing, often for an extended time ▶ observance, observation, scrutiny, watch.

watchman *noun.* —*See* **guard.**

watchtower *noun.* —*See* **lookout** (2).

watchword *noun.* —*See* **cry** (2).

water *verb.* To fill with tears ▶ tear (up), well (up). [*Compare* **flow.**] —*See also* **dilute.**

watercourse *noun.* —*See* **brook¹, river.**

watercraft *noun.* A conveyance that travels over water ▶ bark, barque, boat, craft, ship, vessel.

watered-down *adjective.* —*See* **dilute.**

wateriness *noun.* —*See* **insipidity.**

watering hole *noun.* —*See* **bar** (2).

waterish *adjective.* —*See* **dilute, insipid, pale** (2).

waterless *adjective.* —*See* **dry** (1).

waterlogged *adjective.* —*See* **wet.**

waterloo *noun.* A disastrous defeat or ruin ▶ collapse, fall, downfall. —*See also* **defeat.**

watershed *noun.* The region drained by a river system ▶ drainage basin, watershed.

watery *adjective.* —*See* **dilute, insipid, pale** (2).

wattle *verb.* —*See* **weave.**

wave *verb.* **1.** To have or cause to have a curved or wavy surface ▶ corrugate, curl, curve, ripple, undulate. [*Compare* **bend, fold.**] **2.** To move or cause to move about while being fixed at one edge ▶ flap, flutter, fly. **3.** To wield boldly and dramatically ▶ brandish, flourish, sweep. [*Compare* **handle.**] —*See also* **blow¹** (2), **flap** (1), **gesture, sway.**

wave *noun.* A ridge or swell of water, or a shape suggestive of such a swell ▶ breaker, comber, ripple, roller, swell, undulation, whitecap. ***Idiom:*** peaks and troughs. —*See also* **gesture.**

waver *verb.* To shift from one attitude, interest, condition, or emotion to another ▶ dilly-dally, swing, vacillate. —*See also* **doubt, hesitate, sway.**

wavering *adjective.* —*See* **doubtful** (2), **insecure** (2).

wavy *adjective.* Having a curved or ridged surface ▶ corrugated, curly, curvy, rippled, sinusoidal, waggly, wiggly.

wax¹ *noun.* —*See* **finish.**

wax *verb.* —*See* **finish** (2).

wax² *verb.* —*See* **become** (1), **increase.**

waxen *or* **waxy** *adjective.* —*See* **pale** (1).

way *noun.* **1.** The approach that is used to do something ▶ fashion, formula, manner, method, mode, modus operandi, path, style, system, wise. [*Compare* **approach.**] **2.** A course affording passage from one place to another ▶ alley, avenue, boulevard, canal, channel, course, drive, expressway, footpath, freeway, highway, lane, pass, passage, passageway, path, road, roadway, route, street, superhighway, thoroughfare, thruway, trail, turnpike. —*See also* **behavior** (1), **custom, direction, distance** (1).

✚ **CORE SYNONYMS:** *way, method, system, manner, fashion, mode.* These nouns refer to the approach followed to accomplish a task or attain a goal. *Way* is the most general of these terms: "*It is absurd to think that the only way to tell if a poem is lasting is to wait and see if it lasts*" (Robert Frost). *Method* implies a detailed, logically ordered plan: "*I do not know of a better method for choosing a presidential nominee*" (Harry S. Truman). *System* suggests order, regularity, and coordination of methods: "*Of generalship, of strategic system . . . there was little or none*" (John Morely). *Manner* and *fashion* emphasize personal or distinctive behavior: *a clearly articulated manner of speaking; issuing orders in an arbitrary and abrasive fashion. Mode* often denotes a manner influenced by or arising from tradition or custom: *a nomadic mode of life.*

wayfaring *noun.* —*See* **journey.**

waylay *verb.* —*See* **ambush.**

wayward *adjective.* —*See* **capricious, contrary, erratic, unruly.**

weak *adjective.* **1.** Not physically strong ▶ debilitated, decrepit, delicate, enervated, enfeebled, faint, feeble, flimsy, fragile, frail, infirm, insubstantial, puny, rundown, unsound, unsubstantial, weakly. [*Compare* **insecure, pale, sick, tired.**] **2.** So soft as to be barely audible ▶ faint, feeble. [*Compare* **soft.**] —*See also* **dilute, implausible, ineffectual** (2), **insecure** (2), **pale** (2).

✚ **CORE SYNONYMS:** *weak, feeble, frail, fragile, infirm, decrepit, debilitated.* These adjectives mean lacking or showing a lack of strength. *Weak* is the most widely applicable: "*These poor wretches . . . were so weak they could hardly sit to their oars*" (Daniel Defoe). *Feeble* suggests pathetic or grievous physical or mental weakness or hopeless inadequacy: *a feeble intellect; a feeble effort. Frail* implies delicacy and inability to endure or withstand: "*an aged thrush, frail, gaunt, and small*" (Thomas Hardy). What is *fragile* is easily broken, damaged, or destroyed: *a fragile, expensive vase; a fragile state of mind after the accident. Infirm* implies enfeeblement: "*a poor, infirm, weak, and despis'd old man*" (William Shakespeare). *Decrepit* describes what is weakened, worn out, or broken down by hard use or the passage of time: *a decrepit building slated for demolition. Debilitated* suggests a gradual impairment of energy or strength: *a debilitated constitution further weakened by overwork.*

weaken *verb.* To moderate or change a position or course of action as a result of pressure ▶ back down (*or* off), ease off, relent, slacken, soften, yield. ***Idioms:*** give way (*or* ground). [*Compare* **assent.**] —*See also* **deteriorate, dilute, enervate, fade.**

weakening *noun.* —*See* **debilitation, deterioration** (1).

weak-kneed *adjective.* —*See* **cowardly.**

weakliness *noun.* —*See* **infirmity.**

weakling *noun.* A weak or ineffectual person ▶ pushover. *Informal:* jellyfish, softy. *Slang:* cream puff, doormat, pantywaist, weenie, wimp. [*Compare* **baby, coward.**]

weakly *adjective.* —*See* **weak** (1).

weak-minded *adjective.* —*See* **backward** (1).

weakness *noun.* An imperfection of character ▶ Achilles' heel, failing, fault, foible, frailty, infirmity, shortcoming, weak point. —*See also* **defect, infirmity, taste** (1).

weak point *noun.* —*See* **weakness.**

weal¹ *noun.* A state of health, happiness, and prospering ▶ prosperity, welfare, well-being. [*Compare* **condition, happiness.**]

weal² *noun.* —*See* **welt.**

wealth *noun.* A great amount of accumulated money and precious possessions ▶ affluence, fortune, money, opulence, pelf, riches, treasure. [*Compare* **capital.**] —*See also* **abundance, prosperity** (2), **resources.**

wealthy *adjective.* —*See* **rich** (1).

wear *verb.* —*See* **bear** (3), **display, erode.**

wear down *or* **out** *verb.* —*See* **tire** (1).

wearied *adjective.* —*See* **tired** (1).

weariful *adjective.* —*See* **boring, tired** (1).

weariless *adjective.* —*See* **tireless.**

weariness *noun.* —*See* **dullness, exhaustion.**

wearing *adjective.* Causing fatigue ▶ draining, exhausting, fatiguing, tiring, wearying. [*Compare* **burdensome.**]

wearisome *adjective.* —*See* **boring.**

weary *adjective.* Out of patience ▶ disgusted, fed up, sick, tired. ***Idiom:*** sick and tired. [*Compare* **angry.**] —*See also* **boring, tired** (1).

weary *verb.* —*See* **bore**[2], **tire** (1).

wearying *adjective.* Causing fatigue ▶ draining, exhausting, fatiguing, tiring, wearing. [*Compare* **burdensome.**]

weasel *noun.* One who behaves in a stealthy, furtive way ▶ prowler, skulker, sneak, sneaker. [*Compare* **creep, betrayer.**] —*See also* **creep** (2).

weasel *verb.* —*See* **equivocate** (1).

weasel word *noun.* —*See* **equivocation.**

weather *verb.* —*See* **survive** (1).

weave *verb.* To interlace strips or strands ▶ braid, enlace, entwine, interlace, intertwine, plait, pleach, raddle, splice, twill, twist, twine, wattle. —*See also* **stagger** (1), **sway, wind**[2].

weave *noun.* —*See* **texture, web.**

web *noun.* An open and loosely connected structure, usually interlaced, woven, or knotted ▶ braid, lace, lacing, lattice, mesh, net, netting, network, weave. —*See also* **complex** (1), **tangle, texture.**

web *verb.* —*See* **catch** (1).

wed *verb.* —*See* **combine** (1), **marry.**

wedded *adjective.* —*See* **marital.**

wedding *noun.* The act or ceremony by which two people are married ▶ bridal, espousal, marriage, nuptials, spousals.

wedge *noun.* —*See* **anchor, cut** (2).

wedlock *noun.* —*See* **marriage.**

wee *adjective.* —*See* **tiny.**

weedy *adjective.* —*See* **thin** (1).

weeny *adjective.* —*See* **tiny.**

weep *verb.* —*See* **cry, drip, ooze.**

weeping *noun.* —*See* **cry** (1).

weeping *or* **weepy** *adjective.* —*See* **tearful.**

weigh *verb.* —*See* **choose** (1), **compare, count** (1), **estimate** (1), **ponder.**

weigh down *verb.* —*See* **depress.**

weigh on *or* **upon** *verb.* To come to mind continually ▶ haunt, obsess, torment, trouble.

weight *noun.* **1.** The greatest part or portion ▶ bulk, mass, preponderance, preponderancy. [*Compare* **center.**] **2.** Special attention given to something considered important ▶ accent, accentuation, emphasis, stress, weight. [*Compare* **importance, notice.**] —*See also* **burden**[1] (1), **burden**[1] (2), **cogency, importance, influence, heaviness.**

weight *verb.* —*See* **burden**[1].

weightiness *noun.* **1.** The condition of being grave and of involving serious consequences ▶ graveness, gravity, heaviness, momentousness, seriousness. [*Compare* **severity.**] **2.** Intellectual penetration or range ▶ deepness, depth, profoundness, profundity. [*Compare* **discernment, intelligence, wisdom.**] —*See also* **heaviness, importance.**

weightless *adjective.* Having little weight; not heavy ▶ airy, fluffy, light, lightweight. ***Idioms:*** light as air, light as a feather. [*Compare* **immaterial, sheer**[2].]

weighty *adjective.* —*See* **burdensome, fat** (1), **grave**[2] (1), **heavy** (1), **influential, pregnant** (2).

weird *adjective.* Of an unnatural and usually frightening nature ▶ eerie, freakish, otherworldly, strange, uncanny, unearthly. *Informal:* crawly, creepy, spooky. [*Compare* **mysterious, supernatural.**] —*See also* **eccentric, funny** (3).

✚ **CORE SYNONYMS:** *weird, eerie, uncanny, unearthly.* These adjectives refer to what is of an unnatural, mysterious, and usually frightening nature. *Weird* may suggest the operation of supernatural influences, or merely the odd or unusual: "*The person of the house gave a weird little laugh*" (Charles Dickens). "*There is a weird power in a spoken word*" (Joseph Conrad). Something *eerie* inspires fear or uneasiness and implies a sinister influence: "*At nightfall on the marshes, the thing was eerie and fantastic to behold*" (Robert Louis Stevenson). *Uncanny* refers to what is unnatural and peculiarly unsettling: "*The queer stumps . . . had uncanny shapes, as of monstrous creatures*" (John Galsworthy). Something *unearthly* seems so strange and unnatural as to come from or belong to another world: "*He could hear the unearthly scream of some curlew piercing the din*" (Henry Kingsley).

---

weirdie *or* **weirdo** *noun.* —*See* **crackpot.**

weisenheimer *noun. See* **wisenheimer.**

welcome *noun.* An expression, in words or gestures, marking a meeting of persons ▶ hail, greeting, salutation, salute. *Informal:* hello. —*See also* **acceptance** (2).

welcome *adjective.* —*See* **pleasant.**

welcome *verb.* **1.** To address in a friendly and respectful way ▶ greet, hail, salute. **2.** To receive something given or offered willingly and gladly ▶ accept, embrace, take (up).

welcoming *adjective.* Easily approached ▶ accessible, approachable, responsive. [*Compare* **convenient.**]

welfare *noun.* A state of health, happiness, and prospering ▶ prosperity, weal, well-being. [*Compare* **condition, happiness.**] —*See also* **relief** (2).

well[1] *noun.* —*See* **origin.**

well *verb.* To fill with tears ▶ tear (up), water. —*See also* **flow** (2).

well[2] *adverb.* —*See* **completely** (1), **considerably.**

well *adjective.* —*See* **advisable, healthy.**

well-being *noun.* A state of health, happiness, and prospering ▶ prosperity, weal, welfare. [*Compare* **condition, happiness.**]

wellborn *adjective.* —*See* **noble.**

well-bred *adjective.* —*See* **courteous** (1), **cultured.**

well-considered *adjective.* —*See* **sound[2].**

well-defined *adjective.* —*See* **sharp** (2).

well-developed *adjective.* —*See* **shapely.**

well-fixed *adjective.* —*See* **prosperous.**

well-founded *adjective.* —*See* **sensible, sound[2].**

well-groomed *adjective.* —*See* **neat.**

well-grounded *adjective.* —*See* **sensible, sound[2].**

well-heeled *adjective.* —*See* **prosperous.**

well-kept *adjective.* —*See* **neat.**

well-known *adjective.* —*See* **famous.**

well-liked *adjective.* —*See* **favorite.**

well-mannered *adjective.* —*See* **courteous** (1).

wellness *noun.* —*See* **health** (1).

well-off *adjective.* —*See* **prosperous.**

well-ordered *adjective.* —*See* **neat.**

well-read *adjective.* —*See* **educated.**

well-spoken *adjective.* —*See* **courteous** (1), **eloquent.**

wellspring *noun.* —*See* **origin.**

well-timed *adjective.* —*See* **opportune.**

well-to-do *adjective.* —*See* **prosperous.**

well-worn *adjective.* —*See* **trite.**

welt *noun.* A ridge or bump raised on the flesh as a result of irritation, infection, or injury ▶ blister, boil, pock, wale, wart, weal, wheal, whelk. [*Compare* **bump.**] —*See also* **blow[2].**

welter *verb.* To move about in an indolent or clumsy manner ▶ flounder, roll about, roll around, wallow.

wench *noun.* —*See* **slut.**

wend *verb.* To move along a particular course ▶ go, pass, proceed, push on. ***Idioms:*** make (*or* wend) one's way. [*Compare* **advance, journey, rove.**]

wet *adjective.* Covered with or full of liquid ▶ doused, drenched, dripping, saturated, soaked, soaking, sodden, soggy, sopping, soppy, waterlogged. [*Compare* **damp, sticky.**] —*See also* **rainy.**

wet *verb.* **1.** To make thoroughly wet ▶ douse, drench, saturate, soak, sodden, sop, souse. **2.** To make moist ▶ bathe, dampen, moisten, wash.

wet blanket *noun.* —*See* **killjoy.**

wetland *noun.* —*See* **swamp.**

whack *verb.* —*See* **bang, hit, slap.**

whack *noun. Informal* A brief trial ▶ crack, go, stab, try. *Informal:* fling, shot, whirl. —*See also* **beat** (1), **blow²**, **clash, slap.**

whack *adjective.* —*See* **insane.**

whackiness *adjective. See* **wackiness.**

whacky *adjective. See* **wacky.**

whale *verb.* —*See* **beat** (1).

wham *noun.* A forceful movement causing a loud noise ▶ bang, crash, slam, smash. —*See also* **blow².**

wham *verb.* —*See* **hit.**

whammy *noun.* —*See* **curse** (1).

whatnot *noun.* —*See* **novelty** (3).

wheal *noun.* —*See* **welt.**

wheedle *verb.* —*See* **coax.**

wheel *noun.* —*See* **circle** (1), **revolution** (1).

wheel *verb.* To turn in place, as on a fixed point ▶ pivot, slue, swing, swivel. —*See also* **drive** (1), **turn** (1).

wheeze *verb.* —*See* **gasp, pant.**

whelk *noun.* —*See* **welt.**

whelp *noun.* —*See* **child** (1), **urchin.**

whereabouts *noun.* —*See* **bearing** (3).

wherefore *noun.* —*See* **cause** (2), **reason** (1).

wherewithal *noun.* —*See* **resources.**

whet *verb.* —*See* **sharpen.**

whey-faced *adjective.* —*See* **pale** (1).

whiff *noun.* —*See* **breeze** (1), **shade** (2).

whiff *verb.* —*See* **smell** (1).

while *noun.* —*See* **bit¹** (3), **effort.**

while *verb.* —*See* **idle** (2).

whilom *adjective.* —*See* **late** (2).

whim *noun.* —*See* **fancy.**

whimper *verb.* —*See* **complain, cry.**

whimper *noun.* —*See* **complaint.**

whimsical *adjective.* **1.** Showing invention or whimsy in design ▶ fanciful, fantastic, imaginative. [*Compare* **elaborate, ornate.**] **2.** Determined or marked by whim or caprice rather than reason ▶ arbitrary, capricious. —*See also* **capricious.**

whimsy *noun.* —*See* **fancy.**

whim-whams *noun.* —*See* **jitters.**

whine *verb.* —*See* **complain, cry.**

whine *noun.* —*See* **complaint.**

whiner *noun.* —*See* **grouch.**

whip *verb.* —*See* **agitate** (1), **beat** (2), **beat** (6), **overwhelm** (1).

whippersnapper *noun.* —*See* **nonentity.**

whipping *noun.* —*See* **beating, defeat.**

whipping boy *noun.* —*See* **scapegoat.**

whir *verb.* —*See* **hum.**

whir *noun.* —*See* **hum.**

whirl *verb.* **1.** To move or cause to move like a rapidly rotating current of liquid ▶ eddy, swirl. **2.** To have the sensation of turning in circles ▶ reel, spin, swim, swirl. ***Idiom:*** go round and round. —*See also* **rush, turn** (1).

whirl *noun. Informal* A brief trial ▶ crack, go, stab, try. *Informal:* fling, shot, whack. —*See also* **agitation** (3), **drive** (3), **revolution** (1).

whirlpool *noun.* A rotating, often concave current of liquid ▶ eddy, maelstrom, swirl, vortex. —*See also* **agitation** (3).

whisk *verb.* —*See* **beat** (6), **rush.**

whisker *noun.* —*See* **shade** (2).

whisper *noun.* —*See* **murmur, shade** (2).

whisper *verb.* **1.** To tell in confidence ▶ breathe, confide, share, unbosom. [*Compare* **communicate, reveal, say.**] **2.** To make a low, continuous, and indistinct sound ▶ murmur, rustle, sigh, sough. [*Compare* **burble, hum.**] —*See also* **gossip, mutter.**

whisperer *noun.* —*See* **gossip** (2).

whispery *adjective.* —*See* **soft** (2).

whistleblower *noun.* —*See* **informer.**

whit *noun.* —*See* **bit¹** (1).

whitecap *noun.* —*See* **wave.**

white flag *noun.* —*See* **truce.**

whiten *verb.* —*See* **pale.**

white-tie *adjective.* —*See* **formal.**

whitewash *verb.* —*See* **color** (2), **extenuate.**

whiz *verb.* —*See* **hiss** (1), **hum, rush.**

whiz *noun.* —*See* **expert, hiss** (1), **hum.**

whole *noun.* An amount or quantity from which nothing is left out or held back ▶ aggregate, all, entirety, everything, grand total, gross, sum, total, totality. *Informal:* works. ***Idioms:*** everything but (*or* except) the kitchen sink, lock, stock, and barrel, the lot, the whole ball of wax, the whole kit and caboodle, the whole lot, the whole megillah, the whole nine yards, the whole shebang (*or* schmeer), the works. [*Compare* **completeness.**] —*See also* **system.**

whole *adjective.* No less than; at least ▶ full, good, round. —*See also* **complete** (1), **concentrated** (1), **good** (2), **healthy.**

wholehearted *adjective.* —*See* **implicit** (2).

wholeness *noun.* —*See* **completeness, health** (1), **soundness.**

wholesome *adjective.* —*See* **clean** (2), **healthful, healthy.**

wholly *adverb.* —*See* **completely** (1).

whomp *verb.* —*See* **thud.**

whoop *noun.* —*See* **shout.**

whoop *verb.* —*See* **shout.**

whoosh *verb.* —*See* **hiss** (1).

whoosh *noun.* —*See* **hiss** (1).

whop *verb.* —*See* **hit.**

whop *noun.* —*See* **blow².**

whopper *noun.* —*See* **giant, lie².**

whopping *adjective.* —*See* **enormous.**

whore *noun.* —*See* **prostitute, slut.**

whorish *adjective.* —*See* **wanton** (1).

who's who *noun.* —*See* **society** (1).

why *noun.* —*See* **cause** (2), **intention, reason** (1).

wicked *adjective.* —*See* **evil, malevolent, troublesome** (2).

wickedness *noun.* —*See* **corruption** (1), **crime** (2), **evil** (1).

wide *adjective.* —*See* **broad** (1), **full** (3), **open** (1).

wide-awake *adjective.* Not in a state of sleep or unable to sleep ▶ awake, unsleeping, wakeful. [*Compare* **restless.**] —*See also* **alert.**

widen *verb.* —*See* **broaden.**

wideness *noun.* The extent of something from side to side ▶ breadth, broadness, expanse, width. [*Compare* **distance.**]

wide-ranging *or* **wide-reaching** *adjective.* —*See* **general** (2).

widespread *adjective.* Spread out over a large area ▶ far-flung. [*Compare* **broad.**] —*See also* **common** (1), **general** (2), **prevailing.**

widget *noun.* —*See* **gadget.**

width *noun.* The extent of something from side to side ▶ breadth, broadness, expanse, wideness. [*Compare* **distance.**]

wield *verb.* **1.** To use with or as if with the hands ▶ handle, manipulate, ply. **2.** To bring to bear steadily or forcefully, as influence ▶ exercise, exert, ply. ***Idiom:*** throw one's weight around. —*See also* **operate.**

wife *verb.* —*See* **spouse.**

wiggle *verb.* —*See* **crawl** (1).

wiggly *adjective.* —*See* **insecure** (2), **wavy.**

wild *adjective.* **1.** Unaltered by human intervention; not cultivated or developed ▶ native, natural, rough, uncultivated, undomesticated. **2.** Living outside of human control or intervention;

not domesticated ▶ feral, savage, unbroken, undomesticated, untamed. —*See also* **abandoned, enthusiastic, frantic, rough** (2), **uncivilized, unruly.**

wild *noun.* —*See* **wilderness.**

wilderness *noun.* An uninhabited region left in its natural state ▶ bush, jungle, outback, outdoors, wild, wildness, wilds. [*Compare* **country, desert**[1].]

wildness *noun.* —*See* **abandon** (1), **unruliness, wilderness.**

wilds *noun.* —*See* **wilderness.**

wile *noun.* —*See* **trick** (1).

wile *verb.* —*See* **idle** (2).

wiliness *noun.* —*See* **art.**

will *noun.* **1.** The mental faculty by which one deliberately chooses or decides ▶ free will, volition. [*Compare* **choice, spirit.**] **2.** Unrestricted freedom to choose ▶ convenience, discretion, leisure, pleasure. —*See also* **decision** (2), **liking.**

will *verb.* —*See* **choose** (1), **choose** (2), **leave**[1] (1).

willful *adjective.* —*See* **deliberate** (1), **stubborn** (1), **voluntary.**

willfully *adverb.* Of one's own free will ▶ by choice, freely, spontaneously, voluntarily, willingly. ***Idioms:*** of one's own accord, on one's own volition.

willfulness *noun.* —*See* **stubbornness.**

willies *noun.* —*See* **jitters.**

willing *adjective.* Disposed to accept, agree, or participate ▶ acquiescent, agreeable, amenable, delighted, eager, game, glad, happy, minded, pleased, ready, tickled. [*Compare* **obliging.**] —*See also* **voluntary.**

willingly *adverb.* Of one's own free will ▶ by choice, freely, spontaneously, voluntarily, willfully. ***Idioms:*** of one's own accord, on one's own volition. —*See also* **yes.**

will-o'-the-wisp *noun.* —*See* **illusion.**

willowy *adjective.* —*See* **thin** (1).

willpower *noun.* —*See* **decision** (2).

willy-nilly *adverb.* —*See* **helplessly.**

wilt *verb.* To become limp, as from loss of freshness ▶ droop, flag, sag, wither. —*See also* **slouch** (2), **tire** (2).

wily *adjective.* —*See* **artful.**

wimp *noun.* —*See* **weakling.**

wimpy *adjective.* —*See* **cowardly.**

win *verb.* To achieve victory ▶ be victorious. ***Idioms:*** claim the victory (*or* prize), come out on top, finish (*or* come in) first, take the laurels (*or* palm). [*Compare* **defeat.**] —*See also* **capture, earn** (1), **earn** (2), **get** (1).

win over *verb.* —*See* **charm** (1), **convince.**

win *noun.* —*See* **conquest.**

wince *verb.* —*See* **flinch.**

wince *noun.* —*See* **recoil.**

wind[1] *noun.* A natural movement or current of air ▶ air, blast, blow, gust, waft, zephyr. [*Compare* **breeze.**] —*See also* **breath.**

wind *verb.* To expose to circulating air ▶ aerate, air, freshen, ventilate.

wind[2] *verb.* To move or cause to lie along a repeatedly curving path ▶ coil, corkscrew, curl, entwine, meander, snake, spiral, twine, twist, weave, wrap, wreathe. [*Compare* **turn.**] —*See also* **insinuate.**

wind up *verb.* —*See* **conclude.**

wind down *verb.* —*See* **subside.**

windbreaker *noun.* —*See* **coat** (1).

windiness *noun.* —*See* **wordiness.**

winding *adjective.* Repeatedly curving in alternate directions ▶ anfractuous, convoluted, curvy, flexuous, meandering, meandrous, serpentine, sinuous, snaky, tortuous, twisting, windy. —*See also* **indirect** (1).

winding *noun.* —*See* **curl.**

windless *adjective.* —*See* **airless** (2).

window-dressing *noun.* —*See* **façade** (2).

wind-up *noun.* —*See* **end** (1), **end** (2).

windy *adjective.* —*See* **airy** (3), **inflated, winding.**

wine bar *noun.* —*See* **bar** (2).

wing *noun.* —*See* **branch** (3), **extension** (2).

wing *verb.* To cause bodily damage to a living thing ▶ hurt, injure, traumatize, wound. [*Compare* **cut, break.**] —*See also* **fly** (1), **rush.**

wink *verb.* —*See* **blink, glitter.**

wink at *verb.* —*See* **blink at.**

wink *noun.* —*See* **blink, flash** (1), **flash** (2), **hint** (2).

winner *noun.* One that wins a contest or competition ▶ champion, conqueror, medalist, prizewinner, titleholder, victor. *Informal:* champ. —*See also* **conqueror, hit.**

winning *adjective.* —*See* **attractive, victorious.**

winnow *verb.* To set apart one kind or type from others ▶ separate, sift, sort. ***Idiom:*** separate the sheep from the goats.

wino *noun.* —*See* **drunkard.**

winsome *adjective.* —*See* **attractive.**

wintriness *noun.* —*See* **cold.**

wintry *adjective.* —*See* **cold** (1).

wipe *verb.* —*See* **cancel** (1).

wipe out *verb.* —*See* **annihilate, eliminate, massacre, murder.**

wiped-out *adjective.* —*See* **drugged, tired** (1).

wiretap *verb.* To monitor telephone calls with a concealed device connected to the circuit ▶ bug, tap.

wisdom *noun.* **1.** Deep, thorough, or mature understanding ▶ insight, intelligence, profundity, sagaciousness, sagacity, sageness, sapience. [*Compare* **culture, discernment, illumination, understanding.**] **2.** The sum of what has been perceived, discovered, or inferred ▶ knowledge, lore, understanding. [*Compare* **actuality.**] —*See also* **common sense.**

wise[1] *adjective.* Possessing deep knowledge and understanding ▶ knowing, sagacious, sage, sapient. —*See also* **aware, educated, impudent, sensible, shrewd.**

wise[2] *noun.* —*See* **way** (1).

wiseacre *or* **wisecracker** *noun.* —*See* **smart aleck.**

wisecrack *noun.* —*See* **crack** (3).

wise guy *noun.* —*See* **smart aleck.**

wise man *or* **wise woman** *noun.* —*See* **sage.**

wisenheimer *or* **weisenheimer** *noun.* —*See* **smart aleck.**

wisest *adjective.* —*See* **advisable.**

wish *noun.* —*See* **desire** (1), **dream** (3).

wish *verb.* —*See* **choose** (2), **desire.**

wishy-washiness *noun.* —*See* **insipidity.**

wishy-washy *adjective.* —*See* **insipid.**

wistful *adjective.* —*See* **depressed** (1).

wit *noun.* —*See* **discernment, humor, intelligence, joker.**

witch *noun.* **1.** A woman who practices magic ▶ enchantress, hag, lamia, sorceress. [*Compare* **wizard.**] **2.** An ugly, frightening woman, usually old ▶ beldam, crone, hag. *Slang:* battle-ax, biddy, crow. —*See also* **seductress.**

witch *verb.* —*See* **charm** (2).

witchcraft *noun.* —*See* **magic** (1).

witchery *noun.* —*See* **attraction, magic** (1).

witching *adjective.* —*See* **magic, seductive.**

witching *noun.* —*See* **magic** (1).

withdraw *verb.* To pull back in ▶ draw in, retract. —*See also* **deduct, detach, go** (1), **lift** (2), **remove** (1), **retract** (1), **retreat.**

withdrawal *noun.* —*See* **departure, detachment** (1), **retraction, retreat.**

withdrawn *adjective.* —*See* **cool.**

wither *verb.* —*See* **blast** (2), **dry** (1), **languish, paralyze, slam** (1), **wilt.**

withering *adjective.* —*See* **biting.**

withhold *verb.* —*See* **censor** (2), **decline, deprive, hold** (1), **refrain.**

with-it *adjective.* —*See* **aware, fashionable.**

withstand *verb.* —*See* **endure** (1), **oppose, repel.**

witless *adjective.* —*See* **foolish, stupid.**

witlessness *noun.* —*See* **stupidity.**

witness *noun.* **1.** Someone who sees something occur ▶ audience, eyewitness, seer, viewer. **2.** One who testifies, especially in court ▶ attestant, attester, deponent, testifier. **3.** A formal declaration of truth or fact given under oath ▶ affidavit, deposition, testimony. *—See also* **sign** (1).

witness *verb.* *—See* **certify, indicate** (1), **testify.**

wits *noun.* *—See* **sanity.**

witticism *noun.* *—See* **joke** (1).

wittiness *noun.* *—See* **humor.**

witting *adjective.* *—See* **deliberate** (1).

witty *adjective.* *—See* **clever** (2), **funny** (1).

wizard *noun.* One who practices sorcery or magic ▶ conjurer, enchanter, magician, necromancer, prestidigitator, sorcerer, warlock. [*Compare* **witch.**] *—See also* **expert.**

wizardly *adjective.* *—See* **magic.**

wizardry *noun.* *—See* **magic** (1).

wizen *verb.* *—See* **dry** (1).

wobble *verb.* *—See* **hesitate, stagger** (1), **sway.**

wobbliness *noun.* *—See* **unsteadiness.**

wobbly *adjective.* *—See* **insecure** (2).

woe *noun.* *—See* **curse** (3), **distress, misery.**

woebegone *adjective.* *—See* **miserable, sorrowful, terrible.**

woeful *adjective.* *—See* **deplorable, miserable, sorrowful.**

wolf *noun.* A man who is given to flirting ▶ flirt. *Slang:* masher. [*Compare* **seducer.**] *—See also* **philanderer.**

wolf *verb.* *—See* **gulp.**

womanhood *noun.* Women in general ▶ womankind, womenfolk.

womanish *adjective.* Relating to or characteristic of women ▶ female, feminine, womanly. *—See also* **effeminate.**

womanishness *noun.* *—See* **effeminacy.**

womanizer *noun.* *—See* **philanderer.**

womankind *noun.* Women in general ▶ womanhood, womenfolk.

womanliness *noun.* The quality or condition of being feminine ▶ femaleness, feminineness, femininity.

womanly *adjective.* Relating to or characteristic of women ▶ female, feminine, womanish.

womenfolk *noun.* Women in general ▶ womanhood, womankind.

wonder *noun.* **1.** The emotion aroused by something awe-inspiring or astounding ▶ amaze, amazement, astonishment, awe, marvel, stupefaction, surprise, wonderment. [*Compare* **enthusiasm, surprise.**] **2.** An event inexplicable by the laws of nature ▶ miracle. ***Idiom:*** act of God. *—See also* **doubt, marvel.**

wonder *verb.* To have a feeling of great awe and rapt admiration ▶ admire, marvel. ***Idioms:*** be agog (*or* agape *or* awestruck). [*Compare* **gaze, stagger.**] *—See also* **doubt.**

wonderful *adjective.* *—See* **astonishing, glorious, marvelous.**

wonderment *noun.* *—See* **marvel, wonder** (1).

wondrous *adjective.* *—See* **astonishing, glorious.**

wonkiness *adjective.* *—See* **unsteadiness.**

wont *adjective.* In the habit ▶ accustomed, habituated, used. *—See also* **inclined.**

wont *noun.* *—See* **custom.**

wont *verb.* *—See* **accustom.**

wonted *adjective.* *—See* **common** (1).

woo *verb.* *—See* **court** (2).

wooden *adjective.* Rigidly constrained or formal; lacking grace and spontaneity ▶ buckram, starchy, stiff, stilted. [*Compare* **cool, forced, prudish.**]

woodland *or* **woods** *noun.* A dense growth of trees and underbrush covering an area ▶ backwoods, forest, timberland. [*Compare* **country, wilderness.**]

wooer *noun.* *—See* **beau** (1).

woolgather *verb.* *—See* **dream.**

woolgathering *adjective.* *—See* **dreamy.**

woolly *adjective.* *—See* **ambiguous** (1), **hairy.**

wooziness *noun.* *—See* **dizziness.**

woozy *adjective.* —*See* **dizzy** (1).

word *noun.* Something said ▶ saying, statement, utterance. [*Compare* **language, speech.**] —*See also* **argument, command** (1), **comment, gossip** (1), **message, news, promise** (1), **term.**

word *verb.* —*See* **phrase.**

wordage *noun.* —*See* **wordiness, wording.**

wordbook *noun.* An alphabetical list of words often defined or translated ▶ dictionary, glossary, lexicon, vocabulary.

word-for-word *adjective.* —*See* **literal.**

word-hoard *noun.* All the words of a language ▶ lexicon, vocabulary.

wordiness *noun.* The use of words in excess of those needed for clarity or precision ▶ circumlocution, diffuseness, diffusion, long-windedness, pleonasm, prolixity, redundance, redundancy, verbiage, verboseness, verbosity, windiness, wordage. ***Idiom:*** verbal diarrhea. [*Compare* **bombast.**]

wording *noun.* Choice of words and the way in which they are used ▶ diction, locution, parlance, phrase, phraseology, phrasing, verbalism, wordage. ***Idioms:*** turn of phrase, way of putting it. [*Compare* **expression.**]

wordless *adjective.* —*See* **implicit** (1), **mute, silent** (2), **speechless.**

wordlessness *noun.* —*See* **silence** (2).

word of honor *noun.* —*See* **promise** (1).

word-of-mouth *adjective.* —*See* **oral.**

words *noun.* —*See* **argument.**

wordy *adjective.* **1.** Using or containing an excessive number of words ▶ circumlocutionary, circumlocutory, diffuse, long-winded, periphrastic, pleonastic, prolix, redundant, tautological, verbose. [*Compare* **indirect, talkative.**] **2.** Relating to, consisting of, or having the nature of words ▶ lexical, linguistic, wordy.

✣ **CORE SYNONYMS:** *wordy, diffuse, long-winded, prolix, verbose.* These adjectives mean using or containing an excessive number of words: *a wordy apology; a diffuse historical novel; a long-winded speaker; a prolix, tedious lecturer; verbose correspondence.*

work *noun.* **1.** The technique, style, and quality of working ▶ craft, craftsmanship, workmanship. [*Compare* **approach.**] **2.** Something that is produced by human effort ▶ produce, product, production, manufacture. [*Compare* **good.**] —*See also* **act** (1), **business** (2), **composition** (1), **labor, position** (3), **publication** (2).

work *verb.* **1.** To handle in a way so as to mix, form, and shape ▶ knead, manipulate, squeeze. **2.** To force to work hard ▶ drive, push, task, tax. ***Idiom:*** crack the whip. [*Compare* **force.**] —*See also* **function, insinuate, labor, operate, rub, succeed** (2), **till, use.**

work out *verb.* **1.** To arrive at an answer to a mathematical problem ▶ solve, work. *Informal:* figure out. [*Compare* **calculate.**] **2.** To plan the details or arrangements of ▶ arrange, lay out, prepare, schedule. **3.** To engage in activities in order to strengthen or condition ▶ drill, exercise, practice, train. —*See also* **derive** (2), **design** (1), **succeed** (2).

work over *verb.* —*See* **batter, revise.**

work up *verb.* —*See* **provoke.**

work on *verb.* —*See* **influence.**

workable *adjective.* —*See* **malleable, possible.**

workaday *or* **workday** *adjective.* —*See* **everyday.**

worked up *adjective.* —*See* **thrilled.**

worker *noun.* —*See* **employee, laborer.**

workhorse *noun.* —*See* **drudge** (2).

working *adjective.* —*See* **active, busy** (1), **employed.**

working *noun.* —*See* **behavior** (2).

working girl *noun.* —*See* **harlot, laborer.**

workingman *or* **workingwoman** *noun.* —*See* **laborer.**

workless *adjective.* Having no job ▶ idle, jobless, unemployed, unoccupied. ***Idioms:*** out of a job (*or* work).

workman *or* **workwoman** *noun.* —*See* **laborer.**

workmanship *noun.* The technique, style, and quality of working ▶ craft, craftsmanship, work. [*Compare* **approach.**]

workout *noun.* Energetic physical action ▶ activity, exercise, workout. —*See also* **practice.**

workroom *noun.* An artist's workspace ▶ atelier, studio, workshop.

works *noun.* A building or complex in which an industry is located ▶ factory, mill, plant. —*See also* **whole.**

workshop *noun.* An artist's workspace ▶ atelier, studio, workroom. —*See also* **conference** (1).

workup *noun.* —*See* **examination** (2).

world *noun.* The celestial body where humans live ▶ earth, globe, orb, planet. —*See also* **abundance, area** (1), **environment** (2), **environment** (3), **humankind, universe.**

worldly *adjective.* Experienced in the ways of the world; lacking natural simplicity ▶ cosmopolitan, sophisticated, worldly-wise. [*Compare* **experienced, shrewd, suave.**] —*See also* **earthly, profane** (2).

worldly-wise *adjective.* Experienced in the ways of the world; lacking natural simplicity ▶ cosmopolitan, sophisticated, worldly. [*Compare* **experienced, shrewd, suave.**]

world-shaking *adjective.* —*See* **important.**

worldwide *adjective.* —*See* **universal** (1).

worm *verb.* —*See* **crawl** (1), **insinuate, maneuver** (2).

worm *noun.* —*See* **creep** (2).

worm-eaten *or* **wormy** *adjective.* —*See* **bad** (2).

worn *adjective.* —*See* **haggard, shabby.**

worn-down *adjective.* —*See* **tired** (1).

worn-out *adjective.* —*See* **shabby, tired** (1), **trite.**

worried *adjective.* —*See* **anxious.**

worrisome *adjective.* —*See* **disturbing.**

worry *verb.* To cause anxious uneasiness in ▶ ail, bother, concern, distress, trouble. —*See also* **agitate** (1), **brood, harass.**

worry *noun.* A cause of distress or anxiety ▶ care, concern, stressor, trouble. [*Compare* **burden**[1].] —*See also* **anxiety** (1), **qualm.**

✚ **CORE SYNONYMS:** *worry, ail, distress, trouble.* These verbs mean to cause anxious uneasiness in: *What problems are ailing you today? The bad news from the hospital distressed us. Her high fever worries the doctor. His behavior troubles his parents.*

---

worrywart *noun.* —*See* **pessimist** (2).

worse *noun.* Whatever is destructive or harmful ▶ bad, badness, evil, ill. [*Compare* **harm.**]

worsen *verb.* —*See* **deteriorate.**

worship *noun.* The act of adoring, especially reverently ▶ adoration, idolization, reverence, veneration. [*Compare* **devotion, honor, praise.**] —*See also* **love** (1).

worship *verb.* To feel deep devoted love for ▶ adore, love. ***Idioms:*** be soft (*or* stuck *or* sweet) on, place (*or* put) on a pedestal, worship the ground someone walks on. —*See also* **revere.**

worshipful *adjective.* —*See* **reverent.**

worst *verb.* —*See* **defeat.**

worth *noun.* A measure of those qualities that determine merit, desirability, usefulness, or importance ▶ account, valuation, value. [*Compare* **cost, importance.**] —*See also* **merit.**

worthiness *noun.* —*See* **qualification.**

worthless *adjective.* Lacking worth and value ▶ drossy, empty, good-for-nothing, no-good, valueless. *Informal:* dumb, no-account, nothing, rotten, stupid. [*Compare* **aimless, trivial.**] —*See also* **shoddy.**

worthwhile *adjective.* —*See* **beneficial.**

worthy *adjective.* —*See* **admirable, costly, eligible, good** (1).

worthy *noun.* —*See* **dignitary.**

wound *noun.* Marked tissue damage, especially when produced by physical injury ▶ laceration, lesion, trauma, traumatism. [*Compare* **harm.**] —*See also* **distress.**

wound *verb.* **1.** To cause bodily damage to a living thing ▶ hurt, injure, traumatize, wing. [*Compare* **cut, break, hurt.**] **2.** To inflict physical or mental injury or distress on ▶ shock, traumatize. —*See also* **distress, offend** (1).

wounded *noun.* —*See* **victim.**

wow *noun.* —*See* **hit.**

wrack *noun.* —*See* **destruction, ruin** (2).

wrack *verb.* —*See* **destroy** (1).

wraith *noun.* —*See* **ghost.**

wrangle *verb.* —*See* **argue** (1), **drive** (3), **haggle.**

wrangle *noun.* —*See* **argument.**

wrap *verb.* **1.** To cover completely and closely, as with clothing or bandages ▶ bundle, enfold, envelop, roll, swaddle, swathe. **2.** To surround and cover completely so as to obscure ▶ cloak, clothe, enfold, enshroud, envelop, enwrap, infold, invest, shroud, veil. [*Compare* **conceal, cover, surround.**] —*See also* **wind²**.

wrap up *verb.* To put on warm clothes ▶ bundle up, wrap. —*See also* **conclude, involve** (1).

wrap *noun.* A garment that is worn wrapped about a person ▶ afghan, cloak, muffler, shawl, stole, throw, wrapper. [*Compare* **scarf.**] —*See also* **wrapper.**

wrapper *or* **wrapping** *noun.* The material in which something is wrapped ▶ case, casing, cover, covering, envelope, jacket, packaging, wrap. [*Compare* **frame.**] —*See also* **wrap.**

wrap-up *noun.* —*See* **end** (1), **end** (2), **summary.**

wrath *or* **wrathfulness** *noun.* —*See* **anger.**

wrathful *adjective.* —*See* **angry.**

wreak *verb.* —*See* **inflict.**

wreath *noun.* —*See* **bouquet, circle** (1).

wreathe *verb.* —*See* **wind²**.

wreck *noun.* —*See* **collapse** (2), **crash** (2), **destruction, ruin** (2).

wreck *verb.* **1.** To damage, disable, or destroy a seacraft ▶ shipwreck, sink, run aground. [*Compare* **sink.**] **2.** To injure or destroy property maliciously ▶ vandalize. *Slang:* trash. —*See also* **blast** (2), **botch, crash, destroy** (2), **destroy** (1).

wreckage *noun.* —*See* **damage, destruction, ruin** (2).

wrecker *noun.* —*See* **ruin** (1).

wrench *verb.* **1.** To injure a bodily part by twisting ▶ sprain, strain, turn, twist. [*Compare* **hurt.**] **2.** To move or cause to move with a sudden abrupt motion ▶ jerk, lurch, snap, twitch, yank. [*Compare* **move.**] **3.** To alter the position of by a sharp, forcible twisting or turning movement ▶ twist, wrest, wring. —*See also* **distort, extort, pull** (2).

wrench *noun.* —*See* **jerk.**

wrest *verb.* To alter the position of by a sharp, forcible twisting or turning movement ▶ twist, wrench, wring. —*See also* **distort, extort, pull** (2).

wrestle *verb.* —*See* **contend.**

wretch *noun.* —*See* **unfortunate.**

wretched *adjective.* —*See* **deplorable, despondent, miserable, offensive** (1), **terrible.**

wretchedness *noun.* —*See* **distress, misery.**

wriggle *verb.* —*See* **crawl** (1).

wring *verb.* To alter the position of by a sharp, forcible twisting or turning movement ▶ twist, wrench, wrest. —*See also* **extort.**

wrinkle *noun.* **1.** An indentation or seam on the skin, especially on the face ▶ crease, crinkle, crow's-foot, furrow, line. **2.** *Informal* A clever, unexpected new trick or method ▶ gimmick, trick, twist. *Informal:* kicker. *Slang:* angle, kick. —*See also* **fold** (1).

wrinkle *verb.* To make irregular folds in, especially by pressing or twisting ▶ crimp, crinkle, crumple, rimple, rumple, wrinkle. —*See also* **fold.**

writ *noun.* —*See* **command** (1).

write *verb.* To form letters, characters, or words on a surface with an instrument ▶ chalk, engross, indite, ink, inscribe, pen, pencil, scratch (out), scrawl, scribe. *Informal:* scribble. —*See also* **compose** (1), **publish** (2).

write down *verb.* —*See* **depreciate, list[1].**

write off *verb.* —*See* **drop** (4).

write-down *noun.* —*See* **depreciation.**

write-up *noun.* —*See* **item.**

writhe *verb.* To twist agitatedly, as in pain, struggle, or embarrassment ▶ squirm, toss, twist. [*Compare* **shake.**] —*See also* **crawl** (1).

writing *noun.* —*See* **composition** (1).

written *adjective.* Of or relating to representation by means of writing ▶ calligraphic, graphic, scriptural.

wrong *adjective.* —*See* **erroneous, evil, false, insane, unfair.**

wrong *adverb.* Not in the right way or on the proper course ▶ afield, amiss, astray, awry.

wrong *noun.* —*See* **crime** (2), **evil** (1), **injustice** (1), **injustice** (2).

wrong *verb.* —*See* **abuse** (1), **offend** (1).

✚ **CORE SYNONYMS:** *wrong, afield, amiss, astray, awry.* These adverbs mean not in the right or expected way: *plans for expansion that went wrong; straying far afield; spoke amiss at the debate; afraid the letter would go astray; thinking awry.*

◀ **ANTONYM:** *right*

---

wrongdoer *noun.* —*See* **evildoer.**

wrongdoing *noun.* —*See* **crime** (2), **misbehavior.**

wrongful *adjective.* —*See* **criminal** (1), **illegal.**

wry *adjective.* —*See* **sarcastic.**

XYZ

x *verb.* —*See* **cancel** (1).

yahoo *noun.* —*See* **boor.**

yak *verb.* —*See* **chatter** (1).

yak *noun.* —*See* **chatter.**

yammer *verb.* —*See* **chatter** (1), **complain.**

yammer *noun.* —*See* **chatter, complaint.**

yank *verb.* To move or cause to move with a sudden abrupt motion ▶ jerk, lurch, snap, twitch, wrench. [*Compare* **move.**] —*See also* **pull** (1), **pull** (2).

yank *noun.* —*See* **jerk, pull** (1).

yap *verb.* To utter a shrill, short cry ▶ squeal, yawp, yelp, yip. [*Compare* **cry, shout.**]

yap *noun.* A shrill, short cry ▶ squeal, yawp, yelp, yip. [*Compare* **cry, shout.**] —*See also* **mouth** (1).

yard *noun.* —*See* **court** (1), **pen[2].**

yardstick *noun.* —*See* **standard.**

yarn *noun. Informal* An entertaining and often oral account of a real or fictitious occurrence ▶ anecdote, fable, story, tale. *Informal:* tall tale.

yaw *verb.* —*See* **lurch** (1).

yawn *verb.* **1.** To open the mouth wide with a deep breath, as when tired or bored ▶ gape. **2.** To open wide ▶ gap, gape. [*Compare* **open, widen.**]

yawning *adjective.* Open wide ▶ abysmal, abyssal, cavernous, gaping. [*Compare* **broad, open.**]

yawp *verb.* To utter a shrill, short cry ▶ squeal, yap, yelp, yip. [*Compare* **cry, shout.**]

yawp *noun.* A shrill, short cry ▶ squeal, yap, yelp, yip. [*Compare* **cry, shout.**]

yea *adverb.* —*See* **even** (2), **yes.**

yea *noun.* An affirmative vote or voter ▶ aye, yes.

yeah *adverb.* —*See* **yes.**

year *noun.* A period of time of approximately 12 months, especially that period during which the earth completes a single revolution around the sun ▶ calendar year, season cycle, twelvemonth.

yearn *verb.* —*See* **desire.**

yearning *noun.* —*See* **desire** (1).

years *noun.* —*See* **age** (1), **ages.**

yeast *noun.* —*See* **catalyst, foam.**

yeast *verb.* —*See* **foam.**

yeasty *adjective.* —*See* **foamy.**

yell *verb.* —*See* **shout.**

yell *noun.* —*See* **shout.**

yellow *or* **yellow-bellied** *adjective.* —*See* **cowardly.**

yellow-belly *noun.* —*See* **coward.**

yellow streak *noun.* —*See* **cowardice.**

yelp *verb.* To utter a shrill, short cry or bark ▶ squeal, yap, yawp, yip. [*Compare* **cry, shout.**]

yelp *noun.* A shrill, short cry or bark ▶ squeal, yap, yawp, yip. [*Compare* **cry, shout.**]

yen *noun.* —*See* **desire** (1).

yenta *noun.* —*See* **gossip** (2).

yep *adverb.* —*See* **yes.**

yes *adverb.* It is so; as you say or ask ▶ absolutely, affirmative, agreed, all right, assuredly, aye, gladly, indeed, indubitably, naturally, right, roger, undoubtedly, unquestionably, willingly, yea. *Informal:* OK, uh-huh, yeah, yep, yup. *Slang:* for sure, right on, ten four. ***Idioms:*** you got it, you got that right. [*Compare* **actually, really.**]

yes *noun.* An affirmative vote or voter ▶ aye, yea. —*See also* **acceptance** (1).

yes *verb.* —*See* **assent.**

yes man *noun.* —*See* **sycophant.**

yesterday *or* **yesteryear** *noun.* —*See* **past.**

yet *adverb.* To a more extreme degree ▶ even, ever more so, still. —*See also* **additionally, earlier** (2), **still** (1).

yield *verb.* To conform to the will or judgment of another ▶ bow, defer, submit. ***Idioms:*** give ground, give way. [*Compare* **humor.**] —*See also* **abandon** (1), **produce** (1), **return** (3), **succumb, surrender** (1), **weaken.**

yield *noun.* The amount or quantity produced ▶ garner, output, production. —*See also* **harvest.**

yielding *adjective.* —*See* **deferential, gentle** (3), **passive, soft** (1).

yip *noun.* A shrill, short cry ▶ squeal, yap, yawp, yelp. [*Compare* **cry, shout.**]

yip *verb.* To utter a shrill, short cry ▶ squeal, yap, yawp, yelp. [*Compare* **cry, shout.**]

yoke *noun.* —*See* **bond** (2), **couple, slavery.**

yoke *verb.* —*See* **combine** (1).

yoke with *verb.* —*See* **impose on.**

yokel *noun.* —*See* **clodhopper.**

yore *noun.* —*See* **past.**

young *adjective.* Being in an early period of growth or development ▶ fresh, green, immature, infant, juvenile, puerile, youthful. [*Compare* **childish.**]

young *noun.* **1.** Young people collectively ▶ younger generation, youth. *Informal:* kids, young'uns. **2.** The offspring, as of an animal or bird, for example, that are the result of one breeding season ▶ brood, litter, spawn. [*Compare* **progeny.**]

✚ **CORE SYNONYMS:** *young, youthful, immature, juvenile, puerile, green.* These adjectives mean characteristic of or being in an early period of growth or development. *Young* is the most general of the terms: *The young children took a nap after lunch. Youthful* suggests characteristics, such as enthusiasm, freshness, or energy, that are associated with youth: *The students tackled the task with youthful ardor. Immature* applies to what is not yet fully developed; it sometimes suggests that someone falls short of an expected level of maturity: *The therapist specialized in helping emotionally immature adults. Juvenile* connotes immaturity, often childishness: *The newspaper reported on the juvenile pranks of the conventioneers. Puerile* is used derogatorily to suggest silliness, foolishness, or infantilism: *It was inappropriate to tell such puerile jokes during* *the meeting. Green* implies lack of training or experience and sometimes callowness: *The green recruits couldn't deal with the emergency.*

---

youngster *noun.* —*See* **child** (1).

youth *noun.* **1.** The time of life between childhood and maturity ▶ adolescence, greenness, juvenescence, juvenility, puberty, pubescence, salad days, youthfulness. *Informal:* spring, springtime. [*Compare* **childhood.**] **2.** Young people collectively ▶ young. *Informal:* kids. —*See also* **teenager.**

youthful *adjective.* —*See* **young.**

youthfulness *noun.* —*See* **youth** (1).

yowl *verb.* —*See* **bawl, cry, howl.**

yowl *noun.* —*See* **howl.**

yucky *adjective.* —*See* **unpalatable, unpleasant.**

yuk *verb.* —*See* **laugh.**

yuk *noun.* —*See* **laugh.**

yummy *adjective.* —*See* **delicious.**

yup *adverb.* —*See* **yes.**

zaftig *adjective.* —*See* **fat** (1), **shapely.**

zaniness *noun.* —*See* **foolishness, humor.**

zany *adjective.* —*See* **foolish, funny** (1).

zany *noun.* —*See* **joker.**

zap *verb.* —*See* **kill**[1], **murder.**

zeal *noun.* —*See* **devotion, enthusiasm** (1), **passion.**

zealot *noun.* —*See* **devotee, extremist, fan**[2].

zealous *adjective.* —*See* **enthusiastic, extreme** (2), **pious.**

zealousness *noun.* —*See* **enthusiasm** (1).

zenith *noun.* —*See* **climax.**

zephyr *noun.* —*See* **breeze** (1), **wind**[1].

zero *noun.* —*See* **nonentity, nothing.**

zero in *verb.* —*See* **aim** (1), **concentrate.**

zero hour *noun.* —*See* **crisis.**

zest *noun.* Spirited enjoyment ▶ gusto, relish. [*Compare* **enthusiasm.**] —*See also* **flavor** (1), **skin** (3).

zest *verb.* To impart flavor to ▶ flavor, season, spice (up).

✚ **CORE SYNONYMS:** *zest, gusto, relish.* These nouns denote spirited, hearty enjoyment or pleasure: *ate with zest; telling a joke with gusto; has no relish for repetitive work.*

---

zesty *adjective.* —*See* **spicy.**

zigzag *verb.* —*See* **swerve.**

zigzag *adjective.* —*See* **indirect** (1).

zilch *noun.* —*See* **nonentity, nothing.**

zillion *noun.* —*See* **heap** (2).

zinger *noun.* —*See* **joke** (1).

zip *noun.* —*See* **energy, spirit** (1).

zip *verb.* —*See* **breeze, rush.**

zippy *adjective.* —*See* **energetic.**

zodiac *noun.* —*See* **circle** (1).

zone *noun.* —*See* **area** (2), **territory.**

zonk *verb.* —*See* **daze** (1).

zonked *adjective.* —*See* **drugged, drunk.**

zoom *verb.* —*See* **rush.**